P/E	Price/earnings ratio
P	(1) Stock price; price in Period $t = P_t$; current price $= P_0$
	(2) Sales price per unit of product sold
P_c	Conversion price
$\hat{P}_0$	Expected stock price as PV of expected dividends
P_f	Price of good in foreign country
P_h	Price of good in home country
PI	Profitability index
P_N	A stock's horizon value
PM	Profit margin
PMT	Payment of an annuity
PPP	Purchasing power parity
PV	Present value
PVA_N	Present value of an annuity for N years
Q	Quantity produced or sold
Q_{BE}	Breakeven quantity
r	(1) Percentage interest rate
	(2) Required rate of return
$\bar{r}$	"r bar," actual rate of return
r^*	Real risk-free rate of return
$\hat{r}$	"r hat," expected rate of return
r_d	Required return on debt
r_e	Cost of new common stock including flotation costs
r_f	Interest rate in foreign country
r_h	Interest rate in home country
r_i	Required return for an individual firm or security
r_M	Required return for "the market" or for an "average" stock
r_{NOM}	Nominal rate of interest; also denoted by I_{NOM}
r_p	Required return on portfolio
r_{ps}	Required return on preferred stock
r_{PER}	Periodic rate of return
r_{RF}	Rate of return on a risk-free security
r_s	Required return on common stock
$\bar{r}_{SMB}$	Return on Fama-French small (size) minus big (size) portfolio
$\bar{r}_{HML}$	Return on Fama-French high (B/M) minus big (B/M) portfolio
ρ	Correlation coefficient (lowercase rho)
R	Estimated correlation coefficient for sample data
ROA	Return on assets
ROE	Return on equity
ROIC	Return on invested capital
RP_i	Risk premium for Stock i
RP_M	Market risk premium
RR	Retention rate
S	(1) Sales
	(2) Estimated standard deviation for sample data
	(3) Intrinsic value of stock (i.e., all common equity)
Σ	Summation sign (uppercase sigma)
σ	Standard deviation (lowercase sigma)
σ^2	Variance
SML	Security Market Line
t	Time period
T	Marginal income tax rate
TIE	Times interest earned
TV_N	A stock's horizon, or terminal, value
V	Variable cost per unit
V_B	Bond value
VC	Total variable costs
V_L	Total market value of a levered firm
V_{op}	Value of operations
V_{ps}	Value of preferred stock
V_U	Total market value of an unlevered firm
w	Proportion or weight
w_d	Weight of debt
w_{ps}	Weight of preferred stock
w_s	Weight of common stock
WACC	Weighted average cost of capital
X	Exercise price of option
YTC	Yield to call
YTM	Yield to maturity

Financial Management

Theory & Practice

16e

EUGENE F. BRIGHAM
University of Florida

MICHAEL C. EHRHARDT
University of Tennessee

CENGAGE

Australia • Brazil • Canada • Mexico • Singapore • United Kingdom • United States

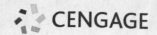

Financial Management: Theory and Practice, 16th Edition

Eugene F. Brigham and Michael C. Ehrhardt

Senior Vice President, Higher Ed Product, Content, and Market Development: Erin Joyner

VP, Product Management: Mike Schenk

Sr. Product Team Manager: Joe Sabatino

Content Manager: Christopher Valentine

Learning Designer: Brittany Waitt

Product Assistant: Renee Schnee

Marketing Manager: Christopher Walz

Marketing Coordinator: Sean Messer

Production Service: MPS Limited

Art Director: Chris Doughman

Text Designer: Ramsdell Design

Cover Designer: Chris Doughman

Cover Image: iStock.com/Gang Zhou

Intellectual Property Analyst: Reba Frederics

Intellectual Property Project Manager: Carly Belcher

For product information and technology assistance, contact us at **Cengage Customer & Sales Support, 1-800-354-9706 or support.cengage.com.**

For permission to use material from this text or product, submit all requests online at **www.cengage.com/permissions.**

Library of Congress Control Number: 2018965690

ISBN: 978-1-337-90260-1

Cengage
200 Pier 4 Boulevard
Boston, MA 02210
USA

Cengage is a leading provider of customized learning solutions with employees residing in nearly 40 different countries and sales in more than 125 countries around the world. Find your local representative at **www.cengage.com.**

To learn more about Cengage platforms and services, register or access your online learning solution, or purchase materials for your course, visit **www.cengage.com.**

Printed in Mexico
Print Number: 04   Print Year: 2022

Brief Contents

Contents

Preface

When we wrote the first edition of *Financial Management: Theory and Practice*, we had four goals: (1) to create a text that would help students make better financial decisions; (2) to provide a book that could be used in the introductory MBA course but that was complete enough for use as a reference text in follow-on case courses and after graduation; (3) to motivate students by demonstrating that finance is both interesting and relevant; and (4) to make the book clear enough so that students could go through the material without wasting either their time or their professors' time trying to figure out what we were saying. We have an additional goal for this edition: to explain and apply the 2017 Tax Cuts and Jobs Act to the topics in this book.

We accomplish our goals through the structure and material in the textbook. In addition, MindTap™ for *Financial Management* is a fully integrated online portfolio of teaching tools and learning solutions that facilitate our objectives.

Intrinsic Valuation as a Unifying Theme

Our emphasis throughout the book is on the actions that a manager can and should take to increase the intrinsic value of the firm. Structuring the book around intrinsic valuation enhances continuity and helps students see how various topics are related to one another.

As its title indicates, this book combines theory and practical applications. An understanding of finance theory is essential for anyone developing and/or implementing effective financial strategies. But theory alone isn't sufficient, so we provide numerous examples in the book and the accompanying *Excel* spreadsheets to illustrate how theory is applied in practice. Indeed, we believe that the ability to analyze financial problems using *Excel* also is essential for a student's successful job search and subsequent career. Therefore, many exhibits in the book come directly from the accompanying *Excel* spreadsheets. Many of the spreadsheets also provide brief "tutorials" by way of detailed comments on *Excel* features that we have found to be especially useful, such as Goal Seek, Tables, and many financial functions.

The book begins with fundamental concepts, including background on the economic and financial environment, financial statements (with an emphasis on cash flows), the time value of money, bond valuation, risk analysis, and stock valuation. With this background, we go on to discuss how specific techniques and decision rules can be used to help maximize the value of the firm. This organization provides four important advantages:

1. Managers should try to maximize the intrinsic value of a firm, which is determined by cash flows as revealed in financial statements. Our early coverage of financial statements helps students see how particular financial decisions affect the various parts of the firm and the resulting cash flow. Also, financial statement analysis provides an excellent vehicle for illustrating the usefulness of spreadsheets.

2. Covering the time value of money early helps students see how and why expected future cash flows determine the value of the firm. Also, it takes time for students to digest TVM concepts and to learn how to do the required calculations, so it is good to cover TVM concepts early and often.

3. Most students—even those who do not plan to major in finance—are interested in investments. The ability to learn is a function of individual interest and motivation, so *Financial Management*'s early coverage of securities and security markets is pedagogically sound.

4. Once basic concepts have been established, it is easier for students to understand both how and why corporations make specific decisions in the areas of capital budgeting, raising capital, working capital management, mergers, and the like.

Intended Market and Use

Financial Management is designed primarily for use in the introductory MBA finance course and as a reference text in follow-on case courses and after graduation. There is enough material for two terms, especially if the book is supplemented with cases and/or selected readings. The book can also be used as an undergraduate introductory text for exceptionally good students or where the introductory course is taught over two terms.

Improvements in the 16th Edition

As in every revision, we updated and clarified materials throughout the text, reviewing the entire book for completeness, ease of exposition, and currency. We made hundreds of small changes to keep the text up to date, with particular emphasis on updating the real-world examples and including the latest changes in the financial environment and financial theory. In addition, we made a number of larger changes. Some affect all chapters, some involve reorganizing sections among chapters, and some modify material covered within specific chapters.

Changes That Affect All Chapters

Following are some of the changes that affect all chapters.

THE 2017 TAX CUT AND JOBS ACT (TCJA)

This is a corporate finance book, and corporate taxes affect many topics. We have fully integrated the 2017 Tax Cut and Jobs Act (TCJA) into the text and all ancillaries.

CHANGES IN MICRODRIVE

For many editions we have used a hypothetical company, MicroDrive, as a running example. This provides continuity in the examples from chapter to chapter and helps students apply the material more quickly. When we changed MicroDrive's tax rate to reflect the TCJA, we lost many of the learning points we had built into MicroDrive. To retain those learning points after incorporating the TCJA, we had to revise several other items in MicroDrive's financial statements.

CONTINUED INTEGRATION WITH *EXCEL*

We have continued to integrate the textbook and the accompanying *Excel Tool Kit* spreadsheet models for each chapter. Many figures in the textbook show the appropriate area from the chapter's *Excel Tool Kit* model. This makes the analysis more transparent to the students and better enables them to follow the analysis in the *Excel* model.

Notable Changes within Selected Chapters

We made too many small improvements within each chapter to mention them all, but some of the more notable ones are discussed here.

CHAPTER 1: AN OVERVIEW OF FINANCIAL MANAGEMENT AND THE FINANCIAL ENVIRONMENT

We added a brief discussion of income-wealth inequality in Section 1-4b (Intrinsic Stock Value Maximization and Social Welfare). We rewrote much of Section 1-4c (Ethics and Intrinsic Stock Value Maximization), including discussion of illegal actions, alleged unethical actions, and whistleblower protections. In Section 1-6a we describe upcoming changes in the London Interbank Offering Rate (LIBOR) due to recent scandals in how it was reported. Also, we describe the Federal Reserve Board's new alternative to LIBOR, the Secured Overnight Financing Rate (SOFR).

CHAPTER 2: FINANCIAL STATEMENTS, CASH FLOW, AND TAXES

We added two new boxes. The first box, "A Matter of Opinion," highlights the leeway companies have in choosing how to present results and how that leeway complicates comparison. The second box, "Financial Statement Fraud," describes the SEC's Financial Reporting and Audit (FRAud) Group, including a recent case.

CHAPTER 4: TIME VALUE OF MONEY

We replaced the opening vignette with one focused on purchasing a car and how time value of money concepts are vital when getting an auto loan. In Section 4-17c we now show how to determine directly the remaining balance on an amortizing loan without building an entire amortization schedule. We added Section 4-17e to explain how the calculation of monthly interest expenses for many auto loans differs from that of mortgages.

CHAPTER 5: BONDS, BOND VALUATION, AND INTEREST RATES

We added a new box describing a 1648 perpetual bond, "You Can Take That to the Bank."

CHAPTER 7: CORPORATE VALUATION AND STOCK VALUATION

We added a section, 7-7d, showing how to calculate the value of operations at each year, not just at the horizon and at t = 0. We also added several new end-of-chapter problems on free cash flow valuation that will be ideal for homework assignments using the algorithmic feature in MindTap.

CHAPTER 9: THE COST OF CAPITAL

We added Section 9-3c, which discusses the difference between the yield to maturity and the expected rate of return based on projected default rates, showing that the difference between the yield and the expected rate of return is so small that it can be ignored for the vast majority of bonds. Sections 9-3d and 9-3e describe how to estimate the after-tax cost for newly issued debt that has large flotation costs.

CHAPTER 11: CASH FLOW ESTIMATION AND RISK ANALYSIS

We revised the example company so that it reflects the TCJA but retains key learning points. We added a description of bonus depreciation to Appendix 11A and used the Scenario Manager to create scenarios in the *Tool Kit* showing the impact of different depreciation methods. We also added bonus depreciation to the Mini-Case and *PowerPoint* show because it is part of the TCJA.

CHAPTER 15: CAPITAL STRUCTURE DECISIONS

We describe the impact that the TCJA's reduced corporate tax rate has on the value of the tax shield with respect to the M&M models and the Miller model. We incorporated the new tax rate into Section 15-6 and our discussion of the optimal capital structure. Due to the TCJA's lower corporate tax rate and its limitation on interest expense deductions, the optimal capital structure will have less debt than before the TCJA. We moved our discussion of bond refunding operations to the new *Web Extension 15B*.

CHAPTER 16: SUPPLY CHAINS AND WORKING CAPITAL MANAGEMENT

We added a new opening vignette focusing on the companies that are best at managing the cash conversion cycle.

CHAPTER 17: MULTINATIONAL FINANCIAL MANAGEMENT

We added a new box, "Meet Me at the Car Wash," describing international bribery by several Brazilian companies. We reorganized and rewrote much of Section 17-3, "Exchange Rates," to explicitly describe exchanges among all combinations of direct and indirect currencies. Section 17-5a, "Determinants of Floating Exchange Rates," now includes Table 17-3 showing U.S. trade balances with key trading partners.

CHAPTER 18: PUBLIC AND PRIVATE FINANCING: INITIAL OFFERINGS, SEASONED OFFERINGS, AND INVESTMENT BANKS

We expanded Section 18-1 to address carried interest, unicorns, investment firms that manage multiple venture capital funds, and publicly traded companies with divisions/subsidiaries that provide funding to start-ups.

CHAPTER 19: LEASE FINANCING

We rewrote Sections 19-2 and 19-3 to reflect the virtual elimination of off-balance sheet accounting due to Accounting Standards Update (ASU) 2016-02. We added a new section, 19-7, to explicitly address the TCJA: "Leases, Taxes, and the 2017 Tax Cuts and Jobs Act."

CHAPTER 20: HYBRID FINANCING: PREFERRED STOCK, WARRANTS, AND CONVERTIBLES

We added a new opening vignette discussing Tesla's convertible bonds, Elon Musk's tweets about going private, and the subsequent actions by the SEC and Tesla.

CHAPTER 22: MERGERS AND CORPORATE CONTROL

We reorganized and rewrote much of the chapter to better integrate changes due to the TCJA. Parts of Section 22-1, "Rationale for Mergers," now include the impact of the TCJA regarding restrictions on carry-forward losses from potential targets and limits on interest expense deductions in highly levered acquisitions. Section 22-2, "Types of Mergers," now includes a brief explanation of roll-up mergers and a new section explaining the relationship between acquisition method (exchange of stock, cash offer to purchase assets, and cash offer to purchase shares) and responsibility for any hidden liabilities. We consolidated our coverage of takeover defenses into Section 22-4b, "Hostile Takeovers." Section 22-13, "Merger Tax Treatments," explains the tax treatments of the types of mergers from Section 22-4.

Digging Deeper with *Web Extensions*

Many chapters have Adobe PDF "appendices" that provide more detailed coverage of specialized topics related to the chapter's content. For example, *Web Extension 9A* explains how to estimate the required rate of return for stocks that have nonconstant dividends and repurchases prior to the forecast horizon.

Four additional chapters are available online for those instructors wishing to cover in depth several other financial issues. For example, a detailed discussion of pension plan management is in *Web Chapter 29*.

Digital Course Solutions for Instructors and Students

MindTap is Cengage Learning's fully online, highly personalized learning experience that combines readings, assessments, multimedia, and activities into a singular Learning Path. Using MindTap, an instructor can easily organize a course that guides students through the class with ease and engagement. Instructors can personalize the Learning Path for their students by customizing the robust suite of *Financial Management's* resources and adding their own content via apps that integrate into the MindTap framework seamlessly with Learning Management Systems.

Instructors: You can access all resources by going to **www.cengage.com/login**, logging in with a faculty account username and password, and using ISBN 9781337902601 to search for and add resources to your account.

Enriching the Student Learning Experience

MindTap provides multiple learning resources that enable students to understand each chapter's concepts and financial applications.

MBA Refresher Pre-/Post-Test

These diagnostic multiple-choice questions will allow students to review specific topics within key prerequisite disciplines—finance, accounting, statistics, economics, and algebra/math—while testing skills in using *Excel* and a financial calculator. Once feedback from the pre-test is reviewed, the post-test will confirm mastery of key topics.

ConceptClips

Available in MindTap and its eBook, finance ConceptClips present fundamental key topics to students in an entertaining and memorable way via short animated video clips. Developed by Mike Brandl of The Ohio State University, these vocabulary animations provide students with a memorable auditory and visual representation of the important terminology for the course.

Excel Tool Kits

Proficiency with spreadsheets is an absolute necessity for all MBA students. With that in mind, we created *Excel* spreadsheets for each chapter, called *Tool Kits*, that calculate all numerical examples, tables, and figures. In addition to greater transparency within numerical examples, the *Tool Kits* explain in detail many of *Excel's* most useful features and functions that students will find invaluable in their courses and careers.

Excel Online

In addition to the *Excel Tool Kit* files that directly explain examples in the text, **Microsoft®** **Excel** Online activities provide students with an opportunity to work auto-gradable, algorithmic homework problems directly in their browser. Students receive instant feedback on their *Excel* work, including the "by hand" calculations and a solution file containing a recommended way of solving the problem. Students' *Excel* work is saved in real time in the cloud; is platform, device, and browser independent; and is always accessible with their homework without cumbersome file uploads and downloads. This unique integration represents a direct collaboration between Cengage and Microsoft to strengthen and support the development of Microsoft Office education skills for success in the workplace.

Blueprint Problems

Blueprint Practice Problems available in MindTap teach students finance concepts and their associated building blocks—going beyond memorization. By going through the problem step by step, they reinforce foundational concepts and allow students to demonstrate their understanding of the problem-solving process and business impact of each topic. Blueprints include rich feedback and explanations, providing students with an excellent learning resource to solidify their understanding.

Exploring Finance

Exploring Finance offers instructors and students interactive visualizations that engage with "lean forward" interactivity. Instructors can use these visual, interactive tools to help students "see" the financial concept being presented directly within MindTap.

Problem Walk-Through Videos

Nearly 260 **Problem Walk-Through** videos are embedded in the online homework. Each video walks students through solving a problem from start to finish, and students can play and replay the tutorials as they work through homework assignments or prepare for quizzes and tests, almost as though they had an instructor by their side the whole time.

Adaptive Test Prep (ATP)

Adaptive Test Prep allows students to create practice quizzes covering multiple chapters in a low-stakes environment. Students receive immediate feedback so they know where they need additional help. In addition, the questions have the same formats as those in the actual test bank, prepare students for what to expect on an exam. With many questions offered per chapter, students can create multiple unique practice quizzes within MindTap.

Classroom Activities

Many of the preceding resources provide an excellent basis for classroom discussions. In addition, each chapter has a Mini Case describing a business situation spanning the chapter's topics. Some professors choose to assign the Mini Cases as graded assignments due at the beginning of class, whereas others use the Mini Cases to provide structure for class discussions or lectures.

Mini Case *PowerPoint* Slides

Each chapter has a set of *PowerPoint* slides that present graphs, tables, lists, and calculations for use in lectures. Although the slides correspond to the Mini Cases at the end of the chapter, the slides are completely self-contained in the sense that they can be used for discussions and lectures regardless of whether students have read the Mini Cases. In fact, we often don't assign the Mini Case, but we do use the *PowerPoint* slides.

Instructors can easily customize the slides and convert them quickly into any *PowerPoint* Design Template.[1] If you add some of your own slides or modify the existing slides to better illustrate important concepts, please share your changes with us—many of our best learning points have come from instructors, and we appreciate all suggestions for ways to improve learning experiences for students.

Mini Case *Excel* Spreadsheets

In addition to the *PowerPoint* slides, we also provide *Excel* spreadsheets that perform the calculations required in the Mini Cases. These spreadsheets are similar to the **Tool Kits** but with two differences. (1) The numbers correspond to the Mini Cases rather than to the chapter examples. (2) We added some features that enable what-if analysis on a real-time basis in class.

We usually begin class with the *PowerPoint* presentation, but after we have explained a basic concept, we "toggle" to the Mini Case *Excel* file and show how the analysis can be done in *Excel*.[2] For example, when teaching bond pricing, we begin with the *PowerPoint* show and cover the basic concepts and calculations. Then we toggle to *Excel* and use a sensitivity-based graph to show how bond prices change as interest rates and time to maturity vary. We encourage students to bring their laptops to class so that they can follow along and do the what-if analysis for themselves.

Evaluating the Student Learning Experience

MindTap provides multiple resources enabling instructors to measure student learning. Some are ideal for online assignments, and others are best as hand-graded cases and exercises.

Algorithmic Homework Assignments That Are Unique to Each Student

One of our favorite MindTap features allows us to quickly create a homework assignment drawn from end-of-chapter problems and test bank problems. We usually include numerical fill-in-the-blank problems that algorithmically generate different inputs for each student.

When our primary objective is to foster learning, we enable students to check their answer for a problem before moving on to the next problem. We allow either three attempts or unlimited attempts, depending on the problem's difficulty. Sometimes we allow a problem to provide hints and feedback if the student's answer is wrong.

---

[1]To convert into a different design template in *PowerPoint* for Office 365, select Design, Theme, and choose a theme. Always double-check the conversion; some templates use fonts of different sizes, which can cause some slide titles to run over their allotted space.

[2]To toggle between two open programs, such as *Excel* and *PowerPoint*, hold the Alt key down and hit the Tab key until you have selected the program you want to show.

When our primary objective is assessment, we disable the multiple attempts feature. We always allow feedback on each question after the assignment's due date.

MindTap automatically grades the assignment and posts grades to the MindTap gradebook. MindTap can also post grades to learning management systems such as Canvas.

We assign homework early and often: Each assignment covers only several class periods and is due shortly after covering those classes. We find that this encourages students to keep up with the course, which enhances their learning experience.

Finance in Action

MindTap offers a series of Finance in Action analytical cases that assess students' ability to perform at a higher level of understanding, critical thinking, and decision making.

End-of-Chapter Spreadsheet Problems

Each chapter has a *Build a Model* problem, where students start with a spreadsheet that contains financial data plus general instructions for solving a specific problem. The *Excel* model is available in MindTap and is partially completed, with headings but no formulas—the student must literally build a model. This structure guides the student through the problem, minimizes unnecessary typing and data entry, and also makes it easy to grade the work because all students' answers are in the same locations on the spreadsheet.

The completed solutions to the *Build a Model*s are located in the Instructor Resource Center.

Cognero™ Test Bank and Testing Software

Cengage Learning Testing Powered by Cognero™ is a flexible online system that allows you to author, edit, and manage test bank content from multiple Cengage Learning solutions; create multiple test versions in an instant; deliver tests from your LMS, your classroom, or wherever you want. The Cognero™ Test Bank contains the same questions that are in the Microsoft *Word* Test Bank. All question content is now tagged according to Tier I (Business Program Interdisciplinary Learning Outcomes) and Tier II (finance-specific) standards topic, Bloom's Taxonomy, and difficulty level.

CengageCompose

More than 100 cases, written by Eugene F. Brigham, Linda Klein, and Chris Buzzard, are available via CengageCompose, Cengage Learning's online case library. These cases are in a customized case database that allows instructors to select cases and create their own customized casebooks. Most of the cases have accompanying spreadsheet models that, while not essential for working the case, do reduce number crunching and thus leave more time for students to consider conceptual issues. The models also show students how computers can be used to make better financial decisions. Cases that we have found particularly useful for the different chapters are listed in the end-of-chapter references. The cases, case solutions, and spreadsheet models can be previewed and ordered by professors at **http://compose.cengage.com.**

Cengage Learning Custom Solutions

Whether you need print, digital, or hybrid course materials, Cengage Learning Custom Solutions can help you create your perfect learning solution. Draw from Cengage Learning's extensive library of texts and collections, add your own original work, and/or create customized media and technology to match your learning and course objectives. Our editorial team will work with you through each step, allowing you to concentrate on the most important thing—your students. Learn more about all our services at **www .cengage.com/custom.**

Solutions Manual

This comprehensive manual contains worked-out solutions to all end-of-chapter questions and problems. It also includes additional explanatory notes with its answers to the end-of-chapter Mini Cases. It is available at the Instructor Resource Center.

ACKNOWLEDGMENTS

This book reflects the efforts of a great many people over a number of years. In addition to our immediate colleagues, we appreciate very much the many helpful comments and suggestions we receive from professors who use our book in their classes. Professors Greg Faulk, Anthony Gu, Andrew Mose, Chee Ng, John Stieven, and Serge Wind have been especially helpful, providing many hints and tips for improving the learning points in our textbook.

Many professors and professionals who are experts on specific topics reviewed earlier versions of individual chapters or groups of chapters, and we are grateful for their insights; in addition, we would like to thank those whose reviews and comments on earlier editions and companion books have contributed to this edition: Mike Adler, Syed Ahmad, Sadhana M. Alangar, Ed Altman, Mary Schary Amram, Anne Anderson, Bruce Anderson, Ron Anderson, Bob Angell, Vince Apilado, Henry Arnold, Nasser Arshadi, Bob Aubey, Abdul Aziz, Gil Babcock, Peter Bacon, Kent Baker, Tom Bankston, Les Barenbaum, Charles Barngrover, Michael Barry, Bill Beedles, Moshe Ben-Horim, Omar M. Benkato, Bill Beranek, Tom Berry, Bill Bertin, Roger Bey, Dalton Bigbee, John Bildersee, Rahul Bishnoi, Eric Blazer, Russ Boisjoly, Keith Boles, Gordon R. Bonner, Geof Booth, Kenneth Boudreaux, Helen Bowers, Oswald Bowlin, Don Boyd, G. Michael Boyd, Pat Boyer, Ben S. Branch, Joe Brandt, Elizabeth Brannigan, Greg Brauer, Mary Broske, Dave Brown, Kate Brown, Bill Brueggeman, Kirt Butler, Robert Button, Chris Buzzard, Bill Campsey, Bob Carleson, Severin Carlson, David Cary, Steve Celec, Don Chance, Antony Chang, Susan Chaplinsky, Jay Choi, S. K. Choudhury, Lal Chugh, Jonathan Clarke, Maclyn Clouse, Margaret Considine, Phil Cooley, Joe Copeland, David Cordell, John Cotner, Charles Cox, David Crary, John Crockett, Roy Crum, Brent Dalrymple, Bill Damon, Joel Dauten, Steve Dawson, Sankar De, Miles Delano, Fred Dellva, Anand Desai, Bernard Dill, Greg Dimkoff, Les Dlabay, Mark Dorfman, Gene Drycimski, Dean Dudley, David Durst, Ed Dyl, Dick Edelman, Charles Edwards, John Ellis, Dave Ewert, John Ezzell, Richard Fendler, Michael Ferri, Jim Filkins, John Finnerty, Susan Fischer, Mark Flannery, Steven Flint, Russ Fogler, E. Bruce Frederickson, Dan French, Tina Galloway, Partha Gangopadhyay, Phil Gardial, Michael Garlington, Sharon H. Garrison, Jim Garvin, Adam Gehr, Jim Gentry, Stuart Gillan, Philip Glasgo, Rudyard Goode, Myron Gordon, Walt Goulet, Bernie Grablowsky, Theoharry Grammatikos, Ed Grossnickle, John Groth, Alan Grunewald, Manak Gupta, Sam Hadaway, Don Hakala, Janet Hamilton, Sally Hamilton, Gerald Hamsmith, William Hardin, John Harris, Paul Hastings, Patty Hatfield, Bob Haugen, Steve Hawke, Del Hawley, Hal Heaton, Robert Hehre, John Helmuth, George Hettenhouse, Hans Heymann, Kendall Hill, Roger Hill, Tom Hindelang, Linda Hittle, Ralph Hocking, J. Ronald Hoffmeister, Jim Horrigan, John Houston, John Howe, Keith Howe, Hugh Hunter, Steve Isberg, Jim Jackson, Vahan Janjigian, Kurt Jesswein, Kose John, Craig Johnson, Keith Johnson, Steve Johnson, Ramon Johnson,

Ray Jones, Manuel Jose, Gus Kalogeras, Mike Keenan, Eric Kelley, Bill Kennedy, Joe Kiernan, Robert Kieschnick, Rick Kish, Linda Klein, Don Knight, Dorothy Koehl, Theodor Kohers, Jaroslaw Komarynsky, Duncan Kretovich, Harold Krogh, Charles Kroncke, Lynn Phillips Kugele, Joan Lamm, P. Lange, Howard Lanser, Martin Laurence, Ed Lawrence, Richard LeCompte, Wayne Lee, Jim LePage, Ilene Levin, Jules Levine, John Lewis, James T. Lindley, Chuck Linke, Bill Lloyd, Susan Long, Judy Maese, Bob Magee, Ileen Malitz, Phil Malone, Terry Maness, Chris Manning, Terry Martell, D. J. Masson, John Mathys, John McAlhany, Andy McCollough, Tom McCue, Bill McDaniel, Robin McLaughlin, Jamshid Mehran, Ilhan Meric, Larry Merville, Rick Meyer, Stuart E. Michelson, Jim Millar, Ed Miller, John Mitchell, Carol Moerdyk, Bob Moore, Hassan Moussawi, Barry Morris, Gene Morris, Fred Morrissey, Chris Muscarella, Stu Myers, David Nachman, Tim Nantell, Don Nast, Bill Nelson, Bob Nelson, Bob Niendorf, Tom O'Brien, Dennis O'Connor, John O'Donnell, Jim Olsen, Robert Olsen, Frank O'Meara, David Overbye, R. Daniel Pace, Coleen Pantalone, Jim Pappas, Stephen Parrish, Pam Peterson, Glenn Petry, Jim Pettijohn, Rich Pettit, Dick Pettway, Hugo Phillips, John Pinkerton, Gerald Pogue, Ralph A. Pope, R. Potter, Franklin Potts, R. Powell, Chris Prestopino, Jerry Prock, Howard Puckett, Herbert Quigley, George Racette, Bob Radcliffe, Allen Rappaport, Bill Rentz, Ken Riener, Charles Rini, John Ritchie, Jay Ritter, Pietra Rivoli, Fiona Robertson, Antonio Rodriguez, E. M. Roussakis, Dexter Rowell, Mike Ryngaert, Jim Sachlis, Abdul Sadik, A. Jon Saxon, Thomas Scampini, Kevin Scanlon, Frederick Schadler, James Schallheim, Mary Jane Scheuer, Carl Schweser, John Settle, Alan Severn, Sol Shalit, Elizabeth Shields, Frederic Shipley, Dilip Shome, Ron Shrieves, Neil Sicherman, J. B. Silvers, Clay Singleton, Joe Sinkey, Stacy Sirmans, Jaye Smith, Steve Smith, Don Sorenson, David Speairs, Ken Stanly, John Stansfield, Ed Stendardi, Alan Stephens, Don Stevens, Jerry Stevens, G. Bennett Stewart, Mark Stohs, Glen Strasburg, Robert Strong, Philip Swensen, Ernie Swift, Paul Swink, Eugene Swinnerton, Robert Taggart, Gary Tallman, Dennis Tanner, Craig Tapley, Russ Taussig, Richard Teweles, Ted Teweles, Andrew Thompson, Jonathan Tiemann, Sheridan Titman, George Trivoli, George Tsetsekos, Alan L. Tucker, Mel Tysseland, David Upton, Howard Van Auken, Pretorious Van den Dool, Pieter Vanderburg, Paul Vanderheiden, David Vang, Jim Verbrugge, Patrick Vincent, Steve Vinson, Susan Visscher, Joseph Vu, John Wachowicz, Mark D. Walker, Mike Walker, Sam Weaver, Kuo Chiang Wei, Bill Welch, Gary R. Wells, Fred Weston, Norm Williams, Tony Wingler, Ed Wolfe, Larry Wolken, Don Woods, Thomas Wright, Michael Yonan, Zhong-guo Zhou, David Ziebart, Dennis Zocco, and Kent Zumwalt.

Special thanks are due to Dana Clark, Susan Whitman, Amelia Bell, and Kirsten Benson, who provided invaluable editorial support; to Joel Houston and Phillip Daves, whose work with us on other books is reflected in this text; and to Lou Gapenski, our past coauthor, for his many contributions.

Our colleagues and our students at the Universities of Florida and Tennessee gave us many useful suggestions, and the Cengage staff—especially Chris Valentine, Brittany Waitt, Joe Sabatino, and Chris Walz—helped greatly with all phases of text development, production, and marketing.

Errors in the Text

At this point, authors generally say something like this: "We appreciate all the help we received from the people just listed, but any remaining errors are, of course, our own responsibility." And in many books, there are plenty of remaining errors. Having experienced difficulties with errors ourselves, both as students and as instructors, we resolved to avoid this problem in *Financial Management*. As a result of our error-detection procedures, we are convinced that the book is relatively free of mistakes.

Partly because of our confidence that few such errors remain, but primarily because we want to detect any errors in the textbook that may have slipped by so that we can correct them in subsequent printings, we decided to offer a reward of $10 per error to the first person who reports a textbook error to us. For purposes of this reward, errors in the textbook are defined as misspelled words, nonrounding numerical errors, incorrect statements, and any other error that inhibits comprehension. Typesetting problems such as irregular spacing and differences in opinion regarding grammatical or punctuation conventions do not qualify for this reward. Also, given the ever changing nature of the Internet, changes in Web addresses do not qualify as errors, although we would appreciate reports of changed Web addresses. Finally, any qualifying error that has follow-through effects is counted as two errors only. **Please report any errors to Michael C. Ehrhardt at the e-mail address shown next in the Conclusion.**

Conclusion

Finance is, in a real sense, the cornerstone of the free enterprise system. Good financial management is therefore vitally important to the economic health of business firms, hence to the nation and the world. Because of its importance, corporate finance should be thoroughly understood. However, this is easier said than done—the field is relatively complex, and it is undergoing constant change in response to shifts in economic conditions. All of this makes corporate finance stimulating and exciting but also challenging and sometimes perplexing. We sincerely hope that *Financial Management: Theory and Practice* will help readers understand and solve the financial problems businesses face today.

Michael C. Ehrhardt
University of Tennessee
Ehrhardt@utk.edu

November 2018

Eugene F. Brigham
University of Florida
Gene.Brigham@cba.ufl.edu

PART 1
The Company and Its Environment

1

An Overview of Financial Management and the Financial Environment

WWW

See http://fortune.com/worlds-most-admired-companies *for updates on the rankings.*

In a global beauty contest for companies, the winner is . . . Apple.

Or at least Apple is the most admired company in the world, according to *Fortune* magazine's annual survey. The others in the global top ten are Amazon.com, Starbucks, Berkshire Hathaway, Disney, Alphabet (formerly Google), General Electric, Southwest Airlines, Facebook, and Microsoft. What do these companies have that separates them from the rest of the pack?

Based on a survey of executives, directors, and security analysts, these companies have very high average scores across nine attributes: (1) innovativeness, (2) quality of management, (3) long-term investment value, (4) social responsibility, (5) people management, (6) quality of products and services, (7) financial soundness, (8) use of corporate assets, and (9) effectiveness in doing business globally. After culling weaker companies, the final rankings are then determined by over 3,800 experts from a wide variety of industries.

What makes these companies special? In a nutshell, they reduce costs by having innovative production processes, they create value for customers by providing high-quality products and services, and they create value for employees by training and fostering an environment that allows employees to utilize all of their skills and talents. As you will see throughout this book, the resulting cash flow and superior return on capital also create value for investors.

This chapter should give you an idea of what financial management is all about, including an overview of the financial markets in which corporations operate. Before going into details, let's look at the big picture.

1-1 The Five-Minute MBA

Okay, we realize you can't get an MBA in five minutes, but we can sketch the key elements of an MBA education. The primary objective of an MBA program is to provide managers with the knowledge and skills they need to run successful companies, so we start there.

First, *successful companies have skilled people* at all levels inside the company, including leaders, managers, and a capable workforce. Skilled people enable a company to identify, create, and deliver products or services that are highly valued by customers—so highly valued that customers choose to purchase from them rather than from their competitors.

Second, *successful companies have strong relationships* with groups outside the company. For example, successful companies develop win–win relationships with suppliers and excel in customer relationship management.

Third, *successful companies have enough funding* to execute their plans and support their growing operations. Companies can reinvest a portion of their earnings, but most growing companies also must raise additional funds externally by some combination of selling stock and/or borrowing in the financial markets. To do this, a company must provide investors with high enough returns to compensate them for the use of their money and their exposure to risk.

To help your company succeed, you must have the skills necessary to evaluate any proposal or idea, whether it relates to marketing, supply chains, production, strategy, mergers, or any other area. In a nutshell, that is what we will do in this book.

SELF-TEST

What are three attributes of successful companies?

What financial skills must every successful manager have?

1-2 Finance from 40,000 Feet Above

A bird's-eye view showing the big picture of finance will help you keep track of its individual components. It all starts with individuals or organizations that have more cash than they presently want to spend (i.e., providers of cash now) and others with opportunities to generate cash in the future (i.e., users of cash now). For example, providers of cash include individuals who are saving for retirement, banks willing to make loans, and many other types of investors. Users of cash include: (1) students wishing to borrow money for tuition and planning to repay it with future earnings after graduating, (2) entrepreneurs with ideas, and (3) corporations with growth plans.

Figure 1-1 shows the relationship between providers and users.

Two problems immediately present themselves. First, how do the providers and users identify one another and exchange cash now for claims on risky future cash? Second, how can potential providers evaluate the users' opportunities? In other words, are the claims on risky future cash flows sufficient to compensate the providers for giving up their cash today? At the risk of oversimplification, **financial markets** are simply ways of connecting providers with users, and **financial analysis** is a tool to evaluate risky opportunities.

FIGURE 1-1
Providers and Users: Cash Now versus Claims on Risky Future Cash

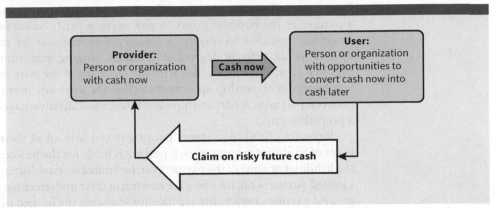

We cover many topics in this book, and it can be easy to miss the forest for the trees. As you read about a particular topic, think about how the topic is related to the role played by financial markets or the tools used to evaluate claims on future cash flows.

We begin with an especially important type of user: companies that are incorporated.

SELF-TEST

What do providers supply? What do providers receive?

What do users receive? What do users offer?

What two problems are faced by providers and users?

1-3 The Corporate Life Cycle

Apple began life in a garage, and Facebook started in a dorm room. How is it possible for such companies to grow into the giants we see today? The following sections describe some typical stages in the corporate life cycle.

1-3a Starting Up as a Proprietorship

Many companies begin as a **proprietorship**, which is an unincorporated business owned by one individual. Starting a business as a proprietor is easy—obtain any required city or state business licenses and begin business operations. The proprietorship has three important advantages: (1) It is easy and inexpensive to start. (2) Relatively few government regulations affect it. (3) It pays no corporate income tax on profits—instead, they are included in the proprietor's personal taxable income.

However, the proprietorship also has three important limitations: (1) It may be difficult for a proprietorship to obtain the funding needed for growth. (2) The proprietor has unlimited personal liability for the business's debts, which can result in losses that exceed the money invested in the company. (Creditors may even be able to seize a proprietor's house or other personal property!) (3) The life of a proprietorship is limited to the life of its founder. Therefore, usually only small businesses operate as sole proprietorships. In fact, about 73% of all companies are proprietorships, accounting for less than 5% of all sales revenue.

1-3b More Than One Owner: A Partnership

Some companies start with more than one owner, and some proprietors decide to add a partner as the business grows. A **partnership** exists whenever two or more persons or entities associate to conduct a noncorporate business for profit. Partnerships may operate under different degrees of formality, ranging from informal, oral understandings to formal agreements filed with the secretary of the state in which the partnership was formed. Partnership agreements define the ways any profits and losses are shared between partners. A partnership's advantages and disadvantages are similar to those of a proprietorship.

Regarding liability, partners potentially can lose all of their personal assets in the event of bankruptcy because each partner is liable for the business's debts. To avoid this, the liabilities of some of the partners can be limited by establishing a **limited partnership**. **Limited partners** can lose only the amount of their investment in the partnership, but the **general partners** have unlimited liability. However, the limited partners typically have no control—which rests solely with the general partners—and their returns are likewise limited. Limited partnerships are common in real estate, oil, equipment-leasing ventures, and venture capital. However, they are not widely used in other businesses because usually no partner is willing to be the general partner due to the risk, and no partners are willing to be limited partners with no control.

In regular and limited partnerships, at least one partner is liable for the partnership's debts. However, in a **limited liability partnership (LLP)** and a **limited liability company (LLC)**, all partners' (or members') potential losses are limited to their investment in the LLP. Of course, this arrangement increases the risk faced by an LLP's lenders, customers, and suppliers.

1-3c Many Owners: A Corporation

Most partnerships have difficulty attracting substantial amounts of capital to support growth. Thus, many growth companies begin as a proprietorship or partnership but subsequently convert to a corporation. Other companies, in anticipation of growth, actually begin as corporations.

A **corporation** is a legal entity created under state laws, and it is separate and distinct from its owners and managers. This separation gives the corporation three major advantages: (1) *unlimited life*—a corporation can continue after its original owners and managers are deceased; (2) *easy transfers of ownership interests*—ownership is divided into shares of stock, which can be transferred far more easily than ownership in a proprietorship or partnership; and (3) *limited liability*—losses are limited to the actual funds invested.

To illustrate limited liability, suppose you invested $10,000 in a partnership that then went bankrupt and owed $1 million. Because partners are liable, you could be held liable for the entire $1 million if your partners could not pay their shares. However, if you invested $10,000 in a corporation's stock, your potential loss in a bankruptcy would be limited to your $10,000 investment.

Unlimited life, easy transfers of ownership, and limited liability make it much easier for corporations to raise money in the financial markets and grow into large companies. Although the corporate form offers significant advantages relative to proprietorships and partnerships, it has two disadvantages: (1) Corporate earnings may be subject to double taxation—the earnings of the corporation are taxed at the corporate level, and then earnings paid out as dividends are taxed again as income to the stockholders. (2) Setting up a corporation involves preparing a charter, writing a set of bylaws, and filing the many required state and federal reports, which is more complex and time-consuming than creating a proprietorship or a partnership.

The **charter** includes the following information: (1) name of the proposed corporation, (2) types of activities it will pursue, (3) amount of capital stock, (4) number of directors, and (5) names and addresses of directors. The charter is filed with the secretary of the state in which the firm will be incorporated, and when it is approved, the corporation is officially in existence.[1] After the corporation begins operating, quarterly and annual employment, financial, and tax reports must be filed with state and federal authorities.

The **bylaws** are a set of rules drawn up by the founders of the corporation. Bylaws specify: (1) how directors are to be elected (all elected each year or perhaps one-third each year for 3-year terms), (2) whether the existing stockholders will have the first right to buy any new shares the firm issues, and (3) procedures for changing the bylaws themselves, should conditions require it.

There are several different types of corporations. Professionals such as doctors, lawyers, and accountants often form a **professional corporation (PC)** or a **professional association (PA)**. These types of corporations do not relieve the participants of professional (malpractice) liability. Indeed, the primary motivation behind the professional corporation was to provide a way for groups of professionals to avoid certain types of unlimited liability yet still be held responsible for professional liability.

Finally, some corporations can elect to be taxed as if the business were a proprietorship or partnership if the corporation meets certain requirements regarding size and number of stockholders. Such firms are called **S corporations**.

1-3d Growing a Corporation: Going Public

After a company incorporates, how does it evolve? When entrepreneurs start a company, they usually provide all the financing from their personal resources, which may include savings, home equity loans, or even credit cards. A fast-growing business must continue to invest in buildings, equipment, technology, and employees. Such investments usually deplete the founders' resources, so they turn to external financing. Many young companies are too risky for banks, so the founders must sell stock to outsiders, including friends, family, private investors (often called "angels"), or venture capitalists.

WWW

For updates on IPO activity, see **www .renaissancecapital .com/IPO-Center.** *Also, see Professor Jay Ritter's Web site for additional IPO data and analysis,* **https:// site.warrington.ufl.edu /ritter/ipo-data/.**

Any corporation can raise funds by selling shares of its stock, but government regulations restrict the number and type of investors who can buy the stock. Also, the shareholders cannot subsequently sell their stock to the general public. Due to these limitations, the shares are called **closely held stock** and the company is a **closely held corporation.**

As it continues to grow, a thriving private corporation may decide to seek approval from the **Securities and Exchange Commission (SEC)**, which regulates stock trading, to sell shares in a public stock market.[2] It does so by filing a **prospectus** with the SEC, which provides relevant information about the company to investors and regulators. In addition to SEC approval, the company applies to be a **listed stock** on

---

[1]About 64% of major U.S. corporations are chartered in Delaware, which has, over the years, provided a favorable legal environment for corporations. It is not necessary for a firm to be headquartered or even to conduct operations in its state of incorporation or even in its country of incorporation.

[2]The SEC is a government agency created in 1934 to regulate matters related to investors, including the regulation of stock markets.

an SEC-registered stock exchange. For example, the company might list on the **New York Stock Exchange (NYSE)**, which is the oldest registered stock exchange in the United States and is the largest exchange in the world when measured by the market value of its listed stocks. Or perhaps the company might list on the **NASDAQ Stock Market**, which has the most stock listings, especially among smaller, high-tech companies.

Going public is called an **initial public offering (IPO)** because it is the first time the company's shares are sold to the general public. In most cases, an **investment bank**, such as Goldman Sachs, helps with the IPO by advising the company. In addition, the investment bank's company usually has a **brokerage firm**, which employs **brokers** who are registered with the SEC to buy and sell stocks on behalf of clients.[3] These brokers help the investment banker sell the newly issued stock to investors.

Most IPOs raise proceeds in the range of $90 million to $140 million. However, some IPOs are huge, such as the $21.7 billion raised by Alibaba when it went public on the NYSE in 2014. Not only does an IPO raise additional cash to support a company's growth, but the IPO also makes it possible for the company's founders and investors to sell some of their own shares, either in the IPO itself or afterward as shares are traded in the stock market. For example, in Facebook's 2012 IPO, the company raised about $6.4 billion by selling 180 million new shares, and the owners received almost $9.2 billion by selling 241 million of their own shares.

Most IPOs are underpriced when they are first sold to the public, based on the initial price paid by IPO investors and the closing price at the end of the first day's trading. For example, in 2017 the average first-day return was around 15%.

Even if you are able to identify a "hot" issue, it is often difficult to purchase shares in the initial offering. In strong markets, these deals generally are oversubscribed, which means that the demand for shares at the offering price exceeds the number of shares issued. In such instances, investment bankers favor large institutional investors (who are their best customers), and small investors find it hard, if not impossible, to get in on the ground floor. They can buy the stock in the aftermarket, but evidence suggests that if you do not get in on the ground floor, the average IPO underperforms the overall market over the long run.[4]

Before you conclude that it isn't fair to let only the best customers have the stock in an initial offering, think about what it takes to become a best customer. Best customers are usually investors who have done lots of business in the past with the investment banking firm's brokerage department. In other words, they have paid large sums as commissions in the past, and they are expected to continue doing so in the future. As is so often true, there is no free lunch—most of the investors who get in on the ground floor of an IPO have, in fact, paid for this privilege.

After the IPO, it is easier for a public firm to raise additional funds to support growth than it is for a private company. For example, a public company raises more funds by selling (i.e., issuing) additional shares of stock through a **seasoned equity offering**, which is much simpler than the original IPO. In addition, publicly traded companies also have better access to the debt markets and can raise additional funds by selling bonds.

---

[3]For example, stockbrokers must register with the **Financial Industry Regulatory Authority (FINRA)**, a nongovernment organization that watches over brokerage firms and brokers. FINRA is the biggest, but there are other self-regulatory organizations (SROs). Be aware that not all self-advertised "investment advisors" are actually registered stockbrokers.

[4]See Jay R. Ritter, "The Long-Run Performance of Initial Public Offerings," *Journal of Finance*, March 1991, pp. 3–27.

1-3e Managing a Corporation's Value

How can managers affect a corporation's value? To answer this question, we first need to ask, "What determines a corporation's value?" In a nutshell, it is *a company's ability to generate cash flows now and in the future.*

In particular, a company's value is determined by three properties of its cash flows: (1) The *size* of the expected future cash flows is important—bigger is better. (2) The *timing* of cash flows counts—cash received sooner is more valuable than cash that comes later. (3) The *risk* of the cash flows matters—safer cash flows are worth more than uncertain cash flows. Therefore, managers can increase their firm's value by increasing the size of the expected cash flows, by speeding up their receipt, and by reducing their risk.

The relevant cash flow is called **free cash flow (FCF)**, not because it is free, but because it is available (or free) for distribution to a company's investors, including creditors and stockholders. You will learn how to calculate free cash flows in Chapter 2, but for now you should know that free cash flow is:

$$\text{FCF} = \frac{\text{Sales}}{\text{revenues}} - \frac{\text{Operating}}{\text{costs}} - \frac{\text{Operating}}{\text{taxes}} - \frac{\text{Required investments}}{\text{in new operating capital}}$$

A company's value depends on its ability to generate free cash flows, but a company must spend money to make money. For example, cash must be spent on R&D, marketing research, land, buildings, equipment, employee training, and many other activities before the subsequent cash flows become positive. Where do companies get this cash? For start-ups, it comes directly from investors. For mature companies, some of it comes directly from new investors, and some comes indirectly from current shareholders when profit is reinvested rather than paid out as dividends. As stated previously, these cash providers expect a rate of return to compensate them for the timing and risk inherent in their claims on future cash flows. This rate of return from an investor's perspective is a cost from the company's point of view. Therefore, the rate of return required by investors is called the **weighted average cost of capital (WACC).**

The following equation defines the relationship between a firm's value, its free cash flows, and its cost of capital:

$$\text{Value} = \frac{\text{FCF}_1}{(1 + \text{WACC})^1} + \frac{\text{FCF}_2}{(1 + \text{WACC})^2} + \frac{\text{FCF}_3}{(1 + \text{WACC})^3} + \cdots + \frac{\text{FCF}_\infty}{(1 + \text{WACC})^\infty} \quad \text{(1-1)}$$

We will explain how to use this equation in later chapters, but for now it is enough to understand that a company's value is determined by the size, timing, and risk of its expected future free cash flows.

If the expected future free cash flows and the cost of capital incorporate all relevant information, then the value defined in Equation 1-1 is called the **intrinsic value**; it is also called the **fundamental value**. If investors have all the relevant information, the **market price**, which is the price that we observe in the financial markets, should be equal to the intrinsic value. Whether or not investors have the relevant information depends on the quality and transparency of financial reporting for the company and for the financial markets. This is an important issue that we will address throughout the book.

1-4 Governing a Corporation

For proprietorships, partnerships, and small corporations, the firm's owners determine strategy and manage day-to-day operations. This is usually not true for a large corporation, which often has many different shareholders who each own a small proportion of the total number of shares. These diffuse shareholders elect directors, who then hire senior executives, who then hire other managers to run the corporation on a day-to-day basis. These **insiders** are elected or hired to work on behalf of the shareholders, but what is to prevent them from acting in their own best interests? This is called an **agency problem** because managers are hired as agents to act on behalf of the owners. Agency problems can be addressed by a company's **corporate governance**, which is the set of rules that control the company's behavior toward its directors, managers, employees, shareholders, creditors, customers, competitors, and community. We will have much more to say about agency problems and corporate governance throughout the book, especially in Chapters 13, 14, and 15.

It is one thing to say that managers should act on behalf of owners, but how can managers put this into practice?

1-4a The Primary Objective of a Corporation: Maximizing Stockholder Wealth

A company's decisions matter to many different **stakeholders**, such as shareholders, employees, local communities, and others who are affected by the company's environmental impact. How should managers address and prioritize stakeholders' different concerns?

First, managers are entrusted with shareholders' property and should be good stewards of this property. Second, good stewardship implies that managers should seek to increase the entrusted property's value. In other words, the primary goal of the corporation should be to maximize stockholder wealth unless the company's charter states differently. This does *not* mean that managers should break laws or violate ethical considerations. This does *not* mean that managers should be unmindful of employee welfare or community concerns. But it does mean that managers should seek to maximize stockholder wealth.

In fact, maximizing shareholder wealth is a fiduciary duty for most U.S. corporations. If companies fail in this duty, they can be sued by shareholders. For example, suppose several different companies make simultaneous offers to acquire a target company. The target's board of directors probably will be sued by shareholders if they don't vote in favor of the highest offer, even if the takeover means that the directors will lose their jobs. Companies can even be sued for maintaining social initiatives (such as purchasing environmentally friendly or locally sourced supplies at higher costs than equivalent imports) if shareholders believe they are too costly to the company.

The situation is different for many non-U.S. companies. For example, many European companies' boards have directors who specifically represent the interests of employees and not just shareholders. Many other international companies have government representatives on their boards or are even completely owned by a government. Such companies obviously represent interests other than shareholders.

In a recent development, some U.S. corporations are choosing a new corporate form called a **benefit corporation (B-corp)**, which expands directors' fiduciary responsibilities to include interests other than shareholders' interests (see the box "Be Nice with a B-Corp").

1-4b Intrinsic Stock Value Maximization and Social Welfare

If a firm attempts to maximize its intrinsic stock value, is this good or bad for society? In general, it is good. Aside from illegal actions such as making or taking bribes, fraudulent accounting, exploiting monopoly power, violating safety codes, or failing to meet environmental standards, *the same actions that maximize intrinsic stock values usually benefit society.*

Be Nice with a B-Corp

In 2010, Maryland became the first state to allow a company, The Big Bad Woof, to be chartered as a benefit corporation (B-corp). As of early 2015, there were more than 1,000 B-corps in 27 states, with legislation pending in 14 other states. B-corps are similar to regular for-profit corporations but have charters that include mandates to benefit the environment and society even if this might not maximize shareholder wealth. For example, The Big Bad Woof, which sells products for companion pets, seeks to purchase merchandise from small, local, minority-owned businesses even if their prices are a bit higher.

B-corps are required to report their progress in meeting the charters' objectives. Many self-report, but some choose to be certified by an independent third party, in much the same way that an independent accounting firm certifies a company's financial statements.

Why would a company become a B-corp? Patagonia founder Yvon Chouinard said, "Benefit corporation legislation creates the legal framework to enable mission-driven companies like Patagonia to stay mission-driven through succession, capital raises, and even changes in ownership, by institutionalizing the values, culture, processes, and high standards put in place by founding entrepreneurs."[a]

Does being a B-corp help or hurt a company's value? Advocates argue that customers will be more loyal and that employees will be prouder, more motivated, and more productive, which will lead to higher free cash flows and greater value. Critics counter that a B-corp will find it difficult to raise cash from additional investors because maximizing shareholder wealth isn't its only objective.

There isn't yet enough data to draw a conclusion, but it will be interesting to see whether B-corps ultimately produce a kinder, gentler form of capitalism.

Note: [a]See **www.patagonia.com/us/patagonia.go?assetid=68413**.

W W W

The Federal Reserve Board conducts surveys of consumer finances every three years. For updates, go to **https://www .federalreserve.gov /econres/scfindex.htm.**

ORDINARY CITIZENS AND THE STOCK MARKET

About 52% of U.S. households own stock, either directly or indirectly through mutual funds or retirement plans. Therefore, when a manager takes actions to maximize intrinsic value, this increases wealth and quality of life for millions of citizens.

Note that about 48% of households *don't directly* benefit from higher stock prices. Even for the stock-owning households, most of the wealth accrues to the rich: (1) 1% of stock-owning households own about 39% of the wealth, (2) the next 9% own about 38%, and (3) the bottom 90% own about 23% (a substantial decrease from the bottom group's 33% share in 1989). If you ask someone whether wealth and income inequality are good or bad for our country, the answer probably depends on the person's political views.

EMPLOYEES AT VALUE-MAXIMIZING COMPANIES

Sometimes a company's stock price increases when it announces plans to lay off employees, but viewed over time, this is the exception rather than the rule. In general, companies that successfully increase stock prices also grow and add more employees, thus benefiting society. Note, too, that many governments across the world, including U.S. federal and state governments, are privatizing some of their state-owned activities by selling these operations to investors. Perhaps not surprisingly, the sales and cash flows of recently privatized companies generally improve. Moreover, studies show that newly privatized companies tend to grow and thus require more employees when they are managed with the goal of stock price maximization.

CONSUMERS AND COMPETITIVE MARKETS

Value maximization requires efficient, low-cost businesses that produce high-quality goods and services at the lowest possible cost. This means that companies must develop products and services that consumers want and need, which leads to new technology and new products. Also, companies that maximize their stock price must generate growth in sales by creating value for customers in the form of efficient and courteous service, adequate stocks of merchandise, and well-located business establishments. Therefore, consumers benefit in competitive markets when companies maximize intrinsic value.

1-4c Ethics and Intrinsic Stock Value Maximization

A firm's commitment to business ethics can be measured by the tendency of its employees, from the top down, to adhere to laws and regulations. But ethical behavior also includes a commitment to (1) appropriate use of confidential information (i.e., not for personal gain), (2) attention to product safety and quality, (3) fair employment practices, (4) fair marketing and selling practices, and (5) community involvement.

The intrinsic value of a company ultimately depends on all of its expected future cash flows, and making a substantive change requires hard work to increase sales, cut costs, or reduce capital requirements. There are very few, if any, *legal and ethical* shortcuts to making significant improvements in the stream of future cash flows, as illustrated by the following examples.

ILLEGAL ACTIONS

Unfortunately, managers at some companies have taken illegal actions to make intrinsic values seem much higher than warranted. For example, ForceField Energy Inc. claimed to be a wholesale distributor of efficient LED lighting products. However, its Chairman of the Board, Richard St. Julien, was arrested in 2015 on charges of security fraud.

Nine others, including brokers and fund managers, were charged in 2016 for taking kickbacks from ForceField in exchange for encouraging investors to purchase the stock even though they knew that the company was in dire financial straits. St. Julien pled guilty and cooperated with investigators in exchange for the possibility of a sentence of less than 40 years. As of mid-2018, five of the others have been sentenced to prison and four have pled guilty. The perpetrators are being punished, but that doesn't restore the $130 million lost by shareholders.

ALLEGED UNETHICAL ACTIONS

Other companies have been accused of unethical actions. For example, Mylan N.V. purchased exclusive rights in 2007 to sell EpiPens, which deliver a dose of epinephrine to reduce the impact of a sudden dangerous allergic reaction. Mylan subsequently increased the price 17 times from $100 per pair to $600 by May 2016. In late August 2016, Mylan was selling about $1 billion in EpiPens and its stock was trading close to $50 per share. However, the steep price increases had touched off outrage from parents and the news media. By fall of 2017, Mylan's stock price had fallen to about $32, a 36% decline. Part of that decline was due to (1) reputational damage, (2) lower revenues because Mylan introduced a generic version of the EpiPen (at $300 per pair), (3) a $467 million settlement with the Justice Department to resolve claims that Mylan had misclassified the EpiPen to avoid paying rebates to Medicaid, and (4) a still unresolved (as of early 2018) class action lawsuit alleging racketeering. As this example shows, even alleged unethical behavior can significantly reduce a company's value.

WHISTLEBLOWER PROTECTIONS

Most illegal or unethical schemes are difficult to hide completely from all other employees. But an employee who believes a company is not adhering to a law or regulation might be hesitant to report it for fear of being fired or otherwise punished by the company. To help address this problem, federal and state governments have created a variety of whistleblower protection programs corresponding to different types of corporate misdeeds.

With respect to financial misdeeds, the Sarbanes-Oxley (SOX) Act of 2002 and the Dodd-Frank Wall Street Reform and Consumer Protection Act of 2010 strengthened protection for whistleblowers who report financial wrongdoing. Under SOX, employees who report corporate financial wrongdoing and subsequently are penalized by the company can ask the Occupational Safety and Health Administration (OSHA) to investigate the situation. If the employee was improperly penalized, the company can be required to reinstate the person, along with back pay and a sizable penalty award. In addition, SOX made it a criminal act for a CEO or CFO to knowingly falsely certify a company's financial position.

WWW

For current information from OSHA, see **www** **.osha.gov/index.html** *and search for "whistleblower investigation data."*

Have these provisions in SOX been successful? There were 202 SOX-related employee complaints in 2017. Only 23% were settled in the employee's favor—the others were withdrawn, dismissed, or kicked out by OSHA. No executives have been jailed for falsely certifying financial statements, even though a significant number of executives have lost their jobs due to their companies' financial misreporting.

The Dodd-Frank Act's establishment of the SEC Office of the Whistleblower has led to dozens of announced awards for reporting wrongdoing by financial firms. In 2017, 13 whistleblowers received a total of $43 million, with one of them receiving $20 million. The awards can be very large because they are based on a percentage of the amount that the SEC fines the wrongdoing corporation. The largest award to an individual was $33 million in 2018.

Taxes and Whistleblowing

The Internal Revenue Service (IRS) has a program to reward whistleblowers for information leading to the recovery of unpaid taxes, and sometimes the rewards are huge. The largest reward was $104 million to Bradley C. Birkenfeld, who discovered schemes that UBS, a large Swiss bank, was using to help its clients avoid U.S. taxes. UBS settled with the U.S. Department of Justice in 2009 by paying $780 million in fines and providing account information for over 4,000 U.S. clients to the IRS. This caused thousands of additional U.S. taxpayers to fear similar exposure and to enter an IRS amnesty program, leading to over $5 billion in collections of unpaid taxes.

Despite the record-setting payout, Birkenfeld and the U.S. government do not have an amicable relationship. The government alleged that Birkenfeld learned about the UBS tax evasion schemes while using them to shelter one of his own clients from taxes. Birkenfeld refused to divulge information about this client during the investigation, so the United States convicted him of fraud. Birkenfeld served 30 months in a medium-security federal prison but still received the $104 million reward.

How much is freedom worth? About $115,000 per day, based on Birkenfeld's reward and prison time served.

Although not a substitute for high individual moral standards, it appears that large and visible rewards to whistleblowers help ethical employees rein in actions being considered by less ethical employees. This leads to less financial misreporting, which in turn helps keep market prices in line with intrinsic value.

SELF-TEST

What is an agency problem? What is corporate governance?

What is the fiduciary duty (i.e., the primary goal) for most U.S. corporations?

How does a benefit corporation's charter differ from that of a typical U.S. corporation?

Explain how individuals, customers, and employees can benefit when a company seeks to maximize its intrinsic value.

What is a whistleblower?

Compare the Sarbanes-Oxley (SOX) Act of 2002 and the Dodd-Frank Wall Street Reform and Consumer Protection Act of 2010 with respect to their impact on whistleblowing.

1-5 An Overview of Financial Markets

At the risk of oversimplification, we can classify providers and users of cash into four groups: individuals, financial organizations (like banks and insurance companies), nonfinancial organizations (like Apple, Starbucks, and Ford), and governments. The following sections explain how these groups interact to allocate capital from providers to users.

1-5a The Net Providers and Users of Capital

In spite of William Shakespeare's advice, most individuals and firms are both borrowers and lenders. For example, an individual might borrow money by having a car loan but might also lend money by having a bank savings account. In the aggregate, however, *individuals are net providers (i.e., savers)* of most funds ultimately used by nonfinancial corporations. In fact, individuals provide a net amount of about $62 *trillion* to users.

Although most nonfinancial corporations own some financial securities, such as short-term Treasury bills, *nonfinancial corporations are net users (i.e., borrowers)* in the aggregate.

In the United States, federal, state, and local *governments are also net users (i.e., borrowers)* in the aggregate, although many foreign governments, such as those of China and oil-producing countries, are actually net providers.

WWW

For current information, see the Federal Reserve Bank of St. Louis's FRED® Economic Data. Take the total financial assets of households (and nonprofit organizations serving households), found at https://fred.stlouisfed .org/series/TFAABSHNO. Then subtract the financial liabilities, found at https://fred .stlouisfed.org/series /TLBSHNO.

Banks and other financial corporations raise money with one hand and invest it with the other. For example, a bank might raise money from individuals in the form of savings accounts and then lend most of that money to business customers. In the aggregate, *financial corporations are net users (i.e., borrowers)* by a slight amount.

1-5b Getting Cash from Providers to Users: The Capital Allocation Process

Because users invest the cash received from providers, it is called "capital." Transfers of capital from providers to users take place in three different ways. Direct transfers of money and securities, as shown in Panel A of Figure 1-2, occur when a business (or government) sells its securities directly to providers. Providers purchase the securities with cash and the business delivers the securities to the providers. For example, a privately held company might sell shares of stock directly to a new shareholder, or the U.S. government might sell a Treasury bond directly to an individual investor.

As shown in Panel B, indirect transfers may go through an investment bank, which *underwrites* the issue. An underwriter serves as a middleman and facilitates the issuance of securities. The company sells its stocks or bonds to the investment bank, which in turn sells these same securities to savers. Because new securities are involved and the corporation receives the proceeds of the sale, this is a "primary" market transaction.

Transfers also can be made through a **financial intermediary** such as a bank or mutual fund, as shown in Panel C. The intermediary obtains funds from providers in exchange for its own securities or ownership of savings accounts. The intermediary then uses this money to purchase the business's securities. For example, an individual might provide dollars to a bank and receive a certificate of deposit; the bank then might lend to a small business, receiving in exchange a legal document from the borrower promising to repay the loan. Thus, intermediaries literally create new types of securities.

There are three important features of the capital allocation process. First, new financial securities are created. Second, different types of financial institutions often act as intermediaries

FIGURE 1-2
Diagram of the Capital Allocation Process

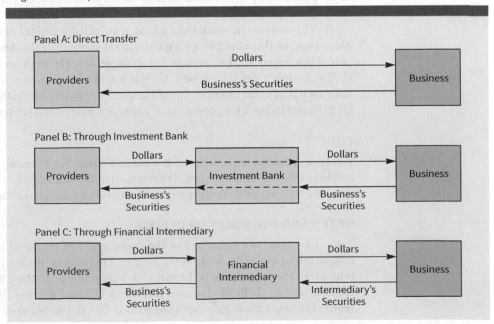

between providers and users. Third, the activities occur in a variety of financial markets. The following sections describe each of these topics, beginning with financial securities.

SELF-TEST

What are the four major groups of providers and users? For each group, state whether it is a net provider or a net user.

Identify three ways that capital is transferred between savers and borrowers.

Distinguish between the roles played by investment banks and financial intermediaries in exchanging cash now for claims on future cash.

1-6 Claims on Future Cash Flows: Types of Financial Securities

Any claim on a future cash flow is called a **financial instrument**. Providers exchange cash for a financial instrument only if they expect an acceptable rate of return. We begin with an overview of financial instruments and then discuss expected returns.

1-6a Type of Claim on Future Cash Flows: Debt and Equity

A **financial security** is a claim that is standardized and regulated by the government (the legal definition is a bit longer). The variety of financial securities is limited only by human creativity, ingenuity, and governmental regulations. At the risk of oversimplification, we can classify most financial securities by the type of claim and the time until maturity.

DEBT

Financial securities are simply documents with contractual provisions that entitle their owners to specific rights and claims on specific cash flows or values. Debt instruments typically have specified payments and a specified maturity. For example, an Alcoa bond might promise to pay $30 semiannually for 30 years, at which time it promises to make a $1,000 principal payment.

If debt matures in more than a year, it is called a *capital market security*. Thus, the Alcoa bond in this example is a capital market security. If the debt matures in less than a year, it is a *money market security*. For example, Google might expect to receive $200,000 in 75 days, but it needs cash now. Google might issue commercial paper, which is essentially an IOU. In this example, Google might agree to pay $200,000 in 75 days in exchange for $199,200 today. Thus, commercial paper is a money market security.

EQUITY

Equity instruments are a claim upon a residual value. For example, Alcoa's stockholders are entitled to the cash flows generated by Alcoa after its bondholders, creditors, and other claimants have been satisfied. Because stock has no maturity date, it is a capital market security.

RATES AND MATURITY OF CLAIMS

Table 1-1 provides a summary of the major types of financial instruments, including risk, original maturity, and rate of return. Three rates of return are especially important. First, the **prime rate** is the rate U.S. banks charge to their most creditworthy customers. Second, **LIBOR** (London Interbank Offered Rate) is the rate that U.K. banks report for loans made to other U.K. banks. Third, the **Secured Overnight Financing**

Rate (SOFR) was introduced by the U.S. Federal Reserve and began trading on April 2, 2018. The SOFR is based on actual overnight loans that use Treasury securities as collateral. The first two rates are important because many financial instruments have returns based on these rates. For example, the rate on a loan might be specified as LIBOR + 2%. Although many loans are tied to LIBOR, the U.K. authority responsible for regulating LIBOR announced in 2016 that it would cease to regulate LIBOR at the end of 2021. As a potential replacement, the U.S. Federal Reserve created the third rate, SOFR, which the Fed began publishing in April, 2018.[5]

TABLE 1-1
Summary of Major Financial Instruments

Instrument	Major Participants	Risk	Original Maturity	Rates of Return on April 4, 2018
U.S. Treasury bills	Sold by U.S. Treasury	Default-free	91 days to 1 year	1.68%
Commercial paper	Issued by financially secure firms to large investors	Low default risk	Up to 270 days	1.90%
Money market mutual funds	Invested in short-term debt; held by individuals and businesses	Low degree of risk	No specific maturity (instant liquidity)	1.72%
Commercial loans	Loans by banks to corporations	Depends on borrower	Up to 7 years	Tied to prime rate (4.75%) or LIBOR (2.31%)
U.S. Treasury notes and bonds	Issued by U.S. government	No default risk, but price falls if interest rates rise	2 to 30 years	2.30% to 3.07%
Mortgages	Loans secured by property	Risk is variable	Up to 30 years	4.4%
Municipal bonds	Issued by state and local governments to individuals and institutions	Riskier than U.S. government bonds, but exempt from most taxes	Up to 30 years	3.01%
Corporate bonds	Issued by corporations to individuals and institutions	Riskier than U.S. government debt; depends on strength of issuer	Up to 40 years (although a few go up to 100 years)	4.64%
Preferred stocks	Issued by corporations to individuals and institutions	Riskier than corporate bonds	Unlimited	4% to 9%
Common stocks	Issued by corporations to individuals and institutions	Riskier than preferred stocks	Unlimited	8% to 15%

Notes:

1. Data for the prime rate and U.S. Treasury bills, notes, and bonds are from the *Federal Reserve Statistical Release* (**www.federalreserve.gov /releases/H15/update**).

2. Data for LIBOR, mortgages, and corporate bonds are from the Federal Reserve Bank of St. Louis's FRED® Economic Data (**https://fred.stlouisfed .org/series/USD3MTD156N, https://fred.stlouisfed.org/series/MORTGAGE30US**, and **https://fred.stlouisfed.org/series/BAA**).

3. Data for money market mutual funds are from Vanguard: **https://personal.vanguard.com/us/funds/snapshot?FundIntExt=INT&FundId =0030&funds_disable_redirect=true**.

4. Data for municipal bonds are from Bloomberg at **www.bloomberg.com/markets/rates-bonds/government-bonds/us**.

5. Common stocks are expected to provide a "return" in the form of dividends and capital gains rather than interest. Of course, if you buy a stock, your *actual* return may be considerably higher or lower than your *expected* return.

_____

[5]There are two related reasons for the demise of LIBOR. First, it is the average of *reported* rates rather than *actual* rates. Second, there were several scandals involving manipulation of the reported rate by U.K. banks. This is why the Fed began publishing SOFR. The transition from LIBOR to SOFR will be gradual, but futures contracts on SOFR began trading on the Chicago Mercantile Exchange not long after the Fed began publishing SOFR rates. We expect rates on most financial securities will be tied to SOFR before 2022.

1-6b Type of Claim on Future Cash Flows: Derivatives and Hybrids

Debt and equity represent claims upon the cash flows generated by real assets, such as the cash flows generated by Alcoa's factories and operations. In contrast, **derivatives** are securities whose values depend on, or are *derived* from, the values of some other traded assets. For example, an option on Alcoa stock and a futures contract to buy wheat are derivatives. We discuss options in Chapter 8 and in **Web Extension 1A**, which provides a brief overview of options and other derivatives.

Some securities are a mix of debt, equity, and derivatives. For example, preferred stock has some features like debt and some like equity, while convertible debt has both debt-like and option-like features. We discuss hybrids in subsequent chapters.

1-6c Type of Claim on Future Cash Flows: Securitized Financial Assets

Some securities are created from packages of other financial assets, a process called **securitization**. The misuse of securitized assets is one of the primary causes of the most recent global financial crisis, so every manager needs to understand the process of securitization.

The details vary for different asset classes, but the processes are similar. For example, a bank might loan money to an individual who purchases a car. The individual signs a loan contract, which entitles the bank to receive future payments from the borrower. The bank can put a large number of these individual contracts into a portfolio (called a *pool*) and transfer the pool into a trust (a separate legal entity). The trust then creates new financial instruments that pay out a prescribed set of cash flows from the pool. The trust registers these new securities and sells them. The bank receives the proceeds from the sale, and the purchasers receive a new financial security that has a claim on the cash flows generated by the pool of auto loans.

Consider the benefits. First, because the bank received cash when it sold the securitized car loans, the bank now has replenished its supply of lendable funds and can make additional loans. Second, the bank no longer bears the risk of the borrowers defaulting. Instead, the securities' purchasers choose to bear that risk in expectation of earning an appropriate return. Third, the purchaser of a security has greater liquidity than the bank had when it owned the loan contract because there is an active secondary market for the securities.

Almost any class of financial assets can be securitized, including car loans, student loans, credit card debt, and home mortgages. We have more to say about securitized mortgages and the Great Recession of 2007 later in this chapter, but first let's take a look at the cost of money.

SELF-TEST

What is a financial instrument? What is a financial security?

What are some differences among the following types of securities: debt, equity, and derivatives?

Describe the process of securitization.

1-7 Claims on Future Cash Flows: The Required Rate of Return (the Cost of Money)

Providers of cash expect more cash back in the future than they originally supply to users. In other words, providers expect a positive rate of return on their investment. We call this a **required rate of return** because the prospect of more money in the future is *required* to induce an investor to give up money today. Keep in mind that an investor's rate of return is a user's cost. For debt, we call this cost the **interest rate**. For equity, we call it the **cost of equity**, which consists of the dividends and capital gains stockholders expect. Therefore, the required rate of return is also called the *cost of money* or the *price of money*.

Notice in Table 1-1 that a financial instrument's rate of return generally increases as its maturity and risk increase. We will have much more to say about the relationships among an individual security's features, risk, and required rate of return later in the book, but first we will examine some fundamental factors and economic conditions that affect all financial instruments.

1-7a Fundamental Factors That Affect the Required Rate of Return (the Cost of Money)

The four most fundamental factors affecting the supply and demand of capital and the resulting cost of money are: (1) production opportunities, (2) time preferences for consumption, (3) risk, and (4) inflation.

PRODUCTION OPPORTUNITIES

Production opportunities are activities that require cash now but have the potential to generate cash in the future. For example, a company might sell stock to build a new factory, or a student might borrow to attend college. In both cases, there are prospects of future cash flows: The company might increase sales, and the new graduate might get a high-paying job. Notice that the size and likelihood of the future cash flows put an upper limit on the amount that can be repaid. All else held equal, improvements in production opportunities will increase this upper limit and create more demand for cash now, which will lead to higher interest rates and required returns.

TIME PREFERENCE FOR CONSUMPTION

Providers can use their current funds for consumption or saving. By saving, they choose not to consume now, expecting to consume more in the future. If providers strongly prefer consumption now, then it takes high interest rates to induce them to trade current consumption for future consumption. Therefore, the time preference for consumption has a major impact on the cost of money. Notice that the time preference for consumption varies for different individuals, for different age groups, and for different cultures. For example, people in Japan have a lower time preference for consumption than those in the United States, which partially explains why Japanese families tend to save more than U.S. families even though interest rates are lower in Japan.

RISK

If an opportunity's future cash flows are very uncertain and might be much lower than expected, providers require a higher expected return to induce them to take the extra risk.

EXPECTED INFLATION

Suppose you just paid $100 for a pair of running shoes that will last a year. If inflation is 3%, then a new pair of running shoes next year will cost $103, assuming shoe prices go up at the same rate as inflation. If you could invest $100 today at 5%, then you would have $105 next year from your investment, could buy new shoes for $103, and still have $2 left for other uses. Notice that part of your $5 return was "used up" by inflation: You will pay $103 for shoes next year instead of today's price of $100, so $3 out of your $5 return simply covered inflation. In terms of additional purchasing power, you gained only $2 from your $100 investment. Therefore, $2 is your real increase in purchasing power, and 2% is your **real rate of return (r_r)** in terms of purchasing power.[6] The 5% return on your investment is called the **nominal rate of return (r_n)** because it is the stated rate shown at the time you make your investment. We will have much more to say about inflation in later chapters, but for now it is enough to understand that if expected inflation goes up, then the nominal interest rate also must go up to maintain the real interest rate.

1-7b Economic Conditions and Policies That Affect the Required Rate of Return (the Cost of Money)

Economic conditions and policies also affect required rates of return. These include: (1) Federal Reserve policy, (2) the federal budget deficit or surplus, (3) the level of business activity, and (4) international factors.

FEDERAL RESERVE POLICY

WWW

The home page for the Board of Governors of the Federal Reserve System can be found at **www .federalreserve.gov**. You can access general information about the Federal Reserve, including press releases, speeches, and monetary policy.

If the Federal Reserve Board wants to stimulate the economy, it most often uses open market operations to purchase Treasury securities held by banks. Because banks are selling some of their securities, the banks will have more cash, which increases their supply of loanable funds, which in turn makes banks willing to lend more money at lower interest rates. In addition, the Fed's purchases represent an increase in the demand for Treasury securities. As with anything for sale, increased demand causes Treasury securities' prices to go up and interest rates to go down. The net result is a reduction in interest rates, which stimulates the economy by making it less costly for companies to borrow for new projects or for individuals to borrow for major purchases or other expenditures.

Unfortunately, there is a downside to stimulation by the Fed. When banks sell their holdings of Treasury securities to the Fed, the banks' reserves go up, which increases the money supply. A larger money supply ultimately leads to an increase in expected inflation, which eventually pushes interest rates up. Thus, the Fed can stimulate the economy in the short term by driving down interest rates and increasing the money supply, but this creates longer-term inflationary pressures. This was exactly the dilemma facing the Fed in mid-2018.

On the other hand, if the Fed wishes to slow down the economy and reduce inflation, the Fed reverses the process. Instead of purchasing Treasury securities, the Fed sells Treasury securities to banks, which reduces banking reserves and causes an increase in short-term interest rates but a decrease in long-term inflationary pressures.

FEDERAL BUDGET DEFICITS OR SURPLUSES

If the federal government spends more than it takes in from tax revenues, then it runs a deficit, and that deficit must be covered either by borrowing or by printing money (increasing the money supply). The government borrows by issuing new Treasury securities. All else held equal, this creates a greater supply of Treasury securities, which leads to lower security prices and higher interest rates. Federal government actions that increase the money supply also increase expectations for future inflation, which drives up

---

[6]The real rate of return is actually found by solving this equation: $(1.05) = (1.03)(1 + r_r)$. With a little algebra, $r_r = (1.05)/(1.03) - 1 = 0.0194 = 1.94\%$. For illustrative purposes, we approximated the calculation as $5\% - 3\% = 2\%$.

FIGURE 1-3
Federal Budget Surplus/Deficits and Foreign Trade Balances (Billions of Dollars)

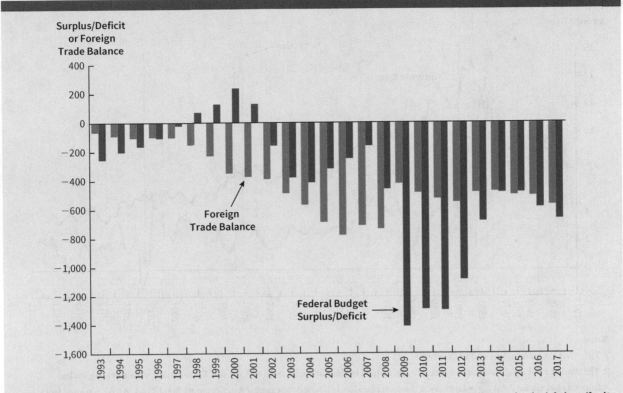

Sources: The raw data are from the Federal Reserve Bank of St. Louis's FRED® Economic Data for fiscal years: **http://research.stlouisfed.org/fred2/series/FYFSD** and **http://research.stlouisfed.org/fred2/series/BOPGSTB?cid=125**.

interest rates. Thus, the larger the federal deficit, other things held constant, the higher the level of interest rates. As shown in Figure 1-3, the federal government has run deficits in 20 of the past 24 years. Annual deficits in the mid-1990s were in the $250 billion range, but they ballooned to well over a trillion dollars in the past recession and are now about $585 billion.

LEVEL OF BUSINESS ACTIVITY

Figure 1-4 shows interest rates, inflation, and recessions. First, notice that interest rates and inflation are presently (late 2017) very low relative to the past 40 years. However, you should never assume that the future will be like the recent past!

Second, notice that interest rates and inflation typically rise prior to a recession and fall afterward. There are several reasons for this pattern. Consumer demand slows during a recession, keeping companies from increasing prices, which reduces price inflation. Companies also cut back on hiring, which reduces wage inflation. Less disposable income causes consumers to reduce their purchases of homes and automobiles, reducing consumer demand for loans. Companies reduce investments in new operations, which reduces their demand for funds. The cumulative effect is downward pressure on inflation and interest rates. The Federal Reserve is also active during recessions, trying to stimulate the economy by driving down interest rates.

FIGURE 1-4
Business Activity, Interest Rates, and Inflation

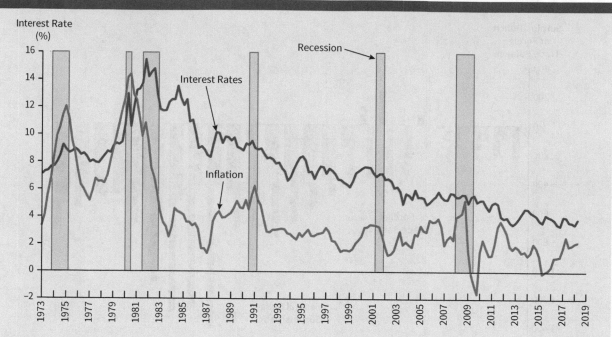

Notes:

1. Tick marks represent January 1 of the year.

2. The shaded areas designate business recessions as defined by the National Bureau of Economic Research; see **www.nber.org/cycles**.

3. Interest rates are for AAA corporate bonds; the source is: Moody's, Moody's Seasoned Aaa Corporate Bond Yield [AAA], retrieved from FRED, Federal Reserve Bank of St. Louis; **https://fred.stlouisfed.org/series/AAA**, April 8, 2018. These rates reflect the average rate during the quarter ending on the date shown.

4. Inflation is measured by the annual rate of change for the Consumer Price Index (CPI) for the preceding 12 months; the source is U.S. Bureau of Labor Statistics, Consumer Price Index for All Urban Consumers: All Items [CPIAUCSL], retrieved from FRED, Federal Reserve Bank of St. Louis; **https://fred.stlouisfed.org/series/CPIAUCSL**, April 8, 2018.

FOREIGN TRADE BALANCE: DEFICITS OR SURPLUSES

Businesses and individuals in the United States buy from and sell to people and firms in other countries. The **foreign trade balance** describes the level of imports relative to exports. If we buy more than we sell (that is, if we import more than we export), we are said to be running a *foreign trade deficit*. When trade deficits occur, they must be financed, and the main source of financing is debt. In other words, if we import $200 billion of goods but export only $90 billion, we run a trade deficit of $110 billion. That $110 billion in the hands of foreign companies won't just sit there as currency. It will be invested, frequently in U.S. Treasury securities, which means those dollars are lent back to the U.S. government. That is, we will probably borrow the $110 billion.[7] Therefore, the larger our trade deficit, the more we must borrow, and the increased borrowing drives up interest rates. Also, international investors are willing to hold U.S. debt only if the risk-adjusted rate paid on this debt is competitive with interest rates in other countries. Therefore, if the Federal

---

[7]The foreign trade deficit could also be financed by selling assets, including gold, corporate stocks, entire companies, and real estate. The United States has financed its massive trade deficits through all of these means in recent years, but the primary method has been by borrowing from foreigners.

Reserve attempts to lower interest rates in the United States, causing our rates to fall below rates abroad (after adjustments for expected changes in the exchange rate), then international investors will sell U.S. bonds, which will depress bond prices and result in higher U.S. rates. Thus, if the trade deficit is large relative to the size of the overall economy, it will hinder the Fed's ability to reduce interest rates and combat a recession.

WWW

If it won't depress you too much, you can see the current value of the national debt at http://treasurydirect.gov/NP/debt/current.

The United States has been running annual trade deficits since the mid-1970s; see Figure 1-3 for recent years. The cumulative effect of trade deficits and budget deficits is that the United States has become the largest debtor nation of all time. In fact, the federal debt exceeds *$21 trillion*! As a result, our interest rates are influenced by interest rates in other countries around the world. Some of the factors that affect foreign interest rates are international changes in tax rates, regulations, currency conversion laws, and currency exchange rates. Foreign investments also include the risk that property will be expropriated by the host government. We discuss these issues in Chapter 17.

Recall that financial markets connect providers and users: Providers supply cash now in exchange for claims on risky future cash. The next section describes how financial institutions connect providers and users.

SELF-TEST

What is a "required rate of return"? Why is it called the "cost of money" or the "price of money"?

What is debt's cost of money called?

What two components make up the cost of money for equity?

What four fundamental factors affect required rates of return (i.e., the cost of money)?

How does Federal Reserve policy affect interest rates now and in the future?

What is a federal budget deficit or surplus? How does this affect interest rates?

What is a foreign trade deficit or surplus? How does this affect interest rates?

1-8 The Functions of Financial Institutions

Direct transfers of funds from individuals to businesses are relatively uncommon in developed economies. Instead, businesses usually find it more efficient to enlist the services of one or more financial institutions to raise capital. Most financial institutions don't compete in a single line of business but instead provide a wide variety of services and products, both domestically and globally. The following sections describe the major types of financial institutions and services, but keep in mind that the dividing lines among them are often blurred.

1-8a Investment Banks and Brokerage Activities

Investment banks help companies raise capital. Such organizations underwrite security offerings, which means they (1) advise corporations regarding the design and pricing of new securities, (2) buy these securities from the issuing corporation, and (3) resell them to investors. Although the securities are sold twice, this process is really one primary market transaction, with the investment banker acting as a facilitator to help transfer capital from savers to businesses. An investment bank often is a division or subsidiary of a larger company. For example, JPMorgan Chase & Co. is a very large financial services firm, with over $2.6 trillion in managed assets. One of its holdings is J.P. Morgan, an investment bank.

In addition to security offerings, investment banks also provide consulting and advisory services, such as merger and acquisition (M&A) analysis and investment management for wealthy individuals.

Most investment banks also provide brokerage services for institutions and individuals (called "retail" customers). For example, Merrill Lynch (acquired in 2008 by Bank of America) has a large retail brokerage operation that provides advice and executes trades for its individual clients. Similarly, J.P. Morgan helps execute trades for institutional customers, such as pension funds.

At one time, most investment banks were partnerships, with income generated primarily by fees from their underwriting, M&A consulting, asset management, and brokering activities. When business was good, investment banks generated high fees and paid big bonuses to their partners. When times were tough, investment banks paid no bonuses and often fired employees. In the 1990s, however, most large investment banks were reorganized into publicly traded corporations (or were acquired and then operated as subsidiaries of public companies). For example, in 1994 Lehman Brothers sold some of its own shares of stock to the public via an IPO. Like most corporations, Lehman Brothers was financed by a combination of equity and debt.

A relaxation of regulations in the 2000s allowed investment banks to undertake much riskier activities than at any time since the Great Depression. The new regulations allowed investment banks to use an unprecedented amount of debt to finance their activities—Lehman used roughly $30 of debt for every dollar of equity. In addition to their fee-generating activities, most investment banks also began trading securities for their own accounts. In other words, they took the borrowed money and invested it in financial securities. If you are earning 12% on your investments while paying 8% on your borrowings, then the more money you borrow, the more profit you make. But if you are leveraged 30 to 1 and your investments decline in value by even 3.33%, your business will fail. This is exactly what happened to Bear Stearns, Lehman Brothers, and Merrill Lynch in the fall of 2008. In short, they borrowed money, used it to make risky investments, and then failed when the investments turned out to be worth less than the amount they owed. Note that it was not their traditional investment banking activities that caused the failure, but the fact that they borrowed so much and used those funds to speculate in the market.

1-8b Deposit-Taking Financial Intermediaries

Some financial institutions are **financial intermediaries** because they take deposits from savers and then lend most of the deposited money to borrowers. Following is a brief description of such intermediaries.

SAVINGS AND LOAN ASSOCIATIONS (S&Ls)

Savings and loan associations (S&Ls) accept deposits from many small savers and then lend this money to home buyers and consumers. **Mutual savings banks (MSBs)** are similar to S&Ls, but they operate primarily in the northeastern states. Today, most S&Ls and MSBs have been acquired by banks.

CREDIT UNIONS

Credit unions are cooperative associations whose members have a common bond, such as being employees of the same firm or living in the same geographic area. Members' savings are loaned only to other members, generally for auto purchases, home-improvement loans, and home mortgages. Credit unions are often the cheapest source of funds available to individual borrowers.

COMMERCIAL BANKS

Commercial banks raise funds from depositors and by issuing stock and bonds to investors. For example, someone might deposit money in a checking account. In return, that person can write checks, use a debit card, and even receive interest on the deposits. Those who buy the banks' stocks and bonds expect to receive dividends and interest payments. Unlike nonfinancial corporations, most commercial banks are highly leveraged in the sense that they owe much more to their depositors and creditors than they raised from stockholders. For example, a typical bank has about $90 of debt for every $10 of stockholders' equity. If the bank's assets are worth $100, we can calculate its equity capital by subtracting the $90 of liabilities from the $100 of assets: Equity capital = $100 − $90 = $10. But if the assets drop in value by 5% to $95, the equity drops to $5 = $95 − $90, a 50% decline.

Banks are vitally important for a well-functioning economy, and their highly leveraged positions make them risky. As a result, banks are more highly regulated than nonfinancial firms. Given the high risk, banks might have a hard time attracting and retaining deposits unless the deposits were insured, so the Federal Deposit Insurance Corporation (FDIC), which is backed by the U.S. government, insures up to $250,000 per depositor. As a result of the great recession of 2007, this insured amount was increased from $100,000 in 2008 to reassure depositors.

Without such insurance, if depositors believed that a bank was in trouble, they would rush to withdraw funds. This is called a "bank run," which is exactly what happened in the United States during the Great Depression of 1929, causing many bank failures and leading to the creation of the FDIC in an effort to prevent future bank runs. Not all countries have their own versions of the FDIC, so international bank runs are still possible. In fact, a bank run occurred in September 2008 at the U.K. bank Northern Rock, leading to its nationalization by the government.

Most banks are small and locally owned, but the largest banks are parts of giant financial services firms. For example, JPMorgan Chase Bank, commonly called Chase Bank, is owned by JPMorgan Chase & Co., and Citibank is owned by Citicorp.

1-8c Investment Funds

At some financial institutions, savers have an ownership interest in a pool of funds rather than owning a deposit account. Examples include mutual funds, hedge funds, and private equity funds.

MUTUAL FUNDS

Mutual funds are organizations that accept money from savers and then pool these funds to buy financial instruments. Most mutual funds belong to a larger company's family of funds. For example, Franklin Resources Inc. is a publicly traded company and manages over $400 billion in more than 200 different mutual funds. Such mutual fund providers achieve economies of scale in analyzing securities, managing portfolios, and buying/selling securities.

Different funds are designed to meet the objectives of different types of savers. Hence, there are bond funds for those who desire safety and stock funds for savers who are willing to accept risks in the hope of higher returns. There are literally thousands of different mutual funds with dozens of different purposes and styles. For example, the Franklin Equity Income fund invests in stocks with high dividends, whereas the Franklin Growth Opportunities fund invests in stock with high growth potential.

Passively managed funds hold a group of stocks in a particular category and then minimize expenses by rarely trading. **Index funds** are passive funds designed to replicate the returns on a particular market index, such as the S&P 500. **Actively managed funds** have higher fees but seek to invest in undervalued securities within a particular category, such as growth stocks.

Money market funds invest in short-term, low-risk securities, such as Treasury bills and commercial paper. Many of these funds offer interest-bearing checking accounts with rates that are greater than those offered by banks, so many people invest in money market funds as an alternative to depositing money in a bank. Note, though, that money market funds are not required to be insured and so are riskier than bank deposits.[8]

Most traditional mutual funds allow investors to redeem their share of the fund only at the close of business. A special type of mutual fund, the **exchange-traded fund (ETF)**, allows investors to sell their share at any time during normal trading hours. ETFs usually have very low management expenses and are rapidly gaining in popularity.

HEDGE FUNDS

Most **hedge funds** are private limited partnerships whose purpose is to raise money from investors and engage in a variety of investment activities. Unlike typical mutual funds, which can have thousands of investors, hedge funds are limited to institutional investors and a relatively small number of high-net-worth individuals. Because these investors are supposed to be sophisticated, hedge funds are much less regulated than mutual funds. Many hedge funds literally try to hedge their bets by forming portfolios of conventional securities and derivatives in such a way as to limit potential losses without sacrificing too much of potential gains. However, many other hedge funds don't hedge as much and instead chase larger but riskier potential returns.

PRIVATE EQUITY FUNDS

Private equity (PE) funds are similar to hedge funds but PE funds own stock (equity) in other companies and often control those companies, whereas hedge funds usually own many types of securities. In contrast to a mutual fund, which might own a small percentage of a publicly traded company's stock, a private equity fund typically purchases the entire company. Before the purchase, the stock may have been privately held or publicly traded. Either way, it is not traded in the public markets after the purchase so it is called "private equity." For example, Staples, Inc. traded on the NASDAQ Stock Market until Sycamore Partners purchased it in 2017 for about $6.9 billion.

The private equity funds' general partners usually sit on their companies' boards and guide their strategies with the goal of later selling the companies for a profit, often through an initial public offering. For example, in 2007 two large private equity firms (Clayton, Dubilier & Rice LLC and KKR & Co LP) jointly purchased U.S. Foodservice, a subsidiary of a publicly traded company (Royal Ahold N.V.). In 2016, the PE firms took the company public as US Foods Holding Corp. in an IPO by selling $1.02 billion in stock.

Most hedge funds and private equity funds belong to a larger company's family of funds. For example, The Blackstone Group manages funds with over $350 billion in assets and Apollo Global Management, LLC, has over $200 billion under management.

---

[8]The U.S. Treasury sold deposit insurance to eligible money market funds between September 2008 and September 2009 to help stabilize the markets during the height of the financial crisis.

1-8d Life Insurance Companies and Pension Funds

Life insurance companies take premiums, invest these funds in stocks, bonds, real estate, and mortgages, and then make payments to beneficiaries. Life insurance companies also offer a variety of tax-deferred savings plans designed to provide retirement benefits.

Traditional **pension funds** are retirement plans funded by corporations or government agencies. Pension funds invest primarily in bonds, stocks, mortgages, hedge funds, private equity, and real estate. Most companies now offer self-directed retirement plans, such as 401(k) plans, as an addition to or substitute for traditional pension plans. In traditional plans, the plan administrators determine how to invest the funds; in self-directed plans, all individual participants must decide how to invest their own funds. Many companies are switching from traditional plans to self-directed plans, partly because this shifts the risk from the company to the employee.

1-8e Regulation of Financial Institutions

In 1933, the **Glass-Steagall Act** was passed with the intent of preventing another great depression. In addition to creating the FDIC to insure bank deposits, the law imposed constraints on banking activities and separated investment banking from commercial banking. The regulatory environment of the post-Depression era included a prohibition on nationwide branch banking, restrictions on the types of assets the institutions could buy, ceilings on the interest rates they could pay, and limitations on the types of services they could provide. Arguing that these regulations impeded the free flow of capital and hurt the efficiency of our capital markets, policymakers took several steps from the 1970s to the 1990s to deregulate financial services companies, culminating with the Gramm–Leach–Bliley Act of 1999, which "repealed" Glass-Steagall's separation of commercial and investment banking.

One result of deregulation was the creation of huge **financial services corporations**, which own commercial banks, S&Ls, mortgage companies, investment-banking houses, insurance companies, pension plan operations, and mutual funds. Many are now global banks with branches and operations across the country and around the world.

WWW

For current bank rankings, go to Global Finance Magazine's Web site, **www.gfmag.com,** *and use the search for "biggest global banks."*

For example, Citigroup combined one of the world's largest commercial banks (Citibank), a huge insurance company (Travelers), and a major investment bank (Smith Barney), along with numerous other subsidiaries that operate throughout the world. Bank of America also made numerous acquisitions of many different financial companies, including Merrill Lynch, with its large brokerage and investment banking operations, and mortgage giant Countrywide Financial.

These conglomerate structures are similar to those of major institutions in China, Europe, Japan, and elsewhere around the globe. Though U.S. banks grew dramatically as a result of recent mergers, they are still relatively small by global standards. The world's largest bank is the Industrial and Commercial Bank of China. Among the world's ten largest world banks, based upon total assets, only one (JPMorgan Chase) is headquartered in the United States.

The great recession of 2007 and continuing global economic weakness caused regulators and financial institutions to rethink the wisdom of deregulating conglomerate financial services corporations. To address some of these concerns, the Dodd-Frank Wall Street Reform and Consumer Protection Act was passed in 2010. As we write this in 2018, Congress is undoing many of the Dodd-Frank's regulations, allowing financial institutions to take on more risk. We discuss Dodd-Frank and other regulatory changes in Section 1-12, where we explain the events leading up to the great recession of 2007.

What were the traditional roles of investment banks prior to the 1990s? What types of activities did investment banks add after that?

Describe the different types of deposit-taking institutions.

What are some similarities and differences among mutual funds, hedge funds, and private equity funds?

Describe a life insurance company's basic activities.

What are traditional pension funds? What are 401(k) plans?

1-9 Financial Markets

Financial markets serve to connect providers of funds with users for the purpose of exchanging cash now for claims on future cash (e.g., securities such as stocks or bonds). In addition, they provide a means for trading securities after they have been issued. We describe different types of markets and trading procedures in the following sections.

1-9a Types of Financial Markets

There are many different ways to classify financial markets, depending upon the types of instruments, customer, or geographic locations. You should recognize the big differences among types of markets, but keep in mind that the distinctions are often blurred.

PHYSICAL ASSETS VERSUS FINANCIAL ASSETS

Physical asset markets (also called "tangible" or "real" asset markets) are those for such products as wheat, autos, real estate, computers, and machinery. **Financial asset markets**, on the other hand, deal with stocks, bonds, notes, mortgages, derivatives, and other financial instruments.

TIME OF DELIVERY: SPOT VERSUS FUTURE

Spot markets are markets where assets are being bought or sold for "on-the-spot" delivery (literally, within a few days). **Futures markets** are for assets whose delivery is at some future date, such as 6 months or a year into the future.

MATURITY OF FINANCIAL ASSET: SHORT VERSUS LONG

Money markets are the markets for short-term, highly liquid debt securities, while **capital markets** are the markets for corporate stocks and debt maturing more than a year in the future. The New York Stock Exchange is an example of a capital market. When describing debt markets, "short term" generally means less than 1 year, "intermediate term" means 1 to 5 years, and "long term" means more than 5 years.

PURPOSE OF LOANS TO INDIVIDUALS: LONG-TERM ASSET PURCHASES VERSUS SHORTER-TERM SPENDING

Mortgage markets deal with loans on residential, agricultural, commercial, and industrial real estate, while **consumer credit markets** involve loans for autos, appliances, education, vacations, and so on.

PRIVATE VERSUS PUBLIC

Private markets are where transactions are worked out directly between two parties. The transactions are called **private placements**. For example, bank loans and private placements of debt with insurance companies are examples of private market transactions. Because these transactions are private, they may be structured in any manner that appeals to the two parties.

Public markets are where standardized contracts are traded on organized exchanges. Because securities that are traded in public markets (for example, common stock and futures contracts) are ultimately held by a large number of individuals, they must have fairly standardized contractual features.

Private market securities are more tailor-made but less liquid, whereas public market securities are more liquid but subject to greater standardization.

GEOGRAPHIC SCOPE

World, national, regional, and local markets also exist. Thus, depending on an organization's size and scope of operations, it may be able to borrow or lend all around the world, or it may be confined to a strictly local, even neighborhood, market.

PRIMARY MARKETS VERSUS SECONDARY MARKETS

Primary markets are the markets in which corporations raise new capital. For example, if a private company has an IPO or if a public company sells a new issue of common stock to raise capital, this would be a primary market transaction. The corporation selling the newly created stock receives the proceeds from such a transaction.

Secondary markets are markets in which existing, already outstanding securities are traded among investors. Thus, if you decided to buy 1,000 shares of Starbucks stock, the purchase would occur in the secondary market. Secondary markets exist for many financial securities, including stocks and bonds.

It is important to remember that the company whose securities are being traded is not involved in a secondary market transaction and thus does not receive any funds from such a sale. However, secondary markets are vital for a well-functioning economy because they provide liquidity and foster entrepreneurship.

1-9b Why Are Secondary Markets Important?

Secondary markets provide liquidity for investors who need cash or who wish to reallocate their investments to potentially more productive opportunities. For example, a parent who owns stock might wish to help pay for a child's college education. Or consider an investor who owns stock in a coal-mining company but who wishes to invest in a manufacturer of solar panels. Without active secondary markets, investors would be stuck with the securities they purchase.

Secondary markets also foster entrepreneurship. For example, it might take a very long time before an entrepreneur can use a start-up company's cash flow for personal spending because the cash flow is needed to support the company's growth. In other words, the company might be successful, but the entrepreneur feels "cash poor." However, if the company goes public, its stock can be traded in the secondary market. The entrepreneur then can sell some personal shares of stock and begin to enjoy the financial rewards of having started a successful company. Without this prospect, entrepreneurs have diminished incentives to start companies.

Secondary markets also provide a measure of value as perceived by buyers and sellers, making it easy to quickly compare different investments.

1-9c Trading Procedures in the Secondary Markets

A **trading venue** is a site (geographical or electronic) where secondary market trading occurs. Although there are many trading venues for a wide variety of securities, we classify their trading procedures along two dimensions: location and method of matching orders.

PHYSICAL LOCATION VERSUS ELECTRONIC NETWORK

In a **physical location exchange** traders actually meet and trade in a specific part of a specific building. For example, the New York Stock Exchange and the London Metals Exchange conduct some trading at physical locations.

In contrast, traders do not physically meet in a **computer/telephone network**. For example, the markets for U.S. Treasury bonds and foreign exchange primarily operate via telephone and/or computer networks. Most stock markets, including the NASDAQ Stock Market, do not have face-to-face trading.

MATCHING ORDERS: OPEN OUTCRY AUCTIONS, DEALER MARKETS, AND AUTOMATED TRADING PLATFORMS

The second dimension is the way orders from sellers and buyers are matched. This can occur in a face-to-face open outcry auction, through dealers, or by automated matching engines.

Open Outcry Auctions An **open outcry auction** occurs when traders actually meet face-to-face and communicate with one another through shouts and hand signals. When a seller and buyer agree on the price and quantity, the transaction is finalized and reported to the organization that manages the auction.

Dealer Markets and Market Makers In a **dealer market**, there are *market makers* who keep an inventory of the stock (or other financial instrument) in much the same way that any merchant keeps an inventory of goods. These dealers list **bid quotes** and **ask quotes**, which are the prices at which they are willing to buy or sell. In a traditional dealer market, computerized quotation systems keep track of all bid and ask quotes, but they don't actually match buyers and sellers. Instead, traders must contact a specific dealer to complete the transaction.

Automated Trading Platforms with Automated Matching Engines An **automated matching engine** is part of a computer system in which buyers and sellers post their orders and then let the computer automatically determine whether a match exists. If a match exists, the computer automatically executes and reports the trade. The entire system is called an **automated trading platform**.

For example, suppose Trader B ("B" is for buyer) places an order to buy 500 shares of GE, but only if the sale occurs within the next hour and at a price of no more than $24.99 per share. The $24.99 is the **bid price** because the buyer is "bidding" $24.99 for a share of GE. The order itself is a **limit order** because the buyer specifies limits with respect to the order's price and duration. The computer will put the information into its **order book**, which is a record of all outstanding orders. Suppose all other bid prices in the order book are less than $24.99. When the computer ranks bids in the order book *from high to low,* Trader B's $24.99 bid will be at the top of the book. In other words, it is the highest bid price of any orders in the book, which is the most anyone currently is willing to pay for GE.

Now suppose Trader S ("S" is for seller) places a limit order to sell 500 shares of GE at a price of at least $25.15. The $25.15 is the **ask price** because the seller is asking for $25.15 per share. Let's suppose that all other ask prices in the computer's order book are greater than $25.15. When the computer ranks ask prices *from low to high*, Trader S's $25.15 ask price will be at the top of the book because it is the *lowest* ask price of any orders in the book. In other words, it is the lowest at which anyone is willing to sell GE.

In this situation, the computer won't find a match—all sellers want at least $25.15, but no buyers will pay more than $24.99. No transactions will occur until sellers reduce their ask prices or buyers increase their bids. The difference between the ask price and the bid price is called the **bid-ask spread**. In this example, it is:

$$\text{Bid-ask spread} = \text{Ask price} - \text{Bid price} = \$25.15 - \$24.99 = \$0.16$$

The order book is updated each time a new order arrives or a limit order expires. New orders arrive frequently, and many times there will be a match.

For example, suppose Trader S worries that prices will fall and would rather sell at $24.99 than wait and hope that prices will come up to the original ask price of $25.15. In this case, Trader S would send in an order to sell at the market price—this is called a **market order** because it asks to transact at the current market price. In this case, the computer would automatically match Trader S and Trader B, execute the trade of 500 shares of GE at $24.99, and notify both participants that the trade has occurred.[9]

Automated trading systems are rapidly replacing face-to-face trading in the secondary stock markets, as we describe in the next section.

SELF-TEST

What is the basic function of a financial market?

Distinguish between (1) physical asset markets and financial asset markets, (2) spot and futures markets, (3) money and capital markets, (4) mortgage and consumer credit markets, (5) private and public markets, and (6) primary and secondary markets.

List three reasons why secondary markets are important.

What is a trading venue?

What are the major differences between physical location exchanges and computer/telephone networks?

What are the differences among open outcry auctions, dealer markets, and automated trading platforms with automated matching engines?

What is a limit order? What is an order book? What is a market order?

1-10 Overview of the U.S. Stock Markets

Because stock markets are so large and important, all managers should have a basic understanding of what the stock markets are and how they function. Before 1970, there was just one major U.S. stock exchange, the NYSE, where the vast majority of stocks were listed and traded. Today, however, the situation is much more fragmented for both listing and trading.

Recall that a publicly traded company first registers with the SEC, applies to be listed at a stock exchange, and then has an IPO, after which its stock can be traded in public

---

[9]Most exchanges have 10 or more types in addition to limit orders and market orders.

TABLE 1-2
Stock Exchange Listings and Total Market Value

Exchange	Number of Listings	Market Value of Listings (Trillions)
NYSE	3,131	$27.9
NASDAQ	3,274	11.3
NYSE MKT	362	0.2
	6,767	$39.4

Source: The NASDAQ Web site provides data for individual companies on these exchanges. The data may be downloaded from the NASDAQ Company List at **www.nasdaq.com/screening/company-list.aspx**. The individual stock data are summarized in this table. The data are for September 12, 2017.

Notes:

These include listings by foreign companies on U.S. exchanges in addition to listings by U.S. companies. In fact, over 35% of the listings are by foreign companies; for the number of U.S. companies on these exchanges, see the World Bank at **https://data.worldbank.org/indicator/CM.MKT.LDOM.NO?locations=US**.

markets. A company can list its stock only at a single SEC-registered stock exchange. In 2017, there were about a dozen active registered exchanges for trading stock, but most stocks were listed on just three—the NYSE, the NASDAQ Stock Market (NASDAQ), and the NYSE MKT (formerly called the American Stock Exchange).[10] As Table 1-2 shows, these three exchanges have almost 6,000 listings with a total value of around $34 *trillion*. NASDAQ has the most listings, but the NYSE's listings have a much bigger market value.

Over 9,000 companies were listed in 1997, about 3,000 more than today. Part of this decline is due to mergers in which two listings become one listing, but the primary reason is that private companies now have much more access to funding, especially from private equity funds.

Does it matter where a stock is listed? It certainly did before the year 2000, when the vast majority of a stock's secondary market trading occurred where it was listed. The two primary trading venues, the NYSE and NASDAQ, had very different trading procedures: NYSE trading took place face-to-face at a physical location (on Wall Street) and NASDAQ trading was a dealer market with a computerized quotation system. The two exchanges also had very different reputations: Only relatively large companies could list at the NYSE, but smaller companies (many of them high-tech) could list at NASDAQ.

The situation today is very different. Although listings are still concentrated at the NYSE (owned by ICE) and NASDAQ (owned by NASDAQ OMX), a company's shares can and do trade at many different venues. In addition, very little stock trading is conducted face-to-face but is instead executed with automated trading platforms.

SELF-TEST

Which exchange has the most listed stocks? Which exchange's listed stocks have the greatest market value?

Are shares of a company's stocks traded only on the exchange where the stock is listed?

---

[10]NASDAQ originally stood for the National Association of Securities Dealers (NASD) Automated Quotation system. However, the NASD became part of the Financial Industry Regulatory Authority (FINRA) and is no longer affiliated with the automated quotation system even though it is still named NASDAQ.

1-11 Trading in the Modern Stock Markets[11]

The NYSE and NASDAQ no longer dominate stock market trading. This section explains how modern stock markets operate.

1-11a Reg NMS: Stock Transactions, Quotes, and the "Market Price"

If an exchange-listed stock is bought or sold at any trading venue, the transaction price and volume (i.e., the number of shares traded) must be reported to the consolidated tape system, which is a computer network.[12] The most recent trade is often called the "market price." Several free sources, including CNBC, report the most recent transaction price. In addition to reporting transactions, registered stock exchanges must also report certain information about limit order bid and ask quotes to a consolidated quote system, as we explain next.

We streamlined the previous example of an automated matching engine by showing quoted limit orders from only one order book. However, there is an order book for each stock at each exchange, and each order book might have different bid and ask prices. To help investors make informed decisions, the SEC adopted **Regulation National Market System (Reg NMS)** in 2005 and implemented it in 2007. Among its provisions, Reg NMS requires all registered stock exchanges to report their best (highest) bid price and best (lowest) ask price for each stock in their order books. After collecting this information from all the exchanges, a computer system identifies and reports the *overall* best bid and best ask. These best overall quotes are called the **National Best Bid and Offer (NBBO)**, which is the overall best (highest) bid price and best (lowest) ask price (the price at which an investor offers to sell stock). In other words, the NBBO represents the best prices at which an investor could buy or sell on any of the exchanges.

If an investor places a market order to buy or sell at the market price, Reg NMS's *order protection rule* requires trading venues to execute the trade at a price that is at least as good as the NBBO quotes. For example, suppose the NBBO quotes for Apple are a bid price of $179.98 and an ask (offer) price of $180.02. If an investor places a market order to sell shares of Apple, the investor must receive at least $179.98, the national best bid price. Or if an investor places a market order to buy Apple stock, the investor must pay no more than $180.02, the national best ask price. As this example illustrates, the NBBO quotes help determine the "market" price in a market order.

What if the investor wants to buy 500 shares of Apple at the market price, but the NBBO ask price of $180.02 is for only 100 shares? In this case, 100 shares might be transacted at the current NBBO price of $180.02, after which the computer systems will announce a new NBBO price, which might be for 100 shares at $180.07. The process would be repeated until the market order to buy 500 shares is completed.

Notice that the average price paid by the buyer might be higher than the original NBBO ask price if there were not enough shares offered for sale at the original NBBO ask price. Therefore, the NBBO is supposed to reflect market conditions, but it might not be very representative of the actual market supply and demand if the number of shares in the NBBO quote is very small. We will have more to say about this when we explain high-frequency trading, but let's first take a look at where stock is traded.

---

[11]The material in this section is relatively technical, and some instructors may choose to skip it.

[12]No tape is involved in the modern consolidated tape system, but the name comes from days in which trades were reported on a thin paper tape that spewed out of a ticker tape machine.

1-11b Where Is Stock Traded?

As mentioned previously, almost all trading occurred on the floor of the NYSE before 1970. Even as recently as 2005, almost 80% of trading in NYSE-listed stocks took place at the NYSE, primarily on the trading floor itself.[13] However, the markets today are very different, with trading taking place at dozens of different venues. Before tackling the different ways that trades are completed, let's take a look at how a trade begins.

HOW A STOCK TRADE BEGINS

Buyers and sellers must have brokerage accounts through which they place orders. These accounts can be with human stockbrokers (Merrill Lynch has over 15,000 brokers) or with computer systems (such as online trading accounts with TD Ameritrade). Either way, investors must pay to have their orders placed, executed, and recorded.

An investor chooses whether or not to place an order, but unless the investor specifies differently, the broker chooses *where* to send the order. This is called *order routing*, and it determines the trading venue. There are three types of trading venues, each differing with respect to the degree of SEC regulation and reporting requirements: (1) standard broker-dealer networks, (2) alternative trading systems, and (3) registered stock exchanges.

Because an investor initiates a trade by placing an order with a broker, we begin by describing broker-dealer networks.

STANDARD BROKER-DEALER NETWORKS

A **broker-dealer** is a broker that is also registered so that it can buy and sell for itself when it acts as a market maker. Broker-dealers can be individuals, companies, or subsidiaries of a larger financial services company. Broker-dealers and individual brokers must also follow state and industry licensing and registration requirements.

When broker-dealers execute trades among themselves, it is called an **off-exchange transaction** because the trades are not executed at a registered stock exchange. Instead, the trades take place within a **broker-dealer network** in which a broker-dealer trades on behalf of its clients or itself.[14] Many years ago, brokers actually would pass physical shares of stock over a counter to a buyer, in much the same way that a fast-food employee now hands a bag of burgers to a customer. Although counters are no longer involved, broker-dealer trades are still called **over-the-counter (OTC) trades**.[15]

About 21% of all stock market trading (based on dollar values) now takes place in broker-dealer networks, as shown in Table 1-3. Broker-dealer networks are less regulated than registered stock exchanges. For example, broker-dealers must report transactions

---

[13]See page 6 in the SEC's Concept Release on Equity Market Structure at **www.sec.gov/rules/concept/2010/34-61358.pdf**.

[14]Most large financial services firms have a subsidiary that acts as a broker-dealer network. Its clients usually are brokers in the financial services firm's other subsidiaries. The network also trades with other broker-dealer networks.

[15]Today the actual certificates for almost all listed stocks and bonds in the United States are stored in a vault, beneath Manhattan, that is operated by the Depository Trust and Clearing Corporation (DTCC). Most brokerage firms have an account with the DTCC, and most investors leave their stocks with their brokers. Thus, when stocks are sold, the DTCC simply adjusts the accounts of the brokerage firms that are involved, and no stock certificates are actually moved.

TABLE 1-3
Stock Trading Venues and Trading Activity

Owner of Trading Venue and Venues	Percentage of Dollar Volume	
Cboe Global Markets: BYX, BZX, EDGA, EDGX	18%	
NASDAQ OMX: NASDAQ[a], NASDAQ BX[b], NASDAQ PSX[c]	22%	
Intercontinental Exchange: NYSE[d], NYSE Arca[e], NYSE American[f]	22%	
Others	3%	
Total trading on all exchanges:		**65%**
Dark pools (ATS): 34	13%	
Broker-dealer networks: Over 250[g]		
Retail trades	8%	
Institutional trades	14%	
Total broker-dealer trades:	*22%*	
Total trading off-exchange:		**35%**

Sources: Data for exchanges are from Bats Global Markets: **http://markets.cboe.com/us/equities/market_share /market/**. The percentages for off-exchange trading are based on the proportions of off-exchange trading for ATSs and non-ATSs shown in an SEC report by Laura Tuttle, which can be found at **www.sec.gov/marketstructure /research/otc_trading_march_2014.pdf**.

Notes:

[a]About 18% trades at NASDAQ.

[b]This was formerly the Boston Stock Exchange.

[c]This was formerly the Philadelphia Stock Exchange.

[d]About 12% trades at NYSE.

[e]This was formerly the Archipelago electronic communications network.

[f]This was formerly the American Stock Exchange.

[g]About half the trades are executed by only seven broker-dealers.

(the price and number of shares) but are not required to report any information about limit orders that have not yet been filled.

Following is a description of how trading works in a broker-dealer network.

Trading in a Standard Broker-Dealer Network Suppose a broker-dealer receives a market order (buy or sell a certain number of shares in a particular company's stock at the market price) from one of its clients, from an independent broker, or from another broker-dealer. In many cases, a broker-dealer will attempt to fill the order in-house without sending it to a stock exchange. For example, Morgan Stanley & Co. LLC is a registered broker-dealer and sometimes facilitates trades for its clients by matching a sell order from one client with a buy order from another client. If no in-house match between clients is available with respect to the company or number of shares, a broker-dealer might act as a dealer and fill the order by selling from or buying for its own inventory. Alternatively, the original broker-dealer might send the order to a "wholesale" broker-dealer who will combine orders from many other broker-dealers and look for a match.

For example, suppose a broker-dealer has a market order to buy 100 shares of Apple and a market order to sell 100 shares of Apple. Recall from Section 1-11a that any transaction must be between the NBBO bid and ask price:

$$\text{NBBO bid} = \$179.98 \le \text{Transaction price} \le \$180.02 = \text{NBBO ask}$$

The broker-dealer can satisfy Reg NMS, provide better prices to clients, and still profit from the transaction. For example, the broker-dealer can buy 100 shares from the selling client at $179.99, which is better than the NBBO bid of $179.98. The selling client actually gets a higher price than the NBBO bid price.

The broker-dealer can then sell the just purchased 100 shares to the buying client at $180.01, which is better than the NBBO ask price of $180.02. Therefore, the buying client gets to purchase shares at a lower price than the NBBO ask price. This process is called **price improvement** because the clients get better deals than the posted NBBO quotes would indicate.

What about the broker-dealer's cash flows? The broker-dealer pays $179.99 per share and then immediately sells for $180.01, pocketing the difference of 2 cents per share: $180.01 − $179.99 = $0.02. This spread is the broker-dealer's compensation for executing the trades.[16]

This process is called **internalization** because the broker-dealer is actually the counterparty for both clients: The broker-dealer buys from one client and sells to the other. Over 200 broker-dealers participate in this network, but only a handful of wholesale broker-dealers actually execute the trades. Some experts estimate that broker-dealers internalize over 90% of all market orders but send almost all limit orders to trading venues outside their own networks.[17]

Retail and Institutional Clients in a Broker-Dealer Network   Broker-dealers facilitate trading by individual investors (often called *retail trading*) and by institutional investors, such as pension funds. Institutions often trade larger quantities of stock than retail clients, which can create a problem.

For example, suppose a pension fund places an order to sell 10,000 shares of Google. (This is called a *block trade* because the quantity is at least 10,000.) A large order like this might create a big addition to the number of shares currently being offered for sale by others. This might create a temporary imbalance in supply and demand, causing the price to fall before the institution can sell all 10,000 shares. To avoid depressing the price, the institution might place many small orders rather than a single large order. Alternatively, the institution might engage the services of a broker-dealer to locate a large counterparty to buy the 10,000 shares. This counterparty might be another institution, or it might be another broker-dealer. In either case, this is called an "upstairs" trade even though no stairs are involved.[18]

Although broker-dealers must publicly report the price and number of shares for each transaction, they do not have to report the names of the traders, making it impossible to identify exactly how much trading is due to retail clients versus institutions. However, large trades of more than 500 shares comprise about 30% of all dealer-broker

---

[16]Some broker-dealers actually pay other brokers or dealers for routing orders their way, which is called "payment for order flow." Dealers do this because the profits from the spread are greater than the payments for flow. Also, the example showed the broker-dealer transacting in prices based on dollars and cents. NBBO quotes must be shown in penny increments, but dealers can actually conduct these transactions using prices that are in increments smaller than pennies as long as the total transaction value (i.e., price multiplied by number of shares) ends up with whole pennies. For example, 1,000 shares could be transacted at $12.00001 because the total value is $12,000.01 = 1,000($12.00001). This means that the client's price improvement relative to the NBBO can be quite small.

[17]See a report by the Chartered Financial Analysts Institute, "Dark Pools, Internalization, and Equity Market Quality," which can be accessed at **www.cfapubs.org/doi/pdf/10.2469/ccb.v2012.n5.1**.

[18]The name came from a time when most trading was on the floor of the NYSE. Block trades were not on the floor, so they were called "upstairs" trades.

trades, and block trades of at least 10,000 shares comprise about 3%.[19] These figures suggest that institutional investors are very active in the upstairs market provided by broker-dealers.

ALTERNATIVE TRADING SYSTEM (ATS): DARK POOLS

Recall that internalization in a standard broker-dealer network means that the broker-dealer is a counterparty in all trades: The broker-dealer buys stock from selling clients and sells the stock to buying clients. However, some broker-dealers also provide a different trading venue in which the broker-dealer is no longer a counterparty in all trades. Instead, buyers can trade directly with sellers. This is called an **alternative trading system (ATS)**.

Broker-dealers must register an ATS with the SEC, which imposes more regulatory requirements than it does for standard broker-dealer networks but fewer than for registered stock exchanges. It is costly for the broker-dealer to provide the infrastructure for an ATS, which usually has an automated matching engine. Therefore, the broker-dealer charges a subscription fee, which entitles a subscriber to trade with other subscribers using the ATS's infrastructure.

Like all trading venues, an ATS must comply with Reg NMS's order protection rule and report completed transactions to the consolidated tape system. However, an ATS is not required to report quotes from its order book to the consolidated quote system.[20] This means that pre-trade information (i.e., bid and ask prices) from an ATS is not available to the general public and is not included when the national best bid and offer (NBBO) prices are reported. Therefore, an ATS is commonly called a **dark pool**.

There are about 30 registered ATSs, accounting for about 13% of total stock market trading (based on dollar value), as shown in Table 1-3.

REGISTERED STOCK EXCHANGES

U.S. stock exchanges must register with the SEC and are more regulated than alternative trading systems or dealer-broker networks. In particular, the SEC requires **registered stock exchanges** to operate in a way that promotes orderly trading and fair dissemination of information, including transactions (price and number of shares) and pre-trade information (i.e., selected quote data from their order books).

As shown in Table 1-2, the NYSE and NASDAQ have the most listed stocks and are probably the most well-known U.S. stock exchanges. Before 2001, neither exchange used automated trading platforms to execute a significant percent of their trading volumes (trading at the NYSE was face-to-face on the floor of the exchange while trading at NASDAQ was through market makers). In response to competition from new exchanges with automated trading platforms, such as Cboe Global Markets, both the NYSE and NASDAQ now execute the majority of their stock trades via automated trading platforms.

---

[19]See two SEC reports by Laura Tuttle: "OTC Trading: Description of Non-ATS OTC Trading in National Market System Stocks," March 2014, and "Alternative Trading Systems: Description of ATS Trading in National Market System Stocks," October 2013. These reports can be accessed at **www.sec.gov/divisions/riskfin /whitepapers/alternative-trading-systems-10-2013.pdf** and **www.sec.gov/marketstructure/research/otc_trading _march_2014.pdf**.

[20]Before 2005, the term "electronic communications network (ECN)" was commonly used to denote any automated trading platform. After Reg NMS was adopted, the definition of ECN was modified to mean an alternative trading system that uses an automated trading platform and that publicly reports order book information in much the same way as a registered stock exchange (i.e., reporting of order book quotes); see Reg NMS §242.600(b)(23) and §242.602(b)(5) at **www.sec.gov/rules/final/34-51808.pdf**. By 2015, all ECNs had been closed or converted to stock exchanges.

Competition has also fragmented trading. From 2005 to 2010, trading on the floor of the NYSE dropped from about 65% of all trading (based on dollar volume) to about 12%. Some of the reduction was due to cannibalization from affiliated exchanges (the NYSE Arca and NYSE MKT), but most was due to gains by other exchanges and by off-exchange trading in dark pools or through broker-dealer internalization.

Table 1-3 shows that about 35% of all trading (based on dollar values) takes place off-exchange, in the less regulated trading venues of dark pools and broker-dealer networks. The combination of technological advances and market fragmentation has led to a phenomenon called "high-frequency trading," as we explain next.

1-11c High-Frequency Trading (HFT)

Investors, broker-dealers, and high-frequency traders all buy and sell stocks. Here are some differences among them.

Most investors purchase stock with the intent of owning it until they think it is no longer a good investment or until they need cash for some other purpose. Some investors, like Warren Buffett, buy and hold for decades. Others, like actively managed mutual funds, buy and hold for about a year, on average. Of course, some investors hold stock only for weeks or days at a time.

In contrast, many broker-dealers often hold stock for a very short period. Recall that when a broker-dealer internalizes orders, it buys stock from one investor and sells to another almost immediately at a higher price. The profit is the broker-dealer's compensation for providing the infrastructure used by the investor to buy or sell shares.

High-frequency trading (HFT) is similar to broker-dealer internalization in that the HF trader buys stock and immediately sells it, profiting if the selling price is higher than the purchase price.[21] Unlike broker-dealer networks, HFT does not provide any infrastructure or other direct service for other buyers and sellers. Because the HFT trader is buying and selling many times a day (or even a second!), the process is called "high-frequency trading." HFT requires expensive computer systems and highly paid programmers, so most HFT is done by firms that are created for this purpose rather than by individual investors.

How does high-frequency trading work? HFT firms pay exchanges, like the NYSE, to let them place computers close to the exchanges' computers, an activity called "colocation." This reduces the time it takes for information about trading at the exchange to reach the HFT computers. HFT firms usually build or lease dedicated high-speed fiber-optic lines between their colocated computers at the different exchanges. Colocation and dedicated lines allow HFT firms to view information from one exchange, process it, and transmit it to another exchange in the blink of an eye. Actually, even a slow blinker can manage two or three blinks per second, whereas HFT computers can send and receive at least several hundred orders per second.

Recall that brokers send most limit orders to exchanges. If an order is large, there might not be big enough buyers at a single exchange to satisfy the order, so brokers often split large orders into smaller orders and send each one to a different exchange. For example, a broker might split an order to buy 600 shares of FedEx at $175 into 6 orders of 100 shares each. However, it might take longer for the order to reach one exchange than another. For example, it might take 1.5 milliseconds to reach the first exchange and 4.2 milliseconds to reach another exchange (there are 1,000 milliseconds in a second) due to slower electronic connections. A person would never notice such a short difference, but this is plenty of time

---

[21]High-frequency trading occurs in many different types of financial markets, but this discussion focuses on the stock market.

for the HFT computers at the first exchange to observe the order. If the trading algorithm decides that the order is just part of several more to come, then the computer might send a faster order over its fiber-optic connections to the other exchange, arriving before the broker's order. This is called "front running" because an order by the HFT gets in front of the order from the broker, even though the broker's order was placed first (albeit at a different exchange).[22] The HFT firm might be able to buy FedEx for $174.99 at the second exchange and then sell it for $175 when the broker's order finally arrives.[23] The net result is that the HFT firm pays $17,499 when it buys the 100 shares at $174.99 and receives $17,500 when it sells 100 shares at $175, for a net profit of $1.

This might look like a lot of effort for a small profit, which could even turn into a loss if the HFT algorithm isn't correct. However, small profits add up if they occur frequently. HFT accounts for 55% of total equity trading, generating about $1.1 billion in revenues for HFT firms in 2016.[24]

What is the net impact of HFT on financial markets? Let's take a look at liquidity, trading costs, and market stability. The total dollar volume of trading has grown from about $33 trillion in 2005 to $74 trillion in 2015, increasing market liquidity and allowing investors to trade more quickly.[25] Much of this increase in volume is due to HFT. However, critics argue that the HFTs provide false liquidity because HFT disappears when markets are falling, which is exactly when the market most needs liquidity.

The average bid-ask spread has shrunk to pennies for many stocks, which reduces costs to investors (and profits to dealers). HFT firms claim this is partially due to their trading, while critics attribute shrinking spreads to more competition and non-HFT advances in technology.

Critics also believe that HFT can destabilize the stock market, pointing to the flash crash of 2010, with the market falling by 9% in a matter of seconds but recovering almost as quickly. The SEC and Commodity Futures Trading Commission concluded that HFT contributed to this disruption but did not cause it. Critics also claim that HFT makes markets more volatile. Most academic studies show that HFT contributes to market volatility but by a relatively small amount.

In summary, the empirical evidence does not clearly show that HFT is especially helpful or harmful to well-functioning markets. However, some HFT revenues, such as those from front running, are direct costs to investors. To put that into perspective, the total value of stock trades in 2015 was about $74 trillion.[26] Based on $1.1 billion in HFT revenues, HFT trading represents an extra "fee" to investors of about 0.001% for each dollar traded ($1.1 billion/$74,000 billion = 0.001%). While HFT might "feel" unfair to non-HFT traders, there is no definitive evidence as to whether the costs of HFT exceed its possible benefits.

1-11d Stock Market Returns

As investors trade, stock prices change. When demand is high (lots of bids at high prices and for large quantities), stock prices go up; when demand is low (bids are only at low prices), stock prices go down.

---

[22]This is just one example among many HFT strategies and computer algorithms.

[23]It is illegal for a broker to front-run by placing a personal order before submitting a client's order, but it is not illegal in HFT because the broker's orders arrive at different exchanges at different times even though they were simultaneously submitted by the broker.

[24]HFT trading volume and revenues peaked in 2009 and have fallen since then, possibly due to increased competition among HFT firms. See **https://fas.org/sgp/crs/misc/R44443.pdf** and **www.bloomberg.com/news/articles/2017-07-13/they-re-the-world-s-fastest-traders-why-aren-t-they-thriving**.

[25]See Table 10 **www.sec.gov/reportspubs/select-sec-and-market-data/secstats2016.pdf**.

[26]See Table 10 in **www.sec.gov/reportspubs/select-sec-and-market-data/secstats2016.pdf**.

Figure 1-5 shows stock market levels and returns, as measured by the S&P 500 Index. Panel A shows that the market was relatively flat in the 1970s, increased somewhat in the 1980s, and has been a roller coaster ever since. Panel B highlights the year-to-year risk by showing total annual returns. Stocks have had positive returns in most years, but there have been several years with very large losses.

FIGURE 1-5
S&P 500 Stock Index Performance

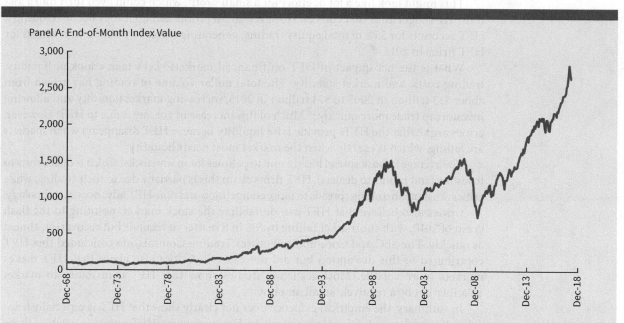

Panel A: End-of-Month Index Value

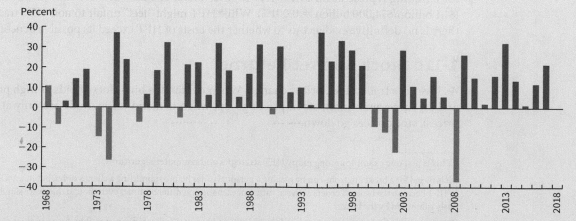

Panel B: Total Annual Returns: Dividend Yield + Capital Gain or Loss

Sources: Data for Panel A are from **http://finance.yahoo.com/quote/%5EGSPC/history?p=^GSPC**; the index is named ^GSPC. In Panel B, total returns prior to 2015 are from various issues of *The Wall Street Journal*. Returns for 2015 and subsequent years are based on the exchange-traded fund ^SP500TR, which replicates total S&P 500 returns; see **http://finance.yahoo.com/quote/%5ESP500TR/history?p=%5ESP500TR**.

SELF-TEST

Briefly describe the NBBO and the order protection rule. What regulation implemented them?

What does it mean to say that a trade was internalized at a broker-dealer?

What is an alternative trading system (ATS)? How does a trade at an ATS differ from an internalized trade at a broker-dealer?

How does the information that a registered stock exchange must display and report differ from that of an ATS? Why is an ATS often called a "dark pool"?

What percentage of stock trading is done off-exchange? On registered exchanges?

What is high-frequency trading? Describe a strategy through which a high-frequency trader makes a profit.

How is high-frequency trading similar to broker-dealer internalization? How is it different?

1-12 Finance and the Great Recession of 2007

Although the Great Recession of 2007 had many causes, mortgage securitization in the 2000s is certainly one culprit, so we begin with it.

1-12a The Globalization of Mortgage Market Securitization

A national TV program ran a documentary on the travails of Norwegian retirees resulting from defaults on Florida mortgages. Your first reaction might be to wonder how Norwegian retirees became financially involved with risky Florida mortgages. Let's start with a single home purchase in Florida.

1. HOME PURCHASE

In exchange for cash, a seller in Florida turned over ownership of a house to a buyer.

2. MORTGAGE ORIGINATION

To get the cash used to purchase the house, the buyer signed a mortgage loan agreement and gave it to an *originator*. Years ago, the originator would probably have been a **savings and loan association (S&L)**, which took in the vast majority of its deposits from individuals who lived in nearby neighborhoods. The S&L would make loans to homebuyers, who signed a contract promising to make interest and principal payments to the S&L, which used these payment to pay interest to its depositors and to issue new mortgages to other homebuyers. More recently, however, the originators have been specialized mortgage brokers who gathered and examined the borrower's credit information, arranged for an independent appraisal of the house's value, handled the paperwork, and received a fee for these services.

3. SECURITIZATION AND RESECURITIZATION

In exchange for cash, the originator sold the mortgage to a securitizing firm. For example, Merrill Lynch's investment banking operation was a major player in securitizing loans. It would bundle large numbers of mortgages into pools and then create new securities that had claims on the pools' cash flows. Some claims were simple, such as a proportional share of a pool; some were more complex, such as a claim on all interest payments during the first 5 years or a claim on only principal payments. More complicated claims were entitled to a fixed payment, while other claims would receive payments only after the senior claimants had been paid. These slices of the pool were called *tranches*, which comes from a French word for "slice."

Some of the tranches were themselves recombined and then subdivided into securities called **collateralized debt obligations (CDOs)**, some of which were themselves combined and subdivided into other securities, commonly called "CDOs-squared." For example, Lehman Brothers often bought different tranches, split them into CDOs of differing risk, and then had the different CDOs rated by an agency like Moody's or Standard & Poor's.

There are three very important points to notice. First, the process didn't change the *total amount of risk* embedded in the mortgages, but it did make it possible to create some securities that were less risky than average and some that were more risky. Second, the complexity of the CDOs spread a little bit of each mortgage's risk to many different investors, making it difficult for investors to determine the aggregate risk of a particular CDO. Third, each time a new security was created or rated, fees were being earned by the investment banks and rating agencies.

4. THE INVESTORS

In exchange for cash, the securitizing firms sold the newly created securities to individual investors, hedge funds, college endowments, insurance companies, and other financial institutions, including a pension fund in Norway. Keep in mind that financial institutions are funded by individuals, so cash begins with individuals and flows through the system until it is eventually received by the seller of the home. If all goes according to plan, payments on the mortgages eventually return to the individuals who originally provided the cash. But in this case, the chain was broken by a wave of mortgage defaults, resulting in problems for Norwegian retirees.

Students and managers often ask, "What happened to all the money?" The short answer is, "It went from investors to home sellers, with fees being skimmed off all along the way."

Although the process is complex, in theory there is nothing inherently wrong with it. In fact, it should, in theory, provide more funding for U.S. home purchasers, and it should allow risk to be shifted to those best able to bear it. Unfortunately, this isn't the end of the story.

1-12b The Dark Side of Securitization: The Sub-Prime Mortgage Meltdown

What caused the financial crisis? Entire books have been written on this subject, but we can identify a few of the culprits.

REGULATORS APPROVED SUB-PRIME STANDARDS

In the 1980s and early 1990s, regulations did not permit a non-qualifying mortgage to be securitized, so most originators mandated that borrowers meet certain requirements, including having at least a certain minimum level of income relative to the mortgage payments and a minimum down payment relative to the size of the mortgage. But in the mid-1990s, Washington politicians wanted to extend home ownership to groups that traditionally had difficulty obtaining mortgages. To accomplish this, regulations were relaxed so that non-qualifying mortgages could be securitized. Such loans are commonly called "sub-prime" or "Alt-A" mortgages. Thus, riskier mortgages were soon being securitized and sold to investors. Again, there was nothing inherently wrong, provided the two following questions were being answered in the affirmative: One, were home buyers making sound decisions regarding their ability to repay the loans? And two, did the ultimate investors recognize the additional risk? We now know that the answer to both questions is a resounding "No." Homeowners were signing mortgages that they could not hope to repay, and investors treated these mortgages as if they were much safer than they actually were.

THE FED HELPED FUEL THE REAL ESTATE BUBBLE

With more people able to get a mortgage, including people who should not have obtained one, the demand for homes increased. This alone would have driven up house prices. However, the Fed also slashed interest rates to historic lows after the terrorist attacks of 9/11 to prevent a recession, and it kept them low for a long time. These low rates made mortgage payments lower, which made home ownership seem even more affordable, again contributing to an increase in the demand for housing. Figure 1-6 shows that the combination of lower mortgage qualifications and lower interest rates caused house prices to skyrocket. Thus, the Fed contributed to an artificial bubble in real estate.

HOME BUYERS WANTED MORE FOR LESS

Even with low interest rates, how could sub-prime borrowers afford the mortgage payments, especially with house prices rising? First, most sub-prime borrowers chose

FIGURE 1-6
The Real Estate Boom: Housing Prices and Mortgage Rates

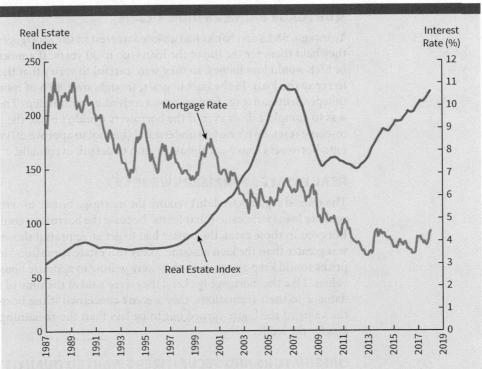

Notes:

1. The real estate index is the Case-Shiller composite index for house prices in 10 real estate markets, not seasonally adjusted, available at the Federal Reserve Bank of St. Louis's FRED® Economic Data: **http:// research.stlouisfed.org/fred2/series/SPCS10RSA**.

2. Interest rates are for 30-year conventional fixed-rate mortgages. Before September 2016, go to **https:// fred.stlouisfed.org/series/MORTG**. After September 2016, go to **www.freddiemac.com/pmms/pmms _archives.html**, scroll down to "Historical Data," and download monthly data for the 30-year fixed rate mortgage.

an adjustable-rate mortgage (ARM) with an interest rate based on a short-term rate, such as that on 1-year Treasury bonds, to which the lender added a couple of percentage points. Because the Fed had pushed short-term rates so low, the initial rates on ARMs were very low.

With a traditional fixed-rate mortgage, the payments remain fixed over time. But with an ARM, an increase in market interest rates triggers higher monthly payments, so an ARM is riskier than a fixed-rate mortgage. However, many borrowers chose an *even riskier* mortgage, the "option ARM," where the borrower can choose to make such low payments during the first couple of years that they don't even cover the interest, causing the loan balance to actually increase each month! At a later date, the payments would be reset to reflect both the current market interest rate and the higher loan balance. For example, in some cases a monthly payment of $948 for the first 32 months was reset to $2,454 for the remaining 328 months.

Why would anyone who couldn't afford to make a $2,454 monthly payment choose an option ARM? Here are three possible reasons. First, some borrowers simply didn't understand the situation and were victims of predatory lending practices by brokers eager to earn fees regardless of the consequences. Second, some borrowers thought that the home price would go up enough to allow them to sell at a profit or else refinance with another low-payment loan. Third, some people were simply greedy and shortsighted, and they wanted to live in a better home than they could afford.

MORTGAGE BROKERS DIDN'T CARE

Years ago, S&Ls and banks had a vested interest in the mortgages they originated because they held them for the life of the loan—up to 30 years. If a mortgage went bad, the bank or S&L would lose money, so they were careful to verify that the borrower would be able to repay the loan. In the bubble years, though, over 80% of mortgages were arranged by independent mortgage brokers who received a commission. Thus, the broker's incentive was to complete deals even if the borrowers couldn't make the payments after the soon-to-come reset. So it's easy to understand (but not to approve of!) why brokers pushed deals onto borrowers who were almost certain to default eventually.

REAL ESTATE APPRAISERS WERE LAX

The relaxed regulations didn't require the mortgage broker to verify the borrower's income, so these loans were called "liar loans" because the borrowers could overstate their income. But even in these cases, the broker had to get an appraisal showing that the house's value was greater than the loan amount. Many real estate appraisers simply assumed that house prices would keep going up, so they were willing to appraise houses at unrealistically high values. Like the mortgage brokers, they were paid at the time of their service. Other than damage to their reputations, they weren't concerned if the borrower later defaulted and the value of the house turned out to be less than the remaining loan balance, causing a loss for the lender.

ORIGINATORS AND SECURITIZERS WANTED QUANTITY, NOT QUALITY

Originating institutions like Countrywide Financial and New Century Mortgage made money when they sold the mortgages, long before any of the mortgages defaulted. The same is true for securitizing firms such as Bear Stearns, Merrill Lynch, and Lehman Brothers. Their incentives were to generate volume through originating loans, not to ensure that the loans were safe investments. This started at the top—CEOs and other top executives received stock options and bonuses based on their firms' profits, and profits depended on volume. Thus, the top officers pushed their subordinates to generate volume, those subordinates pushed the originators to write more mortgages, and the originators pushed the appraisers to come up with high values.

RATING AGENCIES WERE LAX

Investors who purchased the complicated mortgage-backed securities wanted to know how risky they were, so they insisted on seeing the bonds' "ratings." The securitizing firms paid rating agencies to investigate the details of each bond and to assign a rating that reflected the security's risk. For example, Lehman Brothers hired Moody's to rate some of its CDOs. Indeed, the investment banks would actually pay for advice from the rating agencies as they were designing the securities. The rating and consulting activities were extremely lucrative for the agencies, which ignored the obvious conflict of interest: The investment bank wanted a high rating, the rating agency got paid to help design securities that would qualify for a high rating, and high ratings led to continued business for the raters.

INSURANCE WASN'T INSURANCE

To provide a higher rating and make these mortgage-backed securities look even more attractive to investors, the issuers would frequently purchase a type of insurance policy on the security called a **credit default swap (CDS)**. For example, suppose you had wanted to purchase a CDO from Lehman Brothers but worried about the risk. What if Lehman Brothers had agreed to pay an annual fee to an insurance company such as AIG, which would guarantee the CDO's payments if the underlying mortgages defaulted? You probably would have felt confident enough to buy the CDO.

But any similarity to a conventional insurance policy ends here. Unlike home insurance, where there is a single policyholder and a single insurer, totally uninvolved speculators can also make bets on your CDO by either selling or purchasing credit default swaps on the CDO. For example, a hedge fund could buy a credit default swap on your CDO if it thinks the CDO will default, or an investment bank like Bear Stearns could sell a swap, betting that the CDO won't default. In fact, the International Swaps and Derivatives Association estimates that in mid-2008 there was about $54 trillion in credit default swaps. This staggering amount was approximately 7 times the value of all U.S. mortgages, was over 4 times the level of the U.S. national debt, and was over twice the value of the entire U.S. stock market.

Another big difference is that home insurance companies are highly regulated, but there was virtually no regulation in the credit default swap market. The players traded directly among themselves, with no central clearinghouse. It was almost impossible to tell how much risk any of the players had taken on, making it impossible to know whether or not counterparties like AIG would be able to fulfill their obligations in the event of a CDO default. And that made it impossible to know the value of CDOs held by many banks, which in turn made it impossible to judge whether or not those banks were de facto bankrupt.

ROCKET SCIENTISTS HAD POOR REARVIEW MIRRORS AND RISK MANAGERS DROVE BLIND

Financial engineers are brilliant experts, often trained in physics and hired from rocket science firms, who build elegant models to determine the value of a new security. Unfortunately, a model is only as good as its inputs. The experts looked at the high growth rates of recent real estate prices (see Figure 1-6) and assumed that future growth rates also would be high. These high growth rates caused models to calculate very high CDO prices. Perhaps more surprisingly, many risk managers simply did not insist on seeing scenarios in which housing prices fell.

INVESTORS WANTED MORE FOR LESS

In the early 2000s, low-rated debt (including mortgage-backed securities), hedge funds, and private equity funds produced great rates of return. Many investors jumped into this debt to keep up with the Joneses, focusing primarily on returns and largely ignoring risk. In fairness, some investors assumed the credit ratings were accurate, and they trusted the representatives of the investment banks selling the securities. In retrospect, however, Warren Buffett's maxim "I only invest in companies I understand" seems wiser than ever.

THE EMPEROR HAD NO CLOTHES

In 2006, many of the option ARMs began to reset, borrowers began to default, and home prices first leveled off and then began to fall. Things got worse in 2007 and 2008, and by early 2009, almost 1 out of 10 mortgages was in default or foreclosure, resulting in displaced families and virtual ghost towns of new subdivisions. As homeowners defaulted on their mortgages, so did the CDOs backed by the mortgages. That brought down the counterparties like AIG, who had insured the CDOs via credit default swaps. Virtually overnight, investors realized that mortgage-backed security default rates were headed higher and that the houses used as collateral were worth less than the mortgages. Mortgage-backed security prices plummeted, investors quit buying newly securitized mortgages, and liquidity in the secondary market disappeared. Thus, the investors who owned these securities were stuck with pieces of paper worth substantially less than the values reported on their balance sheets.

1-12c From Sub-Prime Meltdown to Liquidity Crisis to Economic Crisis

Like the Andromeda strain, the sub-prime meltdown went viral, and it ended up infecting almost all aspects of the economy. But why did a burst bubble in one market segment, sub-prime mortgages, spread across the globe?

First, securitization allocated the sub-prime risk to many investors and financial institutions. The huge amount of credit default swaps linked to sub-prime-backed securities spread the risk to even more institutions. Unlike previous downturns in a single market, such as the dot-com bubble in 2002, the decline in the sub-prime mortgage values affected many, if not most, financial institutions.

Second, banks were more vulnerable than at any time since the 1929 Depression. Congress had repealed the Glass-Steagall Act in 1999, allowing commercial banks and investment banks to be part of a single financial institution. The SEC compounded the problem in 2004 when it allowed large investment banks' brokerage operations to take on much higher leverage. Some, like Bear Stearns, ended up with $33 of debt for every dollar of its own equity. With such leverage, a small increase in the value of its investments would create enormous gains for the equity holders and large bonuses for the managers; conversely, a small decline would ruin the firm.

When the sub-prime market mortgages began defaulting, mortgage companies were the first to fall. Many originating firms had not sold all of their sub-prime mortgages, and they failed. For example, New Century declared bankruptcy in 2007, IndyMac was placed under FDIC control in 2008, and Countrywide was acquired by Bank of America in 2008 to avoid bankruptcy.

Securitizing firms also crashed, partly because they kept some of the new securities they created. For example, Fannie Mae and Freddie Mac had huge losses on their portfolio assets, causing them to be virtually taken over by the Federal Housing Finance Agency in 2008. In addition to big losses on their own sub-prime portfolios, many investment banks also had losses related to their positions in credit default swaps. Thus, Lehman Brothers was forced into bankruptcy, Bear Stearns was sold to JPMorgan Chase, and Merrill Lynch was sold to Bank of America, with huge losses to stockholders.

Because Lehman Brothers defaulted on some of its commercial paper, investors in the Reserve Primary Fund, a big money market mutual fund, saw the value of its investments "break the buck," dropping to less than a dollar per share. To avoid panic and a total lockdown in the money markets, the U.S. Treasury agreed to insure some investments in money market funds.

AIG was the largest backer of credit default swaps, and it operated worldwide. In 2008 it became obvious that AIG could not honor its commitments as a counterparty, so the Fed effectively nationalized AIG to avoid a domino effect in which AIG's failure would topple hundreds of other financial institutions.

In normal times, banks provide liquidity to the economy and funding for creditworthy businesses and individuals. These activities are crucial for a well-functioning economy. However, the financial contagion spread to commercial banks because some owned mortgage-backed securities, some owned commercial paper issued by failing institutions, and some had exposure to credit default swaps. As banks worried about their survival in the fall of 2008, they stopped providing credit to other banks and businesses. The market for commercial paper dried up to such an extent that the Fed began buying new commercial paper from issuing companies.

Prior to the sub-prime meltdown, many nonfinancial corporations had been rolling over short-term financing to take advantage of low interest rates on short-term lending. When the meltdown began, banks began calling in loans rather than renewing them. In response, many companies began throttling back their capital investment plans.

Anatomy of a Toxic Asset

Consider the dismal history of one particular toxic asset named "GSAMP Trust 2006-NC2." This toxic asset began life as 3,949 individual mortgages issued by New Century in 2006 with a total principal of about $881 million. Almost all were adjustable-rate mortgages, half were concentrated in just two states (California and Florida), and many of the borrowers had previous credit problems. Goldman Sachs bought the mortgages, pooled them into a trust, and divided the trust into 16 "debt" tranches called mortgage-backed securities (MBSs). The tranches had different provisions regarding distribution of payments should there be any defaults, with senior tranches getting paid first and junior tranches getting paid only if funds were available. Despite the mortgages' poor quality and the pool's lack of diversification, Moody's and Standard & Poor's gave most tranches good ratings, with over 79% rated AAA.

Five years later, in July 2011, about 36% of the underlying mortgages were behind in payments, defaulted, or even foreclosed. Not surprisingly, the market prices of the mortgage-backed securities had plummeted. These were very toxic assets indeed!

The story doesn't end here. Fannie Mae and Freddie Mac had purchased some of these toxic assets and taken a beating. In September 2011, the Federal Housing Finance Agency (now the conservator of Fannie Mae and Freddie Mac) sued Goldman Sachs, alleging that Goldman Sachs had knowingly overstated the value of the securities in the prospectuses. The FHFA also alleged that at the very same time Goldman Sachs was selling these and other mortgage-backed securities to Fannie and Freddie, Goldman was (1) trying to get rid of the mortgages by "putting" them back to New Century and (2) was "betting" against the mortgages in the credit default swap market. Goldman settled the suit in 2014 by agreeing to pay $1.2 billion, but it is safe to say that these toxic assets will continue to poison our economy for years to come.

Sources: Adam B. Ashcraft and Til Schuermann, *Understanding the Securitization of Subprime Mortgage Credit*, Federal Reserve Bank of New York Staff Reports, no. 318, March 2008; John Cassidy, *How Markets Fail* (New York: Farrar, Straus and Giroux, 2009), pp. 260–272; and the Federal Housing Finance Agency, **www.fhfa.gov/Media/PublicAffairs/Pages/FHFA-Announces-Settlement-with-Goldman-Sachs.aspx**.

Consumers and small businesses faced a similar situation: With credit harder to obtain, consumers cut back on spending, and small businesses cut back on hiring. Plummeting real estate prices caused a major contraction in the construction industry, putting many builders and suppliers out of work.

What began as a slump in housing prices caused enormous distress for commercial banks, not just mortgage companies. Commercial banks cut back on lending, which caused difficulties for nonfinancial business and consumers. Similar scenarios played out all over the world, resulting in the worst recession in the United States since 1929.

1-12d Responding to the Economic Crisis

Unlike the beginning of the 1929 Depression, the U.S. government did not take a hands-off approach in the most recent crisis. In late 2008, Congress passed the Troubled Asset Relief Plan (TARP), which authorized the U.S. Treasury to purchase mortgage-related assets from financial institutions. The intent was to simultaneously inject cash into the banking system and get these toxic assets off banks' balance sheets. The Emergency Economic Stabilization Act of 2008 (EESA) allowed the Treasury to purchase preferred stock in banks (whether they wanted the investment or not). Again, this injected cash into the banking system. Most of the large banks have already paid back the funding they received from the TARP and EESA financing, although it is doubtful whether all recipients will be able to do so. Fannie Mae and Freddie Mac have also paid the government more than they received in the bailout.

Although TARP and EESA were originally intended for financial institutions, they were subsequently modified so that the Treasury was able to make loans to GM and Chrysler in 2008 and early 2009 so that they could stave off immediate bankruptcy. Both GM and Chrysler went into bankruptcy in the summer of 2009 despite government loans, but they quickly emerged as stronger companies with the government owning some of the newly issued shares of stock. The U.S. government has since sold all of the shares issued to it by Chrysler and GM.

The government also used traditional measures, such as stimulus spending, tax cuts, and monetary policy: (1) The American Recovery and Reinvestment Act of 2009 provided over $700 billion in direct stimulus spending for a variety of federal projects and aid for state projects. (2) In 2010, the government temporarily cut Social Security taxes from 6.2% to 4.2%. (3) In addition to purchasing mortgage-related assets under the TARP program, the Federal Reserve has purchased around $2 trillion in long-term T-bonds from financial institutions, a process called *quantitative easing*.

Did the response work? When we wrote this in mid-2018, real GDP (gross domestic product) was much higher than before the crisis, and the unemployment rate was down to 4.1%, much lower than its 2009 high of 10% and close to its pre-crisis level of 4.4%. In fact, the U.S. recovery has been much stronger than that of Europe.[27]

1-12e Preventing the Next Crisis

Can the next crisis be prevented? Congress passed the **Dodd-Frank Wall Street Reform and Consumer Protection Act** in 2010 as an attempt to do just that. Following is a brief summary of some major elements in the Act.

---

[27]For a comparison of this crisis with 15 previous banking crises, see Serge Wind, "A Perspective on 2000's Illiquidity and Capital Crisis: Past Banking Crises and Their Relevance to Today's Credit Crisis," *Review of Business*, Vol. 31, No. 1, Fall 2010, pp. 68–83.

PROTECT CONSUMERS FROM PREDATORS AND THEMSELVES

Dodd-Frank established the Consumer Financial Protection Bureau, whose objectives include ensuring that borrowers fully understand the terms and risks of the mortgage contracts, that mortgage originators verify borrower's ability to repay, and that originators maintain an interest in the borrowers by keeping some of the mortgages they originate. The Bureau also watches over other areas in which consumers might have been targets of predatory lending practices, such as credit cards, debit cards, and payday loans.

As of 2017, the Bureau has fielded over 1.2 million consumer complaints and has levied over $11.9 billion in fines on financial institutions. The Bureau used the collected fines to provide monetary compensation to over 29 million wronged consumers.

SEPARATE BANKING FROM SPECULATING

The act's **Volcker rule**, named after former Fed chairman Paul Volcker, would greatly limit a bank's proprietary trading, such as investing the banks' own funds into hedge funds. The basic idea is to prevent banks from making highly leveraged bets on risky assets.

INCREASE TRANSPARENCY AND REDUCE RISK DUE TO DERIVATIVES TRADING

Title VII of the Dodd-Frank Act provides for more oversight of hedge funds and credit-rating agencies in an effort to spot potential landmines before they explode. More importantly, it attempts to reduce the financial system's exposure to risk caused by derivative trading, especially the risk stemming from swaps.

A swap is a contract in which one party swaps something with another party. For example, one party might make payments that fluctuate with interest rates to another party (called the "counterparty") in exchange for payments that do not fluctuate—the two parties "swap" payments. Because the swaps are traded directly between two parties, the risk that one party defaults is borne by the other party. The market for swaps is huge, with a value of almost $250 trillion![28] If there is a series of swaps linking various counterparties, then the default by one can trigger financial difficulties for all. Title VII in the Dodd-Frank Act directly addresses this situation.

Rather than two parties entering a custom-made swap contract directly between themselves, Title VII calls for most swaps to be standardized and traded in a public market made by either a *designated contract market (DCM)*, which is like a market maker, or a *swap execution facility (SEF)*, which is an automated trading platform. These markets provide information about trades and market activity, which should provide greater transparency.

In addition, all swap transactions must be sent to a registered *derivatives clearing organization (DCO)*, which "clears" the transaction by agreeing to ensure payments if one of the swap parties defaults. In other words, the risk of default by one party is shifted from the counterparty to the clearinghouse (i.e., the DCO). Of course, the clearinghouse reduces its risk by requiring collateral from each of the swap parties. The SEC and the Commodities Futures Trading Commission also regulate and monitor the clearinghouses.

---

[28]For updates on the swap markets, see **www.cftc.gov/MarketReports/SwapsReports/NotionalOutstanding/index.htm** and select "Cleared Status." This provides information for the swaps most likely to affect banks, including interest rate swaps, credit default swaps, and cross-currency swaps.

In late 2012, about 42% of swaps were cleared; by April 2018, about 63% were cleared. There are still too many uncleared swaps, but the Dodd-Frank Act is improving transparency and reducing the financial system's exposure to swap trading.

HEAD OFF AND REIN IN SYSTEMIC FAILURES AT TOO-BIG-TO-FAIL BANKS

When a bank gets extremely large and has business connections with many other companies, it can be very dangerous to the rest of the economy if the institution fails and goes bankrupt, as the 2008 failure of Lehman Brothers illustrates. In other words, a bank or other financial institution can become "too big to fail." *Systemic risk* is defined as something that affects most companies. When there are a large number of too-big-to-fail institutions and systemic shock hits, the entire world can be dragged into a recession, as we saw in 2008.

Dodd-Frank gives regulators more oversight of too-big-to-fail institutions, including all banks with $50 billion in assets and any other financial institutions that the Financial Stability Oversight Council deems systemically important. In mid-2018, there were 10 nonbank institutions that were designated as systemically important, including insurance companies and clearinghouses.

This oversight includes authority to require additional capital or reductions in leverage if conditions warrant. In addition, these institutions must prepare "transition" plans that would make it easier for regulators to liquidate the institution should it fail. In other words, this provision seeks to reduce the likelihood that a giant financial institution will fail and to minimize the damage if it does fail.

POLITICS AND REGULATION

Is the Dodd-Frank Act needed to prevent future crises or is it regulatory overreach that restricts economic growth? We don't know the answer to that question right now (early 2018), but we do know that the House of Representative passed a bill to repeal Dodd-Frank. The Senate has not voted on the House's bill but has instead introduced its own bill to make major changes in the Dodd-Frank Act. The Senate's bill significantly increases risk by easing constraints, such as redefining a too-big-to-fail financial institution as one with assets greater than $250 billion, significantly more than the previous threshold of $50 billion. By the time you read this, it is likely that the President will have signed a bill that significantly decreases regulatory requirements but that also increases risk. Whether these actions stimulate growth or precipitate another financial crisis remains to be seen.

SELF-TEST

Briefly describe the process that led from a homeowner purchasing a home to an investor purchasing a collateralized debt obligation.

How is a credit default swap like insurance?

Describe some of the motives and mistakes made by the Fed, home buyers, mortgage brokers, real estate appraisers, mortgage originators, mortgage securitizers, financial engineers, and investors.

What triggered the financial crisis and how did it spread to the rest of the economy?

How did the federal government respond to the crisis?

What provisions in the Dodd-Frank Wall Street Reform and Consumer Protection Act are designed to prevent a future financial crisis?

FIGURE 1-7
The Determinants of Intrinsic Value: The Big Picture

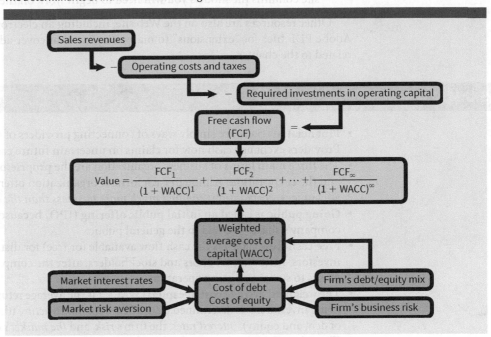

1-13 The Big Picture

Finance has vocabulary and tools that might be new to you. To help you avoid getting bogged down in the trenches, Figure 1-7 presents the big picture. A manager's primary job is to increase the company's intrinsic value, but how exactly does one go about doing that? The equation in the center of Figure 1-7 shows that intrinsic value is the present value of the firm's expected free cash flows, discounted at the weighted average cost of capital. Thus, there are two approaches for increasing intrinsic value: improve FCF or reduce the WACC. Observe that several factors affect FCF and several factors affect the WACC. In the rest of the book's chapters, we will typically focus on only one of these factors, systematically building the vocabulary and tools that you will use after graduation to improve your company's intrinsic value. It is true that every manager needs to understand financial vocabulary and be able to apply financial tools, but successful managers also understand how their decisions affect the big picture. So as you read this book, keep in mind where each topic fits into the big picture.

e-Resources

resource   When we think it might be helpful for you to look at resources on the book's Web site, we'll show an icon in the margin like the one shown here. The Web site contains several types of files that will be helpful to you:

1. It contains *Excel* files, called **Tool Kits**, that provide well-documented models for almost all of the text's calculations. Not only will these **Tool Kits** help you with this finance course, but they also will serve as tool kits for you in other courses and in your career.

2. There are problems at the end of the chapters that require spreadsheets, and the Web site contains the models you will need to begin work on these problems.

Other resources are also on the Web site, including an electronic library that contains Adobe PDF files for "extensions" to many chapters that cover additional useful material related to the chapter.

SUMMARY

- **Financial markets** are simply ways of connecting providers of cash with users of cash. Providers exchange cash now for claims on uncertain future cash.
- The three main forms of business organization are the **proprietorship**, the **partnership**, and the **corporation**. Although each form of organization offers advantages and disadvantages, *corporations conduct much more business than the other forms.*
- **Going public** is called an **initial public offering (IPO)** because it is the first time the company's shares are sold to the general public.
- **Free cash flow (FCF)** is the cash flow available (or free) for distribution to a company's investors, including creditors and stockholders, after the company has made investments to sustain ongoing operations.
- The **weighted average cost of capital (WACC)** is the average return required by all of the firm's investors. It is determined by the firm's *capital structure* (the firm's relative amounts of debt and equity), *interest rates*, the firm's *risk*, and *the market's attitude toward risk.*
- The value of a firm depends on the size of the firm's free cash flows, the timing of those flows, and their risk. If the expected future free cash flows and the cost of capital incorporate all relevant information, then a firm's **fundamental value** (also called **intrinsic value**) is defined by:

$$\text{Value} = \frac{\text{FCF}_1}{(1 + \text{WACC})^1} + \frac{\text{FCF}_2}{(1 + \text{WACC})^2} + \frac{\text{FCF}_3}{(1 + \text{WACC})^3} + \cdots + \frac{\text{FCF}_\infty}{(1 + \text{WACC})^\infty}$$

- The primary objective of management should be to maximize *stockholders' wealth*, and this means *maximizing the company's fundamental value.* Legal actions that maximize stock prices usually increase social welfare.
- Transfers of capital between borrowers and savers take place (1) by direct transfers of money and securities; (2) by transfers through **investment banks**, which act as go-betweens; and (3) by transfers through **financial intermediaries**, which create new securities.
- A **financial security** is a claim on future cash flows that is standardized and regulated. Debt, equity, and derivatives are the primary types of financial securities.
- **Derivatives**, such as options, are claims on other financial securities. In **securitization**, new securities are created from claims on packages of financial assets.
- The prospect of more money in the future is *required* to induce an investor to give up money today. This is a **required rate of return** from an investor's perspective and a cost from the user's point of view.
- Four fundamental factors affect the required rate of return (i.e., the cost of money): (1) production opportunities, (2) time preferences for consumption, (3) risk, and (4) inflation.
- **Spot markets** and **futures markets** are terms that refer to whether the assets are bought or sold for "on-the-spot" delivery or for delivery at some future date.
- **Money markets** are the markets for debt securities with maturities of less than a year. **Capital markets** are the markets for long-term debt and corporate stocks.

- **Primary markets** are the markets in which corporations raise new capital. **Secondary markets** are markets in which existing, already outstanding securities are traded among investors.
- A **trading venue** is a site (geographical or electronic) where secondary market trading occurs.
- Orders from buyers and sellers can be matched in one of three ways: (1) in a face-to-face **open outcry auction**, (2) through a computer network of **dealer markets**, and (3) through **automated trading platforms** with computers that match orders and execute trades.
- Registered stock exchanges (like the NYSE or NASDAQ) must display pre-trade quotes. **Broker-dealer networks** and **alternative trading systems** (ATS) (which are called **dark pools**) conduct **off-exchange** trading and are not required to display pre-trade information.
- The **Dodd-Frank Wall Street Reform and Consumer Protection Act** was passed in 2010 in an effort to prevent financial crises such as the one that triggered the Great Recession of 2007.
- *Web Extension 1A* discusses derivatives.

QUESTIONS

(1-1)   Define each of the following terms:
  a. Proprietorship; partnership; corporation; charter; bylaws
  b. Limited partnership; limited liability partnership; professional corporation
  c. Stockholder wealth maximization
  d. Money market; capital market; primary market; secondary market
  e. Private markets; public markets; derivatives
  f. Investment bank; financial services corporation; financial intermediary
  g. Mutual fund; money market fund
  h. Physical location exchange; computer/telephone network
  i. Open outcry auction; dealer market; automated trading platform
  j. Production opportunities; time preferences for consumption
  k. Foreign trade deficit

(1-2) •   What are the three principal forms of business organization? What are the advantages and disadvantages of each?

(1-3)   What is a firm's fundamental value (which is also called its intrinsic value)? What might cause a firm's intrinsic value to be different from its actual market value?

(1-4)   Edmund Corporation recently made a large investment to upgrade its technology. Although these improvements won't have much of an impact on performance in the short run, they are expected to reduce future costs significantly. What impact will this investment have on Edmund's earnings per share this year? What impact might this investment have on the company's intrinsic value and stock price?

(1-5) •   Describe the ways in which capital can be transferred from suppliers of capital to those who are demanding capital.

(1-6) •   What are financial intermediaries, and what economic functions do they perform?

(1-7)   Is an initial public offering an example of a primary or a secondary market transaction?

(1-8) Contrast and compare trading in face-to-face auctions, dealer markets, and automated trading platforms.

(1-9) Describe some similarities and differences among broker-dealer networks, alternative trading systems (ATS), and registered stock exchanges.

(1-10) What are some similarities and differences between the NYSE and the NASDAQ Stock Market?

MINI CASE

Assume that you recently graduated and have just reported to work as an investment advisor at the brokerage firm of Balik and Kiefer Inc. One of the firm's clients is Michelle DellaTorre, a professional tennis player who has just come to the United States from Chile. DellaTorre is a highly ranked tennis player who would like to start a company to produce and market apparel she designs. She also expects to invest substantial amounts of money through Balik and Kiefer. DellaTorre is very bright, and she would like to understand in general terms what will happen to her money. Your boss has developed the following set of questions you must answer to explain the U.S. financial system to DellaTorre.

a. Why is corporate finance important to all managers?

b. Describe the organizational forms a company might have as it evolves from a start-up to a major corporation. List the advantages and disadvantages of each form.

c. How do corporations go public and continue to grow? What are agency problems? What is corporate governance?

d. What should be the primary objective of managers?
   (1) Do firms have any responsibilities to society at large?
   (2) Is stock price maximization good or bad for society?
   (3) Should firms behave ethically?

e. What three aspects of cash flows affect the value of any investment?

f. What are free cash flows?

g. What is the weighted average cost of capital?

h. How do free cash flows and the weighted average cost of capital interact to determine a firm's value?

i. Who are the providers (savers) and users (borrowers) of capital? How is capital transferred between savers and borrowers?

j. What do we call the cost that a borrower must pay to use debt capital? What two components make up the cost of using equity capital? What are the four most fundamental factors that affect the cost of money, or the general level of interest rates, in the economy?

k. What are some economic conditions that affect the cost of money?

l. What are financial securities? Describe some financial instruments.

m. List some financial institutions.

n. What are some different types of markets?

o. Along what two dimensions can we classify trading procedures?

p. What are the differences between market orders and limit orders?

q. Explain the differences among broker-dealer networks, alternative trading systems, and registered stock exchanges.

r. Briefly explain mortgage securitization and how it contributed to the global economic crisis.

CHAPTER 2

Financial Statements, Cash Flow, and Taxes

Apple generated an operating cash flow of almost $64 billion in 2017! The ability to generate cash flow is the lifeblood of a company and the basis for its fundamental value. How did Apple use this cash flow? It returned over $46 billion to stockholders by paying $13 billion in dividends and by repurchasing $33 billion of its own stock.

Many other companies also reported large cash flows, but they used the money differently. For example, Google generated over $36 billion but returned relatively little to stockholders, paying no dividends and repurchasing only $4 billion of its stock. Instead, Google spent $10 billion on capital expenditures (mostly technology infrastructure). Google also put about $18 billion into short-term investments (such as Treasury securities), saving for a rainy day.

These well-managed companies used their operating cash flows in different ways, including capital expenditures, acquisitions, dividend payments, stock repurchases, and saving for future needs. Which company made the right choices? Only time will tell, but keep these companies and their different cash flow strategies in mind as you read this chapter.

Intrinsic Value, Free Cash Flow, and Financial Statements

In Chapter 1, we told you that managers should strive to make their firms more valuable and that a firm's intrinsic value is determined by the present value of its free cash flows (FCFs) discounted at the weighted average cost of capital (WACC). This chapter focuses on FCF, including its calculation from financial statements and its interpretation when evaluating a company and manager.

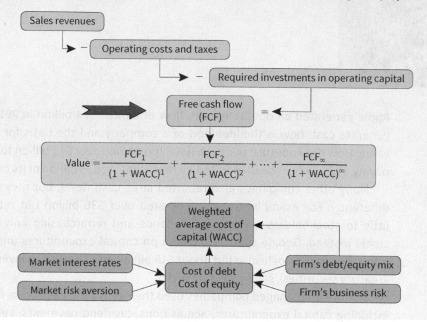

$$\text{Value} = \frac{\text{FCF}_1}{(1 + \text{WACC})^1} + \frac{\text{FCF}_2}{(1 + \text{WACC})^2} + \cdots + \frac{\text{FCF}_\infty}{(1 + \text{WACC})^\infty}$$

resource

*The textbook's Web site contains an Excel file that will guide you through the chapter's calculations. The file for this chapter is **Ch02 Tool Kit.xlsx**, and we encourage you to open the file and follow along as you read the chapter.*

The stream of cash flows a firm is expected to generate in the future determines its fundamental value (also called intrinsic value). But how does an investor go about estimating future cash flows, and how does a manager decide which actions are most likely to increase cash flows? The first step is to understand the financial statements that publicly traded firms must provide to the public. Thus, we begin with a discussion of financial statements, including how to interpret them and how to use them. Value depends on *after-tax cash flows*, so we provide an overview of the federal income tax system and highlight differences between accounting income and cash flow.

2-1 Financial Statements and Reports

www

See the Securities and Exchange Commission's (SEC) Web site for quarterly reports and more detailed annual reports that provide breakdowns for each major division or subsidiary. These reports, called 10-Q and 10-K reports, are available on the SEC's Web site at **www.sec.gov** *under the heading "EDGAR." Once there, you can search by stock ticker symbol.*

A company's **annual report** usually begins with the chairperson's description of the firm's operating results during the past year and a discussion of new developments that will affect future operations. The annual report also presents four basic financial statements—the *balance sheet,* the *income statement,* the *statement of stockholders' equity,* and the *statement of cash flows.*

The quantitative and qualitative written materials are equally important. The financial statements report *what has actually happened* to assets, earnings, dividends, and cash flows during the past few years, whereas the written materials attempt to explain why things turned out the way they did.

SELF-TEST

What is the annual report, and what two types of information does it present?

What four types of financial statements does the annual report typically include?

2-2 The Balance Sheet

For illustrative purposes, we use a hypothetical company, MicroDrive, Inc., which produces memory components for computers and smartphones. Figure 2-1 shows Micro-Drive's most recent **balance sheets**, which represent "snapshots" of its financial position on the last day of each year. Although most companies report their balance sheets only on the last day of a given period, the "snapshot" actually changes daily as inventories are bought and sold, as fixed assets are added or retired, or as loan balances are increased or paid down. Moreover, a retailer will have larger inventories before Christmas than later in the spring, so balance sheets for the same company can look quite different at different times during the year. The following sections explain the accounts shown in Figure 2-1.

The balance sheet begins with assets, which are the "things" the company owns. Assets are listed in order of *liquidity*, or length of time it typically takes to convert them to cash at fair market values. The balance sheet also lists the claims that various groups have against the company's value; these are listed in the order in which they must be paid. For example, suppliers may have claims called *accounts payable* that are due within 30 days, banks may have claims called *notes payable* that are due within 90 days, and bondholders may have claims that are not due for 20 years or more.

Stockholders' claims represent ownership (or equity) and need never be "paid off." These are residual claims in the sense that stockholders may receive payments only if there is value remaining after other claimants have been paid. The nonstockholder claims are

FIGURE 2-1
MicroDrive, Inc.: December 31 Balance Sheets (Millions of Dollars)

	A	B	C	D	E	F	G
26	MicroDrive Inc. December 31 Balance Sheets						
27	(Millions of Dollars)						
28	*Assets*					2019	2018
29	Cash and equivalents					$100	$102
30	Short-term investments					10	40
31	Accounts receivable					500	384
32	Inventories					1,000	774
33	Total current assets					$1,610	$1,300
34	Net property, plant, and equipment (PP&E)					2,000	1,780
35	Total assets					$3,610	$3,080
36							
37	*Liabilities and Equity*						
38	Accounts payable					$200	$180
39	Notes payable					150	28
40	Accruals					400	370
41	Total current liabilities					$750	$578
42	Long-term bonds					520	350
43	Total liabilities					$1,270	$928
44	Preferred stock (1,000,000 shares)					100	100
45	Common stock (60,000,000 shares)					500	500
46	Retained earnings					1,740	1,552
47	Total common equity					$2,240	$2,052
48	Total liabilities and equity					$3,610	$3,080
49							

Source: See the file ***Ch02 Tool Kit.xlsx.*** Numbers are reported as rounded values for clarity but are calculated using *Excel*'s full precision. Thus, intermediate calculations using the figure's rounded values may be inexact.

liabilities from the stockholders' perspective. The amounts shown on the balance sheets are called **book values** because they are based on the amounts recorded by bookkeepers when assets are purchased or liabilities are issued. As you will see throughout this textbook, book values may be very different from **market values**, which are the current values as determined in the marketplace.

The following sections provide more information about specific asset, liability, and equity accounts.

2-2a Assets

Cash, short-term investments, accounts receivable, and inventories are listed as current assets because MicroDrive is expected to convert them into cash within a year. All assets are stated in dollars, but only cash represents actual money that can be spent. Some **marketable securities** mature very soon, and these can be converted quickly into cash at prices close to their book values. Such securities are called *cash equivalents* and are included with cash. Therefore, MicroDrive could write checks for a total of $100 million. Other types of marketable securities have a longer time until maturity (but still less than a year). Their market values are less predictable, so they are not included in cash or cash equivalents.

Because it is helpful in financial analysis, MicroDrive's accountants are careful to separately identify the cash used in daily operations and the cash that is held for other purposes. For example, MicroDrive continuously deposits checks from customers and writes checks to suppliers, employees, and so on. Because inflows and outflows do not coincide perfectly, MicroDrive must keep some cash in its bank account. In other words, Micro-Drive must have some cash on hand to conduct operations, which is the $100 million in cash reported in Figure 2-1.

MicroDrive reports the total of any other cash, cash equivalents, and marketable securities that are not used to support operation in a separate account called short-term investments. For example, Figure 2-1 shows that MicroDrive has $10 million of short-term investments.

We will always distinguish between the cash that is used to support operations and the cash, cash equivalents, and marketable securities that are held for other purposes. However, be alert when looking at the financial statements from sources outside our book because they don't always separately identify the cash used to support operations.

When MicroDrive sells its products to customers but doesn't demand immediate payment, the customers then have obligations to make the payment, which MicroDrive reports as **accounts receivable**. The $500 million shown in accounts receivable is the amount of sales for which MicroDrive has not yet been paid.

Figure 2-1 reports inventories of $1,000 million, which is the amount that Micro-Drive has tied up in raw materials, work-in-process, and finished goods available for sale. MicroDrive uses the **FIFO (first-in, first-out)** inventory accounting method to estimate production costs and the value of remaining inventory. The FIFO method assumes, for accounting purposes only, that the first items placed in inventory are the first ones used in production. In contrast, the **LIFO (last-in, first-out)** method assumes that the items most recently placed in inventory are the first ones used in production. (No matter which method a company chooses for accounting purposes, the company actually can use inventory in any order it wishes.)

During an inflationary period of rising prices, older purchases of materials have lower costs than newer purchases. This means that FIFO will report lower costs of goods sold on the income statement than LIFO (because FIFO assumes that the older items are used first) but will report higher values for remaining inventory on the balance sheet. Because Micro-Drive uses FIFO and because inflation has been occurring: (1) Its balance sheet inventories are higher than they would have been had it used LIFO. (2) Its cost of goods sold is lower than it would have been under LIFO. (3) Its reported profits are therefore higher. Thus, the inventory valuation method can have a significant effect on financial statements, which is important to know when comparing companies that use different methods.

Rather than treat the entire purchase price of a long-term asset (such as a factory, plant, or equipment) as an expense in the purchase year, accountants "spread" the purchase cost over the asset's useful life. The amount they charge each year is called the **depreciation expense**. Some companies report an amount called *gross plant and equipment*, which is the total cost of the long-term assets they have in place, and another amount called *accumulated depreciation*, which is the total amount of depreciation that has been charged on those assets. Some companies, such as MicroDrive, report only net plant and equipment, which is gross plant and equipment less accumulated depreciation. Chapter 11 provides a more detailed explanation of depreciation methods.

2-2b Liabilities and Equity

Accounts payable, notes payable, and accruals are listed as current liabilities because MicroDrive is expected to pay them within a year. When MicroDrive purchases supplies but doesn't immediately pay for them, it takes on obligations called **accounts payable**. Similarly, when MicroDrive takes out a loan that must be repaid within a year, it signs an IOU called a *note payable*.

Most companies use the Accrual Accounting Method, which attempts to match revenues to the periods in which they are earned and expenses to the periods in which the effort to generate income occurred. For example, companies don't pay employees' wages daily, and the amount owed on these items at any point in time usually is reported as a current liability in an account such as "Accrued Wages Payable." Most companies have more than one type of accrued liability, but we combine all such accruals into a single account for MicroDrive to avoid unnecessary complexity. Section 2-5 explains how accruals affect cash flows.

Long-term bonds are also liabilities because they reflect a claim held by someone other than a stockholder. They are not reported as a current liability because the maturity date is more than one year away.

Preferred stock is a hybrid, or a cross between common stock and debt. In the event of bankruptcy, preferred stock ranks below debt but above common stock. Also, the preferred dividend is fixed, so preferred stockholders do not benefit if the company's earnings grow. Most firms do not use much, if any, preferred stock, so "equity" usually means "common equity" unless the words "total" or "preferred" are included.

When a company sells shares of stock, it records the proceeds in the **common stock account**.[1] **Retained earnings** are the cumulative amount of earnings that have not been paid out as dividends. The sum of common stock and retained earnings is called **common equity**, or just *equity*. If a company could actually sell its assets at their book value, and if the liabilities and preferred stock were actually worth their book values, then a company could sell its assets, pay off its liabilities and preferred stock, and the remaining cash would belong to common stockholders. Therefore, common equity is sometimes called the **net worth of shareholders**—it's the assets minus (or "net of") the liabilities and preferred stock.

---

[1]Companies sometimes break the total proceeds into two parts: **par value** and **paid-in capital** (or capital surplus). For example, if a company sells shares of stock for $10, it might record $1 of par and $9 of paid-in capital. For most purposes, the distinction between par and paid-in capital is not important, and most companies now use no-par stock.

Let's Play Hide-and-Seek!

In a shameful lapse of regulatory accountability, banks and other financial institutions were allowed to use so-called structured investment vehicles (SIVs) to hide assets and liabilities and simply not report them on their balance sheets. Here's how SIVs worked and why they subsequently failed. The SIV was set up as a separate legal entity that the bank owned and managed. The SIV would borrow money in the short-term market (backed by the credit of the bank) and then invest in long-term securities. As you might guess, many SIVs invested in mortgage-backed securities. When the SIV paid only 3% on its borrowings but earned 10% on its investments, the managing bank was able to report fabulous earnings, especially if it also earned fees for creating the mortgage-backed securities that went into the SIV.

But this game of hide-and-seek didn't have a happy ending. Mortgage-backed securities began defaulting in 2007 and 2008, causing the SIVs to pass losses through to the banks. SunTrust, Citigroup, Bank of America, and Northern Rock are just a few of the many banks that reported enormous losses in the SIV game. Investors, depositors, and the government eventually found the hidden assets and liabilities, but by then the assets were worth a lot less than the liabilities.

In a case of too little and too late, regulators have closed many of these loopholes, and it doesn't look like there will be any more hidden SIVs in the near future. But the damage has been done, and the entire financial system was put at risk in large part because of this high-stakes game of hide-and-seek.

SELF-TEST

What is the balance sheet, and what information does it provide?

What determines the order of the information shown on the balance sheet?

Why might a company's December 31 balance sheet differ from its June 30 balance sheet?

A firm has $8 million in total assets. It has $3 million in current liabilities, $2 million in long-term debt, and $1 million in preferred stock. What is the reported net worth of shareholders (i.e., the reported common equity)? **($2 million)**

2-3 The Income Statement

resource

See **Ch02 Tool Kit.xlsx** *for details.*

Figure 2-2 shows the **income statements** and selected additional information for Micro-Drive. Income statements can cover any period of time, but they are usually prepared monthly, quarterly, and annually. Unlike the balance sheet, which is a snapshot of a firm at a point in time, the income statement reflects performance during the period. The following sections explain the components of an income statement.

Net sales are the revenues less any discounts or returns. Depreciation and amortization reflect the estimated costs of the assets that wear out in producing goods and services. To illustrate depreciation, suppose that in 2019 MicroDrive purchased a $100,000 machine with a life of 5 years and zero expected salvage value. This $100,000 cost is not expensed in the purchase year but is instead spread out over the machine's 5-year depreciable life.[2] In straight-line depreciation, which we explain in Chapter 11, the depreciation charge for a full year would be $100,000/5 = $20,000. The reported depreciation expense on the income statement is the sum of all the assets' annual depreciation charges.

Depreciation applies to tangible assets, such as plant and equipment, whereas an **amortization expense** applies to intangible assets. For example, if a company acquires another company but pays more than the tangible assets, then the difference is

---

[2]Congress occasionally changes the tax laws regarding depreciation and did so again with the 2017 Tax Cut and Jobs Act. We discuss many of the TCJA's features later in this chapter. See Chapter 11 for a more detailed discussion of depreciation for tax purposes.

FIGURE 2-2

MicroDrive Income Statements (and Selected Additional Information) for Years Ending December 31
(Millions, Except for Per Share Data)

	A	B	C	D	E	F	G
						2019	**2018**
56							
57	Net sales					$5,000	$4,800
58	Costs of goods sold except depreciation					3,900	3,710
59	Depreciation and amortization[a]					200	180
60	Other operating expenses					500	470
61	Earnings before interest and taxes (EBIT)					$400	$440
62	Less interest					60	40
63	Pre-tax earnings					$340	$400
64	Taxes					85	100
65	Net Income before preferred dividends					$255	$300
66	Preferred dividends					7	7
67	Net Income available to common stockholders					$248	$293
68							
69	*Additional Information*						
70	Common dividends					$60.0	$59.4
71	Addition to retained earnings					$188.0	$233.6
72	Number of common shares					60	60
73	Stock price per share					$31.00	$45.00
74							
75	*Per Share Data*						
76	Earnings per share, EPS[b]					$4.13	$4.88
77	Dividends per share, DPS[c]					$1.00	$0.99
78	Book value per share, BVPS[d]					$37.33	$34.20

Source: See the file *Ch02 Tool Kit.xlsx*. Numbers are reported as rounded values for clarity but are calculated using *Excel*'s full precision. Thus, intermediate calculations using the figure's rounded values may be inexact.

Notes:

[a]MicroDrive has no amortization charges.

$$\text{[b]EPS} = \frac{\text{Net income available to common stockholders}}{\text{Common shares outstanding}}$$

$$\text{[c]DPS} = \frac{\text{Dividends paid to common stockholders}}{\text{Common shares outstanding}}$$

$$\text{[d]BVPS} = \frac{\text{Total common equity}}{\text{Common shares outstanding}}$$

called **goodwill**.[3] Other intangible assets include patents, copyrights, trademarks, and similar items. MicroDrive has no amortization charges.

The **cost of goods sold (COGS)** includes labor, raw materials, and other expenses directly related to the production or purchase of the items or services sold in that period. As reported in most financial statements, the COGS includes depreciation because accounting logic defines depreciation as the cost of assets wearing out by producing goods. In contrast, we report depreciation separately so that analysis later in the chapter will be more transparent.

---

[3]The accounting treatment of goodwill resulting from mergers has changed in recent years. Rather than an annual charge, companies are required to periodically evaluate the value of goodwill and reduce net income only if the goodwill's value has decreased materially ("become impaired," in the language of accountants). For example, in 2002 AOL Time Warner wrote off almost $100 billion associated with the AOL merger. It doesn't take too many $100 billion expenses to really hurt net income!

A Matter of Opinion

Investors need to be cautious when they review financial statements. Although companies are required to follow generally accepted accounting principles (GAAP), managers still use a lot of discretion in deciding how and when to report certain transactions. Consequently, two firms in the same operating situation may report financial statements that convey different impressions about their financial strength. Some variations may stem from legitimate differences of opinion about the correct way to record transactions. In other cases, managers may choose to report numbers in a way that helps them present either higher earnings in the current year or more stable earnings over time. As long as they follow GAAP, such actions are not illegal, but these differences make it harder for investors to compare companies and gauge their true performances.

Subtracting COGS (including depreciation) and other operating expenses results in **earnings before interest and taxes (EBIT)**. Many analysts add back depreciation to EBIT to calculate **EBITDA**, which stands for earnings before interest, taxes, depreciation, and amortization. Because neither depreciation nor amortization is paid in cash, some analysts claim that EBITDA is a better measure of financial strength than is net income. MicroDrive's EBITDA is:

$$EBITDA = EBIT + Depreciation \qquad \text{(2-1)}$$

$$= \$400 + \$200 = \$600 \text{ million}$$

Alternatively, EBITDA's calculation can begin with sales:

$$EBITDA = Sales - COGS \text{ excluding depreciation} - Other operating expenses \qquad \text{(2-2)}$$

$$= \$5,000 - \$3,900 - \$500 = \$600 \text{ million}$$

However, as we show later in the chapter, EBITDA is not as useful to managers and analysts as free cash flow, so we usually focus on free cash flow instead of EBITDA.

Subtracting interest expense from EBIT results in **pre-tax income**, which is also called **earning before tax (EBT)**, or **taxable income**. The net income available to common shareholders, which equals revenues less expenses, taxes, and preferred dividends (but before paying common dividends), is generally referred to as **net income**. Net income is also called **accounting income, accounting profit**, **earnings**, or **profit**, particularly in financial news reports. Dividing net income by the number of shares outstanding gives earnings per share (EPS), often called the *bottom line*. Throughout this book, unless otherwise indicated, net income means net income available to common stockholders.[4]

---

[4]Companies also report "comprehensive income," which is the sum of net income and any "comprehensive" income item, such as the change in market value of a financial asset. For example, a decline in a financial asset's value would be recorded as a loss even though the asset has not been sold. We assume that there are no comprehensive income items in our examples.

Some companies also choose to report "pro forma income." For example, if a company incurs an expense that it doesn't expect to recur, such as the closing of a plant, it might calculate pro forma income as though it had not incurred the one-time expense. There are no hard-and-fast rules for calculating pro forma income, so many companies find ingenious ways to make pro forma income higher than traditional income. The SEC and the Public Company Accounting Oversight Board (PCAOB) are taking steps to reduce deceptive uses of pro forma reporting.

What is an income statement, and what information does it provide?

What is often called the "bottom line"?

What is EBITDA?

How does the income statement differ from the balance sheet with regard to the time period reported?

A firm has the following information: $2 million in earnings before taxes. The firm has an, interest expense of $300,000 and depreciation of $200,000; it has no amortization. What is its EBITDA? **($2.5 million)**

Now suppose a firm has the following information: $7 million in sales, $4 million of costs of goods sold excluding depreciation and amortization, and $500,000 of other operating expenses. What is its EBITDA? **($2.5 million)**

2-4 Statement of Stockholders' Equity

resource

See Ch02 Tool Kit.xlsx for details.

Changes in stockholders' equity during the accounting period are reported in the **statement of stockholders' equity**. Figure 2-3 shows that MicroDrive earned $248 million during 2019 and paid out $60 million in common dividends. This means that MicroDrive plowed $188 million back into the business: $248 − $60 = $188. Thus, the balance sheet item "Retained earnings" increased from $1,552 million at year-end 2018 to $1740 million at year-end 2019.[5] The last column shows the beginning stockholders' equity, any changes, and the end-of-year stockholders' equity.

Note that "Retained earnings" is not a pile of money just waiting to be used; it does not represent assets but is instead a *claim against assets*. In 2019, MicroDrive's

FIGURE 2-3
MicroDrive, Inc.: Statement of Stockholders' Equity for Years Ending December 31 (Millions of Dollars and Millions of Shares)

	A	B	C	D	E	F	G	H
99				Preferred	Common	Common	Retained	Total
100				Stock	Shares	Stock	Earnings	Equity
101	Balances, Dec. 31, 2018			$100	60	$500	$1,552	$2,152
102	Changes during year:							
103	Net income						$248	$248
104	Cash dividends						(60)	(60)
105	Issuance/repurchase of stock			0	0	0		
106	Balances, Dec. 31, 2019			$100	60	$500	$1,740	$2,340

Source: See the file *Ch02 Tool Kit.xlsx*. Numbers are reported as rounded values for clarity but are calculated using *Excel*'s full precision. Thus, intermediate calculations using the figure's rounded values may be inexact.

Note: In financial statements, parentheses and red colors denote a negative number.

[5]A more complicated company might require additional columns and rows to report information regarding new issues of stock, treasury stock acquired or reissued, stock options exercised, and unrealized foreign exchange gains or losses.

Financial Analysis on the Web

A wide range of valuable financial information is available on the Web. With just a couple of clicks, an investor can easily find the key financial statements for most publicly traded companies. Here's a partial (by no means complete) list of places you can go to get started.

◆ Try Yahoo! Finance's Web site, **http://finance.yahoo .com.** Here you will find updated market information along with links to a variety of interesting research sites. Enter a stock's ticker symbol, click Search and

select the company, and you will see the stock's current price along with recent news about the company. The panel at the top has links to key statistics and to the company's income statement, balance sheet, statement of cash flows, and more. The Web site also has a list of insider transactions, so you can tell if a company's CEO and other key insiders are buying or selling their company's stock. In addition, there is a message board where investors share opinions about

stockholders allowed it to reinvest $188 million ($248 net income − $60 million dividends) instead of distributing the money as dividends—the "retained earnings of $188 million was spent on new assets. Thus, retained earnings, as reported on the balance sheet, does not represent cash and is not "available" for the payment of dividends or anything else.[6]

SELF-TEST

What is the statement of stockholders' equity, and what information does it provide?

Why do changes in retained earnings occur?

Explain why the following statement is true: "The retained earnings account, as reported on the balance sheet, does not represent cash and is not available for the payment of dividends or anything else."

A firm had a retained earnings balance of $3 million in the previous year. In the current year, its net income is $2.5 million. If it pays $1 million in common dividends in the current year, what is its resulting retained earnings balance? **($4.5 million)**

2-5 Statement of Cash Flows

Even if a company reports a large net income during a year, the *amount of cash* reported on its year-end balance sheet may be the same or even lower than its beginning cash. The reason is that the company can use its net income in a variety of ways, not just keep it as cash in the bank. For example, the firm may use its net income to pay dividends, to increase inventories, to finance accounts receivable, to invest in fixed

---

[6]The amount reported in the retained earnings account is not an indication of the amount of cash the firm has. Cash (as of the balance sheet date) is found in the cash account, an asset account. A positive number in the retained earnings account indicates only that the firm earned some income in the past, but its dividends paid were less than its earnings. Even if a company reports record earnings and shows an increase in its retained earnings account, it still may be short of cash.

The same situation holds for individuals. You might own a new BMW (no loan), lots of clothes, and an expensive stereo and hence have a high net worth. But if you have only 23 cents in your pocket plus $5 in your checking account, you will still be short of cash.

the company. To see a complete list of the company's filings with the SEC, go to **www.sec.gov.**

♦ Other sources for up-to-date market information are **http://money.cnn.com** and **www.zacks.com.** These sites also provide financial statements in standardized formats.

♦ Both **www.bloomberg.com** and **www.marketwatch .com** have areas where you can obtain stock quotes along with company financials, links to Wall Street research, and links to SEC filings.

♦ If you are looking for charts of key accounting variables (e.g., sales, inventory, depreciation and amortization,

and reported earnings), as well as financial statements, take a look at **www.smartmoney.com.**

♦ Another good place to look is **www.reuters.com.** Here you can find links to analysts' research reports, along with the key financial statements.

In addition to this information, you may be looking for sites that provide opinions regarding the direction of the overall market and views regarding individual stocks. Two popular sites in this category are The Motley Fool's Web site, **www.fool.com,** and the Web site for The Street.com, **www .thestreet.com.**

assets, to reduce debt, or to buy back common stock. Indeed, many factors affect a company's *cash position* as reported on its balance sheet. The **statement of cash flows** separates a company's activities into three categories—operating, investing, and financing—and summarizes the resulting cash balance. Look at Figure 2-4 as you read the following sections.

2-5a Operating Activities

Net income is *not* a cash flow! The following sections explain how to determine actual cash flows by adjusting net income and taking into account other short-term operating cash flows.

NONCASH ADJUSTMENTS

Not all revenues and expenses reported on the income statement are received or paid in cash during the year. The most common item is depreciation. As explained in Section 2-2a, depreciation is reported as an expense but is not a cash flow—the cash flow occurred when the asset was purchased, not in the subsequent years.

Other items on the income statement can differ significantly from actual cash flows. For example, companies report one pre-tax income to the public but a different taxable income to the Internal Revenue Service (IRS)! Therefore, a company's reported tax expense can differ significantly from its actual tax payments. For example, Apple's statement of cash flows shows that it paid almost $6 billion less in taxes than it reported in 2017! Most of Apple's differential between taxes reported and taxes paid was due to its foreign earnings, but there are other reasons this can happen.[7] For example, growing companies report lower depreciation expenses to the public than to the IRS. This makes publicly reported taxable income higher than actual taxable income, resulting in higher reported taxes than actual taxes paid.

---

[7]Most of Apple's difference in taxes reported and taxes paid was due to provisions in the 2017 tax code that did not tax foreign income until it was repatriated (i.e., returned) to the United States instead of being invested abroad, even if that investment was simply a foreign bank account. That provision changed for 2018, as we discuss in Section 2-9.

resource

See **Ch02 Tool Kit.xlsx** for details.

FIGURE 2-4

MicroDrive, Inc.: Statement of Cash Flows for Year Ending December 31 (Millions of Dollars)

	A	B	C	D	E	F
118	*Operating Activities*					**2019**
119	**Net Income before preferred dividends**					**$255**
120	*Noncash adjustments*					
121	Depreciation[a]					200
122	*Working capital adjustments*					
123	Increase in accounts receivable[b]					(116)
124	Increase in inventories					(226)
125	Increase in accounts payable					20
126	Increase in accruals					30
127	**Net cash provided (used) by operating activities**					**$163**
128						
129	*Investing Activities*					
130	Cash used to acquire fixed assets[c]					($420)
131	Sale of short-term investments					30
132	**Net cash provided (used) by investing activities**					**($390)**
133						
134	*Financing Activities*					
135	Increase in notes payable					$122
136	Increase in bonds					170
137	Payment of common and preferred dividends					(67)
138	**Net cash provided (used) by financing activities**					**$225**
139						
140	*Summary*					
141	Net change in cash and equivalents					($2)
142	Cash and securities at beginning of the year					102
143	**Cash and securities at end of the year**					**$100**
144						

Source: See the file *Ch02 Tool Kit.xlsx*. Numbers are reported as rounded values for clarity but are calculated using *Excel*'s full precision. Thus, intermediate calculations using the figure's rounded values may be inexact.

Notes:

[a]Depreciation is a noncash expense that is deducted when calculating net income. It must be added back to show cash flow from operations.

[b]An increase in a current asset decreases cash. An increase in a current liability increases cash. See the text in this section for examples and explanations.

[c]The net increase in fixed assets (e.g., net plant and equipment) is $220 million; however, this net amount is after a deduction for the year's depreciation expense. Depreciation expense must be added back to find the increase in gross fixed assets. From the company's income statement, we see that the year's depreciation expense is $200 million; thus, expenditures on fixed assets were actually $420 million.

CHANGES IN WORKING CAPITAL

A firm's investment in current assets—cash, marketable securities, inventory, and accounts receivable—is called **working capital**. Increases in current assets other than cash (such as inventories and accounts receivable) decrease cash, whereas decreases in these accounts increase cash. For example, if inventories are to increase, then the firm must use cash to acquire the additional inventory. Conversely, if inventories decrease, this generally means the firm is selling inventories and not replacing all of them, hence generating cash.

Here's how we keep track of whether a change in assets increases or decreases cash flow: If the amount we *own* goes up (like getting a new laptop computer), it means we have spent money, and our cash goes down. On the other hand, if something we own goes down (like selling a car), our cash goes up.

Now consider a current liability, such as accounts payable. If accounts payable increase, then the firm has received additional credit from its suppliers, which saves cash; however, if payables decrease, this means it has used cash to pay off its suppliers. Therefore, increases in current liabilities such as accounts payable increase cash, whereas decreases in current liabilities decrease cash. To keep track of the cash flow's direction, think about the impact of getting a student loan. The amount you *owe* goes up, and your cash goes up. Now think about paying off the loan: The amount you owe goes down, but so does your cash.

2-5b Investing Activities

Investing activities include transactions involving fixed assets or short-term financial investments. For example, if a company buys new IT infrastructure, its cash goes down at the time of the purchase. On the other hand, if it sells a building or a Treasury bond, its cash goes up.

2-5c Financing Activities

Financing activities include raising cash by issuing short-term debt, long-term debt, or stock. Because dividend payments, stock repurchases, and principal payments on debt reduce a company's cash, such transactions are included here as negative cash flows.

2-5d Putting the Pieces Together

The statement of cash flows is used to help answer questions such as these: Is the firm generating enough cash to purchase the additional assets required for growth? Is the firm generating any extra cash it can use to repay debt or to invest in new products? Such information is useful both for managers and investors, so the statement of cash flows is an important part of the annual report.

Figure 2-4 shows MicroDrive's statement of cash flows as it would appear in the company's annual report. The top section shows cash generated by and used in operations: For MicroDrive, operations provided $163 million. This subtotal is in many respects the most important figure in any of the financial statements. Profits as reported on the income statement can be "doctored" by such tactics as depreciating assets too slowly, not recognizing bad debts promptly, and the like. However, it is far more difficult to simultaneously doctor profits *and* the working capital accounts. It is not uncommon for a company to report positive net income right up to the day it declares bankruptcy, but the cash provided by operations almost always began to deteriorate much earlier, and analysts who kept an eye on cash flow could have predicted trouble. Therefore, if you are ever analyzing a company and are pressed for time, look first at the trend in cash provided by operating activities because it will tell you more than any other single number.

The second section shows investing activities. MicroDrive purchased fixed assets totaling $420 million (a negative cash flow) and sold short-term investments for $30 million (a positive cash flow). Therefore, investing activities *used* a total of $390 million, decreasing MicroDrive's cash.

Filling in the GAAP

While U.S. companies adhere to generally accepted accounting principles (GAAP), when preparing financial statements, most other developed countries use International Financial Reporting Standards (IFRS). The U.S. GAAP system is rules-based, with thousands of instructions, or "guidances," for how individual transactions should be reported in financial statements. IFRS, on the other hand, is a principles-based system in which detailed instructions are replaced by overall guiding principles.

For example, whereas GAAP provides extensive and detailed rules about when to recognize revenue from any conceivable activity, IFRS provides just four categories of revenue and two overall principles for timing recognition. This means that even the most basic accounting measure, revenue, is different under the two standards—total revenue, or sales, under GAAP won't typically equal total revenue under IFRS. Thus, financial statements prepared under GAAP cannot be compared directly to IFRS financial statements, making comparative financial analysis of U.S. and international companies difficult. Perhaps more problematic is that the IFRS principles allow for more company discretion in recording transactions. This means that two companies may treat identical transactions differently when using IFRS, which makes company-to-company comparisons more difficult.

The U.S. Financial Accounting Standards Board (FASB) and the International Accounting Standards Board (IASB) have been working to merge the two sets of standards since 2002. Some of the joint standards are completed, such as the all-important revenue recognition standard, but many other standards had not been adopted as of early 2018. In fact, it seems likely that the adoption of worldwide standards will not happen in the near future.

To keep abreast of developments in IFRS/GAAP convergence, visit the IASB Web site at **www.iasb.org** and the FASB Web site at **www.fasb.org.**

The third section, financing activities, includes borrowing from banks (notes payable), selling new bonds, and paying dividends on common and preferred stock. MicroDrive raised $292 million by taking out short-term loans and issuing new bonds, but it paid $67 million in preferred and common dividends. Therefore, financing activities provided $225 million.

The last section shows the summary. When all of the previous activities are totaled, we see that MicroDrive's cash outflows exceeded its cash inflows by $2 million during 2019; that is, its net change in cash was a *negative* $2 million.

MicroDrive's statement of cash flows should be worrisome to its managers and to outside analysts. The company had $5 billion in sales but generated only $163 million from operations, not nearly enough to cover the $420 million it spent on fixed assets and the $67 million it paid in dividends. It covered these cash outlays by borrowing heavily and by liquidating short-term investments. Obviously, this situation cannot continue year after year, so MicroDrive managers will have to make changes. We will return to MicroDrive throughout the textbook to see what actions its managers are planning.

SELF-TEST

What types of questions does the statement of cash flows answer?

Identify and briefly explain the three categories of activities in the statement of cash flows.

A firm has inventories of $2 million for the previous year and $1.5 million for the current year. What impact does this have on net cash provided by operations? **(Increase of $500,000)**

2-6 Net Cash Flow

Some analysts calculate and use **net cash flow**, which is defined as:

$$\text{Net cash flow} = \text{Net income} - \text{Noncash revenues} + \text{Noncash expenses} \qquad (2\text{-}3)$$

where net income is the net income available for distribution to common shareholders. Depreciation and amortization usually are the largest noncash items, and in many cases the other noncash items roughly net out to zero. For this reason, net cash flow often equals net income plus depreciation and amortization:

$$\text{Net cash flow} = \text{Net income} + \text{Depreciation and amortization} \qquad (2\text{-}4)$$

We can illustrate Equation 2-4 with data for MicroDrive taken from Figure 2-2:

$$\text{Net cash flow} = \$248 + \$200 = \$448 \text{ million}$$

The definition used here is easy to calculate by pen and paper, so it was once used as a performance metric measure to evaluate financial statements. However, advances in technology and finance have made this measure less useful than the other measures of cash flow that we discuss in the remainder of the book. We describe this measure only so that you will be familiar with it if you see it elsewhere.

SELF-TEST

Differentiate between net cash flow and accounting profit.

A firm has net income of $5 million. Assuming that depreciation of $1 million is its only noncash expense, what is the firm's net cash flow? **($6 million)**

2-7 Free Cash Flow: The Cash Flow Available for Distribution to Investors

So far in the chapter we have focused on financial statements as presented in the annual report. When you studied income statements in accounting, the emphasis was probably on the firm's net income. However, the intrinsic value of a company is determined by the stream of cash flows that investors expect to receive now and in the future. A company generates these cash flows through its operating activities. These are called **free cash flows (FCFs)**.

We can calculate FCF in two different ways, by how it is used and by how it is generated. In terms of how it is used, FCF is the cash flow *available for distribution to all the company's investors after the company has made all investments necessary to sustain ongoing operations.* In terms of how it is generated, FCF is equal to *after-tax operating profit minus the amount of new expenditures necessary to sustain the business.* Always keep in mind that the way for managers to make their companies more valuable is to increase free cash flow now and in the future.

Figure 2-5 shows the five steps in calculating free cash flow. As we explain each individual step in the following sections, refer back to Figure 2-5 to keep the big picture in mind.

FIGURE 2-5
Calculating Free Cash Flow

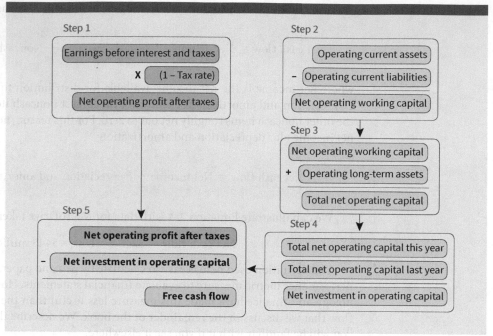

2-7a Net Operating Profit after Taxes (NOPAT)

If two companies have different amounts of debt, thus different amounts of interest charges, they could have identical operating performances but different net incomes: The one with more debt would have a lower net income. Net income is important, but it does not always reflect the true performance of a company's operations or the effectiveness of its managers. A better measure for comparing managers' performance is **net operating profit after taxes (NOPAT)**, which is the amount of profit a company would generate if it had no debt and held no financial assets. NOPAT is defined as follows:[8]

$$\text{NOPAT} = \text{EBIT}(1 - \text{Tax rate}) \qquad (2\text{-}5)$$

Using data from the income statements of Figure 2-2, MicroDrive's 2019 NOPAT is:

$$\text{NOPAT} = \$400(1 - 0.25) = \$300 \text{ million}$$

This means MicroDrive generated an after-tax operating profit of $300 million, less than its previous NOPAT of $440(1 − 0.25) = $330 million.

---

[8]For firms with a more complicated tax situation, it is better to define NOPAT as follows: NOPAT = (Net income before preferred dividends) + (Net interest expense)(1 − Tax rate). Also, if a firm is able to defer paying some taxes, perhaps by the use of accelerated depreciation, then it needs to adjust NOPAT to reflect the taxes it actually paid on operating income. See P. Daves, M. Ehrhardt, and R. Shrieves, *Corporate Valuation: A Guide for Managers and Investors* (Mason, OH: Thomson South-Western, 2004) for a detailed explanation of these and other adjustments.

2-7b Net Operating Working Capital

Most companies need some current assets to support their operating activities. For example, all companies must carry some cash to "grease the wheels" of their operations. If it does not hold any cash, a company might have overdrafts because it is impossible to perfectly time the actual cash in bank accounts due to writing and depositing checks. Companies must also have other current assets, such as inventory and accounts receivable, which are required for normal operations. The short-term assets normally used in a company's operating activities are called **operating current assets**.

Not all current assets are operating current assets. For example, holdings of short-term marketable securities generally result from investment decisions made by the treasurer and not as a natural consequence of operating activities. Therefore, short-term investments are **nonoperating assets** and normally are excluded when calculating operating current assets. A useful rule of thumb is that if an asset pays interest, it should not be classified as an operating asset.

In this textbook, we will always distinguish between the cash needed for operations and the marketable securities held as short-term investments. However, many companies don't make such a clean distinction. For example, Apple reported $22 billion in cash in 2017, in addition to $54 billion in short-term investments. With total assets of $375 billion, Apple certainly doesn't need to have 5.9% ($22/375 = 0.059) of its assets in cash to run its business operations. Therefore, if we were calculating operating current assets for Apple, we would classify about $7 billion as cash and the remainder as short-term investments: $22 − $7 + $54 = $69 billion. The reverse situation is possible, too, where a company reports very little cash but many short-term investments. In such a case, we would classify some of the short-term investments as operating cash when calculating operating current assets.

Some current liabilities—especially accounts payable and accruals—arise in the normal course of operations. Such short-term liabilities are called **operating current liabilities.** Not all current liabilities are operating current liabilities. For example, consider the current liability shown as notes payable to banks. The company could have raised an equivalent amount as long-term debt or could have issued stock, so the choice to borrow from the bank was a financing decision and not a consequence of operations. Again, the rule of thumb is that if a liability charges interest, it is not an operating liability.

If you are ever uncertain about whether an item is an operating asset or operating liability, ask yourself whether the item is a natural consequence of operations or if it is a discretionary choice, such as a particular method of financing or an investment in a particular financial asset. If it is discretionary, then the item is not an operating asset or liability.

Notice that each dollar of operating current liabilities is a dollar that the company does not have to raise from investors in order to conduct its short-term operating activities. Therefore, we define **net operating working capital (NOWC)** as operating current assets minus operating current liabilities. In other words, net operating working capital is the working capital acquired with investor-supplied funds. Here is the definition in equation form:

$$
\begin{array}{c}
\text{Net operating} \\
\text{working capital}
\end{array}
=
\begin{array}{c}
\text{Operating current} \\
\text{assets}
\end{array}
-
\begin{array}{c}
\text{Operating current} \\
\text{liabilities}
\end{array}
\qquad (2\text{-}6)
$$

We can apply these definitions to MicroDrive, using the balance sheet data given in Figure 2-1. Here is its net operating working capital at year-end 2019:

$$
\begin{aligned}
\text{NOWC} &= \text{Operating current assets} - \text{Operating current liabilities} \\
&= (\text{Cash} + \text{Accounts receivable} + \text{Inventories}) \\
&\quad - (\text{Accounts payable} + \text{Accruals}) \\
&= (\$100 + \$500 + \$1,000) - (\$200 + \$400) \\
&= \$1,000 \text{ million}
\end{aligned}
$$

For the previous year, net operating working capital was:

$$
\begin{aligned}
\text{NOWC} &= (\$102 + \$384 + \$774) - (\$180 + \$370) \\
&= \$710 \text{ million}
\end{aligned}
$$

From past experience with our students, we know the terminology can be confusing. Accounting and supply chain management tend to use the term **net working capital**, defined as *all* current assets minus *all* current liabilities. This is quite different from net *operating* working capital, which excludes the impact of items not directly related to operations (e.g., short-term investments and notes payable). Keep this important distinction in mind as you read the rest of this book.

2-7c Total Net Operating Capital

In addition to working capital, most companies also use long-term assets to support their operations. These include land, buildings, factories, equipment, and the like. **Total net operating capital**, also just called **net operating capital** or **operating capital**, is the sum of NOWC and **operating long-term assets** such as net plant and equipment:

$$
\text{Total net operating capital} = \text{NOWC} + \text{Operating long-term assets} \tag{2-7}
$$

Because MicroDrive's operating long-term assets consist only of net plant and equipment, its total net operating capital at year-end 2019 was:

$$
\begin{aligned}
\text{Total net operating capital} &= \$1,000 + \$2,000 \\
&= \$3,000 \text{ million}
\end{aligned}
$$

For the previous year, its total net operating capital was:

$$
\begin{aligned}
\text{Total net operating capital} &= \$710 + \$1,780 \\
&= \$2,490 \text{ million}
\end{aligned}
$$

Notice that we have defined total net operating capital as the sum of net operating working capital and operating long-term assets. In other words, our definition is in terms of operating assets and liabilities. However, we can also calculate total net operating capital by looking at the sources of funds. Total **investor-supplied capital** is defined as the total of funds provided by investors, such as notes payable, long-term bonds, preferred stock, and common equity. For most companies, total investor-supplied capital is:

$$
\begin{array}{c}
\text{Total investor-supplied} \\
\text{capital}
\end{array} = \begin{array}{c}
\text{Notes} \\
\text{payable}
\end{array} + \begin{array}{c}
\text{Long-term} \\
\text{bonds}
\end{array} + \begin{array}{c}
\text{Preferred} \\
\text{stock}
\end{array} + \begin{array}{c}
\text{Common} \\
\text{equity}
\end{array} \tag{2-8}
$$

For MicroDrive, the total capital provided by investors at year-end 2019 was $150 + $520 + $100 + $2,240 = $3,010 million. Of this amount, $10 million was tied up in short-term investments, which are not directly related to MicroDrive's operations. Therefore, we define total **investor-supplied operating capital** as:

$$\begin{matrix} \text{Total investor-supplied} \\ \text{operating capital} \end{matrix} = \begin{matrix} \text{Total investor-supplied} \\ \text{capital} \end{matrix} - \begin{matrix} \text{Short-term} \\ \text{investments} \end{matrix} \qquad (2\text{-}9)$$

MicroDrive had $3,010 - $10 = $3,000 million of investor-supplied operating capital in 2019. Notice that this is exactly the same value as our earlier calculation of total net operating capital for that year. Therefore, we can calculate total net operating capital either from net operating working capital and operating long-term assets or from the investor-supplied funds. We usually base our calculations on operating data because this approach allows us to analyze a division, factory, or work center. In contrast, the approach based on investor-supplied capital is applicable only for the entire company.

The expression "total net operating capital" is a mouthful, so we often call it *operating capital* or even just *capital*. Also, unless we specifically say "investor-supplied capital," we are referring to total net operating capital.

2-7d Net Investment in Operating Capital

As calculated previously, MicroDrive had $2,490 million of total net operating capital at the end of 2018 and $3,000 million at the end of 2019. Therefore, during 2019, it made a **net investment in operating capital** of:

Net investment in operating capital = $3,000 - $2,490 = $510 million

Much of this investment was made in net operating working capital, which rose from $710 million to $1,000 million, or by $290 million. This 41% increase in net operating working capital is very worrying considering that sales grew by only 4.2% (to $5 billion from $4.8 billion), should set off warning bells in your head: Why did MicroDrive tie up so much additional cash in working capital? Is the company gearing up for a big increase in sales, or are inventories not moving and receivables not being collected? We will address these questions in detail in Chapter 3, when we cover ratio analysis.

2-7e Calculating Free Cash Flow

Free cash flow is defined as:

$$\text{FCF} = \text{NOPAT} - \text{Net investment in total operating capital} \qquad (2\text{-}10)$$

MicroDrive's free cash flow in 2019 was:

$$\begin{aligned} \text{FCF} &= \$300 - (\$3,000 - \$2,490) \\ &= \$300 - \$510 \\ &= -\$210 \text{ million} \end{aligned}$$

Although we prefer the approach we just explained, sometimes the financial press calculates FCF differently:

$$FCF = \begin{bmatrix} EBIT(1-T) \\ + \text{Depreciation} \end{bmatrix} - \begin{bmatrix} \text{Gross investment} \\ \text{in fixed assets} \end{bmatrix} - \begin{bmatrix} \text{Investment} \\ \text{in NOWC} \end{bmatrix} \qquad (2\text{-}11)$$

For MicroDrive, this calculation is:

$$FCF = (\$300 + \$200) - \$420 - (\$1{,}000 - \$710) = -\$210$$

Notice that the results are the same for either calculation. To see this, replace $EBIT(1-T)$ with NOPAT in the first bracket of Equation 2-11, and replace Gross investment in fixed assets with Net investment in fixed assets + Depreciation in the second bracket:

$$FCF = \begin{bmatrix} NOPAT \\ + \text{Depreciation} \end{bmatrix} - \begin{bmatrix} \text{Net investment} \\ \text{in fixed assets} \\ + \text{Depreciation} \end{bmatrix} - \begin{bmatrix} \text{Investment} \\ \text{in NOWC} \end{bmatrix} \qquad (2\text{-}11a)$$

Both the first and second brackets have depreciation, so depreciation can be canceled out, leaving:

$$FCF = NOPAT - \begin{bmatrix} \text{Net investment} \\ \text{in fixed assets} \end{bmatrix} - \begin{bmatrix} \text{Investment} \\ \text{in NOWC} \end{bmatrix} \qquad (2\text{-}11b)$$

The last two bracketed terms are equal to the net investment in operating capital, so Equation 2-11b simplifies to Equation 2-10. We usually use Equation 2-10 because it saves us the step of adding depreciation both to NOPAT and to the net investment in fixed assets and also because frequently only net fixed assets and not gross fixed assets are reported on the firm's financial statements.

Financial Statement Fraud

The Securities Exchange Commission (SEC) has a Division of Enforcement that investigates companies and individuals regarding noncompliance with securities laws. Within the Division, the Financial Reporting and Audit (FRAud) Group focuses on financial statement misreporting. Among its tools, the FRAud group utilizes data analytics and advanced algorithms to identify financial reporting that needs additional investigation. When the FRAud Group identifies a violation, it can file a civil suit in a federal court, but usually the matter is settled through an Administrative procedure. The settlement often involves fines, cease-and-desist injunctions, and disgorgement of profits.

For example, the SEC claimed that Bankrate, Inc., its CFO, and other senior executives misreported financial information to the public for the purpose of matching or surpassing analysts' expectations. The company and its officers agreed to pay more than $15 million in fines. However, the story didn't end here. The Justice Department charged the CFO, Hyunjin Lerner, and others for crimes connected with financial fraud. In May 2018, Lerner was sentenced to 5 years in prison and was ordered to pay $21 million in restitution.

Sources: For SEC actions, see **www.sec.gov/divisions/enforce/claims /bankrate-inc.htm**. For Justice Department actions, see **www.justice.gov /criminal-vns/case/hyunjin-lerner/update**.

2-7f The Uses of FCF

Recall that free cash flow (FCF) is the amount of cash that is available for distribution to all investors, including shareholders and debtholders. There are five good uses for FCF:

1. Pay interest to debtholders, keeping in mind that the net cost to the company is the after-tax interest expense.
2. Repay debtholders; that is, pay off some of the debt. Issuing new debt is a "negative use."
3. Pay dividends to shareholders.
4. Repurchase stock from shareholders. Issuing new stock is a "negative use."
5. Buy short-term investments or other nonoperating assets. Selling is a "negative use."

Consider MicroDrive, with its FCF of −$210 million in 2019. How did MicroDrive "use" the FCF?

MicroDrive's income statement shows an interest expense of $60 million. With a tax rate of 25%, the after-tax interest payment for the year is:

$$\text{After-tax interest payment} = \$60(1 - 25\%) = \$45 \text{ million}$$

The net amount of debt that is repaid is equal to the amount at the beginning of the year minus the amount at the end of the year. This includes notes payable and long-term debt. If the amount of ending debt is less than the beginning debt, the company paid down some of its debt. But if the ending debt is greater than the beginning debt, the company actually borrowed additional funds from creditors. In that case, it would be a negative use of FCF. For MicroDrive, the net debt repayment for 2019 is equal to the amount at the beginning of the year minus the amount at the end of the year:

$$\text{Net debt repayment (issuance)} = (\$28 + \$350) - (\$150 + \$520) = -\$292 \text{ million}$$

This is a "negative use" of FCF because it increased the debt balance. This is typical of most companies because growing companies usually add debt each year.

MicroDrive paid $7 million in preferred dividends and $60 in common dividends for a total of:

$$\text{Dividend payments} = \$7 + \$60 = \$67 \text{ million}$$

The net amount of stock that is repurchased is equal to the amount at the beginning of the year minus the amount at the end of the year. This includes preferred stock and common stock. If the amount of ending stock is less than the beginning stock, then the company made net repurchases. But if the ending stock is greater than the beginning stock, the company actually *made* net issuances. In that case, it would be a negative use of FCF. Even though MicroDrive neither issued nor repurchased stock during the year, many companies use FCF to repurchase stocks as a replacement for or supplement to dividends, as we discuss in Chapter 14.

The amount of net purchases of short-term investments is equal to the amount at the end of the year minus the amount at the beginning of the year. If the amount of ending investments is greater than the beginning investments, then the company made net purchases. But if the ending investments are less than the beginning investments, the company actually sold investments. In that case, it would be a negative use of FCF. Micro-Drive's net purchases of short-term investments in 2019 are:

$$\text{Net purchases (sales) of short-term investments} = \$10 - \$40 = -\$30 \text{ million}$$

Notice that this is a negative use because MicroDrive sold short-term investments instead of purchasing them.

We combine these individual uses of FCF to find the total uses:

1. After-tax interest	$45
2. Net debt repayments (issuance)	−$292
3. Dividends	$67
4. Net stock repurchases (sales)	$0
5. Net purchases (sales) of ST investments	−$30
Total uses of FCF	−$210

As it should be, the −$210 total for uses of FCF is identical to the value of FCF from operations that we calculated previously.

Observe that a company does not use FCF to acquire operating assets, because the calculation of FCF already takes into account the purchase of operating assets needed to support growth. Unfortunately, there is evidence to suggest that some companies with high FCF tend to make unnecessary investments that don't add value, such as paying too much to acquire another company. Thus, high FCF can cause waste if managers fail to act in the best interests of shareholders. As discussed in Chapter 1, this is called an agency cost because managers are hired as agents to act on behalf of stockholders. We discuss agency costs and ways to control them in Chapter 13 (where we discuss corporate governance) and in Chapter 15 (where we discuss the choice of capital structure).

2-7g FCF and Corporate Value

Free cash flow is the amount of cash available for distribution to investors; so the fundamental value of a company to its investors depends on the present value of its expected future FCFs, discounted at the company's weighted average cost of capital (WACC). Subsequent chapters will develop the tools needed to forecast FCFs and evaluate their risk. Chapter 7 ties all this together with a model used to calculate the value of a company. Even though you do not yet have all the tools to apply the model, you must understand this basic concept: *FCF is the cash flow available for distribution to investors. Therefore, a company's fundamental value depends primarily on its expected future FCF.*

SELF-TEST

What is net operating working capital? Why does it exclude most short-term investments and notes payable?

What is total net operating capital? Why is it important for managers to calculate a company's capital requirements?

Why is NOPAT a better performance measure than net income?

What is free cash flow? What are its five uses? Why is FCF important?

Suppose a firm has the following information: Sales = $10 million; costs of goods sold (excluding depreciation) = $5 million; depreciation = $1.4 million; other operating expenses = $2 million; interest expense = $1 million. If the tax rate is 25%, what is NOPAT, the net operating profit after taxes? (**$1.2 million**)

Suppose a firm has the following information: Cash = $500,000; short-term investments = $2.5 million; accounts receivable = $1.2 million; inventories = $1 million; and net plant and equipment = $7.8 million. How much is tied up in operating current assets? (**$2.7 million**)

Suppose a firm has the following information: Accounts payable = $1 million; notes payable = $1.1 million; short-term debt = $1.4 million; accruals = $500,000; and long-term bonds = $3 million. What is the amount arising from operating current liabilities? (**$1.5 million**)

Suppose a firm has the following information: Operating current assets = $2.7 million; operating current liabilities = $1.5 million; long-term bonds = $3 million; net plant and equipment = $7.8 million; and other long-term operating assets = $1 million. How much is tied up in net operating working capital (NOWC)? **($1.2 million)** *How much is tied up in total net operating capital?* **($10 million)**

A firm's total net operating capital for the previous year was $9.3 million. For the current year, its total net operating capital is $10 million, and its NOPAT is $1.2 million. What is its free cash flow for the current year? **($500,000)**

2-8 Performance Evaluation

Because free cash flow has such a big impact on value, managers and investors can use FCF and its components to measure a company's performance. The following sections explain three performance measures: return on invested capital, market value added, and economic value added.

2-8a The Return on Invested Capital

Even though MicroDrive had a positive NOPAT, its very high investment in operating assets caused a negative FCF. Is a negative free cash flow always bad? The answer is, "Not necessarily; it depends on why the free cash flow is negative." It's a bad sign if FCF is negative because NOPAT is negative, which probably means the company is experiencing operating problems. However, many high-growth companies have positive NOPAT but negative FCF because they are making large investments in operating assets to support growth. For example, Fabrinet manufactures optical and electromechanical systems and sensors. In 2016, its sales grew 26%, its NOPAT increased by over 30% from 2015, but its FCF was *negative* $5 million. This was an increase from the prior year's FCF, which was negative $15 million. These negative FCFs were due largely to a $40 million investment in working capital in 2015 and a $90 million investment in working capital in 2016 that were required to support sales growth.

There is nothing wrong with value-adding growth, even if it causes negative free cash flows in the short term, but it is vital to determine whether growth is actually adding value. For this, we use the **return on invested capital (ROIC)**, which shows how much NOPAT is generated by each dollar of operating capital:

$$\text{ROIC} = \frac{\text{NOPAT}}{\text{Operating capital}} \qquad (2\text{-}12)$$

As shown in Figure 2-6, MicroDrive's 2019 ROIC is $300/$3,000 = 10%. To determine whether this ROIC is high enough to add value, compare it to the weighted average cost of capital (WACC). Chapter 9 explains how to calculate the WACC; for now, accept that the WACC considers a company's individual risk, as well as overall market conditions. Figure 2-6 shows that MicroDrive's 10% ROIC is less than its 11.5% WACC. Thus, MicroDrive did not generate a sufficient rate of return to compensate its investors for the risk they bore in 2019. This is markedly different from the previous year, in which MicroDrive's 13.25% ROIC was greater than its 11.5% WACC. Not only is the current ROIC too low, but the trend is in the wrong direction. Finally, MicroDrive's ROIC is less than the 13.19% industry average.

FIGURE 2-6
Calculating Performance Measures for MicroDrive, Inc. (Millions of Dollars and Millions of Shares)

	A	B	C	D	E	F	G	H
395						**2019**	**2018**	**Ind. Avg.**
396	*Calculating NOPAT*							
397	EBIT					$400	$440	
398	x (1 – Tax rate)					75%	75%	
399	NOPAT = EBIT(1 – T)					$300	$330	
400								
401	*Calculating Net Operating Working Capital (NOWC)*							
402	Operating current assets					$1,600	$1,260	
403	– Operating current liabilities					600	550	
404	NOWC					$1,000	$710	
405								
406	*Calculating Total Net Operating Capital*							
407	NOWC					$1,000	$710	
408	+ Net plant and equipment					2,000	1,780	
409	Total net operating capital					$3,000	$2,490	
410								
411	*Calculating Return on Invested Capital (ROIC)*							
412	NOPAT					$300	$330	
413	÷ Total net operating capital					3,000	2,490	
414	ROIC = NOPAT/Total net operating capital					10.00%	13.25%	13.19%
415	Weighted average cost of capital (WACC)					11.50%	11.50%	11.20%
416								
417	*Calculating the Operating Profitability Ratio (OP)*							
418	NOPAT					$300	$330	
419	÷ Sales					5,000	4,800	
420	OP = NOPAT/Sales					6.00%	6.88%	6.75%
421								
422	*Calculating Capital Requirement Ratio (CR)*							
423	Total net operating capital					$3,000	$2,490	
424	÷ Sales					5,000	4,800	
425	CR = Total net operating capital/Sales					60.00%	51.88%	51.19%
426								
427	*Calculating Market Value Added (MVA)*							
428	Price per share					$31.00	$45.00	
429	x Number of shares (millions)					60.0	59.4	
430	Market value of equity = P x (# of shares)					$1,860	$2,673	
431	– Book value of equity					2,240	2,052	
432	MVA = Market value Book value					–$380	$621	
433								
434	*Calculating Economic Value Added (EVA)*							
435	Total net operating capital					$3,000.0	$2,490.0	
436	x Weighted average cost of capital (WACC)					11.5%	11.5%	
437	Dollar cost of capital					$345.0	$286.4	
438								
439	NOPAT					$300.0	$330.0	
440	– Dollar cost of capital					345.0	286.4	
441	EVA = NOPAT – Dollar cost of capital					–$45.0	$43.7	

Source: See the file ***Ch02 Tool Kit.xlsx***. Numbers are reported as rounded values for clarity but are calculated using *Excel*'s full precision. Thus, intermediate calculations using the figure's rounded values may be inexact.

Is MicroDrive's ROIC low due to low operating profitability, poor capital utilization, or both? To answer that question, begin with the **operating profitability ratio (OP)**, which measures the percentage operating profit per dollar of sales:

$$\text{Operating profitability ratio (OP)} = \frac{\text{NOPAT}}{\text{Sales}} \qquad (2\text{-}13)$$

MicroDrive's current operating profitability ratio is:

$$\text{OP} = \frac{\$300}{\$5,000} = 6\%$$

and its previous operating profitability ratio was 6.9%. The average operating profitability ratio for companies in MicroDrive's industry is 6.75%, so MicroDrive's operating profitability is trending in the wrong direction and is a bit lower than the 6.75% industry's average.

Let's take a look at how effectively MicroDrive uses its capital. The **capital requirement ratio (CR)** measures how much operating capital is tied up in generating a dollar of sales:

$$\text{Capital requirement ratio (CR)} = \frac{\text{Total net operating capital}}{\text{Sales}} \qquad (2\text{-}14)$$

MicroDrive's current capital requirement ratio is:

$$\text{CR} = \frac{\$3,000}{\$5,000} = 60.0\%$$

and its previous capital requirement ratio was 51.88%. This shows that MicroDrive tied up much more in operating capital needed to generate sales in the current year than it did in the previous year. Even more alarming, MicroDrive's capital requirement ratio is much worse than the industry average of 51.19%.

Although not the case for MicroDrive, in many situations a negative FCF is not necessarily bad. For example, Fabrinet, previously discussed, had a negative FCF in 2016, but its ROIC was about 22.7%. Because its WACC was only 8.5%, Fabrinet's growth was adding value.[9] At some point, its growth will slow, and it will not require such large capital investments. If it maintains a high ROIC, then its FCF will become positive and very large as growth slows.

Neither traditional accounting data nor return on invested capital incorporates stock prices, even though the primary goal of management should be to maximize the firm's intrinsic stock price. In contrast, Market Value Added (MVA) and Economic Value Added (EVA) do attempt to compare intrinsic measures with market measures.[10]

---

[9]If g is the growth rate in capital, then with a little (or a lot of!) algebra, free cash flow is:

$$\text{FCF} = \text{Capital}\left(\text{RIOC} - \frac{g}{1+g}\right)$$

With a little more algebra, this shows that if g > ROIC/(1 − ROIC), then FCF will be negative.

[10]The concepts of EVA and MVA were developed by Joel Stern and Bennett Stewart, co-founders of the consulting firm Stern Stewart & Company. Stern Stewart trademarked the term "EVA," so other consulting firms have given other names to this value, as they have to MVA. Still, EVA and MVA are the terms most commonly used in practice.

2-8b Market Value Added (MVA)

WWW

For an updated estimate of Coca-Cola's MVA, go to **http://finance.yahoo .com,** *enter KO, and click Search. This shows the market value of equity, called Mkt Cap. To get the book value of equity, select Financials and then Balance Sheet.*

One measure of shareholder wealth is the *difference* between the market value of the firm's stock and the cumulative amount of equity capital that was supplied by shareholders. This difference is called the **Market Value Added (MVA):**

$$
\begin{aligned}
\text{MVA} &= \text{Market value of stock} - \text{Equity capital supplied by shareholders} \\
&= (\text{Shares outstanding})(\text{Stock price}) - \text{Total common equity}
\end{aligned}
\tag{2-15}
$$

To illustrate, consider Coca-Cola. In September 2017, its total market equity value, commonly called market capitalization, was \$192 billion, while its balance sheet showed that stockholders had put up only \$22 billion. Thus, Coca-Cola's MVA was \$192 − \$22 = \$170 billion. This \$170 billion represents the difference between the money that Coca-Cola's stockholders have invested in the corporation since its founding—including indirect investment by retaining earnings—and the cash they could get if they sold the business. The higher its MVA, the better the job that management is doing for the firm's shareholders.

MicroDrive's MVA is −\$396 million:

$$
\begin{aligned}
\text{MicroDrive's MVA} &= (\text{Shares outstanding})(\text{Stock price}) - \text{Total common equity} \\
&= (60 \text{ million})(\$31.00) - \$2{,}240 \text{ million} \\
&= \$1{,}844 \text{ million} - \$2{,}240 \text{ million} = -\$380 \text{ million.}
\end{aligned}
$$

As Figure 2-6 shows, MicroDrive's MVA went from a positive value in 2018 to a negative value in 2019. In other words, MicroDrive's current market value is less than the cumulative amount of equity that its shareholders have invested during the company's life.

Sometimes MVA is defined as the total market value of the company minus the total amount of investor-supplied capital:

$$
\begin{aligned}
\text{MVA} &= \text{Total market value} - \text{Total investor-supplied capital} \\
&= (\text{Market value of stock} + \text{Market value of debt}) \\
&\quad - \text{Total investor-supplied capital}
\end{aligned}
\tag{2-16}
$$

For most companies, the total amount of investor-supplied capital is the sum of equity, debt, and preferred stock. We can calculate the total amount of investor-supplied capital directly from their reported values in the financial statements. The total market value of a company is the sum of the market values of common equity, debt, and preferred stock. It is easy to find the market value of equity because stock prices are readily available, but it is not always easy to find the market value of debt. Hence, many analysts use the value of debt reported in the financial statements, which is the debt's book value, as an estimate of the debt's market value.

2-8c Economic Value Added (EVA)

Whereas MVA measures the effects of managerial actions since the inception of a company, **Economic Value Added (EVA)** focuses on managerial effectiveness in a given year. The EVA formula is:

$$EVA = \left(\begin{array}{c} \text{Net operating profit} \\ \text{after taxes} \end{array} \right) - \left(\begin{array}{c} \text{After-tax dollar cost of capital} \\ \text{used to support operations} \end{array} \right) \qquad \text{(2-17)}$$

$$= \text{NOPAT} - (\text{Total net operating capital})(\text{WACC})$$

Economic Value Added is an estimate of a business's true economic profit for the year, and it differs sharply from accounting profit.[11] EVA represents the residual income that remains after the cost of *all* capital, including equity capital, has been deducted, whereas accounting profit is determined without imposing a charge for equity capital. As we will discuss in Chapter 9, equity capital has a cost because shareholders give up the opportunity to invest and earn returns elsewhere when they provide capital to the firm. This cost is an *opportunity* cost rather than an *accounting cost,* but it is real nonetheless.

Note that when calculating EVA we do not add back depreciation. Although it is not a cash expense, depreciation is a cost because worn-out assets must be replaced, and it is therefore deducted when determining both net income and EVA. Our calculation of EVA assumes that the true economic depreciation of the company's fixed assets exactly equals the depreciation used for accounting and tax purposes. If this were not the case, adjustments would have to be made to obtain a more accurate measure of EVA.

Economic Value Added measures the extent to which the firm has increased shareholder value. Therefore, if managers focus on EVA, they will more likely operate in a manner consistent with maximizing shareholder wealth. Note too that EVA can be determined for divisions as well as for the company as a whole, so it provides a useful basis for determining managerial performance at all levels. Consequently, many firms include EVA as a component of compensation plans.

We can also calculate EVA in terms of ROIC:

$$EVA = (\text{Total net operating capital})(\text{ROIC} - \text{WACC}) \qquad \text{(2-18)}$$

As this equation shows, a firm adds value—that is, has a positive EVA—if its ROIC is greater than its WACC. If WACC exceeds ROIC, then growth can actually reduce a firm's value.

Using Equation 2-18, Figure 2-6 shows that MicroDrive's EVA is:

$$EVA = \$300 - (\$3,000)(11.5\%) = \$300 - \$345 = -\$45 \text{ million}$$

This negative EVA reinforces our earlier conclusions that MicroDrive lost value in 2019 due to an erosion in its operating performance. In Chapters 7 and 12, we will determine MicroDrive's intrinsic value and explore ways in which MicroDrive can reverse its downward trend.

2-8d Intrinsic Value, MVA, and EVA

We will have more to say about both MVA and EVA later in the book, but we can close this section with two observations. First, there is a relationship between MVA and EVA, but it is not a direct one. If a company has a history of negative EVAs, then its MVA will

---

[11]The most important reason EVA differs from accounting profit is that the cost of equity capital is deducted when EVA is calculated. Other factors that could lead to differences include adjustments that might be made to depreciation, to research and development costs, to inventory valuations, and so on. These other adjustments also can affect the calculation of investor-supplied capital, which affects both EVA and MVA. See G. Bennett Stewart, III, *The Quest for Value* (New York: HarperCollins, 1991).

probably be negative; conversely, its MVA probably will be positive if the company has a history of positive EVAs. However, the stock price, which is the key ingredient in the MVA calculation, depends more on expected future performance than on historical performance. Therefore, a company with a history of negative EVAs could have a positive MVA, provided investors expect a turnaround in the future.

The second observation is that when EVAs or MVAs are used to evaluate managerial performance as part of an incentive compensation program, EVA is the measure that is typically used. The reasons are as follows: (1) EVA shows the value added during a given year, whereas MVA reflects performance over the company's entire life, perhaps even including times before the current managers were born. (2) EVA can be applied to individual divisions or other units of a large corporation, whereas MVA must be applied to the entire corporation.

SELF-TEST

A company has sales of $200 million, NOPAT of $12 million, net income of $8 million, net operating working capital (NOWC) of $10 million, total net operating capital of $100 million, and total assets of $110 million. What is its operating profitability ratio (OP)? **(6%)** *Its capital requirement ratio (CR)?* **(50%)** *Its return on invested capital (ROIC)?* **(12%)**

Define "Market Value Added (MVA)" and "Economic Value Added (EVA)."

How does EVA differ from accounting profit?

A firm has $100 million in total net operating capital. Its return on invested capital is 14%, and its weighted average cost of capital is 10%. What is its EVA? **($4 million)**

2-9 Corporate Income Taxes

The value of any financial asset (including stocks, bonds, and mortgages), as well as most real assets such as plants or even entire firms, depends on the after-tax stream of cash flows produced by the asset. The following sections describe the key features of corporate and individual taxation.

In December 2017, Congress passed a tax act that is still widely known by the title of its preliminary version, the **2017 Tax Cut and Jobs Act (TCJA)**.[12] We will refer to it as the Tax Cut and Jobs Act, the TCJA, or just the Act. The TCJA made major changes to corporate and personal tax codes. Following are descriptions and example applications of the most important items in the Act that affect corporate taxes.

2-9a The Corporate Tax Rate

Prior to the Act's passage, corporate tax rates were progressive (i.e., the tax rate increased as taxable income increased) up to $18,333,333. Beyond this amount, the tax rate was 35%. The new tax code is not progressive but instead applies a flat 21% rate to taxable income.

For example, consider a company with taxable income of $200 million. Prior to the Act, the tax would have been $70 million. However, the tax on this income is now $(0.21)(\$200) = \$42$ million. This is a 40% reduction in taxes: $(\$70 - \$42)/\$70 = 0.4 = 40\%$.

---

[12]Congress actually passed An Act to Provide for the Reconciliation Pursuant to Titles II and V of the Concurrent Resolution on the Budget for Fiscal Year 2018. It is still widely known by its preliminary version, the Tax Cut and Jobs Act (TCJA), so that is how we will refer to it.

2-9b Limitation on Interest Expense Deduction

Before the Act, interest expense was a fully **deductible expense** because it reduced taxable income. However, the Act put a limit on the amount of interest that could be deducted. For 2018, 2019, 2020, and 2021, the Act reduced the allowable interest expense deduction to 30% of earnings before interest, taxes, depreciation, and amortization (EBITDA). For 2022 and subsequent years, the Act reduced the allowable interest expense deduction to 30% of earnings before interest and taxes (EBIT).[13]

For example, consider a company with EBITDA of $160 million in a year prior to 2022. Even though the company had interest expenses of $80 million, the deductible interest expense for the year is only (0.30)($160) = $48 million. This leaves $80 − $48 = $32 million of unused interest expenses for the current year. However, the company may "carry forward" the unused interest expenses and deduct them in a subsequent year, subject to the 30% limitation. The following section describes the carryforward provision.

2-9c Corporate Loss Carryforward

A corporation's actual tax liability in a current year depends on its current profit *and* its past losses. The Act's **tax loss carryforward** provision allows a company to use prior ordinary operating losses to offset up to 80% of its current taxable income.[14] Any remaining prior operating losses can be carried forward indefinitely and used to offset future taxable income. The purpose of this loss treatment is to avoid penalizing corporations whose incomes fluctuate substantially from year to year.

To illustrate, suppose Apex Corporation lost a cumulative amount of $120 million in 2018 and prior years. (See Table 2-1.) Apex had unadjusted *pre-tax* operating profits of $100 million in 2019 and 2020. Because its 2019 pre-tax income is positive, it may use prior operating losses to offset up to 80% of this income. This limit for Apex is 80%($100) = $80 million. This reduces its 2019 taxable income from $100 million to $20 million and reduces its tax liability from 21%($100) = $21 million to 21%($20) = $4.2 million. Note that Apex has $40 million left in unused prior losses: $120 − $80 = $40 million.

Apex's 2020 pre-tax income is $100 million, and operating losses could offset up to $80 million. However, Apex has only $40 million remaining from cumulative prior operating losses. This is less than the $80 million limit, so Apex can carry forward the full $40 million and reduce its 2020 taxable income.

2-9d Interest and Dividends Received by a Corporation

Interest income received by a corporation is taxed as ordinary income at regular corporate tax rates. The situation is different for dividends. Consider a corporation that receives dividends from another firm. If the corporation subsequently pays a dividend to its own

---

[13]There are situations in which the 30% limitation does not apply. For example, the limitation does not apply to small companies with average annual revenues less than $25 million, based on the current and previous two years. Nor does it apply to investment interest expense, which might be incurred if an investor uses borrowed funds to purchase financial investments, such as stocks and bonds.

Interest on floor financing, which is incurred when auto dealers obtain loans to purchase the vehicles on their lots, is not subject to the limitation. Real estate and farming companies can choose not to be subject to the 30% limitation. However, additional restrictions may be triggered in these situations.

[14]Prior to 2018, firms could carry an operating loss in the current year back to reduce the taxes paid in the prior two years, receiving a tax refund in the current year for taxes paid in the two prior years. The 2017 Act eliminated this carryback provision.

resource

See **Ch02 Tool Kit.xlsx**
for details.

TABLE 2-1

Apex Corporation: Application of $120 Million Loss Carryforward

	2018	2019	2020
Calculation of tax if carryforward losses are ignored			
Taxable operating profit if no carryforward provision		$100.0	$100.0
Tax (21%) if no carryforward provision		$ 21.0	$ 21.0
Calculation of maximum allowed carryforward loss			
Unadjusted taxable operating profit prior to carryforward		$100.0	$100.0
Maximum allowed carryforward loss[a]		$ 80.0	$ 80.0
Cumulative prior unused net operating losses[b]	$120.0	$ 40.0	$ 0.0
Calculation of maximum allowed carryforward loss			
Unadjusted taxable profit prior to carryforward		$100.0	$100.0
Allowed prior unused net operating losses carried forward[c]		$ 80.0	$ 40.0
Adjusted taxable profit after carryforward		$ 20.0	$ 60.0
Tax on adjusted profit (21%) after carryforward		$ 4.2	$ 12.6
Tax savings due to carryforward provision			
Tax if carryforward losses are ignored		$ 21.0	$ 21.0
Tax on adjusted profit (21%) after carryforward		$ 4.2	$ 12.6
Tax savings due to carryforward		$ 16.8	$ 8.4

Notes:

[a]The maximum allowed carryforward loss is limited to 80% of the unadjusted taxable operating profit.

[b]The cumulative prior unused net operating loss for Year$_t$ is equal to its value in Year$_{t-1}$ minus the amount that is used in Year$_t$.

[c]The operating loss that is carried forward is equal to the minimum of the prior unused operating losses and 80% of the current unadjusted operating loss.

investors, then their dividend income is subject to *triple taxation:* (1) The first corporation is taxed on its income before it pays a dividend to the second company. (2) The second corporation is then taxed on the dividends it receives from the first firm. (3) The second firm's investors are taxed on the dividends they receive. To reduce the impact of triple taxation, corporations are allowed to exclude a portion of dividends received, as explained next.

For a company receiving dividends, 50% of the dividends are excluded from taxable income, but the remaining 50% are taxed at the ordinary tax rate.[15] For example, suppose a company has $136.8 million to invest. If it is invested in preferred stock with a 7.31% coupon rate, the dividend payment would be $10 million: 7.31%($136.8 million) = $10 million. The taxes on the dividends would be $1.05 million:

$$\text{Taxes on dividend} = (\text{Dividend payment})(1 - \text{Exclusion rate})(\text{Tax rate})$$
$$= (\$10 \text{ million})(1 - 0.50)(0.21)$$
$$= \$1.05 \text{ million}$$

[15]The size of the dividend exclusion actually depends on the degree of ownership. Before the 2017 TCJA, corporations owning 20% or less of the paying company could exclude 70% of dividends received, but the exclusion is now only 50%. Corporations owning more than 20% but less than 80% of a dividend-paying company can exclude 65% of the dividends, down from 80%. Corporations owing more than 80% can exclude the entire dividend payment. We will assume a 50% dividend exclusion for all subsequent examples.

The after-tax dividend would be $10 − $1.05 = $8.95 million and the effective tax rate on the dividends would be only $10.5/$100 = 10.5%.

Suppose the company in the previous example instead invests in debt with an 8.18% interest rate, which is higher than the preferred stock's 7.31% coupon rate. The company would receive $11.19 million in interest income. The company would pay taxes of $11.19(0.21) = $2.35 million. Its after-tax interest would be $11.19 − $2.35 = $8.84 million. Notice that this is less than the $8.95 million after-tax dividends calculated earlier. Therefore, a corporation with surplus funds might choose to invest in preferred stock rather than interest-paying investments even though the pre-tax rate of return on the preferred stock is lower.[16]

2-9e Interest and Dividends Paid by a Corporation

A firm's operations can be financed with either debt or equity capital. If the firm uses debt, then it must pay interest on this debt. The interest *paid* by a corporation is deducted from its operating income to obtain its taxable income. Therefore, a firm needs $1 of pre-tax income to pay $1 of interest.

In contrast, dividends paid are not deductible. Suppose a firm is in the 24.8% federal-plus-state tax bracket. It must earn $1.33 of pre-tax income for it to have enough after-tax income to pay $1 of dividends:

$$\text{Pre-tax income needed to pay \$1 of dividends} = \frac{\$1}{1 - \text{Tax rate}} = \frac{\$1}{0.752} = \$1.33$$

Working backward, if a company has $1.33 in pre-tax income, it must pay $0.33 in taxes: (0.248)($1.33) = $0.33. This leaves the firm with after-tax income of $1.00.

As this example suggests, companies have a tax incentive to finance with debt and not stock. See Chapter 15 for a more detailed analysis of debt versus equity financing.

2-9f Corporate Capital Gains

A **capital gain** occurs when an asset is sold for more than its book value, and a **capital loss** occurs when the reverse happens. Under current law, corporations' capital gains are taxed at the same rates as their operating income.

2-9g Improper Accumulation to Avoid Payment of Dividends

Corporations could refrain from paying dividends and thus permit their stockholders to avoid personal income taxes on dividends. To prevent this, the Tax Code contains an **improper accumulation** provision stating that earnings accumulated by a corporation are subject to penalty rates *if the purpose of the accumulation is to enable stockholders to avoid personal income taxes.* A cumulative total of $250,000 (the balance sheet item "retained earnings") is by law exempted from the improper accumulation tax for most corporations. This is a benefit primarily to small corporations.

The improper accumulation penalty applies only if the retained earnings in excess of $250,000 are *shown by the IRS to be unnecessary to meet the reasonable needs of the business.*

---

[16]Note that corporations are restricted in their use of borrowed funds to purchase other firms' preferred or common stocks. Without such restrictions, firms could engage in *tax arbitrage* by borrowing and then using the proceeds to purchase preferred stock. As this example shows, the after-tax dividends would be greater than the after-tax interest expense, and the excess amount would be pure after-tax profit. If not for the restriction, firms could generate huge after-tax profits without investing any of their own money: Borrow very large amounts and purchase equally large amounts of preferred stock.

A great many companies do indeed have legitimate reasons for retaining more than $250,000 of earnings. For example, firms may retain and use earnings to pay off debt, finance growth, or provide the corporation with a cushion against possible cash drains caused by losses. How much a firm should be allowed to accumulate for uncertain contingencies is a matter of judgment. We shall consider this matter again in Chapter 14, which deals with corporate dividend policy.

2-9h Consolidated Corporate Tax Returns

If a corporation owns 80% or more of another corporation's stock, then it can aggregate income and file one consolidated tax return; thus, the losses of one company can be used to offset the profits of another. (Similarly, one division's losses can be used to offset another division's profits.) No business ever wants to incur losses (you can go broke losing $1 to save 21¢ in taxes), but tax offsets do help make it more feasible for large, multidivisional corporations to undertake risky new ventures or ventures that will suffer losses during a developmental period.

2-9i Taxes on Overseas Income

Many U.S. corporations have overseas subsidiaries, and those subsidiaries must pay taxes in the countries where they operate. Often, foreign tax rates are lower than U.S. rates. Prior to 2018, no U.S. tax was immediately due on foreign earnings if they were reinvested overseas, even though the "investment" might be a financial asset rather than a physical asset. However, when foreign earnings were repatriated to the U.S. parent for investment here or for dividend payments, they were taxed at the applicable U.S. rate, less a credit for taxes paid to the foreign country. Over the years, this procedure has stimulated overseas investments by U.S. multinational firms; they continued the deferral indefinitely by continuing to reinvest the earnings in their overseas operations (or in overseas bank accounts). As a result, many U.S. corporations such as Google, Coca-Cola, and Microsoft have been able to defer billions of dollars of taxes.

The TCJA made major changes to the taxation of foreign income. U.S. firms with accumulated foreign deferred earnings since 1986 must pay a tax of 15.5% on those earnings that are held in cash and cash equivalents; they must pay 8% on the remainder.[17] After this one-time tax, the United States will not tax any new foreign earnings. The good news is that U.S. tax revenues will increase and that companies with past deferred foreign earnings might now invest them here rather than abroad.

The bad news is that the Act increases incentives for companies to locate production offshore in low-tax countries. After paying the new taxes, companies may choose to reinvest overseas in countries that have lower tax rates than the United States. Doing so will generate higher after-tax profits and free cash flows but won't increase investments and jobs here. If manufacturing in a foreign country is more cost-effective than in the United States, then the Act may not stimulate employment growth for blue-collar workers.

2-9j Taxation of Pass-Through Entities

A **pass-through entity** is a business whose income is not taxed at the business level but is instead passed through to its owners and then is taxed at their individual personal tax rates. (This is true even if the actual cash generated by the pass-through is used by the pass-through rather than being distributed to its owners.) Such businesses include sole proprietorships and partnerships. Another type of pass-through entity is an **S corporation**, which

---

[17]These payments are not all due immediately but may be spread out over 8 years.

receives benefits from the corporate form of organization—especially limited liability—yet is taxed as a proprietorship or partnership. See **Web Extension 2A** for a description of how the TCJA affects the personal taxes of those receiving pass-through income.

2-9k The Corporate Alternative Minimum Tax

In addition to the changes described in the following sections, the TCJA eliminated the corporate Alternative Minimum Tax (AMT). The AMT was an additional method of calculating corporate taxable income that reduced or eliminated some of the various tax credits and deductions used in calculating the normal tax. The corporate AMT's objective was to make it less likely that a company would pay no income taxes.

SELF-TEST

If a corporation has $85,000 in taxable income, what is its tax liability? **($17,150)**

How does the federal income tax system treat dividends received by a corporation?

What is the difference in the tax treatment of interest and dividends paid by a corporation? Does this factor favor debt or equity financing?

Briefly explain how tax loss carryback and carryforward procedures work.

2-10 Personal Taxes

resource

See **Web Extension 2A** on the textbook's Web site for details concerning personal taxation.

Web Extension 2A provides a more detailed treatment of **personal taxes**, but the key elements are presented here based on the 2017 Tax Cut and Job Creation Act. Keep in mind that the TCJA's changes in the corporate tax code will not change unless Congress passes a new tax act. However, most of the changes to the personal tax code are actually suspensions of elements in the prior code and will revert to their former values for the 2026 tax year unless Congress intervenes. In other words, most of the TCJA's changes to the personal tax code are in effect only for tax years 2018–2025.

Ordinary income consists primarily of wages or profits from a proprietorship or partnership, plus investment income *other than* qualified dividends and net long-term capital gains. We describe taxation of qualified dividends and net long-term capital gains in a following section, but for now we will assume that a taxpayer has no qualified dividends or net long-term capital gains. Therefore, the taxable income is just ordinary income.

For the 2018 tax year, individuals with less than the first bracket of $9,525 of taxable income are subject to a federal income tax rate of 10%. Therefore, for someone earning $8,000, the tax is 10%($8,000) = $800. For someone with income of $29,525, which is above the first bracket but below the second of $38,700, the first $9,525 (i.e., the amount less than the first bracket) is taxed at 10% and the remaining $29,525 − $9,525 = $20,000 is taxed at 12%. Because 12% is the rate on each additional dollar between $9,524 and $38,700, it is called a **marginal tax rate**. Total taxes are 10%($9,525) + 12%($20,000) = $3,352.5. As income increases, there are more brackets at higher rates until income exceeds the highest bracket of $500,000 for individuals ($600,000 for married joint filers), at which point the additional income is taxed at 37%. This is called a **progressive tax** because the higher one's income, the larger the percentage paid in taxes.

Prior to the TCJA in 2017, the top bracket was $418,400 for individuals ($470,700 for joint filers), and the top tax rate was 39.6%. In general, the TCJA cut the marginal rates for the brackets and reduced the bracket thresholds. For example, in 2017, the tax on $29,525 of income (the same amount we just used) would be $3,962.50, over $600 more than it would be under the rates and brackets of the TCJA.

As noted, individuals are taxed on investment income as well as earned income, with a few exceptions and modifications. For example, interest received from most municipal bonds issued by state and local government bonds is not subject to federal taxation. However, interest earned on most other bonds or lending is taxed as ordinary income. This means that a lower-yielding muni can provide the same after-tax return as a higher-yielding corporate bond. For a taxpayer in the 37% marginal tax bracket, a muni yielding 5.5% provides the same after-tax return as a corporate bond with a pre-tax yield of 8.73%: 8.73%(1 − 0.37) = 5.5%.

Assets such as stocks, bonds, and real estate are defined as **capital assets**. If you own a capital asset and its price goes up, then your wealth increases, but you are not liable for any taxes on your increased wealth until you sell the asset. If you sell the asset for more than you originally paid, the profit is called a *capital gain*; if you sell it for less, then you suffer a *capital loss*. The length of time you owned the asset determines the tax treatment. If held for less than 1 year, it is a short-term capital gain or loss and is included as part of ordinary income. If held for more than a year, it is a long-term capital gain or loss and is taxed at a lower rate. Dividends are taxed as though they are capital gains, so we will use the term "dividends & gains" when we refer to the combined dividends and net long-term capital gains.[18]

Portions of a capital gain may be taxed at 0%, 15%, and 20%. For an investor with total income (ordinary income plus long-term capital gains) less than $36,800 (the first bracket's threshold), none of the capital gain is taxed. For an investor with *ordinary* income greater than $425,800, all of the capital gains are taxed at 20%. The long-term capital gains rate is 15% for many other situations, but the details are complicated.

Web Extension 2A explains in more detail how to calculate taxes on gains and dividends. It also describes the standard deduction, itemized deductions, personal exemptions (which are not allowed under the TCJA), tax credits, payroll taxes, the net investment income tax, income from pass-through entities, the alternative minimum tax (AMT), gifts, estates, and generation-skipping transfers.

SELF-TEST

Explain what is meant by this statement: "Our tax rates are progressive."

Explain the difference between marginal tax rates and average tax rates.

What are municipal bonds, and how are these bonds taxed?

What are capital gains and losses, and how are they taxed?

SUMMARY

- The four basic statements contained in the **annual report** are the balance sheet, the income statement, the statement of stockholders' equity, and the statement of cash flows.
- The **balance sheet** shows assets and liabilities and equity, or claims against assets. The balance sheet may be thought of as a snapshot of the firm's financial position at a particular point in time.
- The **income statement** reports the results of operations over a period of time, and it shows earnings per share as its "bottom line."
- The **statement of stockholders' equity** shows the change in stockholders' equity, including the change in retained earnings, between balance sheet dates. Retained earnings represent a claim against assets, not assets per se.
- The **statement of cash flows** reports the effect of operating, investing, and financing activities on cash flows over an accounting period.

---

[18]See **Web Extension 2A** for details on how net long-term capital gains are calculated. It also explains which dividends are eligible for treatment as though they are capital gains.

- **Net cash flow** differs from **accounting profit** because some of the revenues and expenses reflected in accounting profits may not have been received or paid out in cash during the year. Depreciation is typically the largest noncash item, so net cash flow is often expressed as net income plus depreciation.
- **Operating current assets** are the current assets that are used to support operations, such as cash, inventory, and accounts receivable. They do not include short-term investments.
- **Operating current liabilities** are the current liabilities that occur as a natural consequence of operations, such as accounts payable and accruals. They do not include notes payable or any other short-term debts that charge interest.
- **Net operating working capital (NOWC)** is the difference between operating current assets and operating current liabilities. Thus, it is the working capital acquired with investor-supplied funds.
- **Operating long-term assets** are the long-term assets used to support operations, such as net plant and equipment. They do not include any long-term investments that pay interest or dividends.
- **Total net operating capital** (which means the same as **operating capital**) is the sum of net operating working capital and operating long-term assets. It is the total amount of capital needed to run the business.
- **NOPAT** is net operating profit after taxes. It is the after-tax profit a company would have if it had no debt and no investments in nonoperating assets. Because NOPAT excludes the effects of financial decisions, it is a better measure of operating performance than is net income.
- **Return on invested capital (ROIC)** is equal to NOPAT divided by total net operating capital. It measures the rate of return that the operations are generating. It is the best measure of operating performance.
- **Free cash flow (FCF)** is the cash flow available for distribution to all of a company's investors after the company has made all investments necessary to sustain ongoing operations. Therefore, *the intrinsic value of a company is directly related to its ability to generate free cash flow.* FCF is defined as NOPAT minus the investment in total net operating capital.
- **Market Value Added (MVA)** represents the difference between the total market value of a firm and the total amount of investor-supplied capital. If the market values of debt and preferred stock equal their values as reported on the financial statements, then MVA is the difference between the market value of a firm's stock and the amount of equity its shareholders have supplied.
- **Economic Value Added (EVA)** is the difference between after-tax operating profit and the total dollar cost of capital, including the cost of equity capital. EVA is an estimate of the value created by management during the year, and it differs substantially from accounting profit because no charge for the use of equity capital is reflected in accounting profit.
- Interest income received by a corporation is taxed as **ordinary income**; however, 50% of the dividends received by one corporation from another are excluded from **taxable income**.
- Interest paid by a corporation is a **deductible expense**, subject to limits established by the 2017 Tax Cut and Jobs Act. However, dividends are not a deductible expense, causing our tax system to favor debt over equity financing.
- The corporate tax code's **carryforward** provision allows a company to carry forward prior cumulative operating losses indefinitely and may be used to offset up to 80% of the taxable income in each future year until the remaining prior cumulative operating losses are all used up.
- **S corporations** are businesses that have the limited-liability benefits of the corporate form of organization yet are taxed as partnerships or proprietorships.
- In the United States, tax rates are **progressive**—the higher one's income, the larger the percentage paid in taxes.

- Assets such as stocks, bonds, and real estate are defined as **capital assets**. If a capital asset is sold for more than its cost, the profit is called a **capital gain**; if the asset is sold for a loss, it is called a **capital loss**. Assets held for more than a year provide long-term gains or losses.
- Dividends are taxed as though they were capital gains in most situations.
- **Personal taxes** are discussed in more detail in *Web Extension 2A*.

QUESTIONS

(2-1) Define each of the following terms:
- a. Annual report; balance sheet; income statement
- b. Common stockholders' equity, or net worth; retained earnings
- c. Statement of stockholders' equity; statement of cash flows
- d. Depreciation; amortization; EBITDA
- e. Operating current assets; operating current liabilities; net operating working capital; total net operating capital
- f. Accounting profit; net cash flow; NOPAT; free cash flow; return on invested capital
- g. Market Value Added; Economic Value Added
- h. Progressive tax; taxable income; marginal and average tax rates
- i. Capital gain or loss; tax loss carryforward
- j. Improper accumulation; S corporation

(2-2) What four statements are contained in most annual reports?

(2-3) If a "typical" firm reports $20 million of retained earnings on its balance sheet, can the firm definitely pay a $20 million cash dividend?

(2-4) Explain the following statement: "Whereas the balance sheet can be thought of as a snapshot of the firm's financial position *at a point in time,* the income statement reports on operations *over a period of time.*"

(2-5) What is operating capital, and why is it important?

(2-6) Explain the difference between NOPAT and net income. Which is a better measure of the performance of a company's operations?

(2-7) What is free cash flow? Why is it the most important measure of cash flow?

(2-8) If you were starting a business, what tax considerations might cause you to prefer to set it up as a proprietorship or a partnership rather than as a corporation?

SELF-TEST PROBLEM   SOLUTION SHOWN IN APPENDIX A

(ST-1)
Net Income, Cash Flow, and EVA

Last year Cole Furnaces had $4 million in operating income (EBIT). The company had a net depreciation expense of $1 million and an interest expense of $1 million; its combined federal and state corporate tax rate is 25%. The company has $14 million in operating current assets and $4 million in operating current liabilities; it has $15 million in net plant and equipment. It estimates that it has an after-tax cost of capital of 10%. Assume that Cole's only noncash item was depreciation.

- a. What was the company's net income for the year?
- b. What was the company's net cash flow?
- c. What was the company's net operating profit after taxes (NOPAT)?
- d. Calculate net operating working capital and total net operating capital for the current year.

e. If total net operating capital in the previous year was $24 million, what was the company's free cash flow (FCF) for the year?

f. What was the return on invested capital?

g. What was the company's Economic Value Added (EVA)?

PROBLEMS ANSWERS ARE IN APPENDIX B

Note: By the time this book is published, Congress may have changed rates and/or other provisions of current tax law. Work all problems on the assumption that the information in the chapter is applicable.

EASY PROBLEMS 1–9

(2-1)
Personal After-Tax Yield
An investor recently purchased a corporate bond that yields 7.68%. The investor is in the 25% federal-plus-state tax bracket. What is the bond's after-tax yield to the investor?

(2-2)
Personal After-Tax Yield
Corporate bonds issued by Johnson Corporation currently yield 8.0%. Municipal bonds of equal risk currently yield 5.5%. At what personal tax rate would an investor be indifferent between these two bonds?

(2-3)
Income Statement
Holly's Art Galleries recently reported $7.9 million of net income. Its EBIT was $13 million, and its federal tax rate was 21% (ignore any possible state corporate taxes). What was its interest expense? (Hint: Write out the headings for an income statement and then fill in the known values. Then divide $7.9 million net income by $1 - T = 0.79$ to find the pre-tax income. The difference between EBIT and taxable income must be the interest expense. Use this procedure to work some of the other problems.)

(2-4)
Income Statement
Nicholas Health Systems recently reported an EBITDA of $25.0 million and net income of $15.8 million. It had $2.0 million of interest expense, and its federal tax rate was 21% (ignore any possible state corporate taxes). What was its charge for depreciation and amortization?

(2-5)
Net Cash Flow
Kendall Corners Inc. recently reported net income of $3.1 million and depreciation of $500,000. What was its net cash flow? Assume it had no amortization expense.

(2-6)
Statement of Retained Earnings
In its most recent financial statements, Del-Castillo Inc. reported $70 million of net income and $900 million of retained earnings. The previous retained earnings were $855 million. How much in dividends did the firm pay to shareholders during the year?

(2-7)
Net Operating Profit after Taxes (NOPAT)
Zucker Inc. recently reported $4 million in earnings before interest and taxes (EBIT). Its federal-plus-state tax rate is 25%. What is its net operating profit after taxes?

(2-8)
Total Net Operating Capital
Jenn Translation (JT) Inc. reported $10 million in operating current assets, $15 million in net fixed assets, and $3 million in operating current liabilities. How much total net operating capital does JT have?

(2-9)
Free Cash Flow (FCF)
Carter Swimming Pools has $16 million in net operating profit after taxes (NOPAT) in the current year. Carter has $12 million in total net operating assets in the current year and had $10 million in the previous year. What is its free cash flow?

INTERMEDIATE PROBLEMS 10–17

(2-10)
Corporate Tax Liability
The Talley Corporation had taxable operating income of $365,000 (i.e., earnings from operating revenues minus all operating costs). Talley also had (1) interest charges of $50,000, (2) dividends received of $15,000, and (3) dividends paid of $25,000. Its federal

tax rate was 21% (ignore any possible state corporate taxes). Recall that 50% of dividends received are tax exempt. What is the taxable income? What is the tax expense? What is the after-tax income?

(2-11)
Corporate Tax
Liability

The Wendt Corporation reported $50 million of taxable income. Its federal tax rate was 21% (ignore any possible state corporate taxes).

a. What is the company's federal income tax bill for the year?

b. Assume the firm receives an additional $1 million of interest income from some bonds it owns. What is the additional tax on this interest income?

c. Now assume that Wendt does not receive the interest income but does receive an additional $1 million as dividends on some stock it owns. Recall that 50% of dividends received are tax exempt. What is the additional tax on this dividend income?

(2-12)
Corporate After-
Tax Yield

The Shrieves Corporation has $10,000 that it plans to invest in marketable securities. It is choosing among AT&T bonds (which yield 6.6%), AT&T preferred stock (with a dividend yield of 6.0%), and state of Florida muni bonds (which yield 5% but are not taxable). The federal tax rate is 21% (ignore any possible state corporate taxes). Recall that 50% of dividends received are tax exempt. Find the after-tax rates of return on all three securities after paying federal corporate taxes.

(2-13)
Net Cash Flows

The Moore Corporation has operating income (EBIT) of $750,000. Its depreciation expense is $200,000. Moore is 100% equity financed. The federal tax rate is 21% (ignore any possible state corporate taxes). What is the company's net income? What is its net cash flow?

(2-14)
Income and Cash
Flow Analysis

The Berndt Corporation expects to have sales of $12 million. Costs other than depreciation are expected to be 75% of sales, and depreciation is expected to be $1.5 million. All sales revenues will be collected in cash, and costs other than depreciation must be paid for during the year. The federal tax rate is 21% (ignore any possible state corporate taxes). Berndt has no debt.

a. Set up an income statement. What is Berndt's expected net income? Its expected net cash flow?

b. Suppose Congress changed the tax laws so that Berndt's depreciation expenses doubled. No changes in operations occurred. What would happen to reported profit and to net cash flow?

c. Now suppose that Congress changed the tax laws such that, instead of doubling Berndt's depreciation, it was reduced by 50%. How would profit and net cash flow be affected?

d. If this were your company, would you prefer Congress to cause your depreciation expense to be doubled or halved? Why?

(2-15)
Net Operating Profit
after Tax (NOPAT)

Use the following income statement of Elliott Game Theory Consulting to determine its net operating profit after taxes (NOPAT). Use 25% as the tax rate.

Elliott Game Theory Consulting Income Statement for Year Ending December 31

	2020
Sales	$800,000
Operating costs excluding depreciation	700,000
Depreciation and amortization	20,000
Earnings before interest and taxes	$ 80,000
Less interest	2,000
Pre-tax income	$ 78,000
Taxes (25%)	19,500
Net income available to common stockholders	$ 58,500

(2-16)
Net Operating
Working Capital
(NOWC)

Using the following balance sheets of Mimi's Gymnastics Inc., what is the net operating working capital (NOWC) for 2020?

Mimi's Gymnastics Inc.: Balance Sheets as of December 31
(Millions of Dollars)

	2020
Assets	
Cash	$ 90
Short-term investments	110
Accounts receivable	1,200
Inventories	900
Total current assets	$2,300
Net plant and equipment	2,200
Total assets	$4,500
Liabilities and Equity	
Accounts payable	$ 600
Accruals	200
Notes payable	180
Total current liabilities	$ 980
Long-term debt	800
Total liabilities	$1,780
Common stock	2,200
Retained earnings	520
Total common equity	$2,720
Total liabilities and equity	$4,500

(2-17)
Investment
in Total Net
Operating Capital

Athenian Venues Inc. just reported the following selected portion of its financial statements for the end of 2020. Your assistant has already calculated the 2020 end-of-year net operating working capital (NOWC) from the full set of financial statements (not shown here), which is $13 million. The total net operating capital for 2019 was $50 million. What was the 2020 net investment in operating capital?

Athenian Venues Inc.: Selected Balance Sheet Information as of December 31
(Millions of Dollars)

	2020
Assets	
Cash	$1
Short-term investments	4
Accounts receivable	8
Inventories	11
Total current assets	$24
Net plant and equipment	51
Total assets	$75

CHALLENGING PROBLEMS 18–19

(2-18)
Free Cash Flows

Rhodes Corporation's financial statements are shown after part f. Suppose the federal-plus-state tax corporate tax is 25%. Answer the following questions.

a. What is the net operating profit after taxes (NOPAT) for 2020?
b. What are the amounts of net operating working capital for both years?
c. What are the amounts of total net operating capital for both years?
d. What is the free cash flow for 2020?
e. What is the ROIC for 2020?
f. How much of the FCF did Rhodes use for each of the following purposes: after-tax interest, net debt repayments, dividends, net stock repurchases, and net purchases of short-term investments? (*Hint:* Remember that a net use can be negative.)

Rhodes Corporation: Income Statements for Year Ending December 31 (Millions of Dollars)

	2020	2019
Sales	$11,000	$10,000
Operating costs excluding depreciation	9,612	8,728
Depreciation and amortization	380	360
Earnings before interest and taxes	$ 1,008	$ 912
Less interest	120	100
Pre-tax income	$ 888	$ 812
Taxes (25%)	222	203
Net income available to common stockholders	$ 666	$ 609
Common dividends	$ 202	$ 200

Rhodes Corporation: Balance Sheets as of December 31 (Millions of Dollars)

	2020	2019
Assets		
Cash	$ 550	$ 500
Short-term investments	110	100
Accounts receivable	2,750	2,500
Inventories	1,650	1,500
Total current assets	$5,060	$4,600
Net plant and equipment	3,850	3,500
Total assets	$8,910	$8,100
Liabilities and Equity		
Accounts payable	$1,100	$1,000
Accruals	550	500
Notes payable	384	200
Total current liabilities	$2,034	$1,700
Long-term debt	1,100	1,000
Total liabilities	$3,134	$2,700
Common stock	4,312	4,400
Retained earnings	1,464	1,000
Total common equity	$5,776	$5,400
Total liabilities and equity	$8,910	$8,100

(2-19)
Loss Carryforward

The Bookbinder Company had $500,000 cumulative operating losses prior to the beginning of *last* year. It had $100,000 in pre-tax earnings *last* year before using the past operating losses and has $300,000 in the *current* year before using any past operating losses. It projects $350,000 pre-tax earnings *next* year.

    a. How much taxable income was there *last* year? How much, if any, cumulative losses remained at the end of the last year?

    b. What is the taxable income in the *current* year? How much, if any, cumulative losses remain at the end of the current year?

    c. What is the projected taxable income for *next* year? How much, if any, cumulative losses are projected to remain at the end of next year?

SPREADSHEET PROBLEMS

(2-20)
Build a Model:
Financial
Statements

resource

Begin with the partial model in the file *Ch02 P20 Build a Model.xlsx* on the textbook's Web site.

    a. Britton String Corp. manufactures specialty strings for musical instruments and tennis racquets. Its most recent sales were $880 million; operating costs (excluding depreciation) were equal to 85% of sales; net fixed assets were $300 million; depreciation amounted to 10% of net fixed assets; interest expenses were $22 million; the state-plus-federal corporate tax rate was 25%; and it paid 40% of its net income out in dividends. Given this information, construct Britton String's income statement. Also calculate total dividends and the addition to retained earnings. Report all dollar figures in millions.

    b. Britton String's partial balance sheets follow. Britton issued $36 million of new common stock in the most recent year. Using this information and the results from part a, fill in the missing values for common stock, retained earnings, total common equity, and total liabilities and equity.

Britton Strings Corp: Balance Sheets as of December 31 (Millions of Dollars)

	2020	2019
Assets		
Cash and cash equivalents	$ 70	$ 60
Short-term investments	46	42
Accounts receivable	120	140
Inventories	$264	$196
Total current assets	$500	$438
Net fixed assets	300	262
Total assets	$800	$700
Liabilities and Equity		
Accounts payable	$ 73	$ 64
Accruals	49	60
Notes payable	30	39
Total current liabilities	$ 152	$ 163
Long-term debt	217	178
Total liabilities	$ 369	$ 341
Common stock	285	$249
Retained earnings	146	110
Total common equity	$431	$359
Total liabilities and equity	$800	$700

    c. Construct the statement of cash flows for 2020.

(2-21)
Build a Model:
Free Cash Flows,
EVA, and MVA

resource

Begin with the partial model in the file *Ch02 P21 Build a Model.xlsx* on the textbook's Web site.

a. Using the financial statements shown here for Lan & Chen Technologies, calculate net operating working capital, total net operating capital, net operating profit after taxes, free cash flow, and return on invested capital for 2020. The federal-plus-state tax rate is 25%.

b. Assume there were 15 million shares outstanding at the end of 2019, the year-end closing stock price was $65 per share, and the after-tax cost of capital was 10%. Calculate EVA and MVA for 2020.

Lan & Chen Technologies: Income Statements for Year Ending December 31 (Millions of Dollars)

	2020	2019
Sales	$945,000	$900,000
Expenses excluding depreciation and amortization	812,700	774,000
EBITDA	$132,300	$126,000
Depreciation and amortization	33,100	31,500
EBIT	$ 99,200	$ 94,500
Interest expense	10,400	8,900
Pre-tax earnings	$ 88,800	$ 85,600
Taxes (25%)	22,200	21,400
Net income	$ 66,600	$ 64,200
Common dividends	$ 43,300	$ 41,230
Addition to retained earnings	$ 23,300	$ 22,970

Lan & Chen Technologies: December 31 Balance Sheets (Thousands of Dollars)

	2020	2019
Assets		
Cash and cash equivalents	$ 47,250	$ 45,000
Short-term investments	3,800	3,600
Accounts receivable	283,500	270,000
Inventories	141,750	135,000
Total current assets	$476,300	$453,600
Net fixed assets	330,750	315,000
Total assets	$807,050	$768,600
Liabilities and Equity		
Accounts payable	$ 94,500	$ 90,000
Accruals	47,250	45,000
Notes payable	17,400	9,000
Total current liabilities	$159,150	$144,000
Long-term debt	90,000	90,000
Total liabilities	$249,150	$234,000
Common stock	$444,600	$444,600
Retained earnings	113,300	90,000
Total common equity	$557,900	$534,600
Total liabilities and equity	$807,050	$768,600

MINI CASE

resource

The following financial statements are available in the file Ch02 Tool Kit. xlsx in the Mini Case tab. Because the statements will be used to project future years, they are organized with the most recent year at the far right.

Jenny Cochran, a graduate of the University of Tennessee with 4 years of experience as an equities analyst, was recently brought in as assistant to the chairman of the board of Computron Industries, a manufacturer of computer components.

During the previous year, Computron had doubled its plant capacity, opened new sales offices outside its home territory, and launched an expensive advertising campaign. Cochran was assigned to evaluate the impact of the changes. She began by gathering financial statements and other data.

Balance Sheets (Millions of Dollars)	2018	2019
Assets		
Cash and equivalents	$ 60	$ 50
Short-term investments	100	10
Accounts receivable	400	520
Inventories	620	820
Total current assets	$ 1,180	$1,400
Gross fixed assets	$ 3,900	$4,820
Less: Accumulated depreciation	1,000	1,320
Net fixed assets	$ 2,900	$3,500
Total assets	$ 4,080	$4,900
Liabilities and Equity		
Accounts payable	$ 300	$ 400
Notes payable	50	250
Accruals	200	240
Total current liabilities	$ 550	$ 890
Long-term bonds	800	1,100
Total liabilities	$ 1,350	$ 1,190
Common stock	1,000	1,000
Retained earnings	1,730	1,910
Total equity	$ 2,730	$ 2,910
Total liabilities and equity	$ 4,080	$ 4,900

Income Statement (Millions of Dollars)	2018	2019
Net sales	$5,500	$6,000
Cost of goods sold (excluding depr. & amort.)	4,300	4,800
Depreciation and amortization[a]	290	320
Other operating expenses	350	420
Total operating costs	$4,940	$5,540
Earnings before interest and taxes (EBIT)	$ 560	$ 460
Less interest	68	108
Pre-tax earnings	$ 492	$ 352
Taxes (25%)	123	88
Net Income	$ 369	$ 264

Note:

[a]Computron has no amortization charges.

Other Data	2018	2019
Stock price	$50.00	$30.00
Shares outstanding (millions)	100	100
Common dividends (millions)	$90	$84
Tax rate	25%	25%
Weighted average cost of capital (WACC)	10.00%	10.00%

Statement of Cash Flows (Millions of Dollars)	2019
Operating Activities	
Net income before preferred dividends	$ 264
Noncash Adjustments	
Depreciation and amortization	320
Due to Changes in Working Capital	
Change in accounts receivable	(120)
Change in inventories	(200)
Change in accounts payable	100
Change in accruals	40
Net cash provided by operating activities	$ 404
Investing Activities	
Cash used to acquire fixed assets	$(920)
Change in short-term investments	90
Net cash provided by investing activities	$(830)
Financing Activities	
Change in notes payable	$ 200
Change in long-term debt	300
Payment of cash dividends	(84)
Net cash provided by financing activities	$ 416
Net change in cash and equivalents	$ (10)
Cash and securities at beginning of the year	60
Cash and securities at end of the year	$ 50

Assume that you are Cochran's assistant and that you must help her answer the following questions:

a. What effect did the expansion have on sales and net income? What effect did the expansion have on the asset side of the balance sheet? What effect did it have on liabilities and equity?

b. What do you conclude from the statement of cash flows?

c. What is free cash flow? Why is it important? What are FCF's five uses?

d. What is Computron's net operating profit after taxes (NOPAT)? What are operating current assets? What are operating current liabilities? How much net operating working capital and total net operating capital does Computron have?

e. What is Computron's free cash flow? What are Computron's "net uses" of its FCF?

f. Calculate Computron's return on invested capital (ROIC). Computron has a 10% cost of capital (WACC). What caused the decline in the ROIC? Was it due to operating profitability or capital utilization? Do you think Computron's growth added value?

g. Cochran also has asked you to estimate Computron's Economic Value Added (EVA). She estimates that the after-tax cost of capital was 10% in both years.
h. What happened to Computron's Market Value Added (MVA)?
i. The Tax Cut and Jobs Act (TCJA) was signed into law in 2017. Briefly describe its key provisions for corporate taxes.
j. Assume that a corporation has $87 million of taxable income from operations. It also received interest income of $8 million and dividend income of $10 million. The federal tax rate is 21%, and the dividend exclusion rate is 50%. What is its taxable income and federal tax liability?
k. Briefly describe the TCJA's key provisions for personal taxes.
l. Assume that you are in the 25% marginal tax bracket and that you have $20,000 to invest. You have narrowed your investment choices down to municipal bonds yielding 7% or equally risky corporate bonds with a yield of 10%. Which one should you choose and why? At what marginal tax rate would you be indifferent?

CHAPTER 3

Analysis of Financial Statements

Even though Twitter Inc. had not yet had a profitable quarter based on generally accepted accounting principles (GAAP), its stock price jumped by 18% on September 26, 2017, when it reported *minus* $21 million in earnings before interest, taxes, depreciation, and amortization (EBITDA). The reason for the positive stock reaction? First, a loss of $21 million was better than the $103 million loss it reported in the previous quarter. Second, Twitter stated that it might report positive EBITDA in its next report.

Most companies guide analysts by providing estimates of future revenues. According to a survey by the National Investors Relations Institute, 94% of respondents in 2014 provided some form of guidance for analysts and investors. Despite the high proportion of companies that provide guidance, a 2015 survey by Integrated Corporate Relations reports that over half of the responding investment professionals don't think guidance is vital for determining whether to recommend purchasing a company's stock. It appears as though many investors rely on other types of information, including ratio analysis.

Source: See the reports at www.cnbc.com/2017/10/26/twitter-earnings-q3-revenue-eps-and-maus.html, http://files.shareholder.com/downloads/AMDA-2F526X/5619402910x0x961127/658476E7-9D8B -4B17-BE5D-B77034D21FCE/TWTR_Q3_17_Earnings_Press_Release.pdf, www.marketwatch.com /news/markets/earningswatch.asp, http://niri.org/Main-Menu-Category/resource/publications/Executive -Alert/2014-Executive-Alert-Archive/NIRI-Guidance-Practices-Survey–2014-Report-102214.aspx, and http://icrinc.com/en/pdfs/xchange/XChange_2015_ICR_Survey.pdf.

Intrinsic Value, Free Cash Flow, and Financial Statements

The intrinsic value of a firm is determined by the present value of the expected future free cash flows (FCFs) when discounted at the weighted average cost of capital (WACC).

This chapter explains how to use financial statements to evaluate a company's profitability, required capital investments, business risk, and mix of debt and equity.

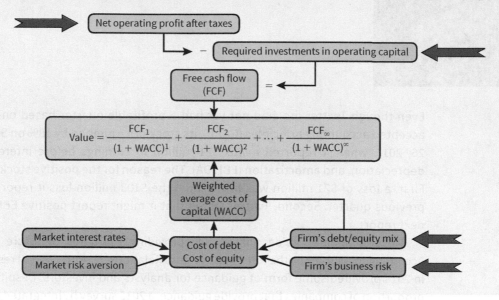

Financial statement analysis involves (1) comparing a firm's performance with that of other firms in the same industry and (2) evaluating trends in the firm's financial position over time. Managers use financial analysis to identify situations needing attention, potential lenders use financial analysis to determine whether a company is creditworthy, and stockholders use financial analysis to help predict future earnings, dividends, and free cash flow. This chapter will explain the similarities and differences among these uses.

3-1 Financial Analysis

When we perform a financial analysis, we conduct the following steps.

3-1a Gather Data

The first step in financial analysis is to gather data. As discussed in Chapter 2, financial statements can be downloaded from many different Web sites. One of our favorites is Zacks Investment Research, which provides financial statements in a standardized format. If you cut and paste financial statements from Zacks into a spreadsheet and then perform a financial analysis, you can quickly repeat the analysis on a different company by pasting that company's financial statements into the same cells of the spreadsheet. In other words, you do not need to reinvent the wheel every time you analyze a company.

3-1b Examine the Statement of Cash Flows

Some financial analysis can be done with virtually no calculations. For example, we always look to the statement of cash flows first, particularly the net cash provided by operating activities. Downward trends or negative net cash flow from operations almost always indicates problems. The statement of cash flows section on investing activities shows whether the company has made a big acquisition, especially when compared with prior years' net cash flows from investing activities. A quick look at the section on financing activities also reveals whether a company is issuing debt or buying back stock; in other words, is the company raising capital from investors or returning it to them?

Recall from the previous chapter (Figure 2-4) that MicroDrive generated $163 million from its operating activities but invested $420 million in new fixed assets. To make these purchases, MicroDrive borrowed heavily.

3-1c Calculate and Examine the Return on Invested Capital and Free Cash Flow

After examining the statement of cash flows, we calculate the net operating profit after taxes (NOPAT) and the total net operating capital. We use these measures to calculate the operating profitability ratio (OP), the capital requirement ratio (CR), the return on invested capital (ROIC), and the free cash flow (FCF), as described in Chapter 2.

The ROIC provides a vital measure of a firm's overall performance. If the ROIC is greater than the company's weighted average cost of capital (WACC), then the company usually is adding value. If the ROIC is less than the WACC, then the company usually has serious problems. No matter what the ROIC tells us about overall performance, it is important to examine specific activities with different financial ratios.

We calculated these measures for MicroDrive in the previous chapter (see Figure 2-6) and report them here for convenience:

MicroDrive (Millions of Dollars)	2018	2019
Net operating working capital (NOWC) =	$710	$1,000
Total net operating capital =	$2,490	$3,000
Net operating profit after taxes (NOPAT) =	$330	$300
Operating profitability ratio (OP) = NOPAT/Sales =	6.88%	6.00%
Capital requirement ratio (CR) = (Total net operating capital/Sales) =	51.88%	60.00%
Return on invested capital (ROIC) = NOPAT/Total net operating capital =	13.3%	10.0%
Free cash flow (FCF) = NOPAT − Net investment in operating capital =	N/A	−$210

MicroDrive's operating profitability fell from 6.88% to 6.00%, and its capital requirement ratio increased from 51.88% to 60%, indicating that MicroDrive is not generating enough in sales from its operating capital. The result is a decline in its ROIC from 13.3% to 10.0%, which is less than MicroDrive's 11.5% cost of capital. We will use ratio analysis in the following sections to identify the root causes of the ROIC's decline.

3-1d Begin Ratio Analysis

Financial ratios are designed to extract important information that might not be obvious simply from examining a firm's financial statements. For example, suppose Firm A owes $5 million in debt while Firm B owes $50 million. Which company is in a stronger financial position? It is impossible to answer this question without first standardizing each firm's debt relative to total assets and earnings. Such standardized comparisons are provided through *ratio analysis*.

We will calculate the 2019 financial ratios for MicroDrive Inc. using data from the balance sheets and income statements given in Figure 3-1; dollar amounts are in millions. Recall from Chapter 2 that MicroDrive reports only net plant, property, and equipment (PP&E) on its balance sheets instead of separately reporting cumulative depreciation and cumulative PP&E. For the sake of clarity, we break down the income statement's costs of goods sold into two components: (1) costs of goods sold excluding depreciation and (2) depreciation (MicroDrive has no amortization charges).

SELF-TEST

What insights does the Statement of Cash Flows provide regarding financial analysis?

What insights are provided by the (1) net operating profit after taxes (NOPAT); (2) operating profitability ratio (OP); (3) capital requirement ratio (CR); (4) return on invested capital (ROIC); and (5) free cash flow (FCF)?

3-2 Profitability Ratios

Profitability is the net result of a number of policies and decisions. The ratios examined thus far provide an overview of a firm's operations, but the **profitability ratios** go on to show the combined effects of liquidity, asset management, and debt on operating *and* financial results.

3-2a Net Profit Margin

The **net profit margin**, also called the **profit margin on sales** or just the **profit margin**, is calculated by dividing net income by sales. It gives the profit per dollar of sales:

$$\text{Net profit margin} = \frac{\text{Net income available to common stockholders}}{\text{Sales}} \qquad (3\text{-}1)$$

MicroDrive's net profit margin is:

$$\text{Net profit margin} = \frac{\$248}{\$5,000} = 4.96 \approx 5.0\%$$

$$\text{Industry average} = 6.2\%$$

MicroDrive's net profit margin is below the industry average, but why is this so? Is it due to inefficient operations, high interest expenses, or both?

Instead of just comparing net income to sales, many analysts also break the income statement into smaller parts to identify the sources of a low net profit margin. For example, the **operating profit margin** is defined as:

$$\text{Operating profit margin} = \frac{\text{EBIT}}{\text{Sales}} \qquad (3\text{-}2)$$

The operating profit margin identifies how a company is performing with respect to its operations before the impact of interest expenses is considered.

FIGURE 3-1

MicroDrive Inc.: Balance Sheets and Income Statements for Years Ending December 31 (Millions of Dollars, Except for Per Share Data)

	A	B	C	D	E
15	*Balance Sheets*			**2019**	**2018**
16	*Assets*				
17	Cash and equivalents			$100	$102
18	Short-term investments			10	40
19	Accounts receivable			500	384
20	Inventories			1,000	774
21	Total current assets			$1,610	$1,300
22	Net property, plant & equipment (PP&E)			2,000	1,780
23	Total assets			$3,610	$3,080
24					
25	*Liabilities and Equity*				
26	Accounts payable			$200	$180
27	Notes payable			150	28
28	Accruals			400	370
29	Total current liabilities			$750	$578
30	Long-term bonds			520	350
31	Total liabilities			$1,270	$928
32	Preferred stock			100	100
33	Common stock			500	500
34	Retained earnings			1,740	1,552
35	Total common equity			$2,240	$2,052
36	Total liabilities and equity			$3,610	$3,080
37					
38	*Income Statements*			**2019**	**2018**
39	Net sales			$5,000	$4,800
40	Costs of goods sold except depreciation			3,900	3,710
41	Depreciation[a]			200	180
42	Other operating expenses			500	470
43	Earnings before interest and taxes (EBIT)			$400	$440
44	Less interest			60	40
45	Pre-tax earnings			$340	$400
46	Taxes (25%)			85	100
47	Net income before preferred dividends			$255	$300
48	Preferred dividends			7	7
49	Net income available to common stockholders			$248	$293
50					
51	*Additional Information*				
52	Common dividends			$60.0	$59.4
53	Addition to retained earnings			$188.0	$233.6
54	Number of common shares			60	60
55	Common stock price per share			$31.00	$45.00
56	Lease payments			$28	$28
57	Bonds' required sinking fund payments			$20	$20
58	Tax rate			25%	25%

Source: See the file *Ch03 Tool Kit.xlsx*. Numbers are reported as rounded values for clarity but are calculated using *Excel*'s full precision. Thus, intermediate calculations using the figure's rounded values will be inexact.

Note:

[a]MicroDrive has no amortization charges, so we omit them from the item name.

MicroDrive's operating margin is:

$$\text{Operating profit margin} = \frac{\$400}{\$5,000} = 8.0\%$$

$$\text{Industry average} = 9.0\%$$

Some analysts drill even deeper by breaking operating costs into their components. For example, the **gross profit margin** is defined as:

$$\text{Gross profit margin} = \frac{\text{Sales} - \text{Cost of goods sold including depreciation}}{\text{Sales}} \tag{3-3}$$

The gross profit margin identifies the gross profit per dollar of sales before any other expenses are deducted.

Rather than calculate each type of profit margin here, later in the chapter we will use common size analysis and percent change analysis to focus on different parts of the income statement. In addition, we will use the DuPont equation to show how the ratios interact with one another.

Sometimes it is confusing to have so many different types of profit margins. To simplify the situation, we will focus primarily on the net profit margin throughout the book and call it the *profit margin*.

3-2b Basic Earning Power (BEP) Ratio

The **basic earning power (BEP) ratio** is calculated by dividing earnings before interest and taxes (EBIT) by total assets:

$$\text{Basic earning power (BEP) ratio} = \frac{\text{EBIT}}{\text{Total assets}} \tag{3-4}$$

The World Might Be Flat, but Global Accounting Is Bumpy! The Case of IFRS versus FASB

In a flat world, distance is no barrier. Work flows to where it can be done most efficiently, and capital flows to where it can be invested most profitably. If a radiologist in India is more efficient than one in the United States, then images will be e-mailed to India for diagnosis; if rates of return are higher in Brazil, then investors throughout the world will provide funding for Brazilian projects. One key to "flattening" the world is agreement on common standards. For example, there are common Internet standards so that users throughout the world are able to communicate.

A glaring exception to standardization is in accounting. The Securities and Exchange Commission (SEC) in the United States requires firms to comply with standards set by the Financial Accounting Standards Board (FASB). But the European Union requires all EU-listed companies to comply with the International Financial Reporting Standards (IFRS), as defined by the International Accounting Standards Board (IASB).

IFRS tends to rely on general principles, whereas FASB standards are rules-based. As we write this in 2018, some progress toward standardizing accounting rules has been made, but it does not seem likely that the United States and the EU will be using the same accounting rules in the near future.

To keep abreast of developments in IFRS/GAAP convergence, visit the IASB Web site at **www.iasb.org** and the FASB Web site at **www.fasb.org**.

For MicroDrive, the ratio is:

$$\text{Basic earning power (BEP) ratio} = \frac{\$400}{\$3,610} = 11.1\%$$

$$\text{Industry average} = 13.8\%$$

This ratio shows the earning power of the firm's assets before the influence of taxes and leverage, and it is useful for comparing firms with different tax situations and different degrees of financial leverage. MicroDrive has a lower BEP than its peers, partly because its profit margin is low and partly because it manages assets inefficiently, as we show in Section 3-3.

3-2c Return on Total Assets

The ratio of net income to total assets measures the **return on total assets (ROA)** after interest and taxes. This ratio is also called the **return on assets** and is defined as follows:

$$\text{Return on assets} = \text{ROA} = \frac{\text{Net income available to common stockholders}}{\text{Total assets}} \qquad (3\text{-}5)$$

For MicroDrive, the ROA is:

$$\text{Return on assets} = \frac{\$248}{\$3,610} = 6.87\% \approx 6.9\%$$

$$\text{Industry average} = 9.6\%$$

MicroDrive's 6.9% return is well below the 9.6% average for the industry. This low return is due to (1) the company's low basic earning power and (2) high interest costs resulting from its above-average use of debt. Both of these factors cause MicroDrive's net income to be relatively low.

3-2d Return on Common Equity

The ratio of net income to common equity measures the **return on common equity (ROE)**, which is often called just the **return on equity**:

$$\text{Return on common equity} = \text{ROE} = \frac{\text{Net income available to common stockholders}}{\text{Common equity}} \qquad (3\text{-}6)$$

MicroDrive's ROE is:

$$\text{Return on equity} = \frac{\$248}{\$2,240} = 11.1\%$$

$$\text{Industry average} = 13.6\%$$

Stockholders invest to earn a return on their money, and this ratio tells how well they are doing in an accounting sense. MicroDrive's 11.1% return is below the 13.6% industry average but not as far below as its return on total assets. This somewhat better result is due to the company's greater use of debt, a point that we explain later in the chapter.

Identify and write out the equations for four profitability ratios.

Why is the basic earning power ratio useful?

Why does the use of debt lower ROA?

What does ROE measure?

Morris Corporation has the following information on its balance sheets: Cash = $40, accounts receivable = $30, inventories = $100, net fixed assets = $500, accounts payable = $20, accruals = $10, short-term debt (matures in less than a year) = $25, long-term debt = $200, and total common equity = $415. Its income statement reports: Sales = $820, costs of goods sold (excluding depreciation) = $450, depreciation = $50, other operating expenses = $100, interest expense = $20, and tax rate = 25%. Calculate the following ratios: Net profit margin **(18.3%)**, *operating profit margin* **(26.8%)**, *basic earning power ratio* **(32.8%)**, *return on total assets* **(22.4%)**, *and return on common equity* **(36.1%)**.

A company has $200 billion of sales and $10 billion of net income. Its total assets are $100 billion, financed half by debt and half by common equity. What is its profit margin? **(5%)** *What is its ROA?* **(10%)** *What is its ROE?* **(20%)** *Would ROA increase if the firm used less leverage?* **(Yes)** *Would ROE increase?* **(No)**

3-3 Asset Management Ratios

Asset management ratios measure how effectively a firm is managing its assets. For this reason, they are also called **efficiency ratios**. If a company has excessive investments in assets, then its operating capital is unduly high, which reduces its free cash flow and ultimately its stock price. On the other hand, if a company does not have enough assets, then it may lose sales, which would hurt profitability, free cash flow, and the stock price. Therefore, it is important to have the *right* amount invested in assets. Ratios that analyze the different types of assets are described in this section.

3-3a Evaluating Total Assets: The Total Assets Turnover Ratio

The **total assets turnover ratio** measures the dollars in sales that are generated for each dollar that is tied up in assets:

$$\text{Total assets turnover ratio} = \frac{\text{Sales}}{\text{Total assets}} \qquad (3\text{-}7)$$

For MicroDrive, the ratio is:

$$\text{Total assets turnover ratio} = \frac{\$5,000}{\$3,610} = 1.39 \approx 1.4$$

$$\text{Industry average} = 1.5$$

MicroDrive's ratio is somewhat below the industry average, indicating that the company is not generating as much business (relative to its peers), given its total asset investment. In other words, MicroDrive uses its assets relatively inefficiently. The following ratios can be used to identify the specific asset classes that are causing this problem.[1]

---

[1]Sales occur throughout the year, but assets are reported at end of the period. For a growing company or a company with seasonal variation, it would be better to use *average* assets held during the year when calculating turnover ratios. However, we use year-end values for all turnover ratios so that we are more comparable with most reported industry averages.

3-3b Evaluating Fixed Assets: The Fixed Assets Turnover Ratio

The **fixed assets turnover ratio** measures how effectively the firm uses its plant and equipment. It is the ratio of sales to net fixed assets:

$$\text{Fixed assets turnover ratio} = \frac{\text{Sales}}{\text{Net fixed assets}} \qquad \text{(3-8)}$$

MicroDrive's fixed assets turnover ratio is:

$$\text{Fixed assets turnover ratio} = \frac{\$5,000}{\$2,000} = 2.5$$

$$\text{Industry average} = 2.7$$

MicroDrive's ratio of 2.5 is a little below the industry average, indicating that the firm is using its fixed assets less intensively than its peers.

Inflation can cause problems when interpreting the fixed assets turnover ratio because fixed assets are reported using the historical costs of the assets instead of current replacement costs that may be higher due to inflation. Therefore, a mature firm with fixed assets acquired years ago might well have a higher fixed assets turnover ratio than a younger company with newer fixed assets that are reported at inflated prices relative to the historical prices of the older assets. However, this would reflect the difficulty accountants have in dealing with inflation rather than inefficiency on the part of the new firm. You should be alert to this potential problem when evaluating the fixed assets turnover ratio.

3-3c Evaluating Receivables: The Days Sales Outstanding

Days sales outstanding (DSO), also called the **average collection period (ACP)**, is used to appraise accounts receivable, and it is calculated by dividing accounts receivable by average daily sales to find the number of days' sales that are tied up in receivables. Thus, the DSO represents the average length of time that the firm must wait after making a sale before receiving cash, which is the average collection period. MicroDrive's DSO is 37, above the 29-day industry average:

$$\text{DSO} = \frac{\text{Days sales}}{\text{outstanding}} = \frac{\text{Receivables}}{\text{Average sales per day}} = \frac{\text{Receivables}}{\text{Annual sales}/365} \qquad \text{(3-9)}$$

MicroDrive's DSO is about 37 days:

$$\text{DSO} = \frac{\$500}{\$5,000/365} = \frac{\$500}{\$13.7} = 36.50 \text{ days} \approx 37 \text{ days}$$

$$\text{Industry average} = 29 \text{ days}$$

MicroDrive's sales terms call for payment within 30 days. The fact that 37 days of sales are outstanding indicates that customers, on average, are not paying their bills on time. As with inventory, high levels of accounts receivable cause high levels of net operating working capital (NOWC), which hurts FCF and stock price.

A customer who is paying late may be in financial trouble, which means MicroDrive may have a hard time collecting the receivable. Therefore, if the trend in DSO has been rising unexpectedly, steps should be taken to review credit standards and to expedite the collection of accounts receivable.

3-3d Evaluating Inventories: The Inventory Turnover Ratio

The **inventory turnover ratio** is defined as costs of goods sold (COGS) divided by inventories.[2] The previous ratios use sales instead of COGS. However, sales revenues include costs and profits, whereas inventory usually is reported at cost. Therefore, the inventory turnover ratio compares inventory with costs rather than sales:

$$\text{Inventory turnover ratio} = \frac{\text{COGS}}{\text{Inventories}} \qquad (3\text{-}10)$$

MicroDrive's income statement in Figure 3-1 separately reports depreciation and the portion of costs of goods sold that is not comprised of depreciation, which is helpful when calculating cash flows. However, we need the total COGS for calculating the inventory turnover ratio. MicroDrive has no amortization charges, and virtually all depreciation is associated with producing its products. MicroDrive's COGS is:

$$\text{COGS} = \text{Costs of goods sold except depreciation} + \text{Depreciation}$$

$$= \$3,900 + \$200 = \$4,100 \text{ million}$$

We can now calculate MicroDrive's inventory turnover:

$$\text{Inventory turnover ratio} = \frac{\text{COGS}}{\text{Inventory}} = \frac{\$4,100}{\$1,000} = 4.1$$

$$\text{Industry average} = 5.3$$

As a rough approximation, each item of MicroDrive's inventory is sold out and restocked, or "turned over," 4.1 times per year.

MicroDrive's turnover of 4.1 is lower than the 5.3 industry average. This suggests that MicroDrive is holding too much inventory. High levels of inventory add to net operating working capital, which reduces FCF, which leads to lower stock prices. In addition, MicroDrive's low inventory turnover ratio makes us wonder whether the firm is holding obsolete goods not worth their stated value.

In summary, MicroDrive's low fixed assets turnover ratio, high DSO, and low inventory turnover ratio each cause MicroDrive's total assets turnover ratio to be lower than the industry average.

SELF-TEST

Identify four ratios that measure how effectively a firm is managing its assets, and write out their equations.

What problem might arise when comparing firms' fixed assets turnover ratios?

---

[2]We calculate the turnover ratio using the ratio of COGS to inventories because most sources report the turnover ratio this way. However, you should be aware that a few sources, such as Dun & Bradstreet, define inventory turnover as the ratio of sales to inventories.

Morris Corporation has the following information on its balance sheets: Cash = $40, accounts receivable = $30, inventories = $100, net fixed assets = $500, accounts payable = $20, accruals = $10, short-term debt (matures in less than a year) = $25, long-term debt = $200, and total common equity = $415. Its income statement reports: Sales = $820, costs of goods sold (excluding depreciation) = $450, depreciation = $50, other operating expenses = $100, interest expense = $20, and tax rate = 25%. Calculate the following ratios: total assets turnover (**1.2**), fixed assets turnover (**1.6**), days sales outstanding (based on a 365-day year) (**13.4**), inventory turnover (**5.0**). (Hint: This is the same company used in the previous Self-Test.)

A firm has $200 million annual sales, $180 million costs of goods sold, $40 million of inventory, and $60 million of accounts receivable. What is its inventory turnover ratio? (**4.5**) What is its DSO based on a 365-day year? (**109.5 days**)

3-4 Liquidity Ratios

resource

See **Ch03 Tool Kit.xlsx** for all calculations.

As shown in Figure 3-1, MicroDrive has current liabilities of $750 million that it must pay off within the coming year. Will it have trouble satisfying those obligations? **Liquidity ratios** attempt to answer this type of question. We discuss two commonly used liquidity ratios in this section.

3-4a The Current Ratio

Current assets normally include cash, marketable securities, accounts receivable, and inventories. Current liabilities consist of accounts payable, short-term notes payable, current maturities of long-term debt, accrued taxes, and other accrued expenses. The **current ratio** measures liquidity by comparing the current assets to the current liabilities:

$$\text{Current ratio} = \frac{\text{Current assets}}{\text{Current liabilities}} \qquad (3\text{-}11)$$

MicroDrive's current ratio is:

$$\text{Current ratio} = \frac{\$1,610}{\$750} = 2.147 \approx 2.1$$

$$\text{Industry average} = 2.3$$

MicroDrive has a slightly lower current ratio than the average for its industry.[3] Is this good or bad? Sometimes the answer depends on who is asking the question. For example, suppose a supplier is trying to decide whether to extend credit to MicroDrive. In general, creditors like to see a high current ratio. If a company starts to experience financial difficulty, it will begin paying its bills (accounts payable) more slowly and borrowing more from its bank, so its current liabilities will be increasing. If current liabilities are rising faster than current assets, then the current ratio will fall, and this could spell trouble. Because the current ratio provides the best single indicator of the extent to which the claims of short-term creditors are covered by assets that are expected to be converted to cash fairly quickly, it is the most commonly used measure of short-term solvency.

Now consider the current ratio from a shareholder's perspective. A high current ratio could mean that the company has a lot of money tied up in nonproductive assets, such as excess cash or marketable securities. Or perhaps the high current ratio is due to large

---

[3]A good source for industry ratios and for S&P 500 ratios is CSIMarket.com: **http://csimarket.com/Industry/industry_Financial_Strength_Ratios.php.**

inventory holdings, which might become obsolete before they can be sold. Thus, shareholders might not want a high current ratio.

An industry average is not a magic number that all firms should strive to maintain—in fact, some well-managed firms will be above the average, while other good firms will be below it. However, if a firm's ratios are far from the averages for its industry, this is a red flag, and analysts should be concerned about why the variance occurs. For example, suppose a low current ratio is traced to low inventories. Is this a competitive advantage resulting from the firm's mastery of just-in-time inventory management, or is it an Achilles' heel that is causing the firm to miss shipments and lose sales? Ratio analysis doesn't answer such questions, but it does point to areas of potential concern.

3-4b The Quick Ratio

The **quick ratio**, also called the **acid test ratio**, is calculated by deducting inventories from current assets and then dividing the remainder by current liabilities:

$$\text{Quick ratio} = \frac{\text{Current assets} - \text{Inventories}}{\text{Current liabilities}} \quad \text{(3-12)}$$

MicroDrive's quick ratio is:

$$\text{Quick ratio} = \frac{\$1,610 - \$1,000}{\$750} = 0.81 \approx 0.8$$

$$\text{Industry average} = 1.0$$

A **liquid asset** is one that trades in an active market, so it can be converted quickly to cash at the going market price. Inventories are typically the least liquid of a firm's current assets; hence, they are the current assets on which losses are most likely to occur in a bankruptcy. Therefore, a measure of the firm's ability to pay off short-term obligations without relying on the sale of inventories is important.

MicroDrive's quick ratio is just below the industry average and is below 1.0. This means that MicroDrive would have to liquidate inventory in order to pay off current liabilities should the need arise.

How does MicroDrive compare to S&P 500 companies? There has been a steady decline in the average liquidity ratios of S&P 500 companies during the past decade. As we write this in 2018, the average current ratio is about 1.5, and the average quick ratio is about 0.6, so MicroDrive and its industry peers are a little more liquid than the typical S&P 500 company.

SELF-TEST

Identify two ratios to use to analyze a firm's liquidity position, and write out their equations.

What are the characteristics of a liquid asset? Give some examples.

Which current asset is typically the least liquid?

A company has the following information on its balance sheets: Cash = $40, accounts receivable = $30, inventories = $100, net fixed assets = $500, accounts payable = $20, accruals = $10, short-term debt (matures in less than a year) = $25, long-term debt = $200, and total common equity = $415. What is its current ratio? **(3.1)** *Its quick ratio?* **(1.3)**

Morris Corporation has current liabilities of $800 million, and its current ratio is 2.5. What is its level of current assets? **($2,000 million)** *If this firm's quick ratio is 2, how much inventory does it have?* **($400 million)**

3-5 Debt Management Ratios

The extent to which a firm uses debt financing is called **financial leverage**. Here are three important implications: (1) Stockholders can control a firm with smaller investments of their own equity if they finance part of the firm with debt. (2) If the firm's assets generate a higher pre-tax return than the interest rate on debt, then the shareholders' returns are magnified, or "leveraged." Conversely, shareholders' losses are also magnified if assets generate a pre-tax return less than the interest rate. (3) If a company has high leverage, even a small decline in performance might cause the firm's value to fall below the amount it owes to creditors. Therefore, a creditor's position becomes riskier as leverage increases. Keep these three points in mind as you consider the impact of financial leverage.

Debt management ratios, which are also called **leverage ratios**, help identify (1) a firm's use of debt relative to equity and (2) its ability to pay interest and principle. These ratios aid in judging the likelihood of default, as explained next.

3-5a How the Firm Is Financed: Leverage Ratios

MicroDrive's two primary types of debt are notes payable and long-term bonds, but more complicated companies also might report the portion of long-term debt due within a year, the value of capitalized leases, and other types of obligations that charge interest. For MicroDrive, total debt is:

$$\text{Total debt} = \text{Notes payable} + \text{Long-term bonds}$$
$$= \$150 + \$520 = \$670 \text{ million}$$

Is this too much debt, not enough, or the right amount? To answer this question, we begin by calculating the percentage of MicroDrive's assets that are financed by debt. The ratio of total debt to total assets is called the **debt-to-assets ratio**. It is sometimes shortened to **debt ratio**. Total debt is the sum of all short-term debt and long-term debt; it does not include other liabilities. The debt ratio is:

$$\text{Debt-to-assets ratio} = \text{Debt ratio} = \frac{\text{Total debt}}{\text{Total assets}} \qquad (3\text{-}13)$$

MicroDrive's debt ratio is 18.6%, which is substantially higher than the 11.7% industry average:

$$\text{Debt-to-assets ratio} = \frac{\$150 + \$520}{\$3,610} = \frac{\$670}{\$3,610} = 18.6\%$$

$$\text{Industry average} = 11.7\%$$

The **debt-to-equity ratio** is defined as:

$$\text{Debt-to-equity ratio} = \frac{\text{Total debt}}{\text{Total common equity}} \qquad (3\text{-}14)$$

MicroDrive's debt ratio is:

$$\text{Debt-to-equity ratio} = \frac{\$150 + \$520}{\$2,240} = \frac{\$670}{\$2,240} = 0.30$$

$$\text{Industry average} = 0.17$$

The debt-to-equity ratio shows that MicroDrive has $0.30 of debt for every dollar of equity, whereas the debt ratio shows that 18.6% of MicroDrive's assets are financed by debt. We find it more intuitive to think about the percentage of the firm that is financed with debt, so we usually use the debt ratio. However, the debt-to-equity ratio is also widely used, so you should know how to interpret it as well.

Be sure you know how a ratio is defined before you use it. Some sources define the debt ratio using only long-term debt instead of total debt; others use investor-supplied capital instead of total assets. Some sources make similar changes in the debt-to-equity ratio, so be sure to check your source's definition.

Sometimes it is useful to express debt ratios in terms of market values. It is easy to calculate the market value of equity, which is equal to the stock price multiplied by the number of shares. MicroDrive's market value of equity is $31(60 million) = $1,860 million. Often it is difficult to estimate the market value of debt, so many analysts use the debt reported in the financial statements. The **market debt ratio** is defined as:

$$\text{Market debt ratio} = \frac{\text{Total debt}}{\text{Total debt} + \text{Market value of equity}} \qquad (3\text{-}15)$$

MicroDrive's ratio is:

$$\text{Market debt ratio} = \frac{\$150 + \$520}{(\$150 + \$520) + (\$31 \times 60)} = 26.5\%$$

$$\text{Industry average} = 11.5\%$$

MicroDrive's market debt ratio in the previous year was 12.3%. The big increase was due to two factors: debt increased and the stock price fell. The stock price reflects a company's prospects for generating future cash flows, so a decline in stock price indicates a likely decline in future cash flows. Thus, the market debt ratio reflects a source of risk that is not captured by the conventional debt ratio.

The ratio of total liabilities to total assets shows the extent to which a firm's assets are not supported by equity. The **liabilities-to-assets ratio** is defined as:

$$\text{Liabilities-to-assets ratio} = \frac{\text{Total liabilities}}{\text{Total assets}} \qquad (3\text{-}16)$$

MicroDrive's ratio is:

$$\text{Liabilities-to-assets ratio} = \frac{\$1,270}{\$3,610} = 35.2\%$$

$$\text{Industry average} = 29.6\%$$

The **equity multiplier** ratio is the factor by which the return on assets is multiplied to determine the return on equity. It is defined as the ratio of total assets to common equity:

$$
\begin{aligned}
\text{Equity multiplier} &= \frac{\text{Return on equity}}{\text{Return on assets}} \\
&= \frac{(\text{Net income})/(\text{Common equity})}{(\text{Net income})/(\text{Total assets})} \\
&= \frac{\text{Total assets}}{\text{Common equity}}
\end{aligned}
\tag{3-17}
$$

MicroDrive's equity multiplier is:

$$
\text{Equity multiplier} = \frac{\$3,610}{\$2,240} = 1.6
$$

$$
\text{Industry average} = 1.4
$$

For a firm without preferred stock, the equity multiplier can also be defined as:

$$
\text{Equity multiplier} = \frac{1}{1 - \text{Liabilities-to-assets ratio}}
\tag{3-17a}
$$

For all the ratios we examined, MicroDrive has more leverage than its industry peers. The next section shows how close MicroDrive might be to serious financial distress.

3-5b Ability to Pay Interest: Times-Interest-Earned Ratio

The **times-interest-earned (TIE) ratio**, also called the **interest coverage ratio**, is determined by dividing earnings before interest and taxes (EBIT in Figure 3-1) by the interest expense:

$$
\text{Times-interest-earned (TIE) ratio} = \frac{\text{EBIT}}{\text{Interest expense}}
\tag{3-18}
$$

MicroDrive's times-interest-earned ratio is:

$$
\text{Times-interest-earned (TIE) ratio} = \frac{\$400}{\$60} = 6.7
$$

$$
\text{Industry average} = 13.3
$$

The TIE ratio measures the extent to which operating income can decline before the firm is unable to meet its annual interest costs. Failure to meet this obligation can bring legal action by the firm's creditors, possibly resulting in bankruptcy. Note that earnings before interest and taxes, rather than net income, is used in the numerator. Because interest is paid with pre-tax dollars, the firm's ability to pay current interest is not affected by taxes.

MicroDrive's interest is covered 6.7 times, which is well above 1, the point at which EBIT isn't sufficient to pay interest. The industry average is 13.3, so even though MicroDrive has enough EBIT to pay interest expenses, it has a lower margin of safety compared to its peers.

3-5c Ability to Service Debt: EBITDA Coverage Ratio

The TIE ratio is useful for assessing a company's ability to meet interest charges on its debt, but this ratio has two shortcomings: (1) Interest is not the only fixed financial charge—companies must also reduce debt on schedule, and many firms lease assets and thus must make lease payments. Failure to repay debt or meet lease payments may force them into bankruptcy. (2) EBIT (earnings before interest and taxes) does not represent all the cash flow available to service debt, especially if a firm has high noncash expenses, like depreciation and/or amortization charges. A better coverage ratio would take all of the "cash" earnings into account in the numerator and the other financial charges in the denominator. The **EBITDA coverage ratio** is:[4]

$$\text{EBITDA coverage ratio} = \frac{\text{EBITDA} + \text{Lease payments}}{\text{Interest} + \text{Principal payments} + \text{Lease payments}} \quad (3\text{-}19)$$

MicroDrive had $400 million of EBIT and $200 million in depreciation, for an EBITDA (earnings before interest, taxes, depreciation, and amortization) of $400 + $200 = $600 million. Also, lease payments of $28 million were deducted when calculating EBITDA. That $28 million was available to meet financial charges; hence, it must be added back, bringing the total available to cover fixed financial charges to $628 million. Fixed financial charges consisted of $60 million of interest, $20 million of sinking fund payments, and $28 million for lease payments, for a total of $108 million.[5]

MicroDrive's EBITDA coverage ratio is:

$$\text{EBITDA coverage ratio} = \frac{(\$400 + 200) + \$28}{\$60 + \$20 + \$28} = \frac{\$628}{\$108} = 5.8$$

$$\text{Industry average} = 12.0$$

MicroDrive covered its fixed financial charges by a factor of 5.8. MicroDrive's ratio is well below the industry average, so again the company seems to have a relatively high level of debt.

The EBITDA coverage ratio is most useful for relatively short-term lenders such as banks, which rarely make loans (except real estate-backed loans) for longer than about 5 years. Over a relatively short period, depreciation-generated funds can be used to service debt. Over a longer time, those funds must be reinvested to maintain the plant and equipment or else the company cannot remain in business. Therefore, banks and other relatively short-term lenders focus on the EBITDA coverage ratio, whereas long-term bondholders focus on the TIE ratio.

[4]Different analysts define the EBITDA coverage ratio in different ways. For example, some omit the lease payment information; others "gross up" principal payments by dividing them by 1 − T because these payments are not tax deductions and so must be made with after-tax cash flows. We included lease payments because they are quite important for many firms, and failing to make them can lead to bankruptcy as surely as failing to make payments on "regular" debt. We did not gross up principal payments because a company's tax rate will probably be zero if it is financially distressed; hence, the gross-up is not necessary whenever the ratio is really important.

[5]A sinking fund is a required annual payment designed to reduce the balance of a bond or preferred stock issue.

How does the use of financial leverage affect current stockholders' control position?

Name six ratios that are used to measure the extent to which a firm uses financial leverage, and write out their equations.

Morris Corporation has the following information on its balance sheets: Cash = $40, accounts receivable = $30, inventories = $100, net fixed assets = $500, accounts payable = $20, accruals = $10, short-term debt (matures in less than a year) = $25, long-term debt = $200, and total common equity = $415. Its income statement reports: Sales = $820, costs of goods sold (excluding depreciation) = $450, depreciation = $50, other operating expenses = $100, interest expense = $20, and tax rate = 40%. Calculate the following ratios: debt-to-assets ratio (33.6%), debt-to-equity ratio (54.2%), liabilities-to-assets ratio (38.1%), and times-interest earned ratio (11.0). (Hint: This is the same company used in the previous Self-Test.)

Suppose Morris Corporation has 100 shares of stock with a price of $15 per share. What is its market debt ratio (assume the market value of debt is close to the book value)? (13.0%) How does this compare with the previously calculated debt-to-assets ratio? Does the market debt ratio imply that the company is more or less risky than the debt-to-assets ratio indicated?

A company has EBITDA of $600 million, interest payments of $60 million, lease payments of $40 million, and required principal payments (due this year) of $30 million. What is its EBITDA coverage ratio? (4.9)

3-6 Market Value Ratios

Market value ratios relate a firm's stock price to its earnings, cash flow, and book value per share. Market value ratios are a way to measure the value of a company's stock relative to that of another company.

3-6a Price/Earnings Ratio

The **price/earnings (P/E) ratio** shows how much investors are willing to pay per dollar of reported profits.

$$\text{Price/earnings (P/E) ratio} = \frac{\text{Price per share}}{\text{Earnings per share}} \qquad (3\text{-}20)$$

MicroDrive has $248 million in net income and 60 million shares, so its earnings per share (EPS) is $4.13 = $248/60. MicroDrive's stock sells for $31, so its P/E ratio is:

$$\text{Price/earnings (P/E) ratio} = \frac{\$31.00}{\$4.13} = 7.5$$

$$\text{Industry average} = 9.4$$

Price/earnings ratios are higher for firms with strong growth prospects, other things held constant, but they are lower for riskier firms. Because MicroDrive's P/E ratio is below the average, this suggests that the company is regarded as being somewhat riskier than most, as having poorer growth prospects, or both. In mid-2018, the average P/E ratio for firms in the S&P 500 was 26.10, indicating that investors were willing to pay $26.10 for every dollar of earnings.[6]

---

[6]There are two reasons why the actual S&P 500 P/E ratio is so much higher than MicroDrive's ratio. As we show in Chapter 7, we assume that MicroDrive's growth slows down to about 5% a year during the next 5 years. We do this so that MicroDrive's forecasted financial statements will fit on one page. However, growth often remains high for many years for S&P 500 companies, which increases their prices relative to their current earnings.

3-6b Price/Free Cash Flow (P/FCF) Ratio

Stock prices depend on a company's ability to generate free cash flow (FCF). Consequently, investors often look at the **price/free cash flow (P/FCF) ratio**:

$$\text{Price/free cash flow ratio} = \frac{\text{Price per share}}{\text{Free cash flow per share}} \qquad (3\text{-}21)$$

MicroDrive's price/free cash flow ratio is:

$$\text{Price/free cash flow ratio} = \frac{\$31.00}{-\$210/60} = -8.9$$

$$\text{Industry average} = 11.1$$

Not only is MicroDrive's price/free cash flow ratio below the industry average, it is negative!

The **price/EBITDA ratio** is defined as price divided by EBITDA. It is a better measure of operating performance than the P/E ratio, which incorporates nonoperating items (i.e., interest expenses and taxes). MicroDrive's EBITDA per share is (EBIT + Depreciation) = ($400 + $200)/60 = $10, so its price/EBITDA is $31/$10 = 3.1. The industry average price/EBITDA ratio is 4.6, so we see again that MicroDrive is below the industry average.

Note that some analysts look at other multiples as well. For example, depending on the industry, some may look at measures such as price/visits (e.g., visits to a Web site) or price/customers. You should view these measures with caution—unless these measures are correlated with cash flow, they are likely to be misleading.

3-6c Market/Book Ratio

The ratio of a stock's market price to its book value gives another indication of how investors regard the company. Companies with relatively high rates of return on equity generally sell at higher multiples of book value than those with low returns. First, we find MicroDrive's **book value per share**:

$$\text{Book value per share} = \frac{\text{Total common equity}}{\text{Shares outstanding}} \qquad (3\text{-}22)$$

MicroDrive's book value per share is:

$$\text{Book value per share} = \frac{\$2,240}{60} = \$37.33$$

Now we divide the market price per share by the book value per share to get a **market/book (M/B) ratio**:

$$\text{Market/book ratio} = \text{M/B} = \frac{\text{Market price per share}}{\text{Book value per share}} \qquad (3\text{-}23)$$

For MicroDrive, the market/book ratio is:

$$\text{Market/book ratio} = \frac{\$31.00}{\$37.33} = 0.8$$

$$\text{Industry average} = 1.3$$

It is also possible to define the market/book ratio as the market value of equity divided by the total common equity reported in the financial statements. The total market value of equity, which is called the **market capitalization** (or just market cap) is:

Market capitalization = (Price per share) (Total number of shares)	(3-24)

For MicroDrive, the market cap is:

Market cap = $31.00(60 million) = $1,860 million

Now we divide the market cap by the total common equity:

$\text{Market/book ratio} = M/B = \dfrac{\text{Market cap}}{\text{Total common equity}}$	(3-24a)

$$= \frac{\$1,860}{\$2,240} = 0.8$$

Both approaches give the same answer, 0.8, which is much lower than the industry average of 1.3. This indicates that investors are willing to pay relatively little for a dollar of MicroDrive's book value.

The book value is a record of the past, showing the cumulative amount that stockholders have invested, either directly by purchasing newly issued shares or indirectly through retaining earnings. In contrast, the market price is forward looking, incorporating investors' expectations of future cash flows. For example, Volkswagon AG had a market/book ratio of 0.88 in late 2017, reflecting its recent scandals involving emission tests, whereas Apple's market/book ratio was 6.83, indicating that investors expected Apple's past successes to continue.

Table 3-1 summarizes selected ratios for MicroDrive. As the table indicates, the company has many problems.

SELF-TEST

Describe three ratios that relate a firm's stock price to its earnings, cash flow, and book value per share, and write out their equations.

What does the price/earnings (P/E) ratio show? If one firm's P/E ratio is lower than that of another, what are some factors that might explain the difference?

How is book value per share calculated? Explain why book values often deviate from market values.

A company has $6 billion in net income, $8 billion of free cash flow, $80 billion of common equity, and one billion shares of stock. If its stock price is $96 per share, what is its price/earnings ratio? **(16)** *Its price/free cash flow ratio?* **(12)** *Its market/book ratio?* **(1.2)**

TABLE 3-1
MicroDrive Inc.: Summary of Selected Financial Ratios (Millions of Dollars)

Ratio	Formula	Calculation	Ratio	Industry Average	Comment
Profitability					
Profit margin on sales	$\dfrac{\text{Net income available to common stockholders}}{\text{Sales}}$	$\dfrac{\$248}{\$5,000} =$	5.0%	6.2%	Poor
Operating profit margin	$\dfrac{\text{Earnings before interest and taxes (EBIT)}}{\text{Sales}}$	$\dfrac{\$400}{\$5,000} =$	8.0%	9.0%	Poor
Return on total assets (ROA)	$\dfrac{\text{Net income available to common stockholders}}{\text{Total assets}}$	$\dfrac{\$248}{\$3,610} =$	6.9%	9.6%	Poor
Return on common equity (ROE)	$\dfrac{\text{Net income available to common stockholders}}{\text{Common equity}}$	$\dfrac{\$248}{\$2,240} =$	11.1%	13.6%	Poor
Asset Management					
Total assets turnover	$\dfrac{\text{Sales}}{\text{Total assets}}$	$\dfrac{\$5,000}{\$3,610} =$	1.4	1.5	Poor
Fixed assets turnover	$\dfrac{\text{Sales}}{\text{Net fixed assets}}$	$\dfrac{\$5,000}{\$2,000} =$	2.5	2.7	Poor
Days sales outstanding (DSO)	$\dfrac{\text{Receivables}}{\text{Annual sales}/365}$	$\dfrac{\$500}{\$5,000/365} =$	36.5	29.0	Poor
Inventory turnover	$\dfrac{\text{COGS}}{\text{Inventories}}$	$\dfrac{\$4,100}{\$1,000} =$	4.1	5.3	Poor
Liquidity					
Current	$\dfrac{\text{Current assets}}{\text{Current liabilities}}$	$\dfrac{\$1,610}{\$750} =$	2.1	2.3	Riskier
Quick	$\dfrac{\text{Current assets} - \text{Inventories}}{\text{Current liabilities}}$	$\dfrac{\$1,610 - \$1,000}{\$750} =$	0.8	1.0	Riskier
Debt Management					
Debt-to-assets ratio	$\dfrac{\text{Total debt}}{\text{Total assets}}$	$\dfrac{\$670}{\$3,610} =$	18.6%	11.7%	Riskier
Times-interest-earned (TIE)	$\dfrac{\text{Earnings before interest and taxes (EBIT)}}{\text{Interest charges}}$	$\dfrac{\$400}{\$60} =$	6.7	13.3	Riskier
Price/earnings (P/E)	$\dfrac{\text{Price per share}}{\text{Earnings per share}}$	$\dfrac{\$31.00}{\$4.13} =$	7.5	9.4	Poor
Market/book (M/B)	$\dfrac{\text{Market price per share}}{\text{Book value per share}}$	$\dfrac{\$31.00}{\$37.33} =$	0.8	1.3	Poor

3-7 Trend Analysis, Common Size Analysis, and Percentage Change Analysis

Trends give clues as to whether a firm's financial condition is likely to improve or deteriorate. To do a **trend analysis**, you examine a ratio over time, as shown in Figure 3-2. This graph shows that MicroDrive's rate of return on assets has been declining since 2017, in contrast to the industry average. All the other ratios could be analyzed similarly.

In a **common size analysis**, all income statement items are divided by sales, and all balance sheet items are divided by total assets. Thus, a common size income statement shows each item as a percentage of sales, and a common size balance sheet shows each item as a percentage of total assets.[7] The advantage of common size analysis is that it facilitates comparisons of balance sheets and income statements over time and across companies.

Common size statements are easy to generate if the financial statements are in a spreadsheet. In fact, if you obtain your data from a source that uses standardized financial statements, then it is easy to cut and paste the data for a new company over your original company's data, and all of your spreadsheet formulas will be valid for the new company. We generated Figure 3-3 in the *Excel* file ***Ch03 Tool Kit.xlsx***. Figure 3-3 shows MicroDrive's 2018 and 2019 common size income statements, along with the composite statement for the industry. (*Note:* Rounding may cause addition/subtraction differences in Figures 3-3, 3-4, and 3-5.) MicroDrive's EBIT is slightly below average, and its interest expenses are slightly above average. The net effect is a relatively low profit margin.

Figure 3-4 shows MicroDrive's common size balance sheets along with the industry composite. Its accounts receivable are slightly higher than the industry average, its inventories are significantly higher, and it uses much more debt than the average firm.

FIGURE 3-2
MicroDrive Inc.: Trend Analysis of Rate of Return on Assets

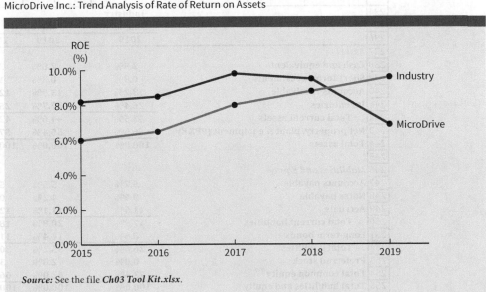

Source: See the file ***Ch03 Tool Kit.xlsx***.

---

[7]Some sources of industry data, such as Risk Management Associates (formerly known as Robert Morris Associates), are presented exclusively in common size form.

FIGURE 3-3
MicroDrive Inc.: Common Size Income Statement

	A	B	C	D	E	F
				Industry		
212				Composite	MicroDrive	
213						
214				2019	2019	2018
215	Net sales			100.0%	100.0%	100.0%
216	Costs of goods sold except depreciation			77.6%	78.0%	77.3%
217	Depreciation[a]			3.9%	4.0%	3.8%
218	Other operating expenses			9.9%	10.0%	9.8%
219	Earnings before interest and taxes (EBIT)			8.7%	8.0%	9.2%
220	Less interest			0.6%	1.2%	0.8%
221	Pre-tax earnings			8.1%	6.8%	8.3%
222	Taxes (25%)			2.0%	1.7%	2.1%
223	Net income before preferred dividends			6.1%	5.1%	6.3%
224	Preferred dividends			0.0%	0.1%	0.1%
225	Net income available to common stockholders			6.1%	5.0%	6.1%
226						

Source: See the file *Ch03 Tool Kit.xlsx.* Numbers are reported as rounded values for clarity but are calculated using *Excel's* full precision. Thus, intermediate calculations using the figure's rounded values will be inexact.

Note:

[a]MicroDrive has no amortization charges so we omit them from the item name.

FIGURE 3-4
MicroDrive Inc.: Common Size Balance Sheet

	A	B	C	D	E
234			Industry		
235			Composite	MicroDrive	
236			2019	2019	2018
237	*Assets*				
238	Cash and equivalents		2.9%	2.8%	3.3%
239	Short-term investments		0.9%	0.3%	1.3%
240	Accounts receivable		13.2%	13.9%	12.5%
241	Inventories		26.4%	27.7%	25.1%
242	Total current assets		43.5%	44.6%	42.2%
243	Net property, plant & equipment (PP&E)		56.5%	55.4%	57.8%
244	Total assets		100.0%	100.0%	100.0%
245					
246	*Liabilities and Equity*				
247	Accounts payable		5.7%	5.5%	5.8%
248	Notes payable		0.6%	4.2%	0.9%
249	Accruals		11.6%	11.1%	12.0%
250	Total current liabilities		17.8%	20.8%	18.8%
251	Long-term bonds		8.8%	14.4%	11.4%
252	Total liabilities		26.6%	35.2%	30.1%
253	Preferred stock		0.0%	2.8%	3.2%
254	Total common equity		73.4%	62.0%	66.6%
255	Total liabilities and equity		100.0%	100.0%	100.0%
256					

Source: See the file *Ch03 Tool Kit.xlsx.* Numbers are reported as rounded values for clarity but are calculated using *Excel's* full precision. Thus, intermediate calculations using the figure's rounded values will be inexact.

FIGURE 3-5
MicroDrive Inc.: Income Statement Percentage Change Analysis

	A	B	C	D
264				**Percent**
265	**Base year = 2018**			**Change in**
266				**2019**
267	Net sales			4.2%
268	Costs of goods sold except depreciation			5.1%
269	Depreciation[a]			11.1%
270	Other operating expenses			6.4%
271	Earnings before interest and taxes (EBIT)			−9.1%
272	Less interest			50.0%
273	Pre-tax earnings			−15.0%
274	Taxes (25%)			−15.0%
275	Net income before preferred dividends			−15.0%
276	Preferred dividends			0.0%
277	Net income available to common stockholders			−15.4%
278				

Source: See the file *Ch03 Tool Kit.xlsx*. Numbers are reported as rounded values for clarity but are calculated using *Excel*'s full precision. Thus, intermediate calculations using the figure's rounded values will be inexact.

In **percentage change analysis**, growth rates are calculated for all income statement items and balance sheet accounts relative to a base year. To illustrate, Figure 3-5 contains MicroDrive's income statement percentage change analysis for 2019 relative to 2018. Sales increased at a 4.2% rate during 2019, but EBIT fell by 9.1%. Part of this decline was due to an increase in depreciation, which is a noncash expense, but the cost of goods sold also increased by more than the growth in sales. In addition, interest expenses grew by 50! We apply the same type of analysis to the balance sheets (see the file *Ch03 Tool Kit.xlsx*), which shows that inventories grew at a whopping 30% rate and accounts receivable grew 29%. With only a 4.2% growth in sales, the extreme growth in receivables and inventories should be of great concern to MicroDrive's managers.

SELF-TEST

What is a trend analysis, and what information does it provide?

What is common size analysis?

What is percentage change analysis?

3-8 Tying the Ratios Together: The DuPont Equation

In ratio analysis, it is sometimes easy to miss the forest for all the trees. In particular, how do managerial actions affecting a firm's profitability, asset efficiency, and financial leverage interact to determine the return on equity, a performance measure that is important for investors? The extended **DuPont equation** provides just such a framework.

$$ROE = \frac{Net\ income}{Common\ equity}$$

The extended DuPont equation reconfigures the ROE into three components (profit margin, total asset turnover, and the equity multiplier):

$$ROE = \frac{Net\ income}{Sales} \times \frac{Sales}{Total\ assets} \times \frac{Total\ assets}{Common\ equity} \qquad (3\text{-}25)$$
$$= (Profit\ margin)(Total\ assets\ turnover)(Equity\ multiplier)$$

As calculated previously, MicroDrive's 2019 profit margin is 4.96%, its total assets turnover ratio is 1.39, and its equity multiplier is 1.61. Applying the DuPont equation to MicroDrive, its return on equity is:

$$ROE = (4.96\%)(1.39)(1.61) = 11.1\%$$

Note that this is the same value calculated previously, as shown in Table 3-1.

Sometimes it is useful to focus just on asset profitability and financial leverage. Notice that the first two terms in the second row of Equation 3-25 are the definition of return on assets. Substituting for these terms in Equation 3-25 provides an expression for ROE in terms of asset profitability and leverage:

$$ROE = \frac{Net\ income}{Total\ assets} \times \frac{Total\ assets}{Common\ equity} \qquad (3\text{-}26)$$
$$= ROA \times Equity\ multiplier$$

Using Equation 3-26, we see that MicroDrive's ROE is 11.1%, the same value given by the extended DuPont equation:

$$ROE = 6.87\% \times 1.61 = 11.1\%$$

The insights provided by the DuPont model are valuable, and the model can be used for "quick and dirty" estimates of the impact that operating changes have on returns. For example, holding all else equal, if MicroDrive can implement lean production techniques and increase to 1.8 its ratio of sales to total assets, then its ROE will improve to 14.4%:

$$ROE = (4.96\%)(1.8)(1.61) = 14.4\%.$$

For a more complete what-if analysis, most companies use a forecasting model such as the one described in Chapter 12.

SELF-TEST

Explain how the extended, or modified, DuPont equation can be used to reveal the basic determinants of ROE.

What is the equity multiplier?

A company has a profit margin of 6%, a total assets turnover ratio of 2, and an equity multiplier of 1.5. What is its ROE? **(18%)**

3-9 Comparative Ratios and Benchmarking

Ratio analysis involves comparisons. A company's ratios are compared with those of other firms in the same industry—that is, with industry average figures. However, like most firms, MicroDrive's managers go one step further: They also compare their ratios with those of a smaller set of the leading computer companies. This technique is called

benchmarking, and the companies used for the comparison are called **benchmark companies**. For example, MicroDrive benchmarks against five other firms that its management considers to be the best-managed companies with operations similar to its own.

Many companies also benchmark various parts of their overall operation against top companies, whether they are in the same industry or not. For example, MicroDrive has a division that sells hard drives directly to consumers through catalogs and the Internet. This division's shipping department benchmarks against Amazon, even though they are in different industries, because Amazon's shipping department is one of the best. MicroDrive wants its own shippers to strive to match Amazon's record for on-time shipments.

Comparative ratios are available from a number of sources, including *Value Line, Dun and Bradstreet* (D&B), and the *Annual Statement Studies* published by Risk Management Associates, which is the national association of bank loan officers. Table 3-2 reports selected ratios from Reuters for Apple and its industry, revealing that Apple has a much higher net profit margin and return on assets than its peers.

Each data-supplying organization uses a somewhat different set of ratios designed for its own purposes. For example, D&B deals mainly with small firms, many of which are proprietorships, and it sells its services primarily to banks and other lenders. Therefore, D&B is concerned largely with the creditor's viewpoint, and its ratios emphasize current assets and liabilities, not market value ratios. So, when you select a comparative data source, you should be sure that your own emphasis is similar to that of the agency whose ratios you plan to use. Additionally, there are often definitional differences in the ratios presented by different sources, so before using a source, be sure to verify the exact definitions of the ratios to ensure consistency with your own work.

TABLE 3-2

Comparative Ratios for Apple Inc., the Computer Hardware Industry, and the Technology Sector

Ratio	Apple	Computer Hardware Industry[a]	Technology Sector[b]
P/E ratio	19.1	15.7	15.8
Market to book	6.7	3.4	2.3
Net profit margin	38.5%	27.1%	42.3%
Quick ratio	1.2	1.4	1.8
Current ratio	1.3	1.7	2.2
Total debt-to-equity[c]	86.3%	64.8%	16.0%
Interest coverage (TIE)[d]	NA	12.4	6.3
Return on assets	13.9%	5.1%	12.4%
Return on equity	36.9%	11.1%	17.2%
Inventory turnover	40.4	16.3	14.8
Assets turnover	0.7	1.2	0.9

Source: Adapted from data at **www.reuters.com/finance/stocks/financial-highlights/AAPL.OQ.com,** November 24, 2017.

Notes:

[a]The computer hardware industry includes such firms as IBM, Dell, Apple, and Silicon Graphics.

[b]The technology sector contains 11 industries, including communications equipment, computer hardware, computer networks, semiconductors, and software and programming.

[c]This is based on book values. Apple's market equity is much bigger than its market debt, but its book equity is small relative to its book debt.

[d]Apple had more interest income than interest expense.

Compare and contrast trend analysis and comparative ratio analysis.

Explain benchmarking.

3-10 Uses and Limitations of Ratio Analysis

Ratio analysis provides useful information concerning a company's operations and financial condition, but it has limitations that necessitate care and judgment. Some potential problems include the following.

1. Many large firms operate different divisions in different industries, and for such companies it is difficult to develop a meaningful set of industry averages. Therefore, industry averages are more meaningful for small, narrowly focused firms than for large, multidivisional ones.

2. To set goals for high-level performance, it is best to benchmark on the industry *leaders'* ratios rather than the industry *average* ratios.

3. Inflation may badly distort firms' balance sheets—reported values are often substantially different from "true" values. Further, because inflation affects depreciation charges and inventory costs, reported profits are also affected. Thus, inflation can distort a ratio analysis for one firm over time or a comparative analysis of firms of different ages.

4. **Seasonal effects** can distort a ratio analysis. For example, the inventory turnover ratio for a food processor will be radically different if the balance sheet figure used for inventory is the one just before versus the one just after the close of the canning season. This problem can be minimized by using monthly averages for inventory (and receivables) when calculating turnover ratios.

5. Firms can employ **window dressing** techniques to make their financial statements look stronger. To illustrate, suppose a company takes out a 2-year loan in late December. Because the loan is for more than 1 year, it is not included in current liabilities even though the cash received through the loan is reported as a current asset. This improves the current and quick ratios and makes the year-end balance sheet look stronger. If the company pays the loan back in January, then the transaction was strictly window dressing.

6. Companies' choices of different accounting practices can distort comparisons. For example, choices of inventory valuation and depreciation methods affect financial statements differently, making comparisons among companies less meaningful.[8]

Ratio Analysis on the Web

A great source for comparative ratios is **www.reuters.com.** Hover over the Markets drop-down box and select U.S. Markets. At the right in the Markets section, select the U.S. tab and enter a company's ticker in the Search box. This brings up a table with the stock quote, company information, and additional links. Select Financials, which brings up a page with a detailed ratio analysis for the company and includes comparative ratios for other companies in the same sector and the same industry. (*Note:* You may have to register to get extra features, but registration is free.)

---

[8]Beginning in December 2018, almost all leases must be reported on the balance sheet as liabilities, and the leased assets must be reported as assets. This is in contrast to the prior rule in which operating leases were reported on the balance sheet, but financial leases were not reported. As we write this in mid-2018, the Financial Accounting Standards Board (FASB) is considering proposals to phase in the requirement over several accounting periods rather than apply it completely in December 2018. For more information, go to **www.fasb.org**, select Standards, Accounting Standards Updates Issued, and click on Update 2016-02.

In summary, conducting ratio analysis in a mechanical, unthinking manner is dangerous. But when ratio analysis is used intelligently and with good judgment, it can provide useful insights into a firm's operations and identify the right questions to ask.

SELF-TEST

List several potential problems with ratio analysis.

3-11 Looking Beyond the Numbers

Sound financial analysis involves more than just calculating and comparing ratios—qualitative factors must be considered. Here are some questions suggested by the American Association of Individual Investors (AAII):

1. To what extent are the company's revenues tied to one key customer or to one key product? To what extent does the company rely on a single supplier? Reliance on single customers, products, or suppliers increases risk.
2. What percentage of the company's business is generated overseas? Companies with a large percentage of overseas business are exposed to risk of currency exchange volatility and political instability.
3. What are the probable actions of current competitors and the likelihood of additional new competitors?
4. Do the company's future prospects depend critically on the success of products currently in the pipeline or on existing products?
5. How do the legal and regulatory environments affect the company?

SELF-TEST

What qualitative factors should analysts consider when evaluating a company's likely future financial performance?

SUMMARY

This chapter explained techniques investors and managers use to analyze financial statements. The key concepts covered are listed here.

- **Profitability ratios** show the combined effects of liquidity, asset management, and debt management policies on operating *and* financial results. They include the **net profit margin, operating profit margin, basic earning power (BEP) ratio, return on total assets (ROA)**, and **return on common equity (ROE)**.
- **Asset management ratios** measure how effectively a firm is managing its assets. These ratios include **inventory turnover, days sales outstanding, fixed assets turnover**, and **total assets turnover**.
- **Liquidity ratios** show the relationship of a firm's current assets to its current liabilities and thus its ability to meet maturing debts. Two commonly used liquidity ratios are the **current ratio** and the **quick ratio** (also called the **acid test ratio**).
- **Debt management ratios** reveal (1) the extent to which the firm is financed with debt and (2) its likelihood of defaulting on its debt obligations. They include the **debt-to-assets ratio** (also called the **debt ratio**), **debt-to-equity ratio, liabilities-to-assets ratio, equity multiplier, times-interest-earned (TIE) ratio**, and **EBITDA coverage ratio**.

- **Market value ratios** relate the firm's stock price to its earnings, cash flow, and **book value per share**, thus giving management an indication of what investors think of the company's past performance and future prospects. These include the **price/earnings (P/E) ratio**, **price/free cash flow (P/FCF) ratio**, and **market/book (M/B) ratio**.
- **Trend analysis**, in which one plots a ratio over time, is important because it reveals whether the firm's condition has been improving or deteriorating.
- The **DuPont equation** shows how the profit margin on sales, the assets turnover ratio, and the use of debt all interact to determine the rate of return on equity.
- **Benchmarking** is the process of comparing a particular company with a group of similar successful companies.

Ratio analysis has limitations, but when used with care and judgment, it can be very helpful.

QUESTIONS

(3-1) Define each of the following terms:
  a. *Liquidity ratios:* current ratio; quick, or acid test, ratio
  b. *Asset management ratios:* inventory turnover ratio; days sales outstanding (DSO); fixed assets turnover ratio; total assets turnover ratio
  c. *Financial leverage ratios:* debt ratio; times-interest-earned (TIE) ratio; EBITDA coverage ratio
  d. *Profitability ratios:* profit margin on sales; basic earning power (BEP) ratio; return on total assets (ROA); return on common equity (ROE)
  e. *Market value ratios:* price/earnings (P/E) ratio; price/free cash flow ratio; market/book (M/B) ratio; book value per share
  f. Trend analysis; comparative ratio analysis; benchmarking
  g. DuPont equation; window dressing; seasonal effects on ratios

(3-2) Financial ratio analysis is conducted by managers, equity investors, long-term creditors, and short-term creditors. What is the primary emphasis of each of these groups in evaluating ratios?

(3-3) Over the past year, M. D. Ryngaert & Co. has realized an increase in its current ratio and a drop in its total assets turnover ratio. However, the company's sales, quick ratio, and fixed assets turnover ratio have remained constant. What explains these changes?

(3-4) Profit margins and turnover ratios vary from one industry to another. What differences would you expect to find between a grocery chain and a steel company? Think particularly about the turnover ratios, the profit margin, and the DuPont equation.

(3-5) How might (a) seasonal factors and (b) different growth rates distort a comparative ratio analysis? Give some examples. How might these problems be alleviated?

(3-6) Why is it sometimes misleading to compare a company's financial ratios with those of other firms that operate in the same industry?

SELF-TEST PROBLEMS SOLUTIONS SHOWN IN APPENDIX A

(ST-1)
Debt Ratio
Argent Corporation has $60 million in current liabilities, $150 million in total liabilities, and $210 million in total common equity; Argent has no preferred stock. Argent's total debt is $120 million. What is the debt-to-assets ratio? What is the debt-to-equity ratio?

(ST-2)
Ratio Analysis

The following data apply to Jacobus and Associates (millions of dollars):

Cash	$ 400
Fixed assets	$ 4,300
Sales	$14,600
Net income	$ 730
Quick ratio	2.0
Current ratio	3.0
DSO	40 days
ROE	12.5%

Jacobus has no preferred stock—only common equity, current liabilities, and long-term debt. Find Jacobus's (1) accounts receivable, (2) current liabilities, (3) current assets, (4) total assets, (5) ROA, (6) common equity, (7) long-term debt, (8) equity multiplier, (9) profit margin, and (10) total asset turnover. Substitute your calculated profit margin, total asset turnover, and equity multiplier into the DuPont equation and verify that resulting ROE is 12.5%.

PROBLEMS ANSWERS ARE IN APPENDIX B

EASY PROBLEMS 1–5

(3-1)
DSO

Greene Sisters has a DSO of 20 days. The company's average daily sales are $20,000. What is the level of its accounts receivable? Assume there are 365 days in a year.

(3-2)
Debt Ratio

Vigo Vacations has $200 million in total assets, $5 million in notes payable, and $25 million in long-term debt. What is the debt ratio?

(3-3)
Market/Book Ratio

Winston Watch's stock price is $75 per share. Winston has $10 billion in total assets. Its balance sheet shows $1 billion in current liabilities, $3 billion in long-term debt, and $6 billion in common equity. It has 800 million shares of common stock outstanding. What is Winston's market/book ratio?

(3-4)
Price/Earnings Ratio

Reno Revolvers has an EPS of $1.50, a free cash flow per share of $3.00, and a price/free cash flow ratio of 8.0. What is its P/E ratio?

(3-5)
ROE

Needham Pharmaceuticals has a profit margin of 3% and an equity multiplier of 2.0. Its sales are $100 million, and it has total assets of $50 million. What is its ROE?

INTERMEDIATE PROBLEMS 6–10

(3-6)
DuPont Analysis

Gardial & Son has an ROA of 12%, a 5% profit margin, and a return on equity equal to 20%. What is the company's total assets turnover? What is the firm's equity multiplier?

(3-7)
Current and Quick Ratios

Ace Industries has current assets equal to $3 million. The company's current ratio is 1.5, and its quick ratio is 1.0. What is the firm's level of current liabilities? What is the firm's level of inventories?

(3-8)
Profit Margin and Debt Ratio

Assume you are given the following relationships for the Haslam Corporation:

Sales/total assets	1.2
Return on assets (ROA)	4%
Return on equity (ROE)	7%

Calculate Haslam's profit margin and liabilities-to-assets ratio. Suppose half its liabilities are in the form of debt. Calculate the debt-to-assets ratio.

(3-9)
Current and
Quick Ratios

The Nelson Company has $1,312,500 in current assets and $525,000 in current liabilities. Its initial inventory level is $375,000, and it will raise funds as additional notes payable and use them to increase inventory. How much can Nelson's short-term debt (notes payable) increase without pushing its current ratio below 2.0? What will be the firm's quick ratio after Nelson has raised the maximum amount of short-term funds?

(3-10)
Times-Interest-
Earned Ratio

The Morrit Corporation has $600,000 of debt outstanding, and it pays an interest rate of 8% annually. Morrit's annual sales are $3 million, its average tax rate is 25%, and its net profit margin on sales is 3%. If the company does not maintain a TIE ratio of at least 5 to 1, then its bank will refuse to renew the loan, and bankruptcy will result. What is Morrit's TIE ratio?

CHALLENGING PROBLEMS 11–14

(3-11)
Balance Sheet
Analysis

Complete the balance sheet and sales information in the table that follows for J. White Industries, using the following financial data:

Total assets turnover: 1.5
Gross profit margin on sales: (Sales − Cost of goods sold)/Sales = 25%
Total liabilities-to-assets ratio: 40%
Quick ratio: 0.80
Days sales outstanding (based on 365-day year): 36.5 days
Inventory turnover ratio: 3.75

Partial Income Statement Information

Sales	_____
Cost of goods sold	_____

Balance Sheet Information

Cash		Accounts payable	_____
Accounts receivable		Long-term debt	50,000
Inventories	_____	Common stock	_____
Fixed assets	_____	Retained earnings	100,000
Total assets	$400,000	Total liabilities and equity	_____

(3-12)
Comprehensive
Ratio Calculations

The Kretovich Company had a quick ratio of 1.4, a current ratio of 3.0, a days sales outstanding of 36.5 days (based on a 365-day year), total current assets of $810,000, and cash and marketable securities of $120,000. What were Kretovich's annual sales?

(3-13)
Comprehensive
Ratio Analysis

Data for Lozano Chip Company and its industry averages follow.

a. Calculate the indicated ratios for Lozano.
b. Construct the extended DuPont equation for both Lozano and the industry.
c. Outline Lozano's strengths and weaknesses as revealed by your analysis.

Lozano Chip Company: Balance Sheet as of December 31, 2019
(Thousands of Dollars)

Cash	$ 225,000	Accounts payable	$ 600,000
Receivables	1,575,000	Notes payable	100,000
Inventories	1,125,000	Other current liabilities	525,000
Total current assets	$2,925,000	Total current liabilities	$1,225,000
Net fixed assets	1,350,000	Long-term debt	400,000
		Common equity	2,650,000
Total assets	$4,275,000	Total liabilities and equity	$4,275,000

Lozano Chip Company: Income Statement for Year Ended December 31, 2019 (Thousands of Dollars)

Sales	$7,500,000
Cost of goods sold	6,375,000
Selling, general, and administrative expenses	933,000
Earnings before interest and taxes (EBIT)	$ 192,000
Interest expense	40,000
Earnings before taxes (EBT)	$ 152,000
Federal and state income taxes (25%)	38,000
Net income	$ 114,000

Ratio	Lozano	Industry Average
Current assets/Current liabilities	_____	2.0
Days sales outstanding (365-day year)	_____	35.0 days
COGS/Inventory	_____	6.7
Sales/Fixed assets	_____	12.1
Sales/Total assets	_____	3.0
Net income/Sales	_____	1.2%
Net income/Total assets	_____	3.6%
Net income/Common equity	_____	9.0%
Total debt/Total assets	_____	30.0%
Total liabilities/Total assets	_____	60.0%

(3-14)
Comprehensive
Ratio Analysis

The Jimenez Corporation's forecasted 2020 financial statements follow, along with some industry average ratios. Calculate Jimenez's 2020 forecasted ratios, compare them with the industry average data, and comment briefly on Jimenez's projected strengths and weaknesses.

Jimenez Corporation: Forecasted Balance Sheet as of December 31, 2020

Assets	
Cash	$ 72,000
Accounts receivable	439,000
Inventories	894,000
Total current assets	$1,405,000
Fixed assets	431,000
Total assets	$1,836,000
Liabilities and Equity	
Accounts payable	$ 332,000
Notes payable	100,000
Accruals	170,000
Total current liabilities	$ 602,000
Long-term debt	404,290
Common stock	575,000
Retained earnings	254,710
Total liabilities and equity	$1,836,000

Jimenez Corporation: Forecasted Income Statement for 2020

Sales	$4,290,000
Cost of goods sold	3,580,000
Selling, general, and administrative expenses	525,456
Earnings before taxes (EBT)	$ 184,544
Interest expense	40,000
Earnings before taxes (EBT)	$ 144,544
Taxes (25%)	36,136
Net income	$ 108,408

Jimenez Corporation: Per Share Data for 2020

EPS	$ 4.71
Cash dividends per share	$ 0.95
P/E ratio	5.0
Market price (average)	$23.57
Number of shares outstanding	23,000

Ratio	Jimenez	Industry Average[a]
Quick ratio		1.0
Current ratio		2.7
Inventory turnover[b]		7.0
Days sales outstanding[c]		32.0 days
Fixed assets turnover[b]		13.0
Total assets turnover[b]		2.6
Return on assets		9.1%
Return on equity		18.2%
Profit margin on sales		3.5%
Debt-to-assets ratio		21.0%
Liabilities-to-assets ratio		50.0%
P/E ratio		6.0
Market/Book ratio		3.5

Notes:

[a]Industry average ratios have been stable for the past 4 years.

[b]Based on year-end balance sheet figures.

[c]Calculation is based on a 365-day year.

SPREADSHEET PROBLEMS

(3-15)
Build a Model:
Ratio Analysis

resource

Start with the partial model in the file ***Ch03 P15 Build a Model.xlsx*** from the textbook's Web site. Joshua & White (J&W) Technology's financial statements are also shown here. Answer the following questions. (*Note:* Industry average ratios are provided in ***Ch03 P15 Build a Model.xlsx***.)

a. Has J&W's liquidity position improved or worsened? Explain.
b. Has J&W's ability to manage its assets improved or worsened? Explain.
c. How has J&W's profitability changed during the last year?

d. Perform an extended DuPont analysis for J&W for 2018 and 2019. What do these results tell you?

e. Perform a common size analysis. What has happened to the composition (that is, percentage in each category) of assets and liabilities?

f. Perform a percentage change analysis. What does this tell you about the change in profitability and asset utilization?

Joshua & White Technology: December 31 Balance Sheets (Thousands of Dollars)

Assets	2019	2018	Liabilities & Equity	2019	2018
Cash	$ 21,000	$ 20,000	Accounts payable	$ 33,600	$ 32,000
Short-term investments	3,759	3,240	Accruals	12,600	12,000
Accounts receivable	52,500	48,000	Notes payable	19,929	6,480
Inventories	84,000	56,000	Total current liabilities	$ 66,129	$ 50,480
Total current assets	$ 161,259	$127,240	Long-term debt	67,662	58,320
Net fixed assets	223,097	200,000	Total liabilities	$ 133,791	$108,800
Total assets	$384,356	$327,240	Common stock	178,440	178,440
			Retained earnings	72,125	40,000
			Total common equity	$250,565	$218,440
			Total liabilities & equity	$384,356	$327,240

Joshua & White Technology: Income Statements for Year Ending on December 31 (Thousands of Dollars)

	2019	2018
Sales	$420,000	$400,000
COGS excluding depr. & amort.	300,000	298,000
Depreciation and amortization	19,660	18,000
Other operating expenses	27,600	22,000
EBIT	$ 72,740	$ 62,000
Interest expense	5,740	4,460
EBT	$ 67,000	$ 57,540
Taxes (25%)	16,750	14,385
Net income	$ 50,250	$ 34,524
Common dividends	$ 18,125	$ 17,262
Additions to retained earnings	$ 32,125	$ 17,262

Other Data	2019	2018
Year-end stock price	$ 90.00	$ 96.00
Number of shares (Thousands)	4,052	4,000
Lease payment (Thousands of Dollars)	$20,000	$20,000
Sinking fund payment (Thousands of Dollars)	$ 5,000	$ 5,000

MINI CASE

The first part of the case, presented in the previous chapter, discussed the situation of Computron Industries after an expansion program. A large loss occurred rather than the expected profit. As a result, its managers, directors, and investors are concerned about the firm's survival.

Jenny Cochran was brought in as assistant to Computron's chairman, who had the task of getting the company back into a sound financial position. Cochran must prepare an analysis of where the company is now, what it must do to regain its financial health, and what actions to take. Your assignment is to help her answer the following questions. Provide clear explanations, not yes or no answers. Use the recent and projected financial information shown next.

Balance Sheets (Millions of Dollars)

	2018	2019	2020E
Assets			
Cash and equivalents	$ 60	$ 50	$ 60
Short-term investments	100	10	50
Accounts receivable	400	520	530
Inventories	620	820	660
Total current assets	$ 1,180	$1,400	$1,300
Net fixed assets	2,900	3,500	3,700
Total assets	$4,080	$4,900	$5,000
Liabilities and equity			
Accounts payable	$ 300	$ 400	$ 330
Notes payable	50	250	100
Accruals	200	240	270
Total current liabilities	$ 550	$ 890	$ 700
Long-term bonds	800	1,100	1,100
Total liabilities	$ 1,350	$ 1,990	$ 1,800
Common stock (100,000 shares)	1,000	1,000	1,000
Retained earnings	1,730	1,910	2,200
Total common equity	$2,730	$ 2,910	$3,200
Total liabilities and equity	$4,080	$4,900	$5,000

Note: "E" denotes the "*estimated* forecast."

Income Statements (Millions of Dollars)

	2018	2019	2020E
Net sales	$5,500	$6,000	$6,600
Cost of goods sold (excluding depr.)	4,300	4,800	5,210
Depreciation	290	320	370
Other operating expenses	350	420	400
Earnings before interest and taxes (EBIT)	$ 560	$ 460	$ 620
Less interest	68	108	100
Pre-tax earnings	$ 492	$ 352	$ 520
Taxes (25%)	123	88	130
Net income	$ 369	$ 264	$ 390

Note: "E" denotes the "*estimated* forecast." Also, Computron has no amortization.

Other Data

	2018	2019	2020E
Per Share Information			
EPS	$ 3.69	$ 2.64	$ 3.90
DPS	$ 0.90	$ 0.84	$ 1.00
Book value per share	$27.30	$ 29.10	$32.00
Additional Information			
Dividends (millions)	$ 90	$ 84	$ 100
Additions to retained earnings (millions)	$ 279	$ 180	$ 290
Year-end shares outstanding (millions)	100	100	100
Year-end common stock price	$50.00	$30.00	$49.00
Lease payments (millions)	$ 20	$ 20	$ 20
Tax rate	25%	25%	25%

Note: "E" denotes the "*estimated* forecast."

Ratio Analysis

Ratio	2018	2019	2020E	Industry Average
Profit margin	6.7%	4.4%		7.2%
Operating profit margin	10.2%	7.7%		10.4%
Basic earning power	13.7%	9.4%		15.6%
ROA	9.0%	5.4%		10.8%
ROE	13.5%	9.1%		15.4%
Inventory turnover	7.4	6.2		9.0
Days sales outstanding	26.5	31.6		28.0
Fixed assets turnover	1.9	1.7		3.0
Total assets turnover	1.348	1.224		1.5
Current	2.1	1.6		2.5
Quick	1.0	0.7		1.4
Debt ratio	20.8%	27.6%		15.0%
Debt-to-equity ratio	0.31	0.46		0.22
Liabilities-to-assets ratio	33.1%	40.6%		30.0%
Earnings multiplier	1.5	1.7		1.5
TIE	8.2	4.3		13.0
EBITDA coverage	9.9	6.3		17.2
Price/earnings (P/E)	13.6	11.4		16.8
Market/book	1.8	1.0		2.6

Note: "E" denotes the "*estimated* forecast."

a. Why are ratios useful? What three groups use ratio analysis and for what reasons?
b. Calculate the projected profit margin, operating profit margin, basic earning power (BEP), return on assets (ROA), and return on equity (ROE). What can you say about these ratios?
c. Calculate the projected inventory turnover, days sales outstanding (DSO), fixed assets turnover, and total assets turnover. How does Computron's utilization of assets stack up against that of other firms in its industry?

d. Calculate the projected current and quick ratios based on the projected balance sheet and income statement data. What can you say about the company's liquidity position and its trend?

e. Calculate the projected debt ratio, debt-to-equity ratio, liabilities-to-assets ratio, times-interest-earned ratio, and EBITDA coverage ratios. How does Computron compare with the industry with respect to financial leverage? What can you conclude from these ratios?

f. Calculate the projected price/earnings ratio and market/book ratio. Do these ratios indicate that investors are expected to have a high or low opinion of the company?

g. Perform a common size analysis and percentage change analysis. What do these analyses tell you about Computron?

h. Use the extended DuPont equation to provide a breakdown of Computron's projected return on equity. How does the projection compare with the previous years and with the industry's DuPont equation?

i. What are some potential problems and limitations of financial ratio analysis?

j. What are some qualitative factors that analysts should consider when evaluating a company's likely future financial performance?

SELECTED ADDITIONAL CASES

The following cases from Cengage Compose cover many of the concepts discussed in this chapter and are available at **http://compose.cengage.com**.

Klein-Brigham Series:

Case 35, "Mark X Company (A)," illustrates the use of ratio analysis in the evaluation of a firm's existing and potential financial positions; Case 36, "Garden State Container Corporation," is similar in content to Case 35; Case 51, "Safe Packaging Corporation," updates Case 36; Case 68, "Sweet Dreams Inc.," also updates Case 36; and Case 71, "Swan-Davis, Inc.," illustrates how financial analysis—based on both historical statements and forecasted statements—is used for internal management and lending decisions.

PART 2
Fixed Income Securities

CHAPTER 4

Time Value of Money

Before you shop for a new car, you will do a lot of research to identify the make and model you want. This will give you a pretty good idea regarding the car's features, ratings, safety record, and various option bundles. If you plan to trade in your current car, you know to leave that car at home until you and the salesperson have agreed on new car's sales price—bundling two transactions into one will reduce transparency, often at the buyer's expense. You know that a factory rebate is paid by the manufacturer, not the dealer, which means that the *dealer's* profit is not affected by the size of the rebate. Knowing this, you won't allow the salesperson to use the rebate as a negotiating point. You put on your best poker face, walk into the dealership, confident that you are ready to negotiate the best possible deal.

After you and the salesperson agree on a price, you will go to the dealer's finance department to conduct the transaction. And this is where it gets *really* tricky! Most dealers offer to finance the purchase themselves and have multiple financing packages involving different interest rates, rebates, down payments, and length of the loan. Sometimes a zero-interest loan is offered by the manufacturer, but it might require that you give up some or all of the factory rebate. Maybe it would be better for you to borrow from your bank rather than the dealer. To make the best financing choice, you need to understand the time value of money, so read on!

Corporate Valuation and the Time Value of Money

In Chapter 1 we explained (1) that managers should strive to make their firms more valuable, and (2) that the value of a firm is determined by the size, timing, and risk of its free cash flows (FCFs). Recall from Chapter 2 that free cash flows are the cash flows available for distribution to all of a firm's investors (stockholders and creditors). We explain how to calculate the weighted average cost of capital (WACC) in Chapter 9, but it is enough for now to think of the WACC as the average rate of return required by all of the firm's investors. The intrinsic value of a company is given by the following diagram. Note that central to this value is discounting the free cash flows at the WACC in order to find the value of the firm. This discounting is one aspect of the time value of money. We discuss time value of money techniques in this chapter.

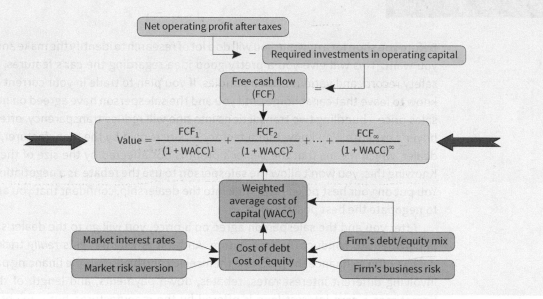

In Chapter 1, we saw that the primary objective of a corporation is to maximize the intrinsic value of its stock. We also saw that stock values depend on the timing of the cash flows investors expect from an investment—a dollar expected sooner is worth more than a dollar expected further in the future. Therefore, it is essential for financial managers to understand the time value of money and its impact on stock prices. In this chapter, we will explain exactly how the timing of cash flows affects asset values and rates of return.

The principles of time value analysis have many applications, including retirement planning, loan payment schedules, and decisions to invest (or not) in new equipment. *In fact, of all the concepts used in finance, none is more important than the* **time value of money (TVM),** *also called* **discounted cash flow (DCF) analysis.** Time value concepts are used throughout the remainder of the book, so it is vital that you understand the material in this chapter and be able to work the chapter's problems before you move on to other topics.

4-1 Time Lines

The first step in a time value analysis is to set up a **time line** to help you visualize what's happening in the particular problem. To illustrate, consider the following diagram, where PV represents $100 that is in a bank account today and FV

resource

*The textbook's Web site contains an Excel file that will guide you through the chapter's calculations. The file for this chapter is **Ch04 Tool Kit.xlsx**, and we encourage you to open the file and follow along as you read the chapter.*

is the value that will be in the account at some future time (3 years from now in this example):

end of year 2 & year 3
beginning of year 3

Periods	0	5%	1		2		3
Cash	PV = $100						FV = ?

The intervals from 0 to 1, 1 to 2, and 2 to 3 are time periods such as years or months. Time 0 is today, and it is the beginning of Period 1; Time 1 is one period from today, and it is both the end of Period 1 and the beginning of Period 2; and so on. In our example, the periods are years, but they could also be quarters or months or even days. Note again that each tick mark corresponds to both the *end* of one period and the *beginning* of the next one. Thus, if the periods are years, the tick mark at Time 2 represents both the end of Year 2 and the beginning of Year 3.

Cash flows are shown directly below the tick marks, and the relevant interest rate is shown just above the time line. Unknown cash flows, which you are trying to find, are indicated by question marks. Here the interest rate is 5%; a single cash outflow, $100, is invested at Time 0; and the Time-3 value is unknown and must be found. In this example, cash flows occur only at Times 0 and 3, with no flows at Times 1 or 2. We will, of course, deal with situations where multiple cash flows occur. Note also that in our example the interest rate is constant for all 3 years. The interest rate is generally held constant, but if it varies, then in the diagram we show different rates for the different periods.

Time lines are especially important when you are first learning time value concepts, but even experts use them to analyze complex problems. Throughout the book, our procedure is to set up a time line to show what's happening, provide an equation that must be solved to find the answer, and then explain how to solve the equation with a regular calculator, a financial calculator, and a computer spreadsheet.

Do time lines deal only with years, or could other periods be used? Quarters/months/days

Set up a time line to illustrate the following situation: You currently have $2,000 in a 3-year certificate of deposit (CD) that pays a guaranteed 4% annually. You want to know the value of the CD after 3 years.

0	4%	1	4%		4%		4%
PV = 2000							FV

4-2 Future Values

A dollar in hand today is worth more than a dollar to be received in the future; if you had the dollar now, you could invest it, earn interest, and end up with more than one dollar in the future. The process of going forward, from **present values (PVs)** to **future values (FVs)**, is called **compounding**. To illustrate, refer back to our 3-year time line and assume that you have $100 in a bank account that pays a guaranteed 5% interest each year. How much would you have at the end of Year 3? We first define some terms, and then we set up a time line and show how the future value is calculated.

PV   =   Present value, or beginning amount. In our example, PV = $100.

FV_N =   Future value, or ending amount, in the account after N periods. Whereas PV is the value *now*, or the *present value*, FV_N is the value N periods into the *future*, after interest earned has been added to the account.

CF_t =   Cash flow. Cash flows can be positive or negative. For a borrower, the first cash flow is positive and the subsequent cash flows are negative, and the reverse holds for a lender. The cash flow for a particular period is often given a subscript, CF_t, where t is the period. Thus, CF_0 = PV = the cash flow at Time 0, whereas CF_3 would be the cash flow at the end of Period 3. In this example the cash flows occur *at the ends* of the periods, but in some problems they occur at the beginning.

I   =   Interest rate earned per year. (Sometimes a lowercase i is used.) Interest earned is based on the balance at the beginning of each year, and we assume that interest is paid at the end of the year. Here I = 5% or, expressed as a decimal, 0.05. Throughout this chapter, we designate the interest rate as I (or I/YR, for interest rate per year) because that symbol is used on most financial calculators. Note, though, that in later chapters we use the symbol "r" to denote the rate because r (for *rate* of return) is used more often in the finance literature. Also, in this chapter we generally assume that interest payments are guaranteed by the U.S. government and hence are riskless (i.e., certain). In later chapters we will deal with risky investments, where the rate actually earned might be different from its expected level.

INT   =   Dollars of interest earned during the year = (Beginning amount) × I. In our example, INT = $100(0.05) = $5 for Year 1, but it rises in subsequent years as the amount at the beginning of each year increases.

N   =   Number of periods involved in the analysis. In our example, N = 3. Sometimes the number of periods is designated with a lowercase n, so both N and n indicate number of periods.

We can use four different procedures to solve time value problems.[1] These methods are described next.

4-2a Step-by-Step Approach

The time line itself can be modified and used to find the FV of $100 compounded for 3 years at 5%, as shown here:

Time	0		1	2	3
		5%			
Amount at beginning of period	$100.00 →		$105.00 →	$110.25 →	$115.76

___

[1]A fifth procedure is called the *tabular approach*, which uses tables that provide "interest factors"; this procedure was used before financial calculators and computers became available. Now, though, calculators and spreadsheets such as *Excel* are programmed to calculate the specific factor needed for a given problem, which is then used to find the FV. This is much more efficient than using the tables. Also, calculators and spreadsheets can handle fractional periods and fractional interest rates. For these reasons, tables are not used in business today; hence we do not discuss them.

We start with $100 in the account, which is shown at t = 0. We then multiply the initial amount, and each succeeding beginning-of-year amount, by $(1 + I) = (1.05)$.

- You earn $100(0.05) = $5 of interest during the first year, so the amount at the end of Year 1 (or at t = 1) is:

$$FV_1 = PV + INT$$
$$= PV + PV(I)$$
$$= PV(1 + I)$$
$$= \$100(1 + 0.05) = \$100(1.05) = \$105$$

- We begin the second year with $105, earn 0.05($105) = $5.25 on the now larger beginning-of-period amount, and end the year with $110.25. Interest during Year 2 is $5.25, and it is higher than the first year's interest, $5, because we earned $5(0.05) = $0.25 interest on the first year's interest. This is called "compounding," and interest earned on interest is called "compound interest."

- This process continues, and because the beginning balance is higher in each successive year, the interest earned each year increases.

- The total interest earned, $15.76, is reflected in the final balance, $115.76.

The step-by-step approach is useful because it shows exactly what is happening. However, this approach is time-consuming, especially if the number of years is large and you are using a calculator rather than *Excel*, so streamlined procedures have been developed.

4-2b Formula Approach

In the step-by-step approach, we multiplied the amount at the beginning of each period by $(1 + I) = (1.05)$. Notice that the value at the end of Year 2 is:

$$FV_2 = FV_1(1 + I)$$
$$= PV(1 + I)(1 + I)$$
$$= PV(1 + I)^2$$
$$= 100(1.05)^2 = \$110.25$$

If N = 3, then we multiply PV by $(1 + I)$ three different times, which is the same as multiplying the beginning amount by $(1 + I)^3$. This concept can be extended, and the result is this key equation:

$$FV_N = PV(1 + I)^N \tag{4-1}$$

We can apply Equation 4-1 to find the FV in our example:

$$FV_3 = \$100(1.05)^3 = \$115.76$$

Equation 4-1 can be used with any calculator, even a nonfinancial calculator that has an exponential function, making it easy to find FVs no matter how many years are involved.

4-2c Financial Calculators

Financial calculators were designed specifically to solve time value problems. First, use the calculator's main menu and choose the time value of money sub-menu. (Many calculators use TVM to denote this sub-menu.). There will be five keys that correspond to the five variables in the basic time value equations. Equation 4-1 has only four variables, but we show the full equation here because it is important for you to understand the negative and positive signs used in calculators. In the following equation, PMT denotes a constant cash flow for all periods:

$$PV(1 + I)^N + PMT\left[\frac{(1 + I)^N - 1}{I}\right] + FV = 0 \qquad \text{(4-2)}$$

If we delete the term with PMT, we get:

$$PV(1 + I)^N + FV = 0 \qquad \text{(4-2a)}$$

We show the inputs for our example above their keys in the following diagram, and the output, which is the FV, below its key. Because there are no periodic payments in this example, we enter 0 for PMT. Assuming that I is less than 100%, either PV or FV must be negative if the left side of Equation 4-2a is to be equal to zero. Think about it like this: If you deposit money today (PV), that is a cash flow out of your pocket; when you withdraw it in the future (FV), that is a cash flow into your pocket. Conversely, if you borrow money today (PV), that is cash into your pocket; when you pay it back in the future (FV), that is cash out of your pocket. We describe the keys in more detail below the diagram.

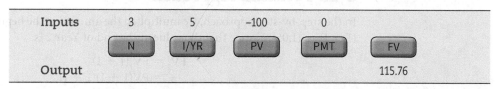

Inputs	3	5	–100	0	
	N	I/YR	PV	PMT	FV
Output					115.76

N = Number of periods = 3. Some calculators use n rather than N.

I/YR = Interest rate per period = 5. Some calculators use i or I rather than I/YR. Calculators are programmed to automatically convert the 5 to the decimal 0.05 before doing the arithmetic.

PV = Present value = 100. In our example we begin by making a deposit, which is an outflow of 100, so the PV is entered with a negative sign. On most calculators you must enter the 100, then press the +/− key to switch from +100 to −100. If you enter −100 directly, this will subtract 100 from the last number in the calculator, which will give you an incorrect answer unless the last number was zero.

PMT = Payment. This key is used if we have a series of equal, or constant, payments. Because there are no such payments in our current problem, we enter PMT = 0. We will use the PMT key later in this chapter.

FV = Future value. In our example, the calculator automatically shows the FV as a positive number because we entered the PV as a negative number. If we had entered the 100 as a positive number, then the FV would have been negative. Calculators automatically assume that either the PV or the FV must be negative.

Hints on Using Financial Calculators

When using a financial calculator, make sure it is set up as indicated below. Refer to your calculator manual or to our calculator tutorial on the textbook's Web site for information on setting up your calculator.

◆ **One payment per period.** Many calculators "come out of the box" assuming that 12 payments are made per year; that is, they assume monthly payments. However, in this book we generally deal with problems in which only one payment is made each year. *Therefore, you should set your calculator at one payment per year and leave it there. See our tutorial or your calculator manual if you need assistance.* We will show you how to solve problems with more than 1 payment per year in Section 4-15.

◆ **End mode.** With most contracts, payments are made at the *end* of each period. However, some contracts call for payments at the *beginning* of each period. You can switch between "End Mode" and "Begin Mode" depending on the problem you are solving. *Because most of the problems in this book call for end-of-period payments, you should return your calculator to End Mode after you work a problem in which payments are made at the beginning of periods.*

◆ **Negative sign for outflows.** There are three cash flows in Equation 4-2: PV, PMT, or FV. Don't forget that at least one of the three cash flows must be negative and at least one must be positive. There are two possible situations: (1) one negative cash flow is out of your pocket and two positive cash flows are into your pocket, or (2) two negative cash flows are out of your pocket and one positive cash flow is into your pocket. *This generally means typing outflows as positive numbers and then pressing the +/− key to convert from + to − before hitting the enter key.*

◆ **Decimal places.** When doing arithmetic, calculators allow you to show from 0 to 11 decimal places on the display. When working with dollars, we generally specify two decimal places. When dealing with interest rates, we generally specify two places if the rate is expressed as a percentage, like 5.25%, but we specify four places if the rate is expressed as a decimal, like 0.0525.

◆ **Interest rates.** For arithmetic operations with a nonfinancial calculator, *the rate 5.25% must be stated as a decimal, .0525.* However, with a financial calculator you must *enter 5.25, not .0525,* because financial calculators are programmed to assume that rates are stated as percentages.

As noted in our example, you first enter the four known values (N, I/YR, PV, and PMT) and then press the FV key to get the answer, FV = 115.76.

4-2d Spreadsheets

resource

See Ch04 Tool Kit.xlsx for all calculations.

Spreadsheets are ideally suited for solving many financial problems, including those dealing with the time value of money.[2] Spreadsheets are obviously useful for calculations, but they can also be used like a word processor to create exhibits like our Figure 4-1, which includes text, drawings, and calculations. We use this figure to show that four methods can be used to find the FV of $100 after 3 years at an interest rate of 5%. The time line on Rows 36 to 37 is useful for visualizing the problem, after which the spreadsheet calculates the required answer. Note that the letters across the top designate columns, the numbers down the left column designate rows, and the rows and columns jointly designate cells.

---

[2]The file **Ch04 Tool Kit.xlsx** on the book's Web site does the calculations in the chapter using *Excel*. We *highly recommend* that you study the models in this *Tool Kit*. Doing so will give you practice with *Excel*, and that will help you tremendously in later courses, in the job market, and in the workplace. Also, going through the models will improve your understanding of financial concepts.

FIGURE 4-1
Alternative Procedures for Calculating Future Values

	A	B	C	D	E	F	G
31	**INPUTS:**						
32		**Investment = CF$_0$ = PV =**	**−\$100.00**				
33		**Interest rate = I =**	**5%**				
34		**No. of periods = N =**	**3**				
35							
36	**Time Line**		**Periods:**	**0**	**1**	**2**	**3**
37			**Cash flow:**	**−\$100.00**	**0**	**0**	**FV = ?**
38							
39	**1. Step-by-Step: Multiply by (1 + I) each step**		**\$100.00 →**	**\$105.00 →**	**\$110.25 →**	**\$115.76**	
40							
41	**2. Formula: FV$_N$ = PV(1+I)^N**			**FV$_3$ =**	**\$100(1.05)^3**	**=**	**\$115.76**
42							
43		**Inputs:**	**3**	**5**	**−100**	**0**	
44	**3. Financial Calculator:**		**N**	**I/YR**	**PV**	**PMT**	**FV**
45		**Output:**					**\$115.76**
46							
47	**4. *Excel* Spreadsheet:**		**FV function:**	**FV$_N$ =**	**=FV(I,N,0,PV)**		
48			**Fixed inputs:**	**FV$_N$ =**	**=FV(0.05,3,0,−100) =**		**\$115.76**
49			**Cell references:**	**FV$_N$ =**	**=FV(C33,C34,0,C32) =**		**\$115.76**

Source: See the file ***Ch04 Tool Kit.xlsx***. Numbers are reported as rounded values for clarity but are calculated using *Excel*'s full precision. Thus, intermediate calculations using the figure's rounded values will be inexact.

Thus, cell C32 shows the amount of the investment, \$100, and it is given a minus sign because it is an outflow.

It is useful to put all inputs in a section of the spreadsheet designated "INPUTS." In Figure 4-1, we put the inputs in the aqua-colored range of cells. Rather than enter fixed numbers into the model's formulas, we enter the cell references for the inputs. This makes it easy to modify the problem by changing the inputs and then automatically use the new data in the calculations.

Time lines are important for solving finance problems because they help us visualize what's happening. When we work a problem by hand, we usually draw a time line, and when we work a problem with *Excel*, we set the model up as a time line. For example, in Figure 4-1 Rows 36 to 37 are indeed a time line. It's easy to construct time lines with *Excel*, with each column designating a different period on the time line.

On Row 39, we use *Excel* to go through the step-by-step calculations, multiplying the beginning-of-year values by (1 + I) to find the compounded value at the end of each period. Cell G39 shows the final result of the step-by-step approach.

We illustrate the formula approach in Row 41, using *Excel* to solve Equation 4-1 to find the FV. Cell G41 shows the formula result, \$115.76. As it must, it equals the step-by-step result.

Rows 43 to 45 illustrate the financial calculator approach, which again produces the same answer, \$115.76.

The last section, in Rows 47 to 49, illustrates *Excel*'s future value (**FV**) function. You can access the function wizard by clicking the *f*_x symbol in *Excel*'s formula bar. Then select the category for Financial functions, and then the **FV** function, which is =**FV(I,N,0,PV)**, as shown in Cell E47.[3] Cell E48 shows how the formula would look with numbers as inputs; the actual function itself is entered in Cell G48, but it shows up in the table as the answer, $115.76. If you access the model and put the pointer on Cell G48, you will see the full formula. Finally, Cell E49 shows how the formula would look with cell references rather than fixed values as inputs, with the actual function again in Cell G49. We generally use cell references as function inputs because this makes it easy to change inputs and see how those changes affect the output. This is called "sensitivity analysis." Many real-world financial applications use sensitivity analysis, so it is useful to form the habit of setting up an input data section and then using cell references rather than fixed numbers in the functions.

When entering interest rates in *Excel,* you can use either actual numbers or percentages, depending on how the cell is formatted. For example, we first formatted Cell C33 to Percentage, and then typed in 5, which showed up as 5%. However, *Excel* uses 0.05 for the arithmetic. Alternatively, we could have formatted C33 as a Number, in which case we would have typed 0.05. If a cell is formatted to Number and you enter 5, then *Excel* would think you meant 500%. Thus, *Excel*'s procedure is different from the convention used in financial calculators.

Sometimes students are confused about the sign of the initial $100. We used +$100 in Rows 39 and 41 as the initial investment when calculating the future value using the step-by-step method and the future value formula, but we used −$100 with a financial calculator and the spreadsheet function in Rows 43 and 48. When must you use a positive value, and when must you use a negative value? The answer is that whenever you set up a time line and use either a financial calculator's time value functions or *Excel*'s time value functions, you must enter the signs that correspond to the "direction" of the cash flows. Cash flows that go out of your pocket (outflows) are negative, but cash flows that come into your pocket (inflows) are positive. In the case of the FV function in our example, if you invest $100 (an outflow and therefore negative) at Time 0, then the bank will make available to you $115.76 (an inflow and therefore positive) at Time 3. In essence, the FV function on a financial calculator or *Excel* answers the question, "If I invest this much now, how much will be available to me at a time in the future?" The investment is an outflow and negative, and the amount available to you is an inflow and positive. If you use algebraic formulas, then you must keep track of whether the value is an outflow or an inflow yourself. When in doubt, refer back to a correctly constructed time line.

4-2e Comparing the Procedures

The first step in solving any time value problem is to understand what is happening and then to diagram it on a time line. Woody Allen said that 90% of success is just showing up. With time value problems, 90% of success is correctly setting up the time line.

After you diagram the problem on a time line, your next step is to pick one of the four approaches shown in Figure 4-1 to solve the problem. Any one approach may be used, but your choice will depend on the particular situation.

---

[3]All functions begin with an equal sign. The third entry is zero in this example, which indicates that there are no periodic payments. Later in this chapter we will use the **FV** function in situations where we have nonzero periodic payments. Also, for inputs we use our own notation, which is similar but not identical to *Excel*'s notation.

All business students should know Equation 4-1 by heart and should also know how to use a financial calculator. So, for simple problems such as finding the future value of a single payment, it is generally easiest and quickest to use either the formula approach or a financial calculator. However, for problems that involve several cash flows, the formula approach usually is time-consuming, so either the calculator or spreadsheet approach would generally be used. Calculators are portable and quick to set up, but if many calculations of the same type must be done, or if you want to see how changes in an input such as the interest rate affect the future value, then the spreadsheet approach is generally more efficient. If the problem has many irregular cash flows, or if you want to analyze alternative scenarios using different cash flows or interest rates, then the spreadsheet approach definitely is the most efficient procedure.

Spreadsheets have two additional advantages over calculators. First, it is easier to check the inputs with a spreadsheet because they are visible; with a calculator the inputs are buried somewhere in the machine. Thus, you are less likely to make a mistake in a complex problem when you use the spreadsheet approach. Second, with a spreadsheet, you can make your analysis much more transparent than you can when using a calculator. This is not necessarily important when all you want is the answer, but if you need to present your calculations to others, like your boss, it helps to be able to show intermediate steps, which enables someone to go through your exhibit and see exactly what you did. Transparency is also important when you must go back, sometime later, and reconstruct what you did.

You should understand the various approaches well enough to make a rational choice, given the nature of the problem and the equipment you have available. In any event, you must understand the concepts behind the calculations, and you also must know how to set up time lines in order to work complex problems. This is true for stock and bond valuation, capital budgeting, lease analysis, and many other types of financial problems.

4-2f Graphic View of the Compounding Process

resource

See Ch04 Tool Kit.xlsx for all calculations.

Figure 4-2 shows how a $100 investment grows (or declines) over time at different interest rates. Interest rates are normally positive, but the "growth" concept is broad enough to include negative rates. We developed the curves by solving Equation 4-1 with different values for N and I. The interest rate is a growth rate: If money is deposited and earns 5% per year, then your funds will grow by 5% per year. Note also that time value concepts can be applied to anything that grows—sales, population, earnings per share, or your future salary. Also, as noted before, the "growth rate" can be negative. For example, Campbell Soup Company had negative revenue growth in 2017.

4-2g Simple Interest versus Compound Interest

As explained earlier, when interest is earned on the interest earned in prior periods, we call it **compound interest**. If interest is earned only on the principal, we call it **simple interest**; it is also called **regular interest**. The total interest earned with simple interest is equal to the principal multiplied by the interest rate times the number of periods: $PV(I)(N)$. The future value is equal to the principal plus the interest: $FV = PV + PV(I)(N)$. For example, suppose you deposit $100 for 3 years and earn simple interest at an annual rate of 5%. Your balance at the end of 3 years would be:

$$FV = PV + PV(I)(N)$$
$$= \$100 + \$100(5\%)(3)$$
$$= \$100 + \$15 = \$115$$

FIGURE 4-2
Growth of $100 at Various Interest Rates and Time Periods

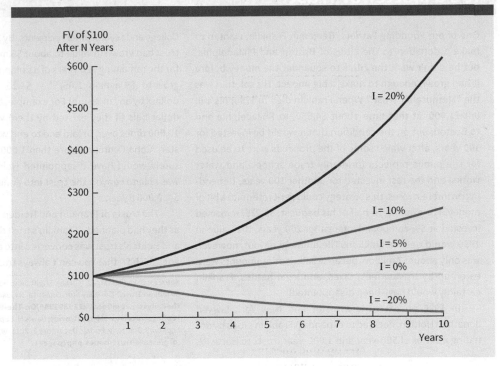

Notice that this is less than the $115.76 we calculated earlier using compound interest. Most applications in finance are based on compound interest, but you should be aware that simple interest is still specified in some legal documents.

SELF-TEST

Explain why this statement is true: "A dollar in hand today is worth more than a dollar to be received next year, assuming interest rates are positive."

What is compounding? What would the future value of $100 be after 5 years at 10% compound interest? **($161.05)**

*Suppose you currently have $2,000 and plan to purchase a 3-year certificate of deposit (CD) that pays 4% interest, compounded annually. How much will you have when the CD matures? **($2,249.73)** How would your answer change if the interest rate were 5%, or 6%, or 20%? (Hint: With a calculator, enter N = 3, I/YR = 4, PV = −2000, and PMT = 0; then press FV to get 2,249.73. Then, enter I/YR = 5 to override the 4% and press FV again to get the second answer. In general, you can change one input at a time to see how the output changes.)* **($2,315.25; $2,382.03; $3,456.00)**

*A company's sales in 2012 were $100 million. If sales grow by 8% annually, what will they be 10 years later? **($215.89 million)** What would they be if they decline by 8% per year for 10 years?* **($43.44 million)**

*How much would $1, growing at 5% per year, be worth after 100 years? **($131.50)** What would FV be if the growth rate were 10%?* **($13,780.61)**

It's a Matter of Trust

One of our Founding Fathers, Benjamin Franklin, wanted to make a donation to the cities of Boston and Philadelphia, but he didn't want the cities to squander the money before it had grown enough to make a big impact. His solution was the "Methuselah Trust." When Franklin died in 1790, his will left £1,000, at that time about $4,550, to Philadelphia and to Boston, but on the condition that it would be invested for 100 years, after which some of the proceeds were to be used for the public projects (primarily trade schools and water works) and the rest invested for another 100 years. Depending on interest rates, this strategy could generate quite a bit of money! For example, if half of his bequest, $2,275, remained invested at 5% compound interest for 200 years, the value in 1990 would be $39.3 million! The ultimate payout, however, was only about $7 million, because substantial amounts were eaten up by trustee fees, taxes, and legal battles. Franklin certainly would have been disappointed!

In 1936 an eccentric investor and New York lawyer, Jonathan Holden, decided to expand on Franklin's idea by donating a series of 500-year and 1,000-year trusts to Hartwick College and several other recipients. By 2008 Hartwick College's trust had grown in value to about $9 million; if invested at 5% for the remaining 928 years of its planned life, its value would grow to ($9 million)(1.05)^{928} = 4.15×10^{26}. That is a lot of dollars by any measure! For example, that amount in million-dollar bills (if they existed by then) would paper the earth 10,000 times over, or laid end to end would reach the nearest star, Alpha Centauri, more than 1,000 times. In a move that surely would have disappointed Holden, Hartwick College was able to convert the trust into annual cash flows of about $450,000 a year.

The trusts of Franklin and Holden didn't turn out exactly as they had planned—Franklin's trust didn't grow adequately, and Holden's trust was converted into annual cash flows. This goes to show that you can't always trust a trust!

Sources: Jake Palmateer, "On the Bright Side: Hartwick College Receives $9 million Trust," *The Daily Star*, Oneonta, NY, January 22, 2008, **http://thedailystar.com/local/x112892349/On-The-Bright-Side-Hartwick-College-receives-9M-trust/print**; Lewis H. Lapham, "Trust Issues," *Lapham's Quarterly*, Friday, December 2, 2011, **www.laphamsquarterly.org/essays/trust-issues.php?page=1.**

4-3 Present Values

Suppose you have some extra money and want to make an investment. A broker offers to sell you a bond that will pay a guaranteed $115.76 in 3 years. Banks are currently offering a guaranteed 5% interest on 3-year certificates of deposit (CDs), and if you don't buy the bond, you will buy a CD. The 5% rate paid on the CD is defined as your **opportunity cost**, or the rate of return you would earn on an alternative investment of similar risk if you don't invest in the security under consideration. Given these conditions, what's the most you should pay for the bond?

4-3a Discounting a Future Value to Find the Present Value

First, recall from the future value example in the last section that if you invested $100 at 5% in a CD, it would grow to $115.76 in 3 years. You would also have $115.76 after 3 years if you bought the bond. Therefore, the most you should pay for the bond is $100—this is its "fair price," which is also its intrinsic, or fundamental, value. If you could buy the bond for *less than* $100, then you should buy it rather than invest in the CD. Conversely, if its price were *more than* $100, you should buy the CD. If the bond's price were exactly $100, you should be indifferent between the bond and the CD.

The $100 is defined as the present value, or PV, of $115.76 due in 3 years when the appropriate interest rate is 5%. In general, *the present value of a cash flow due N years in the future is the amount that, if it were on hand today, would grow to equal the given future*

151

amount. Because $100 would grow to $115.76 in 3 years at a 5% interest rate, $100 is the present value of $115.76 due in 3 years at a 5% rate.

Finding present values is called **discounting**, and as previously noted, it is the reverse of compounding: If you know the PV, you can compound it to find the FV; if instead you know the FV, you can discount it to find the PV. Indeed, we simply solve Equation 4-1, the formula for the future value, for the PV to produce the present value equation. We repeat Equation 4-1 here to see the difference between compounding and discounting:

Compounding to find future values: Future value = $FV_N = PV(1 + I)^N$ (4-1)

Discounting to find present values: Present value = $PV = \dfrac{FV_N}{(1 + I)^N}$ (4-3)

resource

See Ch04 Tool Kit.xlsx for all calculations.

The top section of Figure 4-3 shows inputs and a time line for finding the present value of $115.76 discounted back for 3 years. We first calculate the PV using the step-by-step approach. When we found the FV in the previous section, we worked from left to right, *multiplying* the initial amount and each subsequent amount by (1 + I).

FIGURE 4-3
Alternative Procedures for Calculating Present Values

	A	B	C	D	E	F	G
97	INPUTS:						
98	Future payment = CF_N = FV =		$115.76				
99	Interest rate = I =		5.00%				
100	No. of periods = N =		3				
101							
102	Time Line		Periods:	0	1	2	3
103			Cash flow:	PV = ?	0	0	$115.76
104							
105	1. Step-by-Step:			$100.00	← $105.00	← $110.25	← $115.76
106							
107	2. Formula: PV = $FV_N/(1+I)^N$			PV = $115.76/(1.05)³		=	$100.00
108							
109		Inputs:	3	5		0	115.76
110	3. Financial Calculator:		N	I/YR	PV	PMT	FV
111		Output:			−$100.00		
112							
113	4. *Excel* Spreadsheet:		PV function:	PV =	=PV(I,N,0,FV)		
114			Fixed inputs:	PV =	=PV(0.05,3,0,115.76) =		−$100.00
115			Cell references:	PV =	=PV(C99,C100,0,C98) =		−$100.00

Source: See the file *Ch04 Tool Kit.xlsx*. Numbers are reported as rounded values for clarity but are calculated using *Excel*'s full precision. Thus, intermediate calculations using the figure's rounded values will be inexact.

To find present values, we work backwards, or from right to left, *dividing* the future value and each subsequent amount by (1 + I), with the present value of $100 shown in Cell D105. The step-by-step procedure shows exactly what's happening, and that can be quite useful when you are working complex problems or trying to explain a model to others. However, it's inefficient, especially if you are dealing with more than a year or two.

A more efficient procedure is to use the formula approach in Equation 4-3, simply dividing the future value by $(1 + I)^N$. This gives the same result, as we see in Figure 4-3, Cell G107.

Equation 4-2 is actually programmed into financial calculators. As shown in Figure 4-3, Rows 109 to 111, we can find the PV by entering values for N = 3, I/YR = 5, PMT = 0, and FV = 115.76, and then pressing the PV key to get −100.

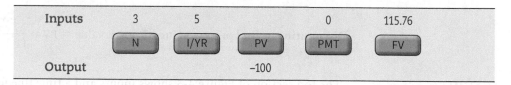

Excel also has a function that solves Equation 4-3—this is the **PV** function, and it is written as **=PV(I,N,0,FV)**.[4] Cell E113 shows the inputs to this function. Next, Cell E114 shows the *Excel* function with fixed numbers as inputs, with the actual function and the resulting −$100 in Cell G114. Cell E115 shows the *Excel* function using cell references, with the actual function and the resulting −$100 in Cell G115.

As with the future value calculation, students often wonder why the result of the present value calculation is sometimes positive and sometimes negative. In the algebraic calculations in Rows 105 and 107 the result is +$100, while the result of the calculation using a financial calculator or *Excel*'s function in Rows 111 and 114 is −$100. Again, the answer is in the signs of a correctly constructed time line. Outflows are negative and inflows are positive. The **PV** function for *Excel* and a financial calculator answer the question, "How much must I invest today in order to have available to me a certain amount of money in the future?" If you want to have $115.76 available in 3 years (an inflow to you and therefore positive), then you must invest $100 today (an outflow and therefore negative). If you use the algebraic functions as in Rows 105 and 107, you must keep track of whether the results of your calculations are inflows or outflows.

The fundamental goal of financial management is to maximize the firm's intrinsic value, and the intrinsic value of a business (or any asset, including stocks and bonds) is the *present value* of its expected future cash flows. Because present value lies at the heart of the valuation process, we will have much more to say about it in the remainder of this chapter and throughout the book.

4-3b Graphic View of the Discounting Process

Figure 4-4 shows that the present value of a sum to be received in the future decreases and approaches zero as the payment date is extended further and further into the future; it also shows that the higher the interest rate, the faster the present value falls. At relatively high rates, funds due far in the future are worth very little today, and even at relatively low rates present values of sums due in the very distant future are quite small. For example, at a 20%

---

[4]The third entry in the **PV** function is zero to indicate that there are no intermediate payments in this example.

FIGURE 4-4
Present Value of $100 at Various Interest Rates and Time Periods

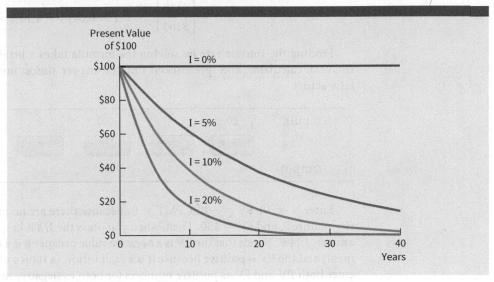

discount rate, $100 due in 40 years would be worth less than 7 cents today. (However, 1 cent would grow to almost $1 million in 100 years at 20%.)

SELF-TEST

What is "discounting," and how is it related to compounding? How is the future value Equation (4-1) related to the present value Equation (4-3)?

How does the present value of a future payment change as the time to receipt is lengthened? As the interest rate increases?

Suppose a risk-free bond promises to pay $2,249.73 in 3 years. If the going risk-free interest rate is 4%, how much is the bond worth today? **($2,000)** *How much is the bond worth if it matures in 5 rather than 3 years?* **($1,849.11)** *If the risk-free interest rate is 6% rather than 4%, how much is the 5-year bond worth today?* **($1,681.13)**

How much would $1 million due in 100 years be worth today if the discount rate were 5%? **($7,604.49)** *What if the discount rate were 20%?* **($0.0121)**

4-4 Finding the Interest Rate, I

We have used Equations 4-1, 4-2, and 4-3 to find future and present values. Those equations have four variables, and if we know three of them, then we (or our calculator or *Excel*) can solve for the fourth. Thus, if we know PV, I, and N, we can solve Equation 4-1 for FV, or if we know FV, I, and N, we can solve Equation 4-3 to find PV. That's what we did in the preceding two sections.

Now suppose we know PV, FV, and N, and we want to find I. For example, suppose we know that a given security has a cost of $100 and that it will return $150 after 10 years. Thus, we know PV, FV, and N, and we want to find the rate of return we will earn if we buy the security. Starting with Equation 4-1 and solving for I gives Equation 4-4:

$$I = \left[\frac{FV_N}{PV}\right]^{(1/N)} - 1 \qquad (4\text{-}4)$$

Using Equation 4-4 with the input values, I is 4.14%:

$$I = \left[\frac{\$150}{\$100}\right]^{(1/10)} - 1 = 0.0414 = 4.14\%$$

Finding the interest rate by solving the formula takes a little time and thought, but financial calculators and spreadsheets find the answer almost instantly. Here's the calculator setup:

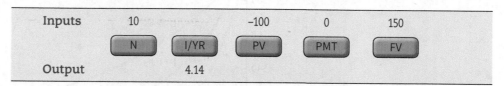

Inputs	10		-100	0	150
	N	I/YR	PV	PMT	FV
Output		4.14			

Enter N = 10, PV = −100, PMT = 0 (because there are no payments until the security matures), and FV = 150. Then, when you press the I/YR key, the calculator gives the answer, 4.14%. Notice that the PV is a negative value because it is a cash outflow (an investment) and the FV is positive because it is a cash inflow (a return of the investment). If you enter both PV and FV as positive numbers (or both as negative numbers), you will get an error message rather than the answer.

resource

See Ch04 Tool Kit.xlsx for all calculations.

In *Excel*, the **RATE** function can be used to find the interest rate: **=RATE(N,PMT,PV,FV)**. For this example, the interest rate is found as **=RATE(10,0,−100,150)** = 0.0414 = 4.14%. See the file ***Ch04 Tool Kit.xlsx*** on the textbook's Web site for an example.

SELF-TEST

*Suppose you can buy a U.S. Treasury bond that makes no payments until the bond matures 10 years from now, at which time it will pay you $1,000. What interest rate would you earn if you bought this bond for $585.43? (**5.5%**) What rate would you earn if you could buy the bond for $550? (**6.16%**) For $600? (**5.24%**)*

*Microsoft earned $0.33 per share in 1997. Fourteen years later, in 2011, it earned $2.75. What was the growth rate in Microsoft's earnings per share (EPS) over the 14-year period? (**16.35%**) If EPS in 2011 had been $2.00 rather than $2.75, what would the growth rate have been? (**13.73%**)*

4-5 Finding the Number of Years, N

We sometimes need to know how long it will take to accumulate a specific sum of money, given our beginning funds and the rate we will earn. For example, suppose we now have $500,000 and the interest rate is 4.5%. How long will it be before we have $1 million? Starting with Equation 4-1 and solving for N gives Equation 4-5:

$$N = \left[\frac{LN(FV_N/PV)}{LN(1 + I)}\right] \tag{4-5}$$

Using Equation 4-5 with the input values, N is:

$$N = \left[\frac{LN(\$1,000,000/\$500,000)}{LN(1 + 0.045)}\right] = 15.7473$$

As you might expect, financial calculator and spreadsheet approaches are easier. Here's the calculator setup:

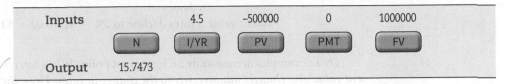

Inputs	4.5	−500000	0	1000000
	N	I/YR	PV	PMT	FV
Output	15.7473			

resource

See *Ch04 Tool Kit.xlsx* for all calculations.

Enter I/YR = 4.5, PV = −500000, PMT = 0, and FV = 1000000. We press the N key to get the answer, 15.7473 years. In *Excel*, we would use the **NPER** function: =**NPER(I,PMT,PV,FV)**. Inserting data, we have =**NPER(0.045,0,−500000,1000000)** = 15.7473. The chapter's tool kit, *Ch04 Tool Kit.xlsx*, shows this example.

SELF-TEST

How long would it take $1,000 to double if it were invested in a bank that pays 6% per year? **(11.9 years)** *How long would it take if the rate were 10%?* **(7.27 years)**

A company's 2013 earnings per share were $2.75, and its growth rate during the prior 14 years was 16.35% per year. If that growth rate were maintained, how long would it take for EPS to double? **(4.58 years)**

4-6 Perpetuities

Section 4-3 showed how to find the present value of a single cash flow occurring N years in the future. However, some types of stocks and bonds pay a fixed amount each period but don't have an ending date.[5] Because the payments are perpetual, this pattern of cash flows is called a **perpetuity**. You can't apply the step-by-step approach because the cash flows never end, but it's easy to find the PV of a perpetuity with the following formula:[6]

$$PV \text{ of a perpetuity} = \frac{PMT}{I} \tag{4-6}$$

For example, suppose the payment is $25 each period and the interest rate is 2.5%. Using Equation 4-6, the PV is:

$$PV = \$25/0.025 = \$1,000$$

What would happen to the present value if interest rates rise to 3%? The present value would fall to $833.33:

$$\text{Present value if rates increase to } 3\% = PV = \$25/0.03 = \$833.33$$

---

[5]Chapters 5 and 7 describe types of bonds and stocks that don't have ending dates for payments.

[6]Here is an intuitive explanation for Equation 4-6. Suppose you deposit an amount equal to PV in a bank that pays an interest rate of I. Each year you would be able to withdraw an amount equal to I × PV. If you left your deposit in forever, you could withdraw a payment of I × PV forever: PMT = I × PV. Rearranging, we get Equation 4-6. This is only an intuitive explanation, so see *Web Extension 4A* on the textbook's Web site for a mathematical derivation of the perpetuity formula.

Note, though, that if interest rates fell to 2%, then the present value would rise to $1,250.00:

$$\text{Present value if rates decline to 2\%} = \$25/0.02 = \$1,250.00$$

These examples demonstrate an important point: *When interest rates change, the present value also changes but inversely to the change in rates.* Thus, the present value **declines** if rates **rise** and **increases** if rates **fall**.

4-7 Annuities

Thus far, we have dealt with a single payment (i.e., a "lump sum") or infinite payments. However, assets such as bonds provide a finite series of cash inflows over time, and obligations such as auto loans, student loans, and mortgages call for a finite series of payments. If the payments are equal and are made at fixed intervals, then we have an **annuity**. For example, $100 paid at the end of each of the next 3 years is a 3-year annuity.

If payments occur at the *end* of each period, then we have an **ordinary annuity**, which is also called a **deferred annuity**. Payments on mortgages, car loans, and student loans are generally made at the ends of the periods and thus are ordinary annuities. If the payments are made at the *beginning* of each period, then we have an **annuity due**. Rental lease payments, life insurance premiums, and lottery payoffs (if you are lucky enough to win one!) are examples of annuities due. Ordinary annuities are more common in finance, so when we use the term "annuity" in this book, you may assume that the payments occur at the ends of the periods unless we state otherwise.

Next we show the time lines for a $100, 3-year, 5%, ordinary annuity and for the same annuity on an annuity due basis. With the annuity due, each payment is shifted back (to the left) by 1 year. In our example, we assume that a $100 payment will be made each year, so we show the payments with minus signs.

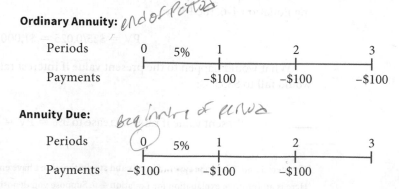

As we demonstrate in the following sections, we can find an annuity's future value, present value, the interest rate built into the contracts, how long it takes to reach a financial goal using the annuity, and, if we know all of those values, the size of the annuity payment. Keep in mind that annuities must have *constant payments* and a *fixed number of periods.* If these conditions don't hold, then the series is not an annuity.

What's the difference between an ordinary annuity and an annuity due?

Why should you prefer to receive an annuity due with payments of $10,000 per year for 10 years than an otherwise similar ordinary annuity?

4-8 Future Value of an Ordinary Annuity

Consider the ordinary annuity whose time line was shown previously, where you deposit $100 at the *end* of each year for 3 years and earn 5% per year. Figure 4-5 shows how to calculate the **future value of the annuity (FVA_N)**, using the same approaches we used for single cash flows.

As shown in the step-by-step section of Figure 4-5, we compound each payment out to Time 3, and then sum those compounded values in Cell F254 to find the annuity's FV, $FVA_3 = \$315.25$ (we ignore the negative signs in the time line to be consistent with the

FIGURE 4-5

Summary: Future Value of an Ordinary Annuity

	A	B	C	D	E	F	G
243	INPUTS:						
244	Payment amount = PMT =		−$100				
245	Interest rate = I =		5.00%				
246	No. of periods = N =		3				
247							
248	1. Step-by-	Periods:	0	1	2	3	
249		Cash flow:		−$100	−$100	−$100	
250				↓	↓	↓	
251				↓	↓	$100.00	
252	Multiply each payment by			↓	L→→	$105.00	
253	$(1+I)^{N-t}$ and sum these FVs to			L→·→→→→→→		$110.25	
254	find FVA_N:					$315.25	
255							
256	2. Formula:						
257							
258	$FVA_N = PMT \times \left(\frac{(1+I)^N}{I} - \frac{1}{I} \right) = PMT \times \left(\frac{(1+I)^N - 1}{I} \right) =$					$315.25	
259							
260							
261		Inputs:	3	5	0	−100	
262	3. Financial Calculator:		N	I/YR	PV	PMT	FV
263	Output:						$315.25
264							
265	4. *Excel* Spreadsheet:	FV function:	$FVA_N =$	=FV(I,N,PMT,PV)			
266		Fixed inputs:	$FVA_N =$	=FV(0.05,3,-100,0)	=	$315.25	
267		Cell references:	$FVA_N =$	=FV(C245,C246,C244,0) =		$315.25	

Source: See the file **Ch04 Tool Kit.xlsx**. Numbers are reported as rounded values for clarity but are calculated using *Excel's* full precision. Thus, intermediate calculations using the figure's rounded values will be inexact.

results from the other methods). The first payment earns interest for two periods, the second for one period, and the third earns no interest because it is made at the end of the annuity's life. This approach is straightforward, but if the annuity extends out for many years, it is cumbersome and time-consuming.

As you can see from the time line diagram, with the step-by-step approach we apply the following equation with N = 3 and I = 5%:

$$FVA_N = PMT(1 + I)^{N-1} + PMT(1 + I)^{N-2} + PMT(1 + I)^{N-3}$$
$$= \$100(1.05)^2 + \$100(1.05)^1 + \$100(1.05)^0$$
$$= \$315.25$$

For the general case, the future value of an annuity is:

$$FVA_N = PMT(1 + I)^{N-1} + PMT(1 + I)^{N-2} + PMT(1 + I)^{N-3} + \cdots + PMT(1 + I)^0$$

As shown in **Web Extension 4A** on the textbook's Web site, the future value of an annuity can be written as follows:[7]

$$FVA_N = PMT\left[\frac{(1 + I)^N}{I} - \frac{1}{I}\right] = PMT\left[\frac{(1 + I)^N - 1}{I}\right] \qquad (4\text{-}7)$$

Using Equation 4-7, the future value of the annuity is $315.25:

$$FVA_3 = \$100\left[\frac{(1 + 0.05)^3 - 1}{0.05}\right] = \$315.25$$

As you might expect, annuity problems can be solved easily using a financial calculator or a spreadsheet. The procedure when dealing with annuities is similar to what we have done thus far for single payments, but the presence of recurring payments means that we must use the PMT key. Here's the calculator setup for our illustrative annuity:

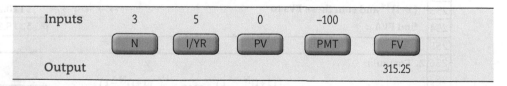

Inputs	3	5	0	–100	
	N	I/YR	PV	PMT	FV
Output					315.25

We enter PV = 0 because we start off with nothing, and we enter PMT = −100 because we will deposit this amount in the account at the end of each of the 3 years. The interest rate is 5%, and when we press the FV key we get the answer, FVA₃ = 315.25.

Because this is an ordinary annuity, with payments coming at the *end* of each year, we must set the calculator appropriately. As noted earlier, most calculators "come out of the box" set to assume that payments occur at the end of each period—that is, to deal with ordinary annuities. However, there is a key that enables us to switch between ordinary annuities and annuities due. For ordinary annuities, the designation "End Mode" or something

---

[7]Section 4-6 shows that the present value of an infinitely long annuity, called a "perpetuity," is equal to PMT/I. The cash flows of an ordinary annuity of N periods are equal to the cash flows of a perpetuity minus the cash flows of a perpetuity that begins at year N + 1. Therefore, the future value of an N-period annuity is equal to the future value (as of year N) of a perpetuity minus the value (as of year N) of a perpetuity that begins at year N + 1. See **Web Extension 4A** on the textbook's Web site for details regarding derivations of Equation 4-7.

The Power of Compound Interest

Assume that you are 26 and just received your MBA. After reading the introduction to this chapter, you decide to start investing in the stock market for your retirement. Your goal is to have $1 million when you retire at age 65. Assuming you earn 10% annually on your stock investments, how much must you invest at the end of each year in order to reach your goal?

The answer is $2,491, but this amount depends critically on the return your investments earn. If your return drops to 8%, the required annual contribution would rise to $4,185. On the other hand, if the return rises to 12%, you would need to put away only $1,462 per year.

What if you are like most 26-year-olds and wait until later to worry about retirement? If you wait until age 40, you will need to save $10,168 per year to reach your $1 million goal, assuming you can earn 10%, but $13,679 per year if you earn only 8%. If you wait until age 50 and then earn 8%, the required amount will be $36,830 per year!

Although $1 million may seem like a lot of money, it won't be when you get ready to retire. If inflation averages 5% a year over the next 39 years, then your $1 million nest egg would be worth only $149,148 in today's dollars. If you live for 20 years after retirement and earn a real 3% rate of return, your annual retirement income in today's dollars would be only $9,733 before taxes. So, after celebrating your graduation and new job, start saving!

calculator

resource

See Ch04 Tool Kit.xlsx for all calculations.

similar is used, while for annuities due, the designator is "Begin," "Begin Mode," "Due," or something similar. If you make a mistake and set your calculator on Begin Mode when working with an ordinary annuity, then each payment will earn interest for 1 extra year, which will cause the compounded amounts, and thus the FVA, to be too large.

The spreadsheet approach uses *Excel*'s **FV** function, **=FV(I,N,PMT,PV)**. In our example, we have **=FV(0.05,3,−100,0)**, and the result is again $315.25.

SELF-TEST

For an ordinary annuity with 5 annual payments of $100 and a 10% interest rate, for how many years will the first payment earn interest, and what is the compounded value of this payment at the end? **(4 years, $146.41)** *Answer these questions for the fifth payment.* **(0 years, $100)**

Assume that you plan to buy a condo 5 years from now, and you estimate that you can save $2,500 per year toward a down payment. You plan to deposit the money in a bank that pays 4% interest, and you will make the first deposit at the end of this year. How much will you have after 5 years? **($13,540.81)** *How would your answer change if the bank's interest rate were increased to 6%, or decreased to 3%?* **($14,092.73; $13,272.84)**

4-9 Future Value of an Annuity Due

Because each payment occurs one period earlier with an annuity due, the payments will all earn interest for one additional period. Therefore, the FV of an annuity due will be greater than that of a similar ordinary annuity.

If you followed the step-by-step procedure, you would see that our illustrative annuity due has a FV of $331.01 versus $315.25 for the ordinary annuity. See ***Ch04 Tool Kit.xlsx*** on the textbook's Web site for a summary of future value calculations.

With the formula approach, we first use Equation 4-7, but because each payment occurs one period earlier, we multiply the Equation 4-7 result by $(1 + I)$:

$$\text{FVA}_{\text{due}} = \text{FVA}_{\text{ordinary}}(1 + I) \tag{4-8}$$

Thus, for the annuity due, $\text{FVA}_{\text{due}} = \$315.25(1.05) = \$331.01$, which is the same result as found with the step-by-step approach.

With a calculator, we input the variables just as we did with the ordinary annuity, but we now set the calculator to Begin Mode to get the answer, $331.01:

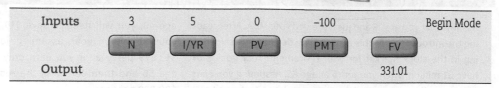

Inputs	3	5	0	−100	Begin Mode
	N	I/YR	PV	PMT	FV
Output					331.01

resource

See *Ch04 Tool Kit.xlsx* for all calculations.

In *Excel*, we still use the FV function, but we must indicate that we have an annuity due. The function is =**FV(I,N,PMT,PV,Type)**, where "Type" indicates the type of annuity. If Type is omitted, then *Excel* assumes that it is 0, which indicates an ordinary annuity. For an annuity due, Type = 1. As shown in *Ch04 Tool Kit.xlsx*, the function is =**FV(0.05,3,−100,0,1)** = $331.01.

SELF-TEST

Why does an annuity due always have a higher future value than an ordinary annuity?

If you know the value of an ordinary annuity, explain why you could find the value of the corresponding annuity due by multiplying by (1 + I).

Assume that you plan to buy a condo 5 years from now and that you need to save for a down payment. You plan to save $2,500 per year, with the first payment being made immediately and deposited in a bank that pays 4%. How much will you have after 5 years? (**$14,082.44**) *How much would you have if you made the deposits at the end of each year?* (**$13,540.81**)

4-10 Present Value of Ordinary Annuities and Annuities Due

The **present value of any annuity (PVA$_N$)** can be found using the step-by-step, formula, calculator, or spreadsheet method. We begin with ordinary annuities.

4-10a Present Value of an Ordinary Annuity

resource

See *Ch04 Tool Kit.xlsx* for all calculations.

See Figure 4-6 for a summary of the different approaches for calculating the present value of an ordinary annuity.

As shown in the step-by-step section of Figure 4-6, we discount each payment back to Time 0, and then sum those discounted values to find the annuity's present value, PVA$_3$ = $272.32. (We ignore the negative signs in the time line to be consistent with the results from the other methods.) This approach is straightforward, but if the annuity extends out for many years, it is cumbersome and time-consuming.

The time line diagram shows that with the step-by-step approach we apply the following equation with N = 3 and I = 5%:

$$PVA_N = PMT/(1 + I)^1 + PMT/(1 + I)^2 + \cdots + PMT/(1 + I)^N$$

The present value of an annuity can be written as:[8]

$$PVA_N = PMT\left[\frac{1}{I} - \frac{1}{I(1 + I)^N}\right]$$

(4-9)

---

[8]See **Web Extension 4A** on the textbook's Web site for details of this derivation.

FIGURE 4-6
Summary: Present Value of an Ordinary Annuity

end

	A	B	C	D	E	F	G
313	INPUTS:						
314	Payment amount = PMT =		–$100				
315	Interest rate = I =		5.00%				
316	No. of periods = N =		3				
317							
318	1. Step-by-	Periods:	0	1	2	3	
319		Cash flow:		–$100	–$100	–$100	
320				↓	↓	↓	
321			$95.24	←←⌐	↓	↓	
322	Divide each payment by		$90.70	←←←←←←	←←⌐	↓	
323	$(1+I)^t$ and sum these PVs to		$86.38	←←←←←←	←←←←←←	←←⌐	
324	find PVA$_N$:		$272.32				
325							
326	2. Formula:						
327							
328		$PVA_N = PMT \times \left(\dfrac{1}{I} - \dfrac{1}{I(1+I)^N}\right) =$				$272.32	
329							
330							
331							
332		Inputs:	3	5		–100	0
333	3. Financial Calculator:		N	I	PV	PMT	FV
334		Output:			272.32		
335							
336	4. *Excel* Spreadsheet:	PV function:	PVA$_N$ =	=PV(I,N,PMT,FV)			
337		Fixed inputs:	PVA$_N$ =	=PV(0.05,3,-100,0) =		$272.32	
338		Cell references:	PVA$_N$ =	=PV(C315,C316,C314,0) =		$272.32	

Source: See the file *Ch04 Tool Kit.xlsx*. Numbers are reported as rounded values for clarity but are calculated using *Excel*'s full precision. Thus, intermediate calculations using the figure's rounded values will be inexact.

For our example annuity, the present value is:

$$PVA_3 = \$100\left[\frac{1}{0.05} - \frac{1}{0.05(1+0.05)^3}\right] = \$272.32$$

Financial calculators are programmed to solve Equation 4-2, so we input the variables and press the PV key, *first making sure the calculator is set to End Mode.* The calculator setup is shown here:

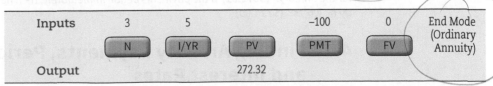

Inputs	3	5		–100	0	End Mode (Ordinary Annuity)
	N	I/YR	PV	PMT	FV	
Output			272.32			

resource

See *Ch04 Tool Kit.xlsx* for all calculations.

The last section of Figure 4-6 shows the spreadsheet solution using *Excel*'s built-in PV function: =**PV(I,N,PMT,FV)**. In our example, we have =**PV(0.05,3,−100,0)** with a resulting value of $272.32.

4-10b Present Value of Annuities Due

Because each payment for an annuity due occurs one period earlier, the payments will all be discounted for one less period. Therefore, the PV of an annuity due must be greater than that of a similar ordinary annuity.

If you went through the step-by-step procedure, you would see that our example annuity due has a PV of $285.94 versus $272.32 for the ordinary annuity. See **Ch04 Tool Kit.xlsx** for this and the other calculations.

With the formula approach, we first use Equation 4-9 to find the value of the ordinary annuity and then, because each payment now occurs one period earlier, we multiply the value given by Equation 4-9 by $(1 + I)$:

$$PVA_{due} = PVA_{ordinary}(1 + I) \tag{4-10}$$

$$PVA_{due} = \$272.32(1.05) = \$285.94$$

With a financial calculator, the inputs are the same as for an ordinary annuity, except you must set the calculator to Begin Mode:

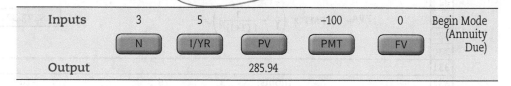

Inputs	3	5		−100	0	Begin Mode (Annuity Due)
	N	I/YR	PV	PMT	FV	
Output			285.94			

In *Excel*, we again use the **PV** function, but now we must indicate that we have an annuity due. The function is now =**PV(I,N,PMT,FV,Type)**, where "Type" is the type of annuity. If Type is omitted then *Excel* assumes that it is 0, which indicates an ordinary annuity; for an annuity due, Type = 1. As shown in **Ch04 Tool Kit.xlsx**, the function for this example is =**PV(0.05,3,−100,0,1)** = $285.94.

Why does an annuity due have a higher present value than an ordinary annuity?

If you know the present value of an ordinary annuity, what's an easy way to find the PV of the corresponding annuity due?

What is the PVA of an ordinary annuity with 10 payments of $100 if the appropriate interest rate is 10%? **($614.46)** *What would the PVA be if the interest rate were 4%?* **($811.09)** *What if the interest rate were 0%?* **($1,000.00)** *What would the PVAs be if we were dealing with annuities due?* **($675.90, $843.53, and $1,000.00)**

Assume that you are offered an annuity that pays $100 at the end of each year for 10 years. You could earn 8% on your money in other equally risky investments. What is the most you should pay for the annuity? **($671.01)** *If the payments began immediately, then how much would the annuity be worth?* **($724.69)**

4-11 Finding Annuity Payments, Periods, and Interest Rates

In the three preceding sections, we discussed how to find the FV and PV of ordinary annuities and annuities due, using these four methods: step-by-step, formula, financial calculator, and *Excel*. Five variables are involved—N, I, PMT, FV, and PV—and if you

Variable Annuities: Good or Bad?

Retirees appreciate stable, predictable income, so they often buy annuities. Insurance companies have been the traditional suppliers, using the payments they receive to buy high-grade bonds, whose interest is then used to make the promised payments. Such annuities were quite safe and stable and provided returns of around 7.5%. However, returns on stocks (dividends plus capital gains) have historically exceeded bonds' returns (interest). Therefore, some insurance companies in the 1990s began to offer *variable annuities*, which were backed by stocks instead of bonds. If stocks earned in the future as much as they had in the past, then variable annuities could offer returns of about 9%; this is better than the return on fixed-rate annuities. If stock returns turned out to be lower in the future than they had been in the past (or even had negative returns), then the variable annuities promised a *guaranteed minimum payment* of about 6.5%. Variable annuities appealed to many retirees, so companies that offered them had a significant competitive advantage.

The insurance company that pioneered variable annuities, The Hartford Financial Services Group, tried to hedge its position with derivatives that paid off if stocks went down. But like so many other derivatives-based risk management programs, this one went awry in 2008 because stock losses exceeded the assumed worst-case scenario. The Hartford, which was founded in 1810 and was one of the oldest and largest U.S. insurance companies at the beginning of 2008, saw its stock price fall from $85.54 per share to $4.16. Because of the general stock market crash, investors feared that The Hartford would be unable to make good on its variable annuity promises, and this would lead to bankruptcy. The company was bailed out by the economic stimulus package, but this venerable old firm will never be the same again.

Source: Leslie Scism and Liam Pleven, "Hartford Aims to Take Risk Out of Annuities," *Online Wall Street Journal*, January 13, 2009.

know any four, you can find the fifth by solving Equation 4-2 for ordinary annuities (for annuities due, substitute PMT(1+I) for PMT in Equation 4-2 and solve for the unknown variable). However, a trial-and-error procedure is generally required to find N or I, and that can be quite tedious if performed manually. Therefore, we discuss only the financial calculator and spreadsheet approaches for finding N and I.

4-11a Finding Annuity Payments, PMT

We need to accumulate $10,000 and have it available 5 years from now. We can earn 6% on our money. Thus, we know that FV = 10,000, PV = 0, N = 5, and I/YR = 6. We can enter these values in a financial calculator and then press the PMT key to find our required deposits. However, the answer depends on whether we make deposits at the end of each year (ordinary annuity) or at the beginning (annuity due), so the mode must be set properly. Here are the results for each type of annuity:

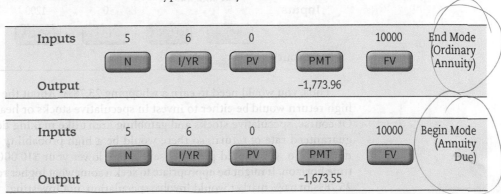

Thus, you must put away $1,773.96 per year if you make payments at the *end* of each year, but only $1,673.55 if the payments begin *immediately*. Finally, note that the required payment for the annuity due is the ordinary annuity payment divided by (1 + I): $1,773.96/1.06 = $1,673.55.

Excel can also be used to find annuity payments, as shown here for the two types of annuities. For end-of-year (ordinary) annuities, "Type" can be left blank or a 0 can be inserted. For beginning-of-year annuities (annuities due), the same function is used but now Type is designated as 1. Here is the setup for the two types of annuities.

resource

See **Ch04 Tool Kit.xlsx** for all calculations.

Function: = **PMT(I,N,PV,FV,Type)**
Ordinary annuity: = **PMT(0.06,5,0,10000)**   = −$1,773.96
Annuity due: = **PMT(0.06,5,0,10000,1)** = − $1,673.55

4-11b Finding the Number of Periods, N

Suppose you decide to make end-of-year deposits, but you can save only $1,200 per year. Again assuming that you would earn 6%, how long would it take you to reach your $10,000 goal? Here is the calculator setup:

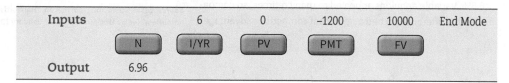

resource

See **Ch04 Tool Kit.xlsx** for all calculations.

With these smaller deposits, it would take 6.96 years, not 5 years, to reach the $10,000 target. If you began the deposits immediately, then you would have an annuity due and N would be slightly less, 6.63 years.

With *Excel*, you can use the **NPER** function: =**NPER(I,PMT,PV,FV, Type)**. For our ordinary annuity example, Type is left blank (or 0 is inserted) and the function is =**NPER(0.06,−1200,0,10000)** = 6.96. If we put in 1 for Type, we would find N = 6.63.

4-11c Finding the Interest Rate, I

Now suppose you can save only $1,200 annually, but you still need to have the $10,000 in 5 years. What rate of return would you have to earn to reach your goal? Here is the calculator setup:

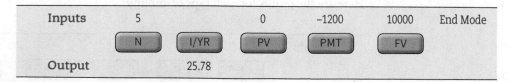

Thus, you would need to earn a whopping 25.78%! About the only way to earn such a high return would be either to invest in speculative stocks or head to a Las Vegas casino. Of course, speculative stocks and gambling aren't like making deposits in a bank with a guaranteed rate of return, so there would be a high probability that you'd end up with nothing. So, you should probably save more, lower your $10,000 target, or extend your time horizon. It might be appropriate to seek a somewhat higher return, but trying to earn 25.78% in a 6% market would involve speculation, not investing.

Using the Internet for Personal Financial Planning

How good are your financial planning skills? For example, should you buy or lease a car? How much and how soon should you begin to save for your children's education? How expensive a house can you afford? Should you refinance your home mortgage? How much must you save each year if you want to retire comfortably? The answers to these questions are often complicated and depend on a number of factors, such as projected housing and education costs, interest rates, inflation, expected family income, and stock market returns.

Fortunately, you should be able to use time value of money concepts and online resources to begin developing

your financial plan. In addition to the online data sources described in Chapter 2, excellent sources of information are available through the National Endowment for Financial Education (NEFE), a not-for-profit foundation whose mission is to provide "educated financial decision making for individuals and families through every stage of life." If you go to their Web site, **www.nefe.org** and scroll to the bottom of the page, look on the right for "*Other NEFE Resources*." These include helpful information, especially Smart About Money (SAM), which has a helpful financial calculator to help you run the numbers for a variety of topics. You can go to this Web site directly at **www.smartaboutmoney.org**.

In *Excel*, you can use the **RATE** function: **=RATE(N,PMT,PV,FV,Type)**. For our example, the function is **=RATE(5,−1200,0,10000)** = 0.2578 = 25.78%. If you decide to make the payments beginning immediately then the required rate of return would decline sharply, to 17.54%.

4-12 Uneven, or Irregular, Cash Flows

The definition of an annuity includes the term *constant payment,* which suggests that annuities involve a set of identical payments over a given number of periods. Although many financial decisions do involve constant payments, many others involve cash flows that differ from year to year. These are called **uneven cash flow streams** or **irregular cash flow streams**. For example, the dividends on common stocks are typically expected to increase over time, and the investments that companies make in new products, expanded production capacity, and replacement machinery almost always generate cash flows that vary from year to year. Throughout the book, we use the term *payment* (PMT) in situations where the cash flows are constant and thus an annuity is involved; if different cash flows occur in different time periods, t, then we use the term CF_t to designate the *cash flow* in period t.

There are two important classes of uneven cash flows: (1) those in which the cash flow stream consists of a series of annuity payments plus an additional final lump sum in Year N and (2) all other uneven streams. Bonds are an instance of the first type, while stocks and capital investments illustrate the second type. Here's an example of each type.

Stream 1. Annuity plus an additional final payment:

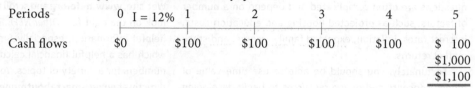

Stream 2. Irregular cash flow stream:

Periods	0	I = 12%	1	2	3	4	5
Cash flows	$0		$100	$300	$300	$300	$500

To find the PV of either stream, you could use the step-by-step procedure of Equation 4-11:

$$PV = \frac{CF_1}{(1+I)^1} + \frac{CF_2}{(1+I)^2} + \cdots + \frac{CF_N}{(1+I)^N} = \sum_{t=1}^{N} \frac{CF_t}{(1+I)^t} \qquad \text{(4-11)}$$

However, as we shall see, the solution process differs significantly for the two types.

4-12a Annuity Plus Additional Final Payment

First, consider Stream 1 and notice that it is a 5-year, 12%, ordinary annuity plus a final payment of $1,000. We can find the PV of the annuity, find the PV of the final payment, and then sum them to get the PV of the stream. Financial calculators are programmed to do this for us—we use all five time value of money (TVM) keys, entering the data for the four known values as shown below, and then pressing the PV key to get the answer:

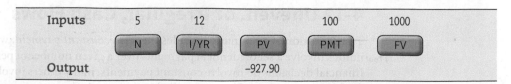

In *Excel*, use the **PV** function: **=PV(I,N,PMT,FV)**. For this example, use **=PV(0.12,5,100,1000)** = −$927.90.

Whether you use a financial calculator or *Excel* to find the present value of the cash flow stream, notice that each approach is similar to the ones used for annuities. The only difference is that there is a nonzero value for FV.

4-12b Irregular Cash Flow Stream

Now consider the irregular stream shown in Figure 4-7. Section 1 shows the basic time line, which contains the inputs, and we first use the step-by-step approach to find PV = $1,016.35. Note that we show the PV of each cash flow directly below the cash flow, and then we sum these PVs to find the PV of the stream.

With a financial calculator, you can't use the TVM sub-menu because the periodic cash flows aren't constant. Instead, go to the calculator's main menu and select the sub-menu for cash flows, which may be labeled "CFLO" or something similar. This sub-menu has a feature—the cash flow register—that allows you to input the individual cash flows in chronological order.[9] Cash flows are designated CF_0, CF_1, CF_2, CF_3, and so on, up to the last cash flow, CF_N. Next, you enter the interest rate, I/YR. At this point, you have substituted in all the known values of Equation 4-11, so when you press the NPV key, you get the PV of the irregular cash flow stream. To input the cash flows for this problem, enter 0 (because $CF_0 = 0$), 100, 300, 300, 300, and 500 in that order into the cash flow register, enter I/YR = 12, and then press NPV to obtain the answer, $1,016.35.

resource

See *Ch04 Tool Kit.xlsx* for all calculations.

FIGURE 4-7
Present Value of an Irregular Cash Flow Stream

	A	B	C	D	E	F	G
466	INPUTS:						
467		Interest rate = I =	12%				
468							
469	1. Step-by-Step:						
470	Periods:	0	1	2	3	4	5
471	Cash flow:	$0.00	$100.00	$300.00	$300.00	$300.00	$500.00
472	of the CFs:		$89.29	$239.16	$213.53	$190.66	$283.71
473	m of PVs =	$1,016.35					
474							
475							
476	2. Financial Calculator:						
477		Enter the cash flows into the cash flow register of a financial calculator, enter I/YR, and then press the NPV key to find the answer.					$1,016.35
478							
479	3. *Excel* Spreadsheet:						
480			Excel NPV function:	=NPV(I,Cash flows)			$1,016.35
481			Fixed inputs:	=NPV(0.12,100,300,300,300,500)			$1,016.35
482			Cell references:	=NPV(C467,C471:G471)			$1,016.35

Source: See the file *Ch04 Tool Kit.xlsx*. Numbers are reported as rounded values for clarity but are calculated using *Excel*'s full precision. Thus, intermediate calculations using the figure's rounded values will be inexact.

---

[9]These instructions are for the HP 10bII+, but most other financial calculators work in a similar manner.

Two points should be noted. First, when dealing with the cash flow register, the calculator uses the term "NPV" rather than "PV." The N stands for "net," so NPV is the abbreviation for "net present value," which is simply the net present value of a series of positive and negative cash flows, including any cash flow at time zero. The **NPV** function will be used extensively when we get to capital budgeting, where CF_0 is generally the cost of the project.

The second point to note is that repeated cash flows with identical values can be entered into the cash flow register more efficiently on some calculators by using the Nj key. In this illustration, you would enter $CF_0 = 0$, $CF_1 = 100$, $CF_2 = 300$, Nj = 3 (which tells the calculator that the 300 occurs 3 times), and $CF_5 = 500$.[10] Then enter I = 12, press the NPV key, and 1,016.35 will appear in the display. Also, note that numbers entered into the cash flow register remain in the register until they are cleared. Thus, if you previously worked a problem with eight cash flows, and then moved to one with only four cash flows, the calculator would simply add the cash flows from the second problem to those of the first problem, and you would get an incorrect answer. Therefore, you must be sure to clear the cash flow register before starting a new problem.

Spreadsheets are especially useful for solving problems with uneven cash flows. You enter the cash flows in the spreadsheet as shown in Figure 4-7 on Row 471. To find the PV of these cash flows without going through the step-by-step process, you would use the *Excel* **NPV** function. First put the cursor on the cell where you want the answer to appear, Cell G482, click the function wizard, choose Financial, scroll down to NPV, and click OK to get the dialog box. Then enter C467 (or 0.12) for Rate and enter either the individual cash flows or the range of cells containing the cash flows, C471:G471, for Value 1. Be very careful when entering the range of cash flows. With a financial calculator, you begin by entering the Time-0 cash flow. With *Excel,* you do *not* include the Time-0 cash flow; instead, you begin with the Time-1 cash flow. Now, when you click OK, you get the PV of the stream, $1,016.35. Note that you can use the **PV** function if the payments are constant, but you must use the **NPV** function if the cash flows are not constant. Finally, note that *Excel* has a major advantage over financial calculators in that you can see the cash flows, which makes it easy to spot data-entry errors. With a calculator, the numbers are buried in the machine, making it harder to check your work.

SELF-TEST

Could you use Equation 4-3, once for each cash flow, to find the PV of an uneven stream of cash flows?

What is the present value of a 5-year ordinary annuity of $100 plus an additional $500 at the end of Year 5 if the interest rate is 6%? **($794.87)** *What would the PV be if the $100 payments occurred in Years 1 through 10 and the $500 came at the end of Year 10?* **($1,015.21)**

What is the present value of the following uneven cash flow stream: $0 at Time 0, $100 at the end of Year 1 (or at Time 1), $200 at the end of Year 2, $0 at the end of Year 3, and $400 at the end of Year 4—assuming the interest rate is 8%? **($558.07)**

Would a "typical" common stock provide cash flows more like an annuity or more like an uneven cash flow stream?

---

[10]On some calculators, instead of entering $CF_5 = 500$, you enter $CF_3 = 500$ because this is the next cash flow *different* from 300.

4-13 Future Value of an Uneven Cash Flow Stream

The future value of an uneven cash flow stream is found by compounding each payment to the end of the stream and then summing the future values:

$$FV = CF_0(1 + I)^N + CF_1(1 + I)^{N-1} + CF_2(1 + I)^{N-2} + \cdots + CF_{N-1}(1 + I) + CF_N$$

$$= \sum_{t=0}^{N} CF_t(1 + I)^{N-t}$$

(4-12)

The future value of this uneven cash flow stream is $1,791.15, as shown in Figure 4-8.

Most financial calculators have a net future value (NFV) key, which, after the cash flows and interest rate have been entered, can be used to obtain the future value of an uneven cash flow stream. If your calculator doesn't have the NFV feature, you can first find the net present value of the stream, and then find its net future value as $NFV = NPV(1 + I)^N$. In the illustrative problem, we find PV = 1,016.35 using the cash flow register and I = 12. Then we use the TVM register, entering N = 5, I = 12, PV = −1016.35, and PMT = 0. When we press FV, we find FV = 1,791.15, which is the same as the value shown on the time line in Figure 4-8. As Figure 4-8 also shows, the same procedure can be used with *Excel*.

SELF-TEST

What is the future value of this cash flow stream: $100 at the end of 1 year, $150 after 2 years, and $300 after 3 years, assuming the appropriate interest rate is 15%? **($604.75)**

FIGURE 4-8
Future Value of an Irregular Cash Flow Stream

	A	B	C	D	E	F	G
498	INPUTS:						
499		Interest rate = I =	12%				
500							
501	1. Step-by-Step:						
502	Periods:	0	1	2	3	4	5
503	Cash flow:	$0.00	$100.00	$300.00	$300.00	$300.00	$500.00
504	of the CFs:		$157.35	$421.48	$376.32	$336.00	$500.00
505						Sum of FV's =	$1,791.15
506							
507							
508	2. Financial Calculator:						
509		Enter the cash flows into the cash flow register of a financial calculator, enter I/YR, and then press the NFV key to find the answer.					$1,791.15
510							
511	3. *Excel* Spreadsheet:						
512		Step 1. Find NPV:			=NPV(C499,C503:G503)		$1,016.35
513		Step 2. Compound NPV to find NFV:			=FV(C499,G502,0,-G512)		$1,791.15

Source: See the file **Ch04 Tool Kit.xlsx**. Numbers are reported as rounded values for clarity but are calculated using *Excel*'s full precision. Thus, intermediate calculations using the figure's rounded values will be inexact.

4-14 Solving for I with Irregular Cash Flows

Before financial calculators and spreadsheets existed, it was *extremely difficult* to find I if the cash flows were uneven. However, with spreadsheets and financial calculators it's easy to find I. If you have an *annuity plus a final lump sum,* you can input values for N, PV, PMT, and FV into the calculator's TVM registers and then press the I/YR key. Here's the setup for Stream 1 from Section 4-12, assuming we must pay $927.90 to buy the asset:

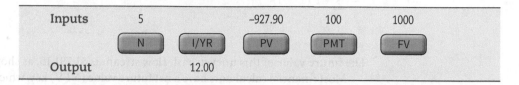

Inputs	5		–927.90	100	1000
	N	I/YR	PV	PMT	FV
Output		12.00			

The rate of return on the $927.90 investment is 12%.

Finding the interest rate for an *irregular cash flow stream* with a calculator is a bit more complicated. Figure 4-9 shows Stream 2 from Section 4-12, assuming a required investment of $CF_0 = -\$1,000$. First, note that there is no simple step-by-step method for finding the rate of return; finding the rate for this investment requires a trial-and-error process, which is terribly time-consuming. Therefore, we always use a financial calculator or a spreadsheet. With a calculator, we would enter the CFs into the cash flow register and then press the IRR key to get the answer. IRR stands for "internal rate of return," and it is the rate of return the investment provides. The investment is the cash flow at Time 0, and it must be entered as a negative number. When we enter those cash flows in the calculator's cash flow register and press the IRR key, we get the rate of return on the $1,000 investment, 12.55%. Finally, note that once you have entered the cash flows in the calculator's register, you can find both the investment's net present value (NPV) and its internal rate of return. For investment decisions, we typically want both of these numbers. Therefore, we generally enter the data once and then find both the NPV and the IRR.

You would get the same answer using *Excel*'s **IRR** function, as shown in Figure 4-9. Notice that when using the **IRR**—unlike using the **NPV** function—you must include all cash flows, including the Time-0 cash flow.

FIGURE 4-9
IRR of an Uneven Cash Flow Stream

	A	B	C	D	E	F	G
545	**Periods:**	0	1	2	3	4	5
546	**Cash flows:**	-$1,000	$100	$300	$300	$300	$500
547							
548	1. Calculator:	You could enter the cash flows into the cash flow register of a financial calculator and then press the IRR key to find the answer.					12.55%
549							
550	2. *Excel* IRR Function:	Cell references:		IRR =	=IRR(B546:G546)		12.55%

Source: See the file **Ch04 Tool Kit.xlsx**. Numbers are reported as rounded values for clarity but are calculated using *Excel*'s full precision. Thus, intermediate calculations using the figure's rounded values will be inexact.

An investment costs $465 now and is expected to produce cash flows of $100 at the end of each of the next 4 years, plus an extra lump-sum payment of $200 at the end of the fourth year. What is the expected rate of return on this investment? **(9.05%)**

An investment costs $465 and is expected to produce cash flows of $100 at the end of Year 1, $200 at the end of Year 2, and $300 at the end of Year 3. What is the expected rate of return on this investment? **(11.71%)**

4-15 Semiannual and Other Compounding Periods

In most of our examples thus far, we assumed that interest is compounded once a year, or annually. This is **annual compounding**. Suppose, however, that you put $1,000 into a bank that pays a 6% annual interest rate but credits interest every 6 months. This is **semiannual compounding**. If you leave your funds in the account, how much would you have at the end of 1 year under semiannual compounding? Note that you will receive $60 of interest for the year with annual compounding. With semiannual compounding, you will receive $30 of it after only 6 months, and you will earn interest on the first $30 during the second 6 months, so you will end the year with more than the $60 you would have had under annual compounding. You would be even better off under quarterly, monthly, weekly, or daily compounding. Note also that virtually all bonds pay interest semiannually; most stocks pay dividends quarterly; most mortgages, student loans, and auto loans involve monthly payments; and most money fund accounts pay interest daily. Therefore, it is essential that you understand how to deal with nonannual compounding.

4-15a Types of Interest Rates

When we move beyond annual compounding, we must deal with the following four types of interest rates:

1. Nominal annual rates, given the symbol I_{NOM}
2. Periodic rates, denoted as I_{PER}
3. Effective annual rates, given the symbol **EAR** or **EFF%**
4. Annual percentage rates, termed **APR** rates

NOMINAL (OR QUOTED) RATE, I_{NOM}[11]

The **nominal annual interest rate** (I_{NOM}), or just the *nominal rate*, is the rate quoted by banks, brokers, and other financial institutions. So, if you talk with a banker, broker, mortgage lender, auto finance company, or student loan officer about rates, the nominal rate is the one he or she will normally quote you. However, to be meaningful, the quoted nominal rate must also include the number of compounding periods per year. For example, a bank might offer you a CD at 6% compounded daily, while a credit union might offer 6.1% compounded monthly.

---

[11]The term *nominal rate* as used here does not have the same meaning as it did in Chapter 1. There, nominal interest rates referred to stated market rates as opposed to real (zero-inflation) rates. In this chapter, the term *nominal rate* means the stated, or quoted, annual rate as opposed to the effective annual rate, which we explain later. In both cases, though, *nominal* means *stated*, or *quoted*, as opposed to some sort of adjusted rate.

Note that we never show the nominal rate on a time line, and we never use it as an input to a financial calculator (except when compounding occurs only once a year).[12] If more frequent compounding occurs, we use periodic rates as explained next.

PERIODIC RATE, I$_{PER}$

The **periodic rate (I$_{PER}$)** is the rate charged by a lender or paid by a borrower each period. It can be a rate per year, per 6 months (semiannually), per quarter, per month, per day, or per any other time interval. For example, a bank might charge 1.5% per month on its credit card loans, or a finance company might charge 3% per quarter on installment loans.

We find the periodic rate as follows:

$$\text{Periodic rate } I_{PER} = I_{NOM}/M \qquad (4\text{-}13)$$

where I$_{NOM}$ is the nominal annual rate and M is the number of compounding periods per year. Thus, a 6% nominal rate with semiannual payments results in a periodic rate of

$$\text{Periodic rate } I_{PER} = 6\%/2 = 3.00\%$$

If only one payment is made per year, then M = 1, in which case the periodic rate would equal the nominal rate: 6%/1 = 6%.

The periodic rate is the rate shown on time lines and used in calculations.[13] To illustrate, suppose you invest $100 in an account that pays a nominal rate of 12%, compounded quarterly, or 3% per period. How much would you have after 2 years if you leave the funds on deposit? First, here is the time line for the problem:

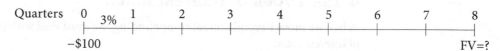

Quarters   0   3%   1   2   3   4   5   6   7   8
            |⸺⸺⸺⸺|⸺⸺⸺⸺|⸺⸺⸺⸺|⸺⸺⸺⸺|⸺⸺⸺⸺|⸺⸺⸺⸺|⸺⸺⸺⸺|⸺⸺⸺⸺|
         −$100   FV=?

To find the FV, we would use this modified version of Equation 4-1:

$$FV_N = PV(1 + I_{PER})^{\text{Number of periods}} = PV\left[\left(1 + \frac{I_{NOM}}{M}\right)\right]^{MN} \qquad (4\text{-}14)$$

$$= \$100\left(1 + \frac{0.12}{4}\right)^{4 \times 2} = \$100(1 + 0.03)^8 = \$126.68$$

---

[12]Some calculators have a feature so that you can input the nominal rate and the number of periods per year. It is easy to make mistakes with this approach, which is why we do not use nominal rates in our calculations.

[13]The only exception is in cases where (1) annuities are involved *and* (2) the payment periods do not correspond to the compounding periods. In such cases—for example, if you are making quarterly payments into a bank account to build up a specified future sum but the bank pays interest on a daily basis—then the calculations are more complicated. For such problems, the simplest procedure is to determine the periodic (daily) interest rate by dividing the nominal rate by 365 (or by 360 if the bank uses a 360-day year), then compound each payment over the exact number of days from the payment date to the terminal point, and then sum the compounded payments to find the future value of the annuity. This is a simple process with a computer.

With a financial calculator, we find the FV using these inputs: N = 4 × 2 = 8, I = 12/4 = 3, PV = −100, and PMT = 0. The result is again FV = $126.68:[14]

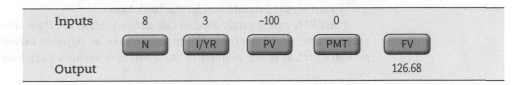

Inputs	8	3	−100	0	
	N	I/YR	PV	PMT	FV
Output					126.68

EFFECTIVE (OR EQUIVALENT) ANNUAL RATE (EAR OR EFF%)

The **effective (or equivalent) annual rate (EAR or EFF%)** is the annual (interest once a year) rate that produces the same final result as compounding at the periodic rate for M times per year. The EAR, also called EFF% (for effective percentage rate), is found as follows:[15]

$$EAR = EFF\% = (1 + I_{PER})^M - 1.0$$

$$= \left(1 + \frac{I_{NOM}}{M}\right)^M - 1.0$$

(4-15)

Here I_{NOM}/M is the periodic rate, and M is the number of periods per year. If a bank would lend you money at a nominal rate of 12%, compounded quarterly, then the EFF% rate would be 12.5509%:

Rate on bank loan: $EFF\% = (1 + 0.03)^4 - 1.0 = (1.03)^4 - 1.0$
$$= 1.125509 - 1.0 = 0.125509 = 12.5509\%$$

It is even easier to use the *Excel* function =**EFF(I_{NOM}, M)**.

To see the importance of the EFF%, suppose that—as an alternative to the bank loan—you could borrow on a credit card that charges 1% per month. Would you be better off using the bank loan or credit card loan? *To answer this question, the cost of each alternative must be expressed as an EFF%.* The cost of the credit card loan, with monthly payments, is:

Credit card loan: $EFF\% = (1 + 0.01)^{12} - 1.0 = (1.01)^{12} - 1.0$
$$= 1.126825 - 1.0 = 0.126825 = 12.6825\%$$

---

[14]Most financial calculators have a feature that allows you to set the number of payments per year and then use the nominal annual interest rate. However, students tend to make fewer errors when using the periodic rate with their calculators set for one payment per year (i.e., per period), so this is what we recommend. Note also that you cannot use a normal time line unless you use the periodic rate.

[15]You could also use the "interest conversion feature" of a financial calculator. Most financial calculators are programmed to find the EFF% or, given the EFF%, to find the nominal rate; this is called "interest rate conversion." You enter the nominal rate and the number of compounding periods per year, and then press the EFF% key to find the effective annual rate. However, we generally use Equation 4-15 because it's easy and because using the equation reminds us of what we are really doing. If you do use the interest rate conversion feature on your calculator, don't forget to reset your settings afterward. Interest conversion is discussed in our calculator tutorials.

Notice that the effective rate is higher for monthly payments than for quarterly payments: 12.6825% versus 12.5509%. This makes sense: Both loans have the same 12% nominal rate, yet you would have to make the first payment after only 1 month on the credit card versus 3 months under the bank loan.

The EFF% rate is rarely used in calculations. *However, it must be used to compare the effective costs of different loans or rates of return on different investments when payment periods differ,* as in our example of the credit card versus a bank loan.

ANNUAL PERCENTAGE RATES (APR)

The **annual percentage rate (APR)** is the nominal annual interest rate actually charged on loans. The APR is especially important for loans that use **add-on interest**, which calculates the total interest to be paid by multiplying the amount borrowed by the quoted rate, dividing this product by the number of times per year that a payment is due, and requiring the first payment due at the time the loan is made.

For example, suppose you buy a refrigerator, stove, and dishwasher for $3,000. The store might offer you one year of financing using an add-on quoted rate of 8%. The total interest is equal to $240: $3,000(0.08) = $240. Add this total interest charge to the $3,000 cost of the kitchen appliances for a total loan of $3,240. Then divide the total loan by 12 to get the monthly payments: $3,240/12 = $270 per month, with the first payment made at the time of purchase. Therefore, you have a 12-month annuity due with payments of $270. Is your cost really the 8% that you were quoted?

To find the APR, set your calculator to Begin Mode, then enter N = 12, PV = 3000, PMT = −270, and FV = 0. When you press the I/YR key, you get the periodic rate, 1.4313%. Multiply this by 12 to get the APR, 17.1758%, which is substantially higher than the 8% quoted rate. The APR might be so high that you decide to decline the in-store financing and ask your bank for a loan.

Before 1968, lenders were not required to tell borrowers the APR. This changed when Congress passed the Consumer Credit Protection Act in 1968. The Act's Truth in Lending provisions require banks and other lenders to disclose the APR. The APR is helpful but not as revealing as the EFF%, which is 18.5945% for the loan with the 17.1758% APR. (We show these calculations using both the calculator and *Excel*, along with a time line that helps visualize what's happening, in the chapter's *Excel **Tool Kit**.*)

Your best bet is to be wary of almost all loan offers and do the math yourself to determine the rate that you really would pay.

4-15b The Result of Frequent Compounding

What would happen to the future value of an investment if interest were compounded annually, semiannually, quarterly, or some other less-than-annual period? Because interest will be earned on interest more often, you should expect higher future values the more frequently compounding occurs. Similarly, you should expect the effective annual rate to increase with more frequent compounding. As Figure 4-10 shows, these results do occur—the future value and the EFF% do increase as the frequency of compounding increases. Notice that the biggest increase in FV (and in EFF%) occurs when compounding goes from annual to semiannual, and notice also that moving from monthly to daily compounding has a relatively small impact. Although Figure 4-10 shows daily compounding as the smallest interval, it is possible to compound even more frequently. At the limit, compounding can occur *continuously*. This is explained in **Web Extension 4B** on the textbook's Web site.

FIGURE 4-10
Effect on $100 of Compounding More Frequently Than Once a Year

	A	B	C	D	E	F	G
568	Frequency of Compounding	Nominal Annual Rate	Number of Periods per Year (M)^a	Periodic Interest Rate (I_{PER})	Effective Annual Rate (EFF%)^b	Future Value^c	Percentage Increase in FV
569	Annual	12%	1	12.0000%	12.0000%	$112.00	
570	Semiannual	12%	2	6.0000%	12.3600%	$112.36	0.32%
571	Quarterly	12%	4	3.0000%	12.5509%	$112.55	0.17%
572	Monthly	12%	12	1.0000%	12.6825%	$112.68	0.12%
573	Daily	12%	365	0.0329%	12.7475%	$112.75	0.06%

Source: See the file *Ch04 Tool Kit.xlsx*. Numbers are reported as rounded values for clarity but are calculated using *Excel*'s full precision. Thus, intermediate calculations using the figure's rounded values will be inexact.

Notes:

^a We used 365 days per year in the calculations.

^b The EFF% is calculated as $(1 + I_{PER})^M - 1$. It can also be calculated using an Excel function: =EFF(I_{NOM},M).

^c The future value is calculated as $100(1 + EFF\%)$.

SELF-TEST

Would you rather invest in an account that pays a 7% nominal rate with annual compounding or with monthly compounding? If you borrowed at a nominal rate of 7%, would you rather make annual or monthly payments? Why?

What is the future value of $100 after 3 years if the appropriate interest rate is 8%, compounded annually? **($125.97)** *Compounded monthly?* **($127.02)**

What is the present value of $100 due in 3 years if the appropriate interest rate is 8%, compounded annually? **($79.38)** *Compounded monthly?* **($78.73)**

Define the following terms: annual percentage rate (APR), effective annual rate (EFF%), and nominal interest rate (I_{NOM}).

A bank pays 5% with daily compounding on its savings accounts. Should it advertise the nominal or effective rate if it is seeking to attract new deposits?

Credit card issuers must by law print their annual percentage rate on their monthly statements. A common APR is 18%, with interest paid monthly. What is the EFF% on such a loan? **(19.56%)**

Some years ago banks weren't required to reveal the rate they charged on credit cards. Then Congress passed a "truth in lending" law that required them to publish their APR rate. Is the APR rate really the most truthful rate, or would the EFF% be even more truthful?

4-16 Fractional Time Periods[16]

So far we have assumed that payments occur at either the beginning or the end of periods, but not *within* periods. However, we occasionally encounter situations that require compounding or discounting over fractional periods. For example, suppose you deposited $100

---

[16]This section is interesting and useful but relatively technical. It can be omitted, at the option of the instructor, without loss of continuity.

in a bank that pays a nominal rate of 10%, compounded daily, based on a 365-day year. How much would you have after 9 months? The answer of $107.79 is found as follows:[17]

$$\text{Periodic rate} = I_{PER} = 0.10/365 = 0.000273973 \text{ per day}$$
$$\text{Number of days} = (9/12)(365) = 0.75(365) = 273.75 \text{ days, rounded to } 274$$
$$\text{Ending amount} = \$100(1.000273973)^{274} = \$107.79$$

Now suppose that instead you borrow $100 at a nominal rate of 10% per year and are charged *simple interest,* which means that interest is not charged on interest. If the loan is outstanding for 274 days (or 9 months), how much interest would you have to pay? The interest owed is equal to the principal multiplied by the interest rate times the number of periods. In this case, the number of periods is equal to a fraction of a year: N = 274/365 = 0.7506849.

$$\text{Interest owed} = \$100(10\%)(0.7506849) = \$7.51$$

Another approach would be to use the daily rate rather than the annual rate and thus to use the exact number of days rather than the fraction of the year:

$$\text{Interest owed} = \$100(0.000273973)(274) = \$7.51$$

You would owe the bank a total of $107.51 after 274 days. This is the procedure most banks use to calculate interest on loans, except that they generally require borrowers to pay the interest on a monthly basis rather than after 274 days; this more frequent compounding raises the EFF% and thus the total amount of interest paid.

SELF-TEST

Suppose a company borrowed $1 million at a rate of 9%, using simple interest, with interest paid at the end of each month. The bank uses a 360-day year. How much interest would the firm have to pay in a 30-day month? **($7,500.00)** *What would the interest be if the bank used a 365-day year?* **($7,397.26)**

Suppose you deposited $1,000 in a credit union that pays 7% with daily compounding and a 365-day year. What is the EFF%? **(7.250098%)** *How much could you withdraw after 7 months, assuming this is 7/12 of a year?* **($1,041.67)**

4-17 Amortized Loans

An extremely important application of compound interest involves loans that are paid off in installments over time. Included are automobile loans, home mortgage loans, student loans, and many business loans. A loan that is to be repaid in equal amounts on a monthly, quarterly, or annual basis is called an **amortized loan.**[18]

---

[17]We assume that these 9 months constitute 9/12 of a year. Also, bank deposit and loan contracts specifically state whether they are based on a 360-day or a 365-day year. If a 360-day year is used, then the daily rate is higher, so the effective rate is also higher. Here we assumed a 365-day year. Finally, note that banks use software with built-in calendars, so they calculate the exact number of days.

Note also that banks often treat such loans as follows: (1) They require monthly payments, and they calculate the interest for the month by multiplying the periodic rate by the beginning-of-month balance times the number of days in the month. This is called "simple interest." (2) The interest for the month is either added to the next beginning of month balance or actually paid by the borrower. In this case, the EFF% is based on 12 compounding periods, not 365 as is assumed in our example.

[18]The word *amortized* comes from the Latin *mors,* meaning "death," so an amortized loan is one that is "killed off" over time.

What You Know Is What You Get: Not in Payday Lending

When money runs low toward the end of a month, many individuals turn to payday lenders. If a borrower's application is approved, the payday lender makes a short-term loan, which will be repaid with the next paycheck. In fact, on the next payday the lender actually transfers the repayment from the borrower's bank account. This repayment consists of the amount borrowed plus a fee.

How costly are payday loans? The lender charges a fee of about $15 to $17 per $100 borrowed. A typical loan is for about $350, so the typical fee is about $56. A typical borrower gets paid about every 2 weeks, so the loan is for a very short amount of time. With a big fee and a short time until repayment, the typical payday loan has an APR of over 400%.

How informed are borrowers? Two professors at the University of Chicago set out to answer this question. When loans are approved, borrowers receive a form to sign that shows the APR. However, subsequent telephone surveys of borrowers show that over 40% of borrowers thought their APR was around 15%; perhaps not coincidentally, these are similar numerals to the fee schedules that are posted prominently in the lender's office.

The professors then did an experiment (with the agreement of 77 payday loan stores) in which they provided more information than just the APR. One group of borrowers received information about the APR of the payday loan as compared to the APRs of other loans, such as car loans. A second group received information about the dollar cost of the payday loan as compared to the dollar cost of other loans, such as car loans. A third group received information about how long it takes most payday borrowers to repay their loans (which is longer than the next payday; borrowers tend to extend the loan for additional pay periods, accruing additional fees).

Compared to a control group with no additional information, the results show that some borrowers with additional information decided not to take the loan; other borrowers reduced the amount that they borrow. These findings suggest that better information helps borrowers make less costly decisions. The more you know, the less you get, at least when it comes to costly payday loans.

Source: Marianne Bertrand and Adair Morse, "Information Disclosure, Cognitive Biases, and Payday Borrowing," *Journal of Finance*, Vol. 66, No. 6, December 2011, pp. 1865–1893.

4-17a Payments

Suppose a company borrows $100,000, with the loan to be repaid in 5 equal payments at the end of each of the next 5 years. The lender charges 6% on the balance at the beginning of each year.

Here's a picture of the situation:

Our task is to find the amount of the payment, PMT, such that the sum of their PVs equals the amount of the loan, $100,000:

$$\$100{,}000 = \frac{PMT}{(1.06)^1} + \frac{PMT}{(1.06)^2} + \frac{PMT}{(1.06)^3} + \frac{PMT}{(1.06)^4} + \frac{PMT}{(1.06)^5} = \sum_{t=1}^{5} \frac{PMT}{(1.06)^t}$$

It is possible to solve the annuity formula, Equation 4-9, for PMT, but it is much easier to use a financial calculator or spreadsheet. With a financial calculator, we insert values as shown below to get the required payments, $23,739.64:

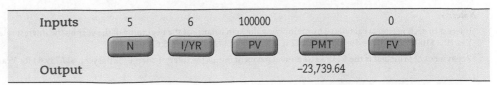

With *Excel*, you would use the **PMT** function: =**PMT(I,N,PV,FV)** =**PMT(0.06,5,100000,0)** = −$23,739.64. Thus, we see that the borrower must pay the lender $23,739.64 per year for the next 5 years.

4-17b Amortization Schedules

Each payment will consist of two parts—part interest and part repayment of principal. This breakdown is shown in the **amortization schedule** given in Figure 4-11. The interest component is relatively high in the first year, but it declines as the loan balance decreases. For tax purposes, the borrower would deduct the interest component while the lender would report the same amount as taxable income. Over the 5 years, the lender will earn 6% on its investment and also recover the amount of its investment.

4-17c Mortgage Payments, Remaining Balances, and Interest Paid

Suppose you buy a house and take out a 30-year home mortgage of $250,000 at an annual rate of 6%. What is the monthly payment? What is the remaining balance after a year? What are the total principal payments and interest payments during the first year? What are the total payments and interest payments over the life of the loan?

FIGURE 4-11
Loan Amortization Schedule, $100,000 at 6% for 5 Years

	A	B	C	D	E	F
675	**INPUTS:**					
676		Amount borrowed:	$100,000			
677		Years:	5			
678		Rate:	6%			
679	**Intermediate calculation:**					
680		PMT:	$23,739.64	=PMT(C678,C677,−C676)		
681	Year	Beginning Amount (1)	Payment (2)	Interest[a] (3)	Repayment of Principal[b] (2) − (3) = (4)	Ending Balance (1) − (4) = (5)
682	1	$100,000.00	$23,739.64	$6,000.00	$17,739.64	$82,260.36
683	2	$82,260.36	$23,739.64	$4,935.62	$18,804.02	$63,456.34
684	3	$63,456.34	$23,739.64	$3,807.38	$19,932.26	$43,524.08
685	4	$43,524.08	$23,739.64	$2,611.44	$21,128.20	$22,395.89
686	5	$22,395.89	$23,739.64	$1,343.75	$22,395.89	$0.00

Source: See the file *Ch04 Tool Kit.xlsx*. Numbers are reported as rounded values for clarity but are calculated using *Excel*'s full precision. Thus, intermediate calculations using the figure's rounded values will be inexact.

Notes:

[a] Interest in each period is calculated by multiplying the loan balance at the beginning of the year by the interest rate. Therefore, interest in Year 1 is $100,000(0.06) = $6,000; in Year 2 it is $82,260.36(0.06) = $4,935.62; and so on.

[b] Repayment of principal is the $23,739.64 annual payment minus the interest charge for the year, $17,739.64 for Year 1.

MONTHLY PAYMENTS

To find the payment, first adjust N and I/YR to reflect monthly payments. The financial calculator inputs are shown below:

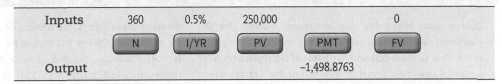

Inputs	360	0.5%	250,000		0
	N	I/YR	PV	PMT	FV
Output				−1,498.8763	

After rounding to cents, the monthly payment is $1,498.88. We will use this rounded value to determine how much you will owe at the end of the first year. In other words, what is your remaining balance after the 12th payment?

REMAINING BALANCE

Imagine you sell the house after the 12th payment. How much would you still owe? In other words, what is the future value of the initial loan amount and the subsequent 12 loan payments at t = 12? Considering this is from the perspective of the lender making a loan of $250,000 and receiving 12 payments of $1,498.88, the financial calculator solution is $246,929.93:

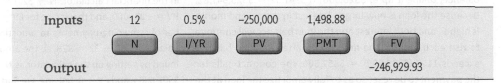

Inputs	12	0.5%	−250,000	1,498.88	
	N	I/YR	PV	PMT	FV
Output					−246,929.93

TOTAL PRINCIPAL PAYMENTS AND INTEREST PAYMENTS DURING THE FIRST YEAR

The total amount of principal repaid in the first year is the difference between the starting principal and the end-of-year principal: $250,000 − $246,929.93 = $3,070.07. The total payments during the year are the product of the 12 months and the monthly payment: 12($1,498.88) = $17,986.56. Therefore, the total interest paid in the year is:

$$\text{Total interest in first year} = \text{Total payments} - \text{Total principal payments}$$
$$= \$17,986.56 - \$3,070.07$$
$$= \$14,916.49.$$

Dividing the total first-year interest ($14,917) by the total first-year payments shows that about 83% of the payments go to interest!

TOTAL PAYMENTS AND INTEREST PAYMENTS DURING THE MORTGAGE'S LIFE

Suppose you don't sell the house. The total amount of your payments is 360($1,498.88) ≈ $539,597. The borrower pays back the borrowed $250,000 over the life of the loan, so the total interest paid is $539,597 − $250,000 = $289,597.

Now consider a 15-year mortgage. To compare apples to apples, assume the interest rate stays at 6%, although it probably would be a bit lower. Changing N to 180, the new payment is $2,109.6421. The total amount of payments is 180($2,109.6421) ≈ $379,736 and the total interest paid is $379,736 − $250,000 = $129,736, a big decrease from the $289,597 paid on the 30-year mortgage. As this example shows, increasing the monthly payment can dramatically reduce the total interest paid and the time required to pay off the mortgage.

An Accident Waiting to Happen: Option Reset Adjustable Rate Mortgages

Option reset adjustable rate mortgages (ARMs) give the borrower some choices regarding the initial monthly payment. One popular option ARM allowed borrowers to make a monthly payment equal to only half of the interest due in the first month. Because the monthly payment was less than the interest charge, the loan balance grew each month. When the loan balance exceeded 110% of the original principal, the monthly payment was reset to fully amortize the now larger loan at the prevailing market interest rates.

Here's an example. Someone borrows $325,000 for 30 years at an initial rate of 7%. The interest accruing in the first month is (7%/12)($325,000) = $1,895.83. Therefore, the initial monthly payment is 50%($1,895.83) = $947.92. Another $947.92 of deferred interest is added to the loan balance, taking it up to $325,000 + $947.92 = $325,947.82. Because the loan is now larger, interest in the second month is higher, and both interest and the loan balance will continue to rise each month. The first month after the loan balance exceeds 110%($325,000) = $357,500, the contract calls for the payment to be reset so as to fully amortize the loan at the then prevailing interest rate.

First, how long would it take for the balance to exceed $357,500? Consider this from the lender's perspective: The lender initially pays out $325,000, receives $947.92 each month, and then would receive a payment of $357,500 if the loan were payable when the balance hit that amount, with interest accruing at a 7% annual rate and with monthly compounding.

We enter these values into a financial calculator: I = 7%/12, PV = −325000, PMT = 947.92, and FV = 357500. We solve for N = 31.3 months, rounded up to 32 months. Thus, the borrower will make 32 payments of $947.92 before the ARM resets.

The payment after the reset depends upon the terms of the original loan and the market interest rate at the time of the reset. For many borrowers, the initial rate was a lower-than-market "teaser" rate, so a higher-than-market rate would be applied to the remaining balance. For this example, we will assume that the original rate wasn't a teaser and that the rate remains at 7%. Keep in mind, though, that for many borrowers the reset rate was higher than the initial rate. The balance after the 32nd payment can be found as the future value of the original loan and the 32 monthly payments, so we enter these values in the financial calculator: N = 32, I = 7%/12, PMT = 947.92, PV = −325000, and then solve for FV = $358,242.84. The number of remaining payments to amortize the $358,242.84 loan balance is 360 − 32 = 328, so the amount of each payment is found by setting up the calculator as N = 328, I = 7%/12, PV = 358242.84, and FV = 0. Solving, we find that PMT = $2,453.94.

Even if interest rates don't change, the monthly payment jumps from $947.92 to $2,453.94 and would increase even more if interest rates were higher at the reset. This is exactly what happened to millions of American homeowners who took out option reset ARMS in the early 2000s. When large numbers of resets began in 2007, defaults ballooned. The accident caused by option reset ARMs didn't wait very long to happen!

4-17d Auto Loans and the Remaining Balance

Auto dealers and manufacturers often offer loans for cars purchased at the dealership. Even if the nominal interest rate, number of payments, and monthly payment amount are the same as those of a regular amortizing loan, the monthly interest charges often differ. Recall that a regular amortizing loan calculates a monthly interest charge by multiplying the beginning loan balance by the periodic rate. An auto loan instead calculates monthly interest charges by multiplying the *total interest charges* by a different predefined percentage each month. These percentages sum to 100%, so the total interest paid is the same for both types of loans. However, the interest portions are larger at the beginning of the loan's life and smaller toward the end. Because the payment is constant, the corresponding principal payments are lower at the beginning months and higher at the later months. However, in every month the beginning balance will be higher than it would have been with a regular amortizing loan. This has two negative consequences. First, if you sell the car before you pay off the loan, you will owe more than you would have with a regular amortizing loan. Second, if you itemize your deductions, your interest rate deductions in the early months will be smaller than they would have been with a regular amortizing loan.

Consider again the example in Figure 4-11. If the loan were amortized over 5 years with 60 equal monthly payments, how much would each payment be, and how would the first payment be divided between interest and principal? **(Each payment would be $1,933.28; the first payment would have $500 of interest and $1,433.28 of principal repayment.)**

Suppose you borrowed $30,000 on a student loan at a rate of 8% and now must repay it in three equal installments at the end of each of the next 3 years. How large would your payments be, how much of the first payment would represent interest and how much would be principal, and what would your ending balance be after the first year? **(PMT = $11,641.01; interest = $2,400; principal = $9,241.01; balance at end of Year 1 = $20,758.99)**

4-18 Growing Annuities[19]

Notice that the term "growing annuity" isn't logical because an annuity is a series of *constant* amounts to be received or paid over a specified number of periods. Despite its name being an oxymoron, a **growing annuity** is a series of amounts either received or paid that grow at a constant rate.

4-18a Example 1: Finding a Constant Real Income

Growing annuities are often used in the area of financial planning, where a prospective retiree wants to determine the maximum constant *real*, or *inflation-adjusted*, withdrawals that he or she can make over a specified number of years. For example, suppose a 65-year-old is contemplating retirement. The individual expects to live for another 20 years, has a $1 million nest egg, expects the investments to earn a nominal annual rate of 6%, expects inflation to average 3% per year, and wants to withdraw a constant *real* amount annually over the next 20 years so as to maintain a constant standard of living. If the first withdrawal is to be made today, what is the amount of that initial withdrawal?

resource

See **Ch04 Tool Kit.xlsx** for all calculations.

This problem can be solved in three ways: (1) Set up a spreadsheet model that is similar to an amortization table, where the account earns 6% per year, withdrawals rise at the 3% inflation rate, and *Excel*'s Goal Seek feature is used to find the initial inflation-adjusted withdrawal. A zero balance will be shown at the end of the 20th year. (2) Use a financial calculator, where we first calculate the real rate of return, adjusted for inflation, and use it for I/YR when finding the payment for an annuity due. (3) Use a relatively complicated and obtuse formula to find this same amount.[20] We will focus on the first two approaches.

We illustrate the spreadsheet approach in the chapter model, **Ch04 Tool Kit.xlsx**. The spreadsheet model provides the most transparent picture because it shows the value of the retirement portfolio, the portfolio's annual earnings, and each withdrawal over the 20-year planning horizon—especially if you include a graph. A picture is worth a thousand numbers, and graphs make it easy to explain the situation to people who are planning their financial futures.

---

[19]This section is interesting and useful but relatively technical. It can be omitted, at the option of the instructor, without loss of continuity. Also, although an annuity is constant, the expression "growing annuity" is widely used. Therefore, we will use it, too, even though it is a self-contradictory term.

[20]For example, the formula used to find the payment of a growing annuity due is shown here. If g = annuity growth rate and r = nominal rate of return on investment, then:

$$\text{PVIF of a growing annuity due} = \text{PVIFGA}_{\text{Due}} = \{1 - [(1 + g)/(1 + r)]^N\} \, [(1 + r)/(r - g)]$$

$$\text{PMT} = \text{PV}/\text{PVIFGA}_{\text{Due}}$$

where PVIF denotes "present value interest factor." Similar formulas are available for growing ordinary annuities.

To implement the calculator approach, we first find the expected *real* rate of return, where r_r is the real rate of return and r_{NOM} the nominal rate of return. The real rate of return is the return that we would see if there were no inflation. We calculate the real rate as:

$$\text{Real rate} = r_r = [(1 + r_{NOM})/(1 + \text{Inflation})] - 1.0 \qquad \text{(4-16)}$$

$$= [1.06/1.03] - 1.0 = 0.029126214 = 2.9126214\%$$

Using this real rate of return, we solve the annuity due problem exactly as we did earlier in the chapter. We set the calculator to Begin Mode, after which we input N = 20, I/YR = real rate = 2.9126214, PV = −1000000, and FV = 0; then we press PMT to get $64,786.88. This is the amount of the initial withdrawal at Time 0 (today), and future withdrawals will increase at the inflation rate of 3%. These withdrawals, growing at the inflation rate, will provide the retiree with a constant real income over the next 20 years—provided the inflation rate and the rate of return do not change.

In our example, we assumed that the first withdrawal would be made immediately. The procedure would be slightly different if we wanted to make end-of-year withdrawals. First, we would set the calculator to End Mode. Second, we would enter the same inputs into the calculator as just listed, including the real interest rate for I/YR. The calculated PMT would be $66,673.87. *However, that value is in beginning-of-year terms*, and because inflation of 3% will occur during the year, we must make the following adjustment to find the inflation-adjusted initial withdrawal:

$$\text{Initial end-of-year withdrawal} = \$66,673.87(1 + \text{Inflation})$$
$$= \$66,673.87(1.03)$$
$$= \$68,674.09$$

Thus, the first withdrawal at the *end* of the year would be $68,674.09; it would grow by 3% per year; and after the 20th withdrawal (at the end of the 20th year), the balance in the retirement fund would be zero.

We also demonstrate the solution for this end-of-year payment example in ***Ch04 Tool Kit.xlsx***. There we set up a table showing the beginning balance, the annual withdrawals, the annual earnings, and the ending balance for each of the 20 years. This analysis confirms the $68,674.09 initial end-of-year withdrawal derived previously.

4-18b Example 2: Initial Deposit to Accumulate a Future Sum

As another example of growing annuities, suppose you need to accumulate $100,000 in 10 years. You plan to make a deposit in a bank now, at Time 0, and then make 9 more deposits at the beginning of each of the following 9 years, for a total of 10 deposits. The bank pays 6% interest, you expect inflation to be 2% per year, and you plan to increase your annual deposits at the inflation rate. How much must you deposit initially? First, we calculate the real rate:

$$\text{Real rate} = r_r = [1.06/1.02] - 1.0 = 0.0392157 = 3.9215686\%$$

Next, because inflation is expected to be 2% per year, in 10 years the target $100,000 will have a real value of:

$$\$100,000/(1 + 0.02)^{10} = \$82,034.83$$

Now we can find the size of the required initial payment by setting a financial calculator to the Begin Mode and then inputting N = 10, I/YR = 3.9215686, PV = 0, and FV = 82034.83. Then, when we press the PMT key, we get PMT = −6598.87. Thus, a deposit of $6,598.87 made at time 0 and growing by 2% per year will accumulate to $100,000 by Year 10 if the interest rate is 6%. Again, this result is confirmed in the chapter's *Tool Kit*. The key to this analysis is to express I/YR, FV, and PMT in real, not nominal, terms.

SELF-TEST

Differentiate between a "regular" and a "growing" annuity.

What three methods can be used to deal with growing annuities?

If the nominal interest rate is 10% and the expected inflation rate is 5%, what is the expected real rate of return? **(4.7619%)**

SUMMARY

Most financial decisions involve situations in which someone makes a payment at one point in time and receives money later. Dollars paid or received at two different points in time are different, and this difference is dealt with using *time value of money (TVM) analysis.*

- **Compounding** is the process of determining the **future value (FV)** of a cash flow or a series of cash flows. The compounded amount, or future value, is equal to the beginning amount plus interest earned.
- Future value of a single payment = $FV_N = PV(1 + I)^N$.
- **Discounting** is the process of finding the **present value (PV)** of a future cash flow or a series of cash flows; discounting is the reciprocal, or reverse, of compounding.

$$\text{Present value of a payment received at the end of Time N} = PV = \frac{FV_N}{(1 + I)^N}.$$

- An **annuity** is defined as a series of equal periodic payments (PMT) for a specified number of periods.
- An annuity whose payments occur at the *end* of each period is called an **ordinary annuity.**

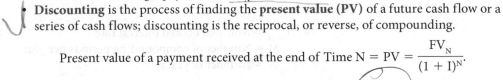

$$\text{Future value of an (ordinary) annuity} = FVA_N = PMT\left[\frac{(1 + I)^N}{I} - \frac{1}{I}\right]$$

$$\text{Present value of an (ordinary) annuity} = PVA_N = PMT\left[\frac{1}{I} - \frac{1}{I(1 + I)^N}\right]$$

- If payments occur at the *beginning* of the periods rather than at the end, then we have an **annuity due.** The PV of each payment is larger, because each payment is discounted back 1 year less, so the PV of the annuity is also larger. Similarly, the FV of the annuity due is larger because each payment is compounded for an extra year. The following formulas can be used to convert the PV and FV of an ordinary annuity to an annuity due:

$$PVA_{due} = PVA_{ordinary}(1 + I)$$
$$FVA_{due} = FVA_{ordinary}(1 + I)$$

- A **perpetuity** is an annuity with an infinite number of payments:

$$\text{Value of a perpetuity} = \frac{\text{PMT}}{I}$$

- To find the PV or FV of an uneven series, find the PV or FV of each individual cash flow and then sum them.
- If you know the cash flows and the PV (or FV) of a cash flow stream, you can determine its interest rate.
- When compounding occurs more frequently than once a year, the nominal rate must be converted to a periodic rate, and the number of years must be converted to periods:

$$\text{Periodic rate } (I_{PER}) = \text{Nominal annual rate} \div \text{Periods per year}$$
$$\text{Number of periods} = \text{Years} \times \text{Periods per year}$$

The periodic rate and number of periods are used for calculations and are shown on time lines.

- If you are comparing the costs of alternative loans that require payments more than once a year, or the rates of return on investments that pay interest more than once a year, then the comparisons should be based on **effective** (or **equivalent**) **rates** of return. Here is the formula:

$$\text{EAR} = \text{EFF\%} = (1 + I_{PER})^M - 1.0 = \left(1 + \frac{I_{NOM}}{M}\right)^M - 1.0$$

- The general equation for finding the future value of a current cash flow (PV) for any number of compounding periods per year is:

$$FV_N = PV(1 + I_{PER})^{\text{Number of periods}} = PV\left(1 + \frac{I_{NOM}}{M}\right)^{MN}$$

where

$$I_{NOM} = \text{Nominal quoted interest rate}$$
$$M = \text{Number of compounding periods per year}$$
$$N = \text{Number of years}$$

- An **amortized loan** is paid off with equal payments over a specified period. An **amortization schedule** shows how much of each payment constitutes interest, how much is used to reduce the principal, and the unpaid balance at the end of each period. The unpaid balance at Time N must be zero.
- A **"growing annuity"** is a stream of cash flows that grows at a constant rate for a specified number of years. The present and future values of growing annuities can be found with relatively complicated formulas or, more easily, with an *Excel* model.
- *Web Extension 4A* provides derivations of the annuity formulas.
- *Web Extension 4B* explains continuous compounding.

QUESTIONS

(4-1)   Define each of the following terms:

a. PV; I; INT; FV$_N$; PVA$_N$; FVA$_N$; PMT; M; I$_{NOM}$
b. Opportunity cost rate
c. Annuity; lump-sum payment; cash flow; uneven cash flow stream
d. Ordinary (or deferred) annuity; annuity due

     e. Perpetuity
     f. Outflow; inflow; time line; terminal value
     g. Compounding; discounting
     h. Annual, semiannual, quarterly, monthly, and daily compounding
     i. Effective annual rate (EAR or EFF%); nominal (quoted) interest rate; APR;
       periodic rate
     j. Amortization schedule; principal versus interest component of a payment; amor-
       tized loan

(4-2)   What is an *opportunity cost rate*? How is this rate used in discounted cash flow analysis, and
where is it shown on a time line? Is the opportunity rate a single number that is used to
evaluate all potential investments?

(4-3)   An *annuity* is defined as a series of payments of a fixed amount for a specific number of
periods. Thus, $100 a year for 10 years is an annuity, but $100 in Year 1, $200 in Year 2,
and $400 in Years 3 through 10 does *not* constitute an annuity. However, the entire series
does contain an annuity. Is this statement true or false?

(4-4)   If a firm's earnings per share grew from $1 to $2 over a 10-year period, the *total growth* would
be 100%, but the *annual growth rate* would be *less than* 10%. True or false? Explain.

(4-5)   Would you rather have a savings account that pays 5% interest compounded semiannually
or one that pays 5% interest compounded daily? Explain.

SELF-TEST PROBLEMS   SOLUTIONS SHOWN IN APPENDIX A

(ST-1)
Future Value

Assume that 1 year from now you plan to deposit $1,000 in a savings account that pays a
nominal rate of 8%.

     a. If the bank compounds interest annually, how much will you have in your account
       4 years from now?
     b. What would your balance be 4 years from now if the bank used quarterly com-
       pounding rather than annual compounding?
     c. Suppose you deposited the $1,000 in 4 payments of $250 each at the end of Years 1,
       2, 3, and 4. How much would you have in your account at the end of Year 4, based on
       8% annual compounding?
     d. Suppose you deposited 4 equal payments in your account at the end of Years 1, 2, 3,
       and 4. Assuming an 8% interest rate, how large would each of your payments have to
       be for you to obtain the same ending balance as you calculated in part a?

(ST-2)
**Time Value
of Money**

Assume that 4 years from now you will need $1,000. Your bank compounds interest at an
8% annual rate.

     a. How much must you deposit 1 year from now to have a balance of $1,000 at Year 4?
     b. If you want to make equal payments at the end of Years 1 through 4 to accumulate
       the $1,000, how large must each of the 4 payments be?
     c. If your father were to offer either to make the payments calculated in part b
       ($221.92) or to give you a lump sum of $750 one year from now, which would you
       choose?
     d. If you will have only $750 at the end of Year 1, what interest rate, compounded an-
       nually, would you have to earn to have the necessary $1,000 at Year 4?
     e. Suppose you can deposit only $186.29 each at the end of Years 1 through 4, but you
       still need $1,000 at the end of Year 4. What interest rate, with annual compounding,
       is required to achieve your goal?

f. To help you reach your $1,000 goal, your father offers to give you $400 one year from now. You will get a part-time job and make 6 additional deposits of equal amounts each 6 months thereafter. If all of this money is deposited in a bank that pays 8%, compounded semiannually, how large must each of the 6 deposits be?

g. What is the effective annual rate being paid by the bank in part f?

(ST-3)
Effective
Annual Rates

Bank A pays 8% interest, compounded quarterly, on its money market account. The managers of Bank B want its money market account's effective annual rate to equal that of Bank A, but Bank B will compound interest on a monthly basis. What nominal, or quoted, rate must Bank B set?

PROBLEMS ANSWERS ARE IN APPENDIX B

EASY PROBLEMS 1–8

(4-1)
Future Value of a
Single Payment

If you deposit $10,000 in a bank account that pays 10% interest annually, how much will be in your account after 5 years?

(4-2)
Present Value of a
Single Payment

What is the present value of a security that will pay $5,000 in 20 years if securities of equal risk pay 7% annually?

(4-3)
Interest Rate on a
Single Payment

Your parents will retire in 18 years. They currently have $250,000, and they think they will need $1 million at retirement. What annual interest rate must they earn to reach their goal, assuming they don't save any additional funds?

(4-4)
Number of Periods
of a Single Payment

If you deposit money today in an account that pays 6.5% annual interest, how long will it take to double your money?

(4-5)
Number of Periods
for an Annuity

You have $42,180.53 in a brokerage account, and you plan to deposit an additional $5,000 at the end of every future year until your account totals $250,000. You expect to earn 12% annually on the account. How many years will it take to reach your goal?

(4-6)
Future Value:
Ordinary Annuity
versus Annuity Due

What is the future value of a 7%, 5-year ordinary annuity that pays $300 each year? If this were an annuity due, what would its future value be?

(4-7)
Present and Future
Value of an Uneven
Cash Flow Stream

An investment will pay $100 at the end of each of the next 3 years, $200 at the end of Year 4, $300 at the end of Year 5, and $500 at the end of Year 6. If other investments of equal risk earn 8% annually, what is this investment's present value? Its future value?

(4-8)
Annuity Payment
and EAR

You want to buy a car, and a local bank will lend you $20,000. The loan would be fully amortized over 5 years (60 months), and the nominal interest rate would be 12%, with interest paid monthly. What is the monthly loan payment? What is the loan's EFF%?

INTERMEDIATE PROBLEMS 9–29

(4-9)
Present and Future
Values of Single
Cash Flows for
Different Periods

Find the following values, *using the equations,* and then work the problems using a financial calculator to check your answers. Disregard rounding differences. (*Hint:* If you are using a financial calculator, you can enter the known values and then press the appropriate key to find the unknown variable. Then, without clearing the TVM register, you can "override" the variable that changes by simply entering a new value for it and then pressing the key for the unknown variable to obtain the second answer. This procedure can be used in parts b and d, and in many other situations, to see how changes in input variables affect the output variable.)

   a. An initial $500 compounded for 1 year at 6%

   b. An initial $500 compounded for 2 years at 6%

   c. The present value of $500 due in 1 year at a discount rate of 6%

   d. The present value of $500 due in 2 years at a discount rate of 6%

(4-10)
Present and Future Values of Single Cash Flows for Different Interest Rates

Use both the TVM equations and a financial calculator to find the following values. See the *Hint* for Problem 4-9.

   a. An initial $500 compounded for 10 years at 6%

   b. An initial $500 compounded for 10 years at 12%

   c. The present value of $500 due in 10 years at a 6% discount rate

   d. The present value of $500 due in 10 years at a 12% discount rate

(4-11)
Time for a Lump Sum to Double

To the closest year, how long will it take $200 to double if it is deposited and earns the following rates? [*Notes:* (1) See the *Hint* for Problem 4-9. (2) This problem cannot be solved exactly with some financial calculators. For example, if you enter PV = −200, PMT = 0, FV = 400, and I = 7 in an HP-12C and then press the N key, you will get 11 years for part a. The correct answer is 10.2448 years, which rounds to 10, but the calculator rounds up. However, the HP10BII gives the exact answer.]

   a. 7%

   b. 10%

   c. 18%

   d. 100%

(4-12)
Future Value of an Annuity

Find the *future value* of the following annuities. The first payment in these annuities is made at the *end* of Year 1, so they are *ordinary annuities*. (*Notes:* See the *Hint* to Problem 4-9. Also, note that you can leave values in the TVM register, switch to Begin Mode, press FV, and find the FV of the annuity due.)

   a. $400 per year for 10 years at 10%

   b. $200 per year for 5 years at 5%

   c. $400 per year for 5 years at 0%

   d. Now rework parts a, b, and c assuming that payments are made at the *beginning* of each year; that is, they are *annuities due.*

(4-13)
Present Value of an Annuity

Find the *present value* of the following *ordinary annuities* (see the *Notes* to Problem 4-12).

   a. $400 per year for 10 years at 10%

   b. $200 per year for 5 years at 5%

   c. $400 per year for 5 years at 0%

   d. Now rework parts a, b, and c assuming that payments are made at the *beginning* of each year; that is, they are *annuities due.*

(4-14)
Uneven Cash Flow Stream

   a. Find the present values of the following cash flow streams. The appropriate interest rate is 8%. (*Hint:* It is fairly easy to work this problem dealing with the individual cash flows. However, if you have a financial calculator, read the section of the manual that describes how to enter cash flows such as the ones in this problem. This will take a little time, but the investment will pay huge dividends throughout the course. Note that, when working with the calculator's cash flow register, you must enter

$CF_0 = 0$. Note also that it is quite easy to work the problem with *Excel*, using procedures described in the file **Ch04 Tool Kit.xlsx**.)

Year	Cash Stream A	Cash Stream B
1	$100	$300
2	400	400
3	400	400
4	400	400
5	300	100

b. What is the value of each cash flow stream at a 0% interest rate?

(4-15)
Effective Rate
of Interest

Find the interest rate (or rates of return) in each of the following situations.

a. You *borrow* $700 and promise to pay back $749 at the end of 1 year.
b. You *lend* $700 and receive a promise to be paid $749 at the end of 1 year.
c. You borrow $85,000 and promise to pay back $201,229 at the end of 10 years.
d. You borrow $9,000 and promise to make payments of $2,684.80 at the end of each of the next 5 years.

(4-16)
Future Value
for Various
Compounding
Periods

Find the amount to which $500 will grow under each of the following conditions.

a. 12% compounded annually for 5 years
b. 12% compounded semiannually for 5 years
c. 12% compounded quarterly for 5 years
d. 12% compounded monthly for 5 years

(4-17)
Present Value
for Various
Compounding
Periods

Find the present value of $500 due in the future under each of the following conditions.

a. 12% nominal rate, semiannual compounding, discounted back 5 years
b. 12% nominal rate, quarterly compounding, discounted back 5 years
c. 12% nominal rate, monthly compounding, discounted back 1 year

(4-18)
Future Value of an
Annuity for Various
Compounding
Periods

Find the future values of the following ordinary annuities.

a. FV of $400 each 6 months for 5 years at a nominal rate of 12%, compounded semiannually
b. FV of $200 each 3 months for 5 years at a nominal rate of 12%, compounded quarterly
c. The annuities described in parts a and b have the same total amount of money paid into them during the 5-year period, and both earn interest at the same nominal rate, yet the annuity in part b earns $101.75 more than the one in part a over the 5 years. Why does this occur?

(4-19)
Effective versus
Nominal
Interest Rates

Universal Bank pays 7% interest, compounded annually, on time deposits. Regional Bank pays 6% interest, compounded quarterly.

a. Based on effective interest rates, in which bank would you prefer to deposit your money?
b. Could your choice of banks be influenced by the fact that you might want to withdraw your funds during the year as opposed to at the end of the year? In answering this question, assume that funds must be left on deposit during an entire compounding period in order for you to receive any interest.

(4-20)
Amortization
Schedule

Consider a $25,000 loan to be repaid in equal installments at the end of each of the next 5 years. The interest rate is 10%.

a. Set up an amortization schedule for the loan.
b. How large must each annual payment be if the loan is for $50,000? Assume that the interest rate remains at 10% and that the loan is still paid off over 5 years.

c. How large must each payment be if the loan is for $50,000, the interest rate is 10%, and the loan is paid off in equal installments at the end of each of the next 10 years? This loan is for the same amount as the loan in part b, but the payments are spread out over twice as many periods. Why are these payments not half as large as the payments on the loan in part b?

(4-21)
Growth Rates

Sales for Hanebury Corporation's just-ended year were $12 million. Sales were $6 million 5 years earlier.

   a. At what rate did sales grow?

   b. Suppose someone calculated the sales growth for Hanebury in part a as follows: "Sales doubled in 5 years. This represents a growth of 100% in 5 years; dividing 100% by 5 results in an estimated growth rate of 20% per year." Explain what is wrong with this calculation.

(4-22)
Expected Rate
of Return

Washington-Pacific (W-P) invested $4 million to buy a tract of land and plant some young pine trees. The trees can be harvested in 10 years, at which time W-P plans to sell the forest at an expected price of $8 million. What is W-P's expected rate of return?

(4-23)
Effective Rate
of Interest

A mortgage company offers to lend you $85,000; the loan calls for payments of $8,273.59 at the end of each year for 30 years. What interest rate is the mortgage company charging you?

(4-24)
Required Lump-
Sum Payment

To complete your last year in business school and then go through law school, you will need $10,000 per year for 4 years, starting next year (that is, you will need to withdraw the first $10,000 one year from today). Your uncle offers to put you through school, and he will deposit in a bank paying 7% interest a sum of money that is sufficient to provide the four payments of $10,000 each. His deposit will be made today.

   a. How large must the deposit be?

   b. How much will be in the account immediately after you make the first withdrawal? After the last withdrawal?

(4-25)
Repaying a Loan

While Mary Corens was a student at the University of Tennessee, she borrowed $12,000 in student loans at an annual interest rate of 9%. If Mary repays $1,500 per year, then how long (to the nearest year) will it take her to repay the loan?

(4-26)
Reaching a
Financial Goal

You need to accumulate $10,000. To do so, you plan to make deposits of $1,250 per year— with the first payment made a year from today—into a bank account that pays 12% annual interest. Your last deposit will be less than $1,250 if less is needed to round out to $10,000. How many years will it take you to reach your $10,000 goal, and how large will the last deposit be?

(4-27)
Present Value of
a Perpetuity

What is the present value of a perpetuity of $100 per year if the appropriate discount rate is 7%? If interest rates in general were to double and the appropriate discount rate rose to 14%, what would happen to the present value of the perpetuity?

(4-28)
PV and Effective
Annual Rate

Assume that you inherited some money. A friend of yours is working as an unpaid intern at a local brokerage firm, and her boss is selling securities that call for 4 payments of $50 (1 payment at the end of each of the next 4 years) plus an extra payment of $1,000 at the end of Year 4. Your friend says she can get you some of these securities at a cost of $900 each. Your money is now invested in a bank that pays an 8% nominal (quoted) interest rate but with quarterly compounding. You regard the securities as being just as safe, and as liquid, as your bank deposit, so your required effective annual rate of return on the securities is the same as that on your bank deposit. You must calculate the value of the securities to decide whether they are a good investment. What is their present value to you?

(4-29)
Loan Amortization

Assume that your aunt sold her house on December 31, and to help close the sale she took a second mortgage in the amount of $10,000 as part of the payment. The mortgage has a quoted (or nominal) interest rate of 10%; it calls for payments every 6 months, beginning on June 30, and is to be amortized over 10 years. Now, 1 year later, your aunt must inform the IRS and the person who bought the house about the interest that was included in the two payments made during the year. (This interest will be income to your aunt and a deduction to the buyer of the house.) To the closest dollar, what is the total amount of interest that was paid during the first year?

CHALLENGING PROBLEMS 30–34

(4-30)
Loan Amortization

Your company is planning to borrow $1 million on a 5-year, 15%, annual payment, fully amortized term loan. What fraction of the payment made at the end of the second year will represent repayment of principal?

(4-31)
Nonannual Compounding

It is now January 1. You plan to make a total of 5 deposits of $100 each, one every 6 months, with the first payment being made *today*. The bank pays a nominal interest rate of 12% but uses *semiannual* compounding. You plan to leave the money in the bank for 10 years.

  a. How much will be in your account after 10 years?
  b. You must make a payment of $1,432.02 in 10 years. To get the money for this payment, you will make five equal deposits, beginning today and for the following 4 quarters, in a bank that pays a nominal interest rate of 12% with *quarterly compounding*. How large must each of the five payments be?

(4-32)
Nominal Rate of Return

Anne Lockwood, manager of Oaks Mall Jewelry, wants to sell on credit, giving customers 3 months to pay. However, Anne will have to borrow from her bank to carry the accounts receivable. The bank will charge a nominal rate of 15% and will compound monthly. Anne wants to quote a nominal rate to her customers (all of whom are expected to pay on time) that will exactly offset her financing costs. What nominal annual rate should she quote to her credit customers?

(4-33)
Required Annuity Payments

Assume that your father is now 50 years old, plans to retire in 10 years, and expects to live for 25 years after he retires—that is, until age 85. He wants his first retirement payment to have the same purchasing power at the time he retires as $40,000 has today. He wants all of his subsequent retirement payments to be equal to his first retirement payment. (Do not let the retirement payments grow with inflation: Your father realizes that if inflation occurs the real value of his retirement income will decline year by year after he retires.) His retirement income will begin the day he retires, 10 years from today, and he will then receive 24 additional annual payments. Inflation is expected to be 5% per year from today forward. He currently has $100,000 saved and expects to earn a return on his savings of 8% per year with annual compounding. To the nearest dollar, how much must he save during each of the next 10 years (with equal deposits being made at the end of each year, beginning a year from today) to meet his retirement goal? (*Note:* Neither the amount he saves nor the amount he withdraws upon retirement is a growing annuity.)

(4-34)
Growing Annuity Payments

You want to accumulate $1 million by your retirement date, which is 25 years from now. You will make 25 deposits in your bank, with the first occurring *today*. The bank pays 8% interest, compounded annually. You expect to receive annual raises of 3%, which will offset inflation, and you will let the amount you deposit each year also grow by 3% (i.e., your second deposit will be 3% greater than your first, the third will be 3% greater than the second, etc.). How much must your first deposit be if you are to meet your goal?

SPREADSHEET PROBLEM

(4-35)
Build a Model:
The Time Value
of Money

resource

Start with the partial model in the file *Ch04 P35 Build a Model.xlsx* from the textbook's Web site. Answer the following questions, using the spreadsheet model to do the calculations.

a. Find the FV of $1,000 invested to earn 10% annually 5 years from now. Answer this question first by using a math formula and then by using the *Excel* function wizard.

b. Now create a table that shows the FV at 0%, 5%, and 20% for 0, 1, 2, 3, 4, and 5 years. Then create a graph with years on the horizontal axis and FV on the vertical axis to display your results.

c. Find the PV of $1,000 due in 5 years if the discount rate is 10% per year. Again, first work the problem with a formula and then by using the function wizard.

d. A security has a cost of $1,000 and will return $2,000 after 5 years. What rate of return does the security provide?

e. Suppose California's population is 30 million people and its population is expected to grow by 2% per year. How long would it take for the population to double?

f. Find the PV of an ordinary annuity that pays $1,000 at the end of each of the next 5 years if the interest rate is 15%. Then find the FV of that same annuity.

g. How would the PV and FV of the above annuity change if it were an annuity due rather than an ordinary annuity?

h. What would the FV and PV for parts a and c be if the interest rate were 10% with *semiannual* compounding rather than 10% with *annual* compounding?

i. Find the PV and FV of an investment that makes the following end-of-year payments. The interest rate is 8%.

Year	Payment
1	$100
2	200
3	400

j. Suppose you bought a house and took out a mortgage for $50,000. The interest rate is 8%, and you must amortize the loan over 10 years with equal end-of-year payments. Set up an amortization schedule that shows the annual payments and the amount of each payment that repays the principal and the amount that constitutes interest expense to the borrower and interest income to the lender.

(1) Create a graph that shows how the payments are divided between interest and principal repayment over time.

(2) Suppose the loan called for 10 years of monthly payments, 120 payments in all, with the same original amount and the same nominal interest rate. What would the amortization schedule show now?

MINI CASE

Assume that you are nearing graduation and have applied for a job with a local bank. The bank's evaluation process requires you to take an examination that covers several financial analysis techniques. The first section of the test addresses discounted cash flow analysis. See how you would do by answering the following questions.

a. Draw time lines for (1) a $100 lump sum cash flow at the end of Year 2, (2) an ordinary annuity of $100 per year for 3 years, and (3) an uneven cash flow stream of −$50, $100, $75, and $50 at the end of Years 0 through 3.

b. (1) What's the *future value* of an initial $100 after 3 years if it is invested in an account paying 10% annual interest?

   (2) What's the *present value* of $100 to be received in 3 years if the appropriate interest rate is 10%?

c. We sometimes need to find out how long it will take a sum of money (or something else, such as earnings, population, or prices) to grow to some specified amount. For example, if a company's sales are growing at a rate of 20% per year, how long will it take sales to double?

d. If you want an investment to double in 3 years, what interest rate must it earn?

e. What's the difference between an ordinary annuity and an annuity due? What type of annuity is shown below? How would you change the time line to show the other type of annuity?

f. (1) What's the future value of a 3-year ordinary annuity of $100 if the appropriate interest rate is 10%?

   (2) What's the present value of the annuity?

   (3) What would the future and present values be if the annuity were an annuity due?

g. What is the present value of the following uneven cash flow stream? The appropriate interest rate is 10%, compounded annually.

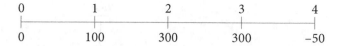

h. (1) Define the stated (quoted) or nominal rate I_{NOM} as well as the periodic rate I_{PER}.

   (2) Will the future value be larger or smaller if we compound an initial amount more often than annually—for example, every 6 months, or *semiannually*—holding the stated interest rate constant? Why?

   (3) What is the future value of $100 after 5 years under 12% annual compounding? Semiannual compounding? Quarterly compounding? Monthly compounding? Daily compounding?

   (4) What is the effective annual rate (EAR or EFF%)? What is the EFF% for a nominal rate of 12%, compounded semiannually? Compounded quarterly? Compounded monthly? Compounded daily?

i. Will the effective annual rate ever be equal to the nominal (quoted) rate?

j. (1) Construct an amortization schedule for a $1,000, 10% annual rate loan with three equal installments.

   (2) During Year 2, what is the annual interest expense for the borrower, and what is the annual interest income for the lender?

k. Suppose that on January 1 you deposit $100 in an account that pays a nominal (or quoted) interest rate of 11.33463%, with interest added (compounded) daily. How much will you have in your account on October 1, or 9 months later?

l. (1) What is the value at the end of Year 3 of the following cash flow stream if the quoted interest rate is 10%, compounded semiannually?

   (2) What is the PV of the same stream?

   (3) Is the stream an annuity?

   (4) An important rule is that you should never show a nominal rate on a time line or use it in calculations unless what condition holds? (*Hint:* Think of annual compounding, when I_{NOM} = EFF% = I_{PER}.) What would be wrong with your answers to parts (1) and (2) if you used the nominal rate of 10% rather than the periodic rate, $I_{NOM}/2$ = 10%/2 = 5%?

m. Suppose someone offered to sell you a note calling for the payment of $1,000 in 15 months. They offer to sell it to you for $850. You have $850 in a bank time deposit that pays a 6.76649% nominal rate with daily compounding, which is a 7% effective annual interest rate, and you plan to leave the money in the bank unless you buy the note. The note is not risky—you are sure it will be paid on schedule. Should you buy the note? Check the decision in three ways: (1) by comparing your future value if you buy the note versus leaving your money in the bank; (2) by comparing the PV of the note with your current bank account; and (3) by comparing the EFF% on the note with that of the bank account.

CHAPTER 5

Bonds, Bond Valuation, and Interest Rates

A lot of bonds have been issued in the United States, and we mean a *lot!* According to the Federal Reserve, in 2017 there were $15.8 trillion of outstanding U.S. Treasury securities, $3.8 trillion of municipal securities, and $5.2 trillion of corporate bonds. Not only is the dollar amount mind-boggling, but so is the variety.

Bonds aren't the only way to borrow. In addition to their bonds, corporations owe $2.9 trillion in short-term debt. Noncorporate businesses, which include small businesses, owe $5.2 trillion.

Let's not ignore households, which owe $3.8 trillion in consumer debt, such as car loans, student loans, and credit cards. This works out to about $30,000 per household, and this doesn't even include the $9.2 trillion in mortgages owed by homeowners.

Given the enormous amount of debt in the modern world, it is vital for everyone to understand debt and interest rates.

Sources: Board of Governors of the Federal Reserve, "Financial Accounts of the United States—Z.1", **www.federalreserve.gov/releases/z1/default.htm;** Federal Reserve Bank of New York at **www.newyorkfed.org/microeconomics/hhdc.html;** and Federal Reserve Bank of St. Louis, "Total Households," **https://fred.stlouisfed.org/series/TTLHH**.

Intrinsic Value and the Cost of Debt

This chapter explains bond pricing and bond risk, which affect the return demanded by a firm's bondholders. A bondholder's return is a cost from the company's point of view. This cost of debt affects the firm's weighted average cost of capital (WACC), which in turn affects the company's intrinsic value. Therefore, it is important for all managers to understand the cost of debt, which we explain in this chapter.

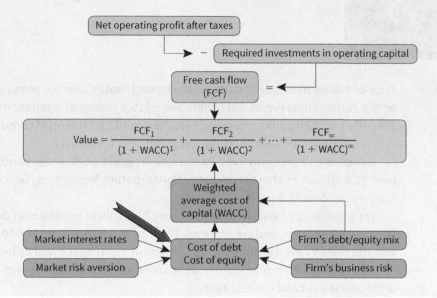

Growing companies must acquire land, buildings, equipment, inventory, and other operating assets. The debt markets are a major source of funding for such purchases. Therefore, every manager should have a working knowledge of the types of bonds that companies and government agencies issue, the terms that are contained in bond contracts, the types of risks to which both bond investors and issuers are exposed, and procedures for determining the values of and rates of return on bonds.

5-1 Who Issues Bonds?

resource

*The textbook's Web site contains an Excel file that will guide you through the chapter's calculations. The file for this chapter is **Ch05 Tool Kit.xlsx**, and we encourage you to open the file and follow along as you read the chapter.*

A **bond** is a long-term contract under which a borrower agrees to make payments of interest and principal, on specific dates, to the holders of the bond. For example, on January 1, 2019, MicroDrive Inc. issued $170 million of bonds.[1] For convenience, we assume that MicroDrive sold 170,000 individual bonds for $1,000 each. (Actually, it could have sold one $170 million bond, 10 bonds with a $17 million face value, or any other combination that totals to $170 million.) In exchange for 170 million, MicroDrive promised to make annual interest payments and to repay the 170 million on a specified maturity date.

Investors have many choices when investing in bonds, but bonds are classified into four main types: Treasury, corporate, municipal, and foreign. Each type differs with respect to expected return and degree of risk.

---

[1]The bonds would actually be issued on the first business day of the year. To reduce unnecessary complications, we will assume that they were issued on January 1.

Treasury bonds (T-bonds) and **Treasury bills (T-bills)**, sometimes referred to as *government bonds,* are issued by the U.S. federal government.[2] It is reasonable to assume that the federal government will make good on its promised payments, so these bonds have almost no default risk. However, Treasury bond prices decline when interest rates rise, so they are not free of all risks.

Federal agencies and other government-sponsored enterprises (GSEs) include the Tennessee Valley Authority, the Small Business Administration, Fannie Mae, Freddie Mac, and the Federal Home Loan Bank System, among others. **Agency debt** and **GSE debt** are not officially backed by the full faith and credit of the U.S. government, but investors assume that the government implicitly guarantees this debt, so these bonds carry interest rates only slightly higher than Treasury bonds. In 2008, the implicit guarantee became much more explicit as the government placed several GSEs into conservatorship, including Fannie Mae and Freddie Mac.

Corporate bonds, as the name implies, are issued by corporations. Unlike Treasury bonds, corporate bonds are exposed to default risk—if the issuing company gets into trouble, it may be unable to make the promised interest and principal payments. Different corporate bonds have different levels of default risk, depending on the issuing company's characteristics and the terms of the specific bond. Default risk is often referred to as "credit risk," and the larger the credit risk, the higher the interest rate the issuer must pay.

Municipal bonds, or "munis," are issued by state and local governments. Like corporate bonds, munis have default risk. However, munis offer one major advantage: The interest earned on most municipal bonds is exempt from federal taxes and also from state taxes if the holder is a resident of the issuing state. Consequently, municipal bonds carry interest rates that are considerably lower than those on corporate bonds with the same default risk.

Foreign bonds are issued by foreign governments or foreign corporations. Foreign corporate bonds are, of course, exposed to default risk, and so are some foreign government bonds, as became apparent in the spring of 2012 when Greece forced its bondholders into an exchange of securities that reduced the value of their holdings of Greek government debt by more than 50%. An additional risk exists if the bonds are denominated in a currency other than that of the investor's home currency. For example, if a U.S. investor purchases a corporate bond denominated in Japanese yen and if the yen subsequently falls relative to the dollar, then the investor will lose money even if the company does not default on its bonds.

SELF-TEST

What is a bond?

What are the four main types of bonds?

Why are U.S. Treasury bonds not riskless?

To what types of risk are investors of foreign bonds exposed?

5-2 Key Characteristics of Bonds

Although all bonds have some common characteristics, they do not always have identical contractual features, as described here.

---

[2]The U.S. Treasury actually issues three types of securities: bills, notes, and bonds. A bond makes an equal payment every 6 months until it matures, at which time it makes an additional payment. If the maturity at the time of issue is less than 10 years, the security is called a note rather than a bond. A T-bill has a maturity of 52 weeks or less at the time of issue, and it makes no payments at all until it matures. Thus, T-bills are sold initially at a discount to their face, or maturity, value.

Betting With or Against the U.S. Government: The Case of Treasury Bond Credit Default Swaps

It might be hard to believe, but there is actually a market for U.S. Treasury bond insurance. In July 2011, investors worried that Congress would not extend the debt ceiling, inducing defaults in Treasury securities. At that time, a credit default swap (CDS) on a 5-year T-bond was selling for 63.5 basis points. (A basis point is 1/100 of a percentage point.) This means that you could pay $6.35 a year to a counterparty who would promise to insure $1,000 of T-bond principal against default. Considering that the T-bond was yielding an amount equal

to about $15 a year, the insurance would eat up a lot of the annual return for an investor who owned the bond. However, most of the trading in this CDS is by speculators and hedgers who don't even own the T-bond but are simply betting for or against the financial soundness of the U.S. government.

But it does make you wonder: "If the United States fails, who will be around to pay off the CDS?"

Note: For updates on the 5-year CDS, go to **www.cnbc.com/id/38451750**, and scroll down to "US CDS 5YR."

5-2a Par Value

The **par value** is the stated face value of the bond; for illustrative purposes, we generally assume a par value of $1,000. In practice, some bonds have par values that are multiples of $1,000 (for example, $5,000), and some have par values of less than $1,000. (Treasury bonds can be purchased in multiples of $100.) The par value generally represents the amount of money the firm borrows and promises to repay on the maturity date.

5-2b Coupon Interest Rate

MicroDrive's bonds require the company to pay a fixed number of dollars of interest every year (or, more typically, every 6 months). When this **coupon payment**, as it is called, is divided by the par value, the result is the **coupon interest rate**. For example, MicroDrive's bonds have a $1,000 par value, and they pay $100 in interest each year. The bond's coupon interest is $100, so its coupon interest rate is $100/$1,000 = 10%. The coupon payment, which is fixed at the time the bond is issued, remains in force during the life of the bond.[3] Typically, at the time a bond is issued, its coupon payment is set at a level that will enable the bond to be issued at or near its par value.

In some cases, a bond's coupon payment will vary over time. For these **floating-rate bonds**, the coupon rate is set for, say, the initial 6-month period, after which it is adjusted every 6 months based on some market rate. Some corporate issues are tied to the Treasury bond rate; other issues are tied to other rates, such as **LIBOR** (the London Interbank Offered Rate). Many additional provisions can be included in floating-rate issues. For example, some are convertible to fixed-rate debt, whereas others have upper and lower limits (*caps* and *floors*) on how high or low the rate can go.

Floating-rate debt is popular with investors who are worried about the risk of rising interest rates because the interest paid on such bonds increases whenever market rates rise. This stabilizes the market value of the debt, and it also provides institutional buyers, such as banks, with income that is better geared to their own obligations. Banks' deposit costs rise with interest rates, so the income on floating-rate loans they have made rises at the

---

[3]At one time, bonds literally had a number of small coupons attached to them, and on each interest payment date the owner would clip off the coupon for that date and either cash it at the bank or mail it to the company's paying agent, who would then mail back a check for the interest. For example, a 30-year, semiannual bond would start with 60 coupons. Today, most new bonds are *registered*—no physical coupons are involved, and interest checks automatically are mailed to the registered owners or directly deposited in their bank accounts.

same time as their deposit costs rise. The savings and loan industry was almost destroyed as a result of its former practice of making fixed-rate mortgage loans but borrowing on floating-rate terms. If you earn 6% fixed but pay 10% floating (which they were), you will soon go bankrupt (which they did). Moreover, floating-rate debt appeals to corporations that want to issue long-term debt without committing themselves to paying a historically high interest rate for the entire life of the loan.

resource

For more on zero coupon bonds, including U.S. Treasury STRIP bonds, see **Web Extension 5A** *on the textbook's Web site.*

Some bonds pay no coupons at all but are offered at a substantial discount below their par values and hence provide capital appreciation rather than interest income. These securities are called **zero coupon bonds** ("zeros"). Most zero coupon bonds are Treasury bonds, although some are issued by banks. Some bonds are issued with a coupon rate too low for the bond to be issued at par, so the bond is issued at a price less than its par value. In general, any bond originally offered at a price significantly below its par value is called an **original issue discount (OID) bond**.

Some bonds don't pay cash coupons but pay coupons consisting of additional bonds (or a percentage of an additional bond). These are called **payment-in-kind (PIK) bonds**. PIK bonds are usually issued by companies with cash flow problems, which makes them risky.

Some bonds have a step-up provision: If the company's bond rating is downgraded, then it must increase the bond's coupon rate. Step-ups are more popular in Europe than in the United States, but that is beginning to change. Note that a step-up is quite dangerous from the company's standpoint. The downgrade means that it is having trouble servicing its debt, and the step-up will exacerbate the problem. This combination has led to a number of bankruptcies.

5-2c Maturity Date

Bonds generally have a specified **maturity date** on which the par value must be repaid. MicroDrive bonds issued on January 1, 2019, will mature on December 31, 2033; thus, they have a 15-year maturity at the time they are issued. Most bonds have an **original maturity** (the maturity at the time the bond is issued) ranging from 10 to 40 years, but any maturity is legally permissible.[4] Of course, the effective maturity of a bond declines each year after it has been issued. Thus, MicroDrive's bonds have a 15-year original maturity, but in 2020, a year later, they will have a 14-year maturity, and so on.

Some bonds have no maturity date. For example, the British government issued some bonds in the mid-1700s with a constant payment each period but without a stated maturity date. The government used the proceeds to pay off other British bonds. Because this action consolidated the government's debt, the new bonds were called "consols." The term stuck, and now any bond that promises to pay interest perpetually is called a **consol**. The terms of the bonds allowed the U.K. to redeem them for a certain amount. Although the consols were around for over 200 years, the U.K. redeemed the last one in 2015. Although the U.K. no longer has consols, some banks in India offer perpetual bonds, though most are callable, a feature described in the next section.

5-2d Provisions to Call or Redeem Bonds

Most corporate bonds contain a **call provision**, which gives the issuing corporation the right to call the bonds for redemption.[5] The call provision generally states that the company

---

[4] In July 1993, Walt Disney Co., attempting to lock in a low interest rate, issued the first 100-year bonds to be sold by any borrower in modern times. Soon after, Coca-Cola became the second company to stretch the meaning of "long-term bond" by selling $150 million of 100-year bonds.

[5] A majority of municipal bonds also contain call provisions. Although the U.S. Treasury no longer issues callable bonds, some past Treasury issues were callable.

You Can Take That to the Bank

To finance canals and dykes in the Netherlands, local communities would band together and create Water Board Authorities. One such board issued a bond in 1648 that had no maturity and would pay 5% interest perpetually. Here's the catch: To collect the interest payment, the bondholder would have to take the bond, written on goatskin, to the board.

As you might expect, many of the boards no longer exist, and many of the goatskin bonds have not survived the years. An exception is the bond purchased by the Beinecke Rare Book & Manuscript Library at Yale in 2003. The bond

had 26 years of accrued interest, so a Yale finance professor took the bond to the Netherlands and collected the interest. Yale keeps the bond in the museum except for infrequent trips to collect the interest. The last trip was in 2015 to collect 12 years of accrued interest, which was about 136 euros. That certainly didn't pay for airfare or other expenses, but it proved that the bond is a living artifact.

Source: See **https://news.yale.edu/2015/09/22/living-artifact -dutch-golden-age-yale-s-367-year-old-water-bond-still -pays-interest**.

must pay the bondholders an amount greater than the par value if they are called. The additional sum, which is termed a **call premium**, is often set equal to 1 year's interest if the bonds are called during the first year, and the premium declines at a constant rate of INT/N each year thereafter (where INT = annual interest and N = original maturity in years). For example, the call premium on a $1,000 par value, 10-year, 10% bond would generally be $100 if it were called during the first year, $90 during the second year (calculated by reducing the $100, or 10%, premium by one-tenth), and so on. However, bonds are often not callable until several years (generally 5 to 10) after they are issued. This is known as a **deferred call**, and the bonds are said to have **call protection**.

Suppose a company sold bonds when interest rates were relatively high. Provided the issue is callable, the company could sell a new issue of low-yielding securities if and when interest rates drop. It could then use the proceeds of the new issue to retire the high-rate issue and thus reduce its interest expense. This process is called a **refunding operation**.

A call provision is valuable to the firm but potentially detrimental to investors. If interest rates go up, the company will not call the bond, and the investor will be stuck with the original coupon rate on the bond, even though interest rates in the economy have risen sharply. However, if interest rates fall, the company *will* call the bond and pay off investors, who then must reinvest the proceeds at the current market interest rate, which is lower than the rate they were getting on the original bond. In other words, the investor loses when interest rates go up but doesn't reap the gains when rates fall. To induce an investor to take this type of risk, a new issue of callable bonds must provide a higher coupon rate than an otherwise similar issue of noncallable bonds.

Bonds that are **redeemable at par** at the holder's option protect investors against a rise in interest rates. If rates rise, the price of a fixed-rate bond declines. However, if holders have the option of turning their bonds in and having them redeemed at par, then they are protected against rising rates. If interest rates have risen, holders will turn in the bonds and reinvest the proceeds at a higher rate.

Event risk is the chance that some sudden event will occur and increase the credit risk of a company, hence lowering the firm's bond rating and the value of its outstanding bonds. Investors' concern over event risk means that those firms deemed most likely to face events that could harm bondholders must pay extremely high interest rates. To reduce this interest rate, some bonds have a covenant called a **super poison put**, which enables a bondholder to turn in, or "put," a bond back to the issuer at par in the event of a takeover, merger, or major recapitalization.

Some callable bonds have a **make-whole provision**. This allows a company to call the bond, but it must pay a call price that is essentially equal to the market value of a similar noncallable bond. This provides companies with an easy way to repurchase bonds as part of a financial restructuring, such as a merger.

5-2e Sinking Funds

Some bonds include a **sinking fund** provision that facilitates the orderly retirement of the bond issue. On rare occasions, the firm may be required to deposit money with a trustee, which invests the funds and then uses the accumulated sum to retire the bonds when they mature. Usually, though, the sinking fund is used to buy back a certain percentage of the issue each year. A failure to meet the sinking fund requirement puts the bond into default, which may force the company into bankruptcy.

In most cases, the firm is given the right to administer the sinking fund in either of two ways.

1. The company can call in for redemption (at par value) a certain percentage of the bonds each year; for example, it might be able to call 5% of the total original amount of the issue at a price of $1,000 per bond. The bonds are numbered serially, and those called for redemption are determined by a lottery administered by the trustee.
2. The company may buy the required number of bonds on the open market.

The firm will choose the less costly method. If interest rates have risen, causing bond prices to fall, then it will buy bonds in the open market at a discount; if interest rates have fallen, it will call the bonds. Note that a call for sinking fund purposes is quite different from a refunding call, as discussed previously. A sinking fund call typically requires no call premium, but only a small percentage of the issue is normally callable in any one year.[6]

Although sinking funds are designed to protect bondholders by ensuring that an issue is retired in an orderly fashion, you should recognize that sinking funds also can work to the detriment of bondholders. For example, suppose that the bond carries a 10% interest rate but that yields on similar bonds have fallen to 7.5%. A sinking fund call at par would require an investor to give up a bond that pays $100 of interest and then to reinvest in a bond that pays only $75 per year. This obviously harms those bondholders whose bonds are called. On balance, however, bonds that have a sinking fund are regarded as being safer than those without such a provision, so at the time they are issued sinking fund bonds have lower coupon rates than otherwise similar bonds without sinking funds.

5-2f Other Provisions and Features

Owners of **convertible bonds** have the option to convert the bonds into a fixed number of shares of common stock. Convertibles offer investors the chance to share in the upside if a company does well, so investors are willing to accept a lower coupon rate on convertibles than on an otherwise identical but nonconvertible bond.

Warrants are options that permit the holder to buy stock at a fixed price, thereby providing a gain if the price of the stock rises. Some bonds are issued with warrants. As with convertibles, bonds with warrants have lower coupon rates than straight bonds.

An **income bond** is required to pay interest only if earnings are high enough to cover the interest expense. If earnings are not sufficient, then the company is not required to pay interest, and the bondholders do not have the right to force the company into bankruptcy. Therefore, from an investor's standpoint, income bonds are riskier than "regular" bonds.

---

[6]Some sinking funds require the issuer to pay a call premium.

Indexed bonds, also called **purchasing power bonds**, first became popular in Brazil, Israel, and a few other countries plagued by high inflation rates. The interest payments and maturity payment rise automatically when the inflation rate rises, thus protecting the bondholders against inflation. In January 1997, the U.S. Treasury began issuing indexed bonds called **Treasury Inflation-Protected Securities (TIPS)**. Later in this chapter we show how TIPS can be used to estimate the real risk-free rate.

5-2g Bond Markets

Corporate bonds are traded primarily in electronic markets rather than in organized exchanges. Most bonds are owned by and traded among a relatively small number of very large financial institutions, including banks, investment banks, life insurance companies, mutual funds, and pension funds. Although these institutions buy and sell very large blocks of bonds, it is relatively easy for bond dealers to arrange transactions because there are relatively few players in this market as compared with stock markets.

Information on bond trades is not widely published, and many bonds trade infrequently, if at all, but a representative group of bonds is listed and traded on the bond division of the NYSE and is reported on the bond market page of *The Wall Street Journal*. The most useful Web site (as of early 2018) is provided by the Financial Industry Regulatory Authority (FINRA) at **www.finra.org**; look for "Investors," "View All Market Data," and then "Bonds."

SELF-TEST

Define "floating-rate bonds" and "zero coupon bonds."

Why is a call provision advantageous to a bond issuer?

What are the two ways a sinking fund can be handled? Which method will be chosen by the firm if interest rates have risen? If interest rates have fallen?

Are securities that provide for a sinking fund regarded as being riskier than those without this type of provision? Explain.

What are income bonds and indexed bonds?

Why do convertible bonds and bonds with warrants have lower coupons than similarly rated bonds that do not have these features?

5-3 Bond Valuation

The value of any financial asset—a stock, a bond, a lease, or even a physical asset such as an apartment building or a piece of machinery—is simply the present value of the cash flows the asset is expected to produce. This is called **discounted cash flow (DCF) analysis**, as described in Chapter 4. The following section applies DCF analysis to a bond.

5-3a Time Line, Cash Flows, and Valuation Formulas for a Bond

For a standard coupon-bearing bond, the cash flows consist of interest payments during the life of the bond plus the amount borrowed when the bond matures (usually a $1,000 par value):

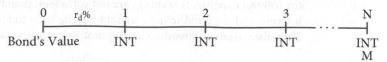

The notation in the time line is explained next.

r_d = The **required rate of return on debt**, which is the rate of return that fairly compensates an investor for purchasing or holding debt, taking into consideration its risk, timing, and the returns available on other similar investments. This is the discount rate that is used to calculate the present value of the bond's cash flows. It is also called the debt's **going interest rate**, **market interest rate**, **quoted interest rate**, **nominal annual interest rate**, or **yield**. Note that r_d is *not* the coupon interest rate. It is equal to the coupon rate only if (as in this case) the bond is selling at par. Generally, most coupon bonds are issued at par, which implies that the coupon rate is set at the r_d prevailing when the bond is issued. Thereafter, interest rates, as measured by r_d, will fluctuate, but the coupon rate is fixed, so after issue r_d will equal the coupon rate only by chance. We use the term "i" or "I" to designate the interest rate for many calculations because those terms are used on financial calculators, but "r," with the subscript "d" to designate the rate on a debt security, is normally used in finance.

N = Number of years until the bond matures. Note that N declines each year after the bond was issued, so a bond that had a maturity of 15 years when it was issued (original maturity = 15) will have N = 14 after 1 year, N = 13 after 2 years, and so on. Note also that for the sake of simplicity we assume in this section that the bond pays interest once a year, or annually, so N is measured in years. We consider bonds with semiannual payments later in the chapter.

INT = Dollars of interest paid each year = (Coupon rate)(Par value). For a bond with a 9% coupon and a $1,000 par value, the annual interest is 0.09($1,000) = $90. In calculator terminology, INT = PMT = 90. If the bond had been a semiannual payment bond, the payment would have been $45 every 6 months.

M = Par, or maturity, value of the bond. This amount must be paid off at maturity, and it is often equal to $1,000.

The following general equation, written in several forms, can be used to find the value of any bond, V_B:

$$V_B = \frac{INT}{(1 + r_d)^1} + \frac{INT}{(1 + r_d)^2} + \cdots + \frac{INT}{(1 + r_d)^N} + \frac{M}{(1 + r_d)^N}$$

$$= \sum_{t=1}^{N} \frac{INT}{(1 + r_d)^t} + \frac{M}{(1 + r_d)^N} \tag{5-1}$$

$$= INT \left[\frac{1}{r_d} - \frac{1}{r_d(1 + r_d)^N} \right] + \frac{M}{(1 + r_d)^N}$$

Observe that the cash flows consist of an annuity of N years plus an additional payment at the end of Year N. Equation 5-1 can be solved by using (1) a formula, (2) a financial calculator, or (3) a spreadsheet.

5-3b Solving for the Bond Price

Recall that MicroDrive issued a 15-year bond with an annual coupon rate of 10% and a par value of $1,000. To find the value of MicroDrive's bond by using a formula, insert values for MicroDrive's bond into Equation 5-1. You could use the first line of Equation 5-1 to discount each cash flow back to the present and then sum these PVs to find the bond's value of $1,000; see Figure 5-1 and Equation 5-1a:

$$V_B = \sum_{t=1}^{15} \frac{\$100}{(1 + 0.10)^t} + \frac{\$1,000}{(1 + 0.10)^{15}} = \$1,000 \tag{5-1a}$$

resource

See *Ch05 Tool Kit.xlsx* on the textbook's Web site.

This procedure is not very efficient, especially if the bond has many years to maturity. Alternatively, you could use the formula in the second line of Equation 5-1 with a simple or scientific calculator:

$$V_B = \$100 \left[\frac{1}{0.10} - \frac{1}{0.10(1 + 0.10)^{15}} \right] + \frac{\$1,000}{(1 + 0.10)^{15}} \tag{5-1b}$$

$$= \$760.61 + \$239.39 = \$1,000$$

As shown in Equation 5-1b, the total bond value of $1,000 is the sum of the coupons' present values ($760.61) and the par value's present value ($239.39). This is easier than the step-by-step approach, but it is still somewhat cumbersome.

A financial calculator is ideally suited for finding bond values. Here is the setup for MicroDrive's bond:

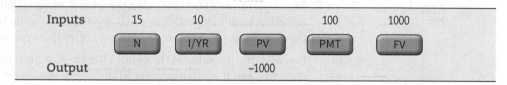

Inputs	15	10		100	1000
	N	I/YR	PV	PMT	FV
Output			−1000		

Input N = 15, I/YR = r_d = 10, INT = PMT = 100, and M = FV = 1000; then press the PV key to find the value of the bond, $1,000. Because the PV is an outflow to the investor, it is shown with a negative sign. The calculator is programmed to solve Equation 5-1: It finds the PV of an annuity of $100 per year for 15 years, discounted at 10%, then it finds the PV of the $1,000 maturity payment, and then it adds these two PVs to find the value of the bond. Notice that even though the bond has a total cash flow of $1,100 at Year 15, you should *not* enter FV = 1100! When you entered N = 15 and PMT = 100, you told the calculator that there is a $100 payment at Year 15. Thus, setting FV = 1000 accounts for any *extra* payment at Year 15, above and beyond the $100 payment.

resource

See *Ch05 Tool Kit.xlsx* on the textbook's Web site.

With *Excel*, it is easiest to use the **PV** function: =PV(I,N,PMT,FV,Type).[7] For MicroDrive's bond, the function is =PV(0.10,15,100,1000,0) with a result of −$1,000. Like the financial calculator solution, the bond value is negative because PMT and FV are positive.

Excel also provides specialized functions for bond prices based on actual dates. For example, in *Excel* you could find the MicroDrive bond value as of the date it was issued by using the function wizard to enter this formula:

=**PRICE(DATE(2019,1,1),DATE(2033,12,31),10%,10%,100,1,1)**

---

[7]In Chapter 4 we note that Type is 0 (or omitted) for payments at the end of the period and 1 for payments at the beginning of the period.

FIGURE 5-1
Finding the Value of MicroDrive's Bond (V$_B$)

	A	B	C	D	E	F	G
20	INPUTS:						
21	Years to maturity = N =		15				
22	Coupon payment = INT =		$100				
23	Par value = M =		$1,000				
24	Required return = r$_d$ =		10%				
25							
26	1. Step-by-Step: Divide each cash flow by (1 + r$_d$)^t						
27	Year (t)	Coupon Payment	PV of Coupon Payment	Par Value	PV of Par Value		
28	1	$100	$90.91				
29	2	$100	$82.64				
30	3	$100	$75.13				
31	4	$100	$68.30				
32	5	$100	$62.09				
33	6	$100	$56.45				
34	7	$100	$51.32				
35	8	$100	$46.65				
36	9	$100	$42.41				
37	10	$100	$38.55				
38	11	$100	$35.05				
39	12	$100	$31.86				
40	13	$100	$28.97				
41	14	$100	$26.33				
42	15	$100	$23.94	$1,000	$239.39		
43		Total =	$760.61				
44							
45	V$_B$ = PV of all coupon payments + PV of par value =			$1,000.00			
46							
47	Inputs:		15	0		100	1000
48	2. Financial Calculator:		N	I/YR	PV	PMT	FV
49	Output:				−$1,000.00		
50							
51	3. Excel:		PV function:	PV$_N$ =	=PV(Rate,Nper,Pmt,Fv,Type)		
52			Fixed inputs:	PV$_N$ =	=PV(10%,15,100,1000)	−$1,000.00	
53			Cell references:	PV$_N$ =	=PV(C24,C21,C22,C23)	−$1,000.00	

Source: See the file *Ch05 Tool Kit.xlsx*. Numbers are reported as rounded values for clarity but are calculated using *Excel*'s full precision. Thus, intermediate calculations using the figure's rounded values will be inexact.

The first two arguments in the function are *Excel*'s **DATE** function. The **DATE** function takes the year, month, and day as inputs and converts them into a date. The first argument is the date on which you want to find the price, and the second argument is the maturity date. The third argument in the **PRICE** function is the bond's coupon rate, followed by the required return on the bond, r$_d$. The fifth argument, 100, is the redemption value of the bond at maturity per $100 of face value; entering "100" means that the bond pays 100% of its face value when it matures. The sixth argument is the number of payments per year. The last argument, 1, tells the program to base the price on the actual number of days in each month and year. This function produces a result based upon a face value of $100. In other words, if the bond pays $100 of face value at maturity, then the **PRICE** function result is the price of the bond. Because MicroDrive's bond pays $1,000 of face value at maturity, we must multiply the **PRICE** function's result by 10. In this example, the **PRICE** function returns a result of $100. When we multiply it by 10, we get the actual price of $1,000.[8] This function is essential if a bond is being evaluated between coupon payment dates. See *Ch05 Tool Kit.xlsx* on the textbook's Web site for an example.[9]

5-3c Interest Rate Changes and Bond Prices

In this example, MicroDrive's bond is selling at a price equal to its par value. Whenever the going market rate of interest, r_d, is equal to the coupon rate, a *fixed-rate* bond will sell at its par value. Normally, the coupon rate is set at the market rate when a bond is issued, causing it to sell at par initially.

The coupon rate remains fixed after the bond is issued, but interest rates in the market move up and down. Looking at Equation 5-1, we see that an *increase* in the market interest rate (r_d) will cause the price of an outstanding bond to *fall*, whereas a *decrease* in rates will cause the bond's price to *rise*. For example, if the market interest rate on MicroDrive's bond increased by 5 percentage points to 15% immediately after it was issued, we would recalculate the price with the new market interest rate as follows:

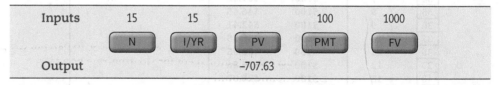

The price would fall to $707.63. Notice that the bond would then sell at a price below its par value. Whenever the going rate of interest *rises above* the coupon rate, a fixed-rate bond's price will *fall below* its par value, and it is called a **discount bond**.

On the other hand, bond prices rise when market interest rates fall. For example, if the market interest rate on MicroDrive's bond decreased by 5 percentage points to 5%, then we would once again recalculate its price:

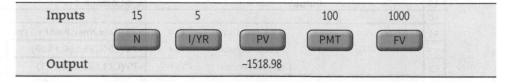

In this case, the price rises to $1,518.98. In general, whenever the going interest rate *falls below* the coupon rate, a fixed-rate bond's price will *rise above* its par value, and it is called a **premium bond**.

---

[8]The value based on the **PRICE** function with these inputs is actually $0.01 lower than the par value because the function finds the price at the end of the settlement day, which means the times to the future payments are shorter than a full year by 1 day.

[9]The bond prices quoted by brokers are calculated as described and are called "clean" prices. However, if you bought a bond between interest payment dates, the amount you would actually have to pay would be the basic price plus accrued interest, which is called the "dirty" price. Thus, if you purchased a MicroDrive bond 6 months after it was issued, your broker would send you an invoice stating that you must pay $1,000 as the basic price of the bond plus $45 interest, representing one-half the annual interest of $90, for a "dirty" price of $1,045. The seller of the bond would receive $1,045. If you bought the bond the day before its interest payment date, you would pay $1,000 + (364/365)($90) = $1,089.75. You would receive an interest payment of $90 at the end of the next day. Unless otherwise stated, all prices quoted in this text are "clean" prices.

Why do the prices of fixed-rate bonds fall if expectations for inflation rise?

What is a discount bond? A premium bond?

A bond that matures in 6 years has a par value of $1,000, an annual coupon payment of $80, and a market interest rate of 9%. What is its price? **($955.14)**

A bond that matures in 18 years has a par value of $1,000, an annual coupon of 10%, and a market interest rate of 7%. What is its price? **($1,301.77)**

5-4 Changes in Bond Values over Time

At the time a coupon bond is issued, the coupon is generally set at a level that will cause the market price of the bond to equal its par value. If a lower coupon were set, investors would not be willing to pay $1,000 for the bond, and if a higher coupon were set, investors would clamor for the bond and bid its price up over $1,000. Investment bankers can judge quite precisely the coupon rate that will cause a bond to sell at its $1,000 par value.

A bond that has just been issued is known as a **new issue bond**. (Investment bankers classify a bond as a new issue for about a month after it has first been issued. New issues are usually actively traded and are called **on-the-run bonds**.) Once the bond has been on the market for a while, it is classified as an **outstanding bond**, also called a **seasoned bond**. Newly issued bonds generally sell very close to par, but the prices of seasoned bonds can vary widely from par. Except for floating-rate bonds, coupon payments are constant, so when economic conditions change, a 10% coupon bond with a $100 coupon that sold at par when it was issued will sell for more or less than $1,000 thereafter, and the annual coupon will remain at $100.

MicroDrive's bonds with a 10% coupon rate were originally issued at par. If r_d remained constant at 10%, what would the value of the bond be 1 year after it was issued? Now the term to maturity is only 14 years—that is, N = 14. With a financial calculator, just override N = 15 with N = 14, press the PV key, and you find a value of $1,000. If we continued, setting N = 13, N = 12, and so forth, we would see that the value of the bond will remain at $1,000 as long as the going interest rate remains equal to the coupon rate, 10%.

Now suppose interest rates in the economy fell drastically after the MicroDrive bonds were issued and, as a result, r_d *fell below the coupon rate*, decreasing from 10% to 5%. Both the coupon interest payments and the maturity value remain constant, but now 5% would have to be used for r_d in Equation 5-1. The value of the bond at the end of the first year would be $1,494.93:

$$V_B = \sum_{t=1}^{14} \frac{\$100}{(1 + 0.05)^t} + \frac{\$1,000}{(1 + 0.05)^{14}}$$

$$= \$100 \left[\frac{1}{0.05} - \frac{1}{0.05(1 + 0.05)^{14}} \right] + \frac{\$1,000}{(1 + 0.05)^{14}}$$

$$= \$1,494.93$$

With a financial calculator, just change r_d = I/YR from 10 to 5, and then press the PV key to get the answer, $1,494.93. Thus, if r_d fell *below* the coupon rate, the bond would sell *above* par, or at a premium.

The arithmetic of the bond value increase should be clear, but what is the logic behind it? Because r_d has fallen to 5%, with $1,000 to invest, you could buy new bonds like Micro-Drive's (every day some 10 to 12 companies sell new bonds), except that these new bonds would pay $50 of interest each year rather than $100. Naturally, you would prefer $100 to $50, so you would be willing to pay more than $1,000 for a MicroDrive bond to obtain its higher coupons. All investors would react similarly; as a result, the MicroDrive bonds would be bid up in price to $1,494.93, at which point they would provide the same 4% rate of return to a potential investor as the new bonds.

Assuming that interest rates remain constant at 5% for the next 14 years, what would happen to the value of a MicroDrive bond? It would fall gradually from $1,494.93 to $1,000 at maturity, when MicroDrive will redeem each bond for $1,000. This point can be illustrated by calculating the value of the bond 1 year later, when it has 13 years remaining to maturity. With a financial calculator, simply input the values for N, I/YR, PMT, and FV, now using N = 13, and press the PV key to find the value of the bond, $1,469.68. Thus, the value of the bond will have fallen from $1,494.93 to $1,469.68, or by $25.25. If you were to calculate the value of the bond at other future dates, the price would continue to fall as the maturity date approached.

Note that if you purchased the bond at a price of $1,494.93 and then sold it 1 year later with r_d still at 5%, you would have a capital loss of $25.25, or a total dollar return of $100.00 − $25.25 = $74.75. Your percentage rate of return would consist of the rate of return due to the interest payment (called the **current yield**) and the rate of return due to the price change (called the **capital gains yield**). This total rate of return is often called the bond yield, and it is calculated as follows:

$$\text{Interest, or current, yield} = \$100/\$1{,}494.93 = 0.0669 = 6.69\%$$
$$\text{Capital gains yield} = -\$25.25/\$1{,}494.93 = -0.0169 = \underline{-1.69\%}$$
$$\text{Total rate of return, or yield} = \$74.75/\$1{,}494.93 = 0.0500 = \underline{\underline{5.00\%}}$$

Had interest rates risen from 10% to 15% during the first year after issue (rather than falling from 10% to 5%), then you would enter N = 14, I/YR = 15, PMT = 100, and FV = 1000, and then press the PV key to find the value of the bond, $713.78. In this case, the bond would sell below its par value, or at a discount. The total expected future return on the bond would again consist of an expected return due to interest and an expected return due to capital gains or capital losses. In this situation, the capital gains yield would be *positive*. The total return would be 15%. To see this, calculate the price of the bond with 13 years left to maturity, assuming that interest rates remain at 15%. With a calculator, enter N = 13, I/YR = 15, PMT = 100, and FV = 1000; then press PV to obtain the bond's value, $720.84.

Note that the capital gain for the year is the difference between the bond's value at Year 2 (with 13 years remaining) and the bond's value at Year 1 (with 14 years remaining), or $720.84 − $713.78 = $7.06. The interest yield, capital gains yield, and total yield are calculated as follows:

$$\text{Interest, or current, yield} = \$100/\$713.78 = 0.1401 = 14.01\%$$
$$\text{Capital gains yield} = \$7.06/\$713.78 = 0.0099 = \underline{0.99\%}$$
$$\text{Total rate of return, or yield} = \$107.06/\$713.78 = 0.1500 = \underline{\underline{15.00\%}}$$

Figure 5-2 graphs the value of the bond over time, assuming that interest rates in the economy (1) remain constant at 10%, (2) fall to 5% and then remain constant at that level, or (3) rise to 15% and remain constant at that level. Of course, if interest rates do *not* remain constant, then the price of the bond will fluctuate. However, regardless of what future interest rates do, the bond's price will approach $1,000 as it nears the maturity date (barring bankruptcy, which might cause the bond's value to fall dramatically).

FIGURE 5-2
Time Path of the Value of a 10% Coupon, $1,000 Par Value Bond When Interest Rates Are 5%, 10%, and 15%

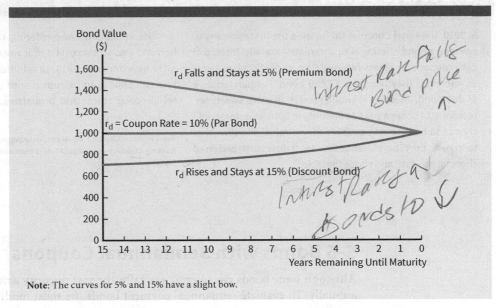

Note: The curves for 5% and 15% have a slight bow.

resource

*See **Ch05 Tool Kit.xlsx** for all calculations.*

Figure 5-2 illustrates the following key points.

1. Whenever the going rate of interest, r_d, is equal to the coupon rate, a *fixed-rate* bond will sell at its par value. Normally, the coupon rate is set equal to the going rate when a bond is issued, causing it to sell at par initially.
2. Interest rates do change over time, but the coupon rate remains fixed after the bond has been issued. Whenever the going rate of interest *rises above* the coupon rate, a fixed-rate bond's price will *fall below* its par value. Such a bond is called a discount bond.
3. Whenever the going rate of interest *falls below* the coupon rate, a fixed-rate bond's price will *rise above* its par value. Such a bond is called a premium bond.
4. Thus, an *increase* in interest rates will cause the prices of outstanding bonds to *fall*, whereas a *decrease* in rates will cause bond prices to *rise*.
5. The market value of a bond will always approach its par value as its maturity date approaches, provided the firm does not go bankrupt.

These points are very important, for they show that bondholders may suffer capital losses or make capital gains depending on whether interest rates rise or fall after the bond is purchased.

SELF-TEST

What is meant by the terms "new issue" and "seasoned issue"?

Last year, a firm issued 30-year, 8% annual coupon bonds at a par value of $1,000. (1) Suppose that 1 year later the going rate drops to 6%. What is the new price of the bonds, assuming that they now have 29 years to maturity? (**$1,271.81**) *(2) Suppose instead that 1 year after issue, the going interest rate increases to 10% (rather than dropping to 6%). What is the price?* (**$812.61**)

Chocolate Bonds

In 2010, the Hotel Chocolat UK became the first company to sweeten a bond offering with chocolate—literally! Instead of cash coupons, investors received 6 boxes of chocolate a year as interest if they bought a £2,000 bond. For purchasing a £4,000 bond, an investor would receive an extra sweetener, receiving 13 boxes a year. At maturity in 2014, investors could choose to be repaid in cash for their original investment or to renew their bonds annually. Most investors preferred chocolate to cash and chose the latter.

The chocolate bond offering raised about £4.2 million and was so successful that Hotel Chocolat decided to offer new bonds in 2014. In addition to chocolate, investors can choose to be repaid with gift certificates to Hotel Chocolat stores and properties, including its hotel in St. Lucia. Sweet!

Sources: Hotel Chocolat's Web site, including **www.hotelchocolat.com/uk /tasting-club/our-story/chocolate-bonds** and **www.hotelchocolat.com /uk/about.**

5-5 Bonds with Semiannual Coupons

Although some bonds pay interest annually, the vast majority actually pay interest semiannually. To evaluate semiannual payment bonds, we must modify the valuation model as follows.

1. Divide the annual coupon interest payment by 2 to determine the dollars of interest paid every 6 months.
2. Multiply the years to maturity, N, by 2 to determine the number of semiannual periods.
3. Divide the nominal (quoted) interest rate, r_d, by 2 to determine the periodic (semiannual) interest rate.

By making these changes, we obtain the following equation for finding the value of a bond that pays interest semiannually:

$$V_B = \sum_{t=1}^{2N} \frac{INT/2}{(1 + r_d/2)^t} + \frac{M}{(1 + r_d/2)^{2N}} \tag{5-2}$$

To illustrate, assume now that MicroDrive's bonds pay $50 interest every 6 months rather than $100 at the end of each year. Each semiannual interest payment is only half as large, but there are twice as many of them. The nominal, or quoted, coupon rate is "10%, semiannual payments."[10]

---

[10]In this situation, the coupon rate of "10% paid semiannually" is the rate that bond dealers, corporate treasurers, and investors generally would discuss. Of course, if this bond were issued at par, then its *effective annual rate* would be higher than its 10% coupon rate:

$$EAR = EFF\% = \left(1 + \frac{r_{NOM}}{M}\right)^M - 1 = \left(1 + \frac{0.10}{2}\right)^2 - 1 = (1.05)^2 - 1 = 10.25\%$$

Notice that this is in contrast to the situation for an otherwise identical bond but with annual coupon payments, which has an effective annual rate equal to its coupon rate.

When the going (nominal) rate of interest is 5% with semiannual compounding, the value of this 15-year bond is found as follows:

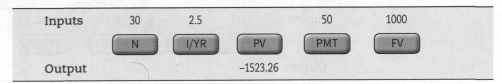

Inputs	30	2.5		50	1000
	N	I/YR	PV	PMT	FV
Output			−1523.26		

Enter N = 30, r_d = I/YR = 2.5, PMT = 50, FV = 1000, and then press the PV key to obtain the bond's value, $1,523.26. The value with semiannual interest payments is slightly larger than the value when interest is paid annually, $1,518.98. This higher value occurs because interest payments are received somewhat sooner under semiannual compounding.

SELF-TEST

Describe how the annual bond valuation formula is changed to evaluate semiannual coupon bonds. Write out the revised formula.

A bond has a 25-year maturity, an 8% annual coupon paid semiannually, and a face value of $1,000. The going nominal annual interest rate (r_d) is 6%. What is the bond's price? **($1,257.30)**

5-6 Bond Yields

Unlike the coupon interest rate, which is fixed, the bond's *yield* varies from day to day depending on current market conditions. Moreover, the yield can be calculated in three different ways, and three "answers" can be obtained. These different yields are described in the following sections.

5-6a Yield to Maturity

Suppose you purchased MicroDrive's bond at a price of $1,494.93 exactly 1 year after it was issued. The bond you now own has a 10% annual coupon, $1,000 par value, and a maturity of 14 years (because you bought it 1 year after it was issued with an original maturity of 15 years). What rate of interest would you earn on your investment if you bought the bond and held it to maturity? This rate is called the bond's **yield to maturity (YTM)**, and it is the interest rate generally discussed by investors when they talk about rates of return. The yield to maturity is usually the same as the market rate of interest, r_d. To find the YTM for a bond with annual interest payments, you must solve Equation 5-1 for r_d:[11]

$$\text{Bond price} = \sum_{t=1}^{N} \frac{\text{INT}}{(1 + \text{YTM})^t} + \frac{M}{(1 + \text{YTM})^N} \qquad (5\text{-}3)$$

For MicroDrive's yield, you must solve this equation:

$$\$1,494.93 = \frac{\$100}{(1 + r_d)^1} + \cdots + \frac{\$100}{(1 + r_d)^{14}} + \frac{\$1,000}{(1 + r_d)^{14}}$$

You could substitute values for r_d until you found a value that "works" and forces the sum of the PVs on the right side of the equal sign to equal $1,494.93, but this would be

---

[11]If the bond has semiannual payments, you must solve Equation 5-2 for r_d.

tedious and time-consuming.[12] As you might guess, it is much easier with a financial calculator. Here is the setup:

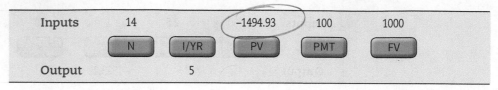

Inputs	14		−1494.93	100	1000
	N	I/YR	PV	PMT	FV
Output		5			

Simply enter N = 14, PV = −1,494.93, PMT = 100, and FV = 1000, and then press the I/YR key for the answer of 5%.

You could also find the YTM with a spreadsheet. In *Excel*, you would use the **RATE** function for this bond, inputting N = 14, PMT = 100, PV = −1494.93, FV = 1000, 0 for Type, and leave Guess blank: **=RATE(14,100,−1494.93,1000,0)**. The result is 5%. The **RATE** function works only if the current date is immediately after either the issue date or a coupon payment date. To find bond yields on other dates, use *Excel*'s **YIELD** function. See the *Ch05 Tool Kit.xlsx* file for an example.

The yield to maturity can be viewed as the bond's *promised rate of return,* which is the return that investors will receive if all the promised payments are made. However, the yield to maturity equals the *expected rate of return* only if: (1) The probability of default is zero. (2) The bond cannot be called. If there is some default risk or if the bond may be called, then there is some probability that the promised payments to maturity will not be received, in which case the calculated yield to maturity will differ from the expected return.

The YTM for a bond that sells at par consists entirely of an interest yield, but if the bond sells at a price other than its par value, then the YTM will consist of the interest yield plus a positive or negative capital gains yield. Note also that a bond's yield to maturity changes whenever interest rates in the economy change, and this is almost daily. If you purchase a bond and hold it until it matures, you will receive the YTM that existed on the purchase date, but the bond's calculated YTM will change frequently between the purchase date and the maturity date.[13]

5-6b Yield to Call

If you purchased a bond that was callable and the company called it, you would not be able to hold the bond until it matured. Therefore, the yield to maturity would not be earned. For example, if MicroDrive's 10% coupon bonds were callable and if interest rates fell from 10% to 5%, then the company could call in the 10% bonds, replace them with 4% bonds, and save $100 − $50 = $50 interest per bond per year. This would be good for the company but not for the bondholders.

---

[12]Alternatively, you can substitute values of r_d into the third form of Equation 5-1 until you find a value that works.

[13]We often are asked by students if the purchaser of a bond will receive the YTM if interest rates subsequently change. The answer is definitely "Yes" provided the question means, "Is the realized rate of return on the investment in the bond equal to the YTM?" This is because the realized rate of return on an investment is by definition the rate that sets the present value of the realized cash flows equal to the price. If instead the question means, "Is the realized rate of return on the investment in the bond and the subsequent reinvestment of the coupons equal to the YTM?" then the answer is definitely "No." Thus, the question really is one about strategy and timing. The bond, in combination with a reinvestment strategy, is really two investments, and clearly the realized rate on this combined strategy depends on the reinvestment rate. (See *Web Extension 5C* for more on investing for a target future value.) For the rest of the book, we assume that an investment in a bond is only an investment in the bond and not a combination of the bond and a reinvestment strategy; this means the investor earns the expected YTM if the bond is held to maturity.

If current interest rates are well below an outstanding bond's coupon rate, then a callable bond is likely to be called, and investors will estimate its expected rate of return as the **yield to call (YTC)** rather than as the yield to maturity. To calculate the YTC, solve this equation for r_d:

$$\text{Price of callable bond} = \sum_{t=1}^{N} \frac{\text{INT}}{(1 + r_d)^t} + \frac{\text{Call price}}{(1 + r_d)^N} \qquad (5\text{-}4)$$

Here N is the number of years until the company can call the bond, r_d is the YTC, and "Call price" is the price the company must pay in order to call the bond (it is often set equal to the par value plus 1 year's interest).

To illustrate, suppose MicroDrive's bonds had a provision that permitted the company, if it desired, to call the bonds 10 years after the issue date at a price of $1,100. Suppose further that 1 year after issuance the going interest rate had declined, causing the price of the bonds to rise to $1,494.93. Here is the time line and the setup for finding the bond's YTC with a financial calculator:

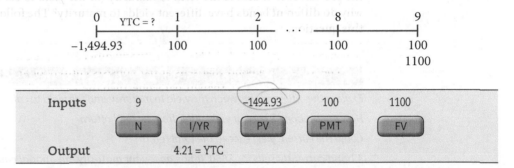

The YTC is 4.21%, which is the return you would earn if you bought the bond at a price of $1,494.93 and it was called 9 years from today. (The bond could not be called until 10 years after issuance, and 1 year has gone by, so there are 9 years left until the first call date.)

Do you think MicroDrive *will* call the bonds when they become callable? MicroDrive's actions will depend on the going interest rate when the bonds become callable. If the going rate remains at $r_d = 5\%$, then MicroDrive could save 10% − 5% = 5%, or $50 per bond per year, by calling them and replacing the 10% bonds with a new 5% issue. There would be costs to the company to refund the issue, but the interest savings would probably be worth the cost, so MicroDrive would probably refund the bonds. Therefore, you would probably earn YTC = 4.21% rather than YTM = 5% if you bought the bonds under the indicated conditions.

In the balance of this chapter, we assume that bonds are not callable unless otherwise noted. However, some of the end-of-chapter problems deal with yield to call.

5-6c Current Yield

If you examine brokerage house reports on bonds, you will often see reference to a bond's current yield. The *current yield* is the annual interest payment divided by the bond's current price. For example, if MicroDrive's bonds with a 10% coupon were currently selling at $985, then the bond's current yield would be $100/$985 = 0.1015 = 10.15%.

Unlike the yield to maturity, the current yield does not represent the rate of return that investors should expect on the bond. The current yield provides information regarding the amount of cash income that a bond will generate in a given year, but it does not provide an accurate measure of the bond's total expected return, the yield to maturity. In fact, here is the relation between current yield, capital gains yield (which can be negative for a capital loss), and the yield to maturity:

$$\text{Current yield} + \text{Capital gains yield} = \text{Yield to maturity} \qquad (5\text{-}5)$$

5-6d The Cost of Debt and Intrinsic Value

The "Intrinsic Value and the Cost of Debt" box at the beginning of this chapter highlights the cost of debt, which affects the weighted average cost of capital (WACC), which in turn affects the company's intrinsic value. The pre-tax cost of debt from the company's perspective is the required return from the debtholder's perspective. Therefore, the pre-tax cost of debt is the yield to maturity (or the yield to call if a call is likely). But why do different bonds have different yields to maturity? The following sections answer this question.

S E L F - T E S T

Explain the difference between the yield to maturity and the yield to call.

How does a bond's current yield differ from its total return?

Could the current yield exceed the total return?

A bond currently sells for $850. It has an 8-year maturity, an annual coupon of $80, and a par value of $1,000. What is its yield to maturity? **(10.90%)** *What is its current yield?* **(9.41%)**

A bond currently sells for $1,250. It pays a $110 annual coupon and has a 20-year maturity, but it can be called in 5 years at $1,110. What are its YTM and its YTC? **(8.38%, 6.85%)** *Is the bond likely to be called if interest rates don't change?*

5-7 The Pre-Tax Cost of Debt: Determinants of Market Interest Rates

Until now we have given you the quoted market interest rate, which is the required rate of return on debt, r_d. But as we showed in Chapter 1, different debt securities often have very different market rates. What explains these differences? In a nutshell, different types of debt have expected future cash flows that differ with respect to timing and risk. We can use a conceptual framework that decomposes the quoted market interest rate into a truly risk-free rate plus several premiums that reflect exposure to inflation risk, price volatility caused by interest rate volatility, default risk, and liquidity risk (stemming from a lack of trading activity):

$$\text{Quoted market interest rate} = r_d = r^* + \text{IP} + \text{MRP} + \text{DRP} + \text{LP} \qquad (5\text{-}6)$$

Here are definitions of the variables in Equation 5-6:

r_d = The quoted market rate, which is the required rate of return on a debt security. There are many different securities and hence many different quoted interest rates.

r^* = Real risk-free interest rate. Pronounced "r-star," r^* is the rate paid each moment on a hypothetical riskless security if zero inflation were expected.

IP = Inflation premium, which is equal to the average expected inflation rate over the life of the security. The expected future inflation rate is not necessarily equal to the current inflation rate, so IP is not necessarily equal to current inflation.

MRP = Maturity risk premium. Changes in market interest rates can cause large changes in the prices of long-term bonds, even Treasury bonds. Lenders charge a maturity risk premium to reflect this risk.

DRP = Default risk premium. This premium reflects the possibility that the issuer will not pay interest or principal at the stated time and in the stated amount. The DRP is zero for U.S. Treasury securities, but it rises as the riskiness of issuers increases.

LP = Liquidity, or marketability, premium. This is a premium charged by lenders to reflect the fact that some securities cannot be converted to cash on short notice at a "reasonable" price. The LP is very low for Treasury securities and for securities issued by large, strong firms, but it is relatively high on securities issued by very small firms.

We discuss the components whose sum makes up the quoted, or nominal, rate on a given security in the following sections.

WWW

See www.bloomberg .com and select MARKETS. Then select RATES AND BONDS for a partial listing of indexed Treasury bonds and their interest rates. See http://online.wsj .com for a complete set of Treasury quotes. See www.treasurydirect .gov/indiv/products /products.htm for a complete listing of all Treasury securities.

SELF-TEST

Write out an equation for the nominal interest rate on any debt security.

5-8 The Risk-Free Interest Rate: Nominal (r_{RF}) and Real (r^*)

The phrases **risk-free interest rate (r_{RF})** and **risk-free rate of return** are used frequently in business and in the financial press, but what do they actually mean? When the term "risk-free rate" is not preceded by "real," people generally mean the **nominal risk-free interest rate (r_{RF})**, which is the market rate observed on a Treasury security. In particular, the T-bill rate is used for the short-term r_{RF}, and a T-bond rate is used for the long-term r_{RF}. Although T-bills and T-bonds are default-free and trade in very active markets, they are not truly riskless. Both are exposed to inflation risk, and T-bonds also experience price volatility due to interest rate volatility.[14]

---

[14]We assume U.S. Treasury securities will not default, but evidence suggests that investors don't always think so. For example, see Srinivas Nippani, Pu Liu, and Craig T. Schulman, "Are Treasury Securities Free of Default?" *Journal of Financial and Quantitative Analysis*, June 2001, pp. 251–266. For more recent evidence, see Srinivas Nippani and Stanley D. Smith, "The Increasing Default Risk of U.S. Treasury Securities due to the Financial Crisis," *Journal of Banking and Finance*, Vol. 34, 2010, pp. 2472–2480. Additionally, on August 5, 2011, S&P downgraded the U.S. credit rating from AAA to AA+. See the box "U.S. Treasury Bonds Downgraded!" later in the chapter for discussion of the downgrade.

In contrast, the **real risk-free interest rate (r*)** is the rate that a hypothetical risk-less security pays each moment if zero inflation were expected. The real risk-free rate is not constant; r* changes over time depending on economic conditions, especially: (1) the rate of return corporations and other borrowers expect to earn on productive assets and (2) people's time preferences for current versus future consumption. Therefore, r* might change from moment to moment.

Even though no such hypothetical security actually exists, it provides a good conceptual basis for understanding why different securities have different yields. We start with r* and add required returns based on a security's probability of default, degree of market liquidity, exposure to inflation, and payment dates. We discuss these sources of risk in the following sections, but we need to immediately address the concept of a risk-free security.

Although there is no security that truly has a real risk-free interest rate, Treasury Inflation-Protected Securities (TIPS) have payments that are indexed to inflation. (For details on how TIPS are adjusted to protect against inflation, see *Web Extension 5B* on the textbook's Web site.) Because the payments (including the principal) are tied to inflation, the yield on a TIPS with 1 year until maturity is a good estimate of the *real* 1-year risk-free rate.[15] In theory, we would like an even shorter maturity to estimate the real risk-free rate, but short-term TIPS are thinly traded and the reported yields are not as reliable.

In early 2018, the YTM was 0.07% on 1-year TIPS. Historically, the real interest rate has averaged around 1.5% to 2.5%. Although unusual, negative real rates are possible and have occurred in the last decade. However, negative *nominal* market rates are impossible (or at least extraordinarily rare) because investors would just hold cash instead of buying a bond that is guaranteed to return less than its cost.

SELF-TEST

What security provides a good estimate of the short-term nominal risk-free rate?

What security provides a good estimate of the long-term nominal risk-free rate?

What security provides a good estimate of the real risk-free rate?

5-9 The Inflation Premium (IP)

Inflation has a major effect on interest rates because it erodes the purchasing power of the dollar and lowers the real rate of return on investments. To illustrate, suppose you invest $3,000 in a default-free zero coupon bond that matures in 1 year and pays a 5% interest rate. At the end of the year, you will receive $3,150—your original $3,000 plus $150 of interest. Now suppose that the inflation rate during the year is 10% and that it affects all items equally. If gas had cost $3 per gallon at the beginning of the year, it would cost $3.30 at the end of the year. Therefore, your $3,000 would have bought $3,000/$3 = 1,000 gallons at the beginning of the year but only $3,150/$3.30 = 955 gallons at the end. In *real*

---

[15]The real rate of interest as discussed here is different from the *current* real rate as often discussed in the press. The current real rate is often estimated as the current interest rate minus the current (or most recent) inflation rate, whereas the real rate, as used here (and in the fields of finance and economics generally) without the word "current," is the current interest rate minus the *expected future* inflation rate over the life of the security. For example, suppose the current quoted rate for a 1-year Treasury bill is 5%, inflation during the previous year was 2%, and inflation expected for the coming year is 4%. Then the *current* real rate would be approximately 5% − 2% = 3%, but the *expected* real rate would be approximately 5% − 4% = 1%.

terms, you would be worse off: You would receive $150 of interest, but it would not be sufficient to offset inflation. You would thus be better off buying 1,000 gallons of gas (or some other storable asset) than buying the default-free bond.

Investors are well aware of inflation's effects on interest rates, so when they lend money, they build in an **inflation premium (IP)** that is approximately equal to the average expected inflation rate over the life of the security.

Consider a U.S. Treasury bill, which is default-free, is very liquid, and has a short maturity. Note that the interest rate on the T-bill ($r_{T\text{-bill}}$) includes the premium for expected inflation:

$$r_{T\text{-bill}} = r^* + IP$$

Therefore, if the real short-term risk-free rate of interest is $r^* = 0.6\%$ and if expected inflation is 1.0% (and hence IP = 1.0%) during the next year, then the quoted rate of interest on 1-year T-bills would be 0.6% + 1.0% = 1.6%.[16]

It is important to note that the inflation rate built into interest rates is *the inflation rate expected in the future,* not the rate experienced in the past. Thus, the latest reported figures might show an annual inflation rate of 2%, but that is for the *past* year. But if people on average expect a 6% inflation rate in the future, then 6% would be built into the current interest rate.

Note also that the inflation rate reflected in the quoted interest rate on any security is the *average rate of inflation expected over the security's life.* Thus, the inflation rate built into a 1-year bond is the expected inflation rate for the next year, but the inflation rate built into a 30-year bond is the average rate of inflation expected over the next 30 years. If I_t is the expected inflation during year t, then the inflation premium for an N-year bond's yield (IP_N) can be approximated as:

$$IP_N = \frac{I_1 + I_2 + \cdots + I_N}{N} \qquad (5\text{-}7)$$

For example, if investors expect inflation to average 3% during Year 1 and 5% during Year 2, then the inflation premium built into a 2-year bond's yield can be approximated by:[17]

$$IP_2 = \frac{I_1 + I_2}{2} = \frac{3\% + 5\%}{2} = 4\%$$

In the previous section, we saw that the yield on an inflation-indexed Treasury bond (TIPS) is a good estimate of the real interest rate. Because a regular (nonindexed) T-bond is similar to a TIPS in all respects except inflation protection, the difference in their yields provides an estimate of the inflation premium. For example, in early 2018, the yield on a 5-year nonindexed T-bond was 2.64%, and the yield on a 5-year TIPS was 0.62%. Thus, the 5-year inflation premium was 2.64% − 0.62% = 2.02%, implying that investors expected

---

[16]This is not technically correct. The quoted rate on the T-bill would be found by solving this equation: $(1 + r_{T\text{-bill}}) = (1 + r^*)(1 + IP)$. For our example, the result would be $r_{T\text{-bill}} = (1.006)(1.01) - 1 = 0.01606 \approx 1.6\%$. This is almost exactly equal to the approximation. Because real rates and inflation rates usually are small, we will continue to use the approximation instead of the exact formula in this footnote.

[17]To be mathematically correct, we should take the *geometric average:* $(1 + IP_2)^2 = (1 + I_1)(1 + I_2)$. In this example, we have $(1 + IP_2)^2 = (1 + 0.03)(1 + 0.05)$. Solving for IP_2 yields 3.9952, which is close to our approximation of 4% in the example.

inflation to average 2.02% per year over the next 5 years.[18] Using the same approach, the results for several different maturities follow:

Yields on:	Maturity		
	1 Year	5 Years	20 Years
Nonindexed U.S. Treasury bond (nominal rate)	2.05%	2.64%	3.00%
TIPS (real rate)	0.07%	0.62%	0.92%
Inflation premium	1.98%	2.02%	2.08%

Expectations for future inflation are closely but not perfectly correlated with rates experienced in the recent past. Therefore, if the inflation rate reported for last month increases, people often raise their expectations for future inflation, and this change in expectations will cause an increase in interest rates.

Note that Germany, Japan, and Switzerland have, over the past several years, had lower inflation rates than the United States, so their interest rates have generally been lower than ours. South Africa, Brazil, and most South American countries have experienced higher inflation, which is reflected in their interest rates.

SELF-TEST

Explain how a TIPS and a nonindexed Treasury security can be used to estimate the inflation premium.

The yield on a 15-year TIPS is 3%, and the yield on a 15-year Treasury bond is 5%. What is the inflation premium for a 15-year bond? **(2%)**

5-10 The Maturity Risk Premium (MRP)

All bonds, even Treasury bonds, are exposed to two additional sources of risk: interest rate risk and reinvestment risk. The net effect of these two sources of risk upon a bond's yield is called the **maturity risk premium (MRP)**. The following sections explain how interest rate risk and reinvestment risk affect a bond's yield.

5-10a Interest Rate Risk

Interest rates go up and down over time, and an increase in interest rates leads to a decline in the value of outstanding bonds. This risk of a decline in bond values due to rising interest rates is called **interest rate risk**. To illustrate, suppose you bought some 15-year 10% MicroDrive bonds at a price of $1,000, and then interest rates rose to 15% in the following year. As we saw earlier, the price of the bonds would fall to $713.78, so you would have a loss of $286.22 per bond.[19] Interest rates can and do rise, and rising rates

---

[18]As we noted in the previous footnote, the mathematically correct approach is to use a *geometric average* and solve the following equation: $(1 + IP)(1 + 0.0062) = 1 + 0.0264$. Solving for IP gives IP = 2.01%, which is very close to our approximation for the 5-year inflation premium in early 2018.

Note, though, that the difference in yield between a T-bond and a TIPS of the same maturity reflects both the expected inflation *and* any risk premium for bearing inflation risk. So the difference in yields is really an upper limit on the expected inflation.

[19]You would have an *accounting* (and tax) loss only if you sold the bond; if you held it to maturity, you would not have such a loss. However, even if you did not sell, you would still have suffered a *real economic loss in an opportunity cost sense* because you would have lost the opportunity to invest at 14% and would be stuck with a 10% bond in a 15% market. In an economic sense, "paper losses" are just as bad as realized accounting losses.

cause a loss of value for bondholders. Thus, bond investors are exposed to risk from changing interest rates.

This point can be demonstrated by showing how the value of a 1-year bond with a 10% annual coupon fluctuates with changes in r_d and then comparing these changes with those on a 25-year bond. The 1-year bond's value for $r_d = 5\%$ is shown here:

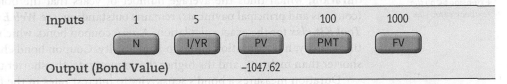

Inputs	1	5		100	1000
	N	I/YR	PV	PMT	FV
Output (Bond Value)			−1047.62		

Using either a calculator or a spreadsheet, you could calculate the bond values for a 1-year and a 25-year bond at several current market interest rates; these results are plotted in Figure 5-3. Note how much more sensitive the price of the 25-year bond is to changes in interest rates. At a 10% interest rate, both the 25-year and the 1-year bonds are valued at $1,000. When rates rise to 15%, the 25-year bond falls to $676.79 but the 1-year bond falls only to $956.52.

resource

See Ch05 Tool Kit.xlsx.

For bonds with similar coupons, this differential sensitivity to changes in interest rates always holds true: The longer the maturity of the bond is, the more its price changes in response to a given change in interest rates. Thus, even if the risk of default on two bonds is exactly the same, the one with the longer maturity is exposed to more risk from a rise in interest rates.

The explanation for this difference in interest rate risk is simple. Suppose you bought a 25-year bond that yielded 10%, or $100 a year. Now suppose interest rates on bonds of comparable risk rose to 15%. You would be stuck with only $100 of interest for the next 25 years. On the other hand, had you bought a 1-year bond, you would have a low return for only 1 year. At the end of the year, you would get your $1,000 back, and you could then

FIGURE 5-3
Value of Long- and Short-Term 10% Annual Coupon Bonds at Different Market Interest Rates

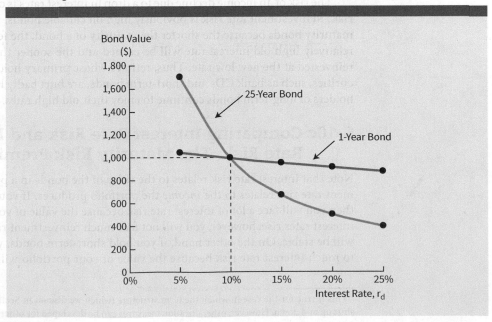

resource

*For more on bond risk, including duration analysis, see **Web Extension 5C** on the textbook's Web site.*

reinvest it and receive a 15% return ($150) for the next year. Thus, interest rate risk reflects the length of time one is committed to a given investment.

In addition to maturity, interest rate sensitivity reflects the size of coupon payments. Intuitively, this is because more of a high-coupon bond's value is received sooner than that of a low-coupon bond of the same maturity. This intuitive concept is measured by **duration**, which finds the average number of years that the bond's PV of cash flows (coupons and principal payments) remains outstanding; see *Web Extension 5C* and *Ch05 Tool Kit.xlsx* for the exact calculation. A zero coupon bond, which has no payments until maturity, has a duration equal to its maturity. Coupon bonds have durations that are shorter than maturity, and the higher the coupon rate, the shorter the duration is.

Duration measures a bond's sensitivity to interest rates in the following sense: Given a change in interest rates, the percentage change in a bond's price is proportional to its duration:[20]

$$\% \text{ change in } V_B = (\% \text{ change in } 1 + r_d)\,(-\text{ Duration})$$

Excel's **DURATION** function provides an easy way to calculate a bond's duration. See *Web Extension 5C* and *Ch05 Tool Kit.xlsx* for more discussion of duration and its use in measuring and managing interest rate risk.

5-10b Reinvestment Rate Risk

As we saw in the preceding section, an *increase* in interest rates will hurt bondholders because it will lead to a decline in the value of a bond portfolio. But can a *decrease* in interest rates also hurt bondholders? The answer is "Yes" because if interest rates fall, then a bondholder may suffer a reduction in his or her income. For example, consider a retiree who has a portfolio of bonds and lives off the income they produce. The bonds, on average, have a coupon rate of 10%. Now suppose that interest rates decline to 5%. The short-term bonds will mature, and when they do, they will have to be replaced with lower-yielding bonds. In addition, many of the remaining long-term bonds may be called, and as calls occur, the bondholder will have to replace 10% bonds with 5% bonds. Thus, our retiree will suffer a reduction of income.

The risk of an income decline due to a drop in interest rates is called **reinvestment rate risk**. Reinvestment rate risk is obviously high on callable bonds. It is also high on short-maturity bonds because the shorter the maturity of a bond, the fewer the years when the relatively high old interest rate will be earned and the sooner the funds will have to be reinvested at the new low rate. Thus, retirees whose primary holdings are short-term securities, such as bank CDs and short-term bonds, are hurt badly by a decline in rates, but holders of long-term bonds continue to enjoy their old high rates.

5-10c Comparing Interest Rate Risk and Reinvestment Rate Risk: The Maturity Risk Premium

Note that interest rate risk relates to the *value* of the bonds in a portfolio, while reinvestment rate risk relates to the *income* the portfolio produces. If you hold long-term bonds, then you will face a lot of interest rate risk because the value of your bonds will decline if interest rates rise; however, you will not face much reinvestment rate risk, so your income will be stable. On the other hand, if you hold short-term bonds, you will not be exposed to much interest rate risk because the value of your portfolio will be stable, but you will

---

[20]This is true for the case in which the term structure (which we discuss in Section 5-13) is flat and can only shift up and down. However, other duration measures can be developed for other term structure assumptions.

be exposed to considerable reinvestment rate risk because your income will fluctuate with changes in interest rates. We see, then, that no fixed-rate bond can be considered totally riskless—even most Treasury bonds are exposed to both interest rate risk and reinvestment rate risk.[21]

Bond prices reflect the trading activities of the marginal investors, defined as those who trade often enough and with large enough sums to determine bond prices. Although one particular investor might be more averse to reinvestment risk than to interest rate risk, the data suggest that the marginal investor is more averse to interest rate risk than to reinvestment risk. To induce the marginal investor to take on interest rate risk, long-term bonds must have a higher expected rate of return than short-term bonds. Holding all else equal, this additional return is the maturity risk premium (MRP).

SELF-TEST

Differentiate between interest rate risk and reinvestment rate risk.

To which type of risk are holders of long-term bonds more exposed? Short-term bondholders?

Assume that the real risk-free rate is r* = 3% and that the average expected inflation rate is 2.5% for the foreseeable future. The applicable MRP is 2% for a 20-year bond. What is the yield on a 20-year T-bond (which is default free and trades in a very active market)? **(7.5%)**

5-11 The Default Risk Premium (DRP)

If the issuer defaults on a payment, investors receive less than the promised return on the bond. The quoted interest rate includes a **default risk premium (DRP)**—the greater the **default risk**, the higher the bond's yield to maturity.[22] The default risk on Treasury securities is virtually zero, but default risk can be substantial for corporate and municipal bonds. In this section, we consider some issues related to default risk.

5-11a Bond Contract Provisions That Influence Default Risk

Default risk is affected by both the financial strength of the issuer and the terms of the bond contract, especially whether collateral has been pledged to secure the bond. Several types of contract provisions are discussed next.

BOND INDENTURES

An **indenture** is a legal document that spells out the rights of both bondholders and the issuing corporation. A **trustee** is an official (usually a bank) who represents the bondholders and makes sure the terms of the indenture are carried out. The indenture may be several hundred pages in length, and it will include **restrictive covenants** that cover such points as the conditions under which the issuer can pay off the bonds prior to maturity, the levels at which certain ratios must be maintained if the company is to issue additional debt, and restrictions against the payment of dividends unless earnings meet certain specifications.

---

[21]Although indexed Treasury bonds are almost riskless, they pay a relatively low real rate. Note also that risks have not disappeared; they have simply been transferred from bondholders to taxpayers.

[22]Suppose two bonds have the same promised cash flows, coupon rate, maturity, liquidity, and inflation exposure, but one bond has more default risk than the other. Investors will naturally pay less for the bond with the greater chance of default. As a result, bonds with higher default risk will have higher yields.

The Securities and Exchange Commission (1) approves indentures and (2) makes sure that all indenture provisions are met before allowing a company to sell new securities to the public. A firm will have different indentures for each of the major types of bonds it issues, but a single indenture covers all bonds of the same type. For example, one indenture will cover a firm's first mortgage bonds, another its debentures, and a third its convertible bonds.

SECURED DEBT AND MORTGAGE BONDS

Secured debt is any debt for which a corporation pledges a particular asset that may be claimed by the secured debtholder in the event of default. The pledged asset is said to have a **lien** against it because the corporation must satisfy the creditor before using proceeds from selling the asset for any other purpose.

A **mortgage bond** is a bond that is secured by property. If this bond is issued before other bonds, it is called a **first-mortgage bond** (also called a **senior mortgage**) and its claims are paid before those of other bonds. The company might also choose to issue **second-mortgage bonds** (also called **junior mortgages**) that are secured by the same assets as the first-mortgage bonds. However, in the event of liquidation, the holders of second-mortgage bonds would receive payments only after the first-mortgage bondholders are paid off in full. All mortgage bonds are subject to an indenture that usually limits the amount of new bonds that can be issued.

DEBENTURES AND SUBORDINATED DEBENTURES

A **debenture** is an unsecured bond, and as such it provides no lien against specific property as security for the obligation. Debenture holders are, therefore, general creditors whose claims are protected by property not otherwise pledged.

There is a definite pecking order among debenture in terms of priority in a bankruptcy. For example, some bonds are called senior bonds because they must be paid before any other general creditors. The term *subordinate* means "below," or "inferior to"; thus, in the event of bankruptcy, subordinated debt has claims on assets only after senior debt has been paid off. **Subordinated debentures** may be subordinated either to designated notes payable (usually bank loans), senior bonds, or to all other debt. In the event of liquidation or reorganization, holders of subordinated debentures cannot be paid until all senior debt, as named in the debentures' indentures, has been paid.

DEVELOPMENT BONDS

Some companies may be in a position to benefit from the sale of either **development bonds** or **pollution control bonds**. State and local governments may set up both *industrial development agencies* and *pollution control agencies*. These agencies are allowed, under certain circumstances, to sell **tax-exempt bonds** and then make the proceeds available to corporations for specific uses deemed (by Congress) to be in the public interest. For example, a Detroit pollution control agency might sell bonds to provide Ford with funds for purchasing pollution control equipment. Because the income from the bonds would be tax exempt, the bonds would have relatively low interest rates. Note, however, that these bonds are guaranteed by the corporation that will use the funds, not by a governmental unit, so their rating reflects the credit strength of the corporation using the funds.

REVENUE BONDS AND PROJECT FINANCING

The payments for some bonds and their claims in the event of bankruptcy are limited to the income produced from a specific project. For example, a **revenue bond** is a type of municipal bond that is secured by the revenues derived from a specific project such as roads

Insuring with Credit Default Swaps: Let the Buyer Beware!

The Global Economic Crisis

A credit default swap (CDS) is like an insurance policy. The purchaser of the CDS agrees to make annual payments to a counterparty that agrees to pay if a particular bond defaults. During the 2000s, investment banks often would purchase CDS for the mortgage-backed securities (MBS) they were creating in order to make the securities more attractive to

investors. But how good was this type of insurance? As it turned out, not very. For example, Lehman Brothers might have bought a CDS from AIG in order to sell a Lehman-created MBS to an investor. But when the MBS began defaulting, neither Lehman nor AIG was capable of making full restitution to the investor.

and bridges, airports, water and sewage systems, and not-for-profit health care facilities. **Project financing** is a method in which a particular project's creditors do not have full recourse against the borrowers; the lenders and lessors must be paid from the project's cash flows and equity. Project financing often is used for large international projects such as oil refineries.

MUNICIPAL BOND INSURANCE

Municipalities can buy **bond insurance**, which means that an insurance company guarantees to pay the coupon and principal payments should the issuer default. This reduces risk to investors, who will thus accept a lower coupon rate for an insured bond than for a comparable but uninsured one. Even though the municipality must pay a fee to have its bonds insured, its savings due to the lower coupon rate often make insurance cost-effective. Keep in mind that the insurers are private companies and that the value added by the insurance depends on the creditworthiness of the insurer. The larger insurers are strong companies, and their own ratings are AAA.

5-11b Bond Ratings

A **bond rating** reflects the probability that a bond will go into default. The three major rating agencies are Moody's Investors Service (Moody's), Standard & Poor's Corporation (S&P), and Fitch Ratings. As shown in Columns (3) and (4) of Table 5-1, triple-A and double-A bonds are extremely safe, rarely defaulting even within 5 years of being assigned a rating. Single-A and triple-B bonds are also strong enough to be called **investment-grade bonds**, and they are the lowest-rated bonds that many banks and other institutional investors are permitted by law to hold. Double-B and lower bonds are speculative bonds and are often called **junk bonds**. These bonds have a significant probability of defaulting.

5-11c Bond Rating Criteria, Upgrades, and Downgrades

Bond ratings are based on both quantitative and qualitative factors, as we describe next.

1. **Financial Ratios.** Many ratios potentially are important, but the return on invested capital, debt ratio, and interest coverage ratio are particularly valuable for predicting financial distress. For example, Columns (1), (5), and (6) in Table 5-1 show a strong relationship between ratings and the return on capital and the debt ratio.
2. **Bond Contract Terms.** Important provisions for determining the bond's rating include whether the bond is secured by a mortgage on specific assets, whether the bond

is subordinated to other debt, any sinking fund provisions, guarantees by some other party with a high credit ranking, and *restrictive covenants* such as requirements that the firm keep its debt ratio below a given level or that it keep its times interest earned ratio above a given level.

3. **Qualitative Factors.** Included here would be such factors as sensitivity of the firm's earnings to the strength of the economy, how it is affected by inflation, whether it is having or is likely to have labor problems, the extent of its international operations (including the stability of the countries in which it operates), potential environmental problems, potential antitrust problems, and so on.

Rating agencies review outstanding bonds on a periodic basis and re-rate if necessary. Columns (7) and (8) in Table 5-1 show the percentages of companies in each rating category that were downgraded or upgraded in 2016 by Fitch Ratings.

Over the long run, ratings agencies have done a reasonably good job of measuring the average credit risk of bonds and of changing ratings whenever there is a significant change in credit quality. However, it is important to understand that ratings do not adjust immediately to changes in credit quality, and in some cases there can be a considerable lag between a change in credit quality and a change in rating. Many abrupt downgrades occurred in 2007 and 2008, leading to calls by Congress and the SEC for changes in rating agencies and the way they rate bonds. Clearly, improvements can be made, but there will always be occasions when completely unexpected information about a company is released, leading to a sudden change in its rating.

TABLE 5-1
Bond Ratings, Default Risk, and Yields

Rating Agency[a]		Percent Defaulting Within:[b]		Median Ratios[c]		Percent Upgraded or Downgraded from 1990–2016[b]		
S&P and Fitch	Moody's	1 year	5 years	Return on capital	Total debt/ Total capital	Up	Down	Yield[d]
(1)	(2)	(3)	(4)	(5)	(6)	(7)	(8)	(9)
Investment-grade bonds								
AAA	Aaa	0.13%	0.39%	27.6%	12.4%	NA%	5.93%	2.99%
AA	Aa	0.05	0.06	27.0	28.3	0.11	9.55	2.78
A	A	0.06	0.30	17.5	37.5	1.73	6.00	3.06
BBB	Baa	0.15	0.80	13.4	42.5	3.16	4.02	3.62
Junk bonds								
BB	Ba	0.73	3.28	11.3	53.7	7.78	8.04	4.28
B	B	2.12	6.87	8.7	75.9	8.47	6.62	5.84
CCC	Caa	21.24	31.61	3.2	113.5	19.75	21.24	10.81

Notes:

[a]The ratings agencies also use "modifiers" for bonds rated below triple-A. S&P and Fitch use a plus and minus system; thus, A+ designates the strongest A-rated bonds and A− the weakest. Moody's uses a 1, 2, or 3 designation, with 1 denoting the strongest and 3 the weakest; thus, within the double-A category, Aa1 is the best, Aa2 is average, and Aa3 is the weakest.

[b]Default data, downgrades, and upgrades are from Fitch Ratings Global Corporate Finance 2016 Transition and Default Study, August 2017: see **www.fitchratings.com**. Default data are for the period 1990–2016. A free registration is required to access the Fitch report.

[c]Median ratios are from Standard & Poor's 2006 Corporate Ratings Criteria, April 23, 2007: see **www.standardandpoors.com/en_US/web/guest /article/-/view/type/HTML/id/785022**. You must register (which is free) and log in to get access to this report.

[d]Data are from BofA Merrill Lynch, retrieved from FRED, Federal Reserve Bank of St. Louis; **https://fred.stlouisfed.org,** December 1, 2017.

U.S. Treasury Bonds Downgraded!

The worsening recession that began at the end of 2007 led Congress to pass a huge economic stimulus package in early 2009. The combination of the stimulus package and the government's bailouts of financial institutions caused the U.S. government to increase its borrowing substantially. The current (October 2016) level of total debt is about $19 trillion, about 101% of gross domestic product (GDP). Any way you look at it, this is a lot of money, even by Washington standards!

With so much debt outstanding and enormous annual deficits continuing, in mid-2011 Congress was faced with the need to increase the amount of debt the federal government is allowed to issue. Although Congress had increased the debt ceiling 74 times previously, and 10 times since 2001, partisan and heated debate seriously delayed approval of the measure and brought the federal government to the brink of default on its obligations by August. At the last minute, Congress approved a debt ceiling increase, narrowly avoiding a partial government shutdown. However, the deficit reduction package that accompanied the legislation was small, doing little to address the structural revenue and spending imbalance the federal government faces going forward.

On August 5, 2011, the combination of a dysfunctional political process apparently incapable of reliably performing basic financial housekeeping chores and the lack of a clear plan to address future deficits raised enough questions about the U.S. government's financial stability to induce Standard & Poor's (S&P), the credit rating agency, to downgrade U.S. public debt from AAA to AA+, effectively removing it from its list of risk-free investments. Financial markets quickly responded to this dark assessment, with the Dow Jones Industrial Average plunging some 13% over the next week. Moody's and Fitch, the other two major rating agencies, however, kept their ratings of U.S. public debt at their highest levels. With two out of three agencies rating U.S. debt at the highest level, is the yield on U.S. debt still a proxy for the riskless rate? Only time will tell, but since the initial downgrade in 2011, a bitterly divided Congress has brought the federal government to the brink of default on its debt obligations several more times. This behavior does not bode well for the prospect of maintaining an AAA rating.

5-11d Bond Ratings and the Default Risk Premium

Why are bond ratings so important? First, most bonds are purchased by institutional investors rather than by individuals, and many institutions are restricted to investment-grade securities. Thus, if a firm's bonds fall below BBB, it will have a difficult time selling new bonds because many potential purchasers will not be allowed to buy them. Second, many bond covenants stipulate that the coupon rate on the bond automatically increases if the rating falls below a specified level. Third, because a bond's rating is an indicator of its default risk, the rating has a direct, measurable influence on the bond's yield. Column (9) of Table 5-1 shows that an AAA bond has a yield of 2.99% and that yields increase as the rating falls. In fact, an investor would earn 10.81% on a CCC bond if it didn't default.

A **bond spread** is the difference between a bond's yield and the yield on some other security of the same maturity. Unless specified differently, the term "spread" generally means the difference between a bond's yield and the yield on a Treasury bond of similar maturity.

Figure 5-4 shows the spreads between an index of AAA bonds and a 10-year Treasury bond; it also shows spreads for an index of BAA bonds relative to the T-bond. Figure 5-4 illustrates three important points. First, the BAA spread always is greater than the AAA spread. This is because a BAA bond is riskier than an AAA bond, so BAA investors require extra compensation for their extra risk. The same is true for other ratings: Lower-rated bonds have higher yields.

Second, the spreads are not constant over time. For example, look at the AAA spread. It was exceptionally low during the boom years of 2005–2007 but rose dramatically as the economy declined in 2008 and 2009.

FIGURE 5-4
Bond Spreads

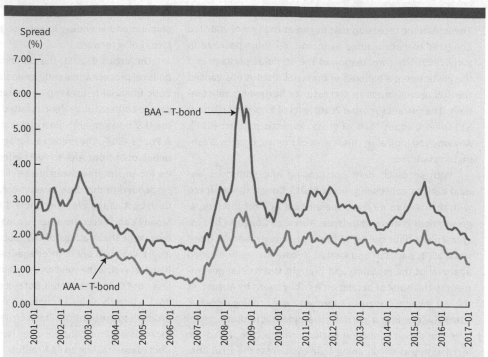

Note: All data are from the Federal Reserve Bank of St. Louis, Moody's Seasoned Aaa and Baa Corporate Bond Yield Relative to Yield on 10-Year Treasury Constant Maturity: **https://fred.stlouisfed.org,** December 1, 2017. The spreads are defined as the yield on the risky bond (AAA or BAA) minus the yield on a 10-year Treasury bond.

Third, the difference between the BAA spread and the AAA spread isn't constant over time. The two spreads were reasonably close to one another in 2005 but were very far apart in early 2009. In other words, BAA investors didn't require much extra return over that of an AAA bond to induce them to take on that extra risk most years, but in 2009 they required a very large risk premium.

The Few, the Proud, the . . . AAA-Rated Companies!

AAA-rated companies are members of an elite group. Over the last 20 years, this cream of the crop has included such powerhouses as 3M, Abbott Labs, BellSouth, ExxonMobil, GE, Kellogg, Microsoft, and UPS. Only large companies with stable cash flows make it into this group, and for years they guarded their AAA ratings vigilantly. In recent years, however, the nonfinancial AAA-rated corporation has become a vanishing breed. In December 2017, Moody's and Standard & Poor's, agreed on the highest rating for only two nonfinancial publicly traded companies: Johnson & Johnson and Microsoft.

Why do so few companies have AAA ratings? One reason may be that the recent financial crisis and recession have hurt the creditworthiness of even large, stable companies. Another reason is that many of the top companies are choosing to be rated by only one or two of the ratings agencies, rather than all three. A third likely explanation is that in recent years, large, stable companies have increased their debt levels to take greater advantage of the tax savings that they afford. With higher debt levels, these companies are no longer eligible for the highest rating. In essence, they have sacrificed their AAA rating for lower taxes. Does this sound like a good trade-off to you? We will discuss how companies choose the level of debt in Chapter 15.

Source: Bond information from the Financial Industry Regulatory Authority, **www.finra.org**.

Fear and Rationality

The following graph shows two measures of fear. One is the "Hi-Yield" spread between the yields on junk bonds and Treasury bonds. The second is the **TED spread**, which is the difference between the 3-month LIBOR rate and the 3-month T-bill rate. Both are measures of risk aversion. The Hi-Yield spread measures the amount of extra compensation investors need to induce them to take on risky junk bonds. The TED spread measures the extra compensation that banks require to induce them to lend to one another. Observe that the spreads were very low from mid-2003 through the end of 2007. During these boom years, investors and bankers had a voracious appetite for risk and simply didn't require much extra return for additional risk. But as the economy began to deteriorate in 2008, investors and bankers reversed course and became extremely risk averse, with spreads skyrocketing. Note that the pre-financial crisis appetite for risk seems to have returned, with spreads again very low. It is hard to reconcile such drastic changes in risk aversion with careful, deliberate, and rational behavior!

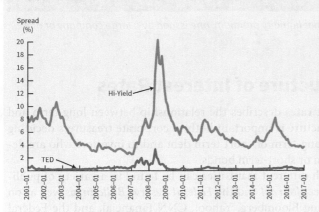

Sources: The TED spread data are retrieved from FRED, Federal Reserve Bank of St. Louis; **https://fred.stlouisfed.org/series/TEDRATE,** December 1, 2017. The Hi-Yield spread data are from BofA Merrill Lynch, BofA Merrill Lynch US High Yield Option-Adjusted Spread [BAMLH0A0HYM2], retrieved from FRED, Federal Reserve Bank of St. Louis; **https://fred.stlouisfed.org/series/BAMLH0A0HYM2,** December 1, 2017.

Not only do spreads vary with the rating of the security, but they also usually increase as maturity increases. This should make sense. If a bond matures soon, investors are able to forecast the company's performance fairly well. But if a bond has a long time until it matures, investors have a difficult time forecasting the likelihood that the company will fall into financial distress. This extra uncertainty creates additional risk, so investors demand a higher required return.

SELF-TEST

Differentiate between mortgage bonds and debentures.

Name the major rating agencies, and list some factors that affect bond ratings.

What is a bond spread?

How do bond ratings affect the default risk premium?

A 10-year T-bond has a yield of 6%. A 10-year corporate bond with a rating of AA has a yield of 7.5%. If the corporate bond has excellent liquidity, what is an estimate of the corporate bond's default risk premium? **(1.5%)**

5-12 The Liquidity Premium (LP)

Financial assets generally have more **liquidity** than real assets, which means that securities can be converted to cash quickly at a "fair market value." However, not all securities have the same degree of liquidity, so investors include a **liquidity premium (LP)** when establishing a security's required rate of return. Although liquidity premiums are difficult to measure accurately, a differential of at least 2 percentage points (and perhaps up to 4 or

5 percentage points) exists between the least liquid and the most liquid financial assets of similar default risk and maturity. Corporate bonds issued by small companies are traded less frequently than those issued by large companies, so small-company bonds tend to have a higher liquidity premium.

For example, liquidity in the market for mortgage-backed securities (MBS) evaporated in 2008 and early 2009. The few transactions that occurred were priced so low that the yields on these MBS were extremely high, which was partially due to a much higher liquidity premium caused by the extremely low liquidity of MBS.

SELF-TEST

Which bond usually will have a higher liquidity premium: one issued by a large company or one issued by a small company?

5-13 The Term Structure of Interest Rates

The **term structure of interest rates** describes the relationship between long-term and short-term rates. The term structure is important both to corporate treasurers deciding whether to borrow by issuing long-term or short-term debt and to investors who are deciding whether to buy long-term or short-term bonds.

Interest rates for bonds with different maturities can be found in a variety of publications, including *The Wall Street Journal* and the *Federal Reserve Bulletin*, as well as on a number of Web sites, including Bloomberg, Yahoo!, CNN Financial, and the Federal Reserve Board. Using interest rate data from these sources, we can determine the term structure at any given point in time. For example, Figure 5-5 presents interest rates for different maturities on three different dates. The set of data for a given date, when plotted on a graph such as Figure 5-5, is called the **yield curve** for that date.

Maturity (yrs.)	March 1980	February 2000	December 2017
0.5	15.0%	6.0%	0.48%
1	14.0%	6.2%	0.63%
5	13.5%	6.7%	1.18%
10	12.8%	6.7%	1.63%
30	12.3%	6.3%	2.34%

As the figure shows, the yield curve changes both in position and in slope over time. In March 1980, all rates were quite high because high inflation was expected. However, the rate of inflation was expected to decline, so the inflation premium (IP) was larger for short-term bonds than for long-term bonds. This caused short-term yields to be higher than long-term yields, resulting in a *downward-sloping* yield curve. By February 2000, inflation had indeed declined and thus all rates were lower. The yield curve had become **humped**—medium-term rates were higher than either short- or long-term rates. In November 2017, all rates were below the 2000 levels. Because short-term rates had dropped below long-term rates, the yield curve was *upward sloping*.

Historically, long-term rates are generally higher than short-term rates owing to the maturity risk premium, so the yield curve usually slopes upward. For this reason, people often call an upward-sloping yield curve a **normal yield curve** and a yield curve that slopes downward an **inverted yield curve** or an **abnormal yield curve**. Thus, in Figure 5-5 the yield curve for March 1980 was inverted, whereas the yield curve in November 2017 was normal. As stated earlier, the February 2000 curve was humped.

FIGURE 5-5
U.S. Treasury Bond Interest Rates on Different Dates

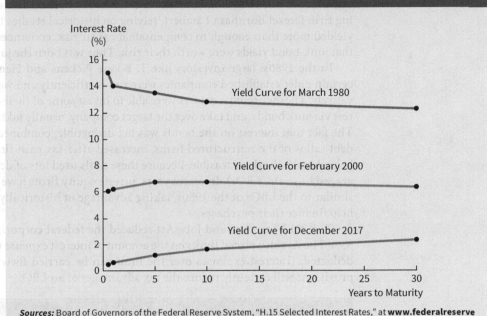

Sources: Board of Governors of the Federal Reserve System, "H.15 Selected Interest Rates," at **www.federalreserve .gov/releases/h15/**. For historical yield curve data, see **www.treasury.gov/resource-center/data-chart-center /interest-rates/Pages/TextView.aspx?data=yield**.

resource

For a discussion of the expectations theory, see Web Extension 5D on the textbook's Web site.

A few academics and practitioners contend that large bond traders who buy and sell securities of different maturities each day dominate the market. According to this view, a bond trader is just as willing to buy a 30-year bond to pick up a short-term profit as to buy a 3-month security. Strict proponents of this view argue that the shape of the yield curve is therefore determined only by market expectations about future interest rates, a position that is called the **pure expectations theory**, or sometimes just the **expectations theory**. If this were true, then the maturity risk premium (MRP) would be zero and long-term interest rates would simply be a weighted average of current and expected future short-term interest rates. See *Web Extension 5D* for a more detailed discussion of the expectations theory.

SELF-TEST

What is a yield curve, and what information would you need to draw this curve?

Distinguish among the shapes of a "normal" yield curve, an "abnormal" curve, and a "humped" curve.

If the interest rates on 1-, 5-, 20-, and 30-year bonds are (respectively) 4%, 5%, 6%, and 7%, then how would you describe the yield curve? How would you describe it if the rates were reversed?

5-14 Financing with Junk Bonds

Recall that bonds rated less than BBB are noninvestment-grade debt, also called junk bonds or high-yield debt. There are two ways that a bond can become a junk bond. First, the bond might have been investment-grade debt when it was issued, but its rating subsequently was cut because the issuing corporation had fallen on hard times. Such bonds are called "fallen angels".

Some bonds are junk bonds at the time they are issued, but this was not always true. Prior to the 1980s, fixed-income investors such as insurance companies were generally unwilling to buy risky bonds. In the late 1970s, Michael Milken of the investment banking firm Drexel Burnham Lambert, relying on historical studies that showed risky bonds yielded more than enough to compensate for their risk, convinced institutional investors that junk-bond yields were worth their risk. Thus was born the junk-bond market.

In the 1980s, large investors like T. Boone Pickens and Henry Kravis thought that certain older established companies were run inefficiently and were financed too conservatively. These corporate raiders were able to invest some of their own money, borrow the rest via junk bonds, and take over the target company, usually taking the company private. The fact that interest on the bonds was tax deductible, combined with the much higher debt ratios of the restructured firms, increased after-tax cash flows to stockholders and helped make the deals feasible. Because these deals used lots of debt, they were called **leveraged buyouts (LBOs)**. In recent years, private equity firms have conducted transactions similar to the LBOs of the 1980s, taking advantage of historically low junk-bond rates to help finance their purchases.

The 2017 Tax Cuts and Jobs Act reduced the federal corporate tax rate to 21% from 35%. The Act also placed limits on the amount of interest expense that can be immediately deducted. (Interest expenses over the limit can be carried forward indefinitely.) These provisions will certainly reduce the tax advantages of an LBO.

What are junk bonds?

5-15 Bankruptcy and Reorganization

A business is **insolvent** if the book values of its liabilities are greater than the market value of its assets or if it does not have enough cash to meet its interest and principal payments. When this occurs, either the creditors or the company may file for **bankruptcy** in the United States Bankruptcy Court. After hearing from the creditors and the company's managers, a federal bankruptcy court judge decides whether to dissolve the firm through **liquidation** or to permit it to remain a viable business through a **reorganization**. **Chapter 7** of the federal bankruptcy statutes addresses liquidation, and **Chapter 11** addresses reorganization.

The decision to force a firm to liquidate versus permit it to reorganize depends on whether the value of the reorganized firm is likely to be greater than the value of the firm's assets if they are sold off piecemeal. In a reorganization, the firm's creditors negotiate with management on the terms of a potential reorganization. The reorganization plan may call for a *restructuring* of the firm's debt, in which case the interest rate may be reduced, the term to maturity may be lengthened, or some of the debt may be exchanged for equity. The point of the restructuring is to reduce the financial charges to a level that the firm's cash flows can support. Of course, the common stockholders also have to give up something: They often see their position diluted as a result of additional shares being given to debtholders in exchange for accepting a reduced amount of debt principal and interest. In fact, the original common stockholders often end up with nothing. The court may appoint a trustee to oversee the reorganization, but usually the existing management is allowed to retain control.

Liquidation occurs if the company is deemed to be too far gone to be saved—if it is worth more dead than alive. If the bankruptcy court orders liquidation, then assets are sold off, and the cash obtained is distributed as specified in Chapter 7 of the Bankruptcy

Act. Here is the priority of claims: (1) past-due property tax liens; (2) secured creditors who are entitled to the proceeds from the sale of collateral; (3) the trustee's costs of administering and operating the bankrupt firm; (4) expenses incurred after bankruptcy was filed; (5) some wages due workers (capped at a maximum amount per worker and limited to wages earned within a specified period prior to the bankruptcy); (6) claims for unpaid contributions to employee benefit plans (capped at a maximum amount per worker and limited to wages earned within a specified period prior to the bankruptcy); (7) unsecured claims for customer deposits (capped at a maximum amount per customer); (8) federal, state, and local taxes due; (9) unfunded pension plan liabilities (although some limitations exist); (10) general unsecured creditors; (11) preferred stockholders (up to the par value of their stock); and (12) common stockholders (although usually nothing is left for them).

Here are the key points for you to know: (1) The federal bankruptcy statutes govern both reorganization and liquidation. (2) Bankruptcies occur frequently. (3) A priority of the specified claims must be followed when distributing the assets of a liquidated firm.

SELF-TEST

Differentiate between a Chapter 7 liquidation and a Chapter 11 reorganization.

List the priority of claims for the distribution of a liquidated firm's assets.

SUMMARY

This chapter described the different types of bonds that governments and corporations issue, explained how bond prices are established, and discussed how investors estimate the rates of return they can expect to earn. The rate of return required by debtholders is the company's pre-tax cost of debt, and this rate depends on the risk that investors face when they buy bonds.

- A **bond** is a long-term promissory note issued by a business or governmental unit. The issuer receives money in exchange for promising to make interest payments and to repay the principal on a specified future date.
- Some special types of long-term financing include **zero coupon bonds**, which pay no annual interest but are issued at a discount; see *Web Extension 5A* for more on zero coupon bonds. Other types are **floating-rate debt**, whose interest payments fluctuate with changes in the general level of interest rates, and **junk bonds**, which are high-risk, high-yield instruments issued by firms that use a great deal of financial leverage.
- A **call provision** gives the issuing corporation the right to redeem the bonds prior to maturity under specified terms, usually at a price greater than the maturity value (the difference is a **call premium**). A firm will typically call a bond if interest rates fall substantially below the coupon rate.
- A **sinking fund** is a provision that requires the corporation to retire a portion of the bond issue each year. The purpose of the sinking fund is to provide for the orderly retirement of the issue. A sinking fund typically requires no call premium.
- The *value of a bond* is found as the present value of an annuity (the interest payments) plus the present value of a lump sum (the principal payment). The bond is evaluated at the appropriate periodic interest rate over the number of periods for which interest payments are made.

- The equation used to find the value of an annual coupon bond is

$$V_B = \sum_{t=1}^{N} \frac{INT}{(1 + r_d)^t} + \frac{M}{(1 + r_d)^N}$$

- An adjustment to the formula must be made if the bond pays interest *semiannually*: divide INT and r_d by 2, and multiply N by 2:

$$\text{Value of semiannual bond} = \sum_{t=1}^{2N} \frac{INT/2}{(1 + r_d/2)^t} + \frac{M}{(1 + r_d/2)^{2N}}$$

- The expected rate of return on a bond held to maturity is defined as the bond's **yield to maturity (YTM)**:

$$\text{Bond price} = \sum_{t=1}^{N} \frac{INT}{(1 + YTM)^t} + \frac{M}{(1 + YTM)^N}$$

- The expected rate of return on a callable bond held to its call date is defined as the **yield to call (YTC)**.
- The **required rate of return on debt (r_d)** is the rate needed to fairly compensate investors for purchasing or holding debt, taking into consideration its cash flows' risk and timing. It is the rate that is observed in the market, so it is also called the **market interest rate**, the **quoted interest rate**, or the **nominal interest rate**.
- The **real risk-free interest rate (r^*)** is the rate that a hypothetical riskless security pays each moment if zero inflation were expected.
- The required rate of return on debt is composed of the real risk-free rate, r^*, plus premiums that reflect inflation (IP), maturity risk (MRP), default risk (DRP), and liquidity (LP):

$$r_d = r^* + IP + MRP + DRP + LP$$

- The **risk-free interest rate (r_{RF})** is the quoted rate on a U.S. Treasury security, which is default-free and very liquid. The short-term risk-free rate is approximated by a T-bill's yield; the long-term risk-free rate is approximated by a T-bond's yield.
- **Treasury Inflation-Protected Securities (TIPS)** are U.S. Treasury bonds that have no inflation risk. See *Web Extension 5B* for more discussion of TIPS.
- The longer the maturity of a bond, the more its price will change in response to a given change in interest rates; this is called **interest rate risk**. However, bonds with short maturities expose investors to high **reinvestment rate risk**, which is the risk that income from a bond portfolio will decline because cash flows received from bonds will be rolled over at lower interest rates.
- **Duration** is a measure of interest rate risk. See *Web Extension 5C* for a discussion of duration.
- Corporate and municipal bonds have **default risk**. If an issuer defaults, investors receive less than the promised return on the bond. Therefore, investors should evaluate a bond's default risk before making a purchase.
- A **bond rating** reflects the probability that a bond will go into default. The highest rating is AAA, and they go down to D. The higher a bond's rating, the lower its risk and therefore its interest rate.
- The relationship between the yields on securities and the securities' maturities is known as the **term structure of interest rates,** and the **yield curve** is a graph of this relationship.

- The shape of the yield curve depends on two key factors: (1) *expectations about future inflation* and (2) *perceptions about the relative risk of securities with different maturities*.
- The yield curve is normally upward sloping; this is called a **normal yield curve**. However, the curve can slope downward (an **inverted yield curve**) if the inflation rate is expected to decline. The yield curve also can be *humped*, which means that interest rates on medium-term maturities are higher than rates on both short- and long-term maturities.
- The **expectations theory** states that yields on long-term bonds reflect expected future interest rates. **Web Extension 5D** discusses this theory.

QUESTIONS

(5-1) Define each of the following terms:

    a. Bond; Treasury bond; corporate bond; municipal bond; foreign bond

    b. Par value; maturity date; coupon payment; coupon interest rate

    c. Floating-rate bond; zero coupon bond; original issue discount bond (OID)

    d. Call provision; redeemable bond; sinking fund

    e. Convertible bond; warrant; income bond; indexed bond (also called a purchasing power bond)

    f. Premium bond; discount bond

    g. Current yield (on a bond); yield to maturity (YTM); yield to call (YTC)

    h. Indentures; mortgage bond; debenture; subordinated debenture

    i. Development bond; municipal bond insurance; junk bond; investment-grade bond

    j. Real risk-free rate of interest, r^*; nominal risk-free rate of interest, r_{RF}

    k. Inflation premium (IP); default risk premium (DRP); liquidity; liquidity premium (LP)

    l. Interest rate risk; maturity risk premium (MRP); reinvestment rate risk

    m. Term structure of interest rates; yield curve

    n. "Normal" yield curve; inverted ("abnormal") yield curve

(5-2) "Short-term interest rates are more volatile than long-term interest rates, so short-term bond prices are more sensitive to interest rate changes than are long-term bond prices." Is this statement true or false? Explain.

(5-3) The rate of return on a bond held to its maturity date is called the bond's yield to maturity. If interest rates in the economy rise after a bond has been issued, what will happen to the bond's price and to its YTM? Does the length of time to maturity affect the extent to which a given change in interest rates will affect the bond's price? Why or why not?

(5-4) If you buy a callable bond and interest rates decline, will the value of your bond rise by as much as it would have risen if the bond had not been callable? Explain.

(5-5) A sinking fund can be set up in one of two ways. Discuss the advantages and disadvantages of each procedure from the viewpoint of both the firm and its bondholders.

SELF-TEST PROBLEM   SOLUTIONS SHOWN IN APPENDIX A

(ST-1)
Bond Valuation

The Pennington Corporation issued a new series of bonds on January 1, 1997. The bonds were sold at par ($1,000), had a 12% coupon, and will mature in 30 years on December 31, 2026. Coupon payments are made semiannually (on June 30 and December 31).

a. What was the YTM on the date the bonds were issued?

b. What was the price of the bonds on January 1, 2002 (5 years later), assuming that interest rates had fallen to 10%?

c. Find the current yield, capital gains yield, and total yield on January 1, 2002, given the price as determined in Part b.

d. Suppose you purchase a Pennington bond for $916.42 on July 1, 2020 (6.5 years before maturity). What are the YTM, the current yield, and the capital gains yield for that date?

e. Suppose instead that you purchase a Pennington bond on March 1, 2020, three months earlier than in Part d. If the going rate for a bond of this risk is 15.5%, how large a check must you write to complete the transaction? (*Hint:* Don't forget the accrued interest.)

PROBLEMS   ANSWERS ARE IN APPENDIX B

EASY PROBLEMS 1–6

(5-1)
Bond Valuation with
Annual Payments

Jackson Corporation's bonds have 12 years remaining to maturity. Interest is paid annually, the bonds have a $1,000 par value, and the coupon interest rate is 8%. The bonds have a yield to maturity of 9%. What is the current market price of these bonds?

(5-2)
Yield to Maturity for
Annual Payments

Wilson Corporation's bonds have 12 years remaining to maturity. Interest is paid annually, the bonds have a $1,000 par value, and the coupon interest rate is 10%. The bonds sell at a price of $850. What is their yield to maturity?

(5-3)
Current Yield for
Annual Payments

Heath Food Corporation's bonds have 7 years remaining to maturity. The bonds have a face value of $1,000 and a yield to maturity of 8%. They pay interest annually and have a 9% coupon rate. What is their current yield?

(5-4)
Determinant of
Interest Rates

The real risk-free rate of interest is 4%. Inflation is expected to be 2% this year and 4% during each of the next 2 years. Assume that the maturity risk premium is zero. What is the yield on 2-year Treasury securities? What is the yield on 3-year Treasury securities?

(5-5)
Default Risk
Premium

A Treasury bond that matures in 10 years has a yield of 6%. A 10-year corporate bond has a yield of 9%. Assume that the liquidity premium on the corporate bond is 0.5%. What is the default risk premium on the corporate bond?

(5-6)
Maturity Risk
Premium

The real risk-free rate is 3%, and inflation is expected to be 3% for the next 2 years. A 2-year Treasury security yields 6.3%. What is the maturity risk premium for the 2-year security?

INTERMEDIATE PROBLEMS 7–20

(5-7)
Bond Valuation
with Semiannual
Payments

Renfro Rentals has issued bonds that have a 10% coupon rate, payable semiannually. The bonds mature in 8 years, have a face value of $1,000, and a yield to maturity of 8.5%. What is the price of the bonds?

(5-8)
Yield to Maturity
and Call with
Semiannual
Payments

Thatcher Corporation's bonds will mature in 10 years. The bonds have a face value of $1,000 and an 8% coupon rate, paid semiannually. The price of the bonds is $1,100. The bonds are callable in 5 years at a call price of $1,050. What is their yield to maturity? What is their yield to call?

(5-9)
Bond Valuation and
Interest Rate Risk

The Garraty Company has two bond issues outstanding. Both bonds pay $100 annual interest plus $1,000 at maturity. Bond L has a maturity of 15 years, and Bond S has a maturity of 1 year.

    a. What will be the value of each of these bonds when the going rate of interest is (1) 5%, (2) 8%, and (3) 12%? Assume that there is only one more interest payment to be made on Bond S.

    b. Why does the longer-term (15-year) bond fluctuate more when interest rates change than does the shorter-term bond (1 year)?

(5-10)
Yield to Maturity
and Required
Returns

The Brownstone Corporation's bonds have 5 years remaining to maturity. Interest is paid annually, the bonds have a $1,000 par value, and the coupon interest rate is 9%.

    a. What is the yield to maturity at a current market price of (1) $829 or (2) $1,104?

    b. Would you pay $829 for one of these bonds if you thought that the appropriate rate of interest was 12%—that is, if $r_d = 12\%$? Explain your answer.

(5-11)
Yield to Call and
Realized Rates
of Return

Goodwynn & Wolf Incorporated (G&W) issued a bond 7 years ago. The bond had a 20-year maturity, a 14% coupon paid annually, a 9% call premium and was issued at par, $1,000. Today, G&W called the bonds. If the original investors had expected G&W to call the bonds in 7 years, what was the yield to call at the time the bonds were issued?

(5-12)
Bond Yields and
Rates of Return

A 10-year, 12% semiannual coupon bond with a par value of $1,000 may be called in 4 years at a call price of $1,060. The bond sells for $1,100. (Assume that the bond has just been issued.)

    a. What is the bond's yield to maturity?

    b. What is the bond's current yield?

    c. What is the bond's capital gain or loss yield?

    d. What is the bond's yield to call?

(5-13)
Yield to Maturity
and Current Yield

You just purchased a bond that matures in 5 years. The bond has a face value of $1,000 and an 8% annual coupon. The bond has a current yield of 8.21%. What is the bond's yield to maturity?

(5-14)
Current Yield
with Semiannual
Payments

A bond that matures in 7 years sells for $1,020. The bond has a face value of $1,000 and a yield to maturity of 10.5883%. The bond pays coupons semiannually. What is the bond's current yield?

(5-15)
Yield to Call, Yield
to Maturity, and
Market Rates

Absalom Energy's 14% coupon rate, semiannual payment, $1,000 par value bonds that mature in 30 years are callable 5 years from now at a price of $1,050. The bonds sell at a price of $1,353.54, and the yield curve is flat. Assuming that interest rates in the economy are expected to remain at their current level, what is the best estimate of the nominal interest rate on new bonds issued in 5 years?

(5-16)
Interest Rate
Sensitivity

A bond trader purchased each of the following bonds at a yield to maturity of 8%. Immediately after she purchased the bonds, interest rates fell to 7%. What is the percentage change in the price of each bond after the decline in interest rates? Fill in the following table:

	Price @ 8%	Price @ 7%	Percentage Change
10-year, 10% annual coupon	_____	_____	_____
10-year zero	_____	_____	_____
5-year zero	_____	_____	_____
30-year zero	_____	_____	_____
Perpetuity, $100 annual coupon	_____	_____	_____

(5-17)
Bond Value as Maturity Approaches

An investor has two bonds in his portfolio. Each bond matures in 4 years, has a face value of $1,000, and has a yield to maturity equal to 9.6%. One bond, Bond C, pays an annual coupon of 10%; the other bond, Bond Z, is a zero coupon bond. Assuming that the yield to maturity of each bond remains at 9.6% over the next 4 years, what will be the price of each of the bonds at the following time periods? Fill in the following table:

T	Price of Bond C	Price of Bond Z
0	_____	_____
1	_____	_____
2	_____	_____
3	_____	_____
4	_____	_____

(5-18)
Determinants of Interest Rates

The real risk-free rate is 2%. Inflation is expected to be 3% this year, 4% next year, and then 3.5% thereafter. The maturity risk premium is estimated to be $0.0005 \times (t - 1)$, where t = number of years to maturity. What is the nominal interest rate on a 7-year Treasury security?

(5-19)
Maturity Risk Premiums

Assume that the real risk-free rate, r^*, is 3% and that inflation is expected to be 8% in Year 1, 5% in Year 2, and 4% thereafter. Assume also that all Treasury securities are highly liquid and free of default risk. If 2-year and 5-year Treasury notes both yield 10%, what is the difference in the maturity risk premiums (MRPs) on the two notes; that is, what is MRP_5 minus MRP_2?

(5-20)
Inflation Risk Premiums

Because of a recession, the inflation rate expected for the coming year is only 3%. However, the inflation rate in Year 2 and thereafter is expected to be constant at some level above 3%. Assume that the real risk-free rate is $r^* = 2\%$ for all maturities and that there are no maturity risk premiums. If 3-year Treasury notes yield 2 percentage points more than 1-year notes, what inflation rate is expected after Year 1?

CHALLENGING PROBLEMS 21–23

(5-21)
Bond Valuation and Changes in Maturity and Required Returns

Suppose Hillard Manufacturing sold an issue of bonds with a 10-year maturity, a $1,000 par value, a 10% coupon rate, and semiannual interest payments.

a. Two years after the bonds were issued, the going rate of interest on bonds such as these fell to 6%. At what price would the bonds sell?

b. Suppose that 2 years after the initial offering, the going interest rate had risen to 12%. At what price would the bonds sell?

c. Suppose that 2 years after the issue date (as in Part a) interest rates fell to 6%. Suppose further that the interest rate remained at 6% for the next 8 years. What would happen to the price of the bonds over time?

(5-22)
Yield to Maturity
and Yield to Call

Arnot International's bonds have a current market price of $1,200. The bonds have an 11% annual coupon payment, a $1,000 face value, and 10 years left until maturity. The bonds may be called in 5 years at 109% of face value (call price = $1,090).

    a. What is the yield to maturity?

    b. What is the yield to call if they are called in 5 years?

    c. Which yield might investors expect to earn on these bonds, and why?

    d. The bond's indenture indicates that the call provision gives the firm the right to call them at the end of each year beginning in Year 5. In Year 5, they may be called at 109% of face value, but in each of the next 4 years the call percentage will decline by 1 percentage point. Thus, in Year 6 they may be called at 108% of face value, in Year 7 they may be called at 107% of face value, and so on. If the yield curve is horizontal and interest rates remain at their current level, when is the latest that investors might expect the firm to call the bonds?

(5-23)
Determinants of
Interest Rates

Suppose you and most other investors expect the inflation rate to be 7% next year, to fall to 5% during the following year, and then to remain at a rate of 3% thereafter. Assume that the real risk-free rate, r^*, will remain at 2% and that maturity risk premiums on Treasury securities rise from zero on very short-term securities (those that mature in a few days) to a level of 0.2 percentage points for 1-year securities. Furthermore, maturity risk premiums increase 0.2 percentage points for each year to maturity, up to a limit of 1.0 percentage point on 5-year or longer-term T-notes and T-bonds.

    a. Calculate the interest rate on 1-, 2-, 3-, 4-, 5-, 10-, and 20-year Treasury securities, and plot the yield curve.

    b. Now suppose ExxonMobil's bonds, rated AAA, have the same maturities as the Treasury bonds. As an approximation, plot an ExxonMobil yield curve on the same graph with the Treasury bond yield curve. (*Hint:* Think about the default risk premium on ExxonMobil's long-term versus short-term bonds.)

    c. Now plot the approximate yield curve of Long Island Lighting Company, a risky nuclear utility.

SPREADSHEET PROBLEM

(5-24)
Build a Model:
Bond Valuation

resource

Start with the partial model in the file *Ch05 P24 Build a Model.xlsx* on the textbook's Web site. A 20-year, 8% semiannual coupon bond with a par value of $1,000 may be called in 5 years at a call price of $1,040. The bond sells for $1,100. (Assume that the bond has just been issued.)

    a. What is the bond's yield to maturity?

    b. What is the bond's current yield?

    c. What is the bond's capital gain or loss yield?

    d. What is the bond's yield to call?

    e. How would the price of the bond be affected by a change in the going market interest rate? (*Hint:* Conduct a sensitivity analysis of price to changes in the going market interest rate for the bond. Assume that the bond will be called if and only if the going rate of interest *falls below* the coupon rate. This is an oversimplification, but assume it for purposes of this problem.)

    f. Now assume the date is October 25, 2020. Assume further that a 12%, 10-year bond was issued on July 1, 2020, pays interest semiannually (on January 1 and July 1), and sells for $1,100. Use your spreadsheet to find the bond's yield.

MINI CASE

Sam Strother and Shawna Tibbs are vice presidents of Mutual of Seattle Insurance Company and co-directors of the company's pension fund management division. An important new client, the North-Western Municipal Alliance, has requested that Mutual of Seattle present an investment seminar to the mayors of the represented cities, and Strother and Tibbs, who will make the actual presentation, have asked you to help them by answering the following questions.

a. What are the key features of a bond?

b. What are call provisions and sinking fund provisions? Do these provisions make bonds more or less risky?

c. How does one determine the value of any asset whose value is based on expected future cash flows?

d. How is the value of a bond determined? What is the value of a 10-year, $1,000 par value bond with a 10% annual coupon if its required rate of return is 10%?

e. (1) What would be the value of the bond described in Part d if, just after it had been issued, the expected inflation rate rose by 3 percentage points, causing investors to require a 13% return? Would we now have a discount or a premium bond?

   (2) What would happen to the bond's value if inflation fell and r_d declined to 7%? Would we now have a premium or a discount bond?

   (3) What would happen to the value of the 10-year bond over time if the required rate of return remained at 13%? If it remained at 7%? (*Hint:* With a financial calculator, enter PMT, I/YR, FV, and N, and then change N to see what happens to the PV as the bond approaches maturity.)

f. (1) What is the yield to maturity on a 10-year, 9% annual coupon, $1,000 par value bond that sells for $887.00? That sells for $1,134.20? What does the fact that a bond sells at a discount or at a premium tell you about the relationship between r_d and the bond's coupon rate?

   (2) What are the total return, the current yield, and the capital gains yield for the discount bond? (Assume the bond is held to maturity and the company does not default on the bond.)

g. How does the equation for valuing a bond change if semiannual payments are made? Find the value of a 10-year, semiannual payment, 10% coupon bond if the nominal $r_d = 13\%$.

h. Suppose a 10-year, 10% semiannual coupon bond with a par value of $1,000 is currently selling for $1,135.90, producing a nominal yield to maturity of 8%. However, the bond can be called after 5 years for a price of $1,050.

   (1) What is the bond's *nominal* yield to call (YTC)?

   (2) If you bought this bond, do you think you would be more likely to earn the YTM or the YTC? Why?

i. Write a general expression for the yield on any debt security (r_d) and define these terms: real risk-free rate of interest (r^*), inflation premium (IP), default risk premium (DRP), liquidity premium (LP), and maturity risk premium (MRP).

j. Define the real risk-free rate (r^*). What security can be used as an estimate of r^*? What is the nominal risk-free rate (r_{RF})? What securities can be used as estimates of r_{RF}?

k. Describe a way to estimate the inflation premium (IP) for a t-year bond.

l. What is a *bond spread* and how is it related to the default risk premium? How are bond ratings related to default risk? What factors affect a company's bond rating?

m. What is *interest rate* (or *price*) *risk?* Which bond has more interest rate risk: an annual payment 1-year bond or a 10-year bond? Why?

n. What is *reinvestment rate risk?* Which has more reinvestment rate risk: a 1-year bond or a 10-year bond?

o. How are interest rate risk and reinvestment rate risk related to the maturity risk premium?

p. What is the term structure of interest rates? What is a yield curve?

q. Briefly describe bankruptcy law. If a firm were to default on its bonds, would the company be liquidated immediately? Would the bondholders be assured of receiving all of their promised payments?

SELECTED ADDITIONAL CASES

The following cases from CengageCompose cover many of the concepts discussed in this chapter and are available at **http://compose.cengage.com.**

Klein-Brigham Series:
Case 3, "Peachtree Securities, Inc. (B)"; Case 72, "Swan Davis"; and Case 78, "Beatrice Peabody."

Brigham-Buzzard Series:
Case 3, "Powerline Network Corporation (Bonds and Preferred Stock)."

PART 3
Stocks and Options

CHAPTER 6

Risk and Return

What a difference a year makes! At the beginning of 2016, many investors purchased shares of stock in the NASDAQ companies Madrigal Pharmaceuticals and Frontier Communications. By year end, Madrigal had gone up by 500% while Frontier had fallen by 87% (yet still remained listed on NASDAQ). Big gains and losses weren't limited to small companies. Investors were feeling good with Vertex Pharmaceuticals, gaining 100% during the year. At the other extreme, Under Armour Inc. went down by 50%.

Did investors in Frontier and Under Armour make bad decisions? Before you answer, suppose you were making the decision back in January 2016, with the information available then. You now know the decision's *outcome* was poor, but that doesn't mean the decision itself was badly made. Investors must have known these stocks were risky, with a chance of a gain or a loss. But given the information available to them, they certainly invested with the expectation of a gain. What about the investors in Madrigal and Vertex? They also realized the stock prices could go down or up but were probably pleasantly surprised that the stocks went up so much.

These examples show that what you expect to happen and what actually happens are often very different—the world is risky! Therefore, it is vital that you understand risk and the ways to manage it. As you read this chapter and think about risk, keep these companies in mind.

Intrinsic Value, Risk, and Return

The intrinsic value of a company is the present value of its expected future free cash flows (FCFs) discounted at the weighted average cost of capital (WACC). This chapter shows you how to measure a firm's risk and the rate of return expected by shareholders, which affects the WACC. All else held equal, higher risk increases the WACC, which reduces the firm's value.

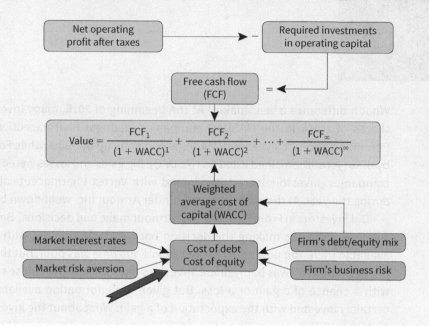

resource

*The textbook's Web site contains an Excel file that will guide you through the chapter's calculations. The file for this chapter is **Ch06 Tool Kit.xlsx**, and we encourage you to open the file and follow along as you read the chapter.*

In this chapter, we start from the basic premise that investors like returns and dislike risk; this is called **risk aversion**. Therefore, people will invest in relatively risky assets only if they expect to receive relatively high returns: the higher the perceived risk, the higher the expected rate of return an investor will demand. In this chapter, we define exactly what the term "risk" means as it relates to investments, we examine procedures used to measure risk, and we discuss more precisely the relationship between risk and required returns. In later chapters, we extend these relationships to show how risk and return interact to determine security prices. Managers must understand and apply these concepts as they plan the actions that will shape their firms' futures, and investors must understand them in order to make appropriate investment decisions.

6-1 Investment Returns and Risk

With most investments, an individual or business spends money today with the expectation of earning even more money in the future. However, most investments are risky. Following are brief definitions of return and risk.

6-1a Returns on Investments

The concept of *return* provides investors with a convenient way to express the financial performance of an investment. To illustrate, suppose you buy 10 shares of a stock for $1,000. The stock pays no dividends, but at the end of 1 year, you sell the stock for $1,100. What is the return on your $1,000 investment?

One way to express an investment's return is in *dollar terms:*

$$\text{Dollar return} = \text{Amount to be received} - \text{Amount invested}$$
$$= \$1,100 - \$1,000$$
$$= \$100$$

If instead, at the end of the year, you sell the stock for only $900, your dollar return will be −$100.

Although expressing returns in dollars is easy, two problems arise: (1) To make a meaningful judgment about the return, you need to know the scale (size) of the investment; a $100 return on a $100 investment is a great return (assuming the investment is held for 1 year), but a $100 return on a $10,000 investment would be a poor return. (2) You also need to know the timing of the return; a $100 return on a $100 investment is a great return if it occurs after 1 year, but the same dollar return after 100 years is not very good.

The solution to these scale and timing problems is to express investment results as *rates of return,* or *percentage returns.* For example, the rate of return on the 1-year stock investment, when $1,100 is received after 1 year, is 10%:

$$\text{Rate of return} = \frac{\text{Amount received} - \text{Amount invested}}{\text{Amount invested}}$$

$$= \frac{\text{Dollar return}}{\text{Amount invested}} = \frac{\$100}{\$1,000}$$

$$= 0.10 = 10\%$$

The rate of return calculation "standardizes" the dollar return by considering the annual return per unit of investment. Although this example has only one outflow and one inflow, the annualized rate of return can easily be calculated in situations where multiple cash flows occur over time by using the time value of money concepts discussed in Chapter 4.

6-1b Stand-Alone Risk versus Portfolio Risk

Risk is defined in *Webster's* as "a hazard; a peril; exposure to loss or injury." Thus, risk refers to the chance that some unfavorable event will occur. For an investment in financial assets or in new projects, the unfavorable event is ending up with a lower return than you expected. An asset's risk can be analyzed in two ways: (1) on a stand-alone basis, where the asset is considered in isolation; and (2) as part of a **portfolio**, which is a collection of assets. Thus, an asset's **stand-alone risk** is the risk an investor would face if she held only this one asset. Most assets are held in portfolios, but it is necessary to understand stand-alone risk in order to understand risk in a portfolio context.

Compare and contrast dollar returns and rates of return.

Why are rates of return superior to dollar returns when comparing different potential investments? (Hint: Think about size and timing.)

If you pay $500 for an investment that returns $600 in 1 year, what is your annual rate of return? **(20%)**

6-2 Measuring Risk for Discrete Distributions

Political and economic uncertainties affect stock market risk. For example, the market went up by over 3% in November 2017. At that time, one scenario might have been continued economic growth and a successful congressional effort to cut corporate taxes. On the other hand, another possible scenario was military conflict with North Korea. At the risk of oversimplification, these outcomes represented distinct (or discrete) scenarios for the market, with each scenario having a very different market return.

Risk can be a complicated topic, so we begin with a simple example that has discrete possible outcomes.[1]

6-2a Probability Distributions for Discrete Outcomes

An event's *probability* is defined as the chance that the event will occur. For example, a weather forecaster might state: "There is a 40% chance of rain today and a 60% chance that it will not rain." If all possible events, or outcomes, are listed, and if a probability is assigned to each event, then the listing is called a **discrete probability distribution**. (Keep in mind that the probabilities must sum to 1.0, or 100%.)

Suppose an investor is facing a situation similar to the debt ceiling crisis and believes there are three possible outcomes for the market as a whole: (1) Best case, with a 30% probability; (2) Most Likely case, with a 40% probability; and (3) Worst case, with a 30% probability. The investor also believes the market would go up by 37% in the Best scenario, go up by 11% in the Most Likely scenario, and go down by 15% in the Worst scenario.

Figure 6-1 shows the probability distribution for these three scenarios. Notice that the probabilities sum to 1.0 and that the possible returns are dispersed around the Most Likely scenario's return.

We can calculate expected return and risk using the probability distribution, as we illustrate in the next sections.

6-2b Expected Rate of Return for Discrete Distributions

The rate-of-return probability distribution is shown in the "Inputs" section of Figure 6-2; see Columns (1) and (2). This portion of the figure is called a *payoff matrix* when the outcomes are cash flows or returns.

If we multiply each possible outcome by its probability of occurrence and then sum these products, as in Column (3) of Figure 6-2, the result is a *weighted average* of outcomes.

FIGURE 6-1

Discrete Probability Distribution for Three Scenarios

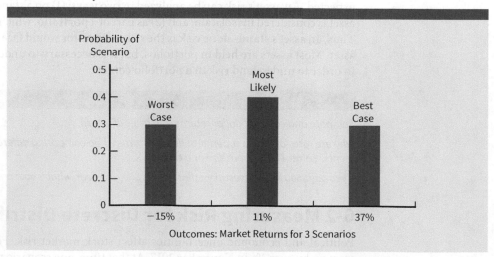

---

[1]The following discussion of risk applies to all random variables, not just stock returns.

FIGURE 6-2
Calculating Expected Returns and Standard Deviations: Discrete Probabilities

	A	B	C	D	E	F	G
61	INPUTS:			Expected Return	Standard Deviation		
62	Scenario	Probability of Scenario (1)	Market Rate of Return (2)	Product of Probability and Return (3) = (1) × (2)	Deviation from Expected Return (4) = (2) − D66	Squared Deviation (5) = (4)²	Prob. × Sq. Dev. (6) = (1) × (5)
63	Best Case	0.30	37%	11.1%	0.2600	0.0676	0.0203
64	Most Likely	0.40	11%	4.4%	0.0000	0.0000	0.0000
65	Worst Case	0.30	−15%	−4.5%	−0.2600	0.0676	0.0203
66		1.00	Exp. ret. =	Sum = 11.0%		Sum = Variance =	0.0406
67						Std. Dev. = Square root of variance =	20.1%

Source: See the file *Ch06 Tool Kit.xlsx.* Calculations are not rounded in intermediate steps.

See *Ch06 Tool Kit.xlsx* on
the textbook's Web site.

resource

The weights are the probabilities, and the weighted average is the **expected rate of return** ($\hat{r}$), called "r-hat," which is the mean of the probability distribution.[2] As shown in cell D66 in Figure 6-2, the expected rate of return is 11%.[3]

The calculation for expected rate of return can also be expressed as an equation that does the same thing as the payoff matrix table:

$$\text{Expected rate of return} = \hat{r} = p_1 r_1 + p_2 r_2 + \cdots + p_n r_n$$
$$= \sum_{i=1}^{n} p_i r_i \tag{6-1}$$

Here r_i is the return if outcome i occurs, p_i is the probability that outcome i occurs, and n is the number of possible outcomes. Thus, $\hat{r}$ is a weighted average of the possible outcomes (the r_i values), with each outcome's weight being its probability of occurrence. Using the data from Figure 6-2, we obtain the expected rate of return as follows:

$$\hat{r} = p_1(r_1) + p_2(r_2) + p_3(r_3)$$
$$= 0.3(37\%) + 0.4(11\%) + 0.3(-15\%)$$
$$= 11\%$$

6-2c Measuring Stand-Alone Risk: The Standard Deviation of a Discrete Distribution

For simple distributions, it is easy to assess risk by looking at the dispersion of possible outcomes: a distribution with widely dispersed possible outcomes is riskier than one with

---

[2] In other chapters, we will use $\hat{r}_d$ and $\hat{r}_s$ to signify expected returns on bonds and stocks, respectively. However, this distinction is unnecessary in this chapter, so we just use the general term $\hat{r}$ to signify the expected return on an investment.

[3] Don't worry about why there is an 11% expected return for the market. We discuss the market return in more detail later in the chapter.

narrowly dispersed outcomes. For example, we can look at Figure 6-1 and see that the possible returns are widely dispersed. But when there are many possible outcomes and we are comparing many different investments, it isn't possible to assess risk simply by looking at the probability distribution—we need a quantitative measure of the tightness of the probability distribution. One such measure is the **standard deviation** (σ), the symbol for which is σ, pronounced "sigma." A large standard deviation means that possible outcomes are widely dispersed, whereas a small standard deviation means that outcomes are more tightly clustered around the expected value.

To calculate the standard deviation, we proceed as shown in Figure 6-2, taking the following steps:

1. Calculate the expected value for the rate of return using Equation 6-1.
2. Subtract the expected rate of return ($\hat{r}$) from each possible outcome (r_i) to obtain a set of deviations about $\hat{r}$, as shown in Column (4) of Figure 6-2:

$$\text{Deviation}_i = r_i - \hat{r}$$

3. Square each deviation as shown in Column (5).
4. Multiply the probability of the occurrence (shown in Column 1) by the squared deviations in Column (5); these products are shown in Column (6).
5. Sum these products to obtain the **variance** of the probability distribution:

$$\text{Variance} = \sigma^2 = \sum_{i=1}^{n} p_i (r_i - \hat{r})^2 \qquad \text{(6-2)}$$

Thus, the variance is essentially a weighted average of the squared deviations from the expected value.

6. Finally, take the square root of the variance to obtain the standard deviation:

$$\text{Standard deviation} = \sigma = \sqrt{\sum_{i=1}^{n} p_i (r_i - \hat{r})^2} \qquad \text{(6-3)}$$

resource

See *Ch06 Tool Kit.xlsx* on the textbook's Web site for all calculations.

The standard deviation provides an idea of how far above or below the expected value the actual value is likely to be. Using this procedure in Figure 6-2, our hypothetical investor believes that the market return has a standard deviation of about 20%.

SELF-TEST

What does "investment risk" mean?

Set up an illustrative probability distribution for an investment.

What is a payoff matrix?

How does one calculate the standard deviation?

An investment has a 20% chance of producing a 25% return, a 60% chance of producing a 10% return, and a 20% chance of producing a −15% return. What is its expected return? **(8%)** *What is its standard deviation?* **(12.9%)**

6-3 Risk in a Continuous Distribution

Investors usually don't estimate discrete outcomes in normal economic times but instead use the scenario approach during special situations, such as the debt ceiling crisis, the European bond crisis, oil supply threats, bank stress tests, and so on. Even in these situations, they would estimate more than three outcomes. For example, an investor might add more scenarios to our example of possible stock market returns; Panel A in Figure 6-3 shows 15 scenarios for the market and has a standard deviation of 20.2%.

Recall that the standard deviation provides a measure of dispersion that provides information about the range of possible outcomes. Panel B of Figure 6-3 shows 15 possible

FIGURE 6-3
Discrete Probability Distributions for 15 Scenarios

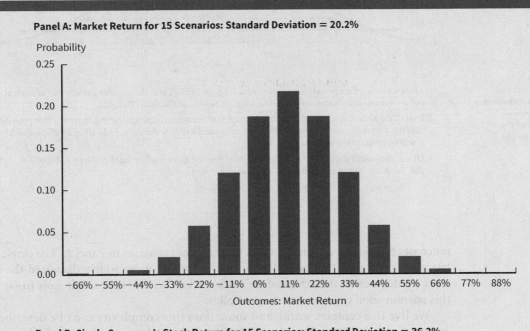

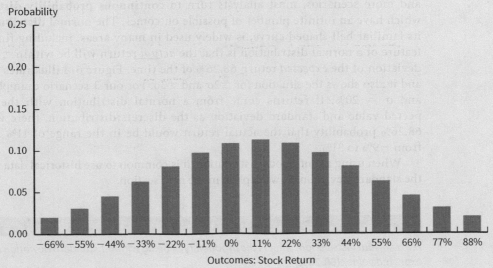

FIGURE 6-4
Probability Ranges for a Normal Distribution

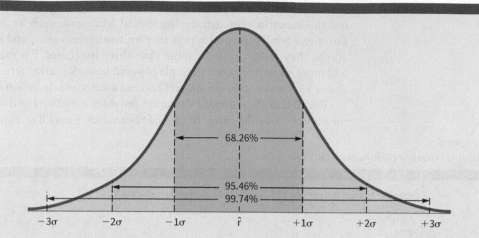

Notes:

1. The area under the normal curve always equals 1.0, or 100%. Thus, the areas under any pair of normal curves drawn on the same scale, whether they are peaked or flat, must be equal.

2. Half of the area under a normal curve is to the left of the mean, $\hat{r}$, indicating that there is a 50% probability that the actual outcome will be less than the mean, and half is to the right, indicating a 50% probability that it will be greater than the mean.

3. Of the area under the curve, 68.26% is within $\pm 1\sigma$ of the mean, indicating that the probability is 68.26% that the actual outcome will be within the range $\hat{r} - \sigma$ to $\hat{r} + \sigma$.

resource

For more discussion of probability distributions, see Web Extension 6A, available on the textbook's Web site.

outcomes for a single company's stock for the same scenarios in Panel A. The single stock has a standard deviation of 36.2%. Notice how much more widely dispersed the single stock's outcomes are than those of the stock market. We will have much more to say about this phenomenon when we discuss portfolios.

We live in a complex world, and sometimes this complexity can't be described adequately with several or even many scenarios. In such cases, instead of adding more and more scenarios, most analysts turn to **continuous probability distributions**, which have an infinite number of possible outcomes. The **normal distribution**, with its familiar bell-shaped curve, is widely used in many areas, including finance. One feature of a normal distribution is that the *actual* return will be within ± 1 standard deviation of the *expected* return 68.26% of the time. Figure 6-4 illustrates this point, and it also shows the situation for $\pm 2\sigma$ and $\pm 3\sigma$. For our 3-scenario example, $\hat{r} = 11\%$ and $\sigma = 20\%$. If returns come from a normal distribution with the same expected value and standard deviation as the discrete distribution, there would be a 68.26% probability that the actual return would be in the range of 11% $\pm$ 20%, or from −9% to 31%.

When using a continuous distribution, it is common to use historical data to estimate the standard deviation, as we explain in the next section.

SELF-TEST

For a normal distribution, what is the probability of being within 1 standard deviation of the expected value? **(68.26%)**

What Does Risk Really Mean?

As explained in the text, the probability of being within 1 standard deviation of the expected return is 68.26%, so the probability of being further than 1 standard deviation from the mean is 100% − 68.26% = 31.74%. There is an equal probability of being above or below the range, so there is a 15.87% chance of being more than 1 standard deviation below the mean, which is roughly equal to a 1 in 6 chance (1 in 6 is 16.67%).

For the average firm listed on the New York Stock Exchange (NYSE), σ has been in the range of 35% to 40% in recent years, with an expected return of around 8% to 12%. One standard deviation below this expected return is about 10% − 35% = −25%. This means that, for a typical stock in a typical year, there is about a 1 in 6 chance of having a 25% loss. You might be thinking that 1 in 6 is a pretty low probability, but what if your chance of getting hit by a car when you crossed a street were 1 in 6? When put that way, 1 in 6 sounds pretty scary.

You might also correctly be thinking that there would be a 1 in 6 chance of getting a return higher than 1 standard deviation above the mean, which would be about 45% for a typical stock. A 45% return is great, but human nature is such that most investors would dislike a 25% loss a whole lot more than they would enjoy a 45% gain.

You might also be thinking that you'll be OK if you hold the stock long enough. But even if you buy and hold a diversified portfolio for 10 years, there is still roughly a 10% chance that you will lose money. If you hold it for 20 years, there is about a 4% chance of losing. Such odds wouldn't be worrisome if you were engaged in a game of chance that could be played multiple times, but you have only one life to live and just a few rolls of the dice.

We aren't suggesting that investors shouldn't buy stocks; indeed, we own stock ourselves. But we do believe investors should understand more clearly how much risk investing entails.

6-4 Using Historical Data to Estimate Risk

Suppose that a sample of returns over some past period is available. These past **realized rates of return ($\bar{r}_t$)** are denoted as $\bar{r}_t$ ("r bar t"), where t designates the time period. The **average return ($\bar{r}_{Avg}$)** over the last T periods is defined as:

$$\bar{r}_{Avg} = \frac{\sum\limits_{t=1}^{T} \bar{r}_t}{T} \tag{6-4}$$

The standard deviation of a sample of returns can then be estimated using this formula:[4]

$$\text{Estimated } \sigma = S = \sqrt{\frac{\sum\limits_{t=1}^{T} (\bar{r}_t - \bar{r}_{Avg})^2}{T - 1}} \tag{6-5}$$

When estimated from past data, the standard deviation is often denoted by S.

---

[4]Because we are estimating the standard deviation from a sample of observations, the denominator in Equation 6-5 is "T − 1" and not just "T." Equations 6-4 and 6-5 are built into all financial calculators. For example, to find the sample standard deviation, enter the rates of return into the calculator and press the key marked S (or S_x) to get the standard deviation. See your calculator's manual for details.

6-4a Calculating the Historical Average and Standard Deviation

To illustrate these calculations, consider the following historical returns for a company:

Year	Return
2017	15%
2018	−5%
2019	20%

Using Equations 6-4 and 6-5, the estimated average and standard deviation, respectively, are:

$$\bar{r}_{Avg} = \frac{15\% - 5\% + 20\%}{3} = 10.0\%$$

$$\text{Estimated } \sigma \text{ (or S)} = \sqrt{\frac{(15\% - 10\%)^2 + (-5\% - 10\%)^2 + (20\% - 10\%)^2}{3 - 1}}$$

$$= 13.2\%$$

The average and standard deviation can also be calculated using *Excel*'s built-in functions, shown here using numerical data rather than cell ranges as inputs:

$$\mathbf{=AVERAGE(0.15, -0.05, 0.20)} = 10.0\%$$
$$\mathbf{=STDEV(0.15, -0.05, 0.20)} = 13.2\%$$

The historical standard deviation is often used as an estimate of future variability. Because past variability is often repeated, past variability may be a reasonably good estimate of future risk. However, it is usually incorrect to use $\bar{r}_{Avg}$ based on a past period as an estimate of $\hat{r}$, the expected future return. For example, just because a stock had a 75% return in the past year, there is no reason to expect a 75% return this year.

6-4b Calculating MicroDrive's Historical Average and Standard Deviation

Figure 6-5 shows 48 months of recent stock returns for two companies, MicroDrive and SnailDrive; the actual data are in the *Excel* file ***Ch06 Tool Kit.xlsx***. A quick glance is enough to determine that MicroDrive's returns are more volatile.

We could use Equations 6-4 and 6-5 to calculate the average return and standard deviation, but that would be quite tedious. Instead, we use *Excel*'s **AVERAGE** and **STDEV** functions and find that MicroDrive's monthly average return was 1.00% and its monthly standard deviation was 14.94%. SnailDrive had an average monthly return of 0.77% and a standard deviation of 9.87%. These calculations confirm the visual evidence in Figure 6-5: MicroDrive had greater stand-alone risk than SnailDrive.

We often use monthly data to estimate averages and standard deviations, but we normally present data in an annualized format. Multiply the monthly average return by 12 to get MicroDrive's annualized average return of 1.00%(12) = 12.0%. As noted earlier, the past average return isn't a good indicator of the future return.

FIGURE 6-5
Historical Monthly Stock Returns for MicroDrive and SnailDrive

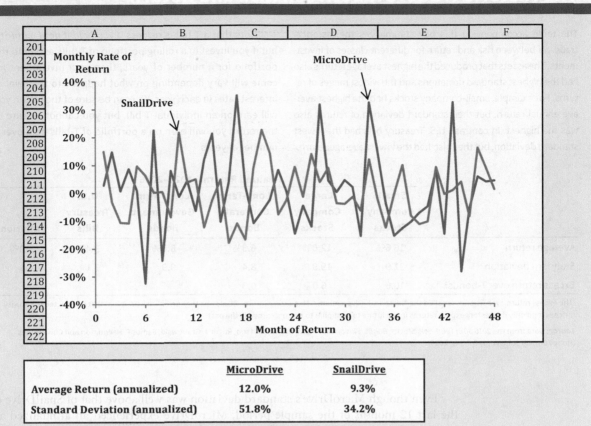

	MicroDrive	SnailDrive
Average Return (annualized)	12.0%	9.3%
Standard Deviation (annualized)	51.8%	34.2%

To annualize the standard deviation, multiply the monthly standard deviation by the square root of 12. MicroDrive's annualized standard deviation was 14.94%($\sqrt{12}$) = 51.8%.[5] SnailDrive's average annual return was 9.3%, and its annualized standard deviation was 34.2%.

Notice that MicroDrive had higher risk than SnailDrive (a standard deviation of 51.8% versus 34.2%) and a higher average return (12.0% versus 9.3%) during the past 48 months. However, a higher return for undertaking more risk isn't guaranteed—if it were, then a riskier investment wouldn't really be risky!

The file **Ch06 Tool Kit.xlsx** calculates the annualized average return and standard deviation using just the most recent 12 months. Here are the results:

Results for Most Recent 12 Months	MicroDrive	SnailDrive
Average return (annual)	−28.9%	11.6%
Standard deviation (annual)	52.4%	31.4%

[5]If we had calculated the monthly variance, we would annualize it by multiplying it by 12, as intuition (and mathematics) suggests. Because standard deviation is the square root of variance, we annualize the monthly standard deviation by multiplying it by the square root of 12.

The Historic Trade-Off between Risk and Return

The table accompanying this box summarizes the historical trade-off between risk and return for different classes of investments. The assets that produced the highest average returns also had the highest standard deviations and the widest ranges of returns. For example, small-company stocks had the highest average annual return, but their standard deviation of returns also was the highest. In contrast, U.S. Treasury bills had the lowest standard deviation, but they also had the lowest average return.

Note that a T-bill is riskless *if you hold it until maturity,* but if you invest in a rolling portfolio of T-bills and hold the portfolio for a number of years, then your investment income will vary depending on what happens to the level of interest rates in each year. You can be sure of the return you will earn on an individual T-bill, but you cannot be sure of the return you will earn on a portfolio of T-bills held over a number of years.

	Realized Returns, 1926–2016					
	Small-Company Stocks	Large-Company Stocks	Long-Term Corporate Bonds	Long-Term Government Bonds	U.S. Treasury Bills	Inflation
Average return	16.6%	12.0%	6.3%	6.0%	3.4%	3.0%
Standard deviation	31.9	19.9	8.4	9.9	3.1	4.1
Excess return over T-bonds[a]	10.6	6.0	0.3			

[a]The excess return over T-bonds is called the "historical risk premium." This excess return will also be the current risk premium that is reflected in security prices if and only if investors expect returns in the future to be similar to returns earned in the past.

Source: Data from the *2016 SBBI Yearbook: Stocks, Bonds, Bills and Inflation,* Roger Ibbotson, Roger J. Grabowski, James P. Harrington and Carla Nunes (Hoboken, NJ: John Wiley & Sons, 2016).

Even though MicroDrive's standard deviation was well above that of SnailDrive over the last 12 months of the sample period, MicroDrive experienced an annualized average loss of almost 29%, while SnailDrive gained almost 12%.[6] MicroDrive's stockholders certainly learned that higher risk doesn't always lead to higher *actual* returns.

SELF-TEST

A stock's returns for the past 3 years were 10%, −15%, and 35%. What is the historical average return? **(10%)** *What is the historical sample standard deviation?* **(25%)**

6-5 Risk in a Portfolio Context

Most financial assets are actually held as parts of portfolios. Banks, pension funds, insurance companies, mutual funds, and other financial institutions are required by law to hold diversified portfolios. Even individual investors—at least those whose security holdings constitute a significant part of their total wealth—generally hold portfolios, not the stock of only one firm, because **diversification** can reduce risk exposure.

6-5a Creating a Portfolio

A portfolio is a collection of assets. The weight of an asset in a portfolio is the percentage of the portfolio's total value that is invested in the asset. For example, if you invest $1,000

---

[6]During the last 12 months, MicroDrive had an average monthly loss of 2.41%, but it had a compound loss for the year of over 34%. We discuss the difference between arithmetic averages and geometric averages (based on compound returns) in Chapter 9.

in each of 10 stocks, your portfolio has a value of $10,000, and each stock has a weight of $1,000/$10,000 = 10%. If instead you invest $5,000 in 1 stock and $1,000 apiece in 5 stocks, the first stock has a weight of $5,000/$10,000 = 50%, and each of the other 5 stocks has a weight of 10%. Usually it is more convenient to talk about an asset's weight in a portfolio rather than the dollars invested in the asset. Therefore, when we create a portfolio, we choose a weight (a percentage) for each asset, with the weights summing to 1.0 (or the percentages summing to 100%).

Suppose we have a portfolio of n stocks. The actual return on a portfolio in a particular period is the weighted average of the actual returns of the stocks in the portfolio, with w_i denoting the weight invested in Stock i:

$$\bar{r}_p = w_1\bar{r}_1 + w_2\bar{r}_2 + \cdots + w_n\bar{r}_n$$

$$= \sum_{i=1}^{n} w_i\bar{r}_i$$

(6-6)

The average portfolio return over a number of periods is also equal to the weighted average of the stock's average returns:

$$\bar{r}_{Avg,p} = \sum_{i=1}^{n} w_i\bar{r}_{Avg,i}$$

Recall from the previous section that SnailDrive had an average annualized return of 9.3% during the past 48 months and MicroDrive had a 12.0% return. A portfolio with 75% invested in SnailDrive and 25% in MicroDrive would have had the following return:

$$\bar{r}_{Avg,p} = 0.75(9.3\%) + 0.25(12\%) = 10.0\%$$

Notice that the portfolio return of 10.0% is between the returns of SnailDrive (9.3%) and MicroDrive (12.0%), as you would expect.

Suppose an investor with stock only in SnailDrive came to you for advice, saying, "I would like more return, but I hate risk!" How do you think the investor would react if you suggested taking 25% of the investment out of the low-risk SnailDrive (with a standard deviation of 34.2%) and putting it into the high-risk MicroDrive (with a standard deviation of 51.8%)? As just shown, the return during the 48-month period would have been 10.0%, well above the return on SnailDrive. But what would have happened to risk?

The file *Ch06 Tool Kit.xlsx* calculates the portfolio return for each month (using Equation 6-6) and calculates the portfolio's standard deviation by applying *Excel's* **STDEV** function to the portfolio's monthly returns. Imagine the investor's surprise in learning that the portfolio's standard deviation is 27.1%, which is *less than* that of SnailDrive's 34.2% standard deviation. In other words, adding a risky asset to a safer asset can reduce risk!

How can this happen? MicroDrive sells high-end memory storage, whereas SnailDrive sells low-end memory, including reconditioned hard drives. When the economy is doing well, MicroDrive has high sales and profits, but SnailDrive's sales lag because customers prefer faster memory. But when times are tough, customers resort to SnailDrive for low-cost memory storage. Take a look at Figure 6-5. Notice that SnailDrive's returns don't move in perfect lockstep with MicroDrive: Sometimes MicroDrive goes up and SnailDrive goes down, and vice versa.

6-5b Correlation and Risk for a Two-Stock Portfolio

The tendency of two variables to move together is called **correlation**, and the **correlation coefficient (ρ)** measures this tendency. The symbol for the correlation coefficient is the Greek letter rho, ρ (pronounced "roe"). The correlation coefficient can range from +1.0, denoting that the two variables move up and down in perfect synchronization, to −1.0, denoting that the variables always move in exactly opposite directions. A correlation coefficient of zero indicates that the two variables are not related to each other at all—that is, changes in one variable are independent of changes in the other.

The estimate of correlation from a sample of historical data is often called "R." Here is the formula to estimate the correlation between stocks i and j ($\bar{r}_{i,t}$ is the actual return for Stock i in period t, and $\bar{r}_{i,Avg}$ is the average return during the T-period sample; similar notation is used for Stock j):

$$\text{Estimated } \rho = R = \frac{\sum_{t=1}^{T} (\bar{r}_{i,t} - \bar{r}_{i,Avg})(\bar{r}_{j,t} - \bar{r}_{j,Avg})}{\sqrt{\left[\sum_{t=1}^{T} (\bar{r}_{i,t} - \bar{r}_{i,Avg})^2\right]\left[\sum_{t=1}^{T} (\bar{r}_{j,t} - \bar{r}_{j,Avg})^2\right]}} \tag{6-7}$$

Fortunately, it is easy to estimate the correlation coefficient with a financial calculator or *Excel*. With a calculator, simply enter the returns of the two stocks and then press a key labeled "r."[7] In *Excel*, use the **CORREL** function. See ***Ch06 Tool Kit.xlsx***, where we calculate the correlation between the returns of MicroDrive and SnailDrive to be −0.13. The negative correlation means that when SnailDrive is having a poor return, MicroDrive tends to have a good return; when SnailDrive is having a good return, MicroDrive tends to have a poor return. This means that adding some of MicroDrive's stock to a portfolio that only had SnailDrive's stock tends to reduce the volatility of the portfolio.

Here is a way to think about the possible benefit of diversification: *If a portfolio's standard deviation is less than the weighted average of the individual stocks' standard deviations, then diversification provides a benefit.* Does diversification always reduce risk? If so, by how much? And how does correlation affect diversification? Let's consider the full range of correlation coefficients, from −1 to +1.

If two stocks have a correlation of −1 (the lowest possible correlation), when one stock has a higher than expected return then the other stock has a lower than expected return, and vice versa. In fact, it would be possible to choose weights such that one stock's deviations from its mean return completely cancel out the other stock's deviations from its mean return.[8] Such a portfolio would have a zero standard deviation but would have an expected return equal to the weighted average of the stock's expected returns. In this situation, diversification can eliminate all risk: *For correlation of −1, the portfolio's standard deviation can be as low as zero if the portfolio weights are chosen appropriately.*

If the correlation were +1 (the highest possible correlation), the portfolio's standard deviation would be the weighted average of the stock's standard deviations. In this case, diversification doesn't help: *For correlation of +1, the portfolio's standard deviation is the weighted average of the stocks' standard deviations.*

---

[7]See your calculator manual for the exact steps. Also, note that the correlation coefficient is often denoted by the term "r." We use ρ to avoid confusion with r, which we use to denote the rate of return.

[8]If the correlation between Stocks 1 and 2 is equal to −1, then the weights for a zero-risk portfolio are $w_1 = \sigma_1/(\sigma_1 + \sigma_2)$ and $w_2 = \sigma_2/(\sigma_1 + \sigma_2)$.

For any other correlation, diversification reduces, but cannot eliminate, risk: *For correlation between −1 and +1, the portfolio's standard deviation is less than the weighted average of the stocks' standard deviations.*

The correlation between most pairs of companies is in the range of 0.2 to 0.3, so diversification reduces risk, but it doesn't completely eliminate risk.[9]

6-5c Diversification and Multi-Stock Portfolios

Figure 6-6 shows how portfolio risk is affected by forming larger and larger portfolios of randomly selected New York Stock Exchange (NYSE) stocks. Standard deviations are plotted for an average one-stock portfolio, an average two-stock portfolio, and so on, up

FIGURE 6-6
Effects of Portfolio Size on Portfolio Risk for Average Stocks

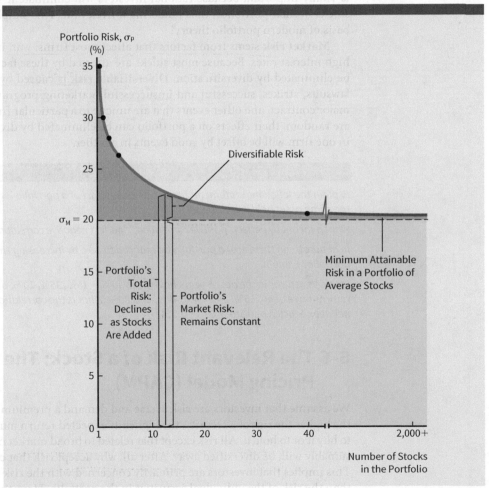

[9]During the period 1968–1998, the average correlation coefficient between two randomly selected stocks was 0.28, while the average correlation coefficient between two large-company stocks was 0.33; see Louis K. C. Chan, Jason Karceski, and Josef Lakonishok, "On Portfolio Optimization: Forecasting Covariance and Choosing the Risk Model," *The Review of Financial Studies,* Vol. 12, No. 5, Winter 1999, pp. 937–974. The average correlation fell from around 0.35 in the late 1970s to less than 0.10 by the late 1990s; see John Y. Campbell, Martin Lettau, Burton G. Malkiel, and Yexiao Xu, "Have Individual Stocks Become More Volatile? An Empirical Exploration of Idiosyncratic Risk," *Journal of Finance,* February 2001, pp. 1–43.

to a portfolio consisting of all 2,000-plus common stocks that were listed on the NYSE at the time the data were plotted. The graph illustrates that, in general, the risk of a portfolio consisting of stocks tends to decline and to approach some limit as the number of stocks in the portfolio increases. According to data from recent years, σ_1, the standard deviation of a one-stock portfolio (or an average stock), is approximately 35%. However, a portfolio consisting of all shares of all stocks, which is called the **market portfolio**, would have a standard deviation, σ_M, of only about 20%, which is shown as the horizontal dashed line in Figure 6-6.

Thus, *almost half of the risk inherent in an average individual stock can be eliminated if the stock is held in a reasonably well-diversified portfolio, which is one containing 40 or more stocks in a number of different industries.* The part of a stock's risk that *cannot* be eliminated is called *market risk*, while the part that *can* be eliminated is called *diversifiable risk*.[10] The fact that a large part of the risk of any individual stock can be eliminated is vitally important because rational investors *will* eliminate it simply by holding many stocks in their portfolios, thus rendering it irrelevant. This simple observation forms the basis of modern portfolio theory!

Market risk stems from factors that affect most firms: war, inflation, recessions, and high interest rates. Because most stocks are affected by these factors, market risk cannot be eliminated by diversification. **Diversifiable risk** is caused by such random events as lawsuits, strikes, successful and unsuccessful marketing programs, winning or losing a major contract, and other events that are unique to a particular firm. Because these events are random, their effects on a portfolio can be eliminated by diversification—bad events in one firm will be offset by good events in another.

SELF-TEST

Explain the following statement: "An asset held as part of a portfolio is generally less risky than the same asset held in isolation."

What is meant by perfect "positive correlation," "perfect negative correlation," and "zero correlation"?

In general, can the risk of a portfolio be reduced to zero by increasing the number of stocks in the portfolio? Explain.

Stock A's returns in the past 5 years have been 10%, −15%, 35%, 10%, and −20%. Stock B's returns have been −5%, 1%, −4%, 40%, and 30%. What is the correlation coefficient for returns between Stock A and Stock B? (−0.35)

6-6 The Relevant Risk of a Stock: The Capital Asset Pricing Model (CAPM)

We assume that investors are risk averse and demand a premium for bearing risk; that is, the higher the risk of a security, the higher its expected return must be to induce investors to buy it or to hold it. All risk except that related to broad market movements can, and presumably will, be diversified away. After all, why accept risk that can be eliminated easily? This implies that investors are primarily concerned with the risk of their *portfolios* rather than the risk of the individual securities in the portfolio. How, then, should the risk of an individual stock be measured?

The **Capital Asset Pricing Model (CAPM)** provides one answer to that question. A stock might be quite risky if held by itself, but—because diversification eliminates about

[10]Diversifiable risk is also known as *company-specific risk* or *unsystematic risk*. Market risk is also known as *nondiversifiable risk* or *systematic risk*; it is the risk that remains after diversification.

half of its risk—the stock's **relevant risk** is its *contribution to a well-diversified portfolio's risk,* which is much smaller than the stock's stand-alone risk.[11]

6-6a Contribution to Market Risk: Beta

A well-diversified portfolio has only market risk. Therefore, the CAPM defines the relevant risk of an individual stock as the amount of risk that the stock contributes to the market portfolio, which is a portfolio containing all stocks.[12] In CAPM terminology, ρ_{iM} is the correlation between Stock i's return and the market return, σ_i is the standard deviation of Stock i's return, and σ_M is the standard deviation of the market's return. The relevant measure of risk is its **beta coefficient (b)**, which is often called just beta; the beta of Stock i, denoted by b_i, is calculated as:[13]

$$b_i = \left(\frac{\sigma_i}{\sigma_M}\right)\rho_{i,M} \qquad (6\text{-}8)$$

This formula shows that a stock with a high standard deviation, σ_i, will tend to have a high beta, which means that, other things held constant, the stock contributes a lot of risk to a well-diversified portfolio. This makes sense because a stock with high stand-alone risk will tend to destabilize a portfolio. Note too that a stock with a high correlation with the market, ρ_{iM}, will also tend to have a large beta and hence be risky. This also makes sense because a high correlation means that diversification does not help much; the stock performs well when the portfolio also performs well, and the stock performs poorly when the portfolio also performs poorly.

Suppose a stock has a beta of 1.4. What does that mean? Specifically, how much risk will this stock add to a well-diversified portfolio? To answer that question, we need two important facts. First, the beta of a portfolio, b_p, is the weighted average of the betas of the stocks in the portfolio, with the weights equal to the same weights used to create the portfolio. This can be written as:

$$b_p = w_1 b_1 + w_2 b_2 + \cdots + w_n b_n$$
$$= \sum_{i=1}^{n} w_i b_i \qquad (6\text{-}9)$$

For example, suppose an investor owns a $100,000 portfolio consisting of $25,000 invested in each of four stocks; the stocks have betas of 0.6, 1.2, 1.2, and 1.4. The weight of each stock in the portfolio is $25,000/$100,000 = 25%. The portfolio's beta will be $b_p = 1.1$:

$$b_p = 25\%(0.6) + 25\%(1.2) + 25\%(1.2) + 25\%(1.4) = 1.1$$

---

[11]Nobel Prizes were awarded to the developers of the CAPM, Professors Harry Markowitz and William F. Sharpe.

[12]In theory, the market portfolio should contain all assets. In practice, it usually contains only stocks. Many analysts use returns on the S&P 500 Index to estimate the market return.

[13]If you express the change in the market portfolio's standard deviation relative to a slight change in the amount of Stock i in the market portfolio (w_i), this differential change is:

$$\frac{\partial \sigma_M}{\partial w_i} = b_i \sigma_M$$

If you compare two stocks with different betas, the stock with the larger beta contributes more risk to the market portfolio, as the preceding equation shows.

The second important fact is that the variance of a well-diversified portfolio is approximately equal to the product of its squared beta and the market portfolio's variance:[14]

$$\sigma_p^2 \approx b_p^2 \, \sigma_M^2 \qquad \text{(6-10)}$$

Now take the square root of each side of Equation 6-10. If we only consider portfolios with positive portfolio betas, which are typical, then the standard deviation of a well-diversified portfolio, σ_p, is approximately equal to the product of the portfolio's beta and the market standard deviation:[15]

$$\sigma_p \approx b_p \, \sigma_M \qquad \text{(6-11)}$$

Equation 6-11 shows three things: (1) A portfolio with a beta greater than 1 will have a bigger standard deviation than the market portfolio. (2) A portfolio with a beta equal to 1 will have the same standard deviation as the market. (3) A portfolio with a beta less than 1 will have a smaller standard deviation than the market. For example, suppose the market standard deviation is 20%. Using Equation 6-11, a well-diversified portfolio with a beta of 1.1 will have a standard deviation of 22%:

$$\sigma_p = 1.1(20\%) = 22\%$$

By substituting Equation 6-9 into Equation 6-11, we can see the impact that each individual stock beta has on the risk of a well-diversified portfolio:

$$\sigma_p \approx (w_1 b_1 + w_2 b_2 + \cdots + w_n b_n)\, \sigma_M$$
$$= \sum_{i=1}^{n} w_i b_i \sigma_M \qquad \text{(6-12)}$$

This means Stock S with beta b_S and weight w_S in a well-diversified portfolio contributes a total of $w_S b_S \sigma_M$ to the portfolio's standard deviation. For a numerical example, consider the four-stock portfolio in our example. Although a well-diversified portfolio would have more than four stocks, let's suppose our portfolio is well diversified. If that is the case, then Figure 6-7 shows how much risk each stock contributes to the portfolio.[16]

---

[14]This relationship is only valid for a very well-diversified portfolio having a large number of stocks with weights that are similar in size. If this is not true, then the portfolio will contain a significant amount of diversifiable risk, and Equation 6-10 will not be a good approximation.

[15]If a portfolio's beta is negative, then the portfolio's standard deviation would depend upon the absolute value of its beta: $\sigma_p \approx |b_p| \, \sigma_M$. However, a portfolio's beta can be negative in only two situations, neither of which occurs in practice. First, the portfolio could be invested heavily in stocks with negative betas. This is not practical because there aren't enough negative beta stocks to create a well-diversified portfolio, which means Equations 6-10 and 6-11 don't apply. Second, it is possible to have a negative portfolio beta if the portfolio has negative weights (which means the stock is sold short) on stocks with large betas and positive weights on stocks with small betas. However, magnitudes of weights necessary for this strategy will result in a portfolio that is not diversified well enough for Equations 6-10 and 6-11 to be good approximations.

[16]If the portfolio isn't well diversified, then $b_p \sigma_M$ (or $|b_p|(\sigma_M)$ if $b_p < 0$) measures the part of the portfolio's standard deviation due to market risk. For undiversified portfolios, $b_i w_i \sigma_M$ measures the amount of the portfolio's standard deviation that is due to the market risk of Stock i.

FIGURE 6-7
The Contribution of Individual Stocks to Portfolio Risk: The Effect of Beta

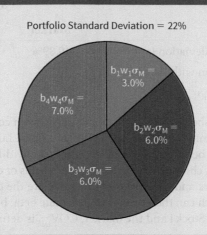

Portfolio Standard Deviation = 22%

$b_1 w_1 \sigma_M = 3.0\%$

$b_2 w_2 \sigma_M = 6.0\%$

$b_3 w_3 \sigma_M = 6.0\%$

$b_4 w_4 \sigma_M = 7.0\%$

Market Standard Deviation = σ_M = 20%

	Stock Beta: b_i	Weight in Portfolio: w_i	Contribution to Portfolio Beta: $b_i \times w_i$	Contribution to Portfolio Risk: $b_i \times w_i \times \sigma_M$
Stock 1	0.6	25.0%	0.150	3.0%
Stock 2	1.2	25.0%	0.300	6.0%
Stock 3	1.2	25.0%	0.300	6.0%
Stock 4	1.4	25.0%	0.350	7.0%
			$b_p = 1.100$	$\sigma_p = 22.0\%$

Out of the total 22% standard deviation of the portfolio, Stock 1 contributes $w_1 b_1 \sigma_M = (25\%)(0.6)(20\%) = 3\%$. Stocks 2 and 3 have betas that are twice as big as Stock 1's beta, so Stocks 2 and 3 contribute twice as much risk as Stock 1. Stock 4 has the largest beta, and it contributes the most risk.

We demonstrate how to estimate beta in the next section, but here are some key points about beta: (1) Beta determines how much risk a stock contributes to a well-diversified portfolio. If all the stocks' weights in a portfolio are equal, then a stock with a beta that is twice as big as another stock's beta contributes twice as much risk. (2) The average of all stocks' betas is equal to 1; the beta of the market also is equal to 1. Intuitively, this is because the market return is the average of all the stocks' returns. (3) A stock with a beta greater than 1 contributes more risk to a portfolio than does the average stock, and a stock with a beta less than 1 contributes less risk to a portfolio than does the average stock. (4) Most stocks have betas that are between about 0.4 and 1.6.

6-6b Estimating Beta

The CAPM is an *ex ante* model, which means that all of the variables represent before-the-fact, *expected* values. In particular, the beta coefficient used by investors should reflect the relationship between a stock's expected return and the market's expected return during some *future* period. However, people generally calculate betas using data from some *past* period and then assume that the stock's risk will be the same in the future as it was in the past.

Many analysts use 4 to 5 years of monthly data, although some use 52 weeks of weekly data. To illustrate, we use the 4 years of monthly returns from *Ch06 Tool Kit.xlsx* and calculate the betas of MicroDrive and SnailDrive using Equation 6-8:[17]

	Market	MicroDrive	SnailDrive
Standard deviation (annual):	19.89%	51.75%	34.17%
Correlation with the market:		0.511	0.264
$b_i = \rho_{iM}(\sigma_i/\sigma_M)$		1.33	0.45

Table 6-1 shows the betas for some well-known companies as provided by two different financial organizations, Yahoo!Finance and Value Line. Notice that their estimates of beta usually differ because they calculate it in slightly different ways. Given these differences, many analysts choose to calculate their own betas or else average the published betas.

Calculators and spreadsheets can calculate the components of Equation 6-8 (ρ_{iM}, σ_i, and σ_M), which can then be used to calculate beta, but there is another way.[18] The covariance between Stock i and the market, COV_{iM}, is defined as:[19]

$$COV_{iM} = \rho_{iM}\sigma_i\sigma_M \qquad \text{(6-13)}$$

TABLE 6-1
Beta Coefficients for Some Actual Companies

Stock (Ticker Symbol)	Value Line	Yahoo! Finance
Amazon.com (AMZN)	1.2	1.39
Apple (AAPL)	0.95	1.34
Coca-Cola (KO)	0.7	0.63
Duke Energy Corp. (DUK)	0.60	0.01
Energen Corp. (EGN)	1.70	2.10
General Electric (GE)	1.05	0.99
Microsoft Corp. (MSFT)	1.10	1.50
Procter & Gamble (PG)	0.70	0.47
Tesla (TSLA)	1.30	0.73

Sources: **www.valueline.com** and **finance.yahoo.com**, December 2017. For Value Line, enter the ticker symbol. For Yahoo!Finance, enter the ticker symbol. When the results page comes up, select Statistics to find beta.

---

[17]As with any estimation, more observations usually lead to tighter confidence intervals. However, a longer estimation period means that beta may change during the period. In our consulting, we use 252 to 504 days of daily data when calculating beta. We have found this to be the best trade-off between tighter confidence intervals due to more observations and the risk due to a changing beta. We use monthly data in this example to reduce the number of observations on the graph and the number of rows in *Ch06 Tool Kit.xlsx*.

[18]For an explanation of computing beta with a financial calculator, see *Web Extension 6B* on the textbook's Web site.

[19]Using historical data, the sample covariance can be calculated as:

$$\text{Sample covariance from historical data} = COV_{iM} = \frac{\sum_{t=1}^{T}(\bar{r}_{i,t} - \bar{r}_{i,Avg})(\bar{r}_{M,t} - \bar{r}_{M,Avg})}{T - 1}$$

Calculating the covariance is somewhat easier than calculating the correlation. So if you have already calculated the standard deviations, it is easier to calculate the covariance and then calculate the correlation as $\rho_{iM} = COV_{iM}/(\sigma_i\sigma_M)$.

Substituting Equation 6-13 into Equation 6-8 provides another frequently used expression for calculating beta:

$$b_i = \frac{COV_{i,M}}{\sigma_M^2} \qquad (6\text{-}14)$$

Suppose you plotted the stock's returns on the y-axis of a graph and the market portfolio's returns on the x-axis. The formula for the slope of a regression line is the same as the formula for beta in Equation 6-14. Therefore, to estimate beta for a security, you can estimate a regression with the stock's returns on the y-axis and the market's returns on the x-axis:

$$r_{i,t} = a_i + b_i\, r_{M,t} + e_{i,t}$$

where $r_{i,t}$ and $r_{M,t}$ are the actual returns for the stock and the market for date t; a_i and b_i are the estimated regression coefficients; and $e_{i,t}$ is the estimated error at date t.[20]

Figure 6-8 illustrates this approach. The blue dots represent each of the 48 data points, with the stock's returns on the y-axis and the market's returns on the x-axis. For reference purposes, the thick black line shows the plot of market versus market. Notice that MicroDrive's returns are generally above the market's returns (the black line) when the market is doing well but below the market when the market is doing poorly, suggesting that MicroDrive is risky.

We used the Trendline feature in *Excel* to show the regression equation and R^2 on the chart (these are colored red): MicroDrive has an estimated beta of 1.33, the same as we calculated earlier using Equation 6-8. It is also possible to use *Excel's* **SLOPE** function to estimate the slope from a regression: =**SLOPE(known_y's,known_x's)**. The **SLOPE** function is more convenient if you are going to calculate betas for many different companies; see *Ch06 Tool Kit.xlsx* for more details.

6-6c Interpreting the Estimated Beta

First, always keep in mind that beta cannot be observed; it can only be estimated. The R^2 value shown in the chart measures the degree of dispersion about the regression line. Statistically speaking, it measures the proportion of the variation that is explained by the regression equation. An R^2 of 1.0 indicates that all points lie exactly on the regression line and hence that all of the variations in the y-variable are explained by the x-variable. Micro-Drive's R^2 is about 0.26, which is a little less than a typical stock's R^2 of 0.32. This indicates that about 26% of the variation in MicroDrive's returns is explained by the market return; in other words, much of MicroDrive's volatility is due to factors other than market gyrations. If we had done a similar analysis for a portfolio of 40 randomly selected stocks, then the points would probably have been clustered tightly around the regression line, and the R^2 probably would have exceeded 0.90. Almost 100% of a well-diversified portfolio's volatility is explained by the market.

Ch06 Tool Kit.xlsx demonstrates how to use the *Excel* function **LINEST** to calculate the confidence interval for MicroDrive's estimated beta and shows that the 95% confidence interval around MicroDrive's estimated beta ranges from about 0.7 to 2.0. This means that we can be 95% confident that MicroDrive's true beta is between 0.7 and 2.0.

---

[20]Theory suggests that the risk-free rate ($r_{RF,t}$) should be subtracted from the stock return and the market return for each observation. However, the estimated coefficients are virtually identical to those estimated without subtracting the risk-free rate, so it is common practice to ignore the risk-free rate when estimating beta with this model, which is called the *market model*.

FIGURE 6-8
Stock Returns of MicroDrive and the Market: Estimating Beta

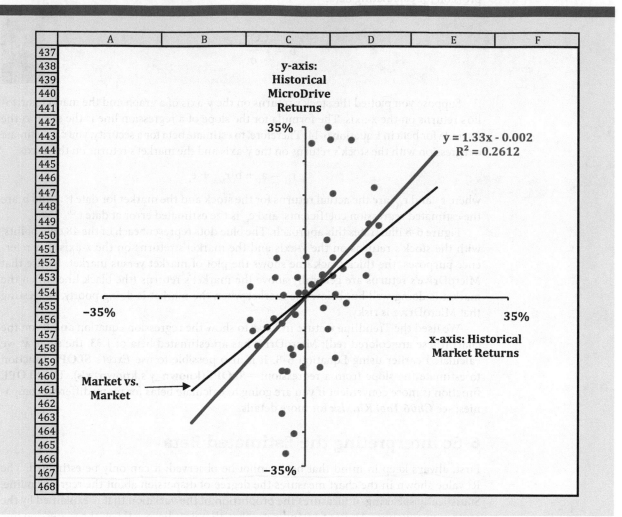

Notice that this is a fairly big range, which is also typical for most stocks. In other words, the estimated beta truly is an estimate!

MicroDrive's estimated beta is about 1.33. What does that mean? By definition, the average beta for all stocks is equal to 1, so MicroDrive contributes 33% more risk to a well-diversified portfolio than does a typical stock (assuming they have the same portfolio weight). Notice also from Figure 6-8 that the slope of the estimated line is about 1.33, which is steeper than a slope of 1. When the market is doing well, a high-beta stock like MicroDrive tends to do better than an average stock, and when the market does poorly, a high-beta stock also does worse than an average stock. The opposite is true for a low-beta stock: When the market soars, the low-beta stock tends to go up by a smaller amount; when the market falls, the low-beta stock tends to fall less than the market.

Finally, observe that the intercept shown in the regression equation on the chart is −0.002. This is a monthly return; the annualized value is 12(−0.2%) = −2.4%. This indicates that MicroDrive lost about 2.4% per year as a result of factors other than general market movements.

The Benefits of Diversifying Overseas

Figure 6-6 shows that an investor can significantly reduce portfolio risk by holding a large number of stocks. The figure accompanying this box suggests that investors may be able to reduce risk even further by holding stocks from all around the world, because the returns on domestic and international stocks are not perfectly correlated.

Source: See Kenneth Kasa, "Measuring the Gains from International Portfolio Diversification," *Federal Reserve Bank of San Francisco Weekly Letter*, No. 94–14 (April 8, 1994).

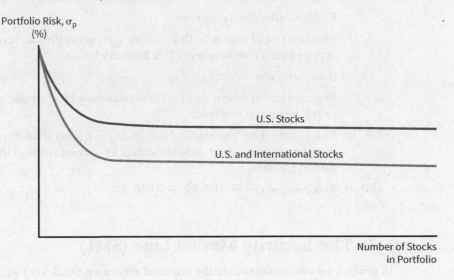

For more on calculating beta, take a look at ***Ch06 Tool Kit.xlsx***, which shows how to download data for an actual company and calculate its beta.

SELF-TEST

What is the average beta? If a stock has a beta of 0.8, what does that imply about its risk relative to the market?

Why is beta the theoretically correct measure of a stock's risk?

If you plotted the returns of a particular stock versus those on the S&P 500 Index over the past 5 years, what would the slope of the regression line tell you about the stock's market risk?

What types of data are needed to calculate a beta coefficient for an actual company?

What does the R^2 measure? What is the R^2 for a typical company?

*An investor has a three-stock portfolio with $25,000 invested in Apple, $50,000 invested in Ford, and $25,000 invested in Walmart. Apple's beta is estimated to be 1.20, Ford's beta is estimated to be 0.80, and Walmart's beta is estimated to be 1.0. What is the estimated beta of the investor's portfolio? (**0.95**)*

6-7 The Relationship between Risk and Return in the Capital Asset Pricing Model

In the preceding section, we saw that beta measures a stock's contribution to the risk of a well-diversified portfolio. The CAPM assumes that the marginal investors (i.e., the investors with enough cash to move market prices) hold well-diversified portfolios. Therefore, beta is the proper measure of a stock's relevant risk. However, we need to quantify how risk affects a stock's **required rate of return**: For a given level of risk as measured by beta, what rate of expected return do investors require to compensate them for bearing that risk? To begin, we define the following terms:

$\hat{r}_i$ = Expected rate of return on Stock i.

r_i = Required rate of return on Stock i. This is the minimum expected return that is required to induce an average investor to purchase the stock.

$\bar{r}$ = Realized, after-the-fact return.

r_{RF} = Risk-free rate of return. In this context, r_{RF} is generally measured by the expected return on long-term U.S. Treasury bonds.

b_i = Beta coefficient of Stock i.

r_M = Required rate of return on a portfolio consisting of all stocks, which is called the *market portfolio*.

RP_M = Risk premium on "the market." $RP_M = (r_M - r_{RF})$ is the additional return over the risk-free rate required to induce an average investor to invest in the market portfolio.

RP_i = Risk premium on Stock i: $RP_i = b_i(RP_M)$.

6-7a The Security Market Line (SML)

In general, we can conceptualize the **required return on Stock i (r_i)** as the risk-free rate plus the extra return (i.e., the risk premium) needed to induce the investor to hold the stock. The CAPM's **Security Market Line (SML)** formalizes this general concept by showing that a stock's risk premium is equal to the product of the stock's beta and the market risk premium:

$$\text{Required return on Stock i} = \text{Risk-free rate} + \left(\begin{array}{c} \text{Risk premium} \\ \text{for Stock i} \end{array} \right)$$

$$\text{Required return on Stock i} = \text{Risk-free rate} + \left(\begin{array}{c} \text{Beta of} \\ \text{Stock i} \end{array} \right)\left(\begin{array}{c} \text{Market risk} \\ \text{premium} \end{array} \right) \qquad \text{(6-15)}$$

$$r_i = r_{RF} + b_i(RP_M)$$
$$= r_{RF} + b_i(r_M - r_{RF})$$

Let's take a look at the three components of required return (the risk-free rate, the market risk premium, and beta) to see how they interact in determining a stock's required return.

THE RISK-FREE RATE

Notice that a stock's required return begins with the **risk-free rate**. To induce an investor to take on a risky investment, the investor will need a return that is at least as big as the risk-free rate. The yield on long-term Treasury bonds is often used to measure the risk-free rate when estimating the required return with the CAPM.

THE MARKET RISK PREMIUM

The **market risk premium (RP$_M$)** is the extra rate of return that investors require to invest in the stock market rather than purchase risk-free securities. It is also called the **equity premium** or the **equity risk premium**.

The size of the market risk premium depends on the degree of risk aversion that investors have on average. When investors as a whole are very risk averse, the market risk premium is high; when investors are less concerned about risk, the market risk premium is low. For example, suppose that investors (on average) need an extra return of 5% before they will take on the stock market's risk. If Treasury bonds yield r_{RF} = 6%, then the required return on the market, r_M, is 11%:

$$r_M = r_{RF} + RP_M = 6\% + 5\% = 11\%$$

If we had instead begun with an estimate of the required market return (perhaps through scenario analysis similar to the example in Section 6-2), then we can find the implied market risk premium. For example, if the required market return is estimated as 11%, then the market risk premium is:

$$RP_M = r_M - r_{RF} = 11\% - 6\% = 5\%$$

We discuss the market risk premium in detail in Chapter 9, but for now you should know that most analysts use a market risk premium in the range of 4% to 7%.

THE RISK PREMIUM FOR AN INDIVIDUAL STOCK

The CAPM shows that the **risk premium for an individual stock (RP$_i$)** is equal to the product of the stock's beta and the market risk premium:

$$\text{Risk premium for Stock i} = RP_i = b_i(RP_M) \tag{6-16}$$

For example, consider a low-risk stock with b_{Low} = 0.5. If the market risk premium is 5%, then the risk premium for the stock (RP$_{Low}$) is 2.5%:

$$RP_{Low} = (5\%)(0.5)$$
$$= 2.5\%$$

Using the SML in Equation 6-15, the required return for our illustrative low-risk stock is then found as follows:

$$r_{Low} = 6\% + 5\%(0.5)$$
$$= 8.5\%$$

If a high-risk stock has b_{High} = 2.0, then its required rate of return is 16%:

$$r_{High} = 6\% + (5\%)2.0 = 16\%$$

An average stock, with b_{Avg} = 1.0, has a required return of 11%, the same as the market return:

$$r_{Avg} = 6\% + (5\%)1.0 = 11\% = r_M$$

Figure 6-9 shows the SML when r_{RF} = 6% and RP_M = 5%. Note the following points:

1. Required rates of return are shown on the y-axis, while risk as measured by beta is shown on the x-axis. This graph is quite different from the regression line shown in Figure 6-8, where the historical returns of the same individual stock were plotted on the y-axis, and historical returns of the market index were plotted on the x-axis.

FIGURE 6-9
The Security Market Line (SML)

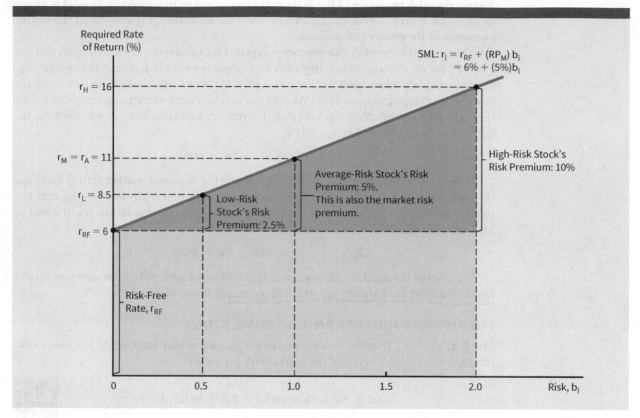

For the SML in Figure 6-9, the *required* (or expected) returns of different stocks (or portfolios) are plotted on the y-axis, and the betas of different stocks (or portfolios) are plotted on the x-axis. In other words, the betas of different stocks are *estimated* in Figure 6-8 but are *used* in Figure 6-9 to determine the required returns.

2. Riskless securities have $b_i = 0$; therefore, r_{RF} is the y-axis intercept in Figure 6-9. If we could construct a portfolio that had a beta of zero, then it would have a required return equal to the risk-free rate.

3. The slope of the SML (5% in Figure 6-9) reflects the degree of risk aversion in the economy: The greater the average investor's aversion to risk, then (a) the steeper the slope of the line, (b) the greater the risk premium for all stocks, and (c) the higher the required rate of return on all stocks.[21]

6-7b The Impact on Required Return due to Changes in the Risk-Free Rate, Risk Aversion, and Beta

The required return depends on the risk-free rate, the market risk premium, and the stock's beta. The following sections illustrate the impact of changes in these inputs.

---

[21]Students sometimes confuse beta with the slope of the SML. The slope of any straight line is equal to the "rise" divided by the "run," or $(Y_1 - Y_0)/(X_1 - X_0)$. Consider Figure 6-9. If we let Y = r and X = beta, and if we go from the origin to b = 1.0, then we see that the slope is $(r_M - r_{RF})/(b_M - b_{RF}) = (11\% - 6\%)/(1 - 0) = 5\%$. Thus, the slope of the SML is equal to $(r_M - r_{RF})$, the market risk premium. In Figure 6-9, $r_i = 6\% + 5\%(b_i)$, so an increase of beta from 1.0 to 2.0 would produce a 5-percentage-point increase in r_i.

THE IMPACT OF CHANGES IN THE RISK-FREE RATE

Suppose that some combination of an increase in real interest rates and in anticipated inflation causes the risk-free interest rate to increase from 6% to 8%. However, real interest rates and inflation don't necessarily affect investors' risk aversion, which is the primary determinant of the market risk premium. Therefore, a change in r_{RF} will not necessarily cause a change in the market risk premium. If there is no change in the market risk premium, then the CAPM shows that an increase in r_{RF} leads to an *identical* increase in the required rate of return on an asset. This applies to all assets, so it also applies to the market return. For this example, the risk-free rate increases by 2 percentage points. Therefore, the required rate of return on the market portfolio, r_M, increases from 11% to 13%.[22] Other risky securities' required returns also rise by 2 percentage points. Figure 6-10 illustrates these points.

CHANGES IN RISK AVERSION

The slope of the Security Market Line reflects the extent to which investors are averse to risk: The greater the average investor's aversion to risk, the steeper the slope

FIGURE 6-10
Shift in the SML Caused by an Increase in the Risk-Free Rate

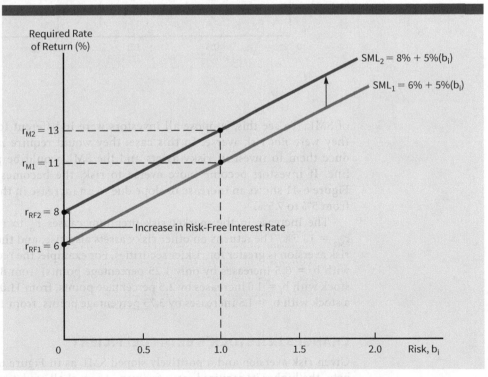

---

[22]Think of a sailboat floating in a harbor. The distance from the ocean floor to the ocean surface is like the risk-free rate, and it moves up and down with the tides. The distance from the top of the ship's mast to the ocean floor is like the required market return: It too moves up and down with the tides. The distance from the mast-top to the ocean surface is like the market risk premium: it stays the same, even though tides move the ship up and down. Thus, other things held constant, a change in the risk-free rate also causes an identical change in the required market return, r_M, resulting in a relatively stable market risk premium, $r_M - r_{RF}$.

FIGURE 6-11
Shift in the SML Caused by Increased Risk Aversion

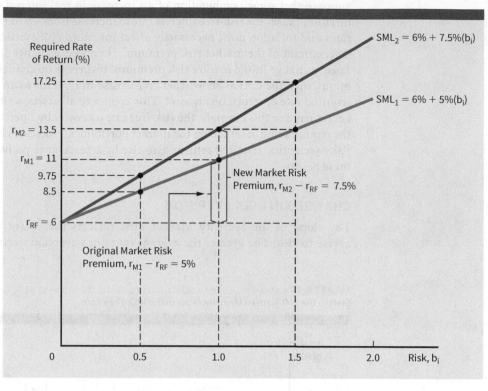

of SML. To see this, suppose all investors were indifferent to risk—that is, suppose they were *not* risk averse. In this case, they would require no risk premium to induce them to invest in risky assets and the SML would be plotted as a horizontal line. If investors become more averse to risk, the becomes steeper. For example, Figure 6-11 shows an increase in slope due to an increase in the market risk premium from 5% to 7.5%.

The increase in the market risk premium causes r_M to rise from $r_{M1} = 11\%$ to $r_{M2} = 13.5\%$. The returns on other risky assets also rise, and the effect of the increased risk aversion is greater for riskier securities. For example, the required return on a stock with $b_i = 0.5$ increases by only 1.25 percentage points, from 8.5% to 9.75%; that on a stock with $b_i = 1.0$ increases by 2.5 percentage points, from 11.0% to 13.5%; and that on a stock with $b_i = 1.5$ increases by 3.75 percentage points, from 13.5% to 17.25%.

CHANGES IN A STOCK'S BETA COEFFICIENT

Given risk aversion and a positively sloped SML as in Figure 6-9, <u>the higher a stock's beta, the higher its required rate of return</u>. As we shall see later in the book, a firm can influence its beta through changes in the composition of its assets and also through its use of debt: <u>Acquiring riskier assets will increase beta</u>, as will a change in capital structure that calls for a higher debt ratio. A company's beta can also change as a result of external factors such as increased competition in its industry, the expiration of basic patents, and the like. When such changes lead to a higher or lower beta, the required rate of return will also change.

6-7c Portfolio Returns and Portfolio Performance Evaluation

The **expected rate of return on a portfolio** ($\hat{r}_p$) is the weighted average of the expected returns on the individual assets in the portfolio. Suppose there are n stocks in the portfolio and the expected return on Stock i is $\hat{r}_i$. The expected return on the portfolio is:

$$\hat{r}_p = \sum_{i=1}^{n} w_i \hat{r}_i \qquad (6\text{-}17)$$

The **required rate of return on a portfolio** (r_p) is the weighted average of the required returns on the individual assets in the portfolio:

$$r_p = \sum_{i=1}^{n} w_i r_i \qquad (6\text{-}18)$$

We can also express the required return on a portfolio in terms of the portfolio's beta:

$$r_p = r_{RF} + b_p RP_M \qquad (6\text{-}19)$$

Equation 6-19 means that we do not have to estimate the beta for a portfolio if we have already estimated the betas for the individual stocks. All we have to do is calculate the portfolio beta as the weighted average of the stock's betas (see Equation 6-9) and then apply Equation 6-19.

This is particularly helpful when evaluating portfolio managers. For example, suppose the stock market has a return for the year of 9% and a particular mutual fund has a 10% return. Did the portfolio manager do a good job or not? The answer depends on how much risk the fund has. If the fund's beta is 2, then the fund should have had a much higher return than the market, which means the manager did not do well. The key is to evaluate the portfolio manager's return against the return the manager should have made given the risk of the investments.

6-7d Required Returns versus Expected Returns: Market Equilibrium

We explained in Chapter 1 that managers should seek to maximize the value of their firms' stocks. We also emphasized the difference between the market price and intrinsic value. Intrinsic value incorporates all *relevant available* information about expected cash flows and risk. This includes information about the company, the economic environment, and the political environment. In contrast to intrinsic value, market prices are based on investors' *selection and interpretation* of information. To the extent that investors don't select all relevant information and don't interpret it correctly, market prices can deviate from intrinsic values. Figure 6-12 illustrates this relationship between market prices and intrinsic value.

When market prices deviate from their intrinsic values, astute investors have profitable opportunities. For example, we saw in Chapter 5 that the value of a bond is the present

Determinants of Intrinsic Values and Market Prices

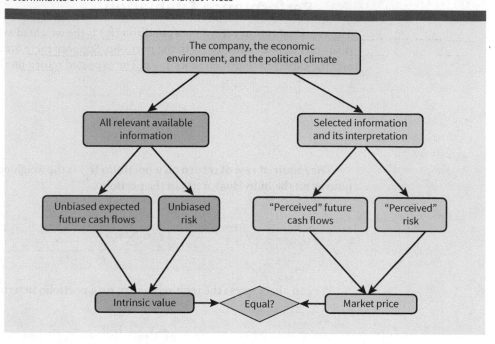

value of its cash flows when discounted at the bond's required return, which reflects the bond's risk. This is the intrinsic value of the bond because it incorporates all relevant available information. Notice that the intrinsic value is "fair" in the sense that it incorporates the bond's risk and investors' required returns for bearing the risk.

What would happen if a bond's market price were lower than its intrinsic value? In this situation, an investor could purchase the bond and receive a rate of return in excess of the required return. In other words, the investor would get more compensation than justified by the bond's risk. If all investors felt this way, then demand for the bond would soar as investors tried to purchase it, driving the bond's price up. But as the price of a bond goes up, its yield goes down. This means that an increase in price would reduce the subsequent return for an investor purchasing (or holding) the bond at the new price.[23] It seems reasonable to expect that investors' actions would continue to drive the price up until the expected return on the bond equaled its required return. After that point, the bond would provide just enough return to compensate its owner for the bond's risk.

If the bond's price were too high compared to its intrinsic value, then investors would sell the bond, causing its price to fall and its yield to increase until its expected return equaled its required return.

A stock's future cash flows aren't as predictable as a bond's, but we show in Chapter 7 that a stock's intrinsic value is the present value of its expected future cash flows, just as a bond's intrinsic value is the present value of its cash flows. If the price of a stock is lower than its intrinsic value, then an investor would receive an expected return greater than the return required as compensation for risk. The same market forces we described for a mispriced bond would drive the mispriced stock's price up. If this process continues until its

---

[23]The original owner of the bond when it was priced too low would reap a nice benefit as the price climbs, but the subsequent purchasers would only receive the now-lower yield.

Another Kind of Risk: The Bernie Madoff Story

In the fall of 2008, Bernard Madoff's massive Ponzi scheme was exposed, revealing an important type of risk that's not dealt with in this chapter. Madoff was a money manager in the 1960s, and apparently through good luck he produced above-average results for several years. Madoff's clients then told their friends about his success, and those friends sent in money for him to invest. Madoff's actual returns then dropped, but he didn't tell his clients that they were losing money. Rather, he told them that returns were holding up well, and he used new incoming money to pay dividends and meet withdrawal requests. The idea of using new money to pay off old investors is called a Ponzi scheme, named after Charles Ponzi, a Bostonian who set up the first widely publicized such scheme in the early 1900s.

Madoff perfected the system, ran his scheme for about 40 years, and attracted about $50 billion of investors' funds. His investors ranged from well-known billionaires to retirees who invested their entire life savings. His advertising

was strictly by word of mouth, and clients telling potential clients about the many wealthy and highly regarded people who invested with him certainly helped. All of his investors assumed that someone else had done the "due diligence" and found the operation to be clean. A few investors who actually did some due diligence were suspicious and didn't invest with him, but for the most part, people just blindly followed the others.

All Ponzi schemes crash when something occurs that causes some investors to seek to withdraw funds in amounts greater than the incoming funds from new investors. Someone tries to get out, can't do it, tells others who worry and try to get out too, and almost overnight the scam unravels. That happened to Madoff in 2008, when the stock market crash caused some of his investors to seek withdrawals and few new dollars were coming in. In the end, his investors lost billions; some lost their entire life savings, and several have committed suicide.

expected return equals its required return, then we say that there is **market equilibrium** (which is also called just **equilibrium**):

Market equilibrium: Expected return = Required return

$$\hat{r} = r$$

We can also express market equilibrium in terms of prices:

Market equilibrium: Market price = Intrinsic value

New information about the risk-free rate, the market's degree of risk aversion, or a stock's expected cash flows (size, timing, or risk) will cause a stock's price to change. But other than periods in which prices are adjusting to new information, is the market usually in equilibrium? We address that question in the next section.

SELF-TEST

Differentiate among the expected rate of return ($\hat{r}$), the required rate of return (r), and the realized, after-the-fact return ($\bar{r}$) on a stock. Which must be larger to get you to buy the stock, $\hat{r}$ or r? Would $\hat{r}$, r, and $\bar{r}$ typically be the same or different for a given company at a given point in time?

What are the differences between the relative returns graph (the regression line in Figure 6-8), where "betas are made," and the SML graph (Figure 6-9), where "betas are used"? Discuss how the graphs are constructed and the information they convey.

What happens to the SML graph in Figure 6-9 when inflation increases or decreases?

What happens to the SML graph when risk aversion increases or decreases? What would the SML look like if investors were completely indifferent to risk—that is, had zero risk aversion?

How can a firm's managers influence market risk as reflected in beta?

A stock has a beta of 0.8. Assume that the risk-free rate is 5.5% and that the market risk premium is 6%. What is the stock's required rate of return? **(10.3%)**

6-8 The Efficient Markets Hypothesis

The **Efficient Markets Hypothesis (EMH)** asserts: (1) Stocks are always in equilibrium. (2) It is impossible for an investor to "beat the market" and consistently earn a higher rate of return than is justified by the stock's risk. In other words, a stock's market price is always equal to its intrinsic value. To put it a little more precisely, suppose a stock's market price is equal to the stock's intrinsic value, but new information that changes the stock's intrinsic value arrives. The EMH asserts that the market price will adjust to the new intrinsic value so quickly that there isn't time for an investor to receive the new information, evaluate the information, take a position in the stock before the market price changes, and then profit from the subsequent change in price.

Here are three points to consider. First, almost every stock is under considerable scrutiny. With 100,000 or so full-time, highly trained, professional analysts and traders, each following about 30 of the roughly 3,000 actively traded stocks (analysts tend to specialize in a specific industry), there are an average of about 1,000 analysts following each stock. Second, financial institutions, pension funds, money management firms, and hedge funds have billions of dollars available for portfolio managers to use in taking advantage of mispriced stocks. Third, SEC disclosure requirements and electronic information networks cause new information about a stock to become available to all analysts virtually simultaneously and almost immediately. With so many analysts trying to take advantage of temporary mispricing due to new information, with so much money chasing the profits due to temporary mispricing, and with such widespread dispersal of information, a stock's market price should adjust quickly from its pre-news intrinsic value to its post-news intrinsic value, leaving only a very short amount of time that the stock is "mispriced" as it moves from one equilibrium price to another. That, in a nutshell, is the logic behind the Efficient Markets Hypothesis.

The following sections discuss forms of the Efficient Markets Hypothesis and empirical tests of the hypothesis.

6-8a Forms of the Efficient Markets Hypothesis

There are three forms of the Efficient Markets Hypothesis, and each focuses on a different type of information availability.

WEAK-FORM EFFICIENCY

The **weak form** of the EMH asserts that all information contained in past price movements is fully reflected in current market prices. If this were true, then information about recent trends in stock prices would be of no use in selecting stocks; the fact that a stock has risen for the past three days, for example, would give us no useful clues as to what it will do today or tomorrow. In contrast, **technical analysts,** also called "chartists," believe that past trends or patterns in stock prices can be used to predict future stock prices.

To illustrate the arguments supporting weak-form efficiency, suppose that after studying the past history of the stock market, a technical analyst identifies the following historical pattern: If a stock has fallen for three consecutive days, its price rose by 10% (on average) the following day. The technician would then conclude that investors could make money by purchasing a stock whose price has fallen three consecutive days.

Weak-form advocates argue that if this pattern truly existed, then surely other investors would soon discover it, and if so, why would anyone be willing to sell a stock after it had fallen for three consecutive days? In other words, why sell if you know that the price is going to increase by 10% the next day? For example, suppose a stock had fallen three consecutive days to $40. If the stock were really likely to rise by 10% to $44 tomorrow, then its price *today*, *right now*, would actually rise to somewhere close to $44, thereby eliminating the trading opportunity. Consequently, weak-form efficiency implies that any information that comes from past stock prices is too rapidly incorporated into the current stock price for a profit opportunity to exist.

SEMISTRONG-FORM EFFICIENCY

The **semistrong form** of the EMH states that current market prices reflect all *publicly available* information. Therefore, if semistrong-form efficiency exists, it would do no good to pore over annual reports or other published data because market prices would have adjusted to any good or bad news contained in such reports back when the news came out. With semistrong-form efficiency, investors should expect to earn returns commensurate with risk, but they should not expect to do any better or worse other than by chance.

Another implication of semistrong-form efficiency is that whenever information is released to the public, stock prices will respond only if the information is different from what had been expected. For example, if a company announces a 30% increase in earnings and if that increase is about what analysts had been expecting, then the announcement should have little or no effect on the company's stock price. On the other hand, the stock price would probably fall if analysts had expected earnings to increase by more than 30%, but it probably would rise if they had expected a smaller increase.

STRONG-FORM EFFICIENCY

The **strong form** of the EMH states that current market prices reflect all pertinent information, whether publicly available or privately held. If this form holds, even insiders would find it impossible to earn consistently abnormal returns in the stock market.

6-8b Is the Stock Market Efficient? The Empirical Evidence

Empirical studies are joint tests of the EMH and an asset pricing model, such as the CAPM. They are joint tests in the sense that they examine whether a particular strategy can beat the market, where "beating the market" means earning a return higher than that predicted by the particular asset pricing model. Before addressing tests of the particular forms of the EMH, let's take a look at market bubbles.

MARKET BUBBLES

The history of finance is marked by numerous instances in which the following string of events occurs: (1) Prices climb rapidly to heights that would have been considered extremely unlikely before the run-up. (2) The volume of trading is much higher than past volume. (3) Many new investors (or speculators?) eagerly enter the market. (4) Prices suddenly fall precipitously, leaving many of the new investors with huge losses. These instances are called *market bubbles*.

The stock market bubbles that burst in 2000 and 2008 suggest that, at the height of these booms, the stocks of many companies—especially in the technology sector in 2000 and the financial sector in 2008—vastly exceeded their intrinsic values, which should not happen if markets are always efficient. Two questions arise. First, how are bubbles formed? Behavioral finance, which we discuss in Section 6-10, provides some possible answers. Second, why do bubbles persist when it is possible to make a fortune when they burst? For example, hedge fund manager Mark Spitznagel reputedly made billions for his Universa funds by betting against the market in 2008. The logic underlying market equilibrium suggests that everyone would bet against an overvalued market and that their actions would cause market prices to fall back to intrinsic values fairly quickly. To understand why this doesn't happen, let's examine the strategies for profiting from a falling market: (1) Sell stocks (or the market index itself) short. (2) Purchase a put option or write a call option. (3) Take a short position in a futures contract on the market index. Following is an explanation for how these strategies work (or fail).

Loosely speaking, selling a stock short means that you borrow a share from a broker and sell it. You get the cash (subject to collateral requirements required by the broker), but you owe a share of stock. For example, suppose you sell a share of Google short at a current price of $500. If the price falls to $400, you can buy a share of the stock at the now-lower $400 market price and return the share to the broker, pocketing the $100 difference between the higher price ($500) when you went short and the lower price ($400) when you closed the position. Of course, if the price goes up, say to $550, you lose $50 because you must replace the share you borrowed (at $500) with one that is now more costly ($550). Even if your broker doesn't require you to close out your position when the price goes up, your broker certainly will require that you put in more collateral.

A put option gives you the option to sell a share at a fixed strike price. For example, suppose you buy a put on Google for $60 with a strike price of $500. If the stock price falls below the strike price, say to $400, you can buy a share at the low price ($400) and sell it at the higher strike price ($500), making a net $40 profit from the decline in the stock price: $40 = −$60 − $400 + $500. However, if the put expires before the stock price falls below the strike price, you lose the $60 you spent buying the put. You can also use call options to bet on a decline. For example, if you write a call option, you receive cash in return for an obligation to sell a share at the strike price. Suppose you write a call option on Google with a strike price of $500 and receive $70. If Google's price stays below the $500 strike price, you keep the $70 cash you received from writing the call. But if Google goes up to $600 and the call you wrote is exercised, you must buy a share at the new high price ($600) and sell it at the lower strike price ($500), for a net loss of $30: $70 − $600 + $500 = −$30.[24]

With a short position in a futures contract on the market index (or a particular stock), you are obligated to sell a share at a fixed price. If the market price falls below the specified price in the futures contract, you make money because you can buy a share in the market and sell it at the higher price specified in the futures contract. But if the market price increases, you lose money because you must buy a share at the now higher price and sell it at the price fixed in the futures contract.[25]

Each of these strategies allows an investor to make a lot of money. And if all investors tried to capitalize on an overvalued market, their actions would soon drive the market back to equilibrium, preventing a bubble from forming. But here is the problem with these strategies. Even if the market is overvalued, it might take months (or even years) before the market falls to its intrinsic value. During this period, an investor would have to spend a lot of cash maintaining the strategies described earlier, including margin calls, settling options, and daily marking to market for futures contracts. These negative cash flows could easily drive an investor into bankruptcy before the investor was eventually proven correct. Unfortunately, there aren't any low-risk strategies for puncturing a market bubble.

Notice that the problem of negative cash flows doesn't exist for the opposite situation of an undervalued market in which the intrinsic value is greater than the market price. Investors can simply buy stock at the too-low market price and hold it until the market price eventually increases to the intrinsic value. Even if the market price continues to go

---

[24]Options are usually settled by cash rather than by actually buying and selling shares of stock.

[25]Futures contracts are actually settled daily and that they are usually settled for cash rather than the actual shares.

down before eventually rising, the investor experiences only paper losses and not actual negative cash flows. Thus, we would not expect "negative" bubbles to persist very long.

TESTS OF WEAK-FORM EFFICIENCY

Most studies suggest that the stock market is highly efficient in the weak form, with two exceptions. The first exception is for long-term reversals, with studies showing that portfolios of stocks with poor past long-term performance (over the past 5 years, for example) tend to do slightly better in the long-term future than the CAPM predicts, and vice versa. The second is momentum, with studies showing that stocks with strong performance in the short-term past (over the past 6 to 9 months, for example) tend to do slightly better in the short-term future than the CAPM predicts, and likewise for weak performance.[26] Strategies based on taking advantage of long-term reversals or short-term momentum produce returns that are in excess of those predicted by the CAPM. However, the excess returns are small, especially when transaction costs are considered.

TESTS OF SEMISTRONG-FORM EFFICIENCY

Most studies show that markets are reasonably efficient in the semistrong form: It is difficult to use publicly available information to create a trading strategy that consistently has returns greater than those predicted by the CAPM. In fact, the professionals who manage mutual fund portfolios, on average, do not outperform the overall stock market as measured by an index like the S&P 500 and tend to have returns lower than predicted by the CAPM, possibly because many mutual funds have high fees.[27]

However, there are two well-known exceptions to semistrong-form efficiency. The first is for small companies, which have had historical returns greater than predicted by the CAPM. The second is related to book-to-market (B/M) ratios, defined as the book value of equity divided by the market value of equity (this is the inverse of the market/book ratio defined in Chapter 3). Companies with high B/M ratios have had higher returns than predicted by the CAPM. We discuss these exceptions in more detail in Section 6-9.

TESTS OF STRONG-FORM EFFICIENCY

The evidence suggests that the strong-form EMH does not hold because those who possessed inside information could make and have (illegally) made abnormal profits. On the other hand, many insiders have gone to jail, so perhaps there is indeed a trade-off between risk and return!

SELF-TEST

What is the Efficient Markets Hypothesis (EMH)?

What are the differences among the three forms of the EMH?

Why is it difficult to puncture a market bubble?

What violations of the EMH have been demonstrated?

What is short-term momentum? What are long-term reversals?

---

[26]For example, see N. Jegadeesh and S. Titman, "Returns to Buying Winners and Selling Losers: Implications for Stock Market Efficiency," *Journal of Finance*, March 1993, pp. 69–91; and W. F. M. DeBondt and R. H. Thaler, "Does the Stock Market Overreact?" *Journal of Finance*, July 1985, pp. 793–808.

[27]For a discussion of the performance of actively managed funds, see Jonathan Clements, "Resisting the Lure of Managed Funds," *The Wall Street Journal*, February 27, 2001, p. C1.

6-9 The Fama-French Three-Factor Model[28]

Take a look at Table 6-2, which reports the returns for 25 portfolios formed by Professors Eugene Fama and Kenneth French. The Fama-French portfolios are based on the company's size as measured by the market value of its equity (MVE) and the company's book-to-market (B/M) ratio, defined as the book value of equity divided by the market value of equity. Each row shows portfolios with similarly sized companies; each column shows portfolios whose companies have similar B/M ratios. Notice that if you look across each row, the average return tends to increase as the B/M ratio increases. In other words, stocks with high B/M ratios have higher returns. If you look up each column (except for the column with the lowest B/M ratios), stock returns tend to increase: Small companies have higher returns.

This pattern alone would not be a challenge to the CAPM if small firms and high-B/M firms had large betas (and thus higher returns). However, even after adjusting for their betas, the small-stock portfolios and the high B/M portfolios earned returns higher than predicted by the CAPM. This indicates that either markets are inefficient or the CAPM isn't the correct model to describe required returns.

In 1992, Fama and French published a study hypothesizing that the SML should have three factors rather than just beta as in the CAPM.[29] The first factor is the stock's CAPM beta, which measures the market risk of the stock. The second is the size of the company, measured by the market value of its equity (MVE). The third factor is the book-to-market (B/M) ratio.

When Fama and French tested their hypotheses, they found that small companies and companies with high B/M ratios had higher rates of return than the average stock, just as they hypothesized. Somewhat surprisingly, however, they found that beta was not useful in explaining returns. After taking into account the returns due to the company's size and B/M ratio, high-beta stocks did not have higher than average returns and low-beta stocks did not have lower than average returns.

TABLE 6-2

Average Annual Returns for the Fama-French Portfolios Based on Size and Book Equity to Market Equity, 1927–2016

Size	Book Equity to Market Equity				
	Low	2	3	4	High
Small	12.1%	18.6%	19.7%	23.4%	29.2%
2	12.5	16.8	17.8	18.8	19.8
3	11.9	15.7	16.1	17.3	19.2
4	12.5	13.4	15.0	16.6	17.6
Big	10.9	12.2	13.5	13.5	16.4

Source: Raw data from Professor Kenneth French, **http://mba.tuck.dartmouth.edu/pages/faculty/ken.french/data_library.html**. These are equal-weighted annual returns. Following is a description from Professor French's Web site describing the construction of the portfolios: "The portfolios, which are constructed at the end of each June, are the intersections of 5 portfolios formed on size (market equity, ME) and 5 portfolios formed on the ratio of book equity to market equity (BE/ME). The size breakpoints for year t are the NYSE market equity quintiles at the end of June of t. BE/ME for June of year t is the book equity for the last fiscal year end in t − 1 divided by ME for December of t − 1. The BE/ME breakpoints are NYSE quintiles. The portfolios for July of year t to June of t + 1 include all NYSE, AMEX, and NASDAQ stocks for which we have market equity data for December of t − 1 and June of t, and (positive) book equity data for t − 1."

---

[28]Some instructors may choose to omit this section with no loss in continuity.

[29]See Eugene F. Fama and Kenneth R. French, "The Cross-Section of Expected Stock Returns," *Journal of Finance*, Vol. 47, 1992, pp. 427–465. In 2013, Eugene Fama was awarded the Nobel Prize in Economics for this and his other work in asset pricing.

In 1993, Fama and French developed a three-factor model based on their previous results.[30] The first factor in the **Fama-French three-factor model** is the market risk premium, which is the market return, $\bar{r}_M$, minus the risk-free rate, $\bar{r}_{RF}$. Thus, their model begins like the CAPM, but they go on to add a second and third factor.[31] To form the second factor, they ranked all actively traded stocks by size and then divided them into two portfolios, one consisting of small stocks and one consisting of big stocks. They calculated the return on each of these two portfolios and created a third portfolio by subtracting the return on the big portfolio from that of the small one. They called this the SMB (small minus big) portfolio. This portfolio is designed to measure the variation in stock returns that is caused by the size effect.

To form the third factor, they ranked all stocks according to their book-to-market (B/M) ratios. They placed the 30% of stocks with the highest ratios into a portfolio they called the H portfolio (for high B/M ratios) and placed the 30% of stocks with the lowest ratios into a portfolio called the L portfolio (for low B/M ratios). Then they subtracted the return of the L portfolio from that of the H portfolio to derive the HML (high minus low) portfolio. Before showing their model, here are the definitions of the variables.

$\bar{r}_{i,t}$ = Historical (realized) rate of return on Stock i in period t.

$\bar{r}_{RF,t}$ = Historical (realized) rate of return on the risk-free rate in period t.

$\bar{r}_{M,t}$ = Historical (realized) rate of return on the market in period t.

$\bar{r}_{SMB,t}$ = Historical (realized) rate of return on the small-size portfolio minus the big-size portfolio in period t.

$\bar{r}_{HML,t}$ = Historical (realized) rate of return on the high-B/M portfolio minus the low-B/M portfolio in period t.

a_i = Vertical axis intercept term for Stock i.

$b_i, c_i,$ and d_i = Slope coefficients for Stock i.

$e_{i,t}$ = Random error, reflecting the difference between the actual return on Stock i in period t and the return as predicted by the regression line.

Their resulting model is shown here:

$$(\bar{r}_{i,t} - \bar{r}_{RF,t}) = a_i + b_i(\bar{r}_{M,t} - \bar{r}_{RF,t}) + c_i(\bar{r}_{SMB,t}) + d_i(\bar{r}_{HML,t}) + e_{i,t} \qquad (6\text{-}20)$$

When this model is applied to actual stock returns, the "extra" return disappears for portfolios based on a company's size or B/M ratio. In fact, the extra returns for the long-term stock reversals that we discussed in Section 6-8 also disappear. Thus, the Fama-French model accounts for many of the major violations of the EMH that we described earlier.

Because the Fama-French model explains so well a stock's actual return given the return on the market, the SMB portfolio, and the HML portfolio, the model is very useful

[30]See Eugene F. Fama and Kenneth R. French, "Common Risk Factors in the Returns on Stocks and Bonds," *Journal of Financial Economics,* Vol. 33, 1993, pp. 3–56.

[31]Although our description captures the essence of their process for forming factors, the actual procedure is a little more complicated. The interested reader should see their 1993 paper, cited in footnote 29.

in identifying the market's reaction to news about a company.[32] For example, suppose a company announces that it is going to include more outsiders on its board of directors. If the company's stock falls by 2% on the day of the announcement, does that mean investors don't want outsiders on the board? We can answer that question by using the Fama-French model to decompose the actual return of the company on the announcement day into the portion that is explained by the environment (i.e., the market and the SMB and HML portfolios) and the portion due to the company's announcement.

To do this, we gather a sample of data ($\bar{r}_{i,t}$, $\bar{r}_{RF,t}$, $\bar{r}_{M,t}$, $\bar{r}_{SMB,t}$, and $\bar{r}_{HML,t}$) for T periods prior to the announcement date and then run a regression using a variation of Equation 2-20:

$$\bar{r}_{i,t} = a_i + b_i\bar{r}_{M,t} + c_i\bar{r}_{SMB,t} + d_i\bar{r}_{HML,t} + e_{i,t}$$

This is similar to the regression approach for estimating beta, described in Section 6-6, except there are three slope coefficients in this multiple regression.[33]

Suppose the estimated coefficients are $a_i = 0.0$, $b_i = 0.9$, $c_i = 0.2$, and $d_i = 0.3$. On the day of the announcement, the stock market had a return of -3%, the SMB portfolio had a return of -1%, and the HML portfolio had a return of -2%. The predicted value of the error term in the Fama-French model, $e_{i,t}$, is by definition equal to zero. Based on these assumptions, the predicted return on the announcement day using the Fama-French three-factor model is:

$$
\begin{aligned}
\text{Predicted return} &= a_i + b_i(\bar{r}_{M,t}) + c_i(\bar{r}_{SMB,t}) + d_i(\bar{r}_{HML,t}) \\
&= 0.0 + 0.9(-3\%) + 0.2(-1\%) + 0.3(-2\%) \\
&= -3.5\%
\end{aligned}
$$

(6-21)

The unexplained return is equal to the actual return less the predicted return:

$$\text{Unexplained return} = -2.0\% - (-3.5\%) = 1.5\%$$

Although the stock price went down by 2% on the announcement day, the Fama-French model predicted that the price should have gone down by 3.5% due to market movements. Thus, the stock had a positive 1.5% reaction on the announcement day. This is just one company, but if we repeated this process for many companies that made similar announcements and calculated the average unexplained reaction, we could draw a conclusion regarding the market's reaction to adding more outside directors. As this example shows, the model is very useful in identifying actions that affect a company's value.

There is no question that the Fama-French three-factor model does a good job in explaining *actual* returns, but how well does it perform in explaining *required* returns? In other words, does the model define a relationship between risk and compensation for bearing risk?

Advocates of the model suggest that size and B/M are related to risk. Small companies have less access to capital markets than do large companies, which exposes small companies to greater risk in the event of a credit crunch—such as the one that occurred during

---

[32]Because the Fama-French model doesn't seem to explain short-term momentum, many researchers also use the four-factor model, which includes a factor for momentum; see Mark Carhart, "On Persistence in Mutual Fund Performance," *Journal of Finance*, Vol. 52, No. 1., March 1997, pp. 57–82.

[33]Notice that the risk-free rate is not used in the regression for the same reasons it is not used in the market model to estimate beta; see footnote 20. Also, the annual risk-free rate is 6% in this example, so the daily rate is 6%/365 = 0.01%, which is so small that it can be ignored.

the global economic crisis that began in 2007. With greater risk, investors would require a higher expected return to induce them to invest in small companies.

Similar arguments apply for companies with high B/M ratios. If a company's prospects are poor, then the company will have a low market value, which causes a high B/M ratio. Lenders usually are reluctant to extend credit to a company with poor prospects, so an economic downturn can cause such a company to experience financial distress. In other words, a stock with a high B/M ratio might be exposed to the risk of financial distress, in which case investors would require a higher expected return to induce them to invest in such a stock.

If a company's sensitivity to the size factor and the B/M factor are related to financial distress risk, then the Fama-French model would be an improvement on the CAPM regarding the relationship between risk and required return. However, the evidence is mixed as to whether financially distressed firms do indeed have higher expected returns as compensation for their risk. In fact, some studies show financially distressed firms actually have *lower* expected returns instead of higher returns.[34]

A number of other studies suggest that the size effect no longer influences stock returns, that there never was a size effect (the previous results were caused by peculiarities in the data sources), that the size effect doesn't apply to most companies, and that the book-to-market effect is not as significant as first supposed.[35]

In summary, the Fama-French model is very useful in identifying the unexplained component of a stock's return. However, the model is less useful when it comes to estimating the required return on a stock because the model does not provide a well-accepted link between risk and required return.

SELF-TEST

What are the factors in the Fama-French model?

How can the model be used to estimate the predicted return on a stock?

Why isn't the model widely used by managers at actual companies?

An analyst has modeled the stock of a company using a Fama-French three-factor model and has estimated that $a_i = 0$, $b_i = 0.7$, $c_i = 1.2$, and $d_i = 0.7$. Suppose that the daily risk-free rate is approximately equal to zero, the market return is 11%, the return on the SMB portfolio is 3.2%, and the return on the HML portfolio is 4.8% on a particular day. The stock had an actual return of 16.9% on that day. What is the stock's predicted return for that day? **(14.9%)** *What is the stock's unexplained return for the day?* **(2%)**

---

[34]For studies supporting the relationship between risk and return as related to size and the B/M ratio, see Nishad Kapadia, "Tracking Down Distress Risk," *Journal of Financial Economics*, Vol. 102, 2011, pp. 167–182; Thomas J. George, "A Resolution of the Distress Risk and Leverage Puzzles in the Cross Section of Stock Returns," *Journal of Financial Economics*, Vol. 96, 2010, pp. 56–79; and Lorenzo Garlappi and Hong Yan, "Financial Distress and the Cross-Section of Equity Returns," *Journal of Finance*, June, 2011, pp. 789–822. For studies rejecting the relationship, see John Y. Campbell, Jens Hilscher, and Jan Szilagyi, "In Search of Distress Risk," *Journal of Finance*, December 2008, pp. 2899–2940; and Ilia D. Dichev, "Is the Risk of Bankruptcy a Systematic Risk?" *Journal of Finance*, June 1998, pp. 1131–1147.

[35]See Peter J. Knez and Mark J. Ready, "On the Robustness of Size and Book-to-Market in the Cross-Sectional Regressions," *Journal of Finance*, September 1997, pp. 1355–1382; Dongcheol Kim, "A Reexamination of Firm Size, Book-to-Market, and Earnings Price in the Cross-Section of Expected Stock Returns," *Journal of Financial and Quantitative Analysis*, December 1997, pp. 463–489; Tyler Shumway and Vincent A. Warther, "The Delisting Bias in CRSP's Nasdaq Data and Its Implications for the Size Effect," *Journal of Finance*, December 1999, pp. 2361–2379; and Tim Loughran, "Book-to-Market across Firm Size, Exchange, and Seasonality: Is There an Effect?" *Journal of Financial and Quantitative Analysis*, September 1997, pp. 249–268.

6-10 Behavioral Finance[36]

A large body of evidence in the field of psychology shows that people often behave irrationally, but in predictable ways. The field of **behavioral finance** focuses on irrational but predictable financial decisions. The following sections examine applications of behavioral finance to market bubbles and to other financial decisions.

6-10a Market Bubbles and Behavioral Finance

We showed in Section 6-8 that strategies for profiting from a punctured bubble expose an investor to possible large negative cash flows if it takes a long time for the bubble to burst. That explains why a bubble can persist, but it doesn't explain how a bubble is created. There are no definitive explanations, but the field of behavioral finance offers some possible reasons, including overconfidence, anchoring bias, and herding.

Many psychological tests show that people are overconfident with respect to their own abilities relative to the abilities of others, which is the basis of Garrison Keillor's joke about a town where all the children are above average. Professor Richard Thaler and his colleague Nicholas Barberis address this phenomenon as it applies to finance:

> Overconfidence may in part stem from two other biases, self-attribution bias and hindsight bias. Self-attribution bias refers to people's tendency to ascribe any success they have in some activity to their own talents, while blaming failure on bad luck, rather than on their ineptitude. Doing this repeatedly will lead people to the pleasing but erroneous conclusion that they are very talented. For example, investors might become overconfident after several quarters of investing success [Gervais and Odean (2001)[37]]. Hindsight bias is the tendency of people to believe, after an event has occurred, that they predicted it before it happened. If people think they predicted the past better than they actually did, they may also believe that they can predict the future better than they actually can.[38]

Psychologists have learned that many people focus too closely on recent events when predicting future events, a phenomenon called **anchoring bias**. Therefore, when the market is performing better than average, people tend to think it will continue to perform better than average. When anchoring bias is coupled with overconfidence, investors can become convinced that their prediction of an increasing market is correct, thus creating even more demand for stocks. This demand drives stock prices up, which serves to reinforce the overconfidence and move the anchor even higher.

There is another way that an increasing market can reinforce itself. Studies have shown that gamblers who are ahead tend to take on more risks (i.e., they are playing with the house's money), whereas those who are behind tend to become more conservative. If this is true for investors, we can get a feedback loop: When the market goes up, investors have gains, which can make them less risk averse, which increases their demand for stock, which leads to higher prices, which starts the cycle again.

Herding behavior occurs when groups of investors emulate other successful investors and chase asset classes that are doing well. For example, high returns in mortgage-backed securities during 2004 and 2005 enticed other investors to move into that asset class. Herding behavior can create excess demand for asset classes that have done well, causing price increases that induce additional herding behavior. Thus, herding behavior can inflate rising markets.

---

[36]Some instructors may choose to omit this section with no loss of continuity.

[37]See Simon Gervais and Terrance Odean, "Learning to Be Overconfident," *Review of Financial Studies,* Spring 2001, pp. 1–27.

[38]See page 1066 in an excellent review of behavioral finance by Nicholas Barberis and Richard Thaler, "A Survey of Behavioral Finance," in *Handbook of the Economics of Finance,* George Constantinides, Milt Harris, and René Stulz, eds. (Amsterdam: Elsevier/North-Holland, 2003), Chapter 18.

Sometimes herding behavior occurs when a group of investors assumes that other investors are better informed—the herd chases the "smart" money. But in other cases, herding can occur even when those in the herd suspect that prices are overinflated. For example, consider the situation of a portfolio manager who believes that bank stocks are overvalued even though many other portfolios are heavily invested in such stocks. If the manager moves out of bank stocks and they subsequently fall in price, then the manager will be rewarded for her judgment. But if the stocks continue to do well, the manager may well lose her job for missing out on the gains. If instead the manager follows the herd and invests in bank stocks, then the manager will do no better or worse than her peers. Thus, if the penalty for being wrong is bigger than the reward for being correct, it is rational for portfolio managers to herd even if they suspect the herd is wrong.

Researchers have shown that the combination of overconfidence and biased self-attribution can lead to overly volatile stock markets, short-term momentum, and long-term reversals.[39] We suspect that overconfidence, anchoring bias, and herding can contribute to market bubbles.

6-10b Other Applications of Behavioral Finance

Psychologists Daniel Kahneman and Amos Tversky show that individuals view potential losses and potential gains very differently.[40] If you ask an average person whether he or she would rather have $500 with certainty or flip a fair coin and receive $1,000 if it comes up heads and nothing if it comes up tails, most would prefer the certain $500 gain, which suggests an aversion to risk—a *sure* $500 gain is better than a risky *expected* $500 gain. However, if you ask the same person whether he or she would rather pay $500 with certainty or flip a coin and pay $1,000 if it's heads and nothing if it's tails, most would indicate that they prefer to flip the coin, which suggests a preference for risk—a risky *expected* $500 loss is better than a *sure* $500 loss. In other words, losses are so painful that people will make irrational choices to avoid sure losses. This phenomenon is called **loss aversion**.

One way that people avoid a loss is by not admitting that they have actually had a loss. For example, in many people's mental bookkeeping, a loss isn't really a loss until the losing investment is actually sold. Therefore, they tend to hold risky losers instead of accepting a certain loss, which is a display of loss aversion. Of course, this leads investors to sell losers much less frequently than winners even though this is suboptimal for tax purposes.[41]

Many corporate projects and mergers fail to live up to their expectations. In fact, most mergers end up destroying value in the acquiring company. Because this is well known, why haven't companies responded by being more selective in their investments? There are many possible reasons, but research by Ulrike Malmendier and Geoffrey Tate suggests that overconfidence leads managers to overestimate their abilities and the quality of their projects.[42] In other words, managers might know that the average decision to merge destroys value, but they are certain that their decision is above average.

---

[39]See Terrance Odean, "Volume, Volatility, Price, and Profit When All Traders are above Average," *Journal of Finance,* December 1998, pp. 1887–1934; and Kent Daniel, David Hirshleifer, and Avanidhar Subrahmanyam, "Investor Psychology and Security Market Under- and Overreactions," *Journal of Finance,* December 1998, pp. 1839–1885.

[40]Daniel Kahneman and Amos Tversky, "Prospect Theory: An Analysis of Decision under Risk," *Econometrica,* March 1979, pp. 263–292.

[41]See Terrance Odean, "Are Investors Reluctant to Realize Their Losses?" *Journal of Finance,* October 1998, pp. 1775–1798.

[42]See Ulrike Malmendier and Geoffrey Tate, "CEO Overconfidence and Corporate Investment," *Journal of Finance,* December 2005, pp. 2661–2700.

Finance is a quantitative field, but good managers in all disciplines must also understand human behavior.[43]

6-11 The CAPM and Market Efficiency: Implications for Corporate Managers and Investors

A company is like a portfolio of projects: factories, retail outlets, R&D ventures, new product lines, and the like. Each project contributes to the size, timing, and risk of the company's cash flows, which directly affect the company's intrinsic value. This means that *the relevant risk and expected return of any project must be measured in terms of its effect on the stock's risk and return.* Therefore, all managers must understand how stockholders view risk and required return in order to evaluate potential projects.

Stockholders should not expect to be compensated for the risk they can eliminate through diversification, only for the remaining market risk. The CAPM provides an important tool for measuring the remaining market risk and goes on to show how a stock's required return is related to the stock's market risk. It is for this reason that the CAPM is widely used to estimate the required return on a company's stock and, hence, the required returns that projects must generate to provide the stock's required return. We describe this process in more detail in Chapters 7 and 9, which cover stock valuation and the cost of capital. We apply these concepts to project analysis in Chapters 10 and 11.

Is the CAPM perfect? No. First, we cannot observe beta but must instead estimate beta. As we saw in Section 6-6, estimates of beta are not precise. Second, we saw that small stocks and stocks with high B/M ratios have returns higher than the CAPM predicts. This could mean that the CAPM is the wrong model, but there is another possible explanation. If the composition of a company's assets were changing over time with respect to the mix of physical assets and growth opportunities (involving, e.g., R&D or patents), then this would be enough to make it *appear* as though there were size and B/M effects. In other words, even if the returns on the individual assets conform to the CAPM, changes in the mix of assets would cause the firm's beta to change over time in such a way that the firm would appear to have size and book-to-market effects.[44] Recent research supports this hypothesis.

Recall that the CAPM asserts that a stock's required return is related to its exposure to systematic risk, not to its diversifiable risk. Therefore, you might expect the CAPM to do a very good job of explaining stock returns when news is announced that affects almost all companies, such as government reports regarding interest rate policy, inflation, and unemployment. Professors Savor and Wilson tested this hypothesis and found an extremely strong relationship between betas and stock returns on announcement days.[45]

---

[43]Excellent reviews of behavioral finance are found in *Advances in Behavioral Finance,* Richard H. Thaler, ed. (New York: Russell Sage Foundation, 1993); and Andrei Shleifer, *Inefficient Markets: An Introduction to Behavioral Finance* (New York: Oxford University Press, 2000).

[44]See Jonathan B. Berk, Richard C. Green, and Vasant Naik, "Optimal Investment, Growth Options, and Security Returns," *Journal of Finance,* October 1999, pp. 1553–1608.

[45]See Pavel Savor and Mungo Wilson, "Asset Pricing: A Tale of Two Days," *Journal of Financial Economics,* Vol. 113, 2014, pp. 171–201.

Based on these results and its widespread use in practice, we will use the CAPM to estimate required returns in subsequent chapters.[46]

Regarding market efficiency, our understanding of the empirical evidence suggests it is very difficult, if not impossible, to beat the market by earning a return that is higher than justified by the investment's risk. This suggests that markets are reasonably efficient for most assets for most of the time. However, we believe that market bubbles do occur and that it is very difficult to implement a low-risk strategy for profiting when they burst.

SELF-TEST

Explain the following statement: "The stand-alone risk of an individual corporate project may be quite high, but viewed in the context of its effect on stockholders' risk, the project's true risk may be much lower."

SUMMARY

This chapter focuses on the trade-off between risk and return. We began by discussing how to estimate risk and return for both individual assets and portfolios. In particular, we differentiated between stand-alone risk and risk in a portfolio context, and we explained the benefits of diversification. We introduced the CAPM, which describes how risk affects rates of return.

- **Risk** can be defined as exposure to the chance of an unfavorable event.
- The risk of an asset's cash flows can be considered on a **stand-alone** basis (each asset all by itself) or in a *portfolio context,* in which the investment is combined with other assets and its risk is reduced through **diversification**.
- Most rational investors hold **portfolios** of assets, and they are more concerned with the risk of their portfolios than with the risk of individual assets.
- The **expected rate of return** on an investment is the mean value of its probability distribution of returns.
- The **required return** on a stock is the minimum expected return that is required to induce an average investor to purchase the stock.
- The *greater the probability* that the actual return will be far below the expected return, the *greater the asset's stand-alone risk.*
- The average investor is **risk averse**, which means that he or she must be compensated for holding risky assets. Therefore, riskier assets have higher required returns than less risky assets.
- An asset's risk has two components: (1) **diversifiable risk**, which can be eliminated by diversification, and (2) **market risk**, which cannot be eliminated by diversification.
- Market risk is measured by the standard deviation of returns on a well-diversified portfolio, one that consists of all stocks traded in the market. Such a portfolio is called the **market portfolio**.
- The **CAPM** defines the **relevant risk** of an individual asset as its contribution to the risk of a well-diversified portfolio. Because market risk cannot be eliminated by diversification, investors must be compensated for bearing it.
- A stock's **beta coefficient (b)** measures how much risk a stock contributes to a well-diversified portfolio.

[46]See Zhi Da, Re-Jin Guo, and Ravi Jagannathan, "CAPM for Estimating the Cost of Equity Capital: Interpreting the Empirical Evidence," *Journal of Financial Economics,* Vol. 103, 2012, pp. 204–220.

- A stock with a beta greater than 1 has stock returns that tend to be higher than the market when the market is up but tend to be below the market when the market is down. The opposite is true for a stock with a beta less than 1. → STOCK RTN ↓ mₖ
- The *beta of a portfolio* is a weighted average of the betas of the individual securities in the portfolio.
- The CAPM's **Security Market Line (SML)** equation shows the relationship between a security's market risk and its required rate of return. The return required for any security i is equal to the **risk-free rate** plus the **market risk premium** multiplied by the security's beta: $r_i = r_{RF} + (RP_M)b_i$.
- In equilibrium, the expected rate of return on a stock must equal its required return. However, a number of things can happen to cause the required rate of return to change: (1) *The risk-free rate can change* because of changes in either real rates or expected inflation. (2) *A stock's beta can change.* (3) *Investors' aversion to risk can change.*
- Because returns on assets in different countries are not perfectly correlated, *global diversification* may result in lower risk for multinational companies and globally diversified portfolios.
- **Market equilibrium** is the condition under which the expected return on a security as seen by the marginal investor is just equal to its required return, $\hat{r} = r$. Also, the stock's intrinsic value must be equal to its market price.
- The **Efficient Markets Hypothesis (EMH)** asserts: (1) Stocks are always in equilibrium. (2) It is impossible for an investor who does not have inside information to consistently "beat the market." Therefore, according to the EMH, stocks are always fairly valued and have a required return equal to their expected return.
- The **Fama-French three-factor model** has one factor for the *market return*, a second factor for the *size effect*, and a third factor for the *book-to-market effect*.
- **Behavioral finance** assumes that investors can behave in predictable but irrational ways. **Anchoring bias** is the human tendency to "anchor" too closely on recent events when predicting future events. **Herding** is the tendency of investors to follow the crowd. When combined with overconfidence, anchoring and herding can contribute to market bubbles.
- Two Web extensions accompany this chapter: *Web Extension 6A* provides a discussion of **continuous probability distributions**, and *Web Extension 6B* shows how to calculate beta with a financial calculator.

QUESTIONS

(6-1)   Define the following terms, using graphs or equations to illustrate your answers where feasible.

    a.   Risk in general; stand-alone risk; probability distribution and its relation to risk
    b.   Expected rate of return, $\hat{r}$
    c.   Continuous probability distribution
    d.   Standard deviation, σ; variance, σ^2
    e.   Risk aversion; realized rate of return, $\bar{r}$
    f.   Risk premium for Stock i, RP_i; market risk premium, RP_M
    g.   Capital Asset Pricing Model (CAPM)
    h.   Expected return on a portfolio, $\hat{r}_p$; market portfolio

    i. Correlation as a concept; correlation coefficient, ρ
    j. Market risk; diversifiable risk; relevant risk
    k. Beta coefficient, b; average stock's beta
    l. Security Market Line (SML); SML equation
    m. Slope of SML and its relationship to risk aversion
    n. Equilibrium; Efficient Markets Hypothesis (EMH); three forms of EMH
    o. Fama-French three-factor model
    p. Behavioral finance; herding; anchoring

(6-2) The probability distribution of a less risky return is more peaked than that of a riskier return. What shape would the probability distribution have for (a) completely certain returns and (b) completely uncertain returns?

(6-3) Security A has an expected return of 7%, a standard deviation of returns of 35%, a correlation coefficient with the market of −0.3, and a beta coefficient of −1.5. Security B has an expected return of 12%, a standard deviation of returns of 10%, a correlation with the market of 0.7, and a beta coefficient of 1.0. Which security is riskier? Why?

(6-4) If investors' aversion to risk *increased*, would the risk premium on a high-beta stock increase by more or less than that on a low-beta stock? Explain.

(6-5) If a company's beta were to double, would its expected return double?

SELF-TEST PROBLEMS   SOLUTIONS SHOWN IN APPENDIX A

(ST-1)
Realized Rates
of Return

Stocks A and B have the following historical returns:

Year	$\bar{r}_A$	$\bar{r}_B$
2015	−18%	−24%
2016	44	24
2017	−22	−4
2018	22	8
2019	34	56

a. Calculate the average rate of return for each stock during the 5-year period. Assume that someone held a portfolio consisting of 50% of Stock A and 50% of Stock B. What would have been the realized rate of return on the portfolio in each year? What would have been the average return on the portfolio for the 5-year period?

b. Now calculate the standard deviation of returns for each stock and for the portfolio. Use Equation 6-5.

c. Looking at the annual returns data on the two stocks, would you guess that the correlation coefficient between returns on the two stocks is closer to 0.8 or to −0.8?

d. If you added more stocks at random to the portfolio, which of the following is the most accurate statement of what would happen to σ_p?

    1. σ_p would remain constant.
    2. σ_p would decline to somewhere in the vicinity of 20%.
    3. σ_p would decline to zero if enough stocks were included.

ECRI Corporation is a holding company with four main subsidiaries. The percentage of its business coming from each of the subsidiaries, and their respective betas, are as follows:

Subsidiary	Percentage of Business	Beta
Electric utility	60%	0.70
Cable company	25	0.90
Real estate	10	1.30
International/special projects	5	1.50

a. What is the holding company's beta?

b. Assume that the risk-free rate is 6% and that the market risk premium is 5%. What is the holding company's required rate of return?

c. ECRI is considering a change in its strategic focus: It will reduce its reliance on the electric utility subsidiary so that the percentage of its business from this subsidiary will be 50%. At the same time, ECRI will increase its reliance on the international/special projects division, and the percentage of its business from that subsidiary will rise to 15%. What will be the shareholders' required rate of return if management adopts these changes?

PROBLEMS   ANSWERS ARE IN APPENDIX B

EASY PROBLEMS 1–4

Your investment club has only two stocks in its portfolio. $20,000 is invested in a stock with a beta of 0.7, and $35,000 is invested in a stock with a beta of 1.3. What is the portfolio's beta?

AA Corporation's stock has a beta of 0.8. The risk-free rate is 4%, and the expected return on the market is 12%. What is the required rate of return on AA's stock?

Suppose that the risk-free rate is 5% and that the market risk premium is 7%. What is the required return on (1) the market, (2) a stock with a beta of 1.0, and (3) a stock with a beta of 1.7?

An analyst gathered daily stock returns for February 1 through March 31, calculated the Fama-French factors for each day in the sample (SMB_t and HML_t), and estimated the Fama-French regression model shown in Equation 6-21. The estimated coefficients were $a_i = 0$, $b_i = 1.2$, $c_i = -0.4$, and $d_i = 1.3$. On April 1, the market return was 10%, the return on the SMB portfolio (r_{SMB}) was 3.2%, and the return on the HML portfolio (r_{HML}) was 4.8%. Using the estimated model, what was the stock's predicted return for April 1?

INTERMEDIATE PROBLEMS 5–10

A stock's return has the following distribution:

Demand for the Company's Products	Probability of This Demand Occurring	Rate of Return if This Demand Occurs (%)
Weak	0.1	−50%
Below average	0.2	−5
Average	0.4	16
Above average	0.2	25
Strong	0.1	60
	1.0	

Calculate the stock's expected return and standard deviation.

(6-6)
Expected
Returns: Discrete
Distribution

The market and Stock J have the following probability distributions:

Probability	r_M	r_J
0.3	15%	20%
0.4	9	5
0.3	18	12

a. Calculate the expected rates of return for the market and Stock J.
b. Calculate the standard deviations for the market and Stock J.

(6-7)
Required Rate
of Return

Suppose $r_{RF} = 5\%$, $r_M = 10\%$, and $r_A = 12\%$.

a. Calculate Stock A's beta.
b. If Stock A's beta were 2.0, then what would be A's new required rate of return?

(6-8)
Required Rate
of Return

As an equity analyst you are concerned with what will happen to the required return for Universal Toddler's stock as market conditions change. Suppose $r_{RF} = 5\%$, $r_M = 12\%$, and $b_{UT} = 1.4$.

a. Under current conditions, what is r_{UT}, the required rate of return on UT stock?
b. Now suppose r_{RF} (1) increases to 6% or (2) decreases to 4%. The market risk premium, RP_M, (i.e., the slope of the SML) remains constant. How would this affect r_M and r_{UT}?
c. Now assume r_{RF} remains at 5% but r_M (1) increases to 14% or (2) falls to 11%. The market risk premium, RP_M, (i.e., the slope of the SML) does not remain constant. How would these changes affect r_{UT}?

(6-9)
Portfolio Beta

Your retirement fund consists of a $5,000 investment in each of 15 different common stocks. The portfolio's beta is 1.20. Suppose you sell one of the stocks with a beta of 0.8 for $5,000 and use the proceeds to buy another stock whose beta is 1.6. Calculate your portfolio's new beta.

(6-10)
Portfolio Required
Return

Suppose you manage a $4 million fund that consists of four stocks with the following investments:

Stock	Investment	Beta
A	$ 400,000	1.50
B	600,000	−0.50
C	1,000,000	1.25
D	2,000,000	0.75

If the market's required rate of return is 14% and the risk-free rate is 6%, what is the fund's required rate of return?

CHALLENGING PROBLEMS 11–14

(6-11)
Portfolio Beta

You have a $2 million portfolio consisting of a $100,000 investment in each of 20 different stocks. The portfolio has a beta of 1.1. You are considering selling $100,000 worth of one stock with a beta of 0.9 and using the proceeds to purchase another stock with a beta of 1.4. What will the portfolio's new beta be after these transactions?

(6-12)
Required Rate
of Return

Stock R has a beta of 1.5, Stock S has a beta of 0.75, the expected rate of return on an average stock is 13%, and the risk-free rate is 7%. By how much does the required return on the riskier stock exceed that on the less risky stock?

(6-13)
Historical Realized
Rates of Return

You are considering an investment in either individual stocks or a portfolio of stocks. The two stocks you are researching, Stock A and Stock B, have the following historical returns:

Year	$\bar{r}_A$	$\bar{r}_B$
2015	−20.00%	−5.00%
2016	42.00	15.00
2017	20.00	−13.00
2018	−8.00	50.00
2019	25.00	12.00

a. Calculate the average rate of return for each stock during the 5-year period.
b. Suppose you had held a portfolio consisting of 50% of Stock A and 50% of Stock B. What would have been the realized rate of return on the portfolio in each year? What would have been the average return on the portfolio during this period?
c. Calculate the standard deviation of returns for each stock and for the portfolio.
d. Suppose you are a risk-averse investor. Assuming Stocks A and B are your only choices, would you prefer to hold Stock A, Stock B, or the portfolio? Why?

(6-14)
Historical Returns:
Expected and
Required Rates
of Return

You have observed the following returns over time:

Year	Stock X	Stock Y	Market
2015	14%	13%	12%
2016	19	7	10
2017	−16	−5	−12
2018	3	1	1
2019	20	11	15

Assume that the risk-free rate is 6% and the market risk premium is 5%.

a. What are the betas of Stocks X and Y?
b. What are the required rates of return on Stocks X and Y?
c. What is the required rate of return on a portfolio consisting of 80% of Stock X and 20% of Stock Y?

SPREADSHEET PROBLEM

(6-15)
Evaluating Risk
and Return

Start with the partial model in the file *Ch06 P15 Build a Model.xlsx* on the textbook's Web site. The file contains data for this problem. Goodman Corporation's and Landry Incorporated's stock prices and dividends, along with the Market Index, are shown here. Stock prices are reported for December 31 of each year, and dividends reflect those paid during the year. The market data are adjusted to include dividends.

resource

	Goodman Corporation		Landry Incorporated		Market Index
Year	Stock Price	Dividend	Stock Price	Dividend	Includes Dividends
2019	$25.88	$1.73	$73.13	$4.50	17,495.97
2018	22.13	1.59	78.45	4.35	13,178.55
2017	24.75	1.50	73.13	4.13	13,019.97
2016	16.13	1.43	85.88	3.75	9,651.05
2015	17.06	1.35	90.00	3.38	8,403.42
2014	11.44	1.28	83.63	3.00	7,058.96

a. Use the data given to calculate annual returns for Goodman, Landry, and the Market Index, and then calculate average annual returns for the two stocks and the index. (*Hint:* Remember, returns are calculated by subtracting the beginning price from the ending price to get the capital gain or loss, adding the dividend to the capital gain or loss, and then dividing the result by the beginning price. Assume that dividends are already included in the index. Also, you cannot calculate the rate of return for 2014 because you do not have 2013 data.)

b. Calculate the standard deviations of the returns for Goodman, Landry, and the Market Index. (*Hint:* Use the sample standard deviation formula given in the chapter, which corresponds to the **STDEV** function in *Excel*.)

c. Construct a scatter diagram graph that shows Goodman's returns on the vertical axis and the Market Index's returns on the horizontal axis. Construct a similar graph showing Landry's stock returns on the vertical axis.

d. Estimate Goodman's and Landry's betas as the slopes of regression lines with stock return on the vertical axis (y-axis) and market return on the horizontal axis (x-axis). (*Hint:* Use *Excel*'s **SLOPE** function.) Are these betas consistent with your graph?

e. The risk-free rate on long-term Treasury bonds is 6.04%. Assume that the market risk premium is 5%. What is the required return on the market? Now use the SML equation to calculate the two companies' required returns.

f. If you formed a portfolio that consisted of 50% Goodman stock and 50% Landry stock, what would be its beta and its required return?

g. Suppose an investor wants to include some Goodman Industries stock in his portfolio. Stocks A, B, and C are currently in the portfolio, and their betas are 0.769, 0.985, and 1.423, respectively. Calculate the new portfolio's required return if it consists of 25% Goodman, 15% Stock A, 40% Stock B, and 20% Stock C.

MINI CASE

Assume that you recently graduated and landed a job as a financial planner with Cicero Services, an investment advisory company. Your first client recently inherited some assets and has asked you to evaluate them. The client owns a bond portfolio with $1 million invested in zero coupon Treasury bonds that mature in 10 years.[47] The client also has $2 million invested in the stock of Blandy, Inc., a company that produces meat-and-potatoes frozen dinners. Blandy's slogan is, "Solid food for shaky times."

Unfortunately, Congress and the president are engaged in an acrimonious dispute over the budget and the debt ceiling. The outcome of the dispute, which will not be resolved until the end of the year, will have a big impact on interest rates one year from now. Your first task is to determine the risk of the client's bond portfolio. After consulting with the economists at your firm, you have specified five possible scenarios for the resolution of the dispute at the end of the year. For each scenario, you have estimated the probability of the scenario occurring and the impact on interest rates and bond prices if the scenario occurs. Given this information, you have

---

[47]The total par value at maturity is $1.79 million and yield to maturity is about 6%, but that information is not necessary for this mini case.

calculated the rate of return on 10-year zero coupon Treasury bonds for each scenario. The probabilities and returns are shown here:

Scenario	Probability of Scenario	Return on a 10-Year Zero Coupon Treasury Bond During the Next Year
Worst Case	0.10	−14%
Poor Case	0.20	−4%
Most Likely	0.40	6%
Good Case	0.20	16%
Best Case	0.10	26%
	1.00	

You have also gathered historical returns for the past 10 years for Blandy and Gour-mange Corporation (a producer of gourmet specialty foods), and the stock market.

Year	Historical Stock Returns		
	Market	Blandy	Gourmange
1	30%	26%	47%
2	7	15	−54
3	18	−14	15
4	−22	−15	7
5	−14	2	−28
6	10	−18	40
7	26	42	17
8	−10	30	−23
9	−3	−32	−4
10	38	28	75
Average return:	8.0%	? 6.4	9.2%
Standard deviation:	20.1%	? 25.2	38.6%
Correlation with the market:	1.00	?	0.678
Beta:	1.00	?	1.30

The risk-free rate is 4%, and the market risk premium is 5%.

a. What are investment returns? What is the return on an investment that costs $1,000 and is sold after 1 year for $1,060?

b. Graph the probability distribution for the bond returns based on the 5 scenarios. What might the graph of the probability distribution look like if there were an infinite number of scenarios (i.e., if it were a continuous distribution and not a discrete distribution)?

c. Use the scenario data to calculate the expected rate of return for the 10-year zero coupon Treasury bonds during the next year.

d. What is the stand-alone risk? Use the scenario data to calculate the standard deviation of the bond's return for the next year.

e. Your client has decided that the risk of the bond portfolio is acceptable and wishes to leave it as it is. Now your client has asked you to use historical returns to estimate the standard deviation of Blandy's stock returns. (*Note:* Many analysts use 4 to 5 years of monthly returns to estimate risk, and many use 52 weeks of weekly returns; some even use a year or less of daily returns. For the sake of simplicity, use Blandy's 10 annual returns.)

f. Your client is shocked at how much risk Blandy stock has and would like to reduce the level of risk. You suggest that the client sell 25% of the Blandy stock and create a portfolio with 75% Blandy stock and 25% in the high-risk Gourmange stock. How do you suppose the client will react to replacing some of the Blandy stock with high-risk stock? Show the client what the proposed portfolio return would have been in each year of the sample. Then calculate the average return and standard deviation using the portfolio's annual returns. How does the risk of this two-stock portfolio compare with the risk of the individual stocks if they were held in isolation?

g. Explain correlation to your client. Calculate the estimated correlation between Blandy and Gourmange. Does this explain why the portfolio standard deviation was less than Blandy's standard deviation?

h. Suppose an investor starts with a portfolio consisting of one randomly selected stock. As more and more randomly selected stocks are added to the portfolio, what happens to the portfolio's risk?

i. (1) Should portfolio effects influence how investors think about the risk of individual stocks? (2) If you decided to hold a one-stock portfolio and consequently were exposed to more risk than diversified investors, could you expect to be compensated for all of your risk; that is, could you earn a risk premium on that part of your risk that you could have eliminated by diversifying?

j. According to the Capital Asset Pricing Model, what measures the amount of risk that an individual stock contributes to a well-diversified portfolio? Define this measurement.

k. What is the Security Market Line (SML)? How is beta related to a stock's required rate of return?

l. Calculate the correlation coefficient between Blandy and the market. Use this and the previously calculated (or given) standard deviations of Blandy and the market to estimate Blandy's beta. Does Blandy contribute more or less risk to a well-diversified portfolio than does the average stock? Use the SML to estimate Blandy's required return.

m. Show how to estimate beta using regression analysis.

n. (1) Suppose the risk-free rate goes up to 7%. What effect would higher interest rates have on the SML and on the returns required on high-risk and low-risk securities? (2) Suppose instead that investors' risk aversion increased enough to cause the market risk premium to increase to 8%. (Assume the risk-free rate remains constant.) What effect would this have on the SML and on returns of high- and low-risk securities?

o. Your client decides to invest $1.4 million in Blandy stock and $0.6 million in Gourmange stock. What are the weights for this portfolio? What is the portfolio's beta? What is the required return for this portfolio?

p. Jordan Jones (JJ) and Casey Carter (CC) are portfolio managers at your firm. Each manages a well-diversified portfolio. Your boss has asked for your opinion regarding their performance in the past year. JJ's portfolio has a beta of 0.6 and had a return of 8.5%; CC's portfolio has a beta of 1.4 and had a return of 9.5%. Which manager had better performance? Why?

q. What does market equilibrium mean? If equilibrium does not exist, how will it be established?

r. What is the Efficient Markets Hypothesis (EMH), and what are its three forms? What evidence supports the EMH? What evidence casts doubt on the EMH?

SELECTED ADDITIONAL CASES

The following cases from CengageCompose cover many of the concepts discussed in this chapter and are available at **compose.cengage.com**.

Klein-Brigham Series:
Case 2, "Peachtree Securities, Inc. (A)."

Brigham-Buzzard Series:
Case 2, "Powerline Network Corporation (Risk and Return)."

Corporate Valuation and Stock Valuation

Stock brokerage companies, mutual fund companies, financial services institutions, pension funds, and financial advisory firms are among the many companies that employ security analysts to estimate the value and risk of stocks.

"Sell-side" analysts work for investment banks and brokerages. They write reports that are distributed to investors, generally through brokers. "Buy-side" analysts work for mutual funds, hedge funds, pension funds, and other institutional investors. Those institutions obtain information from the buy-side analysts, but they also do their own research and ignore analysts if they disagree.

The analysts on both sides generally focus on specific industries, and many of them were hired as analysts after working for a time in the industry they cover. Physics PhDs are often electronics analysts, biologists analyze biotech stocks, and so on. The analysts pore over financial statements and *Excel* models, but they also go on the road and talk with company officials, companies' customers, and their suppliers. The analysts' primary objective is to predict corporate earnings, dividends, and free cash flow—and thus stock prices.

Stock prices are volatile, so it is difficult to estimate a stock's value. However, some analysts are better than others, and the material in this chapter can help you be better than average.

Corporate Valuation and Stock Prices

Free cash flows (FCFs) are the cash flows available for distribution to all of a company's investors; the weighted average cost of capital is the overall return required by all of a company's investors. So the present value of a company's expected free cash flows, discounted by the company's weighted average cost of capital, is the total value of the company to all its investors. It is called the value of operations because operating activities generate the FCF.

We can use this approach to estimate the stock price, but we can do this more directly in some circumstances. Recall that one use of FCF is to pay dividends, which are distributed to stockholders. Chapter 6 showed how to estimate stockholders' required return. Therefore, discounting the expected cash flows to stockholders (the dividends) at the rate required by stockholders determines the stock's value.

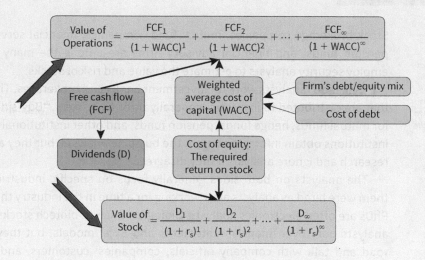

$$\frac{\text{Value of}}{\text{Operations}} = \frac{FCF_1}{(1 + WACC)^1} + \frac{FCF_2}{(1 + WACC)^2} + \cdots + \frac{FCF_\infty}{(1 + WACC)^\infty}$$

$$\frac{\text{Value of}}{\text{Stock}} = \frac{D_1}{(1 + r_s)^1} + \frac{D_2}{(1 + r_s)^2} + \cdots + \frac{D_\infty}{(1 + r_s)^\infty}$$

How much is a company worth? What can managers do to make a company more valuable? Why are stock prices so volatile? This chapter addresses those questions through the application of two widely used valuation models: the free cash flow valuation model and the dividend growth model. But before plunging into stock valuation, we begin with a closer look at what it means to be a stockholder.

7-1 Legal Rights and Privileges of Common Stockholders

Common stockholders are the *owners* of a corporation, and as such they have certain rights and privileges as discussed in this section.

7-1a Control of the Firm

A firm's common stockholders have the right to elect its directors, who, in turn, select the senior executives who manage the business. In a small firm, the largest stockholder typically serves as president and chairperson of the board. In a large, publicly owned firm, the managers typically have some stock, but their personal holdings are generally insufficient to give them voting control. Thus, the managers of most publicly owned firms can be removed by the stockholders if the management team is not effective.

Corporations must hold periodic elections to select directors, usually once a year, with the vote taken at the annual meeting. At some companies, all directors are elected each year for a 1-year term. At other companies, the terms are staggered. For example, one-third of the directors might be elected each year for a 3-year term.

Each share of stock has one vote, so the owner of 1,000 shares has 1,000 votes for each director.[1] Stockholders can appear at the annual meeting and vote in person, but typically they transfer their right to vote to another party by means of a **proxy**. Management always solicits stockholders' proxies and usually gets them. However, if earnings are poor and stockholders are dissatisfied, an outside group may solicit the proxies in an effort to overthrow management and take control of the business. This is known as a **proxy fight**. The proxy ballot is discussed in Chapter 13.

7-1b The Preemptive Right

The **preemptive right** allows current common stockholders to purchase any additional shares sold by the firm. In some states, the preemptive right is automatically included in every corporate charter; in others, it is used only if it is specifically inserted into the charter.

The preemptive right enables current stockholders to maintain control, and it also prevents a transfer of wealth from current stockholders to new stockholders. If not for this safeguard, the management of a corporation could issue additional shares at a low price and purchase these shares itself. Management could thereby seize control of the corporation and steal value from the current stockholders. For example, suppose 1,000 shares of common stock, each with a price of $100, were outstanding, making the total market value of the firm $100,000. If an additional 1,000 shares were sold at $50 a share, or for $50,000, this would raise the total market value to $150,000. When total market value is divided by new total shares outstanding, a value of $75 a share is obtained. The old stockholders thus lose $25 per share, and the new stockholders have an instant profit of $25 per share. Thus, selling common stock at a price below the market value would dilute its price and transfer wealth from the present stockholders to those who were allowed to purchase the new shares. The preemptive right prevents such occurrences.

SELF-TEST

What is a proxy fight?

What are the two primary reasons for using preemptive rights?

7-2 Classified Stock and Tracking Stock

Some corporations have different types of **classified stock**, each with its own dividend rights and voting rights. These are also called **dual class shares** if there are two classes. Typically, one type is designated *Class A*, another *Class B*, and so on, although this is not mandatory. Companies that have dual class shares often issued them in the companies' initial public offerings (IPOs), especially in the tech industry. In 2016, more than 21% of tech IPOs issued dual class shares, much higher than before 2000 and higher than nontech IPOs. In most cases, one class of stock is sold to the public, which receives dividends but cannot vote. The rest, called **founders' shares**, usually preserve all voting rights for the

---

[1]In the situation described, a 1,000-share stockholder could cast 1,000 votes for each of three directors if there were three contested seats on the board. An alternative procedure that may be prescribed in the corporate charter calls for *cumulative voting*. Here the 1,000-share stockholder would get 3,000 votes if there were three vacancies, and he or she could cast all of them for one director. Cumulative voting helps minority stockholders (i.e., those who do not own a majority of the shares) get representation on the board.

founders but have restrictions on dividends. Some, but not all, IPO filings have provisions that ultimately lead to the combination of the classes into a single class.

How valuable is the right to vote? In the United States, which has a legal system with fairly strong protection for minority stockholders (that is, noncontrolling stockholders), voting stock typically sells at a price 4% to 6% above that of otherwise similar nonvoting stock. In countries with legal systems that provide less protection for minority stockholders, the right to vote is far more valuable. For example, voting stock in Israel sells for 45% more on average than nonvoting stock, and voting stock in Italy has an 82% higher value than nonvoting stock.

In 2015, about 7% of the companies listed in the S&P 500 had multiple share classes. A higher percentage of smaller companies had multiple classes. However, this may change in the near future. As we write this in 2017, companies with multiple share classes will no longer be added to the S&P 1500 Index (which includes the S&P 500). This does not apply to companies already included in the index. Also, investors are beginning to revolt against multiple share classes. Chapter 13 describes these developments.

A few companies have multiple lines of business, with each line having different growth prospects. Because cash flows for all business lines are mingled on financial statements, some companies worry that investors are not able to value the high-growth business lines correctly. To separate the cash flows and to allow separate valuations, a company can have classes of stock with dividends tied to a particular part of a company. This is called **tracking stock** or **target stock**. Although this type of stock was once popular, Liberty Media Corp. is one of the few large companies with tracking stocks.

SELF-TEST

What are some reasons why a company might use classified stock?

7-3 Stock Market Reporting

Stock price quotes and other information are readily available from Internet sources, including Zacks, Bloomberg, *The Wall Street Journal*, Yahoo!, and Google.[2] A typical quote shows the ticker symbol (MCDV), where the stock is traded (such as NASDAQ), and a time stamp. If the quote is during trading hours, then some sources report current information about the prices and volumes at which the stock could be bought (the Ask quote) or sold (the Bid quote). Otherwise, the reported quote is the last price at which the stock traded.

Figure 7-1 shows a quote for MicroDrive, which had a closing price of $31.00. Most sources also show the change in the price ($0.75) and the percentage change (1.8%) from the previous day's closing price. This was a relatively slow day of trading for MicroDrive, as shown by the number of shares traded (830,000) versus the 30-day average of 1,356,539. Many sources provide "historical" price information. For example, MicroDrive closed the previous day at $30.25, opened the current day at $30.45 (implying there was positive news prior to the start of trading), went down to $30.20 during the day, increased to $31.29, and finally closed at $32.00. During the past 52 weeks, the price has been as high as $46.22 and as low as $29.50.

Most Web sites also report other data, such as the total market value of common stock (the Market Capitalization, which is commonly called "market cap"), the dividend, the dividend yield, and the most recent "ttm" (trailing twelve months) of earnings per share (EPS).

---

[2]Most free sources actually provide quotes that are delayed by 20 minutes, but if you subscribe to a paid online service or have a brokerage account, you can generally get real-time quotes online.

FIGURE 7-1
Stock Quote for MicroDrive, Inc.

MicroDrive, Inc. (MCDV)

NASDAQ: 12/31/2019, 4:00 PM EST

31.00 ($0.75, 1.8%)

Opening Price:	30.45	52-Week Low:	29.50
Ask Quote:	NA	Dividends per Share (Annual)	1.00
Bid Quote:	NA	Dividend Yield	3.20%
Daily High:	31.29	Earnings per Share, EPS (ttm)	4.13
Daily Low:	30.20	Market Capitalization (Billions)	1.86
Previous Closing Price:	30.25	Volume	830,000
52-Week High:	46.22	30-Day Average Volume	1,356,539

Note: For quotes of other companies, see www.zacks.com/stocks, www.bloomberg.com/markets/stocks, http://finance.yahoo.com, www.google.com/finance, or http://quotes.wsj.com.

Some sites also provide a graph showing the stock's price over time and links to financial statements, research reports, historical ratios, analysts' forecasts of EPS and EPS growth rates, and a wealth of other data.

SELF-TEST

What information is provided on the Internet in addition to the stock's latest price?

7-4 Valuing Common Stocks—Introducing the Free Cash Flow (FCF) Valuation Model

To make good decisions, a manager must be able to estimate the impact that possible strategies, tactics, and projects have on a company's value. In other words, a manager needs a tool that clearly shows the connections between managerial choices and firm value. This is exactly what the **free cash flow (FCF) valuation model** can do. The FCF valuation model defines the value of a company's operations as the present value of its expected free cash flows when discounted at the weighted average cost of capital (WACC).[3] Managerial choices that change operating profitability, asset utilization, or growth also change FCF and, hence, the value of operations. Managerial choices that affect risk, such as implementing riskier strategies or changing the amount of debt financing, also affect the weighted average cost of capital, which affects the company's value. Therefore, the FCF valuation model is an important tool for managers.

Later in this chapter we describe two other valuation approaches, the dividend growth model and market multiples, but we begin with the FCF valuation model because it is applicable in more situations. For example, the FCF valuation model can be applied to all companies, whether or not they pay a dividend and whether they are publicly traded or privately held. It also can be applied to divisions within companies and not just whole companies. The broad applicability and clear links between managerial decisions and

---

[3]The WACC is the rate of return a company must generate in order to fairly compensate investors. We explain how to calculate the WACC in Chapter 9.

value explain why the FCF model is the most widely used valuation model in merger and acquisition analysis.

7-4a Sources of Value and Claims on Value

The total value of a company is called its **entity value**. Companies have two primary sources of value, the value of operations and the value of nonoperating assets. There are three major types of claims on this value: debt, preferred stock, and common stock. Following is a description of these sources and claims.

SOURCES OF VALUE

Recall from Chapter 2 that free cash flow (FCF) is the cash flow available for distribution to *all* of a company's investors. The weighted average cost of capital (WACC) is the overall return required by *all* of a company's investors. Because FCF is generated by a company's operations, the present value of expected FCF when discounted by the WACC is equal to the company's **value of operations (V_{op})**:

$$V_{op} = \frac{FCF_1}{(1 + WACC)^1} + \frac{FCF_2}{(1 + WACC)^2} + \cdots + \frac{FCF_\infty}{(1 + WACC)^\infty}$$

$$= \sum_{t=1}^{\infty} \frac{FCF_t}{(1 + WACC)^t} \tag{7-1}$$

Even though the summation in Equation 7-1 goes to infinity, we can calculate the value of this infinite sum in three situations: (1) The free cash flows are constant forever. (2) The FCF grows at a constant rate forever. (3) The FCF *eventually* grows at a constant rate. Virtually all companies fall into this third situation—free cash flows presently may be growing at nonconstant rates, but product maturation, competition, and market saturation eventually will cause the expected long-term growth rate to level off at a constant rate for all companies. We will apply this second and more realistic situation to several companies later in the chapter, but we start with the simplest situation because this provides a good overview of the valuation process.

Consider B&B Corporation, which owns and manages several bed and breakfast inns located in historic Philadelphia. B&B generated $10 million in free cash flow in the most recent year. B&B's stockholders have strong local ties and do not wish to expand. Therefore, B&B expects to have a constant free cash flow of $10 million each year for the foreseeable future.

B&B's estimated weighted average cost of capital is 10%, which is the rate B&B must earn on its investments to fairly compensate its investors, a combination of debtholders, preferred stockholders, and common stockholders. We will show how to estimate the WACC in Chapter 9, but for now will just accept 10% as B&B's estimated WACC.

The value of operations is the present value of all expected free cash flows discounted at the cost of capital. Because the FCFs are expected to be constant, the cash flow stream is a perpetuity (see Chapter 4 for a review of perpetuities). The present value of a perpetuity is the cash flow divided by the cost of capital:

$$V_{op} \text{ (for a perpetuity)} = \frac{FCF}{WACC} \tag{7-2}$$

Therefore, B&B's value of operations is $100 million:

$$V_{op} \text{ (for a perpetuity)} = \frac{FCF}{WACC} = \frac{\$10}{0.10} = \$100 \tag{7-2a}$$

The primary source of value for most companies is the value of operations. A secondary source of value comes from **nonoperating assets**, which are also called *financial assets*. There are two major types of nonoperating assets: (1) short-term investments, which are very marketable short-term securities (like T-bills) that are temporarily held for future needs rather than to support current operations, and (2) other nonoperating assets, which often are investments in other businesses. For example, in late 2017, Ford Motor Company's automotive operation held about $17.4 billion in marketable securities and $3.2 billion of investments in other businesses, which were reported on the asset side of the balance sheet as "Equity in Net Assets of Affiliated Companies." In total, Ford had $17.4 + $3.2 = $20.6 billion of nonoperating assets, amounting to 20% of its $105.5 billion of total automotive assets. For most companies, the percentage is much lower. For example, Walmart's percentage of nonoperating assets was less than 1%, which is more typical.

We see, then, that for most companies, operating assets are far more important than nonoperating assets. Moreover, companies can influence the values of their operating assets, whereas market forces determine the values of short-term investments and other nonoperating assets.

When using the FCF valuation model, a company's *total intrinsic value* is the value of operations plus the value of short-term investments (assuming the company owns no other nonoperating assets, which is true for most companies). This is called the **intrinsic value** (or **fundamental value**) to distinguish it from the market value. The market value is whatever price the market is willing to pay, but the intrinsic value is estimated from the expected cash flows:

$$\text{Total intrinsic value} = \text{Value of operations} + \text{Short-term investments} \tag{7-3}$$

B&B has $2 million in bank certificates of deposit, earning a little interest while B&B decides how to use the funds. Because B&B does not need the $2 million to run its operations, these should be classified as short-term investments. Therefore, from Equation 7-3 the total intrinsic value of B&B is:

Total intrinsic value = Value of operations + Short-term investments
= $100 + $2 = $102

Because the FCF valuation model determines the total value of the firm before estimating the per share stock price, it is called an **entity valuation model**. The following section explains how to use the estimated entity value (i.e., the total value of the firm) to estimate the value of common stock.

CLAIMS ON VALUE

For a company that is a going concern, debtholders have the first claim on value in the sense that interest and scheduled principal payments must be paid before any preferred or common dividends can be paid. Preferred stockholders have the next claim because preferred dividends must be paid before common dividends. Common shareholders come last in this pecking order and have a residual claim on the company's value.

The estimated *intrinsic value of equity* is the remaining value after subtracting the claims of debtholders and preferred stockholders from the total intrinsic value:[4]

$$\text{Intrinsic value of equity} = \text{Total intrinsic value} - \text{All debt} - \text{Preferred stock} \quad (7\text{-}4)$$

B&B owes a total of $28 million in mortgages and bank loans. B&B also has $4 million of preferred stock outstanding, which was issued to the founders' families early in the company's life. B&B's estimated intrinsic value of equity is:

$$\begin{aligned}
\text{Intrinsic value of equity} &= \text{Total intrinsic value} - \text{All debt} - \text{Preferred stock} \\
&= \$102 - \$28 - \$4 \\
&= \$70
\end{aligned}$$

7-4b The Intrinsic Value per Share of Common Stock

The estimated *intrinsic stock price* is equal to the intrinsic value of equity divided by the number of shares:

$$\text{Intrinsic stock price} = (\text{Intrinsic value of equity})/(\text{Number of shares}) \quad (7\text{-}5)$$

B&B has 5 million shares of common stock outstanding. Therefore, B&B's estimated intrinsic stock price is:

$$\begin{aligned}
\text{Intrinsic stock price} &= \text{Intrinsic value of equity}/\text{Number of shares} \\
&= \$70/5 = \$14 \text{ dollars per share}
\end{aligned}$$

Figure 7-2 summarizes these calculations and shows B&B's two value "pies": One pie shows the sources of value and the other pie shows the "pieces" belonging to debtholders, preferred stockholders, and common stockholders.

SELF-TEST

Why is the free cash flow valuation model so widely used?

Write out the equation for the value of operations.

Explain how to estimate the price per share using the free cash flow valuation model.

A company expects a constant FCF of $240 million per year forever. If the WACC is 12%, what is the value of operations? **($2,000 million)**

A company has a current value of operations of $800 million, and it holds $100 million in short-term investments. If the company has $400 million in debt and has 10 million common shares outstanding, what is the estimated price per share? **($50.00)**

---

[4]In principle, the *market values* rather than book values of the short-term investments in Equation 7-3 and the claims in Equation 7-4 should be used. These market values may differ from the book values. For example, if interest rates have risen since the company's bonds were issued, their market values will have fallen below their book values. Similarly, as yields for comparable preferred stocks change, the market value of preferred stock will change. For simplicity here and in Chapter 12, we will assume that the book values of these items are good estimates of their market values.

FIGURE 7-2

B&B Corporation's Sources of Value and Claims on Value (Millions of Dollars, Except for per Share Data)

Inputs:		Valuation Analysis	
Constant free cash flow (FCF) =	$10	Value of operations	$100
Weighted average cost of capital (WACC) =	10%	+ ST investments	$2
Short-term investments =	$2	Estimated total intrinsic value	$102
Debt =	$28	– All debt	$28
Preferred stock =	$4	– Preferred stock	$4
Number of shares of common stock =	5	Estimated intrinsic value of equity	$70
		÷ Number of shares	5
		Estimated intrinsic stock price	$14

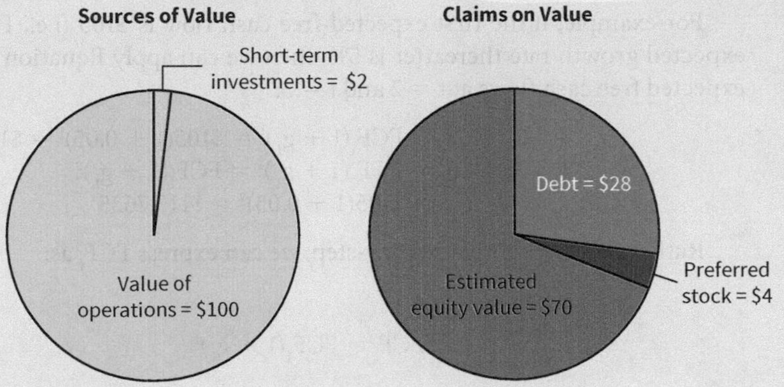

Sources of Value: Short-term investments = $2; Value of operations = $100.

Claims on Value: Debt = $28; Preferred stock = $4; Estimated equity value = $70.

7-5 The Constant Growth Model: Valuation When Expected Free Cash Flow Grows at a Constant Rate

The company in the previous section illustrates the FCF valuation model's steps, but the perpetuity approach is not applicable to most companies because their cash flows aren't constant. In fact, most companies expect to have growing cash flows, often with nonconstant growth rates in the near future. However, even if free cash flows currently are growing at nonconstant rates, the expected *long-term* free cash flows should eventually level off at a constant rate for all companies. To see this, think about the impact of competition and market saturation. For a firm to grow faster than the economy, either the industry must become a bigger part of the economy or the firm must take market share from its competitors. However, market saturation eventually limits the size of the industry, and competition limits the ability to take market share while maintaining profits. This means that, as markets mature, competition and market saturation will tend to limit FCF growth to a constant long-term rate that is approximately equal to the sum of population growth and inflation: Population growth determines the number of units that can be sold when markets are saturated, and inflation determines the growth in prices and profits when there is competition.

Some companies are in growing industries and won't hit their long-term constant growth rate for many years, but some mature firms in saturated industries are already at their constant long-term growth rate. We will address valuation in the presence of nonconstant short-term growth later in the chapter, but we now examine a mature company whose free cash flows are expected to grow at a constant rate.

7-5a Estimating the Value of Operations When Expected Growth Is Constant

Recall that the value of operations is the present value of expected free cash flows, from now to infinity, discounted at the weighted average cost of capital. Even though the cash flows go on forever, we can still calculate their present value if they grow at a *constant rate* forever, g_L. To estimate the cash flow at Year-t (FCF_t), let the previously estimated cash flow grow by g_L:

$$FCF_t = FCF_{t-1}(1 + g_L) \qquad (7\text{-}6)$$

For example, if the first expected free cash flow is \$105 (i.e., FCF_1 = \$105) and the expected growth rate thereafter is 5%, then we can apply Equation 7-6 to determine the expected free cash flows at t = 2 and t = 3:

t = 2: $FCF_2 = FCF_1(1 + g_L)^1 = \$105(1 + 0.05)^1 = \$110.25$
t = 3: $FCF_3 = FCF_2(1 + g_L)^1 = FCF_1(1 + g_L)^2$
$= \$105(1 + 0.05)^2 = \$115.7625$

Rather than repeat this step-by-step, we can express FCF_t as:

$$FCF_t = FCF_1(1 + g_L)^{t-1} \qquad (7\text{-}7)$$

For example, we can use Equation 7-7 to estimate the free cash flow at t = 3, which gives the same result shown previously in the step-by-step process:

$$FCF_3 = FCF_1(1 + g_L)^{3-1} = \$105(1 + 0.05)^2 = \$115.7625$$

Because expected FCF is growing at a constant rate, there is a simple formula for the value of operations, as shown next in Equation 7-8. We will explain the steps used to derive Equation 7-8, but take a look at the formula:

$$
\begin{aligned}
V_{op} \text{ (constant growth)} &= \sum_{t=1}^{\infty} \frac{FCF_t}{(1 + WACC)^t} = \sum_{t=1}^{\infty} \frac{FCF_1(1 + g_L)^{t-1}}{(1 + WACC)^t} = \sum_{t=1}^{\infty} \left[\frac{FCF_1}{1 + g_L}\right]\left[\frac{1 + g_L}{1 + WACC}\right]^t \\
&= FCF_1\left[\frac{1}{1 + g_L}\right] \sum_{t=1}^{\infty} \left[\frac{1 + g_L}{1 + WACC}\right]^t \\
&= FCF_1\left[\frac{1}{1 + g_L}\right]\left[\frac{1 + g_L}{WACC - g_L}\right] \\
&= \frac{FCF_1}{WACC - g_L}
\end{aligned}
\qquad (7\text{-}8)
$$

Look at the first row of Equation 7-8. Its second bracket results from substituting Equation 7-7 into Equation 7-1. The second row uses algebra to factor out some of the variables. Notice that the second row's last bracket is an infinite summation.

However, that infinite summation is replaced with a simple formula in the third row's last bracket. How is this possible? Take a close look at second row's last bracket. If the long-term growth rate of g_L is less than the WACC, then the term in brackets is less than 1. When you compound a number that is less than 1, you get a smaller number. However, the infinite summation of ever shrinking numbers is not necessarily equal to infinity!

For the intuition behind this result, consider the following example. Let's pick a number that is less than 1, compound it, and look at its cumulative compounded sum for several years. The following time line shows the year (t), the compounded value of ½ (which is less than 1) at each year, and the cumulative sum. For example, at Year 1, we have ½ compounded once, which is ½. The cumulative sum is just ½, too, because this is the first year. For Year 2, we have ½ squared, which is ¼. The cumulative sum is the previous sum of ½ plus ¼, which is ¾. The other entries are calculated similarly.

Year t =	1	2	3	4	5
$(1/2)^t =$	1/2	1/4	1/8	1/16	1/32
Cumulative sum of $(1/2)^t =$	1/2	3/4	7/8	15/16	31/32

We stopped after 5 years, but it appears as though the cumulative sum would not grow to infinity even if we continued adding years. In fact, it looks as though the cumulative sum is getting closer and closer to 1, but not exceeding 1. In other words, the cumulative sum is converging to 1.

Web Extension 7A shows that the third row in Equation 7-8 converges to the last row in Equation 7-8, which is called the **constant growth model**. This model provides a simple formula for the present value of an infinite stream of constantly growing free cash flows. However, be alert when using Equation 7-8 because we have seen many students try to apply it prematurely when the growth rate has not yet leveled off to a value less than the WACC, resulting in a *negative* value of operations! This impossible result occurs because they overlook the fact that the last row is valid only if the infinite summation converges, which can happen only if $g_L <$ WACC. In fact, if g_L is greater than or equal to WACC, the bracketed term on the right in the second row of Equation 7-8 is greater than or equal to 1, so its infinite summation is equal to infinity. We really want students to avoid this mistake, so please **don't use Equation 7-8 if $g_L \geq$ WACC!**

There are two related cases for the constant growth model. The first is when constant growth begins at t = 1, and the second is when constant growth begins at t = 0.

CASE 1: APPLICATION OF THE CONSTANT GROWTH MODEL WHEN CONSTANT GROWTH BEGINS AT t = 1

Let's apply the constant growth model to a company with an expected free cash flow of $105 at t = 1 and an expected constant growth rate of 5% thereafter. Suppose the weighted average cost of capital is 9%. The growth rate is less than the cost of capital, so we can use Equation 7-8 to estimate the value of operations:

$$V_{op}(g_L \text{ for } t = 1 \text{ to } \infty) = \frac{FCF_1}{WACC - g_L}$$

$$= \frac{\$105}{0.09 - 0.05} = \$2,625$$

CASE 2: APPLICATION OF THE CONSTANT GROWTH MODEL WHEN CONSTANT GROWTH BEGINS AT t = 0

Equation 7-8 is valid any time we have an estimate of the first cash flow and the expected growth is constant thereafter. But Equation 7-8 is also valid if constant growth begins immediately. In this situation, we can use Equation 7-6 to estimate the first expected free cash flow using the most recent actual free cash flow:

$$FCF_1 = FCF_0(1 + g_L)$$

Substituting this into Equation 7-8 provides a way to calculate the present value of future cash flows if constant growth begins immediately:

$$V_{op,0}(g_L \text{ for } t = 0 \text{ to } \infty) = \frac{FCF_1}{WACC - g_L} = \frac{FCF_0(1 + g_L)}{WACC - g_L} \qquad (7\text{-}9)$$

For example, suppose a company's most recent free cash flow was $200, and it expects FCF to begin growing immediately at a 7% constant growth rate and that the cost of capital is 12%. Again, noting that the growth rate is less than the cost of capital, we can apply the constant growth model in Equation 7-9 to find the value of operations:

$$V_{op,0}(g_L \text{ for } t = 0 \text{ to } \infty) = \frac{FCF_0(1 + g_L)}{WACC - g_L}$$

$$= \frac{\$200(1 + 0.07)}{0.12 - 0.07}$$

$$= \$4,280$$

7-5b How to Avoid Common Mistakes When Applying the Constant Growth Model

Here are three mistakes to avoid when using the constant growth model. First, the model only applies if the expected growth rate is constant *and* is less than the weighted average cost of capital. If growth is greater than the cost of capital, you must use the multistage model that we describe in the next section.

Second, the constant growth models are calculating the present value of all future cash flows from t = 1 to infinity, *not from t = 0 to infinity!* The cash flow at t = 0 has just occurred, so it is in the past and is not included in the present value of *future* cash flows. Even though the numerator of Equation 7-9 shows FCF_0, it is shown there only because it is used to estimate FCF_1, not because FCF_0 is included in the present value of future free cash flows.

Third, don't use Equation 7-9 if constant growth doesn't begin immediately. For example, suppose $FCF_0 = \$963$, FCF_1 is estimated to be $1,040, WACC is 9%, and the expected growth rate from t = 1 and thereafter is 4%. Notice that the growth rate from t = 0 to t = 1 is 8% = ($1040 − $963)/$963. However, the value of operations is the present value of *future* free cash flows, and those future free cash flows beyond t = 1 are growing at a constant rate of 4% even though the current FCF is growing at 8%.

Therefore, you must use Equation 7-8 instead of Equation 7-9 to find the value of operations, as follows:

$$V_{op,0}(g_L \text{ for } t = 1 \text{ to } \infty) = \frac{FCF_1}{WACC - g_L}$$

$$= \frac{\$1,040}{0.09 - 0.04} = \$20,800$$

Now suppose that the current free cash flow is $1,000 and all the other inputs are the same as in the example. The current free cash flow is expected to grow by 4% = ($1,040 − $1,000)/$1,000 from t = 0 to t = 1, and then continue to grow at a constant rate of 4%. In this case, you could use either Equation 7-8 or Equation 7-9 because $FCF_1 = FCF_0(1 + g_L)$.

SELF-TEST

A company expects to have FCF of $300 in 1 year, which is expected to grow at a constant rate of 3% forever. If the WACC is 11%, what is the value of operations? **($3,750)**

A company's most recent free cash flow was $270. The company expects to have a FCF in 1 year of $300, which is expected to grow at a constant rate of 3% forever. If the WACC is 11%, what is the value of operations? **($3,750)**

A company's most recent free cash flow was $600 and is expected to grow at a constant rate of 4% forever. If the WACC is 10%, what is the value of operations? **($10,400)**

7-6 The Multistage Model: Valuation When Expected Short-Term Free Cash Flow Grows at a Nonconstant Rate

The annual growth in expected free cash flows of most companies is nonconstant for years before eventually leveling off at a sustainable long-term constant growth rate. Because the short-term growth rates are nonconstant, we cannot immediately apply the constant growth model from the previous section. However, we can use the **multi-stage valuation model** to estimate the value of operations, as described in the following steps:

STEP 1: Forecast expected free cash flows and calculate the annual growth rates for each year in the forecast. Continue forecasting additional years until the growth rate in FCF is expected to become constant. The last year in the forecast is called the **forecast horizon**. It is also called the **horizon date** or the **terminal date** (because it is at the end of the explicit forecast, not because the free cash flows terminate). For companies in mature, highly competitive markets, you may need to forecast only a few years. For companies in high-growth industries, you may need to forecast 15 to 25 years.

STEP 2: Because expected growth is constant after the horizon date, you can apply the constant growth model from the previous section to estimate the value of operations at the horizon year. This is called the **horizon value**, and it is the value of all free cash flows *beyond* the horizon discounted back to the horizon. In other words, it is how much the operations would be worth if they were sold immediately after receiving the FCF at the horizon date. This is also called the **terminal value** (because it is at the end of the explicit forecast) or the **continuing value** (because it is the value if the operating assets continue to be used rather than be liquidated).

STEP 3: Create a time line with the free cash flows for each year up to the horizon date. The time line should also include the horizon value at the horizon date. This means there will be two cash flows on the horizon date, the free cash flow for that year and the previously calculated horizon value.

STEP 4: Discount the cash flows in the time line using the weighted average cost of capital. The result is the estimated value of operations as of t = 0.

The following example illustrates this approach.

7-6a The Forecast Period and the Horizon Value

We will forecast MicroDrive's free cash flows later in the chapter, but for now let's focus on Thurman Corporation, a fast-growing company in the health care industry. Thurman's expected free cash flows (in millions) for the next four years are shown here:

Year	0	1	2	3	4
FCF		−$20	$80	$100	$110
Growth in FCF				25%	10%

Thurman expects to have a negative FCF in Year 1 due to the company's rapid expansion. Free cash flows become positive at Year 2 and grow rapidly for a couple of years. Thurman expects competition and market saturation to reduce its growth rate after Year 4 to 5% for all years in the foreseeable future. This is why Thurman ends its explicit forecast period at Year 4.

Because growth is constant after Year 4, we can apply the constant growth formula at Year 4 to find the present value of all the cash flows from Year 5 to infinity discounted back to Year 4. This result is the horizon value at Year 4, HV_4. If growth in FCF is expected to be constant after Year t, the general formula for the horizon value at Year t is:

$$HV_t = \frac{FCF_t(1 + g_L)}{WACC - g_L}$$

(7-10)

Thurman's cost of capital is 15%. We can apply Equation 7-10 to estimate Thurman's horizon value at Year 4:

$$HV_4 = \frac{FCF_4(1 + g_L)}{WACC - g_L}$$

$$= \frac{\$110(1 + 0.05)}{0.15 - 0.05}$$

$$= \$1,155 \text{ million}$$

FIGURE 7-3
Thurman Corporation's Value of Operations (Millions of Dollars)

	A	B	C	D	E	F	G	H
228	INPUTS:							
229	g_L =	5%						
230	WACC =	15%		Projections				
231	Year	0	1	2	3	4		
232	FCF		−$20.00	$80.00	$100.00	$110.00	→ → → ↴	
233			↓	↓	↓	↓		↓
234			FCF_1	FCF_2	FCF_3	FCF_4		HV = $V_{op(t=4)}$
235			⎯⎯⎯	⎯⎯⎯	⎯⎯⎯	⎯⎯⎯		↓
236			$(1+WACC)^1$	$(1+WACC)^2$	$(1+WACC)^3$	$(1+WACC)^4$		$FCF_4(1+g_L)$
237			↓	↓	↓	↓		⎯⎯⎯⎯
238			↓	↓	↓	↓		$(WACC-g_L)$
239			↓	↓	↓	↓		↓
240			↓	↓	↓	↓		**$115.500**
241		−$17.391 ← ←↵	↓	↓	↓	↓		10.00%
242	PVs of FCFs	$60.491 ←←←←	←↵	↓	↓	↓		↓
243		$65.752 ←←←←	←←←←	←↵	↓	↓		$1,155.000
244		$62.893 ←←←←	←←←←	←←←←	←↵	↓		↓
245	PV of HV	$660.375 ←←←←	←←←←	←←←←	←←←←	$1,155.000	←←←↵	
246		↓				= ⎯⎯⎯		
247	V_{op} =	$832.12				$(1+WACC)^4$		

Source: See the file ***Ch07 Tool Kit.xlsx***. Numbers are reported as rounded values for clarity but are calculated using *Excel's* full precision. Thus, intermediate calculations using the figure's rounded values will be inexact.

resource

See Ch07 Tool Kit.xlsx for all calculations.

Figure 7-3 summarizes the calculation of the horizon value. We explain the other steps shown in Figure 7-3 in the continuing description of the multistage model.

7-6b The Current Value of Operations

Now that we have estimated Thurman's horizon value, we can lay out a time line of the free cash flows and the horizon value:

Year	0	1	2	3	4
FCF		−$20	$80	$100	$110
Horizon value at Year 4, HV_4					$1,155

The current value of operations ($V_{op,0}$) is the present value of all future free cash flows discounted back to Year 0. We estimate the current value of operations in three steps: (1) Estimate the present value of the free cash flows in the forecast period. (2) Estimate the present value of the horizon value. (3) Add the present value of the free cash flows to the present value of the horizon value. Here is the intuition: The owner of the operations collects the FCF from Year 1 to Year 4 and then immediately sells the operations one second after collecting the FCF at Year 4. The purchaser pays a price at Year 4 equal to the present value of the FCF beyond Year 4 discounted back to Year 4. Therefore, the current value to the owner is the present value of the free cash flows and "sales" price that the owner expects to receive. Notice that this is similar to finding the value of a bond, which is equal to the present value of its coupons plus the present value of the par value paid at maturity.[5]

If the horizon date is Year T, then the current value of operations is:

$$V_{op,0} = \sum_{t=1}^{T} \frac{FCF_t}{(1 + WACC)^t} + \frac{HV_T}{(1 + WACC)^T} \tag{7-11}$$

Let's apply this to Thurman Corporation. The present value of the free cash flows from Years 1 through 4 is:

$$
\begin{aligned}
PV \text{ of } FCF &= \frac{FCF_1}{(1 + WACC)^1} + \frac{FCF_2}{(1 + WACC)^2} + \frac{FCF_3}{(1 + WACC)^3} + \frac{FCF_4}{(1 + WACC)^4} \\
&= \frac{-\$20}{(1 + 0.15)^1} + \frac{\$80}{(1 + 0.15)^2} + \frac{\$100}{(1 + 0.15)^3} + \frac{\$110}{(1 + 0.15)^4} \\
&= \$171.745
\end{aligned}
$$

The present value of the horizon value is:

$$
\begin{aligned}
\text{Present value of } HV_4 &= \frac{HV_4}{(1 + WACC)^4} \\
&= \frac{\$1,155}{(1 + 0.15)^4} = \$660.375
\end{aligned}
$$

The value of operations at Year 0 is equal to the sum of the present value of the horizon value and the present value of the free cash flows. Using Equation 7-11, we can estimate Thurman's value of operations:

$$
\begin{aligned}
V_{op,0} &= \sum_{t=1}^{4} \frac{FCF_t}{(1 + WACC)^t} + \frac{HV_4}{(1 + WACC)^4} \\
&= \$171.745 + \$660.375 \\
&= \$832.12
\end{aligned}
$$

We apply this approach in the next section to estimate MicroDrive's value.[6]

---

[5]You may have noticed that we could have defined the horizon date at Year 3 because we have an estimate of the Year 4 free cash flow, which is expected to grow at a constant rate thereafter. However, we recommend defining the horizon date as the last date in the forecast period even if growth becomes constant at or prior to this date because we have found that doing so leads to fewer errors. For the interested reader, we illustrate this approach in the file *Ch07 Tool Kit.xlsx*.

[6]When using a financial calculator, it requires fewer steps if you combine the free cash flow in the last year and the horizon value into a single cash flow. For example, you could find Thurman's value of operations as:

$$
\begin{aligned}
V_{op,0} &= \frac{FCF_1}{(1 + WACC)^1} + \frac{FCF_2}{(1 + WACC)^2} + \frac{FCF_3}{(1 + WACC)^3} + \frac{(FCF_4 + HV_4)}{(1 + WACC)^4} \\
&= \frac{-\$20}{(1 + 0.15)^1} + \frac{\$80}{(1 + 0.15)^2} + \frac{\$100}{(1 + 0.15)^3} + \frac{(\$110 + \$1,155)}{(1 + 0.15)^4} \\
&= \$832.12
\end{aligned}
$$

This procedure saves a step in the calculations. However, combining cash flows makes it easier to make an error, so we recommend using this approach only if you are extremely careful and confident.

What is the horizon value? Why is it also called the terminal value *or* continuing value?

A company expects to have FCF of $600 at Year 10, which is expected to grow at a constant rate of 4% thereafter. If the WACC is 8%, what is the value of operations at Year 10, HV_{10}? **($15,600)**

A company expects FCF of −$10 million at Year 1 and FCF of $20 million at Year 2; after Year 2, FCF is expected to grow at a 5% rate. If the WACC is 10%, then what is the horizon value of operations, $V_{op(Year\,2)}$? **($420 million)** *What is the current value of operations, $V_{op(Year\,0)}$?* **($354.55 million)**

7-7 Application of the FCF Valuation Model to MicroDrive

We now apply the free cash flow valuation model to MicroDrive, beginning with a simple approach to estimate free cash flows.

7-7a Forecasting MicroDrive's Free Cash Flows

We will forecast MicroDrive's full set of financial statements in Chapter 12, but for purposes of valuation we need only forecast certain components of the financial statements, the ones that determine free cash flows. In particular, we will forecast sales, net operating profit after taxes (NOPAT), and total net operating capital. But before we plunge into the forecast, let's take a look at MicroDrive's current situation.

MICRODRIVE'S CURRENT SITUATION

Figure 7-4 shows MicroDrive's most recent financial statements and selected additional data. Chapters 2 and 3 explain ratio analyses in detail, but here we focus on the items that are required to forecast free cash flows.

resource

See Ch07 Tool Kit.xlsx for all calculations.

Figure 7-5 shows the calculation of free cash flow and other selected performance measures for the previous two years. We can see that MicroDrive's return on invested capital (ROIC) is much lower than that of its industry peers (10.00% versus 13.19%). MicroDrive's operating profitability has fallen so that it is now lower than the industry average (6.00% versus 6.75%). MicroDrive's asset utilization efficiency has drastically worsened, as shown by the increase in its capital requirement ratio (which means that MicroDrive now requires more capital to generate a dollar of sales), and is significantly worse than the industry average (60% versus 51%). We first will forecast MicroDrive's free cash flows assuming that these ratios remain unchanged and then show how MicroDrive's value of operations would be affected by improvements in these operating ratios.

FORECASTING SALES, NET OPERATING PROFIT AFTER TAXES, AND TOTAL NET OPERATING CAPITAL

The first step is to forecast sales. MicroDrive's managers estimate that sales will initially grow at a 10% rate but will decline to a sustainable long-term growth rate of 5% due to market saturation and competition; see Panel A in Figure 7-6 for the forecasted sales growth rates in each year of the five-year forecast period. Had MicroDrive's managers projected nonconstant growth for more than five years, new columns for additional years would be added to Figure 7-6 until the growth rate levels out. Keep in mind that this is just a preliminary estimate and that it is easy to make changes in the *Excel* model (after doing the hard work to build the model!).

MicroDrive's managers initially assume that the operating profitability ratio (OP) and the capital requirement ratio (CR) will remain unchanged. We begin with this Status

FIGURE 7-4

MicroDrive's Most Recent Financial Statements (Millions of Shares and Dollars, Except for per Share Data)

	A	B	C	D	E	F
260	INCOME STATEMENTS			BALANCE SHEETS		
261		2018	2019	*Assets*	2018	2019
262	Net sales	$4,800	$5,000	Cash	$102	$100
263	COGS (excl. depr.)	3,710	3,900	ST Investments	40	10
264	Depreciation	180	200	Accounts receivable	384	500
265	Other operating expenses	470	500	Inventories	774	1,000
266	EBIT	$440	$400	Total CA	$1,300	$1,610
267	Interest expense	40	60	Net PP&E	1,780	2,000
268	Pre-tax earnings	$400	$340	Total assets	$3,080	$3,610
269	Taxes (25%)	100	85			
270	NI before pref. div.	$300	$255	*Liabilities and Equity*		
271	Preferred div.	$7	$7	Accounts payable	$180	$200
272	Net income	$293	$248	Notes payable	28	150
273				Accruals	370	400
274	*Other Data*			Total CL	$578	$750
275	Common dividends	$59.4	$60.0	Long-term bonds	350	520
276	Addition to RE	$234	$188	Total liabilities	$928	$1,270
277	Tax rate	25%	25%	Preferred stock	100	100
278	Number of common shares	60	60	Common stock	500	500
279	Price per share (P)	$45.00	$31.00	Retained earnings	1,552	1,740
280	Earnings per share (EPS)	$4.88	$4.13	Total common equity	$2,052	$2,240
281	Dividends per share (DPS)	$0.99	$1.00	Total liabs. & equity	$3,080	$3,610
282	Dividend yield (DPS/P)	2.2%	3.2%			
283						
284	Weighted average					
285	cost of capital (WACC)	11.50%	11.50%			

Source: See the file *Ch07 Tool Kit.xlsx.* Numbers are reported as rounded values for clarity but are calculated using *Excel*'s full precision. Thus, intermediate calculations using the figure's rounded values will be inexact.

Note: The weighted average cost of capital is the return that the company must generate in order to fairly compensate investors.

resource

See Ch07 Tool Kit.xlsx for all calculations.

Quo scenario (as shown in cell A327), but we also will explore other scenarios later in the chapter. Panel A of Figure 7-6 shows the input ratios, including actual recent values of the ratios for industry peers (the silver section), actual values for MicroDrive's past two years, and forecasted values for MicroDrive's 5-year forecast. The blue section shows inputs for the first year and inputs for any subsequent years that differ from the previous year.

Panel B of Figure 7-6 begins with the forecast of net sales based on the previous year's sales and the forecasted growth rate in sales. For example, the forecast of net sales for 2020 is:

$$\text{Sales}_{2020} = (1 + g_{2019,2020})\text{Sales}_{2019}$$
$$= (1 + 0.10)(\$5,000) = \$5,500$$

The next row shows the forecast of net operating profit after taxes. We will forecast NOPAT's separate components in Chapter 12, but for now we assume that the NOPAT for a particular year will be proportional to the sales for that year. This means we can forecast NOPAT as the product of sales and the operating profitability ratio. For example, the forecast of NOPAT for 2020 is:

$$\text{NOPAT}_{2020} = (\text{Sales}_{2020})(\text{OP}_{2020})$$
$$= (\$5,500)(0.06) = \$330$$

FIGURE 7-5
Key Performance Measures for MicroDrive (Millions, Except for per Share Data)

	A	B	C	D	E	F	G
					MicroDrive		**Industry**
292					2018	2019	2019
293							
294	*Calculating Net Operating Profit after Taxes (NOPAT)*						
295	NOPAT = EBIT(1 – T)				$330	$300	
296	*Calculating Net Operating Working Capital (NOWC)*						
297	Operating current assets				$1,260	$1,600	
298	– Operating current liabilities				$550	$600	
299	NOWC				$710	$1,000	
300	*Calculating Total Net Operating Capital (OpCap)*						
301	NOWC				$710	$1,000	
302	+ Net PP&E				$1,780	$2,000	
303	OpCap				$2,490	$3,000	
304	Investment in operating capital					$510	
305	*Calculating Free Cash Flow (FCF)*						
306	FCF = NOPAT – Investment in operating capital					–$210	
307	*Calculating Return on Invested Capital (ROIC)*						
308	ROIC = NOPAT/Total net operating capital				13.25%	10.00%	13.19%
309	*Calculating the Operating Profitability Ratio (OP)*						
310	OP = NOPAT/Sales				6.88%	6.00%	6.75%
311	*Calculating the Capital Requirement Ratio (CR)*						
312	CR = (Total net operating capital)/Sales				51.88%	60.00%	51.19%

Source: See the file *Ch07 Tool Kit.xlsx*. Numbers are reported as rounded values for clarity but are calculated using *Excel*'s full precision. Thus, intermediate calculations using the figure's rounded values will be inexact.

FIGURE 7-6
MicroDrive's Forecast of Operations for the Selected Scenario (Millions of Dollars, Except for per Share Data)

	A	B	C	D	E	F	G	H	I
	Status Quo	**Industry**	**MicroDrive**			**MicroDrive**			
327		**Actual**	**Actual**			**Forecast**			
328	**Panel A:**								
329	*Operating Ratios*	2019	2018	2019	2020	2021	2022	2023	2024
330	g = Sales growth rate		10%	4%	10%	8%	7%	5%	5%
331	OP = NOPAT/Sales	6.75%	6.9%	6%	6.00%	6.00%	6.00%	6.00%	6.00%
332	CR = OpCap/Sales	51.2%	51.9%	60%	60.00%	60.00%	60.00%	60.00%	60.00%
333	Tax rate	25%	25%	25%	25.00%	25.00%	25.00%	25.00%	25.00%
334	**Panel B:**			**Actual**			**Forecast**		
335	*Operating Items*			*2019*	2020	2021	2022	2023	2024
336	Net sales			*$5,000*	$5,500	$5,940	$6,356	$6,674	$7,007
337	Net operating profit after taxes			*$300*	$330	$356	$381	$400	$420
338	Total net operating capital (OpCap)			*$3,000*	$3,300	$3,564	$3,813	$4,004	$4,204
339	FCF = NOPAT – Investment in OpCap			*–$210*	$30	$92	$132	$210	$220
340	Growth in FCF					208%	43%	59%	5%
341	ROIC = NOPAT/OpCap			*10.00%*	10%	10%	10%	10%	10%

Source: See the file *Ch07 Tool Kit.xlsx*. Numbers are reported as rounded values for clarity but are calculated using *Excel*'s full precision. Thus, intermediate calculations using the figure's rounded values will be inexact.

To support additional sales, we assume that total net operating capital (OpCap) must grow. We forecast OpCap's individual components in Chapter 12, but for now we assume that OpCap will be proportional to sales, so the forecast is equal to sales multiplied by the capital requirement ratio, CR. For example, the forecast of OpCap for 2020 is:

$$OpCap_{2020} = (Sales_{2020})(CR_{2020})$$
$$= (\$5,500)(0.60) = \$3,300$$

With forecasts of NOPAT and total net operating capital, it is straightforward to calculate the forecasted FCF. For example, the forecasted FCF for 2020 is:

$$FCF_{2020} = NOPAT_{2020} - (OpCap_{2020} - OpCap_{2019})$$
$$= \$330 - (\$3,300 - \$3,000)$$
$$= \$330 - \$300$$
$$= \$30$$

Figure 7-6 shows the estimated free cash flows for each year in the forecast period. Notice that FCF is growing at the same rate as sales by the last year in the forecast period and that the input ratios for operating profit and capital utilization have not changed in the two years prior to the end of the forecast period. Therefore, we can be sure that the growth in FCF has leveled off to the long-term growth rate of 5%, and we don't need to forecast any additional years. Had the input ratios and growth rates not been stable by the end of five years, then we would have continued to forecast more years until they were stable.

Notice that the forecasted ROIC of 10% is identical to the most recent actual ROIC. This makes sense, because the forecasted inputs for the operations (i.e., the OP and CR ratios) are the same as those in the most recent year. In other words, if operations aren't changing, then the ROIC shouldn't change.

Although Figure 7-6 reports rounded values to avoid unnecessary distractions, we use *Excel*'s full precision to determine its value of operations; see ***Ch07 Tool Kit.xlsx*** for the actual calculations. Figure 7-7, shown next, applies to MicroDrive the same procedures previously used for Thurman Corporation in Figure 7-3. We begin by estimating the horizon value.

7-7b MicroDrive's Horizon Value

We apply the horizon value formula at the last year in the forecast (2024) because expected growth is constant afterward for the foreseeable future.[7] Recall from Figure 7-4 that MicroDrive's WACC for 2019 and years thereafter is 11.5%. Using Equation 7-10, we estimate MicroDrive's horizon value as the present value of all the cash flows from 2025 to infinity when discounted back to 2024. (We report more significant digits here than in Figures 7-6 and 7-7 to demonstrate that the procedures are correct.) MicroDrive's horizon value is:

$$HV_t = \frac{FCF_t(1 + g_L)}{WACC - g_L}$$

$$HV_{2024} = \frac{FCF_{2024}(1 + g_L)}{WACC - g_L}$$

$$= \frac{\$220.23(1 + 0.05)}{0.115 - 0.05} = \$3,557.6$$

---

[7]We could have defined the horizon date to be 2022 because we have an estimate of the 2023 free cash flow, which is expected to grow at a constant rate thereafter. But as we stated previously, we recommend defining the horizon date as the last date in the forecast period even if growth becomes constant at or prior to this date because we have found that doing so leads to fewer errors.

FIGURE 7-7
MicroDrive, Inc.'s Value of Operations (Millions of Dollars)

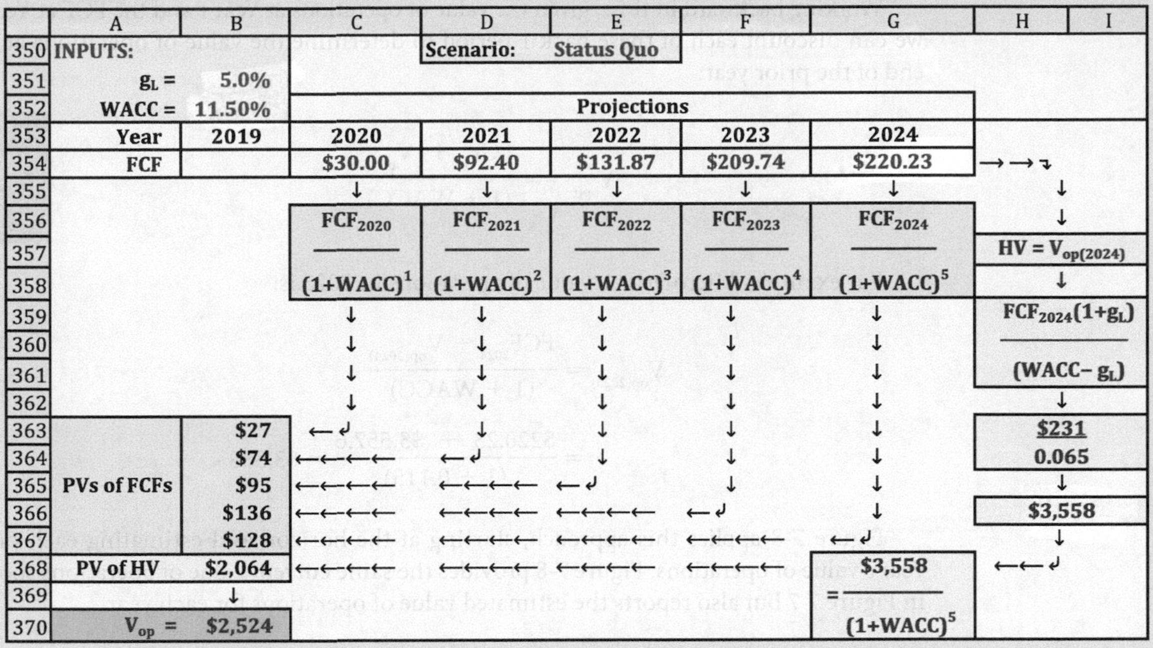

Source: See the file **Ch07 Tool Kit.xlsx**. Numbers are reported as rounded values for clarity but are calculated using *Excel's* full precision. Thus, intermediate calculations using the figure's rounded values will be inexact.

resource

See *Ch07 Tool Kit.xlsx* for all calculations.

7-7c MicroDrive's Current Value of Operations

The current value of operations is the present value of the FCF during the forecast period plus the present value of the horizon value: MicroDrive's current value of operations is shown here and in Figure 7-7:

$$V_{op} = \frac{FCF_1}{(1+WACC)^1} + \frac{FCF_2}{(1+WACC)^2} + \frac{FCF_3}{(1+WACC)^3} + \frac{FCF_4}{(1+WACC)^4} + \frac{FCF_5}{(1+WACC)^5} + \frac{HV_5}{(1+WACC)^5}$$

$$V_{op} = \frac{\$30.00}{(1+0.115)^1} + \frac{\$92.40}{(1+0.115)^2} + \frac{\$131.87}{(1+0.115)^3} + \frac{\$209.74}{(1+0.115)^4} + \frac{\$220.23}{(1+0.115)^5} + \frac{\$3,557.6}{(1+0.115)^5}$$

$$V_{op} = \$460 + \$2,064 = \$2,524$$

7-7d MicroDrive's Projected Annual Value of Operations

Sometimes it is useful to have an estimate of the annual projected value of operations, not just the current value of operations. For example, preparing for a major stock or bond issuance might take well over a year. Therefore, a company might like to have an estimate of its value of operations at the projected issuance date.

By definition, the value of operations at the horizon is equal to the horizon value: Both measures are equal to the present value of all future expected cash flows *beyond* the horizon date. Therefore, if the horizon occurs at Year T, we can use Equation 7-10 to estimate the horizon value at Year T, which also provides the value of operations at Year T.

Working backward in time, given the value of operations at Year t and the FCF at Year t, we can discount each of these back 1 period to determine the value of operations at the end of the prior year:

$$V_{op(t-1)} = \frac{FCF_t + V_{op(t)}}{(1 + WACC)}$$

(7-12)

For example, MicroDrive's value of operations in 2023 is:

$$V_{op(2023)} = \frac{FCF_{2024} + V_{op(2024)}}{(1 + WACC)}$$

$$= \frac{\$220.23 + \$3,557.6}{(1 + 0.115)} = \$3,388$$

Figure 7-8 applies this approach, starting at the horizon and estimating each prior year's value of operations. Figure 7-8 provides the same current value of operations shown in Figure 7-7 but also reports the estimated value of operations for each year.

7-7e MicroDrive's Intrinsic Value per Share of Common Stock

MicroDrive's balance sheets in Figure 7-4 show that it has $10 short-term investments, $150 in notes payable, $520 in long-term bonds, and $100 in preferred stock. We can use these values, along with MicroDrive's value of operations, to estimate its total intrinsic value, intrinsic value of equity, and intrinsic stock price, as shown in the following sections.

FIGURE 7-8

MicroDrive, Inc.'s Projected Annual Value of Operations (Millions of Dollars)

	A	B	C	D	E	F	G
415	INPUTS:			Scenario:	Status Quo		
416	g_L =	5%					
417	WACC =	11.50%			Projections		
418	Year	2019	2020	2021	2022	2023	2024
419	FCF		$30.00	$92.40	$131.87	$209.74	$220.23
420	HV = $V_{op(2024)}$[a]						$3,558
421	$V_{op(t)}$[b]	$2,524	$2,784	$3,012	$3,227	$3,388	$3,558

Source: See the file **Ch07 Tool Kit.xlsx**. Numbers are reported as rounded values for clarity but are calculated using *Excel*'s full precision. Thus, intermediate calculations using the figure's rounded values will be inexact.

Notes:

[a]HV = $[FCF_{2024}(1 + g_L)]/(WACC - g_L)$

[b]$V_{op(t)} = [FCF_{t+1} + V_{op(t+1)}]/(1 + WACC)$

TOTAL INTRINSIC VALUE

A company's total intrinsic value is the value of operations plus the value of short-term investments (assuming the company owns no other nonoperating assets). From Equation 7-3, MicroDrive's total intrinsic value is:

$$\text{Total intrinsic value} = \text{Value of operations} + \text{Short-term investments}$$
$$= \$2,524 + \$10 = \$2,534$$

INTRINSIC VALUE OF EQUITY

The estimated intrinsic value of equity, shown in Equation 7-4, is the remaining value after subtracting the claims of debtholders and preferred stockholders from the total intrinsic value:

$$\text{Intrinsic value of equity} = \text{Total intrinsic value} - \text{All debt} - \text{Preferred stock}$$
$$= \$2,534 - (\$150 + \$520) - \$100$$
$$= \$1,764$$

INTRINSIC STOCK PRICE

From Equation 7-5, the estimated intrinsic stock price is equal to the intrinsic value of equity divided by the number of shares. MicroDrive has 60 million shares of common stock, so the estimated intrinsic stock price is:

$$\text{Intrinsic stock price} = (\text{Intrinsic value of equity})/(\text{Number of shares})$$
$$= \$1,764/60 = \$29.40 \text{ per share}$$

Figure 7-9 summarizes these calculations.

MicroDrive's intrinsic stock price is $29.40, which is about 5% lower than its $31 price observed on December 31, 2019. What can account for this difference? First, keep in mind that MicroDrive's standard deviation of stock returns is about 50%, as estimated in Chapter 6. This high standard deviation makes the 5% difference between the estimated

FIGURE 7-9
MicroDrive, Inc.'s Intrinsic Stock Price (Millions, Except for per Share Data)

	A	B	C	D	E	F	G
474	INPUTS:						
475	g_L =	5%					
476	WACC =	11.50%					
477	Year =	2020	2021	2022	2023	2024	
478	Projected FCF =	$30.00	$92.40	$131.87	$209.74	$220.23	
479							
480	Horizon Value:				Value of operations	$2,524	
481					+ ST investments	$10	
482	$HV_{2024} = \dfrac{FCF_{2024}(1+g_L)}{(WACC - g_L)} =$		$3,558		Estimated total intrinsic value	$2,534	
483					– All debt	$670	
484	Value of Operations:				– Preferred stock	$100	
485	Present value of HV	$2,064.31		Estimated intrinsic value of equity		$1,764	
486	+ Present value of FCF	$459.85		÷ Number of shares		60	
487	Value of operations =	$2,524.16		Estimated intrinsic stock price =		$29.40	

Source: See the file *Ch07 Tool Kit.xlsx*. Numbers are reported as rounded values for clarity but are calculated using *Excel*'s full precision. Thus, intermediate calculations using the figure's rounded values will be inexact.

and actual stock price look pretty small. It could well be that the estimated intrinsic value would have been exactly equal to the actual stock price on a day during the week before or after December 31, 2019. Second, it could be that investors (who determine the price through their buying and selling activities) expect MicroDrive's performance in the future to be better than the Status Quo scenario.

We will address investor expectations in the following sections and use MicroDrive's free cash flow valuation model to answer three important questions. First, how much of a company's value is based on short-term cash flows versus long-term cash flows? Second, how can a company identify the most important factors in its free cash flow valuation model? Third, does high market volatility necessarily imply irrational investors?

SELF-TEST

Cathey Corporation currently has sales of $1,000, which are expected to grow by 10% from Year 0 to Year 1 and by 4% from Year 1 to Year 2. The company currently has an operating profitability ratio (OP) of 7% and a capital requirement ratio (CR) of 50% and expects to maintain these ratios at their current levels. The current level of total net operating capital (OpCap) is $510. Use these inputs to forecast free cash flow (FCF) for Years 1 and 2. (Hint: You must first forecast sales, net operating profit after taxes (NOPAT), and total net operating capital (OpCap) for each year.)
($37.00 and $58.08)

Cathey Corporation has a 12% weighted average cost of capital. Cathey's free cash flows, estimated in the previous question, are expected to grow at 4% beginning at Year 2 and thereafter. What is the horizon value (use Year 2 for the horizon)? What is the current value of operations?
($755.04 and $681.25)

Cathey Corporation has $80 in short-term investments, $20 in short-term debt, $140 in long-term debt, $30 in preferred stock, and 10 shares of common stock outstanding. Use the value of operations from the previous question to estimate the intrinsic common stock price per share. **($57.13)**

7-8 Do Stock Values Reflect Long-Term or Short-Term Cash Flows?

Managers often complain that the stock market is shortsighted and that investors care only about conditions over the next few years. Let's use MicroDrive's valuation to test this assertion. Previously we estimated MicroDrive's current value of operations to be $2,524 million, with $460 of the value due to free cash flows occurring in Years 1 to 5 and $2,064 due to free cash flows beyond Year 5 (i.e., the present value of the horizon value).

If we divide the present value due to cash flows beyond the horizon by the total value of operations, we can identify the percent of value due to long-term cash flows occurring more than 5 years in the future:

$$\text{Percent of value due to long-term cash flows} = \frac{\$2,064}{\$2,524}$$

$$= 0.82 = 82\%$$

This shows that 82% of MicroDrive's value is due to cash flows occurring more than 5 years in the future, which means that managers can affect stock values more by working to increase long-term cash flows than by focusing on short-term flows. This situation holds for most companies, not just MicroDrive. Indeed, a number of professors and consulting firms have used actual company data to show that more than 80% of a typical company's stock price is due to cash flows expected more than 5 years in the future.

This brings up an interesting question. If most of a stock's value is due to long-term cash flows, then why do managers and analysts pay so much attention to quarterly earnings? Part of the answer lies in the information conveyed by short-term earnings. For example, when actual quarterly earnings are lower than expected because a company has increased its research and development (R&D) expenditures and not because of operational problems, studies have shown that the stock price probably won't decline and may actually increase. This makes sense, because R&D should increase future cash flows. On the other hand, if quarterly earnings are lower than expected because customers don't like the company's new products, then this new information will have negative implications for future cash flows and the long-term growth rate. As we show later in this chapter, even small changes in expected long-term growth can lead to large changes in stock prices. Therefore, short-term quarterly earnings themselves might not contribute a large portion to a stock's price, but the information they convey about future prospects can be extremely important.

Another reason many managers focus on short-term earnings is that some firms pay managerial bonuses on the basis of current earnings rather than stock prices (which reflect future cash flows). For these managers, the concern with quarterly earnings is not due to their effect on stock prices—it's due to their effect on bonuses!

Many apparent puzzles in finance can be explained either by managerial compensation systems or by peculiar features of the Tax Code. So, if you can't explain a firm's behavior in terms of economic logic, look to compensation plans or taxes as possible explanations.

SELF-TEST

Are stock values more affected by short-term cash flows or by long-term cash flows?

Describe two reasons why managers might focus on quarterly earnings.

7-9 Value-Based Management: Using the Free Cash Flow Valuation Model to Identify Value Drivers

The key inputs to the free cash flow valuation model are (1) the most recent level of sales; (2) the most recent level of total net operating capital; (3) the projected sales growth rates; (4) the projected operating profitability ratios; (5) the projected capital requirement ratios; and (6) the weighted average cost of capital. Changes to any of these inputs will cause the intrinsic value of operations to change.

Value drivers are the subset of inputs that managers are able to influence through strategic choices and execution of the resulting business plans. Because managers can't change the past, the most recent level of sales and operating capital are *not* value drivers. This means that growth rates, operating profitability, capital requirements, and the cost of capital *are* the value drivers.

Each of these value drivers has an impact on the intrinsic value of operations and the intrinsic stock price. However, the degree of impact varies and depends on each company's particular situation. Therefore, managers must be able to identify the most important value drivers for their companies in order to make good strategic, operating, and financial decisions. **Value-based management** is the systematic use of the free cash flow valuation model to identify value drivers and to guide managerial and strategic decisions.

MicroDrive's managers are considering several possible strategic initiatives. We can apply value-based management techniques to assess these initiatives and identify those that add value. In particular, we can use the free cash flow valuation model we developed for MicroDrive to identify its most important value drivers by estimating how the inputs (sales growth, operating profitability, capital requirements, and cost of capital) affect the value of operations and intrinsic stock price. It is very easy to do this in *Excel* by using the

FIGURE 7-10
Value Drivers for MicroDrive, Inc. (Millions, Except for per Share Data)

	A	B	C	D	E	F	G	H	I
568						Scenario			
569 570 571 572 573			(1) Status Quo	(2) Higher Sales Growth (Only)	(3) Higher Operating Profitability (Only)	(4) Better Capital Utilization (Only)	(5) Improve Growth and OP	(6) Improve Growth and CR	(7) Improve Growth, OP, and CR
574	**Inputs**								
575	Sales growth in 1st year		10%	11%	10%	10%	11%	11%	11%
576	Sales growth in 2nd year		8%	9%	8%	8%	9%	9%	9%
577	Sales growth in 3rd year		7%	8%	7%	7%	8%	8%	8%
578	Long-term sales growth (g_L)		5%	6%	5%	5%	6%	6%	6%
579	Operating profitability (OP)		6%	6%	7%	6%	7%	6%	7%
580	Capital requirement (CR)		60%	60%	60%	51%	60%	51%	51%
581	Weighted average cost of capital (WACC)		11.50%	11.50%	11.50%	11.50%	11.50%	11.50%	11.50%
582	**Results**								
583	Value of operations		$2,524	$2,492	$3,408	$3,344	$3,546	$3,470	$4,524
584	Intrinsic stock price		$29.40	$28.87	$44.13	$43.07	$46.43	$45.17	$62.74
585	Return on invested capital (ROIC)		10.00%	10.00%	11.67%	11.76%	11.67%	11.76%	13.73%

Source: See the file *Ch07 Tool Kit.xlsx*. Numbers are reported as rounded values for clarity but are calculated using *Excel*'s full precision. Thus, intermediate calculations using the figure's rounded values will be inexact.

Scenario Manager feature. The model in ***Ch07 Tool Kit.xlsx*** provides a detailed explanation of the process, but we will only examine the results here.

Figure 7-10 shows seven scenarios. The first is the Status Quo scenario, which we used previously when estimating MicroDrive's value of operations and intrinsic stock price. Figure 7-10 shows the key inputs in the blue section: sales growth rates, operating profitability, capital requirements, and cost of capital. Any inputs that differ from those of the Status Quo scenario are shown in orange. Figure 7-10 reports key results in the green section: the value of operations, the intrinsic stock price, and the return on invested capital that is expected for the long run. (The inputs are stable by the end of the forecast period, so the ROIC in the forecast's last year is the ROIC that is expected to continue into the foreseeable future.)

Recall that MicroDrive's stock price fell from $45 per share in the previous year to $31 in the current year, which is above the estimated intrinsic stock price of $29.40 in the Status Quo scenario. To address this price decline, some of MicroDrive's managers recommended a new marketing campaign to increase the sales growth rates, which would lead to higher FCF growth rates. This Higher Sales Growth scenario is shown next to the Status Quo scenario in Figure 7-10. The managers were surprised to see that the value of operations and intrinsic stock price actually *declined* when sales growth increased, falling from $2,524 to $2,492![8]

The previous example demonstrates that growth doesn't add value for the particular set of ratios used in the Status Quo scenario, but let's examine a more general case to better

---

[8]To avoid unnecessarily complicating these examples, we ignore the cost of the changes. Obviously, additional costs must be taken into account before completing the analysis; see Chapter 12 for details.

understand why this is so. Suppose Year T is the horizon, which means the company has stable ratios and constant expected growth. It is possible (with a lot of algebra!) to express the value of operations in terms of the value drivers:

$$V_{op(\text{at Horizon Year T})} = OpCap_T \left[1 + \frac{\left((1 + g_L) \dfrac{OP_T}{CR_T} - WACC \right)}{WACC - g_L} \right] \qquad (7\text{-}13)$$

The bracket in Equation 7-13 includes the term OP_T/CR_T. This ratio is also equal to the ROIC, as shown next:

$$ROIC_T = \frac{NOPAT_T}{OpCap_T} = \frac{(NOPAT_T/Sales_T)}{(OpCap_T/Sales_T)} = \frac{OP_T}{CR_T} \qquad (7\text{-}14)$$

Substituting Equation 7-14 into Equation 7-13 provides an expression for the horizon value in terms of the return on invested capital (ROIC) and the other value drivers:

$$V_{op(\text{at Horizon Year T})} = OpCap_T \left[1 + \frac{(1 + g_L)\,ROIC_T - WACC}{WACC - g_L} \right] \qquad (7\text{-}15)$$

How do these drivers affect the horizon value? First, an increase in the ROIC, whether due to improvement in operating profitability or in capital utilization, always has a positive effect on the horizon value because it increases the numerator in Equation 7-15. When multistage valuation models must be used due to nonconstant growth, an increase in the ROIC for any year also increases the current value of operations.

Second, a reduction in the cost of capital always increases the numerator and decreases the denominator in the fraction in Equation 7-16, making the fraction larger and the term in brackets larger. This has a positive effect on the horizon value and on the current value of operations even if a multistage model is used.

Third, an increase in the growth rate can have a positive or negative effect on the horizon value. Look at the numerator of the fraction in the bracketed term in Equation 7-15. If the numerator is negative, then the bracketed term is less than 1, causing the intrinsic value of operations at the horizon to be less than the amount invested in operating capital. This happens when ROIC is sufficiently less than WACC. You can think of it as earning a return that isn't enough to compensate the investors for the cost of using their capital. When this happens, the firm's projected operations will destroy value!

In fact, if $ROIC_T$ is so low that:

$$ROIC_T < WACC/(1 + WACC)$$

an increase in growth will make the fraction in Equation 7-15 even more negative, which means that a higher growth rate makes the company even *less* valuable.[9] Mathematically,

---

[9]To see why this is true, take the partial derivative of Equation 7-15 with respect to g_L. This partial derivative is negative for values of $ROIC_T < WACC/(1 + WACC)$.

this is because the denominator of the fraction in Equation 7-15, WACC − g_L, is getting smaller faster than the numerator, $(1 + g_L)\text{ROIC}_T − \text{WACC}$, is getting larger. Intuitively, each new dollar of investment earns an insufficient rate of return to satisfy investors—it is like throwing good money after bad.

The key point to remember is not to implement growth strategies if the return on invested capital is too low. In that situation, managers must improve operating profitability or capital utilization, which will increase the ROIC, before pursuing growth.

Returning to Figure 7-10, Scenarios 3 and 4 improve operating profitability and capital utilization. Notice that these improvements increase the ROIC, which leads to much higher estimates of the value of operations and the intrinsic stock price. Scenarios 5 and 6 show that when improvements in operations increase ROIC, growth adds even more value. Scenario 7 shows the very large increase in value if managers can improve operating profitability, capital utilization, and growth. We will discuss MicroDrive's plans in more detail when we forecast its full financial statements in Chapter 12, but notice now in Figure 7-10 that relatively small operating improvements cause large increases in intrinsic value.

The model in *Ch07 Tool Kit.xlsx* shows an eighth scenario in which the cost of capital is reduced. This increases value substantially, but we defer a discussion of the cost of capital's impact on value until Chapter 15.

SELF-TEST

What are value drivers?

Does an increase in the operating profitability ratio always cause an increase in the value of operations?

Does a decrease in the capital requirement ratio always cause an increase in the value of operations?

Does an increase in the long-term growth rate of free cash flows always cause an increase in the value of operations? Explain your answer.

7-10 Why Are Stock Prices So Volatile?

Recall from Chapter 6 that a typical company's stock returns are very volatile. Because the average stock's standard deviation is about 30%, it should not be surprising that many stocks declined by 80% or more during 2018, and some enjoyed gains of over 100%. At the risk of understatement, the stock market is volatile!

To help understand why stock prices are volatile, look at Figure 7-10. Even though the changes in the value drivers were relatively small, the changes in MicroDrive's intrinsic stock price were very large, with the price ranging from $28.87 to $62.74. This shows that if investors change their expectations regarding future sales growth, operating profitability, capital utilization, or the cost of capital, then the stock price will change. As Figure 7-10 demonstrates, even small changes in the expected value drivers cause large changes in stock prices.

What might cause investors to change their expectations? It could be new information about the company, such as preliminary results for an R&D program, initial sales of a new product, or the discovery of harmful side effects from the use of an existing product. Or new information that will affect many companies could arrive, such as the collapse of the credit markets in 2008. Given the existence of computers and telecommunications networks, new information hits the market on an almost continuous basis, and it causes frequent and sometimes large changes in stock prices. In other words, *readily available information causes stock prices to be volatile.*

If a stock's price is stable, this probably means that little new information is arriving. But if you think it's risky to invest in a volatile stock, imagine how risky it would be to invest in a company that rarely releases new information about its sales or operations. It may be bad to see your stock's price jump around, but it would be a lot worse to see a stable quoted price most of the time and then to see huge moves on the rare days when new information is released.[10] Fortunately, in our economy timely information is readily available, and evidence suggests that stocks—especially those of large companies—adjust rapidly to new information.

SELF-TEST

Why doesn't a volatile stock price necessarily imply irrational pricing?

7-11 Dividend Valuation Models

Free cash flows are the cash flows available for distribution to all of a company's investors (debtholders, preferred stockholders, and common stockholders). The FCF valuation model discounts the cash flows available to *all* investors by the overall rate of return required by *all* investors. This results in a company's primary source of value, the value of operations. Recall that *all* of a company's investors have a claim on this value, with common stockholders having the residual claim.

Rather than finding the total entity value and then determining the residual share that belongs to common stockholders, we can find the intrinsic price per share more directly for companies that pay dividends. The dividends per share are the cash flows that go directly to the owner of a share of common stock, so if you discount dividends at the rate of return required by common stockholders, the result is the intrinsic stock price.

7-11a Definitions of Terms Used in Dividend Valuation Models

We begin by defining key terms:

D_t = Dividend the stockholder *expects* to receive at the end of Year t. D_0 is the most recent dividend, which has already been paid; D_1 is the dividend expected to be paid at Year 1. D_2 is the dividend expected at the end of Year 2; and so forth.[11]

P_0 = Actual *market price* of the stock today.

$\hat{P}_0$ = An investor's estimated *value* of the stock today (pronounced "P hat 0").

$\hat{P}_t$ = Expected price of the stock at the end of each Year t. $\hat{P}_1$ is the price expected at the end of 1 year; and so on.

D_1/P_0 = Expected **dividend yield** is the expected rate of return during the coming year due to dividends.

[10]In geological terms, this would be like *not* having frequent small earthquakes that relieve stress along the fault, instead building up stress for a number of years before a massive earthquake.

[11]Stocks generally pay dividends quarterly, so theoretically we should evaluate them on a quarterly basis. However, in stock valuation, most analysts work on an annual basis because the data generally are not precise enough to warrant refinement to a quarterly model. For additional information on the quarterly model, see Robert Brooks and Billy Helms, "An N-Stage, Fractional Period, Quarterly Dividend Discount Model," *Financial Review,* November 1990, pp. 651–657.

$\dfrac{\hat{P}_1 - P_0}{P_0}$ = Expected **capital gains yield** is the expected rate of return due to the expected change in the stock price at the end of the coming year. It is also equal to the expected stock price growth rate.

g = Expected growth rate in dividends. The expected constant long-term growth is denoted as g_L.

r_s = Required rate of return on the stock that is needed to compensate stockholders for the stock's risk.

$\hat{r}_s$ = Expected rate of return that an investor who buys the stock expects to receive in the future (pronounced "r hat s"). The expected return ($\hat{r}_s$) is equal to the expected dividend yield (D_1/P_0) plus the expected capital gains yield ($[\hat{P}_1 - P_0]/P_0$).

$\bar{r}_s$ = Actual, or realized, *after-the-fact* rate of return, pronounced "r bar s." The actual return can differ considerably from the expected return.

7-11b Expected Dividends as the Basis for Stock Values

What are a shareholder's expected cash flows? To answer this, suppose you buy a share of stock and expect to hold it for 1 year. The stock's value to you, $\hat{P}_0$, is the present value of the dividends during the year plus the present value of the stock's sales price at the end of the year. Its value to the purchaser at that time is $\hat{P}_1$, which is the present value of the dividends expected during Year 2 plus the present value of the stock price at the end of Year 2, which, in turn, will be determined as the present value of another set of future dividends and an even more distant stock price. This process can be continued ad infinitum, and the ultimate result is Equation 7-16:

$$\text{Value of stock} = \hat{P}_0 = \text{PV of expected future dividends}$$

$$= \dfrac{D_1}{(1 + r_s)^1} + \dfrac{D_2}{(1 + r_s)^2} + \cdots + \dfrac{D_\infty}{(1 + r_s)^\infty}$$

$$= \sum_{t=1}^{\infty} \dfrac{D_t}{(1 + r_s)^t}$$

(7-16)

7-11c Valuing a Constant Growth Stock

Later in this section we explain how to determine the value of a firm that is not yet in its long-term constant growth phase, but for now we focus on a mature company whose dividends are expected to constantly grow at g_L. Recall that free cash flow is the source of funds available for distribution to all investors, including dividends to stockholders. Therefore, the long-term growth rate in dividends is equal to the long-term growth rate in free cash flow, g_L. If this constant growth rate is less than the rate of return required by common shareholders (i.e., $g_L < r_s$), then Equation 7-16 can be rewritten as follows:[12]

$$
\begin{aligned}
\hat{P}_0 &= \frac{D_0(1 + g_L)^1}{(1 + r_s)^1} + \frac{D_0(1 + g_L)^2}{(1 + r_s)^2} + \cdots + \frac{D_0(1 + g_L)^\infty}{(1 + r_s)^\infty} \\[2mm]
&= D_0 \sum_{t=1}^{\infty} \frac{(1 + g_L)^t}{(1 + r_s)^t} \\[2mm]
&= \frac{D_0(1 + g_L)}{r_s - g_L} = \frac{D_1}{r_s - g_L}
\end{aligned}
\tag{7-17}
$$

The last term of Equation 7-17 is called the **constant dividend growth model**, or the **Gordon model**, after Myron J. Gordon, who did much to develop and popularize it. Always remember that *if g_L is not less than r_s, then the company is not in its constant growth phase, and Equation 7-17 should not be used!*

Although rare, it is possible for g_L to be less than zero! For example, a mining company might be depleting its reserves faster than it is developing new ones, resulting in smaller dividends each year. Equation 7-17 still applies in such a situation.

Suppose R&R Enterprises just paid a dividend of $1.15 (that is, $D_0 = \$1.15$). Its stock has a required rate of return, r_s, of 13.4% and investors expect the dividend to grow at a constant 8% rate in the future. The expected dividend next year is $1.24: $D_1 = \$1.15(1.08) = \$1.24$. We can use Equation 7-17 to estimate the intrinsic stock price:

$$
\hat{P}_0 = \frac{D_0(1 + g_L)}{r_s - g_L} = \frac{D_1}{r_s - g_L}
$$

$$
= \frac{\$1.15(1.08)}{0.134 - 0.08} = \frac{\$1.242}{0.054} = \$23.00
$$

EXPECTED FUTURE PRICES OF A CONSTANT GROWTH STOCK

Suppose we apply a version of Equation 7-17 that is shifted ahead by 1 year, using D_2 instead of D_1 and solving for $\hat{P}_1$ instead of $\hat{P}_0$. We can estimate the expected Year-2 dividend as $D_2 = D_1(1 + g_L) = \$1.242(1.08) = \$1.3414$. The expected stock price in 1 year is:

$$
\hat{P}_1 = \frac{D_2}{r_s - g_L} = \frac{\$1.3414}{0.134 - 0.08} = \$24.84
$$

The stock price's expected growth rate, which also is its capital gains yield, is:

$$
\frac{\hat{P}_1 - \hat{P}_0}{\hat{P}_0} = \frac{\$24.84 - \$23.00}{\$23.00} = 0.08 = 8\%
$$

If we repeat this process each year, the stock price's expected growth rate will be 8% each year, the same as the dividend growth rate. Thus, the stock price and dividend each grow at g_L, the constant growth rate.

---

[12] See **Web Extension 7A** for a derivation of this result.

EXPECTED RATE OF RETURN ON A CONSTANT GROWTH STOCK

When using Equation 7-17, we estimated the first expected dividend (D_1) and the *required* rate of return (r_s). We used those estimates to determine the stock's intrinsic value. Here we reverse the process: We observe the actual stock price, substitute it into Equation 7-17 for $\hat{P}_0$, and solve for the *expected* rate of return:[13]

$$
\begin{aligned}
\begin{matrix} \text{Expected rate} \\ \text{of return} \end{matrix} = \hat{r}_s &= \frac{D_1}{P_0} + g_L \\
&= \begin{matrix} \text{Expected} \\ \text{dividend yield} \end{matrix} + \begin{matrix} \text{Expected} \\ \text{growth rate} \end{matrix} \\
&= \begin{matrix} \text{Expected} \\ \text{dividend yield} \end{matrix} + \begin{matrix} \text{Expected capital} \\ \text{gains yield} \end{matrix}
\end{aligned}
\tag{7-18}
$$

For example, suppose you buy a stock for a price $P_0 = \$23$. If you expect the stock to pay a dividend of $1.242 in a year and you expect the dividend to grow at a constant rate of 8% in the future, then your expected rate of return will be:

$$
\hat{r}_s = \frac{D_1}{P_0} + g_L = \frac{\$1.242}{\$23} + 8\% = 5.4\% + 8\% = 13.4\%
$$

Notice that the expected dividend yield (D_1/P_0) is 5.4% and the expected capital gains yield (which is equal to g_L) is 8%.

7-11d Valuing Nonconstant Growth Stocks

Most companies are not yet in their constant growth phase. However, the dividend growth rate must eventually level off at a constant growth rate for the same reasons that free cash flow must eventually grow at a constant rate: (1) market saturation and (2) competition from companies in the same industry. We can estimate the intrinsic stock price ($\hat{P}_0$) using the same approach that we used in Section 7-6 to estimate the value of operations ($V_{op,0}$).

Suppose we expect dividends to grow at nonconstant rates for T periods, after which they will grow at a constant rate, g_L. Analogous to the previous examples with the FCF valuation model, T is called the *horizon date* or the *terminal date*. The estimated value of a stock at Time T is the present value of all dividends beyond Time T, discounted back to Time T. Because dividends beyond Time T are expected to grow at a constant long-term rate of g_L, we can use a variation of the constant growth formula, Equation 7-17, to estimate the stock's intrinsic value at Time T. The estimated price at Time T, $\hat{P}_T$, is the horizon value, which also is called the continuing value or terminal value:

$$
\text{Horizon value for stock} = \hat{P}_T = \frac{D_{T+1}}{r_s - g_L} = \frac{D_T(1 + g_L)}{r_s - g_L}
\tag{7-19}
$$

---

[13] Recall from Chapter 6 that if the market is in equilibrium, the expected rate of return will equal the *required* rate of return, $\hat{r}_s = r_s$.

A stock's estimated value today, $\hat{P}_0$, is the present value of the dividends during the nonconstant growth period plus the present value of the horizon value, $\hat{P}_0$:

$$\hat{P}_0 = \left[\frac{D_1}{(1+r_s)^1} + \frac{D_2}{(1+r_s)^2} + \cdots + \frac{D_T}{(1+r_s)^T}\right] + \frac{\hat{P}_T}{(1+r_s)^T}$$

$$= \left[\frac{D_1}{(1+r_s)^1} + \frac{D_2}{(1+r_s)^2} + \cdots + \frac{D_T}{(1+r_s)^T}\right] + \frac{[(D_{T+1})/(r_s - g_L)]}{(1+r_s)^T} \tag{7-20}$$

Suppose R&R, the company from the previous section, was not yet in its constant growth phase. The most recent dividend, D_0, was \$1.15. Dividends are expected to grow at a 30% rate for the first year, 20% for the second year, and 10% for the third year, after which the growth rate is expected to fall to 8% and remain there. The required rate of return, r_s, is 13.4%. Figure 7-11 illustrates the process for valuing a nonconstant growth

FIGURE 7-11
Process for Finding the Value of a Nonconstant Growth Stock

	A	B	C	D	E	F	G
770	**INPUTS:**						
771	D_0 =	\$1.15	Last dividend the company paid.				
772	r_s =	13.4%	Stockholders' required return.				
773	$g_{0,1}$ =	30%	Growth rate for Year 1 only.				
774	$g_{1,2}$ =	20%	Growth rate for Year 2 only.				
775	$g_{2,3}$ =	10%	Growth rate for Year 3 only.				
776	g_L =	8%	Constant long-run growth rate for all years after Year 3.				
777			Projections				
778	Year	0	1	2	3	→∞	
779	Growth rate		30%	20%	10%	8%	
780	Dividend	D_0	$D_0(1+g_{0,1})$	$D_1(1+g_{1,2})$	$D_2(1+g_{1,2})$		
781	D_t	\$1.15	\$1.495	\$1.794	\$1.973		
782			↓	↓	↓		
783			D_1	D_2	D_3		
784						$HV_3 = \hat{P}_3$	
785			$(1+r_s)^1$	$(1+r_s)^2$	$(1+r_s)^3$	↓	
786			↓	↓	↓	$D_3(1+g_L)$	
787			↓	↓	↓	$\hat{P}_3$ =	
788			↓	↓	↓	$(r_s - g_L)$	
789			↓	↓	↓	↓	
790			↓	↓	↓	$\hat{P}_3$ = \$2.131	
791		\$1.318	← ↲	↓	↓	5.400%	
792	PVs of Dividends	\$1.395	← ← ←	← ↲	↓	↓	
793		\$1.353	← ← ←	← ← ←	← ↲	$\hat{P}_3$ = \$39.468	
794						↓	
795	Pv of $\hat{P}_3$	\$27.065	← ← ←	← ← ←	\$39.468		$\hat{P}_3$
796		↓				← ← ←	
797	V_{op} =	\$31.13			$(1+0.134)^3$		$(1+r_s)^3$

Source: See the file ***Ch07 Tool Kit.xlsx***. Numbers are reported as rounded values for clarity but are calculated using *Excel's* full precision. Thus, intermediate calculations using the figure's rounded values will be inexact.

stock. Notice that the dividends are projected using the appropriate growth rate for each year. The estimated horizon value, $\hat{P}_3$, is the value of all dividends from Year 4 through infinity, discounted back to Year 3 by application of the constant growth model at Year 3. The horizon value is actually the value a split-second after D_3 has been paid. Therefore, the estimated value at Time 0 is the present value of the first three dividends plus the present value of $\hat{P}_3$, for an estimated $\hat{P}_0$ of $31.13.

SELF-TEST

What are the two components of most stocks' expected total return?

How does one calculate the capital gains yield and the dividend yield of a stock?

Write out and explain the valuation formula for a constant growth stock.

Are stock prices affected more by long-term or short-term performance? Explain.

What conditions must hold in order for a stock to be evaluated using the constant growth model?

Explain how to find the value of a nonconstant growth stock.

If D_1 = $3.00, P_0 = $50, and $\hat{P}_1$ = $52, what are the stock's expected dividend yield, expected capital gains yield, and expected total return for the coming year? **(6%, 4%, 10%)**

A stock is expected to pay a dividend of $2 at the end of the year. The required rate of return is r_s = 12%. What would the stock's price be if the constant growth rate in dividends were 4%? **($25.00)** What would the price be if g = 0%? **($16.67)**

If D_0 = $4.00, r_s = 9%, and g = 5% for a constant growth stock, what are the stock's expected dividend yield and capital gains yield for the coming year? **(4%, 5%)**

Suppose D_0 = $5.00 and r_s = 10%. The expected growth rate from Year 0 to Year 1 is $g_{0,1}$ = 20%, the expected growth rate from Year 1 to Year 2 is $g_{1,2}$ = 10%, and the constant growth rate beyond Year 2 is g_L = 5%. What are the expected dividends for Year 1 and Year 2? **($6.00 and $6.60)** What is the expected horizon value price at Year 2 ($\hat{P}_3$)? **($138.60)** What is $\hat{P}_0$? **($125.45)**

7-12 The Market Multiple Method

Some analysts use the **market multiple method** to estimate a target company's value. The first step is to identify a group of comparable firms. The second step is to calculate for each comparable firm the ratio of its observed market value to a particular metric, which can be net income, earnings per share, sales, book value, number of subscribers, or any other metric that applies to the target firm and the comparable firms. This ratio is called a *market multiple*. To estimate the target firm's market value, the analyst would multiply the target's metric by the comparable firms' average market multiple.

For example, suppose an analyst chooses earnings per share (EPS) as the metric, identifies a comparable group, and calculates the price/earnings (P/E) ratio for each comparable firm. Multiplying the target company's EPS by the comparable group's average P/E ratio provides an estimate of the target's intrinsic stock price.

To illustrate the concept, suppose Tapley Products is a privately held firm whose forecasted earnings per share are $7.70, and suppose the average P/E ratio for a set of similar publicly traded companies is 12. To estimate the intrinsic value of Tapley's stock we would simply multiply its $7.70 EPS by the multiple 12, obtaining the value $7.70(12) = $92.40.

In the previous example, the EPS belonged to shareholders (because interest had already been paid), so the method used stock price as the measure of value. In contrast, some market multiple methods pick a metric that applies to the total firm and not just shareholders. For example, interest and dividends (as well as taxes) are paid from EBITDA, which is the amount of earnings before interest, taxes, depreciation, and amortization. The EBITDA multiple is the total value of a company (the market value of its equity plus that of its debt) divided by EBITDA. This multiple is based on total value because EBITDA is used to compensate the firm's stockholders and bondholders. Therefore, it is called an **entity multiple**. If you multiply the target firm's EBITDA by the average EBITDA multiple from a group of comparable firms, the result is an estimate of the target's total entity value. To find the estimated intrinsic equity value, you would subtract the values of all debt and preferred stock from total entity value. Dividing this result by the number of outstanding common stock shares provides an estimate of the intrinsic stock price.

In some businesses, such as cable TV and cell phone service, a critical factor is the number of customers the company has. For example, when a phone company acquires a cellular operator, it might pay a price that is based on the number of customers. Managed care companies such as HMOs have applied similar logic in acquisitions, basing valuations primarily on the number of people insured. Some Internet companies have been valued by the number of "eyeballs," which is the number of hits on the site.

SELF-TEST

What is market multiple analysis?

What is an entity multiple?

Dodd Corporation is a private company that earned $4.00 per share for the most recent year. If the average P/E ratio of a group of comparable public companies is 11, what is an estimate of Dodd's stock value on a per share basis? **($44.00)**

*The company in the previous question, Dodd Corporation, has 100,000 shares of common stock owned by its founder. Dodd owes $1,300,000 to its bank. Dodd has 11,400 customers. If the average ratio of total entity value to customers is $500 for a group of comparable public companies, what is Dodd's estimated total entity value? **($5,700,000)** What is its estimated stock value on a per share basis? **($44.00)***

7-13 Comparing the FCF Valuation Model, the Dividend Growth Model, and the Market Multiple Method

The free cash flow valuation model and the dividend growth model give the same estimated stock price if you are very careful to be consistent with the implicit assumptions regarding capital structure when projecting free cash flows and dividends. Which model should you use, since they both give the same answer?

If you were a financial analyst estimating the value of a mature company whose dividends are expected to grow steadily in the future, it would probably be more efficient to use the dividend growth model. In this case, you would need to estimate only the growth rate in dividends, not the entire set of forecasted financial statements.

If a company is paying a dividend but is still in the high-growth stage of its life cycle, you would need to project the future financial statements before you could make a reasonable estimate of future dividends. After you have projected future financial statements, it would be a toss-up as to whether the corporate valuation model or the dividend growth model would be easier to apply.

However, forecasting the entire set of financial statements is more complicated than simply forecasting the operating items and free cash flows, as we did for MicroDrive earlier in this chapter and as we will do in more detail in Chapter 12. Therefore, the free cash flow valuation model is easier to apply for high-growth companies even if they are paying dividends.

If you were trying to estimate the value of a company that has never paid a dividend or a private company (including companies nearing an IPO), then there would be no choice: You would have to estimate future free cash flows and use the corporate valuation model.

The market multiple method is easier to apply than the free cash flow valuation model, but it has two shortcomings. First, it is hard to find companies that are truly comparable. In fact, the sample of comparable companies often has a wide range of values for the market multiple. In these cases, which frequently occur, you must decide if the target company is like the "comparable" companies with high multiples, average multiples, or low multiples. Second, the market multiple method doesn't help you identify the important value drivers or provide much insight into *why* the estimated intrinsic value is high or low or into how the company's managers can increase its value. Therefore, we recommend using the market multiple method only for ballpark estimates or in situations where the free cash flow model requires too many assumptions, such as valuing early-stage start-up companies.

A recent survey of practitioners confirms our recommendation.[14] Managing directors and directors at 11 investment banks all estimate the value in mergers and acquisitions by finding the present value of forecasted cash flows. All used constant growth models *and* market multiples to estimate the horizon value, with the two approaches providing a reality check on one another.

Finally, the free cash flow valuation model can be applied to a division or specific line of business within a company. This is very useful when considering the sale or purchase of a division. It also is useful when setting targets in compensation plans for divisional managers.

SELF-TEST

What situation is ideally suited to valuation with the dividend growth model?

What are the advantages of the free cash flow valuation model relative to the dividend growth model?

What are the advantages of the free cash flow valuation model relative to the market multiple method?

Which method is best suited to determine the value of a division or business unit that is part of a larger company?

7-14 Preferred Stock

Preferred stock is a *hybrid*: It's similar to bonds in some respects and to common stock in others. Like bonds, preferred stock has a par value, and a fixed amount of dividends must be paid on it before dividends can be paid on the common stock. However, if the preferred dividend is not earned, the directors can omit (or "pass") it without throwing the company into bankruptcy. So, although preferred stock has a fixed payment like bonds, a failure to make this payment will not lead to bankruptcy.

The dividends on preferred stock (D_{ps}) are fixed, and if they are scheduled to go on forever, the issue is a perpetuity. If the required rate of return on the preferred stock is r_{ps}, then the value of the preferred stock (V_{ps}) is:

$$V_{ps} = \frac{D_{ps}}{r_{ps}}$$

(7-21)

Notice that Equation 7-21 is just a special case of the constant dividend growth model for which growth is zero.[15]

[14]See W. Todd Brotherson, Kenneth M. Eades, Robert S. Harris, and Robert C. Higgins, "Company Valuation in Mergers and Acquisitions: How Is Discounted Cash Flow Applied by Leading Practitioners?" *Journal of Applied Finance*, No. 2, 2014, pp. 43–51.

[15]See **Web Extension 7A** for a proof of this result.

MicroDrive has preferred stock outstanding that pays a dividend of $8 per year. If the required rate of return on this preferred stock is 8%, then its value is $100:

$$V_{ps} = \frac{\$8.00}{0.08} = \$100.00$$

If we know the current price of a preferred stock and its dividend, we can transpose terms and solve for the expected rate of return as follows:

$$\hat{r}_{ps} = \frac{D_{ps}}{V_{ps}} \qquad\qquad (7\text{-}22)$$

Some preferred stock has a stated maturity, say, 50 years. If a firm's preferred stock matures in 50 years, pays an $8 annual dividend, has a par value of $100, and has a required return of 6%, then we can find its price using a financial calculator: Enter N = 50, I/YR = 6, PMT = 8, and FV = 100. Then press PV to find the price, V_{ps} = $131.52. If you know the price of a share of preferred stock, you can solve for I/YR to find the expected rate of return, $\hat{r}_{ps}$.

Most preferred stock pays dividends quarterly. This is true for MicroDrive, so we could find the effective rate of return on its preferred stock as follows:

$$EFF\% = EAR = \left(1 + \frac{r_{NOM}}{M}\right)^{M} - 1 = \left(1 + \frac{0.08}{4}\right)^{4} - 1 = 8.24\%$$

If an investor wanted to compare the returns on MicroDrive's bonds and its preferred stock, it would be best to convert the nominal rates on each security to effective rates and then compare these "equivalent annual rates."

SELF-TEST

Explain the following statement: "Preferred stock is a hybrid security."

Is the equation used to value preferred stock more like the one used to evaluate perpetual bonds or the one used for common stock? Explain.

A preferred stock has an annual dividend of $5. The required return is 8%. What is the V_{ps}? ($62.50)

SUMMARY

Corporate decisions should be analyzed in terms of how alternative courses of action are likely to affect a firm's value. However, it is necessary to know how stock prices are established before attempting to measure how a given decision will affect a firm's value. This chapter showed how stock values are determined and also how investors go about estimating the rates of return they expect to earn. The key concepts covered are listed here.

- A **proxy** is a document that gives one person the power to act for another, typically the power to vote shares of common stock. A **proxy fight** occurs when an outside group solicits stockholders' proxies in an effort to overthrow the current management.
- Stockholders often have the right to purchase any additional shares sold by the firm. This right, called the **preemptive right**, protects the present stockholders' control and prevents dilution of their value.

- Although most firms have only one type of common stock, in some instances **classified stock** is used to meet the special needs of the company. One type is **founders' shares**. This is stock owned by the firm's founders that carries sole voting rights but restricted dividends for a specified number of years.
- The **free cash flow (FCF) valuation model** estimates the total value of the firm before estimating the per share stock price, so it is called an **entity valuation model**.
- The **value of operations** is the present value of all the future free cash flows (FCFs) expected from operations when discounted at the weighted average cost of capital (WACC):

$$V_{op(at\ time\ 0)} = \sum_{t=1}^{\infty} \frac{FCF_t}{(1 + WACC)^t}$$

- **Nonoperating assets** include short-term investments in marketable securities and noncontrolling interests in the stock of other companies. The value of nonoperating assets is usually close to the figure reported on the balance sheet.
- The total **intrinsic value** is the sum of the value of operations and the nonoperating assets.
- The **horizon date** is the date when there is no need to make additional forecasts because the growth rate in sales, cash flows, and dividends is assumed to be constant thereafter. This is also called the **terminal date**.
- The **horizon value** of operations is the value of operations at the end of the explicit forecast period. It is also called the **terminal value** or **continuing value**, and it is equal to the present value of all free cash flows beyond the forecast period, discounted back to the end of the forecast period at the weighted average cost of capital:

$$\text{Horizon value} = V_{op(at\ time\ T)} = \frac{FCF_{T+1}}{WACC - g} = \frac{FCF_T(1 + g)}{WACC - g}$$

- The estimated *value of equity* is the total value of the company minus the value of the debt and preferred stock. The estimated *intrinsic price per share* is the total value of the equity divided by the number of shares.
- When using the corporate free cash flow valuation model, follow these steps to estimate the *value of operations for a nonconstant growth stock:* (1) Forecast the free cash flows expected during the nonconstant growth period. (2) Estimate the horizon value of operations at the end of the nonconstant growth period. (3) Discount the free cash flows and estimated horizon value of operations back to the present. (4) Sum these PVs to find the current estimated value of operations.
- **Value drivers** are the inputs to the free cash flow valuation model that managers are able to influence through strategic choices and execution of business plans. These include the revenue growth rate (g), the operating profitability ratio (OP), the capital requirement ratio (CR), and the WACC.
- **Value-based management** is the systematic use of the free cash flow valuation model to identify value drivers and to guide managerial and strategic decisions.
- The expected **dividend yield** is the expected dividend divided by the current stock price.
- The expected **capital gains yield** is the expected change in the stock price divided by the current stock price.

- The value of a share of stock is the present value of expected future dividends when discounted at the required return on common stock:

$$\hat{P}_0 = \sum_{t=1}^{\infty} \frac{D_t}{(1 + r_s)^t}$$

- The **constant dividend growth model**, which is also called the **Gordon model**, can be used when dividend growth is constant:

$$\hat{P}_0 = \frac{D_1}{r_s - g_L}$$

- The *horizon value* for a stock is the present value of all dividends *after* the horizon date discounted back to horizon date:

$$\hat{P}_T = \frac{D_{T+1}}{r_s - g_L}$$

- The *expected total rate of return* from a stock consists of an expected dividend yield plus an expected capital gains yield. For a constant growth firm, both the dividend yield and the capital gains yield are expected to remain constant in the future.
- The equation for $\hat{r}_s$, the *expected rate of return on a constant growth stock,* is:

$$\hat{r}_s = \frac{D_1}{P_0} + g$$

- When using the dividend growth model, follow these steps to estimate the *present value of a nonconstant growth stock:* (1) Forecast the dividends expected during the nonconstant growth period. (2) Estimate the projected price of the stock at the end of the nonconstant growth period. (3) Discount the dividends and the projected price back to the present. (4) Sum these PVs to find the current estimated value of the stock, $\hat{P}_0$.
- **Preferred stock** is a hybrid security having some characteristics of debt and some of equity.
- The *value of a share of perpetual preferred stock* is found as the dividend divided by the required rate of return:

$$V_{ps} = \frac{D_{ps}}{r_{ps}}$$

Web Extension 7A provides the derivations of the constant growth formulas for the value of operations (V_{op}) and the intrinsic stock price ($\hat{P}_0$). It also shows the derivation of the perpetual preferred stock valuation model (V_{ps}).

QUESTIONS

(7-1)   Define each of the following terms:

     a. Proxy; proxy fight; preemptive right; classified stock; founders' shares
     b. Free cash flow valuation model; value of operations; nonoperating assets
     c. Constant growth model; horizon date and horizon value
     d. Multistage valuation model
     e. Estimated value ($\hat{P}_0$); market price (P_0)
     f. Required rate of return, r_s; expected rate of return, $\hat{r}_s$; actual, or realized, rate of return, $\bar{r}_s$
     g. Capital gains yield; dividend yield; expected total return
     h. Preferred stock

(7-2) Two investors are evaluating General Electric's stock for possible purchase. They agree on the expected value of D_1 and also on the expected future dividend growth rate. Further, they agree on the risk of the stock. However, one investor normally holds stocks for 2 years and the other normally holds stocks for 10 years. On the basis of the type of analysis done in this chapter, they should both be willing to pay the same price for General Electric's stock. True or false? Explain.

(7-3) A bond that pays interest forever and has no maturity date is a perpetual bond, also called a perpetuity or a consol. In what respect is a perpetual bond similar to (1) a no-growth common stock and (2) a share of preferred stock?

(7-4) Explain how to use the free cash flow valuation model to find the price per share of common equity.

SELF-TEST PROBLEMS   SOLUTIONS SHOWN IN APPENDIX A

(ST-1)
Constant Growth Stock Valuation
Ewald Company's current stock price is $36, and its last dividend was $2.40. In view of Ewald's strong financial position and its consequent low risk, its required rate of return is only 12%. If dividends are expected to grow at a constant rate g in the future, and if r_s is expected to remain at 12%, then what is Ewald's expected stock price 5 years from now?

(ST-2)
Nonconstant Growth Stock Valuation
Snyder Computer Chips Inc. is experiencing a period of rapid growth. Earnings and dividends are expected to grow at a rate of 15% during the next 2 years, at 13% in the third year, and at a constant rate of 6% thereafter. Snyder's last dividend was $1.15, and the required rate of return on the stock is 12%.

a. Calculate the value of the stock today.
b. Calculate $\hat{P}_1$ and $\hat{P}_2$.
c. Calculate the dividend yield and capital gains yield for Years 1, 2, and 3.

(ST-3)
Free Cash Flow Valuation Model
Watkins Inc. has never paid a dividend, and when the firm might begin paying dividends is not known. Its current free cash flow is $100,000, and this FCF is expected to grow at a constant 7% rate. The weighted average cost of capital is WACC = 11%. Watkins currently holds $325,000 of nonoperating marketable securities. Its long-term debt is $1,000,000, but it has never issued preferred stock. Watkins has 50,000 shares of stock outstanding.

a. Calculate Watkins's value of operations.
b. Calculate the company's total value.
c. Calculate the estimated value of common equity.
d. Calculate the estimated per share stock price.

PROBLEMS   ANSWERS ARE IN APPENDIX B

EASY PROBLEMS 1–10

(7-1)
FCF Projections
Ogier Incorporated currently has $800 million in sales, which are projected to grow by 12.5% in Year 1 and by 5% in Year 2. Its operating profitability ratio (OP) is 10%, and its capital requirement ratio (CR) is 80%.

a. What are the projected sales in Years 1 and 2?
b. What are the projected amounts of net operating profit after taxes (NOPAT) for Years 1 and 2?

c. What are the projected amounts of total net operating capital (OpCap) for Years 1 and 2?

d. What is the projected FCF for Year 2?

(7-2)
Value of Operations:
Constant FCF
Growth

EMC Corporation's current free cash flow is $400,000 and is expected to grow at a constant rate of 5%. The weighted average cost of capital is WACC = 12%. Calculate EMC's estimated value of operations.

(7-3)
Horizon Value of
Free Cash Flows

Current and projected free cash flows for Radell Global Operations are shown here. The growth rate from 2021 to 2022 is projected to remain the same for all years beyond 2022. The weighted average cost of capital is 11%. What is the horizon (continuing) value at 2022?

	Actual	Projected		
	2019	2020	2021	2022
Free cash flow (millions of dollars)	$606.820	$667.500	$707.547	$750.000

(7-4)
Value of Operations
of Free Cash Flows

JenBritt Incorporated had a free cash flow (FCF) of $80 million in 2019. The firm projects FCF of $200 million in 2020 and $500 million in 2021. FCF is expected to grow at a constant rate of 4% in 2022 and thereafter. The weighted average cost of capital is 9%. What is the current (i.e., beginning of 2020) value of operations?

(7-5)
Intrinsic Price per
Share Based on FCFs

Blunderbluss Manufacturing's balance sheets report $200 million in total debt, $70 million in short-term investments, and $50 million in preferred stock. Blunderbluss has 10 million shares of common stock outstanding. A financial analyst estimated that Blunderbuss's value of operations is $800 million. What is the analyst's estimate of the intrinsic stock price per share?

(7-6)
DPS Calculation

Thress Industries just paid a dividend of $1.50 a share (i.e., $D_0 = \$1.50$). The dividend is expected to grow 5% a year for the next 3 years and then 10% a year thereafter. What is the expected dividend per share for each of the next 5 years?

(7-7)
Constant Dividend
Growth Valuation

Boehm Incorporated is expected to pay a $1.50 per share dividend at the end of this year (i.e., $D_1 = \$1.50$). The dividend is expected to grow at a constant rate of 6% a year. The required rate of return on the stock, r_s, is 13%. What is the estimated value per share of Boehm's stock?

(7-8)
Constant Dividend
Growth Valuation

Woidtke Manufacturing's stock currently sells for $22 a share. The stock just paid a dividend of $1.20 a share (i.e., $D_0 = \$1.20$), and the dividend is expected to grow forever at a constant rate of 10% a year. What stock price is expected 1 year from now? What is the estimated required rate of return on Woidtke's stock? (Assume the market is in equilibrium with the required return equal to the expected return.)

(7-9)
Nonconstant
Dividend Growth
Valuation

A company currently pays a dividend of $2 per share ($D_0 = \$2$). It is estimated that the company's dividend will grow at a rate of 20% per year for the next 2 years and then at a constant rate of 7% thereafter. The company's stock has a beta of 1.2, the risk-free rate is 7.5%, and the market risk premium is 4%. What is your estimate of the stock's current price?

(7-10)
Preferred Stock
Rate of Return

Nick's Enchiladas has preferred stock outstanding that pays a dividend of $5 at the end of each year. The preferred stock sells for $50 a share. What is the stock's required rate of return? (Assume the market is in equilibrium with the required return equal to the expected return.)

INTERMEDIATE PROBLEMS 11–21

(7-11)
Constant FCF Growth Valuation

Brook Corporation's free cash flow for the current year (FCF_0) was $3.00 million. Its investors require a 13% rate of return on (WACC = 13%). What is the estimated value of operations if investors expect FCF to grow at a constant annual rate of (1) −5%, (2) 0%, (3) 5%, or (4) 10%?

(7-12)
Value of Operations

Kendra Enterprises has never paid a dividend. Free cash flow is projected to be $80,000 and $100,000 for the next 2 years, respectively; after the second year, FCF is expected to grow at a constant rate of 8%. The company's weighted average cost of capital is 12%.

a. What is the terminal, or horizon, value of operations? (*Hint:* Find the value of all free cash flows beyond Year 2 discounted back to Year 2.)
b. Calculate Kendra's value of operations.

(7-13)
Free Cash Flow Valuation

Dozier Corporation is a fast-growing supplier of office products. Analysts project the following free cash flows (FCFs) during the next 3 years, after which FCF is expected to grow at a constant 7% rate. Dozier's weighted average cost of capital is WACC = 13%.

	Year		
	1	**2**	**3**
Free cash flow (millions of dollars)	−$20	$30	$40

a. What is Dozier's horizon value? (*Hint:* Find the value of all free cash flows beyond Year 3 discounted back to Year 3.)
b. What is the current value of operations for Dozier?
c. Suppose Dozier has $10 million in marketable securities, $100 million in debt, and 10 million shares of stock. What is the intrinsic price per share?

(7-14)
Declining FCF Growth Valuation

Brushy Mountain Mining Company's coal reserves are being depleted, so its sales are falling. Also, environmental costs increase each year, so its costs are rising. As a result, the company's free cash flows are declining at the constant rate of 4% per year. If its current free cash flow (FCF_0) is $6 million and its weighted average cost of capital (WACC) is 14%, what is the estimated value of Brushy Mountain's value of operations?

(7-15)
Constant Dividend Growth Rate, g_L

Muller's Investigative Services has stock trading at $80 per share. The stock is expected to have a year-end dividend of $4 per share ($D_1$ = $4), and it is expected to grow at some constant rate, g, throughout time. The stock's required rate of return is 14% (assume the market is in equilibrium with the required return equal to the expected return). What is your forecast of g_L?

(7-16)
Constant Dividend Growth Valuation

Crisp Cookware's common stock is expected to pay a dividend of $3 a share at the end of this year (D_1 = $3.00); its beta is 0.8. The risk-free rate is 5.2%, and the market risk premium is 6%. The dividend is expected to grow at some constant rate g, and the stock currently sells for $40 a share. Assuming the market is in equilibrium, what does the market believe will be the stock's price at the end of 3 years (i.e., what is $\hat{P}_3$)?

(7-17)
Preferred Stock Rate of Return

What is the required rate of return on a preferred stock with a $50 par value, a stated annual dividend of 7% of par, and a current market price of (a) $30, (b) $40, (c) $50, and (d) $70? (Assume the market is in equilibrium with the required return equal to the expected return.)

(7-18)
Nonconstant Dividend Growth Valuation

Assume that the average firm in C&J Corporation's industry is expected to grow at a constant rate of 6% and that its dividend yield is 7%. C&J is about as risky as the average firm in the industry and just paid a dividend (D_0) of $1. Analysts expect that the growth rate of dividends will be 50% during the first year ($g_{0,1}$ = 50%) and 25% during the second year ($g_{1,2}$ = 25%). After Year 2, dividend growth will be constant at 6%. What is the required rate of return on C&J's stock? What is the estimated intrinsic per share?

(7-19)
Nonconstant
Dividend Growth
Valuation

Simpkins Corporation does not pay any dividends because it is expanding rapidly and needs to retain all of its earnings. However, investors expect Simpkins to begin paying dividends, with the first dividend of $0.50 coming 3 years from today. The dividend should grow rapidly—at a rate of 80% per year—during Years 4 and 5. After Year 5, the company should grow at a constant rate of 7% per year. If the required return on the stock is 16%, what is the value of the stock today? (Assume the market is in equilibrium with the required return equal to the expected return.)

(7-20)
Preferred Stock
Valuation

Several years ago, Rolen Riders issued preferred stock with a stated annual dividend of 10% of its $100 par value. Preferred stock of this type currently yields 8%. Assume dividends are paid annually.

a. What is the estimated value of Rolen's preferred stock?
b. Suppose interest rate levels have risen to the point where the preferred stock now yields 12%. What would be the new estimated value of Rolen's preferred stock?

(7-21)
Return on
Common Stock

You buy a share of The Ludwig Corporation stock for $21.40. You expect it to pay dividends of $1.07, $1.1449, and $1.2250 in Years 1, 2, and 3, respectively, and you expect to sell it at a price of $26.22 at the end of 3 years.

a. Calculate the growth rate in dividends.
b. Calculate the expected dividend yield.
c. Assuming that the calculated growth rate is expected to continue, you can add the dividend yield to the expected growth rate to obtain the expected total rate of return. What is this stock's expected total rate of return? (Assume the market is in equilibrium with the required return equal to the expected return.)

CHALLENGING PROBLEMS 22–24

(7-22)
Constant Dividend
Growth Valuation

You are analyzing Jillian's Jewelry (JJ) stock for a possible purchase. JJ just paid a dividend of $1.50 *yesterday*. You expect the dividend to grow at the rate of 6% per year for the next 3 years; if you buy the stock, you plan to hold it for 3 years and then sell it.

a. What dividends do you expect for JJ stock over the next 3 years? In other words, calculate D_1, D_2, and D_3. Note that D_0 = $1.50.
b. JJ stock has a required return of 13%, the rate you'll use to discount dividends. Find the present value of the dividend stream; that is, calculate the PV of D_1, D_2, and D_3, and then sum these PVs.
c. JJ stock should trade for $27.05 3 years from now (i.e., you expect $\hat{P}_3$ = $27.05). Discounted at a 13% rate, what is the present value of this expected future stock price? In other words, calculate the PV of $27.05.
d. If you plan to buy the stock, hold it for 3 years, and then sell it for $27.05, what is the most you should pay for it?
e. Use the constant growth model to calculate the present value of this stock. Assume that g_L = 6% and is constant.
f. Is the value of this stock dependent on how long you plan to hold it? In other words, if your planned holding period were 2 years or 5 years rather than 3 years, would this affect the value of the stock today, $\hat{P}_0$? Explain your answer.

(7-23)
Nonconstant FCF
Growth Valuation

Reizenstein Technologies (RT) has just developed a solar panel capable of generating 200% more electricity than any solar panel currently on the market. As a result, RT is expected to experience a 15% annual growth rate for the next 5 years. By the end of 5 years, other firms will have developed comparable technology, and RT's growth rate will slow to 5% per year indefinitely. RT has a 12% weighted average cost of capital. The most recent annual free cash flow (FCF_0) was $1.75 million.

a. Calculate RT's expected FCFs for $t = 1$, $t = 2$, $t = 3$, $t = 4$, and $t = 5$.
b. What is the horizon value at $t = 5$ (HV_5)?
c. What is the present value of the horizon value?
d. What is the present value of the free cash flows expected at $t = 1$, $t = 2$, $t = 3$, $t = 4$, and $t = 5$?
e. What is the value of operations at $t = 0$?

(7-24)
Nonconstant Dividend Growth Valuation

Conroy Consulting Corporation (CCC) has a current dividend of $D_0 = \$2.5$. Shareholders require a 12% rate of return. Although the dividend has been growing at a rate of 30% per year in recent years, this growth rate is expected to last only for another 2 years ($g_{0,1} = g_{1,2} = 30\%$). After Year 2, the growth rate will stabilize at $g_L = 7\%$.

a. What is CCC's stock worth today?
b. What is the expected stock price at Year 1?
c. What is the Year 1 expected (1) dividend yield, (2) capital gains yield, and (3) total return?
d. What is its expected dividend yield for the second year? The expected capital gains yield? The expected total return?

SPREADSHEET PROBLEMS

(7-25)
Build a Model: Free Cash Flow Valuation Model

resource

Start with the partial model in the file *Ch07 P25 Build a Model.xlsx* on the textbook's Web site. Selected data for the Derby Corporation are shown here. Use the data to answer the following questions.

a. Calculate the estimated horizon value (i.e., the value of operations at the end of the forecast period immediately after the Year-4 free cash flow). Assume growth becomes constant after Year 3.
b. Calculate the present value of the horizon value, the present value of the free cash flows, and the estimated Year-0 value of operations.
c. Calculate the estimated Year-0 price per share of common equity.

INPUTS (In Millions)		Year			
	Current		Projected		
	0	1	2	3	4
Free cash flow		−$20.0	$20.0	$80.0	$84.0
Marketable securities	$40				
Notes payable	$100				
Long-term bonds	$300				
Preferred stock	$50				
WACC	9.00%				
Number of shares of stock	40				

(7-26)
Build a Model: Value Drivers in the Free Cash Flow Valuation Model

Start with the partial model in *Ch07 P26 Build a Model.xlsx* on the textbook's Web site. Traver-Dunlap Corporation has a 15% weighted average cost of capital (WACC). Its most recent sales were $980 million, and its total net operating capital is $970 million. The following table shows estimates of the forecasted growth rates, operating profitability

resource

ratios, and capital requirement ratios for the next three years. All of these ratios are expected to remain constant after the third year. Use this information to answer the following questions:

a. Use the data to forecast sales, net operating profit after taxes (NOPAT), total net operating capital (OpCap), free cash flow (FCF), growth rate in FCF, and return on invested capital (ROIC) for the next 3 years. What is the FCF growth rate for Year 3, and how does it compare with the growth rate in sales? What is the ROIC for Year 3 and how does it compare with the 15% WACC?

b. What is the value of operations at Year 3, $V_{op,3}$? What is the current value of operations, $V_{op,0}$? How does the value of operations at Year 0 compare with the total net operating working capital at Year 3, and what might explain this relationship?

c. Suppose the growth rates for Years 2, 3, and thereafter can be increased to 7%. What is the new value of operations? Did it go up or down? Why did it change in this manner?

d. Return the growth rates to the original values. Now suppose that the capital requirement ratio can be decreased to 60% for all three years and thereafter. What is the new value of operations? Did it go up or down relative to the original base case? Why did it change in this manner?

e. Leave the capital requirement ratios at 60% for all three years and thereafter, but increase the sales growth rates for Years 2, 3, and thereafter to 7%. What is the new value of operations? Did it go up or down relative to the other scenarios? Why did it change in this manner?

Estimated Base Case Data for Traver-Dunlap Corporation

	Forecast Year		
	1	2	3
Annual sales growth rate	20%	6%	6%
Operating profitability (NOPAT/Sales)	12%	10%	10%
Capital requirement (OpCap/Sales)	80%	80%	80%
Tax rate	35%	35%	35%

(7-27)
Build a Model:
Dividend Growth
Valuation Model

resource

Start with the partial model in the file *Ch07 P27 Build a Model.xlsx* on the textbook's Web site. Hamilton Landscaping's dividend growth rate is expected to be 30% in the next year, drop to 15% from Year 1 to Year 2, and drop to a constant 5% for Year 2 and all subsequent years. Hamilton has just paid a dividend of $2.50, and its stock has a required return of 11%.

a. What is Hamilton's estimated stock price today?

b. If you bought the stock at Year 0, what are your expected dividend yield and capital gains for the upcoming year?

c. What are your expected dividend yield and capital gains for the second year (from Year 1 to Year 2)? Why aren't these the same as for the first year?

MINI CASE

Your employer, a midsized human resources management company, is considering expansion into related fields, including the acquisition of Temp Force Company, an employment agency that supplies word processor operators and computer programmers to businesses with temporarily heavy workloads. Your employer is also considering the purchase of Biggerstaff & McDonald (B&M), a privately held company owned by two friends, each with 5 million shares of stock. B&M currently has free cash flow of $24 million, which is expected to grow at a constant rate of 5%. B&M's financial statements report short-term investments of $100 million, debt of $200 million, and preferred stock of $50 million. B&M's weighted average cost of capital (WACC) is 11%. Answer the following questions:

a. Describe briefly the legal rights and privileges of common stockholders.

b. What is free cash flow (FCF)? What is the weighted average cost of capital? What is the free cash flow valuation model?

c. Use a pie chart to illustrate the sources that comprise a hypothetical company's total value. Using another pie chart, show the claims on a company's value. How is equity a residual claim?

d. Suppose the free cash flow at Time 1 is expected to grow at a constant rate of g_L forever. If $g_L <$ WACC, what is a formula for the present value of expected free cash flows when discounted at the WACC? If the most recent free cash flow is expected to grow at a constant rate of g_L forever (and $g_L <$ WACC), what is a formula for the present value of expected free cash flows when discounted at the WACC?

e. Use B&M's data and the free cash flow valuation model to answer the following questions:
   (1) What is its estimated value of operations?
   (2) What is its estimated total corporate value? (This is the entity value.)
   (3) What is its estimated intrinsic value of equity?
   (4) What is its estimated intrinsic stock price per share?

f. You have just learned that B&M has undertaken a major expansion that will change its expected free cash flows to −$10 million in 1 year, $20 million in 2 years, and $35 million in 3 years. After 3 years, free cash flow will grow at a rate of 5%. No new debt or preferred stock was added; the investment was financed by equity from the owners. Assume the WACC is unchanged at 11% and that there are still 10 million shares of stock outstanding.
   (1) What is the company's horizon value (i.e., its value of operations at Year 3)? What is its current value of operations (i.e., at Time 0)?
   (2) What is its estimated intrinsic value of equity on a price-per-share basis?

g. If B&M undertakes the expansion, what percent of B&M's value of operations at Year 0 is due to cash flows from Years 4 and beyond? (*Hint:* Use the horizon value at t = 3 to help answer this question.)

h. Based on your answer to the previous question, what are two reasons why managers often emphasize short-term earnings?

i. Your employer also is considering the acquisition of Hatfield Medical Supplies. You have gathered the following data regarding Hatfield, with all dollars reported in millions: (1) most recent sales of $2,000; (2) most recent total net operating capital, OpCap = $1,120; (3) most recent operating profitability ratio, OP = NOPAT/Sales = 4.5%; and (4) most recent capital requirement ratio, CR = OpCap/Sales = 56%. You estimate that the growth rate in sales from Year 0 to Year 1 will be 10%, from Year 1 to Year 2 will be 8%, from Year 2 to Year 3 will be 5%, and from Year 3 to Year 4 will be 5%. You also estimate that the long-term growth rate beyond Year 4 will be 5%. Assume the operating profitability and capital requirement ratios will not change. Use this information to forecast Hatfield's sales, net operating profit after taxes (NOPAT), OpCap, free cash flow, and return on invested capital (ROIC) for Years 1 through 4. Also estimate the annual growth in free cash flow for Years 2 through 4. The weighted average cost of capital (WACC) is 9%. How does the ROIC in Year 4 compare with the WACC?

j. What is the horizon value at Year 4? What is the total net operating capital at Year 4? Which is larger, and what can explain the difference? What is the value of operations at Year 0? How does the Year-0 value of operations compare with the Year-0 total net operating capital?

k. What are value drivers? What happens to the ROIC and current value of operations if expected growth increases by 1 percentage point relative to the original growth rates (including the long-term growth rate)? What can explain this? (*Hint:* Use Scenario Manager.)

l. Assume growth rates are at their original levels. What happens to the ROIC and current value of operations if the operating profitability ratio increases to 5.5%? Now assume growth rates and operating profitability ratios are at their original levels. What happens to the ROIC and current value of operations if the capital requirement ratio decreases to 51%? Assume growth rates are at their original levels. What is the impact of simultaneous improvements in operating profitability and capital requirements? What is the impact of simultaneous improvements in the growth rates, operating profitability, and capital requirements? (*Hint:* Use Scenario Manager.)

m. What insight does the free cash flow valuation model provide regarding possible reasons for market volatility? (*Hint:* Look at the value of operations for the combinations of ROIC and g_L in the previous questions.)

n. (1) Write out a formula that can be used to value any dividend-paying stock, regardless of its dividend pattern.

(2) What is a constant growth stock? How are constant growth stocks valued?

(3) What happens if a company has a constant g_L that exceeds its r_s? Will many stocks have expected growth greater than the required rate of return in the short run (i.e., for the next few years)? In the long run (i.e., forever)?

o. Assume that Temp Force has a beta coefficient of 1.2, that the risk-free rate (the yield on T-bonds) is 7.0%, and that the market risk premium is 5%. What is the required rate of return on the firm's stock?

p. Assume that Temp Force is a constant growth company whose last dividend (D_0, which was paid yesterday) was $2.00 and whose dividend is expected to grow indefinitely at a 6% rate.

(1) What is the firm's current estimated intrinsic stock price?

(2) What is the stock's expected value 1 year from now?

(3) What are the expected dividend yield, the expected capital gains yield, and the expected total return during the first year?

q. Now assume that the stock is currently selling at $30.29. What is its expected rate of return?

r. Now assume that Temp Force's dividend is expected to experience nonconstant growth of 30% from Year 0 to Year 1, 25% from Year 1 to Year 2, and 15% from Year 2 to Year 3. After Year 3, dividends will grow at a constant rate of 6%. What is the stock's intrinsic value under these conditions? What are the expected dividend yield and capital gains yield during the first year? What are the expected dividend yield and capital gains yield during the fourth year (from Year 3 to Year 4)?

s. What is the market multiple method of valuation? What are its strengths and weaknesses?

t. What are the advantages of the free cash flow valuation model relative to the dividend growth model?

u. What is preferred stock? Suppose a share of preferred stock pays a dividend of $2.10 and investors require a return of 7%. What is the estimated value of the preferred stock?

SELECTED ADDITIONAL CASES

The following cases from CengageCompose cover many of the concepts discussed in this chapter and are available at **http://compose.cengage.com**.

Klein-Brigham Series:

Case 3, "Peachtree Securities, Inc. (B)"; Case 71, "Swan Davis"; Case 78, "Beatrice Peabody"; and Case 101, "TECO Energy."

Brigham-Buzzard Series:

Case 4, "Powerline Network Corporation (Stocks)."

CHAPTER 8

Financial Options and Applications in Corporate Finance

How can someone invest in a stock without buying the stock? If an investor doesn't own a particular stock but expects that stock's price to fall, how can the investor make money? If a company has a big run-up in stock price, how can a shareholder protect the profit without selling the stock? Each question has the same answer: "Use stock options!"

The option market is large and active—about 19 million option contracts traded on average every day in 2018. Most contracts are for 100 shares of stock, so 1.9 billion options traded daily!

Options can take investors on a wild ride. For example, a particular option on Apple stock began trading in late March 2018 at a price of about $2.00. The option price subsequently fell to $0.08 in late April but rebounded to $7.88. It ended up at $5.80 when the option contract reached its expiration date on May 11, 2018.

Keep this activity and volatility in mind as you read the chapter.

The Intrinsic Value of Stock Options

In previous chapters we showed that the intrinsic value of an asset is the present value of its cash flows. This time value of money approach works well for stocks and bonds, but we must use another approach for options and derivatives.

If we can find a portfolio of stocks and risk-free bonds that replicates an option's cash flows, then the intrinsic value of the option must be identical to the value of the replicating portfolio.

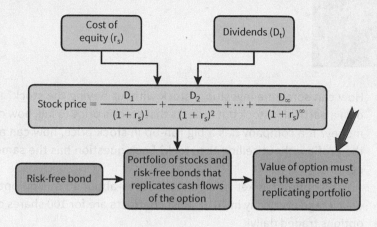

resource

*The textbook's Web site contains an Excel file that will guide you through the chapter's calculations. The file for this chapter is **Ch08 Tool Kit.xlsx**, and we encourage you to open the file and follow along as you read the chapter.*

There are two fundamental approaches to valuing assets. The first is the *discounted cash flow (DCF)* approach, which we covered in previous chapters: An asset's value is the present value of its cash flows. The second is the *option pricing* approach. It is important that all managers understand the basic principles of option pricing for the following reasons. First, many projects allow managers to make strategic or tactical changes in plans as market conditions change. The existence of these "embedded options" often means the difference between a successful project and a failure. Understanding basic financial options can help you manage the value inherent in these real options. Second, many companies use derivatives to manage risk; many derivatives are types of financial options, so an understanding of basic financial options is necessary before tackling derivatives. Third, option pricing theory provides insights into the optimal debt/equity choice, especially when convertible securities are involved. And, fourth, knowing about financial options will help you understand any employee stock options that you receive.

8-1 Overview of Financial Options

In general, an **option** is a contract that gives its owner the right to buy (or sell) an asset at some predetermined price within a specified period of time. However, there are many types of options and option markets.[1] Consider the options reported in Table 8-1, which is an extract from a Listed Options Quotations table as it might appear on a Web site or in a daily newspaper. The first column reports the closing stock price. For example, the table shows that General Computer Corporation's (GCC) stock price closed at $53.50 on January 8, 2019.

---

[1]For an in-depth treatment of options, see Don M. Chance and Robert Brooks, *An Introduction to Derivatives and Risk Management,* 10th ed. (Mason, OH: South-Western, Cengage Learning, 2016); or John C. Hull, *Options, Futures, and Other Derivatives,* 10th ed. (Upper Saddle River, NJ: Prentice-Hall, 2018).

TABLE 8-1
Listed Options Quotations for General Computer Corporation (GCC) on January 8, 2019

		CALLS—LAST QUOTE			PUTS—LAST QUOTE		
Closing Price	Strike Price	February	March	May	February	March	May
53.50	50	4.25	4.75	5.50	0.65	1.40	2.20
53.50	55	1.30	2.05	3.15	2.65	r	4.50
53.50	60	0.30	0.70	1.50	6.65	r	8.00

Note: r means not traded on January 8.

A **call option** gives its owner the right to *buy* a share of stock at a fixed price, which is called the **strike price** (sometimes called the **exercise price** because it is the price at which you exercise the option). A **put option** gives its owner the right to *sell* a share of stock at a fixed strike price. For example, the first row in Table 8-1 is for GCC's options that have a $50 strike price. Observe that the table has columns for call options and for put options with this strike price.

Each option has an **expiration date**, after which the option may not be exercised. Table 8-1 reports data for options that expire in February, March, and May.[2] If the option can be exercised any time before the expiration, it is called an **American option**; if it can be exercised only on its expiration date, it is a **European option**. All of GCC's options are American options. The first row shows that GCC has a call option with a strike price of $50 that expires on Saturday, May 18 (the third Friday in May 2019 is the 17th). The quoted price for this option is $5.50.[3]

When the current stock price is greater than the strike price, the option is **in-the-money**. For example, GCC's $50 (strike) May call option is in-the-money by $53.50 − $50 = $3.50. Thus, if the option were immediately exercised, it would have a payoff of $3.50. On the other hand, GCC's $55 (strike) May call is **out-of-the-money** because the current $53.50 stock price is below the $55 strike price. Obviously, you currently would not want to exercise this option by paying the $55 strike price for a share of stock selling for $53.50. Therefore, the **exercise value**, which is the payoff from immediately exercising a call option, is:[4]

$$\text{Exercise value} = \text{MAX}[\text{Current price of the stock} - \text{Strike price}, 0] \qquad (8\text{-}1)$$

An American option's price always will be greater than (or equal to) its exercise value. If the option's price were less, you could buy the option and immediately exercise it,

---

[2]At its Web site, **www.cboe.com/learncenter/glossary.aspx**, the CBOE defines the expiration date as follows: "The day on which an option contract becomes void. The expiration date for listed stock options is the Saturday after the third Friday of the expiration month. Holders of options should indicate their desire to exercise, if they wish to do so, by this date." The CBOE also defines the expiration time as: "The time of day by which all exercise notices must be received on the expiration date. Technically, the expiration time is currently 5:00 PM on the expiration date, but public holders of option contracts must indicate their desire to exercise no later than 5:30 PM on the business day preceding the expiration date. The times are Eastern Time."

[3]Option contracts are generally written in 100-share multiples, but to reduce confusion we focus on the cost and payoffs of a single option.

[4]MAX means choose the maximum. For example, MAX[15, 0] = 15 and MAX[−10, 0] = 0.

reaping a sure gain. For example, GCC's May call with a $50 strike price sells for $5.50, which is greater than its exercise value of $3.50. Also, GCC's out-of-the-money May call with a strike price of $55 sells for $3.15 even though it would be worthless if it had to be exercised immediately. An option always will be worth more than zero as long as there is still any chance it will end up in-the-money: Where there is life, there is hope! The difference between the option's price and its exercise value is called the **time value** of the option because it represents the extra amount over the option's immediate exercise value that a purchaser will pay for the chance the stock price will appreciate over time.[5] For example, GCC's May call with a $50 strike price sells for $5.50 and has an exercise value of $3.50, so its time value is $5.50 − $3.50 = $2.00.

Suppose you bought GCC's $50 (strike) May call option for $5.50, and then the stock price increased to $60. If you exercised the option by purchasing the stock for the $50 strike price, you could immediately sell the share of stock at its market price of $60, resulting in a payoff of $60 − $50 = $10. Notice that the stock itself had a return of 12.1% = ($60 − $53.50)/$53.50, but the option's return was 81.8% = ($10 − $5.50)/$5.50. Thus, the option offers the possibility of a higher return.

However, if the stock price fell to $50 and stayed there until the option expired, the stock would have a return of −6.5% = ($50.00 − $53.50)/$53.50, but the option would have a 100% loss (it would expire worthless). As this example shows, call options are a lot riskier than stocks. This works to your advantage if the stock price goes up but to your disadvantage if the stock price falls.

Suppose you bought GCC's May put option (with a strike price of $50) for $2.20 and then the stock price fell to $45. The put option gives you the right to sell one share of GCC stock at the strike price, or $50, so you could buy a share of stock for $45 and exercise the put option. This would allow you to use the option to sell the share of stock for $50, and your payoff from exercising the put would be $5 = $50 − $45. Stockholders would lose money because the stock price fell, but a put holder would make money. In this example, your rate of return would be 127.3% = ($5 − $2.20)/$2.20. So if you think a stock price is going to fall, you can make money by purchasing a put option. On the other hand, if the stock price doesn't fall below the strike price of $50 before the put expires, you would lose 100% of your investment in the put option.[6]

Options are traded on a number of exchanges, with the Chicago Board Options Exchange (CBOE) being the oldest and the largest. Existing options can be traded in the secondary market in much the same way that existing shares of stock are traded in secondary markets. But unlike new shares of stock that are issued by corporations, new options can be "issued" by investors. This is called **writing** an option.

For example, you could write a call option and sell it to some other investor. You would receive cash from the option buyer at the time you wrote the option, but you would be obligated to sell a share of stock at the strike price if the option buyer later decided to exercise the option.[7] Thus, each option has two parties, the writer and the buyer, with the CBOE (or some other exchange) acting as an intermediary. Other than commissions, the writer's profits are exactly opposite those of the buyer. An investor who writes call options against stock held in his or her portfolio is said to be selling **covered call options**. Call options sold without the stock to back them up are called **naked call options**.

---

[5]Among traders, an option's market price is also called its "premium." This is particularly confusing because for all other securities the word "premium" means the excess of the market price over some base price. To avoid confusion, we will not use the word "premium" to refer to the option price.

[6]Most investors don't actually exercise an option prior to expiration. If they want to cash in the option's profit or cut its losses, they sell the option to some other investor. As you will see later in the chapter, the cash flow from selling an American option before its expiration is always greater than (or equal to) the profit from exercising the option.

[7]Your broker would require collateral to ensure that you kept this obligation.

In addition to options on individual stocks, options are also available on several stock indexes, such as the NYSE Index and the S&P 100 Index. Index options permit one to hedge (or bet) on a rise or fall in the general market as well as on individual stocks.

The leverage involved in option trading makes it possible for speculators with just a few dollars to make a fortune almost overnight. Also, investors with sizable portfolios can sell options against their stocks and earn the value of the option (less brokerage commissions) even if the stock's price remains constant. Most important, though, options can be used to create *hedges* that protect the value of an individual stock or portfolio.[8]

Conventional options are generally written for 6 months or less, but a type of option called a **Long-Term Equity AnticiPation Security (LEAPS)** is different. Like conventional options, LEAPS are listed on exchanges and are available on both individual stocks and stock indexes. The major difference is that LEAPS are long-term options, having maturities of up to almost 3 years. One-year LEAPS cost about twice as much as the matching 3-month option, but because of their much longer time to expiration, LEAPS provide buyers with more potential for gains and offer better long-term protection for a portfolio.

Corporations on whose stocks the options are written have nothing to do with the option market. Corporations do not raise money in the option market, nor do they have any direct transactions in it. Moreover, option holders do not vote for corporate directors or receive dividends. There have been studies by the SEC and others as to whether option trading stabilizes or destabilizes the stock market and whether this activity helps or hinders corporations seeking to raise new capital. The studies have not been conclusive, but research on the impact of option trading is ongoing.

SELF-TEST

What is an option? A call option? A put option?

Define a call option's exercise value. Why is the market price of a call option always above its exercise value?

Brighton Memory's stock is currently trading at $50 a share. A call option on the stock with a $35 strike price currently sells for $21. What is the exercise value of the call option? **($15.00)** *What is the time value?* **($6.00)**

8-2 The Single-Period Binomial Option Pricing Approach

We can use a model like the Capital Asset Pricing Model (CAPM) to calculate the required return on a stock and then use that required return to discount its expected future cash flows to find its value. No such model exists for the required return on options, so we must use a different approach to find an option's value. In Section 8-5 we describe the Black-Scholes option pricing model, but in this section we explain the binomial option pricing model. The idea behind this model is different from that of the DCF model used for stock valuation. Instead of discounting cash flows at a required return to obtain a price, as we did with the stock valuation model, we will use the option, shares of stock, and the

---

[8]Insiders who trade illegally generally buy options rather than stock because the leverage inherent in options increases the profit potential. However, it is illegal to use insider information for personal gain, and an insider using such information would be taking advantage of the option seller. Insider trading, in addition to being unfair and essentially equivalent to stealing, hurts the economy: Investors lose confidence in the capital markets and raise their required returns because of an increased element of risk, and this raises the cost of capital and thus reduces the level of real investment.

risk-free rate to construct a portfolio whose value we already know and then deduce the option's price from this portfolio's value.

The following sections describe and apply the binomial option pricing model to Western Cellular, a manufacturer of cell phones. Call options exist that permit the holder to buy 1 share of Western at a strike price, X, of $35. Western's options will expire at the end of 6 months (t is the number of years until expiration, so t = 0.5 for Western's options). Western's stock price, P, is currently $40 per share. Given this background information, we will use the binomial model to determine the call option's value. The first step is to determine the option's possible payoffs, as described in the next section.

8-2a Payoffs in a Single-Period Binomial Model

In general, the time until expiration can be divided into many periods, with n denoting the number of periods. But in a single-period model, which we describe in this section, there is only one period. We assume that, at the end of the period, the stock's price can take on only one of two possible values, so this is called the **binomial approach**. For this example, Western's stock will either go up (u) by a factor of 1.25 or go down (d) by a factor of 0.80. If we were considering a riskier stock, then we would have assumed a wider range of ending prices; we will show how to estimate this range later in the chapter. If we let u = 1.25 and d = 0.80, then the ending stock price will be either P(u) = $40(1.25) = $50 or P(d) = $40(0.80) = $32. Figure 8-1 illustrates the stock's possible price paths and contains additional information about the call option that is explained in the text that follows.

resource

See Ch08 Tool Kit.xlsx on the textbook's Web site.

FIGURE 8-1

Binomial Payoffs from Holding Western Cellular's Stock or Call Option

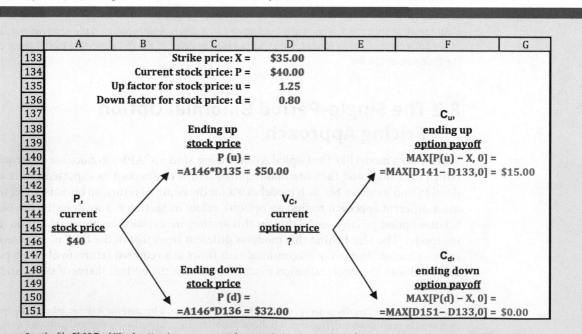

Source: See the file *Ch08 Tool Kit.xlsx*. Numbers are reported as rounded values for clarity but are calculated using *Excel*'s full precision. Thus, intermediate calculations using the figure's rounded values will be inexact.

When the option expires at the end of the period, Western's stock will sell for either $50 or $32. As shown in Figure 8-1, if the stock goes up to $50, then the option will have a payoff, C_u, of $15 at expiration because the option is in-the-money: $50 − $35 = $15. If the stock price goes down to $32, then the option's payoff, C_d, will be zero because the option is out-of-the-money.

8-2b The Hedge Portfolio Approach

Suppose we created a portfolio by writing 1 call option and purchasing 1 share of stock. As Figure 8-1 shows, if the stock price goes up, then our portfolio's stock will be worth $50, but we will owe $15 on the option, so our portfolio's net payoff is $35 = $50 − $15. If the stock price goes down, then our portfolio's stock will be worth only $32, but the amount we owe on the written option also will fall to zero, leaving the portfolio's net payoff at $32. The portfolio's end-of-period price range is smaller than if we had just owned the stock, so writing the call option reduces the portfolio's price risk. Taking this further: Is it possible for us to choose the number of shares held by our portfolio so that it will have the same net payoff whether the stock goes up or down? If so, then our portfolio is hedged and will have a riskless payoff when the option expires. Therefore, it is called a **hedge portfolio**.

We are not really interested in investing in the hedge portfolio, but we want to use it to help us determine the value of the option. The important point to recognize is that if the hedge portfolio has a riskless net payoff when the option expires, then we can find the present value of this payoff by discounting it at the risk-free rate. Our hedge portfolio's current value must equal this present value, which allows us to determine the option's value. The following example illustrates the steps in this approach.

1. FINDING N_s, THE NUMBER OF SHARES OF STOCK IN THE HEDGE PORTFOLIO

We want the portfolio's payoff to be the same whether the stock goes up or down. If we write 1 call option and buy N_s shares of stock, then the portfolio's stock will be worth $N_s(P)(u)$ should the stock price go up, so its net payoff will be $N_s(P)(u) − C_u$. The portfolio's stock will be worth $N_s(P)(d)$ if the stock price goes down, so its net payoff will be $N_s(P)(d) − C_d$. Setting these portfolio payoffs equal to one another (because we want the portfolio to have the same ending value whether the stock goes up or down) and then solving for N_s yields the number of shares of stock to buy for each call option in order to create the hedge portfolio:

$$N_s = \frac{C_u - C_d}{P(u) - P(d)} = \frac{C_u - C_d}{P(u - d)} \tag{8-2}$$

For Western, the hedge portfolio has 0.83333 share of stock:[9]

$$N_s = \frac{C_u - C_d}{P(u) - P(d)} = \frac{\$15 - \$0}{\$50 - \$32} = 0.83333$$

---

[9]An easy way to remember this formula is to notice that N_s is equal to the range in possible option payoffs divided by the range in possible stock prices.

2. FINDING THE HEDGE PORTFOLIO'S PAYOFF

Our next step is to find the hedge portfolio's payoff. Recall that the hedge portfolio has N_s shares of stock and that we have written one call option, so the call option's payoff must be subtracted:

$$
\begin{aligned}
\text{Hedge portfolio's payoff if stock is up} &= N_s P(u) - C_u \\
&= 0.83333(\$50) - \$15 \\
&= \$26.6665
\end{aligned}
$$

$$
\begin{aligned}
\text{Hedge portfolio's payoff if stock is down} &= N_s P(d) - C_d \\
&= 0.83333(\$32) - \$0 \\
&= \$26.6665
\end{aligned}
$$

Figure 8-2 illustrates the payoffs of the hedge portfolio.

3. FINDING THE PRESENT VALUE OF THE HEDGE PORTFOLIO'S PAYOFF

resource

See Ch08 Tool Kit.xlsx on the textbook's Web site.

Because the hedge portfolio's payoff is riskless, the current value of the hedge portfolio must be equal to the present value of its riskless payoff. Suppose the nominal annual risk-free rate, r_{RF}, is 8%. What is the present value of the hedge portfolio's riskless payoff of $26.6665 in 6 months? Recall that the present value depends on how frequently interest is

FIGURE 8-2
Hedge Portfolio with Riskless Payoffs

	A	B	C	D	E	F
180					Strike price: X =	$35.00
181					Current stock price: P =	$40.00
182					Up factor for stock price: u =	1.25
183					Down factor for stock price: d =	0.80
184			Up option payoff: C_u = MAX[0,P(u)-X] =			$15.00
185			Down option payoff: C_d =MAX[0,P(d)-X] =			$0.00
186		Number of shares of stock in portfolio: N_s = (C_u - C_d) / P(u-d) =				0.83333
187						
188			Stock price = P (u) =	$50.00		
189	P,		Portfolio's stock payoff: = P(u)(N_s) =			$41.67
190	current		Subtract option's payoff: C_u =			$15.00
191	stock price		Portfolio's net payoff = P(u)N_s - C_u =			$26.67
192	$40					
193						
194						
195						
196			Stock price = P (d) =	$32.00		
197			Portfolio's stock payoff: = P(d)(N_s) =			$26.67
198			Subtract option's payoff: C_d =			$0.00
199			Portfolio's net payoff = P(d)N_s - C_d =			$26.67
200						

Source: See the file **Ch08 Tool Kit.xlsx**. Numbers are reported as rounded values for clarity but are calculated using *Excel*'s full precision. Thus, intermediate calculations using the figure's rounded values will be inexact.

compounded. Let's assume that interest is compounded daily.[10] We can use a financial calculator to find the present value of the hedge portfolio's payoff by entering N = 0.5(365), because there are 365 days in a year and the contract expires in half a year; I/YR = 8/365 because we want a daily interest rate; PMT = 0; and FV = −$26.6665 because we want to know the amount we would take today in exchange for giving up the payoff when the option expires. Using these inputs, we solve for PV = $25.6210, which is the present value of the hedge portfolio's payoff and which must also be the current value of the components of the hedge portfolio.[11]

4. FINDING THE OPTION'S VALUE

The current value of the hedge portfolio is the value of the stock, $N_s(P)$, less the value of the call option we wrote:

$$\text{Current value of hedge portfolio} = N_s(P) - V_C$$

Because the payoff is riskless, the current value of the hedge portfolio must also equal the present value of the riskless payoff:

$$\text{Current value of hedge portfolio} = \text{Present value of riskless payoff}$$

Substituting for the current value of the hedge portfolio, we get:

$$N_s(P) - V_C = \text{Present value of riskless portfolio}$$

Solving for the call option's value, we get:

$$V_C = N_s(P) - \text{Present value of riskless portfolio}$$

For Western's option, this is:

$$V_C = 0.83333(\$40) - \$25.621$$
$$= \$7.71$$

8-2c Hedge Portfolios and Replicating Portfolios

In our previous derivation of the call option's value, we combined an investment in the stock with writing a call option to create a risk-free investment. We can modify this approach and, instead, create a portfolio that replicates the call option's payoffs. For example, suppose we formed a portfolio by purchasing 0.83333 shares of Western's stock and borrowing $25.621 at the risk-free rate (this is equivalent to selling a T-bill short). In 6 months, we would repay the future value of a $25.621, compounded daily at the risk-free rate. Using a financial calculator, input N = 0.5(365), I/YR = 8/365, PV = −$25.621, and solve for FV = $26.6665.[12] If the stock goes up, our net payoff would be 0.83333($50) − $26.6665 = $15.00. If the stock goes down, our net payoff would be 0.83333($32) − $26.6665 = $0. The portfolio's payoffs are exactly equal to the option's payoffs as shown in Figure 8-1, so our portfolio of 0.83333 shares of stock

---

[10] Option pricing models usually assume continuous compounding, which we discuss in **Web Extension 4B** on the textbook's Web site, but daily compounding works well. We will apply continuous compounding in Sections 8-3 and 8-4.

[11] We could also solve for the present value using the present value equation with the daily periodic interest rate and the number of daily periods: PV = $26.6665/(1+ 0.08/365)^{0.5(365)} = $25.6210.

[12] Alternatively, use the future value equation with daily compounding: $25.621(1 + 0.08/365)^{365(0.5/1)} = $26.6665.

and the $25.621 that we borrowed would exactly replicate the option's payoffs. Therefore, this is called a **replicating portfolio**. Our cost to create this portfolio is the cost of the stock less the amount we borrowed:

$$\text{Cost of replicating portfolio} = 0.83333(\$40) - \$25.621 = \$7.71$$

If the call option did not sell for exactly $7.71, then a clever investor could make a sure profit. For example, suppose the option sold for $8. The investor would write an option, which would provide $8 of cash now but would obligate the investor to pay either $15 or $0 in 6 months when the option expires. However, the investor could use the $8 to create the replicating portfolio, leaving the investor with $8 − $7.71 = $0.29. In 6 months, the replicating portfolio will pay either $15 or $0. Thus, the investor isn't exposed to any risk—the payoffs received from the replicating portfolio exactly offset the payoffs owed on the option. The investor uses none of his own money, has no risk, has no net future obligations, but has $0.29 in cash. This is **arbitrage**, and if such an arbitrage opportunity existed, then the investor would scale it up by writing thousands of options.[13]

Such arbitrage opportunities don't persist for long in a reasonably efficient economy because other investors will also see the opportunity and will try to do the same thing. With so many investors trying to write (i.e., sell) the option, its price will fall; with so many investors trying to purchase the stock, its price will increase. This will continue until the option and replicating portfolio have identical prices. And because our financial markets are really quite efficient, you would never observe the derivative security and the replicating portfolio trading for different prices—they would always have the same price and there would be no arbitrage opportunities. What this means is that, by finding the price of a portfolio that replicates a derivative security, we have also found the price of the derivative security itself!

SELF-TEST

Describe how a risk-free hedge portfolio can be created using stocks and options.

How can such a portfolio be used to help estimate a call option's value?

What is a replicating portfolio, and how is it used to find the value of a derivative security?

What is arbitrage?

Lett Incorporated's stock price is now $50, but it is expected either to rise by a factor of 1.5 or to fall by a factor of 0.7 by the end of the year. There is a call option on Lett's stock with a strike price of $55 and an expiration date 1 year from now. What are the stock's possible prices at the end of the year? **($75 or $35)** *What is the call option's payoff if the stock price goes up?* **($20)** *If the stock price goes down?* **($0)** *If we sell 1 call option, how many shares of Lett's stock must we buy to create a riskless hedged portfolio consisting of the option position and the stock?* **(0.5)** *What is the payoff of this portfolio?* **($17.50)** *If the annual risk-free rate is 6%, then how much is the riskless portfolio worth today (assuming daily compounding)?* **($16.48)** *What is the current value of the call option?* **($8.52)**

---

[13]If the option sold for less than the replicating portfolio, say for $7.50, the investor would raise cash by shorting the portfolio and use the proceeds to purchase the option. To do this, short sell 0.83333 shares of stock at $40 per share for a total of $33.33. Then invest $25.62 in Treasury bills. This leaves $7.71. Use this to purchase the option, leaving $0.21. The combination of the option and the investment in Treasury bills will cover the short position in the stock perfectly and the $0.21 is the investor's arbitrage profit. The investor would scale this up by purchasing thousands of options in this way.

8-3 The Single-Period Binomial Option Pricing Formula[14]

The hedge portfolio approach works well if you only want to find the value of one type of option with one period until expiration. But in all other situations, the step-by-step approach becomes tedious very quickly. The following sections describe a formula that replaces the step-by-step approach.

8-3a The Binomial Option Pricing Formula

With a little (or a lot!) of algebra, we can derive a single formula for a call option. Instead of using daily compounding, we use continuous compounding to make the binomial formula consistent with the Black-Scholes formula (presented in Section 8-5).[15] We also add a new variable, n, which is the number of periods until expiration at time t. We only consider 1 period (i.e., n = 1) in this example, but we consider multiple periods in Section 8-4. Here is the resulting binomial option pricing formula:

$$V_C = \frac{C_u \left[\dfrac{e^{r_{RF}(t/n)} - d}{u - d} \right] + C_d \left[\dfrac{u - e^{r_{RF}(t/n)}}{u - d} \right]}{e^{r_{RF}(t/n)}} \qquad (8\text{-}3)$$

After programming it into *Excel*, which we did for this chapter's ***Tool Kit***, it is easy to change inputs and determine the new value of a call option.

We can apply this formula to Western's call option:

$$V_C = \frac{\$15 \left[\dfrac{e^{0.08(0.5/1)} - 0.80}{1.25 - 0.80} \right] + \$0 \left[\dfrac{1.25 - e^{0.08(0.5/1)}}{1.25 - 0.80} \right]}{e^{0.08(0.5/1)}}$$

$$= \frac{\$15(0.5351) + \$0(0.4649)}{1.04081} = \$7.71$$

Notice that this is the same value that resulted from the step-by-step process shown earlier.

The binomial option pricing formula in Equation 8-3 does not include the actual probabilities that the stock will go up or down, nor does it include the expected stock return. This seems odd to many students since, for every other security we study, the expected return is essential to finding its value, and for options, the higher the stock's expected return, the greater is the chance that the call will be in-the-money at expiration. However,

---

[14]The material in this section is relatively technical, and some instructors may choose to skip it with no loss in continuity.

[15]With daily compounding, the present value is:

$$PV = FV/[(1 + r_{RF}/365)^{365(0.5/1)}]$$

With continuous compounding, the present value is:

$$PV = FV\, e^{-r_{RF}(t/n)}$$

See ***Web Extension 4C*** on the textbook's Web site for more discussion of continuous compounding.

the current stock price already incorporates its expected return as a discount rate, and this is just enough information to find an option price.

8-3b Primitive Securities and the Binomial Option Pricing Formula

If we want to value other Western call options or puts that expire in 6 months, then we can use Equation 8-3, but there is a time-saving approach. Notice that for options with the same time left until expiration, C_u and C_d are the only variables that depend on the option itself. The other variables depend only on the stock process (u and d), the risk-free rate, the time until expiration, and the number of periods until expiration. If we group these variables together, we can then define π_u and π_d as:

$$\pi_u = \frac{\left[\dfrac{e^{r_{RF}(t/n)} - d}{u - d}\right]}{e^{r_{RF}(t/n)}} \tag{8-4}$$

and

$$\pi_d = \frac{\left[\dfrac{u - e^{r_{RF}(t/n)}}{u - d}\right]}{e^{r_{RF}(t/n)}} \tag{8-5}$$

By substituting these values into Equation 8-3, we obtain an option pricing model that can be applied to all of Western's 6-month options:

$$V_C = C_u \pi_u + C_d \pi_d \tag{8-6}$$

In this example, π_u and π_d are:

$$\pi_u = \frac{\left[\dfrac{e^{0.08(0.5/1)} - 0.80}{1.25 - 0.80}\right]}{e^{0.08(0.5/1)}} = 0.5142$$

and

$$\pi_d = \frac{\left[\dfrac{1.25 - e^{0.08(0.5/1)}}{1.25 - 0.80}\right]}{e^{0.08(0.5/1)}} = 0.4466$$

Using Equation 8-6, the value of Western's 6-month call option with a strike price of $35 is:

$$\begin{aligned} V_C &= C_u \pi_u + C_d \pi_d \\ &= \$15(0.5142) + \$0(0.4466) \\ &= \$7.71 \end{aligned}$$

Sometimes π_u and π_d are called *primitive securities* because π_u is the price of a simple security that pays \$1 if the stock goes up and nothing if it goes down; π_d is the opposite. This means that we can use π_u and π_d to find the price of any 6-month option on Western. For example, suppose we want to find the value of a 6-month call option on Western but with a strike price of \$30. Rather than reinvent the wheel, all we have to do is find the payoffs of this option and use the same values of π_u and π_d in Equation 8-6. If the stock goes up to \$50, the option will pay \$50 − \$30 = \$20; if the stock falls to \$32, the option will pay \$32 − \$30 = \$2. The value of the call option is:

$$\text{Value of 6-month call with \$30 strike price} = C_u\pi_u + C_d\pi_d$$
$$= \$20(0.5142) + \$2(0.4466)$$
$$= \$11.18$$

It is a bit tedious initially to calculate π_u and π_d, but once you save them, it is easy to find the value of any 6-month call or put option on the stock. In fact, you can use these values of π to find the value of any security with payoffs that depend on Western's 6-month stock prices, which makes them a very powerful tool.

SELF-TEST

Yegi's Fine Phones has a current stock price of \$30. You need to find the value of a call option with a strike price of \$32 that expires in 3 months. The annual risk-free rate is 6%. Use the binomial model with one period until expiration (i.e., t = 0.25 and n = 1). The factor for an increase in stock price is u = 1.15; the factor for a downward movement is d = 0.85. What are the possible stock prices at expiration? (\$34.50 or \$25.50) *What are the option's possible payoffs at expiration?* (\$2.50 or \$0) *What are π_u and π_d?* (0.5422 and 0.4429) *What is the current value of the option (assume each month is 1/12 of a year)?* (\$1.36)

8-4 The Multi-Period Binomial Option Pricing Model[16]

Clearly, the one-period example is simplified. Although you could duplicate buying 0.8333 share and writing 1 option by buying 8,333 shares and writing 10,000 options, the stock price assumptions are unrealistic—Western's stock price could be almost anything after 6 months, not just \$50 or \$32. However, if we allowed the stock to move up or down more often, then a more realistic distribution of ending prices would result. In other words, dividing the time until expiration into more periods would improve the realism of the resulting prices at expiration. The key to implementing a multi-period binomial model is to keep the stock return's annual standard deviation the same no matter how many periods you have during a year. In fact, analysts typically begin with an estimate of the annual standard deviation and use it to determine u and d. The derivation is beyond the scope of a financial management textbook, but the appropriate equations are:

$$u = e^{\sigma\sqrt{t/n}} \tag{8-7}$$

$$d = \frac{1}{u} \tag{8-8}$$

---

[16]The material in this section is relatively technical, and some instructors may choose to skip it with no loss in continuity.

where

> σ = The annualized standard deviation of the stock's return.
>
> t = The time in years until expiration.
>
> n = The number of periods until expiration.

The standard deviation of Western's stock returns is 0.315573, and application of Equations 8-7 and 8-8 confirms the values of u and d that we used previously:

$$u = e^{0.315573\sqrt{0.5/1}} = 1.25 \qquad \text{and} \qquad d = \frac{1}{1.25} = 0.80$$

Now suppose we allow stock prices to change every 3 months, which means that there are 2 periods until expiration (i.e., n = 2). Using Equations 8-7 and 8-8, we estimate u and d to be

$$u = e^{0.31573\sqrt{0.5/2}} = 1.1709 \qquad \text{and} \qquad d = \frac{1}{1.1709} = 0.8540$$

At the end of the first 3 months, Western's price would either rise to \$40(1.1709) = \$46.84 or fall to \$40(0.8540) = \$34.16. If the price rises in the first 3 months to \$46.84, then it would either go up to \$46.84(1.1709) = \$54.84 or go down to \$46.84(0.8540) = \$40 at expiration. If instead the price initially falls to \$40(0.8540) = \$34.16 during the first 3 months, then it would either go up to \$34.16(1.1709) = \$40 or go down to \$34.16(0.8540) = \$29.17 by expiration. This pattern of stock price movements is called a **binomial lattice** and is shown in Figure 8-3.

Because the interest rate and the volatility (as defined by u and d) are constant for each period, we can calculate π_u and π_d for any period and apply these same values for each period:[17]

$$\pi_u = \frac{\left[\dfrac{e^{0.08(0.5/2)} - 0.8540}{1.1709 - 0.8540}\right]}{e^{0.08(0.5/2)}} = 0.51400$$

$$\pi_d = \frac{\left[\dfrac{1.1709 - e^{0.08(0.5/2)}}{1.1709 - 0.8540}\right]}{e^{0.08(0.5/2)}} = 0.46620$$

These values are shown in Figure 8-3.

The lattice shows the possible stock prices at the option's expiration, and we know the strike price, so we can calculate the option payoffs at expiration, as shown in Figure 8-3. If we focus only on the upper right portion of the lattice shown inside the dotted lines, then it is similar to the single-period problem we solved in Section 8-3. In fact, we can use the binomial option pricing model from Equation 8-6 to determine the value of the option in 3 months given that the stock price increased to \$46.84. As shown in Figure 8-3, the option will be worth \$12.53 in 3 months if the stock price goes up to \$46.84. We can repeat this procedure on the lower right portion of Figure 8-3 to determine the call option's value in 3 months if the stock price falls to \$34.16; in this case, the call's value would be \$2.57. Finally, we can use Equation 8-6 and the 3-month option values just calculated to

---

[17]These values were calculated in *Excel*, so there may be small differences due to rounding in intermediate steps.

FIGURE 8-3
Two-Period Binomial Lattice and Option Valuation

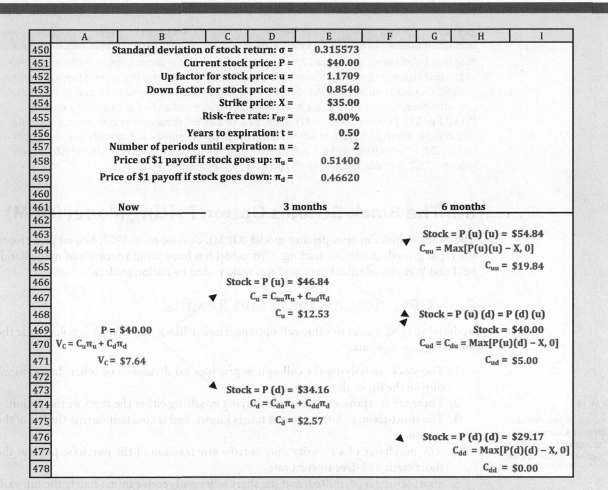

	A	B	C	D	E	F	G	H	I
450		Standard deviation of stock return: σ =			0.315573				
451		Current stock price: P =			$40.00				
452		Up factor for stock price: u =			1.1709				
453		Down factor for stock price: d =			0.8540				
454		Strike price: X =			$35.00				
455		Risk-free rate: r_{RF} =			8.00%				
456		Years to expiration: t =			0.50				
457		Number of periods until expiration: n =			2				
458		Price of $1 payoff if stock goes up: π_u =			0.51400				
459		Price of $1 payoff if stock goes down: π_d =			0.46620				
460									
461		**Now**			**3 months**			**6 months**	
462									
463							Stock = P (u) (u) = $54.84		
464						▼	C_{uu} = Max[P(u)(u) − X, 0]		
465							C_{uu} = $19.84		
466				Stock = P (u) = $46.84					
467			▼	$C_u = C_{uu}\pi_u + C_{ud}\pi_d$					
468				C_u = $12.53			Stock = P (u) (d) = P (d) (u)		
469		P = $40.00					Stock = $40.00		
470	$V_C = C_u\pi_u + C_d\pi_d$						$C_{ud} = C_{du}$ = Max[P(u)(d) − X, 0]		
471	V_C = $7.64						C_{ud} = $5.00		
472									
473			▲	Stock = P (d) = $34.16					
474				$C_d = C_{du}\pi_u + C_{dd}\pi_d$					
475				C_d = $2.57					
476							Stock = P (d) (d) = $29.17		
477						▲	C_{dd} = Max[P(d)(d) − X, 0]		
478							C_{dd} = $0.00		

Source: See the file *Ch08 Tool Kit.xlsx*. Numbers are reported as rounded values for clarity but are calculated using *Excel*'s full precision. Thus, intermediate calculations using the figure's rounded values will be inexact.

resource

See Ch08 Tool Kit.xlsx on the textbook's Web site.

determine the current price of the option, which is $7.64. Thus, we are able to find the current option price by solving three simple binomial problems.

If we broke the year into smaller periods and allowed the stock price to move up or down more often, then the lattice would have an even more realistic range of possible ending stock prices. Of course, estimating the current option price would require solving lots of binomial problems within the lattice, but each problem is simple and computers can solve them rapidly. With more outcomes, the resulting estimated option price is more accurate. For example, if we divide the year into 15 periods, then the estimated price is $7.42. With 50 periods, the price is $7.39. With 100 periods it is still $7.39, which shows that the solution converges to its final value within a relatively small number of steps. In fact, as we break the time to expiration into smaller and smaller periods, the solution for the binomial approach converges to the Black-Scholes solution, which is described in the next section.

The binomial approach is widely used to value options with more complicated payoffs than the call option in our example, such as employee stock options. This is beyond the scope of a financial management textbook, but if you are interested in learning more about the binomial approach, you should take a look at the textbooks by Don Chance and John Hull cited in footnote 1.

SELF-TEST

Ringling Cycle's stock price is now $20. You need to find the value of a call option with a strike price of $22 that expires in 2 months. You want to use the binomial model with 2 periods (each period is a month). Your assistant has calculated that $u = 1.1553$, $d = 0.8656$, $\pi_u = 0.4838$, and $\pi_d = 0.5095$. Draw the binomial lattice for stock prices. What are the possible stock prices after 1 month? **($23.11 or $17.31)** *After 2 months?* **($26.69, $20, or $14.99)** *What are the option's possible payoffs at expiration?* **($4.69, $0, or $0)** *What will the option's value be in 1 month if the stock goes up?* **($2.27)** *What will the option's value be in 1 month if the stock price goes down?* **($0)** *If each month is 1/12 of a year, what is the current value of the option?* **($1.10)**

8-5 The Black-Scholes Option Pricing Model (OPM)

The **Black-Scholes option pricing model (OPM)**, developed in 1973, helped give rise to the rapid growth in options trading. This model has been programmed into many handheld and Web-based calculators, and it is widely used by option traders.

8-5a OPM Assumptions and Results

In deriving their model to value call options, Fischer Black and Myron Scholes made the following assumptions.

1. The stock underlying the call option provides no dividends or other distributions during the life of the option.
2. There are no transaction costs for buying or selling either the stock or the option.
3. The short-term, risk-free interest rate is known and is constant during the life of the option.
4. Any purchaser of a security may borrow any fraction of the purchase price at the short-term, risk-free interest rate.
5. Short selling is permitted, and the short seller will receive immediately the full cash proceeds of today's price for a security sold short.
6. The call option can be exercised only on its expiration date.
7. Trading in all securities takes place continuously, and the instantaneous percentage stock changes (i.e., returns) are distributed normally.

WWW

For a Web-based option calculator, see **www .cboe.com/LearnCenter /OptionCalculator.aspx.**

The derivation of the Black-Scholes model rests on the same concepts as the binomial model, except time is divided into such small increments that stock prices change continuously. The Black-Scholes model for call options consists of the following three equations:

$$V_C = P[N(d_1)] - X e^{-r_{RF}t}[N(d_2)] \tag{8-9}$$

$$d_1 = \frac{\ln(P/X) + [r_{RF} + (\sigma^2/2)]t}{\sigma\sqrt{t}} \tag{8-10}$$

$$d_2 = d_1 - \sigma\sqrt{t} \tag{8-11}$$

The variables used in the Black-Scholes model are as follows.

V_C = Current value of the call option.

P = Current price of the underlying stock.

$N(d_i)$ = Probability that a deviation less than d_i will occur in a standard normal distribution. Thus, $N(d_1)$ and $N(d_2)$ represent areas under a standard normal distribution function.

X = Strike price of the option.

$e \approx 2.7183$.

r_{RF} = Risk-free interest rate.[18]

t = Time until the option expires (the option period).

$\ln(P/X)$ = Natural logarithm of P/X.

σ = Standard deviation of the rate of return on the stock.

The value of the option is a function of five variables: (1) P, the stock's price; (2) t, the option's time to expiration; (3) X, the strike price; (4) σ, the standard deviation of the underlying stock; and (5) r_{RF}, the risk-free rate. We do not derive the Black-Scholes model; the derivation involves some extremely complicated mathematics that go far beyond the scope of this text. However, it is not difficult to use the model. Under the assumptions set forth previously, if the option price is different from the one found by Equation 8-9, then this would provide the opportunity for arbitrage profits, which would force the option price back to the value indicated by the model. As we noted earlier, the Black-Scholes model is widely used by traders because actual option prices conform reasonably well to values derived from the model.

8-5b Application of the Black-Scholes Option Pricing Model to a Call Option

The current stock price (P), the exercise price (X), and the time to maturity (t) can all be obtained from a newspaper, such as *The Wall Street Journal,* or from online sources, such as the CBOE's Web site. The risk-free rate (r_{RF}) is the yield on a Treasury bill with a maturity equal to the option expiration date. The annualized standard deviation of stock returns (σ) can be estimated from daily stock prices. First, find the stock return for each trading day for a sample period, such as each trading day of the past year. Second, estimate the variance of the daily stock returns. Third, multiply this estimated daily variance by the number of trading days in a year, which is

---

[18]The correct process to estimate the risk-free rate for use in the Black-Scholes model for an option with 6 months to expiration is to find the annual nominal rate (compounded continuously) that has the same effective annual rate as a 6-month T-bill. For example, suppose a 6-month T-bill is yielding a 6-month periodic rate of 4.081%. The risk-free rate to use in the Black-Scholes model is $r_{RF} = \ln(1 + 0.0408)/0.5 = 8\%$. Under continuous compounding, a nominal rate of 8% produces an effective rate of $e^{0.08} - 1 = 8.33\%$. This is the same effective rate yielded by the T-bill: $(1+0.0408)^2 - 1 = 8.33\%$. The same approach can be applied for options with different expiration periods. We will provide the appropriate risk-free rate for all problems and examples.

approximately 250.[19] Take the square root of the annualized variance, and the result is an estimate of the annualized standard deviation.

We will use the Black-Scholes model to estimate Western's call option that we discussed previously. Here are the inputs:

$$P = \$40$$
$$X = \$35$$
$$t = 6 \text{ months (0.5 years)}$$
$$r_{RF} = 8.0\% = 0.080$$
$$\sigma = 31.557\% = 0.31557$$

resource

See Ch08 Tool Kit.xlsx on the textbook's Web site for all calculations.

Given this information, we first estimate d_1 and d_2 from Equations 8-10 and 8-11:

$$d_1 = \frac{\ln(\$40/\$35) + [0.08 + ((0.31557^2)/2)](0.5)}{0.31557\sqrt{0.5}}$$

$$= \frac{0.13353 + 0.064896}{0.22314} = 0.8892$$

$$d_2 = d_1 - 0.31557\sqrt{0.5} = 0.6661$$

Note that $N(d_1)$ and $N(d_2)$ represent areas under a standard normal distribution function. The easiest way to calculate this value is with *Excel*. For example, we can use the function =**NORMSDIST(0.8892)**, which returns a value of $N(d_1) = N(0.8892) = 0.8131$. Similarly, the **NORMSDIST** function returns a value of $N(d_2) = 0.7473$. We can use those values to solve Equation 8-9:

$$V_C = \$40[N(0.8892)] - \$35e^{-(0.08)(0.5)}[N(0.6661)]$$
$$= \$7.39$$

Thus, the value of the option is $7.39. This is the same value we found using the binomial approach with 100 periods in the year.

8-5c The Five Factors That Affect Call Option Prices

The Black-Scholes model has five inputs, so five factors affect call option prices. As we will see in the next section, these five inputs also affect put option prices. Figure 8-4 shows how three of Western Cellular's call options are affected by Western's stock price. All three options have a strike price of $35. The first expires in 1 year, the

[19]If stocks traded every day of the year, then each return covers a 24-hour period; you would simply estimate the variance of the 1-day returns with your sample of daily returns and then multiply this estimate by 365 for an estimate of the annual variance. However, stocks don't trade every day because of weekends and holidays. If you measure returns from the close of one trading day until the close of the next trading day (called "trading-day returns"), then some returns are for 1 day (such as Thursday close to Friday close) and some are for longer periods, like the 3-day return from Friday close to Monday close. It might seem reasonable that the 3-day returns have 3 times the variance of a 1-day return and should be treated differently when estimating the daily return variance, but that is not the case. It turns out that the 3-day return over a weekend has only slightly higher variance than a 1-day return (perhaps because of less new information on non-weekdays), and so it is reasonable to treat all of the trading-day returns the same. With roughly 250 trading days in a year, most analysts take the estimate of the variance of daily returns and multiply by 250 (or 252, depending on the year, to be more precise) to obtain an estimate of the annual variance.

FIGURE 8-4
Western Cellular's Call Options with a Strike Price of $35

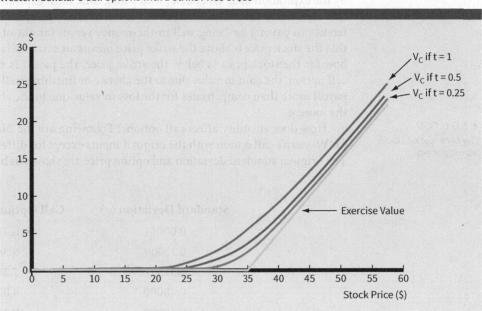

resource

See *Ch08 Tool Kit.xlsx* on
the textbook's Web site.

second in 6 months (0.5 year, like the option in our example), and the third in 3 months (or 0.25 year).

Figure 8-4 offers several insights regarding option valuation. Notice that for all stock prices in the figure, the call option prices are always above the exercise value. If this were not true, then an investor could purchase the call and immediately exercise it for a quick profit.[20]

Also, when the stock price falls far below the strike price, call option prices fall toward zero. In other words, calls lose value as they become more and more out-of-the-money. When the stock price greatly exceeds the strike price, call option prices fall toward the exercise value. Thus, for very high stock prices, call options tend to move up and down by about the same amount as does the stock price.

Call option prices increase if the stock price increases. This is because the strike price is fixed, so an increase in stock price increases the chance that the option will be in-the-money at expiration. Although we don't show it in the figure, an increase in the strike price would obviously cause a decrease in the call option's value because higher strike prices mean a lower chance of being in-the-money at expiration.

The 1-year call option always has a greater value than the 6-month call option, which always has a greater value than the 3-month call option; thus, the longer a call option has until expiration, the greater its value. Here is the rationale for that result. With a long

---

[20]More precisely, this statement is true for all American call options (which can be exercised before expiration) and for European call options written on stocks that pay no dividends. Although European options may not be exercised prior to expiration, investors could earn a riskless profit if the call price were less than the exercise value by selling the stock short, purchasing the call, and investing at the risk-free rate an amount equal to the present value of the strike price. The vast majority of call options are American options, so the call price is almost always above the exercise value.

time until expiration, the stock price has a chance to increase well above the strike price by the expiration date. Of course, with a long time until expiration, there is also a chance that the stock price will fall far below the strike price by expiration. But there is a big difference in payoffs for being well in-the-money versus far out-of-the-money. Every dollar that the stock price is above the strike price means an extra dollar of payoff, but no matter how far the stock price is below the strike price, the payoff is zero. When it comes to a call option, the gain in value due to the chance of finishing well in-the-money with a big payoff more than compensates for the loss in value due to the chance of being far out-of-the-money.

resource
See Ch08 Tool Kit.xlsx for all calculations.

How does volatility affect call options? Following are the Black-Scholes model prices for Western's call option with the original inputs except for different standard deviations. The original standard deviation and option price are shown in bold:

Standard Deviation (σ)	Call Option Price
0.00001	$ 6.37
0.10000	6.38
0.31557	**7.39**
0.40000	8.07
0.60000	9.87
0.90000	12.70

The first row shows the option price if there is very little stock volatility.[21] Notice that as volatility increases, so does the option price. Therefore, the riskier the underlying security, the more valuable the option. To see why this makes sense, suppose you bought a call option with a strike price equal to the current stock price. Suppose also that there is no chance that the stock price will change between now and expiration of the option (volatility is zero in this case). Then there is zero probability of making any money on the option. On the other hand, if you bought a call option on a higher-volatility stock, there would be a higher probability that the stock would increase well above the strike price by the expiration date. Of course, with higher volatility, there also would be a higher probability that the stock price would fall far below the strike price. But as we previously explained, an increase in the price of the stock helps call option holders more than a decrease hurts

---

[21]If a stock's standard deviation is close to zero, then a stock is similar to a risk-free security, and its price will grow at the risk-free rate. Suppose the current price is P_0 and it grows to a value of P_T when it expires at time T. If P_T is greater than the exercise price, the payoff at time T will be $P_T - X$. Because P_T is almost risk-free (due to the very low stock volatility) and X is known with certainty, the payoff should be discounted at the risk-free rate to find the value of the call option. The stock price grew from P_0 to P_T at the risk-free rate, so the present value of P_T is P_0 when discounted at the risk-free rate. Therefore, if stock volatility is very low and P_0 is not too far below the strike price, the value of the call option is approximately equal to the current stock price minus the present value of the option's exercise price. This means that the value of Western's call option would be about $6.37 if the standard deviation is very low (assuming daily compounding):

$$V_C \text{ (for } \sigma = 0.00001) \approx \$40 - \frac{\$35}{\left(1 + \frac{0.08}{365}\right)^{365(0.5)}} = \$6.37$$

Observe that this is the same value given by the Black-Scholes model, even though we calculated it more directly. This approach works only if the volatility is almost zero and the stock price is not too far below the strike price.

them: The greater the stock's volatility, the greater the value of the option. This makes options on risky stocks more valuable than those on safer, low-risk stocks. For example, an option on Cisco should have a greater value than an otherwise identical option on Kroger, the grocery store chain.

The risk-free rate also has a relatively small impact on option prices. Following are the prices for Western's call option with the original inputs except for the risk-free rate, which is allowed to vary.

See *Ch08 Tool Kit.xlsx* for all calculations.

resource

Risk-Free Rate (r_{RF})	Call Option Price
0.0%	$6.41
4.0	6.89
8.0	**7.39**
12.0	7.90
20.0	8.93

As the risk-free rate increases, the value of the option increases. The principal effect of an increase in r_{RF} is to reduce the present value of the exercise price, which increases the current value of the option. Option prices in general are not very sensitive to interest rate changes, at least not to changes within the ranges normally encountered

Myron Scholes and Robert Merton (who also was a pioneer in the field of options) were awarded the 1997 Nobel Prize in Economics, and Fischer Black would have been a co-recipient had he still been living. Their work provided analytical tools and methodologies that are widely used to solve many types of financial problems, not just option pricing. Indeed, the entire field of modern risk management is based primarily on their contributions. Although the Black-Scholes model was derived for a European option that can be exercised only on its maturity date, it also applies to American options that don't pay any dividends prior to expiration. The textbooks by Don Chance and John Hull (cited in footnote 1) show adjusted models for dividend-paying stocks.

SELF-TEST

What is the purpose of the Black-Scholes option pricing model?

Explain what a "riskless hedge" is and how the riskless hedge concept is used in the Black-Scholes OPM.

Describe the effect of a change in each of the following factors on the value of a call option: (1) stock price, (2) exercise price, (3) option life, (4) risk-free rate, and (5) stock return standard deviation (i.e., risk of stock).

Using an Excel worksheet, what is the value of a call option with these data: P = $35, X = $25, r_{RF} = 6%, t = 0.5 (6 months), and σ = 0.6? **($12.05)**

8-6 The Valuation of Put Options

A put option gives its owner the right to sell a share of stock. Suppose a stock pays no dividends and a put option written on the stock can be exercised only upon its expiration date. What is the put's value? Rather than reinventing the wheel, we can establish the price of a put relative to the price of a call.

TABLE 8-2
Portfolio Payoffs

		Payoff at Expiration if:	
		$P_T < X$	$P_T \geq X$
Put		$X - P_T$	0
Stock		P_T	P_T
	Portfolio 1:	X	P_T
Call		0	$P_T - X$
Cash		X	X
	Portfolio 2:	X	P_T

8-6a Put–Call Parity

Consider the payoffs for two portfolios at expiration date T, as shown in Table 8-2. The first portfolio consists of a put option and a share of stock; the second has a call option (with the same strike price and expiration date as the put option) and some cash. The amount of cash is equal to the present value of the strike price discounted at the continuously compounded risk-free rate, which is $Xe^{-r_{RF}t}$. At expiration, the value of this cash will equal the strike price, X.

If P_T, the stock price at expiration date T, is less than X, the strike price, when the option expires, then the payoff of the put option at expiration is $X - P_T$. Therefore, the payoff of Portfolio 1, which contains the put and the stock, is equal to X minus P_T plus P_T, or just X. For Portfolio 2, the payoff of the call is zero at expiration (because the call option is out-of-the-money), and the value of the cash is X, for a total payoff of X. Notice that both portfolios have the same payoffs if the stock price is less than the strike price.

What if the stock price is greater than the strike price at expiration? In this case, the put is worth nothing, so the payoff of Portfolio 1 is equal to P_T, the stock price at expiration. The call option is worth $P_T - X$, and the cash is worth X, so the payoff of Portfolio 2 is P_T. Hence, the payoffs of the two portfolios at expiration are equal regardless of whether the stock price is below or above the strike price.

If the two portfolios have identical payoffs, then they must have identical values. This is known as the **put–call parity relationship**:

Put option + Stock = Call option + PV of exercise price

If V_C is the Black-Scholes value of the call option, then the value of a put is:[22]

$$\text{Put option} = V_C - P + Xe^{-r_{RF}t} \qquad (8\text{-}12)$$

---

[22]This model cannot be applied to an American put option or to a European option on a stock that pays a dividend prior to expiration. For an explanation of valuation approaches in these situations, see the books by Chance and Hull cited in footnote 1.

For example, consider a put option written on the stock discussed in the previous section. If the put option has the same exercise price and expiration date as the call, then its price is:

$$\text{Put option} = \$7.39 - \$40 + \$35\,e^{-0.08(0.5)}$$
$$= \$7.39 - \$40 + \$33.63 = \$1.02$$

It is also possible to modify the Black-Scholes call option formula to obtain a put option formula:

$$\text{Put option} = P[N(d_1) - 1] - Xe^{-r_{RF}t}[N(d_2) - 1] \qquad (8\text{-}13)$$

The only difference between this formula for puts and the formula for calls is the subtraction of 1 from $N(d_1)$ and $N(d_2)$ in the call option formula.

8-6b The Five Factors That Affect Put Option Prices

Just as with call options, the exercise price, the underlying stock price, the time to expiration, the stock's standard deviation, and the risk-free rate affect the price of a put option. Because a put pays off when the stock price declines below the exercise price, the impact on the put of the underlying stock price, exercise price, and risk-free rate are opposite that of the call option. That is, put prices are higher when the stock price is lower and when the exercise price is higher. Put prices are also lower when the risk-free rate is higher, mostly because a higher risk-free rate reduces the present value of the exercise price, which for a put is a payout to the option holder when the option is exercised.

On the other hand, put options are affected by the stock's standard deviation just like call options. Both put and call option prices are higher when the stock's standard deviation is higher. This is true for put options because the higher the standard deviation is, the bigger the chance of a large stock price decline and a large put payoff.

The effect of the time to maturity on the put option price is indeterminate. A call option is more valuable the longer the maturity, but some puts are more valuable the longer to maturity, and some are less valuable. For example, consider an in-the-money put option (the stock price is below the exercise price) on a stock with a low standard deviation. In this case, a longer maturity put option is less valuable than a shorter maturity put option because the longer the time to maturity, the more likely the stock is to grow and erode the put's payoff. But if the stock's standard deviation is high, then the longer maturity put option will be more valuable because the likelihood of the stock declining even more and resulting in a high payoff to the put is greater.

SELF-TEST

In words, what is put-call parity?

A put option written on the stock of Taylor Enterprises (TE) has an exercise price of $25 and 6 months remaining until expiration. The risk-free rate is 6%. A call option written on TE has the same exercise price and expiration date as the put option. TE's stock price is $35. If the call option has a price of $12.05, then what is the price (i.e., value) of the put option? **($1.31)**

Explain why both put and call options are worth more if the stock return standard deviation is higher but put and call options are affected oppositely by the stock price.

8-7 Applications of Option Pricing in Corporate Finance

Option pricing is used in four major areas of corporate finance: (1) real options analysis for project evaluation and strategic decisions, (2) risk management, (3) capital structure decisions, and (4) compensation plans.

8-7a Real Options

Suppose a company has a 1-year proprietary license to develop a software application for use in a new generation of wireless cellular telephones. Hiring programmers and marketing consultants to complete the project will cost $30 million. If consumers love the new cell phones, there will be a tremendous demand for the software. If not, the company might lose $30 million.

Because the company has a license, it has the option of waiting for a year, at which time it might have a much better insight into market demand for the new cell phones. If demand is high in a year, then the company can spend the $30 million and develop the software. If demand is low, it can avoid losing the $30 million development cost by simply letting the license expire. Notice that the license is analogous to a call option: It gives the company the right to buy something (in this case, software for the new cell phones) at a fixed price ($30 million) at any time during the next year. The license gives the company a **real option**, because the underlying asset (the software) is a real asset and not a financial asset.

There are many other types of real options that are analogous to calls and put, including the option to increase capacity at a plant, to expand into new geographical regions, to introduce new products, and to abandon a project.

8-7b Risk Management

Suppose a company plans to issue $400 million of bonds in 6 months to pay for a new plant now under construction. The plant will be profitable if interest rates remain at current levels, but if rates rise, then it will be unprofitable. To hedge against rising rates, the company could purchase a put option on Treasury bonds. If interest rates go up, then the company would "lose" because its bonds would carry a high interest rate, but it would have an offsetting gain on its put options. Conversely, if rates fall, then the company would "win" when it issues its own low-rate bonds, but it would lose on the put options. By purchasing puts, the company has hedged the risk due to possible interest rate changes that it would otherwise face. Thus, financial options and their valuation techniques play key roles in risk management.

8-7c Capital Structure Decisions

Consider a firm with debt requiring a final principal payment of $60 million in 1 year. If the company's value 1 year from now is $61 million, then it can pay off the debt and have $1 million left for stockholders. If the firm's value is less than $60 million, then it may well file for bankruptcy and turn over its assets to creditors, resulting in stockholders' equity of zero. In other words, the value of the stockholders' equity is analogous to a call option: The equity holders have the right to buy the assets for $60 million (which is the face value of the debt) in 1 year (when the debt matures). Chapter 15 discusses this in more detail.

Another example is convertible debt, which gives bondholders the option to convert their debt into stock if the value of the company turns out to be higher than expected.

In exchange for this option, bondholders charge a lower interest rate than for nonconvertible debt.

8-7d Compensation Plans

Many companies use stock options as a part of their compensation plans. It is important for boards of directors to understand the value of these options before they grant them to employees. We discuss compensation issues associated with stock options in more detail in Chapter 13.

SELF-TEST

Describe four ways that option pricing is used in corporate finance.

SUMMARY

In this chapter we discussed option pricing topics, which included the following:

- Financial **options** are instruments that (1) are created by exchanges rather than by firms, (2) are bought and sold primarily by investors, and (3) are of importance to both investors and financial managers.
- The two primary types of financial options are: (1) **call options**, which give the holder the right to purchase a specified asset at a given price (the **exercise price**, which is also called the **strike price**) for a given period of time, and (2) **put options**, which give the holder the right to sell an asset at a given price for a given period of time.
- A call option's **exercise value** is defined as the maximum of zero or the current price of the stock less the strike price.
- The **Black-Scholes option pricing model (OPM)** or the **binomial approach** can be used to estimate the value of a call option.
- The five inputs to the Black-Scholes model are (1) P, the current stock price; (2) X, the strike price; (3) r_{RF}, the risk-free interest rate; (4) t, the remaining time until expiration; and (5) σ, the standard deviation of the stock's rate of return.
- A call option's value increases if P increases, X decreases, r_{RF} increases, t increases, or σ increases.
- The **put–call parity relationship** states that:

$$\text{Put option} + \text{Stock} = \text{Call option} + \text{PV of exercise price}$$

QUESTIONS

(8-1)   Define each of the following terms:

   a. Option; call option; put option
   b. Exercise value; strike price
   c. Black-Scholes option pricing model

(8-2)   Why do options sell at prices higher than their exercise values?

(8-3)   Describe the effect on a call option's price that results from an increase in each of the following factors: (1) stock price, (2) strike price, (3) time to expiration, (4) risk-free rate, and (5) standard deviation of stock return.

SELF-TEST PROBLEMS   SOLUTIONS SHOWN IN APPENDIX A

(ST-1)
Binomial Option Pricing

The current price of a stock is $40. In 1 year, the price will be either $60 or $30. The annual risk-free rate is 5%. Find the price of a call option on the stock that has an exercise price of $42 and that expires in 1 year. (*Hint:* Use daily compounding.)

(ST-2)
Black-Scholes Model

Use the Black-Scholes model to find the price for a call option with the following inputs: (1) current stock price is $22, (2) strike price is $20, (3) time to expiration is 6 months, (4) annualized risk-free rate is 5%, and (5) standard deviation of stock return is 0.7.

PROBLEMS   ANSWERS ARE IN APPENDIX B

EASY PROBLEMS 1–2

(8-1)
Options

A call option on the stock of Bedrock Boulders has a market price of $7. The stock sells for $30 a share, and the option has a strike price of $25 a share. What is the exercise value of the call option? What is the option's time value?

(8-2)
Options

The exercise price on one of Flanagan Company's call options is $15, its exercise value is $22, and its time value is $5. What are the option's market value and the price of the stock?

INTERMEDIATE PROBLEMS 3–4

(8-3)
Black-Scholes Model

Assume that you have been given the following information on Purcell Corporation's call options:

Current stock price = $15	Strike price of option = $15
Time to maturity of option = 6 months	Risk-free rate = 6%
Variance of stock return = 0.12	
d_1 = 0.24495	$N(d_1)$ = 0.59675
d_2 = 0.00000	$N(d_2)$ = 0.50000

According to the Black-Scholes option pricing model, what is the option's value?

(8-4)
Put–Call Parity

The current price of a stock is $33, and the annual risk-free rate is 6%. A call option with a strike price of $32 and with 1 year until expiration has a current value of $6.56. What is the value of a put option written on the stock with the same exercise price and expiration date as the call option?

CHALLENGING PROBLEMS 5–7

(8-5)
Black-Scholes Model

Use the Black-Scholes model to find the price for a call option with the following inputs: (1) current stock price is $30, (2) strike price is $35, (3) time to expiration is 4 months, (4) annualized risk-free rate is 5%, and (5) variance of stock return is 0.25.

(8-6)
Binomial Model
The current price of a stock is $20. In 1 year, the price will be either $26 or $16. The annual risk-free rate is 5%. Find the price of a call option on the stock that has a strike price of $21 and that expires in 1 year. (*Hint:* Use daily compounding.)

(8-7)
Binomial Model
The current price of a stock is $15. In 6 months, the price will be either $18 or $13. The annual risk-free rate is 6%. Find the price of a call option on the stock that has a strike price of $14 and that expires in 6 months. (*Hint:* Use daily compounding.)

SPREADSHEET PROBLEM

(8-8)
Build a Model:
Black-Scholes
Model

resource

Start with the partial model in the file *Ch08 P08 Build a Model.xlsx* on the textbook's Web site. You have been given the following information for a call option on the stock of Puckett Industries: P = $65.00, X = $70.00, t = 0.50, r_{RF} = 5.00%, and σ = 0.50.

a. Use the Black-Scholes option pricing model to determine the value of the call option.

b. Suppose there is a put option on Puckett's stock with exactly the same inputs as the call option. What is the value of the put?

MINI CASE

Assume that you have just been hired as a financial analyst by Triple Play Inc., a mid-sized California company that specializes in creating high-fashion clothing. Because no one at Triple Play is familiar with the basics of financial options, you have been asked to prepare a brief report that the firm's executives can use to gain a cursory understanding of the topic.

To begin, you gathered some outside materials on the subject and used these materials to draft a list of pertinent questions that need to be answered. In fact, one possible approach to the report is to use a question-and-answer format. Now that the questions have been drafted, you have to develop the answers.

a. What is a financial option? What is the single most important characteristic of an option?

b. Options have a unique set of terminology. Define the following terms:
   (1) Call option
   (2) Put option
   (3) Strike price or exercise price
   (4) Expiration date
   (5) Exercise value
   (6) Option price
   (7) Time value
   (8) Writing an option
   (9) Covered option
   (10) Naked option
   (11) In-the-money call
   (12) Out-of-the-money call
   (13) LEAPS

c. Consider Triple Play's call option with a $25 strike price. The following table contains historical values for this option at different stock prices:

Stock Price	Call Option Price
$25	$ 3.00
30	7.50
35	12.00
40	16.50
45	21.00
50	25.50

   (1) Create a table that shows (a) stock price, (b) strike price, (c) exercise value, (d) option price, and (e) the time value, which is the option's price less its exercise value.

   (2) What happens to the time value as the stock price rises? Why?

d. Consider a stock with a current price of P = $27. Suppose that over the next 6 months the stock price will either go up by a factor of 1.41 or down by a factor of 0.71. Consider a call option on the stock with a strike price of $25 that expires in 6 months. The risk-free rate is 6%.

   (1) Using the binomial model, what are the ending values of the stock price? What are the payoffs of the call option?

   (2) Suppose you write one call option and buy N_s shares of stock. How many shares must you buy to create a portfolio with a riskless payoff (i.e., a hedge portfolio)? What is the payoff of the portfolio?

   (3) What is the present value of the hedge portfolio? What is the value of the call option?

   (4) What is a replicating portfolio? What is arbitrage?

e. In 1973, Fischer Black and Myron Scholes developed the Black-Scholes option pricing model (OPM).

   (1) What assumptions underlie the OPM?

   (2) Write out the three equations that constitute the model.

   (3) According to the OPM, what is the value of a call option with the following characteristics?

      Stock price = $27.00

      Strike price = $25.00

      Time to expiration = 6 months = 0.5 years

      Risk-free rate = 6.0%

      Stock return standard deviation = 0.49

f. What impact does each of the following parameters have on the value of a call option?

   (1) Current stock price

   (2) Strike price

   (3) Option's term to maturity

   (4) Risk-free rate

   (5) Variability of the stock price

g. What is put–call parity?

Projects and Their Valuation

CHAPTER 9

The Cost of Capital

When companies consider investing in new projects, the cost of capital plays a major role. Sunny Delight Beverage Co. is making big investments to upgrade its juice factories, but would this happen if low interest rates had not driven down the cost of capital? According to CEO Billy Cyr, "When the cost of capital goes up, it is harder to justify an equipment purchase." The opposite is true when the cost of capital goes down.

Among its businesses, Phoenix Stamping Group LLC produces components for equipment used in agriculture and transportation. After modernizing two factories, Phoenix President Brandyn Chapman said, "The cost of capital certainly helps that decision."

For these and many other companies, the historically low cost of capital is making possible major investments in machinery, equipment, and technology. Many of these investments are designed to increase productivity, which will lead to lower prices for consumers and higher cash flows for shareholders. On the other hand, productivity gains mean not as many employees are needed to run the business.

Think about these issues as you read this chapter.

Source: Adapted from Timothy Aeppel, "Man vs. Machine, a Jobless Recovery—Companies Are Spending to Upgrade Factories but Hiring Lags; Robots Pump Out Sunny Delight," *The Wall Street Journal,* January 17, 2012, B1.

Corporate Valuation and the Cost of Capital

In Chapter 1, we told you that managers should strive to make their firms more valuable and that the value of a firm is determined by the size, timing, and risk of its free cash flows (FCFs). Indeed, a firm's intrinsic value is estimated as the present value of its FCFs, discounted at the weighted average cost of capital (WACC). In previous chapters, we examined the major sources of financing (stocks, bonds, and preferred stock) and the costs of those instruments. In this chapter, we put those pieces together and estimate the WACC that is used to determine intrinsic value.

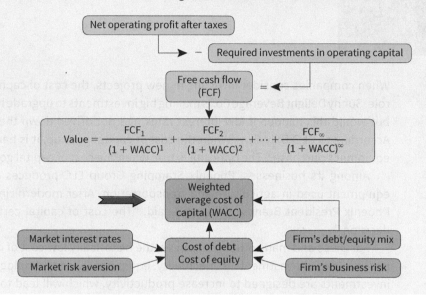

Businesses require capital to develop new products, build factories and distribution centers, install information technology, expand internationally, and acquire other companies. For each of these actions, a company must estimate the total investment required and then decide whether the expected rate of return exceeds the cost of the capital. The cost of capital is also a factor in compensation plans, with bonuses dependent on whether the company's return on invested capital exceeds the cost of that capital. This cost is also a key factor in choosing the firm's mixture of debt and equity and in decisions to lease rather than buy assets. As these examples illustrate, the cost of capital is a critical element in many business decisions.[1]

9-1 The Weighted Average Cost of Capital

The value of a company's operations is the present value of the expected free cash flows (FCFs) discounted at the weighted average cost of capital (WACC):

$$V_{op} = \sum_{t=1}^{\infty} \frac{FCF_t}{(1 + WACC)^t} \tag{9-1}$$

[1]The cost of capital is also an important factor in the regulation of electric, gas, and water companies. These utilities are natural monopolies in the sense that one firm can supply service at a lower cost than could two or more firms. Because it has a monopoly, an unregulated electric or water company could exploit its customers. Therefore, regulators determine the cost of the capital and set rates designed to permit the company to earn its cost of capital, no more and no less.

We define free cash flow (FCF) in Chapter 2; we explain how to find present values in Chapter 4; and we apply the free cash flow valuation model in Chapter 7 to determine the value of operations. In this chapter, we will explain how to estimate the **weighted average cost of capital (WACC):**

$$\text{WACC} = r_d(1 - T)w_d + r_{std}(1 - T)w_{std} + r_{ps}w_{ps} + r_sw_s \qquad \text{(9-2)}$$

Some of these variables should be familiar to you from previous chapters, but some are new. All are defined as follows:

r_d = Required rate of return on debt, which is the coupon rate on *new* long-term debt being issued by the firm or the yield to maturity on *existing* debt, as defined in Chapter 5.

T = The firm's effective marginal tax rate.

r_{std} = Required rate of return on short-term debt, such as notes payable. Because the debt matures soon, r_{std} is approximately equal to the interest rate being charged on the debt.

r_{ps} = Required rate of return on preferred stock, as defined in Chapter 7.

r_s = Required rate of return on common stock, as defined in Chapter 7.

w = w_d, w_{std}, w_{ps}, and w_s = weights of long-term debt, short-term debt, preferred stock, and common stock. These **target capital structure** weights are the percentages of the different sources of capital the firm plans to use on a regular basis, with the percentages based on the market values of those sources. The weights should be chosen to minimize the WACC, as described in Chapter 15.

In the following sections, we explain how to estimate the WACC of a specific company, MicroDrive, Inc., but let's begin with a few general concepts. First, companies are financed by several sources of investor-supplied capital, which are called **capital components**. We have included short-term debt and preferred stock because some companies use them as sources of funding, but most companies use only two major sources of investor-supplied capital: long-term debt and common stock.

Second, investors providing the capital components require rates of return (r_d, r_{std}, r_{ps}, and r_s) commensurate with the risks of the components in order to induce them to make the investments. Previous chapters defined those required returns from an investor's view, but those returns are costs from a company's viewpoint. That is why we call the WACC a *cost* of capital. Because the cost of capital is used to calculate the present value of after-tax cash flows, the cost of capital is the after-tax cost to the company of providing investors' required returns. For example, interest expenses can be deducted for tax purposes, making the after-tax *cost* of debt less than its required rate of return.

Third, recall that FCF is the cash flow available for distribution to all investors. Therefore, the free cash flows must provide an overall rate of return sufficient to compensate investors for their exposure to risk. Intuitively, it makes sense that this overall return should be a weighted average of the capital components' required returns. This intuition is confirmed by applying algebra to the definitions of required returns, free cash flow, and the value of operations: The discount rate used in Equation 9-1 is equal to the WACC as defined in Equation 9-2. In other words, the correct rate for estimating the present value of a company's (or project's) free cash flows is the *weighted* average cost of capital.

Identify a firm's major capital structure components, and give the symbols for their respective costs and weights.

What is a component cost?

9-2 Choosing Weights for the Weighted Average Cost of Capital

Figure 9-1 reports selected data for MicroDrive, including (1) liabilities and equity (L&E) from the balance sheets, (2) percentages of total L&E comprised by each liability or equity account, (3) book values (as reported on the balance sheets) and percentages of financing from investor-supplied capital, (4) current market values and percentages of financing from investor-supplied capital, and (5) target capital structure weights.

Notice that we exclude accounts payable and accruals from capital structure weights. Capital is provided by *investors*—interest-bearing debt, preferred stock, and common equity. Accounts payable and accruals arise from operating decisions, not from financing decisions. Recall that the impact of payables and accruals is incorporated into a firm's free cash flows and a project's cash flows rather than into the cost of capital. Therefore, we consider only investor-supplied capital when discussing capital structure weights.

Figure 9-1 reports percentages of financing based on book values, market values, and target weights. Book values are a record of the cumulative amounts of capital supplied by

FIGURE 9-1
MicroDrive, Inc.: Selected Capital Structure Data (Millions of Dollars, December 31, 2019)

	A	B	C	D	E	F	G	H	I	J
30						Investor-Supplied Capital				
31						Book		Market		Target
32				Percent	Book	Percent	Market	Percent		Capital
33	*Liabilities and Equity*			of Total	Value	of Total	Value	of Total		Structure
34	Accounts payable		$ 200	5.5%						
35	Notes payable		150	4.2%	$ 150	5.0%	$ 150	5.7%	w_{std} =	4%
36	Accruals		400	11.1%						
37	Total C.L.		$ 750	20.8%						
38	Long-term debt		520	14.4%	520	17.3%	520	19.8%	w_d =	20%
39	Total liabilities		$1,270	35.2%						
40	Preferred stock		100	2.8%	100	3.3%	100	3.8%	w_{ps} =	2%
41	Common stock		500	13.9%						
42	Retained earnings		1,740	48.2%						
43	Total common equity		$2,240	62.0%	$2,240	74.4%	$1,860	70.7%	w_s =	74%
44	Total		$3,610	100.0%	$3,010	100.0%	$2,630	100.0%		100%
45										

Source: See the file *Ch09 Tool Kit.xlsx*. Numbers are reported as rounded values for clarity but are calculated using *Excel*'s full precision. Thus, intermediate calculations using the figure's rounded values will be inexact.

Notes:

[1] The market value of the notes payable is equal to the book value. Some of the long-term bonds sell at a discount, and some sell at a premium, but their aggregate market value is approximately equal to their aggregate book value.

[2] The common stock price is $31 per share. There are 60 million shares outstanding, for a total market value of equity of $31(60) = $1,860 million.

[3] The preferred stock price is $100 per share. There are 1 million shares outstanding, for a total market value of preferred stock of $100(1) = $100 million.

investors over the life of the company. For equity, stockholders have supplied capital directly when MicroDrive issued stock, but they have also supplied capital indirectly when MicroDrive retained earnings instead of paying bigger dividends. The WACC is used to find the present value of *future* cash flows, so it would be inconsistent to use weights based on the *past* history of the company.

Stock prices are volatile, so current market values of total common equity often change dramatically from day to day. Companies certainly don't try to maintain the weights in their capital structures daily by issuing stock, repurchasing stock, issuing debt, or repaying debt in response to changes in their stock price. Therefore, the capital structure weights based on the current market values might not be a good estimate of the capital structure that the company will have on average during the future.

The target capital structure is defined as the average capital structure weights (based on market values) that a company will have during the future, which should be the weights that minimize the company's WACC. MicroDrive has chosen a target capital structure composed of 4% short-term debt, 20% long-term debt, 2% preferred stock, and 74% common equity. MicroDrive presently has more debt and preferred stock in its actual capital structure (using either book values or market values), but it intends to move toward its target capital structure in the near future. We explain how firms choose their capital structures in Chapter 15, but for now just accept the given target weights for MicroDrive.

The following sections explain how to estimate the required returns for the capital structure components.

What is a target capital structure?

9-3 The Cost of Debt

A creditor's required rate of return on short-term debt is the interest rate it charges, and an investor's required rate of return on long-term debt is its yield to maturity. However, a company's after-tax cost of debt is *not equal* to the required rate of return because interest expenses are deductible from taxable income. If the tax rate is 25%, each additional dollar of interest expense will cause taxes to fall by $0.25. In other words, the government subsidizes part of the interest expense.

Therefore, the **after-tax cost of debt** is equal to the investors' required rate of return on debt less the issuer's tax savings due to interest expense deductions:

$$\text{After-tax cost of debt} = \text{Required return} - \text{Tax savings}$$
$$= r_{std}(1 - T) \ \textit{or} \ r_d(1 - T)$$

(9-3)

Equation 9-3 assumes that debt is issued at par and that no costs are incurred when issuing the debt. We address those issues in the following sections, but we begin with a direct application of Equation 9-3 to determine the after-tax costs of short-term and long-term debt.

9-3a After-Tax Cost of Short-Term Debt: $r_{std}(1 - T)$

Short-term debt should be included in the capital structure only if it is a permanent source of financing in the sense that the company plans to continually repay and refinance the short-term debt. This is the case for MicroDrive, whose bankers charge 8% on notes payable.

Therefore, MicroDrive's short-term lenders have a required return of r_{std} = 8%, which is MicroDrive's before-tax cost of short-term debt.[2]

MicroDrive's federal-plus-state tax rate is 25%. Using Equation 9-3, the after-tax cost of short-term debt is:

$$\text{After-tax cost} = r_{std}(1 - T)$$
$$= 8\%(1 - 0.25) = 6.0\%$$

9-3b The After-Tax Cost of Long-Term Debt: $r_d(1 - T)$

Estimating long-term debt's after-tax cost is conceptually straightforward, but some problems arise in practice. Companies use both fixed-rate and floating-rate debt, both straight debt and convertible debt, as well as debt with and without sinking funds. Each type of debt may have a somewhat different cost.

It is unlikely that the financial manager will know at the beginning of a planning period the exact types and amounts of debt that will be used during the period. The type or types used will depend on the specific assets to be financed and on capital market conditions as they develop over time. Even so, managers do know what types of debt are typical for their firms. For example, MicroDrive typically issues 15-year bonds to raise long-term debt used to help finance its capital budgeting projects, so MicroDrive's treasurer uses the cost of 15-year bonds in her WACC estimate.

Assume it is January 2020 and that MicroDrive's treasurer is estimating the WACC for the coming year. How should she calculate the component cost of debt? Most financial managers begin by discussing current and prospective interest rates with their investment bankers. MicroDrive's investment bankers believe that a new, 15-year, noncallable, straight bond issue would require a 10% coupon rate with semiannual payments. It can be offered to the public at its $1,000 par value. Therefore, their estimate of r_d is 10%.[3]

Note that the 10% rate on new debt is often called the **marginal rate**. The rate on new debt probably will not be the same as the average rate on MicroDrive's previously issued debt, which is called the **historical rate** or the **embedded rate**. The embedded rate is important for some decisions but not for others. For example, the embedded rate determines the actual coupon payments that a company must make to its debtholders, so the embedded rate is used by regulators when they determine the rate of return that a public utility should be allowed to earn. However, market forces determine the required rate of return that a typical company must provide to its investors if it expects to attract more investment when it undertakes new projects. Therefore, *a company should use the marginal rate when it estimates its WACC!*

Investors require a 10% rate of return on MicroDrive's long-term debt. Using Equation 9-3, the after-tax cost of long-term debt is:

$$r_d(1 - T) = 10\%(1 - 0.25)$$
$$= 7.5\%$$

Suppose a firm does not wish to seek the advice of an investment banker. There are three alternative methods to estimate its cost of debt: (1) The firm can use the coupon rate on any recently issued debt that is trading at par. (2) The firm can calculate the yield to maturity on its previously issued debt even if it is not trading at par. (3) If the firm doesn't have any previously issued publicly traded debt, it can estimate the yield it would have on debt by using the average yield that comparable publicly traded companies have on their debt. Following are examples of the first two methods.

---

[2]Some large companies also use commercial paper as a source of short-term financing, which we explain in Chapter 16.

[3]Because it is a semiannual bond, the effective annual rate is $(1 + 0.10/2)^2 - 1 = 10.25\%$, but MicroDrive and most other companies use nominal rates for all component costs.

MicroDrive's outstanding bonds were recently issued and have a 10% coupon, paid semiannually. The bonds mature in 15 years and have a par value of $1,000. Since interest rates in the economy haven't changed much since the bonds were issued, they are still trading at $1,000. Therefore, the yield to maturity should be equal to the 10% coupon rate. To confirm this, let's calculate the yield. The bonds still have 30 remaining payments (2 payments per year for 15 years) and pay a $50 coupon each payment date ($100 per year divided by 2 payments per year). We can find the yield to maturity by using a financial calculator with these inputs: N = 30, PV = −1000, PMT = 50, and FV = 1000. Solving for the rate, we find I/YR = 5.0%. This is a semiannual periodic rate, so the nominal annual rate is 10.0%. This is equal to the coupon rate and is consistent with the investment bankers' estimated rate, so 10% is a reasonable estimate for r_d.

Suppose a company's previously issued debt isn't trading at par. In that case, the yield to maturity is a good estimate of the return required to satisfy investors. For example, consider a company that issued 15-year bonds with a 9% coupon rate. Market interest rates subsequently changed, causing the market price to fall to $923.14. We can find the yield to maturity with a financial calculator using these inputs: N = 30, PV = −923.14, PMT = 45, and FV = 1000. Solving for the rate, we find I/YR = 5%, which implies a hypothetical nominal annual rate of 10%. This is the coupon rate (and yield to maturity) that the company would have to offer if it issued new bonds at par. As this hypothetical example illustrates, it is not necessary for the bond to trade at par in order to estimate the cost of debt.

The preceding methods are appropriate in most circumstances. However, there are situations in which additional adjustments and factors should be considered. We discuss them in the following sections, beginning with flotation costs.

9-3c Yield to Maturity versus Expected Rate of Return

Although the yield to maturity is also the coupon rate for new debt issued at par, it isn't the bond investor's expected return. This is because the coupon and principal cash flows the bond promises to pay are really the *maximum* cash flows the investor will receive. If MicroDrive gets into financial distress and defaults, the bondholders will receive less. Thus, if there is any chance that MicroDrive will default, then the expected cash flows must be less than the promised payments. Therefore, the investor's expected return must be less than the yield to maturity (i.e., the return based on promised cash flows).

For example, reconsider MicroDrive's 15-year semiannual bonds that can be issued at par if the coupon rate is 10%. As shown previously, the nominal annual yield to maturity is 10%. But suppose investors believe there is a significant chance that MicroDrive will default. To keep the example simple, suppose investors believe that the bonds will default in 14 years and that the recovery rate on the par value will be 70%. Here are the new inputs: N = 2(14) = 28, PV = −1000, PMT = 50, and FV = 0.70(1000) = 700. Solving for the rate, we find I/YR = 4.44%, implying an annual expected return of 8.88%, which is significantly less than the yield to maturity of 10%.

Should a company use the yield to maturity or the expected return when calculating its cost of debt? To answer this question, recall the reason a company calculates its cost of debt: The cost of debt is used to calculate the WACC, which is used to select projects that generate sufficient expected future cash flows. Specifically, the expected cash flows should be enough to cover the contractual bond payments and provide shareholders a fair return. Therefore, the yield to maturity is the appropriate rate to use for the cost of debt because it is based on the contractual bond payments. In other words, when we discuss the WACC, the *required return on debt*, r_d, is the *yield to maturity* because this is the rate of return the company requires in order to meet its debt obligations.

9-3d The After-Tax Cost of Debt: Flotation Costs

In the previous sections, we ignored **flotation costs**, which are the commissions, legal expenses, fees, and any other costs that a company incurs when it issues new securities. The **percentage flotation cost for debt (F)** is the total dollar value of flotation costs divided by the issue's total par value.

For illustrative purposes, suppose a bond is issued at par ($1,000) and has 10 years until maturity, an 8% annual coupon rate, and semiannual payments. The tax rate is 25%, and the flotation percentage cost is 2.8%. The flotation cost per bond is:

$$\text{Flotation cost} = \text{F(Par value)} = 2.8\%(\$1,000) = \$28$$

The **net issue price** is the amount per bond that the issuing company actually receives after it pays the flotation costs. In this example, the net issue price is:

$$\begin{aligned} \text{Net issue price} &= \text{Issue price} - \text{Flotation cost} \\ &= \$1,000 - \$28 = \$972 \end{aligned}$$

THE CONSTANT YIELD METHOD

Many analysts use the **constant yield method**. To find the after-tax cost of debt using this method, calculate the yield to maturity but replace the bond's actual issue price with the *net issue price*. The after-tax cost of debt is the after-tax yield to maturity: $\text{YTM}(1 - T)$.

The first step in the constant yield method is to calculate the yield to maturity with $N = 10(2) = 20$, $\text{PMT} = 8\%(1,000)/2 = 40$, $\text{PV} = -972$, and $\text{FV} = 1000$; solving for RATE results in 4.2099%, which is 8.4198% on an annual basis. The after-tax cost of debt in the constant yield method is:

$$\begin{aligned} \text{YTM}(1 - T) &= 8.4198\%(1 - 0.25) \\ &= 6.31485\% \approx 6.31\% \end{aligned}$$

The constant yield method is correct for many situations. However, it only provides an approximate after-tax cost of debt in others. We recommend using the constant yield method because it is the correct method in most situations and it provides a very close approximation in the others. The following sections explain this in more detail.

AFTER-TAX COST OF DEBT FOR A PAR BOND: FLOTATION COSTS ≥ DE MINIMIS

The after-tax cost of debt depends upon flotation costs, but it also depends upon whether or not the flotation cost per bond is greater than **de minimis**, which is defined as:

$$\text{de minimis} = 0.25\%(\text{Original years until maturity})(\text{Par value}) \qquad (9\text{-}4)$$

For this example, de minimis is:

$$\text{de minimis} = 0.25\%(10)(\$1,000) = 0.0025(10)(\$1,000) = \$25$$

The bond has a flotation cost of $28 per bond, which is greater than the $25 de minimis. Therefore, the constant yield method provides the correct after-tax cost of debt.

AFTER-TAX COST OF DEBT FOR A PAR BOND: FLOTATION COSTS < DE MINIMIS

Now consider a bond exactly like the one in the previous example except that the bond has 28 years until maturity. The de minimis is $70: $0.0025(28)(\$1,000) = \$70$. This is greater than the $28 flotation cost, so the allocation method must be used. The basic idea is to allocate the flotation costs in equal portions to each payment period, determine the issuer's after-tax payments, and then find the yield to maturity using the after-tax payments.

The first step is to calculate the issuer's after-tax cost of making interest payments. As shown previously, the pre-tax interest payment is $40. The payment is deductible, so it reduces the taxes that are owed by the issuer. Therefore, the after-tax cost of making an interest payment is $30:

$$\text{After-tax coupon payment} = (\text{Coupon rate})(\text{Par value})(1 - T)/(2)$$
$$= 8\%(\$1,000)(1 - 0.25)/(2)$$
$$= \$30.00$$

The second step is to allocate the flotation cost in equal proportions to each payment date and determine the impact on taxes. There are 56 semiannual payments: $2(28) = 56$. The flotation cost didn't change, so it is still $28. Therefore, the amount allocated to each payment date is $28/56 = $0.50. Notice that this is a noncash expense. Each dollar of a noncash expense reduces taxes by $0.25 (because the tax rate is 25%), the same as if it were a cash expenses. But because it is a noncash expense, its only impact on cash flows is to reduce taxes. The tax savings each period are $0.125:

$$\text{Tax savings per period} = T(\text{Flotation costs}/\text{Number of periods})$$
$$= 0.25(\$28/56) = \$0.125$$

The total after-tax cost of making an interest payment is the after-tax coupon payment ($30.00) minus the tax savings due to the flotation costs ($0.125) which is $29.875: $30.00 − $0.125 = $29.875.

The after-tax cost of debt is equal to the yield to maturity of the bond's after-tax cash flows. Using a financial calculator, enter N = 2*28 = 56, PMT = $29.875, PV = −(1000 − $28) = −972, and FV = 1000. Solving for I/YR, we find $I/YR = r_d(1 - T) = 3.09330\%$, which is the semiannual after-tax component cost of debt. The annual after-tax cost of debt is 6.187%.

Suppose a financial analyst mistakenly ignored the allocation of flotation costs and instead used the constant yield method. In this case, N = 56, PMT = 40, PV = −972, and FV = 1000. Solving for the rate, the semiannual yield to maturity is 4.128995%. The annual yield is 8.25799%. The after-tax yield is 8.25799%(1 − 0.25) = 6.193%. Recall that the correct value previously found by incorporating the after-tax impact due to the allocation of flotation costs is 6.187%. The difference between the correct value (6.187%), and the incorrect value (6.193%) is just −0.006%. Most analysts would consider this too small a difference to matter and would apply the constant yield method instead, which is what we recommend.

9-3e The After-Tax Cost of Debt When Bonds Are Issued at a Premium or a Discount

As we discussed in Chapter 5, not all bonds are issued at par. Some are issued at a premium (i.e., the issue price is above the par value) and some are issued at a discount (i.e., the issue price is below the bond's par value). What impact does this have on the after-tax cost of capital? To answer this question, we use an approach that is analogous to the one we applied to flotation costs.

Suppose a bond is issued at a discount (i.e., the issue price is less than the par value). The **total net discount** is equal to the flotation costs plus the par value minus the issue price. To estimate the after-tax cost of debt, apply the same approach previously described for a par bond with flotation costs, except replace flotation costs with the total net discount. In other words, use the constant yield method if the total net discount is greater than de minimis; otherwise, use the allocation method.

Now suppose a bond is issued at a premium (i.e., the issue price is greater than the par value). Subtract the flotation cost from the premium bond's issue price. If the result is below par, the bond has a total net discount; calculate the after-tax cost of debt as we just explained. If the result is greater than par, then the **total net premium** is equal to the flotation costs plus the par value minus the issue price. Use the constant yield method to calculate the after-tax cost of debt.

Why is the after-tax cost of debt, rather than its before-tax required rate of return, used to calculate the weighted average cost of capital?

Is the relevant cost of debt, when calculating the WACC, the interest rate on already outstanding *debt or the rate on* new *debt? Why?*

A company has outstanding long-term bonds with a face value of $1,000, a 10% coupon rate, 25 years remaining until maturity, and a current market value of $1,214.82. If it pays interest semiannually, then what is the nominal annual pre-tax required rate of return on debt? **(8%)** *If the company's tax rate is 25%, what is the after-tax cost of debt?* **(6%)**

9-4 Cost of Preferred Stock, r_{ps}

Many firms (including MicroDrive) use, or plan to use, preferred stock as part of their financing mix. Preferred dividends are not tax deductible, so the company bears their full cost. Therefore, *no tax adjustment is used when calculating the cost of preferred stock*. Some preferred stocks are issued without a stated maturity date, but today most have a sinking fund that effectively limits their life. Finally, although it is not mandatory that preferred dividends be paid, firms generally have every intention of doing so because otherwise: (1) They cannot pay dividends on their common stock. (2) They will find it difficult to raise additional funds in the capital markets. (3) In some cases preferred stockholders can take control of the firm.

The component **cost of preferred stock (r_{ps})** is the cost used in the WACC calculation. Equation 9-5 shows how to calculate the cost of preferred stock; D_{ps} is the dividend per share, and P_{ps} is the par price per share. The percentage flotation cost of preferred stock is calculated and denoted the same as for a bond issue.[4]

For preferred stock without a stated maturity date, r_{ps} is:

$$\text{Component cost of preferred stock} = r_{ps} = \frac{D_{ps}}{P_{ps}(1 - F)} \qquad (9\text{-}5)$$

To illustrate the calculation, assume MicroDrive has preferred stock that pays a $7 dividend per share and sells for $100 per share. If MicroDrive issued new shares of preferred stock, it would incur an underwriting (or flotation) cost of 2.1%, or $2.10 per share, so it would net $97.90 per share. Therefore, MicroDrive's cost of preferred stock is 7.15%:

$$r_{ps} = \$7/\$97.90 = 7.15\%$$

If we had not incorporated flotation costs, we would have incorrectly estimated $r_{ps} = \$7/\$100 = 7.0\%$, which is too big a difference to ignore. Therefore, analysts usually include flotation costs when estimating the firm's cost of preferred stock.

Although preferred stock is riskier than debt, MicroDrive's preferred stock has a lower return to investors than does its long-term debt: 7% versus 10%. However, recall that most preferred stock is held by other companies, which are allowed to exclude at least 50% of preferred stocks' dividends from taxation. Thus, the after-tax return to these investors is higher for preferred stock than for debt, which is consistent with preferred stock being riskier than debt.

Some preferred stock has a stated maturity date, just like bonds. To estimate the cost of preferred stock with a maturity date, use the same approach as in Section 9-3 for the

---

[4]We ignore the tax treatment of flotation costs for preferred stock because they have a small impact on the cost of preferred stock.

cost of debt. However, keep in mind that a firm cannot deduct preferred dividends and therefore has no tax savings associated with dividend payments.

SELF-TEST

Does the component cost of preferred stock include or exclude flotation costs? Explain.

Why is no tax adjustment made to the cost of preferred stock?

A company's preferred stock currently trades for $50 per share and pays a $3 annual dividend. Flotation costs are equal to 3% of the gross proceeds. If the company issues preferred stock, what is the cost of that stock? **(6.19%)**

9-5 Cost of Common Stock: The Market Risk Premium, RP$_M$

The **required rate of return on stock (r_s)** is the rate that shareholders require to be fairly compensated for the risk they bear. The **cost of common stock** is the cost a company incurs providing shareholders with their required returns. Therefore, r_s is both a cost and a required return.

Before addressing the required return for an individual stock, let's start with the big picture, which is the required return for the entire stock market. In other words, how much return do investors require to induce them to invest in stocks? It often is more convenient to focus on the extra return that investors require to induce them to invest in risky equities over and above the return on a Treasury bond. As Chapter 6 explained, this extra return is called the market risk premium, RP$_M$. Sometimes this is called the equity risk premium, or just the equity premium.

Unfortunately, the required return on the market and hence the equity premium are not directly observable. Three approaches may be used to estimate the market risk premium: (1) Calculate historical premiums and use them to estimate the current premium. (2) Survey experts. (3) Use the current value of the market to estimate forward-looking premiums. Following are descriptions of each approach.

9-5a Historical Risk Premium

Historical risk premium data for U.S. securities, updated annually, are available from many sources, including Ibbotson Associates.[5] Using data from 1926 through the most recent year, Ibbotson calculates the actual realized rate of return each year for the stock market and for long-term government bonds. Ibbotson defines the annual equity risk premium as the difference between the historical realized returns on stocks and the historical yields to maturity on long-term T-bonds.[6] Ibbotson recently reported a 6.0% arithmetic average historical risk premium.[7] How should these data be used?

---

[5]For the most recent estimates, see Roger Ibbotson, Roger J. Grabowski, James P. Harrington, and Carla Nunes, *2018 SBBI Yearbook: Stocks, Bonds, Bills and Inflation* (Hoboken: John Wiley & Sons, 2018).

[6]The risk premium should be defined using the yield on T-bonds. As a proxy for yield, Ibbotson uses the return on 20-year T-bonds that is due to coupons. This underestimates yield for discount bonds and overstates yield for premium bonds, but the error probably averages out to zero in most years.

[7]The arithmetic average often is used as an estimate of next year's risk premium; this is most appropriate if investor risk aversion had actually been constant during the sample period. On the other hand, the geometric average would be most appropriate to estimate the longer-term risk premium, say, for the next 20 years. Using the data in *Ch09 Tool Kit.xlsx*, the geometric average is 3.6%, which is less than the arithmetic average of 5.1% for the same time period.

First, stock returns are quite volatile, which leads to low statistical confidence in estimated averages. For example, the estimated historical average premium is 6%, but based on the market return's standard deviation of around 20%, the 95% confidence interval ranges about plus or minus 3% from 6%. In other words, the historical average is helpful in deciding whether the risk premium is on the order of 6% or 20%, but it isn't very helpful in deciding whether the premium should be 4% or 6%.

Second, the historical average is sensitive to the period over which it is calculated. For example, we provide annual data for the period 1968–2017 in the file *Ch09 Tool Kit.xlsx*. For this period, the estimated historic risk premium is 5.1%.

Third, changes in the risk premium can occur if investors' tolerance for risk changes. This causes problems in interpreting historical returns because a change in the required risk premium causes an *opposite change in the observed* premium. For example, an increase in the required premium means that investors have become more risk averse and require a higher return on stocks. But applying a higher discount rate to a stock's future cash flows causes a decline in stock price. Thus, an *increase* in the required premium causes a simultaneous *decrease* in the observed premium. Part of the market's precipitous decline in 2008 and 2009 surely was due to investors' increased risk aversion.

9-5b Surveys of Experts

What do the experts think about the market risk premium? Two professors at Duke University, John Graham and Campbell Harvey (working in conjunction with *CFO* magazine), have surveyed CFOs quarterly beginning in 2000.[8] One survey question asks CFOs what they expect the S&P 500 return to be over the next 10 years; the CFOs are also given the yield on a 10-year T-bond. Their average response in the March 2018 survey implied an average expected risk premium of about 3.71%.

Professors from the IESE Business School regularly survey professors, analysts, and companies.[9] For 2017, based on the average U.S. responses, experts predicted a premium of 5.7%.

9-5c Forward-Looking Risk Premiums

An alternative to the historical risk premium is the forward-looking, or *ex ante*, risk premium. This method makes the same two assumptions as the constant dividend growth model from Equation 7-18 in Chapter 7: (1) All distributions are dividends (i.e., no stock repurchases and no short-term investment purchases). (2) Dividends will grow at a constant rate. Using the market's expected total dividend (instead of a single company's dividend) and the market dividend's expected constant growth rate (instead of a single company's growth rate), the expected market rate of return, $\hat{r}_M$, is:

$$\hat{r}_M = \frac{D_1}{P_0} + g \qquad (9\text{-}6)$$

If we also assume that the market is in equilibrium, then required return on the market, r_M, is equal to the expected return, $\hat{r}_M$. Thus, the required return on the market can be

---

[8]See www.cfosurvey.org/2018q1/US-Banners.pdf, page 363.

[9]See Pablo Fernández, Vitaly Pershin, and Isabel Fernández Acín, "Discount Rate (Risk-Free Rate and Market Risk Premium) Used for 41 Countries in 2017: A Survey," at https://papers.ssrn.com/sol3/papers.cfm?abstract_id52954142.

estimated as the sum of the market's expected dividend yield plus the expected constant growth rate in dividends.

SIMPLIFIED ILLUSTRATION OF ESTIMATING A FORWARD-LOOKING RISK PREMIUM

resource

*For current estimates, see instructions in **Ch09 Tool Kit.xlsx**.*

Following is an illustration for how to use Equation 9-6 to estimate the required return on the market. First, you need an estimate of the expected dividend. In May 2018, Standard & Poor's Web site reported a projected dividend yield of 2.00% for the S&P 500, based on declared dividends. Second, you need an estimate of the constant dividend growth rate, g. One approach is to use the historical average growth rate in dividends for the S&P 500, which is about 4.99% (for 1988–2017). Using these estimates produces an estimate of the required market return:

$$r_M = \hat{r}_M = \frac{D_1}{P_0} + g$$
$$= 2.00\% + 4.99\%$$
$$= 6.99\%$$

At the time we estimated r_M, the 10-year T-bond yield was 2.97%. Using the previously estimated r_M of 6.99%, the estimated forward-looking market risk premium is:

$$RP_M = r - r_{RF}$$
$$= 6.99\% - 2.97\%$$
$$= 4.02\%$$

COMPLICATIONS WHEN ESTIMATING A FORWARD-LOOKING RISK PREMIUM

We made numerous simplifying assumptions in the previous example regarding three complications that arise in practice. First, the growth rate in dividends probably will not be constant in the near future but might instead take many years before leveling out. Second, the historical average growth rate in dividends might not be a good estimate of the expected long-term dividend growth rate. Long-term growth in dividends is probably related to long-term sales and profits, which in turn depend on inflation (which affects the reported dollar value of sales), population growth (which affects the unit volume of sales), and productivity (which affects profits). Third, the model is based on dividends per share, but it ignores the impact of stock repurchases on the number of outstanding shares (which then changes the growth rate of dividends per share).

Fortunately, there are ways to address these technical issues, including the use of a multistage growth model. The interested reader should see *Web Extension 9A* and the corresponding worksheet, *Web9A*, in *Ch09 Tool Kit.xlsx*.

9-5d Our View on the Market Risk Premium

After reading the previous sections, you might well be confused about the best way to estimate the market risk premium. Here's our opinion: The risk premium is driven primarily by investors' attitudes toward risk, and there are good reasons to believe that investors' risk aversion changes over time. The introduction of pension plans, Social Security, health insurance, and disability insurance over the last 50 years means that people today can take more chances with their investments, which should make them less risk averse. Moreover, many households have dual earners, allowing households to take more chances. Therefore, we think the risk premium is lower now than it was 50 years ago.

In our consulting, we currently (spring 2018) use a risk premium of about 4.5% to 6%, but we would have a hard time arguing with someone who used a risk premium anywhere in the range of 3% to 7%. We believe that investors' aversion to risk is relatively stable much of the time, but it is not absolutely constant from year to year and is certainly not constant during periods of great stress, such as during the 2008–2009 financial crisis. When stock prices are relatively high, investors feel less risk averse, so we use a risk premium at the low end of our range. Conversely, when prices are depressed, we use a premium at the high end of the range. The bottom line is that there is no way to prove that a particular risk premium is either right or wrong, though we'd be suspicious of an estimated market premium that is less than 3% or greater than 7%.

SELF-TEST

Explain both the historical and the forward-looking approaches to estimating the market risk premium.

9-6 Using the CAPM to Estimate the Cost of Common Stock, r_s

Before estimating the return required by MicroDrive's shareholders, r_s, it is worth considering the two ways that a company can raise common equity: (1) Sell newly issued shares to the public. (2) Reinvest (retain) earnings by not paying out all net income as dividends.

Does new equity capital raised by reinvesting earnings have a cost? The answer is a resounding, "Yes!" If earnings are reinvested, then stockholders will incur an *opportunity cost:* The earnings could have been paid out as dividends or used to repurchase stock, and in either case stockholders would have received funds that they could reinvest in other securities. *Thus, the firm should earn on its reinvested earnings at least as much as its stockholders could earn on alternative investments of equivalent risk.*

What rate of return could stockholders expect to earn on equivalent-risk investments? The answer is r_s because they could presumably earn that return by simply buying the stock of the firm in question or that of a similar firm. *Therefore, r_s is the cost of common equity raised internally via reinvested earnings.* If a company can't earn at least r_s on reinvested earnings, then it should pass those earnings on to its stockholders as dividends and let them invest the money themselves in assets that do yield r_s.

9-6a The Capital Asset Pricing Model

To estimate the cost of common stock using the Capital Asset Pricing Model (CAPM) as discussed in Chapter 6, we proceed as follows:

1. Estimate the risk-free rate, r_{RF}.
2. Estimate the current market risk premium, RP_M, which is the required market return in excess of the risk-free rate.
3. Estimate the stock's beta coefficient, b_i, which measures the stock's relevant risk, which is determined by the amount of risk the stock contributes to a well-diversified portfolio. The subscript i signifies Stock i's beta.
4. Use these three values to estimate the stock's required rate of return:

$$r_s = r_{RF} + (RP_M)b_i \qquad (9\text{-}7)$$

Equation 9-7 shows that the CAPM estimate of r_s begins with the risk-free rate, r_{RF}.[10] We then add a risk premium that is equal to the risk premium on the market, RP_M, scaled up or down to reflect the particular stock's risk as measured by its beta coefficient. The following sections explain how to implement this four-step process.

9-6b Estimating the Risk-Free Rate, r_{RF}

www

To find the rate on a T-bond, go to **www .federalreserve.gov**. *Select "Economic Research & Data" and then select "Statistical Releases and Historical Data." Click on "Daily" for "H.15: Selected Interest Rates."*

The starting point for the CAPM cost-of-equity estimate is r_{RF}, the risk-free rate. There is no such thing as a truly riskless asset in the U.S. economy. Treasury securities are essentially free of default risk; however, nonindexed long-term T-bonds will suffer capital losses if interest rates rise, indexed long-term bonds will decline if the real rate rises, and a portfolio of short-term T-bills will provide a volatile earnings stream because the rate earned on T-bills varies over time.

Because we cannot, in practice, find a truly riskless rate on which to base the CAPM, what rate should we use? Keep in mind that our objective is to estimate the cost of capital, which will be used to discount a company's free cash flows or a project's cash flows. Free cash flows occur over the life of the company, and many projects last for many years. Because the cost of capital will be used to discount relatively long-term cash flows, it seems appropriate to use a relatively long-term risk-free rate, such as the yield on a 10-year Treasury bond. Indeed, a survey of highly regarded companies shows that about two-thirds of them use the rate on 10-year Treasury bonds.[11]

T-bond rates can be found in *The Wall Street Journal*, the *Federal Reserve Bulletin*, or on the Internet. Although most analysts use the yield on a 10-year T-bond as a proxy for the risk-free rate, yields on 20-year or 30-year T-bonds are also reasonable proxies.

9-6c Estimating the Market Risk Premium, RP_M

We described three approaches for estimating the market risk premium, RP_M, in Section 9-5: (1) Use historical averages. (2) Survey experts. (3) Estimate forward-looking expected market returns. All three approaches provide estimates in the same ballpark, around 3% to 7%. The final choice really boils down to judgment informed by the current state of the market and the estimates provided by the three approaches. We will use a market risk premium of 6% in this example.

9-6d Estimating Beta, b_i

www

To find an estimate of beta, go to **www .valueline.com** *and then enter the ticker symbol for a stock quote. (You may need to register, which is free.)*

Recall from Chapter 6 that a stock's beta, b_i, can be estimated as:

$$b_i = \left(\frac{\sigma_i}{\sigma_M}\right)\rho_{iM} \qquad (9\text{-}8)$$

where ρ_{iM} is the correlation between Stock i's return and the market return; σ_i is the standard deviation of Stock i's return; and σ_M is the standard deviation of the market's return. This definition is also equal to the estimated slope coefficient in a regression, with the company's stock returns on the y-axis and market returns on the x-axis.

---

[10]In Chapter 6 we used the subscript i (r_i) to denote the required return for Stock i so that we could differentiate it from required return on other stocks. Because we focus on only a single company in this chapter, we use the subscript s (r_s) to denote the return required on stock relative to other capital components.

[11]See Robert E. Bruner, Kenneth M. Eades, Robert S. Harris, and Robert C. Higgins, "Best Practices in Estimating the Cost of Capital: Survey and Synthesis," *Financial Practice and Education,* Spring/Summer 1998, pp. 13–28.

It is easy to gather historical returns from the Web and then estimate your own beta, as we show in the *Tool Kit* for Chapter 6. Also, many Web sources provide estimates of beta. The good news is that there is no shortage of beta estimates; the bad news is that many estimates differ from one another. We will discuss this in the next section.

9-6e An Illustration of the CAPM Approach: MicroDrive's Cost of Equity, r_s

Following is an application of the CAPM approach to MicroDrive. As estimated in Chapter 6, MicroDrive's beta, b_i, is 1.33. We assume that the market risk premium, RP_M, is about 6%. For this example, assume that the risk-free rate, r_{RF}, is 5.02%. Using Equation 9-7, we estimate MicroDrive's required return as about 13%:

$$r_s = 5.02\% + (6\%)(1.33)$$
$$= 13.00\%$$

This estimate of 13% is a required return from an investor's point of view, but it is a cost of equity from a company's perspective.

Always keep in mind that the estimated cost of equity is indeed an estimate, for several reasons. First, the yield on any long-term T-bond would be an appropriate estimate of the risk-free rate, and different yields would lead to different estimates of r_s. Second, no one truly knows the correct market risk premium. We can narrow the estimated RP_M down to a fairly small range, but different estimates in this range would lead to different estimates of r_s. Third, estimates of beta are inexact. In addition to a large range of the confidence interval around an estimated beta, using slightly different time periods to estimate beta can lead to rather large differences in the estimated beta.

Still, in our judgment, it is possible to develop "reasonable" estimates of the required inputs, and we believe that the CAPM can be used to obtain reasonable estimates of the cost of equity. Indeed, despite the difficulties we have noted, surveys indicate that the CAPM is by far the most widely used method. Although most firms use more than one method, almost 74% of respondents in one survey (and 85% in another) used the CAPM.[12] This is in sharp contrast to a 1982 survey, which found that only 30% of respondents used the CAPM.[13]

SELF-TEST

What are the two primary sources of equity capital?

Explain why there is a cost to using reinvested earnings; that is, why aren't reinvested earnings a free source of capital?

Which is generally considered the more appropriate estimate of the risk-free rate: the yield on a short-term T-bill or the yield on a 10-year T-bond?

A company's beta is 1.4, the yield on a 10-year T-bond is 4%, and the market risk premium is 4.5%. What is r_s? **(10.3%)**

---

[12]See John R. Graham and Campbell Harvey, "The Theory and Practice of Corporate Finance: Evidence from the Field," *Journal of Financial Economics*, 2001, pp. 187–243, and the paper cited in footnote 10. It is interesting that a growing number of firms (about 34%) also are using CAPM-type models with more than one factor. Of these firms, over 40% include factors for interest rate risk, foreign exchange risk, and business cycle risk (proxied by gross domestic product). More than 20% of these firms include a factor for inflation, size, and exposure to particular commodity prices. Less than 20% of these firms make adjustments due to distress factors, book-to-market ratios, or momentum factors.

[13]See Lawrence J. Gitman and Vincent Mercurio, "Cost of Capital Techniques Used by Major U.S. Firms: Survey Analysis of *Fortune's* 1000," *Financial Management*, 1982, pp. 21–29.

9-7 Using the Dividend Growth Approach to Estimate the Cost of Common Stock

In Chapter 7, we saw that if an investor expects dividends to grow at a constant rate and if the company makes all payouts in the form of dividends (the company does not repurchase stock), then the price of a stock can be found as follows:

$$\hat{P}_0 = \frac{D_1}{r_s - g_L} \qquad (9\text{-}9)$$

Here $\hat{P}_0$ is the intrinsic value of the stock for the investor; D_1 is the dividend expected to be paid at the end of Year 1; g_L is the expected constant growth rate in dividends; and r_s is the required rate of return. For the marginal investor, the required return is equal to the expected return. If this investor is the marginal investor, then $\hat{P}_0 = P_0$, the market price of the stock, and we can solve for r_s to obtain the required rate of return on common equity:

$$\hat{r} = r_s = \frac{D_1}{P_0} + \text{Expected } g_L \qquad (9\text{-}10)$$

Thus, investors expect to receive a dividend yield, D_1/P_0, plus a capital gain, g_L, for a total expected return of $\hat{r}$. In equilibrium, this expected return is also equal to the required return, r_s. Henceforth, we will assume that markets are at equilibrium (which means that $r_s = \hat{r}_s$), and this permits us to use the terms r_s and $\hat{r}_s$ interchangeably.

This method of estimating the cost of equity is called the **dividend growth approach** because it is based on constant growth dividends. It is also called the **dividend capitalization method** because it is based on the idea of determining a stock's price by "capitalizing" its dividends.

9-7a Estimating Inputs for the Dividend Growth Approach

Three inputs are required to use the dividend growth approach: the current stock price, the current dividend, and the marginal investor's expected dividend growth rate. The stock price and the dividend are easy to obtain, but the expected growth rate is difficult to estimate, as we will see in the following sections.

HISTORICAL GROWTH RATES

If earnings and dividend growth rates have been relatively stable in the past, and if investors expect these trends to continue, then the past realized growth rate may be used as an estimate of the expected future growth rate. Unfortunately, such situations occur only at a handful of very mature, slow-growing companies, which precludes the usefulness of historical growth rates as predictors of future growth rates for most companies.

RETENTION GROWTH MODEL

Most firms pay out some of their net income as dividends and reinvest, or retain, the rest. Companies will grow faster if they reinvest more or if they earn a higher rate of return on equity. We can use these facts to estimate the expected growth rate of a company's earnings and dividends. We begin by defining the payout ratio and the retention ratio.

The **payout ratio (POR)** is the percent of net income that the firm pays out in dividends:

$$
\begin{aligned}
\text{Payout ratio} &= \text{Dividends/Net income} \\
&= \text{Dividends per share/Earnings per share} \\
&= \text{DPS/EPS}
\end{aligned}
\tag{9-11}
$$

The **retention ratio** is the percent of net income that is reinvested and added to retained earnings:

$$
\begin{aligned}
\text{Retention ratio} &= \text{Addition to retained earnings/Net income} \\
&= (\text{Net income} - \text{Dividends})/\text{Net income} \\
&= 1 - (\text{Dividends per share/Earnings per share}) \\
&= 1 - \text{Payout ratio}
\end{aligned}
\tag{9-12}
$$

Consider Aldabra Corporation, a mature company. Aldabra's payout ratio has averaged 63% over the past 15 years, so its retention rate has averaged $1.0 - 0.63 = 0.37 = 37\%$. Also, Aldabra's return on equity (ROE) has averaged 14.5% over the past 15 years. We know that, other things held constant, the earnings growth rate depends on the amount of reinvestment in the firm, which comes from the income the firm reinvests and from the rate of return it earns on those reinvested earnings. The **retention growth equation** shows how growth is related to reinvestment and is expressed as follows:

$$
\begin{aligned}
g_L &= \text{ROE(Retention ratio)} \\
&= \text{ROE}(1 - \text{Payout ratio})
\end{aligned}
\tag{9-13}
$$

Using Aldabra's 14.5% average ROE and its 37% retention rate, we can use Equation 9-13 to find the estimated g:

$$
g_L = 14.5\%(0.37) = 5.365\% \approx 5.4\%
$$

Although easy to implement, this approach requires four major assumptions: (1) The payout rate and therefore the retention rate remain constant. (2) The ROE on new investments remains constant and equal to the ROE on existing assets. (3) The firm is not expected to repurchase or issue new common stock, or, if it does, this new stock will be sold at a price equal to its book value. (4) Future projects are expected to have the same degree of risk as the firm's existing assets. Unfortunately, these assumptions apply in very few situations, limiting the usefulness of the retention growth model.

ANALYSTS' FORECASTS

A third technique calls for using security analysts' forecasts. As we discussed earlier, analysts publish growth rate estimates for most of the larger publicly owned companies. For example, *Value Line* provides such dividend forecasts on about 1,700 companies. Several sources compile analysts' earnings forecasts on a regular basis, and these earnings growth rates can be used as proxies for dividend growth rates.

However, analysts usually forecast nonconstant growth in earnings, which limits the usefulness of the constant growth model. Instead, a multistage model must be used. See *Web Extension 9A* on the textbook's Web site for an explanation of how to calculate a required return on equity using the multistage approach; all calculations are in the worksheet *Web 9A* in the file *Ch09 Tool Kit.xlsx*.

9-7b An Illustration of the Dividend Growth Approach

To illustrate the dividend growth approach, suppose Aldabra's stock sells for $32, its next expected dividend is $1.82, and its expected constant growth rate is 5.4%. Aldabra is not expected to repurchase any stock. Aldabra's stock is thought to be in equilibrium, so its expected and required rates of return are equal. Based on these assumptions, its estimated cost of common equity is 11.1%:

$$\hat{r}_s = \frac{\$1.82}{\$32.00} + 5.4\%$$
$$= 5.7\% + 5.4\%$$
$$= 11.1\%$$

As previously noted, it is difficult to apply the dividend growth approach because dividends do not grow at a constant rate for most companies. Surveys show that 16% of responding firms use this approach, down from 31% in 1982.[14]

SELF-TEST

What inputs are required for the dividend growth approach?

What are three ways to estimate the expected dividend growth rate?

A company's estimated growth rate in dividends is 6%, its current stock price is $40, and its expected annual dividend is $2. Using the dividend growth approach, what is the firm's r_s? **(11%)**

9-8 The Weighted Average Cost of Capital (WACC)

As we mentioned earlier in this chapter, each firm has an optimal capital structure, which is defined as the mix of debt, preferred stock, and common equity that maximizes its stock price. Therefore, a value-maximizing firm must attempt to find its *target (or optimal) capital structure* and then raise new capital in a manner that will keep the actual capital structure on target over time. In this chapter, we assume that the firm has identified its optimal capital structure, that it uses this optimum as the target, and that it finances so as to remain constantly on target. How the target is established is examined in Chapter 15. The target proportions of debt, preferred stock, and common equity, along with the component costs of capital, are used to calculate the WACC, as shown previously in Equation 9-2:

$$\text{WACC} = w_d r_d (1 - T) + w_{std} r_{std} (1 - T) + w_{ps} r_{ps} + w_s r_s \qquad (9\text{-}2)$$

Here w_d, w_{std}, w_{ps}, and w_s are the target weights for long-term debt, short-term debt, preferred stock, and common equity, respectively.

To illustrate, we first note that MicroDrive has a target capital structure calling for 20% long-term debt, 4% short-term debt, 2% preferred stock, and 74% common equity. MicroDrive's before-tax cost of long-term debt, r_d, is 10%; its before-tax cost of short-term debt, r_{std}, is 8%; its cost of preferred stock, r_{ps}, is 7.15%; its cost of common equity, r_s, is 13.00%; and its marginal tax rate is 25%. We can now calculate MicroDrive's weighted average cost of capital as follows:

$$\text{WACC} = 0.20(10.0\%)(1 - 0.25) + 0.04(8.0\%)(1 - 0.25) + 0.02(7.15\%) + 0.74(13.00\%)$$
$$= 11.5\%$$

---

[14]See the sources cited in footnotes 12 and 13.

Three points should be noted. First, the WACC is the cost the company would incur to raise each new, or *marginal*, dollar of capital; it is not the average cost of dollars raised in the past. Second, the percentages of each capital component, called *weights,* should be based on management's target capital structure, not on the particular sources of financing in any single year. Third, the target weights should be based on market values and not on book values. The following sections explain these points.

9-8a Marginal Rates versus Historical Rates

The required rates of return for a company's investors, whether they are new or old, are always marginal rates. For example, a stockholder might have invested in a company last year when the risk-free interest rate was 6% and the required return on equity was 12%. If the risk-free rate subsequently falls and is now 4%, then the investor's required return on equity is now 10% (holding all else constant). This is the same required rate of return that a new equity holder would have, whether the new investor bought stock in the secondary market or through a new equity offering. In other words, whether the shareholders are already equity holders or are brand-new equity holders, they all have the same required rate of return, which is the current required rate of return on equity. The same reasoning applies for the firm's bondholders. All bondholders, whether old or new, have a required rate of return equal to today's yield on the firm's debt, which is based on current market conditions.

Because investors' required rates of return are based on *current* market conditions, not on market conditions when they purchased their securities, it follows that the cost of capital depends on current conditions and not on past market conditions.

9-8b Target Weights versus Annual Financing Choices

We have heard managers (and students!) say, "Our debt has a 5% after-tax cost versus a 10% WACC and a 14% cost of equity. Therefore, because we will finance only with debt this year, we should evaluate this year's projects at a 5% cost." There are two flaws in this line of reasoning.

First, suppose the firm exhausts its capacity to issue low-cost debt this year to take on projects with after-tax returns as low as 5.1% (which is slightly higher than the after-tax cost of debt). Then next year, when the firm must finance with common equity, it will have to turn down projects with returns as high as 13.9% (which is slightly lower than the cost of equity). It doesn't make any economic sense for the order in which projects are considered to matter so much; to avoid this problem, a firm that plans to remain in business indefinitely should evaluate all projects using the 10% WACC.

Second, both existing and new investors have claims on *all* future cash flows. For example, if a company raises debt and also invests in a new project that same year, the new debtholders don't have a specific claim on that specific project's cash flows (assuming it is not non-recourse project financing). In fact, new debtholders receive a claim on the cash flows being generated by existing as well as new projects, while old debtholders (and equity holders) have claims on both new and existing projects. Thus, the decision to take on a new project should depend on the project's ability to satisfy all of the company's investors, not just the new debtholders, even if only debt is being raised that year.

9-8c Weights for Component Costs: Book Values versus Market Values versus Targets

Our primary reason for calculating the WACC is to use it in capital budgeting or corporate valuation. In particular, we need to compare the expected returns on projects and stocks with investors' required returns to determine whether investors are compensated fairly for the risk they bear. The total amount of required compensation depends both on the *rate of return required* by investors and the *amount* they have at stake.

Global Variations in the Cost of Capital

For U.S. firms to be competitive with foreign companies, they must have a cost of capital no greater than that faced by their international competitors. In the past, many experts argued that U.S. firms were at a disadvantage. In particular, Japanese firms enjoyed a very low cost of capital, which lowered their total costs and thus made it hard for U.S. firms to compete with them. Recent events, however, have considerably narrowed cost-of-capital differences between U.S. and Japanese firms. In particular, the U.S. stock market has outperformed the Japanese market in recent years, which has made it easier and cheaper for U.S. firms to raise equity capital.

As capital markets become increasingly integrated, cross-country differences in the cost of capital are declining. Today, most large corporations raise capital throughout the world; hence, we are moving toward one global capital market instead of a distinct capital market in each country. Government policies and market conditions can affect the cost of capital within a given country, but this primarily affects smaller firms that do not have access to global capital markets, and even these differences are becoming less important as time passes. What matters most is the risk of the individual firm, not the market in which it raises capital.

Regarding the rate of return required by investors, the previous sections showed that investors require a rate of return equal to the current rate they could get on alternative investments of equivalent risk. In other words, the required rate is the opportunity cost.

Regarding the amount that investors have at stake, we again apply the "opportunity" concept. Investors have the opportunity to sell their investment at the market value, so this is the amount that investors have at stake. Notice that the amount at stake is not equal to the book values as reported on the financial statements. Book values are a record of historical investments, not the current market value of the investment. Because the WACC is used to discount future cash flows, the weights should be based on the market value weights expected on average in the future, not necessarily the current weights based on current market values.

In summary, the weights should not be based on book values but instead should be based on the market value weights in the target capital structure. Obviously, the target capital structure must be realistic: Companies can't take on so much debt that they will almost certainly go bankrupt. Also, a company must try to adjust its market value weights toward the target weights; otherwise, the average weights over time might differ significantly from those in the target capital structure. We discuss how fast companies adjust their weights in Chapter 15.

SELF-TEST

How is the weighted average cost of capital calculated? Write out the equation.

Should the weights used to calculate the WACC be based on book values, market values, or something else? Explain.

A firm has the following data: target capital structure = 25% debt, 10% preferred stock, and 65% common equity; tax rate = 25%; r_d = 7%; r_{ps} = 7.5%; and r_s = 11.5%. Assume the firm will not issue new stock. What is this firm's WACC? **(9.54%)**

9-9 Adjusting the Cost of Equity for Flotation Costs

Few firms with moderate or slow growth issue new shares of common stock through public offerings.[15] In fact, fewer than 2% of all new corporate funds come from the external public equity market, for two very good reasons: (1) negative signaling and (2) direct costs. We discuss signaling in Chapter 15, but we address direct costs here.

---

[15]A few companies issue new shares through new-stock dividend reinvestment plans, which we discuss in Chapter 14. Many companies sell stock to their employees, and companies occasionally issue stock to finance huge projects or mergers. Also, some utilities regularly issue common stock.

TABLE 9-1
Average Flotation Costs for Debt and Equity

Amount of Capital Raised (Millions of Dollars)	Average Flotation Cost for Common Stock (% of Total Capital Raised)	Average Flotation Cost for New Debt (% of Total Capital Raised)
2–9.99	13.28%	4.39%
10–19.99	8.72	2.76
20–39.99	6.93	2.42
40–59.99	5.87	2.32
60–79.99	5.18	2.34
80–99.99	4.73	2.16
100–199.99	4.22	2.31
200–499.99	3.47	2.19
500 and up	3.15	1.64

Source: Inmoo Lee, Scott Lochhead, Jay Ritter, and Quanshui Zhao, "The Costs of Raising Capital," *The Journal of Financial Research,* Spring 1996, pp. 59–74.

Table 9-1 shows the average flotation costs for debt and equity U.S. corporations issued in the 1990s. Notice that flotation costs, as a *percentage* of capital raised, fall as the *amount* of capital raised increases. The common stock flotation costs are for non-IPO issues. For IPOs, flotation costs are higher—about 17% higher if less than $10 million is raised and higher still as issue size increases. The data in Table 9-1 include both utility and nonutility companies; if utilities had been excluded, the reported flotation costs would have been higher. Table 9-1 shows that flotation costs are significantly higher for equity than for debt. One reason for higher equity flotation costs is that corporate debt is sold mainly in large blocks to institutional investors, whereas common stock is sold in smaller amounts to many different investors; this imposes higher costs on the investment banks, which pass these costs on to the issuing company. Also, stock values are harder to estimate than debt values, which makes selling stock more difficult, again leading to higher costs for the investment banks.

For companies that do issue new common stock, the **cost of new external common equity** (r_e), which is raised externally, is higher than the cost of common stock raised internally by reinvesting earnings, r_s, because of the flotation costs involved in issuing new common stock. What rate of return must be earned on new investments to make issuing stock worthwhile? Put another way, what is the cost of new common equity?

The answer, for a constant growth firm, is found by applying this formula:

$$r_e = \hat{r}_e = \frac{D_1}{P_0(1-F)} + g_L \qquad (9\text{-}14)$$

In Equation 9-14, F is the percentage flotation cost incurred in selling the new stock, so $P_0(1-F)$ is the net price per share received by the company.

Here is an example. In Section 9-7b, we estimated Aldabra's cost of common equity using the dividend growth approach to be 11.1%, assuming Aldabra didn't issue new equity. Now assume that Aldabra must issue new equity with a flotation cost of 12.5%. The cost of new outside equity is calculated as follows:

$$r_e = \frac{\$1.82}{\$32(1-0.125)} + 5.4\%$$

$$= 6.5\% + 5.4\% = 11.9\%$$

Because of flotation costs, Aldabra must earn 11.9% on the new equity capital in order to provide shareholders the 11.1% they require.

As we noted previously, most analysts use the CAPM to estimate the cost of equity. How would the analyst incorporate flotation costs into a CAPM cost estimate? If application of the dividend growth approach gives a cost of internally generated equity of 11.1% but a cost of 11.9% when flotation costs are involved, then the flotation costs add 0.8 percentage points to the cost of equity. To incorporate flotation costs into the CAPM estimate, we would simply add 0.8% to the CAPM estimate.

As an alternative to adjusting the cost of equity for flotation costs, many companies simply include the flotation costs as a negative cash flow when they perform project analysis. See Chapter 11 for a description of cash flow estimation for projects.

SELF-TEST

What are flotation costs?

Why are flotation costs higher for stock than for debt?

A firm has common stock with D_1 = $3.00; P_0 = $30; g = 5%; and F = 4%. If the firm must issue new stock, what is its cost of external equity, r_e? **(15.42%)**

9-10 Privately Owned Firms and Small Businesses

So far, our discussion of the cost of capital has been focused on publicly owned corporations. Privately owned firms and small businesses have different situations, calling for slightly different approaches.

9-10a Estimating the Cost of Stock by the Comparison Approach

When we estimated the rate of return required by public stockholders, we use stock returns to estimate beta as an input for the CAPM approach and stock prices as input data for the dividend growth approach. But how can one measure the cost of equity for a firm whose stock is not traded? Most analysts begin by identifying one or more publicly traded firms that are in the same industry and that are approximately the same size as the privately owned firm.[16] The analyst then estimates the betas for these publicly traded firms and uses their average beta as an estimate of the beta of the privately owned firm.

9-10b Own-Bond-Yield-Plus-Judgmental-Risk-Premium Approach

From Chapter 5, we know that a company's cost of debt is above the risk-free rate due to the default risk premium. We also know that a company's cost of stock should be greater than its cost of debt because equity is riskier than debt. Therefore, some analysts use a subjective, ad hoc procedure to estimate a firm's cost of common equity: They simply add a judgmental risk premium of 3% to 5% to the cost of debt. In this approach:

$$r_s = r_d + \text{Judgmental risk premium} \qquad (9\text{-}15)$$

---

[16]In Chapter 15, we show how to adjust if these comparison firms have differences in capital structures.

For example, consider a privately held company with a 10% cost of debt. Using 4% as the judgmental risk premium (because it is the mid-point of the 3%–5% range), the estimated cost of equity is 14%:

$$r_s = 10\% + 4\% = 14\%$$

9-10c Adjusting for Lack of Liquidity

The stock of a privately held firm is less liquid than that of a publicly held firm. As we explained in Chapter 5, investors require a liquidity premium on thinly traded bonds. Therefore, many analysts make an ad hoc adjustment to reflect this lack of liquidity by adding 1 to 3 percentage points to the firm's cost of equity. This rule of thumb is not theoretically satisfying because we don't know exactly how large the liquidity premium should be, but it is logical and is also a common practice.

9-10d Estimating the Actual Weights in a Privately Owned Company's Capital Structure

Suppose a privately held firm wonders whether its current actual capital structure is consistent with its target capital structure. The first step for a publicly traded company would be to estimate the actual capital structure weights based on current market values and compare these actual weights with its target weights. However, a privately held firm can't directly observe its market value, so it can't directly observe its actual market value weights.

To resolve this problem, many analysts begin by making a trial guess about the value of the firm's equity. The analysts then use this estimated value of equity to determine the estimated market value weights and the cost of capital based on these estimated weights. They then use this cost of capital to estimate the value of the firm. Finally, they complete the circle by using the estimated value of the firm to estimate the value of its equity. If this newly estimated equity value is different from their trial guess, analysts repeat the process but start the iteration with the newly estimated equity value as the trial value of equity. After several iterations, the trial value of equity and the resulting estimated equity value usually converge.

If the current actual weights estimated from this process aren't equal to the firm's target weights, then the firm should recapitalize to change its actual capital structure to match its target capital structure. We discuss the selection of target weights and the process of recapitalization in Chapter 15.

SELF-TEST

Identify problems that occur when estimating the cost of capital for a privately held firm. What are some solutions to these problems?

Explain the reasoning behind the bond-yield-plus-judgmental-risk-premium approach.

A company's bond yield is 7%. If the appropriate own-bond-yield risk premium is 3.5%, then what is r_s? **(10.5%)**

9-11 The Divisional Cost of Capital

As we have calculated it, the weighted average cost of capital reflects the average risk and overall capital structure of the entire firm. No adjustments are needed when using the WACC as the discount rate when estimating the value of an entire company by discounting its cash flows. However, adjustments for risk are often needed when evaluating a division or project. For example, what if a firm has divisions in several business lines that differ in risk? It is not logical to use the overall cost of capital to discount divisional cash flows that don't have the same risk as the company's average cash flows. The following sections explain how to adjust the cost of capital for divisions that differ in risk. Chapter 11 explains how to measure project risk and adjust the cost of capital for projects that differ in risk.

9-11a Using the CAPM to Estimate the Divisional Cost of Capital

Consider Starlight Sandwich Shops, a company with two divisions—a bakery operation and a chain of cafes. The bakery division is low risk and has a 10% WACC. The cafe division is riskier and has a 14% WACC. Each division is approximately the same size, so Starlight's overall cost of capital is 12%. The bakery manager has a project with an 11% expected rate of return, and the cafe division manager has a project with a 13% expected return. Should these projects be accepted or rejected? Starlight will create value if it accepts the bakery's project because its rate of return is greater than its cost of capital (11% > 10%), but the cafe project's rate of return is less than its cost of capital (13% < 14%), so it should reject that project. However, if management simply compared the two projects' returns with Starlight's 12% overall cost of capital, then the bakery's value-adding project would be rejected while the cafe's value-destroying project would be accepted.

To prevent this from happening, many firms estimate a separate **divisional cost of capital** for each of their business segments using the following approach. Recall that the CAPM expresses the risk–return relationship as follows:

$$r_s = r_{RF} + (RP_M)b_i$$

As an example, consider the case of Huron Steel Company, an integrated steel producer operating in the Great Lakes region. For simplicity, assume that Huron has only one division and uses only equity capital, so its cost of equity is also its corporate cost of capital, or WACC. Huron's beta = b = 1.1, r_{RF} = 5%, and RP_M = 6%. Thus, Huron's cost of equity (and WACC) is 11.6%:

$$r_s = 5\% + (6\%)1.1 = 11.6\%$$

This suggests that investors should be willing to give Huron money to invest in new, average-risk projects if the company expects to earn 11.6% or more on this money. By "average risk," we mean projects having risk similar to the firm's existing division.

Now suppose Huron creates a new transportation division consisting of a fleet of barges to haul iron ore, and suppose barge operations typically have betas of 1.5 rather than 1.1. The barge division, with b = 1.5, has a 14.0% cost of capital:

$$r_{Barge} = 5\% + (6\%)1.5 = 14.0\%$$

On the other hand, if Huron adds a low-risk division, such as a new distribution center with a beta of only 0.5, then that division's cost of capital would be 8%:

$$r_{Center} = 5\% + (6\%)0.5 = 8.0\%$$

A firm itself may be regarded as a "portfolio of assets," and because the beta of a portfolio is a weighted average of the betas of its individual assets, adding the barge and distribution center divisions will change Huron's overall beta. The exact value of the new corporate beta would depend on the size of the investments in the new divisions relative to Huron's original steel operations. If 70% of Huron's total value ends up in the steel division, 20% in the barge division, and 10% in the distribution center, then its new corporate beta would be calculated as follows:

$$\text{New beta} = 0.7(1.1) + 0.2(1.5) + 0.1(0.5) = 1.12$$

Thus, investors in Huron's stock would require a return of:

$$r_{Huron} = 5\% + (6\%)1.12 = 11.72\%$$

Even though investors require an overall return of 11.72%, they should expect a rate of return on projects in each division at least as high as the division's required return. In particular, they should expect a return of at least 11.6% from the steel division, 14.0% from the barge division, and 8.0% from the distribution center.

Our example suggests a level of precision that is much higher than firms can obtain in the real world. Still, managers should be aware of this example's logic, and they should strive to measure the required inputs as accurately as possible.

9-11b Techniques for Measuring Divisional Betas

In Chapter 6, we discussed the estimation of betas for stocks and indicated how difficult it is to measure beta precisely. Estimating divisional betas is much more difficult, primarily because divisions do not have their own publicly traded stock. Therefore, we must estimate the beta that the division would have if it were an independent, publicly traded company. Two approaches can be used to estimate divisional betas: the pure play method and the accounting beta method.

THE PURE PLAY METHOD

In the **pure play method**, the company tries to find the betas of several publicly held specialized companies in the same line of business as the division being evaluated, and it then averages those betas to determine the cost of capital for its own division. For example, suppose Huron found three companies devoted exclusively to operating barges, and suppose that Huron's management believes its barge division would be subject to the same risks as those firms. Then Huron could use the average beta of those firms as an estimate of its barge division's beta.[17]

THE ACCOUNTING BETA METHOD

As noted earlier, it may be impossible to find specialized publicly traded firms suitable for the pure play approach. If that is the case, we may be able to use the **accounting beta method**. Betas are normally found by regressing the returns of a particular company's *stock* against returns on a *stock market index*. However, we could run a regression of the division's *accounting return on assets* against the *average return on assets* for a large sample of companies, such as those included in the S&P 500. Betas determined in this way (that is, by using accounting data rather than stock market data) are called **accounting betas**.

9-12 Estimating the Cost of Capital for Individual Projects

There are three ways to view a project's risk: stand-alone risk, corporate risk, and market risk.

1. A project's **stand-alone risk** is due to the variability of its cash flows. It is the risk that a company would have if the company had only this one project. As we show in Chapter 11, it is often measured by the standard deviation of the project's cash flows.

---

[17]If the pure play firms employ different capital structures than that of Huron, then this must be addressed by adjusting the beta coefficients. See Chapter 15 for a discussion of this aspect of the pure play method. For a technique that can be used when pure play firms are not available, see Yatin Bhagwat and Michael Ehrhardt, "A Full Information Approach for Estimating Divisional Betas," *Financial Management*, Summer 1991, pp. 60–69.

2. **Corporate risk**, which is also called **within-firm risk**, is the variability the project contributes to the corporation's returns, giving consideration to the fact that the project represents only one asset of the firm's portfolio of assets and so some of its risk will be diversified away by other projects within the firm.

3. **Market risk**, which is also called **beta risk**, is the risk of the project as seen by a well-diversified stockholder who owns many different stocks. A project's market risk is measured by its effect on the firm's overall beta coefficient.

Taking on a project with a high degree of either stand-alone or corporate risk will not necessarily increase the company's divisional betas or its overall beta. However, if the project has highly uncertain returns and if those returns are highly correlated with returns on the firm's other assets and with most other assets in the economy, then the project will have a high degree of all types of risk.

Of the three measures, market risk is theoretically the most relevant because of its direct effect on stock prices. Unfortunately, the market risk for a project is also the most difficult to estimate. In practice, most decision makers consider all three risk measures subjectively.

The first step is to determine the divisional cost of capital. The second step is to establish risk categories—such as high, average, and low—for projects being considered by the division. After estimating a project's stand-alone risk (using the tools in Chapter 11) and comparing the project's stand-alone risk to that of other projects in the division, the company will assign the project to one of the risk categories. Third, the company will use the divisional cost of capital and the project's risk category to determine the project's **risk-adjusted cost of capital, r**, which is also called the **project cost of capital**. It is sometimes called the **hurdle rate** because a project's expected return must get over (i.e., be greater than) this rate in order to be accepted.

For example, if a division's WACC were 10%, its managers might use 10% to evaluate average-risk projects in the division, 12% for high-risk projects, and 8% for low-risk projects. Although this approach is better than ignoring project risk, these adjustments are necessarily subjective and somewhat arbitrary. Unfortunately, given the data, there is no completely satisfactory way to specify exactly how much higher or lower we should go in setting risk-adjusted costs of capital.

SELF-TEST

Based on the CAPM, how would one adjust the corporation's overall cost of capital to establish the required return for most projects in a low-risk division and in a high-risk division?

Describe the pure play and the accounting beta methods for estimating divisional betas.

What are the three types of risk to which projects are exposed? Which type of risk is theoretically the most relevant? Why?

Describe a procedure firms can use to establish costs of capital for projects with differing degrees of risk.

9-13 Managerial Issues and the Cost of Capital

We describe several managerial issues in this section, starting with how managerial decisions affect the cost of capital.

9-13a How Managerial Decisions Affect the Cost of Capital

The cost of capital is affected by some factors that are under a firm's control and some that are not.

FOUR FACTORS THE FIRM CANNOT CONTROL

Four factors are beyond managerial control: (1) interest rates, (2) credit crises, (3) the market risk premium, and (4) tax rates.

Interest Rates Interest rates in the economy affect the costs of both debt and equity, but they are beyond a manager's control. Even the Fed can't control interest rates indefinitely. For example, interest rates are heavily influenced by inflation, and when inflation hit historic highs in the early 1980s, interest rates followed. Rates trended mostly down for 25 years through the recession accompanying the 2008 financial crisis. Strong actions by the federal government in the spring of 2009 brought rates even lower, which contributed to the official ending of the recession in June 2009. Since then, rates have trended up a bit as the economy has slowly recovered. These actions encouraged investment, and there is little doubt that they will eventually lead to stronger growth. However, many observers fear that the government's actions will also reignite long-run inflation, which would lead to substantially higher interest rates.

Credit Crisis Although rare, sometimes credit markets are so disrupted that it is virtually impossible for a firm to raise capital at reasonable rates. This happened in 2008 and 2009, before the U.S. Treasury and the Federal Reserve intervened to open up the capital markets. During such times, firms tend to cut back on growth plans; if they must raise capital, its cost can be extraordinarily high.

Market Risk Premium Investors' aversion to risk determines the market risk premium. Individual firms have no control over the RP_M, which affects the cost of equity and thus the WACC.

Tax Rates Tax rates, which are influenced by the president and set by Congress, have an important effect on the cost of capital. They are used when we calculate the after-tax cost of debt for use in the WACC.

THREE FACTORS THE FIRM CAN CONTROL

A firm can affect its cost of capital through (1) its capital structure policy, (2) its dividend policy, and (3) its investment (capital budgeting) policy.

Capital Structure Policy In this chapter, we assume the firm has a given target capital structure, and we use weights based on that target to calculate its WACC. However, a firm can change its capital structure, and such a change can affect the cost of capital. For example, the after-tax cost of debt is lower than the cost of equity, so if the firm decides to use more debt and less common equity, then this increase in debt will tend to lower the WACC. However, an increased use of debt will increase the risk of debt and the equity, offsetting to some extent the effect due to a greater weighting of debt. At some point, the increased debt will cause the WACC to increase. In Chapter 15 we demonstrate that the optimal capital structure (1) minimizes the WACC and (2) maximizes the intrinsic value of the stock.

Dividend Policy As we will see in Chapter 14, the percentage of earnings paid out in dividends may affect a stock's required rate of return, r_s. Also, if the payout ratio is so high that the firm must issue new stock to fund its capital budget, then the resulting flotation costs will also affect the WACC.

Investment Policy When we estimate the cost of capital, we use as the starting point the required rates of return on the firm's outstanding stocks and bonds, which reflect the risks inherent in the existing assets. Therefore, we are implicitly assuming that new capital will be invested in assets with the same degree of risk as existing assets. This assumption is generally correct because most firms invest in assets similar to those they currently use. However, the equal risk assumption is incorrect if a firm dramatically changes its investment policy. For example, if a company invests in an entirely new line of business, then its marginal cost of capital should reflect the risk of that new business. For example, we can see with hindsight that GE's huge investments in the TV and movie businesses, as well as its investment in mortgages, increased its risk and thus its cost of capital.

9-13b Four Mistakes to Avoid

We often see managers and students make the following mistakes when estimating the cost of capital. Although we have discussed these errors previously at separate places in the chapter, they are worth repeating here.

1. *Never base the cost of debt on the coupon rate on a firm's existing debt.* The cost of debt must be based on the interest rate the firm would pay if it issued new debt today.

2. *When estimating the market risk premium for the CAPM method, never use the historical average return on stocks in conjunction with the current return on T-bonds.* The historical average return on bonds should be subtracted from the past average return on stocks to calculate the *historical market risk premium*. On the other hand, it is appropriate to subtract today's yield on T-bonds from an estimate of the expected future return on stocks to obtain the *forward-looking market risk premium*. A case can be made for using either the historical or the current risk premium, but it would be wrong to take the *historical* rate of return on stocks, subtract from it the *current* rate on T-bonds, and then use the difference as the market risk premium.

3. *Never use the current book value capital structure to obtain the weights when estimating the WACC.* Your first choice should be to use the firm's target capital structure for the weights. However, if you are an outside analyst and do not know the target weights, it would probably be best to estimate weights based on the current market values of the capital components. If the company's debt is not publicly traded, then it is reasonable to use the book value of debt to estimate the weights because book and market values of debt, especially short-term debt, are usually close to one another. However, stocks' market values in recent years have generally been at least 2–3 times their book values, so using book values for equity could lead to serious errors. The bottom line: If you don't know the target weights, then use the market value, not the book value, of equity when calculating the WACC.

4. *Always remember that capital components are funds that come from investors.* If it's not from an investor, then it's not a capital component. Sometimes the argument is made that accounts payable and accruals should be included in the calculation of the WACC. However, these funds are not provided by investors, but instead they arise from operating relationships with suppliers and employees. As such, the impact of accounts payable and accruals is incorporated into the calculations of free cash flows and project cash flows. Therefore, accounts payable and accruals should not be included as capital components when we calculate the WACC.

SUMMARY

This chapter discussed how the cost of capital is developed for use in capital budgeting. The key points covered are listed here.

- The **weighted average cost of capital** is the opportunity cost of capital used in capital budgeting. It is a weighted average of the types of capital the firm uses—typically long-term debt, short-term debt, preferred stock, and common equity.
- The **after-tax cost of debt** is found by multiplying the required rate of return on debt by $1 - T$, where T is the firm's marginal tax rate: $r_d(1 - T)$.
- Most debt is raised directly from lenders without the use of investment bankers; hence, very low **flotation costs** are incurred. However, a *debt flotation cost adjustment* should be made if large flotation costs are incurred. If the bond's flotation costs are greater than **de minimis** of $0.25\% \times$ Maturity $\times$ Par value, then we reduce the bond's issue price by the flotation expenses, calculate the yield to maturity based on this reduced price, and multiply by $(1 - T)$. This is called the **constant yield method**. If the bond's flotation costs are less than de minimis, then we reduce the bond's cash flows to reflect taxes, including the linear amortization of the discount, and then solve for the after-tax yield to maturity.
- The component **cost of preferred stock** is calculated as the preferred dividend divided by the net price the firm receives after deducting flotation costs: $r_{ps} = D_{ps}/[P_{ps}(1 - F)]$. Flotation costs on preferred stock are usually fairly high, so we typically include the impact of flotation costs when estimating r_{ps}.
- The **cost of common stock, r_s**, also called the *cost of common equity,* is the rate of return required by the firm's stockholders.
- To use the *CAPM approach,* we take the following steps: (1) Estimate the firm's beta. (2) Multiply this beta by the market risk premium to obtain the firm's risk premium. (3) Add the firm's risk premium to the risk-free rate to obtain its cost of common stock: $r_s = r_{RF} + (RP_M)b_i$.
- The best proxy for the *risk-free rate* is the yield on long-term T-bonds. Many analysts use the yield on a 10-year T-bond.
- The **dividend growth approach**, which is often called the **dividend capitalization method** (and which is sometimes called the *dividend-yield-plus-growth-rate* approach or the *discounted cash flow (DCF)* approach), adds the firm's expected dividend growth rate to its expected dividend yield to estimate the required return on stock: $r_s = \hat{r} = D_1/P_0 + g$. **Web Extension 9A** shows how to apply this model to estimate the required rate of return (and the market risk premium) if dividends are not growing at a constant rate.
- The growth rate for use in the dividend capitalization model can be based on historical growth rates of earnings and dividends, the **retention growth equation**, which assumes $g = (1 - \text{Payout})(\text{Return on equity})$, or on security analysts' forecasts.

- The *own-bond-yield-plus-judgmental-risk-premium approach* calls for adding a subjective risk premium of 3 to 5 percentage points to the interest rate on the firm's own long-term debt: r_s = Bond yield + Judgmental risk premium.
- When calculating the **cost of new external common equity, r_e**, the dividend capitalization model can be used to estimate the flotation cost. For a constant growth stock, the flotation-adjusted cost can be expressed as $r_e = \hat{r} = D_1/[P_0(1 - F)] + g_L$. Note that flotation costs cause r_e to be greater than r_s. We can find the difference between r_e and r_s and then add this differential to the CAPM estimate of r_s to find the CAPM estimate of r_e.
- Each firm has a **target capital structure**, which is defined as the mix of debt, preferred stock, and common equity that minimizes its **weighted average cost of capital (WACC)**:

$$\text{WACC} = w_d r_d (1 - T) + w_{std} r_{std} (1 - T) + w_{ps} r_{ps} + w_s r_s$$

- Various factors affect a firm's cost of capital. Some are determined by the financial environment, but the firm can influence others through its financing, investment, and dividend policies.
- Many firms estimate the **divisional cost of capital** that reflects a division's risk and capital structure.
- The **pure play** and **accounting beta methods** can be used to estimate betas for large projects or for divisions.
- A project's **stand-alone risk** is the risk the project would have if it were the firm's only asset and if stockholders held only that one stock. Stand-alone risk is measured by the variability of the asset's expected returns.
- **Corporate risk**, which is also called **within-firm risk**, reflects the effect of a project on the firm's risk, and it is measured by the project's effect on the firm's earnings variability.
- **Market risk**, which is also called **beta risk**, reflects the effects of a project on stockholders' risk, assuming they hold diversified portfolios. Market risk is measured by the project's effect on the firm's beta coefficient.
- Most decision makers consider all three risk measures in a subjective manner and then classify projects into risk categories. Using the firm's WACC as a starting point, risk-adjusted costs of capital are developed for each category. The **risk-adjusted cost of capital (r)** is the cost of capital appropriate for a given project, given its risk. The greater a project's risk, the higher its cost of capital.

The cost of capital as developed in this chapter is used in the next two chapters to evaluate potential capital budgeting projects, and it is used later in the text to determine the value of a corporation.

QUESTIONS

(9-1)   Define each of the following terms:

    a. Weighted average cost of capital, WACC; after-tax cost of debt, $r_d(1 - T)$; after-tax cost of short-term debt, $r_{std}(1 - T)$

    b. Cost of preferred stock, r_{ps}; cost of common equity (or cost of common stock), r_s

    c. Target capital structure

    d. Flotation cost, F; cost of new external common equity, r_e

(9-2)   How can the WACC be both an average cost and a marginal cost?

(9-3)   How would each of the factors in the following table affect a firm's cost of debt, $r_d(1 - T)$, its cost of equity, r_s, and its weighted average cost of capital, WACC? Indicate by a plus (+), a minus (−), or a zero (0) if the factor would increase, reduce, or have an indeterminate effect on the item in question. Assume that all other factors are held constant. Be prepared to justify your answer, but recognize that several of the parts probably have no single correct answer; these questions are designed to stimulate thought and discussion.

	Effect on:		
	$r_d(1-T)$	r_s	WACC
a. The corporate tax rate is lowered.	_____	_____	_____
b. The Federal Reserve tightens credit.	_____	_____	_____
c. The firm uses more debt.	_____	_____	_____
d. The firm doubles the amount of capital it raises during the year.	_____	_____	_____
e. The firm expands into a risky new area.	_____	_____	_____
f. Investors become more risk averse.	_____	_____	_____

(9-4)   Distinguish between beta (i.e., market) risk, within-firm (i.e., corporate) risk, and stand-alone risk for a potential project. Of the three measures, which is theoretically the most relevant, and why?

(9-5)   Suppose a firm estimates its overall cost of capital for the coming year to be 10%. What might be reasonable costs of capital for average-risk, high-risk, and low-risk projects?

SELF-TEST PROBLEM   SOLUTION SHOWN IN APPENDIX A

(ST-1)   Longstreet Communications Inc. (LCI) has the following capital structure, which it consid-
WACC   ers to be optimal: debt = 25% (LCI has only long-term debt), preferred stock = 15%, and common stock = 60%. LCI's tax rate is 25%, and investors expect earnings and dividends to grow at a constant rate of 6% in the future. LCI paid a dividend of $3.70 per share last year (D_0), and its stock currently sells at a price of $60 per share. Ten-year Treasury bonds yield 6%, the market risk premium is 5%, and LCI's beta is 1.3. The following terms would apply to new security offerings.

Preferred stock: New preferred stock could be sold to the public at a price of $100 per share, with a dividend of $9. Flotation costs of $5 per share would be incurred.

Debt: Debt could be sold at an interest rate of 8%.

Common stock: All new common equity will be raised internally by reinvesting earnings.

a. Find the component costs of debt, preferred stock, and common stock.
b. What is the WACC?

PROBLEMS   ANSWERS ARE IN APPENDIX B

EASY PROBLEMS 1-8

(9-1)   Calculate the after-tax cost of debt under each of the following conditions:
After-Tax Cost
of Debt
a. r_d of 13%, tax rate of 0%
b. r_d of 13%, tax rate of 20%
c. r_d of 13%, tax rate of 35%

(9-2)
After-Tax Cost
of Debt

LL Incorporated's currently outstanding 11% coupon bonds have a yield to maturity of 8.4%. LL believes it could issue new bonds at par that would provide a similar yield to maturity. If its marginal tax rate is 25%, what is LL's after-tax cost of debt?

(9-3)
Cost of Preferred
Stock

Duggins Veterinary Supplies can issue perpetual preferred stock at a price of $50 a share with an annual dividend of $4.50 a share. Ignoring flotation costs, what is the company's cost of preferred stock, r_{ps}?

(9-4)
Cost of Preferred
Stock with
Flotation Costs

Burnwood Tech plans to issue some $60 par preferred stock with a 6% dividend. A similar stock is selling on the market for $70. Burnwood must pay flotation costs of 5% of the issue price. What is the cost of the preferred stock?

(9-5)
Cost of Equity:
Dividend Growth

Summerdahl Resort's common stock is currently trading at $36 a share. The stock is expected to pay a dividend of $3.00 a share at the end of the year (D_1 = $3.00), and the dividend is expected to grow at a constant rate of 5% a year. What is its cost of common equity?

(9-6)
Cost of Equity:
CAPM

Booher Book Stores has a beta of 0.8. The yield on a 3-month T-bill is 4%, and the yield on a 10-year T-bond is 6%. The market risk premium is 5.5%, and the return on an average stock in the market last year was 15%. What is the estimated cost of common equity using the CAPM?

(9-7)
WACC

Shi Import-Export's balance sheet shows $300 million in debt, $50 million in preferred stock, and $250 million in total common equity. Shi's tax rate is 25%, r_d = 6%, r_{ps} = 5.8%, and r_s = 12%. If Shi has a target capital structure of 30% debt, 5% preferred stock, and 65% common stock, what is its WACC?

(9-8)
WACC

David Ortiz Motors has a target capital structure of 40% debt and 60% equity. The yield to maturity on the company's outstanding bonds is 9%, and the company's tax rate is 25%. Ortiz's CFO has calculated the company's WACC as 9.9%. What is the company's cost of equity capital?

INTERMEDIATE PROBLEMS 9–14

(9-9)
Bond Yield
and After-Tax
Cost of Debt

A company's 6% coupon rate, semiannual payment, $1,000 par value bond that matures in 30 years sells at a price of $515.16. The company's federal-plus-state tax rate is 25%. What is the firm's after-tax component cost of debt for purposes of calculating the WACC? (*Hint:* Base your answer on the *nominal* rate.)

(9-10)
Cost of Equity

The earnings, dividends, and stock price of Shelby Inc. are expected to grow at 7% per year in the future. Shelby's common stock sells for $23 per share, its last dividend was $2.00, and the company will pay a dividend of $2.14 at the end of the current year.

a. Using the discounted cash flow approach, what is its cost of equity?
b. If the firm's beta is 1.6, the risk-free rate is 9%, and the expected return on the market is 13%, then what would be the firm's cost of equity based on the CAPM approach?
c. If the firm's bonds earn a return of 12%, then what would be your estimate of r_s using the own-bond-yield-plus-judgmental-risk-premium approach? (*Hint:* Use a 4% risk premium.)
d. On the basis of the results of parts a–c, what would be your estimate of Shelby's cost of equity?

(9-11)
Cost of Equity

Radon Homes' current EPS is $6.50. It was $4.42 5 years ago. The company pays out 40% of its earnings as dividends, and the stock sells for $36.

a. Calculate the historical growth rate in earnings. (*Hint:* This is a 5-year growth period.)

      b. Calculate the *next* expected dividend per share, D_1. (*Hint:* $D_0 = 0.4(\$6.50) = \$2.60$.)
Assume that the past growth rate will continue.

      c. What is Radon's cost of equity, r_s?

(9-12)
Calculation of
g_L and EPS

Spencer Supply's stock is currently selling for $60 a share. The firm is expected to earn $5.40 per share this year and to pay a year-end dividend of $3.60.

      a. If investors require a 9% return, what rate of growth must be expected for Spencer?

      b. If Spencer reinvests earnings in projects with average returns equal to the stock's expected rate of return, then what will be next year's EPS? (*Hint:* $g_L = $ ROE $\times$ Retention ratio.)

(9-13)
The Cost of Equity
and Flotation Costs

Messman Manufacturing will issue common stock to the public for $30. The expected dividend and the growth in dividends are $3.00 per share and 5%, respectively. If the flotation cost is 10% of the issue's gross proceeds, what is the cost of external equity, r_e?

(9-14)
The Cost of Debt
and Flotation Costs

Suppose a company will issue new 20-year debt with a par value of $1,000 and a coupon rate of 9%, paid annually. The issue price will be $1,000. The tax rate is 25%. If the flotation cost is 2% of the issue proceeds, then what is the after-tax cost of debt? What if the flotation costs were 10% of the bond issue?

CHALLENGING PROBLEMS 15–17

(9-15)
WACC Estimation

On January 1, the total market value of the Tysseland Company was $60 million. During the year, the company plans to raise and invest $30 million in new projects. The firm's present market value capital structure, shown here, is considered to be optimal. There is no short-term debt.

Debt	$30,000,000
Common equity	30,000,000
Total capital	$60,000,000

New bonds will have an 8% coupon rate, and they will be sold at par. Common stock is currently selling at $30 a share. The stockholders' required rate of return is estimated to be 12%, consisting of a dividend yield of 4% and an expected constant growth rate of 8%. (The next expected dividend is $1.20, so the dividend yield is $1.20/$30 = 4%.) The marginal tax rate is 25%.

      a. In order to maintain the present capital structure, how much of the new investment must be financed by common equity?

      b. Assuming there is sufficient cash flow for Tysseland to maintain its target capital structure without issuing additional shares of equity, what is its WACC?

      c. Suppose now that there is not enough internal cash flow and the firm must issue new shares of stock. Qualitatively speaking, what will happen to the WACC? No numbers are required to answer this question.

(9-16)
Market Value
Capital Structure

Suppose the Schoof Company has this *book value* balance sheet:

Current assets	$30,000,000	Current liabilities	$20,000,000
		Notes payable	10,000,000
Fixed assets	70,000,000	Long-term debt	30,000,000
		Common stock (1 million shares)	1,000,000
		Retained earnings	39,000,000
Total assets	$100,000,000	Total liabilities and equity	$100,000,000

The notes payable are to banks, and the interest rate on this debt is 10%, the same as the rate on new bank loans. These bank loans are not used for seasonal financing but instead are part of the company's permanent capital structure. The long-term debt consists of 30,000 bonds, each with a par value of $1,000, an annual coupon interest rate of 6%, and a 20-year maturity. The going rate of interest on new long-term debt, r_d, is 10%, and this is the present yield to maturity on the bonds. The common stock sells at a price of $60 per share. Calculate the firm's *market value* capital structure.

(9-17)
WACC Estimation

The following table gives the current balance sheet for Travellers Inn Inc. (TII), a company that was formed by merging a number of regional motel chains.

Travellers Inn (Millions of Dollars)

Cash	$ 10	Accounts payable	$ 10
Accounts receivable	20	Accruals	15
Inventories	20	Short-term debt	0
Current assets	$ 50	Current liabilities	$ 25
Net fixed assets	50	Long-term debt	30
		Preferred stock (50,000 shares)	5
		Common equity	
		Common stock (3,800,000 shares	$ 10
		Retained earnings	30
		Total common equity	$ 40
Total assets	$100	Total liabilities and equity	$100

The following facts also apply to TII.

(1) The long-term debt consists of 29,412 bonds, each having a 20-year maturity, semi-annual payments, a coupon rate of 7.6%, and a face value of $1,000. Currently, these bonds provide investors with a yield to maturity of 11.8%. If new bonds were sold, they would have an 11.8% yield to maturity.

(2) TII's perpetual preferred stock has a $100 par value, pays a quarterly dividend per share of $2, and has a yield to investors of 10%. New perpetual preferred stock would have to provide the same yield to investors, and the company would incur a 3.85% flotation cost to sell it.

(3) The company has 3.8 million shares of common stock outstanding, a price per share = $P_0 = \$20$, dividend per share = $D_0 = \$1$, and earnings per share = $EPS_0 = \$5$. The return on equity (ROE) is expected to be 10%.

(4) The stock has a beta of 1.6. The T-bond rate is 6%, and RP_M is estimated to be 5%.

(5) TII's financial vice president recently polled some pension fund investment managers who hold TII's securities regarding what minimum rate of return on TII's common would make them willing to buy the common rather than TII bonds, given that the bonds yielded 11.8%. The responses suggested a risk premium over TII bonds of 3 percentage points.

(6) TII is in the 25% federal-plus-state tax bracket.

Assume that you were recently hired by TII as a financial analyst and that your boss, the treasurer, has asked you to estimate the company's WACC under the assumption that no new equity will be issued. Your cost of capital should be appropriate for use in evaluating projects that are in the same risk class as the assets TII now operates. Based on your analysis, answer the following questions.

a. What are the current market value weights for debt, preferred stock, and common stock? (*Hint:* Do your work in dollars, not millions of dollars. When you calculate the market values of debt and preferred stock, be sure to round the market price per bond and the market price per share of preferred to the nearest penny.)

b. What is the after-tax cost of debt?

c. What is the cost of preferred stock?

d. What is the required return on common stock using CAPM?

e. Use the retention growth equation to estimate the expected growth rate. Then use the expected growth rate and the dividend growth model to estimate the required return on common stock.

f. What is the required return on common stock using the own-bond-yield-plus-judgmental-risk-premium approach?

g. Use the required return on stock from the CAPM model, and calculate the WACC.

SPREADSHEET PROBLEMS

(9-18)
Build a Model:
WACC

resource

Start with the partial model in the file *Ch09 P18 Build a Model.xlsx* on the textbook's Web site. The stock of Gao Computing sells for $50, and last year's dividend was $3.13. Security analysts are projecting that the common dividend will grow at a rate of 7% a year. A flotation cost of 10% would be required to issue new common stock. Gao's preferred stock sells for $32.61, pays a dividend of $3.30 per share, and new preferred stock could be sold with a flotation cost of 8%. The firm has outstanding bonds with 20 years to maturity, a 12% annual coupon rate, semiannual payments, $1,000 par value. The bonds are trading at $1,171.59. The tax rate is 25%. The market risk premium is 6%, the risk-free rate is 6.5%, and Gao's beta is 1.2. In its cost-of-capital calculations, Gao uses a target capital structure with 45% debt, 5% preferred stock, and 50% common equity.

a. Calculate the cost of each capital component—in other words, the after-tax cost of debt, the cost of preferred stock (including flotation costs), and the cost of equity (ignoring flotation costs). Use both the CAPM method and the dividend growth approach to find the cost of equity.

b. Calculate the cost of new stock using the dividend growth approach.

c. Assuming that GAO will not issue new equity and will continue to use the same target capital structure, what is the company's WACC?

MINI CASE

During the last few years, Jana Industries has been too constrained by the high cost of capital to make many capital investments. Recently, though, capital costs have been declining, and the company has decided to look seriously at a major expansion program proposed by the marketing department. Assume that you are an assistant to Leigh Jones, the financial vice president. Your first task is to estimate Jana's cost of capital. Jones has provided you with the following data, which she believes may be relevant to your task:

• The firm's tax rate is 25%.

• The current price of Jana's 12% coupon, semiannual payment, noncallable bonds with 15 years remaining to maturity is $1,153.72. There are 70,000 bonds. Jana does not use short-term interest-bearing debt on a permanent basis. New bonds would be privately placed with no flotation cost.

- The current price of the firm's 10%, $100 par value, quarterly dividend, perpetual preferred stock is $116.95. There are 200,000 outstanding shares. Jana would incur flotation costs equal to 5% of the proceeds on a new issue.
- Jana's common stock is currently selling at $50 per share. There are 3 million outstanding common shares. Its last dividend (D_0) was $3.12, and dividends are expected to grow at a constant rate of 5.8% in the foreseeable future. Jana's beta is 1.2, the yield on T-bonds is 5.6%, and the market risk premium is estimated to be 6%. For the own-bond-yield-plus-judgmental-risk-premium approach, the firm uses a 3.2% risk premium.

To help you structure the task, Leigh Jones has asked you to answer the following questions:

a. (1) What sources of capital should be included when you estimate Jana's weighted average cost of capital?

   (2) Should the component costs be figured on a before-tax or an after-tax basis?

   (3) Should the costs be historical (embedded) costs or new (marginal) costs?

b. What is the market interest rate on Jana's debt, and what is the component cost of this debt for WACC purposes?

c. (1) What is the firm's cost of preferred stock?

   (2) Jana's preferred stock is riskier to investors than its debt, yet the preferred stock's yield to investors is lower than the yield to maturity on the debt. Does this suggest that you have made a mistake? (*Hint:* Think about taxes.)

d. (1) What are the two primary ways companies raise common equity?

   (2) Why is there a cost associated with reinvested earnings?

   (3) Jana doesn't plan to issue new shares of common stock. Using the CAPM approach, what is Jana's estimated cost of equity?

e. (1) What is the estimated cost of equity using the dividend growth approach?

   (2) Suppose the firm has historically earned 15% on equity (ROE) and has paid out 62% of earnings, and suppose investors expect similar values to obtain in the future. How could you use this information to estimate the future dividend growth rate, and what growth rate would you get? Is this consistent with the 5.8% growth rate given earlier?

   (3) Could the dividend growth approach be applied if the growth rate were not constant? How?

f. What is the cost of equity based on the own-bond-yield-plus-judgmental-risk-premium method?

g. What is your final estimate for the cost of equity, r_s?

h. Jana's target capital structure is 30% long-term debt, 10% preferred stock, and 60% common equity. How does this compare with the current market value capital structure?

i. Use Jana's target weights to calculate the weighted average cost of capital (WACC).

j. What factors influence a company's WACC?

k. Should the company use its overall WACC as the hurdle rate for each of its divisions?

l. What procedures can be used to estimate the risk-adjusted cost of capital for a particular division? What approaches are used to measure a division's beta?

m. Jana is interested in establishing a new division that will focus primarily on developing new Internet-based projects. In trying to determine the cost of capital for this new division, you discover that specialized firms involved in similar projects have, on average, the following characteristics: Their capital structure is 10% debt and 90% common equity; their cost of debt is typically 12%; and they have a beta of 1.7. Given this information, what would your estimate be for the new division's cost of capital?

n. What are three types of project risk? How can each type of risk be considered when thinking about the new division's cost of capital?

o. Explain in words why new common stock that is raised externally has a higher percentage cost than equity that is raised internally by reinvesting earnings.

p. What four common mistakes in estimating the WACC should Jana avoid?

SELECTED ADDITIONAL CASES

The following cases from CengageCompose cover many of the concepts discussed in this chapter and are available at **http://compose.cengage.com**.

Klein-Brigham Series:
Case 42, "West Coast Semiconductor"; Case 54, "Ace Repair"; Case 55, "Premier Paint & Body"; Case 6, "Randolph Corporation"; Case 75, "The Western Company"; and Case 81, "Pressed Paper Products."

Brigham-Buzzard Series:
Case 5, "Powerline Network Corporation (Determining the Cost of Capital)."

CHAPTER 10

The Basics of Capital Budgeting: Evaluating Cash Flows

Nothing runs like a Deere, according to Deere & Co., the manufacturer of the iconic green tractors and agricultural equipment. Commonly known as John Deere, the company is indeed running fast—from the fall of 2016 to early 2018, its stock price more than doubled, going up by 111%! During this same period, the S&P 500 increased by 46%. That's not a shabby return, but it doesn't come close to Deere's return.

Much of Deere's success is due to heavy capital expenditures from 2011 to 2017. During this period, Deere reinvested about 80% of its cash flow from operations, upgrading its U.S. factories and opening others overseas. Deere's CEO, Sam Allen, stated in late 2017 that "even as we find continued ways to make our operations more efficient and profitable, we are focused on the future through investments in technology and advanced products and selective acquisitions that complement our strengths and expand our global presence."

As you read this chapter, think about how capital budgeting methods are a vital part of the capital expenditure process.

Source: See *CEO Business Overview*, December 2017–January 2018, p. 5, at **https://s22.q4cdn.com/253594569 /files/doc_presentations/2017/12/CEO-Presentation_Dec17-Jan18.pdf.**

Corporate Valuation and Capital Budgeting

You can calculate the cash flows (CFs) for a project in much the same way as you do for a firm. When the project's cash flows are discounted at the appropriate risk-adjusted weighted average cost of capital ("r" for simplicity), the result is the project's value. When valuing an entire firm, you discount its free cash flows at the overall weighted average cost of capital, but when valuing a project, you discount its cash flows at the project's own risk-adjusted cost of capital. The firm's free cash flows are the total of all the net cash flows from its ongoing projects. Thus, if a

project is accepted and put into operation, it will provide cash flows that add to the firm's free cash flows and thus to the firm's value.

Subtracting the initial cost of the project from the discounted future expected cash flows gives the project's net present value (NPV). A project that has a positive NPV adds value to the firm. In fact, the firm's Market Value Added (MVA) is the sum of all its projects' NPVs. The key point, though, is that the process of evaluating projects, or capital budgeting, is critical to a firm's success.

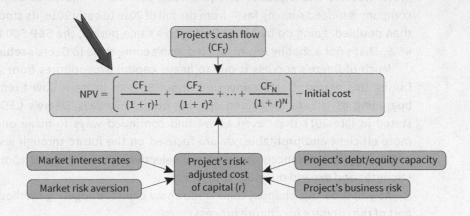

In Chapters 10 and 11, we discuss *capital budgeting*. Here *capital* refers to long-term assets used in production, and a *budget* is a plan that outlines projected expenditures during a future period. Thus, the *capital budget* is a summary of planned investments of assets that will last for more than a year, and **capital budgeting** is the whole process of analyzing projects and deciding which ones to accept and thus include in the capital budget. Chapter 10 explains the measures companies use to evaluate projects, including the measures' strengths and weaknesses. The chapter also describes several other issues that arise in the capital budgeting process. Chapter 11 explains how to estimate cash flows and evaluate project risk.

10-1 An Overview of Capital Budgeting

A firm's ability to remain competitive and to survive depends on a constant flow of ideas for new products, improvements in existing products, and ways to operate more efficiently. Therefore, it is vital for a company to evaluate proposed projects accurately. However, analyzing project proposals requires skill, effort, and time. For certain types of projects, an extremely detailed analysis may be warranted, whereas simpler procedures are adequate for other projects. Accordingly, firms generally categorize projects and analyze those in each category somewhat differently:

1. *Replacement needed to continue profitable operations.* An example would be replacing an essential pump on a profitable offshore oil platform. The platform manager could make this investment without an elaborate review process.
2. *Replacement to reduce costs.* An example would be the replacement of serviceable but obsolete equipment in order to lower costs. A fairly detailed analysis would be needed, with more detail required for larger expenditures.
3. *Expansion of existing products or markets.* These decisions require a forecast of growth in demand, so a more detailed analysis is required. Go/no-go decisions are generally made at a higher level in the organization than are replacement decisions.
4. *Expansion into new products or markets.* These investments involve strategic decisions that could change the fundamental nature of the business. A detailed analysis is required, and top officers make the final decision, possibly with board approval.
5. *Contraction decisions.* Especially during bad recessions, companies often find themselves with more capacity than they are likely to need. Rather than continue to operate plants at, say, 50% of capacity and incur losses as a result of excessive fixed costs, management decides to downsize. That generally requires payments to laid-off workers and additional costs for shutting down selected operations. These decisions are made at the board level.
6. *Safety and/or environmental projects.* Expenditures necessary to comply with environmental orders, labor agreements, or insurance policy terms fall into this category. How these projects are handled depends on their size, with small ones being treated much like the Category 1 projects and large ones requiring expenditures that might even cause the firm to abandon the line of business.
7. *Other.* This catchall includes items such as office buildings, parking lots, and executive aircraft. How they are handled varies among companies.
8. *Mergers.* Buying a whole firm (or division) is different from buying a machine or building a new plant. Still, basic capital budgeting procedures are used when making merger decisions.

Relatively simple calculations and only a few supporting documents are required for most replacement decisions, especially maintenance investments in profitable plants. More detailed analyses are required as we move on to more complex expansion decisions, especially for investments in new products or areas. Also, within each category, projects are grouped by their dollar costs: Larger investments require increasingly detailed analysis and approval at higher levels. Thus, a plant manager might be authorized to approve maintenance expenditures up to $10,000 using a simple payback analysis, but the full board of directors might have to approve decisions that involve either amounts greater than $1 million or expansions into new products or markets.

If a firm has capable and imaginative executives and employees, and if its incentive system is working properly, then many ideas for capital investment will be forthcoming. Some ideas will be good and should be funded, but others should be killed. The following sections explain how to evaluate a project's cash flows.

SELF-TEST

Identify the major project classification categories, and explain how and why they are used.

10-2 The First Step in Project Analysis

In the sections that follow, we will evaluate two projects that Guyton Products Company (GPC) is considering. GPC is a high-tech "lab-bench-to-market" development company that takes cutting-edge research advances and translates them into consumer products. GPC has recently licensed a nano-fabrication coating technology from a university that promises to significantly increase the efficiency with which solar energy can be harvested and stored as heat. GPC is considering using this technology in two different product lines. In the first, code-named "Project S" for "solid," the technology would be used to coat rock and concrete structures to be used as passive heat sinks and sources for energy-efficient residential and commercial buildings. In the second, code-named "Project L" for "liquid," it would be used to coat the collectors in a high-efficiency solar water heater. GPC must decide whether to undertake either of these two projects.

The first step in project analysis is to estimate the project's expected cash flows. We will explain cash flow estimation for Project L in Chapter 11, including the impact of depreciation, taxes, and salvage values. However, we want to focus now on evaluation measures, so we will specify the cash flows used in the following examples.[1]

Recall from Chapter 9 that a company's weighted average cost of capital (WACC) reflects the average risk of all the company's projects and that the appropriate cost of capital for a particular project may differ from the company's WACC. Chapter 11 explains how to estimate a project's risk-adjusted cost of capital, but for now assume that Projects L and S are equally risky and that both have a 10% cost of capital.

resource

See Ch10 Tool Kit.xlsx on the textbook's Web site.

Figure 10-1 shows the inputs for GPC's Projects S and L, including the projects' cost of capital and the time line of expected cash flows (with the initial cost shown at Year 0). Although Projects S and L are GPC's "solid" and "liquid" coating projects, you may also

FIGURE 10-1
Cash Flows and Selected Evaluation Measures for Projects S and L (Millions of Dollars)

	A	B	C	D	E	F
19	Panel A: Inputs for Project Cash Flows and Cost of Capital, r					
20						
21	INPUTS:					
22		r = 10%				
23			Initial Cost and Expected Cash Flows			
24	Year	0	1	2	3	4
25	Project S	−$10,000	$5,300	$4,300	$1,874	$1,500
26	Project L	−$10,000	$1,600	$2,364	$2,469	$8,400
27						
28	Panel B: Summary of Selected Evaluation Measures					
29			Project S	Project L		
30	Net present value, NPV		$804.38	$1,000.57		
31	Internal rate of return, IRR		14.7%	13.5%		
32	Modified IRR, MIRR		12.1%	12.7%		
33	Profitability index, PI		1.08	1.10		
34	Payback		2.21	3.42		
35	Discounted payback		3.21	3.83		

Source: See the file **Ch10 Tool Kit.xlsx**. Numbers are reported as rounded values for clarity but are calculated using *Excel*'s full precision. Thus, intermediate calculations using the figure's rounded values will be inexact.

---

[1]We will see in Chapter 11 that project cash flows are, in fact, free cash flows as calculated in Chapter 2 and used in Chapter 7 to estimate corporate value.

find it helpful to think of S and L as standing for *Short* and *Long*. Project S is a short-term project in the sense that its biggest cash inflows occur relatively soon; Project L has more total cash inflows, but its largest cash flows occur in the later years.

The second step in project analysis is to calculate the evaluation measures, which are shown in Panel B of Figure 10-1: (1) net present value (NPV), (2) internal rate of return (IRR), (3) modified internal rate of return (MIRR), (4) profitability index (PI), (5) regular payback, and (6) discounted payback. The following sections explain how each measure is calculated.

SELF-TEST

What is the first step in project analysis?

10-3 Net Present Value (NPV)

The **net present value (NPV)** is defined as the present value of a project's expected cash flows (including its initial cost) discounted at the appropriate risk-adjusted rate. The NPV measures how much wealth the project contributes to shareholders. When deciding which projects to accept, NPV is generally regarded as the best single criterion.

10-3a Calculating NPV

We can calculate NPV with the following steps.

1. Calculate the present value of each cash flow discounted at the project's risk-adjusted cost of capital, which is r = 10% in our example.
2. The sum of the discounted cash flows is defined as the project's NPV.

The equation for the NPV is:

$$NPV = CF_0 + \frac{CF_1}{(1 + r)^1} + \frac{CF_2}{(1 + r)^2} + \cdots + \frac{CF_N}{(1 + r)^N}$$

$$= \sum_{t=0}^{N} \frac{CF_t}{(1 + r)^t}$$

(10-1)

Applying Equation 10-1 to Project S, we have:

$$NPV_S = -\$10,000 + \frac{\$5,300}{(1.10)^1} + \frac{\$4,300}{(1.10)^2} + \frac{\$1,874}{(1.10)^3} + \frac{\$1,500}{(1.10)^4}$$

$$= -\$10,000 + \$4,818.18 + \$3,553.72 + \$1,407.96 + \$1,024.52$$

$$= \$804 \text{ million}$$

Here CF_t is the expected net cash flow at Time t, r is the project's risk-adjusted cost of capital (or WACC), and N is its life. Projects generally require an initial investment—for example, developing the product, buying the equipment needed to make it, building a factory, and stocking inventory. The initial investment is a negative cash flow. For Projects S and L, only CF_0 is negative; large projects often have outflows for several years before cash inflows begin.

Figure 10-2 shows the cash flow time line for Project S as taken from Figure 10-1. The initial cash flow is −$10,000, which is not discounted because it occurs at t = 0. The PV

FIGURE 10-2
Finding the NPV for Projects S and L (Millions of Dollars)

	A	B	C	D	E	F
46	INPUTS:					
47	r =	10%				
48			Initial Cost and Expected Cash Flows			
49	Year	0	1	2	3	4
50	Project S	−$10,000	$5,300	$4,300	$1,874	$1,500
51		4,818	←← ↵	↓	↓	↓
52		3,554	←←←← ←← ←←↵		↓	↓
53		1,408	←←←← ←← ←←←← ←←←←↵			↓
54		1,025	←←←← ←← ←←←← ←←←←←← ←← ←←↵			
55	NPV$_S$ =	$804	Long way:			
56			Sum the PVs of the CFs to find NPV			
57			Initial Cost and Expected Cash Flows			
58	Year	0	1	2	3	4
59	Project L	−$10,000	$1,600	$2,364	$2,469	$8,400
60	NPV$_L$ =	$1,001	Short way: Use *Excel*'s NPV function.			
61			=NPV(B47,C59:F59)+B59			

Source: See the file **Ch10 Tool Kit.xlsx**. Numbers are reported as rounded values for clarity but are calculated using *Excel*'s full precision. Thus, intermediate calculations using the figure's rounded values will be inexact.

of each cash inflow and the sum of the PVs are shown in Column B. You could find the PVs of the cash flows with a calculator or with *Excel*, and the result would be the numbers in Column B. When we sum the PVs of the inflows and subtract the cost, the result is $804, which is NPV$_S$. The NPV for Project L, $1,001, can be found similarly, but there is a much easier way. The bottom section of Figure 10-2 shows how to use *Excel*'s NPV function to calculate Project L's NPV. Notice that the NPV function uses the range of cash flows beginning with the Year 1 cash flow, not the Year 0 cash flow. Therefore, you must add the Year 0 cash flow to the result of the NPV function to calculate the net present value.

It is also possible to calculate the NPV with a financial calculator. As we discuss in Chapter 4, all calculators have a "cash flow register" that can be used to evaluate uneven cash flows such as those for Projects S and L. Equation 10-1 is programmed into these calculators, and all you need to do is enter the cash flows (with the correct signs) along with r = I/YR = 10. Once you have entered the data, press the NPV key to get the answer, 804.38, on the screen.[2]

10-3b Applying NPV as an Evaluation Measure

Before using these NPVs in the decision process, we need to know whether Projects S and L are **independent** or **mutually exclusive**. The cash flows for independent projects are not affected by other projects. For example, if Walmart were considering a new store in Boise and another in Atlanta, those projects would be independent. If both had positive NPVs, Walmart should accept both.

---

[2]The keystrokes for finding the NPV are shown for several calculators in the calculator tutorials provided on the textbook's Web site.

Mutually exclusive projects, on the other hand, are two different ways of accomplishing the same result, so if one project is accepted, then the other must be rejected. A conveyor belt system to move goods in a warehouse and a fleet of forklifts for the same purpose would be mutually exclusive—accepting one implies rejecting the other.

What should the decision be if Projects S and L are independent? In this case, both should be accepted because both have positive NPVs and thus add value to the firm. However, if they are mutually exclusive, then Project L should be chosen because it has the higher NPV and thus adds more value than S. We can summarize these criteria with the following rules:

1. *Independent projects.* If NPV exceeds zero, accept the project. Because S and L both have positive NPVs, accept them both if they are independent.
2. *Mutually exclusive projects.* Accept the project with the highest positive NPV. If no project has a positive NPV, then reject them all. If S and L are mutually exclusive, the NPV criterion would select L.

Projects must be either independent or mutually exclusive, so one or the other of these rules applies to every project.[3]

SELF-TEST

Why is NPV the primary capital budgeting decision criterion?

What is the difference between "independent" and "mutually exclusive" projects?

Projects SS and LL have the following cash flows:

	End-of-Year Cash Flows			
	0	1	2	3
SS	−700	500	300	100
LL	−700	100	300	600

If the cost of capital is 10%, then what are the projects' NPVs? **(NPV$_{SS}$ = \$77.61; NPV$_{LL}$ = \$89.63)**

What project or set of projects would be in your capital budget if SS and LL were (a) independent or (b) mutually exclusive? **(Both; LL)**

10-4 Internal Rate of Return (IRR)

In Chapter 5 we discussed the yield to maturity on a bond, and we explained that if you hold a bond to maturity, then you will earn the yield to maturity on your investment. The YTM is the discount rate that forces the present values of a bond's coupon payments and maturity payment to equal the price of the bond. This same concept is used in capital budgeting when we calculate a project's **internal rate of return (IRR)**, which is the discount rate that forces the PV of the expected future cash flows to equal the initial cash flow. The IRR is equivalent to the discount rate that forces the NPV to equal zero.

---

[3]You might argue that a pair of projects might be somewhere between independent and mutually exclusive if they affect each other but that accepting one doesn't exclude the other. For example, Apple recently introduced the HomePod, a wireless speaker system. Subscribers to Apple Music, a streaming service, will create demand for the HomePod. Also, the existence of HomePods will boost subscriptions to Apple Music. In this type of situation, you actually have three mutually exclusive options to consider: Project A, Project B, or the combined Project A&B whose cash flows are not the same as the sum of Project A's cash flows and Project B's cash flows. This is an example of an externality, and we discuss these in Chapter 11.

Why is the discount rate that causes a project's NPV to equal zero helpful as an evaluation measure? The reason is that the IRR is an estimate of the rate of return the company would actually earn if it invested in the project. If this return exceeds the opportunity cost of the funds used to finance the project, then the difference benefits the firm's stockholders. On the other hand, if the IRR is less than the cost of capital, stockholders suffer a loss in value.

10-4a Calculating the IRR

To calculate the IRR, begin with Equation 10-1 for the NPV, replace r in the denominator with the term "IRR," and choose a value of IRR so that the NPV is equal to zero. This transforms Equation 10-1 into Equation 10-2, the one used to find the IRR. The rate that forces NPV to equal zero is the IRR.[4]

$$NPV = CF_0 + \frac{CF_1}{(1 + IRR)^1} + \frac{CF_2}{(1 + IRR)^2} + \cdots + \frac{CF_N}{(1 + IRR)^N} = 0$$

$$= \sum_{t=0}^{N} \frac{CF_t}{(1 + IRR)^t} = 0$$

(10-2)

For Project S, we have:

$$NPV_s = 0 = -\$10,000 + \frac{\$5,300}{(1 + IRR)^1} + \frac{\$4,300}{(1 + IRR)^2} + \frac{\$1,874}{(1 + IRR)^3} + \frac{\$1,500}{(1 + IRR)^4}$$

resource

See **Ch10 Tool Kit.xlsx** on the textbook's Web site.

Figure 10-3 illustrates the process for finding the IRR of Project S. Three procedures can be used to find the IRR:

1. *Trial-and-error.* We could use a trial-and-error procedure: Try a discount rate, see if the equation solves to zero, and if it doesn't, try a different rate. Continue until you find the rate that forces the NPV to zero, and that rate will be the IRR. This procedure is rarely used, however. IRR usually is calculated using either a financial calculator or *Excel* (or some other computer program), as is now described.

2. *Calculator solution.* Enter the cash flows into the calculator's cash flow register just as you did to find the NPV, and then press the calculator key labeled "IRR." Instantly, you get the internal rate of return. Here are the values for Projects S and L:

$$IRR_S = 14.7\%$$
$$IRR_L = 13.5\%$$

3. *Excel solution.* It is even easier to find IRRs using *Excel*, as Figure 10-3 shows for Project L. Notice that with *Excel's* IRR function, the range in the function includes the initial cash flow at Year 0. This is in contrast to the NPV function's range, which starts with the Year 1 cash flow. Be alert to this difference when you use these functions because it is easy to mis-specify the range of inputs.

---

[4]For a large, complex project like a power plant, costs are incurred for several years before cash inflows begin. That simply means that we have a number of negative cash flows before the positive cash flows begin.

FIGURE 10-3
Finding the IRR for Projects S and L (Millions of Dollars)

	A	B	C	D	E	F
73	INPUTS:					
74		**Initial Cost and Expected Cash Flows**				
75	**Year**	**0**	**1**	**2**	**3**	**4**
76	**Project S**	−$10,000	$5,300	$4,300	$1,874	$1,500
77		4,621.33	←← ↵	↓	↓	↓
78		3,269.26	←←←← ←←←← ↵		↓	↓
79		1,242.34	←←←← ←←←←←← ←←←← ↵			↓
80		867.07	←←←← ←←←←←←←← ←←←←←← ←←←← ↵			
81			Long way: Try a value for r, sum the PVs of the CFs to			
82	**NPV_S =**	**$0.00**	find NPV. If NPV is not zero, try another value for r.			
83			Or use Goal Seek to find the value of r that makes the NPV = 0.			
84	**IRR_S = r =**	**14.7%**	Value of r that makes NPV = 0.			
85						
86		**Initial Cost and Expected Cash Flows**				
87	**Year**	**0**	**1**	**2**	**3**	**4**
88	**Project L**	−$10,000	$1,600	$2,364	$2,469	$8,400
89	**IRR_L =**	**13.5%**	Short way: Use *Excel*'s IRR function =IRR(B88:F88)			
90						

Source: See the file *Ch10 Tool Kit.xlsx*. Numbers are reported as rounded values for clarity but are calculated using *Excel*'s full precision. Thus, intermediate calculations using the figure's rounded values will be inexact.

10-4b A Potential Problem with the IRR: Multiple Internal Rates of Return[5]

If a project has a **normal cash flow** pattern, which is one or more cash outflows followed only by cash inflows (or the reverse, one or more cash inflows followed only by outflows), then the project can have at most one positive IRR. Here are some examples of normal cash flow patterns:

$$\text{Normal:} - + + + \quad \text{or} \quad - - + + + \quad \text{or} \quad + + - -$$

Notice that the sign of the cash flows changes only once for any of these examples, either from negative to positive or from positive to negative.

However, some projects have cash flows with signs that change more than once. For example, consider a strip coal mine where the company first spends money to buy the property and prepare the site for mining. The mining company has positive inflows for several years and then spends more money to return the land to its original condition. For this project, the cash flow sign goes from negative to positive and then changes again from positive to negative. This is a **nonnormal cash flow** pattern. Here are some examples:

$$\text{Nonnormal:} - + + + + - \quad \text{or} \quad - + + + - + + +$$

---

[5] This section is relatively technical, and some instructors may choose to omit it without loss of continuity.

If a project's cash flows have a nonnormal pattern (i.e., the cash flows have more than one sign change), it is possible for the project to have more than one positive IRR—that is, **multiple IRRs**.[6]

To illustrate multiple IRRs, suppose a firm is considering a potential strip mine (Project M) that has a cost of $1.6 million and will produce a cash flow of $10 million at the end of Year 1; however, the firm must spend $10 million to restore the land to its original condition at the end of Year 2. Therefore, the project's expected net cash flows are as follows (in millions):

Year	0	1	2
Cash flows	−$1.6	+$10	−$10

We can substitute these values into Equation 10-2 and then solve for the IRR:

$$\text{NPV} = \frac{-\$1.6 \text{ million}}{(1 + \text{IRR})^0} + \frac{\$10 \text{ million}}{(1 + \text{IRR})^1} + \frac{-\$10 \text{ million}}{(1 + \text{IRR})^2} = 0$$

resource

See Ch10 Tool Kit.xlsx on the textbook's Web site for all calculations.

For Project M's cash flows, the NPV equals zero when IRR = 25%, but it also equals zero when IRR = 400%.[7] Therefore, Project M has one IRR of 25% and another of 400%. Is either of these IRRs helpful in deciding whether to proceed with Project M? No! To see this, look at Figure 10-4, which shows Project M's NPV for different costs of capital. Notice that Project M has a negative NPV for costs of capital less than 25%. Therefore, Project M should be rejected for reasonable costs of capital.

When you evaluate a project, always look at the projected cash flows and count the number of times that the sign changes. If the sign changes more than once, don't even calculate the IRR because it is at best useless and at worst misleading.

10-4c Potential Problems When Using the IRR to Evaluate Mutually Exclusive Projects

Potential problems can arise when using the IRR to choose among mutually exclusive projects. Projects S and L are independent, but suppose for illustrative purposes that they are mutually exclusive. Their NPVs and IRRs are:

	NPV	IRR
Project S	$804	14.7%
Project L	$1,001	13.5%

---

[6]Equation 10-2 is a polynomial of degree n, so it has n different roots, or solutions. All except one of the roots are imaginary numbers when investments have normal cash flows (one or more cash outflows followed by cash inflows), so in the normal case only one value of IRR appears, and it may be positive, negative, or zero. However, the possibility of multiple real roots and hence of multiple IRRs arises when negative net cash flows occur after the project has been placed in operation.

[7]If you attempt to find Project M's IRR with an HP calculator, you will get an error message, whereas TI calculators give only the IRR closest to zero. When you encounter either situation, you can find the approximate IRRs by first calculating NPVs using several different values for r = I/YR, constructing a graph with NPV on the vertical axis and cost of capital on the horizontal axis, and then visually determining approximately where NPV = 0. The intersection with the x-axis gives a rough idea of the IRRs' values. With some calculators and with *Excel*, you can find both IRRs by entering guesses, as we explain in our calculator and *Excel* tutorials.

FIGURE 10-4
Graph for Multiple IRRs: Project M (Millions of Dollars)

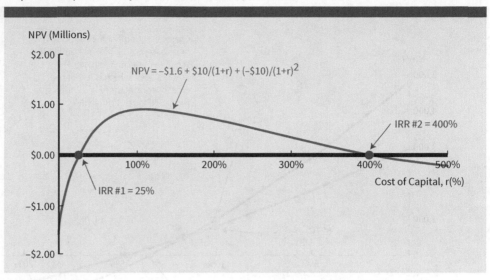

If using NPV as a decision criterion, Project L is preferred. But Project S is preferred if using IRR as a decision criterion. How do we resolve this conflict?

RESOLVING A CONFLICT BETWEEN THE IRR AND NPV FOR MUTUALLY EXCLUSIVE PROJECTS: PICK THE PROJECT WITH THE HIGHEST NPV

Consider these two hypothetical games we offer our students in class. In Game 1, we offer to give a student $2 at the end of class if the student will give us $1 at the beginning. Assuming we can be trusted, Game 1 has a 100% rate of return. In Game 2, we offer to give a student $25 at the end of class in exchange for $20 at the beginning of class. The games are mutually exclusive and may not be repeated: A student can choose only one game and can play it only once. Which game would you choose? If you are like our students, you would choose Game 2 because your wealth goes up by $5, which is better than the $1 increase in wealth offered by Game 1. So even though Game 1 has a higher rate of return, people prefer more wealth to less wealth.

The same is true for the shareholders. If projects are mutually exclusive, managers should choose the project that provides the greatest increase in wealth (as measured by the NPV), even though it may not have the highest rate of return (as measured by the IRR). Therefore, if Projects S and L were mutually exclusive, managers would choose Project L because it has a higher NPV and generates more wealth for shareholders.

THE CAUSES OF POSSIBLE CONFLICTS BETWEEN THE IRR AND NPV FOR MUTUALLY EXCLUSIVE PROJECTS: TIMING AND SCALE DIFFERENCES

Figure 10-5 illustrates the situation with a **net present value profile** for each project. This profile has a project's NPV plotted on the y-axis for different costs of capital. Notice the IRR for each project, which is the point at which the project has a zero NPV (it is also the place where the curve crosses the x-axis). As the figure shows, Project S has the largest IRR (the curve for Project S crosses the x-axis to the right of Project L's curve). Notice the NPV for each project when the cost of capital is 10%. Project L's NPV is above that of Project S.

FIGURE 10-5
NPV Profiles for Projects S and L

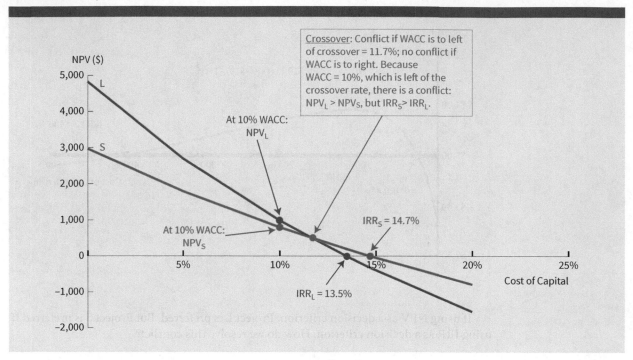

The two NPV profile lines cross at a cost of capital of 11.7%, which is called the **crossover rate**. Find the crossover rate by calculating the IRR of the differences in the projects' cash flows, as demonstrated here:

	Year				
	0	**1**	**2**	**3**	**4**
Project S:	−$10,000	$5,300	$4,300	$1,874	$1,500
Project L:	−10,000	1,600	2,364	2,470	8,400
$\Delta = CF_S - CF_L$:	$0	$3,700	$1,936	−$596	−$6,900

$$IRR\ \Delta = 11.7\%$$

If the cost of capital is *less* than the crossover rate, Project L has the higher NPV. But if the cost of capital is *greater* than the crossover rate, Project S has the higher NPV.

Many projects don't have different rankings: If a project has a larger NPV, it may very well have a higher IRR. But for projects whose rankings conflict, there must be a crossover rate. For a crossover rate to exist, the difference in cash flows between the two projects must have a normal pattern, as described in the previous section: The cash flows must have one and only one sign change. This happens when the cash flows have timing differences, size (or scale) differences, or some combination.[8] For example, consider the cash

---

[8]Also, if mutually exclusive projects have different lives (as opposed to different cash flow patterns over a common life), further complications arise; thus, for meaningful comparisons, some mutually exclusive projects must be evaluated over a common life. This point is discussed later in the chapter.

flows of Project Sooner and Project Later. Both have a 10% cost of capital; their cash flows are shown here:

	Year			Result	
	0	1	2	NPV	IRR
Project Sooner:	−$1,000	$1,020	$ 120	$26	12.7%
Project Later:	−1,000	120	1,120	$35	12.0%
$\Delta = CF_S - CF_L$:	$0	$900	−$1,000		11.1%

Both projects have the same scale (each requires an initial investment of $1,000), so the difference in their initial cost is zero. However, Project Sooner has most of its future cash flows in Year 1, and Project Later has most of its future cash flows in Year 2. This causes their difference in Year 1 to be positive and their difference in Year 2 to be negative. In other words, there is one and only one sign change in the difference between the two projects, so a crossover rate exists. As this illustrates, projects with the same scale must have timing differences in future cash flows for there to be one and only one sign change.

What about a situation in which projects don't have timing differences but do have a scale difference? Projects Smaller and Larger each have a 10% cost of capital, and their cash flows are shown here:

	Year			Result	
	0	1	2	NPV	IRR
Smaller	−$90	$12	$112	$13	18.4%
Larger	−1,000	120	1,120	$35	12.0%
$\Delta = CF_S - CF_L$	$910	−$108	−$1,008		11.3%

There are no timing differences in the future cash flows; in fact, Project Smaller's future cash flows are 10% of Project Larger's. However, there is a scale difference because Project Smaller's initial cost is much less than that of Project Larger. The scale difference causes the difference in the initial cash flow to be positive. However, the differences in the future cash flows are negative. This causes one and only one sign change, so a crossover rate exists.

10-4d Applying IRR as an Evaluation Measure

When using the IRR, it is important to distinguish between independent projects and mutually exclusive projects.

If you are evaluating an independent project with normal cash flows, then the NPV and IRR criteria always lead to the same accept/reject decision: If NPV says accept, then IRR also says accept, and vice versa. To see why this is so, look at Figure 10-5. The IRR rule says accept Project S if the cost of capital (10%) is less than (or to the left of) the IRR (14.7%). Note that if the cost of capital is less than the IRR, then the NPV must be positive. Thus, if the cost of capital is less than 14.7%, then both the NPV and IRR criteria accept Project S; if the cost of capital is greater than 14.7%, then both methods reject the project. A similar statement can be made for Project L, or any other normal project, and we would always reach the same conclusion: For normal, independent projects, if the IRR says to accept it, then so will the NPV.

Now assume that Projects S and L are mutually exclusive rather than independent. Therefore, we can choose either S or L or we can reject both, but we can't accept both. Now look at Figure 10-5 and note these points.

- $IRR_S > IRR_L$, so the IRR decision rule would say to accept Project S over Project L.
- As long as the cost of capital is *greater than* the crossover rate of 11.7%, both methods agree that Project S is better: $NPV_S > NPV_L$ and $IRR_S > IRR_L$. Therefore, if r is *greater* than the crossover rate, no conflict occurs.
- However, if the cost of capital is *less than* the crossover rate, a conflict arises: NPV ranks L higher, but IRR ranks S higher. In this situation, select the project with the highest NPV even if it has a lower IRR.

SELF-TEST

In what sense is a project's IRR similar to the YTM on a bond?

The cash flows for Projects SS and LL are as follows:

	End-of-Year Cash Flows			
	0	1	2	3
SS	−700	500	300	100
LL	−700	100	300	600

Assume that the firm's WACC = r = 10%. What are the two projects' IRRs? (IRR_{SS} = 18.0%; IRR_{LL} = 15.6%)

Which project would the IRR method select if the firm has a 10% cost of capital and the projects are (a) independent or (b) mutually exclusive? (Both; SS)

What condition regarding cash flows would cause more than one IRR to exist?

Project MM has the following cash flows:

	End-of-Year Cash Flows		
0	1	2	3
−$1,000	$2,000	$2,000	−$3,350

Calculate MM's NPV at discount rates of 0%, 10%, 12.2258%, 25%, 122.147%, and 150%. (−$350; −$46; $0; $165; $0; −$94) *What are MM's IRRs?* (12.23% and 122.15%)

If the cost of capital were 10%, should the project be accepted or rejected? (Rejected because NPV < 0)

Describe in words how an NPV profile is constructed. How do you determine the intercepts for the x-axis and the y-axis?

What is the crossover rate, and how does it interact with the cost of capital to determine whether or not a conflict exists between NPV and IRR?

What two characteristics can lead to conflicts between the NPV and the IRR when evaluating mutually exclusive projects?

10-5 Modified Internal Rate of Return (MIRR)

Recall from Chapter 5 that an investor who purchases a bond and holds it to maturity (assuming no default) will receive the bond's yield to maturity (YTM) even if interest rates change. This happens because the realized rate of return on an investment is by definition the rate that sets the present value of the realized cash flows equal to the purchase price. However, the realized rate of return on the investment in the bond and the subsequent reinvestment of the coupons will equal the YTM only if the coupons are reinvested at a rate equal to the YTM. Similar reasoning can be applied to a project: The project's expected return is equal to its IRR, but the expected return on the project plus any return on reinvested cash flows is equal to the IRR only if the cash flows are reinvested at a rate equal to the IRR.

If a manager wishes to evaluate a project based on the return expected from the project and its reinvested cash flows, then the IRR miscalculates this return because it is more likely that the project's future cash flows can be reinvested at the cost of capital and not at the project's IRR. The **modified IRR (MIRR)** is similar to the regular IRR, except it is based on the assumption that cash flows are reinvested at the WACC (or some other explicit rate if that is a more reasonable assumption). Refer to Figure 10-6 as you read the following steps that explain the MIRR's calculation.

resource

See Ch10 Tool Kit.xlsx on the textbook's Web site.

1. Project S has just one outflow, a negative $10,000 at t = 0. Because it occurs at Time 0, it is not discounted, and its PV is −$10,000. If the project had additional outflows, we would find the PV at t = 0 for each one and then sum them for use in the MIRR calculation.

FIGURE 10-6
Finding the MIRR for Projects S and L

	A	B	C	D	E	F	G
293	INPUTS:						
294		r = 10%					
295				Initial Cost and Expected Cash Flows			
296	Year	0	1	2	3	4	
297	Project S	−$10,000	$5,300	$4,300	$1,874	$1,500	
298		↓	↓	↓	↳→→	$2,061	
299		↓	↓	↳→→ →→→→→→		$5,203	
300	Present Value	↓	↳→→ →→→→	→→→→→→		$7,054	
301	of Negative CF	−$10,000	Terminal Value of Positive CF (TV) =			$15,819	
302							
303	Calculator: N = 4, PV = −10000, PMT = 0, FV = 15819. Press I/YR to get:					MIRR$_S$ =	12.15%
304	*Excel* Rate function–Easier:	= RATE(F296,0,B301,F301)				MIRR$_S$ =	12.15%
305	*Excel* MIRR function–Easiest:	= MIRR(B297:F297,B294,B294)				MIRR$_S$ =	12.15%
306							
307	Year	0	1	2	3	4	
308	Project L	−$10,000	$1,600	$2,364	$2,469	$8,400	
309							
310	For Project L, using the MIRR function: = MIRR(B308:F308,B294,B294)					MIRR$_L$ =	12.65%

Source: See the file *Ch10 Tool Kit.xlsx*. Numbers are reported as rounded values for clarity but are calculated using *Excel*'s full precision. Thus, intermediate calculations using the figure's rounded values will be inexact.

Notes:

1. The terminal value (TV) is the future value of all positive cash flows. The present value (PV) is the present value of all negative cash flows.

2. Find the discount rate that forces the TV of the positive cash flows to equal the PV of the negative cash flows. That discount rate is defined as the MIRR.

$$\text{PV of the negative cash flows} = (\text{TV of the positive cash flows})/(1+\text{MIRR})^N$$

$$\$10,000 = \$15,819/(1+\text{MIRR})^4$$

We can find the MIRR with a calculator or *Excel*.

2. Next, we find the future value of each *inflow*, compounded at the WACC out to the *terminal year*, which is the year the last inflow is received. We assume that cash flows are reinvested at the WACC. For Project S, the first cash flow, $5,300, is compounded at WACC = 10% for 3 years, and it grows to $7,054. The second inflow, $4,300, grows to $5,203, and the third inflow, $1,874, grows to $2,061. The last inflow, $1,500, is received at the end, so it is not compounded at all. The sum of the future values, $15,819, is called the *terminal value,* or *TV.*

3. We now have the PV at t = 0 of all negative cash flows, −$10,000, and the TV at Year 4 of all positive cash flows, $15,819. There is some discount rate that will cause the PV of the terminal value to equal the cost. *That interest rate is defined as the Modified Internal Rate of Return (MIRR).* In a calculator, enter N = 4, PV = −10000, PMT = 0, and FV = 15819. Then pressing the I/YR key yields the MIRR, 12.15%.

4. Note that *Excel* and some of the better calculators have a built-in MIRR function that streamlines the process. We explain how to use the MIRR function in our calculator tutorials, and we explain how to find MIRR with *Excel* in this chapter's *Excel Tool Kit.*[9]

The MIRR has two significant advantages over the regular IRR. First, the MIRR assumes that cash flows are reinvested at the cost of capital (or some other explicit rate) rather than at the IRR. Because reinvestment at the IRR is generally not correct, the MIRR is usually a better indicator of the rate of return on the project and its reinvested cash flows. Second, the MIRR eliminates the multiple IRR problem: There can never be more than one MIRR, and it can be compared with the cost of capital when deciding to accept or reject projects.

Our conclusion is that the MIRR is better than the regular IRR; however, this question remains: Is MIRR as good as the NPV? Here is our take on the situation.

- For *independent* projects, the NPV, IRR, and MIRR always reach the same accept/reject conclusion, so the three criteria are equally good when evaluating independent projects.
- However, if projects are *mutually exclusive* and if they differ in size, conflicts can arise. In such cases the NPV is best because it selects the project that maximizes value.[10]

---

[9]If we let COF$_t$ and CIF$_t$ denote cash outflows and inflows, respectively, then we can substitute the PV of inflows for NPV on the left-hand side of Equation 10-2 and the FV of outflows as the only future cash flow on the right-hand side. Using this logic, Equations 10-2a and 10-2b summarize the steps just described:

$$\sum_{t=0}^{N} \frac{COF_t}{(1+r)^t} = \frac{\sum_{t=0}^{N} CIF_t(1+r)^{N-t}}{(1+MIRR)^N} \qquad (10\text{-}2a)$$

$$PV\ costs = \frac{TV}{(1+MIRR)^N} \qquad (10\text{-}2b)$$

Also, note that there are alternative definitions for the MIRR. One difference relates to whether negative cash flows after the positive cash flows begin should be compounded and treated as part of the TV or discounted and treated as a cost. A related issue is whether negative and positive flows in a given year should be netted or treated separately. For more discussion, see David M. Shull, "Interpreting Rates of Return: A Modified Rate of Return Approach," *Financial Practice and Education,* Fall 1993, pp. 67–71.

[10]For projects of equal size but different lives, the MIRR will always lead to the same decision as the NPV if the MIRRs are both calculated using as the terminal year the life of the longer project. (Fill in zeros for the shorter project's missing cash flows.)

- Our overall conclusions are that (1) the MIRR is superior to the regular IRR as an indicator of a project's "true" rate of return, but (2) NPV is better than either IRR or MIRR when choosing among competing projects. If managers want to know the expected rates of return on projects, it would be better to give them MIRRs than IRRs because MIRRs are more likely to be the rates that are actually earned if the projects' cash flows are reinvested in future projects.

SELF-TEST

What's the primary difference between the MIRR and the regular IRR?

Projects A and B have the following cash flows:

| | End of Year Cash Flows | | |
Project	0	1	2
A	−$1,000	$1,150	$100
B	−$1,000	$100	$1,300

The cost of capital is 10%. What are the projects' IRRs, MIRRs, and NPVs? (IRR$_A$ = 23.1%, IRR$_B$ = 19.1%; MIRR$_A$ = 16.8%, MIRR$_B$ =18.7%; NPV$_A$ = $128.10, NPV$_B$ = $165.29)

Which project would each method select? (IRR: A; MIRR: B; NPV: B)

10-6 Profitability Index (PI)

The **profitability index (PI)** measures how much value a project creates for each dollar of the project's cost. The PI is calculated as:

$$PI = \frac{PV \text{ of future cash flows}}{\text{Initial cost}} = \frac{\sum_{t=1}^{N} \frac{CF_t}{(1+r)^t}}{CF_0} \qquad (10\text{-}3)$$

Here CF_t represents the expected future cash flows, and CF_0 represents the initial cost. As we can see from Figure 10-7, the PI for Project S, based on a 10% cost of capital, is

resource

See Ch10 Tool Kit.xlsx on the textbook's Web site.

FIGURE 10-7
Profitability Index (PI)

	A	B	C	D	E
332	**Project S:**		PI$_S$ = PV of future cash flows	÷	Initial cost
333			PI$_S$ = $10,804	÷	$10,000
334			PI$_S$ = 1.08		
335					
336	**Project L:**		PI$_L$ = PV of future cash flows	÷	Initial cost
337			PI$_L$ = $11,001	÷	$10,000
338			PI$_L$ = 1.10		

Source: See the file *Ch10 Tool Kit.xlsx*. Numbers are reported as rounded values for clarity but are calculated using Excel's full precision. Thus, intermediate calculations using the figure's rounded values will be inexact.

$10,804/\$10,000 = 1.08$; the PI for Project L is 1.10. Thus, Project S is expected to produce $1.08 of present value for each $1 of investment, whereas L should produce $1.10 for each dollar invested.

A project is acceptable if its PI is greater than 1.0. Projects with higher PIs should be ranked above projects with lower PIs. Projects S and L would be accepted by the PI criterion if they were independent, and L would be ranked ahead of S if they were mutually exclusive.

Mathematically, the NPV, IRR, MIRR, and PI methods will always lead to the same accept/reject decisions for *normal, independent* projects: If a project's NPV is positive, its IRR and MIRR will always exceed r, and its PI will always be greater than 1.0. However, these methods can give conflicting rankings for *mutually exclusive* projects if the projects differ in size or in the timing of cash flows. If the PI ranking conflicts with the NPV, then the NPV ranking should be used.

SELF-TEST

Explain how the PI is calculated. What does it measure?

A project has the following expected cash flows: $CF_0 = -\$500$, $CF_1 = \$200$, $CF_2 = \$200$, and $CF_3 = \$400$. If the project's cost of capital is 9%, what is the PI? **(1.32)**

10-7 Payback Period

NPV and IRR are the most commonly used methods today, but historically the first selection criterion was the **payback period**, defined as the number of years required to recover the funds invested in a project from its operating cash flows. Equation 10-4 is used for the calculation, and the process is diagrammed in Figure 10-8. We start with the project's cost, a negative number, and then add the cash inflow for each year until the cumulative cash flow turns positive. The payback year is the year *prior to* full recovery, plus a fraction equal to the shortfall at the end of the prior year divided by the cash flow during the year when full recovery occurs:[11]

$$\text{Payback} = \begin{array}{c}\text{Number of}\\ \text{years prior to}\\ \text{full recovery}\end{array} + \frac{\begin{array}{c}\text{Unrecovered cost}\\ \text{at start of year}\end{array}}{\begin{array}{c}\text{Cash flow during}\\ \text{full recovery year}\end{array}} \qquad (10\text{-}4)$$

The cash flows for Projects S and L, together with their paybacks, are shown in Figure 10-8. Project S's payback is 2.21 years, and L's is 3.4 years. The shorter the payback, the better the project. Therefore, if the firm requires a payback of 3 years or less, then S would be accepted, but L would be rejected. If the projects were mutually exclusive, S would be ranked over L because of its shorter payback.

The regular payback has three flaws: (1) Dollars received in different years are all given the same weight—that is, the time value of money is ignored. (2) Cash flows beyond the payback year are given no consideration whatsoever, regardless of how large they might be. (3) Unlike the NPV or the IRR, which tell us how much wealth a project adds or how much a project's rate of return exceeds the cost of capital, the payback merely tells us how long it takes to recover our investment. There is no necessary relationship between a given

---

[11]Equation 10-4 assumes that cash flows come in uniformly during the full recovery year.

FIGURE 10-8
Payback Period

	A	B	C	D	E	F	G
365	Project S	Year	0	1	2	3	4
366		Cash flow	−$10,000	$5,300	$4,300	$1,874	$1,500
367		Cumulative cash flow	−$10,000	−$4,700	−$400	$1,474	$2,974
368	Intermediate calculation		—	—	2.21	—	
369						↑	
370	Payback S = 2 + $400/$1,874 =		2.21			↑	
371					Intermediate calculation:		
372	*Excel* calculation of Payback S =		2.21		=IF(AND(E367<=0,F367>=0),E365+ABS(E367/F366),"—")		
373							
374	Project L	Year	0	1	2	3	4
375		Cash flow	−$10,000	$1,600	$2,364	$2,469	$8,400
376		Cumulative cash flow	−$10,000	−$8,400	−$6,036	−$3,567	$4,833
377							
378	Payback L = 3 + $3,567/$8,400 =		3.42			Payback switches from negative to	
379	Alternative *Excel*					positive cash flow.	
380	calculation of Payback L =		3.42	=PERCENTRANK(C376:G376,0,6)*G374			

Source: See the file *Ch10 Tool Kit.xlsx*. Numbers are reported as rounded values for clarity but are calculated using *Excel's* full precision. Thus, intermediate calculations using the figure's rounded values will be inexact.

Note: The calculation of payback in Cell D380 uses the *Excel* function **PERCENTRANK**. If the cash flows are *nonnormal*, then don't use the **PERCENTRANK** function! It yields the correct answer *only* if cash flows are normal. See the file *Ch10 Tool Kit.xlsx* (Cells J360:O426) for a detailed explanation of the **PERCENTRANK** function.

resource

See *Ch10 Tool Kit.xlsx* on the textbook's Web site.

payback period and investor wealth, so we don't know how to specify an acceptable payback. The firm might use 2 years, 3 years, or any other number as the minimum acceptable payback, but the choice is arbitrary.

To counter the first criticism, financial analysts developed the **discounted payback**, where cash flows are discounted at the WACC, and then those discounted cash flows are used to find the payback. In Figure 10-9, we calculate the discounted paybacks for S and L, assuming both have a 10% cost of capital. Each inflow is divided by $(1 + r)^t = (1.10)^t$, where t is the year in which the cash flow occurs, and r is the project's cost of capital, and then those PVs are used to find the payback. Project S's discounted payback is 3.21 years, and L's is 3.83 years.

Note that the payback is a "break-even" calculation in the sense that if cash flows come in at the expected rate, then the project will at least break even. However, because the regular payback doesn't consider the cost of capital, it doesn't specify the true break-even year. The discounted payback does consider capital costs, but it disregards cash flows beyond the payback year, which is a serious flaw. Further, if mutually exclusive projects vary in size, both payback methods can conflict with the NPV, and that might lead to poor decisions. Finally, there is no way to determine how short the payback periods must be to justify accepting a project.

Although the payback methods have faults as ranking criteria, they do provide information about *liquidity* and *risk*. The shorter the payback, other things held constant, the greater the project's liquidity. This factor is often important for smaller firms that don't have ready access to the capital markets. Also, cash flows expected in the distant future are generally riskier than near-term cash flows, so the payback period is also a risk indicator.

FIGURE 10-9
Discounted Payback

	A	B	C	D	E	F	G
393	Project r =	10%					
394	Project S	Year	0	1	2	3	4
395		Cash flow	−$10,000	$5,300	$4,300	$1,874	$1,500
396		Discounted cash flow	−$10,000	$4,818	$3,554	$1,408	$1,025
397		Cumulative discounted CF	−$10,000	−$5,182	−$1,628	−$220	$804
398							
399	Discounted Payback S = 3 + $220/$1,025 =			3.21		Switches from negative to	
400	*Excel* calculation of Discounted Payback S =					positive cash flow.	
401	=PERCENTRANK(C397:G397,0,6)*G394			3.21			
402							
403	Project L	Year	0	1	2	3	4
404		Cash flow	−$10,000	$1,600	$2,364	$2,469	$8,400
405		Discounted cash flow	−$10,000	$1,455	$1,954	$1,855	$5,737
406		Cumulative discounted CF	−$10,000	−$8,545	−$6,592	−$4,737	$1,001
407							
408	Discounted Payback L = 3 + $4,737/$5,737 =			3.83		Switches from negative to	
409	*Excel* calculation of Discounted Payback L =					positive cash flow.	
410	=PERCENTRANK(C406:G406,0,6)*G403 =			3.83			

Source: See the file *Ch10 Tool Kit.xlsx*. Numbers are reported as rounded values for clarity but are calculated using *Excel*'s full precision. Thus, intermediate calculations using the figure's rounded values will be inexact.

Note: The calculation of payback in Cell D410 uses the *Excel* function **PERCENTRANK**. If the cash flows are *nonnormal*, then don't use the **PERCENTRANK** function! It yields the correct answer *only* if cash flows are normal. See the file *Ch10 Tool Kit.xlsx* (Cells J360:O426) for a detailed explanation of the **PERCENTRANK** function.

S E L F - T E S T

What two pieces of information does the payback method provide that are absent from the other capital budgeting decision methods?

What three flaws does the regular payback method have? Does the discounted payback method correct all of those flaws? Explain.

Project P has a cost of $1,000 and cash flows of $300 per year for 3 years plus another $1,000 in Year 4. The project's cost of capital is 15%. What are P's regular and discounted paybacks? **(3.10, 3.55)** *If the company requires a payback of 3 years or less, would the project be accepted? Would this be a good accept/reject decision, considering the NPV and/or the IRR?* **(NPV = $256.72, IRR = 24.78%)**

10-8 How to Use the Different Capital Budgeting Methods

We have discussed six capital budgeting decision criteria: NPV, IRR, MIRR, PI, payback, and discounted payback. We compared these methods and highlighted their strengths and weaknesses. In the process, we may have created the impression that "sophisticated" firms should use only one method, the NPV. However, virtually all capital budgeting decisions are analyzed by computer, so it is easy to use all six methods. In making the accept/reject decision, most firms usually calculate and consider all six because each method provides a somewhat different piece of information about the decision.

10-8a A Comparison of the Methods

NPV is the single best criterion because it provides a direct measure of the value a project adds to shareholder wealth. IRR and MIRR measure profitability expressed as a percentage rate of return, which decision makers like to consider. The PI also measures profitability but in relation to the amount of the investment. Further, IRR, MIRR, and PI all contain information concerning a project's "safety margin." To illustrate, consider a firm whose WACC is 10% and that must choose between these two mutually exclusive projects: SS (for "small") has a cost of $10,000 and is expected to return $16,500 at the end of 1 year; LL (for "large") has a cost of $100,000 and is expected to return $115,550 at the end of 1 year. SS has a huge IRR, 65%, while LL's IRR is a more modest 15.6%. The NPV paints a somewhat different picture: At the 10% cost of capital, SS's NPV is $5,000 while LL's is $5,045. By the NPV rule, we would choose LL. However, SS's IRR indicates that it has a much larger margin for error: Even if its cash flow were only 66.6% of the $16,500 forecast, the project would still have a barely positive NPV. On the other hand, if LL's inflow were to fall by a much smaller percentage, to just 95.1% of its forecasted $115,550, it would have a negative NPV.

The modified IRR has all the virtues of the IRR, but it avoids the problem of multiple rates of return that can occur with the IRR. The MIRR also measures the expected return of the project and its reinvested cash flows, which provides additional insight into the project. So if decision makers want to know projects' rates of return, the MIRR is a better indicator than the regular IRR.

The PI tells a similar story to the IRR. Here PI_{LL} is only 1.05 while PI_{SS} is 1.50. As with the IRR, this indicates that Project SS is less risky: Its cash inflow could decline by 33.3% before the PI is unacceptable, whereas a decline of only 4.8% in LL's cash flows would result in an unacceptable PI.

Payback and discounted payback provide indications of a project's *liquidity* and *risk*. A long payback means that investment dollars will be locked up for a long time; hence the project is relatively illiquid. In addition, a long payback means that cash flows must be forecast far into the future, and that probably makes the project riskier than one with a shorter payback. A good analogy for this is bond valuation. An investor should never compare the yields to maturity on two bonds without also considering their terms to maturity because a bond's risk is influenced significantly by its maturity. The same holds true for capital projects.

In summary, the different measures provide different types of useful information. It is easy to calculate all of them: Simply put the cost of capital and the cash flows into an *Excel* model like the one provided in this chapter's **Tool Kit**, and the model will instantly calculate all six criteria. Therefore, most sophisticated companies consider all six measures when making capital budgeting decisions. For most decisions, the greatest weight should be given to the NPV, but it would be foolish to ignore the information provided by the other criteria.

10-8b The Decision Process: What Is the Source of a Project's NPV?

Just as it would be foolish to ignore these capital budgeting methods, it would also be foolish to make decisions based *solely* on them. One cannot know at Time 0 the exact cost of future capital or the exact future cash flows. These inputs are simply estimates, and if they turn out to be incorrect, then so will be the calculated NPVs and IRRs. Thus, *quantitative methods provide valuable information, but they should not be used as the sole criteria for accept/reject decisions* in the capital budgeting process. Rather, managers should use quantitative methods in the decision-making process but should also consider the likelihood that actual results will differ from the forecasts. Qualitative factors, such as the chances of a tax increase, a war, or a major product liability suit, should also be considered. In summary, *quantitative methods such as NPV and IRR should be considered as an aid to making informed decisions but not as a substitute for sound managerial judgment.*

In this same vein, managers should ask sharp questions about any project that has a large NPV, a high IRR, or a high PI. In a perfectly competitive economy, there would be no positive-NPV projects: All companies would have the same opportunities, and competition would quickly eliminate any positive NPV. The existence of positive-NPV projects must be predicated on some imperfection in the marketplace, and the longer the life of the project, the longer that imperfection must last. Therefore, managers should be able to identify the imperfection and explain why it will persist before accepting that a project will really have a positive NPV. Valid explanations might include patents or proprietary technology, which is how pharmaceutical and software firms create positive-NPV projects. Gilead's Sovaldi (a drug for treating hepatitis-C) and Microsoft's Windows 10 operating system are examples. Companies can also create positive NPV by being the first entrant into a new market or by creating new products that meet some previously unidentified consumer needs. Post-it notes invented by 3M are an example. Similarly, Dell developed procedures for direct sales of microcomputers and, in the process, created projects with enormous NPV. Also, companies such as Southwest Airlines have trained and motivated their workers better than their competitors, and this has led to positive-NPV projects. In all of these cases, the companies developed some source of competitive advantage, and that advantage resulted in positive-NPV projects.

These examples illustrate three points: (1) If you can't identify the reason a project has a positive projected NPV, then its actual NPV will probably not be positive. (2) Positive-NPV projects don't just happen; they result from hard work to develop some competitive advantage. At the risk of oversimplification, the primary job of a manager is to find and develop areas of competitive advantage. (3) Some competitive advantages last longer than others, with their durability depending on competitors' ability to replicate them. Patents, the control of scarce resources, or large size in an industry where strong economies of scale exist can keep competitors at bay. However, it is relatively easy to replicate product features that cannot be patented. The bottom line is that managers should strive to develop nonreplicable sources of competitive advantage. If such an advantage cannot be demonstrated, then you should question projects with high NPV—especially if they have long lives.

10-8c Decision Criteria Used in Practice

Table 10-1 reports survey evidence and shows that a large majority of companies use NPV and IRR. As suggested in the previous section, other methods are also used.

The table also reports the factors CEOs consider important in allocating capital within the firm. The ranking of projects by NPV is the factor that most CEOs consider important. Interestingly, CEOs also consider the manager who is proposing the project, in terms of both the manager's past success and the manager's confidence in the project. Confidence is often expressed through the range of possible outcomes for the project, with smaller ranges conveying more confidence. Chapter 11 explains how to estimate such confidence intervals.

SELF-TEST

Describe the advantages and disadvantages of the six capital budgeting methods.

Should capital budgeting decisions be made solely on the basis of a project's NPV, with no regard to the other criteria? Explain your answer.

What are some possible reasons that a project might have a high NPV?

TABLE 10-1
Capital Budgeting in Practice

Quantitative Measures Used by Companies	Percentage Using	Factors Considered Important by CEOs When Allocating Capital within the Company	Percentage Agreeing
NPV	75%	Project's ranking based on NPV	78.6%
IRR	76	Proposing manager's track record	71.3
Payback	57	Proposing manager's confidence in project	68.8
Discounted payback	29	Timing of project's cash flows	65.3
		Project's ability to protect market share	51.9
		Proposing division's track record	51.2

Sources: The percentages of companies using particular quantitative measures are from John R. Graham and Campbell R. Harvey, "The Theory and Practice of Corporate Finance: Evidence from the Field," *Journal of Financial Economics,* 2001, pp. 187–244. The percentages of CEOs agreeing with the capital allocation factors are from John R. Graham, Campbell R. Harvey, and Manju Puri, "Capital Allocation and Delegation of Decision Making Authority within Firms," NBER Working Paper 1730, 2011, **www.nber.org/papers/w17370**.

10-9 Other Issues in Capital Budgeting

Three other issues in capital budgeting are discussed in this section: (1) how to deal with mutually exclusive projects whose lives differ; (2) the potential advantage of terminating a project before the end of its physical life; and (3) the optimal capital budget when the cost of capital rises as the size of the capital budget increases.

10-9a Mutually Exclusive Projects with Unequal Lives

When choosing between two mutually exclusive alternatives with significantly different lives, an adjustment is necessary. For example, suppose a company is planning to modernize its production facilities and is considering either a conveyor system (Project C) or a fleet of forklift trucks (Project F) for moving materials. The first two sections of Figure 10-10 show the expected net cash flows, NPVs, and IRRs for these two mutually exclusive alternatives. We see that Project C, when discounted at the firm's 12% cost of capital, has the higher NPV and thus appears to be the better project.

Although the NPVs shown in Figure 10-10 suggest that Project C should be selected, this analysis is incomplete, and the decision to choose Project C is actually incorrect. Since the company will require a means of moving materials around in the plant for at least 6 years, if we choose Project F, we will have to make a similar investment in 3 years when Project F wears out. If cost and revenue conditions continue at the levels shown in Figure 10-10, then this second investment will also be profitable. However, if we choose Project C, we cannot make this second investment. Two approaches can be used to compare Projects C and F, as shown in Figure 10-10 and discussed next.

REPLACEMENT CHAINS

The key to the **replacement chain (common life) approach** for projects that will have to be repeated in the future is to analyze both projects over an equal life. In our example, Project C has a 6-year life, so we assume that Project F will be repeated after 3 years and then analyze it over the same 6-year period. We can then calculate the NPV of C and compare it to the extended-life NPV of Project F. The NPV for Project C, as shown in Figure 10-10, is already based on the 6-year common life. For Project F, however, we must

FIGURE 10-10
Analysis of Projects C and F (r = 12%)

	A	B	C	D	E	F	G	H
438	Project r =	12.0%						
439								
440	**Data on Project C, Conveyor System:**							
441	Year	0	1	2	3	4	5	6
442	Cash flows for C	−$40,000	$8,000	$14,000	$13,000	$12,000	$11,000	$10,000
443		NPV$_C$ =	$6,491		IRR$_C$ =	17.5%		
444								
445	**Data on Project F, Forklifts:**							
446	Year	0	1	2	3			
447	Cash flows for F	−$20,000	$7,000	$13,000	$12,000			
448		NPV$_F$ =	$5,155		IRR$_F$ =	25.2%		
449								
450	**Common Life Approach with F Repeated (Project FF):**							
451	Year	0	1	2	3	4	5	6
452	CF$_t$ for 1st F	−$20,000	$7,000	$13,000	$12,000			
453	CF$_t$ for 2nd F				−$20,000	$7,000	$13,000	$12,000
454	All CFs for FF	−$20,000	$7,000	$13,000	−$8,000	$7,000	$13,000	$12,000
455		NPV$_{FF}$ =	$8,824		IRR$_{FF}$ =	25.2%		

Source: See the file *Ch10 Tool Kit.xlsx*. Numbers are reported as rounded values for clarity but are calculated using *Excel*'s full precision. Thus, intermediate calculations using the figure's rounded values will be inexact.

resource

See Ch10 Tool Kit.xlsx on the textbook's Web site.

add in a second version of it to extend the overall life to 6 years. The time line for this extended project, denoted as "All CFs for FF," is shown in Figure 10-10. Here we assume: (1) that Project F's cost and annual cash inflows will not change if the project is repeated in 3 years and (2) that the cost of capital will remain at 12%.

The NPV of this extended Project F is $8,824, and its IRR is 25.2%. (The IRR of two Project Fs is the same as the IRR for one Project F.) However, the $8,824 extended NPV of Project F is greater than Project C's $6,491 NPV, so Project F should be selected.

Alternatively, we could recognize that Project F has an NPV of $5,155 at Time 0 and a second NPV of that same amount at Time 3, find the PV of the second NPV at Time 0, and then sum the two to find Project F's extended-life NPV of $8,824.

EQUIVALENT ANNUAL ANNUITIES (EAA)

Electrical engineers designing power plants and distribution lines were the first to encounter the unequal life problem. They could install transformers and other equipment that had relatively low initial costs but short lives, or they could use equipment that had higher initial costs but longer lives. The services would be required into the indefinite future, so this was the issue: Which choice would result in a higher NPV in the long run? The engineers converted the annual cash flows under the alternative investments into a constant cash flow stream whose NPV was equal to or equivalent to the NPV of the initial stream. This was called the **equivalent annual annuity (EAA) method**.

To apply the EAA method to Projects C and F, for each project find the constant payment streams that the projects' NPVs ($6,491 for C and $5,155 for F) would provide over their respective lives. Project C's 6-year life and NPV of $6,491 is equivalent to a 6-year annuity of $1,579 per year. To find this using a financial calculator, we enter N = 6, I/YR = 12,

PV = −6491, and FV = 0. Then, when we press the PMT key, we find EAA$_C$ = $1,579. For Project F, we enter N = 3, I/YR = 12, PV = −5155, and FV = 0; solving for PMT, we find EAA$_F$ = $2,146. Thus, whether Project F is repeated once, twice, or more times, it is equivalent to cash flow of $2,146 per year for the total length of the project. Project F would thus produce a higher annual cash flow, so it is the better project.

CONCLUSIONS ABOUT UNEQUAL LIVES

When should we worry about analysis of unequal lives? The unequal life issue (1) does not arise for independent projects but (2) can arise if mutually exclusive projects with significantly different lives are being compared. However, even for mutually exclusive projects, it is not always appropriate to extend the analysis to a common life. This should be done if and only if there is a high probability that the projects will actually be repeated at the end of their initial lives.

We should note several potentially serious weaknesses in this type of analysis. (1) If inflation occurs, then replacement equipment will have a higher price. Moreover, both sales prices and operating costs would probably change. Thus, the static conditions built into the analysis would be invalid. (2) Replacements that occur down the road would probably employ new technology, which in turn might change the cash flows. (3) It is difficult enough to estimate the lives of most projects, and even more so to estimate the lives of a series of projects. In view of these problems, no experienced financial analyst would be too concerned about comparing mutually exclusive projects with lives of, say, 8 years and 10 years. Given all the uncertainties in the estimation process, we would assume that such projects would, for all practical purposes, have the same life. Still, it is important to recognize that a problem exists if mutually exclusive projects have substantially different lives.

When we encounter situations with significant differences in project lives, we first use a computer spreadsheet to build expected inflation and/or possible efficiency gains directly into the cash flow estimates and then use the replacement chain approach. We prefer the replacement chain approach for two reasons. First, it is easier to explain to those who are responsible for approving capital budgets. Second, it is easier to build inflation and other modifications into a spreadsheet and then go on to make the replacement chain calculations.

10-9b Economic Life versus Physical Life

Projects are normally evaluated under the assumption that the firm will operate them over their full physical lives. However, this may not be the best plan; it may be better to terminate a project before the end of its potential life. For example, the cost of maintenance for trucks and machinery can become quite high if they are used for too many years, so it might be better to replace them before the end of their potential lives.

Figure 10-11 provides data for an asset with a physical life of 3 years. However, the project can be terminated at the end of any year and the asset sold at the indicated salvage values. All of the cash flows are after taxes, and the firm's cost of capital is 10%. The undiscounted cash flows are shown in Columns C and D in the upper part of the figure, and the present values of these flows are shown in Columns E and F. We find the project's NPV under different assumptions about how long it will be operated. If the project is operated for its full 3-year life, it will have a negative NPV. The NPV will be positive if it is operated for 2 years and then the asset is sold for a relatively high salvage value; the NPV will be negative if the asset is disposed of after only 1 year of operation. Therefore, the project's optimal life is 2 years.

This type of analysis is used to determine a project's **economic life**, which is the life that maximizes the NPV and thus shareholder wealth. For our project, the economic

FIGURE 10-11
Economic Life versus Physical Life

	A	B	C	D	E	F	G
495	r =	10%			PVs of the Cash Flows		
496			Operating	Salvage	Operating	Salvage	
497		Year	Cash Flow	Value	Cash Flow	Value	
498		0	−$4,800				
499		1	2,000	$3,000	$1,818.18	$2,727.27	
500		2	2,000	1,650	1,652.89	1,363.64	
501		3	1,750	0	1,314.80	0.00	
502					PV of		PV of
503	NPV at Different Operating Lives	Initial Cost		+	Operating	+	Salvage
504					Cash Flows		Value
505	Operate for 3 Years:						
506	NPV$_3$:	−$14.12	−$4,800	+	$4,785.88	+	$0.00
507	Operate for 2 Years:						
508	NPV$_2$:	$34.71	−$4,800	+	$3,471.07	+	$1,363.64
509	Operate for 1 Year:						
510	NPV$_1$:	−$254.55	−$4,800	+	$1,818.18	+	$2,727.27

Source: See the file **Ch10 Tool Kit.xlsx**. Numbers are reported as rounded values for clarity but are calculated using *Excel*'s full precision. Thus, intermediate calculations using the figure's rounded values will be inexact.

Note: The project is profitable if and only if it is operated for just 2 years.

resource

See *Ch10 Tool Kit.xlsx* on the textbook's Web site.

life is 2 years versus the 3-year **physical life**, or **engineering life**. Note that this analysis was based on the expected cash flows and the expected salvage values, and it should always be conducted as a part of the capital budgeting evaluation if salvage values are relatively high.

10-9c The Optimal Capital Budget

The **optimal capital budget** is defined as the set of projects that maximizes the value of the firm. Finance theory states that all independent projects with positive NPVs should be accepted, as should the mutually exclusive projects with the highest NPVs. Therefore, the optimal capital budget consists of that set of projects. However, two complications arise in practice: (1) The cost of capital might increase as the size of the capital budget increases, making it hard to know the proper discount rate to use when evaluating projects. (2) Sometimes firms set an upper limit on the size of their capital budgets, which is also known as *capital rationing.*

AN INCREASING COST OF CAPITAL

The cost of capital may increase as the capital budget increases; this is called an increasing **marginal cost of capital**. As we discussed in Chapter 9, flotation costs associated with issuing new equity can be quite high. This means that the cost of capital will increase once a company has invested all of its internally generated cash and must sell new common stock. In addition, once a firm has used up its normal credit lines and must seek additional debt capital, it may encounter an increase in its cost of debt. This means that a project might have a positive NPV if it is part of a $10 million capital budget, but the same project might have a negative NPV if it is part of a $20 million capital budget because the cost of capital might increase.

FIGURE 10-12
IOS and MCC Schedules

	A	B	C	D	E	F
517	**Investment Opportunity Schedule (IOS)**			**Marginal Cost of Capital (MCC)**		
518			**Highest to**	**Cumulative**	**Lowest to**	
519	**Projects**	**Cost**	**Lowest IRR**	**Cost**	**Highest WACC**	
520	A	$100	14.0%	$100	9.0%	
521	B	$100	13.0%	$200	9.0%	
522	C	$100	11.5%	$300	9.0%	
523	D	$100	10.0%	$400	10.0%	
524	E	$50	9.5%	$450	11.0%	
525	F	$50	9.0%	$500	12.0%	
526	G	$100	8.5%	$600	15.0%	

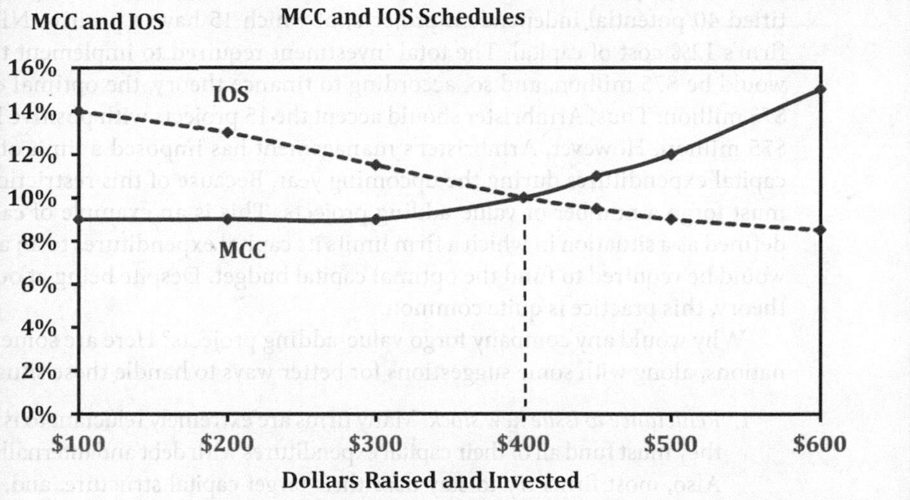

Source: See the file **Ch10 Tool Kit.xlsx**. Numbers are reported as rounded values for clarity but are calculated using *Excel*'s full precision. Thus, intermediate calculations using the figure's rounded values will be inexact.

Note: Use WACC = 10% as the base rate for finding base risk-adjusted project WACCs.

resource

See *Ch10 Tool Kit.xlsx* on
the textbook's Web site.

Fortunately, these problems rarely occur for most firms, especially those that are stable and well established. When a rising cost of capital is encountered, we would proceed as indicated here. You can look at Figure 10-12 as you read through our points.

- Find the IRR (or MIRR) on all potential projects, arrange them in rank order (along with their initial costs), and then plot them on a graph with the IRR on the vertical axis and the cumulative costs on the horizontal axis. The firm's data are shown in Figure 10-12, and the IRRs are plotted in the graph. The line is called the *Investment Opportunity Schedule (IOS)*, and it shows the marginal return on capital.
- Next, determine how much capital can be raised before it is necessary to issue new common stock or go to higher-cost sources of debt, and identify the amounts of higher-cost capital to be used. Use this information to calculate the WACC that corresponds to the different amounts of capital raised. In this example, the firm can raise $300 before the WACC rises, and the WACC increases as additional capital is raised. The increasing WACC represents the marginal cost of capital, and its graph is called the *Marginal Cost of Capital (MCC)* schedule.

- The intersection of the IOS and MCC schedules indicates the amount of capital the firm should raise and invest, and it is analogous to the familiar marginal cost versus marginal revenue schedule discussed in introductory economics courses. In our example, the firm should have a capital budget of $400; if it uses a WACC of 10%, then it will accept projects A, B, C, and D, which have a cumulative cost of $400. The 10% WACC should be used for average-risk projects, but it should be scaled up or down for more or less risky projects, as discussed in Chapter 9.

Our example illustrates the case of a firm that cannot raise all the money it needs at a constant WACC. Firms should not try to be too precise with this process—the data are not good enough for precision—but they should be aware of the concept and get at least a rough idea of how raising additional capital will affect the WACC.

CAPITAL RATIONING

Armbrister Pyrotechnics, a manufacturer of fireworks and lasers for light shows, has identified 40 potential independent projects, of which 15 have a positive NPV based on the firm's 12% cost of capital. The total investment required to implement these 15 projects would be $75 million, and so, according to finance theory, the optimal capital budget is $75 million. Thus, Armbrister should accept the 15 projects with positive NPVs and invest $75 million. However, Armbrister's management has imposed a limit of $50 million for capital expenditures during the upcoming year. Because of this restriction, the company must forgo a number of value-adding projects. This is an example of **capital rationing**, defined as a situation in which a firm limits its capital expenditures to an amount less than would be required to fund the optimal capital budget. Despite being at odds with finance theory, this practice is quite common.

Why would any company forgo value-adding projects? Here are some potential explanations, along with some suggestions for better ways to handle these situations.

1. *Reluctance to issue new stock.* Many firms are extremely reluctant to issue new stock, so they must fund all of their capital expenditures with debt and internally generated cash. Also, most firms try to stay near their target capital structure, and, when combined with the limit on equity, this limits the amount of debt that can be added during any one year without raising the cost of that debt, as well as the cost of equity. The result can be a serious constraint on the amount of funds available for investment in new projects.

   The reluctance to issue new stock could be based on some sound reasons: (a) Flotation costs can be very expensive; (b) investors might perceive new stock offerings as a signal that the company's equity is overvalued; and (c) the company might have to reveal sensitive strategic information to investors, thereby reducing some of its competitive advantages. To avoid these costs, many companies simply limit their capital expenditures.

   However, rather than placing a somewhat artificial limit on capital expenditures, companies might be better off explicitly incorporating the costs of raising external capital into their costs of capital along the lines shown in Figure 10-12. If there still are positive-NPV projects even with the higher cost of capital, then the company should go ahead and raise external equity and accept the projects.

2. *Constraints on nonmonetary resources.* Sometimes a firm simply doesn't have the necessary managerial, marketing, or engineering talent to immediately accept all positive-NPV projects. In other words, the potential projects may be independent from a demand standpoint but not from an internal standpoint because accepting them all would raise the firm's costs. To avoid potential problems due to spreading existing talent too thin, many firms simply limit the capital budget to a size that can be accommodated by their current personnel.

A better solution might be to employ a technique called **linear programming**. Each potential project has an expected NPV, and each potential project requires a certain level of support by different types of employees. A linear program can identify the set of projects that maximizes NPV *subject to the constraint* that the total amount of support required for these projects does not exceed the available resources.

3. *Controlling estimation bias.* Many managers become overly optimistic when estimating the cash flows for a project. Some firms try to control this estimation bias by requiring managers to use an unrealistically high cost of capital. Others try to control the bias by limiting the size of the capital budget. Neither solution is generally effective because managers quickly learn the rules of the game and then increase their own estimates of project cash flows, which might have been biased upward to begin with.

A better solution is to implement a **post-audit** program and to link the accuracy of forecasts to the compensation of the managers who initiated the projects.

SELF-TEST

Briefly describe the replacement chain (common life) approach, and differentiate it from the equivalent annual annuity (EAA) approach.

Differentiate between a project's physical life and its economic life.

What factors can lead to an increasing marginal cost of capital? How might this affect capital budgeting?

What is capital rationing?

What are three explanations for capital rationing? How might firms otherwise handle these situations?

SUMMARY

This chapter has described six techniques used in capital budgeting analysis: NPV, IRR, MIRR, PI, payback, and discounted payback. Each approach provides a different piece of information, so in this age of computers, managers often look at all of them when evaluating projects. However, NPV is the best single measure, and almost all firms now use NPV. The key concepts covered in this chapter are listed here.

- **Capital budgeting** is the process of analyzing potential projects. Capital budgeting decisions are probably the most important ones that managers must make.
- The **net present value (NPV)** is calculated by discounting of the project's cash flows at the project's cost of capital and then summing those cash flows. The project should be accepted if the NPV is positive because such a project increases shareholders' value.
- The **internal rate of return (IRR)** is defined as the discount rate that forces a project's NPV to equal zero. The project should be accepted if the IRR is greater than the cost of capital.
- The NPV and IRR methods make the same accept/reject decisions for **independent projects,** but if projects are **mutually exclusive,** then ranking conflicts can arise. In such cases, the NPV method should generally be relied upon.
- It is possible for a project to have more than one IRR if the project's cash flows change signs more than once.

- Unlike the IRR, a project never has more than one **modified IRR (MIRR)**. MIRR requires finding the terminal value (TV) of the cash inflows by compounding them at the firm's cost of capital to the end of the project, and then determining the discount rate that forces the present value of the TV to equal the present value of the outflows.
- The **profitability index (PI)** is calculated by dividing the present value of cash inflows by the initial cost, so it measures relative profitability—that is, the amount of the present value per dollar of investment.
- The regular **payback period** is defined as the number of years required to recover a project's cost. The regular payback method has three flaws: It ignores cash flows beyond the payback period, it does not consider the time value of money, and it doesn't give a precise acceptance rule. The payback method does, however, provide an indication of a project's risk and liquidity because it shows how long the invested capital will be tied up.
- The **discounted payback** is similar to the regular payback except that it discounts cash flows at the project's cost of capital. It considers the time value of money, but it still ignores cash flows beyond the payback period.
- If mutually exclusive projects have unequal lives, it may be necessary to adjust the analysis to put the projects on an equal-life basis. This can be done using the **replacement chain (common life) approach** or the **equivalent annual annuity (EAA) method**.
- A project's true value may be greater than the NPV based on its **physical life** if it can be terminated at the end of its **economic life**.
- Flotation costs and increased risk associated with unusually large expansion programs can cause the **marginal cost of capital** to increase as the size of the capital budget increases.
- **Capital rationing** occurs when management places a constraint on the size of the firm's capital budget during a particular period.

QUESTIONS

(10-1) Define each of the following terms:

- a. Capital budgeting; payback period; discounted payback period
- b. Independent projects; mutually exclusive projects
- c. Net present value (NPV) method; internal rate of return (IRR) method; profitability index (PI)
- d. Modified internal rate of return (MIRR) method
- e. NPV profile; crossover rate
- f. Nonnormal cash flow projects; normal cash flow projects; multiple IRRs
- g. Reinvestment rate assumption
- h. Replacement chain; economic life; capital rationing; equivalent annual annuity (EAA)

(10-2) What types of projects require the least detailed and the most detailed analyses in the capital budgeting process?

(10-3) Explain why the NPV of a relatively long-term project, defined as one for which a high percentage of its cash flows are expected in the distant future, is more sensitive to changes in the cost of capital than is the NPV of a short-term project.

(10-4) When two mutually exclusive projects are being compared, explain why the short-term project might be ranked higher under the NPV criterion if the cost of capital is high, whereas the long-term project might be deemed better if the cost of capital is low. Would changes in the cost of capital ever cause a change in the IRR ranking of two such projects? Why or why not?

(10-5)   Suppose a firm is considering two mutually exclusive projects. One has a life of 6 years and the other a life of 10 years. Would the failure to employ some type of replacement chain analysis bias an NPV analysis against one of the projects? Explain.

SELF-TEST PROBLEM   SOLUTION APPEARS IN APPENDIX A

(ST-1)
Project Analysis

You are a financial analyst for the Hittle Company. The director of capital budgeting has asked you to analyze two proposed capital investments, Projects X and Y. Each project has a cost of $10,000, and the cost of capital for each is 12%. The projects' expected net cash flows are as follows:

	Expected Net Cash Flows	
Year	Project X	Project Y
0	−$10,000	−$10,000
1	6,500	3,500
2	3,000	3,500
3	3,000	3,500
4	1,000	3,500

a. Calculate each project's payback period, net present value (NPV), internal rate of return (IRR), modified internal rate of return (MIRR), and profitability index (PI).
b. Which project or projects should be accepted if they are independent?
c. Which project should be accepted if they are mutually exclusive?
d. How might a change in the cost of capital produce a conflict between the NPV and IRR rankings of these two projects? Would this conflict exist if r were 5%? (*Hint:* Plot the NPV profiles.)
e. Why does the conflict exist?

PROBLEMS   ANSWERS APPEAR IN APPENDIX B

EASY PROBLEMS 1–7

(10-1)
NPV

A project has an initial cost of $40,000, expected net cash inflows of $9,000 per year for 7 years, and a cost of capital of 11%. What is the project's NPV? (*Hint:* Begin by constructing a time line.)

(10-2)
IRR

Refer to Problem 10-1. What is the project's IRR?

(10-3)
MIRR

Refer to Problem 10-1. What is the project's MIRR?

(10-4)
Profitability Index

Refer to Problem 10-1. What is the project's PI?

(10-5)
Payback

Refer to Problem 10-1. What is the project's payback period?

(10-6)
Discounted Payback

Refer to Problem 10-1. What is the project's discounted payback period?

(10-7)
NPV

Your division is considering two investment projects, each of which requires an up-front expenditure of $15 million. You estimate that the investments will produce the following net cash flows:

Year	Project A	Project B
1	$ 5,000,000	$20,000,000
2	10,000,000	10,000,000
3	20,000,000	6,000,000

a. What are the two projects' net present values, assuming the cost of capital is 5%? 10%? 15%?

b. What are the two projects' IRRs at these same costs of capital?

INTERMEDIATE PROBLEMS 8–18

(10-8)
NPVs, IRRs,
and MIRRs for
Independent
Projects

Edelman Engineering is considering including two pieces of equipment, a truck and an overhead pulley system, in this year's capital budget. The projects are independent. The cash outlay for the truck is $17,100, and that for the pulley system is $22,430. The firm's cost of capital is 14%. After-tax cash flows, including depreciation, are as follows:

Year	Truck	Pulley
1	$5,100	$7,500
2	5,100	7,500
3	5,100	7,500
4	5,100	7,500
5	5,100	7,500

Calculate the IRR, the NPV, and the MIRR for each project, and indicate the correct accept/reject decision for each.

(10-9)
NPVs and IRRs
for Mutually
Exclusive Projects

Davis Industries must choose between a gas-powered and an electric-powered forklift truck for moving materials in its factory. Because both forklifts perform the same function, the firm will choose only one. (They are mutually exclusive investments.) The electric-powered truck will cost more, but it will be less expensive to operate; it will cost $22,000, whereas the gas-powered truck will cost $17,500. The cost of capital that applies to both investments is 12%. The life for both types of truck is estimated to be 6 years, during which time the net cash flows for the electric-powered truck will be $6,290 per year, and those for the gas-powered truck will be $5,000 per year. Annual net cash flows include depreciation expenses. Calculate the NPV and IRR for each type of truck, and decide which to recommend.

(10-10)
Capital Budgeting
Methods

Project S has a cost of $10,000 and is expected to produce benefits (cash flows) of $3,000 per year for 5 years. Project L costs $25,000 and is expected to produce cash flows of $7,400 per year for 5 years. Calculate the two projects' NPVs, IRRs, MIRRs, and PIs, assuming a cost of capital of 12%. Which project would be selected, assuming they are mutually exclusive, using each ranking method? Which should actually be selected?

(10-11)
MIRR and NPV

Your company is considering two mutually exclusive projects, X and Y, whose costs and cash flows are shown here:

Year	X	Y
0	−$5,000	−$5,000
1	1,000	4,500
2	1,500	1,500
3	2,000	1,000
4	4,000	500

The projects are equally risky, and their cost of capital is 12%. You must make a recommendation, and you must base it on the modified IRR (MIRR). Which project has the higher MIRR?

(10-12)
NPV and IRR
Analysis

After discovering a new gold vein in the Colorado mountains, CTC Mining Corporation must decide whether to go ahead and develop the deposit. The most cost-effective method of mining gold is sulfuric acid extraction, a process that could result in environmental damage. Before proceeding with the extraction, CTC must spend $900,000 for new mining equipment and pay $165,000 for its installation. The mined gold will net the firm an estimated $350,000 each year for the 5-year life of the vein. CTC's cost of capital is 14%. For the purposes of this problem, assume that the cash inflows occur at the end of the year.

a. What are the project's NPV and IRR?
b. Should this project be undertaken if environmental impacts were not a consideration?
c. How should environmental effects be considered when evaluating this or any other project? How might these concepts affect the decision in part b?

(10-13)
NPV and IRR
Analysis

Cummings Products is considering two mutually exclusive investments whose expected net cash flows are as follows:

	Expected Net Cash Flows	
Year	Project A	Project B
0	−$ 400	−$650
1	−528	210
2	−219	210
3	−150	210
4	1,100	210
5	820	210
6	990	210
7	−325	210

a. Construct NPV profiles for Projects A and B.
b. What is each project's IRR?

c. If each project's cost of capital were 10%, which project, if either, should be selected? If the cost of capital were 17%, what would be the proper choice?

d. What is each project's MIRR at the cost of capital of 10%? At 17%? (*Hint:* Consider Period 7 as the end of Project B's life.)

e. What is the crossover rate, and what is its significance?

(10-14)
Timing Differences

The Ewert Exploration Company is considering two mutually exclusive plans for extracting oil on property for which it has mineral rights. Both plans call for the expenditure of $10 million to drill development wells. Under Plan A, all the oil will be extracted in 1 year, producing a cash flow at t = 1 of $12 million; under Plan B, cash flows will be $1.75 million per year for 20 years.

a. What are the annual incremental cash flows that will be available to Ewert Exploration if it undertakes Plan B rather than Plan A? (*Hint:* Subtract Plan A's flows from B's.)

b. If the company accepts Plan A and then invests the extra cash generated at the end of Year 1, what rate of return (reinvestment rate) would cause the cash flows from reinvestment to equal the cash flows from Plan B?

c. Suppose a firm's cost of capital is 10%. Is it logical to assume that the firm would take on all available independent projects (of average risk) with returns greater than 10%? Further, if all available projects with returns greater than 10% have been taken, would this mean that cash flows from past investments would have an opportunity cost of only 10% because all the firm could do with these cash flows would be to replace money that has a cost of 10%? Finally, does this imply that the cost of capital is the correct rate to assume for the reinvestment of a project's cash flows?

d. Construct NPV profiles for Plans A and B, identify each project's IRR, and indicate the crossover rate.

(10-15)
Scale Differences

The Pinkerton Publishing Company is considering two mutually exclusive expansion plans. Plan A calls for the expenditure of $50 million on a large-scale, integrated plant that will provide an expected cash flow stream of $8 million per year for 20 years. Plan B calls for the expenditure of $15 million to build a somewhat less efficient, more labor-intensive plant that has an expected cash flow stream of $3.4 million per year for 20 years. The firm's cost of capital is 10%.

a. Calculate each project's NPV and IRR.

b. Set up a Project Δ by showing the cash flows that will exist if the firm goes with the large plant rather than the smaller plant. What are the NPV and the IRR for this Project Δ?

c. Graph the NPV profiles for Plan A, Plan B, and Project Δ.

(10-16)
Unequal Lives

Shao Airlines is considering the purchase of two alternative planes. Plane A has an expected life of 5 years, will cost $100 million, and will produce net cash flows of $30 million per year. Plane B has a life of 10 years, will cost $132 million, and will produce net cash flows of $25 million per year. Shao plans to serve the route for only 10 years. Inflation in operating costs, airplane costs, and fares are expected to be zero, and the company's cost of capital is 12%. By how much would the value of the company increase if it accepted the better project (plane)? What is the equivalent annual annuity for each plane?

(10-17)
Unequal Lives

The Perez Company has the opportunity to invest in one of two mutually exclusive machines that will produce a product it will need for the foreseeable future. Machine A costs $10 million but realizes after-tax inflows of $4 million per year for 4 years. After 4 years, the machine must be replaced. Machine B costs $15 million and realizes after-tax inflows of $3.5 million per year for 8 years, after which it must be replaced. Assume that machine prices are not expected to rise because inflation will be offset by cheaper components used in the machines. The cost of capital is 10%. By how much would the value of the company increase if it accepted the better machine? What is the equivalent annual annuity for each machine?

(10-18)
Unequal Lives

Filkins Fabric Company is considering the replacement of its old, fully depreciated knitting machine. Two new models are available: Machine 190-3, which has a cost of $190,000, a 3-year expected life, and after-tax cash flows (labor savings and depreciation) of $87,000 per year; and Machine 360-6, which has a cost of $360,000, a 6-year life, and after-tax cash flows of $98,300 per year. Knitting machine prices are not expected to rise because inflation will be offset by cheaper components (microprocessors) used in the machines. Assume that Filkins's cost of capital is 14%. Should the firm replace its old knitting machine? If so, which new machine should it use? By how much would the value of the company increase if it accepted the better machine? What is the equivalent annual annuity for each machine?

CHALLENGING PROBLEMS 19–22

(10-19)
Multiple Rates
of Return

The Ulmer Uranium Company is deciding whether or not to open a strip mine whose net cost is $4.4 million. Net cash inflows are expected to be $27.7 million, all coming at the end of Year 1. The land must be returned to its natural state at a cost of $25 million, payable at the end of Year 2.

a. Plot the project's NPV profile.
b. Should the project be accepted if r = 8%? If r = 14%? Explain your reasoning.
c. Can you think of some other capital budgeting situations in which negative cash flows during or at the end of the project's life might lead to multiple IRRs?
d. What is the project's MIRR at r = 8%? At r = 14%? Does the MIRR method lead to the same accept–reject decision as the NPV method?

(10-20)
Present Value
of Costs

The Aubey Coffee Company is evaluating the within-plant distribution system for its new roasting, grinding, and packing plant. The two alternatives are (1) a conveyor system with a high initial cost but low annual operating costs and (2) several forklift trucks, which cost less but have considerably higher operating costs. The decision to construct the plant has already been made, and the choice here will have no effect on the overall revenues of the project. The cost of capital for the plant is 8%, and the projects' expected net costs are listed in the following table:

Year	Expected Net Cost	
	Conveyor	Forklift
0	−$500,000	−$200,000
1	−120,000	−160,000
2	−120,000	−160,000
3	−120,000	−160,000
4	−120,000	−160,000
5	−20,000	−160,000

a. What is the IRR of each alternative?
b. What is the present value of the costs of each alternative? Which method should be chosen?

(10-21)
Payback, NPV,
and MIRR

Your division is considering two investment projects, each of which requires an up-front expenditure of $25 million. You estimate that the cost of capital is 10% and that the investments will produce the following after-tax cash flows (in millions of dollars):

Year	Project A	Project B
1	5	20
2	10	10
3	15	8
4	20	6

a. What is the regular payback period for each of the projects?
b. What is the discounted payback period for each of the projects?
c. If the two projects are independent and the cost of capital is 10%, which project or projects should the firm undertake?
d. If the two projects are mutually exclusive and the cost of capital is 5%, which project should the firm undertake?
e. If the two projects are mutually exclusive and the cost of capital is 15%, which project should the firm undertake?
f. What is the crossover rate?
g. If the cost of capital is 10%, what is the modified IRR (MIRR) of each project?

(10-22)
Economic Life

The Scampini Supplies Company recently purchased a new delivery truck. The new truck cost $22,500, and it is expected to generate net after-tax operating cash flows, including depreciation, of $6,250 per year. The truck has a 5-year expected life. The expected salvage values after tax adjustments for the truck are given here. The company's cost of capital is 10%.

Year	Annual Operating Cash Flow	Salvage Value
0	−$22,500	$22,500
1	6,250	17,500
2	6,250	14,000
3	6,250	11,000
4	6,250	5,000
5	6,250	0

a. Should the firm operate the truck until the end of its 5-year physical life? If not, then what is its optimal economic life?
b. Would the introduction of salvage values, in addition to operating cash flows, ever *reduce* the expected NPV and/or IRR of a project?

SPREADSHEET PROBLEM

(10-23)
Build a Model:
Capital Budgeting
Tools

Start with the partial model in the file *Ch10 P23 Build a Model.xlsx* on the textbook's Web site. Gardial Fisheries is considering two mutually exclusive investments. The projects' expected net cash flows are as follows:

resource

	Expected Net Cash Flows	
Year	Project A	Project B
0	−$375	−$575
1	−300	190
2	−200	190
3	−100	190
4	600	190
5	600	190
6	926	190
7	−200	0

a. If each project's cost of capital is 12%, which project should be selected? If the cost of capital is 18%, what project is the proper choice?

b. Construct NPV profiles for Projects A and B.

c. What is each project's IRR?

d. What is the crossover rate, and what is its significance?

e. What is each project's MIRR at a cost of capital of 12%? At r = 18%? (*Hint:* Consider Period 7 as the end of Project B's life.)

f. What is the regular payback period for these two projects?

g. At a cost of capital of 12%, what is the discounted payback period for these two projects?

h. What is the profitability index for each project if the cost of capital is 12%?

MINI CASE

You have just graduated from the MBA program of a large university, and one of your favorite courses was Today's Entrepreneurs. In fact, you enjoyed it so much you have decided you want to "be your own boss." While you were in the master's program, your grandfather died and left you $1 million to do with as you please. You are not an inventor, and you do not have a trade skill that you can market; however, you have decided that you would like to purchase at least one established franchise in the fast-foods area, maybe two (if profitable). The problem is that you have never been one to stay with any project for too long, so you figure that your time frame is 3 years. After 3 years you will go on to something else.

You have narrowed your selection down to two choices: (1) Franchise L, Lisa's Soups, Salads & Stuff, and (2) Franchise S, Sam's Fabulous Fried Chicken. The net cash flows that follow include the price you would receive for selling the franchise in Year 3 and the forecast of how each franchise will do over the 3-year period. Franchise L's cash flows will start off slowly but will increase rather quickly as people become more health-conscious, while Franchise S's cash flows will start off high but will trail off as other chicken competitors enter the marketplace and as people become more health-conscious and avoid fried foods. Franchise L serves breakfast and lunch, whereas Franchise S serves only dinner, so it is possible for you to invest in both franchises. You see these franchises as perfect complements to one another: You could attract both the lunch and dinner crowds and the health-conscious and not-so-health-conscious crowds without the franchises directly competing against one another.

Here are the net cash flows (in thousands of dollars):

	Expected Net Cash Flows	
Year	Franchise L	Franchise S
0	−$100	−$100
1	10	70
2	60	50
3	80	20

Depreciation, salvage values, net working capital requirements, and tax effects are all included in these cash flows.

You also have made subjective risk assessments of each franchise and concluded that both franchises have risk characteristics that require a return of 10%. You must now determine whether one or both of the franchises should be accepted.

a. What is capital budgeting?
b. What is the difference between independent and mutually exclusive projects?
c. (1) Define the term "net present value (NPV)." What is each franchise's NPV?
   (2) What is the rationale behind the NPV method? According to NPV, which franchise or franchises should be accepted if they are independent? Mutually exclusive?
   (3) Would the NPVs change if the cost of capital changed?
d. (1) Define the term "internal rate of return (IRR)." What is each franchise's IRR?
   (2) How is the IRR on a project related to the YTM on a bond? For example, suppose the initial cost of a project is $100 and it has cash flows of $40 each year at Years 1, 2, and 3. What is its IRR? Use the *Excel* **RATE** function as though the project were a bond.
   (3) What is the logic behind the IRR method? According to IRR, which franchises should be accepted if they are independent? Mutually exclusive?
   (4) Would the franchises' IRRs change if the cost of capital changed?
e. (1) Draw NPV profiles for Franchises L and S. At what discount rate do the profiles cross?
   (2) Look at your NPV profile graph without referring to the actual NPVs and IRRs. Which franchise or franchises should be accepted if they are independent? Mutually exclusive? Explain. Are your answers correct at any cost of capital less than 23.6%?
f. What is the underlying cause of ranking conflicts between NPV and IRR?
g. Define the term "modified IRR (MIRR)." Find the MIRRs for Franchises L and S.
h. What does the profitability index (PI) measure? What are the PIs of Franchises S and L?
i. (1) What is the payback period? Find the paybacks for Franchises L and S.
   (2) What is the rationale for the payback method? According to the payback criterion, which franchise or franchises should be accepted if the firm's maximum acceptable payback is 2 years and if Franchises L and S are independent? If they are mutually exclusive?
   (3) What is the difference between the regular and discounted payback periods?
   (4) What is the main disadvantage of discounted payback? Is the payback method of any real usefulness in capital budgeting decisions?
j. As a separate project (Project P), you are considering sponsorship of a pavilion at the upcoming World's Fair. The pavilion would cost $800,000, and it is expected to result in $5 million of incremental cash inflows during its single year of operation.

However, it would then take another year and $5 million of costs to demolish the site and return it to its original condition. Thus, Project P's expected net cash flows look like this (in millions of dollars):

Year	Net Cash Flows
0	−$0.8
1	5.0
2	−5.0

The project is estimated to be of average risk, so its cost of capital is 10%.

(1) What are normal and nonnormal cash flows?

(2) What is Project P's NPV? What is its IRR? Its MIRR?

(3) Draw Project P's NPV profile. Does Project P have normal or nonnormal cash flows? Should this project be accepted?

k. In an unrelated analysis, you have the opportunity to choose between the following two mutually exclusive projects, Project T (which lasts for 2 years) and Project F (which lasts for 4 years):

	Expected Net Cash Flows	
Year	Project T	Project F
0	−$100,000	−$100,000
1	60,000	33,500
2	60,000	33,500
3	—	33,500
4	—	33,500

The projects provide a necessary service, so whichever one is selected is expected to be repeated into the foreseeable future. Both projects have a 10% cost of capital.

(1) What is each project's initial NPV without replication?

(2) What is each project's equivalent annual annuity?

(3) Apply the replacement chain approach to determine the projects' extended NPVs. Which project should be chosen?

(4) Assume that the cost to replicate Project T in 2 years will increase to $105,000 due to inflation. How should the analysis be handled now, and which project should be chosen?

l. You are also considering another project that has a physical life of 3 years—that is, the machinery will be totally worn out after 3 years. However, if the project were terminated prior to the end of 3 years, the machinery would have a positive salvage value. Here are the project's estimated cash flows:

Year	Initial Investment and Operating Cash Flows	End-of-Year Net Salvage Value
0	−$5,000	$5,000
1	2,100	3,100
2	2,000	2,000
3	1,750	0

Using the 10% cost of capital, what is the project's NPV if it is operated for the full 3 years? Would the NPV change if the company planned to terminate the project at the end of Year 2? At the end of Year 1? What is the project's optimal (economic) life?

SELECTED ADDITIONAL CASES

The following cases from CengageCompose cover many of the concepts discussed in this chapter and are available at **http://compose.cengage.com**.

Klein-Brigham Series:

Case 11, "Chicago Valve Company."

Brigham-Buzzard Series:

Case 6, "Powerline Network Corporation (Basics of Capital Budgeting)."

Cash Flow Estimation and Risk Analysis

Procter & Gamble, Unilever, and the Thales Group are among the many companies that understand the importance of cash flow estimation and risk analysis. For example, P&G conducts risk analysis on a wide variety of capital budgeting projects, from routine cost savings proposals at domestic facilities to cross-border facility location choices. P&G's Associate Director for Investment Analysis, Bob Hunt, says that risk analysis, especially the use of decision trees, "has been very useful in helping us break complex projects down into individual decision options, helping us understand the uncertainties, and ultimately helping us make superior decisions."

Unilever created its Decision Making Under Uncertainty (DMUU) approach to avoid overlooking risk during its project selection process. Unilever applies DMUU to conduct risk analysis for many types of projects, but especially when it must choose among multiple proposals.

Project evaluation is always difficult, but it is even more so when rapidly evolving technology is involved. For firms bidding for government and business contracts, the bidding process itself ramps up the already difficult task of project evaluation. The Thales Group competes in this market by providing communication systems for the defense and aerospace industries. Not only does Thales use risk analysis to better identify the expected levels and risks of project cash flows, but it also uses risk analysis to better understand and manage the risks associated with submitting bids for projects.

Keep these companies in mind as you read the chapter.

Source: Palisade Corporation is a leading developer of software for risk evaluation and decision analysis. For examples of companies using risk analysis, see the case analyses at **www.palisade.com/cases**.

451

Project Valuation, Cash Flows, and Risk Analysis

When we estimate a project's cash flows (CF) and then discount them at the project's risk-adjusted cost of capital (r), the result is the project's NPV, which tells us how much the project increases the firm's value. This chapter focuses on how to estimate the size and risk of a project's cash flows.

Note too that project cash flows, once a project has been accepted and placed in operation, are added to the firm's free cash flows from other sources. Therefore, projects' cash flows essentially determine the firm's free cash flows as discussed in Chapter 6 and thus form the basis for the firm's market value and stock price.

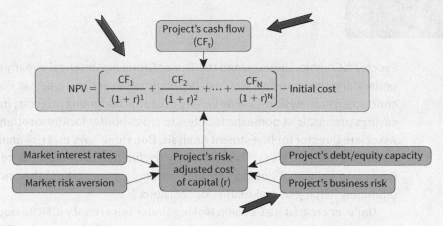

resource

*The textbook's Web site contains an Excel file that will guide you through the chapter's calculations. The file for this chapter is **Ch11 Tool Kit.xlsx**, and we encourage you to open the file and follow along as you read the chapter.*

Chapter 10 assumed that a project's cash flows had already been estimated. Now we cover cash flow estimation and identify the issues a manager faces in producing relevant and realistic cash flow estimates. In addition, cash flow estimates are just that: estimates! It is crucial for a manager to incorporate uncertainty into project analysis if a company is to make informed decisions regarding project selection. We begin with a discussion of procedures for estimating relevant and realistic cash flows.

11-1 Identifying Relevant Cash Flows

The most important—and difficult—step in capital budgeting is estimating a proposal's relevant **project cash flows**, which are the differences between the cash flows the firm will have if it implements the project versus the cash flows it will have if it rejects the project. These are called **incremental cash flows**:

$$\text{Incremental cash flows} = \frac{\text{Company's cash flows}}{\textit{with} \text{ the project}} - \frac{\text{Company's cash flows}}{\textit{without} \text{ the project}}$$

Estimating incremental cash flows might sound easy, but there are many potential pitfalls. In this section, we identify the key concepts that will help you avoid these pitfalls and then apply the concepts to an actual project to illustrate their application to cash flow estimation.

11-1a Project Cash Flow versus Accounting Income

We saw in Chapter 2 that free cash flow differs from accounting income: Free cash flow is the cash flow that is available for distribution to all investors, making free cash flow the basis of a firm's value. It is common in finance to speak of a firm's free cash flow and project cash flow, but these are based on the same concepts. In fact, project cash flow is identical to the project's free cash flow, and a firm's total cash flow from all projects is equal to the firm's free cash flow. We will follow the typical convention and refer to a project's free cash flow simply as project cash flow, but keep in mind that the two concepts are identical.[1]

Because net income is not equal to the cash flow available for distribution to all investors, in the last chapter we discounted *cash flows*, not accounting income, to find projects' NPVs. *For capital budgeting purposes it is the project's cash flow, not its accounting income, that is relevant.* Therefore, when analyzing a proposed capital budgeting project, disregard the project's net income and focus exclusively on its cash flow. Be especially alert to the following differences between cash flow and accounting income.

THE CASH FLOW EFFECT OF ASSET PURCHASES AND DEPRECIATION

Most projects require assets, and asset purchases represent *negative* cash flows. Even though the acquisition of assets results in a cash outflow, accountants do not show the purchase of fixed assets as a deduction from accounting income. Instead, they deduct a depreciation expense each year throughout the life of the asset. Depreciation shelters income from taxation, and this has an impact on cash flow, but depreciation itself is not a cash flow. Therefore, depreciation must be added back when estimating a project's cash flow.

Depreciation is the most common noncash charge, but there are many other noncash charges that might appear on a company's financial statements. Just as with depreciation, all other noncash charges should be added back when calculating a project's cash flow.

CHANGES IN NET OPERATING WORKING CAPITAL

Normally, additional inventories are required to support a new operation, and expanded sales tie up additional funds in accounts receivable. However, payables and accruals increase as a result of the expansion, and this reduces the cash needed to finance inventories and receivables. The difference between the required increase in operating current assets and the increase in operating current liabilities is the change in net operating working capital. If this *change* is positive, as it generally is for expansion projects, then additional financing—beyond the cost of the fixed assets—will be needed.

Toward the end of a project's life, inventories will be used but not replaced, and receivables will be collected without corresponding replacements. As these changes occur, the firm will receive cash inflows; as a result, the investment in net operating working capital will be returned by the end of the project's life.

INTEREST CHARGES ARE *NOT* INCLUDED IN PROJECT CASH FLOWS

Interest is a cash expense, so at first blush it would seem that interest on any debt used to finance a project should be deducted when we estimate the project's cash flows. However, this is not correct. Recall from Chapter 10 that we discount a project's cash flows by its **risk-adjusted discount rate** (which is also called the **risk-adjusted cost of capital** and the **project cost of capital**), which is a weighted average (WACC) of the costs of debt, preferred stock, and common equity, adjusted for the project's risk and debt capacity. This is the rate

---

[1]A cash flow by any other name is not always the same. When the financial press refers to a firm's "net cash flow," it is almost always equal to the definition of net cash flow we provide in Chapter 2 (which simply adds back depreciation and any other noncash charges to net income). This is a quick and dirty measure and is not very helpful to managers or to analysts. We will occasionally speak of a "project's net cash flow." When we do, we mean the project's free cash flow and not the accounting definition of net cash flow.

of return necessary to satisfy *all* of the firm's investors, including stockholders and debtholders. A common mistake made by many students and financial managers is to subtract interest payments when estimating a project's cash flows. This is a mistake because the cost of debt is already embedded in the cost of capital, so subtracting interest payments from the project's cash flows would amount to double-counting interest costs. Therefore, *you should not subtract interest expenses when finding a project's cash flows.*

11-1b Timing of Cash Flows: Yearly versus Other Periods

In theory, in capital budgeting analyses we should discount cash flows based on the exact moment when they occur. Therefore, one could argue that daily cash flows would be better than annual flows. However, it would be costly to estimate daily cash flows and laborious to analyze them. In general, the analysis would be no better than one using annual flows because we simply can't make accurate forecasts of daily cash flows more than a couple of months into the future. Therefore, it is generally appropriate to assume that all cash flows occur at the end of the various years. We would analyze projects with highly predictable cash flows, such as constructing a building and then leasing it on a long-term basis (with monthly payments) to a financially sound tenant, using monthly periods.

11-1c Expansion Projects and Replacement Projects

Two types of projects can be distinguished: (1) *expansion projects,* in which the firm makes an investment in, for example, a new Home Depot store in Seattle; and (2) *replacement projects*, in which the firm replaces existing assets, generally to reduce costs. In expansion projects, the cash expenditures on buildings, equipment, and required working capital are obviously incremental, as are the sales revenues and operating costs associated with the project. The incremental costs associated with replacement projects are not so obvious. For example, Home Depot might replace some of its delivery trucks to reduce fuel and maintenance expenses. Replacement analysis is complicated by the fact that most of the relevant cash flows are the cash flow differences between the existing project and the replacement project. For example, the fuel bill for a more efficient new truck might be $10,000 per year versus $15,000 for the old truck. The $5,000 fuel savings would be an incremental cash flow associated with the replacement decision. We analyze an expansion and replacement decision later in the chapter.

11-1d Sunk Costs

A **sunk cost** is an outlay related to the project that was incurred in the past and that cannot be recovered in the future regardless of whether or not the project is accepted. Therefore, sunk costs are *not incremental costs* and thus are not relevant in a capital budgeting analysis.

To illustrate, suppose FedEx spent $2 million to investigate sites for a potential new distribution center. That $2 million is a sunk cost—the money is gone, and it won't come back regardless of whether or not a new distribution center is built. Therefore, the $2 million should not be included in a capital budgeting decision.

Improper treatment of sunk costs can lead to bad decisions. For example, suppose FedEx completed the analysis for a new center and found that it must spend an additional (or incremental) $17 million to build and supply the center, on top of the $2 million already spent on the site study. Suppose the present value of future cash flows is $18 million. Should the project be accepted? If the sunk costs are mistakenly included, the NPV is −$2 million + (−$17 million) + $18 million = −$1 million, and the project would be rejected. However, *that would be a bad decision*. The real issue is whether the *incremental* $17 million would result in enough *incremental* cash flow to produce a positive NPV. If the $2 million sunk cost were disregarded, as it should be, then the NPV on an incremental basis would be a *positive* $1 million.

11-1e Opportunity Costs Associated with Assets the Firm Already Owns

Another conceptual issue is the **opportunity cost** related to assets the firm already owns. Continuing our example, suppose FedEx already owns land with a current market value of $2 million that can be used for a new distribution center. If FedEx goes forward with the project, only another $15 million will be required, not the full $17 million, because it will not need to buy the required land. Does this mean that FedEx should use the $15 million incremental cost as the cost of the new center? The answer is definitely "No." If the new store is *not* built, then FedEx could sell the land and receive a cash flow of $2 million. This $2 million is an *opportunity cost*—it is cash that FedEx would not receive if the land is used for the new center. Therefore, the $2 million must be charged to the new project, and failing to do so would cause the new project's calculated NPV to be too high.

11-1f Externalities

Externalities are the effects of a project on other parts of the firm or on the environment. As explained in what follows, there are three types of externalities: negative within-firm externalities, positive within-firm externalities, and environmental externalities.

NEGATIVE WITHIN-FIRM EXTERNALITIES

In late 2017, Apple opened its second store in Brooklyn on Flatbush Avenue. Some customers who would have purchased products at the Apple Store on Bedford Avenue probably instead bought them at the Flatbush location. Therefore, the new store's incremental cash flow must be reduced by the amount of the cash flow lost by the previous store. This type of externality is called **cannibalization**, because the new business eats into the company's existing business. Ignoring cannibalization can cause a company to overestimate the value of a project.

POSITIVE WITHIN-FIRM EXTERNALITIES

Cannibalization occurs when a new product competes with an old one. However, a new project can also be *complementary* to an old one, in which case cash flows in the old operation will be *increased* when the new one is introduced. For example, each new model of Nike shoes gets customers into the store, where they are likely to also purchase Nike clothing. Consideration of positive externalities often changes a project's NPV from negative to positive.

ENVIRONMENTAL EXTERNALITIES

The most common type of negative externality is a project's impact on the environment. Government rules and regulations constrain the minimal amount of environmental protection companies are required to provide, but firms have some flexibility in dealing with environmental issues over and above this minimum amount. For example, suppose a manufacturer is studying a proposed new plant. The company could meet current environmental regulations at a cost of $1 million, but the plant would still emit fumes that would cause some bad will in its neighborhood. Those ill feelings would not show up in the cash flow analysis, but they should be considered. Perhaps a relatively small additional expenditure would reduce the emissions substantially, make the plant look good relative to other plants in the area, and provide goodwill that in the future would help the firm's sales and its negotiations with governmental agencies.

Of course, all firms' profits ultimately depend on the Earth remaining healthy, so companies have some incentive to do things that protect the environment even though those actions are not currently required. However, if one firm decides to take actions that are good for the environment but quite costly, then it must either raise its prices or suffer a decline in earnings. If its competitors decide to get by with less costly but environmentally unfriendly processes, they can price their products lower and make more money. Of course, the more environmentally friendly companies can advertise their environmental efforts, and this might—or might not—offset their higher costs. All this illustrates why government regulations are often necessary. Finance, politics, and the environment are all interconnected.

SELF-TEST

Why should companies use a project's cash flows rather than accounting income when determining a project's NPV?

Explain the following terms: incremental cash flow, sunk cost, opportunity cost, externality, cannibalization, and complementary project.

Provide an example of a "good" externality—that is, one that increases a project's true NPV over what it would be if just its own cash flows were considered.

11-2 Analysis of an Expansion Project

Guyton Products Company (GPC) is considering a new project, which is the application of a radically new liquid nano-coating technology to a new type of solar water heater module. GPC has a 3-year license from a university, after which the license is open to all companies. It's not clear how well the water heater will work, how strong demand for it will be, how long it will be before the product becomes obsolete, or how competition will affect cash flows after the license is open for all. Still, the water heater has the potential for being profitable, though it could also fail miserably. GPC is a relatively large company, and this is one of many projects, so a failure would not bankrupt the firm but would hurt profits.

11-2a Base Case Inputs and Key Results

resource

See *Ch11 Tool Kit.xlsx* on the textbook's Web site.

We used *Excel* to do the analysis. We could have used a calculator and paper, but *Excel* is *much* easier to use for capital budgeting problems. You don't need to know *Excel* to understand our discussion, but if you plan to work in finance—or, really, in any business field—you must know how to use *Excel*, so we recommend that you open the *Excel* **Tool Kit** for this chapter and scroll through it as the textbook explains the analysis.

Figure 11-1 shows Part 1 of the *Excel* model used in this analysis; see the first worksheet in *Ch11 Tool Kit.xlsx*, named *1-Base-Case*. The base-case inputs are in the blue section. For example, the cost of required equipment to manufacture the water heaters is $10,000 and is shown in the blue input section. (All dollar values in Figure 11-1 and in our discussion here are reported in thousands, so the equipment actually costs $10,000,000.) The actual number-crunching takes place in Part 2 of the model, shown in Figure 11-2. Part 2 takes

FIGURE 11-1

Analysis of an Expansion Project: Inputs and Key Results (Thousands of Dollars)

	A	B	C	D	E	F	G	H	I
54	Part 1. Inputs and Key Results								
55					Scenario:				
56	Inputs				Base-Case		Key Results		
57	Equipment cost				$10,000		NPV		$1,070
58	Salvage value, equipment, Year 4				$1,000		IRR		13.8%
59	Opportunity cost				$0		MIRR		12.4%
60	Externalities (cannibalization)				$0		PI		1.09
61	Units sold, Year 1				10,000		Payback		2.94
62	Units sold, Year 2, Pct. change from Year 1				20%		Discounted payback		3.65
63	Units sold, Year 3, Pct. change from Year 1				20%				
64	Units sold, Year 4, Pct. change from Year 1				−30%				
65	Sales price per unit, Year 1				$2.00				
66	Annual change in sales price, after Year 1				4%				
67	Variable cost per unit (VC), Year 1				$1.56				
68	Annual change in VC, after Year 1				3%				
69	Nonvariable cost (Non-VC), Year 1				$1,107				
70	Annual change in Non-VC, after Year 1				3%				
71	Project WACC				10%				
72	Tax rate				25%				
73	Working capital as % of next year's sales				10%				

Source: See the file ***Ch11 Tool Kit.xlsx***. Numbers are reported as rounded values for clarity but are calculated using *Excel*'s full precision. Thus, intermediate calculations using the figure's rounded values will be inexact.

the inputs from the blue section of Figure 11-1 and generates the project's cash flows. Part 2 of the model also performs calculations of the project performance measures discussed in Chapter 10 and then reports those results in the orange section of Figure 11-1. This structure allows you (or your manager) to change an input and instantly see the impact on the reported performance measures.

We have saved these base-case inputs in ***Ch11 Tool Kit.xlsx*** with *Excel*'s Scenario Manager. If you change some inputs but want to return to the original base-case inputs, you can select Data, What-If Analysis, Scenario Manager, pick the scenario named "Base-Case" and click Show. This will replace any changes with the original inputs. Scenario Manager is a very useful tool and we will have more to say about it later in this chapter.

11-2b Cash Flow Projections: Intermediate Calculations

Figure 11-2 shows Part 2 of the model. When setting up *Excel* models, we prefer to have more rows but shorter formulas. So instead of having very complicated formulas in the section for cash flow forecasts, we put intermediate calculations in a separate section. The blue section of Figure 11-2 shows these intermediate calculations for the GPC project, as we explain in the following sections.

ANNUAL UNIT SALES, UNIT PRICES, UNIT COSTS, AND INFLATION

Rows 87–90 in Figure 11-2 show annual unit sales, unit sale prices, unit variable costs, and nonvariable costs. Notice that the prices and costs are projected to grow at the rates assumed in Part 1 of the model in Figure 11-1. For example, unit sales are expected to grow

FIGURE 11-2
Analysis of an Expansion Project: Cash Flows and Performance Measures (Thousands of Dollars)

	A	B	C	D	E	F	G	H	I
84	Part 2. Cash Flows and Performance Measures								
85	Scenario: Base-Case								
86	Intermediate Calculations				0	1	2	3	4
87	Unit sales					10,000	12,000	12,000	7,000
88	Sales price per unit					$2.000	$2.080	$2.163	$2.250
89	Variable cost per unit (excl. depr.)					$1.560	$1.607	$1.655	$1.705
90	Nonvariable costs (excl. depr.)					$1,107	$1,140	$1,174	$1,210
91	Sales revenues = Units × Price/unit					$20,000	$24,960	$25,958	$15,748
92	NOWC$_t$ = 10%(Revenues$_{t+1}$)				$2,000	$2,496	$2,596	$1,575	$0
93	Basis for depreciation				$10,000				
94	Annual depreciation rate (MACRS)					33.33%	44.45%	14.81%	7.41%
95	Annual depreciation expense					$3,333	$4,445	$1,481	$741
96	Remaining undepreciated value (book value)					$6,667	$2,222	$741	$0
97	Forecast Project Cash Flows								
98					0	1	2	3	4
99	Sales revenues = Units × Price/unit					$20,000	$24,960	$25,958	$15,748
100	Variable costs = Units × Cost/unit					$15,600	$19,282	$19,860	$11,933
101	Nonvariable costs (excluding depr.)					$1,107	$1,140	$1,174	$1,210
102	Depreciation					$3,333	$4,445	$1,481	$741
103	Earnings before int. and taxes (EBIT)					−$40	$93	$3,443	$1,865
104	Taxes on operating profit (25% rate)					−$10	$23	$861	$466
105	Net operating profit after taxes					−$30	$70	$2,582	$1,399
106									
107					0	1	2	3	4
108	Net operating profit after taxes					−$30	$70	$2,582	$1,399
109	Add back depreciation					$3,333	$4,445	$1,481	$741
110	Equipment purchases				−$10,000				
111	Salvage value								$1,000
112	Cash flow due to tax on salv. val.								−$250
113	Cash flow due to change in NOWC				−$2,000	−$496	−$100	$1,021	$1,575
114	Opportunity cost, after taxes				$0	$0	$0	$0	$0
115	After-tax externalities					$0	$0	$0	$0
116	Project cash flows: Time Line				−$12,000	$2,807	$4,415	$5,084	$4,464
117	Project Evaluation Measures								
118	NPV		$1,070	=NPV(E71,F116:I116)+E116					
119	IRR		13.75%	=IRR(E116:I116)					
120	MIRR		12.37%	=MIRR(E116:I116,E71,E71)					
121	Profitability index		1.09	=NPV(E71,F116:I116)/(-E116)					
122	Payback		2.94	=PERCENTRANK(E125:I125,0,6)*I124					
123	Disc. payback		3.65	=PERCENTRANK(E127:I127,0,6)*I124					
124	Calculations for Payback			Year:	0	1	2	3	4
125	Cumulative cash flows for payback				−$12,000	−$9,193	−$4,778	$306	$4,771
126	Disc. cash flows for disc. payback				−$12,000	$2,552	$3,649	$3,820	$3,049
127	Cumulative discounted cash flows				−$12,000	−$9,448	−$5,799	−$1,980	$1,070

Source: See the file *Ch11 Tool Kit.xlsx*. Numbers are reported as rounded values for clarity but are calculated using *Excel*'s full precision. Thus, intermediate calculations using the figure's rounded values will be inexact.

by 20% from Year 1 to Year 2 ($g_{1,2}$), 20% from Year 1 to Year 3 ($g_{1,3}$), and −30% from Year 1 to Year 4 ($g_{1,4}$) as competitors enter the market after expiration of GPC's exclusive license. Therefore, projected unit sales in Cell G87 for Year 2 are 12,000:

$$\text{Year-2 unit sales} = (1 + g_{1,2})(\text{Year-1 units sold})$$
$$= (1 + 0.20)(10,000) = 12,000$$

Using the same process, unit sales in Year 3 and Year 4 are:

$$\text{Year-3 unit sales} = (1 + g_{1,3})(\text{Year-1 units sold})$$
$$= (1 + 0.20)(10,000) = 12,000$$

and

$$\text{Year-4 unit sales} = (1 + g_{1,4})(\text{Year-1 units sold})$$
$$= (1 - 0.30)(10,000) = 7,000$$

Notice that we specified the growth (or decline) of unit sales each year relative to Year 1. Doing so will be helpful when we do risk analysis later in the chapter.

GPC expects the unit price after Year 1 to grow by 4% each year. The price per unit in Year 2 is $2.08, shown in Cell G88:

$$\text{Year-2 unit price} = (1 + \text{growth in unit price})(\text{Year-1 unit price})$$
$$= (1 + 0.04)(\$2.00) = \$2.08$$

Applying the same process, the sales price in Year 3 is:

$$\text{Year-3 unit price} = (1 + 0.04)(\$2.08) = \$2.163$$

We applied the same process for Year 3 and Year 4. We also used the same approach in Rows 89 and 90 to determine the variable costs per unit and the nonvariable costs.

Notice that we estimated unit sales after Year 1 as a percentage of Year-1 unit sales. In contrast, we estimated future sales prices using a constant year-to-year growth rate of 4%. As we previously mentioned, this will be helpful in risk analysis. We know you must have questions about why we used a different approach for units sold and sales price per unit, and we will answer them later in the chapter. For now, let's focus on the projections and resulting cash flows.

The Year-2 sales revenues in Cell G91 are equal to the units sold multiplied by the price per unit:

$$\text{Year-2 sales revenue} = (\text{Year-2 units sold})(\text{Year-2 price per unit})$$
$$= (12,000)(\$2.08) = \$24,960$$

It is important to incorporate expected inflation rates, which are the percentage changes (i.e., growth) in costs and in revenues. This is important because the WACC includes inflation. (Recall from Chapter 5 that the cost of debt includes an inflation premium. Also, the capital asset pricing model from Chapter 6 defines the cost of equity as the sum of the risk-free rate and a risk premium. Like the cost of debt, the risk-free rate also has an inflation premium.) Because inflation increases the WACC, the estimated cash flows must also include inflation.[2] Otherwise, you will *underestimate* the project's cash flows and hence underestimate its NPV.

---

[2]It is theoretically possible to ignore inflation when estimating the cash flows and adjust the WACC so that it, too, doesn't incorporate inflation, but we have never seen this accomplished correctly in practice. Therefore, you should always include the expected growth rates in prices and costs when estimating cash flows.

NET OPERATING WORKING CAPITAL (NOWC)

Virtually all projects require working capital, and this one is no exception. For example, raw materials must be purchased and replenished each year as they are used. In Part 1 of Figure 11-1 we assume that GPC must have an amount of net operating working capital (NOWC) on hand equal to 10% of the upcoming year's sales revenues. For example, in Year 0, GPC must have:

$$\text{Year-0 NOWC sales revenue} = 10\%(\$20{,}000) = \$2{,}000$$

As sales grow, so does the required working capital. Rows 91–92 in Figure 11-2 show the annual sales revenues and required working capital.

DEPRECIATION EXPENSE

Rows 93–96 report intermediate calculations related to depreciation, beginning with the depreciation basis, which is the cost of acquiring and installing a project. The basis for GPC's project is $10,000. (Regardless of which depreciation method is used, the basis is not adjusted by the expected salvage value when calculating actual taxable income, which is different from calculations for financial reporting purposes.) The depreciation expense for a year is the product of the basis and that year's depreciation rate. Depreciation rates depend on the type of property and its Internal Revenue Service (IRS) classification, such as 3-year property versus 5-year property.

Before proceeding, let's take a quick look at depreciation methods. With the **straight-line depreciation method**, annual depreciation expenses are equal to the basis divided by the project's life. For example, an asset with a $100,000 basis and 5-year life has an annual depreciation expense of $100,000/5 = $20,000. However, the **half-year convention** calculates depreciation expenses as though the asset is placed into service halfway through the year. Therefore, the first-year depreciation expense is $20,000/2 = $10,000 in this example. Depreciation is $20,000 in each of the next 4 years, and $10,000 in the sixth year. Notice that there are depreciation expenses for 6 years even though the property is classified as 5-year property.

Guyton Products will use the **modified accelerated cost recovery system (MACRS)**, which allows faster depreciation than the straight-line method; see Appendix 11A and the worksheet *Appendix A* in this chapter's *Tool Kit* for an explanation of MACRS and other depreciation methods.

Even though GPC's project will operate for 4 years, it is classified as 3-year property for tax purposes. The depreciation rates in Row 94 are for 3-year property using MACRS rates. The remaining undepreciated value is equal to the original basis less the accumulated depreciation; this is called the **book value** of the asset.

The **salvage value** of an asset is the market value at which a used asset can be sold. Both the salvage value and book value are used when determining the after-tax cash flow if a used asset is sold, as we illustrate later in the project's analysis.

Before continuing the analysis, you should know that the **2017 Tax Cut and Jobs Act (TCJA)** includes **bonus depreciation**, which allows projects to be depreciated even more quickly than the MACRS rates we use here. Bonus depreciation is scheduled to be phased out after 2026, but your career will last much longer, so we don't use bonus depreciation in our analysis of GPC's cash flows. See Appendix 11A for an explanation of bonus depreciation.

resource

See *Ch11 Tool Kit.xlsx* on the textbook's Web site.

11-2c Cash Flow Projections: Estimating Net Operating Profit after Taxes (NOPAT)

The yellow section in the middle of Figure 11-2 shows the steps in calculating the project's net operating profit after taxes (NOPAT). Projected sales revenues are on Row 99. Multiply annual variable unit costs (Row 89) by the number of units sold (Row 87) to determine total variable costs (Row 100). Nonvariable costs are on Row 101, and depreciation expenses are on Row 102. Subtract variable costs, nonvariable costs, and depreciation expenses from sales revenues to calculate earnings before interest and taxes (EBIT) for Row 103.

When discussing a company's income statement, interest expense is subtracted from operating profit to determine taxable income. Remember, though, that we do not subtract interest when estimating a project's cash flows, because the project's WACC is the overall rate of return required by *all* the company's investors and not just shareholders. This means that the project's corresponding cash flows also must be the ones available to *all* investors, including lenders, and not just shareholders. Therefore, we do not subtract interest expense when estimating a project's cash flows.

We calculate operating taxes in Row 104 by multiplying the taxable income by the tax rate. We subtract taxes from taxable income to get the project's net operating profit after taxes (NOPAT) on Row 105. Notice that the project has negative earnings before interest and taxes in Year 1. When multiplied by the 25% tax rate, Cell F104 shows negative taxes. This negative tax is subtracted from EBIT and actually makes the after-tax operating profit larger than the pre-tax profit! For example, the EBIT in Year 1 is −$40 and the reported tax is −$10, leading to an after-tax loss of −$40 − (−$10) = −$30. In other words, it is as though the IRS is sending GPC a check for $30. How can this be correct?

Recall the basic concept underlying the relevant cash flows for project analysis—what are the company's cash flows with the project versus the company's cash flows without the project? If GPC expects to have other taxable income in excess of $30 in Year 1, then this project will shelter GPC's other income from $10 in taxes. Therefore, the project's NOPAT in Year 1 will only be −$30 instead of −$40.[3] The tax shelter is small in this example, but it can be quite large in other situations.

11-2d Project Cash Flows: Completing the Calculations

To determine the project cash flow, we must include NOPAT, depreciation, asset purchases, after-tax salvage values, changes in working capital, opportunity costs, and externalities. We have already calculated NOPAT, so we enter it on Row 108 before addressing the other components.

IMPACT OF DEPRECIATION

We subtracted depreciation on Row 102 when calculating taxes, even though depreciation is a noncash expense. If we had not done so, we would have overstated EBIT on Row 103, causing us to overstate taxes on Row 104. For example, if we had incorrectly ignored the Year-2 depreciation of $4,445, the pre-tax income (EBIT) for Year 2 would have been $4,538: $24,960 − $19,282 − $1,140 = $4,538. The tax expense would have been 25%($4,538) = $1,134.5, much higher than the actual tax of $23 in Cell G104. In other words, the depreciation saved $1,111.5 in taxes: $1,134.5 − $23 = $1,111.5. As this shows, it is important that cash flows should reflect the actual taxes. Therefore, we subtract noncash depreciation expense when calculating NOPAT, but we add back depreciation expense on Row 109 to reflect the actual after-tax cash flow.[4]

---

[3]If GPC doesn't expect to have other taxable income in Year 1, then GPC would report zero taxes for the project in Year 1 and carry forward the loss indefinitely until GPC does have taxable income. Prior to the TCJC act, companies could carry forward losses for only 20 years but could carry back losses for 2 years and receive a tax refund.

[4]The tax savings due to depreciation may be directly calculated as the product of the tax rate and the depreciation expense: 25%($4,445) = $1,111.5. However, we find that students make fewer errors in project cash flows if they go through the steps in Figure 11-2.

THE IMPACT OF ASSET PURCHASES AND DISPOSITIONS

GPC purchased the equipment at the beginning of the project for $10,000, which is a negative cash flow shown on Row 110. Had GPC purchased additional assets in other years, we would report those purchases too.

GPC expects to salvage the investment at Year 4 for $1,000 (Row 111). In our example, GPC's project was fully depreciated by the end of the project, so the $1,000 salvage value is a taxable profit. At a 25% tax rate, GPC will owe 25%($1,000) = $250 in taxes at Year 4 (Row 112).

Suppose instead that GPC terminates operations before the equipment is fully depreciated. The after-tax salvage value depends on the price at which GPC can sell the equipment *and* on the book value of the equipment (i.e., the original basis less all previous depreciation charges). Suppose GPC terminates the project at Year 2, at which time the book value is $2,222, as shown on Row 96. We consider two cases, gains and losses. In the first case, the salvage value is $2,570, and there is a reported gain of $2,570 − $2,222 = $348. This gain is taxed as ordinary income, so the tax is 25%($348) = $87. The after-tax cash flow is equal to the sales price less the tax: $2,570 − $87 = $2,483.

Now suppose the salvage value at Year 2 is only $522. In this case, there is a reported loss: $522 − $2,222 = −$1,700. This is treated as an ordinary expense, so its tax is 25%(−$1,700) = −$425. This "negative" tax acts as a credit if GPC has other taxable income, so the net after-tax cash flow is $522 − (−$425) = $947.

THE IMPACT OF NET OPERATING WORKING CAPITAL

As discussed previously, GPC must maintain a level of net operation working capital equal to 10% of the next year's sales. Row 92 shows this level each year. Row 113 shows the *incremental* investment in net operating working capital (NOWC) required to maintain the necessary levels each year. We have found that students easily understand the necessary *amounts* of NOWC but sometimes have difficulty determining the *cash flows* due to NOWC. To make sure that you don't have the same problem, suppose the entire amount of NOWC is comprised of raw materials. Cell E92 shows that GPC's project needs an additional $2,000 of raw materials at the start of the project so that it can manufacture the solar water heating modules. Because GPC didn't already have these materials on hand, it must purchase them for $2,000, which is a cash outflow (i.e., a negative cash flow). Therefore, Cell E113 shows a cash flow of −$2,000 at Year 0, the start of the project.

GPC will use this raw material inventory during the year to manufacture the products that are sold at Year 1. GPC will recoup its raw material expenditures, as well as its other Year-1 expenses, when the products are sold at Year 1 for $12,000. Focusing just on the Year-0 raw materials, it is as though GPC is being "repaid" $2,000 for its initial raw materials expenditures. This "repayment" is a positive cash flow of $2,000 at Year 1.

However, GPC will need to purchase more materials at Year 1 to manufacture the products sold at Year 2. Cell F92 shows that GPC must have $2,496 in raw materials at Year 1. Therefore, GPC must purchase the materials, which is a cash outflow of −$2,496 at Year 1.

Rather than report the positive $2,000 cash from selling the initial materials at Year 1 and the negative $2,496 due to purchasing new materials at Year 1 as separate line items, we combine them into the net cash flow in Cell F113: $2,000 − $2,496 = −$496. The cash flow due to NOWC is calculated similarly for the remaining years.

Notice that NOWC goes down from Year 2 to Year 3 due to lower sales revenues in Year 4. Using the values in Row 92 for the amounts of NOWC, the cash flow due to NOWC at Year 3 is: $NOWC_2 − NOWC_3 = \$2,596 − \$1,575 = \$1,021$. This is a positive cash flow because GPS is selling more of its materials than it is purchasing. GPC doesn't need any additional NOWC at Year 4 because the project has ended. Using the values in Row 92 for the amounts of NOWC, the cash flow due to NOWC at Year 4 is: $NOWC_3 - NOWC_4 = \$1,575 - \$0 = \$1,575$.

Of course, not all NOWC is due to raw materials. It also includes finished goods, accounts payable (because GPC doesn't pay its suppliers immediately), accounts receivable (because GPC doesn't collect from its customers immediately), and some cash on hand, as explained in Chapter 2. If we had made monthly projections, then much of the NOWC would have been comprised of these components. For the sake of clarity, we instead show annual projections and assume all working capital amounts are based on the next year's sales revenues.

THE IMPACT OF SUNK COSTS, OPPORTUNITY COSTS, AND EXTERNALITIES

GPC's project doesn't have any sunk costs, opportunity costs, or externalities, but the following sections show how we would adjust the cash flows if GPC did have some of these issues.

Sunk Costs   Suppose that last year GPC spent \$1,500 on a marketing and feasibility study for the project. Should \$1,500 be included in the project's cost? The answer is "No!" That money already has been spent and accepting or rejecting the project will not change that fact.

Opportunity Costs   Now suppose GPC's new equipment will be installed in a building that GPC now owns but that the space could be leased to another company for \$200 per year after taxes if the project is rejected. The \$200 per year would be an *opportunity cost*, and it should be reflected as a reduction in the calculated annual cash flows.

Externalities   As noted earlier, the solar water heater project does not cause any cannibalization effects. Suppose instead that it would reduce the net after-tax cash flows of another GPC division by \$50 per year and that no other firm could take on this project if GPC turns it down. In this case, we would report the cannibalization on Row 115, deducting \$50 each year. As a result, the project would have a lower NPV. On the other hand, if the project would cause additional inflows to some other GPC division because it was complementary to that other division's products (i.e., if a positive externality exists), then those after-tax inflows should be attributed to the water heater project and thus shown as a positive inflow on Row 115.

11-2e Evaluating Project Cash Flows

We sum Rows 108 to 115 in Figure 11-2 to get the project's annual cash flows, set up as a time line on Row 116. These cash flows are then used to calculate NPV, IRR, MIRR, PI, payback, and discounted payback. These performance measures are shown in the orange portion at the bottom of Figure 11-2.

PRELIMINARY EVALUATION OF THE BASE-CASE SCENARIO

Based on this analysis, the preliminary evaluation indicates that the project is acceptable. The net present value (NPV) is \$1,070, which is fairly large when compared to the initial investment of \$12,000. Its internal rate of return (IRR) and modified internal rate of return (MIRR) are both greater than the 10% WACC, and the profitability index (PI) is larger than 1.0. The payback is just less than 3 years and discounted payback is almost as long as the project's life, which is somewhat concerning, and is something that needs to be explored by conducting a risk analysis of the project.

SCENARIO MANAGER

Excel's Scenario Manager is a very powerful and useful tool. We illustrate its use here as we examine two topics: the impact of forgetting to include inflation and the impact of depreciation methods. To use Scenario Manager in the worksheet named *1-Base-Case* in *Ch11 Tool Kit.xlsx,* make sure you are showing the Home menu, then select Data, What-If Analysis, and Scenario Manager. There are five scenarios: (1) Base-Case, (2) Base-Case but Ignore inflation, (3) Use MACRS Depreciation, (4) Use Bonus Depreciation, and (5) Use Straight-Line Depreciation (see Appendix A at the end of the chapter for descriptions of depreciation methods). The first two scenarios change the inputs in Cells E56:E73 and Cells F94:I94. The last three scenarios change only Cell E56 and the depreciation rates in Cells F94:I94. Notice that all scenarios include Cell E56, the scenario's name. We have painfully learned how important this is, so please learn from our bad experiences rather than from your own.

Notice that the first two scenarios include all changing cells but that the last three include only the scenario name and the depreciation rates. The advantage of having all changing cells in each scenario is that you only have to select a single scenario to show all the desired inputs in the model. The disadvantage is that each scenario can get complicated by having many changing cells.

The advantage of having groups of scenarios that don't include all inputs is that you can focus on particular aspects of the analysis, such as the choice of depreciation methods. The disadvantage is that you must know which other scenarios are active in order to properly interpret your results.

For some models it makes sense to have only one group of scenarios in which each scenario has the same changing cells; for other models, it makes sense to have different groups of scenarios. In any case, be sure to have at least one cell in your model that has a written description that changes with each scenario. In our model, Cell E56 shows a name for the current scenario.

The Impact of Inflation   It is easy to overlook inflation, but it is important to include it. For example, had we forgotten to include inflation in the GPC example, the estimated NPV would have dropped from $1,070 to $131. You can see this by changing all the price and cost growth rates to zero and then looking at the NPV. An easier way to do this is with the Scenario Manager—just choose the scenario named "Base-Case but Ignore Inflation." Forgetting to include inflation in a capital budgeting analysis typically causes the estimated NPV to be lower than the true NPV, which could cause a company to reject a project that it should have accepted. You can return to the original inputs by going back into Scenario Manager, selecting "Base-Case," and clicking on Show.

Accelerated Depreciation versus Straight-Line Depreciation   Congress permits firms to choose from several depreciation methods. The results we have discussed thus far were based on accelerated depreciation. To see the impact of using straight-line depreciation, go to the Scenario Manager, select "Base-Case" (to ensure that all other inputs are the base case), and then select "Use Straight-Line Depreciation."

The results indicate that the project's NPV is $967 when using straight-line depreciation, which is lower than the $1,070 NPV when using accelerated depreciation. In general, *profitable firms are better off using accelerated depreciation* because more depreciation is taken in the early years under the accelerated method, so taxes are lower in those years and higher in later years. Total depreciation, total cash flows, and total taxes are the same under both depreciation methods, but receiving the cash earlier under the accelerated method results in a higher NPV, IRR, and MIRR.

The 2017 Tax Cut and Jobs Act allows companies to use bonus depreciation for the tax years 2018 through 2026, as we explain in Appendix A at the end of the chapter. For the tax

Mistakes in Cash Flow Estimation Can Kill Innovation

Estimating a project's relevant incremental cash flows takes work, but the idea is simple: Forecast a company's after-tax cash flows assuming the company takes the project and then forecast cash flows assuming the company doesn't take the project. The difference between the with-the-project cash flows and the without-the-project cash flows defines the project's relevant incremental cash flows. But as Harvard Business School faculty Clayton Christensen, Stephen Kaufman, and Willy Shih show, ignoring or incorrectly applying this simple rule can kill innovation and harm companies.

First, managers sometimes implicitly assume the company will operate in the future as it has in the past. For example, consider a new product introduction. The analysis might include only the cash flows directly attributable to the new product. But suppose the company's cash flows would decline due to obsolescence or competition if the new product were not introduced. Ignoring this fact would cause the company to underestimate the *incremental* cash flows of the new product and perhaps incorrectly reject a value-adding project.

Second, some managers focus too much on the short term. For example, consider a manager faced with the choice of expanding production by using the company's existing technology or by using a newer and more efficient technology

with a longer expected life. The initial cost of the old technology might be less, but a reduction in operating costs over the long run might make the new technology a better choice. If managers don't consider long-term cash flows, they will underestimate the value of long-lived assets.

Third, some managers' bonuses are based on reported earnings per share (EPS) rather than a market-based measure of performance. These managers may (and do) take actions to maximize EPS (and their bonus!) rather than shareholder value. For example, research and development expenses and start-up costs for new products reduce net income and EPS in the short term, leading some managers to cut these expenses and maximize their current bonuses. However, this kills the pipeline for new products, which reduces the company's expected long-term cash flows. Changing the link for executive compensation from EPS to market-based measures that take long-run expected cash flows into account can improve managers' incentives to invest for the long term.

The moral of the story is that ignoring or misapplying the capital budgeting principles developed in this chapter can cause a manager to destroy value rather than create it!

Note: See Clayton M. Christensen, Stephen P. Kaufman, and Willy C. Shih, "Innovation Killers: How Financial Tools Destroy Your Capacity to Do New Things," *Harvard Business Review*, January 2008, pp. 98–105.

years 2018 through 2022, companies can use a 100% depreciation rate for Year 1. To see its impact on GPC's project, go to the Scenario Manager, select "Base-Case" (to ensure that all other inputs are the base case), and then select "Use Bonus Depreciation." The resulting NPV is $1,262, which makes the project more attractive.

Be sure to return the scenarios to "Base-Case" when you leave this section.

SELF-TEST

In what way is the setup for finding a project's cash flows similar to the projected income statements for a new, single-product firm? In what way would the two statements be different?

Would a project's NPV for a typical firm be higher or lower if the firm used accelerated rather than straight-line depreciation? Explain.

How could the analysis in Figure 11-2 be modified to consider cannibalization, opportunity costs, and sunk costs?

Why do the annual changes in cash flow due to net working capital appear with both negative and positive values in Figure 11-2?

11-3 Risk Analysis in Capital Budgeting[5]

One objective of risk analysis is to determine whether a project's risk differs from that of an average project at the company (or division). If so, the project's cash flows should be discounted at a risk-adjusted cost of capital instead of at the company's overall weighted average cost of capital.

---

[5]Some professors may choose to cover some of the risk sections and skip others. We offer a range of choices, and we tried to make the exposition clear enough that interested and self-motivated students can read these sections on their own if they are not assigned.

Recall from Chapter 6 that there are three ways to view a project's risk: stand-alone risk, corporate risk, and market risk. **Market risk** is the most relevant because it is the one that determines a company's required return on equity when using the capital asset pricing model (CAPM), which is an important factor when estimating the intrinsic stock value. Unfortunately, a project's market risk is also the most difficult to measure, primarily because new projects don't have "market prices" that can be related to stock market returns. **Corporate risk** is important because it is the risk that a project contributes to the company's cash flows. Corporate risk is also difficult to measure. However, **stand-alone risk** reflects the uncertainty of a project's cash flows, and it can be estimated with the tools we present in the following sections.

Most decision makers first conduct a preliminary analysis and estimate the project's value using a risk-adjusted cost of capital that is based on their experience with similar past projects; this is what Guyton Products did in the previous section's project analysis. Second, they conduct a *quantitative* analysis of the project's stand-alone risk using the methods we describe in the following sections. Third, they consider corporate and market risk in a *qualitative* manner. Fourth, they assign a risk-adjusted cost of capital to the projects based on the risk assessment. If the newly assigned risk-adjusted cost of capital differs from the original estimate used in the preliminary analysis, they re-estimate the project's value using the newly assigned cost of capital.

The following sections apply quantitative risk analyses to the project from the previous section.

SELF-TEST

What are the three types of project risk?

Which type is theoretically the most relevant? Why?

Describe a process that firms often use to determine a project's risk-adjusted costs of capital.

11-4 Measuring Stand-Alone Risk

A project's stand-alone risk reflects uncertainty about its cash flows. Using the GPC project discussed in previous sections, first-year sales are projected at 10,000 units to be sold at a price of $2.00 per unit (recall that all dollar values are reported in thousands). However, unit sales will almost certainly be somewhat higher or lower than 10,000, and the price will probably turn out to be different from the projected $2.00 per unit. Similarly, the other variables would probably differ from their indicated values. Indeed, *all the inputs are expected values, not known values, and actual values can and do vary from expected values.* That's what risk is all about!

Three techniques are used in practice to assess stand-alone risk: (1) sensitivity analysis, (2) scenario analysis, and (3) Monte Carlo simulation. We discuss them in the sections that follow.

SELF-TEST

What does a project's stand-alone risk reflect?

What three techniques are used to assess stand-alone risk?

11-5 Sensitivity Analysis

Intuitively, we know that a change in a key input variable such as units sold or the sales price will cause the NPV to change. **Sensitivity analysis** *measures the change in NPV that results from a given percentage change in one input variable when other inputs are held at* *their expected values*. This is by far the most commonly used type of risk analysis. It begins with a base-case scenario in which the project's NPV is found using the base-case value for each input variable. GPC's base-case inputs were given in Figure 11-1, but it's easy to imagine changes in the inputs, and any changes would result in a different NPV. See the worksheet *2-Sens* in *Ch11 Tool Kit.xlsx* for all calculations in the following sections.

11-5a Sensitivity Graph

When GPC's senior managers review a capital budgeting analysis, they are interested in the base-case NPV, but they always go on to ask a series of "what if" questions: "What if unit sales fall to 9,000?" "What if market conditions force us to price the product at $1.90, not $2.00?" "What if variable costs are higher than we have forecasted?" Sensitivity analysis is designed to provide answers to such questions. Each variable is increased or decreased by a specified percentage from its expected value, holding other variables constant at their base-case levels. Then the NPV is calculated using the changed input. Finally, the resulting set of NPVs is plotted to show how sensitive NPV is to changes in the different variables.

Figure 11-3 shows GPC's project's sensitivity graph for four key variables. The data below the graph give the NPVs based on different values of the inputs, and those NPVs

resource

See *Ch11 Tool Kit.xlsx* on the textbook's Web site.

FIGURE 11-3
Sensitivity Graph for Solar Water Heater Project (Thousands of Dollars)

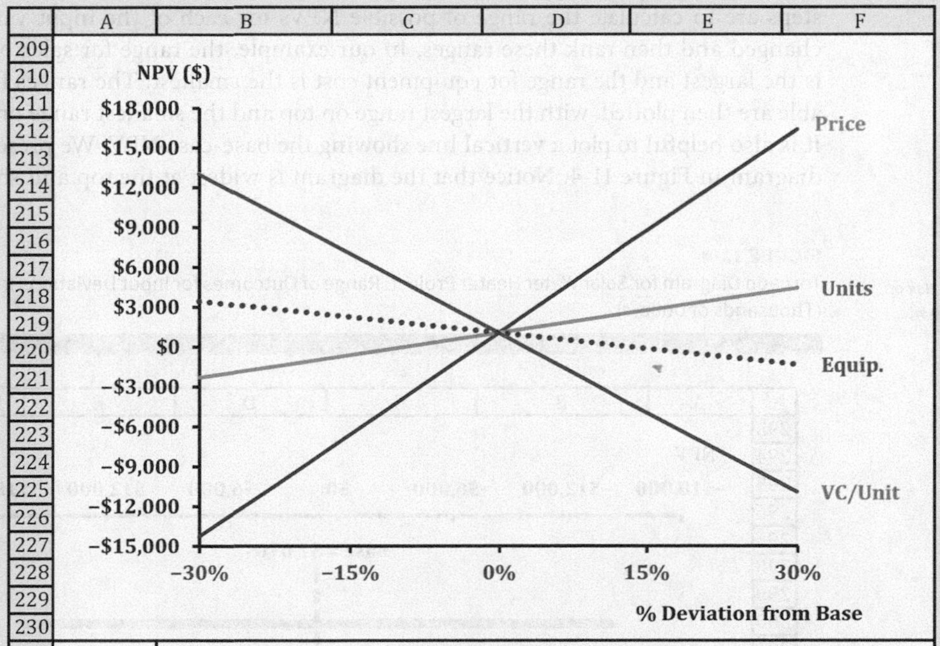

	Data for Sensitivity Graph			
Deviation from Base	NPV with Variables at Different Deviations from Base			
	Equip.	Price	Units	VC/Unit
−30%	$3,446	−$14,264	−$2,296	$13,037
0%	$1,070	$1,070	$1,070	$1,070
30%	−$1,306	$16,403	$4,436	−$10,898
Range	$4,752	$30,667	$6,732	$23,935

Source: See the file *Ch11 Tool Kit.xlsx*. Numbers are reported as rounded values for clarity but are calculated using *Excel*'s full precision. Thus, intermediate calculations using the figure's rounded values will be inexact.

were then plotted to make the graph. Figure 11-3 shows that, as unit sales and the sales price are increased, the project's NPV increases; in contrast, increases in variable costs, nonvariable costs, and equipment costs reduce the project's NPV. The slopes of the lines in the graph and the ranges in the table below the graph indicate how sensitive NPV is to each input: *The larger the range, the steeper the variable's slope, and the more sensitive the NPV is to this variable.* We see that NPV is extremely sensitive to changes in the sales price, fairly sensitive to changes in variable costs and units sold, but not especially sensitive to changes in the equipment's cost. Management should, of course, try especially hard to obtain accurate estimates of the variables that have the greatest impact on the NPV.

If we were comparing two projects, then the one with the steeper sensitivity lines would be riskier (other things held constant), because relatively small changes in the input variables would produce large changes in the NPV. Thus, sensitivity analysis provides useful insights into a project's risk. Note, however, that even though NPV may be highly sensitive to certain variables, if those variables are not likely to change much from their expected values, then the project may not be very risky in spite of its high sensitivity. Also, if several of the inputs change at the same time, the combined effect on NPV can be much greater than sensitivity analysis suggests.

11-5b Tornado Diagrams

Tornado diagrams are another way to present results from sensitivity analysis. The first steps are to calculate the range of possible NPVs for each of the input variables being changed and then rank these ranges. In our example, the range for sales price per unit is the largest and the range for equipment cost is the smallest. The ranges for each variable are then plotted, with the largest range on top and the smallest range on the bottom. It is also helpful to plot a vertical line showing the base-case NPV. We present a tornado diagram in Figure 11-4. Notice that the diagram is widest at the top and smallest at the

resource

See *Ch11 Tool Kit.xlsx* on the textbook's Web site.

FIGURE 11-4

Tornado Diagram for Solar Water Heater Project: Range of Outcomes for Input Deviations from Base Case (Thousands of Dollars)

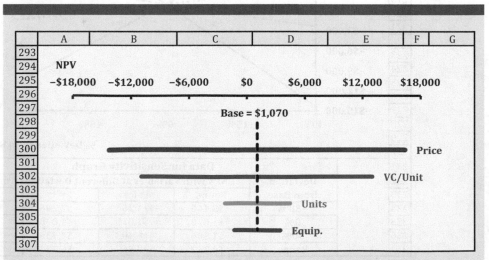

Source: See the file *Ch11 Tool Kit.xlsx*. Numbers are reported as rounded values for clarity but are calculated using *Excel*'s full precision. Thus, intermediate calculations using the figure's rounded values will be inexact.

resource

See *Ch11 Tool Kit.xlsx* on
the textbook's Web site.

TABLE 11-1

NPV Break-Even Analysis (Thousands of Dollars)

Input	Input Value That Produces Zero NPV (All Else Held Constant)
Equipment	$11,351
Units sold, Year 1	9,047
Sales price per unit, Year 1	$1.958
Variable cost per unit (VC), Year 1	$1.602
Nonvariable cost (Non-VC), Year 1	$1,539
Project WACC	14.47%

bottom, resembling a tornado. The tornado diagram makes it immediately obvious which inputs have the greatest impact on NPV—sales price and variable costs, in this case.

11-5c NPV Break-Even Analysis

A special application of sensitivity analysis is called NPV **break-even analysis**. In break-even analysis, we find the level of an input that produces an NPV of exactly zero. We used *Excel*'s Goal Seek feature to do this. See *Ch11 Tool Kit.xlsx* on the textbook's Web site for an explanation of how to use this *Excel* feature.

Table 11-1 shows the values of the inputs discussed previously that produce a zero NPV. For example, the number of units sold in Year 1 can drop to 9,047 before the project's NPV falls to zero. Break-even analysis is helpful in determining how bad things can get before the project has a negative NPV.

11-5d Extensions of Sensitivity Analysis

In our examples, we showed how one output, NPV, varied with a change in a single input. Sensitivity analysis can easily be extended to show how multiple outputs, such as NPV and IRR, vary with a change in an input. See *Ch11 Tool Kit.xlsx* on the textbook's Web site for an example showing how to use *Excel*'s Data Table feature to present multiple outputs.

It is also possible to use a Data Table to show how a single output, such as NPV, varies for changes in two inputs, such as the number of units sold and the sales price per unit. See *Ch11 Tool Kit.xlsx* on the textbook's Web site for an example of this Two-Dimensional Data Table. However, when we examine the impact of a change in more than one input, we usually use scenario analysis, which is described in the following section.

SELF-TEST

What is sensitivity analysis?

Briefly explain the usefulness of a sensitivity graph.

Discuss the following statement: "A project may not be very risky in spite of its high sensitivity to certain variables."

11-6 Scenario Analysis

In the sensitivity analysis just described, we changed one variable at a time. However, it is useful to know what would happen to the project's NPV if several of the inputs turn out to be better or worse than expected, and this is what we do in a **scenario analysis**. Also, scenario analysis allows us to assign probabilities to the base (or most likely) case, the best case, and the worst case; then we can find the *expected value and standard deviation* of the project's NPV to get a better idea of the project's risk.

In a scenario analysis, we begin with the base-case scenario, which uses the most likely value for each input variable. We then ask marketing, engineering, and other operating managers to specify a worst-case scenario (low unit sales, low sales price, high variable costs, and so on) and a best-case scenario. Often, the best and worst cases are defined as having a 25% probability of occurring, with a 50% probability for the base-case conditions. Obviously, conditions could take on many more than three values, but such a scenario setup is useful to help get some idea of the project's riskiness.

After much discussion with the marketing staff, engineers, accountants, and other experts in the company, a set of worst-case and best-case values were determined for several key inputs. Figure 11-5, taken from worksheet *3a-Scen* of the chapter *Tool Kit* model,

resource

See *Ch11 Tool Kit.xlsx* on the textbook's Web site.

FIGURE 11-5
Inputs and Key Results for Each Scenario (Thousands of Dollars)

	A	B	C	D	E	F	G
34						**Scenarios:**	
35	**Scenario Name**				**Worst-Case**	**Base-Case**	**Best-Case**
36	**Probability of Scenario**				25%	50%	25%
37	**Inputs:**						
38	**Equipment cost**				$11,000	$10,000	$9,000
39	**Salvage value of equip. in Year 4**				$1,000	$1,000	$1,000
40	**Opportunity cost**				$0	$0	$0
41	**Externalities (cannibalization)**				$0	$0	$0
42	**Units sold, Year 1**				$8,500	$10,000	$11,500
43	**Units sold, Year 2, Pct. change from Year 1**				20%	20%	20%
44	**Units sold, Year 3, Pct. change from Year 1**				20%	20%	20%
45	**Units sold, Year 4, Pct. change from Year 1**				-30%	-30%	-30%
46	**Sales price per unit, Year 1**				$1.80	$2.00	$2.20
47	**%Δ in sales price, after Year 1**				3%	4%	5%
48	**Var. cost per unit (VC), Year 1**				$1.72	$1.56	$1.40
49	**%Δ in VC, after Year 1**				4%	3%	2%
50	**Nonvar. cost (Non-VC), Year 1**				$941	$1,107	$1,273
51	**%Δ in Non-VC, after Year 1**				3%	3%	3%
52	**Project WACC**				10%	10%	10%
53	**Tax rate**				25%	25%	25%
54	**NOWC as % of next year's sales**				10%	10%	10%
55	**Key Results:**						
56				NPV	-$9,795	$1,070	$15,073
57				IRR	-32.6%	13.8%	57.5%
58				MIRR	-24.8%	12.4%	35.6%
59			Profitability index		0.22	1.09	2.31
60				Payback	Not found	2.94	1.61
61			Discounted payback		Not found	3.65	1.81

Source: See the file *Ch11 Tool Kit.xlsx*. Numbers are reported as rounded values for clarity but are calculated using *Excel*'s full precision. Thus, intermediate calculations using the figure's rounded values will be inexact.

Note:

The rows with red font indicate the variables that are changing in the scenarios.

shows the probability and inputs assumed for the base-case, worst-case, and best-case scenarios, along with selected key results.

The project's cash flows and performance measures under each scenario are calculated; see the worksheet *3a-Scen* in the *Tool Kit* for the calculations. The cash flows for each scenario are shown in Figure 11-6, along with a probability distribution of the possible outcomes for NPV. If the project is highly successful, then a low initial investment, high sales price, high unit sales, and low production costs would combine to result in a very high NPV, $15,073. However, if things turn out badly, then the NPV would be a *negative* $9,795. This wide range of possibilities, and especially the large potential negative value, suggests that this is a risky project. If bad conditions materialize, the project will not bankrupt the company—this is just one project for a large company. Still, losing $9,795 (actually $9,795,000, as the units are thousands of dollars) would certainly hurt the company's value and the reputation of the project's manager.

resource

See *Ch11 Tool Kit.xlsx* on the textbook's Web site.

FIGURE 11-6

Scenario Analysis: Expected NPV and Its Risk (Thousands of Dollars)

	A	B	C	D	E	F	G	H	I
103			**Predicted Cash Flows for Alternative Scenarios**						
104		**Prob:**	**0**	**1**	**2**	**3**	**4**	**WACC**	**NPV**
105	Best →	25%	−$11,530	$6,037	$8,986	$10,646	$8,330	10.00%	$15,073
106									
107	① → Base→	50%	−$12,000	$2,807	$4,415	$5,084	$4,464	10.00%	$1,070
108									
109	Worst →	25%	−$12,530	$360	$938	$813	$1,496	10.00%	−$9,795
110							Expected NPV =		$1,854
111							Standard Deviation (SD) =		$8,827
112				Coefficient of Variation (CV) = Std. Dev./Expected NPV =					4.76
113									
114									
115		**Probability Distribution of Scenarios:**							
116		**Outcomes and Probabilities**							

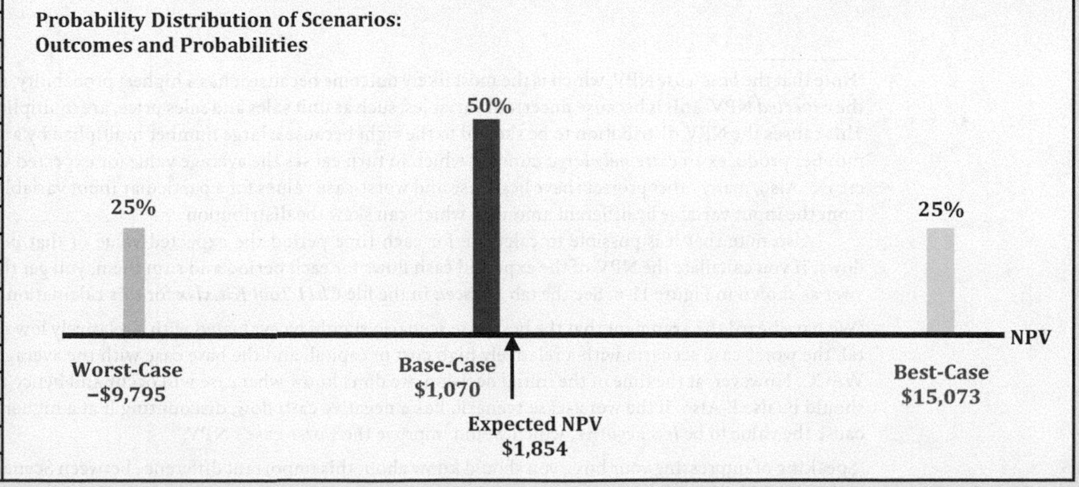

Source: See the file *Ch11 Tool Kit.xlsx.* Numbers are reported as rounded values for clarity but are calculated using *Excel*'s full precision. Thus, intermediate calculations using the figure's rounded values will be inexact.

If we multiply each scenario's probability by the NPV for that scenario and then sum the products, we will have the project's expected NPV of $1,854, as shown in Figure 11-6.[6] We also calculate the standard deviation of the expected NPV; it is $8,827. Dividing the standard deviation by the expected NPV yields the **coefficient of variation**, 4.76, which is a measure of stand-alone risk. The coefficient of variation measures the amount of risk per dollar of NPV, so the coefficient of variation can be helpful when comparing the risk of projects with different NPVs. GPC's average project has a coefficient of variation of about 2.5, so the 4.76 CV indicates that this project is riskier than most of GPC's other typical projects.

GPC's corporate WACC is 9%, so that rate should be used to find the NPV of an average-risk project. However, the water heater project is riskier than GPC's average project, which is why GPC is evaluating the project with a 10% project cost of capital.[7]

Note that the base-case results are the same in our sensitivity and scenario analyses, but in the scenario analysis the worst case is much worse than in the sensitivity analysis and the best case is much better. This is because in scenario analysis all of the variables are set at their best or worst levels, whereas in sensitivity analysis only one variable is adjusted and all the others are left at their base-case levels.

It might be helpful to examine more scenarios, especially ones in which some inputs improve and some get worse, which is more realistic than the previous scenarios. However, it becomes cumbersome to manage more than a couple of scenarios if you create a separate model for each scenario, as we did in the worksheet *3a-Scen*. Fortunately, the analysis can be simplified and automated by using *Excel*'s Scenario Manager to keep track of multiple scenarios. See the worksheet *3b-ScenMgr* in the *Tool Kit* for an explanation of how to use the Summary feature in *Excel*'s Scenario Manager. If you master it, you certainly will be able to impress your boss![8]

Even with Scenario Manager, two problems arise. First, it is relatively easy to determine best-case and worst-case scenarios, but how can managers choose the inputs for a large number of scenarios? Second, it quickly becomes tedious to add a large number of scenarios. Simulation analysis can solve these problems, as we explain in the next section.

---

[6]Note that the *base-case* NPV, which is the most likely outcome because it has a highest probability, differs from the *expected* NPV. This is because uncertain variables, such as unit sales and sales price, are multiplied together. This causes the NPV distribution to be skewed to the right because a large number multiplied by another large number produces an *extremely large* number, which in turn causes the average value (or expected value) to increase. Also, many other projects have best-case and worst-case values for a particular input variable that differ from the input variable by different amounts, which can skew the distribution.

   Also note that it is possible to calculate for each time period the expected value of that period's cash flows. If you calculate the NPV of the expected cash flows for each period and sum them, you get the same answer as shown in Figure 11-6. See the tab *3a-Scen* in the file *Ch11 Tool Kit.xlsx* for this calculation.

[7]We have heard the argument that the best-case scenario should be evaluated with a relatively low cost of capital, the worst-case scenario with a relatively high cost of capital, and the base case with the average corporate WACC. However, at the time of the initial decision, we don't know what case will occur and hence a single rate should be used. Also, if the worst-case scenario has a negative cash flow, discounting it at a higher rate would cause the value to be *less negative*, which would improve the worst-case's NPV.

[8]Speaking of impressing your boss, you should know about this important difference between Scenario Manger and Data Tables if you want to keep your job. Data Tables are dynamic in that, if you change your model, the Data Table will automatically update with new values. Scenario Manager, on the other hand, is static! Once you run Scenario Manager and create a Scenario Summary, that Summary is set in stone. Its values won't change if you change your model. If you want the Scenario Summary to reflect changes you make in your model, you have to run it again and create a new Scenario Summary! Don't show your boss a Scenario Summary that has old data in it if you have changed your model!

What is scenario analysis?

Differentiate between sensitivity analysis and scenario analysis. What advantage does scenario analysis have over sensitivity analysis?

11-7 Monte Carlo Simulation Analysis[9]

Monte Carlo simulation analysis ties together sensitivities, probability distributions, and correlations among the input variables. It grew out of work in the Manhattan Project to build the first atomic bomb and was so named because it utilized the mathematics of casino gambling. Although Monte Carlo simulation is considerably more complex than scenario analysis, simulation software packages make the process manageable. Many of these packages can be used as add-ins to *Excel* and other spreadsheet programs.

In a simulation analysis, a probability distribution is assigned to each input variable—sales in units, the sales price, the variable cost per unit, and so on. The computer begins by picking a random value for each variable from its probability distribution. Those values are then entered into the model, the project's NPV is calculated, and the NPV is stored in the computer's memory. This is called a trial. After completing the first trial, a second set of input values is selected from the input variables' probability distributions, and a second NPV is calculated. This process is repeated many times. The NPVs from the trials can be charted on a histogram, which shows an estimate of the project's outcomes. The average of the trials' NPVs is interpreted as a measure of the project's expected NPV, with the standard deviation (or the coefficient of variation) of the trials' NPV as a measure of the project's risk.

Using this procedure, we conducted a simulation analysis of GPC's solar water heater project. To compare apples and apples, we focused on the same seven variables that were allowed to change in the previously conducted scenario analysis. We assumed that each variable can be represented by its own continuous normal distribution with means and standard deviations that are consistent with the base-case scenario. For example, we assumed that the units sold in Year 1 come from a normal distribution with a mean equal to the base-case value of 10,000. We used the probabilities and outcomes of the three scenarios from Section 11-6 to estimate the standard deviation (all calculations are in the *Tool Kit*). The standard deviation of units sold in Year 1 is 1,061, as calculated using the scenario values. We made similar assumptions for all variables. In addition, we assumed that the annual change in unit sales will be positively correlated with unit sales in the first year: If demand is higher than expected in the first year, GPC will be able to increase prices by greater amounts in subsequent years. In particular, we assume a correlation of 0.6 between units sold in the first year and growth in units sold in later years. For all other variables, we assumed zero correlation. Figure 11-7 shows the inputs used in the simulation analysis.

Figure 11-7 also shows the current set of random variables that were drawn from the distributions at the time we created the figure for the textbook—you will see different values for the key results when you look at the *Excel* model because the values are updated every time the file is opened. We used a two-step procedure to create the random variables for the inputs. First, we used *Excel*'s RAND and NORM.S.INV functions to generate standard normal random variables with a mean of 0 and a standard deviation of 1; these are shown in Cells E54:E66.[10] To create the random values for the inputs used in the analysis, we multiplied a random standard normal variable by the standard deviation and added

[9]This section is relatively technical, and some instructors may choose to skip it with no loss in continuity.

[10] See the *Tool Kit* for detailed explanations on using *Excel to* generate random variables.

FIGURE 11-7
Inputs and Key Results for the Current Simulation Trial (Thousands of Dollars)

	A	B	C	D	E	F
49			**Inputs for Simulation**		**Random Variables Used in**	
50			**Probability Distributions**		**Current Simulation Trial**	
51				**Standard**	**Standard**	
52			**Expected**	**Deviation of**	**Normal**	**Value Used in**
53			**Value of Input**	**Input**	**Random**	**Current Trial**
54	Equipment cost		$10,000	$707	−1.034	$9,269
55	Salvage value of equip. in Year 4		—	—		$1,000
56	Opportunity cost		—	—		$0
57	Externalities (cannibalization)		—	—		$0
58	Units sold, Year 1		10,000	1,061	1.378	11,461
59	Units sold, Year 2		—	—		13,754
60	Units sold, Year 3		—	—		13,754
61	Units sold, Year 4		—	—		8,023
62	Sales price per unit, Year 1		$2.00	$0.14	0.065	$2.01
63	%Δ in sales price, after Year 1		4.00%	0.71%	0.903	4.64%
64	Var. cost per unit (VC), Year 1		$1.56	$0.11	0.220	$1.58
65	%Δ in VC, after Year 1		3.00%	0.71%	69.95%	3.49%
66	Nonvar. cost (Non-VC), Year 1		$1,107	$117	0.879	$1,210.16
67	%Δ in Non-VC, after Year 1		—	—		3%
68	Project WACC		—	—		10.00%
69	Tax rate		—	—		25.00%
70	NOWC as % of next year's sales		—	—		15.00%
71	Assumed correlation between units sold in					
72	Year 1 and annual change in units sold in					
73	later years:		ρ = 0.60			
74	**Key Results Based on Current Trial**					
75		NPV	$2,358			
76		IRR	17.25%			
77		MIRR	14.78%			
78		PI	1.19			
79		Payback	2.86			
80		Discounted payback	$3.36			

Source: See the file *Ch11 Tool Kit.xlsx*. Numbers are reported as rounded values for clarity but are calculated using *Excel*'s full precision. Thus, intermediate calculations using the figure's rounded values will be inexact.

resource

See *Ch11 Tool Kit.xlsx* on the textbook's Web site.

the expected value. For example, *Excel* drew the value for first-year unit sales (Cell E58) from a standard normal distribution. We calculated the value for first-year unit sales to use in the current trial as 10,000 + 1,061(1.378) = 11,462. If there is no rounding in intermediate steps, the actual value is 11,461, which is shown in Cell F58.[11]

We used the inputs in Cells F54:F70 to generate cash flows and to calculate performance measures for the project (the calculations are in the *Tool Kit*). For the trial reported in Figure 11-7, the NPV is $2,358. We used a Data Table in the *Tool Kit* to generate additional trials. For each trial, the Data Table saved the value of the input variables and the value of the trial's NPV. Figure 11-8 presents selected results from the simulation for 10,000 trials. (The worksheet *4a-Sim100* in the *Tool Kit* shows only 100 trials; the worksheet

---

[11] There may be slight rounding differences because *Excel* doesn't round in intermediate steps. We used a slightly more complicated procedure to generate a random variable for the annual change in sales to ensure that the annual percentage change in sales has 0.65 correlation with the first-year units sold. See the *Tool Kit* for details.

4b-Sim10000 has the ability to perform 10,000 simulations, but we have turned off the Data Table in that worksheet because simulating 10,000 trials reduces *Excel*'s speed when performing other calculations in the file.)

After running a simulation, the first thing we do is verify that the results are consistent with our assumptions. The resulting sample mean and standard deviation of units sold in the first year are 10,017 and 1,059, which are virtually identical to our assumptions in Figure 11-7. The same is true for all the other inputs, so we can be reasonably confident that the simulation is doing what we are asking.

Figure 11-8 also reports summary statistics for the project's NPV. The mean is $783, which suggests that the project should be accepted. However, the range of outcomes is quite large, from a loss of $17,427 to a gain of $20,373, so the project is clearly risky. The standard deviation of $4,959 indicates that losses could easily occur, which is consistent

resource

See Ch11 Tool Kit.xlsx on the textbook's Web site.

FIGURE 11-8
Summary of Simulation Results (Thousands of Dollars)

	A	B	C	D	E	F	G	H	I
154	**Number of Trials:**	**10,000**				**Input Variables**			
155					**Sales**		**Var. cost**	**% Δ in**	**Nonvar.**
156					**price per**	**% Δ in sales**	**per unit**	**VC,**	**cost (Non-**
157	**Summary Statistics for**		**Equip-**	**Units sold,**	**unit,**	**price, after**	**(VC),**	**after**	**VC),**
158	**Simulated Input Variables**		**ment cost**	**Year 1**	**Year 1**	**Year 1**	**Year 1**	**Year 1**	**Year 1**
159	**Average**		$9,990	10,017	$2.00	4.0%	$1.56	3.0%	$1,107
160	**Standard deviation**		$704	1,059	$0.14	0.7%	$0.11	0.7%	$118
161	**Maximum**		$12,958	14,754	$2.52	6.6%	$2.00	5.4%	$1,560
162	**Minimum**		$7,284	5,889	$1.46	1.6%	$1.17	0.0%	$629
163	**Correlation with unit sales**					0.60			
164	**Summary Statistics for**								
165	**Simulated Results**		**NPV**						
166	**Average**		$783						
167	**Standard deviation**		$4,959						
168	**Maximum**		$20,373						
169	**Minimum**		−$17,427						
170	**Median**		$636						
171	**Probability of NPV > 0**		55.1%						
172	**Coefficient of variation**		6.34						

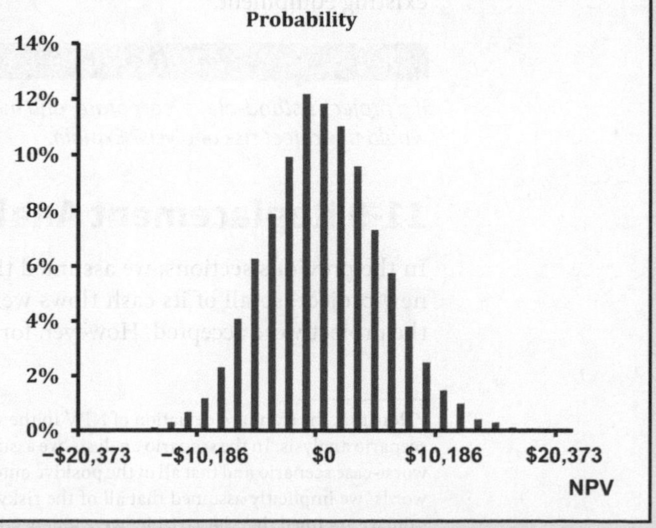

Source: See the file **Ch11 Tool Kit.xlsx**. Numbers are reported as rounded values for clarity but are calculated using *Excel*'s full precision. Thus, intermediate calculations using the figure's rounded values will be inexact.

with this wide range of possible outcomes.[12] Figure 11-8 also reports a median NPV of $636, which means that half the time the project will have an NPV of less than $636. In fact, there is only a 55.1% probability that the project will have a positive NPV.

A picture is worth a thousand words, and Figure 11-8 shows the probability distribution of the outcomes. Note that the distribution of outcomes is slightly skewed to the right. As the figure shows, the potential downside losses are not as large as the potential upside gains. Our conclusion is that this is a very risky project, as indicated by the coefficient of variation, but it does have a positive expected NPV and the potential to be a "home run."

SELF-TEST

What is Monte Carlo simulation?

11-8 Project Risk Conclusions

After conducting a risk analysis using quantitative measures, we can generally say with a fair degree of confidence that a particular project has more, less, or about the same stand-alone risk as the firm's average project. Because stand-alone risk and corporate risk usually are correlated, the project's stand-alone risk is a reasonably good measure of its corporate risk. Similarly, corporate risk and market risk usually are correlated, which means that a company's market risk usually is correlated with its projects' stand-alone risks. Therefore, risk analysis is very helpful to managers when deciding to accept or reject a potential project.

Always remember that it is important to consider qualitative factors in addition to the quantitative project analysis. Sometimes important factors are impossible to quantify, but managers must include them when deciding to accept or reject a potential project. This is especially true if a project's stand-alone risk might not be highly correlated with market risk.

If GPC decides to go ahead with the project, senior management should also identify possible contingency plans for responding to changes in market conditions. We discuss this in Sections 11-10 and 11-11, but now we explain how to evaluate the decision to replace existing equipment.

SELF-TEST

If a project's stand-alone, corporate, and market risk are known to be highly correlated, how would this affect risk analysis? Explain.

11-9 Replacement Analysis

In the previous sections, we assumed that the solar water heater project was an entirely new project, so all of its cash flows were incremental—they would occur if and only if the project were accepted. However, for replacement projects we must find the cash flow

---

[12]Note that the standard deviation of NPV in the simulation is much smaller than the standard deviation in the scenario analysis. In the scenario analysis, we assumed that all of the poor outcomes would occur together in the worst-case scenario and that all of the positive outcomes would occur together in the best-case scenario. In other words, we implicitly assumed that all of the risky variables were perfectly positively correlated. In the simulation, we assumed that the variables were independent (except for the correlation between unit sales and growth). The independence of variables in the simulation reduces the range of outcomes. For example, in the simulation, sometimes the sales price is high but the sales growth is low. In the scenario analysis, a high sales price is always coupled with high growth. Because the scenario analysis assumption of perfect correlation is unlikely, simulation may provide a better estimate of project risk. However, if the standard deviations and correlations used as inputs in the simulation are inaccurately estimated, then the simulation output will likewise be inaccurate.

differentials between the new and old projects, and these differentials are the *incremental cash flows* that we must analyze.

We evaluate a replacement decision in Figure 11-9, which is set up much like Figures 11-1 and 11-2 but with data on both a new, highly efficient machine and data on the old machine; see the worksheet *5-Replmt* in the *Tool Kit.* In Part 1 we show the key inputs in the analysis, including depreciation on the new and old machines. In Part 2 we find the cash flows the firm will have if it continues to use the old machine, and in Part 3 we find the cash flows if the firm replaces the old machine. Then, in Part 4, we subtract the old

resource

See *Ch11 Tool Kit.xlsx* on
the textbook's Web site.

FIGURE 11-9
Replacement Analysis

	A	B	C	D	E	F	G	H	I
15	Part 1. Inputs:					Applies to:			
16					Both	Old	New		
17					Machines	Machine	Machine		
18	Cost of new machine						$2,000		
19	After-tax salvage value old machine					$400			
20	Sales revenues (fixed)				$2,500				
21	Annual operating costs except depr.					$1,000	$280		
22	Tax rate				25%				
23	WACC				10%				
24	Depreciation			1	2	3	4	Totals:	
25	Depr. rates (new machine)			33.33%	44.45%	14.81%	7.41%	100%	
26	Depreciation on new machine			$666.60	$889.00	$296.20	$148.20	$2,000	
27	Depreciation on old machine			$267	$133	$0	$0	$400	
28	Part 2. Cash Flows before Replacement: Old Machine								
29					0	1	2	3	4
30	Sales revenues					$2,500	$2,500	$2,500	$2,500
31	Operating costs except depreciation					1,000	1,000	1,000	1,000
32	Depreciation					267	133	0	0
33	Total operating costs					$1,267	$1,133	$1,000	$1,000
34	Operating income					$1,233	$1,367	$1,500	$1,500
35	Taxes (25%)					308	342	375	375
36	After-tax operating income					$925	$1,025	$1,125	$1,125
37	Add back depreciation					267	133	0	0
38	Cash flows <u>before</u> replacement				$0	$1,192	$1,158	$1,125	$1,125
39	Part 3. Cash Flows after Replacement: New Machine								
40					0	1	2	3	4
41	New machine cost:				−$2,000				
42	After-tax salvage value, old machine				$400				
43	Sales revenues					$2,500	$2,500	$2,500	$2,500
44	Operating costs except depreciation					$280	$280	$280	$280
45	Depreciation					$667	$889	$296	$148
46	Total operating costs					$947	$1,169	$576	$428
47	Operating income					$1,553	$1,331	$1,924	$2,072
48	Taxes 25%					$388	$333	$481	$518
49	After-tax operating income					$1,165	$998	$1,443	$1,554
50	Add back depreciation					$667	$889	$296	$148
51	Cash flows <u>after</u> replacement				−$1,600	$1,832	$1,887	$1,739	$1,702
52	Part 4. Incremental CF: Row 51 − Row 38				−$1,600	$640	$729	$614	$577
53	Part 5. Evaluation			NPV =	$439.70	IRR =	22.45%	MIRR =	16.88%

Source: See the file *Ch11 Tool Kit.xlsx*. Numbers are reported as rounded values for clarity but are calculated using *Excel*'s full precision. Thus, intermediate calculations using the figure's rounded values will be inexact.

flows from the new to arrive at the *incremental cash flows,* and we evaluate those flows in Part 5 to find the NPV, IRR, and MIRR. Replacing the old machine appears to be a good decision.[13]

In some instances, replacements add capacity as well as lower operating costs. In this case, sales revenues in Part 3 would be increased, and if that leads to a need for more working capital, then this would be shown as a Time-0 expenditure along with a recovery at the end of the project's life. These changes would, of course, be reflected in the incremental cash flows on Row 52.

11-10 Phased Decisions and Decision Trees

Up to this point we have focused primarily on techniques for estimating a project's risk. Although this is an integral part of capital budgeting, managers are just as interested in *reducing* risk as in *measuring* it. One way to reduce risk is to structure projects so that expenditures can be made in stages over time rather than all at once. This gives managers the opportunity to reevaluate decisions using new information and then to either invest additional funds or terminate the project, as we explain next.

11-10a The Basic Decision Tree

GPC's analysis of the solar water heater project thus far has assumed that the project cannot be abandoned once it goes into operation, even if the worst-case situation arises. However, GPC is considering the possibility of terminating (abandoning) the project at Year 2 if the demand is low. The net after-tax cash flow from salvage, legal fees, liquidation of working capital, and all other termination costs and revenues is $6,000. Using these assumptions, GPC ran a new scenario analysis; the results are shown in Figure 11-10, which is a simple **decision tree**. It is called a decision tree because there are branches beginning at Year 0 (the three scenarios) and because managers can make a decision at a future time, which leads to additional branches based on that decision.

Here we assume that if the worst case materializes, then this will be recognized after the low Year-1 cash flow and GPC can abandon the project. Rather than continue to realize low cash flows in Years 2, 3, and 4, the company will shut down the operation and liquidate the project for $6,000 at t = 2. Now the expected NPV rises from $1,854 to $2,492, and the CV declines from 4.76 to 3.22. Securing the right to abandon the project if things don't work out raised the project's expected return and reduced its risk.

The right to abandon the project is a type of **real option** because it involves real cash flows and real assets instead of financial assets in contrast to the financial options in

[13]The same sort of risk analysis discussed in previous sections can be applied to replacement decisions.

FIGURE 11-10

Simple Decision Tree: Abandoning Project in Worst-Case Scenario

	A	B	C	D	E	F	G	H	I
123			Predicted Cash Flows for Alternative Scenarios						
124		**Prob:**	**0**	**1**	**2**	**3**	**4**	**WACC**	**NPV**
125	Best→	25%	−$11,530	$6,037	$8,986	$10,646	$8,330	10%	$15,073
126									
127	① →Base→	50%	−$12,000	$2,807	$4,415	$5,084	$4,464	10%	$1,070
128									
129			−$12,530	$360	$938	$813	$1,496		
130	Worst→	25%							
131			−$12,530	$360 ②	$6,000	$0	$0	10%	−$7,244
132	**If abandon project at t = 2, can liquidate for $6,000.**								
133							**Expected NPV =**		$2,492
134							**Standard Deviation (SD) =**		$8,017
135					**Coefficient of Variation (CV) = Std. Dev./Expected NPV =**				3.22

Source: See the file ***Ch11 Tool Kit.xlsx***. Numbers are reported as rounded values for clarity but are calculated using *Excel*'s full precision. Thus, intermediate calculations using the figure's rounded values will be inexact.

resource

See Ch11 Tool Kit.xlsx on the textbook's Web site.

Chapter 8.[14] The example in Figure 11-10 is a type of real option called an **abandonment option** because the company can abandon the project if demand is low. In general, opportunities for managers to respond to changing circumstances also are called **managerial options**, **strategic options** (because they are often associated with large, strategic projects rather than routine maintenance projects), and **embedded options** (because they are a part of the project).

The abandonment option in the decision tree reduced the project's risk, which might have changed the project's required return. A decision tree is a very useful tool to determine the approximate value for most projects, but it is less useful for large strategic decisions. For those situations, managers should treat the decision tree as a real option and use financial option pricing techniques to properly estimate the project's value.

11-10b Staged Decision Tree

After the management team thought about the decision-tree approach, other ideas for improving the project emerged. The marketing manager stated that he could undertake a study that would give the firm a better idea of demand for the product. If the marketing study found favorable responses to the product, the design engineer stated that she could build a prototype solar water heater to gauge consumer reactions to the actual product. After assessing consumer reactions, the company could either go ahead with the project or abandon it. This type of evaluation process is called a **staged decision tree** and is shown in Figure 11-11.

Decision trees such as the one in Figure 11-11 often are used to analyze multistage, or sequential, decisions. Each circle represents a decision point, also known as a **decision node**.

---

[14]For more on real option valuation, see M. Amram and N. Kulatilaka, *Real Options: Managing Strategic Investment in an Uncertain World* (Boston, MA: Harvard Business School Press, 1999); H. Smit and L. Trigeorgis, *Strategic Investments: Real Options and Games* (Princeton, NJ: Princeton University Press, 2004); and J. Mun, *Real Options Analysis, 3rd ed.* (Dublin, CA: Real Option Valuation, Inc., 2016).

FIGURE 11-11
Decision Tree with Multiple Decision Points

	A	B	C	D	E	F	G	H	I	J	K
154	Firm can abandon the project at t = 1 and at t =2.									WACC =	10%
155	Time Periods, Cash Flows, Probabilities, and Decision Points									WACC =	10%
156	0		1		2	3	4	5	6	WACC =	10%
157	1st Invest-ment	Prob.	2nd Invest-ment	Prob.	3rd Invest-ment	Inflow	Inflow	Inflow	Inflow	NPV	Joint Prob.
158											
159			↱	45%	−$11,530 ③	$6,037	$8,986	$10,646	$8,330	$11,902	36%
160			↑								
161	↱	80%	−$500 ② ⇥	40%	−$12,000 ③	$2,807	$4,415	$5,084	$4,464	$330	32%
162	↑		↓								
163	−$100 ①		↳	15%	Stop ③	$0	$0	$0	$0	−$555	12%
164	↓										
165	↳	20%	Stop ②			$0	$0	$0	$0	−$100	20%
166											100%
167								Expected NPV =		$4,304	
168							Standard Deviation (SD) =			$5,705	
169					Coefficient of Variation (CV) = Std. Dev./Expected NPV =					1.33	

Source: See the file *Ch11 Tool Kit.xlsx*. Numbers are reported as rounded values for clarity but are calculated using *Excel*'s full precision. Thus, intermediate calculations using the figure's rounded values will be inexact.

resource

See *Ch11 Tool Kit.xlsx* on the textbook's Web site.

The dollar value to the left of each decision node represents the cash flow at that point, and the cash flows shown under t = 3, 4, 5, and 6 represent the cash inflows if the project is pushed on to completion. Each diagonal line leads to a **branch of the decision tree**, and each branch has an estimated probability. For example, if the firm decides to "go" with the project at Decision Point 1, then it will spend $100,000 on the marketing study. Management estimates that there is a 0.8 probability that the study will produce *positive* results, leading to the decision to make an additional investment and thus move on to Decision Point 2. There is a 0.2 probability that the marketing study will produce *negative* results, indicating that the project should be canceled after Stage 1. If the project is canceled, the cost to the company will be the $100,000 spent on the initial marketing study.

If the marketing study yields positive results, then the firm will spend $500,000 on the prototype water heater module at Decision Point 2. Management estimates (even before making the initial $100,000 investment) that there is a 45% probability of the pilot project yielding good results, a 40% probability of average results, and a 15% probability of bad results. If the prototype yields good or average results, then the firm will invest more at Decision Point 3 to build a production plant, buy the necessary inventory, and commence operations; otherwise, it will abandon the project. The cash flows over the project's 4-year life will be good, average, or bad, and these cash flows are shown under Years 3 through 6.

The column of joint probabilities in Figure 11-11 gives the probability of occurrence of each branch—and hence of each NPV. Each joint probability is obtained by multiplying together all the probabilities on that particular branch. For example, the probability that the company will, if Stage 1 is undertaken, move through Stages 2 and 3, and that a strong demand will produce the indicated cash flows, is (0.8)(0.45) = 0.36 = 36.0%. There is a 32% probability of average results, a 12% probability of building the prototype and then abandoning it due to poor results, and a 20% probability of getting bad news from the marketing study and abandoning the project before building a prototype.

The NPV of the top (most favorable) branch as shown in Column J is $11,092, calculated as follows:

$$\text{NPV} = -\$100 - \frac{\$500}{(1.10)^1} - \frac{\$11,530}{(1.10)^2} + \frac{\$6,037}{(1.10)^3} + \frac{\$8,986}{(1.10)^4} + \frac{\$10,646}{(1.10)^5} + \frac{\$8,330}{(1.10)^6}$$

$$= \$11,902$$

The NPVs for the other branches are calculated similarly.[15]

The last column in Figure 11-11 shows the joint probability for each branch, which is the probability of reaching the end of that particular path. The expected NPV is calculated by multiplying each branch's NPV by its joint probability and then summing these products for all the branches. Based on the expectations used to create Figure 11-11 and a cost of capital of 10%, the project's expected NPV is $4,304, or $4.304 million.[16] In addition, the CV declines from 4.67 in the original decision tree to 1.33. The maximum losses are $100 at t = 0 and $500 at t = 2 and the present value of these losses is a manageable −$555. At this point, the solar water heater project looked good, and GPC's management decided to accept it.

This project incorporates two real options. Both are **investment timing options** because they allow GPC to delay large investments until additional information is available. Keep in mind, though, that the *option to delay* is valuable only if it more than offsets any harm that might result from delaying. For example, while one company delays, some other company might establish a loyal customer base that makes it difficult for the first company to enter the market later. The option to delay is usually the most valuable to firms with proprietary technology, patents, licenses, or other barriers to entry because these factors lessen the threat of competition. The option to delay is valuable when market demand is uncertain, but it is also valuable during periods of volatile interest rates because the ability to wait can allow firms to delay raising capital for a project until interest rates are lower.

Before we discuss other types of real options, note that decision-tree analysis requires managers to articulate explicitly the types of risk a project faces and to develop responses to potential scenarios. This process improves the qualitative analysis even before managers conduct a decision tree analysis. In addition, sequential options are hard to evaluate using financial option techniques, making decision trees an even more important technique for project evaluation.

SELF-TEST

What is a decision tree? A branch? A node?

If a firm can structure a project such that expenditures can be made in stages rather than all at the beginning, how would this affect the project's risk and expected NPV? Explain.

What are real options? What is an abandonment option? What is an investment timing option?

---

[15]The calculations in *Excel* use nonrounded annual cash flows, so there may be small differences when calculating by hand with rounded annual cash flows.

[16]As we mentioned previously when discussing the abandonment option, the presence of the real options in Figure 11-11 might cause the discount rate to change.

11-11 Other Real Options

In addition to the abandonment option and the investment timing option described in the previous section, there are several other important types of real options, including growth options and flexibility options.

11-11a Growth Options

A **growth option** allows a company to increase its capacity if market conditions are better than expected. There are several types of growth options. One lets a company *increase the capacity of an existing product line.* A "peaking unit" electric power plant illustrates this type of growth option. Such units are less expensive to build, can be started up quickly, but have high variable costs. They are used to produce additional power only if demand (and electricity prices) is high.

The second type of growth option allows a company to *expand into new geographic markets.* Many companies are investing in China, Eastern Europe, and Russia even though standard NPV analysis produces negative NPVs. However, if these developing markets really take off, the option to open more facilities could be quite valuable.

The third type of growth option is the opportunity to *add new products,* including complementary products and successive "generations" of the original product. For example, auto companies are losing money on their first electric autos, but the manufacturing skills and consumer recognition those cars will provide should help turn subsequent generations of electric autos into moneymakers.

11-11b Flexibility Options

Many projects offer **flexibility options** that permit the firm to alter operations depending on how conditions change during the life of the project. Typically, either inputs or outputs (or both) can be changed.

For example, many auto assembly plants are configured to switch production from one model to another, depending on demand. Building such a facility is more expensive, but the flexibility can really pay off if consumer tastes change.

Electric power plants provide an example of input flexibility. Utilities can build plants that generate electricity by burning coal, oil, or natural gas. Because these input costs are quite volatile, many power companies build more expensive but more flexible plants, especially ones that could switch from oil to gas and back again depending on relative fuel prices.

11-11c Valuing Real Options

A full treatment of real option valuation is beyond the scope of this chapter, but there are some things we can say. First, if a project has an embedded real option, then management should at least recognize and articulate its existence. Second, we know that a financial option is more valuable if it has a long time until maturity or if the underlying asset is very risky. If either of these characteristics applies to a project's real option, then management should know that its value is probably relatively high. Third, management might be able to model the real option along the lines of a decision tree, as we described in previous sections.

SELF-TEST

Identify some different types of real options and differentiate among them.

SUMMARY

In this chapter, we developed a framework for analyzing a project's cash flows and its risk. The key concepts covered are listed here.

- The most important (and most difficult) step in analyzing a capital budgeting project is estimating the after-tax **incremental cash flows** the project will produce.
- **Project cash flow** is different from its accounting income. Project cash flow reflects: (1) cash outlays for fixed assets, (2) sales revenues, (3) operating costs, (4) the tax shield provided by depreciation, and (5) cash flows due to changes in net working capital. A project's cash flow does *not* include interest payments, because they are accounted for by the discounting process. If we deducted interest and then discounted cash flows at the WACC, this would double-count interest charges.
- In determining incremental cash flows, **opportunity costs** (the cash flows forgone by using an asset) must be included, but **sunk costs** (cash outlays that have been made and that cannot be recouped) are not included. Any **externalities** (effects of a project on other parts of the firm) should also be reflected in the analysis. Externalities can be *positive* or *negative* and may be *environmental*.
- **Cannibalization** is an important type of externality that occurs when a new project leads to a reduction in sales of an existing product.
- The tax code affects cash flow analysis in two ways: (1) Taxes reduce cash flows. (2) Tax codes determine the depreciation expense that can be taken in each year.
- Price level changes (inflation or deflation) must be considered in project analysis. The best procedure is to build expected price changes into the cash flow estimates. Recognize that output prices and costs for a particular product can decline over time even though the overall economy is experiencing inflation.
- The chapter illustrates *expansion projects*, in which the investment generates new sales, and *replacement projects*, where the primary purpose of the investment is to operate more efficiently and thus reduce costs.
- We discuss three types of risk: **stand-alone risk**, **corporate risk** (or **within-firm risk**), and **market risk**. Stand-alone risk does not consider diversification at all; corporate risk considers risk among the firm's own assets; and market risk considers risk at the stockholder level, where stockholders' own diversification is considered.
- Risk is important because it affects the discount rate used in capital budgeting; in other words, a project's WACC depends on its risk.
- Assuming the CAPM holds true, **market risk** is the most important risk because (according to the CAPM) it is the risk that affects stock prices. However, usually *it is difficult to measure a project's market risk*.
- **Corporate risk** is important because it influences the firm's ability to use low-cost debt, to maintain smooth operations over time, and to avoid crises that might consume management's energy and disrupt its employees, customers, suppliers, and community. Also, a project's corporate risk is generally easier to measure than its market risk. Because corporate and market risks usually are generally correlated, corporate risk can often serve as a proxy for market risk.
- **Stand-alone risk** is easier to measure than either market or corporate risk. Also, most of a firm's projects' cash flows are correlated with one another, and the firm's total cash flows are correlated with those of most other firms. These correlations mean that a project's stand-alone risk generally can be used as a proxy for hard-to-measure market and corporate risk. As a result, most risk analysis in capital budgeting focuses on stand-alone risk.

- **Sensitivity analysis** is a technique that shows how much a project's NPV will change in response to a given change in an input variable, such as sales, when all other factors are held constant.
- **Scenario analysis** is a risk analysis technique in which the best- and worst-case NPVs are compared with the project's base-case NPV.
- **Monte Carlo simulation** is a risk analysis technique that uses a computer to simulate future events and thereby estimate a project's profitability and riskiness.
- The **risk-adjusted discount rate** (which is also called the **risk-adjusted cost of capital** and the **project cost of capital**) is the rate used to evaluate a particular project. It is based on the corporate WACC, a value that is increased for projects that are riskier than the firm's average project and decreased for less risky projects.
- A **decision tree** shows how different decisions during a project's life can affect its value.
- A **staged decision tree** divides the analysis into different phases. At each phase a decision is made either to proceed or to stop the project. These decisions are represented on the decision trees by circles and are called **decision nodes**.
- Opportunities to respond to changing circumstances are called **real options** or **managerial options** because they give managers the option to influence the returns on a project. They are also called **strategic options** if they are associated with large, strategic projects rather than routine maintenance projects. Finally, they are also called "real" options because they involve "real" (or "physical") rather than "financial" assets. Many projects include a variety of these **embedded options** that can dramatically affect the true NPV.
- An **investment timing option** involves the possibility of delaying major expenditures until more information on likely outcomes is known. The opportunity to delay can dramatically change a project's estimated value.
- A **growth option** occurs if an investment creates the opportunity to make other potentially profitable investments that would not otherwise be possible. These include (1) options to expand the original project's output, (2) options to enter a new geographical market, and (3) options to introduce complementary products or successive generations of products.
- An **abandonment option** is the ability to discontinue a project if the cash flow turns out to be lower than expected. It reduces the risk of a project and increases its value. Instead of total abandonment, some options allow a company to reduce capacity or temporarily suspend operations.
- A **flexibility option** is the option to modify operations depending on how conditions develop during a project's life, especially the type of output produced or the inputs used.

QUESTIONS

(11-1)   Define each of the following terms:
   a. Project cash flow; accounting income
   b. Incremental cash flow; sunk cost; opportunity cost; externality; cannibalization; expansion project; replacement project
   c. Net operating working capital changes; salvage value
   d. Stand-alone risk; corporate (within-firm) risk; market (beta) risk

    e. Sensitivity analysis; scenario analysis; Monte Carlo simulation analysis

    f. Risk-adjusted discount rate; project cost of capital

    g. Decision tree; staged decision tree; decision node; branch

    h. Real options; managerial options; strategic options; embedded options

    i. Investment timing option; growth option; abandonment option; flexibility option

(11-2)   Cash flows, rather than accounting profits, are used in project analysis. What is the basis for this emphasis on cash flows as opposed to net income?

(11-3)   Why is it true, in general, that a failure to adjust expected cash flows for expected inflation biases the calculated NPV downward?

(11-4)   Explain why sunk costs should not be included in a capital budgeting analysis but opportunity costs and externalities should be included.

(11-5)   Explain how net operating working capital is recovered at the end of a project's life and why it is included in a capital budgeting analysis.

(11-6)   How do simulation analysis and scenario analysis differ in the way they treat very bad and very good outcomes? What does this imply about using each technique to evaluate project riskiness?

(11-7)   Why are interest charges not deducted when a project's cash flows are calculated for use in a capital budgeting analysis?

(11-8)   Most firms generate cash inflows every day, not just once at the end of the year. In capital budgeting, should we recognize this fact by estimating daily project cash flows and then using them in the analysis? If we do not, will this bias our results? If it does, would the NPV be biased up or down? Explain.

(11-9)   What are some differences in the analysis for a replacement project versus that for a new expansion project?

(11-10)   Distinguish among beta (or market) risk, within-firm (or corporate) risk, and stand-alone risk for a project being considered for inclusion in a firm's capital budget.

(11-11)   In theory, market risk should be the only "relevant" risk. However, companies focus as much on stand-alone risk as on market risk. What are the reasons for the focus on stand-alone risk?

SELF-TEST PROBLEMS   SOLUTIONS SHOWN IN APPENDIX A

(ST-1)
New-Project
Analysis

You have been asked by the president of the Farr Construction Company to evaluate the proposed acquisition of a new earth mover. The mover's basic price is $50,000, and it would cost another $10,000 to modify it for special use. Assume that the mover falls into the MACRS 3-year class (see Appendix 11A), that it would be sold after 3 years for $20,000, and that it would require an increase in net working capital (spare parts inventory) of $2,000 at the start of the project. This working capital will be recovered at Year 3. The earth mover would have no effect on revenues, but it is expected to save the firm $20,000 per year in before-tax operating costs, mainly labor. The firm's marginal federal-plus-state tax rate is 25%.

    a. What are the Year-0 cash flows?

    b. What are the operating cash flows in Years 1, 2, and 3?

    c. What are the additional (nonoperating) cash flows in Year 3?

    d. If the project's cost of capital is 10%, should the earth mover be purchased?

(ST-2)
Corporate Risk
Analysis

The staff of Porter Manufacturing has estimated the following net after-tax cash flows and probabilities for a new manufacturing process:

	Net After-Tax Cash Flows		
Year	P = 0.2	P = 0.6	P = 0.2
0	−$100,000	−$100,000	−$100,000
1	20,000	30,000	40,000
2	20,000	30,000	40,000
3	20,000	30,000	40,000
4	20,000	30,000	40,000
5	20,000	30,000	40,000
5*	0	20,000	30,000

Line 0 gives the cost of the process, Lines 1 through 5 give operating cash flows, and Line 5* contains the estimated salvage values. Porter's cost of capital for an average-risk project is 10%.

a. Assume that the project has average risk. Find the project's expected NPV. (*Hint:* Use expected values for the project cash flow in each year.)

b. Find the best-case and worst-case NPVs. What is the probability of occurrence of the worst case if the cash flows are perfectly dependent (perfectly positively correlated) over time? If they are independent over time?

c. Assume that all the cash flows are perfectly positively correlated. That is, assume there are only three possible cash flow streams over time—the worst case, the most likely (or base) case, and the best case—with respective probabilities of 0.2, 0.6, and 0.2. These cases are represented by each of the columns in the table. Find the expected NPV, its standard deviation, and its coefficient of variation.

PROBLEMS ANSWERS ARE IN APPENDIX B

EASY PROBLEMS 1–4

(11-1)
Investment Outlay

Talbot Industries is considering launching a new product. The new manufacturing equipment will cost $17 million, and production and sales will require an initial $5 million investment in net operating working capital. The company's tax rate is 25%.

a. What is the initial investment outlay?

b. The company spent and expensed $150,000 on research related to the new product last year. What is the initial investment outlay?

c. Rather than build a new manufacturing facility, the company plans to install the equipment in a building it owns but is not now using. The building could be sold for $1.5 million after taxes and real estate commissions. What is the initial investment outlay?

(11-2)
Project Cash Flow

The financial staff of Cairn Communications has identified the following information for the first year of the roll-out of its new proposed service:

Projected sales	$18 million
Operating costs (not including depreciation)	$9 million
Depreciation	$4 million
Interest expense	$3 million

The company faces a 25% tax rate. What is the project's cash flow for the first year (t = 1)?

(11-3)
Net Salvage Value

Allen Air Lines must liquidate some equipment that is being replaced. The equipment originally cost $12 million, of which 75% has been depreciated. The salvage value is $4 million. The federal-plus-state tax rate is 25%. What is the equipment's after-tax net salvage value of $4 million?

(11-4)
Replacement Analysis

Although the Chen Company's milling machine is old, it is still in relatively good working order and would last for another 10 years. It is inefficient compared to modern standards, though, and so the company is considering replacing it. The new milling machine, at a cost of $110,000 delivered and installed, would also last for 10 years and would produce after-tax cash flows (labor savings and depreciation tax savings) of $19,000 per year. It would have zero salvage value at the end of its life. The project cost of capital is 10%, and its marginal tax rate is 25%. Should Chen buy the new machine?

INTERMEDIATE PROBLEMS 5–10

(11-5)
Depreciation Methods

Wendy's boss wants to use straight-line depreciation for the new expansion project because he said it will give higher net income in earlier years and give him a larger bonus. The project will last 4 years and requires $1,700,000 of equipment. The company could use either straight line or the 3-year MACRS accelerated method. Under straight-line depreciation, the cost of the equipment would be depreciated evenly over its 4-year life. (Ignore the half-year convention for the straight-line method.) The applicable MACRS depreciation rates are 33.33%, 44.45%, 14.81%, and 7.41%, as discussed in Appendix 11A. The project cost of capital is 10%, and its tax rate is 25%.

a. What would the depreciation expense be each year under each method?
b. Which depreciation method would produce the higher NPV, and how much higher would it be?
c. Why might Wendy's boss prefer straight-line depreciation?

(11-6)
New-Project Analysis

The Campbell Company is considering adding a robotic paint sprayer to its production line. The sprayer's base price is $920,000, and it would cost another $20,000 to install it. The machine falls into the MACRS 3-year class, and it would be sold after 3 years for $500,000. The MACRS rates for the first three years are 0.3333, 0.4445, and 0.1481. The machine would require an increase in net working capital (inventory) of $15,500. The sprayer would not change revenues, but it is expected to save the firm $304,000 per year in before-tax operating costs, mainly labor. Campbell's marginal tax rate is 25%.

a. What is the Year-0 cash flow?
b. What are the cash flows in Years 1, 2, and 3?
c. What is the additional Year-3 cash flow (i.e., the after-tax salvage and the return of working capital)?
d. If the project's cost of capital is 12%, what is the NPV?

(11-7)
New-Project Analysis

The president of your company, MorChuck Enterprises, has asked you to evaluate the proposed acquisition of a new chromatograph for the firm's R&D department. The equipment's basic price is $70,000, and it would cost another $15,000 to modify it for special use by your firm. The chromatograph, which falls into the MACRS 3-year class, would be sold after 3 years for $30,000. The MACRS rates for the first three years are 0.3333, 0.4445, and 0.1481. Use of the equipment would require an increase in net working capital (spare parts inventory) of $4,000. The machine would have no effect on revenues, but it is expected to save the firm $25,000 per year in before-tax operating costs, mainly labor. The firm's marginal federal-plus-state tax rate is 25%.

a. What is the Year-0 cash flow?
b. What are the cash flows in Years 1, 2, and 3?
c. What is the additional (nonoperating) cash flow in Year 3?
d. If the project's cost of capital is 10%, should the chromatograph be purchased?

(11-8)
Inflation
Adjustments

The Rodriguez Company is considering an average-risk investment in a mineral water spring project that has an initial after-tax cost of $170,000. The project will produce 1,000 cases of mineral water per year indefinitely, starting at Year 1. The Year-1 sales price will be $138 per case, and the Year-1 cost per case will be $105. The firm is taxed at a rate of 25%. Both prices and costs are expected to rise after Year 1 at a rate of 6% per year due to inflation. The firm uses only equity, and it has a cost of capital of 15%. Assume that cash flows consist only of after-tax profits because the spring has an indefinite life and will not be depreciated.

   a. What is the present value of future cash flows? (*Hint:* The project is a growing perpetuity, so you must use the constant growth formula to find its NPV.) What is the NPV?

   b. Suppose that the company had forgotten to include future inflation. What would they have incorrectly calculated as the project's NPV?

(11-9)
Replacement
Analysis

The Gilbert Instrument Corporation is considering replacing the wood steamer it currently uses to shape guitar sides. The steamer has 6 years of remaining life. If kept, the steamer will have depreciation expenses of $650 for 5 years and $325 for the sixth year. Its current book value is $3,575, and it can be sold on an Internet auction site for $4,150 at this time. If the old steamer is not replaced, it can be sold for $800 at the end of its useful life.

Gilbert is considering purchasing the *Side Steamer 3000*, a higher-end steamer, which costs $12,000 and has an estimated useful life of 6 years with an estimated salvage value of $1,500. This steamer falls into the MACRS 5-year class, so the applicable depreciation rates are 20.00%, 32.00%, 19.20%, 11.52%, 11.52%, and 5.76%. The new steamer is faster and allows for an output expansion, so sales would rise by $2,000 per year; the new machine's much greater efficiency would reduce operating expenses by $1,900 per year. To support the greater sales, the new machine would require that inventories increase by $2,900, but accounts payable would simultaneously increase by $700. Gilbert's marginal federal-plus-state tax rate is 25%, and the project cost of capital is 15%. Should it replace the old steamer?

(11-10)
Replacement
Analysis

St. Johns River Shipyard's welding machine is 15 years old, fully depreciated, and has no salvage value. However, even though it is old, it is still functional as originally designed and can be used for quite a while longer. A new welder will cost $182,500 and have an estimated life of 8 years with no salvage value. The new welder will be much more efficient, however, and this enhanced efficiency will increase earnings before depreciation from $27,000 to $74,000 per year. The new machine will be depreciated over its 5-year MACRS recovery period, so the applicable depreciation rates are 20.00%, 32.00%, 19.20%, 11.52%, 11.52%, and 5.76%. The applicable corporate tax rate is 25%, and the project cost of capital is 12%. What is the NPV if the firm replaces the old welder with the new one?

CHALLENGING PROBLEMS 11–17

(11-11)
Scenario Analysis

Shao Industries is considering a proposed project for its capital budget. The company estimates the project's NPV is $12 million. This estimate assumes that the economy and market conditions will be average over the next few years. The company's CFO, however, forecasts there is only a 50% chance that the economy will be average. Recognizing this uncertainty, she has also performed the following scenario analysis:

Economic Scenario	Probability of Outcome	NPV
Recession	0.05	−$70 million
Below average	0.20	−25 million
Average	0.50	12 million
Above average	0.20	20 million
Boom	0.05	30 million

What are the project's expected NPV, standard deviation, and coefficient of variation?

(11-12)
New-Project
Analysis

Madison Manufacturing is considering a new machine that costs $350,000 and would reduce pre-tax manufacturing costs by $110,000 annually. Madison would use the 3-year MACRS method to depreciate the machine, and management thinks the machine would have a value of $33,000 at the end of its 5-year operating life. The applicable depreciation rates are 33.33%, 44.45%, 14.81%, and 7.41%. Working capital would increase by $35,000 initially, but it would be recovered at the end of the project's 5-year life. Madison's marginal tax rate is 25%, and a 10% cost of capital is appropriate for the project.

a. Calculate the project's NPV, IRR, MIRR, and payback.
b. Assume management is unsure about the $110,000 cost savings—this figure could deviate by as much as plus or minus 20%. What would the NPV be under each of these extremes?
c. Suppose the CFO wants you to do a scenario analysis with different values for the cost savings, the machine's salvage value, and the working capital (WC) requirement. She asks you to use the following probabilities and values in the scenario analysis:

Scenario	Probability	Cost Savings	Salvage Value	WC
Worst case	0.35	$ 88,000	$28,000	$40,000
Base case	0.35	110,000	33,000	35,000
Best case	0.30	132,000	38,000	30,000

Calculate the project's expected NPV, its standard deviation, and its coefficient of variation. Would you recommend that the project be accepted?

(11-13)
Replacement
Analysis

The Everly Equipment Company's flange-lipping machine was purchased 5 years ago for $55,000. It had an expected life of 10 years when it was bought, and its remaining depreciation is $5,500 per year for each year of its remaining life. As older flange-lippers are robust and useful machines, this one can be sold for $20,000 at the end of its useful life.

A new high-efficiency, digital-controlled flange-lipper can be purchased for $120,000, including installation costs. During its 5-year life, it will reduce cash operating expenses by $30,000 per year, although it will not affect sales. At the end of its useful life, the high-efficiency machine is estimated to be worthless. MACRS depreciation will be used, and the machine will be depreciated over its 3-year class life rather than its 5-year economic life, so the applicable depreciation rates are 33.33%, 44.45%, 14.81%, and 7.41%.

The old machine can be sold today for $35,000. The firm's tax rate is 25%, and the appropriate cost of capital is 16%.

a. If the new flange-lipper is purchased, what is the amount of the initial cash flow at Year 0?
b. What are the incremental cash flows that will occur at the end of Years 1 through 5?
c. What is the NPV of this project? Should Everly replace the flange-lipper?

(11-14)
Replacement
Analysis

DeYoung Entertainment Enterprises is considering replacing the latex molding machine it uses to fabricate rubber chickens with a newer, more efficient model. The old machine has a book value of $450,000 and a remaining useful life of 5 years. The current machine would be worn out and worthless in 5 years, but DeYoung can sell it now to a Halloween mask manufacturer for $135,000. The old machine is being depreciated by $90,000 per year for each year of its remaining life. If DeYoung doesn't replace the old machine, it will have no salvage value at the end of its useful life.

The new machine has a purchase price of $775,000, an estimated useful life and MACRS class life of 5 years, and an estimated salvage value of $105,000. The applicable depreciation rates are 20.00%, 32.00%, 19.20%, 11.52%, 11.52%, and 5.76%. Being highly efficient, it is expected to economize on electric power usage, labor, and repair costs, and, most importantly, to reduce the number of defective chickens. In total, an annual savings of $185,000 will be realized if the new machine is installed. The company's marginal tax rate is 25%, and the project cost of capital is 12%.

a. What is the initial cash flow if the new machine is purchased and the old one is replaced?

b. What is the incremental depreciation tax shield (i.e., the change taxes due to the change in depreciation expenses) if the replacement is made? (*Hint:* First calculate the annual depreciation expense for the new machine and compare it to the depreciation on the old machine.)

c. What is the after-tax salvage value at Year 5?

d. What are the total incremental project cash flows in Years 0 through 5? What is the NPV?

(11-15)
Risky Cash Flows

The Bartram-Pulley Company (BPC) must decide between two mutually exclusive investment projects. Each project costs $6,750 and has an expected life of 3 years. Annual cash flows from each project begin 1 year after the initial investment is made and have the following probability distributions:

Project A		Project B	
Probability	**Cash Flows**	**Probability**	**Cash Flows**
0.2	$6,000	0.2	$ 0
0.6	6,750	0.6	6,750
0.2	7,500	0.2	18,000

BPC has decided to evaluate the riskier project at a 12% rate and the less risky project at a 10% rate.

a. What are the expected values of the annual cash flows from each project? What is the coefficient of variation (CV) for each project? (*Hint:* $\sigma_B = \$5,798$ and $CV_B = 0.76$.)

b. What is the risk-adjusted NPV of each project?

c. If it were known that Project B is negatively correlated with other cash flows of the firm whereas Project A is positively correlated, how would this affect the decision? If Project B's cash flows were negatively correlated with gross domestic product (GDP), would that influence your assessment of its risk?

(11-16)
Simulation

Singleton Supplies Corporation (SSC) manufactures medical products for hospitals, clinics, and nursing homes. SSC may introduce a new type of X-ray scanner designed to identify certain types of cancers in their early stages. There are a number of uncertainties about the proposed project, but the following data are believed to be reasonably accurate:

Probability	Developmental Costs	Random Numbers
0.3	$2,000,000	00–29
0.4	4,000,000	30–69
0.3	6,000,000	70–99

Probability	Project Life	Random Numbers
0.2	3 years	00–19
0.6	8 years	20–79
0.2	13 years	80–99

Probability	Sales in Units	Random Numbers
0.2	100	00–19
0.6	200	20–79
0.2	300	80–99

Probability	Sales Price	Random Numbers
0.1	$13,000	00–09
0.8	13,500	10–89
0.1	14,000	90–99

Probability	Cost per Unit (Excluding Developmental Costs)	Random Numbers
0.3	$5,000	00–29
0.4	6,000	30–69
0.3	7,000	70–99

SSC uses a cost of capital of 15% to analyze average-risk projects such as this one. The firm is in the 25% federal-plus-state income tax bracket.

a. What is the project's NPV? Could you estimate σ_{NPV} without either simulation or a complex statistical analysis?

b. What is the expected IRR for the X-ray scanner project? Base your answer on the expected values of the variables. Also, assume the after-tax "profits" figure that you develop is equal to annual cash flows. All facilities are leased, so depreciation may be disregarded. Can you determine the value of σ_{IRR} short of actual simulation or complex statistical analysis?

c. Show the process by which a computer would perform a simulation analysis for this project. Assume the computer has generated the random numbers used in parts (1) and (2).

(1) Use the random numbers 17 and 44 to determine the project's life and development costs; these will be the same for all sample years.

(2) Use 16, 58, and 1 as random numbers to determine the unit sales, sales price per unit, and cost per unit in the first year, respectively. Calculate the net income. Repeat this for Year 2 by using the random values 79, 83, and 86 to determine the unit sales, sales price per unit, and cost per unit in the second year. Repeat this for Year 3 by using the random values 19, 62, and 37 to determine the unit sales, sales price per unit, and cost per unit in the third year, respectively.

(3) What is the NPV for this sample?

(11-17)
Decision Tree

The Yoran Yacht Company (YYC), a prominent sailboat builder in Newport, may design a new 30-foot sailboat based on the "winged" keels first introduced on the 12-meter yachts that raced for the America's Cup.

First, YYC would have to invest $10,000 at t = 0 for the design and model tank testing of the new boat. YYC's managers believe there is a 60% probability that this phase will be successful and the project will continue. If Stage 1 is not successful, the project will be abandoned with zero salvage value.

The next stage, if undertaken, would consist of making the molds and producing two prototype boats. This would cost $500,000 at t = 1. If the boats test well, YYC would go into production. If they do not, the molds and prototypes could be sold for $100,000. The managers estimate the probability is 80% that the boats will pass testing and that Stage 3 will be undertaken.

Stage 3 consists of converting an unused production line to produce the new design. This would cost $1 million at t = 2. If the economy is strong at this point, the net value of sales would be $3 million; if the economy is weak, the net value would be $1.5 million. Both net values occur at t = 3, and each state of the economy has a probability of 0.5. YYC's corporate cost of capital is 12%.

a. Assume this project has average risk. Construct a decision tree and determine the project's expected NPV.
b. Find the project's standard deviation of NPV and coefficient of variation of NPV. If YYC's average project had a CV of between 1.0 and 2.0, would this project be of high, low, or average stand-alone risk?

SPREADSHEET PROBLEMS

(11-18)
Build a Model:
Issues in Capital
Budgeting

resource

Start with the partial model in the file *Ch11 P18 Build a Model.xlsx* on the textbook's Web site. Webmasters.com has developed a powerful new server that would be used for corporations' Internet activities. It would cost $10 million at Year 0 to buy the equipment necessary to manufacture the server. The project would require net working capital at the beginning of each year in an amount equal to 10% of the year's projected sales; for example, $NWC_0 = 10\%(Sales_1)$. The servers would sell for $24,000 per unit, and Webmasters believes that variable costs would amount to $18,000 per unit. After Year 1, the sales price and variable costs will increase at the inflation rate of 3%. The company's nonvariable costs would be $1 million at Year 1 and would increase with inflation.

The server project would have a life of 4 years. If the project is undertaken, it must be continued for the entire 4 years. Also, the project's returns are expected to be highly correlated with returns on the firm's other assets. The firm believes it could sell 1,000 units per year.

The equipment would be depreciated over a 5-year period, using MACRS rates. The estimated market value of the equipment at the end of the project's 4-year life is $500,000. Webmasters.com's federal-plus-state tax rate is 25%. Its cost of capital is 10% for average-risk projects, defined as projects with a coefficient of variation of NPV between 0.8 and 1.2. Low-risk projects are evaluated with an 8% project cost of capital and high-risk projects at 13%.

a. Develop a spreadsheet model, and use it to find the project's NPV, IRR, and payback.
b. Now conduct a sensitivity analysis to determine the sensitivity of NPV to changes in the sales price, variable costs per unit, and number of units sold. Set these variables' values at 10% and 20% above and below their base-case values. Include a graph in your analysis.
c. Now conduct a scenario analysis. Assume that there is a 25% probability that best-case conditions, with each of the variables discussed in Part b being 20% better than its base-case value, will occur. There is a 25% probability of worst-case conditions, with the variables 20% worse than base, and a 50% probability of base-case conditions.
d. If the project appears to be more or less risky than an average project, find its risk-adjusted NPV, IRR, and payback.
e. On the basis of information in the problem, would you recommend the project should be accepted?

MINI CASE

Shrieves Casting Company is considering adding a new line to its product mix, and the capital budgeting analysis is being conducted by Sidney Johnson, a recently graduated MBA. The production line would be set up in unused space in the main plant. The machinery's invoice price would be approximately $200,000, another $10,000 in shipping charges would be required, and it would cost an additional $30,000 to install the equipment. The machinery has an economic life of 4 years, and Shrieves has obtained a special tax ruling that places the equipment in the MACRS 3-year class. The machinery is expected to have a salvage value of $25,000 after 4 years of use.

The new line would generate incremental sales of 1,000 units per year for 4 years at an incremental cost of $100 per unit in the first year, excluding depreciation. Each unit can be sold for $200 in the first year. The sales price and cost are both expected to increase by 3% per year due to inflation. Further, to handle the new line, the firm's net working capital would have to increase by an amount equal to 12% of sales revenues. The firm's tax rate is 25%, and its overall weighted average cost of capital, which is the risk-adjusted cost of capital for an average project (r), is 10%.

a. Define "incremental cash flow."
   (1) Should you subtract interest expense or dividends when calculating project cash flow?
   (2) Suppose the firm spent $100,000 last year to rehabilitate the production line site. Should this be included in the analysis? Explain.
   (3) Now assume the plant space could be leased out to another firm at $25,000 per year. Should this be included in the analysis? If so, how?
   (4) Finally, assume that the new product line is expected to decrease sales of the firm's other lines by $50,000 per year. Should this be considered in the analysis? If so, how?

b. Disregard the assumptions in Part a. What is the depreciable basis? What are the annual depreciation expenses?

c. Calculate the annual sales revenues and costs (other than depreciation). Why is it important to include inflation when estimating cash flows?

d. Calculate annual net operating profit after sales (NOPAT). Then calculate the operating cash flows.

e. Estimate the required net operating working capital (NOWC) for each year and the cash flow due to changes in NOWC.

f. Calculate the after-tax salvage cash flow.

g. Calculate the project cash flows for each year. Based on these cash flows and the average project cost of capital, what are the project's NPV, IRR, MIRR, PI, payback, and discounted payback? Do these indicators suggest that the project should be undertaken?

h. What does the term "risk" mean in the context of capital budgeting; to what extent can risk be quantified; and, when risk is quantified, is the quantification based primarily on statistical analysis of historical data or on subjective, judgmental estimates?

i. (1) What are the three types of risk that are relevant in capital budgeting?
   (2) How is each of these risk types measured, and how do they relate to one another?
   (3) How is each type of risk used in the capital budgeting process?

j. (1) What is sensitivity analysis?

   (2) Perform a sensitivity analysis on the cost per unit, unit sales, and salvage value. Assume each of these variables can vary from its base-case, or expected, value by plus or minus 10%, 20%, and 30%. Include a sensitivity graph, and discuss the results.

   (3) What is the primary weakness of sensitivity analysis? What is its primary usefulness?

k. Assume that Sidney Johnson is confident of her estimates of all the variables that affect the project's cash flows except unit sales and sales price: If product acceptance is poor, unit sales would be only 800 units a year and the unit price would only be $160; a strong consumer response would produce sales of 1,200 units and a unit price of $240. Sidney believes that there is a 25% chance of poor acceptance, a 25% chance of excellent acceptance, and a 50% chance of average acceptance (the base case).

   (1) What is scenario analysis?

   (2) What is the worst-case NPV? The best-case NPV?

   (3) Use the worst-, base-, and best-case NPVs and probabilities of occurrence to find the project's expected NPV, as well as the NPV's standard deviation and coefficient of variation.

l. Are there problems with scenario analysis? Define simulation analysis, and discuss its principal advantages and disadvantages.

m. (1) Assume the company's average project has a coefficient of variation in the range of 0.2 to 0.4. Would the new line be classified as high risk, average risk, or low risk? What type of risk is being measured here?

   (2) Shrieves typically adds or subtracts 3 percentage points to the overall cost of capital to adjust for risk. Should the new line be accepted?

   (3) Are there any subjective risk factors that should be considered before the final decision is made?

n. What is a real option? What are some types of real options?

SELECTED ADDITIONAL CASES

The following cases from CengageCompose cover many of the concepts discussed in this chapter and are available at **http://compose.cengage.com**.

Klein-Brigham Series:
Case 12, "Indian River Citrus Company (A)," Case 44, "Cranfield, Inc. (A)," and Case 14, "Robert Montoya, Inc.," focus on cash flow estimation. Case 13, "Indian River Citrus (B)," Case 45, "Cranfield, Inc. (B)," Case 58, "Tasty Foods (B)," Case 60, "Heavenly Foods," and Case 15, "Robert Montoya, Inc. (B)," illustrate project risk analysis. Cases 75, 76, and 77, "The Western Company (A and B)," are comprehensive cases.

Brigham-Buzzard Series:
Case 7, "Powerline Network Corporation (Risk and Real Options in Capital Budgeting)."

Depreciation for Tax Purposes

Congress changes the permissible tax depreciation methods from time to time. Prior to 1954, the straight-line method was required for tax purposes, but in 1954 **accelerated depreciation methods** (double-declining balance and sum-of-years'-digits) were permitted. Then, in 1981, the old accelerated methods were replaced by a simpler procedure known as the Accelerated Cost Recovery System (ACRS). The ACRS was changed again by the 1986 Tax Reform Act, and it is now known as the **modified accelerated cost recovery system (MACRS)**; a 1993 tax law made further changes in this area. The 2017 Tax Cut and Jobs Act (TCJA) includes provisions for **bonus depreciation,** which specifies much higher depreciation rates in the first year of depreciation. The 2017 Act's bonus depreciation rates gradually phase out during 2018–2026.

MACRS has simple (relatively speaking) guidelines that created several classes of assets, each with a prescribed life called a *recovery period* or *class life*. The MACRS class lives bear only a rough relationship to assets' actual expected useful economic lives. Table 11A-1 shows property categories and the property life classifications. Property in the 27.5- and 39-year categories (real estate) must be depreciated by the straight-line method, but 3-, 5-, 7-, and 10-year property (personal property) can be depreciated either by the accelerated method set forth in Table 11A-2 or by the straight-line method.

TABLE 11A-1
Major Classes and Asset Lives for MACRS

Class	Type of Property
3-year	Certain special manufacturing tools
5-year	Automobiles, light-duty trucks, computers, and certain special manufacturing equipment
7-year	Most industrial equipment, office furniture, and fixtures
10-year	Certain longer-lived types of equipment
27.5-year	Residential rental real property such as apartment buildings
39-year	All nonresidential real property, including commercial and industrial buildings

Table 11A-2 reports the MACRS depreciation percentages (depreciation rates) for selected property classes. As we saw earlier in the chapter, higher depreciation expenses result in lower taxes in the early years and hence lead to a higher present value of cash flows. Therefore, because firms have the choice of using straight-line rates or the accelerated rates shown in Table 11A-2, most elect to use the accelerated rates.

TABLE 11A-2
MACRS Depreciation Percentages

	Class of Investment			
Ownership Year	3-Year	5-Year	7-Year	10-Year
1	33.33%	20.00%	14.29%	10.00%
2	44.45	32.00	24.49	18.00
3	14.81	19.20	17.49	14.40
4	7.41	11.52	12.49	11.52
5		11.52	8.93	9.22
6		5.76	8.92	7.37
7			8.93	6.55
8			4.46	6.55
9				6.56
10				6.55
11				3.28
	100%	100%	100%	100%

Note:

Residential rental property (apartments) is depreciated over a 27.5-year life, whereas commercial and industrial structures are depreciated over 39 years. In both cases, straight-line depreciation must be used. The depreciation allowance for the first year is based, pro rata, on the month the asset was placed in service, with the remainder of the first year's depreciation being taken in the 28th or 40th year. A half-month convention is assumed; that is, an asset placed in service in February would receive 10.5 months of depreciation in the first year.

The yearly recovery allowance, or depreciation expense, is determined by multiplying each asset's *depreciable basis* by the applicable recovery percentage shown in Table 11A-2. As we explained previously, the half-year convention causes an asset's depreciable life to be 1 year greater than the asset's property class.

resource

See *Ch11 Tool Kit.xlsx* on the textbook's Web site for all calculations.

For example, suppose a property has a $100,000 basis. If it has a 3-year classification, the depreciation expenses in the first two years are $100,000(0.3333) = $33,330 and $100,000(0.4445) = $44,450.

What is the impact of the 2017 TCJA's bonus depreciation provisions? For property acquired in 2018 through 2022, companies may depreciate 100% of the asset in the first year. After that, the amount of bonus depreciation in the first year falls by 20% per year. It is 80% in 2023, 60% in 2024, 40% in 2025, 20% in 2026, and 0% in 2027. To illustrate, suppose that in 2023 a company acquires 3-year property with a basis of $100,000. The depreciation expense in 2023 includes bonus depreciation of 80%($100,000) = $80,000, which leaves $20,000 of undepreciated property, which is the property's new basis. It is 3-year property and has a MACRS rate of 33.33% in Year 1. Applying that rate to the new basis of $20,000, the additional depreciation expense in Year 1 is 33.33%($20,000) = $6,666. The total depreciation is the sum of the bonus and the MACRS depreciations: $80,000 + $6,666 = $86,666. In Year 2, there is only MACRS depreciation, which is 44.45%($20,000) = $8,890. A similar process is applied for Years 3 and 4.

SELF-TEST

What do the acronyms "ACRS" and "MACRS" stand for?

Briefly describe the tax depreciation system under MACRS.

What is bonus depreciation?

CHAPTER 12

Corporate Valuation and Financial Planning

A survey of CFOs disclosed a paradox regarding financial planning. On the one hand, almost all CFOs stated that financial planning is both important and highly useful for allocating resources. On the other hand, 45% also said that budgeting is "contentious, political, and time-consuming," and 53% went on to say that the budgeting process can encourage undesirable behavior among managers as they negotiate budgets to meet their own rather than the company's objectives. They also said that instead of basing growth and incentive compensation targets on an analysis of what markets and competitors are likely to do in the future, firms often set their targets at last year's levels plus a percentage increase, which is dangerous in a dynamic economy.

To resolve these issues, many companies use *demand-pull budgeting*, which links the budget to a sales forecast and updates the sales forecast to reflect changing economic conditions. This approach is often augmented with a *rolling forecast,* in which companies make 1-year and 5-year forecasts but then modify the 1-year forecast each month as new operating results become available.

Another survey shows that high-performance companies also focus on the links between forecasting, planning, and business strategy rather than on just cost management and cost accounting. According to John McMahan of the Hackett Group, such changes are leading to greater forecasting accuracy, higher employee morale, and better corporate performance. These issues are often thought of as "management" rather than "finance," but this is a false distinction. Much of finance is numbers-oriented, but as any CFO will tell you, his or her primary job is to help the firm as a whole achieve good results. The procedures discussed in this chapter can help firms improve their operations and results.

Sources: J. McCafferty, "Planning for the Best," *CFO*, February 2007, p. 24; and Don Durfee, "Alternative Budgeting," *CFO*, June 2006, p. 28.

Corporate Valuation and Financial Planning

The value of a firm is determined by the size, timing, and risk of its expected future free cash flows (FCFs). Managers use projected financial statements to estimate the impact that different operating plans have on intrinsic value. Managers also use projected statements to identify deficits that must be financed in order to implement the operating plans. This chapter explains how to project financial statements that incorporate operating assumptions and financial policies.

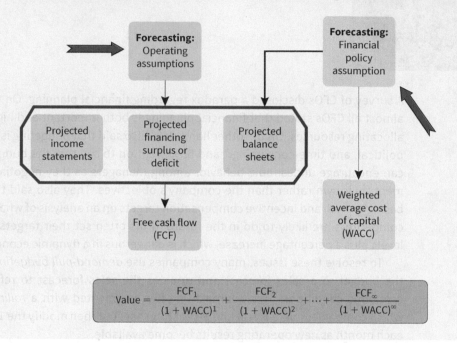

$$Value = \frac{FCF_1}{(1 + WACC)^1} + \frac{FCF_2}{(1 + WACC)^2} + \cdots + \frac{FCF_\infty}{(1 + WACC)^\infty}$$

resource

*The textbook's Web site contains an Excel file that will guide you through the chapter's calculations. The file for this chapter is **Ch12 Tool Kit.xlsx**, and we encourage you to open the file and follow along as you read the chapter.*

Our primary objective in this book is to explain how financial managers can make their companies more valuable. However, value creation is impossible unless the company has well-designed operating and financial plans. As Yogi Berra once said, "You've got to be careful if you don't know where you're going, because you might not get there."

A vital step in financial planning is to forecast financial statements, which are called **projected financial statements** or **pro forma financial statements**. Managers use projected financial statements in four ways: (1) By looking at projected statements, they can assess whether the firm's anticipated performance is in line with the firm's own general targets and with investors' expectations. (2) Pro forma statements can be used to estimate the effect of proposed operating changes, enabling managers to conduct what-if analyses. (3) Managers use pro forma statements to anticipate the firm's future financing needs. (4) Managers forecast free cash flows under different operating plans, forecast their capital requirements, and then choose the plan that maximizes shareholder value. Security analysts make the same types of projections, forecasting future earnings, cash flows, and stock prices.

12-1 Overview of Financial Planning

The two most important components of financial planning are the operating plan and the financial plan.

12-1a The Operating Plan

As its name suggests, an operating plan provides detailed implementation guidance for a firm's operations, including the firm's choice of market segments, product lines, sales and marketing strategies, production processes, and logistics. An operating plan can be developed for any time horizon, but most companies use a 5-year horizon, with the plan being quite detailed for the first year but less and less specific for each succeeding year. The plan explains who is responsible for each particular function and when specific tasks are to be accomplished.

An important part of the operating plan is the forecast of sales, production costs, inventories, and other operating items. In fact, this part of the operating plan actually is a forecast of the company's expected free cash flow. Recall from Chapters 2 and 7 that free cash flow is defined as net operating profit after taxes (NOPAT) minus the investment in total net operating capital.

Free cash flow is the primary source of a company's value. Using what-if analysis, managers can analyze different operating plans to estimate their impact on value. In addition, managers can apply sensitivity analysis, scenario analysis, and simulation to estimate the risk of different operating plans, which is an important part of risk management.

12-1b The Financial Plan

By definition, a company's operating assets can grow only by the purchase of additional assets. Therefore, a growing company must continually obtain cash to purchase new assets. Some of this cash might be generated internally by its operations, but some might have to come externally from shareholders or debtholders. This is the essence of financial planning: forecasting the additional sources of financing required to fund the operating plan.

There is a strong connection between financial planning and free cash flow. A company's operations generate the free cash flow, but the financial plan determines how the company will use the free cash flow. Recall from Chapter 2 that free cash flow can be used in five ways: (1) pay dividends, (2) repurchase stock, (3) pay the net after-tax interest on debt, (4) repay debt, or (5) purchase financial assets such as marketable securities. A company's financial plan must use free cash flow differently if FCF is negative than if FCF is positive.

If free cash flow is positive, the financial plan must identify how much FCF to allocate among its investors (shareholders or debtholders) and how much to put aside for future needs by purchasing short-term investments. If free cash flow is negative, either because the company is growing rapidly (which requires large investments in operating capital) or because the company's NOPAT is too low, then the total uses of free cash flow must also be negative. For example, instead of repurchasing stock, the company might have to issue stock; instead of repaying debt, the company might have to issue debt.

Therefore, the financial plan must incorporate: (1) the company's dividend policy, which determines the targeted size and method of cash distributions to shareholders, and (2) the capital structure, which determines the targeted mix of debt and equity used to finance the firm, which in turn determines the relative mix of distributions to shareholders and payments to debtholders.

SELF-TEST

Briefly describe the key elements of an operating plan.

Identify the five uses of free cash flow and how these uses are related to a financial plan.

12-2 Financial Planning at MicroDrive Inc.

As we described in Chapters 2, 3, and 7, MicroDrive's operating performance and stock price have declined in recent years. As a result, MicroDrive's board recently installed a new management team: A new CEO, CFO, marketing manager, sales manager, inventory manager, and credit manager—only the production manager was retained. The new team met for a 3-day retreat with the goal of developing a plan to improve the company's performance.

In preparation for the retreat, the new CFO developed a very simple *Excel* model to forecast free cash flows. Using this forecast, the model estimates the **value of operations**, which is the present value of all future free cash flows when discounted back at the weighted average cost of capital (WACC). The model also estimates the **intrinsic value (or price)** of the stock, which is based on (1) the estimated value of operations, (2) current levels of short-term investments, debt, and preferred stock, and (3) the number of common shares. Recall that the intrinsic (or fundamental) value incorporates all relevant information regarding expected future cash flows and risk but that it may differ from the actual market price.

The CFO used the model to identify the impact on MicroDrive's value of operations and intrinsic stock price due to different value drivers (sales growth rates, operating profitability, capital requirements, and WACC); see Chapter 7 for this analysis. The CFO then created a more detailed model to incorporate a complete operating plan and financial plan based on the status quo to give the management team a better idea of where the company is now and where it will be if they don't make changes; refer to *Ch12 Tool Kit.xlsx* as we explain MicroDrive's financial planning.

resource

See **Ch12 Tool Kit.xlsx** *on the textbook's Web site.*

The CFO's first step in creating this more detailed model was to examine the current and recent historical data. Figure 12-1 shows MicroDrive's most recent financial

FIGURE 12-1

MicroDrive's Most Recent Financial Statements (Millions, Except for per Share Data)

	A	B	C	D	E	F	G
13	INCOME STATEMENTS			BALANCE SHEETS			
14		2018	2019	*Assets*		2018	2019
15	Net sales	$4,800	$5,000	Cash		$102	$100
16	COGS (excl. depr.)	3,710	3,900	ST Investments		40	10
17	Depreciation	180	200	Accounts receivable		384	500
18	Other operating expenses	470	500	Inventories		774	1,000
19	EBIT	$440	$400	Total CA		$1,300	$1,610
20	Interest expense	40	60	Net PP&E		1,780	2,000
21	Pre-tax earnings	$400	$340	Total assets		$3,080	$3,610
22	Taxes (25%)	100	85				
23	NI before pref. div.	$300	$255	*Liabilities and equity*			
24	Preferred div.	7	7	Accounts payable		$180	$200
25	Net income	$293	$248	Notes payable		28	150
26				Accruals		370	400
27	*Other Data*			Total CL		$578	$750
28	Common dividends	$59.4	$60.0	Long-term bonds		350	520
29	Addition to RE	$233.6	$188.0	Total liabilities		$928	$1,270
30	Tax rate	25%	25%	Preferred stock		100	100
31	Shares of common stock	60	60	Common stock		500	500
32	Earnings per share	$4.88	$4.13	Retained earnings		1,552	1,740
33	Dividends per share	$0.99	$1.00	Total common equity		$2,052	$2,240
34	Price per share	$45.00	$31.00	Total liabs. & equity		$3,080	$3,610
35							

Source: See the file **Ch12 Tool Kit.xlsx**. Numbers are reported as rounded values for clarity but are calculated using *Excel's* full precision. Thus, intermediate calculations using the figure's rounded values will be inexact.

statements and selected additional data; see Chapters 2 and 3 for a full discussion of the process used to assess MicroDrive's current position and trends.

The CFO's second step was to choose a forecasting framework. Many companies, including MicroDrive, forecast their entire financial statements as part of the planning process. This approach is called **forecasted financial statements (FFS) method** of financial planning.

Figure 12-2 shows the inputs MicroDrive uses to forecast its operating plan and financial plan. The inputs shown are for the Status Quo scenario, which assumes most of MicroDrive's operating activities and financial policies remain unchanged. (We will look at strategic initiatives in other scenarios after analyzing the Status Quo; the initiatives' costs are shown at the end of Section 1.) In contrast to the analysis in Chapter 7, which forecast NOPAT and total net operating capital as only two line items, Figure 12-1 shows inputs for all the individual financial statement line items needed to forecast free cash flows.

resource

*See **Ch12 Tool Kit.xlsx** on the textbook's Web site.*

Figure 12-2 shows industry peer actual values of the inputs for forecasting (the silver section), actual values for MicroDrive's past 2 years, and forecasted values for MicroDrive's 5-year forecast. The blue section shows inputs for the first year and inputs

FIGURE 12-2
MicroDrive's Forecast: Inputs for the Status Quo Scenario

	A	B	C	D	E	F	G	H	I
59	Status Quo	Industry	MicroDrive			MicroDrive			
60	Inputs	Actual	Actual			Forecast			
61	*1. Operations*	2019	2018	2019	2020	2021	2022	2023	2024
62	Sales growth rate	5%	10.0%	4.2%	10.0%	8.0%	7.0%	5.0%	5.0%
63	(COGS excl. depr.)/Sales	76%	77.3%	78.0%	78.0%	78.00%	78.0%	78.0%	78.0%
64	Depreciation/(Net PP&E)	9%	10.1%	10.0%	10.0%	10.0%	10.0%	10.0%	10.0%
65	(Other op. exp.)/Sales	10%	9.8%	10.0%	10.0%	10.0%	10.0%	10.0%	10.0%
66	Cash/Sales	1%	2.1%	2.0%	2.0%	2.0%	2.0%	2.0%	2.0%
67	(Acc. rec.)/Sales	8%	8.0%	10.0%	10.0%	10.0%	10.0%	10.0%	10.0%
68	Inventory/Sales	15%	16.1%	20.0%	20.0%	20.0%	20.0%	20.0%	20.0%
69	(Net PP&E)/Sales	33%	37.1%	40.0%	40.0%	40.0%	40.0%	40.0%	40.0%
70	(Acc. pay.)/Sales	4%	3.8%	4.0%	4.0%	4.0%	4.0%	4.0%	4.0%
71	Accruals/Sales	7%	7.7%	8.0%	8.0%	8.0%	8.0%	8.0%	8.0%
72	Tax rate	25%	25.0%	25.0%	25.0%	25.0%	25.0%	25.0%	25.0%
73	Cost of strategic initiatives	NA	NA	NA	$0	$0	$0	$0	$0
74	*2. Capital Structure*	Actual Market Weights			Target Market Weights				
75	% Short-term debt	4%	0.9%	5.7%	4%	4%	4%	4%	4%
76	% Long-term debt	20%	11.0%	19.8%	20%	20%	20%	20%	20%
77	% Preferred stock	2%	3.1%	3.8%	2%	2%	2%	2%	2%
78	% Common stock	74%	85.0%	70.7%	74%	74%	74%	74%	74%
79	% Line of credit	0%	0.0%	0.0%	0%	0%	0%	0%	0%
80	*3. Costs of Capital*						Forecast		
81	Rate on ST debt				8.0%	8.0%	8.0%	8.0%	8.0%
82	Rate on LT debt				10.0%	10.0%	10.0%	10.0%	10.0%
83	Rate on preferred stock (ignoring flotation costs)				7.0%	7.0%	7.0%	7.0%	7.0%
84	Flotation cost of new preferred stock				2.1%	2.1%	2.1%	2.1%	2.1%
85	Cost of equity				13.0%	13.0%	13.0%	13.0%	13.0%
86	Additional rate on line of credit vs. ST debt				1.5%	1.5%	1.5%	1.5%	1.5%
87	*4. Target Dividend Policy*		Actual				Forecast		
88	Growth rate of dividends		11%	1.0%	5%	5%	5%	5%	5%

Source: See the file ***Ch12 Tool Kit.xlsx***. Numbers are reported as rounded values for clarity but are calculated using *Excel's* full precision. Thus, intermediate calculations using the figure's rounded values will be inexact.

for any subsequent years that differ from the previous year. Section 1 shows the ratios required to project the items required for an operating plan, Section 2 shows the inputs related to the capital structure, Section 3 shows the costs of the capital components, and Section 4 shows the target dividend policy. We will describe each of these sections as they are applied to the forecast, beginning with the forecast of operations.

12-3 Forecasting Operations

The first row in Section 1 of Figure 12-2 shows the forecast of the sales growth rate. After discussions with teams from marketing, sales, product development, and production, MicroDrive's CFO projected a growth rate of 10% for the next year. Keep in mind that this is just a preliminary estimate and that it is easy to make changes later in the *Excel* model. Notice that MicroDrive is forecasting sales growth to decline and level off by the end of the forecast. Recall from Chapter 7 that the growth rate for a company's sales and free cash flows must level off at some future date in order to apply the constant growth model at the forecast horizon. Had MicroDrive's managers projected nonconstant growth for more than 5 years, Figure 12-2 would need to be extended until growth does level out.

In Chapter 7's projections, MicroDrive's CFO included only the sales growth rates, operating profitability (OP) ratio, and capital requirement (CR) ratio. In contrast, the comprehensive financial plan presented here includes the individual financial statement accounts that comprise operating profitability and capital requirements, as shown in Figure 12-2. MicroDrive's managers initially assumed that all the operating ratios other than growth would remain constant for the entire forecast period. However, it would be quite easy to modify the model so that future ratios changed, with one caveat. The operating ratios must level off by the end of the forecast period, or else the free cash flows *will not* be growing at a constant rate by the end of the forecast period even if sales *are* growing at a constant rate.

The following sections explain how MicroDrive uses the ratios in Figure 12-2 to forecast its operations. Panel A of Figure 12-3 repeats the operating inputs for convenience; Panel B reports the resulting operating forecast.

12-3a Sales Revenues

Section B1 of Figure 12-3 shows the forecast of net sales based on the previous year's sales and the forecasted growth rate in sales. For example, the forecast of net sales for 2020 is:

$$\text{Sales}_{2020} = (1 + g_{2019,2020})(\text{Sales}_{2019})$$
$$= (1 + 0.10)(\$5,000) = \$5,500$$

12-3b Operating Assets

Section B2 of Figure 12-3 shows the forecast of operating assets. As noted earlier, MicroDrive's assets must increase if sales are to increase, and some types of assets grow proportionately to sales, including cash.

MicroDrive writes and deposits checks every day. Because its managers don't know exactly when all of the checks will clear, they can't predict exactly what the balance in their checking accounts will be on any given day. Therefore, they must maintain a balance of cash and cash equivalents (such as very short-term marketable securities) to avoid

resource

See **Ch12 Tool Kit.xlsx** *on the textbook's Web site.*

FIGURE 12-3

MicroDrive's Forecast of Operations for the Status Quo Scenario (Millions of Dollars, Except for per Share Data)

	A	B	C	D	E	F	G	H	I
127	**Status Quo**	**Industry**	**MicroDrive**		**MicroDrive**				
128	**Panel A: Inputs**	**Actual**	**Actual**		**Forecast**				
129	*A1. Operations*	2019	2018	2019	2020	2021	2022	2023	2024
130	Sales growth rate	5%	*10%*	*4%*	10.0%	8.0%	7.0%	5.0%	5.0%
131	(COGS excl. depr.)/Sales	76%	*77%*	*78%*	78.0%	78.0%	78.0%	78.0%	78.0%
132	Depreciation/(Net PP&E)	9%	*10%*	*10%*	10.0%	10.0%	10.0%	10.0%	10.0%
133	(Other op. exp.)/Sales	10%	*10%*	*10%*	10.0%	10.0%	10.0%	10.0%	10.0%
134	Cash/Sales	1%	*2%*	*2%*	2.0%	2.0%	2.0%	2.0%	2.0%
135	(Acc. rec.)/Sales	8%	*8%*	*10%*	10.0%	10.0%	10.0%	10.0%	10.0%
136	Inventory/Sales	15%	*16%*	*20%*	20.0%	20.0%	20.0%	20.0%	20.0%
137	(Net PP&E)/Sales	33%	*37%*	*40%*	40.0%	40.0%	40.0%	40.0%	40.0%
138	(Acc. pay.)/Sales	4%	*4%*	*4%*	4.0%	4.0%	4.0%	4.0%	4.0%
139	Accruals/Sales	7%	*8%*	*8%*	8.0%	8.0%	8.0%	8.0%	8.0%
140	Tax rate	25%	*25%*	*25%*	25.0%	25.0%	25.0%	25.0%	25.0%
141	Cost of strategic initiatives	NA	*NA*	*NA*	$0	$0	$0	$0	$0
142	**Panel B: Results**			Actual		Forecast			
143	*B1. Sales Revenues*			*2019*	2020	2021	2022	2023	2024
144	Net sales			*$5,000*	$5,500	$5,940	$6,356	$6,674	$7,007
145	*B2. Operating Assets and Operating Liabilities*								
146	Cash			*$100*	$110	$119	$127	$133	$140
147	Accounts receivable			*$500*	$550	$594	$636	$667	$701
148	Inventories			*$1,000*	$1,100	$1,188	$1,271	$1,335	$1,401
149	Net PP&E			*$2,000*	$2,200	$2,376	$2,542	$2,669	$2,803
150	Accounts payable			*$200*	$220	$238	$254	$267	$280
151	Accruals			*$400*	$440	$475	$508	$534	$561
152	*B3. Operating Income*								
153	COGS (excl. depr.)			*$3,900*	$4,290	$4,633	$4,958	$5,205	$5,466
154	Depreciation			*$200*	$220	$238	$254	$267	$280
155	Other operating expenses			*$500*	$550	$594	$636	$667	$701
156	Cost of strategic initiatives			*NA*	$0	$0	$0	$0	$0
157	EBIT			*$400*	$440	$475	$508	$534	$561
158	Net operating profit after taxes			*$300*	$330	$356	$381	$400	$420
159	*B4. Free Cash Flows*								
160	Net operating working capital			*$1,000*	$1,100	$1,188	$1,271	$1,335	$1,401
161	Total net operating capital			*$3,000*	$3,300	$3,564	$3,813	$4,004	$4,204
162	FCF = NOPAT − Δ net op capital			*−$210*	$30	$92	$132	$210	$220
163	*B5. Estimated Intrinsic Value*								
164	Target WACC				11.50%	11.50%	11.50%	11.50%	11.50%
165	OP ratio: NOPAT/Sales			6%	6.0%	6.0%	6.0%	6.0%	6.0%
166	CR ratio: (Total op. cap.)/Sales			61%	60.0%	60.0%	60.0%	60.0%	60.0%
167	ROIC: NOPAT/(Total op. cap.)			10.0%	10.0%	10.0%	10.0%	10.0%	10.0%
168	Growth in FCF					208.0%	42.7%	59.1%	5.0%
169									

170	Value of Operations (12/31/2024)		Estimated intrinsic stock price (12/31/2019)	
171			Value of operations	$2,524
172	$HV_{2024} = \dfrac{FCF_{2024}(1+g_L)}{(WACC - g_L)}$ =	$3,558	+ ST investments	$10
173			Estimated total intrinsic value	$2,534
174	Value of Operations (12/31/2019)		− All debt	$670
175	Present value of HV	$2,064	− Preferred stock	$100
176	+ Present value of FCF	$460	Estimated intrinsic value of equity	$1,764
177	Value of operations =	$2,524	÷ Number of shares	$60.00
178			Estimated intrinsic stock price =	$29.40

Source: See the file *Ch12 Tool Kit.xlsx*. Numbers are reported as rounded values for clarity but are calculated using *Excel's* full precision. Thus, intermediate calculations using the figure's rounded values will be inexact.

overdrawing their accounts. We discuss the issue of cash management in Chapter 16, but MicroDrive's CFO assumed that the cash required to support MicroDrive's operations is proportional to its sales. For example, the forecasted cash in 2020 is:

$$\text{Cash}_{2020} = (\text{Cash/Sales ratio in 2020})(\text{Sales}_{2020})$$
$$= 2\%(\$5,500) = \$110$$

The CFO applied the same process to project cash in subsequent years.

Unless a company changes its credit policy or has a change in its customer base, accounts receivable should be proportional to sales. The CFO assumed that the credit policy and customers' paying patterns would remain constant and so projected accounts receivable to be 10%($5,500) = $550.

As sales increase, firms generally must carry more inventories. The CFO assumed here that inventory would be proportional to sales. (Chapter 16 will discuss inventory management in detail.) The projected inventory is 20%($5,500) = $1,100.

It might be reasonable to assume that cash, accounts receivable, and inventories will be proportional to sales, but will the amount of net property, plant, and equipment go up and down as sales go up and down? The correct answer could be either yes or no. When companies acquire fixed assets, they often install more capacity than they currently need due to economies of scale in building capacity. Moreover, even if a plant is operating at its maximum-rated capacity, most companies can produce additional units by reducing downtime for scheduled maintenance, by running machinery at a higher than optimal speed, or by adding a second or third shift. Therefore, at least in the short run, sales and net PP&E may not have a close relationship.

However, some companies do have a close relationship between sales and net PP&E, even in the short term. For example, new stores in many retail chains achieve the same sales during their first year as the chain's existing stores. The only way such retailers can grow (beyond inflation) is by adding new stores. Such companies therefore have a strong proportional relationship between fixed assets and sales.

Finally, in the long term there is a close relationship between sales and net PP&E for virtually all companies: Few companies can continue to increase sales unless they also add capacity. Therefore, it is reasonable to assume that the long-term ratio of net PP&E to sales will be constant.

For the first years in a forecast, managers generally build in the actual planned expenditures on plant and equipment. If those estimates are not available, it is generally best to assume a constant ratio of net PP&E to sales.

MicroDrive is a relatively large company and makes capital expenditures every year, so the CFO forecast net PP&E as a percentage of sales. The projected net PP&E is 40%($5,500) = $2,200.

12-3c Operating Liabilities

Section B2 of Figure 12-3 shows the forecast of operating liabilities. Some types of liabilities grow proportionately to sales; these are called **spontaneous liabilities**, as we explain next.

As sales increase, so will purchases of raw materials, and those additional purchases will spontaneously lead to a higher level of accounts payable. MicroDrive's forecast of accounts payable in 2020 is 4%($5,500) = $220.

Higher sales require more labor, and higher sales normally result in higher taxable income and thus taxes. Therefore, accrued wages and taxes both increase as sales increase. The projection of accruals is 8%($5,500) = $440.

12-3d Operating Income

For most companies, the cost of goods sold (COGS) is highly correlated with sales, and MicroDrive is no exception. As shown in Section B3 of Figure 12-3, MicroDrive's forecast of COGS (excluding depreciation) for 2020 is 78%($5,500) = $4,290.

Because depreciation depends on an asset's depreciable basis, as described in Chapter 11, it is more reasonable to forecast depreciation as a percent of net plant and equipment rather than of sales. MicroDrive's projection of depreciation in 2020 is 10%(2020 Net PP&E) = 10%($2,200) = $220.

MicroDrive's other operating expenses include items such as salaries of executives, insurance fees, and marketing costs. These items tend to be related to a company's size, which is related to sales. MicroDrive's projection is 10%($5,500) = $550.

MicroDrive will consider several strategic initiatives in other scenarios, so the forecast includes a line item for these costs. For the Status Quo scenario, this cost is zero.

Subtracting the COGS, depreciation, other operating expenses, and the cost of strategic initiatives from net sales gives earnings before interest and taxes (EBIT). Recall from Chapter 2 that net operating profit after taxes (NOPAT) is defined as EBIT(1 − T), where T is the tax rate.

12-3e Free Cash Flow (FCF)

Section B4 in Figure 12-3 calculates free cash flow (FCF) using the process described in Chapter 2. The first row in Section B4 begins with a calculation of net operating working capital (NOWC), which is defined as operating current assets minus operating current liabilities. Operating current assets is the sum of cash, accounts receivable, and inventories; operating current liabilities is the sum of accounts payable and accruals. The second row shows the forecast of total net operating capital, which is NOWC plus net PP&E. All of the items required for these calculations were previously forecast in Section B2.

Recall from Chapter 2 that free cash flow is equal to NOPAT minus the investment in total net operating capital; the forecast of NOPAT is in Section B3, and the forecast of total net operating capital is in the second row of Section B4.

12-3f Estimated Intrinsic Value

Section B5 begins with the estimated target WACC, calculated using the inputs from Sections 2 and 3 of Figure 12-2. These values are the same ones we used in Chapter 9 to estimate MicroDrive's weighted average cost of capital. The weighted average cost of capital is calculated based on the target capital structure. MicroDrive's CFO decided to use the target capital structure for all scenarios but to modify the projections later if the board decides to change the capital structure.

The second, third, and fourth rows of Section B5 in Figure 12-3 report the operating profitability ratio, the capital requirement ratio, and the return on invested capital (ROIC) for easy comparison to their values in previous years. The forecasted values for OP, CR, and ROIC do not change because the input ratios in the Status Quo scenario don't change. Also, notice that the ROIC is less than the WACC, which will influence the choice of strategic initiatives, described later in this analysis.

The fifth row of Section B5 in Figure 12-3 shows the growth rate in FCF. Notice that the growth rate is very high in the early years of the forecast due to high sales growth but then levels out at the sustainable growth rate of sales, 5%. Had it not done so, the forecast period would need to be extended until the growth in FCF became constant.

Using the estimated FCF, WACC, and long-term constant growth rate in FCF, Section B5 shows the calculation of the **horizon value** using the constant growth formula from Chapter 7. Recall that the horizon value is the value of all cash flows *beyond* the horizon when discounted back to the horizon. In other words, it is the value of operations at the horizon date.

To find the value of operations, it is necessary to find the present value of the horizon value and the present value of the forecasted free cash flows and then sum them. The lower left corner of Figure 12-3 shows that MicroDrive's estimated value of operations is $2,524.

The panel on the lower right of Section B5 estimates the intrinsic stock price using the approach in Chapter 7. For the Status Quo forecast, the estimated intrinsic value is $29.40.

12-3g Enhancements to the Basic Model

Although the assumption that operating assets and operating liabilities grow proportionally to sales is a very good approximation for most companies, a few circumstances might require more complicated modeling techniques. We describe four possible refinements in Section 12-8: economies of scale, nonlinear relationships, lumpy purchases of assets, and excess capacity adjustments. However, always keep in mind that additional complexity in a model might not be worth the incremental improvement in accuracy.

SELF-TEST

Which items comprise operating current assets? Why is it reasonable to assume that they grow proportionally to sales?

What are some reasons that net PP&E might grow proportionally to sales, and what are some reasons that it might not?

What are spontaneous liabilities?

12-4 Evaluating MicroDrive's Strategic Initiatives

Based on the analysis in the previous section, MicroDrive's estimated intrinsic stock value is $29.40, which is lower than its actual market price of $31 by about 5%. There are three possible reasons for this difference: (1) MicroDrive's standard deviation of stock returns is about 52%, as estimated in Chapter 6, so a 5% difference between the estimated intrinsic value and the observed stock price could be due to the stock's day-to-day volatility. (2) The model's assumptions might be too pessimistic relative to MicroDrive's most likely future operating performance. (3) The market's assumptions might be too optimistic, which implies that the stock is overvalued and that investors should sell the stock.

MicroDrive's managers identified key value drivers in Chapter 7, but they must flesh out the operating plans here. In particular, they will examine three strategic initiatives. The first, focusing on revenue growth, will cost $50 million to implement and will boost sales growth rates, as shown in Figure 12-4, Panel A, Column (2). A second plan, shown in Column (3), will focus on improving operations and will cost $100 million to implement. Column (4) reports a third plan to simultaneously improve operation and boost revenue growth but that will cost $150 million. Each plan's inputs that differ from the Status Quo are shown in rose-colored cells.

Panel B of Figure 12-4 reports key results. The first seven rows report operating measures for the last year in the forecast, after the inputs' changes have stabilized at their long-term values. The last two rows show the estimated value of operations and the intrinsic stock price.

resource

See **Ch12 Tool Kit.xlsx** on the textbook's Web site.

FIGURE 12-4
Key Inputs and Operating Results for Possible Strategic Initiatives (Millions of Dollars, Except for per Share Data)

	A	B	C	D	E	F
194				Scenario		
195				(2)	(3)	
196			(1)	Higher	Improve	(4)
197			Status	Sales	Operations	Operations
198			Quo	Growth	(Only)	and Growth
199	**Panel A: Key Inputs**					
200	Sales growth (Year 1)		10.0%	11.0%	10.0%	11.0%
201	Sales growth (Year 2)		8.0%	9.0%	8.0%	9.0%
202	Sales growth (Year 3)		7.0%	8.0%	7.0%	8.0%
203	Long-term sales growth (g_L)		5.0%	6.0%	5.0%	6.0%
204	(COGS excl. depr.)/Sales (Year 1)		78.0%	78.0%	78.0%	78.0%
205	(COGS excl. depr.)/Sales (Year 2)		78.0%	78.0%	77.1%	77.1%
206	Inventory/Sales for (Year 1)		20.0%	20.0%	18.0%	18.0%
207	Inventory/Sales for (Year 2)		20.0%	20.0%	15.0%	15.0%
208	(Net PP&E)/Sales (Year 1)		40.0%	40.0%	38.0%	38.0%
209	(Net PP&E)/Sales (Year 2)		40.0%	40.0%	36.0%	36.0%
210	Cost of strategic initiatives		$0	$50	$100	$150
211	Weighted average cost of capital (WACC)		11.50%	11.50%	11.50%	11.50%
212	**Panel B: Key Operating Plan Results**					
213	OP, operating profitability (Year 5)		6.0%	6.0%	7.0%	7.0%
214	CR, capital requirement (Year 5)		60.0%	60.0%	51.0%	51.0%
215	ROIC, return on invested capital (Year 5)		10.00%	10.00%	13.72%	13.72%
216	Sales (Year 5)		$7,007	$7,341	$7,007	$7,341
217	NOPAT (Year 5)		$420	$440	$490	$514
218	Total net operating capital ((Year 5)		$4,204	$4,405	$3,574	$3,744
219	FCF (Year 5)		$220	$191	$320	$302
220	Value of operations (Year 0)		$2,524	$2,458	$4,091	$4,353
221	Intrinsic stock price (Year 0)		$29.40	$28.31	$55.52	$59.88

Source: See the file *Ch12 Tool Kit.xlsx*. Numbers are reported as rounded values for clarity but are calculated using *Excel's* full precision. Thus, intermediate calculations using the figure's rounded values will be inexact.

Note: Operating improvements will be sustained at the Year-2 values.

Notice that the Higher Sales Growth scenario in Column (2) has a lower value of operations ($2,458 versus $2,524) and intrinsic stock price ($28.31 versus $29.40) than the Status Quo scenario. Part of the reason is due to the $50 million cost of implementing the growth initiative, but part is because the ROIC is too low. Recall from Chapter 7 that growth can have a positive or negative effect on value, depending on the relative sizes of the return on invested capital at the horizon, $ROIC_T$, the long-term growth rate, g_L, and the cost of capital. If $ROIC_T < WACC/(1 + g_L)$, then the value of operations will be less than the value of total net operating capital. If the $ROIC_T$ is so low that $ROIC_T < WACC/(1 + WACC)$, then an increase in growth will make the company *less* valuable. Intuitively, this is because the new projects that cause growth will have negative NPVs. With a higher growth rate, the company will be adding negative NPV projects more often. This is the case for MicroDrive: $10\% < 11.5\%/(1 + 11.5\%) = 10.31\%$.

The key point to remember is not to implement growth strategies if the return on invested capital is too low. In that situation, managers must improve operating profitability or capital utilization, which will increase the ROIC, before pursuing growth.

Based on the analysis in Chapter 7, MicroDrive learned that its key value drivers were operating profitability and capital requirements. After much discussion, the management team concluded that, because of licensing fees and other costs, it was not feasible for MicroDrive to reduce its COGS/Sales ratio in the next year. However, the director of R&D explained that the new products in the pipeline will have higher profit margins. If Micro-Drive can fund some extra field tests, the new products can reach the market in a year and drive the ratio of COGS/Sales down to 77.1% from its current level of 78%.

The production, sales, and purchasing managers are jointly responsible for inventory in MicroDrive's supply chain. With some additional funding for technology to improve channels of information among suppliers and customers, MicroDrive can reduce inventory levels without hurting product availability. They estimated that the improved technology would push the Inventory/Sales ratio down to 15% over the next two years from its current level of 20%.

The production and human resource managers stated that productivity could be increased with new training programs so that employees can better utilize the new production equipment that had been added the previous year. They estimated that the increased productivity would cause the ratio of PP&E/Sales to fall from its current level of 40% to 36% in the next 2 years.

Managers from marketing, supply chain management, accounting, and finance estimated that the total cost for these improvement programs would be about $100 million.

The CFO entered these new inputs (including the cost to implement the operating improvement initiatives) into the model; see Figure 12-4, Column (3). The value of operations increased from $2,524 million to $4,091 million and the intrinsic stock price increased from $29.40 to $55.52. The big increase in value is primarily due to the increase in ROIC from 10.0% to 13.7%, which is well above the 11.5% WACC.

Given the improved ROIC, the CFO wondered whether growth might now generate value. Using the inputs and combined costs for the improved operations and higher sales growth scenarios, the CFO created a fourth scenario named Operations and Growth; the results are shown in Column (4) of Figure 12-4. Relative to only improving operations, the value of operations increased from $4,091 million to $4,353 million, and the intrinsic stock price increased from $55.52 to $59.88. Notice that growth now adds value because the ROIC has been improved.

If MicroDrive stays with the Status Quo, what will happen to its dividend payouts and its debt levels? Implementing any of the other plans will require additional expenditures. Should MicroDrive be willing to incur these costs? If so, how can MicroDrive fund the additional expenditures? The following sections address these questions.

SELF-TEST

Will improvements in the long-term growth rate of sales always add value? Explain your answer.

12-5 Projecting MicroDrive's Financial Statements

A key output of a financial plan is the set of projected financial statements. The basic approach in projecting statements is a simple, three-step process: (1) Forecast the operating items. (2) Forecast the amounts of debt, equity, and dividends that are determined by the company's preliminary short-term financial policy. (3) Ensure that the company has sufficient but not excess financing to fund the operating plan.

Despite the simple process, projecting financial statements can be similar to peeling onions—but not because it smells bad and brings tears to your eyes! Just as there are many different onions (white, purple, large, small, sweet, sour, etc.), there are many different variations on the basic approach. And just as onions have many layers, a financial plan can have many layers of complexity. It would be impossible for us to cover all the different methods and details used when projecting financial statements, so we are going to focus on the straightforward method MicroDrive's CFO uses, which is applicable to most companies.

Here are the three steps in this method:

1. MicroDrive will project all the operating items that are part of the operating plan.
2. For the initial forecast, MicroDrive's CFO applied the following preliminary short-term financial policy: (1) MicroDrive will not issue any long-term bonds, preferred stock, or common stock in the upcoming year. (2) MicroDrive will not pay off or increase notes payable. (3) MicroDrive will increase regular dividends at the sustainable 5% long-term growth rate. (4) MicroDrive will sell its short-term investments. (5) Regarding Micro-Drive's total of $60 million of interest payments in 2019, $10 million was for notes payable and $20 million was for bonds.
3. Suppose the short-term financial policies described in Step 2 do not provide sufficient additional financing to fund the additional operating assets needed by the operating plan described in Step 1. If so, MicroDrive will draw on a special **line of credit (LOC)**, which is an arrangement in which a bank agrees now to lend up to a specified maximum amount of funds during a future designated period. If the financial policies provide surplus financing, MicroDrive will pay a special dividend.

12-5a Forecast the Accounts from the Operating Plan

Figure 12-5 shows MicroDrive's projected financial statements for the Status Quo scenario for the upcoming year. MicroDrive's CFO forecast the operating plan in Section 12-3, so it is an easy matter to replicate the process and forecast the corresponding operating items on the financial statement accounts. Column C shows the most recent year, Column D shows the inputs from Figure 12-2, Columns E and F describe how the inputs are applied, and Column G shows the forecast for the upcoming year. Notice that the forecasts for the operating items in Figure 12-5 are identical to those in Figure 12-3.

12-5b Forecast Items Determined by the Preliminary Short-Term Financial Policy

MicroDrive has a target capital structure and target dividend growth, shown in Figure 12-2, Sections 2–4. Like most companies, MicroDrive is willing to deviate from those targets in the short term. For the purpose of this initial forecast, MicroDrive has a preliminary short-term financial policy that sets the projected values for notes payable, long-term debt, preferred stock, and common stock equal to their previous values. In other words, the preliminary short-term financial policy does not call for any change in these items. Keep in mind that financial planning is an iterative process—specify a plan, look at the results, modify if needed, and repeat the process until the plan is acceptable and achievable.

The pale silver rows with blue print in Figure 12-5 show the items determined by the preliminary short-term financial policy. Section 1 shows the projected balance sheets, with the projected values for notes payable, long-term debt, preferred stock, and common stock unchanged from their previous values. The basic approach for projecting financial statements would remain unchanged if the preliminary short-term financial policy had called for changes in these items, such as issuing new debt or equity. In fact, after the preliminary forecast has been analyzed, MicroDrive's CFO plans on presenting long-term recommendations to the board regarding the possibility of issuing additional common stock, preferred stock, or long-term bonds.

resource

See **Ch12 Tool Kit.xlsx** on the textbook's Web site.

FIGURE 12-5
MicroDrive's Projected Financial Statements for the Status Quo Scenario (Millions of Dollars, Except for per Share Data)

	A	B	C	D	E	F	G
262	**Status Quo**						
263	*1. Balance Sheets*		**Most Recent**				**Forecast**
264	*Assets*		**2019**	**Input**	**Basis for 2020 Forecast**		**2020**
265	Cash		$100.0	2.00%	× 2020 Sales		$110.00
266	Short-tem investments		10.0		Set to zero		$0.00
267	Accounts receivable		500.0	10.00%	× 2020 Sales		$550.00
268	Inventories		1,000.0	20.00%	× 2020 Sales		$1,100.00
269	Total current assets		$1,610.0				$1,760.00
270	Net PP&E		2,000.0	40.00%	× 2020 Sales		$2,200.00
271	Total assets (TA)		$3,610.0				$3,960.00
272	*Liabilities and equity*						
273	Accounts payable		$200.0	4.00%	× 2020 Sales		$220.00
274	Notes payable		150.0		Carry over from previous year		$150.00
275	Accruals		400.0	8.00%	× 2020 Sales		$440.00
276	Line of credit		0.0		Draw on LOC if financing deficit		$78.00
277	Total CL		$750.0				$888.00
278	Long-term bonds		520.0		Carry over from previous year		$520.00
279	Total liabilities		$1,270.0				$1,408.00
280	Preferred stock		$100.0		Carry over from previous year		$100.00
281	Common stock		500.0		Carry over from previous year		$500.00
282	Retained earnings		1,740.0		Previous RE + Add. to RE		$1,952
283	Total common equity		$2,240.0				$2,452
284	Total liabs. & equity		$3,610.0				$3,960
285					Check: TA − Total Liab. & Eq. =		$0.00
286	*2. Income Statement*		**Most Recent**				**Forecast**
287			**2019**	**Input**	**Basis for 2020 Forecast**		**2020**
288	Net sales		$5,000.0	110%	× 2019 Sales		$5,500.00
289	COGS (excl. depr.)		3,900.0	78.00%	× 2020 Sales		4,290.00
290	Depreciation		200.0	10.00%	× 2020 Net PP&E		220.00
291	Other operating expenses		500.0	10.00%	× 2020 Sales		550.00
292	Cost of strategic initiatives		0.0		Cost of implementation		0.00
293	EBIT		$400.0				$440.00
294	Less: Interest on notes		10.0	8.00%	× Avg notes		$12.00
295	Interest on bonds		50.0	10.00%	× Avg bonds		$52.00
296	Interest on LOC		0.0	9.50%	× Beginning LOC		$0.00
297	Pre-tax earnings		$340.0				$376.00
298	Taxes (25%)		85.0	25.00%	× Pre-tax earnings		$94.00
299	NI before pref. div.		$255.0				$282.00
300	Preferred dividend		7.0	7.00%	× Avg pref. stock		$7.00
301	Net income		$248.0				$275.00
302	Regular common dividends		$60.0	105%	× 2019 Dividend		$63.00
303	Special dividends		$0.0		Pay if financing surplus		$0.00
304	Addition to RE		$188.0		Net income − Dividends		$212.00
305	*3. Elimination of the Financial Deficit or Surplus*						
306	Increase in spontaneous liabilities (accounts payable and accruals)						$60.00
307	+ Increase in notes payable, long-term bonds, preferred stock, and common stock						$0.00
308	+ Net income minus regular common dividends						$212.00
309	− Previous line of credit						$0.00
310	Increase in financing						$272.00
311	− Increase in total assets						$350.00
312	Amount of deficit or surplus financing:						−$78.00
313	If deficit in financing (negative), draw on line of credit					Line of credit	$78.00
314	If surplus in financing (positive), pay special dividend					Special dividend	$0.00

Source: See the file *Ch12 Tool Kit.xlsx*. Numbers are reported as rounded values for clarity but are calculated using *Excel's* full precision. Thus, intermediate calculations using the figure's rounded values will be inexact.

Section 2 of Figure 12-5 shows the projected income statement. The interest expense on notes payable is projected as the interest rate on notes payable multiplied by the average value of the notes payable outstanding during the year. For example, MicroDrive's notes payable balance was $150 at the end of 2019 and was projected to be $150 at the end of 2020, so the average balance during the year is $150 = ($150 + $150)/2. If MicroDrive's plans had called for borrowing an additional $40 in notes payable during the year (resulting in an end-of-year balance of $320), the average balance would have been $300 = ($150 + $320)/2. The same process is applied to long-term bonds and preferred stock.

Basing interest expense on the average amount of debt outstanding during the year implies that the debt is added (or repaid) smoothly during the year. However, if debt is not added until the last day of the year, that year's interest expense should be based on just the debt at the beginning of the year (i.e., the debt at the end of the previous year) because virtually no interest would have accrued on the new debt. On the other hand, if the new debt is added on the first day of the year, interest would accrue all year, so the interest expense should be based on the amount of debt shown at the end of the year.

MicroDrive's preliminary short-term financial policy calls for its regular common dividends to grow by 5%. Preferred dividends are projected by multiplying the average balance of preferred stock by the preferred dividend rate.

The only items on the projected statements that have not been forecast by the operating plan or the preliminary short-term financial plan are the line of credit (LOC), interest on the LOC, and the item for special dividends. These projections are red and are in the pale silver rows in Figure 12-5. We explain how to complete the financial forecast next.

12-5c Identify and Eliminate the Financing Deficit or Surplus in the Projected Balance Sheets

At this point in the projection, it would be extremely unlikely for the balance sheets to balance because the increase in assets required by the operating plan probably is not equal to the increase in liabilities and financing generated by the operating plan and the preliminary short-term financial policy. There will be a **financing deficit** if the additional financing is less than the additional assets, and a **financing surplus** if the additional financing is greater than the additional assets. If there is a financing deficit, MicroDrive will not be able to afford its operating plan; if there is a financing surplus, MicroDrive must use it in some manner. Therefore, a realistic projection requires balance sheets that balance.

How should a company handle a financing deficit or surplus? There are an infinite number of possible answers to that question, which is why financial modeling can be complicated. MicroDrive's CFO chose a simple but effective approach. If there is a deficit, draw on a line of credit even though it has a relatively high interest rate of 9.5% (the rate on the LOC is 1.5 percentage points higher than the rate on notes payable). If there is a surplus, pay a special dividend. Keep in mind that this is a preliminary plan and that MicroDrive might choose a different source of financing in its final plan.

The first step in implementing this approach is to identify the preliminary amounts of net additional financing. The second step is to identify the required additional assets. The third step is to identify the resulting financing deficit or surplus. The fourth step is to eliminate the financing deficit or surplus. We explain these steps next.

STEP 1: IDENTIFY THE NET ADDITIONAL FINANCING

Preliminary additional financing comes from three sources: (1) spontaneous liabilities, (2) external financing (such as issuing new long-term bonds or common equity), and (3) internal financing (which is the amount of earnings that are reinvested rather than paid out as dividends). In addition, the preliminary financial plan assumes no line of credit. Following is an explanation of how to calculate the additional financing for MicroDrive.

Section 3 in Figure 12-5 begins by adding up the additional financing in the forecast year relative to the previous year. For example, MicroDrive's spontaneous liabilities (accounts payable and accruals) went from a total of $600 to $660, an increase of $60. Due to MicroDrive's preliminary short-term financial policy, there were no changes in the external financing provided by notes payable, long-term bonds, preferred stock, or common stock. MicroDrive's preliminary policy calls for no changes in external financing, but it would be easy to modify this assumption. In fact, the CFO did make changes in external financing in a final plan that we discuss later. The preliminary amount of internal financing available is the difference between net income and regular common dividends; this is the amount of earnings that are being reinvested.

The preliminary plan assumes that there is no line of credit. Therefore, if there is a balance on a line of credit for the previous year, this must be subtracted before estimating the net additional financing. In other words, MicroDrive must pay off any previous line of credit by the end of the year before drawing on a new line of credit. This is called a **cleanup clause**, a common feature with many lines of credit. In general, a line of credit is intended to help a company with short-term liquidity needs rather than serve as a permanent source of financing, so banks often require the LOC to have a zero balance at some point in the year.

Based on the preliminary operating and financing plans, MicroDrive projects a total increase in financing of $272, as shown in Section 3 of Figure 12-5.

STEP 2: IDENTIFY THE REQUIRED ADDITIONAL ASSETS

The second step is to calculate the required additional assets. MicroDrive's forecast calls for total assets to grow from $3,610 to $3,960, for a net increase in assets of $350: $3,960 − $3,610 = $350.

STEP 3: IDENTIFY THE FINANCING DEFICIT OR SURPLUS

The third step is to determine whether there is a financing deficit or surplus. The difference between MicroDrive's increase in financing and its increase in projected assets is $272 − $350 = −$78. This amount is negative because the increase in MicroDrive's projected assets is greater than the increase in MicroDrive's projected financing. Therefore, Micro-Drive has a preliminary financing deficit—MicroDrive needs more financing to support its operating plan and will need to draw on a line of credit. Had this value been positive, MicroDrive would have had a financing surplus and would have had funds available to pay a special dividend. The last two rows in Section 3 of Figure 12-5 apply this logic and show an amount for a line of credit *or* a special dividend, but not both.

STEP 4: ELIMINATE THE FINANCING DEFICIT OR SURPLUS

The fourth step is to adjust the financial statements to eliminate the financing deficit or surplus. MicroDrive has a financing deficit, which is called the **additional financing needed (AFN)**. This is the amount of funding that will be needed to implement the operating plan, given the preliminary choices of capital structure and dividend payout.

MicroDrive will need to draw on a line of credit (LOC). The cell for the LOC in the balance sheet in Section 1 (Cell G276) is linked to the cell for the necessary amount of the LOC that is identified in Section 3 (G313). Notice that this adjustment increases the total liabilities so that the balance sheets now balance.

MicroDrive's balance sheets now show $78 for the line of credit. Does this mean that MicroDrive needs to adjust the interest expense on its income statement? MicroDrive's CFO made a simplifying assumption for the preliminary projection: The LOC will be drawn upon on the last day of the year. Therefore, the LOC will not accrue interest, so the interest expense on the LOC is equal to the interest rate multiplied by the balance of the LOC at the beginning of the year rather than the end of the year.

The CFO realizes that the projected interest expense will understate the true interest expense if MicroDrive draws on the LOC earlier in the year. However, the CFO wanted to keep the model simple for the preliminary presentations at the retreat. The CFO actually made more realistic assumptions in another (but more complex) model, which we describe later in the chapter.

Now that the hard work of projecting the financial statements is done, it is time for MicroDrive's managers to discuss the projections and finalize their plans.

SELF-TEST

How are operating items projected on financial statements?

How are preliminary levels of debt, preferred stock, common stock, and dividends projected?

What is the financing surplus or deficit? How is it calculated?

12-6 Analysis and Selection of a Strategic Plan

The CFO forecast the financial statements for all scenarios for the next five-year period; see *Ch12 Tool Kit.xlsx* for the estimated financial statements for all four scenarios. Figure 12-6 summarizes the estimated impact of each plan on financing needs not included in the preliminary financial policies (shown by the line of credit). It also shows any special dividends.

Column (1) of Figure 12-6 shows that the Status Quo plan requires drawing on the line of credit in the first year, has a maximum draw of $113 million but does not require the LOC by Year 5. This plan maintains regular dividends but does not pay any special dividends until Year 5. However, the plan would be unable to pay regular dividends in Years 1–4 if it did not draw on the LOC. Column (2) reports the Higher Sales Growth scenario. It requires a $143 million LOC in Year 1, which peaks at $248 million and is down to $169 by Year 5.

The management team quickly rejected the Status Quo and Higher Sales Growth scenarios but spent several hours discussing the other two plans. Neither the Improve Operations (Only) plan nor the Operations and Growth plan requires drawing on the line of credit. This is because both plans improve asset utilization, allowing MicroDrive to reduce its inventories (which generates positive cash flow) and make only a much smaller investment in new PP&E in the upcoming year (see the *Tool Kit* for details). As a consequence, neither plan needs to draw on the LOC. However, there are some important differences between the plans—the Improve Operations (Only) plan pays more in special dividends during the next five years, but the Operations and Growth plan has a greater value of operations and stock price.

Think about why the plans have different expected outcomes. The Operations and Growth plan has higher sales growth rates, which means its investments in operating capital are greater, especially in the first couple of years. The net result is lower free cash flow during the forecast period but higher projected free cash flow beyond the forecast horizon, giving it a much larger horizon value.

FIGURE 12-6

Key Inputs and Financial Plan Outcomes for Possible Strategic Initiatives (Millions of Dollars, Except for per Share Data)

	A	B	C	D	E	F
					Scenario	
428						
429				**(2)**	**(3)**	
430			**(1)**	**Higher**	**Improve**	**(4)**
431			**Status**	**Sales**	**Operations**	**Operations**
432			**Quo**	**Growth**	**(Only)**	**and Growth**
433	**Panel A: Key Inputs**					
434	Sales growth (Year 1)		10.0%	11.0%	10.0%	11.0%
435	Sales growth (Year 2)		8.0%	9.0%	8.0%	9.0%
436	Sales growth (Year 3)		7.0%	8.0%	7.0%	8.0%
437	Long-term sales growth (g_L)		5.0%	6.0%	5.0%	6.0%
438	(COGS excl. depr.)/Sales (Year 1)		78.0%	78.0%	78.0%	78.0%
439	(COGS excl. depr.)/Sales (Year 2)		78.0%	78.0%	77.1%	77.1%
440	Inventory/Sales for (Year 1)		20.0%	20.0%	18.0%	18.0%
441	Inventory/Sales for (Year 2)		20.0%	20.0%	15.0%	15.0%
442	(Net PP&E)/Sales (Year 1)		40.0%	40.0%	38.0%	38.0%
443	(Net PP&E)/Sales (Year 2)		40.0%	40.0%	36.0%	36.0%
444	Cost of strategic initiatives		$0	$50	$100	$150
445	Weighted average cost of capital		11.5%	11.5%	11.5%	11.5%
446	**Panel B: Key Financial Plan Results**					
447	Line of credit (Year 1)		$78	$143	$0	$0
448	Line of credit (Year 5)		$0	$169	$0	$0
449	Minimum LOC in forecast		$0	$143	$0	$0
450	Maximum LOC in forecast		$113	$248	$0	$0
451	Regular dividends (Year 1)		$63	$63	$63	$63
452	Regular dividends (Year 5)		$77	$77	$77	$77
453	Special dividends (Year 1)		$0	$0	$75	$13
454	Special dividends (Year 5)		$47	$0	$189	$170
455	Total special dividends in forecast		$47	$0	$894	$751
456	Value of operations (Year 0)		$2,524	$2,458	$4,091	$4,353
457	Intrinsic stock price (Year 0)		$29.40	$28.31	$55.52	$59.88

Source: See the file *Ch12 Tool Kit.xlsx*. Numbers are reported as rounded values for clarity but are calculated using *Excel's* full precision. Thus, intermediate calculations using the figure's rounded values will be inexact.

resource

See **Ch12 Tool Kit.xlsx** on the textbook's Web site.

MicroDrive's managers have a long-term perspective, so they chose the Operations and Growth plan. This is an example of **value-based management** because MicroDrive is using the **free cash flow valuation model** to identify value drivers and guide managerial and strategic decisions.

Figure 12-7 shows selected operating results and financial outcomes for the Operations and Growth plan. After the initial major expenditure on the strategic initiative in 2020, the ROIC rebounds to 13.5% in subsequent years, well above the WACC.[1] Based on the ratios at the end of the forecast period, MicroDrive still has a bit more debt than the industry average (causing a lower than average time-interest-earned ratio) and pays out a higher proportion of its net income. We will examine payout and debt policies in Chapters 14 and 15.

resource

See **Ch12 Tool Kit.xlsx** on the textbook's Web site.

---

[1]Accounting rules require that the expenditures to implement this operating plan must be considered an expense, although common sense suggests that they are an investment because they are expected to produce future benefits. Some compensation plans actually spread this cost over several future years (smoothing out its impact on ROIC) when creating "financial statements" used for calculating bonuses.

FIGURE 12-7
Operating Results and Financial Outcomes for the Operations and Growth Plan (Millions of Dollars, Except for per Share Data)

	A	B	C	D	E	F	G	H
468	**Improve Operations and Growth**	**Industry**				**MicroDrive**		
469		Actual	Actual			Forecast		
470	**Panel A: Inputs**	2019	2019	2020	2021	2022	2023	2024
471	Sales growth rate	5%	4%	11%	9%	8%	6%	6%
472	(COGS excl. depr.)/Sales	76%	78%	78%	77%	77%	77%	77%
473	Inventory/Sales	15%	20%	18%	15%	15%	15%	15%
474	(Net PP&E)/Sales	33%	40%	38%	36%	36%	36%	36%
475	Cost of strategic initiatives	NA	NA	$150	$0	$0	$0	$0
476		**Industry**				**MicroDrive**		
477	**Panel B: Key Output**	Actual	Actual			Forecast		
478		2019	2019	2020	2021	2022	2023	2024
479	Return on invested capital	15.0%	10.00%	7.36%	13.72%	13.72%	13.72%	13.72%
480	Free cash flow	NA	−$210	$121	$446	$210	$285	$302
481	Line of credit	NA	$0	$0	$0	$0	$0	$0
482	Special dividends	NA	$0	$13	$325	$86	$157	$170
483	(Total debt)/TA	25.0%	18.6%	17.8%	17.6%	16.3%	15.4%	14.5%
484	Times interest earned	10.0	3.3	4.8	8.8	9.5	10.1	10.7
485	Return on assets (ROA)	11.0%	5.2%	4.6%	9.7%	9.8%	9.8%	9.9%
486	Return on equity (ROE)	19.0%	8.4%	7.4%	15.9%	15.7%	15.6%	15.4%
487	Earnings per share	NA	$3.13	$2.90	$6.14	$6.70	$7.16	$7.64
488	Payout ratio	35.0%	31.9%	43.6%	106.2%	38.6%	53.5%	53.8%
489	Regular dividends per share	NA	$1.00	$1.05	$1.10	$1.16	$1.22	$1.28
490	Special dividends per share	NA	$0.00	$0.21	$5.42	$1.43	$2.61	$2.84
491								
492	**Panel C: Valuation**							
493			Weighted average cost of capital =		11.50%			
494		12/31/2019	Estimated value of operations =		$4,353			
495		12/31/2019	Estimated intrinsic stock price =		$59.88			

Source: See the file *Ch12 Tool Kit.xlsx*. Numbers are reported as rounded values for clarity but are calculated using *Excel's* full precision. Thus, intermediate calculations using the figure's rounded values will be inexact.

SELF-TEST

What is value-based management and how is it used?

12-7 The CFO's Model[2]

The CFO's final model, shown in the worksheet named *CFO Model* in the file *Ch12 Tool Kit.xlsx*, has several refinements to the basic model presented in the previous sections, including the incorporation of financing feedback and implementation of the target capital structure.

12-7a Financing Feedback

The basic model assumed that no interest would accrue on the line of credit because the LOC would be added at the end of the year. However, if interest is calculated

---

[2]This section is relatively technical, and some instructors may choose to skip it with no loss in continuity.

on the LOC's average balance during the year, which is more realistic, here is what happens:

1. The line of credit required to make the balance sheets balance is added to the balance sheet.
2. Interest expense increases due to the additional LOC.
3. Net income decreases because interest expenses are higher.
4. Internally generated financing decreases because net income decreases.
5. The financing deficit increases because internally generated financing decreases.
6. An additional amount of the LOC is added to the balance sheets to make them balance.
7. Go to Step 2 and repeat the loop.

This loop is called **financing feedback** because the additional financing feeds back and causes a need for more additional financing. If programmed into *Excel,* there will be a circular reference. Sometimes *Excel* can handle this (if the iteration feature is enabled), but sometimes *Excel* freezes up. Fortunately, there is a simple way to modify the required line of credit by scaling it up so that no iterations are required. If this piques your interest, take a look at the *CFO Model* in the *Tool Kit*.

12-7b Implementing the Target Capital Structure

The preliminary financial policy chosen by the CFO during the managers' retreat held external financing constant—with no additional borrowing or repayment of debt (other than the line of credit) and no new issues or repurchases of preferred stock or common stock. However, this ignores the target capital structure. Fortunately, there is a simple way to implement the target capital structure in the projected statements.

In order to implement its target capital structure, MicroDrive must first find the total value of the firm (the value of operations) each year in order to determine the amount of short-term and long-term debt to be consistent with this target. This is easy to do for the last year of projections where MicroDrive can find the horizon value using the target WACC and the projected FCF. We will do this for the Status Quo scenario as an example, and Figure 12-3 has the horizon value calculations. Note that management would do this for their final plan instead of the Status Quo scenario, and we will provide instructions for viewing this scenario at the end of this section. Continuing with the example, MicroDrive's horizon value from the Status Quo plan at the end of 2024 is $3,558, shown at the bottom of Figure 12-3. If MicroDrive's target weight for long-term debt, w_d, is 20%, then the amount of debt required at the end of 2024 is 20%($3,558) = $712.

To find the required level of debt for the rest of the forecast years, MicroDrive next estimates its value of operations for *each year* of the forecast, starting at the horizon and working backward. The value of operations at the horizon, 2024, is equal to the horizon value, $3,558. Note that this is really the value of all free cash flows from 2025 and beyond, discounted back to 2024. The value of operations at 2023, 1 year before the horizon, is equal to the value of all FCFs beyond 2023, discounted at the WACC back to 2023. But we have already found the value of all FCFs beyond 2024 discounted back to 2024 to be $3,558, and we know the FCF in 2024 is $220. Therefore, we can discount the 2024 value of operations and the 2024 free cash flow back 1 year to get the 2023 value of operations: Value at 2023 = ($3,558 + $220)/(1 + 0.115) = $3,388. We can work our way back to the current date by repeating this process, providing estimates of the yearly values of operations.

We also know the weights in the target capital structure for each year. Here, the target weight for long-term debt, w_d, is 20%. We can multiply this target weight by the value of operations each year to obtain the amount of long-term debt that conforms to the target capital structure. In 2024, this is $712: $w_d(V_{op,2024}) = 20\%(\$3,558) = \$712$. In 2023, this would be 20%($3,388) = $678 if the target weight for debt that year were also 20%. Repeating this process for all the capital components each year provides the amounts of external funding that match the target capital structure.

To see the forecast debt levels for the final plan rather than the Status Quo scenario, select the Operations and Growth scenario in the *Chapter* worksheet in the *Tool Kit* and then open the *CFO Model* worksheet. This worksheet implements a modified version of this procedure for the scenario selected in the *Chapter* worksheet. Instead of setting the actual capital structure weights equal to the target weights in the first year of the forecast, the CFO's model allows the actual weights in the capital structure each year to move smoothly from the actual current values to the target values at the horizon. See the *CFO model* in the *Tool Kit* for details.

SELF-TEST

Suppose a company's return on invested capital is less than its WACC. What happens to the value of operations if the sales growth rate increases? Explain your answer.

12-8 Additional Funds Needed (AFN) Equation

A complete financial plan includes projected financial statements, but the **additional funds needed (AFN) equation** provides a simple way to get a ballpark estimate of the additional external financing that will be required. The AFN approach identifies the financing surplus or deficit in much the same way as we did in the previous sections: (1) Identify the amount of additional funding required by the additional assets due to growth in sales. (2) Identify the amount of spontaneous liabilities (which reduces the amount of external financing that is required to support the additional assets). (3) Identify the amount of funding generated internally from net income that will be available for reinvestment in the company after paying dividends. (4) Assume no new external financing (similar to the preliminary financial policy in the Status Quo scenario). The difference between the additional assets and the sum of spontaneous liabilities and reinvested net income is the amount of additional financing needed from external sources. Following are explanations and applications of these steps.

12-8a Required Increase in Assets

In a steady-state situation in which no excess capacity exists, the firm must have additional plant and equipment, more delivery trucks, higher inventories, and so forth if sales are to increase. In addition, more sales will lead to more accounts receivable, and those receivables must be financed from the time of the sale until they are collected. Therefore, both fixed and current assets must increase if sales are to increase. Of course, if assets are to increase, liabilities and equity must also increase by a like amount to make the balance sheet balance.

12-8b Spontaneous Liabilities

The first sources of expansion funding are the "spontaneous" increases that will occur in MicroDrive's accounts payable and accruals, which consist of accrued wages and accrued taxes. The company's suppliers give it 10 days to pay for inventory purchases, and because purchases will increase with sales, accounts payable will automatically rise. For example, if sales rise by 10%, then inventory purchases will also rise by 10%, and this will cause accounts payable to rise spontaneously by the same 10%. Similarly, because the company pays workers every 2 weeks, more workers and a larger payroll will mean more accrued wages payable. Finally, higher expected income will mean more accrued income taxes, and its higher wage bill will mean more accrued withholding taxes. Normally no interest is paid on these spontaneous funds, but their amount is limited by credit terms, contracts with workers, and tax laws. Therefore, *spontaneous funds will be used to the extent possible, but there is little flexibility in their usage.*

12-8c Addition to Retained Earnings

The second source of funds for expansion comes from net income. Part of MicroDrive's profit will be paid out in dividends, but the remainder will be reinvested in operating assets, as shown in the Assets section of the balance sheet; a corresponding amount will be reported as an addition to retained earnings in the Liabilities and Equity section of the balance sheet. There is some flexibility in the amount of funds that will be generated from new reinvested earnings because dividends can be increased or decreased, but if the firm plans to hold its dividend steady or to increase it at a target rate, as most do, then flexibility is limited.

12-8d Calculating Additional Funds Needed (AFN)

If we start with the required new assets and then subtract both spontaneous funds and additions to retained earnings, we are left with the additional funds needed, or AFN. The AFN must come from *external sources;* hence, it is sometimes called EFN. The typical sources of external funds are bank loans, new long-term bonds, new preferred stock, and newly issued common stock. The mix of the external funds used should be consistent with the firm's financial policies, especially its target debt ratio.

12-8e Using MicroDrive's Data to Implement the AFN Equation

Equation 12-1 summarizes the logic underlying the AFN equation. Figure 12-8 defines the notation in Equation 12-1 and applies it to identify MicroDrive's AFN. The **additional funds needed (AFN) equation** is:

$$
\begin{array}{l}
\text{Additional} \quad \text{Required} \quad \text{Increase in} \quad \text{Increase in} \\
\text{funds} \;=\; \text{increase} \;-\; \text{spontaneous} \;-\; \text{retained} \\
\text{needed} \qquad \text{in assets} \qquad \text{liabilities} \qquad \text{earnings}
\end{array}
\tag{12-1}
$$

$$
\text{AFN} = (A_0^*/S_0)\Delta S - (L_0^*/S_0)\Delta S - S_1 \times M \times \left(1 - \dfrac{\text{Payout}}{\text{ratio}}\right)
$$

We see from Part B of Figure 12-8 that for sales to increase by \$500 million, Micro-Drive must increase assets by \$360 million. Therefore, liabilities and capital must also increase by \$360 million. Of this total, \$60 million will come from spontaneous liabilities, and another \$206.8 million will come from new retained earnings. The remaining \$93.2 million must be raised from external sources—probably some combination of short-term bank loans, long-term bonds, preferred stock, and common stock. Notice that the AFN from this model is close to the surplus financing required in the Status Quo model for the projected financial statements because both methods assume that the operating ratios for MicroDrive will not change. However, the AFN model also assumes that short-term investments will remain unchanged. In contrast, the Status Quo model assumes that the short-term investments will be liquidated and used to support growth in operating assets.

resource

See **Ch12 Tool Kit.xlsx** *on the textbook's Web site.*

FIGURE 12-8
Additional Funds Needed (AFN) (Millions of Dollars)

	A	B	C	D	E	F	G	H	I
510	*Panel A. Inputs and Definitions*								
511	S_0:		Most recent year's sales =						$5,000
512	g:		Forecasted growth rate in sales =						10.0%
513	S_1:		Next year's sales: $S_0 \times (1 + g) =$						$5,500
514	gS_0:		Forecasted change in sales = $S_1 - S_0 = \Delta S =$						$500
515	A_0^*:		Most recent year's operating assets =						$3,600
516	A_0^*/S_0:		Required assets per dollar of sales =						72.00%
517	L_0^*:		Most recent year's spontaneous liabilities =						$600
518	L_0^*/S_0:		Spontaneous liabilities per dollar of sales =						12.00%
519	Profit margin (M):		Most recent profit margin = NI/sales =						4.96%
520	Payout ratio (POR):		Most recent year's dividends/NI = % of income paid out =						24.19%
521	*Panel B. Additional Funds Needed (AFN) to Support Growth*								
522									
523	Additional		Required		Increase in			Increase in	
524	funds =		increase	−	spontaneous		−	retained	
525	needed		in assets		liabilities			earnings	
526									
527	AFN =		$(A_0^*/S_0)\Delta S$	−	$(L_0^*/S_0)\Delta S$		−	$S_1 \times M \times (1 - POR)$	
528									
529	=		$(A_0^*/S_0)(gS_0)$	−	$(L_0^*/S_0)(gS_0)$		−	$(1+g)S_0 \times M \times (1 - POR)$	
530									
531	=		(0.72)($500)	−	(0.12)($500)		−	$5,500(0.0496)(1 − 0.2419)	
532	=		$360	−	$60.00		−	$206.80	
533									
534	AFN =	$93.20							

Source: See the file *Ch12 Tool Kit.xlsx*. Numbers are reported as rounded values for clarity but are calculated using *Excel's* full precision. Thus, intermediate calculations using the figure's rounded values will be inexact.

12-8f Key Factors in the AFN Equation

The AFN equation shows that external financing requirements depend on five key factors:

1. Sales **growth rate (g)**. Rapidly growing companies require large increases in assets and a corresponding large amount of external financing, other things held constant.
2. **Capital intensity ratio (A_0^*/S_0)**. The amount of assets required per dollar of sales, A_0^*/S_0, has a major effect on capital requirements. Companies with relatively high assets-to-sales ratios require a relatively large number of new assets for any given increase in sales; hence, they have a greater need for external financing. If a firm can find a way to lower this ratio—for instance, by adopting a just-in-time inventory system, by going to two shifts in its manufacturing plants, or by outsourcing rather than manufacturing parts—then it can achieve a given level of growth with fewer assets and thus less new external capital.
3. **Spontaneous liabilities-to-sales ratio (L_0^*/S_0)**. If a company can increase its spontaneously generated liabilities (L_0^*), this will reduce its need for external financing. One way of raising this ratio is by paying suppliers in, say, 20 days rather than 10 days. Such a change may be possible but, as we shall see in Chapter 16, it would probably have serious adverse consequences.

4. **Profit margin (M)**. The profit margin, M, is equal to net income divided by sales. As the profit margin increases, more net income is available to support an increase in assets, which reduces the need for external financing. A firm's profit margin is normally as high as management can get it, but sometimes a change in operations can boost the sales price or reduce costs, thus raising the margin further. If so, this will permit a faster growth rate with less external capital.

5. **Payout ratio (POR)**. The payout ratio is equal to dividends per share divided by earnings per share. As the payout ratio increases, dividends go up and there is less income to fund growing assets, which increases need for external capital. Companies typically like to keep their dividends stable or to increase them at a steady rate—stockholders like stable, dependable dividends, so such a dividend policy will generally lower the cost of equity and thus maximize the stock price. So even though reducing the dividend is one way a company can reduce its need for external capital, companies generally resort to this method only if they are under financial duress.

12-8g The Self-Supporting Growth Rate

One useful question is, "What is the maximum growth rate the firm could achieve if it had no access to external capital?" This rate is called the *self-supporting growth rate*, and it can be found as the value of g that, when used in the AFN equation, results in an AFN of zero. We first replace ΔS in the AFN equation with gS_0 and S_1 with $(1 + g)S_0$ so that the only unknown is g; we then solve for g to obtain the following equation for the self-supporting growth rate:

$$\text{Self-supporting } g = \frac{M(1 - POR)(S_0)}{A_0^* - L_0^* - M(1 - POR)(S_0)} \qquad (12\text{-}2)$$

The definitions of the terms used in this equation are shown in Figure 12-8.

resource

See **Ch12 Tool Kit.xlsx** *on the textbook's Web site for details.*

If the firm has any positive earnings and pays out less than 100% in dividends, then it will have some additions to retained earnings, and those additions could be combined with spontaneous funds to enable the company to grow at some rate without having to raise external capital. As explained in the chapter's *Excel Tool Kit*, this value can be found either algebraically or with *Excel*'s **Goal Seek** function. For MicroDrive, the self-supporting growth rate is 6.7%; this means it could grow at that rate even if capital markets dried up completely, with everything else held constant.

SELF-TEST

If all ratios are expected to remain constant, an equation can be used to forecast AFN. Write out the equation and briefly explain it.

Describe how the following factors affect external capital requirements: (1) payout ratio, (2) capital intensity, (3) profit margin.

In what sense do accounts payable and accruals provide "spontaneous funds" to a growing firm?

Is it possible for the calculated AFN to be negative? If so, what would this imply?

Refer to data in the MicroDrive example presented, but now assume that MicroDrive's growth rate in sales is forecasted to be 15% rather than 10%. If all ratios remain constant, what would the AFN be? **($233.8 million)**

12-9 Forecasting When the Ratios Change

The versions of the percentage of sales forecasting model and the AFN method assumed that the forecasted items could be estimated as a percentage of sales. This implies that each of the accounts for assets, spontaneous liabilities, and operating costs is proportional to sales. In graph form, this implies the type of relationship shown in Panel A of Figure 12-9, a relationship whose graph (1) is linear and (2) passes through the origin. Under those conditions, if a company's sales increase from $200 million to $400 million, or by 100%, then inventory will also increase by 100%, from $100 million to $200 million.

The assumption of constant ratios and identical growth rates is appropriate at times, but there are times when it is incorrect. We describe three such situations in the following sections.

FIGURE 12-9
Four Possible Ratio Relationships (Millions of Dollars)

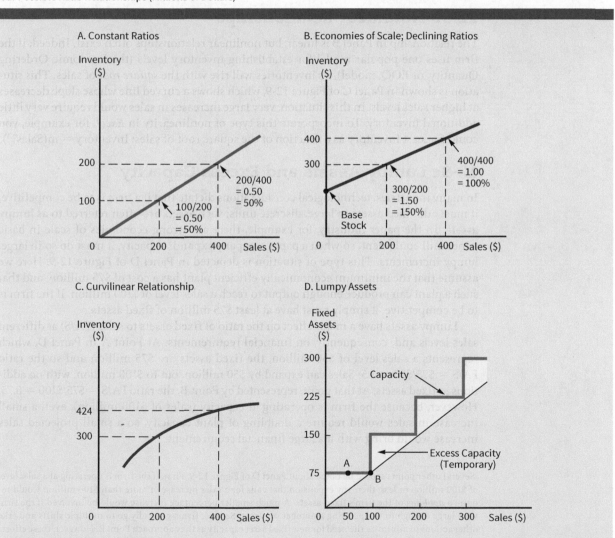

Source: Eugene F. Brigham, Phillip R. Daves, and Michael C. Ehrhardt for use in both Intermediate Financial Management and Financial Management: Theory and Practice.

12-9a Economies of Scale

There are economies of scale in the use of many kinds of assets, and when economies of scale occur, the ratios are likely to change over time as the size of the firm increases. For example, retailers often need to maintain base stocks of different inventory items even if current sales are quite low. As sales expand, inventories may then grow less rapidly than sales, so the ratio of inventory to sales declines. This situation is depicted in Panel B of Figure 12-9. Here we see that the inventory/sales ratio is 1.5 (or 150%) when sales are $200 million but declines to 1.0 (or 100%) when sales climb to $400 million.

It is easy in *Excel* to incorporate this type of scale economy in the forecast. For example, the basic method forecasts inventory as Inventory = m(Sales), where m is a constant. With economies of scale, forecast Inventory as: Inventory = b + m(Sales), where m is the constant slope and b is the intercept.

12-9b Nonlinear Relationships

The relationship in Panel B is linear, but nonlinear relationships often exist. Indeed, if the firm uses one popular model for establishing inventory levels (the Economic Ordering Quantity, or EOQ, model), its inventories will rise with the *square root* of sales. This situation is shown in Panel C of Figure 12-9, which shows a curved line whose slope decreases at higher sales levels. In this situation, very large increases in sales would require very little additional inventory. To incorporate this type of nonlinearity in *Excel,* for example, you could forecast inventory as a function of the square root of sales: Inventory = $m(\text{Sales}^{0.5})$.

12-9c Lumpy Assets and Excess Capacity

In many industries, technological considerations dictate that if a firm is to be competitive, it must add fixed assets in large, discrete units; such assets are often referred to as **lumpy assets**. In the paper industry, for example, there are strong economies of scale in basic paper mill equipment, so when a paper company expands capacity, it must do so in large, lumpy increments. This type of situation is depicted in Panel D of Figure 12-9. Here we assume that the minimum economically efficient plant has a cost of $75 million, and that such a plant can produce enough output to reach a sales level of $100 million. If the firm is to be competitive, it simply must have at least $75 million of fixed assets.

Lumpy assets have a major effect on the ratio of fixed assets to sales (FA/S) at different sales levels and, consequently, on financial requirements. At Point A in Panel D, which represents a sales level of $50 million, the fixed assets are $75 million and so the ratio FA/S = $75/$50 = 1.5. Sales can expand by $50 million, out to $100 million, with no additions to fixed assets. At that point, represented by Point B, the ratio FA/S = $75/$100 = 0.75. However, because the firm is operating at capacity (sales of $100 million), even a small increase in sales would require a doubling of plant capacity, so a small projected sales increase would bring with it a large financial requirement.[3]

---

[3]Several other points should be noted about Panel D of Figure 12-9. First, if the firm is operating at a sales level of $100 million or less, then any expansion that calls for a sales increase of more than $100 million would require a *doubling* of the firm's fixed assets. A much smaller percentage increase would be involved if the firm were large enough to be operating a number of plants. Second, firms generally go to multiple shifts and take other actions to minimize the need for new fixed asset capacity as they approach Point B. However, these efforts can only go so far, and eventually a fixed asset expansion will be required. Third, firms often arrange to share excess capacity with other firms in their industry. For example, the situation in the electric utility industry is very much like that depicted in Panel D. However, electric companies often build plants jointly, or they "take turns" building plants. Then they buy power from or sell power to other utilities to avoid building new plants that would be underutilized.

If assets are lumpy and a firm makes a major purchase, the firm will have excess capacity, which means that sales can grow before the firm must add capacity. The level of full capacity sales is:

$$\text{Full capacity sales} = \frac{\text{Actual sales}}{\text{Percentage of capacity at which fixed assets were operated}} \qquad (12\text{-}3)$$

For example, consider MicroDrive and use the data from its financial statements in Figure 12-1, but now assume that excess capacity exists in fixed assets. Specifically, assume that fixed assets in 2019 were being utilized to only 96% of capacity. If fixed assets had been used to full capacity, then 2019 sales could have been as high as $5,208 million versus the $5,000 million in actual sales:

$$\text{Full capacity sales} = \frac{\text{Actual sales}}{\text{Percentage of capacity at which fixed assets were operated}}$$

$$= \frac{\$5,000 \text{ million}}{0.96} = \$5,208 \text{ million}$$

The target fixed assets/sales ratio can be defined in terms of the full capacity sales:

$$\text{Target fixed assets/Sales} = \frac{\text{Actual fixed assets}}{\text{Full capacity sales}} \qquad (12\text{-}4)$$

If we assume, then, that MicroDrive will tend to operate at full capacity, then its target FA/Sales ratio should be 38.4% rather than 40%:

$$\text{Target FA/Sales} = \frac{\text{Actual fixed assets}}{\text{Full capacity sales}}$$

$$= \frac{\$2,000}{\$5,208} = 0.384 = 38.4\%$$

The required level of fixed assets depends upon this target FA/Sales ratio:

$$\begin{array}{c} \text{Required level} \\ \text{of fixed assets} \end{array} = \left(\frac{\text{Target fixed assets}}{\text{Sales}} \right) \left(\begin{array}{c} \text{Projected} \\ \text{sales} \end{array} \right) \qquad (12\text{-}5)$$

Therefore, if MicroDrive's sales increase to $5,500 million, its fixed assets would have to increase to $2,112 million:

$$\begin{array}{c} \text{Required level} \\ \text{of fixed assets} \end{array} = \left(\frac{\text{Target fixed assets}}{\text{Sales}} \right) \left(\begin{array}{c} \text{Projected} \\ \text{sales} \end{array} \right)$$

$$= 0.384(\$5,500) = \$2,112 \text{ million}$$

We previously forecast that MicroDrive would need to increase fixed assets at the same rate as sales, or by 10%. That meant an increase of $200 million, from $2,000 million to $2,200 million under the old assumption of no excess capacity. Under the new assumption of excess capacity, the actual required increase in fixed assets is only from $2,000 million to $2,112 million, which is an increase of $112 million. Thus, the capacity-adjusted forecast is less than the earlier forecast: $200 − $112 = $88 million. With a smaller fixed asset requirement, the projected AFN would decline from an estimated $93 million to $93 − $88 = $5 million.

Note also that when excess capacity exists, sales can grow to the capacity sales as previously calculated with no increase in fixed assets, but sales beyond that level would require additions of fixed assets as in our example. The same situation could occur with respect to inventories, and the required additions would be determined in exactly the same manner as for fixed assets. Theoretically, the same situation could occur with other types of assets, but as a practical matter excess capacity normally exists only with respect to fixed assets and inventories.

SELF-TEST

How do economies of scale and lumpy assets affect financial forecasting?

SUMMARY

This chapter explained how to forecast operations, required financings, and financial statements. The key concepts covered are listed here.

- The **additional financing needed (AFN)** is the amount of extra funding required to implement an operating plan, given the preliminary choices of capital structure and dividend payout.
- The **forecasted financial statements (FFS) method** of financial planning forecasts the entire set of financial statements. It usually begins with a forecast of the firm's sales and then projects many items on the financial statements as a percent of sales.
- The **additional funds needed (AFN) equation** is a simple way to get a ballpark estimate of the additional external financing that will be required in the upcoming year. It assumes that all asset-to-sales ratios are identical, all spontaneous liabilities-to-sales ratios are identical, and all cost-to-sales ratios are identical. Given these assumptions, the AFN is equal to the required increase in assets minus the increase in spontaneous liabilities minus the increase in retained earnings.
- The higher a firm's sales **growth rate (g)** and the higher its **payout ratio (POR)**, the greater its need will be for additional financing.
- There are two major applications of forecasted financial statements. First, the forecasted free cash flows can be used to estimate the impact that changes in operating plans have on the firm's estimated intrinsic value of operations and stock price. Second, the forecasted financing surplus or deficit allows the firm to identify its future financing needs.
- Adjustments must be made if *economies of scale* exist in the use of assets, if *excess capacity* exists, or if growth must occur in large increments (**lumpy assets**).
- *Excess capacity adjustments* can be used to forecast asset requirements in situations in which assets are not expected to grow at the same rate as sales.

QUESTIONS

(12-1)   Define each of the following terms:

a. Operating plan; financial plan
b. Spontaneous liabilities; profit margin; payout ratio
c. Additional funds needed (AFN); AFN equation; capital intensity ratio; self-supporting growth rate
d. Forecasted financial statement approach using percentage of sales
e. Excess capacity; lumpy assets; economies of scale
f. Full capacity sales; target fixed assets to sales ratio; required level of fixed assets

(12-2)   Some liability and net worth items increase spontaneously with increases in sales. Put a check (✓) by the following listed items that typically increase spontaneously:

Accounts payable	_____	Long-term bonds	_____
Notes payable to banks	_____	Common stock	_____
Accrued wages	_____	Retained earnings	_____
Accrued taxes	_____		

(12-3)   The following equation is sometimes used to forecast financial requirements:

$$AFN = (A_0^*/S_0)(\Delta S) - (L_0^*/S_0)(\Delta S) - MS_1(1 - POR)$$

What key assumption do we make when using this equation? Under what conditions might this assumption not hold true?

(12-4)   Name five key factors that affect a firm's external financing requirements.

(12-5)   What is meant by the term "self-supporting growth rate"? How is this rate related to the AFN equation, and how can that equation be used to calculate the self-supporting growth rate?

(12-6)   Suppose a firm makes the following policy changes listed. If a change means that external, nonspontaneous financial requirements (AFN) will increase, indicate this by a (+); indicate a decrease by a (−); and indicate no effect or an indeterminate effect by a (0). Think in terms of the immediate effect on funds requirements.

a. The dividend payout ratio is increased.   _____
b. The firm decides to pay all suppliers on delivery rather than after a 30-day delay in order to take advantage of discounts for rapid payment.   _____
c. The firm begins to offer credit to its customers, whereas previously all sales had been on a cash basis.   _____
d. The firm's profit margin is eroded by increased competition, although sales hold steady.   _____
e. The firm sells its manufacturing plants for cash to a contractor and simultaneously signs an outsourcing contract to purchase from that contractor goods that the firm formerly produced.   _____
f. The firm negotiates a new contract with its union that lowers its labor costs without affecting its output.   _____

(ST-1)
Self-Supporting Growth Rate

The Barnsdale Corporation has the following ratios: $A_0^*/S_0 = 1.6$; $L_0^*/S_0 = 0.4$; profit margin = 0.10; and dividend payout ratio = 0.45, or 45%. Sales last year were $100 million. Assuming that these ratios will remain constant, use the AFN equation to determine the firm's self-supporting growth rate—in other words, the maximum growth rate Barnsdale can achieve without having to employ nonspontaneous external funds.

(ST-2)
AFN Equation

Refer to Problem ST-1, and suppose Barnsdale's financial consultants report (1) that the inventory turnover ratio (sales/inventory) is 3, compared with an industry average of 4, and (2) that Barnsdale could reduce inventories and thus raise its turnover ratio to 4 without affecting its sales, profit margin, or other asset turnover ratios. Under these conditions, use the AFN equation to determine the amount of additional funds Barnsdale would require during each of the next 2 years if sales grow at a rate of 20% per year.

(ST-3)
Excess Capacity

Van Auken Lumber's 2019 financial statements are shown here.

Van Auken Lumber: Balance Sheet as of December 31, 2019
(Thousands of Dollars)

Cash	$ 1,800	Accounts payable	$ 7,200
Receivables	10,800	Notes payable	3,500
Inventories	12,600	Line of credit	0
Total current assets	$25,200	Accruals	2,520
Net fixed assets	21,600	Total current liabilities	$ 13,220
		Long-term bonds	5,000
		Common stock	2,000
		Retained earnings	26,580
Total assets	$46,800	Total liabilities and equity	$46,800

Van Auken Lumber: Income Statement for December 31, 2019
(Thousands of Dollars)

Sales	$36,000
Operating costs	30,600
Earnings before interest and taxes	$ 5,400
Interest	720
Pre-tax earnings	$ 4,680
Taxes (25%)	1,170
Net income	$ 3,510
Dividends (60%)	$ 2,016
Addition to retained earnings	$ 1,404

a. Assume that the company was operating at full capacity in 2019 with regard to all items *except* fixed assets, which in 2019 were being utilized to only 75% of capacity. By what percentage could 2020 sales increase over 2019 sales without the need for an increase in fixed assets?

b. Now suppose that 2020 sales increase by 25% over 2019 sales. Use the forecasted financial statement method to forecast a 12/31/20 balance sheet and 2020 income statement, assuming that: (1) The historical ratios of (operating costs)/sales, cash/sales, receivables/sales, inventories/sales, (accounts payable)/sales, and accruals/sales remain constant. (2) Van Auken cannot sell any of its fixed assets. (3) Any required financing is done at the *end* of 2020 through a line of credit. (4) The firm earns no interest on its cash. (5) The interest rate on all of its debt is 10%. (6) The firm pays out 60% of its net income as dividends. (7) The firm has a tax rate of 25%.

What is Van Auken's financing deficit or surplus? (*Hints:* Assume any additional financing through the line of credit will be drawn on the last day of the year. Therefore, the line of credit will not accrue interest expense during the year because any new line of credit is added at the end of the year; also, use the forecasted income statement to determine the addition to retained earnings for use in the balance sheet.)

PROBLEMS   ANSWERS ARE IN APPENDIX B

EASY PROBLEMS 1–3

(12-1)
AFN Equation
Broussard Skateboard's sales are expected to increase by 15% from $8 million in 2019 to $9.2 million in 2020. Its assets totaled $5 million at the end of 2019.

Broussard is already at full capacity, so its assets must grow at the same rate as projected sales. At the end of 2019, current liabilities were $1.4 million, consisting of $450,000 of accounts payable, $500,000 of notes payable, and $450,000 of accruals. The after-tax profit margin is forecasted to be 6%, and the forecasted payout ratio is 40%. Use the AFN equation to forecast Broussard's additional funds needed for the coming year.

(12-2)
Projected
Operating Assets
Berman & Jaccor Corporation's current sales and partial balance sheet are shown here. Sales are expected to grow by 10% next year. Assuming no change in operations from this year to next year, what are the projected total operating assets?

	This year
Sales	$1,000
Balance Sheet: Assets	
Cash	$ 100
Short-term investments	$80
Accounts receivable	$ 200
Inventories	$ 200
Total current assets	$ 580
Net fixed assets	$ 500
Total assets	$1,080

(12-3)
Projected
Spontaneous
Liabilities
Smiley Corporation's current sales and partial balance sheet are shown here. Sales are expected to grow by 10% next year. Assuming no change in operations from this year to next year, what are the projected spontaneous liabilities?

	This year
Sales	$10,000
Balance Sheet: Liabilities	
Accounts payable	$ 1,000
Notes payable	$ 2,000
Accruals	$ 1,000
Total current liabilities	$ 4,000
Long-term bonds	$ 2,000
Total liabilities	$ 6,000
Common stock	$ 1,000
Retained earnings	$ 3,000
Total common equity	$ 4,000
Total liabilities & equity	$10,000

INTERMEDIATE PROBLEMS 4–6

(12-4)
Self-Supporting Growth Rate

Maggie's Muffins Bakery generated $5 million in sales during 2019, and its year-end total assets were $2.5 million. Also, at year-end 2019, current liabilities were $1 million, consisting of $300,000 of notes payable, $500,000 of accounts payable, and $200,000 of accruals. Looking ahead to 2020, the company estimates that its operating assets must increase at the same rate as sales, its spontaneous liabilities will increase at the same rate as sales, its profit margin will be 7%, and its payout ratio will be 80%. How large a sales increase can the company achieve without having to raise funds externally—that is, what is its self-supporting growth rate?

(12-5)
Long-Term Financing Needed

At year-end 2019, Wallace Landscaping's total assets were $2.17 million, and its accounts payable were $560,000. Sales, which in 2019 were $3.5 million, are expected to increase by 35% in 2020. Total assets and accounts payable are proportional to sales, and that relationship will be maintained. Wallace typically uses no current liabilities other than accounts payable. Common stock amounted to $625,000 in 2019, and retained earnings were $395,000. Wallace has arranged to sell $195,000 of new common stock in 2020 to meet some of its financing needs. The remainder of its financing needs will be met by issuing new long-term debt at the end of 2020. (Because the debt is added at the end of the year, there will be no additional interest expense due to the new debt.) Its net profit margin on sales is 5%, and 45% of earnings will be paid out as dividends.

a. What were Wallace's total long-term debt and total liabilities in 2019?
b. How much new long-term debt financing will be needed in 2020? (*Hint:* AFN − New stock = New long-term debt.)

(12-6)
Additional Funds Needed

The Booth Company's sales are forecasted to double from $1,000 in 2019 to $2,000 in 2020. Here is the December 31, 2019, balance sheet:

Cash	$ 100	Accounts payable	$ 50
Accounts receivable	200	Notes payable	150
Inventories	200	Accruals	50
Net fixed assets	500	Long-term debt	400
		Common stock	100
		Retained earnings	250
Total assets	$1,000	Total liabilities and equity	$1,000

Booth's fixed assets were used to only 50% of capacity during 2019, but its current assets were at their proper levels in relation to sales. All assets except fixed assets must increase at the same rate as sales, and fixed assets would also have to increase at the same rate if the current excess capacity did not exist. Booth's after-tax profit margin is forecast to be 5% and its payout ratio to be 60%. What is Booth's additional funds needed (AFN) for the coming year?

CHALLENGING PROBLEMS 7–9

(12-7)
Forecasted Statements and Ratios

Upton Computers makes bulk purchases of small computers, stocks them in conveniently located warehouses, ships them to its chain of retail stores, and has a staff to advise customers and help them set up their new computers. Upton's balance sheet as of December 31, 2019, is shown here (millions of dollars):

Cash	$ 3.5	Accounts payable	$ 9.0
Receivables	26.0	Notes payable	18.0
Inventories	58.0	Line of credit	0
Total current assets	$ 87.5	Accruals	8.5
Net fixed assets	35.0	Total current liabilities	$ 35.5
		Mortgage loan	6.0
		Common stock	15.0
		Retained earnings	66.0
Total assets	$122.5	Total liabilities and equity	$122.5

Sales for 2019 were $350 million, and net income for the year was $10.5 million, so the firm's profit margin was 3.0%. Upton paid dividends of $4.2 million to common stockholders, so its payout ratio was 40%. Its tax rate was 25%, and it operated at full capacity. Assume that all assets/sales ratios, (spontaneous liabilities)/sales ratios, the profit margin, and the payout ratio remain constant in 2020.

a. If sales are projected to increase by $70 million, or 20%, during 2020, use the AFN equation to determine Upton's projected external capital requirements.
b. Using the AFN equation, determine Upton's self-supporting growth rate. That is, what is the maximum growth rate the firm can achieve without having to employ nonspontaneous external funds?
c. Use the forecasted financial statement method to forecast Upton's balance sheet for December 31, 2020. Assume that all additional external capital is raised as a line of credit at the end of the year. (Because the debt is added at the end of the year, there will be no additional interest expense due to the new debt.) Assume Upton's profit margin and dividend payout ratio will be the same in 2020 as they were in 2019. What is the amount of the line of credit reported on the 2020 forecasted balance sheets? (*Hint:* You don't need to forecast the income statements because the line of credit is taken out on the last day of the year and you are given the projected sales, profit margin, and dividend payout ratio; these figures allow you to calculate the 2020 addition to retained earnings for the balance sheet without actually constructing a full income statement.)

(12-8)
Financing Deficit
Stevens Textile Corporation's 2019 financial statements are shown here. Stevens grew rapidly in 2019 and financed the growth with notes payable and long-term bonds. Stevens expects sales to grow by 15% in the next year but will finance the growth with a line of credit, not notes payable or long-term bonds. Use the forecasted financial statement method to forecast a balance sheet and income statement for December 31, 2020. The interest rate on all debt is 10%, and cash earns no interest income. The line of credit is added at the end of the year, which means that you should base the forecasted interest expense on the balance of debt at the beginning of the year. Use the forecasted income statement to determine the addition to retained earnings. Assume that the company was operating at full capacity in 2019, that it cannot sell off any of its fixed assets, and that assets, spontaneous liabilities, and operating costs are expected to increase by the same percentage as sales.

a. What is the projected value for earnings before interest and taxes?
b. What is the projected value for pre-tax earnings?
c. What is the projected net income?
d. What is the projected addition to retained earnings?
e. What is the projected value of total current assets?
f. What is the projected value of total assets?
g. What is the projected sum of accounts payable, accruals, and notes payable?
h. What is the forecasted line of credit?

Balance Sheet as of December 31, 2019 (Thousands of Dollars)

Cash	$ 1,080	Accounts payable	$ 4,320
Receivables	6,480	Accruals	2,880
Inventories	9,000	Line of credit	0
Total current assets	$16,560	Notes payable	2,100
Net fixed assets	12,600	Total current liabilities	$ 9,300
		Mortgage bonds	3,500
		Common stock	3,500
		Retained earnings	12,860
Total assets	$29,160	Total liabilities and equity	$29,160

Income Statement for December 31, 2019 (Thousands of Dollars)

Sales	$36,000
Operating costs	34,000
Earnings before interest and taxes	$ 2,000
Interest	160
Pre-tax earnings	$ 1,840
Taxes (25%)	460
Net income	$ 1,380
Dividends	552
Addition to retained earnings	$ 828

(12-9)
Financing Deficit   Garlington Technologies Inc.'s 2019 financial statements are shown here. Suppose that in 2020 sales increase to $4.4 million and that 2020 dividends will increase to $200,000. Forecast the financial statements using the forecasted financial statement method. Assume the firm operated at full capacity in 2019. The long-term bonds have an interest rate of 12%. New financing will be with a line of credit. Assume it will be added at the end of the year. Cash does not earn any interest income.

Income Statement for December 31, 2019

Sales	$4,000,000
Operating costs	3,200,000
EBIT	$ 800,000
Interest	120,000
Pre-tax earnings	$ 680,000
Taxes (25%)	170,000
Net income	$ 510,000
Dividends	$ 190,000

Balance Sheets as of December 31, 2019

Cash	$ 160,000	Accounts payable	$ 360,000
Receivables	360,000	Line of credit	0
Inventories	720,000	Accruals	200,000
Total CA	$1,240,000	Total CL	$ 560,000
Fixed assets	4,000,000	Long-term bonds	$1,000,000
		Common stock	$1,100,000
		RE	$2,580,000
Total assets	$5,240,000	Total L&E	$5,240,000

SPREADSHEET PROBLEMS

(12-10)
Build a Model:
Forecasting
Financial
Statements

resource

Start with the partial model in the file *Ch12 P10 Build a Model.xlsx* on the textbook's Web site, which contains the 2019 financial statements of Zieber Corporation. Forecast Zieber's 2020 income statement and balance sheets. Use the following assumptions: (1) Sales grow by 6%. (2) The ratios of expenses to sales, depreciation to fixed assets, cash to sales, accounts receivable to sales, and inventories to sales will be the same in 2020 as in 2019. (3) Zieber will not issue any new stock or new long-term bonds. (4) The interest rate is 11% for long-term debt, and the interest expense on long-term debt is based on the average balance during the year. (5) No interest is earned on cash. (6) Regular dividends grow at an 8% rate. (7) The tax rate is 25%.

Calculate the additional funds needed (AFN). If new financing is required, assume it will be raised by drawing on a line of credit with an interest rate of 12%. Assume that any draw on the line of credit will be made on the last day of the year, so there will be no additional interest expense for the new line of credit. If surplus funds are available, pay a special dividend.

a. What are the forecasted levels of the line of credit and special dividends? (*Hints:* Create a column showing the ratios for the current year; then create a new column showing the ratios used in the forecast. Also, create a preliminary forecast that doesn't include any new line of credit or special dividends. Identify the financing deficit or surplus in this preliminary forecast and then add a new column that shows the final forecast that includes any new line of credit or special dividend.)

b. Now assume that the growth in sales is only 3%. What are the forecasted levels of the line of credit and special dividends?

(12-11)
Build a Model:
Forecasting and
Valuation

Start with the partial model in the file *Ch12 P11 Build a Model.xlsx* on the textbook's Web site, which contains Henley Corporation's most recent financial statements. Use the following ratios and other selected information for the current and projected years to answer the questions that follow.

	Actual	Projected			
	12/31/ 2019	12/31/ 2020	12/31/ 2021	12/31/ 2022	12/31/ 2023
Sales growth rate		15%	10%	6%	6%
Costs/Sales	72%	72	72	72	72
Depreciation/(Net PPE)	10	10	10	10	10
Cash/Sales	1	1	1	1	1
(Accounts receivable)/Sales	10	10	10	10	10
(Inventories)/Sales	20	20	20	20	20
(Net PPE)/Sales	75	75	75	75	75
(Accounts payable)/Sales	2	2	2	2	2
Accruals/Sales	5	5	5	5	5
Tax rate	40	40	40	40	40
Weighted average cost of capital (WACC)	10.5	10.5	10.5	10.5	10.5

a. Forecast the parts of the income statement and balance sheet that are necessary for calculating free cash flow.

b. Calculate free cash flow for each projected year. Also calculate the growth rates in free cash flow each year to ensure that there is constant growth (that is, the same as the constant growth rate in sales) by the end of the forecast period.

c. Calculate the return on invested capital (ROIC = NOPAT/[Total net operating capital]) and the growth rate in free cash flow. What is the ROIC in the last year of the forecast? What is the long-term constant growth rate in free cash flow (g_L is the growth rate in FCF in the last forecast period because all ratios are constant)? Do you think that Hensley's value would increase if it could add growth without reducing its ROIC? (*Hint:* Growth will add value if the ROIC > WACC/[1 + WACC]). Do you think that the company will have a value of operations greater than its total net operating capital? (*Hint:* Is ROIC > WACC/[1 + g_L]?)

d. Calculate the current value of operations. (*Hint:* First calculate the horizon value at the end of the forecast period, which is equal to the value of operations at the end of the forecast period. Assume that the annual growth rate beyond the horizon is equal to the growth rate at the horizon.) How does the current value of operations compare with the current amount of total net operating capital?

e. Calculate the intrinsic price per share of common equity as of December 31, 2019.

MINI CASE

Hatfield Medical Supply's stock price had been lagging its industry averages, so its board of directors brought in a new CEO, Jaiden Lee. Lee had brought in Ashley Novak, a finance MBA who had been working for a consulting company, to replace the old CFO, and Lee asked Novak to develop the financial planning section of the strategic plan. In her previous job, Novak's primary task had been to help clients develop financial forecasts, and that was one reason Lee hired her.

Novak began by comparing Hatfield's financial ratios to the industry averages. If any ratio was substandard, she discussed it with the responsible manager to see what could be done to improve the situation. The following data show Hatfield's latest financial statements plus some ratios and other data that Novak plans to use in her analysis.

Hatfield Medical Supply (Millions of Dollars, Except per Share Data)

Balance Sheet, 12/31/2019		Income Statement, Year Ending 2019	
Cash	$ 90	Sales	$9,000.9
Accounts receivable	1,260	Op costs (excl. depr.)	8,100.9
Inventories	1,440	Depreciation	360.0
Total CA	$2,790	EBIT	$ 540.0
Net fixed assets	3,600	Interest	144.0
Total assets	$6,390	Pre-tax earnings	$ 396.0
		Taxes (25%)	99.0
Accts. pay. & accruals	$1,620	Net income	$ 297.0
Line of credit	0		
Total CL	$1,620	*Additional Information*	
Long-term debt	1,800	Dividends	$ 100
Total liabilities	$3,420	Additions to RE	$ 197
Common stock	2,100	Common shares	50
Retained earnings	870	EPS	$ 5.94
Total common equity	$2,970	DPS	$ 2.00
Total liab. & equity	$6,390	Ending stock price	$ 40.00

Selected Additional Data for 2019

	Hatfield	Industry		Hatfield	Industry
(Op. costs)/Sales	90%	88%	Profit margin (M)	3.30%	5.60%
Depr./FA	10%	12%	Return on assets (ROA)	4.6%	9.5%
Cash/Sales	1%	1%	Return on equity (ROE)	10.0%	15.1%
Receivables/Sales	14%	11%	Sales/Assets	1.41	1.69
Inventories/Sales	16%	15%	Asset/Equity	2.15	1.59
Fixed assets/Sales	40%	32%	Debt/TA	28.2%	16.9%
(Acc. pay. & accr.)/Sales	18%	12%	(Total liabilities)/(Total assets)	53.5%	37.3%
Tax rate	25%	25%	Times interest earned	3.8	11.7
Target WACC	10%	11%	P/E ratio	6.7	16.0
Interest rate on debt	8%	7%	OP ratio: NOPAT/Sales	4.5%	6.1%
			CR ratio: (Total op. capital)/Sales	53.0%	47.0%
			ROIC	8.5%	13.0%

a. Using Hatfield's data and its industry averages, how well run would you say Hatfield appears to be in comparison with other firms in its industry? What are its primary strengths and weaknesses? Be specific in your answer and point to various ratios that support your position. Also, use the DuPont equation (see Chapter 3) as one part of your analysis.

b. Use the AFN equation to estimate Hatfield's required new external capital for 2020 if the sales growth rate is 11.1%. Assume that the firm's 2019 ratios will remain the same in 2020. (*Hint:* Hatfield was operating at full capacity in 2019.)

c. Define the term *capital intensity*. Explain how a decline in capital intensity would affect the AFN, other things held constant. Would economies of scale combined with rapid growth affect capital intensity, other things held constant? Also, explain how changes in each of the following would affect AFN, holding other things constant: the growth rate, the amount of accounts payable, the profit margin, and the payout ratio.

d. Define the term *self-supporting growth rate*. What is Hatfield's self-supporting growth rate? Would the self-supporting growth rate be affected by a change in the capital intensity ratio or the other factors mentioned in the previous question? Other things held constant, would the calculated capital intensity ratio change over time if the company were growing and were also subject to economies of scale and/or lumpy assets?

e. Use the following assumptions to answer the following questions: (1) Operating ratios remain unchanged. (2) Sales will grow by 11.1%, 8%, 5%, and 5% for the next 4 years. (3) The target weighted average cost of capital (WACC) is 10%. This is the No Change scenario because operations remain unchanged.

   (1) For each of the next 4 years, forecast the following items: sales, cash, accounts receivable, inventories, net fixed assets, accounts payable and accruals, operating costs (excluding depreciation), depreciation, and earnings before interest and taxes (EBIT).

   (2) Using the previously forecasted items, calculate for each of the next 4 years the net operating profit after taxes (NOPAT), net operating working capital, total operating capital, free cash flow (FCF), annual growth rate in FCF, and return on invested capital. What does the forecasted free cash flow in the first year imply about the need for external financing? Compare the forecasted ROIC with the WACC. What does this imply about how well the company is performing?

   (3) Assume that FCF will continue to grow at the growth rate for the last year in the forecast horizon. (*Hint:* $g_L = 5\%$.) What is the horizon value at 2023? What is the

present value of the horizon value? What is the present value of the forecasted FCF? (*Hint:* Use the free cash flows for 2020 through 2023.) What is the current value of operations? Using information from the 2019 financial statements, what is the current estimated intrinsic stock price?

f. Continue with the same assumptions for the No Change scenario from the previous question, but now forecast the balance sheet and income statements for 2020 (but not for the following 3 years) using the following preliminary financial policy. (1) Regular dividends will grow by 10%. (2) No additional long-term debt or common stock will be issued. (3) The interest rate on all debt is 8%. (4) Interest expense for long-term debt is based on the average balance during the year. (5) If the operating results and the preliminary financing plan cause a financing deficit, eliminate the deficit by drawing on a line of credit. The line of credit would be tapped on the last day of the year, so it would create no additional interest expenses for that year. (6) If there is a financing surplus, eliminate it by paying a special dividend. After forecasting the 2020 financial statements, answer the following questions.

   (1) How much will Hatfield need to draw on the line of credit?
   (2) What are some alternative ways than those in the preliminary financial policy that Hatfield might choose to eliminate the financing deficit?

g. Repeat the analysis performed in the previous question, but now assume that Hatfield is able to improve the following inputs: (1) Reduce operating costs (excluding depreciation) to sales to 89.4% at a cost of $40 million. (2) Reduce inventories/sales to 14% at a cost of $10 million. (3) Reduce net fixed assets/sales to 38% at a cost of $20 million. This is the Improve scenario.

   (1) Should Hatfield implement the improvement plan? How much value would it add to the company?
   (2) How much can Hatfield pay as a special dividend in the Improve scenario? What else might Hatfield do with the financing surplus?

SELECTED ADDITIONAL CASES

The following cases from CengageCompose cover many of the concepts discussed in this chapter and are available at **http://compose.cengage.com**.

Klein-Brigham Series:
Case 37, "Space-Age Materials, Inc."; Case 38, "Automated Banking Management, Inc."; Case 52, "Expert Systems"; and Case 69, "Medical Management Systems, Inc."

CHAPTER 13

Corporate Governance

Citigroup CEO Vikram Pandit has had a wild ride regarding compensation. In 2007, Pandit sold his hedge fund to Citigroup and made a reported $167 million profit (the fund was shut down later due to poor performance). Citi appointed Pandit CEO in late 2007 and paid him about $1.2 million in cash and over $39 million in stocks and options during 2007 and 2008. But as the global economic crisis worsened, Pandit offered to take only $1 a year in salary and did so during 2009 and 2010.

The year 2011 was much better financially for Pandit as he received a base salary of about $1.75 million and a retention bonus of over $23 million. Citi's board recommended that Pandit's salary be increased to $15 million at the 2012 board meeting. In addition, the board recommended a bonus plan in which Citi's top five executives could earn $18 million in 2012 if the combined 2011–2012 pretax income at Citi exceeded $12 billion.

Shareholders reacted angrily to these proposals and voted against the proposed compensation plans. What prompted such a reaction? It could have been that Citi earned $19.9 billion in pretax income in 2011, so the executives would still receive the proposed bonus even if Citi *lost* over $7 billion in pretax income in 2012!

Shareholder votes are nonbinding, and Citi's board ignored the vote. Shortly after, a large shareholder sued Citi's board for a breach of duty. Perhaps not surprisingly, Pandit resigned in 2012.

Similar scenes are being played out at many other companies in the United States and overseas. Keep this example of corporate governance in mind as you read this chapter.

Source: Francesco Guerrera, "Citigroup's Pay Fiasco: Wake-Up Call for Board," *The Wall Street Journal,* April 24, 2012, p. C1.

Corporate Governance and Corporate Valuation

A company's managers make decisions that affect operations, financing, corporate culture, and many other organizational characteristics. These decisions affect the operating and financing choices the company makes, which in turn affect free cash flow and risk.

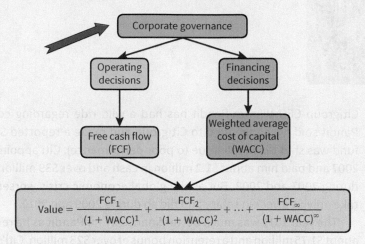

There is no conflict at a one-person company—the owner makes all the decisions, does all the work, reaps all the rewards, and suffers all the losses. This situation changes as the owner begins hiring employees because the employees don't fully share in the owner's rewards and losses. The situation becomes more complicated if the owner sells some shares of the company to an outsider, and even more complicated if the owner hires someone else to run the company. In this situation, there are many potential conflicts between owners, managers, employees, and creditors. These **agency conflicts** occur whenever owners authorize someone else to act on their behalf as their agents. The degree to which agency problems are minimized often depends on a company's **corporate governance**, which is the set of laws, rules, and procedures that influence the company's operations and the decisions its managers make. This chapter addresses these topics, beginning with agency conflicts.

13-1 Agency Conflicts

An **agency relationship** arises whenever someone, called a **principal**, hires someone else, called an **agent**, to perform some service, and the principal delegates decision-making authority to the agent. In companies, the primary agency relationships are between (1) stockholders and creditors, (2) inside owner/managers (managers who own a controlling interest in the company) and outside owners (who have no control), and (3) outside stockholders and hired managers.[1] These conflicts lead to **agency costs**, which are the reductions in a company's value due to agency conflicts. The following sections describe the agency conflicts, the costs, and methods to minimize the costs.

---

[1]One of the first and most important papers in finance and economics to address agency conflicts was written by Michael Jensen and William Meckling, titled "Theory of the Firm: Managerial Behavior, Agency Costs and Ownership Structure," *Journal of Financial Economics*, Vol. 3, 1976, pp. 305–360.

13-1a Conflicts between Stockholders and Creditors

Creditors have a claim on the firm's earnings stream, and they have a claim on its assets in the event of bankruptcy. However, stockholders have control (through the managers) of decisions that affect the firm's riskiness. Therefore, creditors allocate decision-making authority to someone else, creating a potential agency conflict.

Creditors lend funds at rates based on the firm's perceived risk at the time the credit is extended, which in turn is based on (1) the risk of the firm's existing assets, (2) expectations concerning the risk of future asset additions, (3) the existing capital structure, and (4) expectations concerning future capital structure changes. These are the primary determinants of the risk of the firm's cash flows and hence the safety of its debt.

Suppose the firm borrows money, then sells its relatively safe assets and invests the proceeds in assets for a large new project that is far riskier. The new project might be extremely profitable, but it also might lead to bankruptcy. If the risky project is successful, most of the benefits go to the stockholders, because creditors' returns are fixed at the original low-risk rate. However, if the project is unsuccessful, the bondholders take a loss. From the stockholders' point of view, this amounts to a game of "heads, I win; tails, you lose," which obviously is not good for the creditors. Thus, the increased risk due to the asset change will cause the required rate of return on the debt to increase, which in turn will cause the value of the outstanding debt to fall. This is called *asset switching* or *bait-and-switch*.

A similar situation can occur if a company borrows and then issues additional debt, using the proceeds to repurchase some of its outstanding stock, thus increasing its financial leverage. If things go well, the stockholders will gain from the increased leverage. However, the value of the debt will probably decrease because now there will be a larger amount of debt backed by the same amount of assets. In both the asset switch and the increased leverage situations, stockholders have the potential for gaining, but such gains are made at the expense of creditors.

There are two ways that lenders address the potential of asset switching or subsequent increases in leverage. First, creditors may charge a higher rate to protect themselves in case the company engages in activities that increase risk. However, if the company doesn't increase risk, then its weighted average cost of capital (WACC) will be higher than is justified by the company's risk. This higher WACC will reduce the company's intrinsic value (recall that intrinsic value is the present value of free cash flows discounted at the WACC). In addition, the company will reject projects that it otherwise would have accepted at the lower cost of capital. Therefore, this potential agency conflict has a cost, an agency cost.

The second way that lenders address the potential agency problems is by writing detailed debt covenants specifying what actions the borrower can and cannot take. Most debt covenants prohibit the borrower from (1) increasing debt ratios above specified levels, (2) repurchasing stock or paying dividends unless profits and retained earnings are above specified amounts, and (3) reducing liquidity ratios below specified levels. These covenants can cause agency costs if they restrict a company from value-adding activities. For example, a company may not be able to accept an unexpected but particularly good investment opportunity if it requires temporarily adding debt above the level specified in the bond covenant. In addition, the costs incurred to write the covenant and monitor the company to verify compliance also are agency costs.

13-1b Conflicts between Inside Owner/Managers and Outside Owners

If a company's owner also runs the company, the owner/manager will presumably operate it so as to maximize his or her own welfare. This welfare obviously includes the increased wealth due to increasing the value of the company, but it also includes perquisites (or "perks") such as more leisure time, luxurious offices, executive assistants, expense accounts, limousines, corporate jets, and generous retirement plans. However, if the owner/manager incorporates the business and then sells some of the stock to outsiders, a potential conflict of interest immediately arises. Notice that the value of the perquisites still accrues to the owner/manager, but the cost of the perquisites is now partially born by the outsiders. This might even induce the owner/manager to increase consumption of the perquisites because they are relatively less expensive now that the outsider is sharing their costs.

This agency problem causes outsiders to pay less for a share of the company and require a higher rate of return. This is exactly why dual class stock (see Chapter 7) that doesn't have voting rights has a lower price per share than voting stock.

13-1c Conflicts between Managers and Shareholders

Shareholders want companies to hire managers who are able and willing to take legal and ethical actions to maximize intrinsic stock prices.[2] This obviously requires managers with technical competence, but it also requires managers who are willing to put forth the extra effort necessary to identify and implement value-adding activities. However, managers are people, and people have both personal and corporate goals. Logically, therefore, managers can be expected to act in their own self-interests, and if their self-interests are not aligned with those of stockholders, then corporate value will not be maximized. There are six ways in which a manager's behavior might harm a firm's intrinsic value.

1. Managers might not expend the time and effort required to maximize firm value. Rather than focusing on corporate tasks, they might shirk their duties and spend too much time on external activities, such as serving on boards of other companies, or on nonproductive activities, such as golf, gourmet meals, and travel.
2. Managers might use corporate resources on activities that benefit themselves rather than shareholders. For example, they might spend company money on such perquisites as lavish offices, memberships at country clubs, museum-quality art for corporate apartments, large personal staffs, and corporate jets. Because these perks are not actually cash payments to the managers, they are called **nonpecuniary benefits**.
3. Managers might avoid making difficult but value-enhancing decisions that harm friends in the company. For example, a manager might not close a plant or terminate a project if the manager has personal relationships with those who are adversely affected by such decisions, even if termination is the economically sound action.
4. Managers might take on too much risk, or they might not take on enough risk. For example, a company might have the opportunity to undertake a risky project with a positive NPV. If the project turns out badly, then the manager's reputation will be harmed, and the manager might even be fired. Thus, a manager might choose to avoid risky projects even if they are desirable from a shareholder's point of view. On the other hand, a manager might take on projects with too much risk. Consider a project that is not living up to expectations. A manager might be tempted to invest even more

---

[2]Notice that we said both legal and ethical actions. The accounting frauds perpetrated by Enron, WorldCom, and others that were uncovered in 2002 raised stock prices in the short run but only because investors were misled about the companies' financial positions. Then, when Enron finally revealed the correct financial information, the stocks tanked. Investors who bought shares based on the fraudulent financial statements lost tens of billions of dollars. Releasing false financial statements is illegal. Aggressive earnings management and the use of misleading accounting tricks to pump up reported earnings is unethical, and executives can go to jail as a result of their shenanigans. When we speak of taking actions to maximize stock prices, we mean making operational or financial changes designed to maximize intrinsic stock value, not fooling investors with false or misleading financial reports.

money in the project rather than admit that the project is a failure. Or a manager might be willing to take on a second project with a negative NPV if it has even a slight chance of a very positive outcome because hitting a home run with this second project might cover up the first project's poor performance. In other words, the manager might throw good money after bad.

5. If a company is generating positive free cash flow, a manager might "stockpile" it in the form of marketable securities instead of returning FCF to investors. This potentially harms investors because it prevents them from allocating these funds to other investments with good expected returns. Even worse, positive FCF often tempts a manager into paying too much for the acquisition of another company. In fact, most mergers and acquisitions end up as break-even deals, at best, for the acquiring company because the premiums paid for the targets are often very large.

Why would a manager be reluctant to return cash to investors? First, extra cash on hand reduces the company's risk, which appeals to many managers. Second, a large distribution of cash to investors is an admission that the company doesn't have enough good investment opportunities. Slow growth is normal for a maturing company, but this isn't very exciting for a manager to admit. Third, there is a lot of glamour associated with making a large acquisition, and this can provide a large boost to a manager's ego. Fourth, compensation usually is higher for executives at larger companies; cash distributions to investors make a company smaller, not larger.

6. Managers might not release all the information that investors desire. Sometimes, they might withhold information to prevent competitors from gaining an advantage. Other times, they might try to avoid releasing bad news. For example, they might "massage" the data or "manage the earnings" so that the news doesn't look so bad. If investors are unsure about the quality of information managers provide, they tend to discount the company's expected free cash flows at a higher cost of capital, which reduces the company's intrinsic value.

If senior managers believe there is little chance they will be removed, the company has a problem with **entrenchment**. Such a company faces a high risk of being poorly run, because entrenched managers are able to act in their own interests rather than in the interests of shareholders.

resource

For excellent discussions of corporate governance, see the Web pages of CalPERS (the California Public Employees' Retirement System), www.calpers.org, and TIAA-CREF (Teachers Insurance and Annuity Association College Retirement Equity Fund), www.tiaa-cref.org.

SELF-TEST

What are agency conflicts? What groups can have agency conflicts?

Name six types of managerial behaviors that can reduce a firm's intrinsic value.

13-2 Corporate Governance

Agency conflicts can decrease the value of stock owned by outside shareholders. Corporate governance can mitigate this loss in value. Corporate governance can be defined as the set of laws, rules, and procedures that influence a company's operations and the decisions its managers make. At the risk of oversimplification, most corporate governance provisions come in two forms, sticks and carrots. The primary stick is the *threat of removal*, either as a decision by the board of directors or as the result of a hostile **takeover** in which the company is acquired by outsiders. If a firm's managers are maximizing the value of the resources entrusted to them, they need not fear the loss of their jobs. On the other hand, if managers are not maximizing value, they should be removed by their own boards of directors, by dissident stockholders, or by other companies seeking to profit by installing a better management team. The main carrot is *compensation*. Managers have greater incentives to maximize intrinsic stock value if their compensation is linked to the firm's performance rather than being strictly in the form of salary.

Almost all corporate governance provisions affect either the threat of removal or compensation. Some provisions are internal to a firm and are under its control.[3] These internal provisions and features can be divided into five areas: (1) monitoring and discipline by the board of directors, (2) charter provisions and bylaws that affect the likelihood of hostile takeovers, (3) compensation plans, (4) capital structure choices, and (5) accounting control systems. In addition to the corporate governance provisions that are under a firm's control, there are also environmental factors outside of a firm's control, such as the regulatory environment, block ownership patterns, competition in the product markets, the media, and litigation. Our discussion begins with the internal provisions.

13-2a Monitoring and Discipline by the Board of Directors

Shareholders are a corporation's owners, and they elect the board of directors to act as agents on their behalf. In the United States, it is the board's duty to monitor senior managers and discipline them if they do not act in the interests of shareholders, either by removal or by a reduction in compensation.[4] This is not necessarily the case outside the United States. For example, many companies in Europe are required to have board members who represent interests other than those of shareholders, such as employee representatives. Also, many European and Asian companies have bank representatives on the board. But even in the United States, many boards fail to act in the shareholders' best interests. How can this be?

Consider the election process. The board of directors has a nominating committee that selects one candidate per open board seat. Although outside candidates can run a "write-in" campaign, usually, only those candidates named by the board's nominating committee are on the ballot.[5] At many companies, the CEO is also the chair of the board and has so much influence on the nominating committee that the slate of nominees is, in effect, chosen by the CEO. Thus, the nominating process often results in a board that is handpicked by the CEO. Because prestige and high compensation accompany directorships, many directors are grateful to the CEO and wish to be nominated again at the ends of their terms. Given this process, it should be no surprise that many directors act in the best interests of the CEO rather than shareholders.

At most companies, a candidate is elected simply by having a majority of votes cast. The proxy ballot usually lists all candidates, with a box for each candidate to check if the shareholder votes "For" the candidate and a box to check if the shareholder "Withholds" a vote on the candidate—you can't actually vote "No"; you can only withhold your vote. In theory, a candidate could be elected with a single "For" vote if all other votes were withheld. In practice, though, most shareholders either vote "For" or assign to management their right to vote (*proxy* is defined as the authority to act for another, which is why it is

---

[3]We have adapted this framework from the one provided by Stuart L. Gillan, "Recent Developments in Corporate Governance: An Overview," *Journal of Corporate Finance*, June 2006, pp. 381–402. Gillan provides an excellent discussion of the issues associated with corporate governance, and we highly recommend this article to the reader who is interested in an expanded discussion of the issues in this section.

[4]There are a few exceptions to this rule. For example, some states have laws allowing the board to consider the interests of other stakeholders, such as employees and members of the community.

[5]As of late 2016, 40% of S&P 500 firms allow shareholders to nominate candidates for board positions and have these candidates listed on the proxy. This is called *proxy access*. See Harvard Law School on Corporate Governance and Financial Regulation, **https://corpgov.law.harvard.edu/2016/07/13/proxy-access-momentum-in-2016/**.

called a "proxy statement"). In practice, then, the nominated candidates virtually always receive a majority of votes and are thus elected.

Occasionally there is a "Just vote no" campaign in which a large investor (usually an institution such as a pension fund) urges stockholders to withhold their votes for one or more directors. Although such campaigns do not directly affect the director's election, they do provide a visible way for investors to express their dissatisfaction. Empirical evidence shows that "Just vote no" campaigns at poorly performing firms lead to better performance and a greater probability that the CEO will be dismissed.[6]

Voting procedures also affect the ability of outsiders to gain positions on the board. If the charter specifies cumulative voting, then each shareholder is given a number of votes equal to his or her shares multiplied by the number of board seats up for election. For example, the holder of 100 shares of stock will receive 1,000 votes if 10 seats are to be filled. Then, the shareholder can distribute those votes however he or she sees fit. One hundred votes could be cast for each of 10 candidates, or all 1,000 votes could be cast for one candidate. If noncumulative voting is used, the hypothetical stockholder cannot concentrate votes in this way: No more than 100 votes can be cast for any candidate, and the stockholder may do this for as many seats as there are to be filled.

With noncumulative voting, if management controls 51% of the shares, then they can fill every seat on the board, leaving dissident stockholders without any representation on the board. With cumulative voting, however, if 10 seats are to be filled, then dissidents could elect a representative, provided they have 10% plus 1 additional share of the stock.

Note also that bylaws specify whether the entire board is to be elected annually or if directors are to have **staggered terms** with, say, one-third of the seats to be filled each year and directors to serve 3-year terms. With staggered terms, fewer seats come up each year, making it harder for dissidents to gain representation on the board. Staggered boards are also called **classified boards**.

Many boards have **inside directors**—that is, people who hold managerial positions within the company, such as the CFO, and who also are board members. Because insiders report to the CEO, it may be difficult for them to oppose the CEO at a board meeting. To help mitigate this problem, several exchanges, such as the NYSE and NASDAQ, now require that listed companies have a majority of **outside directors** who are supposed to have no other affiliation or financial interest with the company.

However, some "outside" board members often have strong connections with the CEO through professional relationships, personal friendships, and consulting or other fee-generating activities. In fact, outsiders sometimes have very little expert business knowledge but have "celebrity" status from nonbusiness activities. Some companies also have **interlocking boards of directors**, where Company A's CEO sits on Company B's board and B's CEO sits on A's board. In these situations, even the outside directors are not truly independent and impartial.

Large boards (those with more than about 10 members) often are less effective than smaller boards. As anyone who has been on a committee can attest, individual participation tends to fall as committee size increases. Thus, there is a greater likelihood that members of a large board will be less active than those on smaller boards.

The compensation of board members has an impact on the board's effectiveness. When board members have exceptionally high compensation, the CEO also tends to have exceptionally high compensation. This suggests that such boards tend to be too lenient with

---

[6]See Diane Del Guercio, Laura Seery, and Tracie Woidtke, "Do Boards Pay Attention When Institutional Investor Activists 'Just Vote No'?" *Journal of Financial Economics,* October 2008, pp. 84–103.

the CEO.[7] The form of board compensation also affects board performance. Rather than compensating board members with only salary, many companies now include restricted stock grants or stock options in an effort to better align board members with stockholders.

Studies show that corporate governance usually improves under the following circumstances: (1) The CEO is not also the chairman of the board. (2) The board has a majority of true outsiders who bring some type of business expertise to the board and are not too busy with other activities. (3) The board is not too large. (4) Board members are compensated appropriately (not too high and not all cash, but including exposure to equity risk through options or stock). The good news for the shareholder is that the boards at many companies have made significant improvements in these directions during the past decade. Fewer CEOs are also board chairs, and, as power has shifted from CEOs to boards as a whole, there has been a tendency to replace insiders with strong, independent outsiders. Today, the typical board has about one-third insiders and two-thirds outsiders, and most outsiders are truly independent. Moreover, board members are compensated primarily with stock or options rather than a straight salary. These changes clearly have decreased the patience of boards with poorly performing CEOs. Within the past several years, the CEOs of Sprint Nextel, Hewlett-Packard, Home Depot, Citigroup, Pfizer, Groupon, Siemens, J.C. Penney, Men's Warehouse, and Barnes & Noble, to name just a few, have been removed by their boards. This would not have occurred 30 years ago.

13-2b Charter Provisions and Bylaws That Affect the Likelihood of Hostile Takeovers

Hostile takeovers usually occur when managers have not been willing or able to maximize the profit potential of the resources under their control. In such a situation, another company can acquire the poorly performing firm, replace its managers, increase free cash flow, and improve MVA. The following paragraphs describe some provisions that can be included in a corporate charter to make it harder for poorly performing managers to remain in control.[8]

A shareholder-friendly charter should ban **targeted share repurchases**, also known as **greenmail**. For example, suppose a company's stock is selling for $20 per share. Now a hostile bidder, or raider, who plans to replace management if the takeover is successful, buys 5% of the company's stock at the $20 price.[9] The raider then makes an offer to purchase the remainder of the stock for $30 per share. The company might offer to buy back the raider's stock at a price of, say, $35 per share. This is called a targeted share repurchase because the stock will be purchased only from the raider and not from any other shareholders. A raider who paid only $20 per share for the stock would be making a quick profit of $15 per share, which could easily total several hundred million dollars. As a part of the deal, the raider would sign a document promising not to attempt to take over the

---

[7]See I. E. Brick, O. Palmon, and J. Wald, "CEO Compensation, Director Compensation, and Firm Performance: Evidence of Cronyism?" *Journal of Corporate Finance*, June 2006, pp. 403–423.

[8]Some states have laws that go further than others to protect management. This is one reason that many companies are incorporated in manager-friendly Delaware. Some companies have even shifted their state of incorporation to Delaware because their managers felt that a hostile takeover attempt was likely. Note that a "shareholder-friendly charter" could and would waive the company's right to strong anti-takeover protection, even if the state allowed it.

[9]Someone can, under the law, acquire up to 5% of a firm's stock without announcing the acquisition. Once the 5% limit has been hit, the acquirer has 10 days to "announce" the acquisition by filing Schedule 13D with the SEC. Schedule 13D reports not only the acquirer's number of shares but also his or her intentions, such as a passive investment or a takeover. These reports are monitored closely, so as soon as one is filed, management is alerted to the possibility of an imminent takeover.

company for a specified number of years; hence, the buyback also is called greenmail. Greenmail hurts shareholders in two ways. First, they are left with $20 stock when they could have received $30 per share. Second, the company purchased stock from the bidder at $35 per share, which represents a direct loss by the remaining shareholders of $15 for each repurchased share.

Managers who buy back stock in targeted repurchases typically argue that their firms are worth more than the raiders offered and that, in time, the "true value" will be revealed in the form of a much higher stock price. This situation might be true if a company were in the process of restructuring itself, or if new products with high potential were in the pipeline. But absent compelling evidence, one should question whether the true purpose of the buyback was to protect stockholders or management.

Another characteristic of a stockholder-friendly charter is that it does not contain a **shareholder rights provision**, better described as a **poison pill**. These provisions give the shareholders of target firms the right to buy a specified number of shares in the company at a very low price if an outside group or firm acquires a specified percentage of the firm's stock. Therefore, if a potential acquirer tries to take over a company, its other shareholders will be entitled to purchase additional shares of stock at a bargain price, thus seriously diluting the holdings of the raider. For this reason, these clauses are called poison pills because if they are in the charter, the acquirer will end up swallowing a poison pill if the acquisition is successful. Obviously, the existence of a poison pill makes a takeover more difficult, and this helps to entrench management.

A third management entrenchment tool is a **restricted voting rights** provision, which automatically cancels the voting rights of any shareholder who owns more than a specified amount of the company's stock. The board can grant voting rights to such a shareholder, but this is unlikely if that shareholder plans to take over the company.

13-2c Using Compensation to Align Managerial and Shareholder Interests

The typical CEO's compensation is comprised of (1) a fixed salary, (2) cash bonuses awarded by the board of directors (often to a new CEO at the time of the hire or to the current CEO for successfully completing a specific task), (3) stock awards, (5) stock option awards, (6) non-equity incentive awards based on the firm's operating performance, and (7) miscellaneous compensation such as deferred compensation and contributions to pension/retirement accounts. Senior executives and board directors usually have some of these items in their own compensation plans.

Non-equity incentive awards often are based upon short-term operating factors, such as this year's growth in earnings per share or improvements in certain traditional ratios, such as the return on equity and the return on assets. Incentive awards will align managers' and shareholders' interests to the extent that the performance metrics actually reflect changes in the stock's intrinsic value. Unfortunately, humans are creative (especially accountants) and managers often find ways of maximizing these awards without significantly increasing intrinsic value.

As a result, companies today are shifting to the performance metrics described in Chapter 2, such as the return on invested capital (ROIC), economic value added (EVA), and market value added (MVA).[10] For example, increases in EVA are closely linked to

---

[10]For a discussion of EVA, see Al Ehrbar, *EVA: The Real Key to Creating Wealth* (New York: John Wiley & Sons, 1998); and Pamela P. Peterson and David R. Peterson, *Company Performance and Measures of Value Added* (The Research Foundation of the Institute of Chartered Financial Analysts, 1996).

increases in intrinsic value. Also, it is much more difficult to manipulate EVA in ways that don't also increase intrinsic value; the same cannot be said about earnings per share.

EQUITY-BASED COMPENSATION

Equity-based compensation can be in the form of (1) restricted stock awards, (2) restricted stock units (RSUs), or (3) stock options. These forms of compensation increase if the stock price increases, which seems to align the interests of managers and shareholders. We will have more to say later in this section, but first let's take a look at the forms of equity-based compensation.

Restricted stock awards (or grants) allow the recipient to vote and collect dividends, but they may not be sold until after some specified period (the **vesting period**), which is usually 1 to 5 years. Some grants have **cliff vesting**, with all stocks in the grant vesting at the same date, such as 3 years after the grant. Other grants have **annual vesting**, which means that a certain percentage vests each year. For example, one-third of the stocks in the grant might vest each year.

Restricted stock units (RSUs) are similar to restricted stocks in that they entitle the recipient to shares of stock after vesting. However, the recipient does not collect dividends or vote. Usually the RSUs are paid with shares of stock after vesting, but sometimes they are paid with the cash equivalent. In addition, there are tax issues associated with the RSUs versus restricted stock awards.

Chapter 8 explains option valuation in detail, but here we discuss how a typical **stock option compensation plan** works. Suppose IBM decides to grant an option to an employee, allowing her to purchase a specified number of IBM shares at a fixed price, called the **strike price** (or **exercise price**), regardless of the actual price of the stock. The strike price is usually set equal to the current stock price at the time the option is granted. Thus, if IBM's current price were $100, then the option would have an exercise price of $100. Like restricted stock and RSUs, options usually cannot be exercised until after vesting.

The options have an **expiration date**, usually 10 years after issue. For our IBM example, assume that the options have cliff vesting in 3 years and an expiration date in 10 years. Thus, the employee can exercise the option 3 years after issue or wait as long as 10 years. Of course, the employee would not exercise unless IBM's stock is above the $100 exercise price, and if the price never rose above $100, the option would expire unexercised. However, if the stock price were above $100 on the expiration date, the option would surely be exercised.

Suppose the stock price had grown to $134 after 5 years, at which point the employee decided to exercise the option. She would buy stock from IBM for $100, so IBM would get only $100 for stock worth $134. The employee would (probably) sell the stock the same day she exercised the option and hence would receive in cash the $34 difference between the $134 stock price and the $100 exercise price. There are two important points to note in this example. First, most employees sell stock soon after exercising the option. Thus, the incentive effects of an option grant typically end when the option is exercised. Second, option pricing theory shows that it is not optimal to exercise a conventional call option on stock that does not pay dividends before the option expires: An investor is always better off selling the option in the marketplace rather than exercising it. But because employee stock options are not tradable, grantees often exercise the options well before they expire. For example, people often time the exercise of options to coincide with the purchase of a new home or some other large expenditure. But early exercise occurs not just for liquidity reasons, such as needing cash to purchase a house, but also because of behavioral reasons. For example, exercises occur more frequently after stock run-ups, which suggests that grantees view the stock as overpriced.

DOES EQUITY-BASED COMPENSATION ALIGN THE INTERESTS OF MANAGERS AND SHAREHOLDERS?

In theory, equity-based compensation should align a manager's interests with those of shareholders, influencing the manager to behave in ways that maximize the company's value. But in practice, this does not always occur for two reasons. We illustrate these reasons using stock options, but the same logic also applies to restricted stock and RSU grants.

First, suppose a CEO is granted options on 1 million shares. If we use the same stock prices as in our previous example, then at expiration the grantee would receive $34 for each option, or a total of $34 million. But take a closer look at this example. If the risk-free rate is 5.5%, the market risk premium is 6%, and IBM's beta is 1.19, then the expected return, based on the CAPM, is 5.5% + 1.19(6%) = 12.64%. IBM's dividend yield is only 0.8%, so the expected annual price appreciation must be about 11.84% (12.64% − 0.8% = 11.84%). Now note that if IBM's stock price grew from $100 to $134 over 5 years, this would translate to an annual growth rate of only 6%, not the 11.84% shareholders expected. Thus, the executive would receive $34 million for helping run a company that performed below shareholders' expectations. As this example illustrates, standard stock options do not necessarily link executives' wealth with that of shareholders.

Second, and even worse, the events of the early 2000s showed that some executives were willing to illegally falsify financial statements in order to drive up stock prices just prior to exercising their stock options.[11] In some notable cases, the subsequent stock price drop and loss of investor confidence have forced firms into bankruptcy. Such behavior is certainly not in shareholders' best interests!

Just as "all ships rise in a rising tide," so too do most stocks rise in a bull market such as that of 2011–2018. In a strong market, even the stocks of companies whose performance ranks in the bottom 10% of their peer group can rise and thus trigger handsome executive bonuses. This situation is leading to compensation plans that are based on *relative* as opposed to *absolute* stock price performance. For example, some compensation plans have indexed options whose exercise prices depend on the performance of the market or a subset of competitors.

Finally, the empirical results from academic studies show that the correlation between executive compensation and corporate performance is mixed. Some studies suggest that the type of compensation plan used affects company performance, while others find little effect, if any. But we can say with certainty that managerial compensation plans will continue to receive lots of attention from researchers, the popular press, and boards of directors.

13-2d Capital Structure and Internal Control Systems

Capital structure decisions can affect managerial behavior. As the debt level increases, so does the probability of bankruptcy. This increased threat of bankruptcy affects managerial behavior in two ways. First, as discussed earlier in this chapter, managers may waste money on unnecessary expenditures and perquisites. This behavior is more likely when times are good and firms are flush with cash; it is less likely in the face of high

---

[11]Several academic studies show that option-based compensation leads to a greater likelihood of earnings restatements (which means having to refile financial statements with the SEC because there was a material error) and outright fraud. See A. Agrawal and S. Chadha, "Corporate Governance and Accounting Scandals," *Journal of Law and Economics*, 2006, pp. 371–406; N. Burns and S. Kedia, "The Impact of Performance-Based Compensation on Misreporting," *Journal of Financial Economics,* January 2006, pp. 35–67; and D. J. Denis, P. Hanouna, and A. Sarin, "Is There a Dark Side to Incentive Compensation?" *Journal of Corporate Finance,* June 2006, pp. 467–488.

The Dodd-Frank Act and "Say on Pay"

The Dodd-Frank Act requires corporations to hold a non-binding vote to approve or reject the company's executive compensation plan. As of October 2016, 1,972 companies in the Russell 3000 have held say on pay votes since 2011 when the vote was first required. Since then, 93% have passed with at least 70% shareholder support. There have been some notable exceptions, however, with shareholders rejecting compensation plans at companies such as

Navistar International, RadioShack, Abercrombie & Fitch, and Big Lots.

In addition to say on pay, shareholders are also concerned with other issues, submitting proposals on topics dealing with political lobbying, social responsibility and takeover defenses.

Source: Selmer Brossy "2016 Say on Pay Results," published by Semler Brossy and available at **http://www.semlerbrossy.com/sayonpay**.

debt levels and possible bankruptcy. Thus, high levels of debt tend to reduce managerial waste. Second, however, high levels of debt may also reduce a manager's willingness to undertake positive-NPV but risky projects. Most managers have their personal reputation and wealth tied to a single company. If that company has a lot of debt, then a particularly risky project, even if it has a positive NPV, may be just too risky for the manager to tolerate because a bad outcome could lead to bankruptcy and loss of the manager's job. Stockholders, on the other hand, are diversified and would want the manager to invest in positive-NPV projects even if they are risky. When managers forgo risky but value-adding projects, the resulting **underinvestment problem** reduces firm value. So increasing debt might increase firm value by reducing wasteful expenditures, but it also might reduce value by inducing underinvestment by managers. Empirical tests have not been able to establish exactly which effect dominates.

Internal control systems have become an increasingly important issue since the passage of the Sarbanes-Oxley Act of 2002. Section 404 of the act requires companies to establish effective internal control systems. The Securities and Exchange Commission, which is charged with the implementation of Sarbanes-Oxley, defines an effective internal control system as one that provides "reasonable assurance regarding the reliability of financial reporting and the preparation of financial statements for external purposes in accordance with generally accepted accounting principles." In other words, investors should be able to trust a company's reported financial statements.

13-2e Environmental Factors outside a Firm's Control

As noted earlier, corporate governance is also affected by environmental factors that are outside a firm's control, including the regulatory/legal environment, block ownership patterns, competition in the product markets, the media, and litigation.

REGULATIONS AND LAWS

The regulatory/legal environment includes the agencies that regulate financial markets, such as the SEC. Even though the fines and penalties levied on firms for financial misrepresentation by the SEC are relatively small, the damage to a firm's reputation can have significant costs, leading to extremely large reductions in the firm's value.[12] Thus, the regulatory system has an enormous impact on corporate governance and firm value.

---

[12]For example, see Jonathan M. Karpoff, D. Scott Lee, and Gerald S. Martin, "The Cost to Firms of Cooking the Books," *Journal of Financial and Quantitative Analysis,* September 2008, pp. 581–612.

The Sarbanes-Oxley Act of 2002 and Corporate Governance

In 2002, Congress passed the Sarbanes-Oxley Act, known in the industry as SOX, as a measure to improve transparency in financial accounting and to prevent fraud. SOX consists of 11 chapters, or *titles*, which establish wide-ranging new regulations for auditors, CEOs and CFOs, boards of directors, investment analysts, and investment banks. These regulations are designed to ensure the following: (1) Companies that perform audits are sufficiently independent of the companies that they audit. (2) A key executive in each company *personally* certifies that the financial statements are complete and accurate. (3) The board of directors' audit committee is relatively independent of management. (4) Financial analysts are relatively independent of the companies they analyze. (5) Companies publicly and promptly release all important information about their financial condition. The individual titles are briefly summarized as follows.

Title I establishes the Public Company Accounting Oversight Board, whose charge is to oversee auditors and to establish quality control and ethical standards for audits.

Title II requires that auditors be independent of the companies that they audit. Basically this means they can't provide consulting services to the companies they audit. The purpose is to remove financial incentives for auditors to help management "cook the books."

Title III requires that the board of directors' audit committee must be composed of "independent" members. Section 302 requires that the CEO and CFO must review the annual and quarterly financial statements and reports and personally certify that they are complete and accurate. Penalties for certifying reports that executives know are false range up to a $5 million fine, 20 years in prison, or both. Under Section 304, if the financial statements turn out to be false and must be *restated,* then certain bonuses and equity-based compensation that executives earn must be reimbursed to the company.

Title IV's Section 401(a) requires prompt disclosure of and more extensive reporting on off-balance sheet transactions. Section 404 requires that management evaluate its internal financial controls and report whether they are "effective." The external auditing firm must also indicate whether it agrees with management's evaluation of its internal controls. Section 409 requires that a company disclose to the public promptly and *in plain English* any material changes to its financial condition. Title IV also places restrictions on the loans that a company can make to its executives.

Title V addresses the relationship between financial analysts, the investment banks they work for, and the companies they cover. It requires that analysts and brokers who make stock recommendations disclose any conflicts of interest they might have concerning the stocks they recommend.

Titles VI and VII are technical in nature, dealing with the SEC's budget and powers and requiring that several studies be undertaken by the SEC.

Title VIII establishes penalties for destroying or falsifying audit records. It also provides "whistleblower protection" for employees who report fraud.

Title IX increases the penalties for a variety of white-collar crimes associated with securities fraud, such as mail and wire fraud. Section 902 also makes it a crime to alter, destroy, or hide documents that might be used in an investigation. It also makes it a crime to conspire to do so.

Title X requires that the CEO sign the company's federal income tax return.

Title XI provides penalties for obstructing an investigation and grants the SEC authority to remove officers or directors from a company if they have committed fraud.

The regulatory/legal environment also includes the laws and legal system under which a company operates. These vary greatly from country to country. Studies show that firms located in countries with strong legal protection for investors have stronger corporate governance and that this is reflected in better access to financial markets, a lower cost of equity, increases in market liquidity, and less nonsystematic volatility in stock returns.[13]

---

[13]For example, see R. La Porta, F. Lopez-de-Silanes, A. Shleifer, and R. Vishny, "Legal Determinants of External Finance," *Journal of Finance,* January 1997, pp. 1131–1150; Hazem Daouk, Charles M. C. Lee, and David Ng, "Capital Market Governance: How Do Security Laws Affect Market Performance?" *Journal of Corporate Finance,* June 2006, pp. 560–593; and Li Jin and Stewart C. Myers, "R² Around the World: New Theory and New Tests," *Journal of Financial Economics,* February 2006, pp. 257–292.

International Corporate Governance

Corporate governance includes the following factors: (1) the likelihood that a poorly performing firm can be taken over, (2) whether the board of directors is dominated by insiders or outsiders, (3) the extent to which most of the stock is held by a few large "blockholders" versus many small shareholders, and (4) the size and form of executive compensation. An interesting study compared corporate governance in Germany, Japan, and the United States.

First, note from the accompanying table that the threat of a takeover serves as a stick in the United States but not in Japan or Germany. This threat, which reduces management entrenchment, should benefit shareholders in the United States relative to the other two countries. Second, German and Japanese boards are larger than those in the United States. Japanese boards consist primarily of insiders, unlike German and American boards, which have similar inside/outside mixes. It should be noted, though, that the boards of most large German corporations include representatives of labor, whereas U.S. boards represent only shareholders. Thus, it would appear that U.S. boards, with a higher percentage of outsiders, would have interests most closely aligned with those of shareholders.

German and Japanese firms are also more likely to be controlled by large blocks of stock than those in the United States. Although institutional investors such as pension and mutual funds are increasingly important in the United States, block ownership is still less prevalent than in Germany and Japan. In both Germany and Japan, banks often own large blocks of stock, something that is not permitted by law in the United States, and corporations also own large blocks of stock in other corporations. In Japan, combinations of companies, called **keiretsus**, have cross-ownership of stock among the member companies, and these interlocking blocks distort the definition of an outside board member. For example, when the performance of a company in a keiretsu deteriorates, new directors are often appointed from the staffs of other members of the keiretsu. Such appointees might be classified officially as insiders, but they represent interests other than those of the troubled company's CEO.

In general, large blockholders are better able to monitor management than are small investors, so one might expect the blockholder factor to favor German and Japanese shareholders. However, these blockholders have other relationships with the company that might be detrimental to outside shareholders. For example, if one company buys from another, transfer pricing might be used to shift wealth to a favored company, or a company might be forced to buy from a sister company in spite of the availability of lower-cost resources from outside the group.

Executive compensation packages differ dramatically across the three countries, with U.S. executives receiving by

BLOCK OWNERSHIP PATTERNS

Prior to the 1960s, most U.S. stocks were owned by large numbers of individual investors, each of whom owned a diversified portfolio of stocks. Because each individual owned a small amount of any given company's stock, there was little that he or she could do to influence its operations. Also, with such a small investment, it was not cost effective for the investor to monitor companies closely. Indeed, dissatisfied stockholders would typically just "vote with their feet" by selling the stock. This situation began to change as institutional investors such as pension funds and mutual funds gained control of larger and larger shares of investment capital—and as they then acquired larger and larger percentages of all outstanding stock. Given their large block holdings, it now makes sense for institutional investors to monitor management, and they have the clout to influence the board. In some cases, they have actually elected their own representatives to the board. For example, when TIAA-CREF, a huge private pension fund, became frustrated with the performance and leadership of Furr's/Bishop, a cafeteria chain, the fund led a fight that ousted the entire board and then elected a new board consisting only of outsiders.

In general, activist investors with large blocks in companies have been good for all shareholders. They have searched for firms with poor profitability and then replaced management with new teams that are well versed in value-based management techniques,

far the highest compensation. However, compensation plans are remarkably similar in terms of how sensitive total compensation is to corporate performance.

Which country's system of corporate governance is best from the standpoint of a shareholder whose goal is stock price maximization? There is no definitive answer. U.S. stocks have had the best performance in recent years. Moreover, German and Japanese companies are slowly moving toward the U.S. system with respect to size of compensation, and compensation plans in all three countries are being linked ever more

closely to performance. At the same time, however, U.S. companies are moving toward the others in the sense of having larger ownership blocks; because those blocks are primarily held by pension and mutual funds (rather than banks and related corporations), they better represent the interests of shareholders.

Source: Steven N. Kaplan, "Top Executive Incentives in Germany, Japan, and the USA: A Comparison," in *Executive Compensation and Shareholder Value,* Jennifer Carpenter and David Yermack, eds. (Boston: Kluwer Academic Publishers, 1999), pp. 3–12.

International Characteristics of Corporate Governance

	Germany	Japan	United States
Threat of a takeover	Moderate	Low	High
Board of directors			
Size of board	26	21	14
Percent insiders	27%	91%	33%
Percent outsiders	73%	9%	67%
Are large blocks of stock typically owned by			
A controlling family?	Yes	No	No
Another corporation?	Yes	Yes	No
A bank?	Yes	Yes	No
Executive compensation			
Amount of compensation	Moderate	Low	High
Sensitivity to performance	Low to moderate	Low to moderate	Low to moderate

thereby improving profitability. Not surprisingly, stock prices usually rise on the news that a well-known activist investor has taken a major position in an underperforming company.

Note that activist investors can improve performance even if they don't go so far as to take over a firm. More often, they either elect their own representatives to the board or simply point out the firm's problems to other board members. In such cases, boards become less tolerant of management behavior when they realize that the management team is not acting to increase shareholder value. Moreover, the firm's top managers recognize what will happen if they don't whip the company into shape, and they go about doing just that.

COMPETITION IN PRODUCT MARKETS

The degree of competition in a firm's product market has an impact on its corporate governance. For example, companies in industries with lots of competition don't have the luxury of tolerating poorly performing CEOs. As might be expected, CEO turnover is higher in competitive industries than in those with less competition.[14] When most firms in an industry are similar, you might expect it to be easier to find a qualified replacement

---

[14]See M. De Fond and C. Park, "The Effect of Competition on CEO Turnover," *Journal of Accounting and Economics,* Vol. 27, 1999, pp. 35–56; and T. Fee and C. Hadlock, "Management Turnover and Product Market Competition: Empirical Evidence from the U.S. Newspaper Industry," *Journal of Business,* April 2000, pp. 205–243.

from another firm for a poorly performing CEO. This is exactly what the evidence shows: As industry homogeneity increases, so does the incidence of CEO turnover.[15]

THE MEDIA AND LITIGATION

Corporate governance, especially compensation, is a hot topic in the media. The media can have a positive impact by discovering or reporting corporate problems, such as the Enron scandal. Another example is the extensive coverage that was given to option back-dating, in which the exercise prices of executive stock options were set *after* the options officially were granted. Because the exercise prices were set at the lowest stock price during the quarter in which the options were granted, the options were in-the-money and more valuable when their "official" lives began. Several CEOs lost their jobs over this practice.

However, the media can also hurt corporate governance by focusing too much attention on a CEO. Such "superstar" CEOs often command excessive compensation packages and spend too much time on activities outside the company, resulting in too much pay for too little performance.[16]

In addition to penalties and fines from regulatory bodies such as the SEC, civil litigation also occurs when companies are suspected of fraud. Research indicates that such suits lead to improvements in corporate governance.[17]

SELF-TEST

What are the two primary forms of corporate governance provisions that correspond to the stick and the carrot?

What factors improve the effectiveness of a board of directors?

What are three provisions in many corporate charters that deter takeovers?

Describe how a typical stock option plan works. What are some problems with a typical stock option plan?

13-3 Employee Stock Ownership Plans (ESOPs)

WWW

See www .esopassociation.org for updates on ESOP statistics.

Studies show that 90% of the employees who receive stock under option plans sell the stock as soon as they exercise their options, so the plans motivate employees only for a limited period.[18] Moreover, many companies limit their stock option plans to key managers and executives. To help provide long-term productivity gains and improve retirement incomes for all employees, Congress authorized the use of **Employee Stock Ownership Plans (ESOPs)**. As of 2018, there were over 7,000 ESOP plans representing 14 million employees. Typically, the ESOP's major asset is shares of the common stock of the company that created it, and of the 10,000 total ESOPs, about half of them actually own a majority of their company's stock.[19]

---

[15]See R. Parrino, "CEO Turnover and Outside Succession: A Cross-Sectional Analysis," *Journal of Financial Economics,* Vol. 46, 1997, pp. 165–197.

[16]See U. Malmendier and G. A. Tate, "Superstar CEOs," *Quarterly Journal of Economics,* November 2009, pp. 1593–1638.

[17]For example, see D. B. Farber, "Restoring Trust after Fraud: Does Corporate Governance Matter?" *Accounting Review,* April 2005, pp. 539–561; and Stephen P. Ferris, Tomas Jandik, Robert M. Lawless, and Anil Makhija, "Derivative Lawsuits as a Corporate Governance Mechanism: Empirical Evidence on Board Changes Surrounding Filings," *Journal of Financial and Quantitative Analysis,* March 2007, pp. 143–166.

[18]See Gary Laufman, "To Have and Have Not," *CFO,* March 1998, pp. 58–66.

[19]For current information on ESOPs and other equity-based compensation, see The National Center for Employee Ownership's Web page at **www.nceo.org**. See also **www.esop.org**.

To illustrate how an ESOP works, consider Gallagher & Abbott Inc. (G&A), a construction company located in Knoxville, Tennessee. G&A's simplified balance sheet follows:

G&A's Balance Sheet Prior to ESOP (Millions of Dollars)

Assets		Liabilities and Equity	
Cash	$ 10	Debt	$100
Other	190	Equity (1 million shares)	100
Total	$200	Total	$200

Now G&A creates an ESOP, which is a new legal entity. The company issues 500,000 shares of new stock at $100 per share, or $50 million in total, which it sells to the ESOP. The company's employees are the ESOP's stockholders, and each employee receives an ownership interest based on the size of his or her salary and years of service. The ESOP borrows the $50 million to buy the newly issued stock.[20] Financial institutions are willing to lend the ESOP the money because G&A signs a guarantee for the loan. Here is the company's new balance sheet:

G&A's Balance Sheet after the ESOP (Millions of Dollars)

Assets		Liabilities and Equity	
Cash	$ 60	Debt[a]	$100
Other	190	Equity (1.5 million shares)	150
Total	$250	Total	$250

[a]The company has guaranteed the ESOP's loan, and it has promised to make payments to the ESOP sufficient to retire the loan, but this does not show up on the balance sheet.

The company now has an additional $50 million of cash and $50 million more of book equity, but it has a de facto liability due to its guarantee of the ESOP's debt. It could use the cash to finance an expansion, but many companies use the cash to repurchase their own common stock, so we assume that G&A will do likewise. The company's new balance sheets, and that of the ESOP, are as follows:

G&A's Balance Sheet after the ESOP and Share Repurchase (Millions of Dollars)

Assets		Liabilities and Equity	
Cash	$ 10	Debt	$100
Other	190	Equity (1 million shares)	150
		Treasury stock	(50)
Total	$200	Total	$200

ESOP's Initial Balance Sheet (Millions of Dollars)

Assets		Liabilities and Equity	
G&A stock	$50	Debt	$50
		Equity	0
Total	$50	Total	$50

---

[20]Our description is simplified. Technically, the stock would be placed in a suspense account and then be allocated to employees as the debt is repaid.

Note that, although the company's balance sheet looks exactly as it did initially, there is actually a huge difference: The company has guaranteed the ESOP's debt, and hence it has an off–balance sheet liability of $50 million. Moreover, because the ESOP has no equity, the guarantee is very real indeed. Finally, observe that operating assets have not been increased at all, but the total debt outstanding supported by those assets has increased by $50 million.[21]

If this were the whole story, then there would be no reason to have an ESOP. However, G&A has promised to make payments to the ESOP in sufficient amounts to enable the ESOP to pay interest and principal charges on the debt, amortizing it over 15 years. Thus, after 15 years, the debt will be paid off, and the ESOP's equity holders (the employees) will have equity with a book value of $50 million and a market value that could be much higher if G&A's stock increases, as it should over time. Then, as employees retire, the ESOP will distribute a pro rata amount of the G&A stock to each employee, who can then use it as a part of his or her retirement plan.

An ESOP is clearly beneficial for employees, but why would a company want to establish one? There are five primary reasons.

1. Congress passed the enabling legislation in hopes of enhancing employees' productivity and thus making the economy more efficient. In theory, employees who have equity in the enterprise will work harder and smarter. Note too that if employees are more productive and creative, then this will benefit outside shareholders because productivity enhancements that benefit ESOP shareholders also benefit outside shareholders.

2. The ESOP represents additional compensation to employees: In our example, there is a $50 million (or more) transfer of wealth from existing shareholders to employees over the 15-year period. Presumably, if the ESOP were not created, then some other form of compensation would have been required, and that alternative compensation might not have the secondary benefit of enhancing productivity. Also note that the ESOP's payments to employees (as opposed to the payment by the company) come primarily at retirement, and Congress wanted to boost retirement incomes.

3. Depending on when an employee's rights to the ESOP are vested, the ESOP may help the firm retain employees.

4. There are strong tax incentives that encourage a company to form an ESOP. First, Congress decreed that when the ESOP owns 50% or more of the company's common stock, financial institutions that lend money to ESOPs can exclude from taxable income 50% of the interest they receive on the loan. This improves the financial institutions' after-tax returns, which allows them to lend to ESOPs at below-market rates. Therefore, a company that establishes an ESOP can borrow through the ESOP at a lower rate than would otherwise be available; in our example, the $50 million of debt would be at a reduced rate.

    There is also a second tax advantage. If the company were to borrow directly, it could deduct interest but not principal payments from its taxable income. However, companies typically make the required payments to their ESOPs in the form of cash dividends. Dividends are not normally deductible from taxable income, but *cash dividends paid on ESOP stock are deductible if the dividends are paid to plan participants or are used to repay the loan.* Thus, companies whose ESOPs own 50% of their stock can in effect borrow on ESOP loans at subsidized rates and then

---

[21]We assumed that the company used the $50 million paid to it by the ESOP to repurchase common stock and thus to increase its de facto debt. It could have used the $50 million to retire debt, in which case its true debt ratio would remain unchanged, or it could have used the money to support an expansion.

deduct both the interest and principal payments made on the loans. American Airlines and Publix Supermarkets are two of the many firms that have used ESOPs to obtain this benefit, along with motivating employees by giving them an equity interest in the enterprise.

5. A less desirable use of ESOPs is to help companies avoid being acquired by another company. The company's CEO or someone appointed by the CEO typically acts as trustee for its ESOP, and the trustee is supposed to vote the ESOP's shares according to the will of the plan participants. Moreover, the participants, who are the company's employees, usually oppose takeovers because they frequently involve labor cutbacks. Therefore, if an ESOP owns a significant percentage of the company's shares, then management has a powerful tool for warding off takeovers. This is not good for outside stockholders.

Are ESOPs good for a company's shareholders? In theory, ESOPs motivate employees by providing them with an ownership interest. That should increase productivity and thereby enhance stock values. Moreover, tax incentives mitigate the costs associated with some ESOPs. However, an ESOP can be used to help entrench management, and that could hurt stockholders. How do the pros and cons balance out? The empirical evidence is not entirely clear, but certain findings are worth noting. First, if an ESOP is established to help defend against a takeover, then the firm's stock price typically falls when plans for the ESOP are announced. The market does not like the prospect of entrenching management and having to give up the premium normally associated with a takeover. However, if the ESOP is established for tax purposes and/or to motivate employees, the stock price generally goes up at the time of the announcement. In these cases, the company typically has a subsequent improvement in sales per employee and other long-term performance measures, which stimulates the stock price. Indeed, a study showed that companies with ESOPs enjoyed a 26% average annual stock return compared to a return of only 19% for peer companies without ESOPs.[22] It thus appears that ESOPs, if used appropriately, can be a powerful tool for creating shareholder value.

SELF-TEST

What are ESOPs? What are some of their advantages and disadvantages?

SUMMARY

- An **agency relationship** arises whenever an individual or group, called a **principal**, hires someone called an **agent** to perform a service and the principal delegates decision-making power to the agent.
- Important agency relationships include those between stockholders and creditors, owner/managers and outside shareholders, and stockholders and managers.
- An **agency conflict** refers to a conflict between principals and agents. For example, managers, as agents, may pay themselves excessive salaries, obtain unreasonably large stock options, and the like, at the expense of the principals, the stockholders.
- **Agency costs** are the reductions in a company's value due to actions by agents, including the costs that principals incur (such as monitoring costs) trying to modify their agents' behaviors.
- **Corporate governance** involves the manner in which shareholders' objectives are implemented, and it is reflected in a company's policies and actions.

---

[22]See Daniel Eisenberg, "No ESOP Fable," *Time*, May 10, 1999, p. 95.

- The two primary mechanisms used in corporate governance are (1) the threat of removal of a poorly performing CEO and (2) the type of plan used to compensate executives and managers.
- Poorly performing managers can be removed either by a takeover or by the company's own board of directors. Provisions in the corporate charter affect the difficulty of a successful takeover, and the composition of the board of directors affects the likelihood of a manager being removed by the board.
- Managerial **entrenchment** is most likely to occur when a company has a weak board of directors coupled with strong anti-takeover provisions in its corporate charter. In this situation, the likelihood that badly performing senior managers will be fired is low.
- **Nonpecuniary benefits** are noncash perks such as lavish offices, memberships at country clubs, corporate jets, foreign junkets, and the like. Some of these expenditures may be cost effective, but others are wasteful and simply reduce profits. Such fat is almost always cut after a hostile takeover.
- **Targeted share repurchases**, also known as **greenmail**, occur when a company buys back stock from a potential acquirer at a price higher than the market price. In return, the potential acquirer agrees not to attempt to take over the company.
- **Shareholder rights provisions**, also known as **poison pills**, allow existing shareholders to purchase additional shares of stock at a price lower than the market value if a potential acquirer purchases a controlling stake in the company.
- A **restricted voting rights** provision automatically deprives a shareholder of voting rights if he or she owns more than a specified amount of stock.
- **Interlocking boards of directors** occur when the CEO of Company A sits on the board of Company B and B's CEO sits on A's board.
- A **stock option** provides for the purchase of a share of stock at a fixed price, called the **exercise price**, no matter what the actual price of the stock is. Stock options have an **expiration date**, after which they cannot be exercised.
- An **Employee Stock Ownership Plan (ESOP)** is a plan that facilitates employees' ownership of stock in the company for which they work.

QUESTIONS

(13-1)   Define each of the following terms:
  a. Agent; principal; agency relationship
  b. Agency cost
  c. Basic types of agency conflicts
  d. Managerial entrenchment; nonpecuniary benefits
  e. Greenmail; poison pills; restricted voting rights
  f. Stock option; ESOP

(13-2)   What is the possible agency conflict between inside owner/managers and outside shareholders?

(13-3)   What are some possible agency conflicts between borrowers and lenders?

(13-4)   What are some actions an entrenched management might take that would harm shareholders?

(13-5)   How is it possible for an employee stock option to be valuable even if the firm's stock price fails to meet shareholders' expectations?

MINI CASE

Suppose you decide (as did Steve Jobs and Mark Zuckerberg) to start a company. Your product is a software platform that integrates a wide range of media devices, including laptop computers, desktop computers, digital video recorders, and cell phones. Your initial market is the student body at your university. Once you have established your company and set up procedures for operating it, you plan to expand to other colleges in the area and eventually to go nationwide. At some point, hopefully sooner rather than later, you plan to go public with an IPO and then to buy a yacht and take off for the South Pacific to indulge in your passion for underwater photography. With these issues in mind, you need to answer for yourself, and potential investors, the following questions.

a. What is an agency relationship? When you first begin operations, assuming you are the only employee and only your money is invested in the business, would any agency conflicts exist? Explain your answer.

b. If you expanded and hired additional people to help you, might that give rise to agency problems?

c. Suppose you need additional capital to expand, and you sell some stock to outside investors. If you maintain enough stock to control the company, what type of agency conflict might occur?

d. Suppose your company raises funds from outside lenders. What type of agency costs might occur? How might lenders mitigate the agency costs?

e. Suppose your company is very successful, and you cash out most of your stock and turn the company over to an elected board of directors. Neither you nor any other stockholders own a controlling interest (this is the situation at most public companies). List six potential managerial behaviors that can harm a firm's value.

f. What is corporate governance? List five corporate governance provisions that are internal to a firm and under its control.

g. What characteristics of the board of directors usually lead to effective corporate governance?

h. List three provisions in the corporate charter that affect takeovers.

i. Briefly describe the use of stock options in a compensation plan. What are some potential problems with stock options as a form of compensation?

j. What is block ownership? How does it affect corporate governance?

k. Briefly explain how regulatory agencies and legal systems affect corporate governance.

CHAPTER 14

Distributions to Shareholders: Dividends and Repurchases

Apple's sales grew by over 65% in 2011 to $108 billion. In mid-2012, Apple's sales for the first two quarters of 2012 exceeded $85 billion. With a stock price of close to $600 per share, Apple had a market capitalization of well over $500 billion and was sitting on about $110 billion in cash. To put that amount into perspective, Apple had enough cash to pay for California's general state budget for the entire year of 2012!

Apple's founder and former CEO, Steve Jobs (who passed away in 2011), continually shocked the technology community with innovations such as the iPod, the MacBook Air, the iPhone, and the iPad. His successor, Timothy Cook, shocked the investment community by announcing that Apple would begin to pay a quarterly dividend, which totaled over $10 billion in annual dividends during 2013, the first full year of the policy. In addition, Apple repurchased over $22 billion of its stock that year, returning over $32 billion to its shareholders.

Fast forward to 2017, during which Apple paid $12.5 billion in dividends and repurchased $33 billion of its stock. If you think that's a lot of money, consider the first quarter after the 2017 Tax Cuts and Jobs Act. In just the first three months of 2018, Apple repurchased a whopping $23.5 billion of its stock! This is in addition to $3.2 billion in dividends. To top it off, Apple announced that it plans to repurchase an additional $100 billion!

As you read this chapter, think about Apple's reasons for initiating regular dividend payments and for repurchasing its stock.

Uses of Free Cash Flow: Distributions to Shareholders

Free cash flow is generated from operations and is available for distribution to all investors. This chapter focuses on the distributions of FCF to shareholders in the form of dividends and stock repurchases.

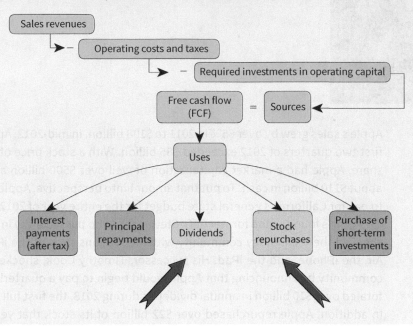

Because a company's value depends on its ability to generate free cash flow (FCF), most of this book has focused on aspects of FCF generation, including measurement, forecasts, and risk analysis. In contrast, this chapter focuses on the use of FCF for cash distributions to shareholders. Here are the central issues addressed in this chapter: Can a company increase its value through its choice of **distribution policy**, defined as: (1) the *level* of distributions, (2) the *form* of distributions (cash dividends versus stock repurchases), and (3) the *stability* of distributions? Do different groups of shareholders prefer one form of distribution over the other? Do shareholders perceive distributions as signals regarding a firm's risk and expected future free cash flows?

Before addressing these questions, let's take a look at the big picture regarding cash distributions.

14-1 An Overview of Cash Distributions

At the risk of stating the obvious, a company must have cash before it can make a cash distribution to shareholders, so we begin by examining a company's sources of cash.

14-1a Sources of Cash

Occasionally the cash comes from a recapitalization or the sale of an asset, but in most cases it comes from the company's internally generated free cash flow. Recall that FCF is defined as the amount of cash flow available for distribution to investors after expenses, taxes, and the necessary investments in operating capital. Thus, the *source* of FCF depends on a company's investment opportunities and its effectiveness in turning those opportunities into realities. Notice that a company with many opportunities will have large investments in operating capital and might have negative FCF even if it is profitable. When growth begins to slow, a profitable company's FCF will be positive and very large. Home Depot and Microsoft are good examples of once-fast-growing companies that are now generating large amounts of free cash flows.

14-1b Uses of Cash

There are only five potentially "good" ways to use free cash flow: (1) Pay interest expenses (after tax). (2) Pay down the principal on debt. (3) Pay dividends. (4) Repurchase stock. (5) Buy short-term investments or other nonoperating assets.[1] If a company's FCF is negative, then its "uses" of FCF must also be negative. For example, a growing company often issues new debt rather than repays debt; it issues new shares of stock rather than repurchases outstanding shares. Even after FCF becomes positive, some of its "uses" can be negative, as we explain next.

PAY INTEREST, REPAY DEBT, OR ISSUE NEW DEBT

A company's capital structure choice determines its payments for interest expenses and debt principal.[2] A company's value typically increases over time, even if the company is mature, which implies its debt will also increase over time if the company maintains a target capital structure. If a company instead were to pay off its debt, then it would lose valuable tax shields associated with the deductibility of interest expenses. Therefore, most companies make net additions to debt over time rather than net repayments, even if FCF is positive. The addition of debt is a "negative use" of FCF, which provides even more FCF for other uses. This "negative use" of FCF is, in an economic sense, a "source" of FCF, but we will continue to call it a "negative use" and reserve the term "source" for NOPAT minus investment in operating capital.

PURCHASE OR SELL SHORT-TERM INVESTMENTS

A company's working capital policies determine its level of short-term investments, such as T-bills or other marketable securities. Chapter 16 discusses short-term investments in more detail, but for now, you should recognize that the decision involves a trade-off between the benefits and costs of holding a large amount of short-term investments. In terms of benefits, a large holding reduces the risk of financial distress should there be an economic downturn. Also, if growth opportunities turn out to be better than expected, short-term investments provide a ready source of funding that does not incur the flotation or signaling costs due to raising external funds. However, there is a potential agency cost: If a company has a large investment in marketable securities, then managers might be tempted to squander the money on perks (such as corporate jets) or high-priced acquisitions.

However, many companies have much bigger short-term investments than the previous reasons can explain. For example, in early 2018 Apple had almost $43 billion. At the end of 2017, Microsoft had a staggering $130 billion in short-term investments! The most rational explanation is that such companies are using short-term investments temporarily until deciding how to use the cash.

---

[1]Recall from Chapter 2 that the company's cost of paying interest is on an after-tax basis. Recall also that a company doesn't *spend* FCF on operating assets (such as the acquisition of another company), because those expenditures were already deducted when calculating FCF. In other words, the purchase of an operating asset (even if it is another company) is not a *use* of FCF; instead, it is a *source* of FCF (albeit a "negative source").

[2]We discuss capital structure choices in more detail in Chapter 15.

Purchasing short-term investments is a positive use of FCF, and selling short-term investments is negative use. If a particular use of FCF is negative, then some other use must be larger than it otherwise would have been.

PAY DIVIDENDS, REPURCHASE STOCK, OR ISSUE NEW SHARES OF STOCK

In summary, a company's investment opportunities and operating plans determine its level of FCF. The company's capital structure policy determines the amount of debt and interest payments. Working capital policy determines the investment in marketable securities. The remaining FCF should be distributed to shareholders, with the only question being how much to distribute in the form of dividends versus stock repurchases.

Obviously this is a simplification, because companies (1) sometimes scale back their operating plans for sales and asset growth if such reductions are needed to maintain an existing dividend, (2) temporarily adjust their current financing mix in response to market conditions, and (3) often use marketable securities as shock absorbers for fluctuations in short-term cash flows. Still, there is an interdependence among operating plans (which have the biggest impact on free cash flow), financing plans (which have the biggest impact on the cost of capital), working capital policies (which determine the target level of marketable securities), and shareholder distributions.

SELF-TEST

What are the five uses of free cash flows?

How do a company's investment opportunities, capital structure, and working capital policies affect its distributions to shareholders?

14-2 Procedures for Cash Distributions

Companies can distribute cash to shareholders via cash dividends or stock repurchases. We describe the actual procedures used to make cash distributions in this section.

14-2a Dividend Payment Procedures

Companies normally pay dividends quarterly, and, if conditions permit, increase the dividend once each year. For example, Katz Corporation paid a $0.50 dividend per share in each quarter of 2019, for an annual dividend per share of $2.00. In common financial parlance, we say that in 2019 Katz's *regular quarterly dividend* was $0.50, and its *annual dividend* was $2.00. In late 2019, Katz's board of directors met, reviewed projections for 2020, and decided to keep the 2020 dividend at $2.00. The directors announced the $2 rate, so stockholders could count on receiving it unless the company experienced unanticipated operating problems.

The actual payment procedure is as follows.

1. *Declaration date.* On the **declaration date**—say, on Thursday, November 21—the directors meet and declare the regular dividend, issuing a statement similar to the following: "On November 21, 2019, the directors of Katz Corporation met and declared the regular quarterly dividend of 50 cents per share, payable to holders of record as of Friday, December 20, payment to be made on Friday, January 10, 2020." For accounting purposes, the declared dividend becomes an actual liability on the declaration date. If a balance sheet were constructed, an amount equal to $0.50 \times n_0$, where n_0 is the number of shares outstanding, would appear as a current liability, and retained earnings would be reduced by a like amount.

2. *Holder-of-record date.* At the close of business on the **holder-of-record date**, December 20, the company closes its stock transfer books and makes up a list of shareholders as of that date. If Katz Corporation is notified of the sale before 5 p.m. on December 20, then the new owner receives the dividend (even if the new owner subsequently sells the stock before the actual dividend payment). However, if notification is received after 5 p.m. on December 20, the previous owner gets the dividend check (even though the previous owner no longer owns the stock).

3. *Ex-dividend date.* Suppose Jean Buyer buys 100 shares of stock from John Seller on December 12. Will the company be notified of the transfer in time to list Buyer as the new owner and thus pay the dividend to her? To avoid conflict, the securities industry has set up a convention under which the right to the dividend remains with the stock until *two business days prior to the holder-of-record date*; on the second day before the holder-of-record date, the right to the dividend no longer goes with the shares. The date when the right to the dividend leaves the stock is called the **ex-dividend date**. In this case, the ex-dividend date is two days prior to December 20, which is December 18. We show a summary of key dates next:

November 21, 2019:	**Declaration date**—board announces holder-of-record date, payment date, and dividend amount.
December 17, 2019:	**One business day prior to ex-dividend date**—owner of stock at closing time on this day will receive dividend on payment date even if the owner sells the stock the next day.
December 18, 2019:	**Ex-dividend date**—two business days prior to the announced holder-of-record date. Any purchaser on or after this date will not get dividend.
December 19, 2019:	Purchaser on or after this date doesn't get the dividend because it is after the ex-dividend date.
December 20, 2019:	**Holder-of-record date**—used to determine ex-dividend date. Purchaser on or after this date will not get the dividend because it is after the ex-dividend date.
January 10, 2020:	**Payment date**—Dividend is paid to whoever owned the stock at closing the day prior to the ex-dividend date.

Therefore, if Buyer is to receive the dividend, she must buy the stock on or before December 17 and own it at the close of business on December 17 so that she will be the holder-of-record on December 20 (even if she sells the stock on December 18, 19, or 20). If she buys it on December 18 or later, Seller who is holder-of-record (i.e., the owner at the close of business on December 17) will receive the dividend. In other words, the holder-of-record date is important because it determines the ex-dividend date, which determines who gets the dividend.

Katz's dividend amounts to $0.50, so the ex-dividend date is important. Barring fluctuations in the stock market, we would normally expect the price of a stock to drop by approximately the amount of the dividend on the ex-dividend date. Thus, if Katz closed at $30.50 on December 17, it would probably open at about $30 on December 18.

4. *Payment date.* The company actually pays the dividend on January 10, which is the **payment date**, to those owning the stock on December 17.

14-2b Stock Repurchase Procedures

Stock repurchases occur when a company buys some of its own outstanding stock.[3] Three situations can lead to stock repurchases. First, a company may decide to increase its leverage by issuing debt and using the proceeds to repurchase stock; we discuss recapitalizations in more detail in Chapter 15. Second, many firms have given their employees stock options, and companies often repurchase their own stock to sell to employees when employees exercise the options. In this case, the number of outstanding shares reverts to its pre-repurchase level after the options are exercised. Third, a company may have excess cash. This may be due to a one-time cash inflow, such as the sale of a division, or the company may simply be generating more free cash flow than it needs to service its debt.[4]

Stock repurchases are usually made in one of three ways. (1) A publicly owned firm can buy back its own stock through a broker on the open market.[5] (2) The firm can make a tender offer, under which it permits stockholders to send in (that is, "tender") shares in exchange for a specified price per share. In this case, the firm generally indicates it will buy up to a specified number of shares within a stated time period (usually about two weeks). If more shares are tendered than the company wants to buy, purchases are made on a pro rata basis. (3) The firm can purchase a block of shares from one large holder on a negotiated basis. This is a targeted stock repurchase, as discussed in Chapter 13.

14-2c Patterns of Cash Distributions

The use of dividends versus stock repurchases has changed dramatically during the past 30 years. First, the percentage of cash distributions relative to net income was around 27% until the early 2000s, but it has dramatically increased since then. In fact, the combined payout ratio of dividends and repurchases for S&P 500 stocks has exceeded 90% since 2012.[6] The relative sizes of dividends and repurchases have also changed. Since 1998, repurchases have exceeded dividends. The average dividend yield in 2017 was 1.84%, and the repurchase yield was 2.28%, for a whopping total of 4.12%.

Second, the percentage of companies paying a dividend has changed over time. In 1978, about 66.5% of NYSE, AMEX, and NASDAQ firms paid a dividend. In 1999, only 20.8% paid a dividend. Part of this reduction can be explained by the large numbers of IPOs in the 1990s because young firms rarely pay dividends. The percentage climbed

---

[3]The repurchased stock is called "treasury stock" and is shown as a negative value on the company's detailed balance sheet. On the consolidated balance sheet, treasury shares are deducted to find shares outstanding, and the price paid for the repurchased shares is deducted when determining common equity.

[4]See Benton Gup and Doowoo Nam, "Stock Buybacks, Corporate Performance, and EVA," *Journal of Applied Corporate Finance,* Spring 2001, pp. 99–110. The authors show that the firms that repurchase stock have superior operating performance to those that do not buy back stock, which is consistent with the notion that firms buy back stock when they generate additional free cash flow. They also show that operating performance improves in the year after the buyback, indicating that the superior performance is sustainable.

[5]Many firms announce their plans to repurchase stock on the open market. For example, a company might announce it plans to repurchase 4 million shares of stock. However, companies usually don't buy back all the shares they announce but instead repurchase only about 80% of the announced number. See Clifford Stephens and Michael Weisbach, "Actual Share Reacquisitions in Open-Market Repurchase Programs," *Journal of Finance,* February 1998, pp. 313–333.

[6]See Gustavo Grullon and Roni Michaely, "Dividends, Share Repurchases, and the Substitution Hypothesis," *Journal of Finance,* August 2002, pp. 1649–1684; and Eugene Fama and Kenneth French, "Disappearing Dividends: Changing Firm Characteristics or Lower Propensity to Pay?" *Journal of Applied Corporate Finance,* Spring 2001, pp. 67–79. For updates, go to the S&P Dow Jones press room at **https://us.spindices.com/resource-center/press-room/**, search for "buybacks," and scroll down until you find "S&P 500 Stock Buybacks." For even more information, find the S&P 500 Q4 report.

TABLE 14-1
Dividend Payouts (as a Percent of Net Income) and Dividend Yields

Company	Industry	Dividend Payout	Dividend Yield
Duke Energy Corp. (DUK)	Electric utility	83%	4.80%
Rayonier Inc. (RYN)	Forest products	83	2.62
Tiffany and Company (TIF)	Specialty retail	66	1.47
WD-40 Company (WDFC)	Household products	51	1.37
Harley-Davidson Inc. (HOG)	Recreational products	49	3.31
Altria Group Inc. (MO)	Tobacco products	47	2.63
Regions Financial Corp. (RF)	Regional banks	32	1.69
Ingles Markets Inc. (IMKTA)	Retail (grocery)	12	2.25
Amazon.com Inc. (AMZN)	Catalog and mail order	0	0.00

Source: **finance.yahoo.com**, June 2018.

after 2000, with 46% of firms paying a dividend in 2017. This reflects the change in the number and composition of publicly traded companies. There are now fewer but larger publicly traded companies. Part of this is due to mergers and part is because many small start-up firms that would have had an IPO are being acquired by private equity firms.[7]

Third, Table 14-1 shows there is considerable variation in distribution policies, with some companies paying a high percentage of their income as dividends and others paying none. The next section discusses some theories about distribution policies.

S E L F - T E S T

Explain the procedures used to actually pay the dividend.

Why is the ex-dividend date important to investors?

What are the three ways in which a company can repurchase stock?

14-3 Cash Distributions and Firm Value

A company can change its intrinsic value of operations only if it changes its cost of capital or expected future free cash flows. This is true for all corporate decisions, including the distribution policy. Is there an **optimal distribution policy** that maximizes a company's intrinsic value?

The answer depends in part on investors' preferences for returns in the form of dividend yields versus capital gains. The relative mix of dividend yields and capital gains is determined by the **target distribution ratio**, which is the percentage of net income distributed to shareholders through cash dividends or stock repurchases, and the **target payout ratio**, which is the percentage of net income paid as a cash dividend. Notice that the payout ratio must be less than the distribution ratio because the distribution ratio includes stock repurchases as well as cash dividends.

The combination of a high distribution ratio and a high payout ratio means that a company pays large dividends and has small (or zero) stock repurchases. In this situation, the dividend yield is relatively high and the expected capital gain is low. If a company has a

---

[7]See Gustavo Grullon and David Ikenberry, "What Do We Know about Stock Repurchases?" *Journal of Applied Corporate Finance,* Spring 2000, pp. 31–51.

large distribution ratio but a small payout ratio, then it pays low dividends but regularly repurchases stock, resulting in a low dividend yield but a higher expected capital gain yield. If a company has a low distribution ratio, then it must also have a relatively low payout ratio, again resulting in a low dividend yield and, it is hoped, a relatively high capital gain yield.

In this section, we examine three theories of investor preferences for dividend yield versus capital gains: (1) the dividend irrelevance theory, (2) the dividend preference theory (also called the "bird-in-the-hand" theory), and (3) the tax effect theory.

14-3a Dividend Irrelevance Theory

The original proponents of the **dividend irrelevance theory** were Merton Miller and Franco Modigliani (MM).[8] They argued that the firm's value is determined only by its basic earning power and its business risk. In other words, MM argued that the value of the firm depends only on the income produced by its assets, not on how this income is split between dividends and retained earnings.

To understand MM's argument, recognize that any shareholder can in theory construct his own dividend policy. For example, if a firm does not pay dividends, a shareholder who wants a 5% dividend can "create" it by selling 5% of his stock. Conversely, if a company pays a higher dividend than an investor desires, the investor can use the unwanted dividends to buy additional shares of the company's stock. If investors could buy and sell shares and thus create their own dividend policy without incurring costs, then the firm's dividend policy would truly be irrelevant.

In developing their dividend theory, MM made a number of important assumptions, especially the absence of taxes and brokerage costs. If these assumptions are not true, then investors who want additional dividends must incur brokerage costs to sell shares and must pay taxes on any capital gains. Investors who do not want dividends must incur brokerage costs to purchase shares with their dividends. Because taxes and brokerage costs certainly exist, dividend policy may well be relevant. We will discuss empirical tests of MM's dividend irrelevance theory shortly.

14-3b Dividend Preference (Bird-in-the-Hand) Theory

The principal conclusion of MM's **dividend irrelevance theory** is that dividend policy does not affect a stock's value or risk. Therefore, it does not affect the required rate of return on equity, r_s. In contrast, Myron Gordon and John Lintner both argued that a stock's risk declines as dividends increase: A return in the form of dividends is a sure thing, but a return in the form of capital gains is risky. In other words, a **bird in the hand** is worth more than two in the bush. Therefore, shareholders prefer dividends and are willing to accept a lower required return on equity.[9]

The presence of agency costs leads to a similar conclusion. First, high payouts reduce the risk that managers will squander cash because there is less cash on hand. Second, a high-payout company must raise external funds more often than a low-payout company, all else held equal. If a manager knows that the company will receive frequent scrutiny

---

[8]See Merton H. Miller and Franco Modigliani, "Dividend Policy, Growth, and the Valuation of Shares," *Journal of Business,* October 1961, pp. 411–433. However, their conclusion is valid only if investors expect managers eventually to pay out the equivalent of the present value of all future free cash flows; see Harry DeAngelo and Linda DeAngelo, "The Irrelevance of the MM Dividend Irrelevance Theorem," *Journal of Financial Economics,* Vol. 79, 2006, pp. 293–315.

[9]Myron J. Gordon, "Optimal Investment and Financing Policy," *Journal of Finance,* May 1963, pp. 264–272; and John Lintner, "Dividends, Earnings, Leverage, Stock Prices, and the Supply of Capital to Corporations," *Review of Economics and Statistics,* August 1962, pp. 243–269.

from external markets, then the manager will be less likely to engage in wasteful practices. Therefore, high payouts reduce the risk of agency costs. With less risk, shareholders are willing to accept a lower required return on equity.

14-3c Tax Effect Theory: Capital Gains Are Preferred

Before 2003, individual investors paid ordinary income taxes on dividends but lower rates on long-term capital gains. The Jobs and Growth Act of 2003 changed this, reducing the tax rate on dividend income to the same as on long-term capital gains.[10] However, there are two reasons why stock price appreciation still is taxed more favorably than dividend income. First, an increase in a stock's price isn't taxable until the investor sells the stock, whereas a dividend payment is taxable immediately; a dollar of taxes paid in the future has a lower effective cost than a dollar paid today because of the time value of money. So even when dividends and gains are taxed equally, capital gains are never taxed sooner than dividends. Second, if a stock is held until the shareholder dies, then no capital gains tax is due at all: The beneficiaries who receive the stock can use its value on the date of death as their cost basis and thus completely escape the capital gains tax.

If dividends are taxed more highly than capital gains, there is a **dividend tax penalty**, causing investors to require a higher pre-tax rate of return on dividend-paying stocks relative to non-dividend stocks. All else equal, investors should be willing to pay more for low-payout companies than for otherwise similar high-payout companies.[11] Therefore, the **tax effect theory** states that investors prefer that companies minimize dividends.

14-3d Empirical Evidence on Distribution Policies

It is very difficult to construct a perfect empirical test of the relationship between payout policy and the required rate of return on stock. First, all factors other than distribution level should be held constant; that is, the sample companies should differ only in their distribution levels. Second, each firm's cost of equity should be measured with a high degree of accuracy. Unfortunately, we cannot find a set of publicly owned firms that differ only in their distribution levels, nor can we obtain precise estimates of the cost of equity. Therefore, no one has yet identified a completely unambiguous relationship between the distribution level and the cost of equity or firm value.

Although none of the empirical tests is perfect, comparing a company's dividend yield with its required rate of return shows that firms with higher dividend payouts also have higher required returns.[12] In other words, investors require a higher pre-tax return to

---

[10]Of course, nothing involving taxes is quite this simple. Following are the rules provided by the 2017 Tax Cuts and Jobs Act. First, it must be a qualified dividend, which means that it must be from a domestic company and that the investor must own the stock for more than 60 days during the 121-day period beginning 60 days before the ex-dividend date. There are additional restrictions for dividends other than regular cash dividends. For single filers in 2018, no taxes are due on dividends if the filer's taxable income is less than $38,600. The tax rate on dividends is 20% for taxable income over $425,800. The situation is much more complicated for taxable income between $38,600 and $425,800; see **Web Extension 2A** on the textbook's Web site for more details. In addition, higher income filers will pay an additional 3.8% on net investment income tax (NIIT), making their effective capital gains rate 23.8%. Also, the Alternative Minimum Tax (AMT) increases the effective tax rate on dividends and capital gains by 7% for some moderately high-income earners. See Leonard Burman, William Gale, Greg Leiserson, and Jeffrey Rohaly, "The AMT: What's Wrong and How to Fix It," *National Tax Journal,* September 2007, pp. 385–405.

[11]For more on tax-related issues, see Eli Talmor and Sheridan Titman, "Taxes and Dividend Policy," *Financial Management,* Summer 1990, pp. 32–35; and Rosita P. Chang and S. Ghon Rhee, "The Impact of Personal Taxes on Corporate Dividend Policy and Capital Structure Decisions," *Financial Management,* Summer 1990, pp. 21–31.

[12]See A. Naranjo, N. Nimalendran, and M. Ryngaert, "Stock Returns, Dividend Yields, and Taxes," *Journal of Finance,* December 1998, pp. 2029–2057.

induce them to buy the stock. This tends to support the tax effect hypothesis, although the size of the required return is too high to be fully explained by taxes.

Another way to test the hypothesis is to compare companies in countries with different tax codes. Empirical evidence shows that if a country has a relatively small dividend tax penalty, more companies tend to pay dividends and the dividend payments tend to be larger. In contrast, if a country has a relatively high dividend tax penalty, more companies tend to repurchase stock.[13] This evidence is consistent with the tax effect theory.

A different way to test for tax effects is to examine payout policies immediately before tax codes are scheduled to change, such as late 2010 and 2012. Given the previous conflicts within Congress and the conflicts between Congress and President Obama, investors had good reasons to expect that no new tax code would be passed, which meant that previous tax codes with reduced taxes on dividends would expire on December 31. To avoid higher taxes if the tax breaks expired, many companies made unusually large one-time **special dividend** payments late in 2010 and 2012, totaling about $7 billion *more* than were paid in late 2009 and 2011.[14] In addition, around 176 companies moved up their payment dates from the first months of the upcoming year (which would be after the dividend-friendly tax laws expired) to months at the end of the current year, totaling over $12 billion in sooner-than-normal payments. Interestingly, these activities are more pronounced for companies whose insiders own larger proportions of the company's stock. It appears as though insiders are trying to avoid taxes on their own stock holdings as well as minimize taxes for the outside shareholders.

The previous evidence suggests that investor prefer to avoid the taxes associated with dividends. However, low dividend payments mean that managers have more discretionary cash and might squander it on perquisites or value-destroying acquisitions. Such agency costs should be most severe in countries with poor investor protection. In such countries, companies with high dividend payouts should be more highly valued than those with low payouts because high payouts limit the extent to which managers can expropriate shareholder wealth. Research shows that this is the case, which supports the dividend preference hypothesis in the case of companies with severe agency problems.[15]

The evidence shows that companies definitely take taxation into account when setting dividend policies. However, agency costs can be worse than taxes in some countries, so the evidence is mixed regarding the impact of dividend policy on value.

Although the evidence is not as clear as to whether the *average* investor uniformly prefers either higher or lower distribution levels, other research does show that *individual* investors have strong preferences. Also, other research shows that investors prefer stable, predictable dividend payouts (regardless of the payout level) and that they interpret dividend changes as signals about firms' future prospects. We discuss these issues in the next several sections.

SELF-TEST

What did Modigliani and Miller assume about taxes and brokerage costs when they developed their dividend irrelevance theory?

How did the bird-in-the-hand theory get its name?

What have been the results of empirical tests of the dividend theories?

---

[13]See M. Jacob and M. Jacob, "Taxation, Dividends, and Share Repurchases: Taking Evidence Global," *Journal of Financial and Quantitative Analysis,* August 2013, pp. 1241–1269.

[14]See M. Hanlon and J. L. Hoopes, "What Do Firms Do When Dividend Tax Rates Change? An Examination of Alternative Payout Responses," *Journal of Financial Economics,* October 2014, pp. 105–124.

[15]See L. Pinkowitz, R. Stulz, and R. Williamson, "Does the Contribution of Corporate Cash Holdings and Dividends to Firm Value Depend on Governance? A Cross-Country Analysis," *Journal of Finance*, December 2006, pp. 2725–2751.

14-4 Clientele Effect

As we indicated earlier, different groups, or *clienteles,* of stockholders prefer different dividend payout policies. For example, retired individuals, pension funds, and university endowment funds generally prefer cash income, so they may want the firm to pay out a high percentage of its earnings. Such investors are often in low or even zero tax brackets, so taxes are of no concern. On the other hand, stockholders in their peak earning years might prefer reinvestment, because they have less need for current investment income and would simply reinvest dividends received—after first paying income taxes on those dividends.

W W W

For updates of industry payout ratios, go to **www.reuters.com /finance/stocks.** After picking a company, select Financials tab.

If a firm retains and reinvests income rather than paying dividends, those stockholders who need current income would be disadvantaged. The value of their stock might increase, but they would be forced to go to the trouble and expense of selling some of their shares to obtain cash. Also, some institutional investors (or trustees for individuals) would be legally precluded from selling stock and then "spending capital." On the other hand, stockholders who are saving rather than spending dividends might favor the low-dividend policy: The less the firm pays out in dividends, the less these stockholders will have to pay in current taxes, and the less trouble and expense they will have to go through to reinvest their after-tax dividends. Therefore, investors who want current investment income should own shares in high-dividend payout firms, while investors with no need for current investment income should own shares in low-dividend payout firms. For example, investors seeking high cash income might invest in the household products industry, which averaged a 59% payout in June 2018, while those favoring growth could invest in the consumer electronics industry, which paid out only 16% during the same time period.

To the extent that stockholders can switch firms, a firm can change from one dividend payout policy to another and then let stockholders who do not like the new policy sell to other investors who do. However, frequent switching would be inefficient because of (1) brokerage costs, (2) the likelihood that stockholders who are selling will have to pay capital gains taxes, and (3) a possible shortage of investors who like the firm's newly adopted dividend policy. Thus, management should be hesitant to change its dividend policy, because a change might cause current shareholders to sell their stock, forcing the stock price down. Such a price decline might be temporary but might also be permanent—if few new investors are attracted by the new dividend policy, then the stock price would remain depressed. Of course, the new policy might attract an even larger clientele than the firm had before, in which case the stock price would rise.

Evidence from several studies suggests that there is, in fact, a **clientele effect**. For example, low-tax or tax-free institutions hold relatively more high-dividend stocks than do taxable investors, and taxable institutions hold fewer high-dividend stocks than do non-taxed investors.[16]

There is additional evidence regarding clientele effects at mutual funds based on the tax status of investors.[17] Some mutual fund investors are sheltered from taxes because their investments are made through **401(k) retirement plans**. In 401(k) plans, employees' contributions, matching contributions from the sponsoring employer (if these are included in the plan), and profits on the investments are not taxable until withdrawn. These are called **defined contribution (DC)** plans because the contributions are known

---

[16]For example, see R. Richardson Pettit, "Taxes, Transactions Costs and the Clientele Effect of Dividends," *Journal of Financial Economics,* December 1977, pp. 419–436; and William J. Moser and Andy Puckett, "Dividend Tax Clienteles: Evidence from Tax Law Changes," *Journal of the American Taxation Association,* Spring 2009, pp. 1–22.

[17]See C. Sialm and L. Starks, "Mutual Fund Tax Clienteles," *Journal of Finance,* August 2012, pp. 1397–1422.

but the future benefits depend on the plans' investments, which often include mutual funds. For tax-liable investors, the dividends paid on stocks held by a mutual fund are taxable income, as are any capital gains recognized when the fund sells stocks for a profit. The evidence shows that mutual funds with a high proportion of taxable investors (i.e., the funds with relatively few DC investors) tend to choose investment strategies that have lower tax burdens than those chosen by funds with a high proportion of DC investors. In other words, the fund managers cater to their investment strategies to be consistent with the tax liabilities of their investors.[18]

MM and others have argued that one clientele is as good as another, so the existence of a clientele effect does not necessarily imply that one dividend policy is better than any other. However, MM may be wrong, and neither they nor anyone else can prove that the aggregate makeup of investors permits firms to disregard clientele effects. This issue, like most others in the dividend arena, is still up in the air.

SELF-TEST

Define the clientele effect, and explain how it affects dividend policy.

14-5 Signaling Hypothesis

When MM set forth their dividend irrelevance theory, they assumed that everyone—investors and managers alike—has identical information regarding a firm's future earnings and dividends. In reality, however, different investors have different views on both the level of future dividend payments and the uncertainty inherent in those payments, and managers have better information about future prospects than public stockholders.

It has been observed that an increase in the dividend is often accompanied by an increase in the price of a stock and that a dividend cut generally leads to a stock price decline. Some have argued this indicates that investors prefer dividends to capital gains. However, MM saw this differently. They noted the well-established fact that corporations are reluctant to cut dividends, which implies that corporations do not raise dividends unless they anticipate higher earnings in the future. Thus, MM argued that a higher-than-expected dividend increase is a signal to investors that the firm's management forecasts good future earnings. Conversely, a dividend reduction, or a smaller-than-expected increase, is a signal that management is forecasting poor earnings in the future. Thus, MM argued that investors' reactions to changes in dividend policy do not necessarily show that investors prefer dividends to retained earnings. Rather, they argue that price changes following dividend actions simply indicate that dividend changes convey information. This is called the dividend **signaling hypothesis**; it is also called the dividend **information content hypothesis**.

The initiation of a dividend by a firm that formerly paid no dividend is certainly a significant change in distribution policy. It appears that initiating firms' future earnings and cash flows are less risky than before the initiation. However, the evidence is mixed regarding the future profitability of initiating firms: Some studies find slightly higher earnings after the initiation but others find no significant change in earnings.[19]

---

[18]Interestingly, the mutual funds with a high proportion of DC clients have lower expense ratios, suggesting that sponsoring companies are more concerned about (or more aware of) expenses than are individual investors.

[19]See Edward Dyl and Robert Weigand, "The Information Content of Dividend Initiations: Additional Evidence," *Financial Management,* Autumn 1998, pp. 27–35; P. Asquith and D. Mullins, "The Impact of Initiating Dividend Payments on Shareholders' Wealth," *Journal of Business,* January 1983, pp. 77–96; and P. Healy and K. Palepu, "Earnings Information Conveyed by Dividend Initiations and Omissions," *Journal of Financial Economics,* September 1988, pp. 149–175.

What happens when firms with existing dividends unexpectedly increase or decrease the dividend? Early studies, using small data samples, concluded that unexpected dividend changes did not provide a signal about future earnings.[20] However, more recent data with larger samples provide mixed evidence.[21] On average, firms that cut dividends had poor earnings in the years directly preceding the cut but actually improved earnings in subsequent years. Firms that increased dividends had earnings increases in the years preceding the increase but did not appear to have subsequent earnings increases. However, neither did they have subsequent declines in earnings, so it appears that the increase in dividends is a signal that past earnings increases were not temporary. Also, a relatively large number of firms that expect a large permanent increase in cash flow (as opposed to earnings) do in fact increase their dividend payouts in the year prior to the cash flow increase.

All in all, there is clearly some information content in dividend announcements: Stock prices tend to fall when dividends are cut, even if they don't always rise when dividends are increased. However, this doesn't necessarily validate the signaling hypothesis, because it is difficult to tell whether any stock price change following a change in dividend policy reflects only signaling effects or reflects both signaling and dividend preferences.

SELF-TEST

Define signaling content, and explain how it affects dividend policy.

14-6 Implications for Dividend Stability

The clientele effect and the information content in dividend announcements definitely have implications regarding the desirability of stable versus volatile dividends. For example, many stockholders rely on dividends to meet expenses, and they would be seriously inconvenienced if the dividend stream were unstable. Further, reducing dividends to make funds available for capital investment could send incorrect signals to investors, who might push down the stock price because they interpret the dividend cut to mean that the company's future earnings prospects have been diminished. Thus, maximizing its stock price probably requires a firm to maintain a steady dividend policy. Because sales and earnings are expected to grow for most firms, a stable dividend policy means a company's regular cash dividends should also grow at a steady, predictable rate.[22] But, as we explain in the next section, most companies will probably move toward small, sustainable, regular cash dividends that are supplemented by stock repurchases.

---

[20]For example, see N. Gonedes, "Corporate Signaling, External Accounting, and Capital Market Equilibrium: Evidence of Dividends, Income, and Extraordinary Items," *Journal of Accounting Research,* Spring 1978, pp. 26–79; and R. Watts, "The Information Content of Dividends," *Journal of Business,* April 1973, pp. 191–211.

[21]See Shlomo Benartzi, Roni Michaely, and Richard Thaler, "Do Changes in Dividends Signal the Future or the Past?" *Journal of Finance,* July 1997, pp. 1007–1034; and Yaron Brook, William Charlton Jr., and Robert J. Hendershott, "Do Firms Use Dividends to Signal Large Future Cash Flow Increases?" *Financial Management,* Autumn 1998, pp. 46–57.

[22]For more on announcements and stability, see Jeffrey A. Born, "Insider Ownership and Signals—Evidence from Dividend Initiation Announcement Effects," *Financial Management,* Spring 1988, pp. 38–45; Chinmoy Ghosh and J. Randall Woolridge, "An Analysis of Shareholder Reaction to Dividend Cuts and Omissions," *Journal of Financial Research,* Winter 1988, pp. 281–294; C. Michael Impson and Imre Karafiath, "A Note on the Stock Market Reaction to Dividend Announcements," *Financial Review,* May 1992, pp. 259–271; James W. Wansley, C. F. Sirmans, James D. Shilling, and Young-jin Lee, "Dividend Change Announcement Effects and Earnings Volatility and Timing," *Journal of Financial Research,* Spring 1991, pp. 37–49; and J. Randall Woolridge and Chinmoy Ghosh, "Dividend Cuts: Do They Always Signal Bad News?" *Midland Corporate Finance Journal,* Summer 1985, pp. 20–32.

Why do the clientele effect and the information content hypotheses imply that investors prefer stable dividends?

14-7 Setting the Target Distribution Level: The Residual Distribution Model

When deciding how much cash to distribute to stockholders, two points should be kept in mind: (1) The overriding objective is to maximize shareholder value. (2) The firm's cash flows really belong to its shareholders, so a company should not retain income unless managers can reinvest that income to produce returns higher than shareholders could themselves earn by investing the cash in investments of equal risk. On the other hand, recall from Chapter 9 that internal equity (reinvested earnings) is cheaper than external equity (new common stock issues) because it avoids flotation costs and adverse signals. This encourages firms to retain earnings so as to avoid having to issue new stock.

When establishing a distribution policy, one size does not fit all. Some firms produce a lot of cash but have limited investment opportunities—this is true for firms in profitable but mature industries in which few opportunities for growth exist. Such firms typically distribute a large percentage of their cash to shareholders, thereby attracting investment clienteles that prefer high dividends. Other firms generate little or no excess cash because they have many good investment opportunities. Such firms generally don't distribute much cash but do enjoy rising earnings and stock prices, thereby attracting investors who prefer capital gains.

As Table 14-1 suggests, dividend payouts and dividend yields for large corporations vary considerably. Generally, firms in stable, cash-producing industries (e.g., utilities, financial services, and tobacco) pay relatively high dividends, whereas companies in rapidly growing industries (e.g., computer software) tend to pay lower dividends.

For a given firm, the optimal distribution ratio is a function of four factors: (1) investors' preferences for dividends versus capital gains, (2) the firm's investment opportunities, (3) its target capital structure, and (4) the availability and cost of external capital. The last three elements are combined in what we call the **residual distribution model**. Under this model a firm follows these four steps when establishing its target distribution ratio: (1) It determines the optimal capital budget. (2) It determines the amount of equity needed to finance that budget, given its target capital structure (we explain the choice of target capital structures in Chapter 15). (3) It uses reinvested earnings to meet equity requirements to the extent possible. (4) It pays dividends or repurchases stock only if more earnings are available than are needed to support the optimal capital budget.[23] The word *residual* implies "leftover," and the residual policy implies that distributions are paid out of "leftover" earnings.

If a firm rigidly follows the residual distribution policy, then distributions paid in any given year can be expressed as follows:

$$\text{Distributions} = \text{Net income} - \begin{array}{c} \text{Additions to retained earnings} \\ \text{needed to finance new investments} \end{array}$$
$$= \text{Net income} - [(\text{Target equity ratio}) \times (\text{Total capital budget})] \qquad (14\text{-}1)$$

---

[23]The residual dividend model is based on the simplifying assumption that net income is equal to cash flow. Section 14-9 explains a much more realistic model.

As an illustration, consider the case of Texas and Western (T&W) Transport Company, which forecasts $60 million in net income and has a target capital structure of 60% equity and 40% debt.

If T&W forecasts poor investment opportunities, then its estimated capital budget will be only $40 million. To maintain the target capital structure, 40% ($16 million) of this capital must be raised as debt and 60% ($24 million) must be equity. If it followed a strict residual policy, T&W would retain $24 million of its $60 million earnings to help finance new investments and then distribute the remaining $36 million to shareholders:

$$\text{Distributions} = \text{Net income} - [(\text{Target equity ratio})(\text{Total capital budget})]$$
$$= \$60 - [(60\%)(\$40)]$$
$$= \$60 - \$24 = \$36$$

Under this scenario, the company's distribution ratio would be $36 million ÷ $60 million = 0.6 = 60%. These results are shown in Table 14-2.

In contrast, if the company's investment opportunities are average, its optimal capital budget would rise to $70 million. Here it would require $42 million of retained earnings, so distributions would be $60 − $42 = $18 million, for a ratio of $18/$60 = 30%. Finally, if investment opportunities are good, then the capital budget would be $150 million, which would require 0.6($150) = $90 million of equity. In this case, T&W would retain all of its net income ($60 million) and thus make no distributions. Moreover, because the required equity exceeds the retained earnings, the company would have to issue some new common stock to maintain the target capital structure.

Because investment opportunities and earnings will surely vary from year to year, a strict adherence to the residual distribution policy would result in unstable distributions. One year the firm might make no distributions because it needs the money to finance good investment opportunities, but the next year it might make a large distribution because investment opportunities are poor and so it does not need to retain much. Similarly, fluctuating earnings could also lead to variable distributions, even if investment opportunities were stable. Until now, we have not addressed whether distributions should be in the form of dividends, stock repurchases, or some combination of these. The next sections discuss specific issues associated with dividend payments and stock repurchases; this is followed by a comparison of their relative advantages and disadvantages.

TABLE 14-2

T&W's Distribution Ratio with $60 Million of Net Income and a 60% Target Equity Ratio When Faced with Different Investment Opportunities (Millions of Dollars)

	Investment Opportunities		
	Poor	Average	Good
Capital budget	$40	$70	$150
Required equity (0.6 × Capital budget)	$24	$42	$90
Net income	$60	$60	$60
Required equity (from above)	$24	$42	$90
Distributions paid (NI − Required equity)	$36	$18	−$30[a]
Distribution ratio (Dividend/NI)	60%	30%	0%

Note:

[a]With a $150 million capital budget, T&W would retain all of its earnings and also issue $30 million of new stock.

Explain the logic of the residual dividend model and the steps a firm would take to implement it.

Hamilton Corporation has a target equity ratio of 65%, and its forecasted capital budget is $2 million. If Hamilton has net income of $1.6 million and follows a residual distribution model, how much will its distribution be? ($300,000)

14-8 The Residual Distribution Model in Practice

If distributions were solely in the form of dividends, then rigidly following the residual policy would lead to fluctuating, unstable dividends. Because investors dislike volatile regular dividends, the required return on stock (r_s) would be high and the stock price low. Therefore, firms should proceed as follows:

1. Estimate earnings and investment opportunities, on average, for the next 5 or so years.
2. Use this forecasted information and the target capital structure to find the average residual model distributions and dollars of dividends during the planning period.
3. Set a *target payout ratio* based on the average projected data.

Thus, *firms should use the residual policy to help set their long-run target distribution ratios, but not as a guide to the distribution in any one year.*

Companies often use financial forecasting models in conjunction with the residual distribution model discussed here to help understand the determinants of an optimal dividend policy. Most large corporations forecast their financial statements over the next 5 to 10 years. Information on projected capital expenditures and working capital requirements is entered into the model, along with sales forecasts, profit margins, depreciation, and the other elements required to forecast cash flows. The target capital structure is also specified, and the model shows the amount of debt and equity that will be required to meet the capital budgeting requirements while maintaining the target capital structure. Then, dividend payments are introduced. Naturally, the higher the payout ratio, the greater the required external equity. Most companies use the model to find a dividend pattern over the forecast period (generally 5 years) that will provide sufficient equity to support the capital budget without forcing them to sell new common stock or move the capital structure ratios outside their optimal range.

Some companies set a very low "regular" dividend and then supplement it with an **extra dividend** when times are good, such as Microsoft now does. This **low-regular-dividend-plus-extras policy** ensures that the regular dividend can be maintained "come hell or high water" and that stockholders can count on receiving that dividend under all conditions. Then, when times are good and profits and cash flows are high, the company can either pay a specially designated extra dividend or repurchase shares of stock. Investors recognize that the extras might not be maintained in the future, so they do not interpret them as a signal that the companies' earnings are going up permanently; nor do they take the elimination of the extra as a negative signal.

Why is the residual model more often used to establish a long-run payout target than to set the actual year-by-year dividend payout ratio?

How do firms use planning models to help set dividend policy?

14-9 A Tale of Two Cash Distributions: Dividends versus Stock Repurchases

Benson Conglomerate, a prestigious publishing house with several Nobel laureates among its authors, recently began generating positive free cash flow and is analyzing the impact of different distribution policies. Benson anticipates extremely stable cash flows and will use the residual model to determine the level of distributions, but it has not yet chosen the form of the distribution. In particular, Benson is comparing distributions via dividends versus repurchases and wants to know the impact the different methods will have on financial statements, shareholder wealth, the number of outstanding shares, and the stock price. Benson's weighted average cost of capital (WACC) is 11.5%.

14-9a The Impact on Financial Statements

Consider first the case in which distributions are in the form of dividends. We begin by forecasting financing statements using the method described in Chapter 12. Figure 14-1 shows inputs in Section 1, the most recent and forecasted financial statements in Sections 2 and 3, and the identification of the preliminary financing surplus or deficit in Section 4.[24] Figure 14-1 shows the most recent financial statements and the forecasted financial statements for the next 2 years. (The file *Ch14 Tool Kit.xlsx* shows 4 years of projected statements.) Benson has no debt, so its interest expense is zero. If there is a preliminary financing deficit, Benson will draw on a line of credit. If there is a surplus, Benson will pay a special dividend.

We show balance sheets in Figure 14-1 for both December 30 and 31 of each year to better illustrate the impact of the distribution, which we assume occurs once each year on December 31.[25] We assume that the financing surplus is temporarily used to purchase short-term investments that are held until the distribution to shareholders. At the time of the distribution, all short-term investments will be converted to cash and paid out as special dividends. Thus, the 2020 short-term investments are $627.5 on December 30 and drop to zero on December 31, when they are distributed to investors.[26] Observe that the retained earnings account also drops by $627.5 on December 31 as funds that were previously retained are paid out as dividends.[27]

---

[24]The increase in financing is the sum of the increase in spontaneous financing (the sum of accounts payable and accruals), external financing (the increase in long-term debt and common stock), and internal financing (net income less any regular dividends); also, we subtract any beginning-of-year balance for the line of credit because Benson must pay off the line of credit each year even if it draws on it the next year. The increase in operating assets is the increase in all assets except the short-term investments. We subtract the increase in operating assets from the increase in financing. If the difference is negative, there is a financing deficit that must be met by drawing on the line of credit. If the difference is positive, there is a financing surplus that will be used by paying a special dividend.

[25]As we noted earlier in the chapter, when dividends are declared, a new current liability called "dividends payable" would be added to current liabilities and then retained earnings would be reduced by that amount. To simplify the example, we ignore that provision and assume that there is no balance sheet effect on the declaration date.

[26]As explained previously, there is a difference between the actual payment date and the exdividend date. To simplify the example, we assume that the dividends are paid on the ex-dividend date to the shareholder owning the stock the day before it goes ex-dividend.

[27]The observation that retained earnings drops when the dividend is paid might lead some to think that dividends are "paid out of retained earnings." They are not. Retained earnings, as do all liability accounts, records where money invested in the firm originally came from. It does not reflect a pile of money available to spend. A better way to think about it is that dividends are paid out of earnings, and that reduces the amount of earnings recorded in the retained earnings account.

FIGURE 14-1

Projecting Benson Conglomerate's Financial Statements: Distributions as Dividends (Millions of Dollars)

	A	B	C	D	E	F
74	**1. Inputs**	**Actual**	**Projected**			
75		**12/31/2019**	**2020**		**2021**	
76	Sales growth rate			5%		5%
77	Costs / Sales	75.00%	75.00%		75.00%	
78	Depreciation / Net PPE	10.00%	10.00%		10.00%	
79	Cash / Sales	1.00%	1.00%		1.00%	
80	Acct. rec. + Inv. / Sales	27.00%	27.00%		27.00%	
81	Net PPE / Sales	85.00%	85.00%		85.00%	
82	Acct. pay. + Accr. / Sales	10.00%	10.00%		10.00%	
83	Tax rate	25%	25%		25%	
84	**2. Income Statement**	**12/31/2019**	**12/31/2020**		**12/31/2021**	
85	Net Sales	$8,000.0		$8,400.0		$8,820.0
86	Costs (except depr.)	6,000.0		6,300.0		6,615.0
87	Depreciation	680.0		714.0		749.7
88	EBIT	$1,320.0		$1,386.0		$1,455.3
89	Interest expense[a]	0.0		0.0		0.0
90	Pre-tax earnings	$1,320.0		$1,386.0		$1,455.3
91	Taxes	330.0		346.5		363.8
92	Net income	$990.0		$1,039.5		$1,091.5
93	Regular dividends	$0.0		$0.0		$0.0
94	Special dividends			$627.5		$658.9
95	Addition to RE			$412.0		$432.6
96	**3. Balance Sheets**	**12/31/2019**	**2020**		**2021**	
97	*Assets*		**12/30**	**12/31**	**12/30**	**12/31**
98	Cash	$80.0	$84.0	$84.0	$88.2	$88.2
99	Short-term investments[b]	0.0	627.5	0.0	658.9	0.0
100	Acct. rec. + Inv.	2,160.0	2,268.0	2,268.0	2,381.4	2,381.4
101	Total current assets	$2,240.0	$2,979.5	$2,352.0	$3,128.5	$2,469.6
102	Net plant and equipment	6,800.0	7,140.0	7,140.0	7,497.0	7,497.0
103	Total assets	$9,040.0	$10,119.5	$9,492.0	$10,625.5	$9,966.6
104	*Liabilities & Equity*					
105	Acct. pay. + Accr.	$800.0	$840.0	$840.0	$882.0	$882.0
106	Line of credit	0.0	0.0	0.0	0.0	0.0
107	Total current liabilities	$800.0	$840.0	$840.0	$882.0	$882.0
108	Long-term debt	0.0	0.0	0.0	0.0	0.0
109	Total liabilities	$800.0	$840.0	$840.0	$882.0	$882.0
110	Common stock	2,400.0	2,400.0	2,400.0	2,400.0	2,400.0
111	Retained earnings[c]	5,840.0	6,879.5	6,252.0	7,343.5	6,684.6
112	Total common equity	$8,240.0	$9,279.5	$8,652.0	$9,743.5	$9,084.6
113	Total liabilities & equity	$9,040.0	$10,119.5	$9,492.0	$10,625.5	$9,966.6
114	Check for balancing:		Yes	Yes	Yes	Yes
115	**4. Financial Deficit or Surplus**		**12/30/20**	**12/31/20**	**12/30/21**	**12/31/21**
116	Incr. spon. liab.		$40.0		$42.0	
117	+ Incr. LT debt and stock		$0.0		$0.0	
118	– Previous line of credit		$0.0		$0.0	
119	+ NI minus regular dividends		$1,039.5		$1,091.5	
120	Increase in financing		$1,079.5		$1,133.5	
121	– Increase in operating assets		$452.0		$474.6	
122	Amount of deficit or surplus financing:		$627.5		$658.9	
123	Line of credit		$0.0	$0.0	$0.0	$0.0
124	Short-term investment		$627.5	$0.0	$658.9	$0.0
125	Special dividend		$0.0	$627.5	$0.0	$658.9

Source: See the file ***Ch14 Tool Kit.xlsx***. Numbers are reported as rounded values for clarity but are calculated using *Excel's* full precision. Thus, intermediate calculations using the figure's rounded values will be inexact.

Notes:

[a]To simplify the example, we assume any short-term investments are held for only part of the year and earn no interest.

[b]If there is a financial surplus, it is shown as a short-term investment on December 30. These funds are distributed to investors on December 31, so the balance of short-term investments goes to zero on December 31.

[c]Because no special dividends have been paid out as of December 30, the retained earnings balance for that date is equal to the previous year's retained earnings balance plus the current year's net income less the regular dividends. When short-term investments are sold and their proceeds are used to make the special cash dividend payments on December 31, the balance of retained earnings is reduced by the amount of the total dividend payments (which is equal to the regular dividend and the reduction in short-term investments that funded the special dividend).

Now let's consider the case of stock repurchases. The projected income statements and asset portion of the balance sheets are the same whether the distribution is in the form of dividends or repurchases, but this is not true for the liabilities-and-equity side of the balance sheet. Figure 14-2 reports the case in which distributions are in the form of stock repurchases. As in the case of dividend distributions, the December 30 balance of the retained earnings account is equal to the previous retained earnings balance plus the year's net income, because all income is retained. However, when funds in the short-term investments account are used to repurchase stock on December 31, the repurchase is shown as a negative entry in the treasury stock account.

To summarize, the projected income statements and assets are identical whether the distribution is made in the form of dividends or stock repurchases. There also is no difference in liabilities. However, distributions as dividends reduce the retained earnings account, whereas stock repurchases reduce the treasury stock account.

FIGURE 14-2

Projecting Benson Conglomerate's Liabilities and Equity: Distributions as Stock Repurchases (Millions of Dollars)

	A	B	C	D	E	F
142		Actual	Projected			
143		12/31/2019	2020		2021	
144	**Liabilities & Equity**		12/30	12/31	12/30	12/31
145	**Acct. pay. + Accr.**	$800.0	$840.0	$840.0	$882.0	$882.0
146	**Line of credit**	0.0	0.0	0.0	0.0	0.0
147	**Total current liabilities**	$800.0	$840.0	$840.0	$882.0	$882.0
148	**Long-term debt**	0.0	0.0	0.0	0.0	0.0
149	**Total liabilities**	$800.0	$840.0	$840.0	$882.0	$882.0
150	**Common stock**	2,400.0	2,400.0	2,400.0	2,400.0	2,400.0
151	**Treasury stock**[a]	0.0	0.0	−627.5	−627.5	−1,286.4
152	**Retained earnings**[b]	$5,840.0	$6,879.5	$6,879.5	$7,971.0	$7,971.0
153	**Total common equity**	$8,240.0	$9,279.5	$8,652.0	$9,743.5	$9,084.6
154	**Total liabilities & equity**	$ 9,040.0	$10,119.5	$ 9,492.0	$10,625.5	$ 9,966.6
155	**Check for balancing:**		Yes	Yes	Yes	Yes

Source: See the file ***Ch14 Tool Kit.xlsx***. Numbers are reported as rounded values for clarity but are calculated using *Excel's* full precision. Thus, intermediate calculations using the figure's rounded values will be inexact.

Notes:

[a]When distributions are made as repurchases, a negative entry equal to the dollar amount of the repurchase is made in the treasury stock account at the time of the repurchase, which occurs when short-term investments are liquidated and used to repurchase stock.

[b]No funds are paid out in dividends, so the retained earnings balance is equal to the previous balance plus the year's net income (all net income is being retained).

14-9b The Residual Distribution Model: Application to Full Financial Statements

Figures 14-1 and 14-2 illustrate the residual distribution model in Equation 14-1 as applied to entire financial statements. The projected capital budget is equal to the net addition to total operating capital from the projected balance sheets in Figure 14-1. For example, for 2020 the capital budget is:

$$
\begin{aligned}
\text{Capital budget} = &\ \Delta\text{Cash} + \Delta(\text{Acct. rec.} + \text{Inv.}) \\
&+ \Delta(\text{Net plant \& equipment}) \\
&- \Delta(\text{Accounts payable} + \text{Accruals}) \\
= &\ (\$84 - \$80) + (\$2{,}268 - \$2{,}160) + (\$7{,}140 - \$6{,}800) \\
&- (\$840 - \$800) \\
= &\ \$412
\end{aligned}
$$

With a 100% target equity ratio and net income of $1,039.5, the residual distribution is:

$$
\begin{aligned}
\text{Distribution} &= \text{Net income} - [(\text{Target equity ratio})(\text{Total capital budget})] \\
&= \$1{,}039.5 - [(100\%)(\$412)] \\
&= \$1{,}039.5 - \$412 = \$627.5
\end{aligned}
$$

Notice that this is the same as the financial surplus we calculated in Figure 14-1.

14-9c The Impact of Distributions on Intrinsic Value

What is the impact of cash distributions on intrinsic value? We use Benson Conglomerate to illustrate the answer to that question next.

FREE CASH FLOW

We begin by calculating expected free cash flows and performance measures as shown in Figure 14-3. Notice that Benson's expected 12.62% return on invested capital is greater than its 11.5% WACC, indicating that the managers are creating value for their shareholders. Also notice that the company is beyond its high-growth phase, so FCF is positive and growing at a constant rate of 5%. Therefore, Benson has cash flow available for distribution to investors.

THE VALUE OF OPERATIONS

Figure 14-3 also shows the horizon value at 2023, which is the value immediately after the payment of the FCF at 2023—it is the value of all FCF from 2024 and beyond discounted back to 12/31/2023. We can use the projected FCFs to determine the horizon value at the end of the projections and then estimate the value of operations for each year prior to the horizon. For Benson, the horizon value on December 31, 2023, is:

$$
\begin{aligned}
\text{HV}_{12/31/23} &= \frac{\text{FCF}_{12/31/23}\,(1 + g_{\text{L}})}{\text{WACC} - g_{\text{L}}} \\[2mm]
&= \frac{\$726.41\,(1 + 0.05)}{0.115 - 0.05} = \$11{,}734.3
\end{aligned}
$$

The value of operations on 12/31/2023 is the present value of all FCF from 2024 and beyond discounted back to 12/31/2023, which is exactly the definition of the horizon value on 12/31/2023. Therefore, the value of operations on 12/31/2023 is $11,734.3.

To estimate the value of operations at dates prior to the horizon, consider the following logic. Suppose you own the operations on 12/31/2022 and have just received the 2022 FCF.

FIGURE 14-3
Benson Conglomerate's Value of Operations (Millions of Dollars)

	A	B	C	D	E	F	G	H	I	J
195	WACC =	11.50%				Projected				
196		12/31/2019	12/31/2020		12/31/2021		12/31/2022		12/31/2023	
197	**1. Calculation of Free Cash Flow**									
198	Operating current assets[a]	$2,240.00	$2,352.00		$2,469.60		$2,593.08		$2,722.73	
199	Operating current liabilitie	800.00	840.00		882.00		926.10		972.41	
200	NOWC[c]	$1,440.00	$1,512.00		$1,587.60		$1,666.98		$1,750.33	
201	Net plant & equipment	6,800.00	7,140.00		7,497.00		7,871.85		8,265.44	
202	Total net operating capital	$8,240.00	$8,652.00		$9,084.60		$9,538.83		$10,015.77	
203	NOPAT[e]	$990.00	$1,039.50		$1,091.48		$1,146.05		$1,203.35	
204	Inv. in operating capital[f]		412.00		432.60		454.23		476.94	
205	Free cash flow (FCF)[g]		$627.50		$658.88		$691.82		$726.41	
206	**2. Performance Measures**	12/31/2019	12/31/2020		12/31/2021		12/31/2022		12/31/2023	
207	Expected ROIC[h]		12.62%		12.62%		12.62%		12.62%	
208	Growth in FCF		na		5.00%		5.00%		5.00%	
209	Growth in sales		5.00%		5.00%		5.00%		5.00%	
210	**3. Valuation**	12/31/2019	12/31/2020		12/31/2021		12/31/2022		12/31/2023	
211	Horizon value at 12/31/2023 (after FCF paid)[i]								$11,734.31	
212	Value of operations[j]	$9,653.85	$10,136.54		$10,643.37		$11,175.53		$11,734.31	

Source: See the file **Ch14 Tool Kit.xlsx**. Numbers are reported as rounded values for clarity but are calculated using *Excel*'s full precision. Thus, intermediate calculations using the figure's rounded values will be inexact.

Notes:

[a]Sum of cash, accounts receivable, and inventories.

[b]Sum of accounts payable and accruals.

[c]Net operating working capital is equal to operating current assets minus operating current liabilities.

[d]Sum of NOWC and net plant & equipment.

[e]Net operating profit after taxes = (EBIT)(1 − T). In this example, NOPAT is equal to net income because there is no interest expense or interest income.

[f]Change in net operating capital from previous year.

[g]FCF = NOPAT − Investment in operating capital.

[h]Expected return on invested capital = NOPAT divided by beginning capital.

[i]Horizon value at 2023 is immediately after the FCF at 2023 has been paid, which makes the horizon value at 2023 the present value of all FCF from 2024 and beyond when discounted back to 12/31/2023: $HV_{2022} = [FCF_{2023}(1 + g_L)]/(WACC − g_L)$.

[j]Value of operations before horizon = $V_{op(t)} = (V_{op(t+1)} + FCF_{t+1})/(1 + WACC)$.

You plan to sell the operations in a year, after receiving the 2023 FCF. Your expected cash flows would be the 2023 FCF and the value at which you expect to sell the operations on 12/31/2023. What is the expected sales price of the operations on 12/31/23? It is the value of all cash flows in 2024 and beyond, discounted back to 12/31/2023, which is the definition of the previously calculated value of 12/31/2023 value of operations. Therefore, the value of operations on 12/31/2022 (immediately after the 2022 FCF has been paid) is the sum of the 12/31/2023 FCF and value of operations, discounted back 1 year at the WACC:

$$V_{op(12/31/22)} = \frac{FCF_{12/31/23} + V_{op(12/31/23)}}{(1 + WACC)}$$

$$= \frac{\$726.41 + \$11,734.3}{1 + 0.115} = \$11,175.5$$

We can repeat this process to obtain the current value of operations (i.e., as of December 31, 2019): $9,653.85.

Notice that the choice of how to distribute the residual does not affect the value of operations because the distribution choice does not affect the projected free cash flows.

THE INTRINSIC STOCK PRICE: DISTRIBUTIONS AS DIVIDENDS

Figure 14-4 shows the intrinsic stock price each year using the corporate FCF valuation approach described in Chapters 7 and 12. Section 1 provides calculations assuming cash is distributed via dividends. (See *Ch14 Tool Kit.xlsx* for projections for 4 years.) Notice that on December 31 the intrinsic value of equity drops because the firm no longer owns the short-term investments. This causes the intrinsic stock price also to drop. In fact, the drop in stock price is equal to the dividend per share. For example, the 2020 dividend per share (DPS) is $0.63 and the drop in stock price is $10.76 − $10.14 = $0.62 ≈ $0.63. (The penny difference here is due to rounding in intermediate steps.)

Notice that if the stock price did *not* fall by the amount of the DPS, then there would be an opportunity for arbitrage. If the price were to drop by less than the DPS—say, by $0.50 to $10.26—you could buy the stock on December 30 for $10.76, receive a DPS of $0.63 on December 31, and then immediately sell the stock for $10.26, reaping a sure profit of −$10.76 + $0.63 + $10.26 = $0.13. Of course, you'd want to implement this strategy with a million shares, not just a single share. But if everyone tried to use this strategy, the increased demand would drive up the stock price on December 30 until there was no more sure profit to be made. The reverse would happen if investors expected the stock price to fall by more than the DPS.[28]

Here is an important observation: Even though the stock price falls, shareholder wealth does not fall. For example, on December 30, a shareholder owns stock worth $10.76. On December 31, the shareholder owns stock worth $10.14 but has cash of $0.63 from the dividend, for total wealth of $10.77 ≈ $10.76 (subject to rounding differences). Thus, the shareholder's wealth is the same before and after the dividend payment, with the only difference being that part of the shareholder's wealth is in the form of cash from the dividend payment.

THE INTRINSIC STOCK PRICE: DISTRIBUTIONS AS REPURCHASES

Section 2 of Figure 14-4 provides calculations of intrinsic value for the case in which stock is repurchased. Observe that the intrinsic value of equity is the same for both methods of distributions, but the analysis of a repurchase is a little more complicated because the number of shares changes. The key to solving this additional complexity is to recognize that the repurchase does not change the stock price. If the price did change due to the repurchase, then there would be an arbitrage opportunity. For example, suppose the stock price is expected to increase after the repurchase. If this were true, then it should be possible for an investor to buy the stock the day before the repurchase and then reap a reward the very next day. Current stockholders would realize this and would refuse to sell the stock unless they were paid the price that is expected immediately after the repurchase. Now suppose the stock price is expected to fall immediately after the repurchase. In this case, current shareholders should try to sell the stock prior to the repurchase, but their actions would drive the price down to the price that is expected after the repurchase. As you can see, the repurchase itself does not change the stock price.

In summary, the events leading up to a repurchase generate cash (the sale of a division, a recapitalization, or the generation of high free cash flows from operations). Generating

---

[28]We ignore taxes in this description. Empirical evidence suggests that the actual drop in stock price is equal to about 90% of the DPS, with all pre-tax profit being eliminated by taxes.

FIGURE 14-4
Benson Conglomerate's Intrinsic Stock Price for Each Method of Distribution (Millions of Dollars)

	A	B	C	D	E	F
258	**Section 1. Distribute as Dividends**			**Projected**		
259				2020		2021
260		12/31/19	12/30	12/31	12/30	12/31
261	**Value of operations**	$9,654	$10,137	$10,137	$10,643	$10,643
262	**+ Value of nonoperating assets**	$0	$628	$0	$659	$0
263	**Total intrinsic value of firm**	$9,654	$10,764	$10,137	$11,302	$10,643
264	**− Debt**	$0	$0	$0	$0	$0
265	**− Preferred stock**	$0	$0	$0	$0	$0
266	**Intrinsic value of equity**	$9,654	$10,764	$10,137	$11,302	$10,643
267	**÷ Number of shares**	$1,000	$1,000	$1,000	$1,000	$1,000
268	**Intrinsic price per share**[a]	$9.65	$10.76	$10.14	$11.30	$10.64
269	**Dividend per share**			$0.63		$0.66
270						
271	**Section 2. Distribute as Repurchase**			2020		2021
272		12/31/19	12/30	12/31	12/30	12/31
273	**Value of operations**	$9,654	$10,137	$10,137	$10,643	$10,643
274	**+ Value of nonoperating assets**	$0	$628	$0	$659	$0
275	**Total intrinsic value of firm**	$9,654	$10,764	$10,137	$11,302	$10,643
276	**− Debt**		$0	$0	$0	$0
277	**− Preferred stock**	$0	$0	$0	$0	$0
278	**Intrinsic value of equity**	$9,654	$10,764	$10,137	$11,302	$10,643
279	**÷ Number of shares**[b]	1,000	$1,000	$942	$942	$887
280	**Intrinsic price per share**[a]	$9.65	$10.76	$10.76	$12.00	$12.00

Source: See the file ***Ch14 Tool Kit.xlsx***. Numbers are reported as rounded values for clarity but are calculated using *Excel*'s full precision. Thus, intermediate calculations using the figure's rounded values will be inexact.

Notes:

[a]The projected intrinsic stock prices for 4 years are shown in ***Ch14 Tool Kit.xlsx***.

[b]The number of shares after the repurchase is $n_{Post} = n_{Prior} - (Cash_{Rep}/P_{Prior})$. In this example, the entire amount of ST investments (i.e., the balance of nonoperating assets) is used to repurchase stock.

cash can certainly change the stock price, but the repurchase itself doesn't change the stock price. We can use this fact to determine the number of shares repurchased. First, though, we must define some notation.

n_{Prior} = The number of shares outstanding prior to the repurchase

n_{Post} = The number of shares outstanding after the repurchase

S_{Prior} = The intrinsic value of equity prior to the repurchase

S_{Post} = The intrinsic value of equity after the repurchase

P_{Prior} = The intrinsic stock price prior to the repurchase

P_{Post} = The intrinsic stock price after the repurchase

$P = P_{Prior} = P_{Post}$ = The intrinsic stock price during, before, and after the repurchase

$Cash_{Rep}$ = The amount of cash used to repurchase shares

As we explained, the repurchase itself doesn't change the stock price. Therefore, the number of shares repurchased is equal to the amount of cash used to repurchase stocks divided by the stock price:

$$\text{Number of shares repurchased} = n_{Prior} - n_{Post} = \frac{Cash_{Rep}}{P_{Prior}} \qquad (14\text{-}2)$$

We can rewrite Equation 14-2 to find an expression for the number of shares after the repurchase:

$$
\begin{aligned}
n_{Post} &= n_{Prior} - \frac{Cash_{Rep}}{P_{Prior}} \\[2mm]
&= n_{Prior} - \frac{Cash_{Rep}}{S_{Prior}/n_{Prior}} \\[2mm]
&= n_{Prior}\left(1 - \frac{Cash_{Rep}}{S_{Prior}}\right)
\end{aligned}
\qquad (14\text{-}3)
$$

For example, as shown in Section 2 of Figure 14-4, the intrinsic stock price on December 30, 2020, the day before the repurchase, is $10.76, and there are 1,000 shares of stock. Using Equation 14-3, the number of shares after the repurchase is equal to:

$$
\begin{aligned}
n_{Post} &= n_{Prior} - \frac{Cash_{Rep}}{P_{Prior}} \\[2mm]
&= 1{,}000 - \frac{\$627.5}{\$10.76} \\[2mm]
&\approx 941.70 \text{ without rounding in intermediate steps}
\end{aligned}
$$

Section 2 of Figure 14-4 also shows that on December 31, 2020, the intrinsic value of equity prior to the repurchase, S_{Prior}, drops from \$10,764.04 to a value after the repurchase, S_{Post}, of \$10,136.54. This decrease in the intrinsic value of equity is equal to the amount of the cash used in the repurchase, \$627.5. However, the stock price remains at \$10.76 after the repurchase because the number of shares also drops:

$$P_{Post} = \frac{S_{Post}}{n_{Post}} = \frac{\$10,136.54}{941.70} = \$10.76$$

How does the repurchase affect shareholder wealth? The aggregate value of outstanding stock drops after the repurchase, but the aggregate wealth of the shareholders remains unchanged. Before the repurchase, shareholders own a total of equity worth S_{Prior}, \$10,764.04. After the repurchase, shareholders own a total of equity worth S_{Post}, \$10,136.54, but they also own cash (received in the repurchase) in the amount of \$627.5, for a total wealth of \$10,764.04. Thus, the repurchase does not change shareholders' aggregate wealth; it only changes the form in which they hold wealth (all stock versus a combination of stock and cash).

COMPARING INTRINSIC STOCK PRICES: DIVIDENDS VERSUS REPURCHASES

The chart at the top of Figure 14-4 shows the projected intrinsic stock prices for the two different distribution methods. Notice that the prices begin at the same level (because Benson has not yet begun making any distributions). The price for the repurchase scenario climbs smoothly and grows to a higher level than does the price for the dividend scenario, which drops by the DPS each time it is paid. However, the number of shares falls in the repurchase scenario. As shown in Rows 266 and 278 of the figure, the intrinsic values of equity are identical for both distribution methods.

This example illustrates three key results: (1) Ignoring possible tax effects and signals, the total market value of equity will be the same whether a firm pays dividends or repurchases stock. (2) The repurchase itself does not change the stock price (compared with using the cash to buy marketable securities) at the time of the repurchase, although it does reduce the number of outstanding shares. (3) Because a company that repurchases stock will have fewer shares than an otherwise identical company that pays dividends, the stock price of a repurchasing company will climb faster than that of the dividend-paying company. However, the total return to the two companies' shareholders will be the same.[29]

SELF-TEST

Explain how a repurchase changes the number of shares but not the stock price.

A firm's most recent FCF was \$2.4 million, and its FCF is expected to grow at a constant rate of 5%. The firm's WACC is 14%, and it has 2 million shares outstanding. The firm has \$12 million in short-term investments that it plans to liquidate and then distribute in a stock repurchase; the firm has no other financial investments or debt. Verify that the value of operations is \$28 million.

---

[29]For more on repurchases, see David J. Denis, "Defensive Changes in Corporate Payout Policy: Share Repurchases and Special Dividends," *Journal of Finance*, December 1990, pp. 1433–1456; Gerald D. Gay, Jayant R. Kale, and Thomas H. Noe, "Share Repurchase Mechanisms: A Comparative Analysis of Efficacy, Shareholder Wealth and Corporate Control Effects," *Financial Management*, Spring 1991, pp. 44–59; Jeffry M. Netter and Mark L. Mitchell, "Stock-Repurchase Announcements and Insider Transactions after the October 1987 Stock Market Crash," *Financial Management*, Autumn 1989, pp. 84–96; William Pugh and John S. Jahera, Jr., "Stock Repurchases and Excess Returns: An Empirical Examination," *The Financial Review*, February 1990, pp. 127–142; and James W. Wansley, William R. Lane, and Salil Sarkar, "Managements' View on Share Repurchase and Tender Offer Premiums," *Financial Management*, Autumn 1989, pp. 97–110.

Immediately prior to the repurchase, what are the intrinsic value of equity and the intrinsic stock price? **($40 million; $20/share)** *How many shares will be repurchased?* **(0.6 million)** *How many shares will remain after the repurchase?* **(1.4 million)** *Immediately after the repurchase, what are the intrinsic value of equity and the intrinsic stock price?* **($28 million; $20/share)**

14-10 The Pros and Cons of Dividends and Repurchases

The advantages of repurchases can be listed as follows:

1. Repurchase announcements are viewed as positive signals by investors because the repurchase is often motivated by management's belief that the firm's shares are undervalued.[30]
2. Stockholders have a choice when the firm distributes cash by repurchasing stock—they can sell or not sell. Those stockholders who need cash can sell back some of their shares while others can simply retain their stock. With a cash dividend, on the other hand, stockholders must accept a dividend payment.
3. Dividends are "sticky" in the short run because management is usually reluctant to raise the dividend if the increase cannot be maintained in the future, and cutting cash dividends is always avoided because of the negative signal it gives. Hence, if the excess cash flow is thought to be only temporary, management may prefer making the distribution in the form of a stock repurchase to declaring an increased cash dividend that cannot be maintained.
4. Companies can use the residual model to set a *target cash distribution* level and then divide the distribution into a *dividend component* and a *repurchase component*. The dividend payout ratio will be relatively low, but the dividend itself will be relatively secure, and it will grow as a result of the declining number of shares outstanding. The company has more flexibility in adjusting the total distribution than it would if the entire distribution were in the form of cash dividends, because repurchases can be varied from year to year without giving adverse signals.
5. Repurchases can be used to produce large-scale changes in capital structures. For example, PepsiCo borrowed $4 billion to use in its stock repurchase plan. The repurchases totaled over 4% of the firm's market value, allowing PepsiCo to quickly change its capital structure.
6. Companies that use stock options as an important component of employee compensation usually repurchase shares in the secondary market and then use those shares when employees exercise their options. This technique allows companies to avoid issuing new shares and thus diluting earnings.

Repurchases have three principal disadvantages:

1. Stockholders may not be indifferent between dividends and capital gains, and the price of the stock might benefit more from cash dividends than from repurchases. Cash dividends are generally dependable, but repurchases are not.
2. The *selling* stockholders may not be fully aware of all the implications of a repurchase, or they may not have all the pertinent information about the corporation's present and future activities. However, in order to avoid potential stockholder suits, firms generally announce repurchase programs before embarking on them.

[30]This is not true for firms that make regular repurchases, but it is true for occasional repurchasers, which are able to buy back stock at a price that is lower than the average price in the surrounding months. See A. Dittmar and L. Field, "Can Managers Time the Market? Evidence Using Repurchase Price Data," *Journal of Financial Economics*, Vol. 115, 2015, pp. 261–282.

3. The corporation may pay too much for the repurchased stock—to the disadvantage of remaining stockholders. If the firm seeks to acquire a relatively large amount of its stock, then the price may be bid above its equilibrium level and then fall after the firm ceases its repurchase operations.

When all the pros and cons on stock repurchases versus dividends have been considered, where do we stand? Our conclusions may be summarized as follows:

1. Because of the deferred tax on capital gains, repurchases have a tax advantage over dividends as a way to distribute income to stockholders. This advantage is reinforced by the fact that repurchases provide cash to stockholders who want cash while allowing those who do not need current cash to delay its receipt. On the other hand, dividends are more dependable and thus are better suited for those who need a steady source of income.

2. The danger of signaling effects requires that a company not have volatile dividend payments, which would lower investors' confidence in the company and adversely affect its cost of equity and its stock price. However, cash flows vary over time, as do investment opportunities, so the "proper" dividend in the residual model varies. To get around this problem, a company can set its dividend low enough to keep dividend payments from constraining operations and then use repurchases on a more or less regular basis to distribute excess cash. Such a procedure will provide regular, dependable dividends plus additional cash flow to those stockholders who want it.

3. Repurchases are also useful when a firm wants to make a large shift in its capital structure, wants to distribute cash from a one-time event such as the sale of a division, or wants to obtain shares for use in an employee stock option plan.

SELF-TEST

What are some advantages and disadvantages of stock repurchases?

How can stock repurchases help a company operate in accordance with the residual distribution model?

Dividend Yields around the World

Dividend yields vary considerably in different stock markets throughout the world. In 2016, dividend yields varied from 0.60% in South Korea to 2.23% in the United States to 3.75% in the European Union, to 4.42% in the United Kingdom and to a high of 5.42% in Australia. Some of this variability can be explained by differences in the various corporate tax laws' treatment of dividends. In the United States, dividends are somewhat penalized by double taxation in that the income used to pay dividends is taxed first at the corporate level at a rate of up to 39%, and then the dividends themselves are taxed at the individual level at a rate of up to 20%. In Korea, this dividend penalty is even greater for higher-income recipients with individual tax rates on dividends ranging up to 48%. To top it off, Korea's tax laws also provide an even stronger incentive not to pay out dividends by allowing an exemption of up to 75% of capital gains for shares held at least 4 years. At the other end of the spectrum, Australia's tax code has aggressively removed double taxation of the income used to pay dividends by providing a credit to dividend recipients of the corporate taxes paid on the dividends received. This process is called "franking" and makes dividends much more attractive to investors, explaining in part why Australian firms have dividend yields that are double those of U.S. firms.

Sources: Jonathan Hill, "Australia," **https://www2.deloitte.com /content/dam/Deloitte/us/Documents/Tax/us-tax-ice-country -highlights-australia.pdf**; "Taxation and Investment in Korea 2016," published by Deloitte Touche Tohmatsu Limited, **https://www2 .deloitte.com/content/dam/Deloitte/global/Documents/Tax/dttl -tax-koreaguide-2016.pdf**; and David L. Ruff, "The Dividend Signal, Uncovering Global Growth Opportunities," Salientpartners.com, March 2016, **www.salientpartners.com/wp-content/uploads/salient -the-dividend-signal-white-paper.pdf**.

14-11 Other Factors Influencing Distributions

In this section, we discuss several other factors that affect the dividend decision. These factors may be grouped into two broad categories: (1) constraints on dividend payments and (2) availability and cost of alternative sources of capital.

14-11a Constraints

Constraints on dividend payments can affect distributions, as the following examples illustrate.

1. *Bond indentures.* Debt contracts often limit dividend payments to earnings generated after the loan was granted. Also, debt contracts often stipulate that no dividends can be paid unless the current ratio, times-interest-earned ratio, and other safety ratios exceed stated minimums.

2. *Preferred stock restrictions.* Typically, common dividends cannot be paid if the company has omitted its preferred dividend. The preferred arrearages must be satisfied before common dividends can be resumed.

3. *Impairment of capital rule.* Dividend payments cannot exceed the balance sheet item "retained earnings." This legal restriction, known as the "impairment of capital rule," is designed to protect creditors. Without the rule, a company in trouble might distribute most of its assets to stockholders and leave its debtholders out in the cold. (*Liquidating dividends* can be paid out of capital, but they must be indicated as such and must not reduce capital below the limits stated in debt contracts.)

4. *Availability of cash.* Cash dividends can be paid only with cash, so a shortage of cash in the bank can restrict dividend payments. However, the ability to borrow can offset this factor.

5. *Penalty tax on improperly accumulated earnings.* To prevent wealthy individuals from using corporations to avoid personal taxes, the Tax Code provides for a special surtax on improperly accumulated income. Thus, if the IRS can demonstrate that a firm's dividend payout ratio is being deliberately held down to help its stockholders avoid personal taxes, the firm is subject to heavy penalties. This factor is generally relevant only to privately owned firms.

14-11b Alternative Sources of Capital

The second factor that influences the dividend decision involves the cost and availability of alternative sources of capital.

1. *Cost of selling new stock.* If a firm needs to finance a given level of investment, it can obtain equity by retaining earnings or by issuing new common stock. If flotation costs (including any negative signaling effects of a stock offering) are high, then the required return on new equity, r_e, will be well above the required return on internally generated equity, r_s, making it better to set a low payout ratio and to finance through retention rather than through the sale of new common stock. On the other hand, a high dividend payout ratio is more feasible for a firm whose flotation costs are low. Flotation costs differ among firms—for example, the flotation percentage is generally higher for small firms, so they tend to set low payout ratios.

2. *Ability to substitute debt for equity.* A firm can finance a given level of investment with either debt or equity. As just described, low stock flotation costs permit a more flexible dividend policy because equity can be raised either by retaining earnings or by selling new stock. A similar situation holds for debt policy: If the firm can adjust

its debt ratio without raising the cost of capital sharply, then it can pay the expected dividend—even if earnings fluctuate—by increasing its debt ratio.

3. *Control.* If management is concerned about maintaining control, it may be reluctant to sell new stock; hence, the company may retain more earnings than it otherwise would. However, if stockholders want higher dividends and a proxy fight looms, then the dividend will be increased.

What constraints affect dividend policy?
How do the availability and cost of outside capital affect dividend policy?

14-12 Summarizing the Distribution Policy Decision

In practice, the distribution decision is made jointly with capital structure and capital budgeting decisions. The underlying reason for joining these decisions is asymmetric information—managers know more than investors know about their company's prospects. Here is how asymmetric information influences managerial actions.

1. In general, managers do not want to issue new common stock. First, new common stock involves issuance costs—commissions, fees, and so on—and those costs can be avoided by reinvesting earnings to finance equity needs. Second, as we will explain in Chapter 15, asymmetric information causes investors to view new common stock issues as negative signals and thus lowers expectations regarding the firm's future prospects. The end result is that the announcement of a new stock issue usually leads to a decrease in the stock price. Considering the total costs due to issuance and asymmetric information, managers prefer to use retained earnings as the primary source of new equity.

2. Dividend changes provide signals about managers' beliefs concerning their firms' future prospects. Thus, dividend reductions generally have a significant negative effect on a firm's stock price. Because managers recognize this, they try to set dollar dividends low enough so there is only a remote chance the dividend will have to be reduced in the future.

The effects of asymmetric information suggest that, to the extent possible, managers should avoid both new common stock sales and dividend cuts, because both actions tend to lower the stock price. Thus, in setting distribution policy, managers should begin by considering the firm's future investment opportunities relative to its projected internal sources of funds. The target capital structure also plays a part, but because it is a *range*, firms can vary their actual capital structures somewhat from year to year. Because it is best to avoid issuing new common stock, the target long-term payout ratio should be designed to permit the firm to meet all of its equity capital requirements by retaining earnings. In effect, *managers should use the residual model to set dividends, but in a long-term framework.* Finally, the current dollar dividend should be set so that there is an extremely low probability that the dividend, once set, will ever have to be lowered or omitted.

Of course, the dividend decision is made during the planning process, so there is uncertainty about future investment opportunities and operating cash flows. The actual payout ratio in any year will therefore likely be above or below the firm's long-range target. However, the dollar dividend should be maintained, or increased as planned, unless the firm's financial condition deteriorates to the point at which the planned policy simply cannot be maintained. A steady or increasing stream of dividends over the long run signals that the firm's financial condition is under control. Moreover, investor uncertainty is decreased by stable dividends, so a steady dividend stream reduces the negative effect of a new stock issue—should one become absolutely necessary.

In general, firms with superior investment opportunities should set lower payouts, and hence retain more earnings, than firms with poor investment opportunities. The degree of uncertainty also influences the decision. If there is a great deal of uncertainty regarding the forecasts of free cash flows, which are defined here as the firm's operating cash flows minus mandatory equity investments, then it is best to be conservative and to set a lower current dollar dividend. Also, firms with postponable investment opportunities can afford to set a higher dollar dividend, because in times of stress investments can be postponed for a year or two, thus increasing the cash available for dividends. Finally, firms whose cost of capital is largely unaffected by changes in the debt ratio can also afford to set a higher payout ratio, because in times of stress they can more easily issue additional debt to maintain the capital budgeting program without having to cut dividends or issue stock.

The net result of these factors is that many firms' dividend policies are consistent with the life-cycle theory in which younger firms with many investment opportunities but relatively low cash flows reinvest their earnings so that they can avoid the large flotation costs associated with raising external capital.[31] As firms mature and begin to generate more cash flow, they tend to pay more dividends and issue more debt as a way to "bond" their cash flows (as described in Chapter 15) and thereby reduce the agency costs of free cash flow.

What do executives think? A recent survey indicates financial executives believe that it is extremely important to *maintain* dividends but much less important to initiate or increase dividend payments. In general, they view the cash distribution decision as being much less important than capital budgeting decisions. Managers like the flexibility provided by repurchases instead of regular dividends. They tend to repurchase shares when they believe their stock price is undervalued, and they believe that shareholders view repurchases as positive signals. In general, the different taxation of dividends and repurchases is not a major factor when a company chooses how to distribute cash to investors.[32]

SELF-TEST

Describe the decision process for distribution policy and dividend payout. Be sure to discuss all the factors that influence this decision.

14-13 Stock Splits and Stock Dividends

The rationale for stock splits and dividends can best be explained through an example. We will use Porter Electronic Controls Inc., a $700 million electronic components manufacturer, for this purpose. Since its inception, Porter's markets have been expanding, and the company has enjoyed growth in sales and earnings. Some of its earnings have been paid out in dividends, but some are also retained each year, causing its earnings per share and stock price to grow. The company began its life with only a few thousand shares outstanding, and after some years of growth the stock price was high. Porter's CFO thought

---

[31]For a test of the life-cycle theory, see Harry DeAngelo, Linda DeAngelo, and René Stulz, "Dividend Policy and the Earned/Contributed Capital Mix: A Test of the Life-Cycle Theory," *Journal of Financial Economics*, August 2006, pp. 227–254.

[32]See Alon Brav, John R. Graham, Campbell R. Harvey, and Roni Michaely, "Payout Policy in the 21st Century," *Journal of Financial Economics*, September 2005, pp. 483–527.

this high price limited the number of investors who could buy the stock, which reduced demand for the stock and thus kept the firm's total market value below what it could be if there were more shares, at a lower price, outstanding. To correct this situation, Porter "split its stock," as we describe next.

14-13a Stock Splits

Although there is little empirical evidence to support the contention, there is neverthe-less a widespread belief in financial circles that an *optimal price range* exists for stocks. "Optimal" means that if the price is within this range, the firm's value will be maximized. Many observers, including Porter's management, believe the best range for most stocks is from $20 to $80 per share. Accordingly, if the price of Porter's stock rose to $80, manage-ment would probably declare a 2-for-1 **stock split**, thus doubling the number of shares outstanding, halving the earnings, dividends, and free cash flow per share, and thereby lowering the stock price. Each stockholder would have more shares, but each share would be worth less. If the post-split price were $40, then Porter's stockholders would be exactly as well off as before the split. However, if the stock price were to stabilize above $40, stock-holders would be better off. Stock splits can be of any size—for example, the stock could be split 2-for-1, 3-for-1, 1.5-for-1, or in any other way.

Sometimes a company will have a **reverse split**. For example, the financial services company Citigroup (C) was trading in the $55 per share range in 2007 prior to the global financial meltdown. After the meltdown, the stock traded as low as $1 in 2009 and had recovered only to $4.52 per share by May 6, 2011. On May 9, 2011 Citigroup had a 1-10 reverse stock split before trading began, with its shareholders exchanging 10 shares of stock for a single new share. In theory, the stock price should have increased by a factor of 10, to around $45.20, and Citigroup indeed closed that day at a price of $44.16. Even though Citigroup was again trading in the same per share price range as it did before the global financial meltdown, with only 1/10 the number of shares outstanding, its market value of equity was still less than 10% of what it had been in 2007.

14-13b Stock Dividends

Stock dividends are similar to stock splits in that they "divide the pie into smaller slices" without affecting the fundamental position of the current stockholders. For example, with a 5% stock dividend, the holder of 100 shares would receive an additional 5 shares (without cost) and with a 20% stock dividend, the same holder would receive 20 new shares. Again, the total number of shares is increased, so earnings, dividends, free cash flow, and price per share all decline.

If a firm wants to reduce the price of its stock, should it use a stock split or a stock dividend? Stock splits are generally used after a sharp price run-up to produce a large price reduction. Stock dividends used on a regular annual basis will keep the stock price more or less constrained. For example, if a firm's earnings, dividends, and free cash flow were growing at about 10% per year, its stock price would tend to go up at about the same rate, and it would soon be outside the desired trading range. A 10% annual stock dividend would maintain the stock price within the optimal trading range. Note, however, that small stock dividends create bookkeeping problems and unnecessary expenses, so firms today use stock splits far more often than stock dividends.[33]

---

[33]Accountants treat stock splits and stock dividends somewhat differently. For example, in a 2-for-1 stock split, the number of shares outstanding is doubled and the par value is halved. With a stock dividend, a bookkeeping entry is made transferring "retained earnings" to "common stock." Neither a stock split nor a stock dividend is taxable to investors.

14-13c Effect on Stock Prices

If a company splits its stock or declares a stock dividend, will this increase the market value of its stock? Many empirical studies have sought to answer this question. Here is a summary of their findings.

1. On average, the price of a company's stock rises shortly after it announces a stock split or a stock dividend.
2. However, these price increases are probably due to signaling rather than a desire for stock splits or dividends per se. Only managers who think future earnings will be higher tend to split stocks, so investors often view the announcement of a stock split as a positive signal. Thus, it is the signal of favorable prospects for earnings and dividends that causes the price to increase.
3. If a company announces a stock split or stock dividend, its price will tend to rise. However, if during the next few months it does not announce an increase in earnings and dividends, then its stock price will drop back to the earlier level.
4. As we noted earlier, brokerage commissions are generally higher in percentage terms on lower-priced stocks. This means that it is more expensive to trade low-priced than high-priced stocks—which, in turn, means that stock splits may reduce the liquidity of a company's shares. This particular piece of evidence suggests that stock splits/dividends might actually be harmful, although a lower price does mean that more investors can afford to trade in round lots (100 shares), which carry lower commissions than do odd lots (fewer than 100 shares).

What can we conclude from all this? From a purely economic standpoint, stock dividends and splits are just additional pieces of paper. However, they provide management with a relatively low-cost way of signaling that the firm's prospects look good.[34] Further, we should note that since few large, publicly owned stocks sell at prices above several hundred dollars, we simply do not know what the effect would be if Microsoft, Walmart, Starbucks, and other highly successful firms had never split their stocks and consequently sold at prices in the thousands or even tens of thousands of dollars. All in all, it probably makes sense to employ stock splits (or stock dividends) when a firm's prospects are favorable, especially if the price of its stock has gone beyond the normal trading range.[35]

SELF-TEST

What are stock splits and stock dividends?

How do stock splits and dividends affect stock prices?

In what situations should managers consider the use of stock splits?

In what situations should managers consider the use of stock dividends?

Suppose you have 1,000 common shares of Burnside Bakeries. The EPS is $6.00, the DPS is $3.00, and the stock sells for $90 per share. Burnside announces a 3-for-1 split. Immediately after the split, how many shares will you have? **(3,000)** *What will the adjusted EPS and DPS be?* **($2 and $1)** *What would you expect the stock price to be?* **($30)**

---

[34]For more on stock splits and stock dividends, see H. Kent Baker, Aaron L. Phillips, and Gary E. Powell, "The Stock Distribution Puzzle: A Synthesis of the Literature on Stock Splits and Stock Dividends," *Financial Practice and Education*, Spring/Summer 1995, pp. 24–37; Maureen McNichols and Ajay Dravid, "Stock Dividends, Stock Splits, and Signaling," *Journal of Finance*, July 1990, pp. 857–879; and David R. Peterson and Pamela P. Peterson, "A Further Understanding of Stock Distributions: The Case of Reverse Stock Splits," *Journal of Financial Research*, Fall 1992, pp. 189–205.

[35]It is interesting to note that Berkshire Hathaway (controlled by billionaire Warren Buffett) has never had a stock split, and its stock (BRKa) sold on the NYSE for $255,040 per share in February 2017. Yet in response to investment trusts that were being formed in 1996 to sell fractional units of the stock and thus—in effect—split it, Buffett himself created a new class of Berkshire Hathaway stock (Class B) now worth about 1/1,500 of a Class A (regular) share.

14-14 Dividend Reinvestment Plans

During the 1970s, most large companies instituted **dividend reinvestment plans (DRIPs)**, under which stockholders can choose to automatically reinvest their dividends in the stock of the paying corporation. Today most large companies offer DRIPs; participation rates vary considerably, but about 25% of the average firm's shareholders are enrolled. There are two types of DRIPs: (1) plans that involve only "old stock" that is already outstanding and (2) plans that involve newly issued stock. In either case, the stockholder must pay taxes on the amount of the dividends, even though stock rather than cash is received.

Under both types of DRIPs, stockholders choose between continuing to receive dividend checks or having the company use the dividends to buy more stock in the corporation. Under the "old stock" type of plan, if a stockholder elects reinvestment, then a bank, acting as trustee, takes the total funds available for reinvestment, purchases the corporation's stock on the open market, and allocates the shares purchased to the participating stockholders' accounts on a pro rata basis. The transaction costs of buying shares (brokerage costs) are low because of volume purchases, so these plans benefit small stockholders who do not need cash dividends for current consumption.

The "new stock" type of DRIP uses the reinvested funds to buy newly issued stock; hence, these plans raise new capital for the firm. AT&T, Union Carbide, and many other companies have used new stock plans to raise substantial amounts of new equity capital. No fees are charged to stockholders, and many companies offer stock at a discount of 3% to 5% below the actual market price. The companies offer discounts as a trade-off against flotation costs that would have been incurred if new stock had been issued through investment bankers instead of through the dividend reinvestment plans.

One interesting aspect of DRIPs is that they cause corporations to re-examine their basic dividend policies. A high participation rate in a DRIP suggests that stockholders might be better off if the firm simply reduced cash dividends, which would save stockholders some personal income taxes. Quite a few firms are surveying their stockholders to learn more about their preferences and to find out how they would react to a change in dividend policy. A more rational approach to basic dividend policy decisions may emerge from this research.

Note that companies start or stop using new stock DRIPs depending on their need for equity capital. For example, Union Carbide and AT&T stopped offering new stock DRIPs with a 5% discount because their needs for equity capital declined.

Some companies have expanded their DRIPs by moving to "open enrollment," whereby anyone can purchase the firm's stock directly and thus bypass brokers' commissions. ExxonMobil not only allows investors to buy their initial shares at no fee but also lets them pick up additional shares through automatic bank account withdrawals. Several plans, including ExxonMobil's, offer dividend reinvestment for individual retirement accounts, and some, such as U.S. West's, allow participants to invest weekly or monthly rather than on the quarterly dividend schedule. In all of these plans, and many others, stockholders can invest more than the dividends they are forgoing—they simply send a check to the company and buy shares without a brokerage commission. According to First Chicago Trust, which handles the paperwork for 13 million shareholder DRIP accounts, at least half of all DRIPs will offer open enrollment, extra purchases, and other expanded services within the next few years.

SELF-TEST

What are dividend reinvestment plans?

What are their advantages and disadvantages from both the stockholders' and the firm's perspectives?

SUMMARY

In this chapter, we discussed the various ways a firm can distribute cash to its shareholders and how this choice affects firm value.

- **Distribution policy** involves three issues: (1) What fraction of earnings should be distributed? (2) Should the distribution be in the form of cash dividends or stock repurchases? (3) Should the firm maintain a steady, stable dividend growth rate?
- The **optimal distribution policy** strikes a balance between current dividends and future growth so as to maximize the firm's stock price.
- Miller and Modigliani (MM) developed the **dividend irrelevance theory**, which holds that a firm's dividend policy has no effect on either the value of its stock or its cost of capital.
- The **dividend preference theory**, also called the **bird-in-the-hand theory**, holds that the firm's value will be maximized by a high dividend payout ratio, because investors regard cash dividends as being less risky than potential capital gains.
- The **tax effect theory** states that because long-term capital gains are subject to lower taxes than dividends, investors prefer to have companies retain earnings rather than pay them out as dividends.
- Dividend policy should take account of the **signaling hypothesis**, which is also called the **information content hypothesis**. The signaling effect stems from investors regarding an unexpected dividend change as a signal of management's forecast of future earnings.
- The **clientele effect** suggests that a firm will attract investors who like the firm's dividend payout policy.
- In practice, dividend-paying firms follow a policy of paying a steadily increasing dividend. This policy provides investors with stable, dependable income, and departures from it give investors signals about management's expectations for future earnings.
- Most firms use the **residual distribution model** to set the long-run target distribution ratio at a level that will permit the firm to meet its equity requirements with retained earnings.
- Under a **stock repurchase plan**, a firm buys back some of its outstanding stock, thereby decreasing the number of shares but leaving the stock price unchanged.
- Legal constraints, investment opportunities, availability and cost of funds from other sources, and taxes are also considered when firms establish dividend policies.
- A **stock split** increases the number of shares outstanding. Normally, splits reduce the price per share in proportion to the increase in shares because splits merely "divide the pie into smaller slices." However, firms generally split their stocks only if: (1) The price is quite high. (2) Management thinks the future is bright. Therefore, stock splits are often taken as positive signals and thus boost stock prices.
- A **stock dividend** is a dividend paid in additional shares rather than in cash. Both stock dividends and splits are used to keep stock prices within an "optimal" trading range.
- A **dividend reinvestment plan (DRIP)** allows stockholders to have the company automatically use dividends to purchase additional shares. DRIPs are popular because they allow stockholders to acquire additional shares without brokerage fees.

QUESTIONS

(14-1) Define each of the following terms:
   a. Optimal distribution policy
   b. Dividend irrelevance theory; bird-in-the-hand theory; tax effect theory
   c. Signaling hypothesis; clientele effect
   d. Residual distribution model; extra dividend
   e. Declaration date; holder-of-record date; ex-dividend date; payment date
   f. Dividend reinvestment plan (DRIP)
   g. Stock split; stock dividend; stock repurchase

(14-2) How would each of the following changes tend to affect aggregate payout ratios (that is, the average for all corporations), other things held constant? Explain your answers.
   a. An increase in the personal income tax rate
   b. A liberalization of depreciation for federal income tax purposes—that is, faster tax write-offs
   c. A rise in interest rates
   d. An increase in corporate profits
   e. A decline in investment opportunities
   f. Permission for corporations to deduct dividends for tax purposes as they now do interest charges
   g. A change in the Tax Code so that both realized and unrealized capital gains in any year were taxed at the same rate as dividends

(14-3) What is the difference between a stock dividend and a stock split? As a stockholder, would you prefer to see your company declare a 100% stock dividend or a 2-for-1 split? Assume that either action is feasible.

(14-4) One position expressed in the financial literature is that firms set their dividends as a residual after using income to support new investments. Explain what a residual policy implies (assuming that all distributions are in the form of dividends), illustrating your answer with a table showing how different investment opportunities could lead to different dividend payout ratios.

(14-5) Indicate whether the following statements are true or false. If the statement is false, explain why.
   a. If a firm repurchases its stock in the open market, the shareholders who tender the stock are subject to capital gains taxes.
   b. If you own 100 shares in a company's stock and the company's stock splits 2-for-1, then you will own 200 shares in the company following the split.
   c. Some dividend reinvestment plans increase the amount of equity capital available to the firm.
   d. The Tax Code encourages companies to pay a large percentage of their net income in the form of dividends.
   e. A company that has established a clientele of investors who prefer large dividends is unlikely to adopt a residual dividend policy.
   f. If a firm follows a residual dividend policy then, holding all else constant, its dividend payout will tend to rise whenever the firm's investment opportunities improve.

SELF-TEST PROBLEMS SOLUTIONS SHOWN IN APPENDIX A

(ST-1)
Residual Dividend

Components Manufacturing Corporation (CMC) has 1 million shares of stock outstanding. CMC has a target capital structure with 60% equity and 40% debt. The company projects net income of $5 million and investment projects requiring $6 million in the upcoming year.

    a. CMC uses the residual distribution model and pays all distributions in the form of dividends. What is the projected DPS?

    b. What is the projected payout ratio?

(ST-2)
Repurchase or
Dividend

Burns & Kennedy Corporation (BK) has a value of operations equal to $2,100, short-term investments of $100, debt of $200, and 100 shares of stock.

    a. What is BK's estimated intrinsic stock price?

    b. If BK converts its short-term investments to cash and pays a total of $100 in dividends, what is the resulting estimated intrinsic stock price?

    c. If BK converts its short-term investments to cash and repurchases $100 of its stock, what is the resulting estimated intrinsic stock price and how many shares remain outstanding?

PROBLEMS ANSWERS ARE IN APPENDIX B

EASY PROBLEMS 1–5

(14-1)
Residual
Distribution
Model

Puckett Products is planning for $5 million in capital expenditures next year. Puckett's target capital structure consists of 60% debt and 40% equity. If net income next year is $3 million and Puckett follows a residual distribution policy with all distributions as dividends, what will be its dividend payout ratio?

(14-2)
Residual
Distribution
Policy

Petersen Company has a capital budget of $1.2 million. The company wants to maintain a target capital structure that is 60% debt and 40% equity. The company forecasts that its net income this year will be $600,000. If the company follows a residual distribution model and pays all distributions as dividends, what will be its payout ratio?

(14-3)
Dividend Payout

The Wei Corporation expects next year's net income to be $15 million. The firm is currently financed with 40% debt. Wei has $12 million of profitable investment opportunities, and it wishes to maintain its existing debt ratio. According to the residual distribution model (assuming all payments are in the form of dividends), how large should Wei's dividend payout ratio be next year?

(14-4)
Stock Repurchase

A firm has 10 million shares outstanding with a market price of $20 per share. The firm has $25 million in extra cash (short-term investments) that it plans to use in a stock repurchase; the firm has no other financial investments or any debt. What is the firm's value of operations, and how many shares will remain after the repurchase?

(14-5)
Stock Split

JPix management is considering a stock split. JPix currently sells for $120 per share and a 3-for-2 stock split is contemplated. What will be the company's stock price following the stock split, assuming that the split has no effect on the total market value of JPix's equity?

INTERMEDIATE PROBLEMS 6–9

(14-6)
External Equity
Financing

Gardial GreenLights, a manufacturer of energy-efficient lighting solutions, has had such success with its new products that it is planning to substantially expand its manufacturing capacity with a $15 million investment in new machinery. Gardial plans to maintain its current 30% debt-to-total-assets ratio for its capital structure and to maintain its dividend policy in which at the end of each year it distributes 55% of the year's net income. This year's net income was $8 million. How much external equity must Gardial seek now to expand as planned?

(14-7)
Stock Split

Suppose you own 2,000 common shares of Laurence Incorporated. The EPS is $10.00, the DPS is $3.00, and the stock sells for $80 per share. Laurence announces a 2-for-1 split. Immediately after the split, how many shares will you have, what will the adjusted EPS and DPS be, and what would you expect the stock price to be?

(14-8)
Stock Split

Fauver Enterprises declared a 3-for-1 stock split last year, and this year its dividend is $1.50 per share. This total dividend payout represents a 6% increase over last year's pre-split total dividend payout. What was last year's dividend per share?

(14-9)
Residual
Distribution
Policy

Harris Company must set its investment and dividend policies for the coming year. It has three independent projects from which to choose, each of which requires a $3 million investment. These projects have different levels of risk, and therefore different costs of capital. Their projected IRRs and costs of capital are as follows:

Project A:	Cost of capital = 17%;	IRR = 20%
Project B:	Cost of capital = 13%;	IRR = 10%
Project C:	Cost of capital = 7%;	IRR = 9%

Harris intends to maintain its 35% debt and 65% common equity capital structure, and its net income is expected to be $4,750,000. If Harris maintains its residual dividend policy (with all distributions in the form of dividends), what will its payout ratio be?

CHALLENGING PROBLEMS 10–12

(14-10)
Alternative
Dividend Policies

Boehm Corporation has had stable earnings growth of 8% a year for the past 10 years, and in 2019 Boehm paid dividends of $4 million on net income of $10 million. However, net income is expected to grow by 28% in 2020, and Boehm plans to invest $7.5 million in a plant expansion. This one-time unusual earnings growth won't be maintained, though, and after 2020 Boehm will return to its previous 8% earnings growth rate. Its target debt ratio is 34%. Boehm has 1 million shares of stock.

a. Calculate Boehm's dividends per share for 2020 under each of the following policies:
   (1) Its 2020 dividend payment is set to force dividends to grow at the long-run growth rate in earnings.
   (2) It continues the 2019 dividend payout ratio.
   (3) It uses a pure residual policy with all distributions in the form of dividends (34% of the $7.5 million investment is financed with debt).
   (4) It employs a regular-dividend-plus-extras policy, with the regular dividend being based on the long-run growth rate and the extra dividend being set according to the residual policy.

b. Which of the preceding policies would you recommend? Restrict your choices to the ones listed, but justify your answer.

(14-11)
Residual
Distribution
Model

Kendra Brown is analyzing the capital requirements for Reynold Corporation for next year. Kendra forecasts that Reynold will need $15 million to fund all of its positive-NPV projects and her job is to determine how to raise the money. Reynold's net income is $11 million, and it has paid a $2 dividend per share (DPS) for the past several years (1 million shares of common stock are outstanding); its shareholders expect the dividend to remain constant for the next several years. The company's target capital structure is 30% debt and 70% equity.

a. Suppose Reynold follows the residual model and makes all distributions as dividends. How much retained earnings will it need to fund its capital budget?

b. If Reynold follows the residual model with all distributions in the form of dividends, what will be its dividend per share and payout ratio for the upcoming year?

c. If Reynold maintains its current $2 DPS for next year, how much retained earnings will be available for the firm's capital budget?

d. Can Reynold maintain its current capital structure, maintain its current dividend per share, and maintain a $15 million capital budget *without* having to raise new common stock? Why or why not?

e. Suppose management is firmly opposed to cutting the dividend; that is, it wishes to maintain the $2 dividend for the next year. Suppose also that the company is committed to funding all profitable projects and is willing to issue more debt (along with the available retained earnings) to help finance the company's capital budget. Assume the resulting change in capital structure has a minimal impact on the company's composite cost of capital, so that the capital budget remains at $15 million. What portion of this year's capital budget would have to be financed with debt?

f. Suppose once again that management wants to maintain the $2 DPS. In addition, the company wants to maintain its target capital structure (30% debt, 70% equity) and its $15 million capital budget. What is the minimum dollar amount of new common stock the company would have to issue in order to meet all of its objectives?

g. Now consider the case in which management wants to maintain the $2 DPS and its target capital structure but also wants to avoid issuing new common stock. The company is willing to cut its capital budget in order to meet its other objectives. Assuming the company's projects are divisible, what will be the company's capital budget for the next year?

h. If a firm follows the residual distribution policy, what actions can it take when its forecasted retained earnings are less than the retained earnings required to fund its capital budget?

(14-12)
Stock Repurchase
Bayani Bakery's most recent FCF was $48 million; the FCF is expected to grow at a constant rate of 6%. The firm's WACC is 12%, and it has 15 million shares of common stock outstanding. The firm has $30 million in short-term investments, which it plans to liquidate and distribute to common shareholders via a stock repurchase; the firm has no other nonoperating assets. It has $368 million in debt and $60 million in preferred stock.

a. What is the value of operations?

b. Immediately prior to the repurchase, what is the intrinsic value of equity?

c. Immediately prior to the repurchase, what is the intrinsic stock price?

d. How many shares will be repurchased? How many shares will remain after the repurchase?

e. Immediately after the repurchase, what is the intrinsic value of equity? The intrinsic stock price?

SPREADSHEET PROBLEMS

(14-13)
Build a Model:
Distributions
as Dividends or
Repurchases

resource

Start with the partial model in the file *Ch14 P13 Build a Model.xlsx* on the textbook's Web site. J. Clark Inc. (JCI), a manufacturer and distributor of sports equipment, has grown until it has become a stable, mature company. Now JCI is planning its first distribution to shareholders. (See the file for the most recent year's financial statements and projections for the next year, 2020; JCI's fiscal year ends on June 30.) JCI plans to liquidate and distribute $500 million of its short-term securities on July 1, 2020, the first day of the next fiscal year, but it has not yet decided whether to distribute with dividends or with stock repurchases.

    a. Assume first that JCI distributes the $500 million as dividends. Fill in the missing values in the file's balance sheet column for July 1, 2020, which is labeled "Distribute as Dividends." (*Hint:* Be sure that the balance sheets balance after you fill in the missing items.) Assume that JCI did not have to establish an account for dividends payable prior to the distribution.

    b. Now assume that JCI distributes the $500 million through stock repurchases. Fill in the missing values in the file's balance sheet column for July 1, 2020, which is labeled "Distribute as Repurchase." (*Hint:* Be sure that the balance sheets balance after you fill in the missing items.)

    c. Calculate JCI's projected free cash flow; the tax rate is 25%.

    d. What is JCI's current intrinsic stock price (the price on 6/30/2019)? What is the projected intrinsic stock price for 6/30/2020?

    e. What is the projected intrinsic stock price on 7/1/2020 if JCI distributes the cash as dividends?

    f. What is the projected intrinsic stock price on 7/1/2020 if JCI distributes the cash through stock repurchases? How many shares will remain outstanding after the repurchase?

MINI CASE

Integrated Waveguide Technologies (IWT) is a 6-year-old company founded by Hunt Jackson and David Smithfield to exploit metamaterial plasmonic technology to develop and manufacture miniature microwave frequency directional transmitters and receivers for use in mobile Internet and communications applications. IWT's technology, although highly advanced, is relatively inexpensive to implement, and its patented manufacturing techniques require little capital as compared to many electronics fabrication ventures. Because of the low capital requirement, Jackson and Smithfield have been able to avoid issuing new stock and thus own all of the shares. Because of the explosion in demand for its mobile Internet applications, IWT must now access outside equity capital to fund its growth, and Jackson and Smithfield have decided to take the company public. Until now, Jackson and Smithfield have paid themselves reasonable salaries but routinely reinvested all after-tax earnings in the firm, so dividend policy has not been an issue. However, before talking with potential outside investors, they must decide on a dividend policy.

Your new boss at the consulting firm Flick and Associates, which has been retained to help IWT prepare for its public offering, has asked you to make a presentation to Jackson and Smithfield in which you review the theory of dividend policy and discuss the following issues.

    a. (1) What is meant by the term "distribution policy"? How has the mix of dividend payouts and stock repurchases changed over time?

       (2) The terms "irrelevance," "dividend preference" (or "bird-in-the-hand"), and "tax effect" have been used to describe three major theories regarding the way dividend payouts affect a firm's value. Explain these terms, and briefly describe each theory.

       (3) What do the three theories indicate regarding the actions management should take with respect to dividend payouts?

       (4) What results have empirical studies of the dividend theories produced? How does all this affect what we can tell managers about dividend payouts?

b. Discuss the effects on distribution policy consistent with: (1) the signaling hypothesis (also called the information content hypothesis) and (2) the clientele effect.

c. (1) Assume that IWT has completed its IPO and has a $112.5 million capital budget planned for the coming year. You have determined that its present capital structure (80% equity and 20% debt) is optimal, and its net income is forecasted at $140 million. Use the residual distribution approach to determine IWT's total dollar distribution. Assume for now that the distribution is in the form of a dividend. Suppose IWT has 100 million shares of stock outstanding. What is the forecasted dividend payout ratio? What is the forecasted dividend per share? What would happen to the payout ratio and DPS if net income were forecasted to decrease to $90 million? To increase to $160 million?

(2) In general terms, how would a change in investment opportunities affect the payout ratio under the residual distribution policy?

(3) What are the advantages and disadvantages of the residual policy? (*Hint:* Don't neglect signaling and clientele effects.)

d. (1) Describe the procedures a company follows when it makes a distribution through dividend payments.

(2) What is a stock repurchase? Describe the procedures a company follows when it makes a distribution through a stock repurchase.

e. Discuss the advantages and disadvantages of a firm repurchasing its own shares.

f. Suppose IWT has decided to distribute $50 million, which it presently is holding in liquid short-term investments. IWT's value of operations is estimated to be about $1,937.5 million; it has $387.5 million in debt and zero preferred stock. As mentioned previously, IWT has 100 million shares of stock outstanding.

(1) Assume that IWT has not yet made the distribution. What is IWT's intrinsic value of equity? What is its intrinsic stock price per share?

(2) Now suppose that IWT has just made the $50 million distribution in the form of dividends. What is IWT's intrinsic value of equity? What is its intrinsic stock price per share?

(3) Suppose instead that IWT has just made the $50 million distribution in the form of a stock repurchase. Now what is IWT's intrinsic value of equity? How many shares did IWT repurchase? How many shares remained outstanding after the repurchase? What is its intrinsic stock price per share after the repurchase?

g. Describe the series of steps that most firms take when setting dividend policy.

h. What are stock splits and stock dividends? What are the advantages and disadvantages of each?

i. What is a dividend reinvestment plan (DRIP), and how does it work?

SELECTED ADDITIONAL CASES

The following cases from CengageCompose cover many of the concepts discussed in this chapter and are available at **http://compose.cengage.com**.

Klein-Brigham Series:
Case 19, "Georgia Atlantic Company"; Case 20, "Bessemer Steel Products, Inc."; Case 47, "Floral Fragrance, Inc."; and Case 80, "The Western Company."

Brigham-Buzzard Series:
Case 9, "Powerline Network Corporation (Dividend Policy)."

CHAPTER 15

Capital Structure Decisions

A bankruptcy and a liquidity crisis are very different. An *economic* bankruptcy means that the intrinsic value of a company's assets (which is determined by the cash flows those assets are expected to produce) is less than the amount owed to creditors. A *legal* bankruptcy occurs when a company files in bankruptcy court for protection from its creditors until it can arrange an orderly reorganization or liquidation. A *liquidity crisis* occurs when a company doesn't have access to enough cash to make payments to creditors as the payments come due in the near future. In normal times, a strong company (one whose market value of assets far exceeds the amount owed to creditors) can usually borrow money in the short-term credit markets to meet any urgent liquidity needs. Thus, a liquidity crisis usually doesn't trigger a bankruptcy.

However, 2008 and 2009 were anything but usual. Many companies had loaded up on debt during the boom years prior to 2007, and much of that was short-term debt. When the mortgage crisis began in late 2007 and spread like wildfire through the financial sector, many financial institutions virtually stopped providing short-term credit as they tried to stave off their own bankruptcies. As a result, many nonfinancial companies faced liquidity crises. Even worse, consumer demand began to drop and investors' risk aversion began to rise, leading to falling market values of assets and triggering economic and legal bankruptcy for many companies.

The economic crisis drove many companies into bankruptcy, including Lehman Brothers, Washington Mutual, General Motors, Chrysler, Pilgrim's Pride, and Circuit City. Many other companies scrambled to reduce their liquidity problems. For example, Black & Decker (B&D) issued about $350 million in 5-year notes and used the proceeds to pay off some of its commercial paper. Even though the interest rate on Black & Decker's 5-year notes was higher than the rates on its commercial paper, B&D did not have to repay the note for five years, whereas it had to refinance the commercial paper each time it came due.

As you read the chapter, think of these companies that suffered or failed because they mismanaged their capital structure decisions.

Sources: See **www.bankruptcydata.com** and the Black & Decker press release of April 23, 2009.

Corporate Valuation and Capital Structure

A firm's financing choices obviously have a direct effect on the weighted average cost of capital (WACC). Financing choices also have an indirect effect on the costs of debt and equity because they change the risk and required returns of debt and equity. Financing choices can also affect free cash flows if the probability of bankruptcy becomes high. This chapter focuses on the debt–equity choice and its effect on value.

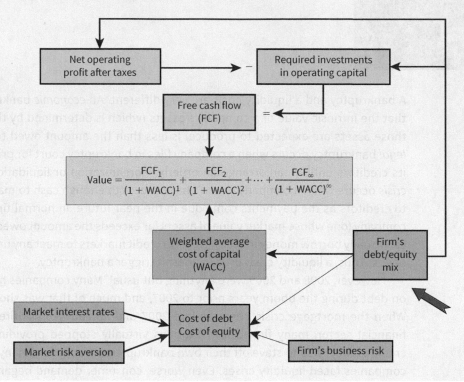

resource

The textbook's Web site contains an Excel file that will guide you through the chapter's calculations. The file for this chapter is Ch15 Tool Kit.xlsx, and we encourage you to open the file and follow along as you read the chapter.

As explained in Chapters 12 and 13, growth in sales requires growth in operating capital, and this often requires that external funds be raised through a combination of equity and debt. The firm's mixture of debt and equity is called its **capital structure**. Although actual levels of debt and equity may vary somewhat over time, most firms try to keep their financing mix close to a **target capital structure**. A firm's **capital structure decision** includes its choice of a target capital structure, the average maturity of its debt, and the specific types of financing it decides to use at any particular time. As with operating decisions, managers should make capital structure decisions that are designed to maximize the firm's intrinsic value.

15-1 An Overview of Capital Structure

The value of a firm's operations is the present value of its expected future free cash flows (FCFs) discounted at its weighted average cost of capital (WACC):

$$V_{op} = \sum_{t=1}^{\infty} \frac{FCF_t}{(1 + WACC)^t}$$

(15-1)

The WACC of a firm financed only by debt and common stock depends on the percentages of debt and common stock (w_d and w_s), the cost of debt (r_d), the cost of stock (r_s), and the corporate tax rate (T):

$$WACC = w_d(1 - T)r_d + w_s r_s$$

(15-2)

As these equations show, the only way any decision can change the value of operations is by changing either expected free cash flows or the cost of capital. As you read the chapter, think about the ways the capital structure choices can affect FCF or the WACC.

Table 15-1 shows that the average long-term debt-to-equity ratio diverges widely for different business sectors, ranging from 7% in Non-Cyclical Goods and Services to 107% in Utilities. However, sub-sector industries within a sector also have a wide dispersion of ratios. For example, the Cyclical Consumer Goods and Services sector's average is 38%, but two of its sub-sectors are *Hotels, Motels & Cruise Lines* and *Apparel and Accessories (A&A)*, which have average ratios of 55% and 19%, respectively. Companies within a sub-sector also have considerable variation: Foot Locker Inc. and Tiffany & Co. are in the *A&A* sub-sector, but Tiffany has a 27% ratio while Foot Locker has a 5% ratio. Why do we see such variation across companies and business sectors? Can a company make itself more valuable through its choice of debt ratio? We address these questions in the rest of this chapter, beginning with a description of business risk and financial risk.

SELF-TEST

What are some ways in which the capital structure decisions can affect the value of operations?

TABLE 15-1
Long-Term Debt-to-Equity Ratios for Business Sectors, Selected Sub-Sectors, and Selected Firms

Name of Sector	Long-Term Debt-to-Equity Ratio		
	Company	Sub-Sector	Sector
Cyclical Consumer Goods and Services			38%
Selected Sub-Sectors in Cyclical Consumer Goods:			
Hotels, Motels & Cruise Lines		55%	
Apparel and Accessories Retailers (A&A):		19%	
Selected Companies in A&A			
Foot Locker (FL)	5%		
Tiffany & Co. (TIF)	27%		
Utilities			107%
Industrials			86%
Telecommunications Services			74%
Financials			33%
Energy			31%
Materials			24%
Health Care			13%
Technology			9%
Non-Cyclical Goods and Services			7%

Source: For updates on a company's ratio, go to **www.reuters.com** and enter the ticker symbol for a stock quote. Click the Financials tab for updates on company and sector ratios.

15-2 Business Risk and Financial Risk

Business risk and financial risk combine to determine the total risk of a firm's future return on equity, as we explain in the next sections.

15-2a Business Risk and Operating Leverage

Business risk is the risk a firm's common stockholders would face if the firm had no debt. In other words, it is the risk inherent in the firm's operations, which arises from uncertainty about future operating profits and capital requirements.

Business risk depends on a number of factors, beginning with variability in product demand and production costs. If a high percentage of a firm's costs are fixed and hence do not decline when demand falls, then the firm has high *operating leverage,* which increases its business risk.

A high degree of **operating leverage** implies that a relatively small change in sales results in a relatively large change in earnings before interest and taxes (EBIT), net operating profits after taxes (NOPAT), return on invested capital (ROIC), return on assets (ROA), and return on equity (ROE). Other things held constant, the higher a firm's fixed costs, the greater its operating leverage. Higher fixed costs are generally associated with (1) highly automated, capital-intensive firms; (2) businesses that employ highly skilled workers who must be retained and paid even when sales are low; and (3) firms with high product development costs that must be maintained to complete ongoing R&D projects.

To illustrate the relative impact of fixed versus variable costs, consider Garcia Technology, a manufacturer of components used in scientific instruments. Garcia is considering several different operating technologies and several different financing alternatives. We will analyze its financing choices in the next section, but for now we will focus on its operating plans.

Garcia is comparing two plans, each requiring a capital investment of $200 million; assume for now that Garcia will finance its choice entirely with equity. Each plan is expected to produce 110 million units (Q) per year at a sales price (P) of $2 per unit. As shown in Figure 15-1, Plan A's technology requires a smaller annual fixed cost (F) than Plan U's, but Plan A has higher variable costs (V). (We denote the second plan with U because it has no financial leverage, and we denote the third plan with L because it does have financial leverage; Plan L is discussed in the next section.) Figure 15-1 also shows the projected income statements and selected performance measures for the first year. Notice that Plan U's performance measures are superior to Plan A's if the expected sales occur.

The projections in Figure 15-1 are based on the 100 million units expected to be sold. But what if demand is lower than expected? It often is useful to know how far sales can fall before operating profits become negative. The **operating break-even point** occurs when earnings before interest and taxes (EBIT) equal zero:[1]

$$EBIT = PQ - VQ - F = 0 \qquad \text{(15-3)}$$

---

[1]This definition of the break-even point does not include any fixed financial costs because it focuses on operating profits. We could also examine net income, in which case a firm with debt would have negative net income even at the operating break-even point. We introduce financial costs shortly.

FIGURE 15-1

Illustration of Operating and Financial Leverage (Millions of Dollars and Millions of Units, Except Per Unit Data)

	A	B	C	D	E
			Plan A	Plan U	Plan L
14	*1. Input Data*				
15	Required operating current assets		$3	$3	$3
16	Required long-term assets		$199	$199	$199
17	Total assets		$202	$202	$202
18	Resulting operating current liabilities		$2	$2	$2
19	Required capital (TA – Op. CL)		$200	$200	$200
20	Book equity		$200	$200	$150
21	Debt		$0	$0	$50
22	Interest rate		8%	8%	8%
23	Sales price (P)		$2.00	$2.00	$2.00
24	Tax rate (T)		25%	25%	25%
25	Expected units sold (Q)		100	100	100
26	Fixed costs (F)		$20	$60	$60
27	Variable costs (V)		$1.50	$1.00	$1.00
28	*2. Income Statements*		Plan A	Plan U	Plan L
29	Sales revenue (P x Q)		$200.0	$200.0	$200.0
30	Fixed costs		20.0	60.0	60.0
31	Variable costs (V x Q)		150.0	100.0	100.0
32	EBIT		$30.0	$40.0	$40.0
33	Interest		0.0	0.0	4.0
34	Pre-tax earnings		$30.0	$40.0	$36.0
35	Tax		7.5	10.0	9.0
36	Net income		$22.5	$30.0	$27.0
37	*3. Key Performance Measures*		Plan A	Plan U	Plan L
38	NOPAT = EBIT(1 – T)		$22.5	$30.0	$30.0
39	ROIC = NOPAT/Capital		11.3%	15.0%	15.0%
40	ROA = NI/Total assets		11.1%	14.9%	13.4%
41	ROE = NI/Equity		11.3%	15.0%	18.0%

Source: See the file *Ch15 Tool Kit.xlsx*. Numbers are reported as rounded values for clarity but are calculated using *Excel*'s full precision. Thus, intermediate calculations using the figure's rounded values will be inexact.

Note:

ROA is not exactly equal to ROE for Plan L or Plan U because total assets are not quite equal to equity for these plans. This is because the operating current liabilities, such as accounts payable and accruals, reduce the required equity capital investment.

If we solve for the break-even quantity, Q_{BE}, we get this expression:

$$Q_{BE} = \frac{F}{P - V}$$

(15-4)

The break-even quantities for Plans A and U are:

$$\text{Plan A: } Q_{BE} = \frac{\$20 \text{ million}}{\$2.00 - \$1.50} = 40 \text{ million units}$$

$$\text{Plan U: } Q_{BE} = \frac{\$60 \text{ million}}{\$2.00 - \$1.00} = 60 \text{ million units}$$

Plan A will be profitable if unit sales are above 40 million, whereas Plan U requires sales of 60 million units before it is profitable. This difference occurs because Plan U

FIGURE 15-2
Operating Leverage and Financial Leverage

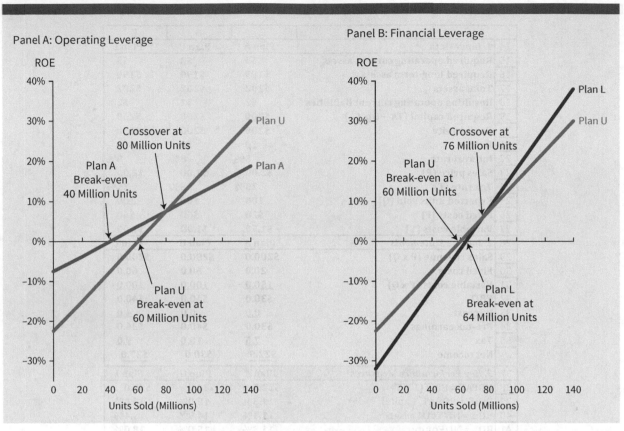

has higher fixed costs, so more units must be sold to cover these fixed costs. Panel A of Figure 15-2 illustrates the operating profitability of these two plans for different levels of unit sales. Because these companies have no debt, the return on assets and the return on equity measure operating profitability; we report ROE instead of ROA to facilitate comparisons when we discuss financial risk in the next section.

Suppose sales are at 80 million units. In this case, the ROE is identical for each plan. As unit sales begin to climb above 80 million, both plans increase in profitability, but ROE increases more for Plan U than for Plan A. If sales fall below 80 million, then both plans become less profitable, but ROE decreases more for Plan U than for Plan A. This illustrates that the combination of higher fixed costs and lower variable costs of Plan U magnifies its gain or loss relative to Plan A. In other words, because Plan U has higher operating leverage, it also has greater business risk.

15-2b Financial Risk and Financial Leverage

Financial risk is the additional risk placed on the common stockholders as a result of the decision to finance with debt.[2] Conceptually, stockholders face a certain amount of risk that is inherent in a firm's operations—this is its business risk, which is defined as the uncertainty in projections of future EBIT, NOPAT, and ROIC. If a firm uses debt (financial leverage),

---

[2]Preferred stock also adds to financial risk. To simplify matters, we examine only debt and common equity in this chapter.

then the business risk is concentrated on the common stockholders. To illustrate, suppose 10 people decide to form a corporation to manufacture flash memory drives. There is a certain amount of business risk in the operation. If the firm is capitalized only with common equity and if each person buys 10% of the stock, then each investor shares equally in the business risk. However, suppose the firm is capitalized with 50% debt and 50% equity, with five of the investors putting up their money by purchasing debt issued by the company and the other five putting up their money by purchasing equity. In this case, the five debtholders are paid before the five stockholders, so *virtually all* of the business risk is borne by the stockholders. Thus, the use of debt, or **financial leverage**, concentrates business risk on stockholders.[3]

To illustrate the impact of financial risk, we can extend the Garcia Electronics example. Garcia initially decided to use the technology of Plan U, which is unlevered (financed with all equity), but now it's considering financing the technology with $150 million of equity and $50 million of debt at an 8% interest rate, as shown for Plan L in Figure 15-1 (recall that L denotes leverage). Figure 15-1 also shows that Plan L's NOPAT and ROIC are identical to those of Plan U—financing choices don't affect operations. However, Plan L has lower net income ($27 versus $30) because it must pay interest. Despite the lower net income, Plan L has a higher ROE (18% versus 15%) because the net income is shared by a smaller equity base.

But there is more to the story than just a higher ROE with financial leverage. Just as operating leverage adds risk, so does financial leverage. We used the Data Table feature in the file **Ch15 Tool Kit.xlsx** to generate performance measures for plans U and L at different levels of unit sales. Panel B of Figure 15-2 shows the ROE of Plans U and L versus quantity sold.

When 76 million units are sold, the crossover point in Panel B of Figure 15-2 has an ROE of 6%. Note this ROE is equal to the 6% ROIC of each plan and also is equal to the 6% after-tax cost of debt: 8%(1 − 0.25) = 6%. To see why this is so, notice that Plan L's capital providers are debtholders and stockholders, each receiving a 6% after-tax return. Plan U's capital providers are all stockholders and they, too, receive a 6% return. What happens if unit sales increase such that each plan has an 8% ROIC? Plan U's stockholders receive this 8% return. Plan L's debtholders receive only 6% even though the capital they provided earned 8%. The difference in the amount the debtholder's capital earns and the amount debtholders receive accrues to the stockholders, boosting their ROE.

What happens if sales fall below 76 million units, causing the each plan's ROIC to fall to 4%? Plan L's debtholders still receive a 6% after-tax return on the capital they provided even though the capital is earning only 4%. This difference must come from earnings on capital provided by stockholders, which drives down ROE. Thus, financial leverage magnifies the ROE for good or ill, increasing the risk born by shareholders in a levered firm.

We see, then, that using leverage has both good and bad effects: If expected ROIC is greater than the after-tax cost of debt, then higher leverage increases expected ROE but also increases risk.

SELF-TEST

What is business risk, and how can it be measured?

What are some determinants of business risk?

How does operating leverage affect business risk?

What is financial risk, and how does it arise?

Explain this statement: "Using leverage has both good and bad effects."

A firm has fixed operating costs of $100,000 and variable costs of $4 per unit. If it sells the product for $6 per unit, what is the break-even quantity? **(50,000)**

---

[3]Holders of corporate debt generally do bear some business risk, because they may lose some of their investment if the firm goes bankrupt. We discuss this in more depth later in the chapter.

15-3 Capital Structure Theory: The Modigliani and Miller Models

In the previous section, we showed how capital structure choices affect a firm's ROE and its risk. For a number of reasons, we would expect capital structures to vary considerably across industries. For example, pharmaceutical companies generally have very different capital structures than airline companies. Moreover, capital structures vary among firms within a given industry. What factors explain these differences? In an attempt to answer this question, academics and practitioners have developed a number of theories, and the theories have been subjected to many empirical tests. We discuss theories and empirical evidence in the following sections, beginning with the work of Professors Franco Modigliani and Merton Miller.[4]

15-3a Modigliani and Miller: No Taxes

Modern capital structure theory began in 1958, when Modigliani and Miller (hereafter, MM) published what has been called the most influential finance article ever written.[5] MM's study was based on some strong assumptions, which included the following:

1. There are no brokerage costs.
2. There are no taxes.
3. There are no bankruptcy costs.
4. Investors can borrow at the same rate as corporations.
5. All investors have the same information as management about the firm's future investment opportunities.
6. Earnings before interest and taxes (EBIT) do not grow and are not affected by the use of debt.

Modigliani and Miller imagined two hypothetical portfolios. The first contains all the equity of an unlevered firm, so the portfolio's value is V_U, **the value of an unlevered firm**. Because the firm has no growth (which means it does not need to invest in any new net assets) and because it pays no taxes, the firm can pay out all of its EBIT in the form of dividends. Therefore, the cash flow from owning this first portfolio is equal to EBIT.

Now consider a second firm that is identical to the unlevered firm *except* that it is partially financed with debt. The second portfolio contains all of the **levered firm's stock (S_L)** and debt (D), so the portfolio's value is V_L, **the total value of the levered firm**. If the interest rate is r_d, then the levered firm pays out interest in the amount r_dD. Because the firm is not growing and pays no taxes, it can pay out dividends in the amount EBIT $- r_dD$. If you owned all of the firm's debt and equity, your cash flow would be equal to the sum of the interest and dividends: $r_dD + (EBIT - r_dD) = EBIT$. Therefore, the cash flow from owning this second portfolio is equal to EBIT.

---

[4]For additional discussion of capital structure theories, see John C. Easterwood and Palani-Rajan Kadapakkam, "The Role of Private and Public Debt in Corporate Capital Structures," *Financial Management,* Autumn 1991, pp. 49–57; Gerald T. Garvey, "Leveraging the Underinvestment Problem: How High Debt and Management Shareholdings Solve the Agency Costs of Free Cash Flow," *Journal of Financial Research,* Summer 1992, pp. 149–166; Milton Harris and Artur Raviv, "Capital Structure and the Informational Role of Debt," *Journal of Finance,* June 1990, pp. 321–349; and Ronen Israel, "Capital Structure and the Market for Corporate Control: The Defensive Role of Debt Financing," *Journal of Finance,* September 1991, pp. 1391–1409.

[5]Franco Modigliani and Merton H. Miller, "The Cost of Capital, Corporation Finance, and the Theory of Investment," *American Economic Review,* June 1958, pp. 261–297. Modigliani and Miller each won a Nobel Prize for their work.

Notice that the cash flow of each portfolio is equal to EBIT. Thus, MM concluded that two portfolios producing the same cash flows must have the same value:[6]

$$V_L = V_U = S_L + D \tag{15-5}$$

Given their assumptions, MM proved that a firm's value is unaffected by its capital structure.[7] This result is often called the **MM Proposition I** without taxes.

MM assumed that debt doesn't affect EBIT, and they proved that debt doesn't affect value. Therefore, debt doesn't affect the weighted average cost of capital (WACC). Recall that the WACC is a combination of the cost of debt and the relatively higher cost of equity, r_s. As leverage increases, more weight is given to low-cost debt, but equity becomes riskier, which drives up r_s by exactly enough to keep the WACC constant.

MM showed that a constant WACC implies that the cost of equity to a levered firm, r_{sL}, is equal to:

$$r_{sL} = r_{sU} + (r_{sU} - r_d)(D/E) \tag{15-6}$$

Here r_{sU} **(unlevered cost of equity)** is the cost of equity to an otherwise identical but unlevered firm, D is the market value of debt, S is the market value of equity, and r_d is the cost of debt (which is assumed to be constant for all degrees of leverage). Equation 15-6 is called the **MM Proposition II** without taxes.

Taken together, the two MM propositions imply that using more debt in the capital structure will not increase the value of the firm, because the benefits of cheaper debt will be exactly offset by an increase in the riskiness of the equity and hence in its cost. Thus, MM argued that, *in a world without taxes, both the value of a firm and its WACC would be unaffected by its capital structure.*

Even though some of their assumptions are obviously unrealistic, MM's irrelevance result is extremely important. By indicating the conditions under which capital structure is irrelevant, MM also provided us with clues about what is required for capital structure to be relevant and hence to affect a firm's value. The work of MM marked the beginning of modern capital structure research, and subsequent research has focused on relaxing the MM assumptions in order to develop a more realistic theory of capital structure.

Modigliani and Miller's thought process was just as important as their conclusion. It seems simple now, but their idea that two portfolios with identical cash flows must also have identical values changed the entire financial world because it led to the development of options and derivatives. It is no surprise that Modigliani and Miller received Nobel awards for their work.

---

[6]They actually showed that if the values of the two portfolios differed, then an investor could engage in riskless arbitrage: The investor could create a trading strategy (buying one portfolio and selling the other short) that had no risk, required none of the investor's own cash, and resulted in a positive cash flow for the investor. This would be such a desirable strategy that everyone would try to implement it. But if everyone tries to buy the same portfolio, its price will be driven up by market demand, and if everyone tries to short sell a portfolio, its price will be driven down. The net result of the trading activity would be to change the portfolios' values until they were equal and no more arbitrage was possible.

[7]See **Web Extension 15A** for a more formal derivation of this result and for derivations of the other MM and Miller models.

15-3b Modigliani and Miller: The Effect of Corporate Taxes

In 1963, MM published a follow-up paper in which they relaxed the assumption that there are no corporate taxes.[8] The Tax Code allows corporations to deduct interest payments as an expense, but dividend payments to stockholders are not deductible. The differential treatment encourages corporations to use debt in their capital structures. This means that interest payments reduce the taxes a corporation pays, and if a corporation pays less to the government, then more of its cash flow is available for investors. In other words, the tax deductibility of the interest payments shields the firm's pre-tax income.

To illustrate, look at Figure 15-1 and see that Plan U (with no debt) pays taxes of $10, but Plan L (with leverage) pays taxes of only $9. What happens to the difference of $1 = $10 − $9? This extra amount is paid out to investors! Notice that Plan U has $30 of net income for shareholders. However, Plan L has $4 of interest for debtholders and $27 of net income for shareholders, a combined total of $31, which is exactly $1 more than Plan U. With more cash flows available for investors, a levered firm's total value should be greater than that of an unlevered firm, and this is what MM showed.

As in their earlier paper, MM introduced a second important way of looking at the effect of capital structure: The value of a levered firm is the value of an otherwise identical unlevered firm plus the value of any "side effects." While others have expanded on this idea by considering other side effects, MM focused on the **tax savings due to interest** (TS_t), which are the reductions in Year-t taxes due to the tax deductibility of interest expenses. They defined the **interest tax shield** ($V_{Tax\ shield}$), often shortened to the **tax shield**, as the present value of the tax savings due to interest when discounted at the interest rate. MM expressed the value of a levered firm as:

$$
\begin{aligned}
V_L &= V_U + \text{Value of side effects} \\
&= V_U + \text{Present value of annual tax savings} \\
&= V_U + \text{Tax shield} \\
&= V_U + V_{Tax\ shield}
\end{aligned}
\tag{15-7}
$$

Yogi Berra on the MM Proposition

When a waitress asked Yogi Berra, Baseball Hall of Fame catcher for the New York Yankees, whether he wanted his pizza cut into four pieces or eight, Yogi replied: "Better make it four. I don't think I can eat eight."[a]

Yogi's quip helps convey the basic insight of Modigliani and Miller. The firm's choice of leverage "slices" the distribution of future cash flows in a way that is like slicing a pizza. MM recognized that holding a company's investment activities fixed is like fixing the size of the pizza; no information costs means that everyone sees the same pizza; no taxes means the

IRS gets none of the pie; and no "contracting costs" means nothing sticks to the knife.

So, just as the substance of Yogi's meal is unaffected by whether the pizza is sliced into four pieces or eight, the economic substance of the firm is unaffected by whether the liability side of the balance sheet is sliced to include more or less debt—at least under the MM assumptions.

[a]Lee Green, *Sportswit* (New York: Fawcett Crest, 1984), p. 228.

Source: "Yogi Berra on the MM Proposition," *Journal of Applied Corporate Finance,* Winter 1995, p. 6. Stern Stewart Management.

---

[8]Franco Modigliani and Merton H. Miller, "Corporate Income Taxes and the Cost of Capital: A Correction," *American Economic Review,* June 1963, pp. 433–443.

Under their assumptions, they showed that the tax shield is equal to the corporate tax rate, T, multiplied by the amount of debt, D:

$$V_L = V_U + TD \qquad (15\text{-}8)$$

This is the MM Proposition I with corporate taxes. Before the 2017 TCJA, the combined federal plus state tax rate was about 40%. This implied that every dollar of debt added about 40 cents of value to the firm and that the optimal capital structure was virtually 100% debt.

The TCJA's federal-plus-state tax rate now is about 25%, which reduces the value added per dollar of debt from 40 cents to 25 cents, a reduction of 37.5%: ($0.40 − $0.25)/40% = 0.375.

Recall from Chapter 2 that there is now a limit on the amount of interest expense that can be deducted each year (30% of EBITDA for 2018–2021 and 30% of EBIT for subsequent years), with any excess being carried forward to future tax years. Using the MM assumptions (r_d is the correct discount rate for tax shields and g = 0) and reasonable values of interest rates (r_{su} = 12% and r_d = 8%), a company can deduct all its interest expenses in a single year only for capital structures containing less than 52% debt.[9] If w_d exceeds this threshold, then the excess interest expenses may be carried forward to offset future taxes. If EBIT remains low, then a company might never get to use past excess interest expenses. We will have more to say about this in the following sections.

Using Equation 15-8, MM also showed that the WACC falls as debt is added. This is because the cost of equity, r_s, doesn't increase quite as fast as it would if there were no taxes. Equation 15-9 is a version of Proposition II with corporate taxes included:

$$r_{sL} = r_{sU} + (r_{sU} − r_d)(1 − T)(D/S) \qquad (15\text{-}9)$$

As we explained previously, the limit on interest expense deductibility begins with w_d = 52%. This means that if D/S in Equation 15-9 exceeds 1.09, then additional debt does not provide any additional tax shields in the current year.

15-3c Miller: The Effect of Corporate and Personal Taxes

Merton Miller (this time without Modigliani) later brought in the effects of personal taxes.[10] The income from bonds is usually interest, which is taxed at personal income rates (T_d) going up to 35%, while income from stocks generally comes partly from dividends and partly from capital gains. *Web Extension 2A* provides more details regarding personal taxes on dividends and gains under the 2017 Tax Cut and Jobs Act (TCJA), but we describe the least complicated situations here and their implications for firm value.

---

[9]Using definitions and algebra, the ratio of interest expense to EBIT is:

$$\text{Int/EBIT} = [w_d(1 − T)r_d]/[\{r_{su}(1 − w_dT)]$$

Setting Int/EBIT to 0.3 and solving for w_d provides an expression for the maximum w_d that still allows the immediate deduction of interest expenses:

$$\text{Max } w_d = (0.3r_{su})/[\{(1 − T)r_d\} + (0.3r_{su}T)]$$

If r_{su} = 12%, T = 25%, and r_d = 8%, then the maximum w_d is 52%. Interest expense from additional debt will not be deductible for tax purposes in the year it occurs because Int/EBIT exceeds 30%.

[10]See Merton H. Miller, "Debt and Taxes," *Journal of Finance*, May 1977, pp. 261–275.

Instead of being taxed at the personal rate, long-term capital gains and dividends are taxed at a rate of 20% for high-income investors, most of whom also pay a 3.8% Net Investment Income Tax.

However, capital gains are not taxed until the stock is sold, whereas dividends are taxed when they are received. Also, if stock is held until the owner dies, the estate pays no capital gains tax unless the estate is worth more than $11.2 million for individual decedents.[11] The net effect is that stock returns are taxed at lower effective rates, T_s, than are interest payments.

Miller argued that investors are willing to accept relatively low *before-tax* returns on stock compared to the *before-tax* returns on bonds because the effective tax rate on stocks is lower. (The situation here is similar to that with tax-exempt municipal bonds, discussed in Chapter 5, and preferred stocks held by corporate investors, discussed in Chapter 7.) For example, if stocks and debt were taxed identically, an investor might require a 8% before-tax return on bonds and a 16% before-tax return on stock. Because stock returns have a lower effective tax rate, investors might require only a 14% pre-tax return on stock.

Thus, as Miller pointed out, the tax code has two opposite implications. First, the *corporate deductibility of interest* favors the use of debt financing. Second, the *more favorable personal tax treatment of income from stock* lowers the required rate of return on stock and thus favors the use of equity financing.

Miller showed that the net impact of corporate and personal taxes is given by this equation, which is called the **Miller model**:

$$V_L = V_U + \left[1 - \frac{(1 - T_c)(1 - T_s)}{(1 - T_d)} \right] D$$

(15-10)

Here T_c is the corporate tax rate, T_s is the effective personal tax rate on income from stocks, and T_d is the tax rate on income from debt. Miller argued that the marginal tax rates on stock and debt balance out in such a way that the bracketed term in Equation 15-10 is zero. Therefore, leverage would not add value: $V_L = V_U$.

However, reasonable assumptions for the tax rates in 2017 indicated that debt added some value. For example, suppose the marginal corporate federal-plus-state tax rate was 40%, the marginal rate on debt was 33%, and the marginal rate on stock was 12%. Substituting these values into Equation 15-10 results in:

$$V_L = V_U + 0.21D$$

This shows that personal taxes reduced the debt advantage to 21 cents per dollar, lower than the 40 cents per dollar in 2017 if personal taxes were ignored.

However, the TCJA tax rates made a dramatic impact on application of the Miller model. Today, reasonable estimates for tax rates are $T_c = 25\%$, $T_d = 32\%$, and $T_s = 12\%$. Substituting these values into Equation 15-10 results in:

$$V_L = V_U + 0.03D$$

When applied today, the Miller model indicates that every dollar of debt adds only 3 cents of value. Thus it appears that the presence of personal taxes significantly reduces but does not completely eliminate the advantage of debt financing.

---

[11]This is the threshold for 2018.

The Miller model has several important implications, as we show next.

1. The bracketed term in Equation 15-10 is:

$$\left[1 - \frac{(1 - T_c)(1 - T_s)}{(1 - T_d)} \right]$$

When multiplied by D, it shows the gain from leverage. Recall that the earlier MM model with only corporate taxes is: $V_L = V_U + TD$. Thus, the bracketed term replaces the corporate tax rate, T, in the model that ignores personal taxes.

2. If we ignore all taxes (i.e., if $T_c = T_s = T_d = 0$), then the bracketed term is zero, so in this case Equation 15-10 is the same as the original MM model without taxes.

3. If we ignore personal taxes (i.e., if $T_s = T_d = 0$), then the bracketed term reduces to $[1 - (1 - T_c)] = T_c$, so in this case Equation 15-10 is the same as the MM model with corporate taxes.

4. If the effective personal tax rates on stock and bond incomes were equal (i.e., if $T_s = T_d$), then $(1 - T_s)$ and $(1 - T_d)$ would cancel, and so the bracketed term would again reduce to T_c.

5. If $(1 - T_c)(1 - T_s) = (1 - T_d)$, then the bracketed term would be zero, and so the value of using leverage would also be zero. This implies that the tax advantage of debt to the firm would be exactly offset by the personal tax advantage of equity. Under this condition, capital structure would have no effect on a firm's value or its cost of capital, so we would be back to MM's original zero-tax proposition.

6. It is possible for the bracketed term to be negative. This was true when Miller proposed the model, but tax rates were such that it was very unlikely that the bracketed term would be negative. That was also true in 2017, but the TCJA's tax rates now make it seem more likely that debt might reduce a firm's value.

SELF-TEST

What does the MM theory with no taxes state about the value of a levered firm versus the value of an otherwise identical but unlevered firm? What does this imply about the optimal capital structure?

Why does the MM theory with corporate taxes lead to 100% debt?

What does the Miller model with personal and corporate taxes imply about value relative to the MM model with just corporate taxes?

15-4 Capital Structure Theory: Beyond the Modigliani and Miller Models

The MM models are important because they guided subsequent research in terms of methodology: Compare levered firms with unlevered firms and look for side effects. Also, the unrealistic MM assumptions provided a place for subsequent researchers to extend the MM models by relaxing the assumptions. The following sections describe the important developments in capital structure theory.

15-4a Trade-Off Theory

The results of Modigliani and Miller also depend on the assumption that there are no **bankruptcy costs**. However, bankruptcy can be quite costly. Firms in bankruptcy have very high legal and accounting expenses, and they also have a hard time retaining customers, suppliers, and employees. Moreover, bankruptcy often forces a firm to liquidate or sell assets for less than they would be worth if the firm were to continue operating.

For example, if a steel manufacturer goes out of business, it might be hard to find buyers for the company's blast furnaces. Such assets are often illiquid because they are configured to a company's individual needs and also because they are difficult and very expensive to disassemble and move.

Note, too, that the *threat of bankruptcy,* not just bankruptcy per se, causes **financial distress costs**. Key employees jump ship, suppliers refuse to grant credit, customers seek more stable suppliers, and lenders demand higher interest rates and impose more restrictive loan covenants if potential bankruptcy looms. Therefore, even the threat of bankruptcy can cause free cash flows to fall, causing further declines in a company's value.

Bankruptcy-related problems are most likely to arise when a firm includes a great deal of debt in its capital structure. Therefore, bankruptcy costs discourage firms from pushing their use of debt to excessive levels.

Bankruptcy-related costs have two components: (1) the probability of financial distress and (2) the costs that would be incurred if financial distress does occur. Firms whose earnings are more volatile, all else equal, face a greater chance of bankruptcy and should therefore use less debt than more stable firms. This is consistent with our earlier point that firms with high operating leverage, and thus greater business risk, should limit their use of financial leverage. Likewise, firms that would face high costs in the event of financial distress should rely less heavily on debt. For example, firms whose assets are illiquid and thus would have to be sold at "fire sale" prices should limit their use of debt financing.

The preceding arguments led to the development of what is called the trade-off theory of leverage, in which firms trade off the benefits of debt financing (favorable corporate tax treatment) against higher interest rates and bankruptcy costs. In essence, the **trade-off theory** says that the value of a levered firm is equal to the value of an unlevered firm plus the value of any side effects, which include the tax shield and the expected costs due to financial distress. A summary of the trade-off theory is expressed graphically in Figure 15-3, and a list of observations about the figure follows here:

1. Under the assumptions of the MM model with corporate taxes, a firm's value increases linearly for every dollar of debt. The line labeled "MM Result Incorporating the Effects of Corporate Taxation" in Figure 15-3 expresses the relationship between value and debt under those assumptions.

2. There is some threshold level of debt, labeled D_1 in Figure 15-3, below which the probability of bankruptcy is so low as to be immaterial. Beyond D_1, however, expected bankruptcy-related costs become increasingly important, and they reduce the tax benefits of debt at an increasing rate. In the range from D_1 to D_2, expected bankruptcy-related costs reduce but do not completely offset the tax benefits of debt, so the stock price rises (but at a decreasing rate) as the debt ratio increases. However, beyond D_2, expected bankruptcy-related costs exceed the tax benefits, so from this point on increasing the debt ratio lowers the value of the stock. Therefore, D_2 is the optimal capital structure. Of course, D_1 and D_2 vary from firm to firm, depending on their business risks and bankruptcy costs.

3. Although theoretical and empirical work confirms the general shape of the curve in Figure 15-3, this graph must be taken as an approximation and not as a precisely defined function.

15-4b Signaling Theory

MM assumed that investors have the same information about a firm's prospects as its managers—this is called **symmetric information**. However, managers in fact often have better information than outside investors. This is called **asymmetric information**, and it

FIGURE 15-3
Effect of Financial Leverage on Value

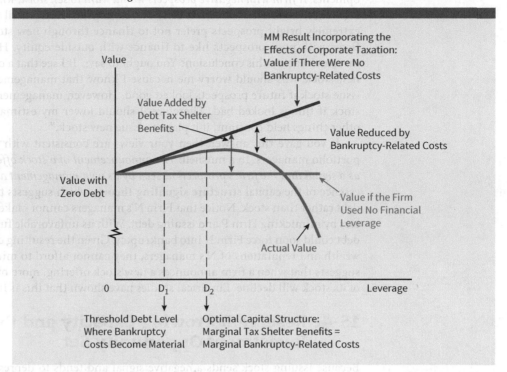

has an important effect on the optimal capital structure. To see why, consider two situations, one in which the company's managers know that its prospects are extremely positive (Firm P) and one in which the managers know that the future looks negative (Firm N).

Suppose, for example, that Firm P's R&D labs have just discovered a cure for the common cold. Firm P can't provide investors with any details about the product because that might give competitors an advantage. But if they don't provide details, then investors will underestimate the value of the discovery. Given the inability to provide accurate, verifiable information to the market, how should Firm P's management raise the needed capital?

Suppose Firm P issues stock. When profits from the new product start flowing in, the price of the stock would rise sharply and the purchasers of the new stock would make a bonanza. The current stockholders (including the managers) would also do well, but not as well as they would have done if the company had not sold stock before the price increased, because then they would not have had to share the benefits of the new product with the new stockholders. Therefore, *we should expect a firm with very positive prospects to avoid selling stock and instead to raise required new capital by other means, including debt usage beyond the normal target capital structure.*[12]

Now let's consider Firm N. Suppose its managers have information that new orders are off sharply because a competitor has installed new technology that has improved its products' quality. Firm N must upgrade its own facilities, at a high cost, just to maintain its current sales. As a result, its return on investment will fall (but not by as much as if it took no action, which would lead to a 100% loss through bankruptcy). How should Firm N raise the needed capital? Here the situation is just the reverse of that facing Firm P,

---

[12]It would be illegal for Firm P's managers to personally purchase more shares on the basis of their inside knowledge of the new product.

which did not want to sell stock so as to avoid having to share the benefits of future developments. *A firm with negative prospects would want to sell stock, which would mean bringing in new investors to share the losses!*[13] The conclusion from all this is that firms with extremely bright prospects prefer not to finance through new stock offerings, whereas firms with poor prospects like to finance with outside equity. How should you, as an investor, react to this conclusion? You ought to say: "If I see that a company plans to issue new stock, this should worry me because I know that management would not want to issue stock if future prospects looked good. However, management *would* want to issue stock if things looked bad. Therefore, I should lower my estimate of the firm's value, other things held constant, if it plans to issue new stock."

If you gave this answer, then your views are consistent with those of sophisticated portfolio managers. In a nutshell: *The announcement of a stock offering is generally taken as a signal that the firm's prospects as seen by its own management are not good*. This is the essence of the capital structure **signaling theory**, which suggests that firms should issue debt rather than stock. Notice that Firm N's managers cannot make a false signal to investors by mimicking Firm P and issuing debt. With its unfavorable future prospects, issuing debt could soon force Firm N into bankruptcy. Given the resulting damage to the personal wealth and reputations of N's managers, they cannot afford to mimic Firm P. All of this suggests that when a firm announces a new stock offering, more often than not the price of its stock will decline. Empirical studies have shown that this is indeed true.

15-4c Reserve Borrowing Capacity and the Investment Opportunity Set

Because issuing stock sends a negative signal and tends to depress the stock price even if the company's true prospects are bright, a company should try to maintain a **reserve borrowing capacity** so that debt can be used if an especially good investment opportunity comes along. This is especially important if the investment opportunity set has high-risk, high-NPV potential investments. High debt and the resulting lack of reserve borrowing capacity can be doubly costly. First, high debt increases expected financial distress and bankruptcy costs. Second, the lack of reserve borrowing capacity means that a company may be unable to finance potentially profitable investments. The net result is that *firms should, in normal times, use more equity and less debt than is suggested by the tax benefit–bankruptcy cost trade-off model depicted in Figure 15-3.*

15-4d The Investment Opportunity Set and Reserve Borrowing Capacity

Bankruptcy and financial distress are costly, and, as just reiterated, this can discourage highly levered firms from undertaking risky new investments. If potential new investments, although risky, have positive net present values, then high levels of debt can be doubly costly—the expected financial distress and bankruptcy costs are high, and the firm loses potential value by not making some potentially profitable investments. On the other hand, if a firm has very few profitable investment opportunities, then high levels of debt can keep managers from wasting money by investing in poor projects. For such companies, increases in the debt ratio can actually increase the value of the firm.

Thus, in addition to the tax, signaling, bankruptcy, and managerial constraint effects discussed previously, the firm's optimal capital structure is related to its set of investment

---

[13]Of course, Firm N would have to make certain disclosures when it offered new shares to the public, but it might be able to meet the legal requirements without fully disclosing management's worst fears.

opportunities. Firms with many profitable opportunities should maintain their ability to invest by using low levels of debt, which is also consistent with maintaining reserve borrowing capacity. Firms with few profitable investment opportunities should use high levels of debt (which have high interest payments) to impose managerial constraint.

15-4e The Pecking Order Hypothesis

The **pecking order hypothesis** asserts that the presence of flotation costs or asymmetric information may cause a firm to raise different types of capital in a sequence that minimizes these costs. To do so, a firm first raises capital internally by reinvesting its net income and selling its short-term marketable securities. When that supply of funds has been exhausted, the firm will issue debt and perhaps preferred stock. Only as a last resort will the firm issue common stock.[14]

15-4f Using Debt Financing to Reduce Agency Costs

Agency costs may arise if managers and shareholders have different objectives. Such conflicts are particularly likely when the firm's managers have too much cash at their disposal. Managers often use excess cash to finance pet projects or for perquisites such as nicer offices, corporate jets, and skyboxes at sports arenas—none of which have much to do with maximizing stock prices. Even worse, managers might be tempted to pay too much for an acquisition, something that could cost shareholders hundreds of millions of dollars. By contrast, managers with limited "excess cash flow" are less able to make wasteful expenditures.

Firms can reduce excess cash flow in a variety of ways. One way is to funnel some of it back to shareholders through higher dividends or stock repurchases. Another alternative is to shift the capital structure toward more debt in the hope that higher debt service requirements will force managers to be more disciplined. If debt is not serviced as required, then the firm will be forced into bankruptcy, in which case its managers would likely lose their jobs. Therefore, a manager is less likely to buy an expensive new corporate jet if the firm has large debt service requirements that could cost the manager his or her job. In short, high levels of debt *bond the cash flow*, because much of it is precommitted to servicing the debt.[15]

A **leveraged buyout (LBO)** is one way to bond cash flow. In an LBO, a large amount of debt and a small amount of cash are used to finance the purchase of a company's shares, after which the firm "goes private." The first wave of LBOs was in the mid-1980s; private equity funds led the buyouts of the late 1990s and early 2000s. Many of these LBOs were specifically designed to reduce corporate waste. As noted, high debt payments force managers to conserve cash by eliminating unnecessary expenditures.

Of course, increasing debt and reducing the available cash flow has its downside: It increases the risk of bankruptcy. Ben Bernanke, former chairman of the Fed, has argued that adding debt to a firm's capital structure is like putting a dagger into the steering wheel of a car.[16] The dagger—which points toward your stomach—motivates you to drive more carefully, but you may get stabbed if someone runs into you even if you are being careful.

---

[14]For more information, see Jonathon Baskin, "An Empirical Investigation of the Pecking Order Hypothesis," *Financial Management*, Spring 1989, pp. 26–35.

[15]See Michael J. Barclay and Clifford W. Smith Jr., "The Capital Structure Puzzle: Another Look at the Evidence," *Journal of Applied Corporate Finance*, Spring 1999, pp. 8–20.

[16]See Ben Bernanke, "Is There Too Much Corporate Debt?" *Federal Reserve Bank of Philadelphia Business Review*, September/October 1989, pp. 3–13.

The analogy applies to corporations in the following sense: Higher debt forces managers to be more careful with shareholders' money, but even well-run firms could face bankruptcy (get stabbed) if some event beyond their control occurs: a war, an earthquake, a strike, or a recession. To complete the analogy, the capital structure decision comes down to deciding how long a dagger stockholders should use to keep managers in line.

Finally, too much debt may overly constrain managers. A large portion of a manager's personal wealth and reputation is tied to a single company, so managers are not well diversified. When faced with a positive-NPV project that is risky, a manager may decide that it's not worth taking on the risk even though well-diversified stockholders would find the risk acceptable. The more debt the firm has, the greater the likelihood of financial distress and thus the greater the likelihood that managers will forgo risky projects even if they have positive NPVs. This is called the **underinvestment problem**.

15-4g The Market Timing Theory

If markets are efficient, then security prices should reflect all available information; hence, they are neither underpriced nor overpriced (except during the time it takes prices to move to a new equilibrium caused by the release of new information). The *market timing theory* states that managers don't believe this and hypothesizes instead that stock prices and interest rates are sometimes either too low or too high relative to their true fundamental values. In particular, the theory suggests that managers issue equity when they believe stock market prices are abnormally high and issue debt when they believe interest rates are abnormally low. In other words, they try to time the market.[17] Notice that this differs from signaling theory because no asymmetric information is involved. These managers aren't basing their beliefs on insider information, just on a different opinion than the market consensus.

SELF-TEST

Explain how asymmetric information *and* signals *affect capital structure decisions.*

What is meant by reserve borrowing capacity, *and why is it important to firms?*

How can the use of debt serve to discipline managers?

15-5 Capital Structure Evidence and Implications

As the previous sections show, there are a lot of capital structure theories! Which ones are correct and which ones are important for managers? As we show in the following sections, each of the theories provides useful insights and guidelines for managers making capital structure decisions.

15-5a Empirical Evidence[18]

There have been hundreds, perhaps even thousands, of papers testing the capital structure theories described in the previous section. We can cover only the highlights here, beginning with the empirical evidence.[19]

---

[17]See Malcolm Baker and Jeffrey Wurgler, "Market Timing and Capital Structure," *Journal of Finance*, February 2002, pp. 1–32.

[18]All of the empirical results described in this section are based on market values of leverage, not book values.

[19]This section also draws heavily from Barclay and Smith, "The Capital Structure Puzzle," cited in footnote 17; Jay Ritter, ed., *Recent Developments in Corporate Finance* (Northampton, MA: Edward Elgar Publishing Inc., 2005); and a presentation by Jay Ritter at the 2003 FMA meeting, "The Windows of Opportunity Theory of Capital Structure."

THE TRADE-OFF BETWEEN TAX BENEFITS AND BANKRUPTCY COSTS

Recent studies by Professors Van Binsbergen, Graham, and Yang and by Professor Korteweg suggest that the average net benefits of leverage (i.e., the value of the tax shield less the expected cost of financial distress) make up about 3% to 6% of a levered firm's value.[20] To put this into perspective, let's look at the impact of debt on an average company's value. The average company is financed with about 25% to 35% debt, so let's suppose that the company has $25 of debt and $75 of equity, just to keep the arithmetic simple. The total net benefit of debt is about $5, based on the recent research. This implies that each dollar of debt added (on average) about $0.20 of value ($5/$25 = 0.2) to the company. The first dollar of debt adds a bigger net benefit because bankruptcy risk is low when debt is low. By the time the 25th dollar of debt is added, its incremental net benefit is close to zero—the incremental expected costs of financial distress are about equal to the incremental expected tax shield.

These studies also showed that the net benefits of debt increase slowly until reaching the optimal level but decline rapidly thereafter. In other words, it isn't very costly to be somewhat below the optimal level of debt, but it is costly to exceed it.

A particularly interesting study by Professors Mehotra, Mikkelson, and Partch examined the capital structure of firms that were spun off from their parent companies.[21] The financing choices of existing firms might be influenced by their past financing choices and by the costs of moving from one capital structure to another, but because spin-offs are newly created companies, managers can choose a capital structure without regard to these issues. The study found that more profitable firms (which have a lower expected probability of bankruptcy) and more asset-intensive firms (which have better collateral and thus a lower cost of bankruptcy should one occur) have higher levels of debt.

The Miller model hypothesizes that the value of a levered firm is affected by personal tax rates as well as corporate tax rates. Therefore, a cut in the tax rate on dividends should reduce the value of leverage, all else held equal. Professors Lin and Flannery examined the 2003 tax cut on dividends and found that leverage decreases as the personal effective tax rate on stock decreases, which is consistent with the Miller model's prediction. In addition, the impact of the tax cut was more pronounced for companies with a high proportion of individual owners (who are subject to personal income tax) than for companies with a high proportion of institutional owners (such as pension funds that might not be liable for personal taxes).[22]

The empirical evidence clearly shows that corporate taxes, personal taxes, and bankruptcy costs matter when it comes to choosing a capital structure. In particular, companies do consider the trade-off between tax benefits and bankruptcy costs.

A DYNAMIC TRADE-OFF THEORY

However, there is also evidence that is inconsistent with the static optimal target capital structure implied by the trade-off theory. For example, stock prices are volatile, which frequently causes a firm's actual market-based debt ratio to deviate from its target. However, such deviations don't cause firms to immediately return to their target by issuing or repurchasing securities. Instead, Professors Flannery and Rangan show that firms tend to make a partial adjustment each year, moving about 30% of the way toward their target capital

---

[20]See Jules H. Van Binsbergen, John H. Graham, and Jie Yang, "The Cost of Debt," *Journal of Finance*, Vol. 65, No. 6, December 2010, pp. 2089–2135; also see Arthur Korteweg, "The Net Benefits to Leverage," *Journal of Finance*, Vol. 65, No. 6, December 2010, pp. 2137–2169.

[21]See V. Mehotra, W. Mikkelson, and M. Partch, "The Design of Financial Policies in Corporate Spin-Offs," *Review of Financial Studies*, Winter 2003, pp. 1359–1388.

[22]See L. Lin and M. J. Flannery, "Do Personal Taxes Affect Capital Structure? Evidence from the 2003 Tax Cut," *Journal of Financial Economics*, Vol. 109, 2013, pp. 549–565.

structure. In a more recent study, Professors Faulkender, Flannery, Hankins, and Smith show that the speed of adjustment depends on a company's cash flows—companies with high cash flows adjust by about 50%. This effect is even more pronounced if the company's leverage exceeds its target—high cash flow companies in this situation have a 70% speed of adjustment. This is consistent with the idea that it is more costly to exceed the target debt ratio than to be lower than the target.[23]

MARKET TIMING

As we mentioned in Chapter 14, companies with infrequent stock repurchase activity are able to repurchase stock at a lower average price than the average price in the months surrounding the repurchase, indicating the ability to time the market with respect to repurchases. This supports the idea that a firm's managers have better information than investors regarding their stock's value, implying that managers would issue stock when it is overvalued. We see evidence of this when a company has had a big stock run-up. This reduces the market-based leverage ratio, so the trade-off theory suggests that the firm should issue debt to return to its target. However, firms tend to do the opposite, issuing stock after big run-ups. This is much more consistent with the market timing theory, with managers trying to time the market by issuing stock when they perceive the market to be overvalued.

Furthermore, firms tend to issue debt when stock prices and interest rates are low. The maturity of the issued debt seems to reflect an attempt to time interest rates: Firms tend to issue short-term debt if the term structure is upward sloping but long-term debt if the term structure is flat. Again, these facts suggest that managers try to time the market.

SIGNALING AND THE PECKING ORDER

When a firm announces a seasoned equity offering, the stock price tends to fall by around 2% to 4%, all else held equal, suggesting that investors believe that firms issue equity when it is overvalued.[24] For seasoned nonconvertible debt offerings, the stock price tends to fall a little, but not by a significant amount.[25] Asymmetric information is a significant problem in stock and bond issues but is less likely when a company announces a large credit agreement with a bank—in fact, the stock price reaction is positive.[26] These results suggest that signaling is important, especially when informational asymmetry is high.

Given these results, it is no surprise that firms issue equity much less frequently than debt. On the surface, this seems to support both the pecking order hypothesis and the signaling hypothesis. The pecking order hypothesis predicts that firms with a high level of informational asymmetry, which causes equity issuances to be costly, should issue debt before issuing equity. Yet we often see the opposite, with high-growth firms (which usually have greater informational asymmetry) issuing more equity than debt. Also, many highly profitable firms could afford to issue debt (which comes before equity in the pecking order) but instead choose to issue equity. With respect to the signaling hypothesis, consider the

[23]See Mark Flannery and Kasturi Rangan, "Partial Adjustment toward Target Capital Structures," *Journal of Financial Economics*, Vol. 79, 2006, pp. 469–506. Also see Michael Faulkender, Mark Flannery, Kristine Hankins, and Jason Smith, "Cash Flows and Leverage," *Journal of Financial Economics*, Vol. 103, 2012, pp. 632–646.

[24]For the first studies to document this phenomenon, see W. Mikkelson and M. Partch, "Valuation Effects of Security Offerings and the Issuance Process," *Journal of Financial Economics*, Vol. 15, 1986, pp. 31–60; and R. Masulis and A. Korwar, "Seasoned Equity Offerings," *Journal of Financial Economics*, Vol. 15, 1986, pp. 91–118.

[25]See B. E. Eckbo, "Valuation Effects of Corporate Debt Offerings," *Journal of Financial Economics*, Vol. 15, 1986, pp. 119–151.

[26]As the old saying goes, "If you borrow $1,000, you have a banker; if you borrow $10 million, you have a partner." See C. James, "Some Evidence on the Uniqueness of Bank Loans," *Journal of Financial Economics*, Vol. 19, 1987, pp. 217–235.

case of firms that have large increases in earnings that were unanticipated by the market. If managers have superior information, then they will anticipate these upcoming performance improvements and issue debt before the increase. Such firms do, in fact, tend to issue debt slightly more frequently than other firms, but the difference isn't economically meaningful.

RESERVE BORROWING CAPACITY

Many firms have less debt than might be expected, and many have large amounts of short-term investments. This is especially true for firms with high market/book ratios (which indicate many growth options as well as informational asymmetry). This behavior is consistent with the hypothesis that investment opportunities influence attempts to maintain reserve borrowing capacity. It is also consistent with tax considerations, because low-growth firms (which have more debt) are more likely to benefit from the tax shield. This behavior is not consistent with the pecking order hypothesis, where low-growth firms (which often have high free cash flow) would be able to avoid issuing debt by raising funds internally.

SUMMARY OF EMPIRICAL TESTS

To summarize these results, it appears that firms try to capture debt's tax benefits while avoiding financial distress costs. However, they also allow their debt ratios to deviate from the static optimal target ratio implied by the trade-off theory. In fact, Professors Harry DeAngelo, Linda DeAngelo, and Toni Whited extend the dynamic trade-off model by showing that firms often deliberately issue debt to take advantage of unexpected investment opportunities, even if this causes them to exceed their target debt ratio.[27] Firms often maintain reserve borrowing capacity, especially firms with many growth opportunities or problems with informational asymmetry.[28] There is a little evidence indicating that firms follow a pecking order and use security issuances as signals, but there is some evidence in support of the market timing theory.

15-5b Implications for Managers

Empirical research shows that tax effects and financial distress costs are important. In addition, many firms take advantage of refinancing opportunities when interest rates are low.

TAKE ADVANTAGE OF THE INTEREST TAX SHIELD

Managers should explicitly consider tax benefits when making capital structure decisions. Firms can utilize tax loss carryforwards but the time value of money means that tax benefits are more valuable for firms with stable, positive pre-tax income. Therefore, a firm whose sales are relatively stable can safely take on more debt and incur higher fixed charges than a company with volatile sales. Other things being equal, a firm with less operating leverage is better able to employ financial leverage because it will have less business risk and less volatile earnings.

---

[27]See Harry DeAngelo, Linda DeAngelo, and Toni Whited, "Capital Structure Dynamics and Transitory Debt," *Journal of Financial Economics*, Vol. 99, 2011, pp. 235–261.

[28]For more on empirical tests of capital structure theory, see Gregor Andrade and Steven Kaplan, "How Costly Is Financial (Not Economic) Distress? Evidence from Highly Leveraged Transactions That Became Distressed," *Journal of Finance*, Vol. 53, 1998, pp. 1443–1493; Malcolm Baker, Robin Greenwood, and Jeffrey Wurgler, "The Maturity of Debt Issues and Predictable Variation in Bond Returns," *Journal of Financial Economics*, November 2003, pp. 261–291; Murray Z. Frank and Vidhan K. Goyal, "Testing the Pecking Order Theory of Capital Structure," *Journal of Financial Economics*, February 2003, pp. 217–248; and Michael Long and Ileen Malitz, "The Investment-Financing Nexus: Some Empirical Evidence," *Midland Corporate Finance Journal*, Fall 1985, pp. 53–59.

DON'T UNDERESTIMATE FINANCIAL DISTRESS COSTS

Managers should also consider the expected cost of financial distress, which depends on the probability and cost of distress. Notice that stable sales and lower operating leverage provide tax benefits but also reduce the *probability* of financial distress. One *cost* of financial distress comes from lost investment opportunities. Firms with profitable investment opportunities need to be able to fund them, either by holding higher levels of marketable securities or by maintaining excess borrowing capacity.

Another cost of financial distress is the possibility of being forced to sell assets to meet liquidity needs. General-purpose assets that can be used by many businesses are relatively liquid and make good collateral, in contrast to special-purpose assets. Thus, real estate companies are usually highly leveraged, whereas companies involved in technological research are not.

Asymmetric information also has a bearing on capital structure decisions. For example, suppose a firm has just successfully completed an R&D program, and it forecasts higher earnings in the immediate future. However, the new earnings are not yet anticipated by investors and hence are not reflected in the stock price. This company should not issue stock—it should finance with debt until the higher earnings materialize and are reflected in the stock price. Then it could issue common stock, retire the debt, and return to its target capital structure.

Managers should consider conditions in the stock and bond markets. For example, during a recent credit crunch, the junk bond market dried up and there was simply no market at a "reasonable" interest rate for any new long-term bonds rated below BBB. Therefore, low-rated companies in need of capital were forced to go to the stock market or to the short-term debt market, regardless of their target capital structures. When conditions eased, however, these companies sold bonds to get their capital structures back on target.

Finally, managers should always consider lenders' and rating agencies' attitudes. For example, Moody's and Standard & Poor's told a large utility that its bonds would be downgraded if it issued more debt. This influenced the utility's decision to finance its expansion with common equity. This doesn't mean that managers should never increase debt if it will cause their bond rating to fall, but managers should always factor this into their decision making.[29]

CONSIDER REFINANCING DEBT WHEN RATES ARE LOW

When current market rates are sufficiently low relative to rates on a firm's outstanding debt, managers should consider a **refunding operation**, in which a company calls old debt and issues new debt after interest rates have fallen. Even though the new interest rate is lower, initial costs and tax implications must be evaluated before undertaking a refunding operation. The process is similar to project analysis because managers must estimate the incremental after-tax cash flows associated with the refunding and find their net present value. If the value is positive, then managers should refinance the debt unless there is a compelling reason to wait. See **Web Extension 15B** for a complete description of this process.

SELF-TEST

Which capital structure theories does the empirical evidence seem to support?

What issues should managers consider when making capital structure decisions?

[29]For some insights into how practicing financial managers view the capital structure decision, see John Graham and Campbell Harvey, "The Theory and Practice of Corporate Finance: Evidence from the Field," *Journal of Financial Economics*, Vol. 60, 2001, pp. 187–243; Ravindra R. Kamath, "Long-Term Financing Decisions: Views and Practices of Financial Managers of NYSE Firms," *The Financial Review*, May 1997, pp. 331–356; and Edgar Norton, "Factors Affecting Capital Structure Decisions," *The Financial Review*, August 1991, pp. 431–446.

15-6 Estimating the Optimal Capital Structure

Capital structure matters. Adding debt decreases taxes (because interest expenses are deductible) but also increases the cost of debt (because the additional debt is riskier). Additional debt also increases shareholder risk as measured by beta and the cost of equity. Managers should identify the **optimal capital structure**, which is the percentage of debt (w_d) that maximizes shareholder wealth. Managers should implement the optimal capital structure unless there are other compelling reasons (e.g., information asymmetry, current market conditions, etc.).

15-6a Estimating a Company's Current Value and Capital Structure

The following sections illustrate how to estimate the optimal capital structure using Strasburg Electronics Company, a manufacturer of specialty components for cell phones. First, let's take a look at Strasburg's current situation. The blue section of Figure 15-4 shows the input data. The green section shows the calculations needed to determine the

FIGURE 15-4

Strasburg's Current Value and Capital Structure (Millions of Dollars, Except for Per Share Data)

	A	B	C	D	E
288	**Input Data**		**Capital Structure and Cost of Capital**		
289	Stock price (P)	$22.50	Market value of equity (S = P x n)		$2,250
290	# of shares (n)	100	Total value (V = D + S)		$2,500
291	Market value of debt (D)	$250.00	% financed with debt (w_d = D/V)		10.00%
292	Tax rate	25%	% financed with stock (w_s = S/V)		90.00%
293	EBIT	$400	Cost of equity: $r_s = r_{RF} + b(RP_M)$		12.67%
294	Net operating capital	$2,000			
295	Growth rate (g_L)	0%	Weighted average cost of capital:		
296	Cost of debt (r_d)	8.00%	WACC = $r_d (1 - T)(w_d) + r_s (w_s)$		12.00%
297	Beta (b)	1.01			
298	Risk-free rate (r_{RF})	6.67%			
299	Mkt. risk prem. (RP_M)	5.94%			
300	**ROIC and Free Cash Flow**		**Estimated Intrinsic Value**		
301	NOPAT = EBIT(1 − T)	$300	V_{op} = [FCF(1 + g_L)]/(WACC − g_L):		$2,500.00
302	ROIC = NOPAT/Op. Cap.	15%	+ Value of ST investments		$0.00
303	Inv. in Op. Cap. = Δ Cap.	$0	Estimated total intrinsic value		$2,500.00
304			− Debt		$250.00
305	Free cash flow:		Estimated intrinsic value of equity		$2,250.00
306	FCF = NOPAT − Δ Cap.	$300	÷ Number of shares		$100.00
307			Estimated intrinsic price per share		$22.50

Source: See the file *Ch15 Tool Kit.xlsx*. Numbers are reported as rounded values for clarity but are calculated using *Excel*'s full precision unless otherwise noted. Thus, intermediate calculations using the figure's rounded values will be inexact.

Notes:

1. The weighted average cost of capital is rounded to 4 decimal places.

2. Strasburg's sales, earnings, and assets are not growing, so it does not need investments in operating capital. Therefore, FCF = NOPAT − Investment in operating capital = EBIT(1 − T) − $0 = EBIT(1 − T). The growth in FCF also is 0.

current capital structure and the weighted cost of capital (WACC). The yellow section shows the calculations needed to estimate the return on invested capital (ROIC) and the free cash flow (FCF). The orange section shows the calculations to estimate the intrinsic stock price.

Notice that the 15% ROIC in Figure 15-4 is greater than the 12% WACC, indicating that Strasburg's managers are doing a good job. But is this the optimal capital structure? We will address that question in the following sections.

15-6b Preliminary Steps to Identify the Optimal Capital Structure

The process to identify the optimal capital structure begins with some preliminary steps. First, choose the percentage of debt, w_d, that corresponds with each capital structure to be considered. Strasburg's managers wish to evaluate capital structures with the following percentages of debt, w_d, based on market values: 0%, 10%, 20%, 30%, 40%, and 50%.

Second, theory and empirical evidence demonstrate that beta and the cost of equity increase with financial leverage. To estimate the cost of equity at different capital structures, start with the **unlevered beta (b_U)**, which is the beta a company would have if it had no debt. Use the unlevered beta to determine the beta and cost of equity for each capital structure. Note that the unlevered beta is a measure of a firm's "basic business risk," whereas beta also includes financial risk.

The **Hamada equation** specifies the relationship between financial leverage and beta, b:[30]

$$b = b_U[1 + (1 - T)(D/S)] \tag{15-11}$$

Here D is the market value of the debt, and S is the market value of the equity. The left-hand side of the equation, b, is the firm's **levered beta** because it reflects the financial leverage due to the choice of D/S.

Sometimes it is more convenient to work with the percentages of debt and equity, w_d and w_s, rather than the dollar values of D and S. Since $w_d = D/(D + S)$ and $w_s = S/(D + S)$, the ratio D/S is equal to w_d/w_s. Substituting these values gives us another form of the Hamada equation:

$$b = b_U[1 + (1 - T)(w_d/w_s)] \tag{15-11a}$$

Often we know the current capital structure and beta but wish to know the unlevered beta. We find this by rearranging Equation 15-11a as follows:

$$b_U = b/[1 + (1 - T)(w_d/w_s)] \tag{15-12}$$

---

[30]See Robert S. Hamada, "Portfolio Analysis, Market Equilibrium, and Corporation Finance," *Journal of Finance,* March 1969, pp. 13–31. For a comprehensive framework, see Robert A. Taggart Jr., "Consistent Valuation and Cost of Capital Expressions with Corporate and Personal Taxes," *Financial Management,* Autumn 1991, pp. 8–20.

Strasburg has a current capital structure with $w_d = 10\%$ and $w_s = (1 - w_d) = 90\%$. Strasburg's beta is 1.01, so the unlevered beta is:

$$b_U = 1.01/[1 + (1 - 0.25)(0.1/0.9)]$$
$$= 0.9323$$

15-6c Estimating the Weighted Average Cost of Capital for Different Capital Structures

To identify the optimal capital structure, apply the following steps to each capital structure under consideration: (1) Estimate the levered beta and cost of equity. (2) Estimate the interest rate and cost of debt. (3) Calculate the weighted average cost of capital. (4) Calculate the value of operations, which is the present value of free cash flows discounted by the new WACC. The objective is to find the amount of debt financing that maximizes the value of operations. As we will show, this capital structure also maximizes shareholder wealth and the intrinsic stock price. The following sections illustrate Step 1 through Step 3.

ESTIMATING THE LEVERED BETA AND COST OF EQUITY (r_s)

Use the previously calculated unlevered beta (0.9323) and Equation 15-11a to determine the levered beta for each of the capital structures being considered. For example, the levered beta for a capital structure with 20% debt is:

$$b = b_U[1 + (1 - T)(w_d/w_s)]$$
$$= 0.9323\,[1 + (1 - 0.25)(0.20/0.80)]$$
$$= 1.107$$

Recall from Figure 15-4 that the risk-free rate is 6.67% and the market risk premium is 5.94%. Use these values and the previously estimated beta for $w_d = 20\%$ to estimate this capital structure's cost of equity:

$$r_s = r_{RF} + b(RP_M)$$
$$= 6.67\% + 1.107(5.94\%) = 13.25\%$$

Figure 15-5 graphs Strasburg's required return on equity for each capital structure under consideration. As expected, Strasburg's cost of equity increases as its debt increases. Observe that the cost of equity consists of the 6.67% risk-free rate, a constant premium for business risk in the amount of $RP_M(b_U) = 5.54\%$, and a premium for financial risk in the amount of $RP_M(b - b_U)$ that starts at zero (because $b = b_U$ for zero debt) but rises at an increasing rate as the debt ratio increases.

ESTIMATING THE COST OF DEBT (r_d)

The CFO asked Strasburg's investment bankers to estimate the cost of debt at different capital structures. They began by analyzing industry conditions and prospects. They next appraised Strasburg's business risk based on its past financial statements and its current technology and customer base. The bankers also forecast financial statements with different capital structures and analyzed such key ratios as the current ratio and the times-interest-earned ratio. Finally, they factored in current conditions in the financial markets, including interest rates paid by firms in Strasburg's industry.

FIGURE 15-5
Strasburg's Required Rate of Return on Equity at Different Debt Levels

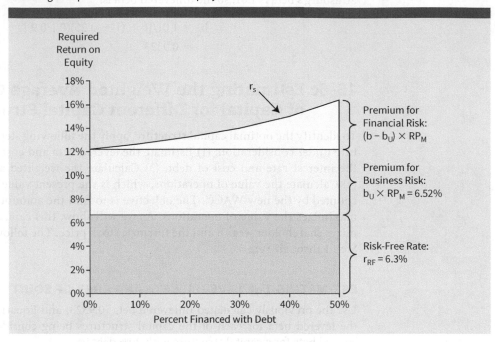

Based on their analysis and judgment, they estimated interest rates at various capital structures, starting with a 7.8% cost of debt for a capital structure with zero debt.[31] This rate increases to 12.2% if the firm finances 50% of its capital structure with debt. (*Note:* These are the average rates for all of Strasburg's possible debt levels, not the marginal rates for the next dollar of debt.)

Figure 15-6 reports the estimated costs of debt as well as the previously estimated betas and costs of equity. Strasburg's current situation is in Column C and is shown in blue. The following sections explain the remaining rows in Figure 15-6.

THE WEIGHTED AVERAGE COST OF CAPITAL AT DIFFERENT LEVELS OF DEBT

Line 6 of Figure 15-6 shows Strasburg's weighted average cost of capital, WACC, at different capital structures. As the debt ratio increases, the costs of both debt and equity rise, at first slowly but then at an accelerating rate. Eventually, the increasing costs of these two components offset the fact that more debt (which is still less costly than equity) is being used. At 30% debt, Strasburg's WACC hits a minimum of 11.75%; Column E is shown in silver to indicate that it is the capital structure with the minimum WACC. Notice that the WACC begins to increase for capital structures with more than 30% debt. Figure 15-7 shows how the WACC changes as debt increases.

Also note that even though the component cost of equity is always higher than that of debt, financing with almost nothing but debt would not maximize value. If Strasburg were to issue more than 30% debt, then the costs of both debt and equity would increase in such

---

[31]For a description of a technique for estimating the cost of debt, see Jules H. Van Binsbergen, John H. Graham, and Jie Yang, "An Empirical Model of Optimal Capital Structure," *Journal of Applied Corporate Finance*, Vol. 23, No. 4, Fall, 2011, pp. 34–59. They also provide an approach for estimating the optimal capital structure that explicitly incorporates the tax benefits of debt net of the financial distress costs and other costs.

FIGURE 15-6

Estimating Strasburg's Optimal Capital Structure (Millions of Dollars)

	A	B	C	D	E	F	G
443		Percent of Firm Financed with Debt (w$_d$)					
444		0%	10%	20%	30%	40%	50%
445	1. w$_s$	100.00%	90.00%	80.00%	70.00%	60.00%	50.00%
446	2. b	0.932	1.010	1.107	1.232	1.398	1.632
447	3. r$_s$	12.21%	12.67%	13.25%	13.99%	14.98%	16.36%
448	4. r$_d$	7.80%	8.00%	8.20%	8.70%	10.10%	12.20%
449	5. r$_d$ (1−T)	5.85%	6.00%	6.15%	6.53%	7.58%	9.15%
450	6. WACC	12.21%	12.00%	11.83%	11.75%	12.02%	12.76%
451	7. V$_{op}$	$2,457.00	$2,500.00	$2,535.93	$2,553.19	$2,495.84	$2,351.10
452	8. Debt	$0.00	$250.00	$507.19	$765.96	$998.34	$1,175.55
453	9. Equity	$2,457.00	$2,250.00	$2,028.74	$1,787.23	$1,497.50	$1,175.55
454	10. # Shares	111.33	100.00	88.75	77.60	66.68	55.95
455	11. Stock price	$22.07	$22.50	$22.86	$23.03	$22.46	$21.011
456	12. Net income	$300.00	$285.00	$268.81	$250.02	$224.38	$192.44
457	13. EPS	$2.69	$2.85	$3.03	$3.22	$3.37	$3.44

Source: See the file *Ch15 Tool Kit.xlsx*. Numbers are reported as rounded values for clarity but are calculated using *Excel*'s full precision unless otherwise noted. Thus, intermediate calculations using the figure's rounded values will be inexact.

Notes:

1. The percent financed with equity is w$_s$ = 1 − w$_d$.

2. The levered beta for each proposed capital structure is estimated by Hamada's formula with a 25% federal-plus-state tax rate, the unlevered beta (0.9323), and the proposed capital structure: b = b$_U$ [1 + (1 − T)(w$_d$/w$_s$)].

    The unlevered beta is found by using a version of Hamada's formula with the current capital structure (w$_d$ = 10%) and current levered beta (1.01) as shown in the blue range of cells: b$_U$ = b/[1 + (1 − T)(w$_d$/w$_s$)].

3. The cost of equity is estimated using the CAPM formula with a risk-free rate of 6.67% and a market risk premium of 5.94%:
    r$_s$ = r$_{RF}$ + b(RP$_M$).

4. The cost of debt, r$_d$, is obtained from investment bankers. This is the resulting average rate on all debt, not the marginal rate on new debt.

5. The after-tax cost of debt is r$_d$(1 − T).

6. The weighted average cost of capital is calculated as WACC = w$_d$r$_d$(1 − T) + w$_s$r$_s$. It is rounded to 4 decimal places.

7. The value of the firm's operations is calculated as V$_{op}$ = [FCF(1 + g$_L$)]/(WACC − g$_L$), where FCF = $300 million and g$_L$ = 0.

8. Debt = w$_d$ × V$_{op}$.

9. The intrinsic value of equity after the recapitalization and repurchase is S$_{Post}$ = V$_{op}$ − Debt = w$_s$ × V$_{op}$.

10. The number of shares after the recap has been completed is found using this equation: n$_{Post}$ = n$_{Prior}$ × [(V$_{opNew}$ − D$_{New}$)/(V$_{opNew}$ − D$_{Old}$)]. The subscript "Old" indicates values from the original capital structure, where w$_d$ = 10%; the subscript "New" indicates values at the current capital structure after the recap and repurchase; and the subscript "Post" indicates values after the recap and repurchase.

11. The price after the recap and repurchase is P$_{Post}$ = S$_{Post}$/n$_{Post}$, but we can also find the price as P$_{Post}$ = (V$_{opNew}$ − D$_{Old}$)/n$_{Prior}$.

12. EBIT is $400 million; see Figure 15-4. Net income is NI = (EBIT − r$_d$D)(1 − T).

13. Earnings per share is EPS = NI/n$_{Post}$.

a way that the overall WACC would increase, because the cost of debt would increase by more than the cost of equity.

15-6d Estimating Value and Identifying the Optimal Capital Structure

As we showed previously, Strasburg currently has a $2,500 million intrinsic value of operations: w$_d$ = 10%, WACC = 12.00%, FCF = $300 million, and zero growth in FCF. Using the same approach as in Section 15-6a, we can use the data in Figure 15-6 to estimate

FIGURE 15-7
Effects of Capital Structure on the Cost of Capital

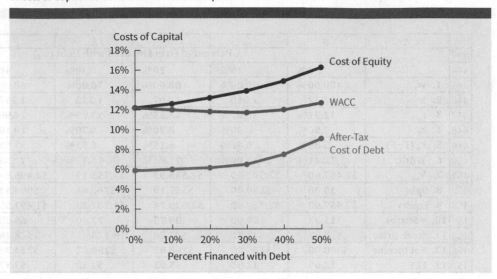

Strasburg's value of operations at different capital structures; these results are reported in Line 7 of Figure 15-6 and are graphed in Figure 15-8.[32] The maximum value of $2,553 million occurs at a capital structure with 30% debt, which also is the capital structure that minimizes the WACC.

Notice that the value of the firm initially increases but then begins to fall. As discussed earlier, the value initially rises because the WACC initially falls. But the rising costs of equity and debt eventually cause the WACC to increase, causing the value of the firm to fall. Notice how flat the curve is around the optimal level of debt. Thus, it doesn't make a great deal of difference whether Strasburg's capital structure has 20% debt or 30% debt.

Also, notice that the maximum value is about 4% greater than the value with no debt. Although this example is for a single company, the results are not unrealistic: The optimal capital structure for most firms can add 3% to 10% more value relative to zero debt, and there is a fairly wide range of w_d (from about 15% to 40%) over which value changes very little.

One of the reasons that debt increases value by a relatively small amount is the 2017 Tax Cuts and Jobs Act (TCJA), which cut the federal corporate tax rate from 35% to 21%. This change increases free cash flows but reduces the value of the tax shield provided by debt. In addition, the Act limits interest expense deductions to 30% of EBITDA in 2018–2021 and 30% of EBIT for subsequent years, which in turn reduces the value of the tax shield for many companies.

Figures 15-6 and 15-8 also show the values of debt and equity for each capital structure. The value of debt is found by multiplying the value of operations by the percentage of the firm that is financed by debt: Debt $= w_d \times V_{op}$. The intrinsic value of equity is found in a similar manner: S $= V_{op} -$ Debt $= w_s \times V_{op}$. Even though the intrinsic value of equity falls as debt increases, the wealth of shareholders is maximized at the maximum value of operations, as we explain in the next section.

---

[32]In this analysis we assume that Strasburg's expected EBIT and FCF are constant for the various capital structures. In a more refined analysis, we might try to estimate any possible declines in FCF at high levels of debt as the threat of bankruptcy becomes imminent.

FIGURE 15-8
Effects of Capital Structure on the Value of Operations (Millions of Dollars)

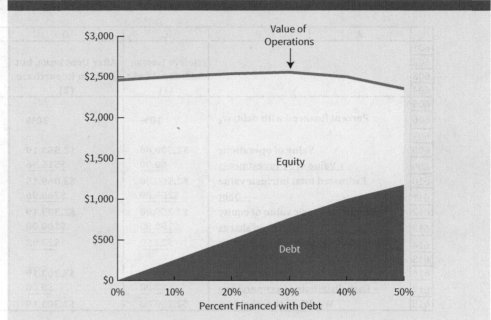

What happens to the costs of debt and equity when leverage increases? Explain.

JAB Industry's capital structure has 20% debt. Use the following data to calculate its cost of equity: levered beta = b_L = 1.1, r_{RF} = 6%, and RP_M = 5%. **(11.5)**

Use the Hamada equation to calculate JAB's unlevered beta and unlevered cost of equity. The tax rate is 20%. **(0.926, 10.63)**

What would its cost of equity be if JAB changes its capital structure to 35% debt? **(12.5%)**

15-7 Anatomy of a Recapitalization

Strasburg should issue enough additional debt to optimize its capital structure, and then use the debt proceeds to repurchase stock, a process known as a **recapitalization**. As shown in Figure 15-6, a capital structure with 30% debt is optimal. But before tackling the recap, as it is commonly called, let's consider the sequence of events, starting with the situation before Strasburg issues any additional debt. Figure 15-4 shows the valuation analysis of Strasburg at a capital structure consisting of 10% debt and 90% equity. These results are repeated in Column 1 of Figure 15-9, along with the shareholder wealth, which consists of $2,250 million in stock before the repurchase. The next step is to examine the impact of Strasburg's debt issuance.

15-7a Strasburg Issues New Debt but Has Not Yet Repurchased Stock

The next step in the recap is to issue debt and announce the firm's intent to repurchase stock with the newly issued debt. At the optimal capital structure of 30% debt, the value of the firm's operations is $2,553.19 million, as calculated in Figure 15-6 and repeated in

FIGURE 15-9
Anatomy of a Recapitalization (Millions, Except for Per Share Data)

	A	B	C	D	E
			Before Issuing Additional Debt (1)	**After Debt Issue, but Prior to Repurchase (2)**	**Post Repurchase (3)**
606		Percent financed with debt: w_d	10%	30%	30%
608		Value of operations	$2,500.00	$2,553.19	$2,553.19
609		+ Value of ST investments	$0.00	$515.96	$0.00
610		Estimated total intrinsic value	$2,500.00	$3,069.15	$2,553.19
611		− Debt	$250.00	$765.96	$765.96
612		Estimated intrinsic value of equity	$2,250.00	$2,303.19	$1,787.23
613		÷ Number of shares	$100.00	$100.00	$77.60
614		Estimated intrinsic price per share	$22.50	$23.03	$23.03
616		Value of stock	$2,250.00	$2,303.19	$1,787.23
617		+ Cash distributed in repurchase	$0.00	$0.00	$515.96
618		Wealth of shareholders	$2,250.00	$2,303.19	$2,303.19

Source: See the file *Ch15 Tool Kit.xlsx*. Numbers are reported as rounded values for clarity but are calculated using *Excel*'s full precision. Thus, intermediate calculations using the figure's rounded values will be inexact.

Notes:

1. The value of ST investments in Column 2 is equal to the amount of cash raised by issuing additional debt. This cash has not yet been used to repurchase shares, so it is held in the form of short-term investments: ST investments = $D_{New} - D_{Old}$.

2. The value of ST investments in Column 3 is zero because the funds have been used to repurchase shares of stock.

3. The number of shares in Column 3 reflects the shares repurchased: $n_{Post} = n_{Prior} - (Cash_{Rep}/P_{Prior}) = n_{Prior} - [(D_{New} - D_{Old})/P_{Prior}]$.

Column 2 of Figure 15-9. This value of operations is greater than the $2,500 million value of operations for w_d = 10% because the WACC is lower. Notice that Strasburg raised its debt from $250 million to $765.96 million, an increase of $515.96 million: $765.96 − $250 = $515.96. Because Column 2 reports data prior to the repurchase, Strasburg has short-term investments in the amount of $515.96 million, the amount that was raised in the debt issuance but that has not yet been used to repurchase stock.[33] As Figure 15-9 shows, Strasburg's intrinsic value of equity is $2,303.19 million:

$$Equity = V_{op} + ST\ investments - Debt$$
$$= \$2,553.19 + \$515.96 - \$765.96$$
$$= \$2,303.19\ million$$

Because Strasburg has not yet repurchased any stock, it still has 100 million shares outstanding. Therefore, the price per share after the debt issue but prior to the repurchase is:

$$P_{Prior} = S_{Prior}/n_{Prior}$$
$$= \$2,303.19/100 = \$23.03$$

---

[33]These calculations are shown in the *Excel* file *Ch15 Tool Kit.xlsx* on the textbook's Web site. The values reported in the text are rounded, but the values used in calculations in the spreadsheet are not rounded.

Column 2 of Figure 15-9 summarizes these calculations and also shows the wealth of the shareholders. Since the shareholders own Strasburg's equity, their total wealth is now $2,303.19 million. Notice that the increase in wealth of $53.19 million ($2,303.19 − $2,250 = $53.19) is identical to the increase in the value of operations. The increase in value comes from reducing the amount of taxes Strasburg pays and represents a transfer of value from the government to Strasburg's shareholders. By increasing the level of debt, interest expenses increase and taxes go down. Notice also that the debt issuance caused the intrinsic stock price to increase from $22.50 to $23.03.[34]

Summarizing these results, we see that the issuance of debt and the resulting change in the optimal capital structure caused (1) the WACC to decrease, (2) the value of operations to increase, (3) shareholder wealth to increase, and (4) the stock price to increase.

15-7b Strasburg Repurchases Stock

What happens to the stock price during the repurchase? In Chapter 14, we discussed repurchases and showed that a repurchase does not change the stock price. It is true that the additional debt will change the WACC and the stock price prior to the repurchase (P_{Prior}), but the subsequent repurchase itself will not affect the post-repurchase stock price (P_{Post}).[35] Therefore, $P_{Post} = P_{Prior}$. (Keep in mind that P_{Prior} is the price immediately prior to the repurchase, not the price prior to announcing the recapitalization and issuing the debt.)

Strasburg uses the entire amount of cash raised by the debt issue to repurchase stock. The total cash raised is equal to $D_{New} − D_{Old}$. The number of shares repurchased is equal to the cash raised by issuing debt divided by the repurchase price:

$$\text{Number of shares repurchased} = \frac{D_{New} - D_{Old}}{P_{Prior}} \tag{15-13}$$

The number of remaining shares after the repurchase, n_{Post}, is equal to the initial number of shares minus the number that is repurchased:

$$
\begin{aligned}
n_{Post} &= \text{Number of outstanding shares remaining after the repurchase} \\
&= n_{Prior} - \text{Number of shares repurchased} \\
&= n_{Prior} - \frac{D_{New} - D_{Old}}{P_{Prior}}
\end{aligned}
\tag{15-14}
$$

For Strasburg, the number of remaining shares after the repurchase is:

$$
\begin{aligned}
n_{Post} &= n_{Prior} - (D_{New} - D_{Old})/P_{Prior} \\
&= 100 - (\$765.96 - \$250)/\$23.03 \\
&= 77.6 \text{ million}
\end{aligned}
$$

[34]The increase in value is, in principle, the present value of the new tax shields as in Equation 15-8. Hamada's formula for levering beta, Equation 15-11, was developed for the special case in which debt is risk free. Since $r_d > r_{Rf}$ in this example, the additional value doesn't exactly equal the present value of the tax shields. It is possible to develop an equation similar to Equation 15-11 that deals with risky debt, and when it is used to lever and unlever beta, the additional value from a recapitalization is precisely equal to the present value of the new tax shields.

[35]As we discuss in Chapter 14, a stock repurchase may be a signal of a company's future prospects or it may be the way a company "announces" a change in capital structure, and either of these situations could have an impact on estimated free cash flows or WACC. However, neither situation applies to Strasburg.

Column 3 of Figure 15-9 summarizes these post-repurchase results. The repurchase doesn't change the value of operations, which remains at \$2,553.19 million. However, the short-term investments of \$515.96 are sold and the cash is used to repurchase stock. Strasburg is left with no short-term investments, so the intrinsic value of equity is:[36]

$$S_{Post} = \$2,553.19 - \$765.96 = \$1,787.23 \text{ million}$$

After the repurchase, Strasburg has 77.6 million shares of stock. We can verify that the intrinsic stock price has not changed:

$$P_{Post} = S_{Post}/n_{Post} = \$1,787.23/77.6 = \$23.03$$

Shareholders now own an equity position in the company worth only \$1,787.23 million, but they have received a cash distribution in the amount of \$515.96 million, so their total wealth is equal to the value of their equity plus the amount of cash they received: \$1,787.23 + \$515.96 = \$2,303.19, which is what it was in Column 2 before the repurchase but after issuing the debt.

Here are some points worth noting. As shown in Column 3 of Figure 15-9, the change in capital structure clearly added wealth to the shareholders, increased the price per share, and increased the cash (in the form of short-term investments) temporarily held by the company. However, the repurchase itself did not affect shareholder wealth or the price per share. The repurchase did reduce the cash held by the company and the number of shares outstanding, but shareholder wealth stayed constant. After the repurchase, shareholders directly own the funds used in the repurchase; before the repurchase, shareholders indirectly own the funds. In either case, shareholders own the funds. The repurchase simply takes them out of the company's account and puts them into the shareholders' personal accounts.

Figure 15-6 reports the number of shares and the intrinsic price per share in Lines 10–11. Notice that the number of shares goes down as debt goes up because the debt proceeds are used to buy back stock. Notice also that the capital structure that maximizes stock price, $w_d = 30\%$, is the same capital structure that optimizes the WACC and the value of operations.

Figure 15-6 also reports the earnings per share for the different levels of debt. Figure 15-10 graphs the intrinsic price per share and the earnings per share. Notice that the maximum earnings per share is at 50% debt even though the optimal capital structure is at 30% debt. This means that *maximizing EPS will not maximize shareholder wealth*.

15-7c Recapitalization: A Post-Mortem

In Chapter 12, we saw how a company can increase its value by improving its operations. There is good news and bad news regarding this connection. The good news is that small improvements in operations can lead to huge increases in value. The bad news is that it's often difficult to improve operations, especially if the company is already well managed and is in a competitive industry.

If instead you seek to increase a firm's value by changing its capital structure, we again have good news and bad news. The good news is that changing capital structure is easy—just call an investment banker and issue debt (or issue equity if the firm has too much debt). The bad news is that this will add only a relatively small amount of value. Of course,

---

[36]There may be a small rounding difference due to using rounded numbers in intermediate steps. See the *Excel* file **Ch16 Tool Kit.xlsx** for the exact calculations.

FIGURE 15-10
Effects of Capital Structure on Stock Price and Earnings per Share

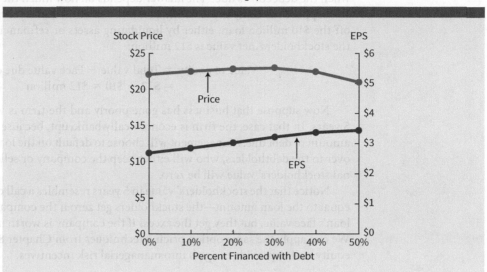

any additional value is better than none, so it's hard to understand why there are some mature firms with zero debt.

Finally, some firms have more debt than is optimal and should recapitalize to a lower debt level. This is called *deleveraging*. We can use exactly the same approach and the same formulas we used for Strasburg. The difference is that the debt will go down and the number of shares will go up. In other words, the company will issue new shares of stock and then use the proceeds to pay off debt, resulting in a capital structure with less debt and lower interest payments.

The TCJA's lower tax rate and limits on interest expense deductibility should cause many companies to reassess their capital structures and deleverage. Keep on the lookout for this to happen.

SELF-TEST

A firm's value of operations is equal to $800 million after a recapitalization. (The firm had no debt before the recap.) The firm raised $200 million in new debt and used this to buy back stock. The firm had no short-term investments before or after the recap. After the recap, $w_d = 25\%$. The firm had 10 million shares before the recap. Its federal-plus-state tax rate is 25%. What is S (the value of equity after the recap)? **($600 million)** *What is P_{Post} (the stock price after the recap)?* **($80/share)** *What is n_{Post} (the number of remaining shares after the recap)?* **(7.5 million)**

15-8 Risky Debt and Equity as an Option

In the previous sections, we evaluated equity and debt using the standard discounted cash flow techniques. However, we saw in Chapter 11 that if there is an opportunity for management to make a change as a result of new information after a project or investment has been started, then there might be an option component to the project or investment being evaluated. This type of opportunity also applies to managers of levered firms.

For example, consider Kunkel Inc., a small manufacturer of electronic wiring harnesses and instrumentation located in Minot, North Dakota. Kunkel has just issued some zero coupon bonds that mature in 5 years and have a $10 million face value. Kunkel plans to invest the debt proceeds in several new projects. What decision will management make when the debt comes due? The answer depends on how much the firm is worth in 5 years.

Suppose the company is worth a total of $22 million in 5 years. In this case, it will pay off the $10 million loan, either by liquidating assets or refinancing the debt. Either way, the stockholders' net value is $12 million:

$$\text{Value of equity} = \text{Total value} - \text{Face value due on debt}$$
$$= \$22 - \$10 = \$12 \text{ million}$$

Now suppose that business has gone poorly and the firm is worth only $9 million in 5 years. In that case, the firm is economically bankrupt, because its value is less than the amount of debt due. Management will choose to default on the loan and turn the company over to the debtholders, who will either keep the company or sell it. Either way, the original stockholders' value will be zero.

Notice that the stockholders' value in 5 years resembles a call option with a strike price equal to the loan amount—the stockholders get zero if the company is worth less than the loan's face value, but they get the excess if the company is worth more than the face value. We can apply the same option pricing techniques from Chapter 8 to estimate the value of equity and to provide insights into managerial risk incentives.

15-8a Using the Black-Scholes Option Pricing Model to Value Equity

Recall from Chapter 8 that the value of a call option depends on five factors: the price of the underlying asset, the strike price (X), the risk-free rate (r_{RF}), the time to expiration (T), and the volatility of the market value of the underlying asset (σ). When applied to a levered firm, the underlying asset is the total value of the firm (denoted here by P instead of V_L to show how it is used in the Black-Scholes model). The strike price is the face value of the debt, and the expiration date is the bond's maturity date.

resource

See Ch15 Tool Kit.xlsx on the textbook's Web site for all calculations.

The total value of the firm at the time it issues the debt but before it has yet invested the proceeds is the value of operations (which reflects expected future free cash flows of existing assets and growth plans) plus the proceeds from issuing debt. For Kunkel, the total value is $20 million when the debt is issued, the volatility is 40%, and the risk-free rate is 6%. The inputs for the Black-Scholes model are as follows:

$$P = \$20 \text{ million}$$
$$X = \$10 \text{ million}$$
$$t = 5 \text{ years}$$
$$r_{RF} = 6\%$$
$$\sigma = 40\%$$

The value of a European call option, as shown in Chapter 8, is:

$$V_0 = P[N(d_1)] - Xe^{-r_{RF}t}[N(d_2)] \tag{15-15}$$

where

$$d_1 = \frac{\ln(P/X) + (r_{RF} + \sigma^2/2)t}{\sigma\sqrt{t}} \quad \text{and} \quad d_2 = d_1 - \sigma\sqrt{t} \tag{15-16}$$

Using the inputs for Kunkel, the values of d_1 and d_2 are:

$$d_1 = \frac{\ln(20/10) + (0.06 + 0.40^2/2)5}{0.40\sqrt{5}} = 1.5576$$

$$d_2 = 1.5576 - 0.40\sqrt{5} = 0.6632$$

Using the *Excel* **NORMSDIST** function gives $N(d_1) = N(1.5576) = 0.9403$, $N(d_2) = N(0.6632) = 0.7464$. Using Equation 15-18, the Black-Scholes value is:

$$V = \$20(0.9403) - \$10e^{-0.06(5)}(0.7464) = \$13.28 \text{ million}$$

This means that the value of Kunkel's equity at the time it issues debt is $13.28 million. Because the values of debt and equity must sum to the total value of $20 million, the value of Kunkel's debt (at the issue date) is:

$$\text{Debt value} = \text{Total value} - \text{Equity value}$$
$$= \$20 - \$13.28 = \$6.72 \text{ million}$$

Recall that we can determine the rate (I) on a single future value (FV) at Year N if we know the present value (PV):

$$I = [(FV/PV)^{(1/N)}] - 1 \tag{15-17}$$

The rate on the zero coupon bond is its yield to maturity, so we can apply Equation 15-20 to determine the yield on the bond at the time it is issued:

$$\text{Yield on debt} = [(\$10/\$6.72)^{(1/5)}] - 1 = 0.0827 = 8.27\%$$

Thus, when Kunkel issues the debt, it receives $6.72 million and the yield on the debt is 8.27%. Notice that the yield on the debt, 8.27%, is greater than the 6% risk-free rate because the debt has default risk. In particular, the debtholders expect Kunkel to invest in projects with a total volatility of 40%, which means it is possible that the company will be worth less than $10 million when the debt matures.

15-8b Managerial Risk Incentives

The debt's yield depends on debtholders' perception of Kunkel's risk, which is determined in part by what debtholders expect management to do with the $6.72 million debt proceeds. Suppose Kunkel's management can find a way to increase future free cash flow volatility without reducing the value of operations (i.e., invest in projects that maintain NPV but that have higher risk). This will not change the total value of the firm, but it will change the relative values of debt and equity because the value of equity is like a call option on the firm's value (recall from Chapter 8 that options are worth more when volatility is higher). Table 15-2 shows different levels of volatility that correspond to management's choice of projects. For each volatility level, the table reports the total value, the value of equity, and the value of debt.

Notice in Table 15-2 that the total value remains constant because management is accepting projects with identical NPVs even though they have different risk levels. The row for 40% volatility (shown in a blue font) reports the values expected by the lenders *before* the debt is issued. However, suppose management instead undertakes projects

TABLE 15-2
The Value of Kunkel's Debt and Equity for Various Levels of Volatility (Millions of Dollars)

Standard Deviation of Total Value	Total Value	Value of Equity	Value of Debt
20%	$20	$12.62	$7.38
40	**20**	**13.28**	**6.72**
60	20	14.51	5.49
80	20	15.81	4.19
100	20	16.96	3.04

Source: Numbers in the table are shown as rounded values for clarity in reporting. However, unrounded values are used for all calculations. See the *Excel Tool Kit* for this chapter.

that increase its risk from a volatility of 40% to a volatility of 80% *after* the debt is issued. This will cause Kunkel's equity to increase in value by $2.53 million to $15.81 million, which is a 19% gain. Notice that the value of debt will decrease by the same dollar amount. Therefore, increasing risk causes a transfer of wealth from bondholders to stockholders. The reverse occurs if Kunkel undertakes projects that are safer than originally planned.

Investing borrowed funds in riskier assets than anticipated by lenders is called **bait-and-switch** because the firm obtains the money by promising one investment policy and then switches to another policy. The bait-and-switch problem is more severe when a firm's value is low relative to its level of debt. For example, suppose total value immediately falls to $11 million due to an unexpected change in the business environment. If the volatility remains at 40%, the value of equity drops to $5.25 million, and the value of debt drops to $5.75 million (see the *Tool Kit* for all calculations). If management now doubles volatility, the equity value increases to $7.69 million, an increase of 46%, coming at the expense of debtholders.[37] Therefore, the incentive for management to "roll the dice" with borrowed funds can be enormous—if management owns many stock options, then their payoff from rolling the dice is even greater than the payoff to stockholders!

Bondholders are aware of these incentives and write covenants into debt issues that restrict management's ability to invest in riskier projects than originally promised. However, their attempts to protect themselves are not always successful, as the failures of Toys "R" Us, Inc., Sports Authority, Inc., and Nine West Holdings demonstrate. The combination of a risky industry, high levels of debt, and option-based compensation has proven to be very dangerous.

---

[37]For extremely high volatilities, the yield on the debt is much higher than any reasonable required return on stock; see the *Tool Kit* for calculations. When debt is supposedly safer than equity, why would its yield be so high? There are two answers. First, the yield to maturity is high because debtholders get only the face value of the debt when the company does well. But when the company does poorly, the debtholders only get to take over a poorly performing company. As the volatility increases, the probability of receiving ownership of a poorly performing company instead of the face value of debt increases, driving down the value of the debt. In the limit, as the volatility continues to increase, the value of the debt is driven to zero, and the yield to maturity is driven to infinity. The second and more important answer is that the yield to maturity on debt is not equal to its expected or required return (unless the debt is risk free) and so is not what you should compare to the required return on stock in the first place. The calculated yield to maturity is actually the *maximum* return a bondholder will receive—not the expected return. If the company defaults, the actual yield received will be lower than the yield to maturity, and so the expected return on debt will always be less than the yield to maturity. We show an expected return on debt calculation in the *Tool Kit*.

Discuss how equity can be viewed as an option. Who has the option, and what decision can they make?

Why would management want to increase the riskiness of the firm? Why would this make bondholders unhappy?

What can bondholders do to limit management's ability to bait and switch?

15-9 Managing the Maturity Structure of Debt

In conjunction with choosing how much debt to have in its capital structure, firms must choose the maturities of the various securities that make up its debt. The following sections explain the factors associated with the choice of maturity structure.

15-9a Maturity Matching

Assume that Consolidated Tools, a Cincinnati machine tool manufacturer, made the decision to float a $25 million nonconvertible bond issue to help finance its 2018 capital budget. It must choose a maturity for the issue, taking into consideration the shape of the yield curve, management's own expectations about future interest rates, and the maturity of the assets being financed. To illustrate how asset maturities affect the choice of debt maturities, suppose Consolidated's capital projects consist primarily of new milling machinery. This machinery has an expected economic life of 10 years (even though it falls into the MACRS 5-year class life). Should Consolidated use debt with a 5-year, 10-year, 20-year, 30-year, or some other maturity?

Note that some of the new capital will come from common equity, which is permanent capital. On the other hand, debt maturities can be specified at the time of issue. If Consolidated financed its capital budget with 10-year sinking fund bonds, it would be matching asset and liability maturities. The cash flows resulting from the new machinery could be used to make the interest and sinking fund payments on the issue, so the bonds would be retired as the machinery wore out.

If instead Consolidated used 1-year debt, then it would have to pay off this debt with cash flows derived from assets other than the machinery in question, because the machinery doesn't produce enough cash in 1 year to pay off the loan. Of course, the 1-year debt could probably be rolled over year after year, out to the 10-year asset maturity. However, if interest rates rose, then Consolidated would have to pay a higher rate when it rolled over its debt, and if the company experienced difficulties, then it might not be able to refund the debt at a reasonable rate. Conversely, if it used 20-year or 30-year debt, it would have to service the debt long after the assets that were purchased with the funds had been scrapped and had ceased providing cash flows. This would worry lenders.

For all these reasons, *the safest all-around financing strategy is to match debt maturities with asset maturities.* In recognition of this fact, firms generally place great emphasis on maturity matching, and this factor often dominates the debt maturity decision.

15-9b Effects of Interest Rate Levels and Forecasts

Financial managers also consider interest rate levels and forecasts, both absolute and relative, when making financing decisions. For example, if long-term interest rates are high by historical standards and are expected to fall, managers will be reluctant to issue long-term debt, which would lock in those costs for long periods. We already know that one solution to this problem is to use a call provision, because callability permits refunding should interest rates drop. This flexibility comes at a cost, however, because of the call premium and also because the firm must set a higher coupon on callable debt. Floating-rate debt could be used, but another alternative would be to finance with short-term debt whenever long-term rates are historically high, and then, assuming that interest rates subsequently fall, sell a long-term issue to replace the short-term debt. Of course, this strategy has its risks: If interest rates move even higher, the firm will be forced to renew its short-term debt at higher and higher rates or to replace the short-term debt with a long-term bond that costs even more than it would have when the original decision was made.

15-9c Information Asymmetries

Consider two types of firms that need to raise funds to finance projects but that have high degrees of asymmetric information. The first type of firm has better prospects than investors expect, and the second has worse prospects. How does the information asymmetry affect maturity choice?

In the first situation, managers may be reluctant to issue common stock because this might be taken as a negative signal. But if they issue debt, the interest rate will be too high because it reflects investors' expectations (which are too pessimistic compared to the better informed expectations of management). Rather than locking in a high rate for a long period, the firm can issue short-term debt. It also will have a too-high interest rate, but it can be refinanced at a lower rate when it comes due and the firm's excellent prospects have been realized.

In the second situation, a company with poorer prospects than expected by the market would wish to issue stock but would also be worried about the negative signal (which is justified in this case). It would prefer to lock in a better interest rate than its true situation warrants, so it would want to issue long-term debt.[38]

15-9d Amount of Financing Required

Obviously, the amount of financing required will influence the financing decision. This is mainly because of flotation costs. A $5 million debt financing, which is small in Wall Street terms, would most likely be done with a term loan or a privately placed bond issue, whereas a firm seeking $2 billion of new debt would most likely use a public offering of long-term bonds.

15-9e Availability of Collateral

Generally, secured debt is less costly than unsecured debt. Thus, firms with large amounts of marketable fixed assets are likely to use a relatively large amount of long-term debt, especially mortgage bonds. Additionally, each year's financing decision would be influenced by the amount of qualified assets available as security for new bonds.

16-9f Evidence on Debt Maturity in Practice

Professors Custódio, Ferreira, and Laureano show that the ratio of total debt to total assets (based on book values) has remained relatively stable at about 27% for the past 40 years for publicly traded companies.[39] However, the mix of long-term debt and short-term debt has

---

[38]If the market expects firms in these two situations to behave as described, then it will interpret the choice of short-term debt versus long-term debt as a signal regarding the quality of the issuer. See M. Flannery, "Asymmetric Information and Risky Debt Maturity Choice," *Journal of Financial Economics,* Vol. 41, 1986, pp. 19–37.

[39]For more details, see C. Custódio, M. Ferreira, and L. Laureano, "Why Are US Firms Using More Short-Term Debt?" *Journal of Financial Economics,* Vol. 108, 2013, pp. 182–212.

changed dramatically. Long-term debt (maturing in more than 5 years) comprised about 62% of all debt financing in 1976 but has dropped to about 40% in recent years. In addition, the average original maturity of publicly issued debt has dropped from over 25 years to 11 years in that same period. What has caused this shift?

Part of the explanation is due to the changing nature of public companies. Before 1990, most IPOs were for relatively mature companies with a strong record of earnings. Since then, many smaller and riskier companies have gone public. Just as fewer of these companies pay dividends (as described in Chapter 14), fewer issue long-term debt. In fact, the maturity mix of debt issued by older companies has not changed significantly.

In general, many public companies today (mature and new) have high levels of informational asymmetry because they compete in complex product environments, including information technology, biotechnology, and pharmaceuticals. Theory suggests that such firms should raise capital from debt rather than equity and should raise short-term debt rather than long-term debt, and this is what the evidence shows.

SELF-TEST

What are some factors that financial managers consider when choosing the maturity structure of their debt?

How do information asymmetries affect financing decisions?

SUMMARY

This chapter examined the effects of financial leverage on stock prices, earnings per share, and the cost of capital. The key concepts covered are listed here.

- A firm's **optimal capital structure** is the mix of debt and equity that maximizes the stock price. At any point in time, management has a specific **target capital structure** in mind, presumably the optimal one, but this target may change over time.
- **Business risk** is the risk inherent in the firm's operations if it uses no debt. A firm will have little business risk if the demand for its products is stable, if the prices of its inputs and products remain relatively constant, if it can adjust its prices freely if costs increase, and if a high percentage of its costs are variable and hence will decrease if sales decrease. Other things the same, the lower a firm's business risk, the higher its optimal debt ratio.
- **Financial leverage** is the extent to which fixed-income securities (debt and preferred stock) are used in a firm's capital structure. **Financial risk** is the added risk borne by stockholders as a result of financial leverage.
- **Operating leverage** is the extent to which fixed costs are used in a firm's operations. In business terminology, a high degree of operating leverage, other factors held constant, implies that a relatively small change in sales results in a large change in ROIC.
- If there are no corporate or personal taxes, Modigliani and Miller showed that the value of a levered firm is equal to the value of an otherwise identical but unlevered firm:

$$V_L = V_U$$

- If there are only corporate taxes, Modigliani and Miller showed that a firm's value increases as it adds debt due to the interest rate deductibility of debt:

$$V_L = V_U + TD$$

- If there are personal and corporate taxes, Miller showed that:

$$V_L = V_U + \left[1 - \frac{(1 - T_c)(1 - T_s)}{(1 - T_d)}\right]D$$

- The **Hamada equation** shows the effect of financial leverage on beta as follows:

$$b = b_U[1 + (1 - T)(D/S)]$$

Firms can use their current beta, tax rate, and debt/equity ratio to derive their **unlevered beta, b_U,** as follows:

$$b_U = b/[1 + (1 - T)(D/S)] = b/[1 + (1 - T)(w_d/w_s)]$$

- The **trade-off theory** of capital structure states that debt initially adds value because interest is tax deductible but that debt also brings costs associated with actual or potential bankruptcy. The optimal capital structure strikes a balance between the tax benefits of debt and the costs associated with bankruptcy.
- **Signaling hypothesis** assumes that there is **asymmetric information** because managers have more complete information than investors. A stock issue is viewed as a negative signal, whereas a bond issue is a neutral (or small negative) signal. As a result, companies try to avoid having to issue stock by maintaining a **reserve borrowing capacity**, and this means using less debt in "normal" times than the trade-off theory would suggest.
- A firm's owners may decide to use a relatively large amount of debt to constrain the managers. A *high debt ratio raises the threat of bankruptcy,* which not only carries a cost but also forces managers to be more careful and less wasteful with shareholders' money. Many of the corporate takeovers and leveraged buyouts in recent years were designed to improve efficiency by reducing the cash flow available to managers.
- When debt is risky, management may choose to default. If the debt is zero coupon debt, then this makes equity like an option on the value of the firm with a strike price equal to the face value of the debt.
- When a firm has risky debt and equity is like an option, management has an incentive to increase the firm's risk in order to increase the equity value at the expense of the debt value. This is called **bait-and-switch**.
- *Web Extension 15A* provides proofs of the MM propositions.
- *Web Extension 15B* illustrates bond refunding operations.

QUESTIONS

(15-1)   Define each of the following terms:

a. Capital structure; business risk; financial risk
b. Operating leverage; financial leverage; break-even point
c. Reserve borrowing capacity

(15-2)   What term refers to the uncertainty inherent in projections of future ROIC?

(15-3)   Firms with relatively high nonfinancial fixed costs are said to have a high degree of what?

(15-4)   "One type of leverage affects both EBIT and EPS. The other type affects only EPS." Explain this statement.

(15-5)   Why is the following statement true? "Other things being the same, firms with relatively stable sales are able to carry relatively high debt ratios."

(15-6)   Why do public utility companies usually have capital structures that are different from those of retail firms?

(15-7)   Why is EBIT generally considered to be independent of financial leverage? Why might EBIT be influenced by financial leverage at high debt levels?

(15-8)   If a firm went from zero debt to successively higher levels of debt, why would you expect its stock price to first rise, then hit a peak, and then begin to decline?

(15-9)   Your firm's CEO has just learned about options and how your firm's equity can be viewed as an option. Why might he want to increase the riskiness of the firm, and why might the bondholders be unhappy about this?

SELF-TEST PROBLEMS   SOLUTIONS SHOWN IN APPENDIX A

(ST-1)
Optimal Capital Structure   The Rogers Company is currently in this situation: (1) EBIT = $4.7 million; (2) tax rate, T = 25%; (3) value of debt, D = $2 million; (4) r_d = 10%; (5) r_s = 15%; (6) shares of stock outstanding, n = 600,000; and (7) stock price, P = $30. The firm's market is stable and it expects no growth, so all earnings are paid out as dividends. The debt consists of perpetual bonds.

a. What is the total market value of the firm's stock, S, and the firm's total market value, V?
b. What is the firm's weighted average cost of capital?
c. Suppose the firm can increase its debt by issuing debt and repurchasing stock so that its capital structure will have 50% debt, based on market values. At this level of debt, its cost of equity rises to 18.5% and its interest rate on all debt will rise to 12%. (It will have to call and refund the old debt.) What is the WACC under this capital structure? What is the total value? How much debt will it issue, and what is the stock price after the repurchase? How many shares will remain outstanding after the repurchase?

(ST-2)
Hamada Equation   Lighter Industrial Corporation (LIC) is considering a large-scale recapitalization. Currently, LIC is financed with 25% debt and 75% equity. LIC is considering increasing its level of debt until it is financed with 60% debt and 40% equity. The beta on its common stock at the current level of debt is 1.5, the risk-free rate is 6%, the market risk premium is 4%, and LIC faces a 25% federal-plus-state tax rate.

a. What is LIC's current cost of equity?
b. What is LIC's unlevered beta?
c. What will be the new beta and new cost of equity if LIC recapitalizes?

PROBLEMS   ANSWERS ARE IN APPENDIX B

EASY PROBLEMS 1–9

(15-1)
Break-Even Quantity   Shapland Inc. has fixed operating costs of $500,000 and variable costs of $50 per unit. If it sells the product for $75 per unit, what is the break-even quantity?

(15-2)
Unlevered Beta   Counts Accounting's beta is 1.2 and its tax rate is 25%. If it is financed with 21% debt, what is its unlevered beta?

(15-3)
Premium for
Financial Risk

Ethier Enterprise has an unlevered beta of 1.0. Ethier is financed with 50% debt and has a levered beta of 1.6. If the risk-free rate is 5.5% and the market risk premium is 6%, how much is the additional premium that Ethier's shareholders require to be compensated for financial risk?

(15-4)
MM Model with
Zero Taxes

Quillpen Company is unlevered and has a value of $40 billion. An otherwise identical but levered firm finances 25% of its capital structure with debt. Under the MM zero-tax model, what is the value of the levered firm?

(15-5)
MM Model with
Corporate Taxes

Walkrun Inc. is unlevered and has a value of $400 billion. An otherwise identical but levered firm finances 25% of its capital structure with debt at an 8% interest rate. No growth is expected. Assume the corporate tax rate is 25%. Use the MM model with corporate taxes to determine the value of the levered firm.

(15-6)
Miller Model with
Corporate and
Personal Taxes

Cruz Corporation has $100 billion of debt outstanding. An otherwise identical firm has no debt and has a market value of $500 billion. Under the Miller model, what is Cruz's value if the federal-plus-state corporate tax rate is 28%, the effective personal tax rate on stock is 17%, and the personal tax rate on debt is 29%?

(15-7)
Value of Equity after
Recapitalization

Nichols Corporation's value of operations is equal to $500 million after a recapitalization (the firm had no debt before the recap). It raised $200 million in new debt and used this to buy back stock. Nichols had no short-term investments before or after the recap. After the recap, w_d = 40%. What is S (the value of equity after the recap)?

(15-8)
Stock Price after
Recapitalization

Lee Manufacturing's value of operations is equal to $900 million after a recapitalization. (The firm had no debt before the recap.) Lee raised $300 million in new debt and used this to buy back stock. Lee had no short-term investments before or after the recap. After the recap, w_d = 1/3. The firm had 30 million shares before the recap. What is P (the stock price after the recap)?

(15-9)
Shares
Remaining after
Recapitalization

Dye Trucking raised $150 million in new debt and used this to buy back stock. After the recap, Dye's stock price is $7.50. If Dye had 60 million shares of stock before the recap, how many shares does it have after the recap?

INTERMEDIATE PROBLEMS 10–11

(15-10)
Break-Even Point

Schweser Satellites Inc. produces satellite earth stations that sell for $100,000 each. The firm's fixed costs, F, are $2 million, 50 earth stations are produced and sold each year, profits total $500,000, and the firm's assets (all equity financed) are $5 million. The firm estimates that it can change its production process, adding $4 million to assets and $500,000 to fixed operating costs. This change will reduce variable costs per unit by $10,000 and increase output by 20 units. However, the sales price on all units must be lowered to $95,000 to permit sales of the additional output. The firm has tax loss carryforwards that render its tax rate zero, its cost of equity is 16%, and it uses no debt.

 a. What is the incremental profit? To get a rough idea of the project's profitability, what is the project's expected rate of return for the next year (defined as the incremental profit divided by the investment)? Should the firm make the investment? Why or why not?

 b. Would the firm's break-even point increase or decrease if it made the change?

 c. Would the new situation expose the firm to more or less business risk than the old one?

(15-11)
Capital Structure Analysis

The Rivoli Company has no debt outstanding, and its financial position is given by the following data:

Expected EBIT	$600,000
Growth rate in EBIT, g_L	0%
Cost of equity, r_s	10%
Shares outstanding, n_0	200,000
Tax rate, T (federal-plus-state)	25%

a. What is Rivoli's intrinsic value of operations (i.e., its unlevered value)? What is its intrinsic stock price? Its earnings per share?

b. Rivoli is considering selling bonds and simultaneously repurchasing some of its stock. If it moves to a capital structure with 30% debt based on market values, its cost of equity, r_s, will increase to 12% to reflect the increased risk. Bonds can be sold at a cost, r_d, of 7%. Based on the new capital structure, what is the new weighted average cost of capital? What is the levered value of the firm? What is the amount of debt?

c. Based on the new capital structure, what is the new stock price? What is the remaining number of shares? What is the new earnings per share?

CHALLENGING PROBLEMS 12–15

(15-12)
Capital Structure Analysis

Pettit Printing Company (PPC) has a total market value of $100 million, consisting of 1 million shares selling for $50 per share and $50 million of 10% perpetual bonds now selling at par. The company's EBIT is $13.24 million, and its tax rate is 15%. Pettit can change its capital structure by either increasing its debt to 70% (based on market values) or decreasing it to 30%. If it decides to *increase* its use of leverage, it must call its old bonds and issue new ones with a 12% coupon. If it decides to *decrease* its leverage, it will call its old bonds and replace them with new 8% coupon bonds. The company will sell or repurchase stock at the new equilibrium price to complete the capital structure change.

PPC expects no growth in its EBIT, so g_L is zero. Its current cost of equity, r_s, is 14%. If it increases leverage, r_s will be 16%. If it decreases leverage, r_s will be 13%. What is the firm's WACC and total corporate value under each capital structure?

(15-13)
Optimal Capital Structure with Hamada

Beckman Engineering and Associates (BEA) is considering a change in its capital structure. BEA currently has $20 million in debt carrying a rate of 8%, and its stock price is $40 per share with 2 million shares outstanding. BEA is a zero-growth firm and pays out all of its earnings as dividends. The firm's EBIT is $16 million, and it faces a 25% federal-plus-state tax rate. The market risk premium is 4%, and the risk-free rate is 6%. BEA is considering increasing its debt level to a capital structure with 40% debt, based on market values, and repurchasing shares with the extra money that it borrows. BEA will have to retire the old debt in order to issue new debt, and the rate on the new debt will be 9%. BEA has a beta of 1.0.

a. What is BEA's unlevered beta? Use market value D/S (which is the same as w_d/w_s) when unlevering.

b. What are BEA's new beta and cost of equity if it has 40% debt?

c. What are BEA's WACC and total value of the firm with 40% debt?

(15-14)
WACC and Optimal Capital Structure

F. Pierce Products Inc. is considering changing its capital structure. F. Pierce currently has no debt and no preferred stock, but it would like to add some debt to take advantage of the tax shield. Its investment banker has indicated that the pre-tax cost of debt under various possible capital structures would be as follows:

Market Debt-to-Value Ratio (w_d)	Market Equity-to-Value Ratio (w_s)	Market Debt-to-Equity Ratio (D/S)	Before-Tax Cost of Debt (r_d)
0.0	1.0	0.00	6.0%
0.10	0.90	0.1111	6.4
0.20	0.80	0.2500	7.0
0.30	0.70	0.4286	8.2
0.40	0.60	0.6667	10.0

F. Pierce uses the CAPM to estimate its cost of common equity, r_s and at the time of the analysis the risk-free rate is 5%, the market risk premium is 6%, and the company's tax rate is 25%. F. Pierce estimates that its beta now (which is "unlevered" because it currently has no debt) is 0.8. Based on this information, what is the firm's optimal capital structure, and what would be the weighted average cost of capital at the optimal capital structure?

(15-15)
Equity Viewed as an Option

A. Fethe Inc. is a custom manufacturer of guitars, mandolins, and other stringed instruments and is located near Knoxville, Tennessee. Fethe's current value of operations, which is also its value of debt plus equity, is estimated to be $100 million. Fethe has $50 million face value, zero coupon debt that is due in 10 years. The risk-free rate is 6%, and the standard deviation of returns for companies similar to Fethe is 50%. Fethe's owners view their equity investment as an option, and they would like to know the value of their investment.

a. Using the Black-Scholes option pricing model, how much is Fethe's equity worth?
b. How much is the debt worth today? What is its yield?
c. How would the equity value and the yield on the debt change if Fethe's managers could use risk management techniques to reduce its volatility to 30%? Can you explain this?

SPREADSHEET PROBLEMS

(15-16)
Build a Model: WACC and Optimal Capital Structure

resource

Start with the partial model in the file *Ch15 P16 Build a Model.xlsx* on the textbook's Web site. Reacher Technology has consulted with investment bankers and determined the interest rate it would pay for different capital structures, as shown in the following table. Data for the risk-free rate, the market risk premium, an estimate of Reacher's unlevered beta, and the tax rate are also shown. Reacher expects zero growth. Based on this information, what is the firm's optimal capital structure, and what is the weighted average cost of capital at the optimal structure?

Percent Financed with Debt (w_d)	Before-Tax Cost Debt (r_d)	Input Data	
0%	6.0%	Risk-free rate	4.5%
5%	6.1%	Market risk premium	5.5%
10%	6.3%	Unlevered beta	1.1
15%	6.7%	Tax rate	25.0%
20%	10.0%		
30%	12.5%		
35%	15.5%		
40%	18.0%		

(15-17)
Build a Model:
Equity Viewed
as an Option

resource

Higgs Bassoon Corporation is a custom manufacturer of bassoons and other wind instruments. Its current value of operations, which is also its value of debt plus equity, is estimated to be $200 million. Higgs has zero coupon debt outstanding that matures in 3 years with $110 million face value. The risk-free rate is 5%, and the standard deviation of returns for similar companies is 60%. The owners of Higgs Bassoon view their equity investment as an option and would like to know its value. Start with the partial model in the file *Ch15 P17 Build a Model.xlsx* on the textbook's Web site, and answer the following questions:

a. Using the Black-Scholes option pricing model, how much is the equity worth?

b. How much is the debt worth today? What is its yield?

c. How would the equity value change if the company used risk management techniques to reduce its volatility to 45%? Can you explain this?

d. Graph the yield to maturity on debt versus the face value of debt for values of the face value from $10 to $160 million.

e. Graph the values of debt and equity for volatilities from 0.10 to 0.90 when the face value of the debt is $110 million.

MINI CASE

Assume you have just been hired as a business manager of PizzaPalace, a regional pizza restaurant chain. The company's EBIT was $120 million last year and is not expected to grow. PizzaPalace is in the 25% state-plus-federal tax bracket, the risk-free rate is 6 percent, and the market risk premium is 6 percent. The firm is currently financed with all equity, and it has 10 million shares outstanding.

   When you took your corporate finance course, your instructor stated that most firms' owners would be financially better off if the firms used some debt. When you suggested this to your new boss, he encouraged you to pursue the idea. If the company were to recapitalize, then debt would be issued, and the funds received would be used to repurchase stock. As a first step, assume that you obtained from the firm's investment banker the following estimated costs of debt for the firm at different capital structures:

Percent Financed with Debt, w_d	r_d
0%	—
20	8.0%
30	8.5
40	10.0
50	12.0

a. Using the free cash flow valuation model, show the only avenues by which capital structure can affect value.

b. (1) What is business risk? What factors influence a firm's business risk?

   (2) What is operating leverage, and how does it affect a firm's business risk? Show the operating break-even point if a company has fixed costs of $200, a sales price of $15, and variable costs of $10.

c. Explain the difference between financial risk and business risk.

d. To illustrate the effects of financial leverage for PizzaPalace's management, consider two hypothetical firms: Firm U (which uses no debt financing) and Firm L (which uses $4,000 of 8% interest rate debt). Both firms have $20,000 in net operating capital, a 25% tax rate, and an expected EBIT of $2,400.

(1) Construct partial income statements, which start with EBIT, for the two firms.

(2) Calculate NOPAT, ROIC, and ROE for both firms.

(3) What does this example illustrate about the impact of financial leverage on ROE?

(4) Why did leverage increase ROE in this example?

e. What happens to ROE for Firm U and Firm L if EBIT falls to $1,600? What happens if EBIT falls to $1,200? What is the after-tax cost of debt? What does this imply about the impact of leverage on risk and return?

f. What does capital structure theory attempt to do? What lessons can be learned from capital structure theory? Be sure to address the MM models.

g. What does the empirical evidence say about capital structure theory? What are the implications for managers?

h. With the preceding points in mind, now consider the optimal capital structure for PizzaPalace.

(1) For each capital structure under consideration, calculate the levered beta, the cost of equity, and the WACC.

(2) Now calculate the corporate value for each capital structure.

i. Describe the recapitalization process and apply it to PizzaPalace. Calculate the resulting value of the debt that will be issued, the resulting market value of equity, the price per share, the number of shares repurchased, and the remaining shares. Considering only the capital structures under analysis, what is PizzaPalace's optimal capital structure?

j. Liu Industries is a highly levered firm. Suppose there is a large probability that Liu will default on its debt. The value of Liu's operations is $4 million. The firm's debt consists of 1-year, zero coupon bonds with a face value of $2 million. Liu's volatility, σ, is 0.60, and the risk-free rate r_{RF} is 6%.

Because Liu's debt is risky, its equity is like a call option and can be valued with the Black-Scholes Option Pricing Model (OPM). (See Chapter 8 for details of the OPM.)

(1) What are the values of Liu's stock and debt? What is the yield on the debt?

(2) What are the values of Liu's stock and debt for volatilities of 0.40 and 0.80? What are yields on the debt?

(3) What incentives might the manager of Liu have if she understands the relationship between equity value and volatility? What might debtholders do in response?

k. How do companies manage the maturity structure of their debt?

SELECTED ADDITIONAL CASES

The following cases from CengageCompose cover many of the concepts discussed in this chapter and are available at **http://compose.cengage.com**.

Klein-Brigham Series:

Case 9, "Kleen Kar, Inc."; Case 43, "Mountain Springs, Inc."; and Case 57, "Greta Cosmetics, Inc.," each present a situation similar to the Strasburg example in the text. Case 74, "The Western Company"; and Case 99, "Moore Plumbing Supply," explore capital structure policies.

Brigham-Buzzard Series:

Case 8, "Powerline Network Corporation (Operating Leverage, Financial Leverage, and the Optimal Capital Structure)."

CHAPTER 16

Supply Chains and Working Capital Management

What do Apple, Molson Brewing Company, Whirlpool, and Alcoa have in common? Each was a leader in its industry according to the annual *2018 CFO/The Hackett Group Working Capital Scorecard*, which covered the 1,000 largest U.S. publicly traded firms. Each company is rated on its "cash conversion cycle," which is the *net* amount of time between a company's payments to its suppliers and collections from its customers. A shorter cycle is better because it means that a company has more cash to invest or to pay out to its shareholders.

The median industry ratio varies significantly. For example, the median in the pharmaceuticals industry is 125 days, but the median in retail food & staples is only 18. The median airline holds zero days of working capital—its payables are as large as its combined receivables and inventory. But even within an industry, there is considerable variation. For example, Walmart has 6 days but Sears has 68.

There has been a downward trend in the average cash conversion cycle during the past five years. How can companies cut their cycles and free up cash for other uses? Read on to find out.

Sources: See Ramona Dzinkowski, "Working Capital Scorecard: Suppliers Can Wait," *CFO,* July 10, 2018, at the Web site **http://ww2.cfo.com/cash-flow/2018/07/working-capital-scorecard-cash-conversion-cycle/**; for the rankings, see the CFO/Hackett Group Working Capital Scorecard at **ww2.cfo.com/17jul_workingcap_charts/**.

Corporate Valuation and Working Capital Management

Superior working capital management can dramatically reduce required investments in operating capital, which can lead, in turn, to larger free cash flows and greater firm value.

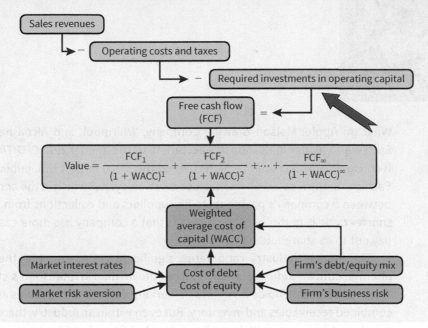

Working capital management involves two basic questions: (1) What is the appropriate amount of working capital, both in total and for each specific account? (2) How should working capital be financed? Note that sound working capital management goes beyond finance. Indeed, improving the firm's working capital position generally comes from improvements in the operating divisions. For example, experts in logistics, operations management, and information technology often work with engineers and production specialists to develop ways to speed up the manufacturing process and thus reduce the goods-in-process inventory. Similarly, marketing managers and logistics experts cooperate to develop better ways to deliver the firm's products to customers. Finance comes into play in evaluating how effective the firm's operating departments are relative to other firms in its industry and also in evaluating the profitability of alternative proposals for improving working capital management. In addition, financial managers decide how much cash their companies should keep on hand and how much short-term financing should be used to finance their working capital.

16-1 Overview of Supply Chain Management

A **supply chain** consists of the network of organizations that convert materials and labor into products or services that ultimately are purchased by consumers. A requirement for effective supply chain management (SCM) is sharing information throughout the chain, all the way from retailers (where consumers make purchases) to wholesalers, to manufacturers, to suppliers, and even back to the suppliers' suppliers. SCM requires special computer software, but even more importantly, it requires cooperation among the different companies and departments in the supply chain.

Consider some of the activities involved in the supply chain of a company that purchases materials, adds value, and then sells the product. The company places an order with a supplier. The supplier ships the order and bills the company. The company either pays immediately or waits, in which case the unpaid amount is called an **account payable**. The newly arrived shipment goes into inventory until it is needed. If the supplier shipped finished products, the company will distribute the goods to its warehouses or retail facilities. If instead the supplier shipped components or raw materials, the company will use the shipment in a manufacturing or assembly process, putting the final product into its finished goods inventory. Items from the finished goods inventory will be shipped either directly to customers or to warehouses for later shipments.

When a customer purchases the product, the company bills the customer and often offers the customer credit. If the customer accepts the credit and doesn't pay immediately, the unpaid balance is called an **account receivable**.[1] At the time a credit sale is made, three events occur: (1) Inventories are reduced by the cost of goods sold. (2) Accounts receivable are increased by the sales price. (3) The difference between the amounts that receivables increase and that inventories decrease is reported immediately as pre-tax profit (even though cash has not yet been received), adjusted for taxes, and then added to the previous retained earnings balance.

If the sale were instead for cash, then the scenario just described would accurately describe cash flow. However, a firm will not receive cash from a credit sale unless and until the account is collected. Firms have been known to encourage credit "sales" to weak customers in order to report high current profits. This might boost the firm's stock price—but only for a short time. Eventually, future credit losses will reduce earnings, at which time the stock price will fall. This is another example of how differences between a firm's stock price and its intrinsic value can arise.

During this supply chain process, companies accrue unpaid wages (because companies don't pay employees daily) and unpaid taxes (because companies don't pay the IRS daily).

Notice that several current assets and current liabilities are involved in this process— *cash* is spent (when actually paying suppliers, employees, taxes, etc.) and collected (when customers pay), *accounts receivable* are created and collected, *inventory* ebbs and flows, *accounts payable* are generated and paid, and *accruals* accumulate until paid. Recall that these are the same operating current assets (cash, accounts receivable, and inventories) and operating current liabilities (accounts payable and accruals) that we have used in previous chapters when calculating **net operating working capital (NOWC)**, which is defined as operating current assets minus operating current liabilities.

In addition to operating current assets and operating current liabilities, there are two other current accounts related to working capital management: short-term investments and short-term debt. We discuss individual current assets and liabilities later in the chapter, but it will be helpful if we first distinguish between cash and short-term investments because this can be a source of confusion.

Many dictionaries define cash as currency (coins and bills) and demand deposit accounts (such as a checking account at a bank). Most companies have very little currency on hand, and most have relatively small checking accounts. However, most companies own a wide variety of short-term financial assets. For example, Apple and Microsoft own (1) checking accounts, (2) U.S. Treasury and agency securities, (3) certificates of deposits and time deposits, (4) commercial paper, (5) money market funds and other mutual funds (with low price volatility), (6) short-term or floating-rate corporate and municipal notes and bonds, and (7) and floating-rate preferred stock. Most of these holdings can be

---

[1]For every account receivable recorded by a seller (which is a current asset), an equal account payable is recorded by the purchaser (which is a liability).

converted into cash very quickly at prices identical or very close to their book values, so sometimes they are called cash equivalents.

Some of these financial assets are held to support current ongoing operations and some are held for future purposes, and this is the distinction we make when defining cash and short-term investments. In particular, we define cash as the total value of the short-term financial assets that are held to support ongoing operations because this is the definition of cash that is required to be consistent with the definition of cash used to calculate NOWC (which is used, in turn, to calculated free cash flow and the intrinsic value of the company). We define short-term investments as the total value of short-term financial assets held for future purposes. Keep these distinctions in mind when we discuss cash management and short-term investments later in the chapter.

You should be aware that the financial press isn't as careful with its definitions. For example, the press often uses **working capital** (or *gross working capital*) to denote current assets used in operations, which ignores the impact operating current liabilities have on cash flow.[2] The press also uses **net working capital** to denote *all* current assets minus *all* current liabilities, which mixes operating assets and liabilities with financing choices. We focus on net operating working capital because NOWC is directly related to free cash flow from operations.

16-2 Using and Financing Operating Current Assets

Operating current assets (CA) are used to support sales. Having too much invested in operating CA is inefficient, but having too little might constrain sales. Many companies have seasonal, growing sales, so they have seasonal, growing operating CA, which has an implication for the pattern of financing that companies choose. The next sections address these issues.

16-2a Efficient Investment in Operating Current Assets

Most companies can influence their levels of operating current assets. Some companies choose a **relaxed policy** and hold a lot of cash, receivables, and inventories relative to sales. On the other hand, if a firm has a **restricted policy**, holdings of current assets are minimized and we say that the firm's policy is *tight* or *lean-and-mean*. A **moderate policy** lies between the two extremes.

We can use the DuPont equation from Chapter 3 to demonstrate how working capital management affects the return on equity:

$$\text{ROE} = \text{Profit margin} \times \text{Total assets turnover} \times \text{Equity multiplier}$$

$$= \text{Profit margin} \times \left[\frac{\text{Sales}}{\text{Assets}}\right] \times \text{Equity multiplier}$$

A relaxed policy means a high level of current assets and hence a low total assets turnover ratio; this results in a low return on equity (ROE), other things held constant. Conversely, a restricted policy results in low current assets, a high turnover, and hence a relatively high ROE. However, the restricted policy exposes the firm to risk, because

---

[2]The term "working capital" originated with the old Yankee peddler, who would load his wagon with pots and pans and then take off to peddle his wares. His horse and wagon were his fixed assets, while his merchandise was sold, or turned over at a profit, and thus was called his *working capital*.

shortages can lead to work stoppages, unhappy customers, and serious long-run problems. The moderate policy falls between the two extremes. The optimal strategy is the one that management believes will maximize the firm's long-run free cash flow and thus the stock's intrinsic value.

Note that changing technologies can lead to changes in the optimal policy. For example, if a new technology makes it possible for a manufacturer to produce a given product in 5 rather than 10 days, then work-in-progress inventories can be cut in half. Similarly, most retailers have inventory management systems that use bar codes on all merchandise. These codes are read at the cash register; this information is transmitted electronically to a computer that adjusts the remaining stock of the item; and the computer automatically places an order with the supplier's computer when the supply falls to a specified level. This process lowers the **safety stock** of inventory held to guard against larger-than-normal sales and/or shipping delays.

16-2b Financing Operating Current Assets

Investments in operating current assets must be financed, and the primary sources of funds include bank loans, credit from suppliers (accounts payable), accrued liabilities, long-term debt, and common equity. Each of those sources has advantages and disadvantages, so a firm must decide which sources are best for it.

To begin, note that most businesses experience seasonal and/or cyclical fluctuations. For example, construction firms tend to peak in the summer, retailers peak around Christmas, and the manufacturers who supply both construction companies and retailers follow related patterns. Similarly, the sales of virtually all businesses increase when the economy is strong, so they increase operating current assets during booms but let inventories and receivables fall during recessions. However, current assets rarely drop to zero—companies maintain some **permanent operating current assets**, which are the operating current assets needed even at the low point of the business cycle. For a growing firm in a growing economy, permanent current assets tend to increase over time. Also, as sales increase during a cyclical upswing, current assets are increased; these extra current assets are defined as **temporary operating current assets** as opposed to permanent current assets. The way permanent and temporary operating current assets are financed is called the firm's **operating current assets financing policy**. Three alternative policies are discussed next.

MATURITY MATCHING APPROACH

The **maturity matching approach**, which is also called the **self-liquidating approach**, calls for matching asset and liability maturities as shown in Panel A of Figure 16-1. All of the fixed assets plus the permanent current assets are financed with long-term capital, but temporary current assets are financed with short-term debt. Inventory expected to be sold in 30 days would be financed with a 30-day bank loan; a machine expected to last for 5 years would be financed with a 5-year loan; a 20-year building would be financed with a 20-year mortgage bond; and so on.

Actually, two factors prevent exact maturity matching: uncertain asset lives and equity financing. For example, a firm might finance inventories with a 30-day bank loan, expecting to sell the inventories and use the cash to retire the loan. But if sales are slow, then the "life" of the inventories would exceed the original 30-day estimate and the cash from sales would not be forthcoming, perhaps causing the firm problems in paying off the loan when it comes due. In addition, some common equity financing must be used, and common equity has no maturity. Still, many firms adopt a short-term financing policy that comes close to matching asset and liability maturities.

FIGURE 16-1
Alternative Approaches to Finance Operating Current Assets

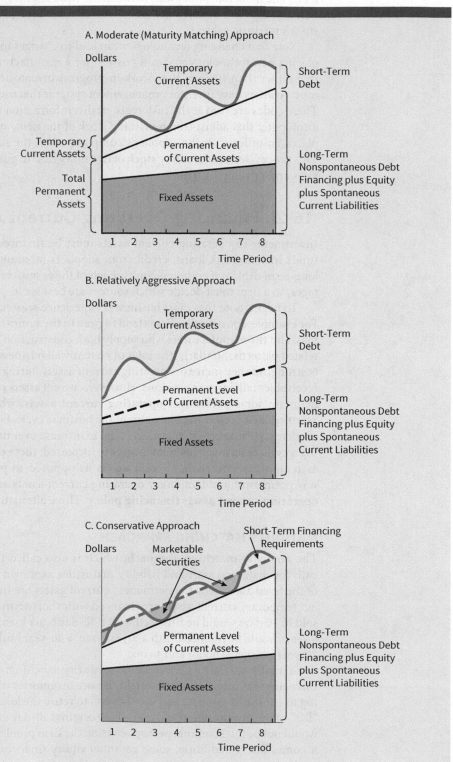

AGGRESSIVE APPROACH

Panel B of Figure 16-1 illustrates the **aggressive approach** in which a firm finances some of its permanent assets with short-term debt. Note that we used the term "relatively" in the title for Panel B because there can be different *degrees* of aggressiveness. For example, the dashed line in Panel B could have been drawn *below* the line designating fixed assets, indicating that all the current assets—both permanent and temporary—and part of the fixed assets were financed with short-term credit. This policy would be highly aggressive, and the firm would be subject to dangers from loan renewal as well as rising interest rates.

The benefit to using short-term debt is overall lower interest rates since most of the time the yield curve is upward sloping. However, as many firms learned during the financial crisis of 2007, a strategy of financing long-term assets with short-term debt is really quite risky. As an illustration, suppose a company borrowed $1 million on a 1-year basis and used the funds to buy machinery that would lower labor costs by $200,000 per year for 10 years.[3] Cash flows from the equipment would not be sufficient to pay off the loan at the end of only 1 year, so the loan would have to be renewed. If the economy were in a recession like that of 2007, the lender might refuse to renew the loan, and that could lead to bankruptcy. Had the firm matched maturities and financed the equipment with a 10-year loan, then the annual loan payments would have been lower and better matched with the cash flows, and the loan renewal problem would not have arisen.

Under some circumstances, even maturity matching can be risky, as many firms that thought they were conservatively financed learned in 2007. If a firm borrowed on a 30-day bank loan to finance inventories that it expected to sell within 30 days but then sales dropped, as they did for many firms in 2007, the funds needed to pay off the maturing bank loan might not be available. If the bank would not extend the loan, then the firm could be forced into bankruptcy. This happened to many firms in 2009, and it was exacerbated by the banks' own problems. The banks lost billions on mortgages, mortgage-backed bonds, and other bad investments, which led them to restrict credit to their normal business customers in order to conserve their own cash.

CONSERVATIVE APPROACH

Panel C of the figure shows the **conservative approach**, with the dashed line *above* the line designating permanent current assets. In this approach, long-term capital is used to finance all permanent assets and also to meet some seasonal needs. The firm uses a small amount of short-term credit to meet its peak requirements, but it also meets a part of its seasonal needs by "storing liquidity" in the form of marketable securities. The humps above the dashed line represent short-term financings, while the troughs below the dashed line represent short-term security holdings. This conservative financing policy is fairly safe, and the wisdom of using it was demonstrated in 2007—when credit dried up, firms with adequate cash holdings were able to operate more effectively than those that were forced to cut back their operations because they couldn't order new inventories or pay their normal workforce.

CHOOSING AMONG THE APPROACHES

Because the yield curve is normally upward sloping, *the cost of short-term debt is generally lower than that of long-term debt.* However, *short-term debt is riskier for the borrowing firm* for two reasons: (1) If a firm borrows on a long-term basis, then its interest costs will

---

[3]We are oversimplifying here. Few lenders would explicitly lend money for 1 year to finance a 10-year asset. What would actually happen is that the firm would borrow on a 1-year basis for "general corporate purposes" and then actually use the money to purchase the 10-year machinery.

be relatively stable over time, but if it uses short-term credit, then its interest expense can fluctuate widely—perhaps reaching such high levels that profits are extinguished.[4] (2) If a firm borrows heavily on a short-term basis, then a temporary recession may drag down its financial ratios, causing a lender to choose not to renew a loan. In a weak financial position, the firm may not be able to find another lender and not be able to repay the loan, forcing it into bankruptcy. Had the debt been long-term, the company would not have faced having to renew the loan at the time.

On the plus side, *short-term loans can generally be negotiated much faster* than long-term loans. Lenders need to make a thorough financial examination before extending long-term credit, and the loan agreement must be spelled out in great detail because a lot can happen during the life of a 10- to 20-year loan.

Finally, *short-term debt generally offers greater flexibility.* If the firm thinks that interest rates are abnormally high and due for a decline, it may prefer short-term credit because prepayment penalties are often attached to long-term debt. Also, if its needs for funds are seasonal or cyclical, then the firm may not want to commit itself to long-term debt because of its underwriting costs and possible prepayment penalties. Finally, long-term loan agreements generally contain provisions, or *covenants,* that constrain the firm's future actions in order to protect the lender, whereas short-term credit agreements generally have fewer restrictions.

All things considered, it is not possible to state that either long-term or short-term financing is generally better. The firm's specific conditions will affect its decision, as will the risk preferences of managers. Optimistic and/or aggressive managers will lean more toward short-term credit to gain an interest cost advantage, whereas more conservative managers will lean toward long-term financing to avoid potential renewal problems. The factors discussed here should be considered, but the final decision will reflect managers' personal preferences and subjective judgments.

SELF-TEST

Identify and explain three alternative current asset investment policies.

Use the DuPont equation to show how working capital policy can affect a firm's expected ROE.

What are the reasons for not wanting to hold too little working capital? For not wanting to hold too much?

Differentiate between permanent operating current assets and temporary operating current assets.

What does maturity matching mean, and what is the logic behind this policy?

What are some advantages and disadvantages of short-term versus long-term debt?

16-3 The Cash Conversion Cycle

All firms follow a "working capital cycle" in which they purchase or produce inventory, hold it for a time, and then sell it and receive cash. This process is known as the **cash conversion cycle (CCC)**.

---

[4]The prime interest rate—the rate banks charge very good customers—hit 21% in the early 1980s. This produced a level of business bankruptcies that was not seen again until 2009. The primary reason for the very high interest rate was that the inflation rate was up to 13%, and high inflation must be compensated by high interest rates. Also, the Federal Reserve was tightening credit in order to hold down inflation, and it was encouraging banks to restrict their lending.

16-3a Calculating the Target CCC

Assume that Great Basin Medical Equipment (GBM) buys medical devices from manufacturers in China and sells them in the United States, Canada, and Mexico. On average, it is 50 days from the time GBM purchases merchandise ($10 million a month) until the time GBM sells to its customers. GBM's suppliers require payment within 40 days, but GBM gives its customers 60 days to pay for their purchases.

GBM's cash conversion cycle shows the *net* amount of time between GBM's payments to suppliers and GBM's collections from customers. The cash conversion cycle has a big impact on GBM's financing costs because GBM takes out bank loans to cover cash shortfalls during this cycle. The following definitions are used in calculating the cycle length:

1. **Inventory conversion period (ICP).** This is the length of time between purchasing material or merchandise from suppliers and recording a sale to customers (which creates an account receivable because GBM offers credit to its customers). GBM's target is 50 days.[5]
2. **Average collection period (ACP).** This is the length of time customers are given to pay for goods following a sale. The ACP is also called the **days sales outstanding (DSO)**. GBM's business plan calls for an ACP of 60 days based on its 60-day credit terms. This is also called the **receivables conversion period** because it's the number of days required to convert receivables into cash.
3. **Payables deferral period (PDP).** This is the length of time GBM takes to pay its suppliers. GBM's suppliers allow it 40 days.[6]

On Day 1, GBM expects to buy merchandise, and it expects to sell the goods and thus convert them to accounts receivable within 50 days. It should then take 60 days to collect the receivables, making a total of 110 days between receiving merchandise and collecting cash. However, GBM is able to defer its own payments for only 40 days. The net number of days in GBM's target cash conversion cycle is shown in the following formula:

$$
\begin{array}{c}
\text{Cash} \\
\text{conversion} \\
\text{cycle}
\end{array}
=
\begin{array}{c}
\text{Inventory} \\
\text{conversion} \\
\text{period}
\end{array}
+
\begin{array}{c}
\text{Average} \\
\text{collection} \\
\text{period}
\end{array}
-
\begin{array}{c}
\text{Payables} \\
\text{deferral} \\
\text{period}
\end{array}
\qquad (16\text{-}1)
$$

$$
= \quad 50 \quad + \quad 60 \quad - \quad 40
$$
$$
= 70 \text{ days}
$$

Figure 16-2 diagrams the activities represented in Equation 16-1. Notice that GBM has a 70-day cash shortfall that it must finance during the cycle.

Although GBM is supposed to pay its suppliers $10 million by the 40th day after making the purchases, GBM does not expect to receive any cash until 110 days into the cycle: $50 + 60 = 110$. Therefore, it will have to borrow the $10 million cost of merchandise from its bank on Day 40, and it does not expect to be able to repay the loan until it collects on Day 110. Thus, during its 70-day ($110 - 40 = 70$) target cash conversion cycle, it will owe the bank $10 million and accrue interest on this debt. All else equal, a shorter cash conversion cycle is preferable because a shorter CCC means lower interest charges.

---

[5]If GBM were a manufacturer, the inventory conversion period would be the time required to convert raw materials into finished goods and then to sell those goods.

[6]GBM's payables deferral period corresponds to its suppliers' average collection period. That is, if GBM takes 40 days to pay, then the supplier has to wait 40 days to collect its account receivable.

FIGURE 16-2
The Cash Conversion Cycle

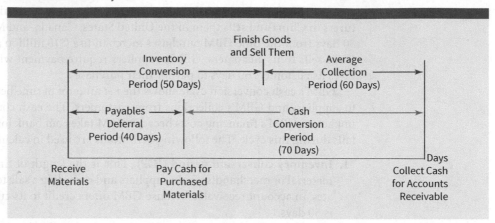

Observe that if GBM could sell goods faster, collect receivables faster, or defer its payables longer without hurting sales or increasing operating costs, then its CCC would decline, its expected interest charges would be reduced, and its expected net income would increase.

16-3b Calculating the Actual Cash Conversion Cycle from Financial Statements

Instead of using *target* values, let's calculate GBM's *actual* cash conversion cycle. The following data were taken from its latest financial statements:

Selected Data (Millions of Dollars)	
Annual sales	$150
Cost of goods sold	122
Inventories	17
Accounts receivable	51
Accounts payable	13

We begin by calculating GBM's actual inventory conversion period. Financial statements record inventory at cost, so we divide inventory by the daily cost of goods sold (and not sales) when calculating the inventory conversion period:

$$\text{Inventory conversion period (ICP)} = \frac{\text{Inventory}}{\text{Cost of goods sold per day}} \quad (16\text{-}2)$$

$$= \frac{\$17}{\$122/365} = 50.9 \text{ days}$$

Thus, it takes GBM 50.9 days to convert inventory into sales, which is very close to its 50-day target.

Receivables are recorded at the sales price because they reflect the cash that is forgone by offering credit to customer. Therefore, we use daily sales (rather than the cost of goods sold per day) to calculate GBM's average collection period:

$$\text{Average collection period (ACP or DSO)} = \frac{\text{Receivables}}{\text{Sales}/365} \qquad (16\text{-}3)$$

$$= \frac{\$51}{\$150/365} = 124.1 \text{ days}$$

Notice that GBM actually takes 124.1 days after a sale to receive cash, which is much higher than its 60-day target.

In contrast to receivables, accounts payable are recorded at purchase price because this reflects the cash payments that can be deferred by accepting credit from the supplier. Therefore, we divide payables by the daily cost of goods sold (and not sales) when calculating the payables deferral period:

$$\text{Payables deferral period (PDP)} = \frac{\text{Payables}}{\text{Daily purchases}} = \frac{\text{Payables}}{\text{Cost of goods sold}/365} \qquad (16\text{-}4)$$

$$= \frac{\$13}{\$122/365} = 38.9 \text{ days}$$

GBM is supposed to pay its suppliers within 40 days, and it is doing so.

We can use Equation 16-1 and the previously calculated individual periods to determine GBM's actual cash conversion cycle:

Cash conversion cycle (CCC) = 50.9 days + 124.1 days − 38.9 days = 136.1 days

Figure 16-3 summarizes the previous calculations and shows that GBM's inventory management and purchasing payment systems are performing as expected. However, its receivables are much higher than targeted, indicating that customers are not paying on time. In fact, they are taking over twice as long to pay as GBM expects. This delay hurts GBM's free cash flows, increases its interest expense, and reduces debt capacity that could be used elsewhere in the company.

16-3c Benefits of Reducing the Cash Conversion Cycle

Later sections provide more detailed analyses of changes in inventory management, receivables management, and payables management, but let's look at the big picture right now. Suppose GBM can improve its business processes so that it reduces the inventory conversion period to 35 days and the average collection period to 40 days. In addition, suppose GBM can negotiate an extension in the suppliers' payment terms to 50 days. The "New Target" column of Figure 16-4 shows the effects of these changes.

As shown in Figure 16-4, GBM's current actual cash conversion cycle is 136.1 days, with the net operating working capital financed during this period by a bank loan charging a 10% annual rate. With an average annual level of $55 million in NOWC, the annual interest paid on the bank loan is $5.5 million: 10%($55) = $5.5. Figure 16-4 shows that NOWC would drop to $11.4 million if GBS can implement the improvements, which would cut the interest expense to about $1.14 million.

FIGURE 16-3
GBM's Target and Actual Cash Conversion Cycle (Millions of Dollars)

	A	B	C	D	E	F	G
35	Panel A. Target CCC: Based on Plans						
36	Target Cash		Planned		Credit Terms		Credit Terms
37	Conversion Cycle	=	Inventory	+	Offered to	−	Offered by
38	(CCC)		Conversion		Customers (ACP)		Suppliers (PDP)
39		=	50	+	60	−	40
40	Target CCC	=	70				
41	Panel B. Actual CCC: Based on Financial Statements						
42							
43	Sales	$150.0					
44	COGS	$122.0					
45	Inventories	$17.0					
46	Receivables	$51.0					
47	Payables	$13.0					
48	Days/year	365					
49	Actual CCC	=	Inventory ÷	+	Receivables ÷	−	Payables ÷
50			(COGS/365)		(Sales/365)		(COGS/365)
51		=	$17 ÷	+	$51 ÷	−	$13 ÷ ($122/365)
52			($122/365)		($150/365)		
53		=	50.9	+	124.1	−	38.9
54	Actual CCC	=	136.1				
55	Panel C. Actual versus Target Components						
56			ICP		ACP		PDP
57	Actual − Target	=	50.9 − 50.0		124.1 − 60.0		38.9 − 40.0
58		=	0.9		64.1		−1.1
59	% Difference	=	1.7%		106.8%		−2.8%
60	Evaluation	=	Ok		Bad		Ok

Source: See the file *Ch16 Tool Kit.xlsx*. Numbers are reported as rounded values for clarity but are calculated using *Excel*'s full precision. Thus, intermediate calculations using the figure's rounded values will be inexact.

Not only does a reduction in NOWC reduce interest expense, but also the reduction itself frees up money to be used elsewhere. Recall from previous chapters that free cash flow (FCF) is equal to net operating profit after taxes (NOPAT) minus the investment in total net operating capital. Therefore, if working capital *decreases* by a given amount while all else remains constant, then FCF *increases* by that same amount. For GBM, free cash flow would increase $43.6 million ($55.0 − $11.4 = $43.6). If sales remained constant in the following years, then this reduction in working capital would be a one-time cash inflow only. However, suppose sales grow in future years. When a company improves its working capital management, the components (inventory conversion period, collection period, and payments period) usually remain at their improved levels, which means the NOWC-to-Sales ratio remains at its new level. With an improved NOWC-to-Sales ratio, less working capital will be required to support future sales, leading to higher annual FCFs than would have otherwise existed.

Thus, an improvement in working capital management creates a large one-time increase in FCF at the time of the improvement as well as higher FCF in future years. Therefore, an improvement in working capital management is a gift that keeps on giving.

These benefits can add substantial value to the company. Professors Hyun-Han Shin and Luc Soenen studied more than 2,900 companies over a 20-year period, finding a strong

FIGURE 16-4
Benefits from Reducing the Cash Conversion Cycle (Millions of Dollars)

	A	B	C	D	E	F
70						
71	**New Targets for Conversion Periods**				**Old (Actual)**	**New Target**
72	Inventory conversion period (ICP, days)				50.9	35.0
73	Average collection period (ACP, days)				124.1	40.0
74	Payable deferral period (PDP, days)				38.9	50.0
75	Cash Conversion Cycle (CCC, days)				136.1	25.0
76	Reduction in Cash Conversion Cycle:			111.1		
77						
78	**Impact of Reduction in CCC**				**Old (Actual)**	**New Target**
79	Annual sales: No change				$150.00	$150.00
80	Costs of goods sold (COGS): No change				$122.00	$122.00
81	Inventory: New level is ICP(COGS/365)				$17.00	$11.70
82	Receivables: New level is ACP(Sales/365)				$51.00	$16.44
83	Payables: New level is PDP(COGS/365)				$13.00	$16.71
84	Net operating working capital:					
85	NOWC = Inventory + Receivables – Payables				$55.00	$11.42
86	Interest rate on NOWC loans (10%)			10%		
87	Interest expense due to NOWC: 10%(NOWC)				$5.50	$1.14
88						
89	**Improvement in Selected Results**					
90	Reduction in NOWC:			$43.6		
91	Increase in free cash flow:			$43.6		
92	Reduction in interest expense:			$4.36		

Source: See the file *Ch16 Tool Kit.xlsx*. Numbers are reported as rounded values for clarity but are calculated using *Excel's* full precision. Thus, intermediate calculations using the figure's rounded values will be inexact.

relationship between a company's cash conversion cycle and its stock performance.[7] For an average company, a 10-day improvement in its CCC was associated with an increase in pre-tax operating profit margin from 12.76% to 13.02%. Moreover, companies with cash conversion cycles 10 days shorter than the average for their industry had annual stock returns that were 1.7 percentage points higher than the average company. Given results like these, it's no wonder firms place so much emphasis on reducing working capital through improved supply chain management![8]

Define the following terms: inventory conversion period, average collection period, and payables deferral period. Give the equation for each term.

What is the cash conversion cycle? What is its equation?

What should a firm's goal be regarding the cash conversion cycle, holding other things constant? Explain your answer.

What are some actions a firm can take to shorten its cash conversion cycle?

A company has $20 million of inventory, $5 million of receivables, and $4 million of payables. Its annual sales revenue is $80 million, and its cost of goods sold is $60 million. What is its CCC? **(120.15)**

[7]Hyun-Han Shin and Luc Soenen, "Efficiency of Working Capital Management and Corporate Profitability," *Financial Practice and Education,* Fall/Winter 1998, pp. 37–45.

[8]For more on the CCC, see James A. Gentry, R. Vaidyanathan, and Hei Wai Lee, "A Weighted Cash Conversion Cycle," *Financial Management,* Spring 1990, pp. 90–99.

Some Firms Operate with Negative Working Capital!

Some firms are able to operate with a zero or even negative cash conversion cycle. For example, when customers order from Amazon, they must provide a credit card number. Amazon receives next-day cash, even before the product is shipped and even before paying their own suppliers. This results in a negative CCC, which means that working capital *provides* cash rather than *uses* it.

Apple is another example. Apple turns over its inventory very quickly and pays its suppliers very slowly, resulting in a

negative CCC. Sky West collects on its receivables (primarily ticket purchases) in a few days, giving it a negative CCC.

In order to grow, companies normally need cash for working capital. However, if the CCC is negative, then growth in sales *provides* cash rather than *uses* it. This cash can be invested in plant and equipment, research and development, or for any other corporate purpose. Analysts recognize this point when they value a company, and it certainly helps their stock prices.

16-4 Inventory Management

Inventory management techniques are covered in depth in production management courses. Still, financial managers have a responsibility for raising the capital needed to carry inventory and for overseeing the firm's overall profitability, so it is appropriate that we cover the financial aspects of inventory management here.

The twin goals of inventory management are (1) ensuring that the inventories needed to sustain operations are available, while (2) holding the costs of ordering and carrying inventories to the lowest possible level. In analyzing improvements in the cash conversion cycle, we identified some of the cash flows associated with a reduction in inventory. In addition to the points made earlier, lower inventory levels reduce costs due to storage and handling, insurance, property taxes, spoilage, and obsolescence.

Before the computer age, companies used simple inventory control techniques such as the **red-line method**, where a red line was drawn around the inside of a bin holding inventory items; when the actual stock declined to the level where the red line showed, inventory would be reordered. Now computers have taken over, and supply chains have been established that provide inventory items just before they are needed—the **just-in-time (JIT) inventory system**. For example, consider Trane Corporation, which makes air conditioners and uses just-in-time procedures. In the past, Trane produced parts on a steady basis, stored them as inventory, and had them ready whenever the company received an order for a batch of air conditioners. However, the company's inventory eventually covered an area equal to three football fields, and it still could take as long as 15 days to fill an order. To make matters worse, occasionally some of the necessary components simply could not be located; in other instances, the components were located but found to have been damaged from long storage.

Then Trane adopted a new inventory policy—it began producing components only after receiving an order and then sending the parts directly from the machines that make them to the final assembly line. The net effect: Inventories fell nearly 40% even as sales were increasing by 30%.

Such improvements in inventory management can free up considerable amounts of cash. In the last section, we examined inventory reductions due to improvements in the inventory conversion period. Many analysts also use the inventory turnover ratio as a performance measure, so you should know how to estimate inventory reductions due to improvements in turnover. Recall from Chapter 3 that the inventory turnover ratio is defined as cost of goods sold (COGS) divided by inventory.[9] If we know the turnover ratio and the COGS, we can determine the inventory level. For example, suppose a company's inventory turnover ratio is 3 and its COGS is $120 million. Starting with the definition of the turnover ratio and solving for inventory yields:

$$\text{Inventory turnover ratio} = \text{COGS/Inventory}$$
$$\text{Inventory} = \text{COGS/(Inventory turnover ratio)}$$
$$= \$120/3 = \$40 \text{ million}$$

If the company can improve its inventory turnover ratio to 4, then its inventory will fall to:

$$\text{Inventory} = \$120/4 = \$30 \text{ million}$$

This $10 million reduction in inventory ($40 − $30 = $10) boosts free cash flow by $10 million.

However, there are costs associated with holding too little inventory, and these costs can be severe. If a business lowers its inventories, then it must reorder frequently, which increases ordering costs. Even worse, if stocks become depleted then firms can miss out on profitable sales and also suffer lost goodwill, which may lead to lower future sales. Therefore, it is important to have enough inventory on hand to meet customer demands but not so much as to incur the costs we discussed previously. Inventory optimization models have been developed, but the best approach—and the one most firms today are following—is to use supply chain management and monitor the system closely.[10]

SELF-TEST

What are some costs associated with high inventories? With low inventories?

What is a "supply chain," and how are supply chains related to just-in-time inventory procedures?

A company has $20 million in cost of goods sold and an inventory turnover ratio of 2.0. If it can reduce its inventory and improve its inventory turnover ratio to 2.5 with no loss in units sold and no change in cost of goods sold, by how much will FCF increase? **($2 million)**

16-5 Receivables Management

Firms would, in general, rather sell for cash than on credit, but competitive pressures force most firms to offer credit for substantial purchases, especially to other businesses. Thus, goods are shipped, inventories are reduced, and receivables are increased. Eventually, customers will pay their bills, at which time the firm's cash will increase and its receivables will decrease.[11] Carrying receivables has both direct and indirect costs, but selling on credit also has an important benefit—increased sales. Balancing these

---

[9]The relationship between the inventory conversion period and the inventory turnover ratio is Inventory conversion period = 365/(Inventory turnover ratio).

[10]For additional insights into the problems of inventory management, see Richard A. Followill, Michael Schellenger, and Patrick H. Marchard, "Economic Order Quantities, Volume Discounts, and Wealth Maximization," *The Financial Review,* February 1990, pp. 143–152.

[11]If the purchaser doesn't pay for the goods in a reasonable amount of time, the adjustments are more complicated and differ between public and tax accounting.

benefits and costs requires an effective credit policy and monitoring system, described in the following sections.[12]

16-5a Credit Policy

The success or failure of a business depends primarily on the demand for its products—as a rule, high sales lead to larger profits and a higher stock price. Sales, in turn, depend on a number of factors: Some, like the state of the economy, are exogenous, but others are under the firm's control. The major controllable factors are sales prices, product quality, advertising, and the firm's **credit policy**. Credit policy, in turn, consists of the following four variables:

1. **Credit period**. A firm might sell on terms of "net 30," which means that the customer must pay within 30 days.
2. **Cash discounts**. Some companies offer a percentage reduction in the sales price (called a **discount percentage**) if the purchaser pays in cash before the end of the specified **discount period**. A company's **credit terms** specify the discount percentage, the discount period, and the full credit period. For example, "2/10, net 30" means that buyers may deduct 2% of the purchase price (the discount percentage) if payment is made within 10 days (the discount period); otherwise, the full amount must be paid within 30 days (the credit period). Cash discounts provide incentives for purchasers to make cash payments more quickly.
3. **Credit standards**. How much financial strength must a customer show to qualify for credit? Lower credit standards boost sales, but they also increase bad debts.
4. **Collection policy**. How tough or lax is a company in attempting to collect slow-paying accounts? A tough policy may speed up collections, but it might also anger customers and cause them to take their business elsewhere.

The credit manager is responsible for administering the firm's credit policy. However, because of the pervasive importance of credit, the credit policy itself is normally established by the executive committee, which usually consists of the president plus the vice presidents of finance, marketing, and production.

16-5b Credit Policy and the Accumulation of Receivables

Credit policies and customer behaviors determine the accumulation of accounts receivable. For example, suppose Boston Lumber Company (BLC), a wholesale distributor of lumber products, had always collected at the time of purchase. BLC had an average collection period of 0 days, but its sales were lower than they would have been if it offered credit sales. Several years ago BLC began offering credit sales on January 1 with the terms "net 30" and all customers bought on credit. Sales increased to $1,000 each day, but what impact did this have on accounts receivable?

At the end of the first day, accounts receivable were $1,000; they rose to $2,000 by the end of the second day; and by January 30, they were $30,000. On January 31, another $1,000 was added to receivables, but $1,000 in payments was collected for sales made on January 1. Therefore, the cumulative accounts receivable remained constant at $30,000.

[12]For more on credit policy and receivables management, see Shehzad L. Mian and Clifford W. Smith, "Extending Trade Credit and Financing Receivables," *Journal of Applied Corporate Finance,* Spring 1994, pp. 75–84; and Paul D. Adams, Steve B. Wyatt, and Yong H. Kim, "A Contingent Claims Analysis of Trade Credit," *Financial Management,* Autumn 1992, pp. 104–112.

Netting out new credit sales and collections each day is accurate but tedious, so we show an easier method next.

We can rewrite Equation 16-3, solving for the level of accounts receivable:

$$\text{Accounts receivable} = \text{Sales per day} \times \text{Average collection period} \qquad (16\text{-}5)$$

BLC's daily sales were $1,000 and its average collection period increased from 0 to 30 days, so its receivables leveled off at:

$$
\begin{aligned}
\text{Accounts receivable} &= \text{Sales per day} \times \text{Average collection period} \\
&= \$1,000 \times 30 \\
&= \$30,000
\end{aligned}
$$

Therefore, modifications in either daily credit sales or the collection period (due to changes in the credit terms or customer behavior) will change the accounts receivable balance, which in turn changes free cash flow.

16-5c Monitoring the Receivables Position

In the previous example, BLC's customers paid on time, but that is not always the case. Analysis along the lines suggested in the following sections can help detect potential problems before they become too serious.

CREDIT TERMS, CUSTOMER BEHAVIOR, AND THE DAYS SALES OUTSTANDING

Suppose Super Set Inc., a manufacturer of ultra-thin televisions, sells 219,000 sets a year at a price of $200 each. Assume that all sales are on credit under the terms 2/10, net 30. Finally, assume that 70% of the customers take the discount and pay on Day 10 and 30% pay on Day 30.[13]

Super Set's average collection period (ACP), which is also called days sales outstanding (DSO), is 16 days:

$$
\begin{aligned}
\text{Average collection period} = \text{DSO} &= 0.7(10 \text{ days}) + 0.3(30 \text{ days}) \\
&= 16 \text{ days}
\end{aligned}
$$

On average, Super Set sells $120,000 per day:

$$
\begin{aligned}
\text{Sales per day} &= \frac{\text{Annual sales}}{365} = \frac{(\text{Units sold})(\text{Sales price})}{365} \\
&= \frac{(219,000)(\$200)}{365} = \$120,000
\end{aligned}
$$

---

[13]Unless otherwise noted, we assume throughout that payments are made either on the *last day* for taking discounts or on the *last day* of the credit period. It would be foolish to pay on (say) the 5th day or on the 20th day if the credit terms were 2/10, net 30.

Using Equation 16-5 and recognizing that the average collection period is the same as the days sales outstanding, Super Set's accounts receivable—assuming a constant, uniform rate of sales throughout the year—will at any point in time be $1,920,000:

$$\begin{array}{ccc} \text{Accounts} \\ \text{receivable} \end{array} = \begin{array}{c} \text{Sales} \\ \text{per day} \end{array} \times \begin{array}{c} \text{Days sales} \\ \text{outstanding} \end{array} \qquad \text{(16-5a)}$$

$$= \$120,000 \times 16$$
$$= \$1,920,000$$

AGING SCHEDULES

An **aging schedule** breaks down a firm's receivables by age of account. Table 16-1 shows the December 31, 2019, aging schedules of two television manufacturers, Super Set and Wonder Vision. Both firms offer the same credit terms, and they have the same total receivables. Super Set's aging schedule indicates that all of its customers pay on time: 70% pay by Day 10 and 30% pay by Day 30. In contrast, Wonder Vision's schedule, which is more typical, shows that many of its customers are not paying on time: 27% of its receivables are more than 30 days old, even though Wonder Vision's credit terms call for full payment by Day 30.

Aging schedules cannot be constructed from the type of summary data reported in financial statements; rather, they must be developed from the firm's accounts receivable ledger. However, well-run firms have computerized accounts receivable records, so it is easy to determine the age of each invoice, to sort electronically by age categories, and thus to generate an aging schedule.

Management should constantly monitor both the DSO and the aging schedule to detect any trends, to see how the firm's collections experience compares with its credit terms, and to see how effectively the credit department is operating in comparison with other firms in the industry. If the DSO starts to lengthen or the aging schedule begins to show an increasing percentage of past-due accounts, then the credit manager should examine why these changes are occurring.

Although increases in the DSO and the aging schedule are warning signs, this does not necessarily indicate the firm's credit policy has weakened. If a firm experiences sharp seasonal variations or if it is growing rapidly, then both the aging schedule and the DSO may be distorted. To see this point, recall that the DSO is calculated as follows:

$$DSO = \frac{\text{Accounts receivable}}{\text{Annual sales}/365}$$

TABLE 16-1
Aging Schedules

Age of Account (Days)	Super Set		Wonder Vision	
	Value of Account	Percentage of Total Value	Value of Account	Percentage of Total Value
0–10	$1,344,000	70%	$902,400	47%
11–30	576,000	30	499,200	26
31–45	0	0	288,000	15
46–60	0	0	192,000	10
Over 60	0	0	38,400	2
Total receivables	$1,920,000	100%	$1,920,000	100%

Receivables at any point in time reflect sales in the past 1 or 2 months, but sales as shown in the denominator are for the past 12 months. Therefore, a seasonal increase in sales will increase the numerator more than the denominator and hence will raise the DSO, even if customers continue to pay just as quickly as before. Similar problems arise with the aging schedule. If sales are rising, then the percentage in the 0–10-day category will be high; the reverse will occur if sales are falling. Therefore, a change in either the DSO or the aging schedule should be taken as a signal to investigate further; it is not necessarily a sign that customers have changed their payment behaviors.

SELF-TEST

Explain how a new firm's receivables balance is built up over time.

Define days sales outstanding (DSO). What can be learned from it? How is it affected by sales fluctuations?

What is an aging schedule? What can be learned from it? How is it affected by sales fluctuations?

A company has annual sales of $730 million. If its DSO is 35, what is its average accounts receivables balance? **($70 million)**

16-6 Accruals and Accounts Payable (Trade Credit)

Recall that net operating working capital is equal to operating current assets minus operating current liabilities. The previous sections discussed the management of operating current assets (cash, inventory, and accounts receivable), and the following sections discuss the two major types of operating current liabilities: accruals and accounts payable.[14]

16-6a Accruals

Firms generally pay employees on a weekly, biweekly, or monthly basis, so the balance sheet will typically show some accrued wages. Similarly, the firm's own estimated income taxes, employment and income taxes withheld from employees, and sales taxes collected are generally paid on a weekly, monthly, or quarterly basis. Therefore, the balance sheet will typically show some accrued taxes along with accrued wages.

These **accruals** can be thought of as short-term, interest-free loans from employees and taxing authorities, and they increase automatically (that is, *spontaneously*) as a firm's operations expand. However, a firm cannot ordinarily control its accruals: The timing of wage payments is set by economic forces and industry norms, and tax payment dates are established by law. Thus, firms generally use all the accruals they can, but they have little control over the levels of these accounts.

16-6b Accounts Payable (Trade Credit)

Firms generally make purchases from other firms on credit, recording the unpaid amount as an *account payable*. Accounts payable, or **trade credit**, is the largest single operating current liability, representing about 40% of the current liabilities for an average nonfinancial corporation. The percentage is somewhat larger for smaller firms: Because small companies often have difficulty obtaining financing from other sources, they rely especially heavily on trade credit.

Trade credit is a spontaneous source of financing in the sense that it arises from ordinary business transactions. For example, suppose a firm makes average purchases of $2,000 a day on terms of net 30, meaning that it must pay for goods 30 days after the

---

[14]For more on accounts payable management, see James A. Gentry and Jesus M. De La Garza, "Monitoring Accounts Payables," *Financial Review*, November 1990, pp. 559–576.

invoice date. On average, it will owe 30 times $2,000, or $60,000, to its suppliers. If its sales, and consequently its purchases, were to double, then its accounts payable would also double, to $120,000. So simply by growing, the firm would spontaneously generate an additional $60,000 of financing. Similarly, if the terms under which the firm buys were extended from 30 to 40 days, then its accounts payable would expand from $60,000 to $80,000 even with no growth in sales. Thus, both expanding sales and lengthening the credit period generate additional amounts of financing via trade credit.

16-6c The Cost of Trade Credit

Suppose that Microchip Electronics sells on terms of 2/10, net 30. The "true price" of Microchip's products is the net price, or 0.98 times the list price, because any customer can purchase an item at that price as long as payment is made within 10 days. Now consider Personal Computer Company (PCC), which buys its memory chips from Microchip. One chip is listed at $100, so its "true" price to PCC is $98. Now if PCC wants an additional 20 days of credit beyond the 10-day discount period, it must incur a finance charge of $2 per chip for that credit. Thus, the $100 list price consists of two components:

$$\text{List price} = \$98 \text{ true price} + \$2 \text{ finance charge}$$

The question PCC must ask before it turns down the discount to obtain the additional 20 days of credit is this: Could credit be obtained at a lower cost from a bank or some other lender? To answer this, we calculate the annualized cost of financing as shown next.

If PCC takes the credit instead of paying on the 10th day, it means that PCC is accepting a $2 finance charge so that it can delay paying the true price of $98 for 20 days. The percentage cost of this delay for the 20-day period is $2/$98 = 2.0408%. To find the annual nominal rate, multiply by the number of 20-day periods in a year, 365/20 = 18.25, to get 37.2%. This rate, 37.2%, is high enough, but the effective annual (that is, compound) rate is even higher:

$$\text{Effective annual rate} = (1.020408)^{18.25} - 1.0 = 1.446 - 1.0 = 44.6\%$$

PCC should take the credit terms only if its effective borrowing costs are greater than 44.6%. Otherwise PCC should pay in 10 days and take the discount, borrowing short-term from a bank if necessary. A compact formula for the nominal annual cost of trade credit is:

$$\begin{aligned}
\frac{\text{Nominal cost}}{\text{of trade credit}} &= \text{Cost per period} \times \text{Number of periods per year} \\[2mm]
&= \frac{\text{Discount percentage}}{100 - \frac{\text{Discount}}{\text{percentage}}} \times \frac{365}{\frac{\text{Days credit is}}{\text{outstanding}} - \frac{\text{Discount}}{\text{period}}}
\end{aligned} \tag{16-6}$$

Using PCC's terms (2/10, net 30), the nominal cost is:

$$\begin{aligned}
\frac{\text{Nominal cost}}{\text{of trade credit}} &= \frac{2}{100 - 2} \times \frac{365}{30 - 10} \\[2mm]
&= 2.0408\% \times 18.25 = 37.2\%
\end{aligned}$$

PCC buys 73,000 of these chips a year. If PCC pays in 10 days and takes the discount, its accounts payable balance will be the discount purchases per day multiplied by the 10 days, which is $98(73,000/365)(10 days) = $196,000. This amount is called **free trade credit** since PCC doesn't have to pay anything to receive this trade credit. If PCC, instead, pays in 30 days, then its accounts payable balance will be $98(73,000/365)(30 days) = $588,000. This additional accounts payable balance, $588,000 − $196,000 = $392,000, is called **costly trade credit** because PCC must pay an effective rate of 44.6% to receive it. In this case, the costly trade credit is very costly indeed![15]

Note, however, that the calculated cost of trade credit can be reduced by paying late. Thus, if PCC could get away with paying in 60 days rather than the specified 30 days, then the effective credit period would become 60 − 10 = 50 days, the number of times the discount would be lost would fall to 365/50 = 7.3, and the nominal cost would drop from 37.2% to 2.0408% × 7.3 = 14.9%. Then the effective annual rate would drop from 44.6% to 15.9%:

$$\text{Effective annual rate} = (1.0204)^{7.3} - 1.0 = 1.1589 - 1.0 = 15.9\%$$

In periods of excess capacity, firms may be able to get away with deliberately paying late, or **stretching accounts payable**. However, they will also suffer a variety of problems associated with being a "slow payer." These problems are discussed later in the chapter.

The costs of the additional trade credit from forgoing discounts under some other purchase terms are taken from the chapter's *Excel **Tool Kit*** model and shown here as Figure 16-5. As these numbers indicate, the cost of not taking discounts can be substantial.

On the basis of the preceding discussion, *firms should always use the free component of trade credit, but they should use the costly component only after analyzing the cost of this credit to make sure it is less than the cost of funds that could be obtained from other sources.* Under the terms of trade found in most industries, the costly component is relatively expensive, so stronger firms generally avoid using it.

Note, though, that firms sometimes offer favorable credit terms in order to stimulate sales. For example, suppose a firm has been selling on terms of 2/10, net 30, with a nominal cost of 37.24%, but a recession has reduced sales and the firm now has excess capacity. It wants to boost the sales of its product without cutting the list price, so it might offer terms of 1/10, net 90, which implies a nominal cost of additional credit of only 4.61%. In this situation, its customers would probably be wise to take the additional credit and reduce their reliance on banks and other lenders. So, turning down discounts is not always a bad decision.

FIGURE 16-5

Varying Credit Terms and Their Associated Costs

	A	B	C	D	E	F
286	**Days in Year: 365**					
287		**Discount**	**Discount**	**Net**	**Cost of Additional Credit**	
288	**Credit Terms**	**Percentage**	**Period**	**period**	**Nominal**	**Effective**
289	1/10, net 20	1%	10	20	36.87%	44.32%
290	1/10, net 30	1%	10	30	18.43%	20.13%
291	1/10, net 90	1%	10	90	4.61%	4.69%
292	2/10, net 20	2%	10	20	74.49%	109.05%
293	2/10, net 30	2%	10	30	37.24%	44.59%
294	3/15, net 45	3%	15	45	37.63%	44.86%

Source: See the file ***Ch16 Tool Kit.xlsx***. Numbers are reported as rounded values for clarity but are calculated using *Excel's* full precision. Thus, intermediate calculations using the figure's rounded values will be inexact.

---

[15]A question arises here: Should accounts payable reflect gross purchases or purchases net of discounts? Generally accepted accounting principles permit either treatment if the difference is not material, but if the discount is material, then the transaction must be recorded net of discounts, or at "true" prices. Then, the higher payment that results from not taking discounts is reported as an expense called "discounts lost." Therefore, *we show accounts payable net of discounts even if the company does not expect to take discounts.*

What are accruals? How much control do managers have over accruals?

What is trade credit?

What's the difference between free trade credit and costly trade credit?

How does the cost of costly trade credit generally compare with the cost of short-term bank loans?

A company buys on terms of 2/12, net 28. What is its nominal cost of trade credit? **(46.6%)** *The effective cost?* **(58.5%)**

16-7 The Cash Budget

Firms must forecast their cash flows. If they are likely to need additional cash, then they should line up funds well in advance. Yet, if they are likely to generate surplus cash, then they should plan for its productive use. The primary forecasting tool is the **cash budget**, illustrated in Figure 16-6, which is based on the chapter's *Excel **Tool Kit*** model. The illustrative company is Educational Products Corporation (EPC), which supplies educational materials to schools and retailers in the Midwest. Sales are cyclical, peaking in September and then declining for the balance of the year.

16-7a Monthly Cash Budgets

Cash budgets can be of any length, but EPC and most companies use a monthly cash budget such as the one in Figure 16-6, but set up for 12 months. We used only 6 months for illustration. The monthly budget is used for longer-range planning, but a daily cash budget is also prepared at the start of each month to provide a more precise picture of the daily cash flows for use in scheduling actual payments on a day-by-day basis.

The cash budget focuses on cash flows, but it also includes information on forecasted sales, credit policy, and inventory management. Because the statement is a forecast and not a report on historical results, actual results could vary from the figures given. Therefore, the cash budget is generally set up as an expected, or base-case, forecast, but it is created with a model that makes it easy to generate alternative forecasts to see what would happen under different conditions.

Figure 16-6 begins with Panel A, a forecast of gross sales for each month. The next row in Panel A shows possible percentage deviations from the forecasted sales. Because we are showing the base-case forecast, no adjustments are made, but the model is set up to show the effects if sales increase or decrease and so result in "adjusted sales" that are above or below the forecasted levels.

The company sells on terms of "2/10, net 60." This means that a 2% discount is given if payment is made within 10 days; otherwise, the full amount is due in 60 days. However, like most companies, EPC finds that some customers pay late. Experience shows that 20% of customers pay during the month of the sale and take the discount. Another 70% pay during the month immediately following the sale, and 10% are late, paying in the second month after the sale.[16] Panel B shows the collections on sales based on these assumed collection rates.

---

[16]Because we are using a monthly forecast instead of a daily forecast, we assume that all purchases are made on the first day of the month. Thus, discounted payments are received in the month of the sale, regular payments are received in the month after the sale, and late payments are received two months after the sale. Obviously, a daily budget would be more accurate. Also, a negligible percentage of sales results in bad debts. The low bad-debt losses evident here result from EPC's careful screening of customers and its generally tight credit policies. However, the cash budget model can show the effects of bad debts, so EPC's CFO could show top management how cash flows would be affected if the firm relaxed its credit policy in order to stimulate sales or if the recession worsened and more customers were forced to delay payments.

FIGURE 16-6
EPC's Cash Budget, July–December 2019 (Millions of Dollars)

	A	B	C	D	E	F	G	H	I	J	K	L	M	N
370	Scenario: Base Case					May	June	July	August	Sept	Oct	Nov	Dec	Jan
371	Panel A: Forecasted sales (manual inputs)													
372	Gross sales					$200	$250	$300	$400	$500	$350	$250	$200	$200
373	Adjustment: % deviation from forecast					0%	0%	0%	0%	0%	0%	0%	0%	0%
374	Adjusted gross sales forecast					$200	$250	$300	$400	$500	$350	$250	$200	$200
375	Panel B: Collections on sales													
376	During month of sales : 0.2 ×(Sales)(1 – Discount %)							$58.8	$78.4	$98.0	$68.6	$49.0	$39.2	
377	During 2nd month = 0.7 ×(Prior month's sales)							$175.0	$210.0	$280.0	$350.0	$245.0	$175.0	
378	Due in 3rd month: = 0.1 ×(Sales 2 months ago)							$20.0	$25.0	$30.0	$40.0	$50.0	$35.0	
379	Less bad debts (BD% × Sales 2 months ago)							$0.0	$0.0	$0.0	$0.0	$0.0	$0.0	
380	Total collections							$253.8	$313.4	$408.0	$458.6	$344.0	$249.2	
381	Panel C: Purchases: 60% of next month's sales		$180.0	$240.0	$300.0					$210.0	$150.0	$120.0	$120.0	
382	Panel D: Payments													
383	Pmt for last month's purchases (30 days of credit)							$180.0	$240.0	$300.0	$210.0	$150.0	$120.0	
384	Wages and salaries							$30.0	$40.0	$50.0	$40.0	$30.0	$30.0	
385	Lease payments							$30.0	$30.0	$30.0	$30.0	$30.0	$30.0	
386	Other payments (interest on LT bonds, dividends, etc.)							$30.0	$30.0	$30.0	$30.0	$30.0	$30.0	
387	Taxes									$30.0			$30.0	
388	Payment for plant construction									$150.0				
389	Total payments							$270.0	$340.0	$590.0	$310.0	$240.0	$240.0	
390	Panel E: Net cash flows													
391	Assumed excess cash on hand at start of forecast					$0.0								
392	Net cash flow: Total collections – Total payments							–$16.2	–$26.6	–$182.0	$148.6	$104.0	$9.2	
393	Cumulative net cash flow							–$16.2	–$42.8	–$224.8	–$76.2	$27.8	$37.0	
394	Panel F: Net cash position before financing or investing													
395	Target cash balance							$10.0	$10.0	$10.0	$10.0	$10.0	$10.0	
396	Surplus cash or loan needed: Cum NCF – Target cash							–$26.2	–$52.8	–$234.8	–$86.2	$17.8	$27.0	
397	Panel G: Maximum loan requirements and investible funds													
398	Max required loan (smallest on Row 396)							$234.8						
399	Max investable funds (largest on Row 396)							$27.0						

Source: See the file *Ch16 Tool Kit.xlsx*. Numbers are reported as rounded values for clarity but are calculated using *Excel*'s full precision. Thus, intermediate calculations using the figure's rounded values will be inexact.

Notes:

1. Although the budget period is July through December, sales and purchases data for May and June are needed to determine collections and payments during July and August.

2. Firms can both borrow and pay off commercial loans on a daily basis, so the $26.2 million loan needed for July would likely be gradually borrowed as needed on a daily basis, and during October the $234.8 million loan that presumably existed at the beginning of the month would be reduced daily to the $86.2 million ending balance—which, in turn, would be completely paid off sometime during November.

3. The data in the figure are for EPC's base-case forecast. Data for alternative scenarios are shown in the chapter's *Excel Tool Kit* model.

Panel C shows forecasted materials purchases, which equal 60% of the following month's sales. EPC buys on terms of net 30, meaning that it receives no discounts and is required to pay for its purchases within 30 days of the purchase date.

Panel D shows forecasted payments for materials purchases (from Panel C), labor, leases, other payments such as dividends and interest on long-term bonds, taxes (due in September and December), and a payment of $150 million in September for enlarging an existing manufacturing facility.

Panel E shows the monthly net cash flows due to the differences between total forecasted payments (from Panel D) and total forecasted collections (from Panel B). Panel E also shows the cumulative monthly net cash flow, including any excess cash on hand at the start of the forecast (which we assume was zero). This cumulative cash flow is the amount of cash the firm would have on hand at the end of the month if it neither borrowed nor invested.

Panel F begins with EPC's target cash balance of $10 million each month. (We explain how companies choose target cash balances later in the chapter.) Subtracting the monthly target cash balances from Panel E's cumulative monthly cash flows provides the monthly *loan requirements or surplus cash available for investment*, as shown in the last row of Panel F. A negative number indicates the need for a loan, whereas a positive number indicates surplus cash that is available for investment or other uses.

Looking back at the last row in Panel E, the cumulative net cash flow is $37 million by the end of December. Because this number is positive, it indicates that EPC's cumulative cash flow is positive. However, Panel G shows that EPC will need to borrow up to $234.8 million at some point in the forecast. If EPC does not conduct a cash budget forecast, EPC might not be able to arrange financing to cover the months of negative cash flow. In particular, EPC needs a line of credit (LOC) that allows it to begin borrowing in July (see the last row in Panel F) and then continue drawing on the LOC through September. Then, when its cash flows turn positive in October, it would start repaying the LOC and completely pay it off sometime in November. Although the forecast is on a monthly basis, EPC would draw and then pay down the LOC on a daily basis.[17]

Under the base-case forecast, the CFO will need to arrange a line of credit so that the firm can borrow up to $234.8 million, increasing the loan over time as funds are needed and repaying it later when cash flows become positive. The treasurer would show the cash budget to the bankers when negotiating for the line of credit. Lenders would want to know how much the firm expects to need, when the funds will be needed, and when the loan will be repaid. The lenders—and EPC's top executives—would question the treasurer about the budget, and they would want to know how the forecasts would be affected if sales were higher or lower than those projected, how changes in customers' payment times would affect the forecasts, and the like. The focus would be on these two questions: *How accurate is the forecast likely to be? What would be the effects of significant errors?* The first question could best be answered by examining historical forecasts, and the second by running different scenarios as we do in the *Excel **Tool Kit*** model.

resource

See *Ch16 Tool Kit.xlsx* on the textbook's Web site for details.

No matter how hard we try, no forecast will ever be exactly correct, and this includes cash budgets. You can imagine the bank's reaction if the company negotiated a loan of $235 million and then came back a few months later saying that it had underestimated its requirements and needed to boost the loan to, say, $260 million. The banker might refuse, thinking the company was not managed very well. Therefore, EPC's treasurer would undoubtedly want to build a cushion into the line of credit—say, a maximum commitment of $260 million rather than the forecasted requirement of $234.8 million. However, as we discuss later in the chapter, banks charge commitment fees for guaranteed lines of credit; thus, the higher the cushion built into the line of credit, the

---

[17]Note that EPC's cash budget ignores interest paid on the LOC and interest earned on positive cash balances. Because the loans will be outstanding for a relatively short period, the impact of neglecting interest payments is small. However, interest expenses and income could be incorporated by adding rows and following steps similar to those used in Chapter 12 to forecast financial statements.

more costly the credit will be. This is another reason why it is important to develop accurate forecasts.

16-7b Cash Budgets versus Income Statements and Free Cash Flows

If you look at the cash budget, it looks similar to an income statement. However, the two statements are quite different. Here are four key differences: (1) In an income statement, the focus would be on sales, not collections. (2) An income statement would show accrued taxes, wages, and so forth—not the actual payments. (3) An income statement would show depreciation as an expense, but it would not show expenditures on new fixed assets. (4) An income statement would show a cost for goods purchased when those goods were sold, not for when they were ordered or paid.

These are obviously large differences, so it would be a big mistake to confuse a cash budget with an income statement. Also, the cash flows shown on the cash budget are different from the firm's free cash flows, because FCF reflects after-tax operating income and the investments required to maintain future operations, whereas the cash budget reflects only the actual cash inflows and outflows during a particular period.

The bottom line is that cash budgets, income statements, and free cash flows are all important and are related to one another, but they are also quite different. Each is designed for a specific purpose, and the main purpose of the cash budget is to forecast the firm's liquidity position, not its profitability.

16-7c Daily Cash Budgets

resource

See **Ch16 Tool Kit.xlsx** on the textbook's Web site for details.

Note that if cash inflows and outflows do not occur uniformly during each month, then the actual funds needed might be quite different from the indicated amounts. The data in Figure 16-6 show the situation on the last day of each month, and we see that the maximum projected loan during the forecast period is $234.8 million. Yet if all payments had to be made on the 1st of the month but most collections came on the 30th, then EPC would have to make $270 million of payments in July before it received the $253.8 million from collections. In that case, the firm would need to borrow about $270 million in July, not the $26.2 million shown in Figure 16-6. This would make the bank unhappy—perhaps so unhappy that it would not extend the requested credit. A daily cash budget would have revealed this situation.

Figure 16-6 was prepared using *Excel,* which makes it easy to change the assumptions. In the ***Tool Kit*** model, we examine the cash flow effects of changes in sales, in customers' payment patterns, and so forth. Also, the effects of changes in credit policy and inventory management could be examined through the cash budget.

SELF-TEST

How could the cash budget be used when negotiating the terms of a bank loan?

How would a shift from a tight credit policy to a relaxed policy be likely to affect a firm's cash budget?

How would the cash budget be affected if our firm's suppliers offered us terms of "2/10, net 30," rather than "net 30," and we decided to take the discount?

Suppose a firm's cash flows do not occur uniformly throughout the month. What effect would this have on the accuracy of the forecasted borrowing requirements based on a monthly cash budget? How could the firm deal with this problem?

16-8 Cash Management and the Target Cash Balance

Companies need cash to pay for expenses related to daily ongoing operations, including labor, raw materials, utility bills, and taxes. Companies also need cash for several other predictable purposes, including major purchases and payments to investors (interest payments, principal payments, and dividend payments). Following are the issues that companies consider when deciding how much cash to hold in support of ongoing operations, which is called the **target cash balance**. We discuss major purchases and payments to investors in Section 16-10.

16-8a Routine (but Uncertain) Operating Transactions

Cash balances are necessary in business operations. Payments must be made in cash, and receipts are deposited in the cash account. Cash balances associated with routine payments and collections are known as **transactions balances**. Cash inflows and outflows are unpredictable, and the degree of predictability varies among firms and industries. Therefore, firms need to hold some cash to meet random, unforeseen fluctuations in inflows and outflows. These "safety stocks" are called **precautionary balances**, and the less predictable the firm's cash flows, the larger such balances should be. Research confirms this and shows that companies with volatile cash flows do in fact hold higher cash balances.[18]

In addition to holding cash for transactions and precautionary reasons, the firm should have sufficient cash to take advantage of trade discounts. Suppliers frequently offer customers discounts for early payment of bills. As shown previously, the cost of not taking discounts is sometimes very high, so firms should have enough cash to permit payment of bills in time to take advantage of discounts.

Many companies have a line of credit to cover unexpected cash needs; we discuss lines of credit in Section 16-11.

16-8b Compensating Balances

A bank makes money by lending out funds that have been deposited with it, so the larger its deposits, the better the bank's profit position. If a bank is providing services to a customer, then it may require that customer to leave a minimum balance on deposit to help offset the costs of providing those services. Also, banks may require borrowers to hold their transactions deposits at the bank. Both types of deposits are called **compensating balances**. In a 1979 survey, 84.7% of responding companies reported they were required to maintain compensating balances to help pay for bank services; only 13.3% reported paying direct fees for banking services.[19] By 1996, those findings were reversed: Only 28% paid for bank services with compensating balances, while 83% paid direct fees.[20]

The use of compensating balances to pay for services has declined, but some companies hold additional cash in such accounts because they believe these balances

---

[18]See Tim Opler, Lee Pinkowitz, René Stulz, and Rohan Williamson, "The Determinants and Implications of Corporate Cash Holdings," *Journal of Financial Economics*, 1999, pp. 3–46.

[19]See Lawrence J. Gitman, E. A. Moses, and I. T. White, "An Assessment of Corporate Cash Management Practices," *Financial Management*, Spring 1979, pp. 32–41.

[20]See Charles E. Maxwell, Lawrence J. Gitman, and Stephanie A. M. Smith, "Working Capital Management and Financial-Service Consumption Preferences of U.S. and Foreign Firms: A Comparison of 1979 and 1996 Preferences," *Financial Practice and Education*, Fall/Winter 1998, pp. 46–52.

improve relationships with their banks. However, this applies primarily to small banks and small companies.

Why is cash management important?

What are the primary motives for holding cash?

16-9 Cash Management Techniques

In terms of dollar volume, most business is conducted by large firms, many of which operate nationally or globally. They collect cash from many sources and make payments from a number of different cities or even countries. For example, companies such as Apple, General Electric, and Ford have manufacturing plants all around the world. Such global companies have sales offices and bank accounts in virtually every city in which they do business. Their collection centers follow sales patterns. However, while some disbursements are made from local offices, most are made in the cities where manufacturing occurs or from the home office. Thus, a major corporation might have hundreds or even thousands of bank accounts located in cities all over the globe, but there is no reason to think that inflows and outflows will balance in each account. Therefore, a system must be in place to transfer funds from where they come in to where they are needed, to arrange loans to cover net corporate shortfalls, and to invest net corporate surpluses without delay.[21] Because cash is an operating asset just like inventory or accounts receivable, companies work to keep on hand only the amount needed to meet their operating needs.

Before describing specific cash management techniques, we begin with a brief overview of payment, clearing, and settlement systems.

16-9a Payment, Clearing, and Settlement Systems[22]

When you make a small, simple, cash deposit in person at your bank, your account balance is increased immediately to show the deposit.[23] However, most financial transactions are not conducted with cash, so a payment infrastructure system is required to enable adjustments to the bank accounts of payers and payees.[24]

For nonfinancial companies and individuals, most payment paths begin with the payer's bank account and end at the payee's account. The primary forms of payment, in

---

[21]For more information on cash management, see Bruce J. Summers, "Clearing and Payment Systems: The Role of the Central Bank," *Federal Reserve Bulletin*, February 1991, pp. 81–91.

[22]The Bank for International Settlements (BIS) and the Committee on Payment and Settlement Systems (CPSS) periodically publish descriptions of payment systems used by many large countries. For more details on the United States payments system, see the BIS/CPSS publication *Payment, Clearing and Settlement Systems in the CPSS Countries,* 2012, Vol. 2, pp. 471–508. It is available at the BIS Web site: **http://www.bis.org/cpmi/publ/d105.htm.**

[23]Most banks will allow you to withdraw your cash deposit later that same day, but this is not required! Instead, a bank is allowed to wait until the next business day before you can access those funds for cash withdrawals or even for settling debit card charges. In fact, the bank can wait until the second business day if you didn't make the deposit in person. For more, see the Consumer Financial Protection Bureau at **www.consumerfinance.gov/askcfpb/1029/i-made-cash-deposit-my-checking-account-i-attempted-withdrawal-later-day-and-was-told-i-could-not-withdraw-until-tomorrow-can-bank-do.html.**

[24]We use the term "bank" here to denote all deposit transaction accounts that allow payments, whether they are at a commercial bank, S&L, or other financial intermediary.

terms of total dollar value transactions, are (1) direct transfers from account to account, (2) paper checks, (3) credit cards, and (4) debit cards.[25] Following is a brief description of each method.

Two automated clearing house (ACH) network operators, the Federal Reserve and The Clearing House, facilitate direct transfers on behalf of users from one bank account to another. For example, many companies make direct deposits to employees' bank accounts for payroll and make direct deposits to suppliers' bank accounts for purchases. Individuals often pre-authorize regular payments from their bank accounts, such as monthly cell phone bills and mortgage payments. In addition, an online purchase can be made by a one-time authorization to deduct funds from the purchaser's bank account. Direct online transfers are often called **wire transfers** because they were first conducted via telegraph.

Even with an ACH transaction, the actual funds in the bank accounts don't change immediately due to the following reasons. First, most banks batch ACH orders several times a day rather submitting each order in real time. Second, after processing ACH orders, a payer's bank puts a hold on the pending amount coming from the payer's account and verifies that the payer has sufficient funds; also, the payee's bank puts a pending credit on the payee's account. Third, **clearing** occurs when the ACH network confirms that the banks themselves have sufficient funds and transmits the confirmation to the banks.[26] Fourth, **settlement** occurs when the payer's bank actually deducts the payment amount from the account balance and the payee's bank actually deposits the amount into the payee's account. The complete process can happen within minutes or it can take 1 to 2 business days, depending on the complexity of the transaction.

Printed checks still make up a large percentage of payments. The Check 21 Act, implemented in 2004, allows banks to exchange digital images of checks rather than the actual pieces of paper. Digital checks may be cleared directly between the payer's and payee's bank, through the Federal Reserve, or through services provided by third-party banks or clearing houses. Before Check 21, clearing could take 2 to 5 days, but now most checks clear in a single day. Keep in mind that clearing and settlement are not the same—clearing is the exchange of information, but funds can't be spent until settlement, which can take another business day or two.

When you use your debit or credit card to make a purchase, the information goes from the purchasing location (which can be face-to-face or online) to the seller's bank, then to the payment card network (such as MasterCard or Visa), and then to the bank that issued your card. If your card's bank approves, you have just made a purchase. However, cash doesn't move instantaneously from your bank account to the seller's bank account, even with most debit card purchases.[27] Similar to the ACH process, orders are batched, holds are placed, and time can lapse before interbank clearing by the payment card network occurs. The payment card network will clear the transaction, but it is up to the banks to settle the transactions.

---

[25]See pages 485–486 in the source cited in footnote 22. These rankings are based on 2010 data. Based on trends, it is likely that debit card transactions will exceed those of credit cards by the time you read this.

[26]The Federal Reserve Board and The Clearing House operate special transfer systems for banks to make large payments on behalf of themselves or their customers.

[27]Some debit card transactions clear and settle at the time of the purchase, but most don't. For more details, see Susan Herbst-Murphy, "Clearing and Settlement of Interbank Card Transactions: A MasterCard Tutorial for Federal Reserve Payments Analysts." This paper is available at the Federal Reserve Bank of Philadelphia: **https://www.philadelphiafed.org/-/media/consumer-credit-and-payments/payment-cards-center/publications/discussion-papers/2013/d-2013-october-clearing-settlement.pdf?la=en.**

Because payments don't occur instantaneously, companies must maintain a sufficient balance in their bank accounts to handle the transactions.[28] The following sections describe different techniques that companies use.

16-9b Synchronizing Cash Flow

If you as an individual were to receive income once a year, then you would probably put it in the bank, draw down your account periodically, and have an average balance for the year equal to about half of your annual income. If instead you received income weekly and paid rent, tuition, and other charges on a daily basis, then your average bank balance would still be about half of your periodic receipts and thus only 1/52 as large as if you received income only once annually.

Exactly the same situation holds for businesses: By timing their cash receipts to coincide with their cash outlays, firms can hold their transactions balances to a minimum. Recognizing this fact, firms such as utilities, oil companies, and credit card companies arrange to bill customers—and to pay their own bills—on regular "billing cycles" throughout the month. This **synchronization of cash flows** provides cash when it is needed and thus enables firms to reduce their average cash balances.

16-9c Using Float

Float is defined as the difference between the balance shown in a firm's (or individual's) checkbook and the balance on the bank's records. Suppose a firm writes and mails, on average, checks in the amount of $5,000 each day, and suppose it takes 6 days for these checks to reach their destination, clear, and be deducted from the firm's bank account. This will cause the firm's own checkbook to show a balance that is $30,000 smaller than the balance on the bank's records; this difference is called **disbursement float**. Now suppose the firm also receives checks in the amount of $5,000 daily but that it loses 4 days while those checks are being deposited and cleared. This will result in $20,000 of **collections float**. The firm's **net float** is the difference between the $30,000 positive disbursement float and the $20,000 negative collections float, which will be $10,000. In sum, collections float is bad, disbursement float is good, and positive net float is even better.

Delays that cause float will occur because it takes time for checks to (1) travel through the mail (mail float), (2) be processed by the receiving firm (processing float), and (3) clear through the banking system (clearing, or availability, float). Basically, the size of a firm's net float is a function of its ability to speed up collections on checks it receives and to slow down collections on checks it writes. Efficient firms go to great lengths to speed up the processing of incoming checks, thus putting the funds to work faster, and they try to stretch their own payments out as long as possible, sometimes by disbursing checks from banks in remote locations.

16-9d Speeding Up Collections

Two major techniques are used to speed collections and to get funds where they are needed: lockboxes and electronic transfers.

LOCKBOXES

A **lockbox system** is one of the oldest cash management tools. In a lockbox system, incoming checks are sent to post office boxes rather than to the firm's corporate headquarters. For example, a firm headquartered in New York City might have its West Coast customers

---

[28]Banks will offer "overdraft" protection, but it is costly.

send their payments to a post office box in San Francisco, its customers in the Southwest send their checks to Dallas, and so on, rather than having all checks sent to New York City. Several times a day, a local bank will empty the lockbox and deposit the checks into the company's local account. The bank then provides the firm with a daily record of the receipts collected, usually via an electronic data transmission system in a format that permits online updating of the firm's accounts receivable records.

A lockbox system reduces the time required to receive incoming checks, to deposit them, and to get them cleared through the banking system. Lockbox services can make funds available as many as 2 to 5 days faster than for checks mailed directly to a company.

ELECTRONIC PAYMENTS

Firms are increasingly demanding payments of larger bills by automatic electronic transfers instead of printed checks. As described in previous sections, clearing and settlement can occur much more quickly with electronic payments.

SELF-TEST

What is float? How do firms use float to increase cash management efficiency?

What are some methods firms can use to accelerate receipts?

16-10 Managing Short-Term Investments

Short-term investments include short-term financial assets such as U.S. Treasury securities, U.S. agency securities, certificates of deposit, time deposits, and commercial paper. There are three reasons companies hold short-term investments: (1) for liquidation just prior to scheduled transactions, (2) for unexpected opportunities, and (3) to reduce the company's risk.

Some future transaction dates and amounts are known with a high degree of certainty. For example, a company knows the dates on which it will need cash to make interest, principal, and dividend payments; if a company has decided to make a major purchase, such as a new machine or even a new factory, the company knows the dates on which it will pay for the purchase. A company's payment isn't complete until the funds have been deducted from the company's bank account and credited to the depositor's bank account. Because a company doesn't actually need a balance in the bank account until the payment is deducted, most companies try to keep their bank account balances (which pay zero or very low interest rates) as low as possible until the day the payment is deducted. For example, if a company has a scheduled dividend payment, the company is likely to hold the amount needed for the payment in the form of short-term investments such as T-bills or other interest-paying short-term securities. The company will liquidate these short-term investments and deposit the proceeds into its bank accounts just prior to the required payment date.

Short-term investments that are designated for making scheduled payments, such as those just described, are temporary in the sense that a company acquires these short-term investments and plans to hold them for a specific period and for a particular use. The following sections describe short-term investments that are less transitory.

Some companies hold short-term investments even though they haven't planned a specific use for them and even though the rate of return on short-term investments is very low. For example, some companies compete in businesses that have growth opportunities that arise unexpectedly. If such a company doesn't have stable cash flows or ready access to credit markets (perhaps because the company is small or doesn't have a high credit rating), it might not be able to take advantage of an unexpected opportunity. Therefore, the company might hold short-term investments, which are **speculative balances** in the sense that the company speculates that it will have an opportunity to use them and subsequently earn much more than the rate on short-term investments. Studies show that such firms do hold relatively high levels of marketable securities. In contrast, cash holdings are less important to large firms with high credit ratings because they have quick and inexpensive access to capital markets. As expected, such firms hold relatively low levels of cash.[29]

Holding short-term investments reduces a company's risk of facing a liquidity crisis, such as the ones that occurred during the economic downturn and credit crunch of the 2007 recession. A stockpile of short-term investments also reduces transaction costs due to issuing securities because the investments can be liquidated instead.

Although there are good reasons many companies hold short-term investments, there are too many companies holding too much cash. As we write this in mid-2018, U.S. nonfinancial companies hold about $3.3 trillion in cash, savings and money market funds, making up about 5% of their total assets. Some companies, such as Apple and Microsoft, have much larger cash-to-assets ratios. Even with the uncertain economic environment, it is hard to believe that investors would not benefit by cash distributions instead of cash stockpiles.

SELF-TEST

Why might a company hold low-yielding marketable securities when it could earn a much higher return on operating assets?

16-11 Short-Term Bank Loans

Earlier in the chapter, we discussed using short-term debt as part of the aggressive approach to financing operating current assets. One source of this short-term debt is loans from a bank. Loans from commercial banks generally appear on balance sheets as notes payable. A bank's importance is actually greater than it appears from the dollar amounts shown on balance sheets because banks provide *nonspontaneous* funds. As a firm's financing needs increase, it requests additional funds from its bank. If the request is denied, the firm may be forced to abandon attractive growth opportunities. The key features of bank loans are discussed in the following paragraphs.

16-11a Maturity

Although banks do make longer-term loans, *the bulk of their lending is on a short-term basis*—about two-thirds of all bank loans mature in a year or less. Bank loans to businesses are frequently written as 90-day notes, so the loan must be repaid or renewed at the end of 90 days. Of course, if a borrower's financial position has deteriorated, then the bank may refuse to renew the loan. This can mean serious trouble for the borrower.

16-11b Promissory Notes

When a bank loan is approved, the agreement is executed by signing a **promissory note**. The note specifies (1) the amount borrowed, (2) the interest rate, (3) the repayment schedule, which can call for either a lump sum or a series of installments, (4) any collateral that

---

[29]See the study by Opler, Pinkowitz, Stulz, and Williamson cited in footnote 18.

might have to be put up as security for the loan, and (5) any other terms and conditions to which the bank and the borrower have agreed. When the note is signed, the bank credits the borrower's checking account with the funds; hence, both cash and notes payable increase on the borrower's balance sheet.

16-11c Compensating Balances

Banks sometimes require borrowers to maintain an average demand deposit (checking account) balance of 10% to 20% of the loan's face amount. This is called a compensating balance, and such balances raise the effective interest rate on the loans. For example, if a firm needs $80,000 to pay off outstanding obligations but it must maintain a 20% compensating balance, then it must borrow $100,000 to obtain a usable $80,000. If the stated annual interest rate is 8%, the effective cost is actually 10%: $8,000 interest divided by $80,000 of usable funds equals 10%.[30]

As we noted earlier in the chapter, recent surveys indicate that compensating balances are much less common now than earlier. In fact, compensating balances are now illegal in many states. Despite this trend, some small banks in states where compensating balances are legal still require their customers to maintain them.

16-11d Line of Credit

A **line of credit (LOC)** is an agreement between a bank and a borrower indicating the maximum credit the bank will extend to the borrower during a specific period and at a specified rate. The borrower does not have to use the full line of credit at the time it is established but instead can draw on the LOC for additional financing as it is needed. The bank charges interest only on outstanding balances. This LOC agreement can be either informal or formal, as explained next.

INFORMAL LINE OF CREDIT

Suppose that on December 31, a bank loan officer indicates to a company's financial manager that the bank regards the firm as being "good" for up to $80,000 during the forthcoming year, provided the borrower's financial condition does not deteriorate. Notice that no documents are signed at that time; hence it is an informal LOC.

Ten days later, the company signs a 90-day promissory note for $15,000. This is called "taking down" $15,000 of the total line of credit. This amount would be credited to the firm's checking account at the bank, and the firm could borrow additional amounts up to a total of $80,000 outstanding at any one time.

FORMAL LINE OF CREDIT (REVOLVING CREDIT AGREEMENT)

Large firms often use a formal line of credit called a **revolving credit agreement**. For example, suppose Texas Petroleum Company negotiates a revolving credit agreement for $100 million with a group of banks. The banks are formally committed for 4 years to lend the firm up to $100 million if the funds were needed.

Texas Petroleum, in turn, pays an annual **commitment fee** of 0.25% on the unused balance of the commitment to compensate the banks for making the commitment. Thus, if Texas Petroleum does not take down any of the $100 million commitment during a

---

[30]Note, however, that the compensating balance may be set as a minimum monthly *average,* and if the firm would maintain this average anyway, then the compensating balance requirement would not raise the effective interest rate. Also, note that these loan compensating balances are *added to* any compensating balances that the firm's bank may require for services performed, such as clearing checks.

year, it would still be required to pay a $250,000 annual fee, normally in monthly install-ments of $20,833.33. If it borrowed $40 million on the first day of the agreement, then the unused portion of the line of credit would fall to $60 million, and the annual fee would fall to $125,000. Of course, interest would also have to be paid on the money Texas Petro-leum actually borrowed. As a general rule, the interest rate on "revolvers" is pegged to the London Interbank Offered Rate (LIBOR), the T-bill rate, or some other market rate, so the cost of the loan varies over time as interest rates change. The interest that Texas Petroleum must pay was set at the prime lending rate plus 1.0%.

Observe that a revolving credit agreement is similar to an informal line of credit but has an important difference: The bank has a *legal obligation* to honor a revolving credit agreement, and it receives a commitment fee. Neither the legal obligation nor the fee exists under the informal line of credit.

Often a line of credit will have a **cleanup clause** that requires the borrower to reduce the loan balance to zero at least once a year. Keep in mind that a line of credit typically is designed to help finance seasonal or cyclical peaks in operations, not as a source of perma-nent capital. For example, our cash budget for Educational Products Corporation showed negative flows from July through September but positive flows from October through December. Also, the cumulative net cash flow goes positive in November, indicating that the firm could pay off its loan at that time. If the cumulative flows were always negative, this would indicate that the firm was using its credit lines as a permanent source of financing.

16-11e Costs of Bank Loans

The costs of bank loans vary for different types of borrowers at any given point in time and for all borrowers over time. Interest rates are higher for riskier borrowers, and rates are also higher on smaller loans because of the fixed costs involved in making and servic-ing loans. A bank publishes its **prime rate**, which is defined as the rate a bank charges its strongest customers, and then scales this rate up for other customers. For example, a small company might get a loan with a rate of "prime plus 1.0%." Despite the prime rate's defi-nition, many bank loans to very large, strong customers are made at rates tied to LIBOR (such as "LIBOR plus 1.5%"), with a net cost often below the prime rate:

Rates on July 12, 2018	
Prime	5.00%
1-Year LIBOR	2.78%

Bank rates vary widely over time depending on economic conditions and Federal Reserve policy. When the economy is weak, loan demand is usually slack, inflation is low, and the Fed makes plenty of money available to the system. As a result, rates on all types of loans are relatively low. Conversely, when the economy is booming, loan demand is typi-cally strong, the Fed restricts the money supply to fight inflation, and the result is high interest rates. As an indication of the kinds of fluctuations that can occur, the prime rate during 1980 rose from 11% to 21% in just 4 months; during 1994, it rose from 6% to 9%.

CALCULATING BANKS' INTEREST CHARGES: REGULAR (OR "SIMPLE") INTEREST

Banks calculate interest in several different ways. In this section, we explain the proce-dure used for most business loans. For illustration purposes, we assume a loan of $10,000 at 5.25%, with a 365-day year. Interest must be paid monthly, and the principal is payable "on demand" if and when the bank wants to end the loan. Such a loan is called a **regular interest** loan or a **simple interest** loan.

We begin by dividing the nominal interest rate by 365 to obtain the rate per day. This rate is expressed as a *decimal fraction*, not as a percentage:

$$\text{Simple interest rate per day} = \frac{\text{Nominal rate}}{\text{Days in year}}$$

$$= 0.0525/365 = 0.0001438356$$

The monthly interest payment is the product of the daily rate, the number of days in the month, and the loan amount. The average month has 30.4167 days (365/12 = 30.4167), so we will use this value to determine the average monthly payment, although the bank would use the actual number of days in each month. The average monthly interest charge is $43.75:

$$\text{Interest charge for month} = (\text{Rate per day})(\text{Amount of loan})(\text{Days in month})$$

$$= (0.0001438356)(\$10,000)(30.4167) = \$43.75$$

The *effective interest rate* on a loan depends on how frequently interest must be paid—the more frequently interest is paid, the higher the effective rate. If interest is paid once per year, then the nominal rate is also the effective rate. However, if interest must be paid monthly, then the effective rate is $(1 + 0.0525/12)^{12} - 1 = 5.378\%$.

CALCULATING BANKS' INTEREST CHARGES: ADD-ON INTEREST

Some lenders sometimes use **add-on interest**. They begin by calculating the total amount of interest that must be repaid. For car loans, this total is often the total interest that would be paid on an amortizing loan, as described in Chapter 4. But some lenders calculate the total interest as the product of the loan's annual interest rate, the number of years until the loan is fully repaid, and the amount that is borrowed. Notice that this second approach ignores the fact that some principal will be repaid with each payment, making the total interest charge much higher than that of an amortizing loan.

It is called *add-on interest* because the total interest charged by the lender is added to the amount borrowed to determine the total amount of payments. This total of interest and principal is divided by the number of payments to get the amount of each equal payment.[31]

To illustrate, suppose you borrow $10,000 on an add-on basis at a nominal rate of 7.25%, with the loan to be repaid in 12 monthly installments. At a 7.25% add-on rate, the total interest payments are $725 = (0.0725)(1 year)($10,000). The total amount of interest and principal is $10,725 = $725 + $10,000, and the monthly payment is $893.75 = $10,725/12.

To find the annual percentage rate (APR), we use *Excel*'s **RATE** function or a financial calculator: N = 12, PV = 10000, PMT = −893.75, and FV = 0. With these inputs,

---

[31]Each payment consists of interest and principal, but the relative amounts are not always calculated like those for an amortizing loan. Instead, many lenders use other methods that often result in higher interest and lower principal in the early life of the loans. Of course, lower principal payments in the early periods of repayments mean that more principal will be owed relative to an amortizing loan if the borrower repays the loan early. One such method is the **Rule of 78**, which allocates interest in the following manner. First, determine the sum of the payment numbers. For example, with 12 payments, the sum of 1 through 12 is 78; with 24 payments, the sum is 300. Second, divide the number of remaining payments (not including the current payment) by the previously calculated total sum to determine the portion of the payment that goes to interest. For example, if 12 payments remain on a 12-month loan, divide 12 by 78 to get 0.1538 = 12/78. For this first month, 15.38% of the payment would be for interest and the remainder would be principal.

the monthly rate is 1.093585%. Multiply the monthly rate by 12 to get 13.12%, which is the APR that a lender would report to the borrower. This is quite a bit above the 7.25% rate, and the effective rate on an add-on loan is even higher. The effective annual rate is $(1.010936)^{12} - 1 = 13.94\%$, which is even higher. As this example shows, add-on interest loans can be very costly for borrowers.

SELF-TEST

What is a promissory note, and what are some terms that are normally included in promissory notes?

What is a line of credit? A revolving credit agreement?

What's the difference between simple interest and add-on interest?

Explain how a firm that expects to need funds during the coming year might make sure that the needed funds will be available.

How does the cost of costly trade credit generally compare with the cost of short-term bank loans?

If a firm borrowed $500,000 at a rate of 10% simple interest with monthly interest payments and a 365-day year, what would be the required interest payment for a 30-day month? **($4,109.59)** *If interest must be paid monthly, what would be the effective annual rate?* **(10.47%)**

If this loan had been made on a 10% add-on basis, payable in 12 end-of-month installments, what would be the monthly payment amount? **($45,833.33)** *What is the annual percentage rate?* **(17.97%)** *The effective annual rate?* **(19.53%)**

16-12 Commercial Paper

W W W

For updates on the outstanding balances of commercial paper and corporate debt, go to www.federalreserve.gov /releases/cp/outstanding .htm. For commercial and industrial bank loans, go to www.federalreserve .gov/releases/h8/current /default.htm

Commercial paper is a type of unsecured promissory note issued by large, strong firms and sold primarily to other business firms, to insurance companies, to pension funds, to money market mutual funds, and to banks. In mid-2018, there was approximately $1.1 trillion of commercial paper outstanding, versus nearly $2.1 trillion of commercial and industrial bank loans. Most, but not all, commercial paper outstanding is issued by financial institutions.

16-12a Maturity and Cost

W W W

For current rates, see www.federalreserve .gov/releases/h15/.

Maturities of commercial paper generally vary from 1 day to 9 months, with an average of about 5 months.[32] The interest rate on commercial paper fluctuates with supply and demand conditions—it is determined in the marketplace, varying daily as conditions change. Recently, commercial paper rates have ranged from 1.5 to 3.5 percentage points below the stated prime rate and up to half of a percentage point above the T-bill rate. For example, in mid-2018, the average rate on 3-month nonfinancial commercial paper was 2.12%, the prime rate was 5.0%, and the 3-month T-bill rate was 1.99%.

16-12b Use of Commercial Paper

The use of commercial paper is restricted to a comparatively small number of very large companies that are exceptionally good credit risks. Even so, Moody's, Standard & Poor's,

---

[32]The maximum maturity without SEC registration is 270 days. Also, commercial paper can be sold only to "sophisticated" investors; otherwise, SEC registration would be required even for maturities of 270 days or less.

and Fitch often assign ratings at the time of issue. This is important because commercial paper issuers very rarely provide collateral.

Dealers prefer to handle the paper of firms whose net worth is $100 million or more and whose annual borrowing exceeds $10 million. One potential problem with commercial paper is that a debtor who has a temporary financial difficulty may receive little help because commercial paper dealings are generally less personal than are bank relationships. Thus, banks are generally more able and willing to help a good customer weather a temporary storm than is a commercial paper dealer. On the other hand, using commercial paper permits a corporation to tap a wide range of credit sources, including financial institutions outside its own area and industrial corporations across the country; this can reduce interest costs.

SELF-TEST

What is commercial paper?

What types of companies can use commercial paper to meet their short-term financing needs?

How does the cost of commercial paper compare with the cost of short-term bank loans? With the cost of Treasury bills?

16-13 Use of Security in Short-Term Financing

A **secured basis loan** is a type of short-term financing that is backed by collateral. Other things held constant, it is better to borrow on an unsecured basis because the bookkeeping and monitoring activities for secured loans can be onerous. However, firms often find that they can borrow only if they put up some type of collateral to protect the lender or that, by using security, they can borrow at a much lower rate.

Companies can employ several different kinds of collateral, including marketable stocks or bonds, land or buildings, equipment, inventory, and accounts receivable. Marketable securities make excellent collateral, but few firms that need loans also hold portfolios of stocks and bonds. Similarly, real property (land and buildings) and equipment are good forms of collateral, but they are generally used as security for long-term loans rather than for working capital loans. Therefore, most secured short-term business borrowing involves the use of accounts receivable and inventories as collateral.

resource

*For a more detailed discussion of secured financing, see **Web Extension 16A** on the textbook's Web site.*

Consider the case of a Chicago hardware dealer who requested a $200,000 bank loan to modernize and expand his store. After examining the business' financial statements, his bank indicated that it would lend him a maximum of $100,000 and that the effective interest rate would be 9%. The owner had a substantial personal portfolio of stocks, and he offered to put up $300,000 of high-quality stocks to support the $200,000 loan. The bank then granted the full $200,000 loan at the prime rate of 3.25%. The store owner might also have used his inventories or receivables as security for the loan, but processing costs would have been high.[33]

SELF-TEST

What is a secured loan?

What are some types of current assets that are pledged as security for short-term loans?

---

[33]The term "asset-based financing" is often used as a synonym for "secured financing." In recent years, accounts receivable have been used as security for long-term bonds, permitting corporations to borrow from lenders such as pension funds rather than just from banks and other traditional short-term lenders.

SUMMARY

This chapter discussed working capital management and short-term financing. The key concepts covered are as follows:

- **Working capital** refers to current assets used in operations, and **net working capital** is defined as current assets minus all current liabilities. **Net operating working capital** is defined as operating current assets minus operating current liabilities.
- Under a **relaxed policy** for current assets, a firm would hold relatively large amounts of each type of current asset. Under a **restricted policy**, the firm would hold minimal amounts of these items.
- **Permanent operating current assets** are the operating current assets the firm holds even during slack times, whereas **temporary operating current assets** are the additional operating current assets needed during seasonal or cyclical peaks. The methods used to finance permanent and temporary operating current assets define the firm's **operating current assets financing policy**.
- A **maturity matching approach** to short-term financing involves matching, to the extent possible, the maturities of assets and liabilities, so that temporary operating current assets are financed with short-term debt and permanent operating current assets and fixed assets are financed with long-term debt or equity. Under an **aggressive approach**, some permanent operating current assets, and perhaps even some fixed assets, are financed with short-term debt. A **conservative approach** would be to use long-term sources to finance all permanent operating capital and some of the temporary operating current assets.
- The **inventory conversion period** is the average time required to convert materials into finished goods and then to sell those goods:

$$\text{Inventory conversion period} = \text{Inventory} \div \text{Cost of goods sold per day}$$

- The **average collection period** is the average length of time required to convert the firm's receivables into cash—that is, to collect cash following a sale:

$$\text{Average collection period} = \text{DSO} = \text{Receivables} \div (\text{Sales}/365)$$

- The **payables deferral period** is the average length of time between the purchase of materials and labor and the payment of cash for them:

$$\text{Payables deferral period} = \text{Payables} \div \text{Cost of goods sold per day}$$

- The **cash conversion cycle (CCC)** is the length of time between the firm's actual cash expenditures to pay for productive resources (materials and labor) and its own cash receipts from the sale of products (that is, the length of time between paying for labor and materials and collecting on receivables):

$$\begin{matrix} \text{Cash} & & \text{Inventory} & & \text{Average} & & \text{Payables} \\ \text{conversion} = & & \text{conversion} + & & \text{collection} - & & \text{deferral} \\ \text{cycle} & & \text{period} & & \text{period} & & \text{period} \end{matrix}$$

- A **cash budget** is a schedule showing projected cash inflows and outflows over some period. The cash budget is used to predict cash surpluses and deficits, and it is the primary cash management planning tool.
- The *primary goal of cash management* is to minimize the amount of cash the firm must hold for conducting its normal business activities while at the same time maintaining a sufficient cash reserve to take discounts, pay bills promptly, and meet any unexpected cash needs.

- The **transactions balance** is the cash necessary to conduct routine day-to-day business; **precautionary balances** are cash reserves held to meet random, unforeseen needs. A **compensating balance** is a minimum checking account balance that a bank requires as compensation either for services provided or as part of a loan agreement.
- The twin goals of *inventory management* are (1) to ensure that the inventories needed to sustain operations are available, but (2) to hold the costs of ordering and carrying inventories to the lowest possible level.
- When a firm sells goods to a customer on credit, an **account receivable** is created.
- A firm can use an **aging schedule** and the **days sales outstanding (DSO)** to monitor its receivables balance and to help avoid an increase in bad debts.
- A firm's **credit policy** consists of four elements: (1) credit period, (2) discounts given for early payment, (3) credit standards, and (4) collection policy.
- **Accounts payable**, or **trade credit**, arises spontaneously as a result of credit purchases. Firms should use all the **free trade credit** they can obtain, but they should use **costly trade credit** only if it is less expensive than other forms of short-term debt. Suppliers often offer discounts to customers who pay within a stated period. The following equation may be used to calculate the nominal cost, on an annual basis, of not taking such discounts:

$$\frac{\text{Nominal annual cost}}{\text{of trade credit}} = \frac{\text{Discount percentage}}{100 - \frac{\text{Discount}}{\text{percentage}}} \times \frac{365}{\frac{\text{Days credit is}}{\text{outstanding}} - \frac{\text{Discount}}{\text{period}}}$$

- The advantages of short-term credit are (1) the *speed* with which short-term loans can be arranged, (2) increased *flexibility,* and (3) generally *lower interest rates* than with long-term credit. The principal disadvantage of short-term credit is the *extra risk* the borrower must bear because (1) the lender can demand payment on short notice; (2) the cost of the loan will increase if interest rates rise.
- Bank loans are an important source of short-term credit. When a bank loan is approved, a **promissory note** is signed. It specifies (1) the amount borrowed, (2) the percentage interest rate, (3) the repayment schedule, (4) the collateral, and (5) any other conditions to which the parties have agreed.
- **Speculative balances** are short-term, highly liquid financial assets held by a company in excess of the amounts needed to support operating activities or to cover expected near-term payments.
- A **line of credit** is an informal agreement between the bank and the borrower indicating the maximum amount of credit the bank will extend to the borrower.
- A **revolving credit agreement** is a formal line of credit often used by large firms; it involves a **commitment fee**.
- A **simple interest** loan is one in which interest must be paid monthly and the principal is payable "on demand" if and when the bank wants to end the loan.
- An **add-on interest loan** is one in which interest is calculated and added to the funds received to determine the face amount of the installment loan.
- **Commercial paper** is unsecured short-term debt issued by large, financially strong corporations. Although the cost of commercial paper is lower than the cost of bank loans, it can be used only by large firms with exceptionally strong credit ratings.
- Sometimes a borrower will find it is necessary to obtain financing with a **secured basis loan**, in which case the borrower pledges assets such as real estate, securities, equipment, inventories, or accounts receivable as collateral for the loan. For a more detailed discussion of secured financing, see *Web Extension 16A.*

QUESTIONS

(16-1)   Define each of the following terms:
  a.   Working capital; net working capital; net operating working capital
  b.   Current asset usage policies: relaxed policy, restricted policy, and moderate policy
  c.   Permanent operating current assets; temporary operating current assets
  d.   Current asset financing policies: maturity matching, aggressive, and conservative
  e.   Inventory conversion period; average collection period; payables deferral period; cash conversion cycle
  f.   Cash budget; target cash balance
  g.   Transactions balances; compensating balances; precautionary balances
  h.   Trade (cash) discounts
  i.   Credit policy; credit period; credit standards; collection policy; cash discounts
  j.   Account receivable; days sales outstanding; aging schedule
  k.   Accruals; trade credit
  l.   Stretching accounts payable; free trade credit; costly trade credit
  m.   Promissory note; line of credit; revolving credit agreement
  n.   Commercial paper; secured loan

(16-2)   What are the two principal reasons for holding cash? Can a firm estimate its target cash balance by summing the cash held to satisfy each of the two reasons?

(16-3)   Is it true that, when one firm sells to another on credit, the seller records the transaction as an account receivable while the buyer records it as an account payable and that, disregarding discounts, the receivable typically exceeds the payable by the amount of profit on the sale?

(16-4)   What are the four elements of a firm's credit policy? To what extent can firms set their own credit policies as opposed to accepting policies that are dictated by its competitors?

(16-5)   What are the advantages of matching the maturities of assets and liabilities? What are the disadvantages?

(16-6)   From the standpoint of the borrower, is long-term or short-term credit riskier? Explain. Would it ever make sense to borrow on a short-term basis if short-term rates were above long-term rates?

(16-7)   Discuss this statement: "Firms can control their accruals within fairly wide limits."

(16-8)   Is it true that most firms are able to obtain some free trade credit and that additional trade credit is often available, but at a cost? Explain.

(16-9)   What kinds of firms use commercial paper?

SELF-TEST PROBLEMS   SOLUTIONS SHOWN IN APPENDIX A

(ST-1)   The Calgary Company is attempting to establish a current assets policy. Fixed assets
Working Capital   are $600,000, and the firm plans to maintain a 50% debt-to-assets ratio. Calgary has no
Policy   operating current liabilities. The interest rate is 10% on all debt. Three alternative current asset policies are under consideration: 40%, 50%, and 60% of projected sales. The company expects to earn 15% before interest and taxes on sales of $3 million. Calgary's effective federal-plus-state tax rate is 25%. What is the expected return on equity under each asset policy?

(ST-2)
Current Asset Financing

Van Press Inc. and the Herr Publishing Company had the following balance sheets for the most recent year (thousands of dollars):

	Van Press	Herr Publishing
Current assets	$100,000	$80,000
Fixed assets (net)	100,000	120,000
Total assets	$200,000	$200,000
Short-term debt	$10,000	$50,000
Long-term debt	50,000	10,000
Common stock	112,000	112,000
Retained earnings	28,000	28,000
Equity	140,000	140,000
Total liabilities and equity	$200,000	$200,000

Earnings before interest and taxes for both firms are $30 million, and the effective federal-plus-state tax rate is 25%.

a. What is the return on equity for each firm if the interest rate on short-term debt is 10% and the rate on long-term debt is 13%?

b. Assume that the short-term rate rises to 20%, that the rate on new long-term debt rises to 16%, and that the rate on existing long-term debt remains unchanged. What would be the return on equity for Van Press and Herr Publishing under these conditions?

c. Which company is in a riskier position? Why?

PROBLEMS ANSWERS ARE IN APPENDIX B

EASY PROBLEMS 1–5

(16-1)
Inventory Management

Williams & Sons last year reported sales of $12 million, cost of goods sold (COGS) of $10 million, and an inventory turnover ratio of 2. The company is now adopting a new inventory system. If the new system is able to reduce the firm's inventory level and increase the firm's inventory turnover ratio to 5 while maintaining the same level of sales and COGS, how much cash will be freed up?

(16-2)
Receivables Investment

Medwig Corporation has a DSO of 17 days. The company averages $3,500 in sales each day (all customers take credit). What is the company's average accounts receivable?

(16-3)
Cost of Trade Credit

What are the nominal and effective costs of trade credit under the credit terms of 3/15, net 30?

(16-4)
Cost of Trade Credit

A large retailer obtains merchandise under the credit terms of 1/15, net 45, but routinely takes 60 days to pay its bills. (Because the retailer is an important customer, suppliers allow the firm to stretch its credit terms.) What is the retailer's effective cost of trade credit?

(16-5)
Accounts Payable

A chain of appliance stores, APP Corporation, purchases inventory with a net price of $500,000 each day. The company purchases the inventory under the credit terms of 2/15, net 40. APP always takes the discount but takes the full 15 days to pay its bills. What is the average accounts payable for APP?

INTERMEDIATE PROBLEMS 6–12

(16-6)
Receivables Investment

Snider Industries sells on terms of 2/10, net 45. Total sales for the year are $1,500,000. Thirty percent of customers pay on the 10th day and take discounts; the other 70% pay, on average, 50 days after their purchases.

    a. What is the days sales outstanding?
    b. What is the average amount of receivables?
    c. What would the new days sales outstanding and average receivables be if Snider toughened its collection policy with the result that all nondiscount customers paid on the 45th day?

(16-7)
Cost of Trade Credit

Calculate the nominal annual cost of trade credit under each of the following terms.
    a. 1/15, net 20
    b. 2/10, net 60
    c. 3/10, net 45
    d. 2/10, net 45
    e. 2/15, net 40

(16-8)
Cost of Trade Credit

Captain Whitman Ship Supplies offers terms of 3/15, net 45.

    a. If a purchaser takes the discount and pays on the 10th day, what is the nominal cost of trade credit?
    b. Now suppose a purchaser actually pays on the 20th day but *still takes the discount*. What is the *actual* nominal cost of the trade credit?

(16-9)
Cost of Trade Credit

Grunewald Industries sells on terms of 2/10, net 40. Gross sales last year were $4,562,500 and accounts receivable averaged $437,500. Half of Grunewald's customers paid on the 10th day and took discounts. What are the nominal and effective costs of trade credit to Grunewald's nondiscount customers? (*Hint:* Calculate daily sales based on a 365-day year, calculate the average receivables for discount customers, and then find the DSO for the nondiscount customers.)

(16-10)
Effective Cost of Trade Credit

The D.J. Masson Corporation needs to raise $500,000 for 1 year to supply working capital to a new store. Masson buys from its suppliers on terms of 3/10, net 90, and it currently pays on the 10th day and takes discounts. However, it could forgo the discounts, pay on the 90th day, and thereby obtain the needed $500,000 in the form of costly trade credit. What is the effective annual interest rate of this trade credit?

(16-11)
Cash Conversion Cycle

Negus Enterprises has an inventory conversion period of 50 days, an average collection period of 35 days, and a payables deferral period of 25 days. Assume that cost of goods sold is 80% of sales.

    a. What is the length of the firm's cash conversion cycle?
    b. If annual sales are $4,380,000 and all sales are on credit, what is the firm's investment in accounts receivable?
    c. How many times per year does Negus Enterprises turn over its inventory?

(16-12)
Working Capital Cash Flow Cycle

Strickler Technology is considering changes in its working capital policies to improve its cash flow cycle. Strickler's sales last year were $3,250,000 (all on credit), and its net profit margin was 7%. Its inventory turnover was 6.0 times during the year, and its DSO was 41 days. Its annual cost of goods sold was $1,800,000. The firm had fixed assets totaling $535,000. Strickler's payables deferral period is 45 days.

    a. Calculate Strickler's cash conversion cycle.
    b. Assuming Strickler holds negligible amounts of cash and marketable securities, calculate its total assets turnover and ROA.

c. Suppose Strickler's managers believe the annual inventory turnover can be raised to 9 times without affecting sale or profit margins. What would Strickler's cash conversion cycle, total assets turnover, and ROA have been if the inventory turnover had been 9 for the year?

CHALLENGING PROBLEMS 13–17

(16-13)
Current Asset Usage Policy

Payne Products had $1.6 million in sales revenues in the most recent year and expects sales growth to be 25% this year. Payne would like to determine the effect of various current assets policies on its financial performance. Payne has $1 million of fixed assets and intends to keep its debt ratio at its historical level of 40%. Payne's debt interest rate is currently 8%. You are to evaluate three different current asset policies: (1) a restricted policy in which current assets are 45% of projected sales, (2) a moderate policy with 50% of sales tied up in current assets, and (3) a relaxed policy requiring current assets of 60% of sales. Earnings before interest and taxes are expected to be 12% of sales. Payne's tax rate is 25%.

a. What is the expected return on equity under each current asset level?
b. In this problem, we have assumed that the level of expected sales is independent of current asset policy. Is this a valid assumption? Why or why not?
c. How would the overall risk of the firm vary under each policy?

(16-14)
Cash Budgeting

Dorothy Koehl recently leased space in the Southside Mall and opened a new business, Koehl's Doll Shop. Business has been good, but Koehl frequently runs out of cash. This has necessitated late payment on certain orders, which is beginning to cause a problem with suppliers. Koehl plans to borrow from the bank to have cash ready as needed, but first she needs a forecast of how much she should borrow. Accordingly, she has asked you to prepare a cash budget for the critical period around Christmas, when needs will be especially high.

Sales are made on a cash basis only. Koehl's purchases must be paid for during the following month. Koehl pays herself a salary of $4,800 per month, and the rent is $2,000 per month. In addition, she must make a tax payment of $12,000 in December. The current cash on hand (on December 1) is $400, but Koehl has agreed to maintain an average bank balance of $6,000—this is her target cash balance. (Disregard the amount in the cash register, which is insignificant because Koehl keeps only a small amount on hand in order to lessen the chances of robbery.)

The estimated sales and purchases for December, January, and February are shown below. Purchases during November amounted to $140,000.

	Sales	Purchases
December	$160,000	$40,000
January	40,000	40,000
February	60,000	40,000

a. Prepare a cash budget for December, January, and February. For each month report the amount that must be borrowed or the amount of the surplus.
b. Suppose that Koehl starts selling on a credit basis on December 1, giving customers 30 days to pay. All customers accept these terms, and all other facts in the problem are unchanged. What would the company's loan requirements be at the end of December in this case? (*Hint:* The calculations required to answer this part are minimal.)

(16-15)
Cash Discounts

Suppose a firm makes purchases of $3.65 million per year under terms of 2/10, net 30, and takes discounts.

a. What is the average amount of accounts payable net of discounts? (Assume the $3.65 million of purchases is net of discounts—that is, gross purchases are $3,724,489.80, discounts are $74,489.80, and net purchases are $3.65 million.)

b. Is there a cost of the trade credit the firm uses?

c. If the firm did not take discounts but did pay on the due date, what would be its average payables and the nominal and effective costs of this nonfree trade credit?

d. What would be the firm's nominal and effective costs of not taking discounts if it could stretch its payments to 40 days?

(16-16)
Trade Credit

The Thompson Corporation projects an increase in sales from $1.5 million to $2 million, but it needs an additional $300,000 of current assets to support this expansion. Thompson can finance the expansion by no longer taking discounts, thus increasing accounts payable. Thompson purchases under terms of 2/10, net 30, but it can delay payment for an additional 35 days—paying in 65 days and thus becoming 35 days past due—without a penalty because its suppliers currently have excess capacity. What is the effective, or equivalent, annual cost of the trade credit?

(16-17)
Bank Financing

The Raattama Corporation had sales of $3.5 million last year, and it earned a 5% return (after taxes) on sales. Recently, the company has fallen behind in its accounts payable. Although its terms of purchase are net 30 days, its accounts payable represents 60 days' purchases. The company's treasurer is seeking to increase bank borrowing in order to become current in meeting its trade obligations (that is, to have 30 days' payables outstanding). The company's balance sheet is as follows (in thousands of dollars):

Cash	$ 100	Accounts payable	$ 600
Accounts receivable	300	Bank loans	700
Inventory	1,400	Accruals	200
Current assets	$1,800	Current liabilities	$1,500
Land and buildings	600	Mortgage on real estate	700
Equipment	600	Common stock, $0.10 par	300
		Retained earnings	500
Total assets	$3,000	Total liabilities and equity	$3,000

a. How much bank financing is needed to eliminate the past-due accounts payable?

b. Assume that the bank will lend the firm the amount calculated in part a. The terms of the loan offered are 8%, simple interest, and the bank uses a 360-day year for the interest calculation. What is the interest charge for 1 month? (Assume there are 30 days in a month.)

c. Now ignore part b and assume that the bank will lend the firm the amount calculated in part a. The terms of the loan are 7.5%, add-on interest, to be repaid in 12 monthly installments.

  (1) What is the total loan amount?
  (2) What are the monthly installments?
  (3) What is the APR of the loan?
  (4) What is the effective rate of the loan?

d. Would you, as a bank loan officer, make this loan? Why or why not?

SPREADSHEET PROBLEMS

(16-18)
Build a Model:
Cash Budgeting

resource

Start with the partial model in the file *Ch16 P18 Build a Model.xlsx* on the textbook's Web site. Rusty Spears, CEO of Rusty's Renovations, a custom building and repair company, is preparing documentation for a line of credit request from his commercial banker. Among the required documents is a detailed sales forecast for parts of 2020 and 2021:

	Sales	Labor and Raw Materials
May 2020	$60,000	$75,000
June	100,000	90,000
July	130,000	95,000
August	120,000	70,000
September	100,000	60,000
October	80,000	50,000
November	60,000	20,000
December	40,000	20,000
January 2021	30,000	NA

Estimates obtained from the credit and collection department are as follows: collections within the month of sale, 15%; collections during the month following the sale, 65%; collections the second month following the sale, 20%. Payments for labor and raw materials are typically made during the month following the one in which these costs were incurred. Total costs for labor and raw materials are estimated for each month as shown in the table.

General and administrative salaries will amount to approximately $15,000 a month; lease payments under long-term lease contracts will be $5,000 a month; depreciation charges will be $7,500 a month; miscellaneous expenses will be $2,000 a month; income tax payments of $25,000 will be due in both September and December; and a progress payment of $80,000 on a new office suite must be paid in October. Cash on hand on July 1 will amount to $60,000, and a minimum cash balance of $40,000 will be maintained throughout the cash budget period.

a. Prepare a monthly cash budget for the last 6 months of 2020.
b. Prepare an estimate of the required financing (or excess funds)—that is, the amount of money Rusty's Renovations will need to borrow (or will have available to invest)— for each month during that period.
c. Assume that receipts from sales come in uniformly during the month (i.e., cash receipts come in at the rate of 1/30 each day) but that all outflows are paid on the 5th of the month. Will this have an effect on the cash budget—in other words, would the cash budget you have prepared be valid under these assumptions? If not, what can be done to make a valid estimate of peak financing requirements? No calculations are required, although calculations can be used to illustrate the effects.
d. Rusty's Renovations produces on a seasonal basis, just ahead of sales. Without making any calculations, discuss how the company's current ratio and debt ratio would vary during the year assuming all financial requirements were met by short-term bank loans. Could changes in these ratios affect the firm's ability to obtain bank credit? Why or why not?
e. If its customers began to pay late, this would slow down collections and thus increase the required loan amount. Also, if sales dropped off, this would have an effect on the required loan amount. Perform a sensitivity analysis that shows the effects of these two factors on the maximum loan requirement.

MINI CASE

Karen Johnson, CFO for Raucous Roasters (RR), a specialty coffee manufacturer, is re-thinking her company's working capital policy in light of a recent scare she faced when RR's corporate banker, citing a nationwide credit crunch, balked at renewing RR's line of credit. Had the line of credit not been renewed, RR would not have been able to make payroll, potentially forcing the company out of business. Although the line of credit was ultimately renewed, the scare has forced Johnson to examine carefully each component of RR's working capital to make sure it is needed, with the goal of determining whether the line of credit can be eliminated entirely. In addition to (possibly) freeing RR from the need for a line of credit, Johnson is well aware that reducing working capital will improve free cash flow.

Historically, RR has done little to examine working capital, mainly because of poor communication among business functions. In the past, the production manager resisted Johnson's efforts to question his holdings of raw materials, the marketing manager resisted questions about finished goods, the sales staff resisted questions about credit policy (which affects accounts receivable), and the treasurer did not want to talk about the cash and securities balances. However, with the recent credit scare, this resistance has become unacceptable and Johnson has undertaken a company-wide examination of cash, marketable securities, inventory, and accounts receivable levels.

Johnson also knows that decisions about working capital cannot be made in a vacuum. For example, if inventories could be lowered without adversely affecting operations, then less capital would be required, and free cash flow would increase. However, lower raw materials inventories might lead to production slowdowns and higher costs, and lower finished goods inventories might lead to stockouts and loss of sales. So, before inventories are changed, it will be necessary to study operating as well as financial effects. The situation is the same with regard to cash and receivables. Johnson has begun her investigation by collecting the ratios shown here. (The partial cash budget shown after the ratios is used later in this mini case.)

	RR	Industry
Current	1.75	2.25
Quick	0.92	1.16
Total liabilities/assets	58.76%	50.00%
Turnover of cash and securities	16.67	22.22
Days sales outstanding (365-day basis)	45.63	32.00
Inventory turnover	10.80	20.00
Fixed assets turnover	7.75	13.22
Total assets turnover	2.60	3.00
Profit margin on sales	2.07%	3.50%
Return on equity (ROE)	10.45%	21.00%
Payables deferral period	30.00	33.00

Cash Budget (Thousands of Dollars)	Nov	Dec	Jan	Feb	Mar	Apr
Sales Forecast						
(1) Sales (gross)	$71,218.00	$68,212.00	$65,213.00	$52,475.00	$42,909.00	$30,524.00
Collections						
(2) During month of sale: (0.2)(0.98)(month's sales)			12,781.75	10,285.10		
(3) During first month after sale: (0.7)(previous month's sales)			47,748.40	45,649.10		
(4) During second month after sale: (0.1)(sales 2 months ago)			7,121.80	6,821.20		
(5) Total collections (Lines 2 + 3 + 4)			$67,651.95	$62,755.40		
Purchases						
(6) (0.85)(forecasted sales 2 months from now)			$44,603.75	$36,472.65	$25,945.40	
Payments						
(7) Payments (1-month lag)			44,603.75	36,472.65		
(8) Wages and salaries			6,690.56	5,470.90		
(9) Rent			2,500.00	2,500.00		
(10) Taxes						
(11) Total payments			$53,794.31	$44,443.55		
NCFs						
(12) Cash on hand at start of forecast			$3,000.00			
(13) NCF: Collections − Payments. = Line 5 − Line 11			$13,857.64	$18,311.85		
(14) Cum NCF: Prior + this mos. NCF			$16,857.64	$35,169.49		
Cash Surplus (or Loan Requirement)						
(15) Target cash balance			1,500.00	1,500.00		
(16) Surplus cash or loan needed			$15,357.64	$33,669.49		

a. Johnson plans to use the preceding ratios as the starting point for discussions with RR's operating team. Based on the data, does RR seem to be following a relaxed, moderate, or restricted current asset usage policy?

b. How can one distinguish between a relaxed but rational working capital policy and a situation in which a firm simply has excessive current assets because it is inefficient? Does RR's working capital policy seem appropriate?

c. Calculate the firm's cash conversion cycle given that annual sales are $660,000 and cost of goods sold represents 90% of sales. Assume a 365-day year.

d. Is there any reason to think that RR may be holding too much inventory?

e. If RR reduces its inventory without adversely affecting sales, what effect should this have on free cash flow: (1) in the short run and (2) in the long run?

f. Johnson knows that RR sells on the same credit terms as other firms in its industry. Use the ratios presented earlier to explain whether RR's customers pay more or less promptly than those of its competitors. If there are differences, does that suggest

RR should tighten or loosen its credit policy? What four variables make up a firm's credit policy, and in what direction should each be changed by RR?

g. Does RR face any risks if it tightens its credit policy?

h. If the company reduces its DSO without seriously affecting sales, what effect would this have on free cash flow (1) in the short run and (2) in the long run?

i. What is the impact of higher levels of accruals, such as accrued wages or accrued taxes? Is it likely that RR could make changes to accruals?

j. Assume that RR purchases $200,000 (net of discounts) of materials on terms of 1/10, net 30, but that it can get away with paying on the 40th day if it chooses not to take discounts. How much free trade credit can the company get from its equipment supplier, how much costly trade credit can it get, and what is the nominal annual interest rate of the costly credit? Should RR take discounts?

k. Cash doesn't earn interest, so why would a company have a positive target cash balance?

l. What might RR do to reduce its target cash balance without harming operations?

m. RR tries to match the maturity of its assets and liabilities. Describe how RR could adopt either a more aggressive or a more conservative financing policy.

n. What are the advantages and disadvantages of using short-term debt as a source of financing?

o. Would it be feasible for RR to finance with commercial paper?

p. In an attempt to better understand RR's cash position, Johnson developed a cash budget for the first 2 months of the year. She has the figures for the other months, but they are not shown. After looking at the cash budget, answer the following questions:

1. What does the cash budget show regarding the target cash level?
2. Should depreciation expense be explicitly included in the cash budget? Why or why not?
3. What are some other potential cash inflows besides collections?
4. How can interest earned or paid on short-term securities or loans be incorporated in the cash budget?
5. In her preliminary cash budget, Johnson has assumed that all sales are collected and thus that RR has no bad debts. Is this realistic? If not, how would bad debts be dealt with in a cash budgeting sense? (*Hint*: Bad debts will affect collections but not purchases.)

SELECTED ADDITIONAL CASES

The following cases from CengageCompose cover many of the concepts discussed in this chapter and are available at **http://compose.cengage.com**.

Klein-Brigham Series:
Case 29, "Office Mates, Inc.," which illustrates how changes in current asset policy affect expected profitability and risk; Case 32, "Alpine Wear, Inc.," which illustrates the mechanics of the cash budget and the rationale behind its use; Case 50, "Toy World, Inc.," and Case 66, "Sorenson Stove Company," which deal with cash budgeting; Case 33, "Upscale Toddlers, Inc.," which deals with credit policy changes; and Case 34, "Texas Rose Company," which focuses on receivables management.

Brigham-Buzzard Series:
Case 11, "Powerline Network Corporation (Working Capital Management)."

CHAPTER 17

Multinational Financial Management*

In early 2014, Medtronic was a quintessential American success story. Founded in Minnesota by two brothers-in-law, Earl Bakken and Palmer Hermundslie, Medtronic began by repairing electronic medical equipment in a garage. When Mr. Bakken invented a heart pacemaker small enough to run on batteries, the business took off. After a near bankruptcy in the early 1960s, a Minnesota venture capital fund provided cash and financial expertise. Medtronic began its global operations in 1967 and its stock went public on the NYSE in 1977. By 2014, sales were over $17 billion and it had a global presence in over 140 countries.

In early 2015, Medtronic continued to grow by acquiring Covidien, an Irish medical technology company less than half its size. However, the American portion of the success story ends there, because Medtronic reincorporated in Ireland as a part of Covidien and moved its executive headquarters to Dublin.

Why? Part of the reason is due to a more favorable tax code in Ireland than in the United States. Medtronic isn't the only company to follow this strategy, which is called a tax inversion.

The 2017 Tax Cuts and Jobs Act changed how corporations are taxed on international income, so read on to learn more.

---

*Earlier editions of this chapter benefited from the help of Professor Roy Crum of the University of Florida and Subu Venkataraman of Morgan Stanley.

Source: For the history of Medtronic, see **www.medtronic.com/wcm/groups/mdtcom_sg/@masterbrand /documents/documents/contrib_176744.pdf**.

Corporate Valuation in a Global Context

The intrinsic value of a firm is determined by the size, timing, and risk of its expected future free cash flows (FCFs). This is true for foreign as well as domestic operations, but the FCF of a foreign operation is affected by exchange rates, cultural differences, and the host country's regulatory environment. In addition, global financial markets and political risk can affect the cost of capital.

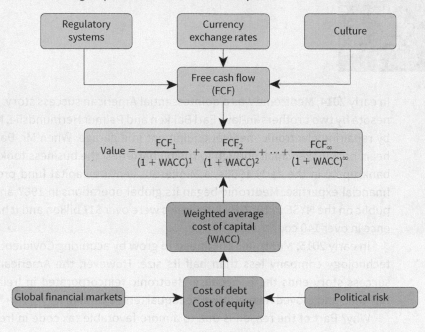

resource

The textbook's Web site contains an Excel file that will guide you through the chapter's calculations. The file for this chapter is **Ch17 Tool Kit.xlsx,** *and we encourage you to open the file and follow along as you read the chapter.*

Managers of multinational companies must deal with a wide range of issues that are not present when a company operates in a single country. In this chapter, we highlight the key differences between multinational and domestic corporations, and we discuss the effects these differences have on the financial management of multinational businesses.

17-1 Multinational, or Global, Corporations

The terms **multinational corporations**, **transnational corporations**, **multinational enterprises**, and **global corporations** are used to describe firms that operate in an integrated fashion in a number of countries. Rather than merely buying resources from and selling goods to foreign nations, multinational firms often make direct investments in fully integrated operations, from extraction of raw materials, through the manufacturing process, and to distribution to consumers throughout the world. Today, multinational corporate networks control a large and growing share of the world's technological, marketing, and productive resources.

Companies "go global" for many reasons, including the following:

1. *To broaden their markets.* For example, Apple has more iPhone users in China than in the United States.
2. *To seek raw materials.* Many U.S. oil companies, such as ExxonMobil, have major subsidiaries around the world to ensure access to the basic resources needed to sustain the companies' primary business lines.

FIGURE 17-1
Employment by U.S. Multinational Corporations

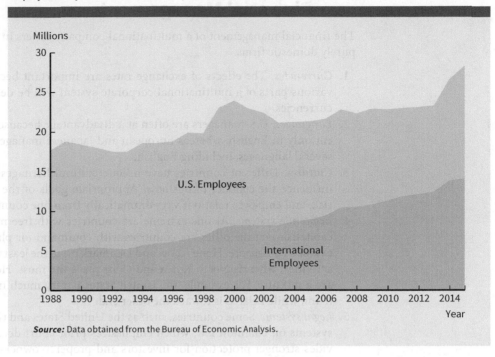

Source: Data obtained from the Bureau of Economic Analysis.

WWW

Interesting reports about the effect of trade on the U.S. economy can be found on the United States Trade Representative's home page at www.ustr.gov.

3. *To seek new technology.* Companies scour the globe for leading scientific and design ideas.
4. *To seek production efficiency.* Ford assembles all its Fusions in Mexico, even the ones sold in the United States, because it is less costly than producing them here.
5. *To avoid political and regulatory hurdles.* This is especially true with respect to the minimization of taxes, a topic we discuss later in the chapter.
6. *To diversify.* Geographic diversification reduces risks because the economic ups and downs of different countries are not perfectly correlated.

Figure 17-1 shows the employment by U.S. multinational companies (MNCs), broken down into U.S. employees and international employees. U.S. employment grew by an average rate of 1.5%, whereas international employment grew by 5.5%. One reason for the slower U.S. growth is due to productivity gains, with the same number of employees producing more goods and services. However, the biggest reason is economic growth in developing markets rather than in the United States, a trend that is likely to continue in the foreseeable future.[1]

What is a multinational corporation?

Why do companies "go global"?

---

[1]The Bureau of Economic Analysis states that the apparent increases in 2013 and 2014 are due to improved data collection processes rather than a true shift in employment.

17-2 Multinational versus Domestic Financial Management

The financial management of a multinational company differs in nine ways from that of purely domestic firms.

1. *Currencies.* The effects of exchange rates are important because the cash flows in various parts of a multinational corporate system will be denominated in different currencies.
2. *Languages.* U.S. managers are often at a disadvantage because they are generally fluent only in English, whereas European and Japanese managers are usually fluent in several languages, including English.
3. *Cultures.* Different countries have unique cultural heritages that shape values and influence the conduct of business. Appropriate goals of the firm, attitudes toward risk, and employee relations vary dramatically from one country to the next.
4. *Economic systems.* At one extreme are countries with free markets (i.e., unfettered capitalism); at the other are countries with command (or planned) economies. For example, Singapore, Hong Kong, and Denmark place the least restrictions on business activities, whereas North Korea and Cuba place the most. However, most countries are a mixture. For example, the United States is very much in the free market spectrum, while Belarus is toward the other end.
5. *Legal systems.* Some countries, such as the United States and the U.K., base their legal systems on **common law**, which emphasizes prior court decisions and usually provides stronger protection for investors and property owners. In contrast, **civil law** legal systems, such as in France, rely on detailed laws and regulations enacted by the government. Different legal systems complicate matters ranging from the simple recording of business transactions to the role played by the judiciary in resolving conflicts. Such differences can even make procedures that are required in one part of the company illegal in another part.
6. *Taxation.* Differences in countries' tax laws can cause strikingly different after-tax cash flows for identical transactions.
7. *Government intervention.* The terms under which companies compete, the actions that must be taken or avoided, the ability to curtail unprofitable operations, and the terms of trade on various transactions often are determined not in the marketplace but by direct negotiation with host governments.
8. *Political risk.* A foreign government might place constraints on the transfer of corporate resources or even expropriate assets within its boundaries. Also, corrupt government officials might expect gifts or bribes.
9. *Terrorism and crime.* Terrorist groups and criminals might threaten a company's property or the safety of its employees. This includes extortion and kidnapping. In fact, some terrorist groups finance substantial portions of their budgets through kidnapping and ransom.

These differences pose challenges for executives who must manage multinational operations—skills and knowledge gained in one country may not be as relevant in another. We address many of these issues in the following sections.

SELF-TEST

Identify and briefly discuss nine major factors that complicate financial management in multinational firms.

Meet Me at the Car Wash

This is not your ordinary car wash. Instead, it is Operation Car Wash that began as an investigation in Brazil into money laundering using small businesses like car washes and has become a global corruption scandal involving over $5 billion in illegal payments to executives and politicians throughout the world. Although other countries are connected to the investigation, it has caused enormous repercussions for Brazilian politicians and companies.

As of late 2017, one former Brazilian president, Luiz Inácio Lula da Silva, has been convicted on corruption charges. His successor, Dilma Rousseff, has been impeached for an unrelated matter. Her replacement, former Vice President Michel

Temer, has been charged with corruption by the attorney general. Dozens of other government officials have also been charged and jailed. And this is just in Brazil.

Most of the bribes were paid by several Brazilian companies, including meatpacker JBS S.A., construction conglomerate Odebrecht S.A., petrochemical company Braskem S.A., and the semi–state-owned petroleum giant Petrobras (the official name for Petrobras is Petróleo Brasileiro S.A.).

Government authorities in Brazil, the United States, Switzerland, and elsewhere have levied over $5 billion in fines. However, more are sure to be issued, making this a long and costly car wash.

17-3 Exchange Rates

WWW

The Bloomberg World Currency Values site provides up-to-the-minute foreign currency values versus the U.S. dollar. The site can be accessed at **www.bloomberg.com /markets/currencies**.

By 1914, the governments of most developed countries were issuing paper currencies that could be redeemed for gold from the government's treasury, so the monetary system was called the **gold standard**.[2] For example, until 1932, gold was worth $20.67 an ounce in the United States and £4.24 in the U.K. ("£" is the symbol for British pounds). Therefore, a British pound was worth about $4.87: ($20.67 per ounce)/(£4.24 per ounce) ≈ $4.87 per British pound. In other words, $4.87 per U.K. pound was the rate at which dollars and pounds could be exchanged. The gold standard is no longer used, but we still have rates for exchanging currencies.

In general, a **foreign exchange rate** specifies the number of units of a given currency that can be purchased with one unit of another currency. The foreign exchange rate is also called the **exchange rate**, the **FX rate**, and the **FOREX rate**.

Importers, exporters, tourists, and governments buy and sell currencies in the foreign exchange market. For example, when a U.S. company imports automobiles from Japan, the payment probably will be made in Japanese yen. To do this, the importer must buy yen (through its bank) in the foreign exchange market, which consists of a network of brokers and banks based in New York, London, Tokyo, and other financial centers. Almost all transactions are conducted by computer and telephone.

Later sections explain how exchange rates are now determined and how different monetary systems work, but in this section we show how exchange rates are used in international transactions. Unless you trade in foreign currencies, the notation can be confusing, so that is where we begin.

---

[2]For a comprehensive history of the international monetary system and details of how it has evolved, consult one of the many economics books on the subject, which include Robert Carbaugh, *International Economics*, 16th ed. (Mason, OH: South-Western Cengage Learning, 2017); Mordechai Kreinin and Don Clark, *International Economics: A Policy Approach*, 2nd ed. (New York: Pearson Learning Solutions, 2013); Jeff Madura, *International Financial Management*, 13th ed. (Mason, OH: Cengage Learning, 2018); and Joseph P. Daniels and David D. Van Hoose, *International Monetary and Financial Economics* (Boston: Pearson, 2014).

17-3a Foreign Exchange Notation

The **euro** is the common currency used by countries in the European Monetary Union (EMU).[3] What does it mean if you see an exchange rate for dollars and euros posted at 1.2500? Does it mean 1 dollar buys 1.2500 euros or that 1 euro buys 1.2500 dollars? Or if you see an exchange rate quote for dollars and the Japan yen of 101.01, what does that mean?

To avoid confusion, the International Organization for Standardization (ISO) defined specific codes for currencies. For example, the U.S. dollar is USD, the Japanese yen is JPY, and the euro is EUR. Suppose you see an FX quote of USD/JPY = 101.01. Here is how to interpret that quote. First, it is *not* the number of dollars per yen, as you might be led to think by the slash mark between USD and JPY—in fact, it is the opposite! *It is the value of one dollar when expressed in yen*, or 101.01 yen per dollar.

If this quote were an equation, you could do some algebra and get:

$$USD/JPY = 101.01$$
$$USD = 101.01 \; JPY$$
$$\$1.00 = ¥101.21$$

where "¥" denotes yen. This means that 1 dollar is worth 101.01 yen.

Just remember that the "fraction" in the notation shows the relative values of the two currencies, and you will be able to keep exchange rates straight. For example, the FX quote of EUR/USD = 1.2500 means two things: (1) The value of a euro expressed in dollars is $1.2500, and (2) the euro is 25% more valuable than the dollar, so 1 euro can buy 1.2500 dollars.

17-3b Direct Quotes versus Indirect Quotes

Sometimes the financial press will talk about a **foreign currency** and the **home currency** (also called the domestic currency). That is pretty straightforward: If you are in the United States and taking a U.S. perspective, then the U.S. dollar is the home currency and all other currencies are foreign currencies. Alternatively, if you are in India and taking a local perspective, the home currency is the rupee.

An FX **direct quote** reports the number of units of the home currency per unit of foreign currency, which is the price of the foreign currency in terms of the home currency. For example, an FX direct quote might be FOREIGN/HOME = 1.2500. Suppose this quote is from a U.S. perspective and the foreign currency is the euro, which is the same situation as in the previous section. The quote EUR/USD = 1.2500 is an FX direct quote because it shows the number of dollars per euro. When not shown in tables, the U.S. financial press often reports a direct quote with a dollar sign. For example, the press would report, "The euro was at $1.2500."

An **indirect quote** reports the number of units of a foreign currency per unit of the home currency. For example, the FX indirect quote might be HOME/FOREIGN = 101.01. Suppose this is the quote from a U.S. perspective and the foreign currency is the yen, which is the same situation as in the previous section. Notice that the FX quote of USD/JPY = 101.01 is an indirect quote from a U.S. perspective. When not shown in tables, the U.S. financial press often reports an indirect quote with the foreign currency symbol. For example, the press would report, "The dollar was at ¥101.01."

---

[3]The European Union (EU) is comprised of over 25 European countries. One of its objectives is to create a unified market in which its member countries have fewer barriers to trade, travel, and intra-country employment. The European Monetary Union is a subset of those countries that use a common currency, the euro. Not all EU countries are also members of the EMU. For example, Sweden is an EU member but uses its own currency. The U.K. also retained its own currency. In fact, U.K. citizens voted (2016) in a non-binding referendum to leave the EU, which is commonly known as Brexit. In 2017, the U.K. government began the formal process of withdrawal from the EU. Unless matters change, the U.K. will leave the EU on March 29, 2019.

Notice that it is easy to convert a direct quote into an indirect quote and vice versa. For example, to convert the direct quote EUR/USD = 1.2500 into an indirect quote, calculate the inverse of the direct quote:

$$EUR/USD = 1.2500$$

$$\frac{1}{EUR/USD} = \frac{1}{1.2500}$$

$$USD/EUR = 0.8000$$

To convert an indirect quote into a direct quote, calculate the inverse of the indirect quote.

For consistency throughout this chapter, we will always take the U.S. perspective. A simple mnemonic device to help you remember is that a *Direct* quote is *Dollars* per unit of foreign currency.

17-3c Reporting Foreign Exchange Rates

Normal practice in currency trading centers is to use direct quotations for British pounds and euros. For all other currencies, the normal convention is to use indirect quotations. This convention eliminates confusion when comparing quotations from one trading center—say, New York—with those from another—say, London or Zurich.

Although traders work with the direct quotes for euros and British pounds, most sources of exchange rate quotes, such as *The Wall Street Journal*, Reuters, Google Finance, and Yahoo!Finance, report direct and indirect quotes for euros and British pounds. To do this, they report the direct quote from traders and then calculate the indirect quote as the inverse of the direct quote.

Other than the euro and British pound, traders work with indirect quotes for all other currencies. Data sources report the indirect quote from traders and convert it into a direct quote by taking the inverse of the indirect quote.

Table 17-1 reports recent exchange rates for several currencies. These are known as **spot rates**, which means the rate paid for delivery of the currency "on the spot."[4] The exchange rates shown in Column 3 are direct quotes and show the number of U.S. dollars required to purchase one unit of a foreign currency. The values in Column 4 are indirect quotes.

17-3d Transactions Involving U.S. Currency

resource

See *Ch17 Tool Kit.xlsx* on the textbook's Web site for all calculations.

We illustrate the role of exchange rates in foreign transactions, beginning here with transactions involving exchanges between the U.S. dollar and other currencies. Four distinct types of U.S. currency transactions are possible. An example of each type follows. We ignore commission and trading fees because they are relatively small for large transactions.

1. CONVERTING U.S. DOLLARS INTO A DIRECT QUOTE CURRENCY (EUROS OR BRITISH POUNDS)

www

Many Web sites provide currency converters—enter two currencies, and it returns the exchange rates. For example, see www.bloomberg.com /markets/currencies or www.google.com /finance/converter.

Suppose a U.S. company wishes to import pharmaceuticals from the U.K. costing £100 million. The U.S. company first must convert dollars into 100 million pounds using the *direct* quote of 1.3071 GBP/USD shown in Table 17-1:

(100 million pounds)(1.3071 dollars per pound) = $130.71 million

Therefore, the U.S. company must exchange $130.71 million for £100 million before completing the purchase.

---

[4]Spot rate transactions are not actually settled immediately but must be settled no more than 2 days after the day of the trade.

TABLE 17-1
Selected Exchange Rates

Country	ISO Currency Code (1)	Currency Name and Symbol (2)	Direct Quote: U.S. Dollars Required to Buy a Unit of Foreign Currency (FOREIGN/HOME) (3)	Indirect Quote: Number of Foreign Currency Units Required to Buy a U.S. Dollar (HOME/ FOREIGN) (4)
Direct Quote Currencies:				
Euro area	EUR	Euro (€)	1.1641	0.8590
U.K.	GPB	U.K. (British) pound (£)	1.3071	0.7651
Indirect Quote Currencies:				
Canada	CAD	Canadian dollar ($)	0.7594	1.3168
China	CNY	Chinese yuan (¥)	0.1488	6.7222
India	INR	Indian rupee (₹)	0.0146	68.4750
Japan	JPY	Japanese yen (¥)	0.0089	112.8400
Mexico	MXN	Mexican peso ($)	0.0529	18.8955
South Korea	KRW	South Korea won (₩)	0.0009	1,131.1600
Switzerland	CHF	Swiss franc (SFr)	1.0011	0.9989

Source: *The Wall Street Journal*, **http://online.wsj.com**; quotes for July 18, 2018.

Note: The financial press usually quotes British pounds and euros as direct quotations, so Column 4 equals 1.0 divided by Column 3 for these currencies. The financial press usually quotes all other currencies as indirect quotations, so Column 3 equals 1.0 divided by Column 4 for these currencies. We use blue to denote a quote that is an inverse of the actual reported quote.

2. CONVERTING A DIRECT QUOTE CURRENCY INTO DOLLARS

A French company wants to import medical equipment from a U.S. company charging $80 million. The French company must convert euros into dollars using the *direct* quote of 1.1641 EUR/USD. Recall that this actually means $1.1641 per euro. To find the required euros, use the following equation:[5]

$$\frac{80 \text{ million dollars}}{1.1641 \text{ euros/dollar}} = 68.72 \text{ million euros}$$

It will cost the French company about €68.72 million to purchase $80 million of U.S. equipment (€ is the euro currency symbol).

---

[5]For a quick refresher in algebra, recall that:

$$\frac{aX}{b\left(\frac{X}{Y}\right)} = \left(\frac{a}{b}\right)\left(\frac{X}{\left(\frac{X}{Y}\right)}\right) = \left(\frac{a}{b}\right)\left(\frac{XY}{X}\right) = \left(\frac{a}{b}\right)Y$$

So if a = 80 million, X = dollars, b = 1.11623, and Y = euros, then

$$\frac{aX}{b\left(\frac{X}{Y}\right)} = \left(\frac{a}{b}\right)Y = \left(\frac{80 \text{ million}}{1.1641}\right) \text{euros} = €68.7226$$

3. CONVERTING DOLLARS INTO AN INDIRECT QUOTE CURRENCY (ANY CURRENCY OTHER THAN EUROS OR BRITISH POUNDS)

A U.S. retailer wants to purchase LED televisions from a South Korean manufacturer. The cost is ₩9 billion ("₩" is the currency symbol for the won). If the won is quoted at 1,131.16 USD/KRW (which is 1,131.16 won per dollar), the U.S. company must spend about $7.96 million:

$$\frac{9,000,000,000 \text{ won}}{1,131.16 \text{ won/dollar}} = 7,956,434 \text{ dollars}$$

4. CONVERTING AN INDIRECT QUOTE CURRENCY INTO U.S. DOLLARS

A jewelry company in India seeks to import precious metals from a U.S. mining company for $37 million. The current exchange rate is 68.475 USD/INR (i.e., 68.475 rupees per dollar). The Indian company must convert rupees to dollars:

$$(37,000,000 \text{ dollars})(68.4750 \text{ rupees per dollar}) = 2,533,575,000.00 \text{ rupees}$$

Therefore, the Indian company must exchange about ₹2.53 billion for $37 million ("₹" is the symbol for the Indian rupee).

17-3e Currency Cross Rates for Transactions Not Involving U.S. Currency

The exchange rate between any two currencies other than dollars is called a **cross rate**. Cross rates are actually calculated on the basis of the two currencies relative to the U.S. dollar. We explain four distinct situations when calculating cross rates in the following sections.

1. CONVERTING A DIRECT QUOTE CURRENCY INTO A DIRECT QUOTE CURRENCY

For example, suppose you wish to convert British pounds into euros. Here is the method:

$$\frac{1.3071 \left(\dfrac{\text{dollars}}{\text{pound}}\right)}{1.1641 \left(\dfrac{\text{dollars}}{\text{euro}}\right)} = \left(\frac{1.3071}{1.1641}\right)\left(\frac{\text{euros}}{\text{pound}}\right) = 1.1228 \text{ euros per pound}$$

Therefore, the cross rate is 1.1228 euros per pound.

2. CONVERTING AN INDIRECT QUOTE CURRENCY INTO AN INDIRECT QUOTE CURRENCY

Suppose you wish to convert Mexican pesos into Japanese yen. Use this approach:

$$\frac{112.84 \left(\dfrac{\text{yen}}{\text{dollar}}\right)}{18.8955 \left(\dfrac{\text{pesos}}{\text{dollar}}\right)} = \left(\frac{112.84}{18.8955}\right)\left(\frac{\text{yen}}{\text{dollar}}\right)\left(\frac{\text{dollars}}{\text{pesos}}\right) = 5.9718 \text{ yen per peso}$$

Using this cross rate, you could exchange 1 peso for 5.9718 yen.

3. CONVERTING A DIRECT QUOTE CURRENCY INTO AN INDIRECT QUOTE CURRENCY

Suppose you wish to exchange euros for pesos. Here is the procedure:

$$18.8955\left(\frac{pesos}{dollar}\right)\left[1.1641\left(\frac{dollars}{euro}\right)\right] = (18.8955)(1.1641)\left(\frac{pesos}{dollar}\right)\left(\frac{dollar}{euro}\right)$$

$$= 21.9963 \text{ pesos per euro}$$

This shows that the cross rate is 21.9963 pesos per dollar.

4. CONVERTING AN INDIRECT QUOTE CURRENCY INTO A DIRECT QUOTE CURRENCY

Suppose you need to convert an indirect currency, such as the peso, into a direct quote currency, such as the euro. The easiest way is to use Situation 3's method to find pesos per euro and then take the inverse. Alternatively, you could take the inverse of the pesos per dollar rate and the inverse of the dollars per euro rate, and multiply them to get the pesos per euro.

Major business publications, such as *The Wall Street Journal*, and Web sites, such as **www.bloomberg.com**, regularly report cross rates among key currencies. Selected cross rates are shown in Table 17-2.

When examining the table, note the following points:

1. *Each column reports indirect exchange rates.* Column 1 has indirect quotes for dollars. For example, Row 5 in Column 1 shows that the exchange rate is 18.8955 Mexican pesos per dollar. Similarly, Column 2 has indirect quotes for the euro; Row 5 shows that the Mexican peso per euro exchange rate is 21.9963.
2. *Each row shows direct quotes.* Row 1 has direct quotes for dollars; Column 2 in Row 1 shows that the exchange rate is 1.1641 dollars per euro. Row 4 shows direct quotes for Japanese yen, and Column 2 reports that the exchange rate is 131.3570 Japanese yen per euro.
3. *The values in the lower diagonal are reciprocals of the corresponding values in the top diagonal.* For example, the value in Row 4, Column 5, is 5.9718 and the value in Row 5, Column 4 is 0.1675. Notice that 0.1675 is the inverse of 5.9718: 0.1675 = (1/5.9718).

TABLE 17-2
Selected Currency Cross Rates

	U.S. Dollar (1)	Euro (2)	U.K. Pound (3)	Japanese Yen (4)	Mexican Peso (5)
(1) U.S. dollar	—	1.1641	1.3071	0.0089	0.0529
(2) Euro	0.8590	—	1.1228	0.0076	0.0455
(3) U.K. pound	0.7651	0.8906	—	0.0068	0.0405
(4) Japanese yen	112.8400	131.3570	147.4932	—	5.9718
(5) Mexican peso	18.8955	21.9963	24.6983	0.1675	—

Source: Derived from Table 17-1; quotes for July 18, 2018.

CONSISTENCY AMONG CROSS RATES

Even though all cross rates are based on the dollar's direct and indirect quotes, currency dealers are constantly trading in exchange rates, seeking small inconsistencies from which they can profit risklessly. This process is known as *arbitrage*. Arbitrage can't last long because everyone would employ the same strategy, resulting in a supply–demand mismatch that would cause exchange rates to change such that arbitrage opportunities disappear. Therefore, the traders' activities ensure that currency markets are always very close to equilibrium and that cross rates are all internally consistent with the dollar's direct and indirect quotes.[6]

17-3f Individuals and Currency Conversion

We hope that you will travel internationally. If so, you will see only cross rates listed at locations providing currency conversion (such as in airports). Other than converting a little currency to use for taxis and tips, most individual travelers use credit cards that automatically take care of currency differences. For example, you may use your card to pay euros for a meal in France, but when you pay your credit card bill, you do so in dollars. In contrast to large business transactions, conversion fees can be up to 5% or more of the transaction amount.[7]

The previous section described how to use exchange rates. The following sections explain how exchange rates are determined under different exchange rate policies.

SELF-TEST

Describe the gold standard monetary system.

What is an exchange rate?

Explain the difference between direct and indirect quotations.

What is a cross rate?

Assume that the indirect quote is for 10.0 Mexican pesos per U.S. dollar. What is the direct quote for dollars per peso? **(0.10 dollars per peso)**

Assume that the indirect quote is for 115 Japanese yen per U.S. dollar and that the direct quote is for 1.25 U.S. dollars per euro. What is the yen per euro exchange rate? **(143.75 yen per euro)**

17-4 The Fixed Exchange Rate System

Recall that the gold standard required a nation to be willing to redeem its currency for gold. An effective worldwide gold standard requires considerable international cooperation regarding (1) the prices at which gold can be redeemed in local currencies and

---

[6]For more discussion of exchange rates, see Jongmoo Jay Choi and Anita Mehra Prasad, "Exchange Risk Sensitivity and Its Determinants: A Firm and Industry Analysis of U.S. Multinationals," *Financial Management,* Autumn 1995, pp. 77–88; Jerry A. Hammer, "Hedging Performance and Hedging Objectives: Tests of New Performance Measures in the Foreign Currency Market," *Journal of Financial Research,* Winter 1990, pp. 307–323; and William C. Hunter and Stephen G. Timme, "A Stochastic Dominance Approach to Evaluating Foreign Exchange Hedging Strategies," *Financial Management,* Autumn 1992, pp. 104–112.

[7]These fees and exchange rates vary considerably by credit card issuer. In July 2017, www.creditcards.com reported the dollar price of a €100 meal was $108.48 at the current exchange rate but ranged from $109.63 if charged on a Visa card to $114.98 if you converted dollars to euros at your local Bank of America branch. In addition to the cost of the currency itself, your credit card will charge a foreign exchange fee of up to 3%. If you withdraw foreign currency at an ATM to pay for the meal, you'll be hit with a fee of up to $5 per withdrawal plus a 3% foreign exchange fee. Some credit cards have lower fees, so it makes sense to comparison shop if you are traveling abroad!

(2) the free flow of gold and trade from one country to another. However, World War I and subsequent depressions caused many governments to cease cooperation, which essentially ended the gold standard.

To restore stability in the international financial system, 44 countries signed the Bretton Woods Agreement in 1944, which called for the creation of the **International Monetary Fund (IMF)**. The IMF's purpose was to promote international trade and prosperity by stabilizing exchange rates, by reducing restrictions on currency exchanges, and by providing short-term financial help to countries with financial crises.

To stabilize exchange rates, the price of gold would be fixed at $35 per ounce, and the Federal Reserve would redeem foreign central banks' dollars for gold at that price. Other currencies would be tied to the dollar. For example, the exchange rate for Swiss francs was set at about SFr 4.37 per dollar.[8] This **fixed exchange rate system** lasted from 1945 to 1971.

As the U.S. money supply expanded in the 1960s to support economic growth, the total dollars in the hands of foreign governments also increased. Also, the U.S. government was actively involved both in extensive foreign aid and in foreign wars, both of which resulted in more dollars being held abroad. These foreign-held dollars could, in principle, be converted to gold, and by 1971 foreign central banks had accumulated more dollars than the value of the U.S. gold reserve, making it impossible for the United States to redeem for gold the foreign central banks' dollars. The threat of a run on the Federal Reserve by foreign governments requesting gold in return for dollars, among other things, forced President Richard Nixon to declare in 1973 that the United States would no longer exchange gold for dollars at a fixed rate and would no longer abide by the Bretton Woods Agreement, ending the era of fixed exchange rates and ushering in the modern era of floating exchange rates.[9]

SELF-TEST

Describe the fixed exchange rate monetary system.

17-5 Floating Exchange Rates

In a monetary system with **floating exchange rates**, the exchange rate between two countries is determined by the relative supply and demand for their currencies rather than by government intervention. The IMF reports that about 30 countries have *free floating currencies* because their central banks rarely intervene. These include the United States and most developed nations, including the U.K., EMU members, Canada, Mexico, Japan, Russia (as of 2015), and Sweden. The IMF also reports another 40 countries that float with only modest central bank intervention to smooth out extreme exchange rate fluctuations. In total, almost all well developed countries have floating exchange rates.

17-5a Determinants of Floating Exchange Rates

Floating rate systems have little government intervention, so exchange rates are determined primarily by international trade and investment activities.

---

[8]Nothing is quite this simple. (1) Only IMF member countries had to abide by the agreement. There were originally 29 members, but by 1971 there were well over 100. (2) Non-dollar currencies were not fixed exactly but were allowed to fluctuate within a narrow range. (3) Several countries changed the rate between their currencies and the dollar during this period. For example, the exchange rate for British pounds changed significantly in 1949 and 1967.

[9]See **https://history.state.gov/milestones/1969-1976/nixon-shock** for a brief description of the events leading up to President Richard Nixon's ending of the convertibility of dollars into gold at a fixed price of $35 per ounce.

TABLE 17-3

U.S. Exports, Imports, and Trade Balances in 2017 (Billions of Dollars)

	Exports (1)	Imports (2)	Trade Balance (3)	Total Bilateral Trade Activity (4)
China	$188	$524	−$336	$712
Canada	$341	$339	$2	$680
Mexico	$277	$345	−$68	$622
Japan	$115	$171	−$56	$286
Germany	$87	$153	−$66	$240
United Kingdom	$126	$111	$15	$237
South Korea	$73	$83	−$10	$156
Seven-country total	$1,207	$1,726	−$519	$2,933
World total	2,351	2,903	−552	5,254
Seven-country total World total	51.3%	59.5%	94.0%	55.8%

Source: Bureau of Economic Analysis. For updates, go to **www.bea.gov/international/index.htm**, select the link named "Trade in Goods and Services Annual Revision," and then download the data in the link named "U.S. Trade in Goods and Services by Selected Countries and Areas, 1999–present."

Note: The Trade Balance in Column 3 is equal to Column 1 (Exports) minus Column 2 (Imports). Column 4 (Total Bilateral Trade Activity) is equal to Column 1 (Exports) plus Column 2 (Imports). The countries are sorted by Total Bilateral Trade Activity.

THE IMPACT OF INTERNATIONAL TRADE ON EXCHANGE RATES

In a floating rate system, bilateral trade is an important determinant of the relative demand between two currencies. Table 17-3 shows the bilateral trade between the United States and each of its seven largest trading partners, ranked by the total value of bilateral trades (Column 4). The table includes exports, imports, and the **foreign trade balance**, which is equal to imports minus exports.[10] (The foreign trade balance is also called the **trade balance** and the **balance of trade**.) If the trade balance is positive, it is called a trade surplus; if negative, it is a trade deficit.

Table 17-3 also shows the exports and imports between the United States and each of its major trading partners. Although the United States exports over $1.2 trillion to these countries, it imports even more (over $1.7 trillion). The United States is running a total trade deficit of over $500 billion with these countries, which represents about 94% of its total worldwide trade deficit. In fact, the U.S. trade deficit with China alone comprises over 60% of the U.S. total trade deficit! In addition to China, the United States runs large trade deficits with Mexico, Japan, and Germany. Notice that the United States exports more to Canada than to any other country.

---

[10]The Bureau of Economic Analysis (BEA) reports the exports and imports of goods (also called "merchandise"). It also reports the exports and imports of services. For example, payments made by foreign tourists in the United States are like U.S. exports because the tourists must use foreign currency to purchase dollars. Payments made by foreign businesses and individuals for professional fees charged by U.S. lawyers and engineers are like exports because the foreigners must convert their currency to dollars. Similarly, payments by foreigners for royalties on U.S. intellectual properties are like exports. Since mid-1993, the BEA has reported the trade balance as the combined trade balances of goods and services.

What impact does the bilateral trade balance have on the exchange rate between two countries? Let's take the United States and the EMU region (i.e., the euro region) as an example. U.S. importers must convert dollars to euros in order to purchase exports from EMU members, and EMU importers must convert euros to dollars in order to purchase U.S. exports to EMU countries. The United States consistently runs a trade deficit with the EMU countries, which increases the demand to purchase euros with dollars relative to the demand to purchase dollars with euros. The excess demand for euros will make the euro more valuable relative to the dollar.

THE IMPACT OF INTERNATIONAL INVESTMENT ACTIVITIES ON EXCHANGE RATES

In addition to trade balances, international investment transactions also affect currency demand. Direct investment occurs when a business or individual starts or purchases a foreign company or establishes a foreign division.[11] For example, Volkswagen Group of America built an auto assembly plant in Tennessee but is owned by a German company. Another example is GE Energy Netherlands, B.V., owned by General Electric.

In contrast to direct investment, purchases and sales of foreign securities are called "portfolio investments." For example, international investors may purchase U.S. government bonds because they are not going to default. To see the effect of international investments on currency demand, suppose Japanese banks, corporations, or individuals want to buy U.S. stocks or bonds. They first must buy dollars with yen and then use those dollars to purchase U.S. securities. This would create greater demand for dollars than for yen, driving up the value of the dollar relative to the yen.

For years, foreign investors have been buying more U.S. investments than U.S. investors have been purchasing foreign investments. In fact, the value of U.S. investments abroad has been lower than the value of foreign investments in the United States since 1985.

Even with the strong demand for U.S. investments from foreign investors, the weak demand for U.S. products (i.e., the trade balance) has reduced the value of the U.S. dollar. Take a look at Figure 17-2, which shows the value of the U.S. dollar relative to eight major currencies since the dollar began to float. There have been some peaks when demand for the dollar was high (such as in the mid-1980s and early 2000s), but the overall trend has been down. This has hurt U.S. exports but has helped consumers with lower prices for imports. The dollar has been increasing since 2011; time will tell whether this is a trend or an aberration.

17-5b Currency Appreciation, Depreciation, and Exchange Rate Risk

Floating rate systems allow exchange rates to go up or down, which exposes businesses and investors to exchange rate risk. We begin by explaining currency appreciation and depreciation.

CURRENCY APPRECIATION

Currency appreciation occurs when one currency gains value relative to another currency—in other words, the appreciating currency can buy more of the other currency than it could before appreciating. For example, suppose the current direct exchange rate for euros is EUR/USD = 1.25, which means that 1 euro can buy (or costs) 1.25 dollars.

---

[11]The purchaser doesn't have to own 100% of the foreign business but must own enough to give the owner substantial influence in decisions. The ownership could be in the form of equity or debt.

FIGURE 17-2
U.S. Dollar Index versus Eight Major Currencies

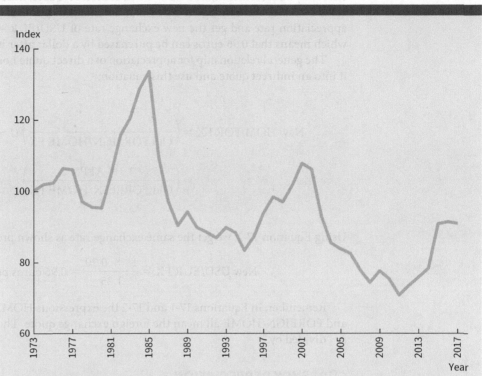

Source: Data obtained from the St. Louis Federal Reserve. The Federal Reserve defines the index as "Averages of daily figures. A weighted average of the foreign exchange value of the U.S. dollar against a subset of the broad index currencies that circulate widely outside the country of issue. The major currency index includes the Euro Area, Canada, Japan, United Kingdom, Switzerland, Australia, and Sweden." See **http://research.stlouisfed .org/fred2/series/TWEXMANL?cid=105**.

Suppose the euro appreciates 20% against the dollar. In this case, the euro would be able to purchase 20% more dollars, so the new exchange rate would be EUR/USD = 1.25(1 + 0.20) = 1.50, which means the euro can purchase 1.50 dollars.

Let APP% denote the appreciation rate, FOR the foreign currency, and HOM the home currency. The general relationship for appreciation of a direct quote foreign currency is:

$$\text{New FOR/HOM FX} = (\text{Old FOR/HOM FX})(1 + \text{APP\%}) \tag{17-1}$$

Using Equation 17-1, the new exchange rate for euros per dollar is:

New EUR/USD FX = 1.25(1 + 0.20) = 1.5 euros per dollar

It is easy to get mixed up when calculating rates of appreciation, so here are some suggestions. Notice that two currencies are involved (euros and dollars) and that the euro is the one appreciating. This means we need to express the exchange rate as the number of dollars per euro to find the number of dollars per euro after the appreciation.

Now consider a situation in which the dollar appreciates 20% versus the euro. This means the dollar now can purchase 20% more euros, so we need to express the exchange rate as the number of euros that can be purchased by a dollar. We can't use the direct quote of \$1.25 (which is EUR/USD = 1.25) because it is the number of dollars that can be purchased by a euro. Instead, we need to find the indirect quote, which is 1/(1.25): USD/EUR = 1/1.25 = 0.80, the number of euros that a dollar can purchase. Now we apply the 20% appreciation rate and get the new exchange rate of USD/EUR = 0.80(1 + 0.20) = 0.96, which means that 0.96 euros can be purchased by a dollar after its appreciation.

The general relationship for appreciation of a direct quote home currency is to convert it into an indirect quote and use this equation:

$$\text{New HOM/FOR FX} = \left(\frac{1}{\text{Old FOREIGN/HOME FX}} \right)(1 + \text{APP\%})$$

$$= \left(\frac{1 + \text{APP\%}}{\text{Old FOREIGN/HOME FX}} \right)$$

(17-2)

Using Equation 17-2, we get the same exchange rate as shown previously:

$$\text{New USD/EUR FX} = \frac{1 + 0.20}{1.25} = 0.96 \text{ euros per dollar}$$

Remember, in Equations 17-1 and 17-2 the expressions HOME/FOREIGN, USD/EUR, and FOREIGN/HOME all mean the foreign exchange quote. The "/" does not mean "per" or "divided by."

CURRENCY DEPRECIATION

Currency depreciation occurs when one currency loses value relative to another currency—the depreciating currency now buys less of the other currency than it could before depreciating. For example, suppose the dollar depreciates 10% with respect to the Mexican peso. We want to start with the number of pesos that 1 dollar could purchase before depreciating, so this is the indirect quote. Suppose the exchange rate is USD/MXN = 20, which is the number of pesos that can be purchased by 1 dollar. The exchange rate after the dollar depreciates is USD/MXN = 20(1 − 0.10) = 18. Therefore, the dollar is able to purchase only 18 pesos, a 10% decrease from the 20 pesos a dollar originally was able to purchase.

Letting DEP% denote the depreciation rate, the general equation is:

$$\text{New HOM/FOR FX} = (\text{Old HOM/FOR FX})(1 - \text{DEP\%})$$

(17-3)

$$\text{New USD/MXN FX} = 20(1 - 0.10) = 18 \text{ pesos per dollar}$$

Perhaps contrary to intuition, the percentage that one currency appreciates with respect to a second currency usually is not the same as the percentage that the second currency depreciates with respect to the first currency. To see this, suppose the euro appreciated by 20% against the dollar, with the exchange rate changing from EUR/USD = 1.25 to 1.50. Let's calculate by how much the dollar depreciated against the euro. Start by finding the indirect rates: 1/1.25 = 0.80 and 1/1.5 = 0.6667. This means that the dollar could purchase 0.80 euros before the dollar depreciated, and 0.6667 euros after it depreciated, for a change of 16.67%: (0.80 − 0.6667)/0.80 = 0.1667 = 16.67%. This shows that the euro appreciated by 20% and the dollar depreciated by 16.67%. As this example shows, you need to be very careful when analyzing currency appreciation or depreciation.

EXCHANGE RATE RISK

Exchange rate fluctuations can have a profound effect on profits and trade. This is called **exchange rate risk**. For example, in 2014 the euro exchange rate was about $1.33 (i.e., 1.33 dollars per euro), but it subsequently changed to about $1.16 by 2018. Consider the impact this has on profits and trade. For example, a handblown glass from the Italian island of Murano cost about €100 in 2014. Ignoring shipping costs and taxes, a consumer in the United States could have purchased this glass for €100($1.33/€) = $133. Assuming the price in 2018 still was €100, it would cost €100($1.16/€) = $116 to purchase the glass. Thus, the change in exchange rates made Murano glass less expensive to U.S. customers and would help Italian exports to the United States.

On the other hand, suppose it cost a California vineyard $50 in 2014 to produce a fine bottle of Pinot Noir that could be sold for €45 in Europe. In 2014, the profit would have been €45($1.33/€) − $50 = $59.85 − $50 = $9.85. Assuming no change in production costs, the bottle's profit in 2018 is €45($1.16/€) − $50 = $52.20 − $50 = $2.20. Thus, U.S. exporters to Europe have been hurt by the change in exchange rates.

As these examples illustrate, the volatility of exchange rates under a floating system increases the uncertainty of the cash flows for a multinational corporation. We illustrate ways to mitigate this risk later in the chapter.

Non-floating systems can also be risky. But before describing other monetary systems, we explain how governments can and do intervene in currency markets.

SELF-TEST

Define a floating exchange rate system.

How does a trade deficit affect floating exchange rates?

How do international investment activities affect exchange rates?

What is currency appreciation? What is currency depreciation?

What is exchange rate risk?

17-6 Government Intervention in Foreign Exchange Markets

WWW

The International Monetary Fund reports a full listing of exchange rate arrangements. See **www.imf.org/external /data.htm**. *The IMF also publishes a more detailed listing in its* Annual Report on Exchange Arrangements and Exchange Restrictions.

A country's central bank can artificially prop up its currency by using its reserves of gold or foreign currencies to purchase its own currency in the open market. This creates artificial demand for its own currency, thus causing its value to be artificially strong. A central bank can also make its currency artificially weak by selling its own currency in the open markets. This increases the currency's supply, which reduces its price.

What are the outcomes if a country intervenes and keeps its currency artificially weak or strong? The following sections answer this question.

17-6a Currency Intervention: Artificially Weak Currencies

A weak currency makes it less expensive for other nations to purchase the country's goods, which creates jobs in the exporting country. However, an artificially weak currency value can cause inflation due to the following three reasons.

First, a weak currency value means that it costs more in the local currency to purchase imports, causing inflation in prices of imported goods. Second, higher prices for imported goods allow competing domestic manufacturers to raise their prices as well, further boosting inflation. Third, to keep its currency weak, the central bank must keep the currency's supply high by selling more and more of its currency in foreign exchange markets. All else held constant, such increases in the money supply create additional inflationary pressures.

As just explained, an artificially weak currency stimulates exports but usually creates economic problems due to inflation. In addition, a country's artificially weak currency hurts other countries' exports and manufacturing sectors. In retaliation, they may impose tariffs or other trade restrictions, leading to trade wars. History shows that no one wins a trade war: When prices go up for all consumers, demand for products goes down and leads to reductions in manufacturing and employment.

17-6b Currency Intervention: Artificially Strong Currencies

A currency that is artificially strong has the opposite effects of one that is artificially weak. Inflation will be held down, and citizens can purchase imported goods at low domestic prices, but exporting industries are hurt, as are domestic industries that compete with the cheap imports. Because there is relatively little true external demand for the currency, the government will have to create demand by purchasing its own currency with its central bank's gold reserves or its foreign currencies reserves. Over time, this will deplete the gold and foreign currency reserves unless the central bank increases its foreign currency reserves by issuing debt that is denominated in a foreign currency. This is not sustainable in the long run.

17-6c Currency Intervention and Manipulation

There is a difference between intervention and manipulation. Many countries occasionally intervene but don't qualify as manipulators as defined by the U.S. Treasury Department in its annual study of major U.S. trade partners. To be named a **currency manipulator**, the other country must meet each of the three criteria: (1) have a large trade surplus with the United States, (2) have a large current account balance (i.e., a country's worldwide trade surplus plus its worldwide surplus of income generated abroad by its companies and citizens versus net of income generated by foreign entities in its own country), and (3) have large repeated currency interventions that consistently act in one direction (e.g., to reduce its currency's value).

Since beginning this evaluation method in 1988, the Treasury has named only three countries as manipulators: Japan (for 1988), Taiwan (for 1988 and 1992), and China (for 1992–1994). However, the Treasury maintains a Monitoring List for countries that meet two of the three criteria. For 2016, this list named China, Japan, Korea, India, Germany, and Switzerland. Interestingly, Switzerland has been intervening, albeit somewhat unsuccessfully, trying to push its overvalued currency down by purchasing huge amounts of foreign currencies. As of year-end 2017, it had accumulated foreign currency reserves amounting to 112% of its GDP![12]

SELF-TEST

What is the effect on a country's economy of an artificially low exchange rate? Of an artificially high exchange rate?

What is currency manipulation?

---

[12]See the 2018 U.S. Treasury report to Congress for an interesting analysis of each of the countries that is on the monitoring list. You can find it at **https://home.treasury.gov/sites/default/files/2018-04/2018-04-13-Spring-2018-FX-Report-FINAL.pdf**.

17-7 Other Exchange Rate Systems: No Local Currency, Pegged Rates, and Managed Floating Rates

Section 17-5 described floating rate systems. The following sections describe other exchange rate systems, beginning with countries that don't have their own local currency.

17-7a No Local Currency

A few countries don't have their own separate legal tender but instead use the currency of another nation. For example, Ecuador and Panama use the U.S. dollar, and Montenegro and Kosovo use the euro.

Some countries belong to a monetary union that uses a common currency. The Eastern Caribbean Currency Union (ECCU) uses the Eastern Caribbean dollar. Both the West African Economic and Monetary Union (WAEMU) and the Central African Economic and Monetary Community (CAEMC) use the CFA Franc. The European Monetary Union members use the euro, which is allowed to float. This is not true for these other unions, as we describe next.

17-7b Pegged Exchange Rates

In a **pegged exchange rate** system, a country locks, or "pegs," its currency's exchange rate to another currency or basket of currencies. It is common for a country with a pegged exchange rate to allow its currency to vary within specified limits or bands (often set at ±1% of the target rate) before the country intervenes to force the currency back within the limits.

The IMF estimates that almost 70 countries report using some form of a pegged currency. Eight countries peg their currencies directly to the U.S. dollar (such as the Belizian dollar and the Saudi Arabian riyal). Several countries, including Denmark, are linked to the euro.

In addition to individual nations, several different monetary unions peg their unions' currencies. For example, the ECCU's Eastern Caribbean dollar is pegged to the U.S. dollar. The CFA franc (used by both the WAEMU and CAEMC) is pegged to the euro.[13]

CURRENCY DEVALUATION AND REVALUATION

Suppose a country decides to intervene and change the rate it uses when pegging to a currency. For example, consider Honduras. The Honduran lempira was pegged to the U.S. dollar at about 18.9 lempira per dollar in late 2005. It remained at that level until mid-2012, after which the rate has gradually changed until it was about L24.0 per dollar in 2018 ("L" is the symbol for lempira). This type of change is called currency **devaluation**.

Here are some tips to avoid confusion. First, currency *devaluation* doesn't apply to floating rate systems, where a change in exchange rates is called currency *depreciation*. Devaluation is due to government intervention, whereas depreciation is due to market forces. Second, devaluation doesn't apply to the only two direct-quote currencies, the euro and the British pound, because those currencies float. Third, an indirect quote expresses currencies as the number of foreign currency units per dollar (such as lempira per dollar).

---

[13]A few countries, such as Bosnia and Herzegovina, have currency board arrangements. Under this system, a country technically has its own currency but commits to exchange it for a specified foreign money unit at a fixed exchange rate. This requires it to impose domestic currency restrictions unless it has the foreign currency reserves to cover requested exchanges.

An increase to the reported indirect rate means the currency has weakened. For example, the increase in the lempira from L18.9 to L24.0 means that a dollar purchases more lempira and that a lempira purchases fewer dollars. Therefore, an *increase* in the reported indirect rate means that a currency has *weakened*.

Some countries have devalued their currencies in a single large step, such as Argentina in 2002. A large devaluation helps exporters but immediately increases the prices of imported consumer goods and imported factors of production such as oil. A large devaluation also hurts companies and individuals that have borrowed foreign-denominated debt, such as a company in Argentina that borrowed dollars. Foreign-denominated debt payments increase dramatically in terms of the local currency, which must be converted before making payments in the foreign currency. The initial pain caused by devaluation helps explain why many countries with pegged exchange rates tend to postpone needed measures until economic pressures build to explosive levels.

In contrast to Argentina, Honduras increased the exchange rate for the lempira from about L18.9 to L24.0 from 2012 to 2018, but it did so in small steps. This provides time for its economy to adjust to new economic realities.

CURRENCY REVALUATION

Currency **revaluation** means that the pegged exchange rate has changed to make the currency stronger so that it can purchase more units of a foreign currency. This tends to hurt exporters since their products become more expensive for foreigners, to help local consumers since they can purchase imports more cheaply, and to hurt local producers since they face increased competition from cheaper imports.

17-7c Managed Floating Rates

In a **managed floating rate** system, there is significant government intervention to manage the currency's supply and demand. The IMF breaks managed floating rate systems into two categories. The first is a stabilized arrangement in which the currency (1) doesn't float, (2) isn't officially pegged to another currency, yet (3) remains fairly stable for many months. In other words, the currency behaves like a pegged currency, but the country hasn't reported it as such. This category includes Singapore, Costa Rica, Burundi, and about 15 other countries.

The second IMF category of managed floating rates is "Other Managed Arrangement," which is a catch-all for currencies that don't fit into any of the IFM's other groups. Most of the 20 countries in this category are relatively small, such as Algeria, Egypt, and Myanmar. The exception is China.

From 1994 until mid-2005, the Chinese government actively intervened in the currency markets to keep the yuan at about 8.28 yuan per dollar. In July 2005, it announced that it would peg its currency to a basket of other currencies. Although China did not reveal the exact mix of currencies in this basket, the behavior of the yuan indicated that the U.S. dollar was a big component in the basket. However, China still actively intervened in currency markets, so it was a loose peg.

During the worldwide recession that began in 2008, China once again actively intervened, keeping its exchange rate at about 6.83 yuan per dollar. In mid-2010, China modified its policies and took steps to better integrate its foreign exchange markets with international markets. The yuan again behaved more as if it were pegged to a currency basket.

In August 2015, China modified its pegging method to become more market oriented. This change was driven by IMF rules regarding eligibility for inclusion in the IMF Special Drawing Rights (SDR) basket. But what is an SDR? Each country that is a member of the IMF must deposit some of its own currency with the IMF as a reserve. An SDR is a supplemental reserve that includes countries with (1) very large international trade and (2) a "freely traded" currency, as determined by the IMF.[14] The IMF uses its resources to help countries experiencing a monetary crisis. Only five currencies are in the SDR basket: the U.S. dollar, the euro, the Japanese yen, the British pound, and the Chinese yuan. Inclusion is a sign of status and official recognition indicating that a country plays a major role in the international monetary markets and international trade.

17-7d Convertibility of Currency

How easy is it for one country to exchange its currency with that of another country for the purposes of exporting/importing and investing? The answer depends upon the convertibility of the currency, as explained next.

FREELY CONVERTIBLE CURRENCY

A **freely convertible currency** is traded in the international currency markets with no government restrictions. Such a currency is also called a **fully convertible currency** and a **hard currency**. Although there is no officially sanctioned list of fully convertible currencies, most sources report that countries with free floating exchange systems also have fully convertible currencies. In addition, several other floating rate currencies are fully convertible, such as the New Zealand dollar and the Israeli new shekel.[15]

PARTIALLY CONVERTIBLE CURRENCY

A **partially convertible currency** is one that trades in international FOREX markets but that has significant government-imposed restrictions. Most currencies fall into this category.

For example, India has a floating rupee that is actively traded in international FOREX markets. Within India, however, FOREX trading is restricted to trades between the rupee and four other currencies: the U.S. dollar, the euro, the British pound, and the Japanese yen. In addition, the Indian government has specific regulations regarding large international investments. For example, the government has restrictions on the amounts of rupees that may be converted to foreign currencies for purposes of investing abroad. It also restricts the reverse: Foreigners are limited in how many rupees they can use to make investments in India.

NONCONVERTIBLE CURRENCY

A **nonconvertible currency** is one that is not traded in international FOREX markets due to government restrictions. It is also called a **soft currency** or a **blocked currency**. Cuba and North Korea have nonconvertible currencies.

SELF-TEST

What are pegged exchange rates?

What does it mean to say that the dollar is depreciating with respect to the euro?

What is a convertible currency?

Define "partially convertible currency."

Which nations have a nonconvertible currency?

---

[14]A freely traded currency is not the same as a floating currency. A currency can be freely traded even if its government intervenes more actively in the international FOREX market than a government with a floating currency.

[15]The new shekel was implemented in 1986, over 30 years ago—not so new in the United States but a blink of the eye when compared with the history of the Middle East.

17-8 Forward Exchange Rates and Risk Management

WWW

Currency futures prices are available from the Chicago Mercantile Exchange (CME) on its Web site at www.cme.com. Currency spot and forward rates are available from investing.com at https:// www.investing.com /rates-bonds/forward -rates.

Suppose that an importer enters into a contract with a foreign supplier. The contract specifies the quantity and price of the goods with delivery and payment to be made in 30 days. It also specifies that the payment must be in the foreign supplier's currency. The importer knows the current spot rate and the dollar value of the payment if it is made immediately. But what if spot rates change during the 30-day period before payment is due? This will change the amount of foreign currency needed by the importer to pay for the goods, making the deal much riskier.

17-8a Forward Exchange Rates

A **forward exchange rate** is a guaranteed rate at which two currencies can be exchanged for one another at specified future date (usually 30, 90, or 180 days from the current date). This allows an importer or exporter to reduce or eliminate the impact of possible changes in exchange rates that might occur between the time that an order for goods is placed and the time that the goods are delivered and payment is made. Table 17-4 reports forward exchange rates along with the current spot rates for some commonly traded currencies.

If a dollar buys *more* of the foreign currency in the spot market than in the forward market, then the foreign currency is appreciating. Therefore, the forward foreign currency is selling at a **premium**. This is the case for the Japanese yen shown in Table 17-4: A dollar can buy 112.84 yen in the spot market but only 111.27 yen in the 180-day forward market.

If a dollar buys *less* of the foreign currency in the spot market than in the forward market, then the foreign currency is depreciating and the forward foreign currency is selling at a **discount**.

TABLE 17-4
Selected Spot and Forward Exchange Rates, Indirect Quotation: Number of Units of Foreign Currency per U.S. Dollar

| | Spot Rate | Forward Rates[a] | | | Foreign Currency Is: | Forward Currency is Selling at a:[b] |
		30 Days	90 Days	180 Days		
Mexico (Peso)	18.8955	18.8955	18.8955	18.8956	Depreciating	Discount
Japan (Yen)	112.84	112.61	112.12	111.27	Appreciating	Premium
Switzerland (Franc)	0.9989	0.9964	0.9910	0.9822	Appreciating	Premium

Source: Spot rates are from *The Wall Street Journal* for July 18, 2018, as reported in Table 17-1. Forward rates are determined from quotes from Investing.com on July 18, 2018, at **www.investing.com.**

Notes:

[a]Forward rates for pesos and francs are rounded to 4 decimal places, and forward rates for yen are rounded to 2 decimal places to be consistent with reported spot rates.

Traders quote forward rates in pips (percentage in points). A pip is the smallest digit in which a currency is quoted. For example, the Swiss franc is quoted out to 4 decimal places, so 1 pip is equal to 0.0001, which is 1/10,000. The pip divisor is 10,000 for the Swiss franc. For the yen, the pip divisor is 100 (i.e., 1 pip is equal to 0.01) because the yen is quoted only to 2 decimal places. The quote is the number of pips represented by the forward rate minus the spot. For example, the quote for the 30-day forward rate for the Swiss franc was −25.42 pips. This means the forward rate calculation is equal to the spot rate plus pips/divisor: 0.9989 + (−22.52/10,000) = 0.9964, rounded to four decimal places. For the yen, the quote was −22.54 pips. The forward rate calculation is 112.84 + (−22.54/100) = 112.61, rounded to 2 decimal places.

[b]When it takes more units of a foreign currency to buy a dollar in the future, then the value of the foreign currency is less in the forward market than in the spot market; hence, the forward rate is at a *discount* to the spot rate. When it takes fewer units of a foreign currency to buy a dollar in the future, the forward rate is at a *premium*. If using indirect quotes, a higher forward rate is at a discount, and a lower forward rate is at a premium.

17-8b Managing Exchange Rate Risk

For example, suppose that a U.S. firm must pay 500 million yen to a Japanese firm in 30 days and that the current spot rate is 112.84 yen per dollar. If spot rates remain constant, then the U.S. firm will pay the Japanese firm the equivalent of $4.431 million (500 million yen divided by 112.84 yen per dollar) in 30 days. But if the spot rate falls to, say, 102 yen per dollar, then the U.S. firm will have to pay the equivalent of $4.902 million: $4.902 = (500 yen)/(102 ¥ per $). If the spot rate increases to 115, the firm will pay only $4.348 million: $4.348 = (500 yen)/(115 ¥ per $).

The treasurer of the U.S. firm can avoid exposure to this variability by entering into a 30-day forward exchange contract. Suppose this contract promises delivery of yen to the U.S. firm in 30 days at a guaranteed price of 112.61 yen per dollar. No cash changes hands at the time the treasurer signs the forward contract, although the U.S. firm might have to put some collateral down as a guarantee against default. Yet because the firm can use an interest-bearing instrument for the collateral, this requirement is not costly. The counterparty to the forward contract must deliver the yen to the U.S. firm in 30 days, and the U.S. firm is obligated to purchase the 500 million yen at the previously agreed-upon rate of 112.61 yen per dollar. Therefore, the treasurer of the U.S. firm is able to lock in a payment equivalent to $4.440 million = (500 million yen)/(112.61 ¥ per $), no matter what happens to spot rates. This technique is called *hedging*. Notice that the U.S. firm will pay more if it hedges than it would if exchange rates didn't change. However, this extra payment to reduce risk might be well worth it.

SELF-TEST

Differentiate between spot and forward exchange rates.

Explain what it means for a forward currency to sell at a discount and at a premium.

17-9 Interest Rate Parity

Market forces determine whether a currency sells at a forward premium or a discount, and the general relationship between spot and forward exchange rates is specified by a concept called "interest rate parity."

Interest rate parity means that investors should expect to earn the same return on security investments in all countries after adjusting for risk. It recognizes that when you invest in a country other than your home country, you are affected by two factors—returns on the investment itself and changes in the exchange rate. It follows that your overall return will be higher than the investment's stated return if the currency in which your investment is denominated appreciates relative to your home currency. Likewise, your overall return will be lower if the foreign currency that you receive declines in value.

To illustrate interest rate parity, consider the case of a U.S. investor who can buy default-free 180-day Swiss bonds that promise a 4% nominal annual return. The 180-day foreign (Swiss) interest rate, r_f is 4% ÷ 2 = 2% because 180 days is one-half of a 360-day year. Assume also that the indirect quotation for the spot exchange rate is 1.0000 Swiss francs per dollar. Finally, assume that the 180-day forward exchange rate is 0.9951 Swiss francs per dollar, which means that in 180 days the investor can exchange 1 dollar for 0.9951 Swiss francs.

The U.S. investor could receive a 4% annualized return denominated in Swiss francs, but if she ultimately wants to consume goods in the United States, then those Swiss francs must be converted to dollars. The dollar return on the investment depends, therefore, on what happens to exchange rates over the next 6 months. However, the investor can lock in the dollar return by selling the foreign currency in the forward market. For example, the investor could simultaneously do the following:

1. Convert $1,000 to 1,000 Swiss francs in the spot market: $1,000(1.0000 Swiss francs per dollar) = 1,000 Swiss francs.
2. Invest the Swiss francs in a 180-day Swiss bond that has a 4% annual return, or a 2% semiannual return. This investment will pay 1,000(1.02) = 1,020 Swiss francs in 180 days.
3. Agree today to exchange the Swiss francs in 180 days at the forward rate of 0.9951 Swiss francs per dollar, for a total of (1,020 Swiss francs) ÷ (0.9951 Swiss francs per dollar) = $1,025.03.

Hence, this investment has an expected 180-day return in dollars of $1,025.03/$1,000 = 2.50%, which translates into a nominal annual return of 2(2.50%) = 5%. In this case, the expected 5% return consists of 4% from the Swiss bond itself plus 1% because the market believes that the Swiss franc will strengthen relative to the dollar. Observe that, by locking in the forward rate today, the investor has eliminated all exchange rate risk. And because the Swiss bond is assumed to be default-free, the investor is certain to earn a 5% annual dollar return.

Interest rate parity implies that an investment in the United States with the same risk as the Swiss bond should also have a return of 5%. When we express interest rates as periodic rates, we can express interest rate parity by the following equation (later in the chapter we will use a slightly different version of interest rate parity when we consider multi-year cash flows):

$$\frac{\text{Forward exchange rate}}{\text{Spot exchange rate}} = \frac{1 + r_h}{1 + r_f} \qquad (17\text{-}4)$$

Here, r_h is the periodic interest rate in the home country, r_f is the periodic interest rate in the foreign country, and the forward and spot exchange rates are expressed as direct quotations (that is, units of home currency per unit of foreign currency).

The direct spot quotation is 1.0000 dollar per Swiss franc: (1/1.000 Swiss francs per dollar) = 1.0000. The direct 180-day forward quotation is 1.0049 dollars per Swiss franc: (1/0.9951) = 1.0049. Using Equation 17-4, we can solve for the equivalent home rate, r_h:

$$\frac{\text{Forward exchange rate}}{\text{Spot exchange rate}} = \frac{1 + r_h}{1 + r_f}$$

$$\frac{1.0049}{1.0000} = \frac{1 + r_h}{1 + 0.02}$$

$$1 + r_h = \left(\frac{1.0049}{1.0000}\right)(1 + 0.02) = 1.0250$$

The periodic home interest rate is 2.50%, and the annualized home interest rate is (2.50%)(2) = 5.00%, the same value we found previously.

After accounting for exchange rates, interest rate parity states that bonds in the home country and the foreign country must have the same actual rate of return in the investor's currency. In this example, the U.S. bond must yield 5.00% to provide the same return as the 4% Swiss bond. If one country's bond provides a higher return, then investors will sell their low-return bond and flock to the high-return bond. This activity will cause the price of the low-return bond to fall (which pushes up its yield) and the price of the high-return bond to increase (driving down its yield). These effects will continue until the two bonds again have the same returns after accounting for exchange rates.

In other words, interest rate parity implies that a U.S. investment with the same risk as a Swiss bond should have a dollar value return of 5.00%. Solving for r_h in Equation 17-4, we indeed find that the predicted U.S. interest rate is 5.00%, the actual U.S. bond return stated previously.

Interest rate parity shows why a particular currency might be at a forward premium or discount. Note that a currency is at a forward premium whenever domestic interest rates are higher than foreign interest rates. Discounts prevail if domestic interest rates are lower than foreign interest rates. If these conditions do not hold, then arbitrage will soon force interest rates and exchange rates back to parity.

17-10 Purchasing Power Parity

Suppose it is possible buy a product in one country, ship it to another country, sell it there for a higher price, and enjoy a riskless profit (assuming no FOREX transaction fees, transportation costs, transit time, or import/export restrictions). Arbitrage can't last long, so the exchange rate, the goods' prices, or all three must change. The **purchasing power parity (PPP)** equation states that exchange rates and prices of goods adjust so that identical goods cost the same amount in different countries. This relationship is also called the *law of one price.*

To use the purchasing power parity equation, we define P_h as the price of a good in the home country and P_f as the price of an identical good in the foreign country. We are using only the spot exchange rate (i.e., the exchange rate for immediate conversion) and not forward rates because we assume the shipping time is very short. Note that the spot rate is expressed as a direct rate; it is the number of units of home currency that can be exchanged for one unit of foreign currency. The purchasing power parity equation is:

$$P_h = (P_f)(\text{Spot rate}) \qquad \text{(17-5)}$$

It can also be expressed as:

$$\text{Spot rate} = \frac{P_h}{P_f} \qquad \text{(17-6)}$$

For example, suppose you can buy a pair of tennis shoes in the United States for $150 and an identical pair in the U.K. for £100 pounds. Using the PPP equation, the exchange rate must be $1.50 per pound:

$$\text{Spot rate} = \frac{P_h}{P_f} = \frac{\$150}{£100} = \$1.50 \text{ per pound}$$

Purchasing power parity assumes that market forces will eliminate situations in which the same product sells at a different price overseas. For example, if the shoes cost $140 in the United States, then importers/exporters could purchase them in the United States for $140, sell them for 100 pounds in Britain, exchange the 100 pounds for $150 in the foreign exchange market, and earn a profit of $10 on every pair of shoes. Ultimately, this trading activity would increase the demand for shoes in the United States and thus raise P_h, increase the supply of shoes in Britain and thus reduce P_f, and increase the demand for dollars in the foreign exchange market and thus reduce the spot rate. Each of these actions works to restore PPP.

Recall that PPP is based on very strong assumptions: no FOREX transaction fees, transportation costs, transit time, or import/export restrictions. In addition, products in different countries are rarely identical. These reasons explain why PPP often appears to be violated. Still, the concepts of interest rate parity and purchasing power parity are vitally important to those engaged in international activities. Companies and investors must anticipate changes in interest rates, inflation, and exchange rates, and they often try to hedge the risks of adverse movements in these factors. The parity relationships are extremely useful when anticipating future conditions.

SELF-TEST

What is meant by purchasing power parity?

A computer sells for $1,500 U.S. dollars. In the spot market, $1 = 115 Japanese yen. If purchasing power parity holds, what should be the price (in yen) of the same computer in Japan? **(¥172,500)**

Hungry for a Big Mac? Go to Ukraine!

Purchasing power parity (PPP) implies that the same product will sell for the same price in every country after adjusting for current exchange rates. One problem when testing to see if PPP holds is that it assumes that goods consumed in different countries are of the same quality. For example, if you find that a product is more expensive in Switzerland than it is in Canada, one explanation is that PPP fails to hold, but another explanation is that the product sold in Switzerland is of a higher quality and therefore deserves a higher price.

One way to test for PPP is to find goods that have the same quality worldwide. With this in mind, *The Economist* magazine occasionally compares the prices of a well-known good whose quality is the same in over 100 different countries: the McDonald's Big Mac hamburger.

In July 2017, a Big Mac cost about $5.30 in the United States but could be purchased for about $1.70 in Ukraine after converting dollars to the Ukrainian hryvnia. *The Economist* "backed out" the exchange rate implied by the purchasing power parity relationship and calculated that the hryvnia was undervalued by about 68%. At the other extreme, a Big Mac sold for the equivalent of $6.74 in Switzerland. Based on the PPP equation, the Swiss franc is overvalued relative to the dollar by about 27%.

If the PPP relationship holds, then the Big Mac test suggests that there is an opportunity for investors to profit by shorting the Swiss franc and going long in the hryvnia. We don't suggest that you do this, but we do recommend that you avoid Big Macs if you travel in Switzerland.

Source: The Economist, online edition, July 2017, **www.economist.com /content/big-mac-index**.

17-11 Inflation, Interest Rates, and Exchange Rates

W W W

For current international interest rates, go to www.bloomberg.com and select Market Data. Then select "Rates and Bonds."

Many multinational financial decisions are influenced by the difference between the rate of inflation in a foreign country relative to that in the home country. Obviously, relative inflation rates will greatly influence future production costs at home and abroad. Equally important, inflation has a dominant influence on relative interest rates and exchange rates. Both of these factors influence decisions by multinational corporations for financing their foreign investments, and both have an important effect on the profitability of foreign investments.

The currencies of countries with higher inflation rates than that of the United States will by definition *depreciate* over time against the dollar. Countries where this has occurred include Mexico and all the South American nations. On the other hand, the currencies of Switzerland and Japan, which have had less inflation than the United States, have generally *appreciated* against the dollar. In fact, *a foreign currency will, on average, depreciate or appreciate against the U.S. dollar at a percentage rate approximately equal to the amount by which its inflation rate exceeds or is less than the U.S. rate.*

Relative inflation rates also affect interest rates. The interest rate in any country is largely determined by its inflation rate. Therefore, countries currently experiencing higher rates of inflation than the United States also tend to have higher interest rates. The reverse is true for countries with lower inflation rates.

It is tempting for a multinational corporation to borrow in countries with the lowest interest rates. However, this is not always a good strategy. Suppose, for example, that interest rates in Switzerland are lower than those in the United States because of Switzerland's lower inflation rate. A U.S. multinational firm could therefore save interest by borrowing in Switzerland. However, because of relative inflation rates, the Swiss franc will probably appreciate in the future, causing the dollar cost of annual interest and principal payments on Swiss debt to rise over time. Thus, *the lower interest rate could be more than offset by losses from currency appreciation.* Similarly, multinational corporations should not necessarily avoid borrowing in a country such as Brazil, where interest rates have been very high, because future depreciation of the Brazilian real could make such borrowing end up being relatively inexpensive.

SELF-TEST

What effects do relative inflation rates have on relative interest rates?

What happens over time to the currencies of countries with higher inflation rates than that of the United States? To those with lower inflation rates?

Why might a multinational corporation decide to borrow in a country such as Brazil, where interest rates are high, rather than in a country like Switzerland, where interest rates are low?

17-12 International Money and Capital Markets

From World War II through the 1960s, the U.S. capital markets dominated world markets. Now many corporations are finding that international markets often offer better opportunities for raising or investing capital than are available domestically. The growth of the international markets has also opened up opportunities for investors. One way for U.S. citizens to invest in world markets is to buy the stocks of U.S. multinational corporations that invest directly in foreign countries. Another way is to purchase foreign securities—stocks, bonds, or money market instruments issued by foreign companies. Security investments are known as *portfolio investments*, and they are distinguished from *direct investments* in physical assets by U.S. corporations.

17-12a Eurodollar Market

A **Eurodollar** is a U.S. dollar deposited in a bank outside the United States. (Although they are called Eurodollars because they originated in Europe, Eurodollars are actually any dollars deposited in any part of the world other than the United States.) The bank in which the deposit is made may be a non-U.S. bank, such as Barclays Bank in London; the foreign branch of a U.S. bank, such as Citibank's Paris branch; or even a foreign branch of a third-country bank, such as the Barclays Munich branch. Most Eurodollar deposits are for $500,000 or more, and they have maturities ranging from overnight to about 1 year.

The major difference between Eurodollar deposits and regular U.S. time deposits is their geographic locations. The two types of deposits do not involve different currencies—in both cases, dollars are on deposit. However, Eurodollars are outside the direct control of the U.S. monetary authorities, so U.S. banking regulations, including reserve requirements and FDIC insurance premiums, do not apply. The absence of these costs means that the interest rate paid on Eurodollar deposits can be higher than domestic U.S. rates on equivalent instruments.

The dollar is the leading international currency. However, British pounds, euros, Swiss francs, Japanese yen, and other currencies are also deposited outside their home countries; these *Eurocurrencies* are handled in exactly the same way as Eurodollars.

Eurodollars are borrowed by U.S. and foreign corporations for various purposes but especially to pay for goods imported from the United States and to invest in U.S. security markets. Also, U.S. dollars are used as an international currency or medium of exchange, and many Eurodollars are also used for this purpose. It is interesting to note that Eurodollars were actually "invented" by the Soviets in 1946. International merchants did not trust the Soviets or their rubles, so the Soviets bought some dollars (for gold), deposited them in a Paris bank, and then used these dollars to buy goods in the world markets. Others found it convenient to use dollars this same way, and soon the Eurodollar market was in full swing.

Eurodollars are usually held in interest-bearing accounts. The interest rate paid on these deposits depends (1) on the bank's lending rate, because the interest a bank earns on loans determines its willingness and ability to pay interest on deposits, and (2) on rates of return available on U.S. money market instruments. If money market rates in the United States were above Eurodollar deposit rates, then these dollars would be sent back and invested in the United States; if U.S. rates were lower than Eurodollar deposit, which is more often the case, then more dollars would be sent out of the United States to become Eurodollars. Given the existence of the Eurodollar market and the electronic flow of dollars to and from the United States, it is easy to see why interest rates in the United States cannot be insulated from those in other parts of the world.

Interest rates on Eurodollar deposits (and loans) are tied to a standard rate known by the acronym **LIBOR**, which stands for **London Interbank Offered Rate**. LIBOR is the rate of interest offered by the largest and strongest London banks on dollar deposits of significant size.[16] In 2018, LIBOR rates were above domestic U.S. bank rates on time deposits of the same maturity—2.20% for 3-month CDs versus 2.31% for LIBOR CDs. The Eurodollar market is essentially a short-term market; most loans and deposits are for less than 1 year.

---

[16]The U.K. authority responsible for regulating LIBOR announced in 2016 that it would cease to regulate LIBOR at the end of 2021. As a potential replacement, the U.S. Federal Reserve created the Secured Overnight Financing Rate (SOFR) and began publishing it in April 2018.

17-12b International Bond Markets

Any bond sold outside the country of the borrower is called an **international bond**. The Bank for International Settlements reports in 2018 that over $24 trillion international bonds are outstanding, with 44% denominated in dollars and 40% in Euros. British pounds, Japanese yen, Swiss francs, and Australian dollars account for most of the rest. There are two important types of international bonds: foreign bonds and Eurobonds.

Foreign bonds are bonds sold by a foreign borrower but denominated in the currency of the country in which the issue is sold. For instance, Nortel Networks (a Canadian company) may need U.S. dollars to finance the operations of its subsidiaries in the United States. If it decides to raise the needed capital in the United States, then the bond would be underwritten by a syndicate of U.S. investment bankers, denominated in U.S. dollars, and sold to U.S. investors in accordance with SEC and applicable state regulations. Except for the foreign origin of the borrower, this bond would be indistinguishable from those issued by equivalent U.S. corporations. However, because Nortel is a foreign corporation, the bond would be a foreign bond. Furthermore, because it is denominated in dollars and sold in the United States under SEC regulations, it is also called a **Yankee bond**.

The term **Eurobond** is used to designate any bond issued in one country but denominated in the currency of some other country. Examples include a Ford Motor Company issue sold in Germany but denominated in dollars; another is a British firm's sale of bonds in Switzerland but denominated in euros. Issuers include multinational firms, international financial institutions, and national governments. In 2017, General Electric issued about €8 billion worth of bonds in the United States that were denominated in euros. This is called a "reverse Yankee bond" because a U.S. domestic firm issued bonds in the United States that were denominated in a currency other than dollars.

The institutional arrangements for issuing Eurobonds are different from those of purely domestic bond issues, with the most important distinction being a far lower level of required disclosure, especially when compared with bonds issued in the United States. Governments tend to be less strict when regulating securities denominated in foreign currencies because the bonds' purchasers are generally more "sophisticated." The lower disclosure requirements result in lower total transaction costs to issue Eurobonds.

Although centered in Europe, global syndicates of investment banks underwrite and sell Eurobonds to investors from all parts of the world, not just Europe. Eurobonds appeal to investors for several reasons. Generally, they are issued in bearer form rather than as registered bonds, so the names and nationalities of investors are not recorded. Individuals who desire anonymity, whether for privacy reasons or for tax avoidance, like Eurobonds. Similarly, most governments do not withhold taxes on interest payments associated with Eurobonds. If the investor requires an effective yield of 10%, then a Eurobond that is exempt from tax withholding would simply need a coupon rate of 10%. Another type of bond—for instance, a domestic issue subject to a 30% withholding tax on interest paid to foreigners—would need a coupon rate of 14.3% to yield an after-withholding rate of 10%. Investors who desire secrecy would not want to file for a refund of the tax, so they would prefer to hold the Eurobond.

17-12c International Stock Markets

New issues of stock are sold in international markets for a variety of reasons. For example, a non-U.S. firm might sell an equity issue in the United States because it can tap a much larger source of capital than in its home country. Also, a U.S. firm might tap a foreign market because it wants to create an equity market presence to accompany its operations in that country. Large multinational companies also occasionally issue new

Stock Market Indexes around the World

In the United States, the Dow Jones Industrial Average (^DJI) is the most well-known stock market index. Similar indices also exist for each major world financial center.

Hong Kong (^HSI)

In Hong Kong, the primary stock index is the Hang Seng. Created by HSI Services Limited, the Hang Seng index is composed of 33 large stocks.

Great Britain (^FTSE)

The FT-SE 100 Index (pronounced "footsie") is the most widely followed indicator of equity investments in Great Britain. It is a value-weighted index composed of the 100 largest companies on the London Stock Exchange.

Japan (^N225)

In Japan, the principal barometer of stock performance is the Nikkei 225 Index. The index consists of highly liquid equity issues thought to be representative of the Japanese economy.

Germany (^GDAXI)

The Deutscher Aktienindex, commonly called the DAX, is an index composed of the 30 largest companies trading on the Frankfurt Stock Exchange.

India (^BSESN)

Of the 22 stock exchanges in India, the Bombay Stock Exchange (BSE) is the largest, with more than 6,000 listed stocks and approximately two-thirds of the country's total trading volume. Established in 1875, the exchange is also the oldest in Asia. Its yardstick is the BSE Sensex, an index of 30 publicly traded Indian stocks that account for one-fifth of the BSE's market capitalization. (Even though the city of Bombay changed its name to Mumbai in 1995, the stock exchange kept its name.)

Note: For easy access to world indices, see **http://finance.yahoo.com/m2** and use the ticker symbols as shown here in parentheses.

stock simultaneously in multiple countries. For example, Alcan Aluminum, a Canadian company, issued new stock in Canada, Europe, and the United States simultaneously, using different underwriting syndicates in each market.

Stock trading is truly global, with shares of large multinational U.S. companies traded worldwide on multiple international exchanges. U.S. investors can also invest in foreign companies through American Depository Receipts (ADRs), which are certificates representing ownership of foreign stock held in trust. Many ADRs trade on U.S. stock exchanges, including Toyota (Japan), Alibaba (China), and Anheuser-Busch InBev (Belgium).[17]

17-12d Sovereign Debt

Sovereign debt is the total amount that a government owes. Economics courses on public finance cover government debt in detail, but government debt also has an enormous impact on the topics we address in this book, including interest rates, risk, credit availability to nonfinancial corporations, and corporate valuation. Following is a brief overview of sovereign debt, along with some key insights that managers should keep in mind.

Countries with well-developed economies usually issue debt denominated in their own currencies, but lesser developed countries often issue debt denominated in a foreign currency. Some government debt offerings are governed only by the issuing country's judicial system, which often does not provide much protection for lenders. However, most government debt is issued under the auspices of international law (or the laws of the borrowing country), and we focus only on this type of sovereign debt.

---

[17]For an interesting discussion of ADRs and the costs faced by listing companies when the ADR is underwritten by investment banks, see Hsuen-Chi Chen, Larry Fauver, and Pei-Ching Yang, "What Do Investment Banks Charge to Underwrite American Depository Receipts?" *Journal of Banking and Finance,* April 2009, pp. 609–618.

Most government debt is held by financial institutions, pension funds, mutual funds, hedge funds, and individual investors. However, a few governments, such as China, actually own significant amounts of other governments' debt. Let's take a look at some facts, and then draw some implications for managers and investors.

First, how much sovereign debt are we talking about? The total debt for the 20 OECD members reporting at the end of 2017 was over $55 trillion.[18] The United States owes almost 44% of this total, Japan owes over 20%, followed by the U.K., France, and Germany (which together owe almost 15% of the total).

In terms of the United States, the total federal debt in mid-2018 was about $21.3 trillion, with about $15.5 trillion called "public debt" because it is owed to investors; the rest is owed to other U.S. government entities, such as the Social Security Trust fund.[19] Foreign investors own about $6.2 trillion of the public debt, which is about 40% ($6.2/$15.5 = 0.40 = 43%). Japan and China each own about 7% of the U.S. public debt.

Government debt can be used to invest in infrastructure, such as the highways, which are expected to "pay off" in the future with higher productivity, higher gross domestic product (GDP), and higher tax collections. However, governments can also use debt to finance deficit spending on items that aren't really investments. Such stimulus spending can help an economy avoid a recession, but it dampens economic growth in the long run.

How much debt is too much? To put it another way, how much debt is likely to lead to missed payments to lenders, default, or restructuring? One indicator is the ratio of a country's debt to its GDP. Table 17-5 reports estimated ratios for OECD members reporting at the end of 2017. The median ratio of all reported countries is 63.3%. While no particular level of debt/GDP guarantees a problem, it is no coincidence that several of the Eurozone governments facing financial problems (Greece, Portugal, and Italy) have high ratios. Notice that the U.S. ratio is 99.0%, much higher than it was a decade ago.

TABLE 17-5

Government Debt: Public Debt as a Percentage of Gross Domestic Product (Q4-2017)

Country	Public Debt/ GDP (%)	Country	Public Debt/ GDP (%)	Country	Public Debt/ GDP (%)
Japan	196.2	Slovenia	73.5	Canada	45.1
Greece	184.6	Austria	72.3	Germany	41.4
Portugal	134.6	Ireland	70.9	Sweden	39.5
Italy	127.3	New Zealand	65.8	Mexico	35.5
United States	99.0	Iceland	63.3	Denmark	34.7
United Kingdom	90.2	Israel	59.1	Turkey	30.9
Belgium	89.5	Finland	54.2	Norway	24.8
France	89.1	Poland	53.9	Switzerland	18.0
Hungary	73.9	Australia	45.6	Estonia	13.1

Source: See the Organisation for Economic Co-operation and Development (OECD) "National Accounts Statistics" at **www.oecd-ilibrary.org /economics/data/oecd-national-accounts-statistics_na-data-en**.

---

[18]The OECD and the U.S. Treasury define the total U.S. debt a little differently, which might cause small differences in the values reported here and in following paragraphs.

[19]This total does not include debt issued by government-sponsored agencies, for which the U.S. government provides an implicit guarantee.

Japan has been unusual because it has had the highest ratio for many years but has not had a financial crisis. What makes Japan different? First, Japan's debt is overstated because the Japanese government also owns large amounts of foreign assets, making Japan's net debt much lower than the debt value used by the OECD. Second, Japan's central bank (the Bank of Japan) holds large amounts of Japanese debt, which means that holdings by non-Japanese investors are much lower than Japan's reported debt. Third, Japan has had very low interest rates for a long time, so its interest payments are relatively low. Still, you have to wonder how long Japan can maintain its debt levels.

SELF-TEST

Differentiate between foreign portfolio investments and direct foreign investments.

What are Eurodollars?

Has the development of the Eurodollar market made it easier or more difficult for the Federal Reserve to control U.S. interest rates?

Differentiate between foreign bonds and Eurobonds.

Why do Eurobonds appeal to investors?

17-13 Multinational Capital Budgeting

Until now we've discussed the general environment in which multinational firms operate. In the remainder of the chapter, we see how international factors affect key corporate decisions, beginning with capital budgeting. Although the same basic principles apply to capital budgeting for both foreign and domestic operations, there are some key differences. These include the types of risks faced by the firm, cash flow estimation, and project analysis.

17-13a Risk Exposure

Foreign projects may be more or less risky than equivalent domestic projects, and that can lead to differences in the cost of capital. Lower risk might be due to factors including more stable markets, less competition, and favorable legal systems. Higher risk for foreign projects tends to result from several sources in the following sections. Keep in mind that companies can reduce some risks by having operations in multiple countries, which provides a degree of international diversification.

EXCHANGE RATE RISK

Exchange rate risk affects the value of the basic cash flows in the parent company's home currency. Foreign currency cash flows turned over to the parent must be converted into U.S. dollars, so projected cash flows must be translated to dollars at the expected future exchange rates. An analysis should be conducted to ascertain the effects of exchange rate variations on dollar cash flows; then, on the basis of this analysis, an exchange rate risk premium should be added to the domestic cost of capital. It is sometimes possible to hedge against exchange rate risk, but it may not be possible to hedge completely, especially on long-term projects. If hedging is used, then the costs of doing so must be subtracted from the project's operating cash flows.

POLITICAL RISK

Political risk refers to potential actions by a host government that would reduce the value of a company's investment. Foreign governments can impose curbs on currency conversion and restrictions on product prices charged by the subsidiary. Repatriation risk, expropriation risk, and corruption risk are additional exposures, as we explain next.

Repatriation Restrictions Consider a U.S. parent company that converts dollars into a foreign currency and establishes a subsidiary in that country. If its foreign subsidiary is successful, it will generate cash and profits in the local currency. The subsidiary might wish to convert some of the local cash flow into dollars and transfer it back to the parent, a process called **repatriation**. One source of risk is that the host country will impose restrictions on the amount that can be repatriated.

Expropriation Risk **Expropriation risk** is due to possible property seizure by a host government.[20] The risk of expropriation is small in traditionally friendly and stable countries such as Great Britain or Switzerland. However, in Latin America, Africa, the Far East, and Eastern Europe, the risk may be substantial. Past expropriations include those of Anaconda Copper in Chile; Gulf Oil in Bolivia; Occidental Petroleum in Libya; BP, ConocoPhillips, ExxonMobil, and Chevron in Venezuela; and the assets of many companies in Iran and Cuba. Note that companies can take steps to reduce the potential loss from expropriation, including one or more of the following:

1. Finance the subsidiary with local capital.
2. Structure operations so that the subsidiary has value only as a part of the integrated corporate system.
3. Obtain insurance against economic losses from expropriation from a source such as the Overseas Private Investment Corporation (OPIC). If OPIC insurance is purchased, then the premiums paid must be added to the project's cost.

Corruption Risk Several organizations rate countries according to different aspects of risk. For example, Transparency International (TI) ranks countries based on perceived corruption, which is an important part of political risk. Table 17-6 shows the most and least

TABLE 17-6
The 2017 Transparency International Corruption Perceptions Index (CPI)

Top-Ranked Countries		Bottom-Ranked Countries	
Rank	**Country**	**Rank**	**Country**
1	New Zealand	169 (tie)	Iraq
2	Denmark	169 (tie)	Venezuela
3 (tie)	Finland	171 (tie)	Korea, North
3 (tie)	Norway	171 (tie)	Equatorial Guinea
3 (tie)	Switzerland	171 (tie)	Guinea Bissau
6 (tie)	Singapore	171 (tie)	Libya
6 (tie)	Sweden	175 (tie)	Sudan
8 (tie)	Canada	175 (tie)	Yemen
8 (tie)	Luxembourg	177	Afghanistan
8 (tie)	Netherlands	178	Syria
8 (tie)	United Kingdom	179	South Sudan
12	Germany	180	Somalia

Source: See the Transparency International Web site at **www.transparency.org/news/feature/corruption
_perceptions_index_2017#table**.

---

[20]For an interesting article on expropriation, see Arvind Mahajan, "Pricing Expropriation Risk," *Financial Management*, Winter 1990, pp. 77–86.

honest countries. New Zealand and Denmark are the most honest countries, while Somalia is the most dishonest. Note the conspicuous absences of the United States (tied for 16th), China (tied for 77th), and Russia (tied for 135th) from the list of most honest countries.

TAXATION RISK

In addition to foreign taxes, the United States taxes repatriated earnings. The U.S. has had "grace" periods in the past during which it reduced the rate on repatriated earnings. However, these grace periods were uncertain, which created taxation risk.

Prior to the 2017 Tax Cuts and Jobs Act (TCJA), the United States had one of the highest statutory corporate tax rates in the world. If a U.S. company repatriated foreign earnings and it was not a grace period, then it would have to pay corporate taxes on those earnings, less any taxes paid to the foreign government. Because the United States had one of the highest statutory corporate tax rates in the world, many U.S. companies would not repatriate foreign earnings. In fact, the Congressional Joint Committee on Taxation estimated that foreign subsidiaries of U.S. firms held $2.6 trillion in undistributed foreign earnings, much of it in cash or other short-term investments.

The TCJA imposed a tax on undistributed foreign earnings accumulated since 1986. In particular, companies must pay a tax of 15.5% on those earnings that are held in cash and cash equivalents; they must pay 8% on the remainder. These payments are not due immediately but may be spread out over 8 years using the TCJA's schedule of payments. In return for taxes now on unrepatriated earnings, the U.S. will not tax any future foreign income earned after 2017. Thus, the TCJA eliminated a major source of repatriation risk.

17-13b Cash Flow Estimation

Cash flow estimation is more complex for foreign than domestic investments. Most multinational firms set up separate subsidiaries in each foreign country in which they operate, and the relevant cash flows for the parent company are the dividends and royalties paid by the subsidiaries to the parent, translated into dollars. Dividends and royalties are normally taxed by both foreign and home country governments, although the home country may allow credits for some or all of the foreign taxes paid. Furthermore, a foreign government may restrict the amount of the cash that may be repatriated to the parent company. For example, some governments place a ceiling, stated as a percentage of the company's net worth, on the amount of cash dividends that a subsidiary can pay to its parent. Such restrictions normally are intended to force multinational firms to reinvest earnings in the foreign country, although restrictions are sometimes imposed to prevent large currency outflows, which might disrupt the exchange rate.

Whatever the host country's motivation for blocking repatriation of profits, the result is that the parent corporation cannot use cash flows blocked in the foreign country to pay dividends to its shareholders or to invest elsewhere in the business. Hence, from the perspective of the parent organization, the cash flows relevant for foreign investment analysis are the cash flows that the subsidiary is actually expected to send back to the parent. Note, though, that if returns on investments in the foreign country are attractive and if blockages are expected to be lifted in the future, then current blockages may not be bad; however, dealing with this situation does complicate the process of cash flow estimation.

Some companies attempt to circumvent repatriation restrictions (and to lower their taxes) through transfer pricing. For example, a foreign subsidiary might obtain raw materials or other input components from the parent. The price the subsidiary pays the parent is called a **transfer price**. If the transfer price is high, then the foreign subsidiary's costs will be high, leaving little or no profit to repatriate. However, the parent's profit will be higher because it sold to the subsidiary at an inflated transfer price. The net result is that the parent receives cash flows from the subsidiary via transfer pricing rather than as repatriated dividends. Transfer pricing also can be used to shift profits from high-tax to low-tax jurisdictions. Of course, governments are well aware of these possibilities, so governmental auditors are on guard to prevent abusive transfer pricing.

17-13c Project Analysis

Consider a domestic project that requires foreign raw materials or one where the finished product will be sold in a foreign market. Because the operation is based in the United States, any projected nondollar cash flows—costs of raw materials and revenues of the finished product—should be converted into dollars. This conversion does not present much of a problem for cash flows to be paid or received in the short run, but there is a significant problem in estimating exchange rates for converting long-term foreign cash flows into dollars because forward exchange rates are usually not available for more than 180 days into the future.[21] However, long-term expected forward exchange rates can be estimated using the idea behind the interest rate parity relationship. For example, if a foreign cash flow is expected to occur in 1 year, then the 1-year forward exchange rate can be estimated using domestic and foreign government bonds maturing in 1 year. Similarly, the 2-year exchange rate can be estimated using 2-year bonds. Thus, foreign cash flows can be converted into dollars and added to the project's other projected cash flows, and then the project's NPV can be calculated based on its cost of capital.

Now consider a project to be based overseas, so that most expected future cash flows will be denominated in a foreign currency. Two approaches can be used to estimate such a project's NPV. Both begin by forecasting the future cash flows denominated in the foreign currency and then determining the annual repatriations to the United States, denominated in the foreign currency. Under the first approach, we convert the expected future repatriations to dollars (as described earlier) and then find the NPV using the project's cost of capital. Under the second approach, we take the projected repatriations (denominated in the foreign currency) and then discount them at the foreign cost of capital, which reflects foreign interest rates and relevant risk premiums. This produces an NPV denominated in the foreign currency, which can be converted into a dollar denominated NPV using the spot exchange rate.

The following example illustrates the first approach. A U.S. company has the opportunity to lease a manufacturing facility in Great Britain for 3 years. The company must spend £20 million initially to refurbish the plant. The expected net cash flows from the plant for the next 3 years, in millions, are $CF_1 = £7$, $CF_2 = £9$, and $CF_3 = £11$. A similar project in the United States would have a risk-adjusted cost of capital of 10%. The first step is to estimate the expected exchange rates at the end of 1, 2, and 3 years using the multiyear interest rate parity equation:

$$\text{Expected t-year forward exchange rate} = (\text{Spot exchange rate})\left(\frac{1 + r_h}{1 + r_f}\right)^t \qquad (17\text{-}7)$$

---

[21]Investing.com has forward exchange rate quotes for some currency pairs out as long as 30 years. There is very little or no volume, however, in any transactions longer than 5 years, and the long-dated forward quotes have large bid–ask spreads because there are few market participants. Unless the project is very large, a company would probably not actually enter a forward contract to hedge the project's cash flows—the costs would be too great for small transactions, and there is uncertainty in the size of the cash flows that will actually occur, leaving some residual exchange rate risk. Rather, the company will calculate the dollar value of the cash flows based on the forward rates but only hedge them in conjunction with other expected cash flows in that currency if they are large enough to bring the transaction costs down.

The exchange rates in Equation 17-7 are expressed in direct quotations, and the interest rates are expressed as annual rates, not periodic rates. (Recall that the direct quote is for units of home currency per unit of foreign currency.) We are using the interest rate parity equation to estimate expected forward rates because market-based forward rates for maturities longer than a year are generally not available.

Suppose the spot exchange rate is 1.8000 dollars per pound. Also suppose the following data are for interest rates on U.S. and U.K. government bonds, along with the expected forward rate implied by the multi-year interest rate parity relationship in Equation 17-7:

	Maturity (Years)		
	1	2	3
r_h (annualized)	2.0%	2.8%	3.5%
r_f (annualized)	4.6%	5.0%	5.2%
Spot rate ($ per £)	1.8000	1.8000	1.8000
Expected forward rate based on Equation 17-7 ($ per £)	1.7553	1.7254	1.7141

The current dollar cost of the project is £20(1.8000 $ per £) = $36 million. The Year-1 cash flow in dollars is £7(1.7553 $ per £) = $12.29 million. Table 17-7 shows the complete time line and the net present value of $2.18 million.

SELF-TEST

List some key differences in capital budgeting as applied to foreign versus domestic operations.

What are the relevant cash flows for an international investment: the cash flow produced by the subsidiary in the country where it operates, or the cash flows in dollars that it sends to its parent company?

Why might the cost of capital for a foreign project differ from that of an equivalent domestic project? Could it be lower?

What adjustments might be made due to exchange rate risk and political risk to the domestic cost of capital for a foreign investment?

The current exchange rate is 1.1 dollars per euro. A 5-year U.S. government bond has a 3% yield, and a 5-year French government bond has a yield of 4%. What is the expected 5-year forward rate? **(1.0481 dollars per euro)**

The current exchange rate is 0.8000 Swiss francs per dollar. A 5-year U.S. government bond has a 3% yield, and a 5-year Swiss government bond has a yield of 2%. What is the expected 5-year forward rate? **(0.7619 Swiss francs per dollar)** *(Hint: Remember that the interest rate parity equation is for direct quotes.)*

TABLE 17-7
Net Present Value of International Investment (Cash Flows in Millions)

	Year			
	0	1	2	3
Cash flows in pounds	−£20	£7	£9	£11
Expected exchange rates (dollars per pound)	1.8000	1.7553	1.7254	1.7141
Cash flows in dollars	−$36.00	$12.29	$15.53	$18.86
Project cost of capital	10%			
NPV	$2.18			

17-14 International Capital Structures

Corporate capital structures vary among countries. For example, the IMF's calculation of the corporate debt to total assets for reporting countries shows that five countries, including Romania, Portugal, and Israel, have ratios over 60%, which is a lot of debt. Only U.S. and Belgium companies average less than 30%. One problem when interpreting these numbers is that different countries often use different accounting conventions with regard to (1) reporting assets on the basis of historical versus replacement cost, (2) the treatment of leased assets, (3) pension plan funding, and (4) capitalizing versus expensing R&D costs. These differences make it difficult to compare capital structures.

A study by Raghuram Rajan and Luigi Zingales of the University of Chicago applied corrections to account for differences in accounting practices.[22] In their study, Rajan and Zingales used a database that covered fewer firms than the OECD but that provided a more complete breakdown of balance sheet data. They concluded that differences in accounting practices can explain much of the cross-country variation in capital structures.

For example, when Rajan and Zingales measure capital structure as interest-bearing debt to total assets, German firms use less leverage than U.S. firms, a different result compared to the OECD report. What explains these conflicting results? Rajan and Zingales argue that much of the difference is explained by the way German firms account for pension liabilities. German firms generally include all pension liabilities (and their offsetting assets) on the balance sheet, whereas firms in other countries (including the United States) generally "net out" pension assets and liabilities on their balance sheets. To see the importance of this difference, consider a firm with $10 million in liabilities (not including pension liabilities) and $20 million in assets (not including pension assets). Assume that the firm has $10 million in pension liabilities that are fully funded by $10 million in pension assets. Therefore, net pension liabilities are zero. If this firm were in the United States, it would report a ratio of total liabilities to total assets equal to 50% ($10 million/$20 million). By contrast, if this firm operated in Germany, both its pension assets and liabilities would be reported on the balance sheet. The firm would have $20 million in liabilities and $30 million in assets—or a 67% ($20 million/$30 million) ratio of total liabilities to total assets. Total debt is the sum of short-term debt and long-term debt and *excludes* other liabilities, including pension liabilities. Therefore, the measure of total debt to total assets provides a more comparable measure of leverage across different countries.

Rajan and Zingales also make a variety of adjustments that attempt to control for other differences in accounting practices. The effects of these adjustments suggest that companies in Germany and the United Kingdom tend to have less leverage, and that firms in Canada appear to have more leverage, than firms in the United States, France, Italy, and Japan. This conclusion is supported by the average times-interest-earned ratio for firms in a number of different countries. Recall from Chapter 3 that the times-interest-earned ratio is the ratio of operating income (EBIT) to interest expense. This measure indicates how much cash the firm has available to service its interest expense. In general, firms with more leverage have a lower times-interest-earned ratio. The data indicate that this ratio is highest in the United Kingdom and Germany and lowest in Canada.

SELF-TEST

Are there international differences in firms' financial leverage? Explain.

---

[22]See Raghuram Rajan and Luigi Zingales, "What Do We Know about Capital Structure? Some Evidence from International Data," *Journal of Finance*, Vol. 50, No. 5, December 1995, pp. 1421–1460.

17-15 Multinational Working Capital Management

Working capital management in a multinational setting involves more complexity than purely domestic working capital management. We discuss some of these differences in this section.

17-15a Cash Management

The goals of cash management in a multinational corporation are similar to those in a purely domestic corporation: (1) to speed up collections, slow down disbursements, and thus maximize net float; (2) to shift cash as rapidly as possible from those parts of the business where it is not needed to those parts where it is needed; and (3) to maximize the risk-adjusted, after-tax rate of return on temporary cash balances. Multinational companies use the same general procedures for achieving these goals as domestic firms, but the longer distances and more serious mail delays make such devices as lockbox systems and electronic funds transfers especially important.

Although multinational and domestic corporations have the same objectives and use similar procedures, multinational corporations face a far more complex task. As noted earlier in our discussion of political risk, foreign governments often place restrictions on transfers of funds out of the country. So even though IBM can transfer money from its Salt Lake City office to its New York concentration bank just by pressing a few buttons, a similar transfer from its Buenos Aires office is far more complex. Buenos Aires funds must be converted to dollars before the transfer. If there is a shortage of dollars in Argentina or if the Argentinean government wants to conserve dollars so they will be available for the purchase of strategic materials, then conversion, and hence the transfer, may be blocked. Even if no dollar shortage exists in Argentina, the government may still restrict funds outflows if those funds represent profits or depreciation rather than payments for purchased materials or equipment, because many countries—especially those that are less developed—want profits reinvested in the country in order to stimulate economic growth.

Once it has been determined what funds can be transferred, the next task is to get those funds to locations where they will earn the highest returns. Whereas domestic corporations tend to think in terms of domestic securities, multinationals are more likely to be aware of investment opportunities around the world. Most multinational corporations use one or more global concentration banks, located in money centers such as London, New York, Tokyo, Zurich, or Singapore, and their staffs in those cities, working with international bankers, are able to take advantage of the best rates available anywhere in the world.

17-15b Credit Management

Consider the international cash conversion cycle for a foreign company importing from the United States: The order is placed, the goods are shipped, an account payable is created for the importer and an account receivable is created for the exporter, the goods arrive in the foreign country, the importer sells them, and the importer collects on the sales. At some point in this process, the importer pays off the account payable, which is usually before the importer collects on its own sales. Notice that the importer must finance the transaction from the time it pays the account payable until it collects on its sales. In many poorer, less-developed nations, the capital markets are not adequate to enable the importer to finance the cash conversion cycle. Even when foreign capital markets are available, the additional shipping time might lengthen the cash conversion cycle to such an extent that the importer can't afford the financing costs. Thus, there is enormous pressure on the exporter to grant credit, often with very long payment periods.

But now consider the situation from the exporter's point of view. First, it is much more difficult for the exporter to perform a credit analysis on a foreign customer. Second, the exporter also must worry about exchange rate fluctuations between the time of the sale and the time the receivable is collected. For example, if IBM sold a computer to a Japanese customer for 90 million yen when the exchange rate was 90 yen to the dollar, IBM would obtain 90,000,000/90 = $1,000,000 for the computer. However, if it sold the computer on terms of net/60 and if the yen then fell against the dollar, so that 1 dollar would now buy 112.5 yen, IBM would end up realizing only 90,000,000/112.5 = $800,000 when it collected the receivable. Hedging with forward contracts can reduce this exchange rate risk, but what about the credit risk?

One possibility is for the importer to obtain a letter of credit from its bank whereby the bank certifies that the importer will meet the terms of the account payable or else the bank will pay. However, the importer often must pay the bank a relatively large fee for the letter of credit, and letters of credit might not be available to companies in developing countries.

A second option is for the importer essentially to write a check to the exporter at the time of the purchase, but to postdate the check so that it cannot be cashed until the account payable's due date. If the importer's bank promises that it will "accept" the check even if there are insufficient funds in the importer's account, then the check becomes a financial instrument called a **banker's acceptance**. If the bank is strong, then this virtually eliminates the credit risk. In addition, the exporter can then sell this banker's acceptance in the secondary market if it needs funds immediately. Of course, it must sell the banker's acceptance at a discount to reflect the time value of money, because the banker's acceptance is essentially a short-term financial security that pays no interest, similar to a T-bill. Financing an international transaction via a banker's acceptance has many benefits for the exporter, but the importer often must pay the bank a relatively large fee, and this service might not be available to companies in developing countries.

A third alternative is for the exporter to purchase export credit insurance, in which an insurer makes a commitment to pay the exporter even if the importer defaults. Sometimes the "insurer" is a government agency, such as the Japanese Ministry of International Trade and Industry (MITI) or the United States Export-Import Bank. Other times, the insurer is a private insurance company. These large insurance companies have developed expertise in international credit analysis, and they can spread the risk over a large number of customers. These advantages allow them to offer credit insurance at rates that often make it less costly than either letters of credit or bankers' acceptances. In fact, export credit insurance has been so successful that it has virtually killed the market for bankers' acceptances and has become the primary way in which companies manage the credit risk of international sales.

17-15c Inventory Management

As with most other aspects of finance, inventory management for a firm in a multinational setting is similar to but more complex than for a purely domestic firm. First, there is the matter of the physical location of inventories. For example, where should ExxonMobil keep its stockpiles of crude oil and refined products? It has refineries and marketing centers located worldwide, and one alternative is to keep items concentrated in a few strategic spots from which they can then be shipped as needs arise. Such a strategy might minimize the total amount of inventories needed and thus might minimize the investment in inventories. Note, though, that consideration will have to be given to potential delays in getting goods from central storage locations to user locations all around the world. Both working stocks and safety stocks would have to be maintained at each user location, as well as at the strategic storage centers.

Exchange rates also influence inventory policy. If a local currency—say, the Danish krone—were expected to rise in value against the dollar, then a U.S. company operating in Denmark would want to increase stocks of local products before the rise in the krone, and vice versa if the krone were expected to fall.

Another factor that must be considered is the possibility of import or export quotas or tariffs. For example, Apple was buying certain memory chips from Japanese suppliers at a bargain price. Then U.S. chipmakers accused the Japanese of dumping chips in the U.S. market at prices below cost, and they sought to force the Japanese to raise their prices.[23] This led Apple to increase its chip inventory. Then computer sales slacked off, and Apple ended up with an oversupply of obsolete computer chips. As a result, Apple's profits were hurt and its stock price fell, demonstrating once more the importance of careful inventory management.

As mentioned earlier, another danger in certain countries is the threat of expropriation. If that threat is large, then inventory holdings will be minimized and goods will be brought in only as needed. Similarly, if the operation involves extraction of raw materials such as oil or bauxite, processing plants may be moved offshore rather than located close to the production site.

Taxes have two effects on multinational inventory management. First, countries often impose property taxes on assets, including inventories; when this is done, the tax is based on holdings as of a specific date, such as January 1 or March 1. Such rules make it advantageous for a multinational firm: (1) to schedule production so that inventories are low on the assessment date, and (2) if assessment dates vary among countries in a region, to hold safety stocks in different countries at different times during the year.

Finally, multinational firms may consider the possibility of at-sea storage. Oil, chemical, grain, and other companies that deal in a bulk commodity that must be stored in some type of tank can often buy tankers at a cost not much greater—or perhaps even less, considering land cost—than land-based facilities. Loaded tankers can then be kept at sea or at anchor in some strategic location. This eliminates the danger of expropriation, minimizes the property tax problem, and maximizes flexibility with regard to shipping to areas where needs are greatest or prices highest.

This discussion has only scratched the surface of inventory management in the multinational corporation—the task is much more complex than for a purely domestic firm. However, the greater the degree of complexity, the greater the rewards from superior performance, so if you are willing to take challenges along with potentially high rewards, then look to the international arena.

SELF-TEST

What are some factors that make cash management more complicated in a multinational corporation than in a purely domestic corporation?

Why is granting credit riskier in an international context?

Why is inventory management especially important for a multinational firm?

---

[23]Here is an explanation of dumping. Suppose Japanese chipmakers have excess capacity. A particular chip has a variable cost of $25, and its "fully allocated cost," which is the $25 plus total fixed cost per unit of output, is $40. Now suppose the Japanese firm can sell chips in the United States at $35 per unit, but if it charges $40, then it won't make any sales because U.S. chipmakers sell for $35.50. If the Japanese firm sells at $35, it will cover variable costs plus make a contribution to fixed overhead, so selling at $35 makes sense. Continuing, if the Japanese firm can sell in Japan at $40 but U.S. firms are excluded from Japanese markets by import duties or other barriers, then the Japanese will have a huge advantage over U.S. manufacturers. This practice of selling goods at lower prices in foreign markets than at home is called "dumping." U.S. firms are required by antitrust laws to offer the same price to all customers and, therefore, cannot engage in dumping.

SUMMARY

Multinational companies have more opportunities, but they also face more risks than do companies that operate only in their home market. This chapter discussed many of the key trends affecting the global markets today, and it described the most important differences between multinational and domestic financial management. The key concepts are listed here.

- A multinational, transnational, or **global corporation** is a firm that operates in an integrated fashion in a number of countries.
- Companies "go global" for these reasons: (1) to expand their markets, (2) to obtain raw materials, (3) to seek new technology, (4) to lower production costs, (5) to avoid trade barriers, and (6) to diversify.
- Several major factors distinguish financial management as practiced by domestic firms from that practiced by multinational corporations, including different: (1) different currencies, (2) languages, (3) cultures (4) economic systems, (5) legal systems, and (6) tax codes. In addition, there is the threat of (1) government intervention that restricts free market transactions, (2) terrorism/crime, and (3) the **political risk** that the foreign government will take some action that will decrease the value of direct investments
- When discussing **exchange rates**, the number of U.S. dollars required to purchase one unit of a foreign currency is called a **direct quote**, while the number of units of foreign currency that can be purchased for one U.S. dollar is an **indirect quote**.
- Prior to August 1971, the world was on a **fixed exchange rate system** whereby the U.S. dollar was linked to gold and other currencies were then tied to the dollar. After August 1971, the world monetary system changed to a **floating system** under which major world currency rates float with market forces, largely unrestricted by governmental intervention. The central bank of each country does operate in the foreign exchange market, buying and selling currencies to smooth out exchange rate fluctuations, but only to a limited extent.
- **Pegged exchange rates** occur when a country establishes a fixed exchange rate with a major currency. Consequently, the values of pegged currencies move together over time.
- A **convertible currency** is one that may be readily exchanged for other currencies at market prices.
- **Spot rates** are the rates paid for delivery of currency "on the spot," whereas the **forward exchange rate** is the rate paid for delivery at some agreed-upon future date— usually 30, 90, or 180 days from the day the transaction is negotiated. The forward currency can sell at either a **premium** or a **discount** to the spot rate.
- **Interest rate parity** holds that investors should expect to earn the same risk-free return in all countries after adjusting for exchange rates.
- **Purchasing power parity (PPP)**, sometimes referred to as the *law of one price*, implies that the level of exchange rates adjusts so that identical goods cost the same in different countries.
- Granting credit to a supplier is more risky in an international context because, in addition to the normal risks of default, the multinational firm must worry about exchange rates changing between the time a sale is made and the time a receivable is collected.
- Credit policy is important for a multinational firm for two reasons: (1) Much trade is with less-developed nations, and in such situations granting credit is a necessary condition for doing business. (2) The governments of nations such as Japan, whose economic health depends on exports, often help their firms compete by granting credit to foreign customers.

- Foreign investments are similar to domestic investments, but they have **exchange rate risk**, which is the risk that a transaction in a foreign currency will be more costly than anticipated due to possible future fluctuations in exchange rates.
- The relevant cash flows in international capital budgeting are the dollars that can be **repatriated** to the parent company.
- **Eurodollars** are U.S. dollars deposited in banks outside the United States. Interest rates on Eurodollars are tied to **LIBOR**, the **London Interbank Offered Rate**.
- U.S. firms often find that they can raise long-term capital at a lower cost outside the United States by selling bonds in the international capital markets. International bonds may be either (1) **foreign bonds** which are exactly like regular domestic bonds except that the issuer is a foreign company; or (2) **Eurobonds**, which are bonds sold in a foreign country but denominated in the currency of the issuing company's home country.

QUESTIONS

(17-1)   Define each of the following terms:
a. Multinational corporation
b. Exchange rate; fixed exchange rate system; floating exchange rate
c. Trade deficit; devaluation; revaluation
d. Exchange rate risk; convertible currency; pegged exchange rate
e. Interest rate parity; purchasing power parity
f. Spot rate; forward exchange rate; discount on foreign currency forward rate; premium on foreign currency forward rate
g. Repatriation of earnings; political risk
h. Eurodollar; Eurobond; international bond; foreign bond
i. The euro

(17-2)   Under the fixed exchange rate system, what was the currency against which all other currency values were defined? Why?

(17-3)   Exchange rates fluctuate under both the fixed exchange rate and floating exchange rate systems. What, then, is the difference between the two systems?

(17-4)   If the Swiss franc depreciates against the U.S. dollar, can a dollar buy more or fewer Swiss francs as a result?

(17-5)   If the United States imports more goods from abroad than it exports, then foreigners will tend to have a surplus of U.S. dollars. What will this do to the value of the dollar with respect to foreign currencies? What is the corresponding effect on foreign investments in the United States?

(17-6)   Why do U.S. corporations build manufacturing plants abroad when they could build them at home?

(17-7)   Should firms require higher rates of return on foreign projects than on identical projects located at home? Explain.

(17-8)   What is a Eurodollar? If a French citizen deposits $10,000 in Chase Bank in New York, have Eurodollars been created? What if the deposit is made in Barclays Bank in London? Chase's Paris branch? Does the existence of the Eurodollar market make the Federal Reserve's job of controlling U.S. interest rates easier or more difficult? Explain.

(17-9)   Does interest rate parity imply that interest rates are the same in all countries?

(17-10)   Why might purchasing power parity fail to hold?

SELF-TEST PROBLEM   SOLUTION SHOWN IN APPENDIX A

(ST-1)
Cross Rates

Suppose that the exchange rate between U.S. dollars and euros is €0.98 = $1.00 and that the exchange rate between the U.S. dollar and the Canadian dollar is $1.00 = C$1.50. What is the cross rate of euros to Canadian dollars?

PROBLEMS   ANSWERS ARE IN APPENDIX B

EASY PROBLEMS 1–4

(17-1)
Cross Rates

At today's spot exchange rates 1 U.S. dollar can be exchanged for 9 Mexican pesos or for 111.23 Japanese yen. You have pesos that you would like to exchange for yen. What is the cross rate between the yen and the peso; that is, how many yen would you receive for every peso exchanged?

(17-2)
Interest Rate Parity

The nominal yield on 6-month T-bills is 7%, while default-free Japanese bonds that mature in 6 months have a nominal rate of 5.5%. In the spot exchange market, 1 yen equals $0.009. If interest rate parity holds, what is the 6-month forward exchange rate?

(17-3)
Purchasing Power Parity

A computer costs $500 in the United States. The same model costs €550 in France. If purchasing power parity holds, what is the spot exchange rate between the euro and the dollar?

(17-4)
Exchange Rate

If euros sell for $1.50 (U.S.) per euro, what should dollars sell for in euros per dollar?

INTERMEDIATE PROBLEMS 5–8

(17-5)
Currency Appreciation

Suppose that the exchange rate is 0.60 dollars per Swiss franc. If the franc appreciates 10% against the dollar, how many francs would a dollar buy tomorrow?

(17-6)
Cross Rates

Suppose the exchange rate between U.S. dollars and the Swiss franc is SFr1.6 = $1 and the exchange rate between the dollar and the British pound is £1 = $1.50. What then is the cross rate between francs and pounds?

(17-7)
Interest Rate Parity

Assume that interest rate parity holds. In both the spot market and the 90-day forward market, 1 Japanese yen equals 0.0086 dollar. In Japan, 90-day risk-free securities yield 4.6%. What is the yield on 90-day risk-free securities in the United States?

(17-8)
Purchasing Power Parity

In the spot market, 7.8 pesos can be exchanged for 1 U.S. dollar. A pair of headphones costs $15 in the United States. If purchasing power parity holds, what should be the price of the same headphones in Mexico?

CHALLENGING PROBLEMS 9–14

(17-9)
Exchange Gains and Losses

Your Boston-headquartered manufacturing company, Wruck Enterprises, obtained a 50-million-peso loan from a Mexico City bank last month to fund the expansion of your Monterrey, Mexico, plant. The exchange rate was 10 U.S. cents per peso when you took out the loan, but since then the exchange rate has dropped to 9 U.S. cents per peso. Has Wruck Enterprises made a gain or a loss due to the exchange rate change, and how much? Note that your shareholders live in the United States.

(17-10)
Results of Exchange Rate Changes

In 1983, the Japanese yen–U.S. dollar exchange rate (USD/JPY) was 245 yen per dollar, and the dollar cost of a compact Japanese-manufactured car was $8,000. Suppose that now the exchange rate is 80 yen per dollar. Assume there has been no inflation in the yen cost of an automobile so that all price changes are due to exchange rate changes. What would the dollar price of the car be now, assuming the car's price changes only with exchange rates?

(17-11)
Spot and
Forward Rates

Boisjoly Watch Imports has agreed to purchase 15,000 Swiss watches for 1 million francs at today's spot rate. The firm's financial manager, James Desreumaux, has noted the following current spot and forward rates:

	U.S. Dollar/Swiss Franc	Swiss Franc/U.S. Dollar
Spot	1.6590	0.6028
30-day forward	1.6540	0.6046
90-day forward	1.6460	0.6075
180-day forward	1.6400	0.6098

On the same day, Desreumaux agrees to purchase 15,000 more watches in 3 months at the same price of 1 million Swiss francs.

a. What is the cost of the watches in U.S. dollars, if purchased at today's spot rate?
b. What is the cost in dollars of the second 15,000 batch if payment is made in 90 days and the spot rate at that time equals today's 90-day forward rate?
c. If the exchange rate is 0.50 Swiss francs per dollar in 90 days, how much will Desreumaux have to pay (in dollars) for the watches?

(17-12)
Interest Rate Parity

Assume that interest rate parity holds and that 90-day risk-free securities yield 5% in the United States and 5.3% in Germany. In the spot market, 1 euro equals $1.40. What is the 90-day forward rate? Is the 90-day forward rate trading at a premium or a discount relative to the spot rate?

(17-13)
Foreign Investment
Analysis

Chapman Inc.'s Mexican subsidiary, V. Gomez Corporation, is expected to pay to Chapman 50 pesos in dividends in 1 year after all foreign and U.S. taxes have been subtracted. The exchange rate in 1 year is expected to be 0.10 dollars per peso. After this, the peso is expected to depreciate against the dollar at a rate of 4% a year forever due to the different inflation rates in the United States and Mexico. The peso-denominated dividend is expected to grow at a rate of 8% a year indefinitely. Chapman owns 10 million shares of V. Gomez. What is the present value of the dividend stream, in dollars, assuming V. Gomez's cost of equity is 13%?

(17-14)
Foreign Capital
Budgeting

The South Korean multinational manufacturing firm, Nam Sung Industries, is debating whether to invest in a 2-year project in the United States. The project's expected dollar cash flows consist of an initial investment of $1 million with cash inflows of $700,000 in Year 1 and $600,000 in Year 2. The risk-adjusted cost of capital for this project is 13%. The current exchange rate is 1,050 won per U.S. dollar. Risk-free interest rates in the United States and S. Korea are:

	1-Year	2-Year
U.S.	4.0%	4.25%
S. Korea	3.0%	3.25%

a. If this project were instead undertaken by a similar U.S.-based company with the same risk-adjusted cost of capital, what would be the net present value and rate of return generated by this project?

b. What is the expected forward exchange rate 1 year from now and 2 years from now? (*Hint:* Take the perspective of the Korean company when identifying home and foreign currencies and direct quotes of exchange rates.)

c. If Nam Sung undertakes the project, what is the net present value and rate of return of the project for Nam Sung?

SPREADSHEET PROBLEM

(17-15)
Build a Model:
Multinational
Financial
Management

resource

Start with the partial model in the file ***Ch17 P15 Build a Model.xlsx*** on the textbook's Web site. Mark Collins, luthier and businessman, builds and sells custom-made acoustic and electric stringed instruments. Although located in Maryville, Tennessee, he purchases raw materials from around the globe. For example, he constructs his top-of-the line acoustic guitar with onboard electronics, the MC-28, from rosewood and mahogany imported from a distributor in Mexico, spruce harvested in and imported from Canada, and ebony and the electronics imported from a Japanese distributor. He obtains other parts in the United States. When broken down on a per-guitar basis, the component and finishing costs are as follows:

Rosewood and mahogany: 2,750 Mexican pesos
Spruce: 200 Canadian dollars
Ebony and electronics: 12,400 Japanese yen
Other parts plus woodworking labor: $600

Collins sells some of this model in the United States, but the majority of the units are sold in England, where he has developed a loyal following and the guitars have become something of a cult symbol. There, his guitars fetch £1,600, excluding shipping. Mark is concerned about the effect of exchange rates on his materials costs and profit. You will find Tables 17-1 and 17-2 useful for this problem.

a. How much, in dollars, does it cost for Collins to produce his MC-28? What is the dollar sale price of the MC-28 sold in England?

b. What is the dollar profit that Collins makes on the sale of the MC-28? What is the percentage profit?

c. If the U.S. dollar were to depreciate by 10% against all foreign currencies, what would be the dollar profit for the MC-28?

d. If the U.S. dollar were to depreciate by 10% only against the pound and remain constant relative to all other foreign currencies, what would be the dollar and percentage profits for the MC-28?

e. The rate of return on 90-day U.S. Treasury securities is 3.9%, and the rate of return on 90-day U.K. risk-free securities is 5.0%. Using the spot exchange information from Table 17-1, estimate the 90-day forward exchange rate.

f. Assuming that purchasing power parity (PPP) holds, what would be the sale price of the MC-28 if it were sold in France rather than in England? (*Hint:* Assume England is the home country.)

MINI CASE

With the growth in demand for exotic foods, Possum Inc.'s CEO Michael Munger is considering expanding the geographic footprint of its line of dried and smoked low-fat opossum, ostrich, and venison jerky snack packs. Historically, jerky products have performed well in the southern United States, but there are indications of a growing demand for these unusual delicacies in Europe. Munger recognizes that the expansion carries some risk. Europeans may not be as accepting of opossum jerky as initial research suggests, so the expansion will proceed in steps. The first step will be to set up sales subsidiaries in France and Sweden (the two countries with the highest indicated demand), and the second is to set up a production plant in France with the ultimate goal of product distribution throughout Europe.

Possum Inc.'s CFO, Kevin Uram, although enthusiastic about the plan, is nonetheless concerned about how an international expansion and the additional risk that entails will affect the firm's financial management process. He has asked you, the firm's most recently hired financial analyst, to develop a 1-hour tutorial package that explains the basics of multinational financial management. The tutorial will be presented at the next board of directors meeting. To get you started, Uram has supplied you with the following list of questions:

a. What is a multinational corporation? Why do firms expand into other countries?
b. What are the six major factors that distinguish multinational financial management from financial management as practiced by a purely domestic firm?
c. Consider the following illustrative exchange rates:

	U.S. Dollars Required to Buy One Unit of Foreign Currency	Units of Foreign Currency Required to Buy One U.S. Dollar
Euro	1.2500	—
Swedish krona	—	7.0000

   (1) What is a direct quotation? What is the direct quote for euros?
   (2) What is an indirect quotation? What is the indirect quotation for kronor (the plural of krona is kronor)?
   (3) The euro and British pound usually are quoted as direct quotes. Most other currencies are quoted as indirect quotes. How would you calculate the indirect quote for a euro? How would you calculate the direct quote for a krona?
   (4) What is a cross rate? Calculate the two cross rates between euros and kronor.
   (5) Assume Possum Inc. can produce a package of jerky and ship it to France for $1.75. If the firm wants a 50% markup on the product, what should the jerky sell for in France?
   (6) Now assume that Possum Inc. begins producing the same package of jerky in France. The product costs 2 euros to produce and ship to Sweden, where it can be sold for 20 kronor. What is the dollar profit on the sale?
   (7) What is exchange rate risk?
d. Briefly describe the current international monetary system. How does the current system differ from the system that was in place prior to August 1971?
e. What is a convertible currency? What problems arise when a multinational company operates in a country whose currency is not convertible?
f. What is the difference between spot rates and forward rates? When is the foreign currency forward rate selling at a premium to the spot rate? At a discount?
g. What is interest rate parity? Currently, you can exchange 1 euro for 1.25 dollars in the 180-day forward market, and the risk-free rate on 180-day securities is 6% in the United States and 4% in France. Does interest rate parity hold? If not, which securities offer the highest expected return?

h. What is purchasing power parity? If a package of jerky costs $2 in the United States and purchasing power parity holds, what should be the price of the jerky package in France?

i. What effect does relative inflation have on interest rates and exchange rates?

j. Briefly discuss the international capital markets.

k. To what extent do average capital structures vary across different countries?

l. Briefly describe a company's risk exposure if it invests in an international project.

m. Describe the process for evaluating a foreign project. Now consider the following project: A U.S. company has the opportunity to lease a manufacturing facility in Japan for 2 years. The company must spend ¥1 billion initially to refurbish the plant. The expected net cash flows from the plant for the next 2 years, in millions, are CF_1 = ¥500 and CF_2 = ¥800. A similar project in the United States would have a risk-adjusted cost of capital of 10%. In the United States, a 1-year government bond pays 2% interest, and a 2-year bond pays 2.8%. In Japan, a 1-year bond pays 0.05%, and a 2-year bond pays 0.26%. What is the project's NPV?

n. Briefly discuss special factors associated with the following areas of multinational working capital management:

   (1) Cash management
   (2) Credit management
   (3) Inventory management

SELECTED ADDITIONAL CASES

The following case from CengageCompose covers many of the concepts discussed in this chapter and is available at **http://compose.cengage.com**.

Klein-Brigham Series:
Case 18, "Alaska Oil Corporation."

Public and Private Financing: Initial Offerings, Seasoned Offerings, Investment Banks

On May 18, 2012, Facebook went public in one of the most eagerly anticipated initial public offerings (IPO) of the decade. Facebook and some of its founders/investors sold about 421 million shares for $38 each, but subsequent trading on NASDAQ was delayed for 30 minutes due to technological problems. When trading did begin, the price quickly went up to over $42. Although the price rose to $45 during the day, most new investors were selling the stock, putting downward pressure on the price. Morgan Stanley, one of the underwriters, kept the price from plunging by purchasing enough shares itself to create artificial demand. By the end of the day, the price was down to $38.23, barely above the initial price. During the following two weeks, the price fell below $26, and finger-pointing and blaming ensued.

First, analysts and investors complained that shortly before its IPO, Facebook had increased the number of shares it planned to sell and then sold them at a higher-than-expected price. This combination, they said, reduced demand for the stock and hurt the per share value.

Second, there was pandemonium during the day when traders were unable to confirm their trades. For example, UBS (a large Swiss financial institution) claimed it suffered $350 million in losses due to the interruption in information. NASDAQ offered $40 million in compensation to brokerage firms that lost money due to the information interruption, but that is unlikely to satisfy all the traders.

Third, some investors sued Facebook and its underwriters, alleging that they concealed a reduction in projected sales revenues from all but a few favored clients.

We will have more to say about Facebook's IPO later in the chapter, so keep these events in mind.

Sources: Shayndi Raice, Ryan Dexember, and Jacob Bunge, "Facebook's Launch Sputters," *The Wall Street Journal*, May 19, 2012, p. A1; Jonathan Stempel and Dan Levine, www.reuters.com, May 23, 2012.

resource

The textbook's Web site contains an Excel file that will guide you through the chapter's calculations. The file for this chapter is Ch18 Tool Kit.xlsx, and we encourage you to open the file and follow along as you read the chapter.

Previous chapters described how a company selects projects, chooses its capital structure, and implements its dividend policy. These activities determine the amount of new capital a company must raise and the debt/equity mix of that new capital. In this chapter, we describe the actual process of raising capital from the public markets (such as selling stock in an initial public offering) and private markets (such as selling stock to a private investor like a pension fund). We also describe the roles investment banks and regulatory agencies play in raising capital.

18-1 The Financial Life Cycle of a Start-Up Company

Most businesses begin life as proprietorships or partnerships, and if they become successful and grow, at some point they find it desirable to become corporations. Initially, most corporate stock is owned by the firms' founding managers and key employees. Even start-up firms that are ultimately successful usually begin with negative free cash flows because of their high growth rates and product development costs; hence, they must raise capital during these high-growth years. If the founding owner-managers have invested all of their own financial resources in the company, then they must turn to outside sources of capital. Start-up firms generally have high growth opportunities, and they suffer from especially large problems due to asymmetric information. Therefore, as we discussed in Chapter 15, they must raise external capital primarily as equity rather than debt.

To protect investors from fraudulent stock issues, in 1933 Congress enacted the Securities Act, which created the **Securities and Exchange Commission (SEC)** to regulate the financial markets.[1] The Securities Act regulates interstate public offerings, which we explain later in this section, but it also provides several exemptions that allow companies to issue securities through **private placements** that are not registered with the SEC. The rules governing these exemptions are quite complex, but in general they restrict the number and type of investors who may participate in an issue. **Accredited investors** include the officers and directors of the company, high-wealth individuals, and institutional investors. In a nonregistered private placement, the company may issue securities to an unlimited number of accredited investors but to only 35 nonaccredited investors. In addition, none of the investors can sell their securities in the secondary market to the general public.

For most start-ups, the first round of external financing comes through a private placement of equity to one or two individual investors, called **angel investors**. In return for a typical investment in the range of $50,000 to $400,000, the angels receive stock and perhaps also a seat on the board of directors. Because angels can influence the strategic direction of the company, it is best when they bring experience and industry contacts to the table in addition to cash.

As the company grows, its financing requirements may exceed the resources of individual investors, in which case it is likely to turn to a **venture capital fund**. A venture capital fund is a private limited partnership established to invest in start-up companies. It is managed by its **general partners**, who are often called **venture capitalists (VCs)**. The VCs are usually very knowledgeable and experienced in a particular industry, such as health care, information technology, or biotechnology. They screen hundreds of start-ups and ultimately make equity investments in around a dozen, called **portfolio companies**. The VCs or their employees sit on the companies' boards of directors. Some portfolio

---

[1]In addition to federal statutes, which affect transactions that cross state borders, states have "blue sky" laws that regulate securities sold just within the state. These laws were designed to prevent unscrupulous dealers from selling something of little worth, such as the blue sky, to naïve investors.

companies and other start-up companies are called **unicorns** because they have an estimated valuation greater than $1 billion dollars, which is rare among start-ups. Current (early 2018) examples are Uber Technologies, Airbnb, and Reddit.

A fund typically raises around $300 million from a relatively small group of individual and institutional investors, including pension funds, college endowments, and corporations. The general partner usually contributes a relatively modest amount of cash but acts as the fund's manager. In return, the general partner normally receives annual compensation equal to 1% to 2% of the fund's assets plus a 20% share of the fund's eventual profits. As we write this in early 2018, a VC's eventual profits are called **carried interest** and are taxed at the capital gains tax rate, which usually is lower than the ordinary income tax rate. This is a contentious political issue because the VC's original investment is so much smaller than the limited partners' investments, causing some people to regard carried interest as ordinary income rather than capital gains.

Individual venture capital funds may be part of a larger investment firm that serves as the funds' general manager. Such investment firms can be quite large, such as Andreessen Horowitz, with ownership stakes in Airbnb and Pinterest.

Some start-up "funds" are divisions or subsidiaries of publicly traded companies. For example, GV (originally named Google Ventures) is a subsidiary of Alphabet, Inc. (which also owns Google). GV has ownership stakes in Uber and SurveyMonkey.

SELF-TEST

What is a private placement?

What is an angel investor?

What is a venture capital fund? A VC?

18-2 The Decision to Go Public

Going public means selling some of a company's stock to outside investors in an **initial public offering (IPO)** and then letting the stock trade in public markets. For example, Snap, Inc. (the owner of Snapchat), Roku, Inc., and Stitch Fix Inc. all went public in 2018. There are advantages and disadvantages for going public, as explained next.

18-2a Advantages of Going Public

The advantages to going public include the following:

1. *Increases liquidity and allows founders to harvest their wealth.* The stock of a private, or closely held, corporation is illiquid. It may be hard for one of the owners who wants to sell some shares to find a ready buyer, and even if a buyer is located, there is no established price on which to base the transaction.
2. *Permits founders to diversify.* As a company grows and becomes more valuable, its founders often have most of their wealth tied up in the company. By selling some of their stock in a public offering, they can diversify their holdings, thereby reducing the riskiness of their personal portfolios.
3. *Facilitates raising new corporate cash.* If a privately held company wants to raise cash by selling new stock, it must either go to its existing owners, who may not have any money or may not want to put more eggs in this particular basket, or else shop around for wealthy investors. However, it is usually quite difficult to get outsiders to put money into a closely held company: If the outsiders do not have voting control (more than 50% of the stock), then the inside stockholders/managers can take advantage of them. Going public, which brings with it both public disclosure

of information and regulation by the SEC, greatly reduces this problem and thus makes people more willing to invest in the company, which makes it easier for the firm to raise capital.

4. *Establishes a value for the firm.* If a company wants to give incentive stock options to key employees, it is useful to know the exact value of those options. Employees much prefer to own stock, or options on stock, that is publicly traded and therefore liquid. Also, when the owner of a privately owned business dies, state and federal tax appraisers must set a value on the company for estate tax purposes. Often these appraisers set a higher value than that of a similar publicly traded company.

5. *Facilitates merger negotiations.* Having an established market price helps when a company either is being acquired or is seeking to acquire another company in which the payment will be with stock.

6. *Increases potential markets.* Many companies report that it is easier to sell their products and services to potential customers after they become publicly traded.

18-2b Disadvantages of Going Public

The disadvantages associated with going public include the following:

1. *Increases reporting costs.* A publicly owned company must file quarterly and annual reports with the SEC and/or various state agencies. These reports can be a costly burden, especially for small firms. In addition, compliance with the Sarbanes-Oxley Act often requires considerable expense and manpower.

2. *Increases disclosure requirements.* Management may not like the idea of reporting operating data, because these data will then be available to competitors. Similarly, the owners of the company may not want people to know their net worth. But because a publicly owned company must disclose the number of shares its officers, directors, and major stockholders own, it is easy enough for anyone to multiply shares held by price per share to estimate the net worth of the insiders.

3. *Increases risk of having an inactive market and/or low price.* If the firm is very small and if its shares are not traded frequently, then its stock will not really be liquid and so the market price may not represent the stock's true value. Security analysts and stockbrokers simply will not follow the stock, because there will not be sufficient trading activity to generate enough brokerage commissions to cover the costs of following it.

4. *Reduces owner/manager control.* Because of possible tender offers and proxy fights, the managers of publicly owned firms who do not have voting control must be concerned about maintaining control. Further, there is pressure on such managers to produce annual earnings gains, even when it might be in the shareholders' best long-term interests to adopt a strategy that reduces short-term earnings but raises them in future years. These factors have led a number of public companies to "go private" in leveraged buyout deals, where the managers borrow the money to buy out the nonmanagement stockholders. We discuss the decision to go private in a later section.

5. *Increases time spent on investor relations.* Public companies must keep investors abreast of current developments. Many CFOs of newly public firms report that they spend 2 full days a week talking with investors and analysts.

What are the major advantages of going public?

What are the major disadvantages?

18-3 The Process of Going Public: An Initial Public Offering

An initial public offering is complicated, expensive, and time-consuming, as the following explains.

18-3a Selecting an Investment Bank

After a company decides to go public, it faces the problem of how to sell its stock to a large number of investors. Although most companies know how to sell their products, few have experience in selling securities. To help in this process, the company will interview a number of different **investment banks**, also called **underwriters**, and then select one to be the lead underwriter. To understand the factors that affect this choice, it helps to understand exactly what investment banks do in an IPO.

First, the investment bank helps the firm determine the preliminary offering price, or price range, for the stock and the number of shares to be sold. The investment bank's reputation and experience in the company's industry are critical in convincing potential investors to purchase the stock at the offering price. In effect, the investment bank implicitly certifies that the stock is not overpriced, which obviously comforts investors. Second, the investment bank actually sells the shares to its existing clients, which include a mix of institutional investors and retail (that is, individual) customers. Third, the investment bank, through its associated brokerage house, will have an analyst "cover" the stock after it is issued. This analyst will regularly distribute reports to investors describing the stock's prospects, which will help to maintain an interest in the stock. Well-respected analysts increase the likelihood that there will be a liquid secondary market for the stock and that its price will reflect the company's true value.

Some activities in finance involve as much marketing skill as finance expertise. For example, the selection of an underwriter often is described as a bake-off in which the competing investment banks woo the company with their best sales pitch, much like a cake-baking contest in which bakers vie for first prize.

Facebook chose Morgan Stanley to be its lead underwriter, but other investment banks were also involved, as we explain next.

18-3b The Underwriting Syndicate

The firm and its investment bank must next decide whether the bank will work on a **best efforts basis** or will **underwrite** the issue. In a best efforts sale, the bank does not guarantee that the securities will be sold or that the company will get the cash it needs, only that it will put forth its "best efforts" to sell the issue.

In contrast, in an underwritten issue, the company does get a guarantee: The bank agrees to buy the entire issue from the company at a set price per share. The investment bank will then try to sell the newly issued stock to investors. Notice that the company receives the cash it needs even if the investment bank is unable to sell the stock at a price that is high enough to be profitable. Hence, an underwritten offer shifts risk from the company to the investment bank. However, the company pays for this protection because the price per share that it receives from the investment banker is less than the price per share that the investment bank expects to receive when it sells the stock. The following sections explain IPO pricing in more detail.

Except for extremely small issues, virtually all IPOs are underwritten. Investors are required to pay for securities within 10 days, and the investment bank must pay the issuing firm within 4 days of the official commencement of the offering. Typically, the bank sells the stock within a day or two after the offering begins, but on occasion the bank miscalculates, sets the offering price too high, and thus is unable to move the issue. At other times, the market declines during the offering period, forcing the bank to reduce the price of the stock. In either instance, on an underwritten offering the firm receives the price that was agreed upon, so the bank must absorb any losses that are incurred.

Because they are exposed to large potential losses, investment banks typically do not handle the purchase and distribution of issues single-handedly unless the issue is very small. If the sum of money involved is large, then investment banks form **underwriting syndicates** in an effort to minimize the risk each individual bank faces. The banking house that sets up the deal is called the **lead underwriter** or the **managing underwriter**. Syndicated offerings are usually covered by more analysts, which contribute to greater liquidity in the post-IPO secondary market. Thus, syndication provides benefits to both underwriters and issuers.

In addition to the underwriting syndicate, on larger offerings still more investment banks are included in a **selling group**, which handles the distribution of securities to individual investors. The selling group includes all members of the underwriting syndicate plus additional dealers who take relatively small percentages of the total issue from the members of the underwriting syndicate. Thus, the underwriters act as wholesalers while members of the selling group act as retailers. The number of brokerage houses in a selling group depends partly on the size of the issue, but it is normally in the range of 10 to 15.

For example, the lead underwriter for Facebook's IPO was Morgan Stanley, and the sales syndicate included over 30 firms, including Goldman Sachs, Merrill Lynch, Barclays, Citigroup, Credit Suisse Securities, Deutsche Bank Securities, and Wells Fargo.

A new selling procedure has recently emerged that takes advantage of the trend toward institutional ownership of stock. In this type of sale, called an **unsyndicated offering**, the managing underwriter—acting alone—sells the issue entirely to a group of institutional investors, thus bypassing both retail stockbrokers and individual investors. In recent years, about 50% of all stock sold has been by unsyndicated offerings. Behind this phenomenon is a simple motivating force: money. The fees that issuers pay on a syndicated offering, which include commissions paid to retail brokers, can run a full percentage point higher than those on unsyndicated offerings. Moreover, although total fees are lower in unsyndicated offerings, managing underwriters usually come out ahead because they do not have to share the fees with an underwriting syndicate. However, some types of stock do not appeal to institutional investors, so not all firms can use unsyndicated offers.

18-3c Regulation of Securities Sales

WWW

The SEC Web site allows users to search for any filings by a company, including Form S-1. See www.sec.gov/edgar.shtml.

Sales of new securities, and also sales in the secondary markets, are regulated by the Securities and Exchange Commission and, to a lesser extent, by each of the 50 states. There are four primary elements of SEC regulation.

1. *Jurisdiction.* The SEC has jurisdiction over all **interstate public offerings** in amounts of $1.5 million or more.
2. *Registration.* Newly issued securities (stocks and bonds) must be registered with the SEC at least 20 days before they are publicly offered. The **registration statement**, called Form S-1, provides financial, legal, and technical information about the company to the SEC. A **prospectus**, which is embedded in the S-1, summarizes this information for investors. The SEC's lawyers and accountants analyze both the registration

statement and the prospectus; if the information is inadequate or misleading, the SEC will delay or stop the public offering.[2]

Among its disclosures, the S-1 document and subsequent amendments (S-1/A) show the proposed number of shares to be sold (including a breakdown between shares sold by the company and shares sold by current stockholders, including the founders and investors) and a range of possible offering prices (the prices at which the first investors may purchase the stock). For example, Facebook's S-1 filing on February 1, 2012, did not specify either the number of shares or price range, but its amended statement on May 3, 2012, stated that Facebook would offer 337 million shares (180 million from the company and 157 million shares from its current stockholders) at a price between $28 and $35 per share.

3. *Prospectus.* After the SEC declares the registration to be effective, new securities may be advertised, but all sales solicitations must be accompanied by the prospectus. The **preliminary prospectus**, which is also called a **red herring prospectus**, may be distributed to potential buyers during the 20-day waiting period after the registration is effective, but no sales may be finalized during this time. The "red herring" prospectus (so called because it has a standard legal disclaimer printed in red across its cover) contains all the key information that will appear in the final prospectus except the final price, which is generally set after the market closes the day before the new securities are offered to the public.

4. *Truth in reporting.* If the registration statement or prospectus contains misrepresentations or omissions of material facts, then any purchaser who suffers a loss may sue for damages. Severe penalties may be imposed on the issuer or its officers, directors, accountants, engineers, appraisers, underwriters, and all others who participated in the preparation of the registration statement or prospectus.

18-3d The Roadshow and Book-Building

After the registration statement has been filed, the senior management team, the investment banker, and the company's lawyers go on a **roadshow**. The management team will make three to seven presentations each day to potential institutional investors, who typically are existing clients of the underwriters. The institutional investors ask questions during the presentation, but the management team may not give any information that is not in the registration statement. Nor may the management team make any forecasts or express any opinions about the value of their company. These provisions are due to the SEC-mandated **quiet period**. This quiet period begins when the registration statement is made effective and lasts for 40 days after the stock begins trading. Its purpose is to create a level playing field for all investors by ensuring that they all have access to the same information. It is not uncommon for the SEC to delay an IPO if managers violate the quiet period rules. The typical roadshow may last 10 to 14 days, with stops in 10 to 20 different cities. In many ways the process resembles a coming-out party for the company, but it is more grueling and has much higher stakes.

After each presentation, the investment banker asks the investor for an indication of interest based on the offering price range shown in the registration statement. The

---

[2]It is easy to obtain the S-1 form, which typically has 50 to 200 pages of financial statements in addition to a detailed discussion of the firm's business, the risks and opportunities the firm faces, its principal stockholders and managers, what will be done with the funds raised, and the like. The company seeking to go public files the statement with the SEC, which makes it immediately available to investors via the Internet. The SEC staff reviews the filed S-1 and amendments may be issued (labeled S-1/A). The likely range for the offering price will be reported— for example, $13 to $15 per share. If the market strengthens or weakens during the SEC review, the price may be increased or decreased right up until the last day. The SEC Web site for these and other filings is **www.sec.gov**.

investment banker records the number of shares each investor is willing to buy, which is called **book-building**. As the roadshow progresses, an investment bank's "book" shows how demand for the offering is building. Many IPOs are **oversubscribed**, with investors wishing to purchase more shares than are available. In such a case, the investment bank will allocate shares to the investors on a pro rata basis.[3] If demand is high enough, the banks may increase the offering price; if demand is low, they will either reduce the offering price or withdraw the IPO. Sometimes low demand is specifically due to concern over the company's future prospects, but sometimes low demand is caused by a fall in the general stock market. Thus, the timing of the roadshow and offering date are important. As the old saying goes, sometimes it is better to be lucky than good.

18-3e Setting the Offer Price

Before trading can begin, a company must file a final amended registration statement showing the actual number of shares to be sold and the final price range. A company usually announces the actual **offer price** (P_{Offer}) the evening before the IPO. This is the price at which the investment banking syndicate seeks to sell shares to the buyers it lined up during the roadshow. The **gross proceeds** are equal to the offer price multiplied by the number of new shares issued (n_{New}):

$$\text{Gross proceeds} = P_{Offer}(n_{New}) \tag{18-1}$$

However, the company does not receive the gross proceeds because the investment bank collects a percentage of the gross proceeds as a fee. This percentage is called the **underwriting spread (F)**, or just the **spread**. In effect, it is the percentage of the offer price that the underwriter collects for each share of issued stock and often is set at 7%. Therefore, the company receives the **net proceeds**, the amount remaining after the investment bank deducts its fee. The resulting net proceeds are:

$$\begin{aligned}\text{Net proceeds} &= (\text{Gross proceeds})(1 - F) \\ &= P_{Offer}(n_{New})(1 - F)\end{aligned} \tag{18-2}$$

How do the company and its investment bankers set the offering price? It is simple in theory but complicated in practice, so we will start with theory. There are two situations: (1) A company knows how many shares it plans to sell. (2) It knows how much cash it needs to raise.

SETTING THE OFFER PRICE IF THE NUMBER OF NEW SHARES IS KNOWN

A company must decide how much ownership it wishes to sell to new investors, and this depends on the number of shares owned by the founder and previous investors, $n_{Existing}$, and the number of new shares purchased by new investors, n_{New}:

$$\text{Percentage shares owned by new investors} = \frac{n_{New}}{n_{New} + n_{Existing}} \tag{18-3}$$

---

[3]Most underwriting agreements contain an "overallotment option" that permits the underwriter to purchase additional shares from the company, up to 15% of the issue size, to cover promises made to potential buyers. This is called a "green shoe" agreement because it was first used in the 1963 underwriting of a company named Green Shoe.

Given the target percentage to be sold, Equation 18-3 can be solved for the required number of new shares to sell:

$$n_{New} = \frac{(\% \text{ owned by new investors})n_{Existing}}{1 - (\% \text{ owned by new investors})} \tag{18-4}$$

In order to determine the price to require for these new shares, the investment banker and the company must estimate the value of its equity prior to the IPO, $V_{Pre\text{-}IPO}$. Once this is done, you might think the price for the new shares should be the price per share for the existing shares, $V_{Pre\text{-}IPO}/n_{Existing}$. It isn't, though, because of the underwriting costs. To see this, note that the total value of equity after the IPO, $V_{Post\text{-}IPO}$, is the sum of the pre-IPO value and the net proceeds from the IPO:

$$V_{Post\text{-}IPO} = V_{Pre\text{-}IPO} + P_{Offer}(1 - F)n_{New} \tag{18-5}$$

The new investors will buy stock only if the value of their stake after the IPO is at least as big as what they pay for the shares. Their stake is equal to the post-IPO value of the company multiplied by the percentage of the company that they own; the amount they pay is equal to the offer price multiplied by the number of new shares. Applying this observation to Equations 18-4 and 18-5, and then using considerable algebra to solve for P_{Offer}, we get:

$$P_{Offer} = \left[\frac{V_{Pre\text{-}IPO}}{F(n_{New}) + n_{Existing}} \right] \tag{18-6}$$

Noting that underwriting costs are equal to $(P_{Offer})(n_{new})F$, and after even more algebra, we get a new formula for P_{Offer}:

$$P_{Offer} = \left[\frac{V_{Pre\text{-}IPO}}{n_{Existing}} \right] = \left[\frac{\text{Underwriting costs}}{n_{Existing}} \right] \tag{18-7}$$

In other words, the offer price is the pre-IPO price per share less the per share underwriting costs:

$$P_{Offer} = \text{Pre-IPO price per share} - \text{Underwriting fee per share} \tag{18-8}$$

Thus, the pre-IPO shareholders bear all the costs of the IPO, which is reflected in the offer price. If this were not the case, then the new shareholders would refuse to purchase the shares knowing that their value would decline because of the underwriting costs.

For example, Facebook's founders and early investors owned 1.96 billion shares before the IPO, and Facebook sold 0.18 billion new shares in the IPO. If the pre-IPO value of Facebook was $75 billion and if the investment bank's spread was 7%, the offer price should have been:

$$P_{Offer} = \left[\frac{\$75}{(0.07)(0.18) + 1.96} \right] = \$38.02$$

For many new companies without a track record of cash flows, the pre-IPO value is difficult to estimate. One way to get a handle on what a given offer price implies about $V_{Pre-IPO}$ is to use Equation 18-6 to solve for the pre-IPO value implied by the pricing. At Facebook's offer price of $38 per share and a 7% underwriting spread, Facebook's implied pre-IPO value would have been about $75 billion. After the investment banker's spread, Facebook's proceeds would have been about $38.02(1 − 0.07)(0.18 billion) = $6.4 billion. The new investors owned about 8.4% of Facebook: 0.18/(0.18 + 1.96) = 8.4%.[4]

SETTING THE OFFER PRICE IF THE TARGET NET PROCEEDS ARE KNOWN

How does a company set the offer price if it needs a certain amount of net proceeds? To determine the answer, look at the situation from the new investors' perspective. They will invest an amount equal to the gross proceeds: $P_{Offer}(n_{New})$. In return, they expect to own a percentage of the company's shares equal to the percentage of the company's value that they provide. The company's value immediately after the IPO will be equal to the pre-IPO value plus the gross proceeds minus the investment bank's underwriting fee, which is the pre-IPO value plus the net proceeds. Therefore, the percentage ownership required by new investors is:

$$\% \text{ shares required by new investors} = \frac{\text{Gross proceeds}}{\text{Net proceeds} + V_{Pre-IPO}} \qquad (18\text{-}9)$$

Solving Equation 18-2 for gross proceeds and substituting into Equation 18-9 gives:

$$\% \text{ shares required by new investors} = \frac{\text{Net proceeds}}{(1 - F)(\text{Net proceeds} + V_{Pre-IPO})} \qquad (18\text{-}10)$$

For example, suppose a company has a pre-IPO value of $50 million, has 2 million existing shares, needs $9.3 million in net proceeds, and the investment bank charges a 7% spread. Using Equation 18-10, the new investors will require a 16.86341% stake in the company:

$$\% \text{ shares required by new investors} = \frac{\$9.3}{(1 - 0.07)(\$9.3 + \$50)} = 16.86341\%$$

Equation 18-4 can be used to solve for the number of new shares:

$$n_{New} = \frac{(0.1686341)(2,000,000)}{(1 - 0.1686341)} = 405,680$$

Rather than using Equations 18-10 and 18-4 in combination, the number of new shares also can be calculated directly (after considerable algebra) by Equation 18-11:

$$n_{New} = \frac{(n_{Existing})(\text{Net proceeds})}{V_{Pre-IPO} - F(\text{Net proceeds} + V_{Pre-IPO})} \qquad (18\text{-}11)$$

---

[4]Although many offerings have an underwriting fee of 7%, high-profile or exceptionally large IPOs may have lower fees. Facebook sold its shares for $38.00 per share and received $37.582 for them. Solving $38(1 − F) = $37.582 gives F = 1.1%. When Google went public in 2004, the offer price was $85, and they received $82.6161 per share for an underwriting discount of 2.8%. Valvoline, on the other hand, issued its shares at $22 and received $20.845 for an F = 5.25%.

Substituting the values in this example into Equation 18-11, the number of new shares is:

$$n_{New} = \frac{(2 \text{ million})(\$9.3 \text{ million})}{\$50 \text{ million} - 0.07(\$9.3 \text{ million} + \$50 \text{ million})} = 405,680$$

The price per share is found by dividing the new shareholders' investment (which is equal to the gross proceeds) by the number of new shares:

$$P_{Offer} = \$10,000,000/405,680 = \$24.65$$

We can also find this price using Equation 18-8 by noting that the total underwriting costs in millions are (Gross proceeds)F = $10 (7%) = $0.7. Then subtract the underwriting costs per share ($0.7/2 = $0.35) from the per share pre-IPO price($50/2 = $25): $25.00 − $0.35 = $24.65.

CONFLICTS BETWEEN THE COMPANY AND THE INVESTMENT BANK

Although the pricing is simple in theory, there are big conflicts of interest in practice. The issuing company wants the offer price to be high because that will generate more cash in the IPO or reduce the number of shares that must be sold. However, the investment banker in an underwritten IPO is afraid of being stuck with overvalued stock if the offer price is too high. Although rare, some IPOs have been canceled at the last moment because the company and the underwriters could not reach an agreement.

18-3f The First Day of Trading

The first day of trading for many IPOs can be wild and exciting. For example, in 2017 Roku's stock increased by 68% on its first day of trading, but Allena Pharmaceuticals, Inc. was down by over 29%. Professor Jay Ritter of the University of Florida reported that the average first-day return in 2017 was about 12%, a bit lower than the 2000–2017 return of 13.9%.[5]

In one of the most famous IPOs of the recent past, Facebook broke even on the first day, May 18, 2012, and would have fallen if the underwriters had not created artificial demand by purchasing the falling shares. On the second day, Facebook fell by 11%. Facebook's amended filings in the week before its IPO may have contributed to its weak first-day performance. On May 15, 2012, Facebook filed an amended S-1/A increasing the range of prices from $28–$35 to $34–$38. On May 16, Facebook filed another amendment increasing by 84 million shares the amount to be sold by insiders. On May 17, Facebook announced that the offer price would be $38 per share, at the very top of the already higher range. Facebook's stock began trading the next day.

Many analysts were surprised by these increases in the offer price and the number of shares to be sold, especially the proportion of shares from insiders, which rose to 57% of the total sold in the IPO. To put this in perspective, Google's insiders represented about 28% of its IPO, but some insiders don't sell any of their shares in an IPO, like the insiders at Amazon in 1994. It is possible that this increase in supply and cost drove down demand for the stock.

The relation between the ranges in the initial and the final offer prices is an important indicator of first-day returns. During the period 2000–2017, higher-than-expected demand in the roadshows caused about 21% of IPOs to have a final offer price that exceeded the

---

[5]See Jay R. Ritter, **https://site.warrington.ufl.edu/ritter/ipo-data/** and select the first link for "IPO Statistics for 2017 and Earlier Years." The reported data are in Table 1.

top of the initial range.[6] On average, these stocks subsequently went up on the first day by about 37%! For the 35% of IPOs with an offer price below the bottom of the initial range, the average first-day return was about 3%. However, a large percentage of these actually had negative returns. About 44% of IPOs had an offering price within the initial range of the initial filing. For such companies, the average first-day return was about 11%.

You're probably asking yourself two questions. First, how can I get in on these deals? Second, why is the offering price so low on average? Unfortunately, you probably can't get the chance to buy an IPO at its offering price, especially not a "hot" one. Virtually all sales go to institutional investors and preferred retail customers. A few Web-based investment banks are trying to change this, such as the OpenIPO of W. R. Hambrecht & Co., but right now it is difficult for small investors to get in on the first day for hot IPOs.

Various theories have been put forth to explain IPO underpricing. As long as issuing companies don't complain, investment banks have strong incentives to underprice the issue. First, underpricing increases the likelihood of oversubscription, which reduces the risk to the underwriter. Second, most investors who get to purchase the IPO at its offering price are preferred customers of the investment bank, and they became preferred customers by generating lots of commissions in the investment bank's sister brokerage company. Therefore, the IPO is an easy way for the underwriter to reward customers for past and future commissions. Third, the underwriter needs an honest indication of interest when building the book prior to the offering, and underpricing is a possible way to secure this information from the institutional investors.

But why don't issuing companies object to underpricing? Some do, and they are seeking alternative ways to issue securities, such as OpenIPO. However, most seem content to leave some money on the table. The best explanations seem to be that: (1) The company wants to create excitement, and a price run-up on the first day does that. (2) Only a small percentage of the company's stock generally is offered to the public, so current stockholders lose less to underpricing than appears at first glance. (3) IPO companies generally plan to have additional offerings in the future, and the best way to ensure future success is to have a successful IPO, which underpricing guarantees.

Although IPOs on average provide large first-day returns, their long-term returns over the following 3 years are below average. For example, if you could not get in at the IPO price but purchased a portfolio of IPO stocks on their second day of trading, your 3-year return would have been lower than the return on a portfolio of similar but seasoned stocks. In summary, the offering price appears to be too low, but the first-day run-up is generally too high.

18-3g The Costs of Going Public

How much does it cost to go public? Suppose RipleyTech (RT) goes public by selling 5 million shares at an offer price of $20 per share. Investment banks usually charge a 7% spread between the price they pay the issuing company and the price at which they sell shares to the public, although it can be lower for very large IPOs. For RT, the underwriting spread is 7%, and the underwriting fee is $1.40 per share: $20(0.07) = $1.40. Therefore, RT receives only $18.60 per share: $20.00 − $1.40 = $18.60. In total, RT receives $93 million: $18.60(5 million) = $93 million. The total underwriting fee is $7 million: $1.40(5 million) = $7 million.

There are other direct costs as well, with fees for lawyers, external auditing, printing, engraving stock certificates, registration, and filing. For IPOs with gross proceeds less

---

[6]For the source of data in this paragraph, see the source cited in footnote 5. For information on the offer price relative to the range in the initial filing, see Table 7 in footnote 5's source.

than $50 million, the direct costs average over 7% of the gross proceeds.[7] For IPOs raising $50–$100 million, the direct costs are about 4.5% of the proceeds. For larger IPOs, the direct costs are between 1% and 2.5%. Assuming that RT's direct costs are similar to those of other firms its size, the direct costs are $4.5 million: 4.5%($100 million) = $4.5 million.

Last but not least are the indirect costs. First, there is the **money left on the table**, which is equal to the number of shares multiplied by the difference in the first-day closing price and the offering price (assuming the price goes up). During 2017, the average IPO left $34 million on the table, which is about 24% of the average proceeds of $141.[8]

RT's stock had a typical first-day return of 15% and was up at closing by $3: 15%($20) = $3. This suggests that the offer price could have been $23. With an offer price increased by $3, RT could have raised on additional $15 million: $3(5 million shares) = $15 million. In other words, RT left $15 million on the table because its offer price was too low.

In our example, the total of the underwriter fee, direct costs, and money left on the table is $26.5 million: $7 million + $4.5 million + $15 million = $26.5 million. In addition, senior managers spend an enormous amount of time working on the IPO rather than on managing the business, which certainly carries a high cost even if it cannot be easily measured. As you can see, an IPO is quite expensive.[9]

18-3h The Importance of the Secondary Market

An active secondary market after the IPO provides the pre-IPO shareholders with a chance to convert some of their wealth into cash, makes it easier for the company to raise additional capital later, makes employee stock options more attractive, and makes it easier for the company to use its stock to acquire other companies. Without an active secondary market, there would be little reason to have an IPO. Thus, companies should try to ensure that their stock will trade in an active secondary market before they incur the high costs of an IPO.

As part of the IPO process, the stock will be listed on a stock exchange, usually the NYSE or the NASDAQ. To be listed, a company must apply to an exchange, pay a relatively small fee, and meet the exchange's minimum requirements regarding net income, total market value, and "float," which is the number of shares outstanding and in the hands of outsiders (as opposed to the number held by insiders, who generally do not actively trade their stock).[10] Also, the company must agree to disclose certain information to the exchange and to help the exchange track trading patterns and thus ensure that no one is attempting to manipulate the stock's price.

As part of its IPO duties, the investment bank (or its parent company) usually agrees to make a market in a company's stock by holding an inventory of the shares and meeting

---

[7]These estimates are based on survey results in a PWC publication, "Considering an IPO? The Costs of Going and Being Public May Surprise You." See **https://www.strategyand.pwc.com/media/file/Strategyand _Considering-an-IPO.pdf.**

[8]For the source of data in this paragraph, see the source cited in footnote 5. For information on the money left on the table, see Table 1a in that source.

[9]For more on IPOs, see Roger G. Ibbotson, Jody L. Sindelar, and Jay R. Ritter, "The Market's Problems with the Pricing of Initial Public Offerings," *Journal of Applied Corporate Finance*, Spring 1994, pp. 66–74; Chris J. Muscarella and Michael R. Vetsuypens, "The Underpricing of 'Second' Initial Public Offerings," *Journal of Financial Research*, Fall 1989, pp. 183–192; Jay R. Ritter, "The Long-Run Performance of Initial Public Offerings," *Journal of Finance*, March 1991, pp. 3–27; and Jay R. Ritter, "Initial Public Offerings," *Contemporary Finance Digest*, Spring 1998, pp. 5–30.

[10]For additional discussion on the benefits of listing, see H. Kent Baker and Richard B. Edelman, "AMEX-to-NYSE Transfers, Market Microstructure, and Shareholder Wealth," *Financial Management*, Winter 1992, pp. 60–72; and Richard B. Edelman and H. Kent Baker, "Liquidity and Stock Exchange Listing," *The Financial Review*, May 1990, pp. 231–249.

demand in the secondary market by offering to buy or sell the stock. The diligence with which it carries out this task can have a huge effect on the stock's liquidity in the secondary market and thus on the success of the IPO.

18-3i Regulating the Secondary Market

As we stated earlier, a liquid and crime-free secondary market is critical to the success of an IPO or any other publicly traded security. So, in addition to regulating the process for issuing securities, the Securities Exchange Commission also has responsibilities in the secondary markets. The primary elements of SEC regulation are set forth next.

1. *Stock exchanges.* The SEC *regulates all national stock exchanges,* and companies whose securities are listed on an exchange must file annual reports similar to the registration statement with both the SEC and the exchange.
2. *Insider trading.* The SEC has control over trading by corporate *insiders.* Officers, directors, and major stockholders must file monthly reports of changes in their holdings of the stock of the corporation. Any short-term profits from such transactions must be turned over to the corporation.
3. *Market manipulation.* The SEC has the power to *prohibit manipulation* by such devices as pools (large amounts of money used to buy or sell stocks to artificially affect prices) or wash sales (sales between members of the same group to record artificial transaction prices).
4. *Proxy statements.* The SEC has *control over the proxy statement* and the way the company uses it to solicit votes.

Control over credit used to buy securities is exercised by the Federal Reserve Board through **margin requirements**, which specify the maximum percentage of the purchase price someone can borrow. If a great deal of margin borrowing has persisted, then a decline in stock prices can result in inadequate coverages. This could force stockbrokers to issue **margin calls**, which require investors either to put up more money or have their margined stock sold to pay off their loans. Such forced sales further depress the stock market and thus can set off a downward spiral. The required "initial margin" at the time a stock is purchased has been 50% since 1974; required "maintenance margin" after the initial purchase is lower than the initial margin and is set by the individual lender.

The securities industry itself realizes the importance of stable markets, sound brokerage firms, and the absence of stock manipulation.[11] Therefore, the various exchanges work closely with the SEC to police transactions and to maintain the integrity and credibility of the system. Similarly, the **Financial Industry Regulatory Authority (FINRA)** cooperates with the SEC to police trading and broker conduct. These industry groups also cooperate with regulatory authorities to set standards for securities firms, to develop insurance programs to protect the customers of failed brokerage houses, and to provide resolution of complaints made by investors regarding brokers.

In general, government regulation of securities trading, as well as industry self-regulation, is designed to ensure that: (1) Investors receive information that is as accurate as possible. (2) No one artificially manipulates the market price of a given stock. (3) Corporate insiders do not take advantage of their position to profit in their companies' stocks at the

---

[11]It is illegal for anyone to attempt to manipulate the price of a stock. During the 1920s and earlier, syndicates would buy and sell stocks back and forth at rigged prices so the public would believe that a particular stock was worth more or less than its true value. The stock exchanges, with the encouragement and support of the SEC, utilize sophisticated computer programs to help spot any irregularities that suggest manipulation, and they require disclosures to help identify manipulators. This system also helps to identify illegal insider trading. It is now illegal to manipulate a stock's price by spreading false news on the Internet.

expense of other stockholders. The SEC, the state regulators, and the industry itself can't prevent investors from making foolish decisions or from having "bad luck," but they can and do help investors obtain the best data possible for making sound investment decisions.

18-3j Questionable IPO Practices

Among the many revelations to come out during 2002 regarding investment banking was the practice by some investment banking houses of letting CEOs and other high-ranking corporate executives in on "hot" IPOs. In these deals, the demand for the new stock was far greater than supply at the offering price, so the investment banks were virtually certain that the stock would soar far above the offering price.

Some investment banks systematically allocated shares of hot IPOs to executives of companies that were issuing stocks and bonds—and thus generating fees to the banks who underwrote the deals. Bernie Ebbers, the chairman and CEO of WorldCom—one of the biggest sources of underwriting fees for investment banks—was given huge allocations in hot IPOs, and he made millions on these deals. Ebbers is just one example; a lot of this was going on in the late 1990s, at the height of the tech/dot-com bubble.

Government regulators investigated this practice, called "spinning," and corporate executives and investment bankers were charged with something that amounts to a kick-back scheme under which those executives who favored particular investment banks were rewarded with allocations in hot IPOs. Indeed, in 2003 ten Wall Street securities firms agreed to pay $1.4 billion in fines to settle charges of investor abuse, including spinning. The corporate executives were paid to work for their stockholders, so they should have turned over any IPO profits to their companies—not kept those profits for themselves. This practice was found to be a form of bribery by the New York Supreme Court and was ruled to be illegal in 2006.

This kind of unethical and illegal behavior may help to explain past IPO underpricing and money left on the table if executives allowed their IPOs to be underpriced in exchange for allocations of similarly underpriced shares in other IPOs. Whether or not similar activities take place now remains to be seen.

In summary, we have a hard time justifying IPO underpricing during the late 1990s on rational economic grounds. Researchers and analysts have come up with explanations for why companies let their investment banks price their stocks too low in IPOs, but those reasons seem rather weak. However, when coupled with what may have been a kickback scheme, the underpricing is less puzzling (but still ethically troubling). Before closing, we should make it clear that relatively few corporate executives were corrupt. However, just as one rotten apple can spoil an entire barrel, a few bad executives—when combined with lax regulation—can help a bad practice become "the industry standard," and thus become widespread.

SELF-TEST

What is the difference between best efforts and underwriting?

What are some SEC regulations regarding sales of new securities?

What is a roadshow? What is book-building?

What is underpricing? What is leaving money on the table?

What are some of the costs of going public?

A privately held company has an estimated value of equity equal to $100 million. The founders own 10 million shares. If the company goes public and sells 1 million shares with no underwriting costs, how much should the per share offer price be? **($10.00)** *If instead the underwriting spread is 7%, what should the offer price be?* **($9.93)**

A company is planning an IPO. Its underwriters have said the stock will sell at $50 per share. The underwriters will charge a 7% spread. How many shares must the company sell to net $93 million, ignoring any other expenses? (**2 million**)

18-4 Equity Carve-Outs: A Special Type of IPO

In 2016, Ashland sold to the public about 15% of the equity in its Valvoline subsidiary. In this transaction, the subsidiary, like the parent, became publicly owned, but the parent retained full control of the subsidiary by keeping about 85% of the subsidiary's common stock. (Parent companies typically retain at least 80% of the subsidiary's common stock to preserve their ability to file a consolidated tax return.) This type of transaction is called an **equity carve-out** (or **partial public offering**, or **spin-out**).[12] The market's response to Valvoline's carve-out was neutral—the stock price remained flat the first week of trading. The announcement (as opposed to the completion) of a carve-out, however, is typically associated with a stock price increase for the parent company. This leads to an interesting question: Why do carve-out announcements typically result in stock price increases while the announcements of new stock issues by parent corporations generally decrease stock prices?

One possible answer is that carve-outs facilitate the evaluation of corporate growth opportunities on a line-of-business basis. Thus, analysts might have an easier time evaluating Valvoline as a separate company than when it was a part of Ashland. This also applies to providers of capital—Valvoline might be able to raise capital more effectively as a stand-alone company because investors are better able to evaluate its prospects. A third advantage to carve-outs is that they improve the ability of the parent to offer incentives to a subsidiary's managers. Thus, Valvoline can now offer equity incentives to its managers based on its own stock price rather than that of Ashland.

Equity carve-outs do have some associated costs. First, the underwriting commission involved in a carve-out is larger than for an equity offering by the parent. Second, because an equity carve-out is a type of initial public offering, there is a potential for underpricing the new offering. Third, key managers of the subsidiary must spend a significant amount of time marketing the new stock. Fourth, there are costs associated with the minority interest that is created in the carve-out. For example, the subsidiary's new board of directors must monitor all transactions between the subsidiary and the parent to ensure that the minority investors are not being exploited. Finally, there are additional costs such as annual reports, SEC filings, analyst presentations, and so on, which now must be borne both by parent and subsidiary.

SELF-TEST

Explain what is meant by an equity carve-out.

On average, equity carve-outs have increased shareholder wealth. What are some potential explanations for this phenomenon?

18-5 Other Ways to Raise Funds in the Capital Markets

IPOs are exciting and play a vital role in stimulating the entrepreneurship and innovation that are vital for economic growth. However, the funds raised through IPOs are only a small fraction of the total funding raised from commercial banks and capital markets. In

---

[12]For more information on equity carve-outs, see Roni Michaely and Wayne H. Shaw, "The Choice of Going Public: Spin-offs vs. Carve-outs," *Financial Management*, Autumn 1995, pp. 5–21; and Anand Vijh, "Long-Term Returns from Equity Carve-outs," *Journal of Financial Economics*, Vol. 51, 1999, pp. 273–308.

2017, U.S. companies raised over $1,600 billion in bonds and $200 billion in equity.[13] Of this $1,800 billion total debt and equity, only 2% was raised in IPOs. Therefore, it is important to understand other ways that firms raise cash from capital markets.[14]

18-5a Preliminary Decisions

Before raising capital, a firm must make some initial, preliminary decisions, which include the following:

1. *Dollars to be raised.* How much new capital is needed?
2. *Type of securities used.* Should common stock, preferred stock, bonds, hybrid securities, or a combination be used? Should the capital be public securities (which are registered and may be traded freely in the secondary markets) or should it be a private placement that might have restrictions on its subsequent trading? If common stock is to be issued, should it be done as a preemptive rights offering to current shareholders or by a direct sale to the general public?
3. *Competitive bid versus a negotiated deal.* Should the company simply offer a block of its securities for sale to the highest bidder, or should it negotiate a deal with an investment bank? These two procedures are called **competitive bids** and **negotiated deals**, respectively. Only about 100 of the largest firms listed on the NYSE, whose securities are already well known to the investment banking community, are in a position to use the competitive bidding process. The investment banks must do a great deal of investigative work ("due diligence") to bid on an issue unless they are already quite familiar with the firm, and such costs would be too high to make it worthwhile unless the bank was sure of getting the deal. Therefore, except for the largest firms, offerings of stock and bonds are generally on a negotiated basis. The exceptions are utilities, which are able to issue debt through competitive bids because the offerings are relatively easy for the investment banks to value and sell to clients.
4. *Selection of an investment bank.* Most deals are negotiated, so the firm must select an investment bank. This can be an important decision for a firm that is going public. On the other hand, an older firm that has already "been to market" will have an established relationship with an investment bank. However, it is easy to change banks if the firm is dissatisfied. Different investment banking houses are better suited for different companies. For example, Goldman Sachs and Morgan Stanley are the leading tech-IPO underwriters. Investment banking houses sell new issues largely to their own regular brokerage customers, so the nature of these customers has a major effect on the ability of the house to do a good job for corporate issuers. Finally, a major factor in choosing an underwriter is the reputation of the analyst who will cover the stock in the secondary market, because a strong buy recommendation from a well-respected analyst can trigger a sharp price run-up.

18-5b Seasoned Equity Offerings

When a company with publicly traded stock issues additional shares, this is called a **seasoned equity offering**, also known as a *secondary* or *follow-on offering*. Because the stock is already publicly traded, the offering price will be based upon the existing market

---

[13]See the Securities Industry and Financial Markets Association (SIFMA) Web site's research and statistics for these and other interesting data: **www.sifma.org/research**.

[14]For an excellent discussion of the various procedures used to raise capital, see Jay R. Ritter, "Investment Banking and Securities Issuance," in *North-Holland Handbook of the Economics of Finance*, George Constantinides, Milton Harris, and René Stulz, eds. (Amsterdam: North-Holland, 2002). Also see Claudio Loderer, John W. Cooney, and Leonard D. Van Drunen, "The Price Elasticity of Demand for Common Stock," *Journal of Finance*, June 1991, pp. 621–651.

price of the stock. Typically, the investment bank buys the securities at a prescribed number of points below the closing price on the last day of registration. For example, suppose that in August 2019 the stock of Microwave Telecommunications Inc. (MTI) had a price of $28.60 per share and that the stock had traded between $25 and $30 per share during the previous 3 months. Suppose further that MTI and its underwriter agreed that the investment bank would buy 10 million new shares at $1 per share below the closing price on the last day of registration. If the stock closed at $25 on the day the SEC released the issue, then MTI would receive $24 per share. Typically, such agreements have an escape clause that provides for the contract to be voided if the price of the securities drops below some predetermined figure. In the illustrative case, this "upset" price might be set at $24 per share. Thus, if the closing price of the shares on the last day of registration had been $23.50, MTI would have had the option of withdrawing from the agreement.

The investment bank will have an easier job if the issue is priced relatively low. However, the issuer naturally wants as high a price as possible. A conflict of interest on price therefore arises between the investment bank and the issuer. If the issuer is financially sophisticated and makes comparisons with similar security issues, the investment bank will be forced to price close to the market.

As we discussed in Chapter 15, the announcement of a new stock offering by a mature firm is often taken as a negative signal—if the firm's prospects were good, management would not want to issue new stock and thus share the rosy future with new stockholders. Therefore, the announcement of a new offering is taken as bad news. Consequently, the price will probably fall when the announcement is made, so the offering price will probably have to be set at a price below the pre-announcement market price.

One final point is that *if negative signaling effects drive down the price of the stock, then all shares outstanding, not just the new shares, are affected.* Thus, if MTI's stock should fall from $28.60 to $25 per share as a result of the financing and remains at the new level, then the company's shareholders would incur a loss of $3.60 on each of the 50 million shares previously outstanding, or a total market value loss of $180 million. This loss, like underwriting expenses, is a flotation cost, and it should be considered as a cost associated with the stock issue. Of course, if the company's prospects really were poorer than investors thought, then the price decline would have occurred sooner or later anyway. On the other hand, if the company's prospects are really not all that bad (the signal was incorrect), then over time MTI's price should move back to its previous level. Yet even if the price does revert to its former level, there will have been a transfer of wealth from the original shareholders to the new shareholders.

resource

See *Web Extension 18A* on the textbook's Web site for a discussion of rights offerings.

To prevent dilution due to a regular seasoned equity offering, companies occasionally sell additional shares of stock through a **rights offering** (also called a **preemptive rights offering**). The issuing company gives the owner of each share of outstanding stock a "right," which is similar to a stock option: Each right's holder has the option to purchase a specified number of new shares of the company's stock at a specified purchase price on a certain date. The purchase price usually is very low relative to the current stock price, so the rights are valuable and will be exercised. The rights usually are transferable, so a shareholder can sell the right if she so chooses. This allows each shareholder the opportunity to maintain a proportional ownership stake in the company, but it also gives each shareholder a chance to receive cash from selling the right if the shareholder doesn't want to maintain a proportional ownership. See *Web Extension 18A* for more details and numerical examples.

18-5c Shelf Registrations

The selling procedures described so far, including the 20-day waiting period after registration with the SEC, apply to most security sales. However, under the SEC's Rule 415, large, well-known public companies that issue securities frequently may file a master registration statement with the SEC and then update it with a short-form statement just prior to each individual offering. Under this procedure, a company can decide at 10 a.m. to sell securities and have the sale completed before noon. This procedure is known as **shelf registration** because, in effect, the company puts its new securities "on the shelf" and then sells them to investors when it feels the market is "right." Firms with less than $150 million in stock held by outside investors cannot use shelf registrations. The rationale for this distinction is to protect investors who may not be able to obtain adequate financial data about a little-known company in the short time between announcement of a shelf issue and its sale. Shelf registrations have two advantages over standard registrations: (1) lower flotation costs and (2) more control over the timing of the issue.[15]

18-5d Private Placements

Private placements are a very important source of financing. In fact, U.S. companies raise more equity through private placements than through public placements.[16]

The 1933 Securities Act regulates the issuance and subsequent trading of securities. Public offerings must be registered with the SEC, but several exemptions allow companies meeting certain conditions to issue unregistered securities in a process called a private placement. In particular, **Regulation D** is a provision in the Code of Federal Regulations that permits the sale of securities to accredited investors but places restrictions on the subsequent trading of those securities.[17] The basic idea behind Reg D, as it is commonly called, is to enable companies to raise new capital quickly and with lower flotation costs. It also allows smaller companies greater access to the capital markets. Reg D can be used to issue equity or debt and can be used by companies with registered stock.

The following sections describe several different types of private placements.

PRIVATE PLACEMENTS OF EQUITY

Sometimes a privately held firm makes a private placement of equity. For example, Facebook placed $1 billion of common stock with non-U.S. investors in 2011. At other times it is a public company making a private placement. For example, Enbridge, Inc. is a Canadian company that provides energy infrastructure, especially oil pipelines. In late 2017, Enbridge raised 1.5 billion Canadian dollars (about $1 billion U.S. dollars) of equity by selling stock directly to a consortium of investors. Because Enbridge is a publicly held company, this is called a **private investment in public equity (PIPE)**. The most common type of private placement occurs when a company places securities directly with a financial institution, often an insurance company or a pension fund.

Many large companies make equity investments in suppliers or in start-up companies that are developing a related technology. For example, Microsoft's 2017 annual report showed $5.5 billion of investments in the common and preferred stock of other companies.

---

[15]In 2005, the SEC began allowing very large firms, known as "well known seasoned issuers" or WKSIs, even greater flexibility in selling shelf-registered shares. WKSIs may now bypass SEC review and automatically shelf-register an unspecified number of securities to sell at times of their choosing. This speeds up even more the process for these large issuers. For more on shelf registrations, see David J. Denis, "The Costs of Equity Issues since Rule 415: A Closer Look," *Journal of Financial Research,* Spring 1993, pp. 77–88.

[16]See a special SEC report by Scott Bauguess, Rachita Gullapalli, and Vladamir Ivanov, "Capital Raising in the U.S.: An Analysis of the Market for Unregistered Securities Offerings, 2009–2014," October 2015, **https://www.sec.gov/files/unregistered-offering10-2015.pdf**.

[17]See CFR Title 17 Chapter II Part 230 Section 230.501. In addition, Regulation S allows U.S. companies to sell unregistered securities abroad, and Section 4(2) allows the sale of unregistered securities if the purchaser is knowledgeable and agrees not to resell them to the public.

PRIVATE PLACEMENTS OF DEBT

Before 1990, debt could be issued privately (without SEC registration), but the purchasers faced restrictions on their abilities to resell the debt. This changed in 1990 with SEC Rule 144A, which allows qualified institutional buyers to trade unregistered securities among themselves. This opened the door for non-U.S. companies to raise capital in the states. In addition, subsequent amendments permit Rule 144A securities to be registered shortly after they have been issued, providing companies a quicker way to issue debt that ultimately will trade in public markets. The increased liquidity has made private placement of debt the preferred choice, with the majority of debt being placed privately rather than being issued publicly.

18-5e Securitization

In Chapter 1, we discussed securitization in the context of mortgage markets, and now we discuss it in the context of capital formation. As the term is generally used, a **financial security** refers to a publicly traded financial instrument as opposed to a privately placed instrument. Thus, securities have greater liquidity than otherwise similar instruments that are not traded in an open market. The process of creating a financial security is called **securitization**.

Securitization occurs in two ways. First, a debt instrument that formerly was rarely traded becomes actively traded, usually because the size of the market increases and the terms of the debt instrument become more standardized. For example, this has occurred with commercial paper and junk bonds, both of which are now considered to be securities.

Second, a security can be created by the pledging of specific assets, resulting in the creation of **asset-backed securities**. The oldest type of asset securitization was in the mortgage industry, as we described in Chapter 1. Today, many different types of assets are used as collateral, including auto loans and credit card balances.

The asset securitization process involves the pooling and repackaging of loans secured by relatively homogeneous, small-dollar assets (such as an automobile) into liquid securities. Usually several different financial institutions are involved, with each playing a different functional role. For example, an auto dealer might sell a car, the auto manufacturer's lending operation might originate the loan, an investment bank might pool similar car loans and structure the security, a federal agency might insure against credit risk, a second investment bank might sell the securities, and a pension fund might supply the final capital.

A similar process can occur with equipment or cell-tower leases, student loans, or more exotic assets like Miramax's 2011 sale of $550 million of bonds backed by revenues from its library of films, including *Pulp Fiction* and *Good Will Hunting*.[18]

The process of securitization lowers costs and increases the availability of funds to borrowers, with the risk being transferred to the investor. But as we described in Chapter 1, if loans are originated to borrowers with poor credit risk, then the cash flows received by the ultimate investor are likely to be low.

18-5f Syndicated Loans

Large corporations (or even countries) often borrow substantial amounts via **syndicated loans**, in which a group of financial institutions act jointly to fund the loan. The syndicate is created by one or more banks, investment banks, or other financial institutions acting

---

[18]See Liz Moyer and Al Yoon, "Jury Out on Uma-Backed Securities," **www.wsj.com/articles/SB100014240529 70204517204577046381261300406,** November 19, 2011.

as **lead arrangers**. The lead arranger provides some funding for the syndicated loan, but other lenders also join the syndicate and provide additional funds.

There are several advantages for both the borrower and the lenders. First, the amount of the loan might be too much for a single lender. Second, the risk is spread across multiple lenders rather than being borne by a single lender. Third, the original lenders can sell their portions of the syndicated loans later if the need arises. For the borrower, the fees paid to the arrangers are lower than those incurred by alternative methods of raising the same amount.

18-5g Project Financing

Historically, many large projects, such as the Alaska pipeline, have been financed by what is called **project financing**, and investment banks often help put these deals together.[19] Project financing has been used to finance energy explorations, oil tankers, refineries, and electric generating plants. Generally, one or more firms will sponsor the project, putting up the required equity capital, while the remainder of the financing is furnished by lenders or lessors. Most often, a separate legal entity is formed to operate the project. Normally, the project's creditors do not have full recourse against the sponsors. In other words, the lenders and lessors must be paid from the project's cash flows and from the sponsors' equity in the project because the creditors have no claims against the sponsors' other assets or cash flows. Often the sponsors write "comfort" letters, giving general assurances that they will strive diligently to make the project successful. However, these letters are not legally binding, so in project financing the lenders and lessors must focus their analysis on the inherent merits of the project and on the equity cushion provided by the sponsors.[20]

Project financing is not a new development. Indeed, back in 1299 the English Crown negotiated a loan with Florentine merchant banks that was to be repaid with 1 year's output from the Devon silver mines. Essentially, the Italians were allowed to operate the mines for 1 year, paying all the operating costs and mining as much ore as they could. The Crown made no guarantees as to how much ore could be mined or the value of the refined silver.

A more recent example is the 2017 project financing for 271,500 solar panels near Fayetteville, North Carolina. Prudential Capital Group and a division of U.S. Bank provided the financing for Canadian Solar, Inc. to build the facility. In fact, about half of all project financings in recent years have been for electric generating plants, including plants owned by electric utilities and cogeneration plants operated by industrial companies. Project financings are generally characterized by large size and a high degree of complexity. However, because project financing is tied to a specific project, it can be tailored to meet the specific needs of both the creditors and the sponsors. In particular, the financing can be structured so that both the funds provided during the construction phase and the subsequent repayments match the timing of the project's projected cash outflows and inflows.

---

[19]For an excellent discussion of project financing, see Benjamin C. Esty, "Petrozuata: A Case Study on the Effective Use of Project Finance," *Journal of Applied Corporate Finance*, Fall 1999, pp. 26–42.

[20]In another type of project financing, each sponsor guarantees its share of the project's debt obligations. Here the creditors also consider the creditworthiness of the sponsors in addition to the project's own prospects. It should be noted that project financing with multiple sponsors in the electric utility industry has led to problems when one or more of the sponsors has landed in financial trouble. For example, Long Island Lighting, one of the sponsors in the Nine Mile Point nuclear project, became unable to meet its commitments to the project, which forced other sponsors to shoulder an additional burden or else see the project canceled and lose all their investment up to that point. The risk of such default makes many companies reluctant to enter into such projects.

Project financing offers several potential benefits over conventional debt financing. For one, project financing usually restricts the use of the project's cash flows, which means that the lenders—rather than the managers—can decide whether excess cash flows should be reinvested or instead used to reduce the loan balance by more than the minimum required. Conferring this power on the lenders reduces their risks. Project financings also have advantages for borrowers. First, because risks to the lenders are reduced, the interest rate built into a project financing deal may be relatively low. Second, because suppliers of project financing capital have no recourse against the sponsoring firms' other assets and cash flows, project financings insulate the firms' other assets from risks associated with the project being financed. Managers may be more willing to take on a large, risky project if they know that the company's existence would not be threatened if it fails.

Project financings increase the number and type of investment opportunities; hence, they make capital markets "more complete." At the same time, project financings reduce the costs to investors of obtaining information and monitoring the borrower's operations. To illustrate, consider an oil and gas exploration project that is funded using project financing. If the project were financed as an integral part of the firm's normal operations, investors in all the firm's outstanding securities would need information on the project. By isolating the project, the need for information is confined to the investors in the project financing, who need to monitor only the project's operations and not those of the entire firm.

Project financings also permit firms whose earnings are below the minimum requirements specified in their existing bond indentures to obtain additional debt financing. In such situations, lenders look only at the merits of the new project, and its cash flows may support additional debt even though the firm's overall situation does not. Project financings also permit managers to reveal proprietary information to a smaller group of investors, so project financings increase the ability of a firm to maintain confidentiality. Finally, project financings can improve incentives for key managers by enabling them to take direct ownership stakes in the operations under their control. By establishing separate projects, companies can provide incentives that are much more directly based on individual performance than is typically possible within a large corporation.

SELF-TEST

What is the difference between a competitive bid and a negotiated deal?

What is a private placement?

What is shelf registration?

What is Reg D?

What is securitization? What are its advantages to borrowers? What are its advantages to lenders?

What is a syndicated loan? What are its advantages and disadvantages?

What is project financing? What are its advantages and disadvantages?

18-6 Investment Banking Activities

Investment banks underwrite IPOs, underwrite seasoned equity offerings, and manage debt offerings. In other words, investment banks help firms raise capital, and lots of it: Table 18-1 shows that investment banks helped firms raise over *$7 trillion* during 2017. Investment banks also engage in other activities. Because of increasingly relaxed regulations that culminated with the repeal of the Glass-Steagall Act in 1999, there is no longer a clear delineation between investment banks, brokerage firms, and commercial banks. In the following sections, we discuss activities that are primarily associated with the investment banking arm of the financial conglomerates.

TABLE 18-1
Top Five Underwriters of Global Debt and Equity in 2017

Manager	Proceeds (Billions)
Citi	$ 399
JP Morgan	394
Bank of America Merrill Lynch	341
Goldman Sachs	280
Morgan Stanley	279
Industry total	$7,599

Source: See **www.hitc.com/en-gb/2018/01/03/equity-capital-markets-review-2017-thomson-reuters/**.

18-6a Mergers and Acquisitions

Many investment banks are actively involved in mergers and acquisitions (M&As) through three activities.

1. *Matchmaking.* Investment banks often find potential targets for acquirers, sometimes earning a finder's fee if the deal is successful.
2. *Advising.* Both the target and acquirer must document that the deal is "fair" for their stockholders by performing a due diligence valuation analysis. Investment banks often provide consulting advice during this stage of the M&A.
3. *Underwriting.* Most M&As require that new capital be raised. Investment banks underwrite these new issues.

Underwriting is the most lucrative of these activities, but if the deal falls through, then no new securities will be underwritten. This makes one wonder how unbiased investment bankers are when finding targets and providing advice during negotiations.

18-6b Securitization

Investment banks often provide advice to financial institutions regarding the securitization of the institutions' loans or leases. In fact, investment banks frequently provide turnkey service by purchasing an institution's loans, securitizing the loans, and selling the newly created securities. Thus, the investment bank becomes the securitizer, not just the advisor. During the build-up to the 2007 global economic crisis, many investment banks were unable to sell all the mortgage-backed securities they created and were left holding some of them in their own portfolios. When the original borrowers began defaulting, the values of these securities owned by the investment banks plummeted, contributing to the downfall of Bear Stearns, Lehman Brothers, and Merrill Lynch.

18-6c Asset Management

Many investment banking companies create investment funds, such as a limited partnership (LP) that might invest in real estate in developing nations or an LP that might seek to exploit mispricing in various asset classes. In other words, they run their own hedge funds, which can be quite lucrative. Like any other hedge fund, they raise capital for these funds from a variety of sources. But unlike other hedge funds, investment banks often have access to a special source—their own clients!

Here is how that works. Many investment banks have "wealth management" divisions or subsidiaries that provide investment advice to wealthy individuals or institutions such as pension funds. As advisors, they recommend investment strategies, including specific investments, to their clients. Some of these investments might be individual securities or mutual funds managed by other organizations. However, some of the recommended investments might be funds managed by the advisor's own investment bank. These might be great investments, but there is at least the appearance of a conflict of interest when advisors recommend funds managed by their own company.

In addition to managing clients' money, investment banks also invest their own money (actually, the money of their own stockholders and creditors) in financial securities. Sometimes the choice of investment is intentional, but sometimes it is not—as we mentioned previously, some investment banks were unable to sell all the mortgage-backed securities they created and were left holding some in their own portfolios.

18-6d Trading Operations

Many investment banking companies have trading operations through which they actively trade on the behalf of clients. For example, a client might need help in selling a large block of debt. Also, investment banking companies usually make a market in the stock of companies that they took public. Thus, these activities can be viewed as services provided to clients.

However, many investment banks also view their trading operations as profit centers. In other words, the traders try to buy low and sell high, and in the process they sometimes accumulate large positions that become difficult to unload.

What Was the Role of Investment Banks?

There is plenty of blame to spread around for the cause of the 2007 global economic crisis, but investment banks certainly played a special role.

Among their many strategic errors, investment banks morphed from organizations that earned money primarily through fee-generating activities into organizations that earned money as highly leveraged investors. Investing is an inherently risky business, especially when the investments include extremely complicated mortgage-backed securities and credit default swaps. Investing becomes even riskier when you borrow $33 for every $1 of equity, as many investment banks did. This strategy is great if you earn more than you owe on your debt because leverage magnifies returns, and these magnified returns generated gigantic bonuses for senior managers at the investment banks. But it doesn't take too much of a decline in asset values and investment income to cause failure. In essence, the investment bankers were willing to risk it all for the chance of mind-boggling bonuses.

In addition to selling toxic investments (such as complex mortgage-backed securities) to pension funds and other financial institutions, the interconnectedness of failing investment banks threatened the entire world economy. Lehman Brothers had been borrowing short term in the commercial paper market and investing long term in risky assets. When those assets failed, Lehman defaulted on its commercial

paper obligations, many of which were owned by money market funds. This caused some funds, like the large Primary Reserve Fund, to "break the buck," which means that their reported net asset value dropped below $1, something that investors never expected. This led to a run on many money market funds and a huge disruption in the financial commercial paper markets.

Investment banks also were major players in the market for credit default swaps (CDS). If investment banks defaulted on their CDS, then it would cause potentially bankrupting financial distress at many other financial institutions.

Because many investment banks are subsidiaries of bank holding companies, the failure of the investment banks threatened the viability of the holding company and its other subsidiaries, such as commercial banks, which began limiting the credit they provided to their borrowers. In short, the financial crisis spread to the nonfinancial sector as financial institutions began cutting back on the credit they provided to the nonfinancial sector.

The investment banking landscape has certainly changed during the global economic crisis. Bear Stearns was acquired by JP Morgan, Lehman Brothers went bankrupt and was sold piecemeal, Merrill Lynch was acquired by Bank of America, and several investment banks, including Goldman Sachs, rechartered themselves as banks to qualify for TARP funds.

What are some investment banking activities?

18-7 The Decision to Go Private

In a **going private** transaction, the entire equity of a publicly held firm is purchased by a small group of investors, with the firm's current senior management usually maintaining or increasing their ownership stakes. The outside investors typically place directors on the now-private firm's board and arrange for the financing needed to purchase the publicly held stock. When the financing involves substantial borrowing, as it usually does, it is known as a **leveraged buyout (LBO)**. In some cases, the current management group raises the financing and acquires all of the equity of the company; these are called management buyouts (MBOs).

The outside equity in a buyout often comes from a **private equity (PE) fund**, which is a limited liability partnership created to own and manage investments in nontraded equity. Private equity funds raise money from wealthy investors and institutions such as university endowments, pension funds, and insurance companies. The PE funds then take public firms private or invest in firms that already are privately held. Most PE funds plan on improving the companies' performance and then harvesting their investments by selling the company, perhaps in an IPO.[21]

Regardless of the deal's structure, going private initially affects the right-hand side of the balance sheet, the liabilities and capital, and not the assets: Going private simply rearranges the ownership structure. Thus, going private involves no obvious operating economies, yet the new owners are generally willing to pay a large premium over the stock's current price in order to take the firm private.

For example, in 2006 HCA Inc., a large health care corporation, was taken private by the original family owners, the Frists, and a group of private equity firms and investment banks, including Bain Capital and Kohlberg Kravis Roberts & Co. (KKR), for $51 per share. The stock price had been in the low $40s the month prior to the announcement. The investors put up about $4.9 billion in equity and borrowed about $28 billion to fund the purchase of equity and refinance some of the company's debt.

It is hard to believe that these sophisticated investors and managers would knowingly pay too much for the firm. Thus, the investors and managers must have regarded the firm as being grossly undervalued, even at $51 per share, or else thought that they could significantly boost the firm's value under private ownership.

Indeed, after 4 years as a private company HCA went public again in 2011. The owners received $4.3 billion in dividends during 2010 and an additional $1.1 billion in cash from shares they sold in the IPO, almost completely recovering their initial investment. After the IPO, the stock was worth about $16 billion, with about 25% of the company in public hands and 75% (about $12 billion) remaining with the private equity fund. Although the total return the investors ultimately earn depends on how much they receive for the shares they still hold in the company, the $4.9 billion investment has currently reaped cash and stock worth some $16 billion. Not a bad return for a 4-year investment!

This suggests that going private can increase the value of some firms sufficiently to enrich both managers and public stockholders. Other large companies going private

---

[21]For more information on private equity, see Steve Kaplan, "Private Equity: Past, Present, and Future," *Journal of Applied Corporate Finance,* Summer 2007, pp. 8–16; "Morgan Stanley Roundtable on Private Equity and Its Import for Public Companies," *Journal of Applied Corporate Finance,* Summer 2006, pp. 8–37; and Stephen D. Prowse, "The Economics of the Private Equity Market," *Economic Review,* third quarter 1998, pp. 21–33.

recently include Panera Bread (2017), Krispy Kreme Doughnuts (2016), Burger King (2014), and Dell (2013).

The primary advantages to going private are: (1) administrative cost savings, (2) increased managerial incentives, (3) increased managerial flexibility, (4) increased shareholder oversight and participation, and (5) increased use of financial leverage, which of course reduces taxes. We discuss each of these advantages in more detail in the following paragraphs.

1. *Administrative cost savings.* Because going private takes the stock of a firm out of public hands, it saves on the time and costs associated with securities registration, annual reports, SEC and exchange reporting, responding to stockholder inquiries, and so on.

2. *Increased managerial incentives.* Managers' increased ownership and equity incentive plans mean that managers benefit more directly from their own efforts; hence, managerial efficiency tends to increase after going private. If the firm is highly successful, then its managers can easily see their personal net worth increase twentyfold, but if the firm fails, then its managers end up with nothing.

3. *Increased managerial flexibility.* Managers at private companies do not have to worry about what a drop in the next quarter's earnings will do to the firm's stock price, so they can focus on long-term, strategic actions that ultimately will have the greatest positive impact on the firm's value. Managerial flexibility concerning asset sales is also greater in a private firm, because such sales need not be justified to a large number of shareholders with potentially diverse interests.

4. *Increased shareholder oversight and participation.* Going private typically results in replacing a dispersed, largely passive group of public shareholders with a small group of investors who take a much more active role in managing the firm. These new equity investors have a substantial position in the private firm; hence, they have a greater motivation to monitor management and to provide incentives to management than do the typical stockholders of a public corporation. Further, the new nonmanagement equity investors—frequently private equity firms, such as KKR, Carlyle Group, or Blackstone Group—are typically represented on the board, and they bring sophisticated industry and financial expertise and hard-nosed attitudes to the new firm.

5. *Increased financial leverage.* Going private usually entails a drastic increase in the firm's use of debt financing, which has two effects. First, the firm's taxes are reduced because of the increase in deductible interest payments, so more of the operating income flows through to investors. Second, the increased debt service requirements force managers to hold costs down to ensure that the firm has sufficient cash flow to meet its obligations—a highly leveraged firm simply cannot afford any fat.

One might ask why all firms are not privately held. The answer is that, although there are real benefits to private ownership, there are also benefits to being publicly owned. Most notably, public corporations have access to large amounts of equity capital on favorable terms, and for most companies, the advantage of access to public capital markets dominates the advantages of going private. Also, note that most companies that go private end up going public again after several years of operation as private firms. In addition to HCA, for example, Celanese AG, a global chemical company, went public in 1999. It was taken private in 2004 by Blackstone Capital Partners, a PE firm, and then taken public again in 2005.

SELF-TEST

What is meant by the term "going private"?

What is a private equity fund?

What are the main benefits of going private?

Why don't all firms go private to capture these benefits?

SUMMARY

Ready access to new financing is necessary for growing companies and growing economies. This chapter explains some of the ways that companies raise funds to support growth.

- The **Securities and Exchange Commission (SEC)** regulates securities markets.
- **Private placements** are securities offerings to a limited number of investors and are exempt from registration with the SEC.
- **Accredited investors** include the officers and directors of a company, high-wealth individuals, and institutional investors. These investors are eligible to buy securities in private placements.
- An **angel investor** is a wealthy individual who makes an equity investment in a start-up company.
- The managers of a **venture capital fund** are called **venture capitalists (VCs)**. They raise money from investors and make equity investments in start-up companies, called **portfolio companies**. One way venture capitalists are paid is as a percent of the eventual profits known as **carried interest**. A company in a VC fund whose estimated value is at least $1 billion even though it doesn't have a history of profitable operations is called a **unicorn**.
- **Going public** in an **initial public offering (IPO)** facilitates stockholder diversification, increases liquidity of the firm's stock, makes it easier for the firm to raise capital, establishes a value for the firm, and makes it easier for a firm to sell its products. However, reporting costs are high, operating data must be disclosed, management self-dealings are harder to arrange, the price may sink to a low level if the stock is not traded actively, and public ownership may make it harder for management to maintain control.
- **Investment banks** assist in issuing securities by helping the firm determine the size of the issue and the type of securities to be used, by establishing the selling price, by selling the issue, and, in some cases, by maintaining an after-market for the stock.
- An investment bank may sell a security issue on a **best efforts basis**, or it may **underwrite** the issue by agreeing to purchase all stocks in the offering at a previously agreed upon price.
- Before an IPO, the investment bank and management team go on a **roadshow** and make presentations to potential institutional investors.
- An IPO is **oversubscribed** if investors are willing to purchase more shares than are being offered at the IPO price.
- The **spread** is the difference between the price at which an underwriter sells a security and the proceeds that the underwriter gives to the issuing company. In recent years the spread for almost all IPOs has been 7%.
- The **money left on the table** is the increase in the market price on the first day of trading over the issue price.
- An **equity carve-out** (also called a **partial public offering** or **spin-out**) is a special IPO in which a publicly traded company converts a subsidiary into a separately traded public company by selling shares of stock in the subsidiary. The parent typically retains a controlling interest.
- SEC Rule 415, also known as **shelf registration**, allows a company to register an issue and then sell that issue in pieces over time rather than all at once.
- A **seasoned equity offering** occurs when a public company issues additional shares of stock.
- A **rights offering** occurs when a public company gives its stockholders the option to purchase a specified number of the new shares. See *Web Extension 18A* for more details.

- **Regulation D** is a provision in the Code of Federal Regulations that permits the sale of securities to accredited investors but places restrictions on the subsequent trading of those securities.
- A **private equity fund** is a limited liability partnership created to own and manage investments in the nontraded equity of firms.
- **Going private** means that a small group of investors, including the firm's senior management, purchases all of the equity in the company. Such deals usually involve high levels of debt and are commonly called **leveraged buyouts (LBOs)**.
- An **asset-backed security** represents a claim on a specific portfolio of financial assets, such as a portfolio of credit card debts or mortgages.
- Large corporations (or even countries) often borrow substantial amounts via **syndicated loans**, in which a group of financial institutions act jointly to fund the loan.
- **Lead arrangers** are one or more banks, investment banks, or other financial institutions acting jointly to create a syndicated loan. The lead arrangers provide some funding for the syndicated loan, but other lenders join the syndicate and provide additional funds.
- In **project financing**, the payments on debt are secured by the cash flows of a particular project.

QUESTIONS

(18-1)   Define each of the following terms:
  a. Going public; new issue market; initial public offering (IPO)
  b. Public offering; private placement
  c. Venture capitalists; roadshow; spread
  d. Securities and Exchange Commission (SEC); registration statement; shelf registration; margin requirement; insiders
  e. Prospectus; "red herring" prospectus
  f. Best efforts arrangement; underwritten arrangement
  g. Project financing; securitization

(18-2)   Many companies that go public with an IPO don't actually need additional cash to continue growing their operations. Why might such a firm decide to go public?

(18-3)   The SEC attempts to protect investors who are purchasing newly issued securities by making sure that the information put out by a company and its investment banks is correct and is not misleading. However, the SEC does not provide an opinion about the real value of the securities; hence, an investor might pay too much for some new stock and consequently lose heavily. Do you think the SEC should, as a part of every new stock or bond offering, render an opinion to investors on the proper value of the securities being offered? Explain.

(18-4)   How do you think each of the following items would affect a company's ability to attract new capital and the flotation costs involved in doing so?
  a. A decision of a privately held company to go public
  b. The increasing institutionalization of the "buy side" of the stock and bond markets
  c. The trend toward financial conglomerates as opposed to stand-alone investment banking houses
  d. Elimination of the preemptive right
  e. The introduction in 1981 of shelf registration of securities

(18-5) Before entering a formal agreement, investment banks carefully investigate the companies whose securities they underwrite; this is especially true of the issues of firms going public for the first time. Because the banks do not themselves plan to hold the securities but intend to sell them to others as soon as possible, why are they so concerned about making careful investigations?

SELF-TEST PROBLEMS SOLUTIONS SHOWN IN APPENDIX A

(ST-1)
IPO Number of Shares and Offer Price

Kelley Corporation is considering an IPO. Kelley and its underwriter agree that the company is worth $500 million. Kelley's founders and early investors own 20 million shares of stock. Kelley has no debt, preferred stock, or short-term investments. The underwriters will charge a 7% spread. Kelly wishes to sell enough new shares so that the new investor will own 20% of the company after the IPO. Assume that the direct costs of the IPO are negligible.

a. How many shares should Kelley sell?
b. What is the intrinsic value of Kelley's stock price per share before the IPO?
c. What offer price is fair to Kelley's current owners and to the new shareholders?

(ST-2)
IPO Shares and Money Left on Table

Blue Coral Breweries (BCB) is planning an IPO. Its underwriters have said the stock will sell at $20 per share. The direct costs (legal fees, printing, etc.) will be $800,000. The underwriters will charge a 7% spread.

a. How many shares must BCB sell to net $30 million?
b. If the stock price closes the first day at $22, how much cash has BCB left on the table?
c. What are BCB's total costs (direct, indirect, and underwriting) for the IPO?

PROBLEMS ANSWERS ARE IN APPENDIX B

EASY PROBLEMS 1–2

(18-1)
Profit or Loss on New Stock Issue

Beedles Inc. needed to raise $14 million in an IPO and chose Security Brokers Inc. to underwrite the offering. The agreement stated that Security Brokers would sell 3 million shares to the public and provide $14 million in net proceeds to Beedles. The out-of-pocket expenses incurred by Security Brokers in the design and distribution of the issue were $300,000. What profit or loss did Security Brokers incur if the issue were sold to the public at the following average price?

a. $5 per share
b. $6 per share
c. $4 per share

(18-2)
Underwriting and Flotation Expenses

The Beranek Company, whose stock price is now $25, needs to raise $20 million in common stock. Underwriters have informed the firm's management that they must price the new issue to the public at $22 per share because of signaling effects. The underwriters' compensation will be 5% of the issue price, so Beranek will net $20.90 per share. The firm will also incur expenses in the amount of $150,000. How many shares must the firm sell to net $20 million after underwriting and flotation expenses?

INTERMEDIATE PROBLEMS 3–5

(18-3)
Pricing Stock
Issues

Benjamin Garcia's start-up business is succeeding, but he needs $200,000 in additional funding to fund continued growth. Benjamin and an angel investor agree the business is worth $800,000 and the angel has agreed to invest the $200,000 that is needed. Benjamin presently owns all 40,000 shares in his business. What is a fair price per share and how many additional shares must Benjamin sell to the angel? Because the stock will be sold directly to an investor, there is no spread; the other flotation costs are insignificant.

(18-4)
New Stock Issue

Bynum and Crumpton, a small jewelry manufacturer, has been successful and has enjoyed a positive growth trend. Now B&C is planning to go public with an issue of common stock, and it faces the problem of setting an appropriate price for the stock. The company and its investment banks believe that the proper procedure is to conduct a valuation and select several similar firms with publicly traded common stock and to make relevant comparisons.

Several jewelry manufacturers are reasonably similar to B&C with respect to product mix, asset composition, and debt/equity proportions. Of these companies, Abercrombe Jewelers and Gunter Fashions are most similar. When analyzing the following data, assume that the most recent year has been reasonably "normal" in the sense that it was neither especially good nor especially bad in terms of sales, earnings, and free cash flows. Abercrombe is listed on the AMEX and Gunter on the NYSE, while B&C will be traded in the NASDAQ market.

Company Data	Abercrombe	Gunter	B&C
Shares outstanding	5 million	10 million	500,000
Price per share	$35.00	$47.00	NA
Earnings per share	$2.20	$3.13	$2.60
Free cash flow per share	$1.63	$2.54	$2.00
Book value per share	$16.00	$20.00	$18.00
Total assets	$115 million	$250 million	$11 million
Total debt	$35 million	$50 million	$2 million

a. B&C is a closely held corporation with 500,000 shares outstanding. Free cash flows have been low and in some years negative due to B&C's recent high sales growth rates, but as its expansion phase comes to an end, B&C's free cash flows should increase. B&C anticipates the following free cash flows over the next 5 years:

Year	1	2	3	4	5
FCF	$1,000,000	$1,050,000	$1,208,000	$1,329,000	$1,462,000

After Year 5, free cash flow growth will be stable at 7% per year. Currently, B&C has no nonoperating assets, and its WACC is 12%. Using the free cash flow valuation model (see Chapters 7 and 12), estimate the (1) horizon value, (2) intrinsic value of operations, (3) intrinsic value of equity, and (4) intrinsic per share price.

b. Calculate debt to total assets, P/E, market to book, P/FCF, and ROE for Abercrombe, Gunter, and B&C. For calculations that require a price for B&C, use the per share price you obtained with the corporate valuation model in part a.

c. Using Abercrombe's and Gunter's P/E, Market/Book, and Price/FCF ratios, calculate the range of prices for B&C's stock that would be consistent with these ratios. For example, if you multiply B&C's earnings per share by Abercrombe's P/E ratio you get a price. What range of prices do you get? How does this compare with the price you get using the corporate valuation model?

(18-5)
Pricing Stock
Issues in an IPO

Zang Industries has hired the investment banking firm of Eric, Schwartz, & Mann (ESM) to help it go public. Zang and ESM agree that Zang's current value of equity is $60 million. Zang currently has 4 million shares outstanding and will issue 1 million new shares. ESM charges a 7% spread. What is the correctly valued offer price, rounded to the nearest penny? How much cash will Zang raise net of the spread (use the rounded offer price)?

SPREADSHEET PROBLEM

(18-6)
Build a Model:
IPO Terms

resource

Start with the partial model in the file **Ch18 P06 Build a Model.xlsx** on the textbook's Web site. Lingadalli Corporation (LC) is considering an IPO. LC has 12 million shares of common stock owned by its founder and early investors. LC has no preferred stock, debt, or short-term investments. Based on its free cash flow projection, LC's intrinsic value of operations is $210 million. LC wants to raise $30 million (net of flotation costs) in net proceeds. The investment bank charges a 7% underwriting spread. All other costs associated with the IPO are small enough to be neglected in this analysis, and all shares sold in the IPO will be newly issued shares. Answer the following questions.

a. What is the intrinsic stock price per share before the IPO?
b. Given the target net proceeds, what amount of gross proceeds are required?
c. What is the projected total value of LC immediately after the IPO? Based on the total amount paid by the shareholders purchasing new shares in the IPO, what percentage of the total post-IPO value do you think the new shareholders require to justify their stock purchases?
d. How many new shares must be sold in the IPO to provide the percentage of ownership required by the new shareholders? How many total shares will be outstanding after the IPO?
e. Based on number of new shares sold in the IPO and the total amount paid by the new shareholders, what is the offer price?
f. Based on total value of the company after the IPO and the total number of outstanding shares after the IPO, what is the intrinsic price per share after the IPO?
g. Compare the pre-IPO price, the offer price, and the post-IPO price. Explain why they are similar or different. (No calculations are required.)

MINI CASE

Randy's, a family-owned restaurant chain operating in Alabama, has grown to the point that expansion throughout the entire Southeast is feasible. The proposed expansion would require the firm to raise about $18.3 million in new capital. Because Randy's currently has a debt ratio of 50% and because family members already have all their personal wealth invested in the company, the family would like to sell common stock to the public to raise the $18.3 million. However, the family wants to retain voting control. You have been asked to brief family members on the issues involved by answering the following questions:

a. What agencies regulate securities markets?
b. How are start-up firms usually financed?
c. Differentiate between a private placement and a public offering.
d. Why would a company consider going public? What are some advantages and disadvantages?

e. What are the steps of an initial public offering?

f. What criteria are important in choosing an investment bank?

g. Would companies going public use a negotiated deal or a competitive bid?

h. Would the sale be on an underwritten or best efforts basis?

i. The estimated pre-IPO value of equity in the company is about $63 million, and there are 4 million shares of existing shares of stock held by family members. The investment bank will charge a 7% spread, which is the difference between the price the new investor pays and the proceeds to the company. To net $18.3 million, what is the value of stock that must be sold? What is the total post-IPO value of equity? What percentage of this equity will the new investors require? How many shares will the new investors require? What is the estimated offer price per share?

j. What is a roadshow? What is book-building?

k. Describe the typical first-day return of an IPO and the long-term returns to IPO investors.

l. What are the direct and indirect costs of an IPO?

m. What are equity carve-outs?

n. Describe some ways other than an IPO that companies can use to raise funds from the capital markets.

o. What are some other investment banking activities? How did these increase investment banks' risk?

p. What is meant by "going private"? What are some advantages and disadvantages? What role do private equity funds play?

q. What is project financing?

SELECTED ADDITIONAL CASES

The following cases from CengageCompose cover many of the concepts discussed in this chapter and are available at **http://compose.cengage.com**.

Klein-Brigham Series:
Case 21, "Sun Coast Savings Bank," illustrates the decision to go public; Case 22, "Precision Tool Company," emphasizes the investment banking process; and Case 23, "Art Deco Reproductions, Inc.," focuses on the analysis of a rights offering.

CHAPTER 19

Lease Financing

The Forty-Year-Old Virgin, starring Steve Carell, cost $26 million to produce but grossed over $177 million at box offices worldwide. That's a lot of money, but there is a 34-year-old Virgin making even more: Virgin Atlantic, the airline, turned 34 in 2018.

Virgin is privately held by Sir Richard Branson's Virgin Group (with Singapore Airlines owning a 49% share), so we don't know exactly how much money Virgin is making, but in mid-2009 Virgin placed an order for 10 Airbus A330-300 jet airliners that cost about $2.1 billion. Virgin purchased 6 of the jets and then immediately sold them to AerCap Holdings NV, a Dutch company specializing in leasing aircraft. AerCap then leased the jets to back to Virgin. In addition, AerCap purchased 4 of the jets directly from Airbus and then leased them to Virgin. The bottom line is that Virgin didn't have to pony up $2.1 billion to get the 10 jets, but Virgin gets to operate the aircraft because it makes lease payments to AerCap.

Virgin had previously placed orders with Boeing, a U.S. company, for Boeing's 787 Dreamliner. Because Boeing experienced a series of production delays, Virgin turned to Airbus, which is owned by the European Aeronautic Defence and Space Company (EADS). EADS itself was formed in 2000 from a number of smaller companies at the encouragement of many European governments desiring a European company with the size and scope to be a major competitor in the global aviation and defense business.

Thus, the 10 Airbus jets will be produced in Europe by EADS, owned by the Dutch company AerCap, operated by the U.K. company Virgin Atlantic, and flown all over the world. As you read this chapter, think about the ways that leasing helps support global operations.

Firms generally own fixed assets and report them on their balance sheets, but it is the use of assets that is important, not their ownership per se. One way to obtain the *use* of facilities and equipment is to buy them, but an alternative is to lease them. Prior to the 1950s, leasing was generally associated with real estate—land and buildings. Today, however, it is possible to lease virtually any kind of asset, including (1) computer hardware and software, (2) transportation-related assets (e.g., ocean tankers, rail cars, aircraft, trucks, etc.), (3) factory machinery, and (4) equipment used by hospitals, retailers, and other businesses. Because leases are so frequently used by virtually all businesses, it is important for every manager to understand them.

19-1 Types of Leases

Lease transactions involve two parties: the **lessor**, who owns the property, and the **lessee**, who obtains use of the property in exchange for one or more lease, or rental, payments. (Note that the term *lessee* is pronounced "less-ee," not "lease-ee," and *lessor* is pronounced "less-or.") Because both parties must agree before a lease transaction can be completed, this chapter discusses leasing from the perspectives of both the lessor and the lessee.

The following sections describe different types of leases, including their impact on financial statements, taxes, and cash flows. We begin with the two most common types, financial leases and operating leases.

19-1a Finance Leases

Finance leases must meet at least one of the following criteria:[1] (1) The lessee receives ownership of the asset when the lease term expires. (2) The lessee can purchase the property at less than its true market value when the lease expires, or the lessee has an option to buy it for a very low price. (3) The lease's life is at least 75% of the asset's economic life. (3) The present value of lease payments is greater than or equal to 90% of the asset's fair value.[2] Finance leases are sometimes called **capital leases**, but FASB prefers the term "finance lease." All other leases are classified as operating leases.

Finance leases (1) *do not* provide for maintenance service, (2) *are not* cancelable, and (3) *are* fully amortized because the **residual value**, which is the asset's value at the end of the lease, is not guaranteed. (We show how to amortize a lease for financial reporting later in the chapter.)

In a typical arrangement, the firm that will use the equipment (the lessee) selects the specific items it requires, negotiates the price with the manufacturer, arranges to have a leasing company (the lessor) buy the equipment, and enters a lease contract at the same time that the lessor actually makes the purchase.

The lessee is generally given an option to renew the lease at a reduced rate upon expiration of the basic lease. However, the basic lease usually cannot be canceled unless the lessor is paid in full. Also, the lessee generally pays the property taxes and insurance on the leased property. Because the lessor receives a return *after*, or *net of*, these payments, this type of lease is often called a *net, net lease.*

---

[1]See the Financial Accounting Standards Board publication "Statement of Financial Accounting Standards No. 13 Accounting for Leases."

[2]The discount rate used to calculate the present value of the lease payments must be the lower of (1) the rate used by the lessor to establish the lease payments (this rate is discussed later in the chapter) or (2) the rate of interest that the lessee would have to pay for new debt with a maturity equal to that of the lease. Also, note that any maintenance payments embedded in the lease payment must be stripped out prior to checking this condition.

Not all financial leases involve new property. Under a **sale-and-leaseback** arrangement, a firm that owns land, buildings, or equipment sells the property to another company and simultaneously executes an agreement to lease the property back from the company. The lessor could be an insurance company, a commercial bank, a specialized leasing company, the finance arm of an industrial firm, a limited partnership, or an individual investor. Note that the seller immediately receives the purchase price from the lessor while retaining use of the property. The sale-and-leaseback plan is an alternative to a mortgage.

Sale-and-leaseback arrangements are almost the same as financial leases; the major difference is that the leased property is used, not new, and the lessor buys it from the user-lessee instead of a manufacturer.

19-1b Operating Leases

Operating leases differ from financial leases in several ways. For example, they usually require the lessor to maintain and service the leased equipment. Of course, the lessor builds the cost of the maintenance into the contract's lease payments.

An operating lease usually ends much sooner than the expected economic life of the asset. Consequently, payments required by an operating lease are not sufficient for the lessor to recover the full cost of the asset. However, the lessor can expect to recover all its costs either by subsequent renewal payments, releasing the asset to another lessee, or selling the asset.

An operating lease often contains a *cancelation clause* that gives the lessee the right to cancel the lease and return the asset before the expiration of the basic lease agreement. This is an important consideration to the lessee because it means that the asset can be returned if it is rendered obsolete by technological developments or is no longer needed because of a change in the lessee's business.

19-1c Combination Leases

Many lessors offer a wide variety of terms. Therefore, in practice leases often do not fit exactly into the operating lease or financial lease category but combine some features of each. Such leases are called **combination leases**. To illustrate, cancelation clauses are normally associated with operating leases, but many of today's financial leases also contain cancelation clauses. However, in finance leases, these clauses generally include prepayment provisions whereby the lessee must make penalty payments sufficient to enable the lessor to recover the unamortized cost of the leased property.

SELF-TEST

Who are the two parties to a lease transaction?

What is the difference between an operating lease and a financial lease?

What is a sale-and-leaseback transaction?

What is a combination lease?

19-2 Reporting Leases on Financial Statements

Prior to 2019, an operating lease was not reported on the balance sheets even though the company had the right to use the leased asset and had an obligation to make lease payments. This is called **off–balance sheet financing**, which makes it difficult for investors to identify a company's true financial obligations. However, off-balance sheet financing for leases was virtually eliminated by the recent implementation of **Accounting Standards**

Update (ASU) 2016-02.[3] Now a company must **capitalize** any lease lasting more than a year by reporting it on the balance sheets as a liability and as an asset. This is great news for financial transparency!

The following sections explain how to capitalize a lease and report it on financial statements by way of an example. In particular, we examine a lease with a 3-year term and $10,000 annual payments at the end of each year. The appropriate incremental cost of debt for reporting this lease is 6%.

19-2a Preliminary Calculations

resource

See Ch19 Tool Kit.xlsx, for calculations in Excel.

The first step in capitalizing a lease is to determine the initial **lease liability**, which is the present value of all lease payments discounted at the company's cost of debt, r_d. Set up your financial calculator to N = 3, I/YR = 6%, PMT = −10000, FV = 0 and solve for PV = 26,730. This is the initial lease liability.

The imputed interest is equal to the cost of debt multiplied by the previous lease liability. For example, the imputed interest for Year 1 is equal to $1,604: 6%($26,730) = $1,604. The new lease liability is equal to the previous lease liability plus the imputed interest less the amount of the lease payment. For example, the Year-1 lease liability is $18,334: $26,730 + $1,604 − $10,000 = $18,334. The values for Years 2 and 3 are found similarly.

Table 19-1 reports the preliminary calculations for each year in Part 1. The following sections explain the other parts of the table.

19-2b Reporting an Operating Lease

resource

See Ch19 Tool Kit.xlsx, for calculations in Excel.

Suppose that the lease in our example is an operating lease. The financial statements would report a lease liability equal to the lease liability in Part 1 of Table 19-1. A **right-of-use asset** is the reported asset value of the lease. For operating leases, the right-of-use asset is equal to the lease liability. The reported lease expense is equal to the lease payment. See Part 2 for these reported values.

19-2c Reporting a Finance Lease

resource

See Ch19 Tool Kit.xlsx, for calculations in Excel.

Now suppose that the lease in our example is a finance lease. The financial statements would report annual lease liabilities equal to the annual lease liabilities in Part 2 of Table 19-1. The statements would also report the *initial* right-of-use asset equal to the *initial* lease liability, the same as Part 1. However, the similarities end here because the subsequent right-of-use assets and lease expenses are reported differently than for operating leases.

To determine the right-of-use asset for subsequent years, we first need to calculate the annual amortization charge. This is equal to the initial right-of-use asset divided by the length of the lease. In our example, the amortization charge is $8,910: $26,730/3 = $8,910. The right-of-use asset for subsequent years is equal to the previous right-of-use asset minus the amortization charge. For example, the Year-1 right-of-use asset is $17,820: $26,730 − $8,910 = $17,820. The right-of-use assets for a financial lease are reported in Part 3 of Table 19-1.

---

[3]New reporting rules were issued by the Financial Accounting Statements Board (FASB) in Accounting Standards Update No. 2016-02, Leases (Topic 842), which is commonly called **ASU 2016-02**. They apply to all leases lasting for more than one year. The actual implementation date for the new reporting standards was December 15, 2018, so they were in force for the last two weeks of December. See **www.fasb.org/jsp/FASB/Document _C/DocumentPage?cid=1176167901010&acceptedDisclaimer=true**.

TABLE 19-1
Financial Reporting for Leases

Part 1: Preliminary Calculations

	Year 0	Year 1	Year 2	Year 3
Lease liability balance[a]	$26,730	$18,334	$ 9,434	$ 0
Imputed interest expense[b]		$ 1,604	$ 1,100	$ 566
Lease payment		$10,000	$10,000	$10,000

Part 2: Reporting an Operating Lease

	Year 0	Year 1	Year 2	Year 3
Lease liability balance	$26,730	$18,334	$ 9,434	$ 0
Right-of-use asset balance[c]	$26,730	$18,334	$ 9,434	$ 0
Lease expense[d]		$10,000	$10,000	$10,000

Part 3: Reporting a Finance Lease

	Year 0	Year 1	Year 2	Year 3
Lease liability balance	$26,730	$18,334	$ 9,434	$ 0
Right-of-use asset balance[e]	$26,730	$ 17,820	$ 8,910	$ 0
Interest expense[f]		$ 1,604	$ 1,100	$ 566
Amortization expense[g]		$ 8,910	$ 8,910	$8,910
Total lease expense		$ 10,514	$10,010	$9,476

Source: See the file ***Ch19 Tool Kit.xlsx***. Numbers in the table are shown as rounded values for clarity in reporting. However, unrounded values are used for all calculations.

Notes:

[a]The lease liability in Year 0 is equal to the initial lease liability. For subsequent years, the lease liability balance is equal to the previous balance plus the imputed interest minus the lease payment.

[b]The imputed interest for the end of Year t is equal to the cost of debt (r_d) multiplied by the lease liability payment at the beginning of Year t.

[c]The right-of-use asset balance for an operating lease is equal to the lease liability balance.

[d]The lease expense for an operating lease is equal to the lease payment.

[e]The right-of-use balance for a finance lease is equal to the previous balance minus the amortization charge.

[f]The interest expense for a finance lease is equal to the imputed interest .

[g]The amortization charge for a finance lease is equal to initial right-of-use asset divided by the number of years of the lease.

resource

See ***Ch19 Tool Kit.xlsx***, for calculations in Excel.

The reported total lease expense each year is equal to the imputed interest from Part 1 plus the amortization charge. For example, the reported lease expense for Year 1 is $10,514: $1,604 + $8,910 = $10,514.

Part 3 of Table 19-1 shows how a finance lease is reported in financial statements.[4]

Why were some leases referred to as off–balance sheet financing prior to 2019?

What does it mean to capitalize a lease? What is a lease liability?

What is a right-of-use asset? How is it reported on a balance sheet?

Which type of lease reports higher assets in the lease's early years? Which type of lease reports higher lease expenses in the lease's early years.

---

[4]Note that an interest expense reduces the retained earnings reported on the liability side of balance sheets. Therefore, the cumulative effect of reporting annual interest expenses is to reduce the retained earnings account on the liability side of the balance sheet by the cumulative annual interest expenses, all else held constant. The sum of the cumulative interest expenses and the lease liability is equal to the right-of-use asset, ensuring that balance sheets balance.

19-3 Lease Analysis: Determination of Tax Status by the Internal Revenue Service (IRS)

Suppose a company has a potential project that requires the use of new equipment. After conducting a project analysis using the methods in Chapter 11, the company has decided to accept the project. Should the firm obtain financing by leasing the equipment or by borrowing and buying it?[5] The answer often depends upon whether or not the IRS determines that the lease is simply a loan in disguise, which in turn affects the lease's tax treatment.

If the IRS deems it to be a loan in disguise, then it is called a **non-tax-oriented lease**. Otherwise, it is called a **tax-oriented lease**, also known as a **guideline lease** or a **true lease**. Later sections explain the different tax treatments of tax-oriented leases and non-tax-oriented leases, but first we show how the IRS makes its determination. The IRS will classify the contract as a tax-oriented lease if the lease meets each of the following requirements; otherwise, the IRS classifies it as a non-tax-oriented lease.

1. The lease term (including any extensions or renewals at a fixed rental rate) must not exceed 80% of the estimated useful life of the equipment at the commencement of the lease transaction. Thus, an asset with a 10-year life can be leased for no more than 8 years. Further, the remaining useful life must not be less than 1 year. Note that an asset's expected useful life is normally much longer than its MACRS depreciation class life.
2. The equipment's estimated residual value (in real dollars without any increase due to inflation) at the expiration of the lease must be at least 20% of its value at the start of the lease. This requirement can have the effect of limiting the maximum lease term.
3. Neither the lessee nor any related party can have the right to purchase the property at a predetermined fixed price. However, the lessee can be given an option to buy the asset at its fair market value.
4. Neither the lessee nor any related party can pay or guarantee payment of any part of the price of the leased equipment. Simply put, the lessee cannot make any investment in the equipment other than through the lease payments.
5. The leased equipment must not be "limited use" property, defined as equipment that can be used only by the lessee or a related party at the end of the lease.

If the IRS decides that the contract is a tax-oriented lease, then the lessor is entitled to the tax benefits of ownership (i.e., depreciation and any investment tax credits). The lessor also bears the responsibilities of ownership, such as maintenance expenses. The reverse is true for a non-tax-oriented lease: The lessee retains the tax benefits and pays for maintenance.

Notice that IRS guidelines mean that almost all operating leases are tax-oriented leases and almost all finance leases are non-tax-oriented leases. As you will see in the following sections, the actual tax treatments for leases are similar to the financial reporting for leases shown in Table 19-1.

SELF-TEST

What are some lease provisions that would cause a lease to be classified as a non-tax-oriented lease instead of a tax-oriented lease?

What type of lease retains the tax benefits of ownership and the responsibility for maintenance?

---

[5]As you might expect, there are some situations for which the decision to lease can change the results of a capital budgeting analysis, but these situations are very rare. Hence, we do not discuss them here.

19-4 Lease Analysis: Non-Tax-Oriented Leases

resource

See *Ch19 Tool Kit.xlsx* on
the textbook's Web site for
all calculations.

A lease is comparable to a loan in the sense that the firm is required to make a specified
series of payments, and a failure to meet these payments could result in bankruptcy. This
means that $1 of lease financing displaces $1 of debt financing in the firm's capital structure. Therefore, lease analysis should compare the cost of leasing with the cost of debt
financing *regardless* of how the asset purchase is actually financed. This means that the
appropriate discount rate to use in lease analysis is the cost of debt, r_d.

resource

See *Ch19 Tool Kit.xlsx* on
the textbook's Web site
for this analysis.

To illustrate the analysis of a non-tax-oriented lease, consider the CJ&M Corporation,
a very successful consulting firm providing strategic marketing services. CJ&M needs an
asset that costs $36,000 and will use it for four years. The asset is in the 3-year MACRS
class, and those rates will be used to depreciate the asset over its 4-year life, after which it
has no residual value. The asset will require $3,000 per year for maintenance.

If the asset is purchased, the bank would lend CJ&M the $36,000 purchase price at a
rate of 10% on a 4-year amortizing loan with payments at the end of the year. To calculate
the loan payments, set your financial calculator to N = 4, I/YR = 10, PV = 36000, FV =
0 and solve for PMT = −11,356.95.

Alternatively, CJ&M could lease the asset for $11,000 per year with payments made at
the end of the year. Based on the criteria in Section 19-3, the IRS classifies this contract as
a non-tax-oriented lease. This means that CJ&M must pay for maintenance but can claim
the tax shield provided by depreciation. The firm cannot deduct the entire lease payment
but can deduct only the imputed interest based on the lease liability.

CJ&M must evaluate the cost of the lease versus that of borrowing and buying. The
cost of leasing is the present value of the lease's after-tax cash flows, and the cost of owning
is the present value of the after-tax cash flows due to owning. The appropriate discount
rate is the after-tax cost of debt because these are after-tax cash flows. The **net advantage
to leasing (NAL)** is defined by Equation 19-1:

$$\begin{aligned} \text{Net advantage of} \atop \text{leasing (NAL)} &= {\text{Present value of after-tax} \atop \text{leasing cash flows}} - {\text{Present value of after-tax} \atop \text{owning cash flows}} \\[4pt] &= \text{Cost of leasing} - \text{Cost of owning} \end{aligned} \qquad (19\text{-}1)$$

resource

See *Ch19 Tool Kit.xlsx* on
the textbook's Web site
for this analysis.

The *Tool Kit* for this chapter shows how to calculate the NAL for a finance lease in just
30 easy steps. Fortunately, there is a much easier way to determine the NAL for almost all
finance leases. Simply subtract the initial lease liability from the purchase price, and the
result is the NAL:[6]

$$\text{NAL for finance lease} = \text{Purchase price} - \text{Initial lease liability} \qquad (19\text{-}2)$$

Here is the intuition for this result. The present values of the depreciation tax shield
and after-tax maintenance costs are the same whether the asset is purchased or leased, so
they net out to zero when calculating the NAL. The present value of a finance lease's other
after-tax cash flows is equal to the initial lease liability because that is the definition of the

---

[6]This result is valid only if all costs other than the lease payment and loan payment (e.g., maintenance, insurance, etc.) are the same whether the asset is leased or purchased. If that is not true, then you must use the
30-step method shown in this chapter's *Tool Kit*.

initial lease liability. For the case of borrow and purchase, the present value of the loan payments is equal to the purchase price. Therefore, Equation 19-2 results in the correct NAL.

We already know the purchase price ($36,000), but we need to calculate the initial lease liability. Using a financial calculator, the inputs are N = 4, I/YR = r_d = 10%, PMT = −$11,000, and FV = 0. Solving for PV results in an initial lease liability of $34,869.

Applying Equation 19-2 to CJ&M's lease-versus-buy decision, the resulting NAL is $1,131:

$$\text{NAL for finance lease} = \text{Purchase price} - \text{Initial lease liability}$$
$$= \$36,000 - \$34,869$$
$$= \$1,131$$

Why is the NAL positive for this lease? The lease payment is less than the loan payment. If the lease payment is equal to the loan payment, then the initial lease liability is equal to the purchase price, and the result from Equation 19-2 is a zero NAL.

Alternatively, the rate on the loan is greater than the implicit rate in the lease, which is 8.54%: set N = 4, PV = −36000 (the purchase price), PMT = 11000 (the lease payment), FV = 0, and solve for I/YR = 8.54%. If you use the *Excel* model in the ***Tool Kit*** and substitute 8.54% for the loan rate, then the loan payment drops to $11,000, and the NAL drops to zero.[7] We discuss this in more detail when we explain the lessor's analysis in Section 19-6.

19-5 Lease Analysis: Tax-Oriented Lease

The previous section showed that the lessee of a non-tax-oriented lease can deduct only the imputed portion of the lease payment for tax purposes, can deduct depreciation, and must pay for maintenance. In contrast, the lessee of a tax-oriented lease can deduct the entire lease payment, cannot deduct depreciation, and does not have to pay for maintenance. The following sections explain how to determine the net advantage to leasing for a tax-oriented lease.

19-5a The Net Advantage to Leasing for a Tax-Oriented Lease

resource

See *Ch19 Tool Kit.xlsx, for calculations in* Excel.

The Anderson Company is conducting a lease analysis on some assembly line equipment it will procure during the coming year. The following data have been collected:

1. Anderson plans to acquire automated assembly line equipment with a 10-year life at a cost of $10 million, delivered and installed. However, Anderson plans to use the equipment for only 5 years and then discontinue the product line.
2. Anderson can borrow the required $10 million at a pre-tax cost of 10%.
3. The equipment's estimated scrap value is $50,000 after 10 years of use, but its estimated residual value after only 5 years of use is $2,000,000. Thus, if Anderson buys the equipment, it would expect to receive $2,000,000 before taxes when the equipment is sold in 5 years.
4. Anderson can lease the equipment for 5 years for an annual rental charge of $2,600,000, payable at the beginning of each year, but the lessor will own the equipment upon the expiration of the lease. (The lease payment schedule is established by the potential lessor, as described in the next section, and Anderson can accept it, reject it, or negotiate modifications.)

---

[7]Actually, you must substitute the unrounded value of the lease's implicit interest rate.

5. The lease contract stipulates that the lessor will maintain the equipment at no additional charge to Anderson. However, if Anderson borrows and buys, it will have to bear the cost of maintenance, which will be done by the equipment manufacturer at a fixed contract rate of $500,000 per year, payable at the beginning of each year.

6. The equipment falls in the MACRS 5-year class, Anderson's marginal tax rate is 25%, and the lease qualifies as a guideline lease.

COMPLETE ANALYSIS

Figure 19-1 shows the steps involved in the analysis. Part 1 of the table is devoted to the costs of borrowing and buying. The company borrows $10 million and uses it to pay for the equipment, so these two items net out to zero and thus are not shown in the figure. Then, the company makes the *after-tax* payments shown in Line 1. In Year 1, the after-tax interest charge is 0.10($10 million)(1 − 0.25) = $750,000, and other payments are calculated similarly. The $10 million loan is repaid at the end of Year 5. Line 2 shows the maintenance

resource

See Ch19 Tool Kit.xlsx on the textbook's Web site for all calculations.

FIGURE 19-1
Anderson Company: Lease Analysis (Thousands of Dollars)

	A	B	C	D	E	F	G	H
319	**Part 1: Cost of Owning**					Year		
320			**0**	**1**	**2**	**3**	**4**	**5**
321								
322	**1. After-tax loan payments**			−$750	−$750	−$750	−$750	−$10,750
323	**2. Maintenance cost**		−$500	−$500	−$500	−$500	−$500	
324	**3. Maintenance tax savings**		$125	$125	$125	$125	$125	
325	**4. Depreciation tax savings**			$500	$800	$480	$288	$288
326	**5. Residual value**							$2,000
327	**6. Tax on residual value**							−$356
328	**7. Net cash flow of owning**		−$375	−$625	−$325	−$645	−$837	−$8,818
329								
330	**8. PV ownership CF @ 7.5%**		−$8,526					
331	**Part 2: Cost of Leasing**					Year		
332			**0**	**1**	**2**	**3**	**4**	**5**
333	**9. Lease payment**		−$2,600	−$2,600	−$2,600	−$2,600	−$2,600	
334	**10. Tax savings from lease**		$650	$650	$650	$650	$650	
335	**11. Net cash flow of leasing**		−$1,950	−$1,950	−$1,950	−$1,950	−$1,950	$0
336								
337	**12. PV of leasing CF @ 7.5%**		−$8,481					
338	**Part 3: Net advantage to leasing (NAL)**							
339	**13. NAL = PV of leasing − PV of owning =**				$45			

Source: Numbers in the figure are shown as rounded values for clarity in reporting. However, unrounded values are used for all calculations. See the *Excel Tool Kit* for this chapter.

Notes:

1. The after-tax loan payments consist of after-tax interest for Years 1–4 and after-tax interest plus the principal amount in Year 5.

2. The net cash flows shown in Lines 7 and 11 are discounted at the lessee's after-tax cost of debt, 7.5%.

3. The MACRS depreciation allowances are 0.20, 0.32, 0.192, 0.1152, and 0.1152 in Years 1 through 5, respectively. Thus, the depreciation expense is 0.20($10,000) = $2,000 in Year 1, and so on. The depreciation tax savings in each year is 0.25(Depreciation).

4. The residual value is $2,000, while the book value is $576. Thus, Anderson would have to pay 0.25($2,000 − $576) = $356 in taxes. These amounts are shown in Lines 5 and 6 in the cost-of-owning analysis.

5. Maintenance is shown at the beginning of the year to reflect cash that is set aside for routine maintenance throughout the year.

cost. Line 3 gives the maintenance tax savings. Line 4 contains the annual depreciation tax savings, which are the depreciation expenses multiplied by the tax rate. The notes to Figure 19-1 explain the depreciation calculation. Lines 5 and 6 contain the residual (or salvage) value cash flows. The tax is on the excess of the residual value over the asset's book value, not on the full residual value. Line 7 contains the net cash flows, and Line 8 shows the net present value of these flows discounted at the 7.5% after-tax cost of debt.

Part 2 of Figure 19-2 analyzes the lease. The lease payments, shown in Line 9, are $2,600,000 per year; this rate, which includes maintenance, was established by the prospective lessor and offered to Anderson Equipment. If Anderson accepts the lease then the full amount will be a deductible expense, so the annual tax savings, shown in Line 10, are 0.25(Lease payment) = 0.25($2,600,000) = $650,000. Thus, the after-tax cost of the lease payment is Lease payment − Tax savings = $2,600,000 − $650,000 = $1,950,000. This amount is shown in Line 11 for Years 0 through 4. Line 12 shows the cost of leasing, which is the present value of the cash flows discounted at the 7.5% after-tax cost of debt.

Part 3 compares the cost of leasing versus owning. Line 12 shows that the cost of leasing is −$8,481,000, and Line 8 shows that the cost of owning is −$8,526,000. The net advantage to leasing is about $45 thousand (ignoring rounding differences):

$$\begin{aligned} \text{NAL} &= \text{PV of leasing} - \text{PV of owning} \\ &= -\$8,481,000 - (-\$8,526,000) \\ &= \$45,000 \end{aligned}$$

Owning is more costly than leasing, so the NAL is positive. Therefore, Anderson should lease the equipment.

SHORTCUT FOR AFTER-TAX LOAN PAYMENTS

resource

See *Ch19 Tool Kit.xlsx*, for calculations in Excel.

Now that you understand the process, there is a shortcut to determine Line 1, the after-tax cash flows from the loan payments. Look at the line-by-line PVs for the cost of owning as shown here:

Cost of Owning	Present Value
1. After-tax loan payments	−$10,000
2. Maintenance cost	−$2,175
3. Maintenance tax savings	$544
4. Depreciation tax savings	$1,960
5. Residual value	$1,393
6. Tax on residual value	−$248
7. PV ownership	−$8,526

Notice the present values of the line items add up to the same PV of ownership as in Figure 19-1. Now notice that the present value of the after-tax loan payments in Line 1 is equal to the amount of the loan. This should not be surprising, because the loan payments are determined by the loan amount (i.e., the purchase price) and the interest rate. In other words, the purchase price determines the loan payments, so the PV of the payments must equal the purchase price.

Therefore, we can use a shortcut for Line 1. Instead of calculating the after-tax loan payment in each period for Line 1, we can use Equation 19-3.

NPV of after-tax loan payments = Purchase price shown as cost   (19-3)

Instead of calculating the annual after-tax loan payments, replace them with a single cash flow at Year 0, which is the purchase price shown as a cost (i.e., a negative cash flow). See the chapter's *Excel Tool Kit* for an application of this shortcut.

19-5b Purchase at End of Lease for Residual Value

In the previous example, Anderson did not plan on using the equipment beyond Year 5. But if Anderson instead had planned on using the equipment after Year 5, the analysis would be modified. For example, suppose Anderson planned on using the equipment for 10 years and the lease allowed Anderson to purchase the equipment at the residual value. First, how do we modify the cash flows due to owning? Lines 5 and 6 (for residual value and tax on residual value) in Figure 19-1 will be zero at Year 5, because Anderson will not sell the equipment then.[8] However, there will be the additional remaining year of depreciation tax savings in Line 4 for Year 6. There will be no entries for Years 6–10 for Line 1, the after-tax loan payments, because the loan is completely repaid at Year 5. Also, there will be no incremental maintenance costs and tax savings in Lines 2 and 3 for Years 6–10, because Anderson will have to perform its own maintenance on the equipment in those years whether it initially purchases the equipment or whether it leases the equipment for 5 years and then purchases it. Either way, Anderson will own the equipment in Years 6–10 and must pay for its own maintenance.

Second, how do we modify the cash flows if Anderson leases the equipment and then purchases it at Year 5? There will be a negative cash flow at Year 5 reflecting the purchase. Because the equipment was originally classified with a MACRS 5-year life, Anderson will be allowed to depreciate the purchased equipment (even though it is not new) with a MACRS 5-year life. Therefore, in Years 6–10, there will be after-tax savings due to depreciation.[9] Given the modified cash flows, we can calculate the NAL just as we did in Figure 19-1. See *Ch19 Tool Kit.xlsx* for these calculations and results.

In this section, we focused on the dollar cost of leasing versus borrowing and buying, which is analogous to the NPV method used in capital budgeting. A second method that lessees can use to evaluate leases focuses on the percentage cost of leasing and is analogous to the IRR method used in capital budgeting.

SELF-TEST

Explain how the cash flows are structured in order to estimate the net advantage to leasing.

What discount rate should be used to evaluate a lease? Why?

Define the term net advantage to leasing (NAL).

19-6 Evaluation by the Lessor

Thus far, we have considered leasing only from the lessee's viewpoint. It is also useful to analyze the transaction as the lessor sees it: Is the lease a good investment for the party who must put up the money? The lessor will generally be a specialized leasing company, a bank or bank affiliate, an individual or group of individuals organized as a limited partnership or limited liability corporation, or a manufacturer that uses leasing as a sales tool.

---

[8]There might be a salvage value in Line 5 at Year 10 (and a corresponding tax adjustment in Line 6) if the equipment is not completely worn out or obsolete.

[9]There will also be an after-tax cash flow at Year 10 that depends on the salvage value of the equipment at that date.

Any potential lessor needs to know the rate of return on the capital invested in the lease, and this information is also useful to the prospective lessee: Lease terms on large leases are generally negotiated, so the lessee should know what return the lessor is earning. The lessor's analysis involves (1) determining the net cash outlay, which is usually the invoice price of the leased equipment less any lease payments made in advance; (2) determining the periodic cash inflows, which consist of the lease payments minus both income taxes and any maintenance expense the lessor must bear; (3) estimating the after-tax residual value of the property when the lease expires; and (4) determining whether the rate of return on the lease exceeds the lessor's opportunity cost of capital or, equivalently, whether the NPV of the lease exceeds zero.

19-6a Analysis by the Lessor

resource

See *Ch19 Tool Kits.xlsx* on the textbook's Web site for all calculations.

To illustrate the lessor's analysis, we assume the same facts as for the Anderson Company lease, plus the following: (1) The potential lessor is a wealthy individual whose current income is in the form of interest and whose personal marginal federal-plus-state income tax rate, T, is 35%. (2) The investor can buy 5-year bonds that have a 9% yield to maturity, providing an after-tax yield of $(9\%)(1 - T) = (9\%)(0.65) = 5.85\%$. This is the after-tax return the investor can obtain on alternative investments of similar risk. (3) The before-tax residual value is $2,000,000. Because the asset will be depreciated to a book value of $600,000 at the end of the 5-year lease, $1,400,000 of this $2 million will be taxable at the 35% rate by the depreciation recapture rule, so the lessor can expect to receive $2,000,000 - 0.35($1,400,000) = $1,510,000 after taxes from the sale of the equipment after the lease expires.

The lessor's cash flows are developed in Figure 19-2. Here we see that the lease as an investment has a net present value of $93,401. On a present value basis, the investor who

FIGURE 19-2

Lease Analysis from the Lessor's Viewpoint (Thousands of Dollars)

		A	B	C	D	E	F	G	H
460						Year			
461				0	1	2	3	4	5
462									
463	1. Net purchase price			−$10,000					
464	2. Maintenance cost			−$500	−$500	−$500	−$500	−$500	
465	3. Maintenance tax savings[a]			$175	$175	$175	$175	$175	
466	4. Depreciation tax savings[b]				$700	$1,120	$672	$403	$403
467	5. Lease payment			$2,600	$2,600	$2,600	$2,600	$2,600	
468	6. Tax on lease payment			−$910	−$910	−$910	−$910	−$910	
469	7. Residual value								$2,000
470	8. Tax on residual value[c]								−$498
471	9. Net cash flow			−$8,635	$2,065	$2,485	$2,037	$1,768	$1,905
472	10. NPV @ 5.85% =			$93.401					
473	11. IRR =			6.26%					
474	12. MIRR=			6.08%					

Source: Numbers in the figure are shown as rounded values for clarity in reporting. However, unrounded values are used for all calculations. See the *Excel* **Tool Kit** for this chapter.

Notes:

[a]Maintenance tax savings = Maintenance cost × (Tax rate).

[b]Depreciation tax savings = Depreciation × (Tax rate).

[c](Residual value − Book value) × (Tax rate).

invests in the lease rather than in the 9% bonds (5.85% after taxes) is better off by $93,401, indicating that he or she should be willing to write the lease. As we saw earlier, the lease is also advantageous to Anderson Company, so the transaction should be completed.

The investor can also calculate the lease investment's internal rate of return based on the net cash flows shown in Line 9 of Figure 19-2. The IRR of the lease, which is that discount rate that forces the NPV of the lease to zero, is 6.26%. Thus, the lease provides a 6.26% after-tax return to this 35% tax rate investor, which exceeds the 5.85% after-tax return on 9% bonds. So, using either the IRR or the NPV method, the lease would appear to be a satisfactory investment.[10]

19-6b Setting the Lease Payment

So far we have evaluated leases assuming that the lease payments have already been specified. However, in large leases the parties generally sit down and work out an agreement on the size of the lease payments, with these payments being set so as to provide the lessor with some specific rate of return. In situations in which the lease terms are not negotiated, which is often the case for small leases, the lessor must still go through the same type of analysis, setting terms that provide a target rate of return and then offering these terms to the potential lessee on a take-it-or-leave-it basis.

To illustrate all this, suppose the potential lessor described earlier, after examining other alternative investment opportunities, decides that the 5.85% after-tax bond return is too low to use for evaluating the lease and that the required after-tax return on the lease should be 7.0%. What lease payment schedule would provide this return?

To answer this question, note again that Figure 19-2 contains the lessor's cash flow analysis. We used the *Excel* Goal Seek function to set the lessor's IRR equal to 7% by changing the lease payment; see the analysis in *Ch19 Tool Kit.xlsx*. We found that the lessor must set the lease payment at $2,657,773 to obtain an after-tax rate of return of 7.0%. If this lease payment is not acceptable to the lessee, Anderson Company, then it may not be possible to strike a deal. Naturally, competition among leasing companies forces lessors to build market-related returns into their lease payment schedules.[11]

If the inputs to the lessee and the lessor are identical, then a positive NAL to the lessee implies an equal but negative NPV to the lessor. However, *conditions are often such that leasing can provide net benefits to both parties. This situation arises because of differentials in taxes, in borrowing rates, in estimated residual values, or in the ability to bear the residual value risk.* We will explore these issues in detail in the next section.

resource

We discuss leveraged leases in more detail in Web Extension 19B on the textbook's Web site.

Note that the lessor can, under certain conditions, increase the return on the lease by borrowing some of the funds used to purchase the leased asset. Such a lease is called a **leveraged lease**. Whether or not a lease is leveraged has no effect on the lessee's analysis, but it can have a significant effect on the cash flows to the lessor and hence on the lessor's expected rate of return.

SELF-TEST

What discount rate is used in a lessor's NPV analysis?

Under what conditions will the lessor's NPV be the negative of the lessee's NAL?

---

[10]Note that the lease investment is actually slightly more risky than the alternative bond investment because the residual value cash flow is less certain than a principal repayment. Thus, the lessor might require an expected return somewhat above the 5.85% promised on a bond investment.

[11]For a discussion of realized returns on lease contracts, see Ronald C. Lease, John J. McConnell, and James S. Schallheim, "Realized Returns and the Default and Prepayment Experience of Financial Leasing Contracts," *Financial Management*, Summer 1990, pp. 11–20.

19-7 Leases, Taxes, and the 2017 Tax Cuts and Jobs Act

An investment tax credit (ITC) is a direct reduction in taxes when a firm purchases new capital equipment. These credits are authorized by Congress for a specific number of years before they begin phasing out. For example, in 2019, there is a 30% ITC for individuals and companies that purchase and install a new solar energy power system. If a system costs $100,000, the ITC allows the purchaser to reduce federal taxes owed by 30%($100,000) = $30,000. The residential ITC expires at the end of 2021, and the business ITC phases down to 10% for years after 2021.

The 2017 Tax Cuts and Jobs Act (TCJA) made major changes to the tax code, and those changes certainly affect leasing decisions even though the TCJA made minimal direct changes to the tax treatment of leases. First, the TCJA reduced the corporate tax rate to 21%, which in turn should reduce the demand for leases (and for debt financing in general) because the tax savings will be smaller. On the other hand, the reduced tax rate might induce leasing companies to offer better deals because they will be taxed less heavily. Also, companies may invest in more projects because the corporate tax rate is lower, which would increase the demand for leases.

Second, the TCJA allows much more rapid depreciation from now until 2026 through bonus depreciation. Companies can immediately depreciate 100% of an asset's purchase price from now through 2022; afterward, the percentage drops by 20% each year until it is completely phased out. Some companies may not have enough taxable income to utilize this benefit, but many leasing companies with high taxable income will be able to reduce their taxes by using bonus depreciation. This creates some bargaining space in which both the lessee and lessor benefit.

Third, the TCJA put a limit on the amount of interest expense that can be deducted in a year, with any excess interest expense being carried forward to future years. However, it did not impose a limit on the amount of tax-oriented leasing expenses that may be deducted from taxable income. This made leasing more attractive to lessees, but it might reduce the amount of debt financing that a lessor can use.

What is the net impact of the TCJA on leasing? As we write this in 2018, there has not yet been enough time for researchers to conduct empirical tests, so we can't answer that question just yet.

SELF-TEST

What are some ways that the TCJA might affect lessees and lessors?

19-8 Other Issues in Lease Analysis

The basic methods of analysis used by lessees and lessors were presented in the previous sections. However, some other issues warrant discussion.[12]

19-8a Estimated Residual Value

A lessor owns the property upon expiration of a lease, so the lessor has claim to the asset's residual value. If expected residual values are large—as they may be under inflation for certain types of equipment and also if real estate is involved—then competition among leasing companies and other financing sources will force leasing rates down to the point

---

[12]For a description of lease analysis in practice as well as a comprehensive bibliography of the leasing literature, see Tarun K. Mukherjee, "A Survey of Corporate Leasing Analysis," *Financial Management*, Autumn 1991, pp. 96–107.

where potential residual values are fully recognized in the lease contract. Thus, the existence of large residual values is not likely to result in materially higher costs for leasing.

19-8b Increased Credit Availability

Leasing may be a way for firms to increase their financial leverage. First, it is sometimes argued that firms can obtain more money, and for longer terms, under a lease arrangement than under a loan secured by a specific piece of equipment. There may be some truth to these claims for smaller firms but not for large enterprises, which must report detailed financial statements to the public.

If loan covenants prohibit a firm from issuing more debt but fail to restrict lease payments, then the firm could effectively increase its leverage by leasing additional assets. Also, firms that are in poor financial condition and face possible bankruptcy may be able to obtain lease financing at a lower cost than comparable debt financing because (1) lessors often have a more favorable position than lenders should the lessee actually go bankrupt, and (2) lessors that specialize in certain types of equipment may be in a better position to dispose of repossessed equipment than banks or other lenders.

19-8c Real Estate Leases

Many companies acquire the use of real estate property by way of long-term leases. For example, many retailers choose to lease their stores rather than buy the property. In some situations, retailers have no choice but to lease—this is true of locations in malls and certain office buildings.

The type of lease-versus-purchase analysis we discussed in this chapter is just as applicable for real estate as for equipment. Of course, such things as maintenance, who the other tenants will be, what alterations can be made, who will pay for alterations, and the like become especially important with real property.

19-8d Vehicle Leases

For corporations, the key factor involved with transportation is often maintenance and disposal of used vehicles—the leasing companies are specialists here, and many businesses prefer to "outsource" services related to autos and trucks. For individuals, leasing is often more convenient, and it may be easier to justify tax deductions on leased than on owned vehicles. Also, most auto leasing to individuals is through dealers. These dealers (and manufacturers) use leasing as a sales tool, and they often make the terms quite attractive—especially when it comes to the down payment, which may be nonexistent in the case of a lease.

19-8e Synthetic Leases

A **synthetic lease** allows a company to treat the financing as a lease on its reported financial statements but to treat the asset and the financing as a loan when calculating its tax liability. Before 2003, many corporations created synthetic leases by establishing a **special purpose entity (SPE)** that obtained about 97% of its funding from a loan made by a single financial institution and about 3% as equity from a party other than the corporation itself. The SPE would then use the funds to acquire the property and lease it to the corporation, generally for a term of 3 to 5 years but with an option to extend the lease. Unlike a tax-oriented lease, the terms of a synthetic lease were such that, for all practical purposes, the corporate lessee was guaranteeing the SPE's debt. But because of the relatively short term of the lease, it was deemed to be an operating lease and hence did not have to be capitalized and shown on the balance sheet.

Synthetic leases stayed under the radar until 2001 when they were at the heart of several major financial fraud cases that led to bankruptcies and jail terms. To prevent this type of financial fraud, in 2003 the FASB put in place rules that require companies to report on their balance sheets most special purpose entities and synthetic leases, limiting management's opportunity to hide these transactions from shareholders.

But humans are creative and developed multi-asset entities that are very similar to the SPEs. These multi-asset entities provide financing for more than one asset rather than the single asset financing of an SPE, but they are still highly levered with financing provided by multiple financial institutions. Like an SPE, the lease did not have to be reported on financial statements. This changed in 2018, and they now must be reported. Given human ingenuity, we suspect that a new method will be developed so that companies can add leverage via leases that are not reported on financial statements. In financial games of whack a mole, it always seems that regulators are one step behind.

SELF-TEST

How might leasing lead to increased credit availability?

What is a synthetic lease?

How do tax laws affect leasing?

19-9 Other Reasons for Leasing

Up to this point, we have noted that the tax rate or other differentials are generally necessary to make leasing attractive to both the lessee and lessor. If the lessee and lessor are facing different tax situations, including the alternative minimum tax, then it is often possible to structure a lease that is beneficial to both parties. However, there are other reasons that firms might want to lease an asset rather than buy it.

More than half of all commercial aircraft are leased, and smaller airlines, especially in developing nations, lease an especially high percentage of their planes. One of the reasons for this is that airlines can reduce their risks by leasing. If an airline purchased all its aircraft, it would be hampered in its ability to respond to changing market conditions. Because they have become specialists at matching airlines with available aircraft, the aircraft lessors (which are multibillion-dollar concerns) are quite good at managing the changing demand for different types of aircraft. This permits them to offer attractive lease terms. In this situation, *leasing provides operating flexibility.* Leasing is not necessarily less expensive than buying, but the operating flexibility is quite valuable.

Leasing is also an attractive alternative for many high-technology items that are subject to rapid and unpredictable technological obsolescence. Suppose a small rural hospital wants to buy a magnetic resonance imaging (MRI) device. If it buys the MRI equipment, then it is exposed to the risk of technological obsolescence. In a short time some new technology might lower the value of the current system and thus render the project unprofitable. Because it does not use much equipment of this nature, the hospital would bear a great deal of risk if it bought the MRI device. However, a lessor that specializes in state-of-the-art medical equipment would be exposed to significantly less risk. By purchasing and then leasing many different items, the lessor benefits from diversification. Of course, over time some items will probably lose more value than the lessor expected, but this will be offset by other items that retain more value than expected. Also, because such a leasing company will be especially familiar with the market for used medical equipment, it can refurbish the equipment and then get a better price in the resale market than could a remote rural hospital. For these reasons, *leasing can reduce the risk of technological obsolescence.*

Leasing can also be attractive when a firm is uncertain about the demand for its products or services and thus about how long the equipment will be needed. Again, consider the hospital industry. Hospitals often offer services that are dependent on a single staff member—for example, a physician who performs liver transplants. To support the physician's practice, the hospital might have to invest millions in equipment that can be used only for this particular procedure. The hospital will charge for the use of the equipment, and if things go as expected, the investment will be profitable. However, if the physician leaves the hospital and if no replacement can be recruited, then the project is dead and the equipment becomes useless to the hospital. In this case, a lease with a cancelation clause would permit the hospital to simply return the equipment. The lessor would charge something for the cancelation clause, and this would lower the expected profitability of the project, but it would provide the hospital with an option to abandon the equipment, and the value of the option could easily exceed the incremental cost of the cancelation clause. The leasing company would be willing to write this option because it is in a better position to remarket the equipment, either by writing another lease or by selling it outright.

The leasing industry recently introduced a type of lease that even transfers some of a project's operating risk from the lessee to the lessor and also motivates the lessor to maintain the leased equipment in good working order. Instead of making a fixed rental payment, the lessee pays a fee each time the leased equipment is used. This type of lease originated with copy machines, where the lessee pays so much per month plus an additional amount per copy made. If the machine breaks down, no copies are made and the lessor's rental income declines. This motivates the lessor to repair the machine quickly.

This type of lease is also used in the health care industry, where it is called a "per-procedure lease." For example, a hospital might lease an X-ray machine for a fixed fee per X-ray, say, $5. If demand for the machine's X-rays is less than expected by the hospital, then revenues will be lower than expected—but so will the machine's capital costs. Conversely, high demand would lead to higher than expected lease costs—but these would be offset by higher than expected revenues. By using a per-procedure lease, the hospital is converting a fixed cost for the equipment into a variable cost and thereby reducing the machine's operating leverage and break-even point. The net effect is to reduce the project's risk. Of course, the expected cost of a per-procedure lease might be more than the cost of a conventional lease, but the risk reduction benefit could be worth the cost. Note too that if the lessor writes a large number of per-procedure leases then much of the riskiness inherent in such leases can be eliminated by diversification, so the risk premiums that lessors build into per-procedure lease payments could be low enough to attract potential lessees.

Some companies also find leasing attractive because the lessor is able to provide servicing on favorable terms. For example, Virco Manufacturing, a company that makes school desks and other furniture, recently leased 25 truck tractors and 140 trailers that it uses to ship furniture from its plant. The lease agreement, with a large leasing company that specializes in purchasing, maintaining, and then reselling trucks, permitted the replacement of an aging fleet that Virco had built up over the years. "We are pretty good at manufacturing furniture, but we aren't very good at maintaining a truck fleet," said Virco's CFO.

There are other reasons that might cause a firm to lease an asset rather than buy it. Often these reasons are difficult to quantify and so cannot be easily incorporated into an NPV or IRR analysis. Nevertheless, a sound lease decision must begin with a quantitative analysis, and then qualitative factors can be considered before making the final lease-or-buy decision.[13]

SELF-TEST

Describe some economic factors that might provide an advantage to leasing.

[13]For more on leasing, see Thomas J. Finucane, "Some Empirical Evidence on the Use of Financial Leases," *Journal of Financial Research*, Fall 1988, pp. 321–333; and Lawrence D. Schall, "The Evaluation of Lease Financing Opportunities," *Midland Corporate Finance Journal*, Spring 1985, pp. 48–65.

SUMMARY

Leasing is an important financing alternative to borrowing. In this chapter, we discussed the leasing decision from the standpoints of both the lessee and lessor. The key concepts covered are listed here.

- There are several important types of lease agreements: (1) the **operating lease**; (2) the **finance lease**, which is also called a **capital lease**; (3) the **sale-and-leaseback**; (4) the **combination lease**; and (5) the **synthetic lease**.
- The IRS has specific guidelines that apply to lease arrangements. A lease that meets these guidelines is called a **guideline lease**, or a **tax-oriented lease**, because the IRS permits the lessor to deduct the asset's depreciation and allows the lessee to deduct the lease payments. A lease that does not meet the IRS guidelines is called a **non-tax-oriented lease**, in which case ownership for tax purposes resides with the lessee rather than the lessor.
- **ASU 2016-02** requires that companies must **capitalize** virtually all leases longer than one year and reported them on the balance sheets.
- The lessee's analysis consists basically of a comparison of the PV of leasing versus the PV of owning. The difference in these PV's is called the **net advantage to leasing (NAL)**.
- One of the key issues in the lessee's analysis is the appropriate discount rate. A lease is a substitute for debt, cash flows in a lease analysis are stated on an after-tax basis, and cash flows are known with relative certainty, so the appropriate discount rate is the lessee's after-tax cost of debt.
- The lessor evaluates the lease as an investment. If the lease's NPV is greater than zero or if its IRR is greater than the lessor's opportunity cost, then the lease should be written.
- Leasing is motivated by various differences between lessees and lessors. Three of the most important reasons for leasing are: (1) tax rate differentials, (2) leases in which the lessor is better able than the lessee to bear the residual value risk, and (3) situations in which the lessor can maintain the leased equipment more efficiently than the lessee can.
- *Web Extension 19A* explains the percentage cost of leasing, and *Web Extension 19B* explains leveraged leases.

QUESTIONS

(19-1)   Define each of the following terms:
   a. Lessee; lessor
   b. Operating lease; financial lease; sale-and-leaseback; combination lease
   c. Off–balance sheet financing; capitalizing
   d. FASB Statement 13; ASU 2016-02
   e. Guideline lease
   f. Residual value
   g. Lessee's analysis; lessor's analysis
   h. Net advantage to leasing (NAL)

(19-2)   Distinguish between operating leases and financial leases. Would you be more likely to find an operating lease employed for a fleet of trucks or for a manufacturing plant?

(19-3)   Are lessees more likely to be in higher or lower income tax brackets than lessors?

(19-4)   In our Anderson Company example, we assumed that the lease could not be canceled. What effect would a cancelation clause have on the lessee's analysis? On the lessor's analysis?

SELF-TEST PROBLEM SOLUTION APPEARS IN APPENDIX A

(11-1)
Investment Outlay

The Randolph Teweles Company (RTC) has decided to acquire a new tractor. One alternative is to lease the tractor on a 4-year tax-oriented contract for a lease payment of $16,000 per year, with payments to be made at the *beginning* of each year. (*Note:* The tax shelter from the lease payment in Year 0 occurs at Year 0.) The lease would include maintenance. RTC has a marginal federal-plus-state tax rate of 25%.

Alternatively, RTC could purchase the tractor outright for $40,000, financing the purchase by a bank loan for the net purchase price and amortizing the loan over a 4-year period at an interest rate of 8% per year. Under the borrow-to-purchase arrangement, RTC would have to maintain the tractor at a cost of $1,000 per year, payable at year end. The tractor falls into the MACRS 3-year class with depreciation rates for Year 1 through Year 4 equal to 0.3333, 0.4445, 0.1481, and 0.0741. The tractor has a residual value of $10,000, which is the expected market value after 4 years. RTC plans to replace the tractor at the end of Year 4 irrespective of whether it leases or buys.

a. What is RTC's present value of leasing?

b. What is RTC's present value of owning? Should the truck be leased or purchased?

PROBLEMS ANSWERS ARE IN APPENDIX B

EASY PROBLEMS 1–3

(19-1)
Cost of Leasing

Bird Wing Bedding can lease an asset for 4 years with payments of $20,000 due at the beginning of the year. The firm can borrow at a 6% rate and pays a 25% federal-plus-state tax rate. The lease qualifies as a tax-oriented lease. What is the cost of leasing?

(19-2)
Cost of Borrowing

Comey Products has decided to acquire some new equipment having a $200,000 purchase price. The equipment will last 4 years and is in the MACRS 3-year class. (The depreciation rates for Year 1 through Year 4 are equal to 0.3333, 0.4445, 0.1481, and 0.0741.) The firm can borrow at a 9% rate and pays a 25% federal-plus-state tax rate. Comey is considering leasing the property but wishes to know the cost of borrowing that it should use when comparing purchasing to leasing and has hired you to answer this question. What is the correct answer to Comey's question? (*Hint:* Use the shortcut method in Section 19-5a to find the after-tax cost of the loan payments.)

(19-3)
Finance Lease:
Net Advantage
to Leasing

Dunbar Corporation can purchase an asset for $30,000; the asset will be worthless after 14 years. Alternatively, it could lease the asset for 14 years with an annual lease payment of $3,653 paid at the end of each year. The firm's cost of debt is 9%. The IRS classifies the lease as a non-tax-oriented lease. What is the net advantage to leasing?

INTERMEDIATE PROBLEMS 4–6

(19-4)
Financial Statement
Reporting for an
Operating Lease

Harmeling Paint Ball (HPB) Corporation needs a new air compressor that costs $80,000. HPB will need it for only 3 years even though the compressor's economic life is long enough so that the lease is an operating lease. The firm can lease the compressor for 3 years with $15,000 lease payments at the end of each year. HPB's cost of debt is 12%. Answer the following questions. (*Hint:* See Table 19-1.)

a. What is the initial lease liability that must be reported on the balance sheet?

b. What is the initial right-of-use asset?

c. What will HPB report as the Year-1 lease expense?

     d. What is the Year-1 imputed interest expense?

     e. What lease liability must be reported at Year 1?

     f. What right-of-use asset must be reported at Year 1?

(19-5)
Financial Statement
Reporting for a
Finance Lease

Reynolds Construction (RC) needs a piece of equipment that costs $100,000. The equipment has an economic life of 2 years and no residual value. The equipment will not require maintenance because its useful life is so short. RC can borrow the full cost of the equipment at an interest rate of 8% with payments due at the end of the year. Alternatively, RC can lease the equipment for $55,000 with payments due at the end of the year. Assume RC chooses the lease, which is a finance lease for financial reporting purposes. Answer the following questions. (*Hint:* See Table 19-1.)

     a. What is the initial lease liability that must be reported on the balance sheet?

     b. What is the initial right-of-use asset?

     c. What will RC report as an interest expense at Year 1?

     d. What will RC report as an amortization expense at Year 1?

     e. What will RC report as the lease liability at Year 1?

     f. What will RC report as the right-of-use asset at Year 1?

(19-6)
Lease versus Buy

Big Sky Mining Company must install $1.5 million of new machinery in its Nevada mine. It can obtain a bank loan for 100% of the purchase price, or it can lease the machinery. Assume that the following facts apply.

     (1) The machinery falls into the MACRS 3-year class.

     (2) Under either the lease or the purchase, Big Sky must pay for insurance, property taxes, and maintenance.

     (3) The firm's tax rate is 25%.

     (4) The loan would have an interest rate of 15%. It would be nonamortizing, with only interest paid at the end of each year for four years and the principal repaid at Year 4.

     (5) The lease terms call for $400,000 payments at the end of each of the next 4 years.

     (6) Big Sky Mining has no use for the machine beyond the expiration of the lease, and the machine has an estimated residual value of $250,000 at the end of the 4th year.

         a. What is the cost of owning?

         b. What is the cost of leasing?

         c. What is the NAL of the lease?

CHALLENGING PROBLEM 7

(19-7)
Lease versus Buy

Sadik Industries must install $1 million of new machinery in its Texas plant. It can obtain a 6-year bank loan for 100% of the cost at a 14% interest rate with equal payments at the end of each year. Sadik's tax rate is 25%. The equipment falls in the MACRS 3-year class. (The depreciation rates for Year 1 through Year 4 are equal to 0.3333, 0.4445, 0.1481, and 0.0741.)

Alternatively, a Texas investment banking firm that represents a group of investors can arrange a guideline lease calling for payments of $320,000 at the end of each year for 3 years. Under the proposed lease terms, the Sadik must pay for insurance, property taxes, and maintenance.

Sadik must use the equipment if it is to continue in business, so it will almost certainly want to acquire the property at the end of the lease. If it does, then under the lease terms, it can purchase the machinery at its fair market value at Year 3. The best estimate of this market value is $200,000, but it could be much higher or lower under certain circumstances. If purchased at Year 3, the used equipment would fall into the MACRS 3-year class. Sadik would actually be able to make the purchase on the last day of the year (i.e., slightly before Year 3), so Sadik would get to take the first depreciation expense at Year 3 (the remaining depreciation expenses would be from Year 4 through Year 6). On the time line, Sadik would show the cost of purchasing the used equipment at Year 3 *and* its depreciation expenses starting at Year 3.

To assist management in making the proper lease-versus-buy decision, you are asked to answer the following questions:

    a. What is the cost of owning?

    b. What is the cost of leasing?

    c. What is the net advantage to leasing?

    d. Consider the $200,000 estimated residual value. How high could the residual value get before the net advantage of leasing falls to zero?

SPREADSHEET PROBLEM

(19-8)
Build a Model:
Lessee's Analysis

resource

Start with the partial model in the file *Ch19 P08 Build a Model.xlsx* on the textbook's Web site. As part of its overall plant modernization and cost reduction program, Western Fabrics' management has decided to install a new automated weaving loom. In the capital budgeting analysis of this equipment, the IRR of the project was found to be 20% versus the project's required return of 12%.

The loom has an invoice price of $250,000, including delivery and installation charges. The funds needed could be borrowed from the bank through a 4-year amortized loan at a 10% interest rate, with payments to be made at the end of each year. In the event the loom is purchased, the manufacturer will contract to maintain and service it for a fee of $20,000 per year paid at the end of each year. The loom falls in the MACRS 5-year class, and Western's marginal federal-plus-state tax rate is 25%.

Aubey Automation Inc., maker of the loom, has offered to lease the loom to Western for $70,000 upon delivery and installation (at t = 0) plus four additional annual lease payments of $70,000 to be made at the end of Years 1 to 4. (Note that there are five lease payments in total.) The lease agreement includes maintenance and servicing. The loom has an expected life of 8 years, at which time its expected salvage value is zero; however, after 4 years its market value is expected to equal its book value of $42,500. Western plans to build an entirely new plant in 4 years, so it has no interest in either leasing or owning the proposed loom for more than that period.

    a. Should the loom be leased or purchased?

    b. The salvage value is clearly the most uncertain cash flow in the analysis. What effect would a salvage value risk adjustment have on the analysis? (Assume that the appropriate salvage value pre-tax discount rate is 15%.)

    c. Assuming that the after-tax cost of debt should be used to discount all anticipated cash flows, at what lease payment would the firm be indifferent to either leasing or buying?

MINI CASE

Lewis Securities Inc. has decided to acquire a new market data and quotation system for its Richmond home office. The system receives current market prices and other information from several online data services and then either displays the information on a screen or stores it for later retrieval by the firm's brokers. The system also permits customers to call up current quotes on terminals in the lobby.

The equipment costs $1,000,000 and, if it were purchased, Lewis could obtain a term loan for the full purchase price at a 10% interest rate. Although the equipment has a

6-year useful life, it is classified as a special-purpose computer and therefore falls into the MACRS 3-year class. If the system were purchased, a 4-year maintenance contract could be obtained at a cost of $20,000 per year, payable at the beginning of each year. The equipment would be sold after 4 years, and the best estimate of its residual value is $200,000. However, because real-time display system technology is changing rapidly, the actual residual value is uncertain.

As an alternative to the borrow-and-buy plan, the equipment manufacturer informed Lewis that Consolidated Leasing would be willing to write a 4-year guideline lease on the equipment, including maintenance, for payments of $260,000 at the beginning of each year. Lewis's marginal federal-plus-state tax rate is 25%. You have been asked to analyze the lease-versus-purchase decision and, in the process, to answer the following questions.

a. (1) Who are the two parties to a lease transaction?
   (2) What are the four primary types of leases, and what are their characteristics?
   (3) How are leases classified for tax purposes?
   (4) What effect does leasing have on a firm's balance sheet?
   (5) What effect does leasing have on a firm's capital structure?

b. (1) What is the present value of owning the equipment? (*Hint:* Set up a time line that shows the net cash flows over the period t = 0 to t = 4, and then find the PV of these net cash flows, or the PV of owning.)
   (2) What is the discount rate for the cash flows of owning?

c. What is Lewis's present value of leasing the equipment? (*Hint:* Again, construct a time line.)

d. What is the net advantage to leasing (NAL)? Does your analysis indicate that Lewis should buy or lease the equipment? Explain.

e. Now assume that the equipment's residual value could be as low as $0 or as high as $400,000, but $200,000 is the expected value. Because the residual value is riskier than the other relevant cash flows, this differential risk should be incorporated into the analysis. Describe how this could be accomplished. (No calculations are necessary, but explain how you would modify the analysis if calculations were required.) What effect would the residual value's increased uncertainty have on Lewis' lease-versus-purchase decision?

f. The lessee compares the present value of owning the equipment with the present value of leasing it. Now put yourself in the lessor's shoes. In a few sentences, how should you analyze the decision to write or not to write the lease?

g. (1) Assume that the lease payments were actually $280,000 per year, that Consolidated Leasing is also in the 25% tax bracket, and that it also forecasts a $200,000 residual value. Also, to furnish the maintenance support, it would have to purchase a maintenance contract from the manufacturer at the same $20,000 annual cost, again paid in advance. Consolidated Leasing can obtain an expected 10% pre-tax return on investments of similar risk. What are its NPV and IRR of leasing under these conditions?
   (2) What do you think the lessor's NPV would be if the lease payment were set at $260,000 per year? (*Hint:* The lessor's cash flows would be a "mirror image" of the lessee's cash flows.)

h. Lewis's management has been considering moving to a new downtown location, and they are concerned that these plans may come to fruition prior to the equipment lease's expiration. If the move occurs then Lewis would buy or lease an entirely new set of equipment, so management would like to include a cancelation clause in the lease contract. What effect would such a clause have on the riskiness of the lease from Lewis's standpoint? From the lessor's standpoint? If you were the lessor, would you insist on changing any of the other lease terms if a cancelation clause were added? Should the cancelation clause contain provisions similar to call premiums or any restrictive covenants and/or penalties of the type contained in bond indentures? Explain your answer.

i. What are some other issues in lease analysis?

SELECTED ADDITIONAL CASES

The following cases from CengageCompose cover many of the concepts discussed in this chapter and are available at **http://compose.cengage.com**.

Klein-Brigham Series:
Case 25, "Environmental Sciences, Inc.," Case 49, "Agro Chemical Corporation," Case 69, "Friendly Food Stores, Inc.," and Case 26, "Prudent Solutions, Inc.," all examine the lease decision from the perspectives of both the lessee and the lessor.

Brigham-Buzzard Series:
Case 12, "Powerline Network Corporation (Leasing)."

CHAPTER 20

Hybrid Financing: Preferred Stock, Warrants, and Convertibles

Can eight words and one number roil the financial markets? Yes, if they are the tweet by Tesla Inc. CEO Elon Musk on August 7, 2018: "Am considering taking Tesla private at $420. Funding secured." Tesla's stock had closed at $341.99 on August 6 but jumped by 11% to $379.57 by closing on August 7.

Tesla has around $2.3 billion in bonds that allow their owners to exchange a bond for 2.7788 shares of Tesla's stock. The par value of each bond is $1,000, so the break-even stock price is $359.87: $1,000/2.7788 = $359.87. If the stock price is higher than the break-even price, then a debtholder should exchange a bond for the stock. For example, if the stock price is $380, then a debtholder can choose to receive stock worth $1,056: 2.7788($380) = $1,055.94 ≈ $1,056. This is more than the $1,000 par value the investor would receive, so bondholders should convert their bonds into stock. The reverse is true if the stock price is less than $359.87.

About $900 million of Tesla's convertible debt matures in early 2019 and the rest in early 2021. If Tesla's stock price is less than $359.87 when the bonds mature, then bondholders won't convert. Instead, Tesla must come up with cash to repay the par value. This could be a problem because Tesla has a negative cash flow. Unless Tesla can generate a positive cash flow, it will need to secure additional financing to pay bondholders when the bonds mature.

However, news sources soon reported that Tesla did not have funding secured! On August 24, Mr. Musk and Tesla's board of directors announced that Tesla would *not* go private. Its stock had already fallen to from a high of $379.57 to $320 and continued to slide downward for the next two weeks to about $263. Many investors filed lawsuits alleging financial fraud, as did the Securities and Exchange Commission (SEC) on September 27. The SEC suit was settled on October 16, requiring that (1) Mr. Musk and Tesla each pay a $20 million fine, (1) Mr. Musk cannot be Tesla's CEO for three years, (4) Tesla must add two independent board members, (5) and that Tesla must hire a securities lawyer to oversee its social media use. The market must have anticipated a worse settlement, because Tesla's stock went up by over 6% to $276.59, much higher than the market's overall return of 2%.

We don't know what will eventually happen, but we can say for certain that Tesla's stock and convertible bonds are taking a wild ride. Keep Tesla and its convertible bonds in mind as you read this chapter.

resource

*The textbook's Web site contains an Excel file that will guide you through the chapter's calculations. The file for this chapter is **Ch20 Tool Kit.xlsx**, and we encourage you to open the file and follow along as you read the chapter.*

In previous chapters, we examined common stocks and various types of long-term debt. In this chapter, we examine three other securities used to raise long-term capital: (1) *preferred stock*, which is a hybrid security that represents a cross between debt and common equity, (2) *warrants*, which are derivative securities issued by firms to facilitate the issuance of some other type of security, and (3) *convertibles*, which combine the features of debt (or preferred stock) and warrants.

20-1 Preferred Stock

Preferred stock is a hybrid—it is similar to bonds in some respects and to common stock in other ways. Accountants classify preferred stock as equity; hence they show it on the balance sheet as an equity account. However, from a financial perspective preferred stock lies somewhere between debt and common equity: It imposes a fixed charge and thus increases the firm's financial leverage, yet omitting the preferred dividend does not force a company into bankruptcy. Also, unlike interest on debt, preferred dividends are not deductible by the issuing corporation, so preferred stock has a higher cost of capital than debt. We first describe the basic features of preferred stock, after which we discuss the types of preferred stock and the advantages and disadvantages of preferred stock.

20-1a Basic Features, Risks, and Tax Treatments of Preferred Stock

The following sections explain the basic features, risks, and tax treatments of preferred stocks.

FEATURES

Preferred stock has a par (or liquidating) value, often either $25 or $100. The dividend is stated as either a percentage of par, as so many dollars per share, or both ways. For example, several years ago Klondike Paper Company sold 150,000 shares of $100 par value perpetual preferred stock for a total of $15 million. This preferred stock had a stated annual dividend of $12 per share, so the preferred dividend yield was $12/$100 = 0.12, or 12%, at the time of issue. The dividend was set when the stock was issued; it will not be changed in the future.

Although the dividend is fixed, the market price of preferred stock changes as market conditions change. Continuing with Klondike, the required rate of return (r_{ps}) for its preferred currently is 9%. Therefore, the price is now $133.33: $12/0.09 = $133.33. If the required return increased to 15%, the price would fall to $80: $12/0.15 = $80.

Some preferred stocks are similar to perpetual bonds in that they have no maturity date, but most new issues now have specified maturities. For example, many preferred shares have a sinking fund provision that calls for the retirement of 2% of the issue each year, meaning the issue will "mature" in a maximum of 50 years. Also, many preferred issues are callable by the issuing corporation, which can also limit the life of the preferred.[1]

About half of all preferred stock issued in recent years has a feature that allows the owner to convert the preferred stock into common stock. We discuss convertibles in Section 20-3. Corporations own virtually all nonconvertible preferred stock because dividend income is taxed less than interest income. We explain dividend taxation later in this section.

---

[1]Prior to the late 1970s, virtually all preferred stock was perpetual and almost no issues had sinking funds or call provisions. Then insurance company regulators, worried about the unrealized losses the companies had been incurring on preferred holdings as a result of rising interest rates, made changes essentially mandating that insurance companies buy only limited life preferreds. From that time on, virtually no new preferred has been perpetual. This example illustrates the way securities change as a result of changes in the economic environment.

If a company does not have enough income to pay a preferred dividend, the company can omit it without triggering bankruptcy. However, most preferred issues have **cumulative preferred dividends**, meaning that the cumulative total of unpaid preferred dividends must be paid before dividends can be paid on the common stock. Unpaid preferred dividends are called **arrearages**. However, they do not accrue any interest prior to their eventual payment to the preferred stock owners.

Many preferred stocks accrue arrearages for only a limited number of years. For example, the cumulative feature may cease after 3 years. However, the dividends in arrears continue in force until they are paid.

Preferred stock normally has no voting rights. However, most preferred issues stipulate that the preferred stockholders can elect a minority of the directors—say, three of ten—if the preferred dividend is passed (omitted). Some preferreds even entitle their holders to elect a majority of the board.

RISKS

What impact does preferred stock have on the risks faced by issuing companies and investors? Let's start with issuing companies.

Suppose a company is experiencing some temporary problems that it can fix if given a little time. If the company had previously obtained financing as bonds instead of preferred stock, the company could be forced into bankruptcy before it could straighten out its problems. This suggests that financing with preferred stock is less risky than financing with debt.

However, financing with preferred stock does not completely eliminate risk to the issuer. If the issuer's temporary problems are such that it omits preferred dividends, then investors are reluctant to buy new bond issues. Also, investors will not buy new issues of preferred or common stock except at rock-bottom prices. Therefore, an issuing company might not be able to obtain financing that would give itself enough time to weather temporary problems.

Despite the problem a company can have with raising new financing when dividends are in arrears, this is not nearly as bad as triggering bankruptcy by missing a debt payment. Therefore, the net effect for the issuing company is that financing with preferred stock is less risky than financing with bonds.

For an investor, however, preferred stock is riskier than bonds: (1) Preferred stockholders' claims are subordinated to those of bondholders in the event of liquidation. (2) Bondholders are more likely to continue receiving income during hard times than are preferred stockholders. Accordingly, investors require a higher after-tax rate of return on a firm's preferred stock than on its bonds.

Dividend income and interest income are taxed differently, complicating the after-tax comparison of debt versus preferred stock. The next section shows how to determine the after-tax yields.

TAXES

What impact does preferred stock versus debt have on taxes for (1) issuers, (2) corporate investors, and (3) individual investors? We begin with issuers.

Issuers Issuing companies can deduct interest expenses from taxable income but they cannot deduct preferred dividend payments. Letting T_c denote the corporate tax rate, an issuer's after-tax cost of debt is $r_d(1 - T_c)$ and its after-tax cost of preferred stock is r_{ps}. If the cost of preferred stock is less than the after-tax cost of debt, then debt financing is cheaper for an issuer; otherwise, issuing preferred stock is a better choice. We can be more specific and identify the break-even point at which the cost of preferred is equal to the after-tax cost of debt:

$$r_{ps} \text{ break-even} = r_d(1 - T_c)$$

For example, suppose $r_d = 8\%$ and $T_c = 25\%$. The break-even point is 6%:

$$r_{ps} \text{ break-even} = r_d(1 - T_c) = 8\%(1 - 0.25) = 6\%$$

If r_{ps} is greater than 6%, then preferred stock is more costly than debt for the issuing company. Alternatively, if r_{ps} is less than 6%, then debt is less costly for issuers.

Corporate Investors Before the 2017 Tax Cuts and Jobs Act (TCJA), corporations could exclude 70% of dividend income from taxable income. After 2017, the TCJA allows companies to exclude only 50%. This change reduces the tax advantage of receiving preferred dividends instead of interest payments for corporate investors. Keep in mind that the TCJA also cut the corporate tax rate from 35% to 21%. What is the net effect of these changes?

To illustrate the changes with an example, suppose a company receives $100 million in interest income and $100 million in dividend income after implementation of the TCJA. The corporate tax rate is 21% for most corporations, so the after-tax interest income is $79 million: $100(1 − 0.21) = $79. The company can exclude 50% of the dividend from taxes but pays a 21% rate on the remainder. The after-tax dividend is $89.5 million:

$$
\begin{aligned}
\text{Post-TCJA after-tax dividend income} &= \text{Dividend} - \text{Tax on dividend}\\
&= \text{Dividend} - \text{Dividend}(1 - \text{Exclusion rate})(T_c)\\
&= \$100 - \$100(1 - 0.50)(0.21)\\
&= \$89.5 \text{ million}
\end{aligned}
$$

It is easy to calculate the pre-TCJA after-tax dividend and interest income using the same approach. The following table reports the post-TCJA and pre-TCJA results.

	Post-TCJA	Pre-TCJA	Change
After-tax dividend income	$89.5	$89.5	$0.0
After-tax interest income	$79.0	$65.0	$14.0
Advantage to after-tax dividend income	$10.5	$24.5	−$14.0

The last column shows that the TCJA did not change the after-tax dividend income for corporate investors, possibly because this was Congress's intent. However, the TCJA significantly increased the after-tax interest income by $14. The bottom row shows that the TCJA reduced the tax advantage of dividend income by $14. Although corporate investors still receive a tax advantage from dividend income, it has shrunk. It is too soon to tell, but the post-TCJA tax advantage might not be enough to compensate corporate investors for the additional risk due to owning preferred stock relative to owning interest-bearing securities.

There is an additional aspect of dividend income versus interest income for corporate investors. Namely, the TCJA imposed a limit on the amount of net interest expense that may be deducted in a single year. For most companies, the allowable interest expense deduction is 30% of earnings before interest, taxes, depreciation, and amortization (EBITDA) for 2019, 2020, and 2021. After that, the 30% limit will be based on earnings before interest and taxes (EBIT). Any excess interest expense can be carried forward indefinitely to offset future income.

How does this affect a corporate investor? Note that a dollar of interest income offsets a dollar interest expense, hence increasing the amount of interest expense a company can deduct before hitting the limit. Therefore, a highly levered company that is subject to the limitation would prefer interest income instead of dividend income.

Individual Investors   The 2017 Tax Cuts and Jobs Act (TCJA) did not make any significant changes to the tax treatment of dividend income versus interest income. High-wealth individuals pay a 35% tax on ordinary income, which includes interest income. In contrast, they pay a 20% tax on dividend income.[2]

20-1b Other Types of Preferred Stock

In addition to "plain vanilla" preferred stock, there are two primary variations: adjustable rate and market auction preferred stock.[3]

ADJUSTABLE RATE PREFERRED STOCK

Instead of paying fixed dividends, **adjustable rate preferred stock (ARP)** has dividends tied to the rate on Treasury securities. ARPs are issued mainly by utilities and large commercial banks. When ARPs were first developed, they were touted as nearly perfect short-term corporate investments because (1) only 30% of the dividends are taxable to corporations, and (2) the floating-rate feature was supposed to keep the issue trading at near par. The new security proved to be popular as a short-term investment for firms with idle cash, so mutual funds that held ARPs sprouted like weeds (and shares of these funds, in turn, were purchased by corporations). However, the ARPs still had some price volatility due to (1) changes in the riskiness of the issuers (some big banks that had issued ARPs, such as Continental Illinois, ran into serious loan default problems) and (2) fluctuations in Treasury yields between dividend rate adjustment dates. Therefore, the ARPs had too much price instability to be held in the liquid asset portfolios of many corporate investors.

MARKET AUCTION PREFERRED STOCK

In 1984, investment bankers introduced **money market preferred stock**, which is also called **market auction preferred stock**.[4] Here the underwriter conducts an auction on the issue every 7 weeks. (To get the 50% exclusion from taxable income, corporate buyers must hold the stock for at least 46 days.) Holders who want to sell their shares can put them up for auction at par value. Buyers then submit bids in the form of the yields they are willing to accept over the next 7-week period. The yield set on the issue for the coming period is the lowest yield sufficient to sell all the shares being offered at that auction. The buyers pay the sellers the par value; hence holders are virtually assured that their shares

---

[2]There is also a 3.8% Net Investment Income Tax (NIIT), which increases the effective tax rate on interest income and dividend income for many high-wealth individuals.

[3]In addition to the types of preferred stock described in this section, some financially engineered preferred stock has "dividends" that the paying company can deduct for tax purposes in the same way that interest payments are deductible. Therefore, the company is able to pay a higher rate on such preferred stock, making it potentially attractive to individual investors. These securities trade under a variety of colorful names, including MIPS (Modified Income Preferred Securities), QUIPS (Quarterly Income Preferred Securities), TOPrS (Trust Originated Preferred Stock), and QUIDS (Quarterly Income Debt Securities). However, dividends from these hybrid securities are not subject to the 50% corporate exclusion and are taxed as ordinary income for individual investors.

[4]Confusingly, market auction preferred stock is frequently referred to as *auction-rate preferred* stock and with the acronym ARP as well.

can be sold at par. The issuer then must pay a dividend rate over the next 7-week period as determined by the auction. From the holder's standpoint, market auction preferred is a low-risk, largely tax-exempt, 7-week maturity security that can be sold between auction dates at close to par.

In practice, things may not go quite so smoothly. If there are few potential buyers, then an excessively high yield might be required to clear the market. To protect the issuing firms or mutual funds from high dividend payments, the securities have a cap on the allowable dividend yield. If the market-clearing yield is higher than this cap, then the next dividend yield will be set equal to this cap rate, but the auction will fail and the owners of the securities who wish to sell will not be able to do so. This happened in February 2008, and many market auction preferred stockholders were left holding securities they wanted to liquidate.[5]

20-1c Advantages and Disadvantages of Preferred Stock

There are both advantages and disadvantages to financing with preferred stock. Here are the major advantages from the issuer's standpoint.

1. In contrast to bonds, a company may pass (i.e., not pay) a preferred dividend without triggering bankruptcy.
2. By issuing preferred stock, the firm avoids the dilution of common equity that occurs when common stock is sold.
3. Because preferred stock sometimes has no maturity and because preferred sinking fund payments (if present) are typically spread over a long period, preferred issues reduce the cash flow drain from repayment of principal that occurs with debt issues.

There are two major disadvantages.

1. Preferred stock dividends are not normally deductible to the issuer, so the after-tax cost of preferred is typically higher than the after-tax cost of debt. However, the tax advantage of preferreds to corporate purchasers lowers its pre-tax cost and thus its effective cost.
2. Although preferred dividends can be passed, investors expect them to be paid and firms intend to pay them if conditions permit. Thus, preferred dividends are considered to be a fixed cost. As a result, their use—like that of debt—increases financial risk and hence the cost of common equity.

SELF-TEST

Should preferred stock be classified as equity or debt? Explain.

Who are the major purchasers of nonconvertible preferred stock? Why?

Briefly explain the mechanics of adjustable rate and market auction preferred stock.

What are the advantages and disadvantages of preferred stock to the issuer?

A company's preferred stock has a pre-tax dividend yield of 7%, and its debt has a pre-tax yield of 8%. If an investor is in the 35% marginal tax bracket, what are the after-tax yields of the preferred stock and debt? **(6.27% and 5.20%)**

---

[5]For more on preferred stock, see Arthur L. Houston Jr. and Carol Olson Houston, "Financing with Preferred Stock," *Financial Management*, Autumn 1990, pp. 42–54; and Michael J. Alderson and Donald R. Fraser, "Financial Innovations and Excesses Revisited: The Case of Auction Rate Preferred Stock," *Financial Management*, Summer 1993, pp. 61–75.

20-2 Warrants

A **warrant** is a certificate issued by a company that gives the holder the right to buy a stated number of shares of the company's stock at a specified price for some specified length of time. Generally, warrants are issued along with debt, and they are used to induce investors to buy long-term debt with a lower coupon rate than would otherwise be required. For example, when Infomatic Corporation, a rapidly growing high-tech company, wanted to sell $50 million of 20-year bonds in 2019, the company's investment bankers informed the financial vice president that the bonds would be difficult to sell and that a coupon rate of 10% would be required. However, as an alternative the bankers suggested that investors might be willing to buy the bonds with a coupon rate of only 8% if the company would offer 20 warrants with each $1,000 bond, each warrant entitling the holder to buy one share of common stock at a strike price (also called an *exercise price*) of $22 per share. The stock was selling for $20 per share at the time, and the warrants would expire in the year 2029 if they had not been exercised previously.

Why would investors be willing to buy Infomatic's bonds at a yield of only 8% in a 10% market just because warrants were also offered as part of the package? It's because the warrants are long-term *call options* that allow holders to buy the firm's common stock at the strike price regardless of how high the market price climbs. The value of this option offsets the low interest rate on the bonds and makes the package of low-yield bonds plus warrants attractive to investors. (See Chapter 8 for a discussion of options.)

20-2a Initial Market Price of a Bond with Warrants

If Infomatic's bonds had been issued as straight debt, they would have carried a 10% interest rate. However, with warrants attached, the bonds were sold to yield 8%. Someone buying the bonds at their $1,000 initial offering price would thus be receiving a package consisting of an 8%, 20-year bond plus 20 warrants. Because the going interest rate on bonds as risky as those of Infomatic was 10%, we can find the straight-debt value of the bonds, assuming an annual coupon for ease of illustration, as follows:

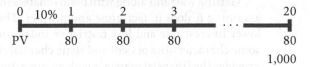

Using a financial calculator, input N = 20, I/YR = 10, PMT = 80, and FV = 1000. Then press the PV key to obtain the bond's value of $829.73, or approximately $830. Thus, a person buying the bonds in the initial underwriting would pay $1,000 and receive in exchange a straight bond worth about $830 plus 20 warrants that are presumably worth about $1,000 − $830 = $170:

$$\begin{array}{c}\text{Price paid for}\\\text{bond with warrants}\end{array} = \begin{array}{c}\text{Straight-debt}\\\text{value of bond}\end{array} + \begin{array}{c}\text{Value of}\\\text{warrants}\end{array} \qquad \text{(20-1)}$$

$$\$1,000 = \$830 + \$170$$

Because investors receive 20 warrants with each bond, each warrant has an implied value of $170/20 = $8.50.

The key issue in setting the terms of a bond-with-warrants deal is valuing the warrants. The straight-debt value can be estimated quite accurately, as we have shown. However, it is more difficult to estimate the value of the warrants. The Black-Scholes option pricing model (OPM), discussed in Chapter 8, can be used to find the value of a call option. There is a temptation to use this model to find the value of a warrant, because call options are similar to warrants in many respects: Both give the investor the right to buy a share of stock at a fixed strike price on or before the expiration date. However, there are major differences between call options and warrants. When call options are exercised, the stock provided to the option holder comes from the secondary market, but when warrants are exercised, the stock provided to the warrant holder is either newly issued shares or treasury stock the company has previously purchased. This means that the exercise of warrants dilutes the value of the original equity, which could cause the value of the original warrant to differ from the value of a similar call option. Also, call options typically have a life of just a few months, whereas warrants often have lives of 10 years or more. Finally, the Black-Scholes model assumes that the underlying stock pays no dividend, which is not unreasonable over a short period but is unreasonable for 5 or 10 years. Therefore, investment bankers cannot use the original Black-Scholes model to determine the value of warrants.

Even though the original Black-Scholes model cannot be used to determine a precise value for a warrant, there are more sophisticated models that work reasonably well.[6] In addition, investment bankers can simply contact portfolio managers of mutual funds, pension funds, and other organizations that would be interested in buying the securities to get an indication of how many they would buy at different prices. In effect, the bankers hold a pre-sale auction and determine the set of terms that will just clear the market. If they do this job properly then they will, in effect, be letting the market determine the value of the warrants.

20-2b Use of Warrants in Financing

Warrants generally are used by small, rapidly growing firms as **sweeteners** when they sell debt or preferred stock. Such firms frequently are regarded by investors as being highly risky, so their bonds can be sold only at extremely high coupon rates and with very restrictive indenture provisions. To avoid such restrictions, firms like Infomatic often offer warrants along with the bonds.

Getting warrants along with bonds enables investors to share in the company's growth, assuming it does in fact grow and prosper. Therefore, investors are willing to accept a lower interest rate and less restrictive indenture provisions. A bond with warrants has some characteristics of debt and some characteristics of equity. It is a hybrid security that provides the financial manager with an opportunity to expand the firm's mix of securities and thereby appeal to a broader group of investors.

Virtually all warrants issued today are **detachable**. In other words, after a bond with attached warrants is sold, the warrants can be detached and traded separately from the

---

[6]For example, see John C. Hull, *Options, Futures, and Other Derivatives*, 10th ed. (Boston, MA: Prentice-Hall, 2018). Hull shows that if there are m warrants outstanding, each of which can be converted into γ shares of common stock at an exercise price of X, as well as n shares of common stock outstanding, then the price ω of a warrant is given by this modification of the Black-Scholes option pricing formula from Chapter 11:

$$\omega = \left(\frac{n\gamma}{n + m\gamma}\right)\left[S^*N(d_1^*) - Xe^{-r_{RF}(T - t)}N(d_2^*)\right] \text{ where } d_1^* = \frac{\ln(S^*/X) + (r_{RF} + \sigma_Q^2/2)(T - t)}{\sigma_Q\sqrt{T - t}}$$

Here $d_2^* = d_1^* - \sigma_Q(T - t)^{1/2}$ and $S^* = S + m\omega/n$, where S is the underlying stock price, T is the maturity date, r_{RF} is the risk-free rate, σ_Q is the volatility of the stock and the warrants together, and N(·) is the cumulative normal distribution function. See Chapter 8 for more on the Black-Scholes option pricing formula. If γ = 1 and n is very much larger than m, so that the number of warrants issued is very small compared to the number of shares of stock outstanding, then this simplifies to the standard Black-Scholes option pricing formula.

bond. Further, even after the warrants have been exercised, the bond (with its low coupon rate) remains outstanding.

The strike price on warrants is generally set some 20% to 30% above the market price of the stock on the date the bond is issued. If the firm grows and prospers, causing its stock price to rise above the strike price at which shares may be purchased, warrant holders could exercise their warrants and buy stock at the stated price. However, without some incentive, warrants would never be exercised prior to maturity—their value in the open market would be greater than their value if exercised, so holders would sell warrants rather than exercise them. There are three conditions that cause holders to exercise their warrants: (1) Warrant holders will surely exercise and buy stock if the warrants are about to expire and the market price of the stock is above the exercise price. (2) Warrant holders will exercise voluntarily if the company raises the dividend on the common stock by a sufficient amount. No dividend is earned on the warrant, so it provides no current income. However, if the common stock pays a high dividend, then it provides an attractive dividend yield but limits stock price growth. This induces warrant holders to exercise their option to buy the stock. (3) Warrants sometimes have **stepped-up strike prices** (also called **stepped-up exercise prices**), which prod owners into exercising them. For example, Williamson Scientific Company has warrants outstanding with a strike price of $25 until December 31, 2023, at which time the strike price rises to $30. If the price of the common stock is over $25 just before December 31, 2023, many warrant holders will exercise their options before the stepped-up price takes effect and the value of the warrants falls.

Another desirable feature of warrants is that they generally bring in funds only if funds are needed. If the company grows, it will probably need new equity capital. At the same time, growth will cause the price of the stock to rise and the warrants to be exercised; hence the firm will obtain the cash it needs. If the company is not successful and it cannot profitably employ additional money, then the price of its stock will probably not rise enough to induce exercise of the warrants.

20-2c The Component Cost of Bonds with Warrants

When Infomatic issued its bonds with warrants, the firm received $1,000 for each bond. The pre-tax cost of debt would have been 10% if no warrants had been attached, and this is the component cost of debt that would have been used for calculating the company's weighted average cost of capital as we did in Chapter 9. However, each Infomatic bond has 20 warrants, each of which entitles its holder to buy one share of stock for $22. The presence of warrants also allows Infomatic to pay only 8% interest on the bonds, obligating it to pay $80 interest for 20 years plus $1,000 at the end of 20 years. So given these complicating factors, what is the component cost of capital for bonds with warrants? As we shall see, the cost is well above the 8% coupon rate on the bonds and is also above the 10% cost if the company had issued straight debt.

The best way to approach this analysis is to break the $1,000 bond with warrants attached into two components, one consisting of an $830 bond and the other consisting of $170 of warrants, and calculate the cost of capital for each of these components. Thus, the $1,000 bond-with-warrants package consists of $830/$1,000 = 0.83 = 83% straight debt and $170/$1,000 = 0.17 = 17% warrant. We will find the cost of capital for the straight bonds and the cost of capital for the warrant, and then weight them to derive the cost of capital for the bond-with-warrants package.

Finding the cost of capital for the straight bond component is easy. The pre-tax component cost of debt is 10% because this is the pre-tax cost of debt for a straight bond. Estimating the cost of capital for the warrant component, however, is fairly complicated in theory, but we can use the following simplified procedure to obtain a reasonable approximation.[7] The basic idea is to estimate the firm's expected dollar cost of satisfying the warrant holders at the time the warrants expire and use this to calculate the warrant holders' expected return from owning the warrants. This expected return will be our component cost of capital for the warrants.

To calculate the firm's expected cost of satisfying the warrants, we need an estimate of the value of the firm's stock price on the warrants' expiration date, T. From the Corporate Valuation Model in Chapter 7, this price will be the expected intrinsic value of the total firm less the value of the debt, all divided by the number of shares. Each of these three pieces is estimated for the date the warrants expire, T:

$$\frac{\text{Estimated}}{\text{price of stock}_T} = \frac{\text{Intrinsic value of equity}_T}{\text{Shares outstanding}_T}$$

$$= \frac{\begin{array}{c}\text{Estimated total} \\ \text{value of firm}_T\end{array} - \begin{array}{c}\text{Estimated value} \\ \text{of debt}_T\end{array}}{\text{Shares outstanding}_T}$$

Assume that the total value of Infomatic's operations and investments, which is $250 million immediately after issuing the bonds with warrants, is expected to grow at 9% per year. When the warrants are due to expire in 10 years, the total value of Infomatic is expected to be $250(1.09)^{10} = $591.841 million.

Infomatic will receive $22 per warrant when exercised; with 1 million warrants, this creates a $22 million cash flow to Infomatic. The total value of Infomatic will be equal to the value of operations plus the value of this cash. This will make the total value of Infomatic equal to $591.84 + $22 = $613.841 million.

When the warrants expire, the bonds will have 10 more years remaining until maturity with a fixed coupon payment of $80. If the expected market interest rate is still 10%, then the time line of cash flows will be:

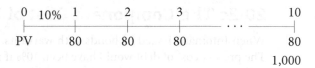

Using a financial calculator, input N = 10, I/YR = 10, PMT = 80, and FV = 1000; then press the PV key to obtain the bond's value, $877.11. The total value of all of the bonds is therefore expected to be 50,000($877.11) = $43.856 million.

The intrinsic value of equity is equal to the total value of the firm minus the value of debt: $613.841 − $43.856 = $569.985 million.

Infomatic had 10 million shares outstanding prior to the warrants' exercise, so it will have 11 million after the 1 million options are exercised. The predicted intrinsic stock price is equal to the intrinsic value of equity divided by the number of shares: $569.985/11 = $51.82 per share.[8] These calculations are summarized in Table 20-1.

To find the component cost of the warrants, consider that Infomatic will have to issue one share of stock worth $51.82 for each warrant exercised and, in return, Infomatic will receive the strike price from the warrant holder, $22. Thus, a purchaser of the bonds with

---

[7]For an exact solution, see P. Daves and M. Ehrhardt, "Convertible Securities, Employee Stock Options, and the Cost of Equity," *The Financial Review*, Vol. 42, 2007, pp. 267–288.

[8]If the stock price had been less than the strike price of $22 at expiration, then the warrants would not have been exercised. Based on the expected growth in the firm's value, there is little chance that the stock price will not be greater than $22.

TABLE 20-1
Valuation Analysis after Exercise of Warrants in 10 Years (Millions of Dollars, Except for Per Share Data)

	Warrants Are Exercised
Expected value of operations and investments[a]	$ 591.841
Plus new cash from exercise of warrants[b]	22.000
Total value of firm	$ 613.841
Minus value of bonds	43.856
Value remaining for shareholders	$ 569.985
Divided by shares outstanding[c]	11
Price per share	$ 51.82

[a]The value of operations and investments is expected to grow from its current $250 million at a rate of 9%: $250(1.09)^{10} = $591.841 million.

[b]The warrants will be exercised only if the stock price at expiration is above $22. If the stock price is less than $22, then the warrants will expire worthless and there will be no new capital. Our calculations show that the expected stock price is much greater than $22, so the warrants are expected to be exercised.

[c]Before the warrants are exercised, there are 10 million shares of stock. After the warrants are exercised, there will be 10 + 1 = 11 million shares outstanding.

warrants, if she holds the complete package, would expect to realize a profit in Year 10 of $51.82 − $22 = $29.82 for each warrant exercised.[9] Because each bond has 20 warrants attached and because each warrant entitles the holder to buy one share of common stock, it follows that warrant holders will have an expected cash flow of 20($29.82) = $596.40 per bond at the end of Year 10. Here is a time line of the expected cash flow stream to a warrant holder:

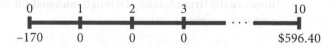

The IRR of this stream is 13.35%, which is an approximation of the warrant holder's expected return on the warrants (r_w) in the bond with warrants. The overall pre-tax cost of capital for the bonds with warrants is the weighted average of the cost of straight debt and the cost of warrants:

$$\text{Pre-tax cost of bonds with warrants} = r_d(\$830/\$1{,}000) + r_w(\$170/\$1{,}000)$$
$$= 10\%(0.83) + 13.35\%(0.17) = 10.57\%$$

The cost of the warrants is higher than the cost of debt because warrants are riskier than debt; in fact, the cost of warrants is greater than the cost of equity because warrants also are riskier than equity. Thus, the cost of capital for a bond with warrants is somewhere between the cost of debt and the much higher cost of equity. This means the overall

[9]It is not strictly accurate to say that the expected profit from the warrant position is the expected stock price less the strike price: $29.82 = $51.82 − $22. This is because if the stock price drops below the strike price, in this case $22, then the warrant profit is $0, regardless of how low the stock price goes. Thus, the expected payoff will be somewhat more than $29.82. Although this expectation can be calculated using options techniques similar to those in Chapter 8, it is beyond the scope of this chapter. However, if there is a very small probability that the stock price will drop below the exercise price, then $29.82 is very close to the true expected payoff.

cost of capital for the bonds with warrants will be greater than the cost of straight debt and will be much higher than the 8% coupon rate on the bonds-with-warrants package.[10]

Bonds with warrants and preferred stock with warrants have become an important source of funding for companies during the global economic crisis. But as our example shows, this form of financing has a much higher cost of capital than its low coupon and preferred dividend might lead you to think.[11]

SELF-TEST

What is a warrant?

Describe how a new bond issue with warrants is valued.

How are warrants used in corporate financing?

The use of warrants lowers the coupon rate on the corresponding debt issue. Does this mean that the component cost of a debt-plus-warrants package is less than the cost of straight debt? Explain.

Shanton Corporation could issue 15-year straight debt at a rate of 8%. Instead, Shanton issues 15-year debt with a coupon rate of 6%, but each bond has 25 warrants attached. The bonds can be issued at par ($1,000 per bond). Assuming annual interest payments, what is the implied value of each warrant? ($6.85)

20-3 Convertible Securities

Convertible securities are bonds or preferred stocks that, under specified terms and conditions, can be exchanged for (that is, converted into) common stock at the option of the holder. Unlike the exercise of warrants, which brings in additional funds to the firm, conversion does not provide new capital; debt (or preferred stock) is simply replaced on the balance sheet by common stock. Of course, reducing the debt or preferred stock will improve the firm's financial strength and make it easier to raise additional capital, but that requires a separate action.

20-3a Conversion Ratio and Conversion Price

resource

See Ch20 Tool Kit.xlsx on the textbook's Web site for details.

The **conversion ratio (CR)** is defined as the number of shares of stock a bondholder will receive upon conversion. The **conversion price (P_c)** is defined as the effective price investors pay for the common stock when conversion occurs. The relationship between the conversion ratio and the conversion price can be illustrated by Silicon Valley Software

---

[10]In order to estimate the after-tax cost of capital, the after-tax cost of each component must be estimated. The after-tax cost of the warrant is the same as the pre-tax cost because warrants do not affect the issuer's tax liability. This is not true for the bond component. **Web Extension 5A** on the textbook's Web site shows that the after-tax cost of debt when the bond is issued at a price less than par is equal to the yield on that debt multiplied by 1 − T, just like when the bond is issued at par. Thus the after-tax cost of Infomatic's bond component is 10%(1 − 0.40) = 6%, assuming a 25% tax rate. We also show this calculation as well as the complete after-tax cost of capital calculation for the bonds with warrants attached in the **Ch20 Tool Kit.xlsx**.

[11]For more on warrant pricing, see Michael C. Ehrhardt and Ronald E. Shrieves, "The Impact of Warrants and Convertible Securities on the Systematic Risk of Common Equity," *Financial Review*, November 1995, pp. 843–856; Beni Lauterbach and Paul Schultz, "Pricing Warrants: An Empirical Study of the Black-Scholes Model and Its Alternatives," *Journal of Finance*, September 1990, pp. 1181–1209; David C. Leonard and Michael E. Solt, "On Using the Black-Scholes Model to Value Warrants," *Journal of Financial Research*, Summer 1990, pp. 81–92; and Katherine L. Phelps, William T. Moore, and Rodney L. Roenfeldt, "Equity Valuation Effects of Warrant-Debt Financing," *Journal of Financial Research*, Summer 1991, pp. 93–103.

Company's convertible debentures issued at their $1,000 par value in July 2018.[12] At any time prior to maturity on July 15, 2038, a debenture holder can exchange a bond for 18 shares of common stock. Therefore, the conversion ratio, CR, is 18. The bond cost a purchaser $1,000, the par value, when it was issued. Dividing the $1,000 par value by the 18 shares received gives a conversion price of $55.56 a share:

$$\text{Conversion price} = P_c = \frac{\text{Par value of bond given up}}{\text{Shares received}} \qquad (20\text{-}2)$$

$$= \frac{\$1,000}{\text{CR}} = \frac{\$1,000}{18} = \$55.56$$

Conversely, by solving for CR, we obtain the conversion ratio:

$$\text{Conversion ratio} = \text{CR} = \frac{\$1,000}{P_c} \qquad (20\text{-}3)$$

$$= \frac{\$1,000}{\$55.56} = 18 \text{ shares}$$

Once CR is set, the value of P_c is established, and vice versa.

Like a warrant's exercise price, the conversion price is typically set some 20% to 30% above the prevailing market price of the common stock on the issue date. Generally, the conversion price and conversion ratio are fixed for the life of the bond, with the exception of protection against dilutive actions the company might take, including stock splits, stock dividends, and the sale of common stock at prices below the conversion price.[13]

The typical protective provision states that if the stock is split or if a stock dividend is declared, the conversion price must be lowered by the percentage amount of the stock dividend or split. For example, if Silicon Valley Software (SVS) were to have a 2-for-1 stock split, then the conversion ratio would automatically be adjusted from 18 to 36 and the conversion price lowered from $55.56 to $27.73. Also, if SVS sells common stock at a price below the conversion price, then the conversion price must be lowered (and the conversion ratio raised) to the price at which the new stock is issued. If protection were not contained in the contract, then a company could always prevent conversion by the use of stock splits and stock dividends. Warrants have similar protection against dilution.

However, this standard protection against dilution from selling new stock at prices below the conversion price can get a company into trouble. For example, SVS's stock was selling for $35 per share at the time the convertible was issued. Now suppose that the market went sour and the stock price dropped to $15 per share. If SVS needs new equity to support operations, a new common stock sale would require the company to lower the conversion price on the convertible debentures from $55.56 to $15. What impact would this have on the existing shareholders?

---

[12]A debenture is a bond that isn't collateralized. It is backed only by the ability of the firm to generate cash flows. The debentures in this example are convertible into common stock. Not all debentures are convertible.

[13]Some convertible bonds have a stepped-up conversion price. For example, a convertible bond might be convertible into 12 shares for the first 10 years, into 11 shares for the next 10, and 10 shares for the remainder of its life. This has the effect of increasing the conversion price over time, so that the holder of a convertible bond won't get rewarded if the stock price grows slowly.

First, think about the value of a convertible bond as consisting of a straight bond and an option to convert. Reducing the conversion price is like reducing the strike price on an option, which would make the option to convert and therefore the convertible bond much more valuable. Second, to see how this impacts the value of equity, recall the approach taken by the free cash flow valuation model to determine the value of equity—start with the value of operations, add the value of any nonoperating assets (like T-bills), and subtract the value of any debt, including convertible bonds. Since reducing the conversion price causes the value of the convertible bond to increase, it must also cause the value of the equity to decrease since this higher bond value is now subtracted from the value of operations to get the value of the equity. This is a transfer of wealth from the existing shareholders to the convertible bondholders. Therefore, the protective reset feature on the conversion price makes it very costly for existing shareholders to raise additional equity in the times when new equity is needed.

20-3b The Component Cost of Convertibles

In the spring of 2018, Silicon Valley Software was evaluating the use of the convertible bond issue described earlier. The issue would consist of 20-year convertible bonds that would sell at a price of $1,000 per bond; this $1,000 would also be the bond's par (and maturity) value. The bonds would pay an 8% annual coupon interest rate, which is $80 per year. Each bond would be convertible into 18 shares of stock, so the conversion price would be $1,000/18 = $55.56. Its stock price was $35. If the bonds were not made convertible then they would have to provide a yield of 10%, given their risk and the general level of interest rates. The convertible bonds would not be callable for 10 years, after which they could be called at a price of $1,050, with this price declining by $5 per year thereafter. If, after 10 years, the conversion value exceeded the call price by at least 20%, management would probably call the bonds.[14]

SVS's cost of equity is 13%, with a 4% dividend yield and expected capital gain of 9% per year. (Silicon Valley Software is a high-risk company with low dividends and occasional stock repurchases, so its stock price has a high expected growth rate.)

Figure 20-1 shows the expectations of both an average investor and the company. Refer to the figure as you consider the following points.

1. The horizontal dashed line at $1,000 represents the par (and maturity) value. Also, $1,000 is the price at which the bond is initially offered to the public.
2. The bond is protected against a call for 10 years. It is initially callable at a price of $1,050; the call price declines thereafter by $5 per year, as shown by the pink line in Figure 20-1.
3. Because the convertible has an 8% coupon rate and because the yield on a nonconvertible bond of similar risk is 10%, it follows that the expected "straight-bond" value of the convertible, B_t, must be less than par. At the time of issue and assuming an annual coupon, B_0 is $830:

$$\text{Straight-debt value at time of issue} = B_0 = \sum_{t=1}^{N} \frac{\text{Coupon interest}}{(1 + r_d)^t} + \frac{\text{Maturity value}}{(1 + r_d)^N} \qquad \textbf{(20-4)}$$

$$= \sum_{t=1}^{20} \frac{\$80}{(1.10)^t} + \frac{\$1,000}{(1.10)^{20}} = \$830$$

---

[14]Calling the bonds in this case would force the bondholders to convert them. We discuss forced conversion later in the chapter.

FIGURE 20-1
Silicon Valley Software: Convertible Bond Model

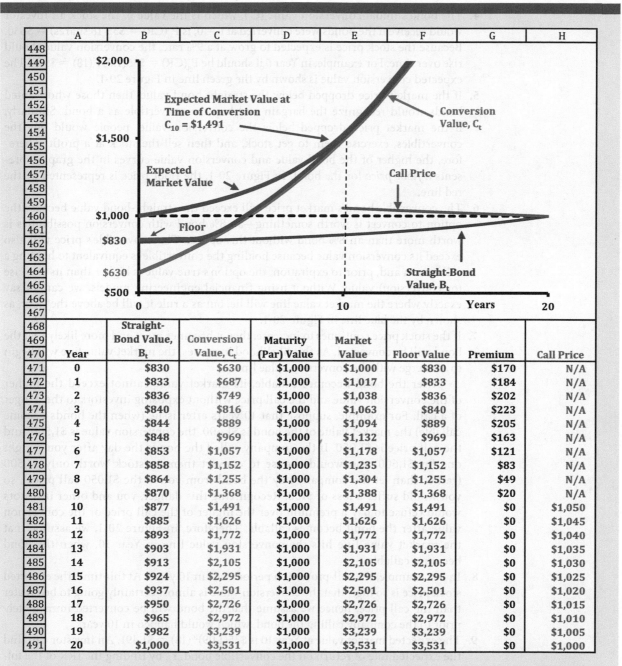

	A	B	C	D	E	F	G	H
468		**Straight-**						
469		**Bond Value,**	**Conversion**	**Maturity**	**Market**			
470	**Year**	**B$_t$**	**Value, C$_t$**	**(Par) Value**	**Value**	**Floor Value**	**Premium**	**Call Price**
471	0	$830	$630	$1,000	$1,000	$830	$170	N/A
472	1	$833	$687	$1,000	$1,017	$833	$184	N/A
473	2	$836	$749	$1,000	$1,038	$836	$202	N/A
474	3	$840	$816	$1,000	$1,063	$840	$223	N/A
475	4	$844	$889	$1,000	$1,094	$889	$205	N/A
476	5	$848	$969	$1,000	$1,132	$969	$163	N/A
477	6	$853	$1,057	$1,000	$1,178	$1,057	$121	N/A
478	7	$858	$1,152	$1,000	$1,235	$1,152	$83	N/A
479	8	$864	$1,255	$1,000	$1,304	$1,255	$49	N/A
480	9	$870	$1,368	$1,000	$1,388	$1,368	$20	N/A
481	10	$877	$1,491	$1,000	$1,491	$1,491	$0	$1,050
482	11	$885	$1,626	$1,000	$1,626	$1,626	$0	$1,045
483	12	$893	$1,772	$1,000	$1,772	$1,772	$0	$1,040
484	13	$903	$1,931	$1,000	$1,931	$1,931	$0	$1,035
485	14	$913	$2,105	$1,000	$2,105	$2,105	$0	$1,030
486	15	$924	$2,295	$1,000	$2,295	$2,295	$0	$1,025
487	16	$937	$2,501	$1,000	$2,501	$2,501	$0	$1,020
488	17	$950	$2,726	$1,000	$2,726	$2,726	$0	$1,015
489	18	$965	$2,972	$1,000	$2,972	$2,972	$0	$1,010
490	19	$982	$3,239	$1,000	$3,239	$3,239	$0	$1,005
491	20	$1,000	$3,531	$1,000	$3,531	$3,531	$0	$1,000

Source: Numbers in the figure are shown as rounded values for clarity in reporting. However, unrounded values are used for all calculations, so columns may not total exactly. See the *Excel Tool Kit* for this chapter.

Note, however, that the bond's straight-debt value must be $1,000 at maturity, so the straight-debt value rises over time; this is plotted by the brown line in Figure 20-1.

4. The bond's initial **conversion value (C_t)**, which is the value of the stock an investor would receive if the bonds were converted at t = 0, is P_0(CR) = $35(18 shares) = $630. Because the stock price is expected to grow at a 9% rate, the conversion value should rise over time. For example, in Year 5 it should be P_5(CR) = $35(1.09)^5(18) = $969. The expected conversion value is shown by the green line in Figure 20-1.

5. If the market price dropped below the straight-bond value, then those who wanted bonds would recognize the bargain and buy the convertible as a bond. Similarly, if the market price dropped below the conversion value, people would buy the convertibles, exercise them to get stock, and then sell the stock at a profit. Therefore, the higher of the bond value and conversion value curves in the graph represents a *floor price* for the bond. In Figure 20-1, the floor price is represented by the red line.

6. The convertible bond's market price will exceed the straight-bond value because the option to convert is worth something—an 8% bond with conversion possibilities is worth more than an 8% bond without this option. The convertible's price will also exceed its conversion value because holding the convertible is equivalent to holding a call option and, prior to expiration, the option's true value is higher than its exercise (or conversion) value. Without using financial engineering models, we cannot say exactly where the market value line will lie, but as a rule it will be above the floor, as shown by the blue line in Figure 20-1.

7. If the stock price continues to increase, then it becomes more and more likely that the bond will be converted. As this likelihood increases, the market value line will begin to converge with the conversion value line.

   After the bond becomes callable, its market value cannot exceed the higher of the conversion value and the call price without exposing investors to the danger of a call. For example, suppose that 10 years after issue (when the bonds become callable) the market value of the bond is $1,600, the conversion value is $1,500, and the call price is $1,050. If the company called the bonds the day after you bought one for $1,600, you would choose to convert them to stock worth only $1,500 (rather than let the company buy the bond from you at the $1,050 call price), so you would suffer a loss of $100. Recognizing this danger, you and other investors would refuse to pay a premium over the higher of the call price or the conversion value after the bond becomes callable. Therefore, in Figure 20-1, we assume that the market value line hits the conversion value line in Year 10, when the bond becomes callable.

8. In our example, the call-protection period ends in 10 years. At this time, the expected stock price is so high that the conversion value is almost certainly going to be greater than the call price; hence we assume that the bond will be converted immediately prior to the company calling the bond, which would happen in 10 years.

9. The expected market value at Year 10 is $35(1.09)^{10}(18) = $1,491. An investor can find the expected rate of return on the convertible bond, r_c, by finding the IRR of the following cash flow stream:

With a financial calculator, we set N = 10, PV = −1000, PMT = 80, and FV = 1491; we then solve for I/YR = r_c = IRR = 10.94%.[15]

10. A convertible bond is riskier than straight debt but less risky than stock, so its cost of capital should be somewhere between the cost of straight debt and the cost of equity. This is true in our example: r_d = 10%, r_c = 10.94%, and r_s = 13%.[16]

20-3c Use of Convertibles in Financing

Convertibles have two important advantages from the issuer's standpoint: (1) Convertibles, like bonds with warrants, offer a company the chance to sell debt with a low coupon rate in exchange for giving bondholders a chance to participate in the company's success if it does well. (2) In a sense, convertibles provide a way to sell common stock at prices higher than those currently prevailing.

Management may know, for example, that earnings are depressed because of start-up costs associated with a new project, but they expect earnings to rise sharply during the next year or so, pulling the price of the stock up with them. Thus, if the company sold stock now, it would be giving up more shares than necessary to raise a given amount of capital. However, if it set the conversion price 20% to 30% above the present market price of the stock, then 20% to 30% fewer shares would be given up when the bonds were converted than if stock were sold directly at the current time.

Note, however, that management is counting on the stock's price to rise above the conversion price, thus making the bonds attractive in conversion. If earnings do not rise and pull the stock price up, and conversion does *not* occur, then the company will be saddled with debt in the face of low earnings, which could be disastrous.

How can the company be sure that conversion will occur if the price of the stock rises above the conversion price? Typically, convertibles contain a call provision that enables the issuing firm to force holders to convert. Suppose the conversion price is $50, the conversion ratio is 20, the market price of the common stock has risen to $60, and the call price on a convertible bond is $1,050. If the company calls the bond, bondholders can either convert into common stock with a market value of 20($60) = $1,200 or allow the company to redeem the bond for $1,050. Naturally, bondholders prefer $1,200 to $1,050, so conversion would occur. The call provision thus gives the company a way to force

---

[15]As in the case with warrants, the expected conversion value is not precisely equal to the expected stock price multiplied by the conversion ratio. Here is the reason. If after 10 years the stock price happens to be low, so that the conversion value is less than the call price, then the bondholders would not choose to convert—instead, they would surrender their bonds if the company called them. In this example, conversion does not occur if the stock price is less than $1,050/18 = $58.33 after 10 years. Because the company makes a call in order to force conversion, it won't call the bonds if the stock price is less than $58.33. So when the stock price is low, the bondholders will keep the bonds, whose value will depend primarily on interest rates at that time. Finding the expected value in this situation is a difficult problem (and is beyond the scope of this text). However, if the expected stock price is much greater than the conversion price when the bonds are called (in this case, $35[1.09]^{10}$ = $82.86 is much more than $58.33), then the difference between the true expected conversion value and the conversion value that we calculated using the expected stock price will be very small. Therefore, we can approximate the component cost reasonably accurately with the approach used in the example.

[16]To find the after-tax cost of the convertible, you can replace the pre-tax coupons with the after-tax coupons paid by the company. If the corporate tax rate is 25%, then we have N = 10, PV = −1000, PMT = 80(1 − 0.25) = 60, and FV = 1491; we solve for I/YR = $r_{c,AT}$ = 9.2%. Notice that this after-tax cost is not equal to $r_c(1 − T)$. Note also that this tax treatment is different from that of bonds with warrants as discussed earlier in this chapter. The company receives no tax benefits from the conversion feature in convertible bonds.

conversion, provided the market price of the stock is greater than the conversion price. Note, however, that most convertibles have a fairly long period of call protection—10 years is typical. Therefore, if the company wants to be able to force conversion early, it will have to set a short call-protection period. This will, in turn, require that it set a higher coupon rate or a lower conversion price.

From the standpoint of the issuer, convertibles have three important disadvantages: (1) Even though the use of a convertible bond may give the company the opportunity to sell stock at a price higher than the current price, if the stock greatly increases in price then, the firm would be better off if it had used straight debt (in spite of its higher cost) and then later sold common stock and refunded the debt. (2) Convertibles typically have a low coupon interest rate, and the advantage of this low-cost debt will be lost when conversion occurs. (3) If the company truly wants to raise equity capital and if the price of the stock does not rise sufficiently after the bond is issued, then the company will be stuck with debt.

20-3d Convertibles and Agency Costs

An important benefit of issuing convertible securities is that they can help reduce costs due to agency problems. Two of these problems are "bait and switch" and information asymmetry. Bait and switch, also known as *asset substitution*, is a conflict between bond-holders and stockholders over a firm's investment choices. For example, suppose a company has been investing in low-risk projects, and because risk is low, bondholders charge a low interest rate. What happens if the company actually invests in a very risky but still profitable venture that potential lenders don't know about? The company has raised low-interest-rate debt and after the investment is made, the value of the debt should fall because its interest rate will be too low to compensate debtholders for the high risk they bear. This is a "heads I win, tails you lose" situation, and it results in a wealth transfer from bondholders to stockholders.

Let's use some numbers to illustrate this scenario. The value of a company, based on the present value of its future free cash flows, is $800 million. It has $300 million of debt, based on market values. Therefore, its equity is worth $800 − $300 = $500 million. The company now undertakes some projects with high but risky expected returns, and its expected NPV remains unchanged. In other words, the actual NPV will probably end up much higher or much lower than under the old situation, but the expected value is the same. Even though its total value is still $800 million, the value of the debt falls because its risk has increased. Debtholders are hurt by the added project risk because if the risky ventures fail, they won't receive their contracted interest and principal payments. But if these ventures are homeruns, they don't receive any benefit more than their contracted coupon and the principal repayment. In other words, risk doesn't give them any upside potential but does expose them to downside losses, so the bondholders' expected value must decline.

With a constant total firm value, if the value of the debt falls from $300 to $200 million, then the value of equity must increase from $500 to $800 − $200 = $600 million. Thus, the bait-and-switch tactic causes a wealth transfer of $100 million from debtholders to stockholders.

If debtholders think a company might employ the bait-and-switch tactic, they will charge a higher interest rate, and this higher interest rate is an agency cost. Debtholders will charge this higher rate even if the company has no intention of engaging in bait-and-switch behavior, because they can't know the company's true intentions. Therefore, they assume the worst and charge a higher interest rate.

Convertible securities can mitigate this type of agency cost. Suppose the debt is convertible and the company does take on the high-risk project. If the value of the company turns out to be higher than expected, then bondholders can convert their debt to equity and benefit from the successful investment. Therefore, bondholders are willing to charge a lower interest rate on convertibles, and this serves to reduce the agency costs.

Note that if a company does not engage in bait-and-switch behavior by swapping low-risk projects for high-risk projects, then the chance of "hitting a home run" is reduced. Because there is less chance of a home run, the convertible bond is less likely to be converted. In this situation, the convertible bonds are actually similar to nonconvertible debt, except that they carry a lower interest rate.

Now consider a different agency cost, one due to asymmetric information between the managers and potential new stockholders. Suppose a firm's managers know that its future prospects are not as good as the market believes, which means the current stock price is too high. Acting in the interests of existing stockholders, managers can issue stock at the current high price. When the poor future prospects are eventually revealed, the stock price will fall, causing a transfer of wealth from the new shareholders to old shareholders.

To illustrate this, suppose the market estimates an $800 million present value of future free cash flows. For simplicity, assume the firm has no nonoperating assets and no debt, so the total value of both the firm and the equity is $800 million. However, its managers know the market has overestimated the future free cash flows and that the true value is only $700 million. When investors eventually discover this, the value of the company will drop to $700 million. But before this happens, suppose the company raises $200 million of new equity. The company uses this new cash to invest in projects with a present value of $200 million, which shouldn't be too hard, because these projects have a zero NPV. Right after the new stock is sold, the company will have a market value of $800 + $200 = $1,000 million, based on the market's overly optimistic estimate of the company's future prospects. Observe that the new shareholders own 20% of the company ($200/$1,000 = 0.20) and the original shareholders own 80%.

Eventually, the market will realize that the value of the company's original projects is only $700 million. The new projects are still worth $200 million, so the total value of the company will fall to $700 + $200 = $900 million. The original shareholders' value is now 80% of $900 million, which is $720 million. Note that this is $20 million *more* than it would have been if the company had issued no new stock. The new shareholders' value is now 0.20($900) = $180 million, which is $20 million *less* than their original investment. The net effect is a $20 million wealth transfer from the new shareholders to the original shareholders.

Because potential shareholders know this might occur, they interpret an issue of new stock as a signal of poor future prospects, which causes the stock price to fall. Note also that this will occur even for companies whose future prospects are actually quite good because the market has no way of distinguishing between companies with good versus poor prospects.

A company with good future prospects might want to issue equity, but it knows the market will interpret this as a negative signal. One way to obtain equity and yet avoid this signaling effect is to issue convertible bonds. Because the company knows its true future prospects are better than the market anticipates, it knows the bonds will likely end up being converted to equity. Thus, a company in this situation is issuing equity "through the back door" when it issues convertible debt.

In summary, convertibles are logical securities to use in at least two situations. First, if a company would like to finance with straight debt but lenders are afraid the funds will be invested in a manner that increases the firm's risk profile, then convertibles are a good choice. Second, if a company wants to issue stock but thinks such a move would cause investors to interpret a stock offering as a signal of tough times ahead, then again convertibles would be a good choice.[17]

What is a conversion ratio? A conversion price? A straight-bond value?

What is meant by a convertible's floor value?

What are the advantages and disadvantages of convertibles to issuers? To investors?

How do convertibles reduce agency costs?

A convertible bond has a par value of $1,000 and a conversion price of $25. The stock currently trades for $22 a share. What are the bond's conversion ratio and conversion value at t = 0? **(40, $880)**

20-4 A Final Comparison of Warrants and Convertibles

Convertible debt can be thought of as straight debt with nondetachable warrants. Thus, at first blush, it might appear that debt with warrants and convertible debt are more or less interchangeable. However, a closer look reveals one major and several minor differences between these two securities.[18] First, as we discussed previously, the exercise of warrants brings in new equity capital, whereas the conversion of convertibles results only in an accounting transfer, albeit one in which the interest and principal payments on the old debt vanish.

A second difference involves flexibility. Most convertibles contain a call provision that allows the issuer either to refund the debt or to force conversion, depending on the relationship between the conversion value and call price. However, most warrants are not callable, so firms must wait until maturity for the warrants to generate new equity capital. Generally, maturities also differ between warrants and convertibles. Warrants typically have much shorter maturities than convertibles, and warrants typically expire before their accompanying debt matures. Warrants also provide for fewer future common shares than do convertibles. Finally, with convertibles all of the debt is converted to stock, whereas debt remains outstanding when warrants are exercised. Together, these facts suggest that debt-plus-warrant issuers are actually more interested in selling debt than in selling equity.

In general, firms that issue debt with warrants are smaller and riskier than those that issue convertibles. One possible rationale for the use of option securities, especially the use of debt with warrants by small firms, is the difficulty investors have in assessing the risk of small companies. If a start-up with a new, untested product seeks debt financing, then it's difficult for potential lenders to judge the riskiness of the venture and so it's difficult to set a fair interest rate. Under these circumstances, many potential investors will be reluctant to invest, making it necessary to set a very high interest rate to attract debt capital. By issuing debt with warrants, investors obtain a package that offers upside potential to offset the risks of loss.

[17]See Craig M. Lewis, Richard J. Rogalski, and James K. Seward, "Understanding the Design of Convertible Debt," *Journal of Applied Corporate Finance*, Vol. 11, No. 1, Spring 1998, pp. 45–53. For more insights into convertible pricing and use, see Paul Asquith and David W. Mullins Jr., "Convertible Debt: Corporate Call Policy and Voluntary Conversion," *Journal of Finance*, September 1991, pp. 1273–1289; Randall S. Billingsley and David M. Smith, "Why Do Firms Issue Convertible Debt?" *Financial Management*, Summer 1996, pp. 93–99; Douglas R. Emery, Mai E. Iskandor-Datta, and Jong-Chul Rhim, "Capital Structure Management as a Motivation for Calling Convertible Debt," *Journal of Financial Research*, Spring 1994, pp. 91–104; T. Harikumar, P. Kadapakkam, and Ronald F. Singer, "Convertible Debt and Investment Incentives," *Journal of Financial Research*, Spring 1994, pp. 15–29; and V. Sivarama Krishnan and Ramesh P. Rao, "Financial Distress Costs and Delayed Calls of Convertible Bonds," *Financial Review*, November 1996, pp. 913–925.

[18]For a more detailed comparison of warrants and convertibles, see Michael S. Long and Stephen F. Sefcik, "Participation Financing: A Comparison of the Characteristics of Convertible Debt and Straight Bonds Issued in Conjunction with Warrants," *Financial Management*, Autumn 1990, pp. 23–34.

Finally, there is a significant difference in issuance costs between debt with warrants and convertible debt. Bonds with warrants typically require issuance costs that are about 1.2 percentage points more than the flotation costs for convertibles. In general, bond-with-warrant financings have underwriting fees that approximate the weighted average of the fees associated with debt and equity issues, whereas underwriting costs for convertibles are more like those associated with straight debt.

What are some differences between debt-with-warrant financing and convertible debt?

Explain how bonds with warrants might help small, risky firms sell debt securities.

20-5 Reporting Earnings When Warrants or Convertibles Are Outstanding

If warrants or convertibles are outstanding, the Financial Accounting Standard Board requires that a firm report basic earnings per share and diluted earnings per share.[19]

1. *Basic EPS* is calculated as earnings available to common stockholders divided by the average number of shares actually outstanding during the period.
2. *Diluted EPS* is calculated as the earnings that would have been available to common shareholders divided by the average number of shares that would have been outstanding if "dilutive" securities had been converted. The rules governing the calculation of diluted EPS are quite complex; here we present a simple illustration using convertible bonds. If the bonds had been converted at the beginning of the accounting period, then the firm's interest payments would have been lower because it would not have had to pay interest on the bonds, and this would have caused earnings to be higher. But the number of outstanding shares of stock also would have increased because of the conversion. If the higher earnings and higher number of shares caused EPS to fall, then the convertible bonds would be defined as dilutive securities because their conversion would decrease (or dilute) EPS. All convertible securities with a net dilutive effect are included when calculating diluted EPS. Therefore, this definition means that diluted EPS always will be lower than basic EPS. In essence, the diluted EPS measure is an attempt to show how the presence of convertible securities reduces common shareholders' claims on the firm.

Under SEC rules, firms are required to report both basic and diluted EPS. For firms with large amounts of option securities outstanding, there can be a substantial difference between the basic and diluted EPS figures. This makes it easier for investors to compare the performance of U.S. firms with their foreign counterparts, which tend to use basic EPS.

What are the three possible methods for reporting EPS when warrants and convertibles are outstanding?

Which methods are most used in practice?

Why should investors be concerned about a firm's outstanding warrants and convertibles?

---

[19]FAS 128 was issued in February of 1997. It simplified the calculations required by firms, made U.S. standards more consistent with international standards, and required the presentation of both basic EPS and diluted EPS for those firms with significant amounts of convertible securities. In addition, it replaced a measure called *primary* EPS with basic EPS. In general, the calculation of primary EPS required the company to estimate whether or not a security was "likely to be converted in the near future" and to base the calculation of EPS on the assumption that those securities would in fact have been converted. In June 2008 the FASB issued FSP APB 14-1, which (although not changing how EPS is reported under FAS 128) requires that convertibles be split into their implied equity and debt components for accounting purposes, in much the same way as we analyze them in this chapter.

SUMMARY

Although common stock and long-term debt provide most of the capital used by corporations, companies also use several forms of "hybrid securities." The hybrids include preferred stock, convertibles, and warrants, and they generally have some characteristics of debt and some of equity. The key concepts covered are listed here.

- **Preferred stock** is a hybrid—it is similar to bonds in some respects and to common stock in other ways.
- **Adjustable rate preferred stocks (ARPs)** pay dividends tied to the rate on Treasury securities. **Market auction (money market) preferred stocks** are low-risk, largely tax-exempt securities of 7-week maturity that can be sold between auction dates at close to par.
- A **warrant** is a long-term call option issued along with a bond. Warrants are generally detachable from the bond, and they trade separately in the market. When warrants are exercised, the firm receives additional equity capital, and the original bonds remain outstanding.
- A **convertible** security is a bond or preferred stock that can be exchanged for common stock at the option of the holder. When a security is converted, debt or preferred stock is replaced with common stock, and no money changes hands.
- Warrant and convertible issues generally are structured so that the **strike price** (also called the **exercise price**) or **conversion price** is 20% to 30% above the stock's price at time of issue.
- Although both warrants and convertibles are option securities, there are several differences between the two, including separability, impact when exercised, callability, maturity, and flotation costs.
- Warrants and convertibles are **sweeteners** used to make the underlying debt or preferred stock issue more attractive to investors. Although the coupon rate or dividend yield is lower when options are part of the issue, the overall cost of the issue is higher than the cost of straight debt or preferred, because option-related securities are riskier.
- For a more detailed discussion of call strategies see *Web Extension 20A* on the textbook's Web site.

QUESTIONS

(20-1)   Define each of the following terms.
- a. Preferred stock
- b. Cumulative dividends; arrearages
- c. Warrant; detachable warrant
- d. Stepped-up price
- e. Convertible security
- f. Conversion ratio; conversion price; conversion value
- g. Sweetener

(20-2)   Is preferred stock more like bonds or common stock? Explain.

(20-3)   What effect does the trend in stock prices (subsequent to issue) have on a firm's ability to raise funds through: (a) convertibles and (b) warrants?

(20-4)   If a firm expects to have additional financial requirements in the future, would you recommend that it use convertibles or bonds with warrants? What factors would influence your decision?

(20-5) How does a firm's dividend policy affect each of the following?
a. The value of its long-term warrants
b. The likelihood that its convertible bonds will be converted
c. The likelihood that its warrants will be exercised

(20-6) Evaluate the following statement: "Issuing convertible securities is a means by which a firm can sell common stock for more than the existing market price."

(20-7) Suppose a company simultaneously issues $50 million of convertible bonds with a coupon rate of 10% and $50 million of straight bonds with a coupon rate of 14%. Both bonds have the same maturity. Does the convertible issue's lower coupon rate suggest that it is less risky than the straight bond? Is the cost of capital lower on the convertible than on the straight bond? Explain.

SELF-TEST PROBLEM   SOLUTION APPEARS IN APPENDIX A

(ST-1)
Warrants
Connor Company recently issued two types of bonds. The first issue consisted of 10-year straight debt with a 6% annual coupon. The second issue consisted of 10-year bonds with a 4.5% annual coupon and attached warrants. Both issues sold at their $1,000 par values. What is the implied value of the warrants attached to each bond?

PROBLEMS   ANSWERS APPEAR IN APPENDIX B

EASY PROBLEMS 1-2

(20-1)
Warrants
Neubert Enterprises recently issued $1,000 par value 15-year bonds with a 5% coupon paid annually and warrants attached. These bonds are currently trading for $1,000. Neubert also has outstanding $1,000 par value 15-year straight debt with a 7% coupon paid annually, also trading for $1,000. What is the implied value of the warrants attached to each bond?

(20-2)
Convertibles
Breuer Investment's convertible bonds have a $1,000 par value and a conversion price of $50 a share. What is the convertible issue's conversion ratio?

INTERMEDIATE PROBLEMS 3–4

(20-3)
Warrants
Maese Industries Inc. has warrants outstanding that permit the holders to purchase 1 share of stock per warrant at a price of $25.

a. Calculate the exercise value of a warrant at each of the following common stock prices: (1) $20, (2) $25, (3) $30, (4) $100. (*Hint:* A warrant's exercise value is the difference between the stock price and the purchase price specified by the warrant if the warrant were to be exercised.)

b. Assume the firm's stock now sells for $20 per share. The company wants to sell some 20-year, $1,000 par value bonds with interest paid annually. Each bond will have attached 50 warrants, each exercisable into 1 share of stock at an exercise price of $25. The firm's straight bonds yield 12%. Assume that each warrant will have a market value of $3 when the stock sells at $20. What coupon interest rate, and dollar coupon, must the company set on the bonds with warrants if they are to clear the market? (*Hint:* The convertible bond should have an initial price of $1,000.)

(20-4)
Convertible
Premiums

The Tsetsekos Company was planning to finance an expansion. The principal executives of the company all agreed that an industrial company such as theirs should finance growth by means of common stock rather than by debt. However, they felt that the current $42 per share price of the company's common stock did not reflect its true worth, so they decided to sell a convertible security. They considered a convertible debenture but feared the burden of fixed interest charges if the common stock did not rise enough in price to make conversion attractive. They decided on an issue of convertible preferred stock, which would pay a dividend of $2.10 per share.

a. The conversion ratio will be 1.0; that is, each share of convertible preferred can be converted into a single share of common. Therefore, the convertible's par value (and also the issue price) will be equal to the conversion price, which in turn will be determined as a premium (i.e., the percentage by which the conversion price exceeds the stock price) over the current market price of the common stock. What will the conversion price be if it is set at a 10% premium? At a 30% premium?

b. Should the preferred stock include a call provision? Why or why not?

CHALLENGING PROBLEMS 5–7

(20-5)
Convertible
Bond Analysis

Fifteen years ago, Roop Industries sold $400 million of convertible bonds. The bonds had a 40-year maturity, a 5.75% coupon rate, and paid interest annually. They were sold at their $1,000 par value. The conversion price was set at $62.75, and the common stock price was $55 per share. The bonds were subordinated debentures and were given an A rating; straight nonconvertible debentures of the same quality yielded about 8.75% at the time Roop's bonds were issued.

a. Calculate the premium on the bonds—that is, the percentage excess of the conversion price over the stock price at the time of issue.

b. What is Roop's annual before-tax interest savings on the convertible issue versus a straight-debt issue?

c. At the time the bonds were issued, what was the value per bond of the conversion feature?

d. Suppose the price of Roop's common stock fell from $55 on the day the bonds were issued to $32.75 now, 15 years after the issue date (also assume the stock price never exceeded $62.75). Assume interest rates remained constant. What is the current price of the straight-bond portion of the convertible bond? What is the current value if a bondholder converts a bond? Do you think it is likely that the bonds will be converted? Why or why not?

e. The bonds originally sold for $1,000. If interest rates on A-rated bonds had remained constant at 8.75% and if the stock price had fallen to $32.75, then what do you think would have happened to the price of the convertible bonds? (Assume no change in the standard deviation of stock returns.)

f. Now suppose that the price of Roop's common stock had fallen from $55 on the day the bonds were issued to $32.75 at present, 15 years after the issue. Suppose also that the interest rate on similar straight debt had fallen from 8.75% to 5.75%. Under these conditions, what is the current price of the straight-bond portion of the convertible bond? What is the current value if a bondholder converts a bond? What do you think would have happened to the price of the bonds?

(20-6)
Warrant/Convertible
Decisions

The Howland Carpet Company has grown rapidly during the past 5 years. Recently, its commercial bank urged the company to consider increasing its permanent financing. Its bank loan under a line of credit has risen to $250,000, carrying an 8% interest rate. Howland has been 30 to 60 days late in paying trade creditors.

Discussions with an investment banker have resulted in the decision to raise $500,000 at this time. Investment bankers have assured the firm that the following alternatives are feasible (flotation costs will be ignored).

- *Alternative 1*: Sell common stock at $8.
- *Alternative 2*: Sell convertible bonds at an 8% coupon, convertible into 100 shares of common stock for each $1,000 bond (i.e., the conversion price is $10 per share).
- *Alternative 3*: Sell debentures at an 8% coupon, each $1,000 bond carrying 100 warrants to buy common stock at $10.

John L. Howland, the president, owns 80% of the common stock and wishes to maintain control of the company. There are 100,000 shares outstanding. The following are extracts of Howland's latest financial statements:

Balance Sheet

		Line of credit	250,000
		Other current liabilities	$150,000
		Long-term debt	0
		Common stock, par $1	100,000
		Retained earnings	50,000
Total assets	$550,000	Total claims	$550,000

Income Statement

Sales	$1,100,000
All costs except interest	990,000
EBIT	$ 110,000
Interest	20,000
Pre-tax earnings	$ 90,000
Taxes (25%)	22,500
Net income	$ 67,500
Shares outstanding	100,000
Earnings per share	$ 0.68
Price/earnings ratio	12.67
Market price of stock	$ 8.55

a. Show the new balance sheet under each alternative. For Alternatives 2 and 3, show the balance sheet after conversion of the bonds or exercise of the warrants. Assume that half of the funds raised will be used to pay off the bank loan and half to increase total assets.

b. Show Mr. Howland's control position under each alternative, assuming that he does not purchase additional shares.

c. What is the effect on earnings per share of each alternative, assuming that profits before interest and taxes will be 20% of total assets?

d. What will be the debt ratio (TL/TA) under each alternative?

e. Which of the three alternatives would you recommend to Howland, and why?

(20-7)
Convertible Bond Analysis

Niendorf Incorporated needs to raise $25 million to construct production facilities for a new type of USB memory device. The firm's straight nonconvertible debentures currently yield 9%. Its stock sells for $23 per share, has an expected constant growth rate of 6%, and has an expected dividend yield of 7%, for a total expected return on equity of 13%. Investment bankers have tentatively proposed that the firm raise the $25 million by issuing convertible debentures. These convertibles would have a $1,000 par value, carry a coupon rate of 8%, have a 20-year maturity, and be convertible into 35 shares of stock. Coupon payments would be made annually. The bonds would be noncallable for 5 years, after which they would be callable at a price of $1,075; this call price would decline by $5 per year in Year 6 and each year thereafter. For simplicity, assume that the bonds may be called or converted only at the end of a year, immediately after the coupon and dividend payments. Also assume that management would call eligible bonds if the conversion value exceeded 20% of par value (not 20% of call price).

a. At what year do you expect the bonds will be forced into conversion with a call? What is the bond's value in conversion when it is converted at this time? What is the cash flow to the bondholder when it is converted at this time? (*Hint:* The cash flow includes the conversion value and the coupon payment, because the conversion occurs immediately after the coupon is paid.)

b. What is the expected rate of return (i.e., the before-tax component cost) on the proposed convertible issue?

SPREADSHEET PROBLEM

(20-8)
Build a Model:
Convertible
Bond Analysis

resource

Start with the partial model in the file *Ch20 P08 Build a Model.xlsx* on the textbook's Web site. Maggie's Magazines (MM) has straight nonconvertible bonds that currently yield 9%. MM's stock sells for $22 per share, has an expected constant growth rate of 6%, and has a dividend yield of 4%. MM plans on issuing convertible bonds that will have a $1,000 par value, a coupon rate of 8%, a 20-year maturity, and a conversion ratio of 32 (i.e., each bond could be convertible into 32 shares of stock). Coupon payments will be made annually. The bonds will be noncallable for 5 years, after which they will be callable at a price of $1,090; this call price would decline by $6 per year in Year 6 and each year thereafter. For simplicity, assume that the bonds may be called or converted only at the end of a year, immediately after the coupon and dividend payments. Management will call the bonds when their conversion value exceeds 25% of their par value (not their call price).

a. For each year, calculate (1) the anticipated stock price, (2) the anticipated conversion value, (3) the anticipated straight-bond price, and (4) the cash flow to the investor assuming conversion occurs. At what year do you expect the bonds will be forced into conversion with a call? What is the bond's value in conversion when it is converted at this time? What is the cash flow to the bondholder when it is converted at this time? (*Hint:* The cash flow includes the conversion value and the coupon payment, because the conversion occurs immediately after the coupon is paid.)

b. What is the expected rate of return (i.e., the before-tax component cost) on the proposed convertible issue?

c. Assume that the convertible bondholders require a 9% rate of return. If the coupon rate remains unchanged, then what conversion ratio will give a bond price of $1,000?

MINI CASE

Paul Duncan, financial manager of EduSoft Inc., is facing a dilemma. The firm was founded 5 years ago to provide educational software for the rapidly expanding primary and secondary school markets. Although EduSoft has done well, the firm's founder believes an industry shakeout is imminent. To survive, EduSoft must grab market share now, and this will require a large infusion of new capital.

Because he expects earnings to continue rising sharply and looks for the stock price to follow suit, Mr. Duncan does not think it would be wise to issue new common stock at this time. On the other hand, interest rates are currently high by historical standards, and the firm's B rating means that interest payments on a new debt issue would be prohibitive. Thus, he has narrowed his choice of financing alternatives to (1) preferred stock, (2) bonds with warrants, or (3) convertible bonds.

As Duncan's assistant, you have been asked to help in the decision process by answering the following questions.

a. How does preferred stock differ from both common equity and debt? Is preferred stock more risky than common stock? What is floating rate preferred stock?

b. How can knowledge of call options help a financial manager to better understand warrants and convertibles?

c. Mr. Duncan has decided to eliminate preferred stock as one of the alternatives and focus on the others. EduSoft's investment banker estimates that EduSoft could issue a bond-with-warrants package consisting of a 20-year bond and 27 warrants. Each warrant would have a strike price of $25 and 10 years until expiration. It is estimated that each warrant, when detached and traded separately, would have a value of $5. The coupon on a similar bond but without warrants would be 10%.

   (1) What coupon rate should be set on the bond with warrants if the total package is to sell at par ($1,000)?

   (2) When would you expect the warrants to be exercised? What is a stepped-up exercise price?

   (3) Will the warrants bring in additional capital when exercised? If EduSoft issues 100,000 bond-with-warrant packages, how much cash will EduSoft receive when the warrants are exercised? How many shares of stock will be outstanding after the warrants are exercised? (EduSoft currently has 20 million shares outstanding.)

   (4) Because the presence of warrants results in a lower coupon rate on the accompanying debt issue, shouldn't all debt be issued with warrants? To answer this, estimate the anticipated stock price in 10 years when the warrants are expected to be exercised, and then estimate the return to the holders of the bond-with-warrants packages. Use the corporate valuation model to estimate the expected stock price in 10 years. Assume that EduSoft's current value of operations is $500 million and it is expected to grow at 8% per year.

   (5) How would you expect the cost of the bond with warrants to compare with the cost of straight debt? With the cost of common stock (which is 13.4%)?

   (6) If the corporate tax rate is 25%, what is the after-tax cost of the bond with warrants?

d. As an alternative to the bond with warrants, Mr. Duncan is considering convertible bonds. The firm's investment bankers estimate that EduSoft could sell a 20-year, 8.5% coupon (paid annually), callable convertible bond for its $1,000 par value, whereas a straight-debt issue would require a 10% coupon (paid annually). The convertibles would be call protected for 5 years, the call price would be $1,100, and the company would probably call the bonds as soon as possible after their conversion value exceeds $1,200. Note, though, that the call must occur on an issue-date anniversary. EduSoft's current stock price is $20, its last dividend was $1, and the dividend is expected to grow at a constant 8% rate. The convertible could be converted into 40 shares of EduSoft stock at the owner's option.

   (1) What conversion price is built into the bond?

   (2) What is the convertible's straight-debt value? What is the implied value of the convertibility feature?

(3) What is the formula for the bond's expected conversion value in any year? What is its conversion value at Year 0? At Year 10?

(4) What is meant by the "floor value" of a convertible? What is the convertible's expected floor value at Year 0? At Year 10?

(5) Assume that EduSoft intends to force conversion by calling the bond as soon as possible after its conversion value exceeds 20% above its par value, or 1.2($1,000) = $1,200. When is the issue expected to be called? (*Hint:* Recall that the call must be made on an anniversary date of the issue.)

(6) What is the expected cost of capital for the convertible to EduSoft? Does this cost appear to be consistent with the riskiness of the issue?

(7) What is the after-tax cost of the convertible bond?

e. Mr. Duncan believes that the costs of both the bond with warrants and the convertible bond are close enough to call them even and that the costs are consistent with the risks involved. Thus, he will make his decision based on other factors. What are some of the factors that he should consider?

f. How do convertible bonds help reduce agency costs?

SELECTED ADDITIONAL CASES

The following cases from CengageCompose cover many of the concepts discussed in this chapter and are available at **http://compose.cengage.com**.

Klein-Brigham Series:
Case 27, "Virginia May Chocolate Company," which illustrates convertible bond valuation, and Case 98, "Levinger Organic Snack," which illustrates the use of convertibles and warrants.

Strategic Finance in a Dynamic Environment

CHAPTER 21

Dynamic Capital Structures and Corporate Valuation

Many companies actively manage their capital structures by several different methods. One way to accomplish this is to issue stock in a secondary public offering (SPO) and use some of the proceeds to reduce debt. For example, Intricon Corporation is a public company that develops and sells wearable health care devices. Their products include miniature hearing aids and small devices that help monitor and manage diabetes. Intricon sold about $100 million in a secondary stock offering in 2018. Some of the proceeds were used to reduce its debt. The net effect was to change the relative proportions of its debt and equity financing.

Tandem Diabetes Care, Inc., and Merit Medical Systems, Inc., each issued over $90 million in equity in 2018 and used the proceeds to reduce debt. Dell Frisco's Restaurant Group, Inc., had borrowed the money it used to acquire Barteca Restaurant Group in 2018 and subsequently raised about $90 million in an SPO to pay down the borrowed funds.

In contrast to these debt-reducing changes in capital structure, many companies increase debt financing. CVS Health Corporation issued about $40 billion in bonds to help finance its $69 billion acquisition of Aetna Incorporated in 2018.

Think about these companies as you read the chapter.

Corporate Valuation and Capital Structure Decisions

A firm's financing choices obviously have a direct effect on its weighted average cost of capital (WACC). Financing choices also have an indirect effect because they change the risk and required return of debt and equity. This chapter focuses on the debt–equity choice and its effect on value in a dynamic environment.

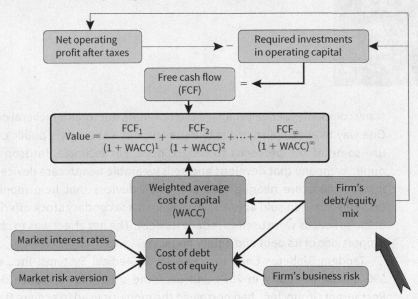

Chapter 15 described capital structure decisions, including the selection of an optimal capital structure. The analysis assumed a static capital structure in the sense that managers have a target and try to keep the actual capital structure equal to the target. However, capital structures often are dynamic. Some variation occurs without managerial actions, such as changes in the stock price due to overall market conditions. Some changes occur due to economies of scale with respect to raising capital—because of transaction costs, companies raise large amounts of capital less frequently instead of small amounts often. Other changes occur as companies deliberately deviate from their target to take advantage of unexpected opportunities, such as acquisition opportunities. Managers need to understand how a dynamic capital structure will affect firm value, which is the question we address in this chapter.

21-1 The Adjusted Present Value (APV) Approach

Before addressing issues arising from dynamic capital structures, we present a general framework for analyzing the impact of capital structure on value.

21-1a The Value of a Levered Firm (V_L)

By definition, the **value of a levered firm (V_L)** is equal to the value of the firm's stock (S_L) plus the value of its debt (D). Alternatively, we can use a conceptual framework that defines the value of a levered firm as the **unlevered value of a firm (V_U)**, which is the value that the firm would have if it had no debt, plus the value of any side effects due to leverage. This is called the **adjusted present value (APV)** approach and is expressed as:

$$V_L = V_U + \text{Value of side effects} \tag{21-1}$$

Recall from Chapter 15 that the **unlevered cost of equity (r_{sU})** is the the cost of equity for the stock of a firm with zero debt. The value of an unlevered firm (assuming that it does not have any nonoperating assets) is the present value of its free cash flows (FCFs) discounted at the weighted average cost of capital (WACC). For an unlevered firm, the WACC is the unlevered cost of equity: WACC = r_{sU}. As we saw in the free cash flow corporate valuation model from Chapter 7, this present value is:

$$V_U = \sum_{t=1}^{\infty} \frac{FCF_t}{(1 + r_{sU})^t} \tag{21-2}$$

As shown in Chapter 7, if FCF grows at a constant rate of g_L, then Equation (21-2) can be simplified:

$$V_U = \sum_{t=1}^{\infty} \frac{FCF_0(1 + g_L)^t}{(1 + r_{sU})^t} = \frac{FCF_1}{r_{sU} - g_L} \tag{21-3}$$

In Chapter 15, we discussed some of the side effects of leverage, including benefits due to deductibility of interest expenses and costs due to financial distress. We will focus on the tax benefits now and address the costs of financial distress later. The gain from leverage is called the **interest tax shield ($V_{\text{Tax shield}}$)** or just the **tax shield**. Therefore, the value of a levered firm is:

$$V_L = V_U + V_{\text{Tax shield}} \tag{21-4}$$

How do you calculate the interest tax shield? First, estimate the annual tax benefits due to leverage. These are the **interest tax savings (TS_t)**, which are the Year-t reductions in taxes due to the deductibility of interest expenses. If r_d is the interest rate on debt, D_t is the amount of debt (which we assume to be constant during the year), and T is the tax rate, then the tax savings in Year t are:

$$TS_t = (\text{Interest expense})(T) = r_d(D_t)(T) \tag{21-5}$$

Second, the value of the tax shield is the present value of all interest tax savings (TS_t), discounted at the appropriate **tax shield discount rate (r_{TS})**:

$$V_{\text{Tax shield}} = \sum_{t=1}^{\infty} \frac{TS_t}{(1 + r_{TS})^t} = \sum_{t=1}^{\infty} \frac{r_d T D_t}{(1 + r_{TS})^t} \tag{21-6}$$

If free cash flows grow at a constant rate and the proportions of debt and equity in the capital structure remain constant, then the annual tax savings grow at a constant rate. Using the constant growth model, the present value of these growing tax savings is:

$$V_{\text{Tax shield}} = \sum_{t=1}^{\infty} \frac{r_d TD_0(1+g_L)^t}{(1+r_{TS})^t}$$

$$= \frac{r_d\,TD_0(1+g_L)}{r_{TS} - g_L}$$

(21-7)

Substituting Equation 21-7 into Equation 21-4 yields a valuation expression that separately identifies the impact of leverage and growth on value:

$$V_L = V_U + \left(\frac{r_d}{r_{TS} - g_L}\right)(T)(D_0)(1+g_L)$$

(21-8)

Equation 21-8 is a very general model of the adjusted present value approach. We will examine some specific applications of this general approach later, but now we address the impact of leverage on the cost of equity.

21-1b The Levered Cost of Equity (r_{sL})

With considerable algebra, the levered cost of equity (r_{sL}) can be expressed in terms of (1) the unlevered cost of equity, (2) the capital structure weights (w_d is the percentage of the firm financed with debt and w_s is the percentage financed with common stock), (3) the cost of debt (r_d), and (4) the discount rate for the tax shield:

$$r_{sL} = r_{sU} + (r_{sU} - r_d)\frac{w_d}{w_s} - (r_{sU} - r_{TS})\left[\frac{r_d T}{r_{TS} - g_L}\right]\frac{w_d}{w_s}$$

(21-9)

The ratio of w_d/w_s in Equation 21-9 is also equal to the ratio D/S, where S is the value of the stock. For some situations it is easier to use the ratio of D/S if you have already calculated D and S; in others, you might have target capital structure weights, so it is easier to use the ratio w_d/w_s. Depending on the situation, we use the form of the leverage ratio (D/S or w_d/w_s) that reduces the number of calculations and saves the most time, so be aware of this as you read the chapter and work problems.

21-1c The Levered Beta (b)

With a little more algebra, we can express a company's beta as a function of the stock's **unlevered beta (b_U)**, **debt beta (b_d)**, and **tax shield beta (b_{TS})**; the betas of the debt and the tax shield reflect their systematic risk. The levered beta of a company is:

$$b = b_U + (b_U - b_d)\frac{w_d}{w_s} - (b_U - b_{TS})\left[\frac{r_d T}{r_{TS} - g_L}\right]\frac{w_d}{w_s}$$

(21-10)

If corporate debt is not riskless, then its beta, b_d, may not be zero. If we assume that bonds lie on the Security Market Line, then a bond's required return, r_d, can be expressed as:

$$r_d = r_{RF} + b_d RP_M.$$

Solving for b_d gives:

$$b_d = (r_d - r_{RF})/RP_M \qquad \text{(21-11)}$$

21-1d The Tax Shield Discount Rate (r_{TS})

Notice that the value of a levered firm (Equation 21-8), the levered cost of equity (Equation 21-9), and the levered beta (Equation 21-10) each depend upon the assumed rate for discounting the tax shield, r_{TS}. Although r_{TS} cannot be directly observed, we can put some bounds on it, as we show next.

If the company will always get to deduct interest expenses, then the tax shield has no risk and should be discounted at the risk-free rate. However, corporate debt is not riskless—firms do occasionally default on their loans if cash flows from operations are so low that the firm's value is less than the debt's value. Even if a company doesn't default on its debt, a company might not be able to use tax savings from interest deductions in the current year. This can happen if the firm has a pre-tax operating loss. This also can happen if interest expense deductions are limited by the 2017 Tax Cuts and Jobs Act (TCJA) Recall from Chapter 2 that the TCJA limits the amount of interest that may be deducted for tax purposes in a single year to 30% of EBITDA for 2018–2021 and 30% of EBIT for subsequent years; any excess may be carried forward indefinitely. Therefore, the discount rate should be greater than the risk-free rate.[1]

How much higher should the discount rate be? The risk that the company will not be able to use future interest rate deductions stems from the risk of its pre-tax operating profit. This suggests that the unlevered cost of equity, which reflects the risk of operations, should be an upper limit for the required return on the tax shield.

The following sections describe some special cases of the adjusted present value model that correspond to particular values of r_{TS}.

SELF-TEST

What does the term "value of an unlevered firm" mean?

What is the tax shield of interest?

How does the value of a levered firm compare to the value of an unlevered firm that is otherwise identical?

---

[1]The discount rate for the tax shield, r_{TS}, must also be greater than the growth rate, g_L. To see this, look at the first row in Equation 21-7. If r_{TS} is less than g_L, then the ratio of $(1 + g_L)/(1 + r_{TS})$ will be greater than 1, causing each term in the infinite series to be greater than the initial tax shield of $r_d(T)(D_0)$ and the sum to be infinite. We know that the value of the tax shield can't be infinite, so r_{TS} must be greater than g_L.

If g_L is high and r_{TS} is barely greater than g_L, then the third term in Equation 21-9 can be larger than the second term, causing the levered cost of equity to be less than the unlevered cost of equity! That makes no economic sense. The combination of a high g_L and relatively low r_{TS} would also cause the value of a levered firm in Equation 21-8 to be very large. Consequently, high-growth firms would choose high levels of leverage, but this is inconsistent with low levels of leverage actually chosen by high-growth firms. Therefore, r_{TS} probably is much larger than g_L. In fact, the levered cost of equity cannot be lower than the unlevered cost of equity if $r_{TS} = r_{sU}$. For a more detailed discussion, see Michael C. Ehrhardt and Phillip R. Daves, "Corporate Valuation: The Combined Impact of Growth and the Tax Shield of Debt on the Cost of Capital and Systematic Risk," *Journal of Applied Finance,* Fall/Winter 2002, pp. 31–38.

21-2 The Modigliani and Miller Models

Recall from Chapter 15 that Modigliani and Miller (MM) developed a model of capital structure based on the assumption of zero growth ($g_L = 0$) and no risk of bankruptcy ($b_d = 0$). In addition, they assumed that the appropriate discount rate for the tax shield is $r_{TS} = r_d$. They made this assumption because the annual tax savings are proportional to the annual debt, which implies that the tax savings have the same risk as debt. MM examined two situations, one with no taxes and one with corporate taxes.

21-2a Modigliani and Miller: No Taxes

In addition to the previous assumptions (including zero growth), MM's first model assumed no taxes. Substituting $g_L = 0$ and $T = 0$ into Equations 21-8, 21-9, and 21-10 provides the MM results for zero taxes from Chapter 15:

$$V_L = V_U \tag{21-12}$$

and

$$r_{sL} = r_{sU} + (r_{sU} - r_d)(w_d/w_s) \tag{21-13}$$

The levered beta is:

$$b = b_U + (b_U - b_d)\frac{w_d}{w_s} \tag{21-14}$$

21-2b Modigliani and Miller: Corporate Taxes

Substituting $g_L = 0$ and $r_{TS} = r_d$ into Equations 21-8 and 21-9 but allowing T to be nonzero provides the MM results when corporate taxes are considered:

$$V_L = V_U + TD \tag{21-15}$$

and

$$r_{sL} = r_{sU} + (r_{sU} - r_d)(1 - T)(w_d/w_s) \tag{21-16}$$

Substituting $g = 0$, $b_d = 0$, and $r_{TS} = r_d$ into Equation 21-10 (and allowing T to be nonzero) provides the Hamada equation from Chapter 15:

$$b = b_U[1 + (1 - T)(w_d/w_s)] \tag{21-17}$$

Therefore, the MM models are special cases of the more general adjusted present value approach. The following section provides another special case that is widely used, the compressed APV model.

Using the adjusted present value model, under what assumptions are the MM (no taxes) results correct?

Using the adjusted present value model, under what assumptions are the MM (with corporate taxes) results correct?

21-3 The Compressed Adjusted Present Value (CAPV) Model

In contrast to the MM models, the **compressed adjusted present value (CAPV)** model allows nonzero growth and risky debt with a nonzero debt beta.[2] It also differs from the MM models in its assumption regarding the appropriate discount rate for the tax shield. In particular, it assumes that $r_{TS} = r_{sU}$.

Substituting $r_{TS} = r_{sU}$ into the general valuation model in Equation 218, we get:

$$V_L = V_U + \left(\frac{r_d T D_1}{r_{sU} - g_L} \right) \tag{21-18}$$

Notice that the gain from leverage (the second term in Equation 21-18) can be larger or smaller than the gain from leverage in the MM model with taxes, depending on the fraction $r_d/(r_{sU} - g_L)$. If the cost of debt is high relative to the spread between the unlevered cost of equity and the growth rate, then a growing tax shield is very valuable. On the other hand, if growth is very low (or zero), then the fraction $r_d/(r_{sU} - g_L)$ is less than 1, which means that the gain from leverage is bigger in the MM model than in the APV model. This makes sense, because the MM model discounts the tax savings at the relatively low cost of debt, r_d, while the CAPV model discounts the tax savings at the relatively high unlevered cost of equity, r_{sU}.

---

[2]It is called the *compressed* APV because it is not necessary to separately discount FCF and the interest tax shield when calculating the value of the levered firm because each is discounted at the unlevered cost of equity. In other words, you can estimate the value of a levered firm as:

$$V_L = \sum_{t=1}^{\infty} \frac{FCF_t + TS_t}{(1 + r_{sU})^t}$$

With a little algebra (and neglecting the subscript t to avoid clutter), it is easy to show that:

FCF + TS = Adjusted net income

= Net income + (Depreciation + Amortization

− Investment in total net operating capital) + Interest expense

Therefore, the value of a levered firm can be estimated by first adjusting forecasted net income as previously shown and then discounting adjusted net income by the unlevered cost of equity.

However, we usually separately discount the forecasted FCF and tax shields so that we can more easily identify the impact on value due to operations versus leverage. For more on the compressed APV, see Steven N. Kaplan and Richard S. Ruback, "The Valuation of Cash Flow Forecasts: An Empirical Analysis," *Journal of Finance,* September 1995, pp. 1059–1093. For evidence showing the effectiveness of the adjusted present value approach, see S. N. Kaplan and R. S. Ruback, "The Market Pricing of Cash Flow Forecasts: Discounted Cash Flow vs. the Method of 'Comparables,'" *Journal of Applied Corporate Finance,* Winter 1996, pp. 45–60.

Substituting $r_{TS} = r_{sU}$ into Equation 21-9 shows that the levered cost of equity is:

$$r_{sL} = r_{sU} + (r_{sU} - r_d) (w_d/w_s) \qquad (21\text{-}19)$$

Although the derivation of Equation 21-19 reflects corporate taxes and growth, neither of these expressions includes the corporate tax rate or the growth rate. This means that the expression for the levered required rate of return, Equation 21-19, is exactly the same as MM's expression for the levered required rate of return *without taxes*, Equation 21-13. The reason the tax rate and the growth rate drop out of these two expressions is that the growing tax shield is discounted at the unlevered cost of equity, r_{sU}, not at the cost of debt as in the MM model. The tax rate drops out because no matter how high the level of T, the total risk of the firm will not be changed—the unlevered cash flows and the tax shield are discounted at the same rate. The growth rate drops out for the same reason—an increasing debt level will not change the combined risk of the debt and equity no matter what rate of growth prevails.

If a company already has leverage, the unlevered cost of equity is not directly observable. Rearranging Equation 21-19 provides an expression for r_{sU}:

$$r_{sU} = w_s r_{sL} + w_d r_d \qquad (21\text{-}20)$$

For many purposes, including corporate valuation using the APV or CAPV model, knowing r_{sU} is sufficient. However, it is also useful to see the relationship between leverage and beta. Substituting $r_{TS} = r_{sU}$ and $b_{TS} = b_U$ into Equation 21-10 shows the levered beta:

$$b = b_U + (b_U - b_d) (w_d/w_s) \qquad (21\text{-}21)$$

Rearranging Equation 21-21, the unlevered beta is:[3]

$$b_U = [b + b_d (w_d/w_s)]/[1 + (w_d/w_s)] \qquad (21\text{-}22)$$

We will use the compressed APV model to determine the value of a company whose capital structure is changing during the forecast period, but first we present a related valuation model, the free cash flow to equity (FCFE) model.

S E L F - T E S T

Using the adjusted present value model, under what assumptions are the compressed APV results correct?

---

[3]You can also calculate b_U directly from the CAPM formula once you have r_{sU} from Equation 21-20: $b_U = (r_{sU} - r_{RF})/RP_M$. This has the advantage of being simple but the disadvantage of not providing any insight into the contribution of risky debt.

21-4 The Free Cash Flow to Equity (FCFE) Model

Free cash flow is the cash flow available for distribution to *all* investors. In contrast, **free cash flow to equity (FCFE)** is the cash flow available for distribution to *common shareholders*. Because FCFE is available for distribution only to shareholders, it should be discounted at the levered cost of equity, r_{sL}. Therefore, the **free cash flow to equity model**, also called the **equity residual model**, discounts the projected FCFE at the cost of equity to determine the value of the equity.

Because FCFE is the cash flow available for distribution to shareholders, it may be used to pay common dividends, repurchase stock, purchase financial assets, or some combination of these uses. In other words, the uses of FCFE include all those of FCF except for distributions to debtholders. Therefore, one way to calculate FCFE is to start with FCF and reduce it by the net after-tax distributions to debtholders:

$$\text{FCFE} = \frac{\text{Free}}{\text{cash flow}} - \frac{\text{After-tax}}{\text{interest expense}} - \frac{\text{Principal}}{\text{payments}} + \frac{\text{Newly issued}}{\text{debt}}$$

$$= \frac{\text{Free}}{\text{cash flow}} - \frac{\text{Interest}}{\text{expense}} + \frac{\text{Tax savings}}{\text{due to interest}} + \frac{\text{Net change}}{\text{in debt}}$$

(21-23)

Alternatively, the FCFE can be calculated as:

$$\text{FCFE} = \text{Net income} - \frac{\text{Investment in total}}{\text{net operating capital}} + \frac{\text{Net change}}{\text{in debt}}$$

(21-24)

Given projections of FCFE, the value of a firm's equity (V_{FCFE}) is:

$$V_{\text{FCFE}} = \sum_{t=1}^{\infty} \frac{\text{FCFEt}}{(1 + r_{sL})^t}$$

(21-25)

The following section explains how to use the FCF model, the CAPV model, and the FCFE model to value companies with constant capital structures and constant long-term growth but with nonconstant growth during the forecast period.

SELF-TEST

What cash flows are discounted in the FCFE model, and what is the discount rate?

21-5 Multistage Valuation When the Capital Structure Is Stable

In this section we briefly review the free cash flow (FCF) valuation model from Chapter 7 and we modify the compressed APV and FCFE models for application to a firm with nonconstant FCF growth in the forecast period (but constant FCF growth after the forecast horizon). To better focus on the impact of leverage due to debt, we assume that the models are being applied to a firm without any preferred stock or non-operating assets.

21-5a A Brief Review of the Multistage FCF Corporate Valuation Model

Recall the free cash flow valuation model from Chapter 7, in which the value of operations (V_{op}) is equal to the present value of expected future free cash flows (FCFs) discounted at the weighted average cost of capital (WACC). FCF growth can be nonconstant *during* the forecast period but the rate of growth (g_L) must become constant *by the end* of the forecast period (Period N), which is called the horizon. The horizon value ($HV_{FCF,N}$) is the present value of all FCF beyond the horizon, discounted back to the horizon date. The horizon value of the FCF at time N ($HV_{FCF,N}$) is:

$$HV_{FCF,N} = \frac{FCF_N(1 + g_L)}{WACC - g_L} \qquad (21\text{-}26)$$

The present value of all FCF is the value of operations (V_{FCF}):[4]

$$V_{FCF} = \sum_{t=1}^{N} \frac{FCF_t}{(1 + WACC)^t} + \frac{HV_{FCF,N}}{(1 + WACC)^N} \qquad (21\text{-}27)$$

Because we assume that there is no preferred stock and that there are no nonoperating assets, the total value of equity is found by subtracting the value of all debt from the total value. The price per share is found by dividing the total value of equity by the number of shares.

21-5b The Multistage Compressed APV Approach

To estimate the unlevered value of operations, V_U, we need the projected free cash flows and the unlevered cost of equity, r_{sU}. It is straightforward to estimate the projected free cash flows, as shown in Chapters 7 and 12. It can be a bit more complicated to estimate the unlevered cost of equity. If the company being analyzed currently has no debt, then its current cost of equity *is* the unlevered cost of equity. If the company already has some debt, then we need to unlever its current cost of equity. The Hamada equation is based on the MM model with corporate taxes, which discounts the tax savings at the cost of debt and which assumes zero growth, making the Hamada equation inappropriate for applications of the compressed APV model.

For the compressed APV model, we use Equation 21-20 to estimate the unlevered cost of equity if we already know the levered cost of equity. If instead we already know the beta, we find the debt beta using Equation 21-11 and the unlevered beta using Equation 21-22. This allows us to use the Capital Asset Pricing Model (CAPM) to estimate the unlevered cost of equity. Given the estimated FCF and unlevered cost of equity, the unlevered value

---

[4]We denoted the value of operations as V_{op} in Chapters 7 and 12, but we use V_{FCF} here to distinguish it from other valuation approaches that we discuss in this chapter.

of operations is the present value of the firm's free cash flows discounted at the unlevered cost of equity:

$$V_U = \sum_{t=1}^{\infty} \frac{FCF_t}{(1 + r_{sU})^t}$$

(21-28)

If the FCFs grow at a nonconstant rate during the forecast period but grow at a constant rate after the forecast horizon, then we first find the horizon value of the unlevered firm ($HV_{U,N}$):

$$HV_{U,N} = \frac{FCF_N(1 + g_L)}{r_{sU} - g_L}$$

(21-29)

The total value of the unlevered firm is:

$$V_U = \sum_{t=1}^{N} \frac{FCF_t}{(1 + r_{s,U})^t} + \frac{HV_{U,N}}{(1 + r_{s,U})^N}$$

(21-30)

As described earlier, the compressed APV discounts the tax savings at the unlevered cost of equity, so the value of the tax shield is:

$$V_{Tax\ shield} = \sum_{t=1}^{\infty} \frac{TS_t}{(1 + r_{sU})^t}$$

(21-31)

If the annual tax shields grow at a nonconstant rate during the forecast period but grow at a constant rate after the forecast horizon, then we first find the horizon value of the tax shields ($HV_{TS,N}$):

$$HV_{TS,N} = \frac{TS_N(1 + g_L)}{r_{sU} - g_L}$$

(21-32)

The total value of the shield is:

$$V_{Tax\ shield} = \sum_{t=1}^{N} \frac{TS_t}{(1 + r_{sU})^t} + \frac{HV_{TS,N}}{(1 + r_{sU})^N}$$

(21-33)

The total value of operations is the sum of the unlevered value and the value of the tax shield. Because we assume that there is no preferred stock and that there are no nonoperating assets, the total value of equity is found by subtracting all debt from the total value of operations. The price per share is found by dividing the total value of equity by the number of shares.

The compressed APV model gets its name from the fact that the annual FCFs and tax savings can be added together before conducting any calculations; in other words, the annual FCFs and tax savings can be "compressed" into a single stream of cash flows. When discounted at the unlevered cost of equity, the present value of this single stream of cash flows is the value of operations.

21-5c The Multistage Free Cash Flow to Equity (FCFE) Model

If we assume constant growth beyond the horizon, then the horizon value of the equity ($HV_{FCFE,N}$) is:

$$HV_{FCFE,N} = \frac{FCFE_{N+1}}{r_{sL} - g_L} = \frac{FCFE_N(1 + g_L)}{r_{sL} - g_L} \qquad \text{(21-34)}$$

The value of equity is the present value of the horizon value and the FCFE during the forecast period, plus the change in debt at t = 0, denoted by ΔD_0. Keep in mind that a company may issue (or retire) debt immediately after the valuation date to maintain its capital structure. That additional debt is available to the shareholders immediately as a free cash flow to equity and must be included as a cash flow at t = 0. In many cases, this term will be zero, but in some cases, like the one in our example in the next sections, it is not. Therefore, the value of equity is:

$$V_{FCFE} = \Delta D_0 + \sum_{t=1}^{N} \frac{FCFE_t}{(1 + r_{sL})^t} + \frac{HV_{FCFE,N}}{(1 + r_{sL})^N} \qquad \text{(21-35)}$$

To get a per share price, simply divide the value of equity by the shares outstanding.[5] Like the FCF corporate valuation model, the FCFE model can be applied only when the capital structure is constant.

Table 21-1 summarizes the three cash flow valuation methods and their assumptions.

Notice that that all three models assume that growth in FCFs must be constant after the horizon date and that the capital structure must be constant after the horizon date. However, only the compressed APV approach is valid if the capital structure is nonconstant during the forecast period. The next section illustrates all three models for the situation in which the capital structure is constant, followed by an example of the compressed APV approach when the capital structure changes during the forecast period.

---

[5]The FCFE model is similar to the dividend growth model in that cash flows are discounted at the cost of equity. The models are equivalent if there is no preferred stock and there are no nonoperating assets.

TABLE 21-1
Summary of Cash Flow Approaches

	Approach		
	Corporate FCF Valuation Model	**Free Cash Flow to Equity Model**	**APV Model**
Cash flow definition	FCF = NOPAT − Net investment in operating capital	FCFE = FCF − Interest expense + Interest tax shield + ΔD_0	(1) FCF and (2) Interest tax savings
Discount rate	WACC	r_{sL} = Cost of equity	r_{sU} = Unlevered cost of equity
Result of present value calculation	Value of operations	Value of equity	(1) Value of unlevered operations and (2) Value of the tax shield; together, these are the value of operations
How to get equity value	Value of operations + Value of nonoperating assets − Value of debt	Value of equity as calculated above	Value of operations + Value of nonoperating assets − Value of debt
Assumption about capital structure during forecast period	Capital structure is stable	Capital structure is stable	None
Requirement for analyst to project interest expense	No interest expense projections needed	Projected interest expense must be based on the assumed capital structure	Interest expense projections are unconstrained
Assumption at horizon	FCF grows at constant rate g_L	FCFE grows at constant rate g_L	FCF and interest tax savings grow at constant rate g_L (because capital structure is stable after horizon)

Note: To better focus on the impact of leverage due to debt, the definitions here assume there is no preferred stock and that there are no nonoperating assets. In general, you must add the value of nonoperating assets. For the Corporate FCF Valuation model and the APV model, you would also subtract the value of preferred stock.

S E L F - T E S T

How do the FCFE, corporate FCF valuation, and compressed APV models differ? How are they similar?

21-6 Illustration of the Three Valuation Approaches for a Constant Capital Structure

To illustrate the three valuation approaches, consider Tutwiler Controls, a small technology company specializing in voice-activated commands. Tutwiler currently has a $154 million market value of equity and $38 million in debt, for a total market value of $192 million. Thus, Tutwiler's current capital structure consists of almost 20% debt: $38/$192 = 19.79\%$. Tutwiler intends to maintain a target capital structure with 20% debt throughout the projection period and thereafter.

Because investors expect Tutwiler to maintain the target capital structure in the future, the current estimates of beta and the cost of debt already reflect the investors' expectations. Tutwiler is a publicly traded company, and its market-determined beta is 1.4.

Given a risk-free rate of 6% and a 5% market risk premium, the Capital Asset Pricing Model produces a required rate of return on equity, r_{sL}, of:

$$r_{sL} = r_{RF} + b(RP_M)$$
$$= 6\% + 1.4(5\%) = 13\%$$

Tutwiler's pre-tax cost of debt is 8%, and its federal-plus-state tax rate is 25%. Its WACC is:

$$WACC = w_d(1 - T)r_d + w_s r_{sL}$$
$$= 0.20(1 - 0.25)(8\%) + 0.80(13\%)$$
$$= 11.6\%$$

What is Tutwiler's intrinsic value? Is the market overvaluing or undervaluing Tutwiler? To determine these answers, we apply the FCF corporate valuation model, the compressed APV model, and the FCFE model in the following sections. As you will see, all three models produce an identical intrinsic value of equity, but keep in mind this is only because the capital structure is constant. If the capital structure were to change during the projection period (before becoming stable after the forecast horizon), then only the compressed APV model could be used. Section 21-7 illustrates application of the compressed APV in the case of a nonconstant capital structure.

21-6a Cash Flow Projections

resource

See *Ch21 Tool Kit.xlsx* for details.

See *Web Extension 21A* for an explanation of the process used to project financial statements with a constant capital structure. All calculations are in the worksheet *Web 21A* in *Ch21 Tool Kit.xlsx*. Figure 21-1 shows projections for the items needed to calculate FCF, interest tax savings, and FCFE. The calculations include projections for the first post-horizon year to verify that the cash flows grow at 5% beyond the horizon.

Panel A of Figure 21-1 shows selected items from the projected financial statements. Panel B shows the calculations for free cash flow, which are used in the corporate FCF valuation model. Row 6 shows net operating profit after taxes (NOPAT), which is equal to EBIT$(1 - T)$. Row 7 shows the net investment in operating capital, which is the annual change in the total net operating capital in Row 5. Free cash flow, shown in Row 8, is equal to NOPAT less the net investment in operating capital.

Panel C shows the cash flows that will be used in the APV model. In particular, Row 10 shows the annual tax savings due to debt, which is equal to the interest expense multiplied by the tax rate. Panel D, using Equation 21-23, provides the calculations for FCFE.

Following are valuations of Tutwiler using all three methods, beginning with the FCF corporate valuation model.

21-6b Valuation Using the Corporate FCF Valuation Model

resource

See *Ch21 Tool Kit.xlsx* on the textbook's Web site for all calculations. Note that rounded intermediate values are shown in the text but all calculations are performed in Excel using nonrounded values.

Tutwiler's free cash flows are shown in Row 8 of Figure 21-1. The horizon value of Tutwiler's free cash flows as of 2024 can be calculated using the constant growth formula shown in Equation 21-26:

$$HV_{FCF,2024} = \frac{FCF_{2025}}{WACC - g_L} = \frac{FCF_{2024}(1 + g_L)}{WACC - g_L}$$

$$= \frac{\$17.0000(1.05)}{0.116 - 0.05} = \$270.4545 \text{ million}$$

FIGURE 21-1
Projections for Tutwiler (Millions of Dollars)

	A	B	C	D	E	F	G	H
56	Panel A: Selected Items from Projected Financial Statements							
57			1/1	12/31	12/31	12/31	12/31	12/31
58			2020	2020	2021	2022	2023	2024
59	1. Net Sales			$155.0000	$170.0000	$185.0000	$200.0000	$210.0000
60	2. EBIT			$24.8000	$27.2000	$29.6000	$32.0000	$33.6000
61	3. Int.[a]			$3.0859	$3.3430	$3.6012	$3.8606	$4.1212
62	4. Debt[b]		$38.5736	$41.7881	$45.0155	$48.2573	$51.5152	$54.0909
63	5. Op. cap.		$114.8000	$127.1000	$139.4000	$151.7000	$164.0000	$172.2000
64	Panel B: Corporate FCF Valuation Model Cash Flows							
65			1/1	12/31	12/31	12/31	12/31	12/31
66			2020	2020	2021	2022	2023	2024
67	6. NOPAT[c]			$18.6000	$20.4000	$22.2000	$24.0000	$25.2000
68	7. – Inv. in op. cap.			$12.3000	$12.3000	$12.3000	$12.3000	$8.2000
69	8. Free cash flow			$6.3000	$8.1000	$9.9000	$11.7000	$17.0000
70	Panel C: CAPV Model Cash Flows							
71			1/1	12/31	12/31	12/31	12/31	12/31
72			2020	2020	2021	2022	2023	2024
73	9. Free cash flow			$6.3000	$8.1000	$9.9000	$11.7000	$17.0000
74	10. Interest(T)			$0.7715	$0.8358	$0.9003	$0.9651	$1.0303
75	Panel D: FCFE Model Cash Flows							
76			1/1	12/31	12/31	12/31	12/31	12/31
77			2020	2020	2021	2022	2023	2024
78	11. Free cash flow			$6.3000	$8.1000	$9.9000	$11.7000	$17.0000
79	12. – Int.(T)			$2.3144	$2.5073	$2.7009	$2.8954	$3.0909
80	13. + Δ debt		$0.5736	$3.2145	$3.2274	$3.2418	$3.2578	$2.5758
81	14. FCFE		$0.5736	$7.2001	$8.8201	$10.4409	$12.0624	$16.4848

Source: See the file **Ch21 Tool Kit.xlsx.** Numbers are reported as rounded values for clarity but are calculated using *Excel's* full precision. Thus, intermediate calculations using the figure's rounded values will be inexact.

Notes:

[a] Interest payments are based on Tutwiler's existing debt and additional debt required to finance annual growth.

[b] Debt is existing debt plus additional debt required to maintain a constant capital structure.

[c] Net operating profit after taxes (NOPAT) is equal to EBIT$(1 - T)$. The tax rate is 25%.

As shown in Equation 21-27, the value of operations is the present value of the free cash flows in the forecast period plus the present value of the horizon value. For January 1, 2020, the value is:

$$V_{FCF} = \frac{\$6.3000}{(1 + 0.116)^1} + \frac{\$8.1000}{(1 + 0.116)^2} + \frac{\$9.9000}{(1 + 0.116)^3}$$

$$+ \frac{\$11.7000}{(1 + 0.116)^4} + \frac{\$17.0000 + \$270.4545}{(1 + 0.116)^5}$$

$$= \$192.8678$$

There are no nonoperating assets, so the intrinsic value of Tutwiler's equity is equal to the value of operations less the value of debt. The debt on 12/31/2019, the date of the valuation, is $38 million, and this is the amount that is subtracted from the value of operations. Note that on 1/1/2020 (the day after the valuation date) Tutwiler will increase its debt by

$0.5736 million to $38.5736 million (as shown in Figure 21-1) to match its target capital structure. This addition of debt will be important in the later APV and FCFE analysis to make the assumed capital structures in all three models consistent with one another. Since the FCF valuation analysis occurs before the new debt of $0.5736 million is added, the value of debt that is used to determine the value of equity is equal to the original debt of $38 million.

$$\text{Intrinsic } S = V_{FCF} - D$$
$$= \$192.8678 - \$38 = \$154.8678 \text{ million}$$

The actual market value of equity is $154 million, which means that the intrinsic value is just a bit higher. This implies that the market is very slightly undervaluing the stock.

21-6c Valuation Using the APV Approach

The APV approach requires an estimate of Tutwiler's unlevered cost of equity. Using Tutwiler's capital structure, levered cost of equity, and cost of debt, Equation 21-20 provides the unlevered cost of equity:

$$r_{sU} = w_s r_{sL} + w_d r_d$$
$$= 0.80(13\%) + 0.20(8\%)$$
$$= 12\%$$

In other words, if Tutwiler had no debt, its cost of equity would be 12%.[6]

To estimate the beta on debt due to systematic risk, we use Equation 21-11:

$$b_d = (r_d - r_{RF})/RP_M$$
$$= (0.08 - 0.06)/0.05$$
$$= 0.04$$

Using this result and Equation 21-23, Tutwiler's unlevered beta is:

$$b_U = [b + b_d(w_d/w_s)]/[1 + (w_d/w_s)]$$
$$= [1.4 + 0.4(0.20/0.80)]/[1 + (0.20/0.80)]$$
$$= 1.2$$

Using the CAPM, the unlevered cost of equity is:

$$r_{sU} = r_{RF} + b_U(RP_M)$$
$$= 6\% + 1.2(5\%) = 12\%$$

This is identical to the value previously estimated. Because this alternative approach requires that we assume that the CAPM is the correct model and because it takes extra steps, we usually use the first method shown in Equation 21-20.

---

[6]Notice that we do not use the Hamada equation to lever or unlever beta, nor do we use the MM model with taxes to lever or unlever the required return on equity. These models assume zero growth, and they assume that the discount rate for the tax shield is the cost of debt, but neither assumption is true for this example. Instead, we use Equations 21-19 and 21-11, which assume that the growing debt tax shield is discounted at the unlevered cost of equity.

The horizon value of Tutwiler's unlevered cash flows ($HV_{U,2024}$) and tax shield ($HV_{TS,2024}$) can be calculated using the constant growth formula with the unlevered cost of equity as the discount rate, as shown in Equations 21-29 and 21-32:[7]

$$HV_{U,2024} = \frac{FCF_{2025}}{r_{sU} - g_L} = \frac{FCF_{2024}(1 + g_L)}{r_{sU} - g_L} = \frac{\$17.0000(1.05)}{0.12 - 0.05} = \$255.0000 \text{ million}$$

$$HV_{TS,2024} = \frac{TS_{2025}}{r_{sU} - g_L} = \frac{TS_{2024}(1 + g_L)}{r_{sU} - g_L} = \frac{\$1.0303(1.05)}{0.12 - 0.05} = \$15.4545 \text{ million}$$

The sum of the two horizon values is $255.0000 + $15.4545 = $270.4545 million. This is the total horizon value of operations. Note that this is the same horizon value of operations we previously obtained using the FCF corporate valuation model.

Row 9 in Figure 21-1 shows the projected free cash flows. Using Equation 21-30, the unlevered value of operations is:

$$V_U = \frac{\$6.3000}{(1 + 0.12)^1} + \frac{\$8.1000}{(1 + 0.12)^2} + \frac{\$9.9000}{(1 + 0.12)^3}$$

$$+ \frac{\$11.7000}{(1 + 0.12)^4} + \frac{\$17.0000 + \$255.0000}{(1 + 0.12)^5}$$

$$= \$180.9046$$

This shows that Tutwiler's operations would be worth $180.9046 million if it had no debt. Row 10 shows the yearly tax savings due to interest deductions. Using Equation 21-33, the value of the tax shield is:

$$V_{Tax\ shield} = \frac{\$0.7715}{(1 + 0.12)^1} + \frac{\$0.8358}{(1 + 0.12)^2} + \frac{\$0.9003}{(1 + 0.12)^3}$$

$$+ \frac{\$0.9651}{(1 + 0.12)^4} + \frac{\$1.0303 + \$15.4545}{(1 + 0.12)^5}$$

$$= \$11.9632 \text{ million}$$

Thus, Tutwiler's operations would be worth only $180.9046 million if it had no debt, but its capital structure contributes $11.9632 million in value due to the tax deductibility of its interest payments. Because Tutwiler has no nonoperating assets, the total value of the firm is the sum of the unlevered value of operations, $180.9046 million, and the value of the tax shield, $11.9632 million, for a total of $192.8678 million. Other than rounding differences, this is the same value given by the corporate valuation model in the previous section. The value of the equity is the total value less Tutwiler's outstanding debt of $38 million: $192.8678 − $38 = $154.8678 million.

Sometimes it is more convenient to use the compressed APV. Recall that this method begins by calculating the sum of the FCF and the tax shield each year. Because the unlevered cost of equity is the appropriate discount rate for the annual FCFs and tax shields,

---

[7]Figure 21-1 reports only four decimal places. All calculations are performed using the full nonrounded values in the *Excel* file *Ch21 Tool Kit.xlsx*.

we can discount their annual sums to determine the value of operations. To apply this process, we calculate the combined total cash flow in each year, denoted by TotalCF$_t$:

	2020	2021	2022	2023	2024
FCF	$6.3000	$8.1000	$9.9000	$11.7000	$17.0000
Tax savings = Interest(T)	$0.7715	$0.8358	$0.9003	$0.9651	$1.0303
TotalCF = FCF + TS	$7.0715	$8.9358	$10.8003	$12.6651	$18.0303

Using the unlevered cost of equity, the horizon value of the total annual cash flows (HV$_{TotalCF}$) is:

$$HV_{TotalCF,2024} = \frac{TotalCF_{2024}(1 + g_L)}{r_{sU} - g_L} = \frac{\$18.0303(1.05)}{0.12 - 0.05} = 270.4545 \text{ million}$$

The total value of operations is:

$$V_{op} = \frac{\$7.0715}{(1 + 0.12)^1} + \frac{\$8.9358}{(1 + 0.12)^2} + \frac{\$10.8003}{(1 + 0.12)^3}$$

$$+ \frac{\$12.6651}{(1 + 0.12)^4} + \frac{\$18.0303 + \$270.4545}{(1 + 0.12)^5}$$

$$= \$192.8678 \text{ million}$$

Note that this is the same value of operations we obtained previously by separately finding the value of unlevered operations and the value of the tax shield. Although this compressed approach requires fewer calculations, we prefer to separately value the FCF and the tax savings because this shows us how much value is being added by the unlevered operations and how much by the choice of capital structure.

21-6d Valuation Using the FCFE Model

The horizon value of Tutwiler's free cash flows to equity can be calculated using the constant growth formula of Equation 21-34:[8]

$$HV_{FCFE,2024} = \frac{FCFE_{2024}(1 + g_L)}{r_{sL} - g_L} = \frac{\$16.4848(1.05)}{0.13 - 0.05}$$

$$= \$216.3630 \text{ million}$$

$$\approx \$216.3636 \text{ million if no rounding}$$

Notice that this horizon value is different from that of the compressed APV model and FCF corporate valuation model. That is because the FCFE horizon value is only for equity, whereas the other two horizon values are for the total value of operations. If the 2024 debt of $54.0909 million shown in Row 4 of Figure 21-1 is added to the horizon value of $216.3636, the result is $270.4545 million, the same horizon value of operations obtained with the FCF corporate valuation model and compressed APV model.

Row 14 in Figure 21-1 shows the yearly projections of FCFE. Notice that the initial FCFE is $0.5763. This is the debt that Tutwiler immediately issued after previously determining

---

[8]Figure 21-1 reports only four decimal places. All calculations are performed using the full nonrounded values in the *Excel* file *Ch21 Tool Kit.xlsx*.

its value of operations with the FCF model. This is the amount of debt that is needed so that the actual capital structure would match the target capital structure. See **Web Extension 21A** for a detailed explanation. The proceeds from this debt issue are available to the shareholders immediately and don't appear in $FCFE_1$ and so must be included as an undiscounted lump sum in Year 0. If Tutwiler's initial debt level of $38 million had been consistent with its target capital structure of 20% debt, then it would not have issued this new debt, and the initial term would have been zero.

Using Equation 21-35, the value of the free cash flow to equity is:

$$V_{FCFE} = \$0.5736 + \frac{\$7.2001}{(1 + 0.13)^1} + \frac{\$8.8201}{(1 + 0.13)^2} + \frac{\$10.4409}{(1 + 0.13)^3}$$

$$+ \frac{\$12.0624}{(1 + 0.13)^4} + \frac{\$16.4848 + \$216.3636}{(1 + 0.13)^5}$$

$$= \$154.8678 \text{ million}$$

resource

*See **Web Extension 21A** and Ch21 Tool Kit.xlsx on the textbook's Web site.*

Because Tutwiler has no nonoperating assets, its total intrinsic equity value is equal to the V_{FCFE} of $154.8678 million. Notice that this is the same value given by the FCF corporate valuation model and the compressed APV approach, other than small rounding differences.

As mentioned previously, the FCF corporate valuation model and the FCFE model are not appropriate if the capital structure is not constant during the forecast period. However, the compressed APV approach is appropriate for such situations, as illustrated in the next section.

SELF-TEST

How do the FCFE, APV, and corporate valuation approaches differ from one another? How are they similar?

21-7 Analysis of a Dynamic Capital Structure

Suppose Tutwiler has decided to increase its debt from a target weight of 20% to 30% over the next 5 years and to maintain the new capital structure thereafter. How would this affect Tutwiler's valuation? The free cash flows and unlevered cost of equity will not change, so the unlevered value will not change. However, the annual interest tax shields and the long-term WACC will change. At a 20% debt level, the interest rate on Tutwiler's debt was 8%. However, at higher debt levels, Tutwiler is more risky, and its average interest rate will rise to 8.5% to reflect this additional risk.[9] Because the capital structure is changing, we can use only the compressed APV for this analysis.

21-7a Application of the CAPV Model

Tutwiler will increase its debt during the first 5 years to reach its long-run target capital structure of 30% debt. With more debt and a higher interest rate, the interest payments will be higher than those shown in Figure 21-1, thus increasing the tax savings. The new interest payments and tax savings with more debt and a higher interest rate are

---

[9]We are assuming for simplicity that its higher risk will not affect the expected free cash flows. In practice, it is extremely difficult to estimate the impact on free cash flow of expected bankruptcy costs. However, these costs can be significant and should be considered when a very high degree of leverage is being used.

projected as follows (see the worksheet *Web21A* in the file *Ch21 Tool Kit.xlsx* for the calculations):

	12/31/19	12/31/20	12/31/21	12/31/22	12/31/23	12/31/24
Debt	$38.0000	$49.0000	$59.0000	$70.0000	$80.1572	$84.1650
Interest		$3.2300	$4.1650	$5.0150	$5.9500	$6.8134
Tax savings		$0.8075	$1.0413	$1.2538	$1.4875	$1.7033

Based on the new tax shields, the tax shield horizon value in 2024 is:

$$HV_{TS,2024} = \frac{TS_{2024}(1 + g_L)}{r_{sU} - g_L} = \frac{\$1.7033(1.05)}{0.12 - 0.05} = \$25.5495$$

$$\approx \$25.5501 \text{ million if no rounding}$$

The total value of the tax shields is:

$$V_{Tax\ shield} = \frac{\$0.8075}{(1 + 0.12)^1} + \frac{\$1.0413}{(1 + 0.12)^2} + \frac{\$1.2538}{(1 + 0.12)^3}$$

$$+ \frac{\$1.4875}{(1 + 0.12)^4} + \frac{\$1.7033 + \$25.5501}{(1 + 0.12)^5}$$

$$= \$18.8532 \text{ million}$$

$$\approx \$18.8531 \text{ million if no rounding}$$

The free cash flows are unchanged, so the value of the unlevered firm is the same as calculated previously in Section 21-6c, which is $180.9046 million. Adding the value of the tax shield of $18.8531 million gives the total value of operations:

$$V_{op} = \$180.9046 + \$18.8531 = \$199.7577 \text{ million}$$

The intrinsic value of equity is:

$$\text{Intrinsic value of equity} = V_{op} + \text{Nonoperating assets} - \text{Debt}$$
$$= \$199.7577 + \$0 - \$38.0000$$
$$= \$161.7577 \text{ million}$$

Increasing the capital structure to 30% debt increases the intrinsic value of equity to $161.7577. Recall that for a constant capital structure with 20% debt, the intrinsic value of equity is $154.8678 million. Therefore, the change in capital structure increased the intrinsic value of equity by about $6.9 million: $161.7577 − $154.8678 = $6.8899 ≈ $6.9 million.

Sometimes a company will know how much debt it wants at the horizon and wishes to know what w_d will be given the FCF and other inputs. For example, suppose Tutwiler wishes to have $100 million of debt at the horizon. Equation 21-36 determines w_d given Tutwiler's choices:

$$w_d = \frac{D_t(r_{sU} - g_L)}{[FCF_t(1 + g_L)] + (D_t - r_d T)} \tag{21-36}$$

Using Tutwiler's inputs, Equation 21-36 shows that w_d will be 35.04% if the debt is $100 million.

$$w_d = \frac{D_t(r_{sU} - g_L)}{[FCF_t(1 + g_L)] + [D_t(r_d)(T)]}$$

$$= \frac{\$100(0.12 - 0.05)}{[\$17(1 + 0.05)] + [\$100(0.085)(0.25)]}$$

$$= 35.04\%$$

21-7b The 2017 Tax Cuts and Jobs Act (TCJA): Interest Expense Limitations

The 2017 Tax Cuts and Jobs Act (TCJA) limits interest expense deductions to 30% of EBITDA for 2018–2021 and 30% of EBIT for subsequent years; any excess may be carried forward indefinitely. Even though none of the previous examples exceeded this limit, it is important to know the maximum amount of debt financing that does not trigger the limitation. Rather than determine this amount by trial-and-error, we can use the following equation, where IntLim is the limit on deductibility (e.g., 30%):

$$w_{dMax} = \frac{IntLim(r_{sU} - g_L)}{\{[r_d(1 - T)/(1 + g_L)x[1 + g_L - g_L(CR/OP)]\} + IntLim(r_d)(T)} \qquad (21\text{-}38)$$

Using the inputs for this example and a limit of 30%, $w_{dMax} = 42.5\%$. See the file **Ch21 Tool Kit.xlsx** for this calculation. Try substituting this value into the input for the analysis of a dynamic capital structure and you will see that Interest/EBIT is in fact 30% by the end of the forecast period.

SELF-TEST

Why is the compressed adjusted present value approach appropriate for situations with a changing capital structure?

Describe the steps required to apply the compressed APV approach.

A company forecasts free cash flow of $400 at Year 1 and $600 at Year 2; after Year 2, the FCFs grow at a constant rate of 5%. The company forecasts the tax savings from interest deductions as $200 in Year 1, $100 in Year 2; after Year 2, the tax savings grow at a constant rate of 5%. The unlevered cost of equity is 9%. What is the horizon value of operations at Year 2? **($15,750.0)** *What is the current unlevered value of operations?* **($14,128.4)** *What is the horizon value of the tax shield at Year 2?* **($2,625.0)** *What is the current value of the tax shield?* **($2,477.1)** *What is the levered value of operations at Year 0?* **($16,605.5)**

SUMMARY

In this chapter we discussed a variety of topics related to capital structure decisions. The key concepts covered are listed here.

- The most general approach to analyzing capital structure effects is the **adjusted present value (APV)** approach, should be in regular font, not bold and colored., which expresses the levered value of a company as the combination of its unlevered value and the value of side effects due to leverage:

$$V_L = V_U + \text{Value of side effects}$$

- MM stated that the primary benefit of debt stems from the *tax deductibility of interest payments*. The present value of the tax savings due to interest expense deductibility is called the **interest tax shield**. If we ignore other side effects, the value of an unlevered firm is:

$$V_L = V_U + V_{Tax\ shield}$$

- The **compressed adjusted present value (CAPV)** model incorporates nonconstant growth and assumes that the tax savings should be discounted at the unlevered cost of equity.
- The levered cost of equity and the levered beta are different in the compressed APV model than in the MM and Hamada models. In the compressed APV model, the relationships are:

$$r_{sL} = r_{sU} + (r_{sU} - r_d)\left(\frac{w_d}{w_s}\right)$$

and

$$b = b_U + (b_U - b_d)\left(\frac{w_d}{w_s}\right)$$

- The **free cash flow to equity (FCFE)** model discounts the cash flows available for distribution to *common shareholders* using the levered cost of equity, resulting in the intrinsic value of equity. It is also called the **equity residual model**.
- *Web Extension 21A* explains how to project financial statements that are consistent with target capital structures.

QUESTIONS

(21-1)   Define each of the following terms:
a. Interest tax shields; value of tax shield
b. Adjusted present value (APV) model
c. Compressed adjusted present value (CAPV) model
d. Free cash flow to equity model

(21-2)   Modigliani and Miller assumed that firms do not grow. How does positive growth change their conclusions about the value of the levered firm and its cost of capital?

SELF-TEST PROBLEM   SOLUTION SHOWN IN APPENDIX A

(ST-1)
Value of a
Levered Firm

The Menendez Corporation forecasts free cash flow of $100 at Year 1 and $120 at Year 2; after Year 2, the FCF is expected to grow at a constant rate of 4%. The company has a tax rate of 25% and $800 in debt at an interest rate of 5%. The company plans to hold debt steady until after Year 2, after which the debt (and tax savings) will grow at a constant rate of 4%. The unlevered cost of equity is 8%. Using the compressed APV model, answer the following questions.

a. What is the unlevered horizon value of operations at Year 2?
b. What is the current unlevered value of operations?

c. What are the tax savings for Year 1 and Year 2 (*Hint:* They are identical because the debt doesn't change.)
d. What is the horizon value of the tax shield at Year 2?
e. What is the current value of the tax shield?
f. What is the levered value of operations at Year 0?

PROBLEMS   ANSWERS ARE IN APPENDIX B

EASY PROBLEMS 1–5

(21-1)
MM Model with Zero Taxes

An unlevered firm has a value of $500 million. An otherwise identical but levered firm has $50 million in debt. Under the MM zero-tax model, what is the value of the levered firm?

(21-2)
MM Model with Corporate Taxes

An unlevered firm has a value of $800 million. An otherwise identical but levered firm has $60 million in debt at a 5% interest rate, which is its pre-tax cost of debt. Its unlevered cost of equity is 11%. No growth is expected. Assuming the federal-plus-state corporate tax rate is 25%, use the MM model with corporate taxes to determine the value of the levered firm.

(21-3)
Compressed APV Model with Constant Growth

An unlevered firm has a value of $800 million. An otherwise identical but levered firm has $60 million in debt at a 5% interest rate, which is its pre-tax cost of debt. Its unlevered cost of equity is 11%. After Year 1, free cash flows and tax savings are expected to grow at a constant rate of 3%. Assuming the corporate tax rate is 25%, use the compressed adjusted present value model to determine the value of the levered firm. (*Hint:* The interest expense at Year 1 is based on the current level of debt.)

(21-4)
Calculation of FCFE

A company has the following information:

Earnings before interest and taxes	$80.00
Interest expense	$8.00
Tax rate	25%
Net change in debt	$12.00
Investment in total capital	$9.00

What is its free cash flow to equity?

(21-5)
FCFE Valuation

A company's most recent free cash flow to equity was $100 and is expected to grow at 5% thereafter. The company's cost of equity is 10%. Its WACC is 8.72%. What is its current intrinsic value?

INTERMEDIATE PROBLEMS 6–7

(21-6)
Business and Financial Risk— MM Model

Air Tampa has just been incorporated, and its board of directors is grappling with the question of optimal capital structure. The company plans to offer commuter air services between Tampa and smaller surrounding cities. Air Tampa believes it would have the same business risk as Jaxair, which is an airline that has been around for a few years and that has had zero growth. Jaxair's market-determined beta is 2.1, and it has a current market value debt ratio (total debt to total assets) of 50% and a federal-plus-state tax rate of 25%. Air Tampa expects to have investment tax credits when it begins business, which reduces its federal-plus-state tax rate to 20%. Air Tampa's owners expect that the total book and market value of the firm's stock, if it uses zero debt, would be $10 million. Air Tampa's CFO believes that the MM and Hamada formulas for the value of a levered firm and the levered firm's cost of capital should be used because zero growth is expected.

a. Estimate the beta of an unlevered firm in the commuter airline business based on Jaxair's market-determined beta.
b. Now assume that $r_d = r_{RF} = 10\%$ and that the market risk premium $RP_M = 5\%$. Find the required rate of return on equity for an unlevered commuter airline.
c. Air Tampa is considering three capital structures: (1) $2 million debt, (2) $4 million debt, and (3) $6 million debt. Estimate Air Tampa's r_s for these debt levels.
d. Suppose Air Tampa's investment tax credits expire, causing it to have a 25% federal-plus-state tax rate. Calculate Air Tampa's r_s at $6 million debt using the new tax rate. Compare this with your corresponding answer to Part c. (*Hint:* The increase in the tax rate causes V_U to drop to $9.375 million.)

(21-7)
MM with
Corporate Taxes

Companies U and L are identical in every respect except that U is unlevered while L has $10 million of 5% bonds outstanding. Assume: (1) All of the MM assumptions are met. (2) Both firms are subject to a 25% federal-plus-state corporate tax rate. (3) EBIT is $2 million. (4) The unlevered cost of equity is 10%.

a. What value would MM now estimate for each firm? (*Hint:* Use Proposition I.)
b. What is r_s for Firm U? For Firm L?
c. Find S_L, and then show that $S_L + D = V_L$ results in the same value as obtained in part a.
d. What is the WACC for Firm U? For Firm L?

CHALLENGING PROBLEMS 8–9

(21-8)
Compressed
Adjusted
Present Value

Schwarzentraub Corporation's expected free cash flow for the year is $500,000; in the future, free cash flow is expected to grow at a rate of 8%. The company currently has no debt, and its cost of equity is 13%. Its tax rate is 25%. Suppose the firm issues $5 million debt at a rate of 7%. Use the compressed adjusted value approach to answer the following questions.

a. Find V_U.
b. Find V_L and r_{sL}. Use the APV model that allows for growth.
c. Start with the value of the unlevered firm, V_U, from part a. Use the MM model (with taxes but with zero growth) to calculate V_L and r_{sL}. (*Hint:* These answers will differ from those in part b due to differences in growth assumptions.)

(21-9)
Compressed APV
with Nonconstant
Growth

Sheldon Corporation projects the following free cash flows (FCFs) and interest expenses for the next 3 years, after which FCF and interest expenses are expected to grow at a constant 7% rate. Sheldon's unlevered cost of equity is 13%; its tax rate is 25%.

	Year		
	1	**2**	**3**
Free cash flow ($ millions)	$20.0	$30.0	$40.0
Interest expense ($ millions)	$12.8	$14.4	$16.0

a. What is Sheldon's unlevered horizon value of operations at Year 3?
b. What is the current unlevered value of operations?
c. What is the horizon value of the tax shield at Year 3?
d. What is the current value of the tax shield?
e. What is the current total value of the company?

SPREADSHEET PROBLEM

(21-10)
Build a Model:
Compressed
Adjusted Value
Model

Start with the partial model in the file *Ch21 P10 Build a Model.xlsx* on the textbook's Web site. Kasperov Corporation has an unlevered cost of equity of 12% and is taxed at a 25% rate. The 4-year forecasts of free cash flow and interest expenses are shown in the following table; free cash flow and interest expenses are expected to grow at a 5% rate after Year 4. Using the compressed APV model, answer the following questions.

INPUTS (In Millions)	Projected			
Year:	1	2	3	4
Free cash flow	$200	$280	$320	$340
Interest expense	$100	$120	$120	$140

a. Calculate the estimated horizon value of unlevered operations at Year 4 (i.e., immediately after the Year-4 free cash flow).
b. Calculate the current value of unlevered operations.
c. Calculate the estimated horizon value of the tax shield at Year 4 (i.e., immediately after the Year-4 free cash flow).
d. Calculate the current value of the tax shield.
e. Calculate the current total value.

MINI CASE

David Lyons, CEO of Lyons Solar Technologies, is concerned about his firm's level of debt financing. The company uses short-term debt to finance its temporary working capital needs, but it does not use any permanent (long-term) debt. Other solar technology companies have debt, and Mr. Lyons wonders why they use debt and what its effects are on stock prices. To gain some insights into the matter, he poses the following questions to you, his recently hired assistant:

a. Who were Modigliani and Miller (MM), and what assumptions are embedded in the MM and Miller models?

b. Assume that Firms U and L are in the same risk class and that both have EBIT = $560,000. Firm U uses no debt financing, and its cost of equity is r_{sU} = 14%. Firm L has $1 million of debt outstanding at a cost of r_d = 8%. There are no taxes. Assume that the MM assumptions hold.
   (1) Find V, S, r_s, and WACC for Firms U and L.
   (2) Graph (a) the relationships between capital costs and leverage as measured by D/V and (b) the relationship between V and D.

c. Now assume that Firms L and U are both subject to a 25% corporate tax rate. Using the data given in part b, repeat the analysis called for in parts b(1) and b(2) using assumptions from the MM model with taxes.

d. Suppose that Firms U and L have the same input values as in Part c except for debt of $980,000. Also, both firms have total net operating capital of $2,000,000 and both firms are expected to grow at a constant rate of 7%. (Assume that the EBIT in part c is expected at t = 1.) Use the compressed adjusted present value (APV) model to estimate the value of U and L. Also estimate the levered cost of equity and the weighted average cost of capital.

e. Suppose the expected free cash flow for Year 1 is $250,000 but it is expected to grow faster than 7% during the next 3 years: $FCF_2 = \$290,000$ and $FCF_3 = \$320,000$, after which it will grow at a constant rate of 7%. The expected interest expense at Year 1 is $128,000, but it is expected to grow over the next couple of years before the capital structure becomes constant: Interest expense at Year 2 will be $152,000, at Year 3 it will be $192,000 and it will grow at 7% thereafter. What is the estimated horizon unlevered value of operations (i.e., the value at Year 3 immediately after the FCF at Year 3)? What is the current unlevered value of operations? What is the horizon value of the tax shield at Year 3? What is the current value of the tax shield? What is the current total value? The tax rate and unlevered cost of equity remain at 25% and 14%, respectively.

SELECTED ADDITIONAL CASES

The following cases from CengageCompose cover many of the concepts discussed in this chapter and are available at **http://compose.cengage.com**.

Klein-Brigham Series:
Case 7, "Seattle Steel Products"; Case 9, "Kleen Kar, Inc."; Case 10, "Aspeon Sparkling Water"; Case 43, "Mountain Springs"; Case 57, "Greta Cosmetics"; Case 74, "The Western Company"; Case 83, "Armstrong Production Company"; Case 99, "Moore Plumbing Supply Company," focus on capital structure theory. Case 8, "Johnson Window Company," and Case 56, "Isle Marine Boat Company," cover operating and financial leverage.

Brigham-Buzzard Series:
Case 8, "Powerline Network Corporation," covers operating leverage, financial leverage, and the optimal capital structure.

CHAPTER 22

Mergers and Corporate Control

Verizon Communications made Verizon Wireless into a wholly owned subsidiary in 2014 with a $130 billion deal to acquire all the Verizon Wireless stock that it did not already own. What does this have to do with Vodafone Group, a UK telecommunications company? The story began in 1999 when Vodafone entered a joint venture with Bell Atlantic, resulting in a mobile technology subsidiary called Verizon Wireless. At about the same time, Bell Atlantic merged with GTE, the largest of the original Bell system companies. The merged companies became Verizon Communications and owned 55% of the Verizon Wireless subsidiary; Vodafone retained a 45% share in Verizon Wireless.

Vodafone soon made news in 2000 with its hostile takeover of Mannesmann AG, a German technology giant, in a deal valued at $161 billion, the largest merger in history. Through acquisitions and growth of its existing operations, Vodafone became one of the two largest wireless phone companies in the world, second only to China Mobile.

Fast-forward to 2014. To obtain Vodafone's 45% interest in Verizon Wireless, Verizon Communications gave Vodafone over 1.2 million shares of Verizon Communications stock (worth about $60.2 billion) and paid around $70 billion in cash (and other financial assets). Vodafone then gave each of its own shareholders a proportional amount of the Verizon Communications stock and paid its shareholders about $24 billion in a cash distribution.

Think about these transactions as you read the chapter.

Most corporate growth occurs by *internal expansion*, which takes place when a firm's existing divisions grow through normal capital budgeting activities. However, the most dramatic examples of growth result from mergers, the first topic covered in this chapter. Other actions that alter corporate control are divestitures—conditions change over time, causing firms to sell off, or divest, major divisions to other firms that can better utilize the divested assets. A *holding company* is another form of corporate control in which one corporation controls other companies by owning some, or all, of their stocks.

22-1 Rationale for Mergers

Many reasons have been proposed by financial managers and theorists to account for the high level of U.S. merger activity. The primary motives behind corporate **mergers** are presented in this section.[1]

22-1a Synergy as a Motivation for Mergers

The primary motivation for most mergers is to increase the value of the combined enterprise. If Companies A and B merge to form Company C and if C's value exceeds that of A and B taken together, then **synergy** is said to exist, and such a merger should be beneficial to both A's and B's stockholders. Synergistic effects can arise from five sources: (1) *operating economies*, which result from **economies of scale** in management, marketing, production, or distribution in which larger companies can reduce costs, increase sales, or both; (2) *differential efficiency*, which implies that the management of one firm is more efficient and that the weaker firm's assets will be more productive after the merger; (3) *financial economies*, including lower borrowing costs, lower transaction/issuing costs, and better coverage by security analysts; (4) *tax effects*, in which case the combined enterprise pays less in taxes than the separate firms would pay; and (5) *increased market power* due to reduced competition.

The first three sources (operating economies, differential efficiency, and financial economies) are economically desirable because they increase productivity, leading to lower prices for consumers and higher returns for investors.

The fourth source, tax effects, also benefits consumers and investors by reducing firms' costs. However, if the government collects less from businesses, then it is likely to make up the loss by raising taxes for individuals, increasing the federal deficit, reducing federal programs, or some combination of the three.

Increased market power (the fifth source of synergy) reduces competition, leading to higher prices for consumers. For example, a **monopoly** is a market structure in which a single firm has enough market power to deter new competitors from entering the market. Without competition, the firm can maximize its profits by increasing prices until decreasing sales offset its gains. If several firms dominate an industry and choose not to compete on the basis of prices, then the market structure is an **oligopoly**. Because the firms jointly behave much like a monopoly, they can charge higher prices to consumers. However, the Antitrust Division of the Justice Department and the Federal Trade Commission are not supposed to approve mergers that significantly reduce competition.[2]

For example, the proposed 2017 merger between health insurance giants Cigna and Anthem was blocked because regulators feared that it would increase prices for consumers. Rather than keep fighting in court, Anthem terminated the deal. Anthem also refused to

---

[1]As we use the term, *merger* means any combination that forms one economic unit from two or more previous ones. For legal purposes, there are distinctions among the various ways these combinations can occur, but our focus is on the fundamental economic and financial aspects of mergers.

[2]The Sherman Act (1890), the Clayton Act (1914), and the Celler Act (1950) make it illegal for firms to combine if the combination tends to lessen competition. For interesting insights into antitrust regulations and mergers, see B. Espen Eckbo, "Mergers and the Value of Antitrust Deterrence," *Journal of Finance*, July 1992, pp. 1005–1029.

pay Cigna the $1.85 billion termination fee specified in their pre-merger agreement. Cigna sued Anthem for refusing to pay the termination fee and asked the courts for another $13 billion in "damages." Cigna needs this to offset its planned merger with Express Scripts in which Cigna will increase its debt obligations by about $15 billion. As we write this in October 2018, the Justice Department and most state regulators had approved the deal.

When mergers are completed, the expected synergies often fail to occur. For example, Triarc Companies (which owned the Arby's fast-food chain) acquired Wendy's International in 2008, forming Wendy's Arby's Group. The former Arby's shareholders retained about $490 million worth of shares in the new company, a little more than they owned prior to the merger. The former Wendy's shareholders received new shares worth about $2 billion. The merger didn't create the hoped-for synergies—Arby's performance prior to the merger had a negative trend that continued after the merger. In 2011, the Wendy's Arby's Group sold Arby's for about $339 million, a significant decrease from its pre-merger value.[3]

22-1b Tax Considerations as a Motivation for Mergers

Tax considerations often cause firms to merge. We describe different tax-related merger motivations and deterrents in the following sections.

REDUCTION IN CORPORATE TAX RATES DUE TO THE 2017 TAX CUTS AND JOBS ACT (TCJA)

Recall from previous chapters that the TCJA reduced the federal corporate tax rate to 21%. All else equal, companies will have lower tax expenses, higher profits, and more free cash flows (FCFs) under the TCJA. It is possible that these changes might induce potential acquirers to seek out merger targets. However, the TCJA has the same impact on a potential target's taxes, profits, and FCFs. With higher FCFs, the potential target's market value should increase, making its acquisition more expensive. Therefore, it is not clear whether the reduction in the corporate tax rate will stimulate merger activity, all else held constant.

ACCUMULATED LOSSES AND INTEREST EXPENSES

A profitable company with a large amount of taxable income could acquire a firm with low or negative income but with large accumulated tax losses. With a merger, the target's accumulated losses could immediately reduce taxes for the merged firms rather than be carried forward and used in the future by the target.[4]

Recall that the TCJA limits the amount of interest expense a firm may deduct, with any excess carried over to future years. Therefore, firms with carried-over interest expenses might be good targets for highly profitable companies because the acquirer could immediately deduct the carried-over interest.

However, the tax shield provided by a target's carryovers of accumulated losses and interest expenses will be smaller because the TCJA corporate tax rate is lower, which reduces the value of the tax shield.

In addition, the TCJA might have a chilling effect on highly leveraged mergers in which acquirers finance a large amount of the deal with debt. In these situations, the acquirer itself might have more interest expenses than it can deduct for tax purposes.

---

[3]The Wendy's Arby's Group reincorporated as the Wendy's Company. Arby's purchaser paid Wendy's $130 million in cash, transferred $19 million worth of stock in the new Arby's to Wendy's, and took on $190 million in Arby's debt, for a total of $339 million. In addition, Wendy's gained about $80 billion in tax breaks resulting from its loss on Arby's.

[4]Congress has made it increasingly difficult for firms to pass along tax savings after mergers by limiting the use of loss carryforwards in a merger.

We believe that the TCJA will reduce the number of highly leveraged mergers, but we are unsure about the Act's overall effect on merger activity. Time will tell whether the positive impact of a target's carried-over interest expenses outweighs the negative impact of reductions in highly levered acquisitions.

ACQUISITIONS VERSUS DISTRIBUTIONS TO SHAREHOLDERS

Another tax-related motive occurs when a firm has more free cash flow (FCF) than it needs to support positive NPV internal investment opportunities. It could pay a special dividend, but its stockholders would have to pay immediate taxes on the distribution. It could repurchase stock, but the selling shareholders would have to pay capital gains taxes. Instead, the firm could spare its stockholders from these negative tax consequences by using the FCF to make an acquisition. Should a firm make a distribution to its shareholders or make an acquisition?

First, recall that high-wealth shareholders usually pay a 20% tax on dividends and long-term capital gains. A 20% tax isn't zero, but it's significantly less than the rate on ordinary income. In addition, most repurchases are for a relatively small percentage of a company's outstanding stock, so relatively few shareholders pay the capital gains tax. Note also that the shareholders who do sell their stock might have other capital losses that offset the gains. Thus, we are highly skeptical of the idea that companies make acquisitions to spare their shareholder from taxes.

In contrast, we believe CEOs and boards of directors will make acquisitions for reasons other than their fiduciary responsibility to act on behalf of shareholders. We discuss empirical evidence related to shareholder value in Section 22-9.

22-1c Breakup Value as a Motivation for Mergers

Some takeover specialists estimate a company's **breakup value**, which is the value of the individual parts of the firm if they were sold off separately. Suppose the breakup value is greater than the value of the firm, which often is true for conglomerates. A takeover specialist could acquire the firm at or even above its current market value, sell it off in pieces, and earn a profit.

22-1d Diversification as a Motivation for Mergers

Managers often cite diversification as a reason for mergers. They contend that diversification helps stabilize a firm's earnings and thus benefits its owners. Stabilization of earnings is certainly beneficial to employees, suppliers, and customers, but its value to stockholders is less obvious. For example, shareholders could diversify by purchasing stock in both firms. Also, research shows that diversified conglomerates are worth significantly *less* than the sum of their individual parts.[5]

The situation is different for the owner-manager of a closely held firm. To diversify, the owner must sell some of the firm's stock and use the proceeds to purchase other investments. However, it is difficult to sell closely held stock, and any profits from the stock sale would be taxed as capital gains. Therefore, a merger might be the best way for an owner to diversify personal wealth.

---

[5]See, for example, Philip Berger and Eli Ofek, "Diversification's Effect on Firm Value," *Journal of Financial Economics*, 1995, pp. 37–65; and Larry Lang and René Stulz, "Tobin's Q, Corporate Diversification, and Firm Performance," *Journal of Political Economy*, December 1994, pp. 1248–1280.

22-1e Purchase of Assets below Their Replacement Cost as a Motivation for Mergers

Sometimes a firm will be touted as an acquisition candidate because the cost of replacing its assets is considerably higher than its market value. This is especially true in the natural resources industry; for example, an oil company's reserves might be worth more on paper than the company's stock. Of course, converting paper value to monetary value isn't always as easy as it sounds.

22-1f Executives' Personal Incentives as a Motivation for Mergers

Many business decisions are based on executives' personal motivations rather than on sound economic analyses. Power, prestige, and higher compensation are associated with running a larger corporation, which plays a prominent role in many mergers.[6] Therefore, some CEOs might advocate an acquisition for personal rather than business reasons.

Some executives and managers of acquired companies often lose their jobs or perks and might oppose a merger for purely personal reasons. For example, on February 17, 2017, Kraft Heinz announced that it was seeking to acquire Unilever, which would create a massive food and consumer goods giant. The offer price was over 17% higher than Unilever's current stock price. The offer must have pleased shareholders because Kraft Heinz's stock price increased by over 10% and Unilever's by 15%. Two days later, Kraft Heinz withdrew its offer due to Unilever's intent to fight the merger. One of Kraft Heinz's largest shareholders, 3G Capital Management, was well known to have a penchant for cost-cutting, including eliminating perks like corporate jets. Perhaps this played a role in Unilever's opposition.

SELF-TEST

Define synergy. Is synergy a valid rationale for mergers? Describe several situations that might produce synergistic gains.

Suppose your firm could purchase another firm for only half of its replacement value. Would that be a sufficient justification for the acquisition? Why or why not?

Discuss the pros and cons of diversification as a rationale for mergers.

What is breakup value?

22-2 Types of Mergers: Business Types, Acquisition Methods, and Hidden Liabilities

We can classify mergers by business types or by purchase method and resulting legal liabilities. We begin with the relationship between the acquirer's businesses and the target's businesses.

22-2a Business Types

Economists classify mergers into four types based on the businesses of the acquirer and target: (1) horizontal, (2) vertical, (3) congeneric, and (4) conglomerate.

In a **horizontal merger**, one firm combines with another in its same line of business; the 2017 merger of Sherwin-Williams with Valspar (painting industry) is an example. A **roll-up merger** is a particular type of horizontal merger in which a firm purchases many small

---

[6]See Randall Morck, Andrei Shleifer, and Robert W. Vishny, "Do Managerial Objectives Drive Bad Acquisitions?" *Journal of Finance*, March 1990, pp. 31–48.

companies in the same industry and "rolls them up" to create a consolidated brand. This has happened in many businesses, including garbage collection (e.g., Waste Connections), used car sales (e.g., AutoNation), and even funeral homes (e.g. Services Corporation International).

In a **vertical merger**, one company's products are used by the other company. The 2017 merger of Tecogen (a manufacturer of clean energy power generation systems for business facilities) and American DG Energy (which owns and manages on-site power generation systems) was a vertical merger.

Congeneric means "allied in nature or action"; hence, a **congeneric merger** involves related enterprises but not producers of the same product (horizontal) and not firms in a producer–supplier relationship (vertical). Verizon's acquisition of Yahoo! is an example.

A **conglomerate merger** occurs when unrelated enterprises combine. Berkshire Hathaway Inc. has completed numerous conglomerate mergers and acquisitions, resulting in a variety of subsidiaries with different operations, including wholesale food, railroads, specialty chemicals, and insurance.

22-2b Acquisition Method and Hidden Legal Liabilities

There are three primary purchase methods: (1) stock offerings to provide target shareholders with stock in the acquirer's post-merger company in exchange for their shares; (2) cash offers to purchase assets; and (3) cash offers to purchase shares. The choice of method affects the acquirer's responsibility for hidden liabilities, which are liabilities that are unknown by the acquirer at the time of the acquisition.

To avoid hidden liabilities, acquirers conduct a thorough investigation of the target. Indeed, in a friendly merger, the acquiring firm would send a team with dozens of financial analysts, accountants, engineers, and so forth to the target firm's headquarters. They would go over its books, estimate required maintenance expenditures, set values on assets such as real estate, petroleum reserves, and the like. This process is an essential part of any merger analysis and is called **due diligence**.

In a cash purchase of assets, the acquirer and the target specify which assets and liabilities go to the acquirer and which remain with the target. After the acquirer pays its debtors, creditors, and the IRS, it usually pays a liquidating dividend to its shareholders from the remaining cash. In general, the acquirer is not responsible for hidden liabilities if it purchases the target's assets. In contrast, the acquirer generally is responsible for hidden liabilities if the acquisition is an exchange of stock or a cash purchase of the target shareholder's stock.

There are two types of hidden liabilities. First, a target's liability may be unforeseen by both the acquirer and target. For example, future lawsuits might later arise from something in the target's past. This most often occurs with product liabilities such as revelations that one of the target's pre-merger products is unsafe.

The second type of hidden liability is known by the target's senior managers but is hidden from the acquirer. This includes products that the target knows are unsafe and fraudulent accounting by the target's senior managers.

Sometimes a liability is known but is grossly underestimated at the time of the merger. For example, Bayer AG acquired Monsanto Co. by means of a cash offer purchase of its stock on June 7, 2018. Bayer knew prior to the acquisition that there was the possibility of legal action against Monsanto due to accusations that its herbicide Roundup caused cancer but still proceeded with the merger.

As events later showed, Bayer misjudged its potential liability. A California resident dying from cancer after exposure to Roundup was awarded $289 million on August 10, 2018 in a lawsuit against Bayer. After trading at €100 (about $118) at the time of the acquisition, Bayer's stock plummeted to €77 (about $87.50) when the verdict was announced.

What are the four types of business combinations through mergers?

What are three types of acquisition methods?

Is an acquirer responsible for the target's hidden liabilities?

22-3 Level of Merger Activity

The number and value of mergers tend to rise and fall through the years in a cycle, known as **merger waves**. There have been at least five merger waves: (1) Around 1900, horizontal mergers (e.g., oil and steel industries) created monopolies. (2) In the 1920s, many mergers consolidated industries (e.g., autos and utilities) and created oligopolies; others created vertically integrated supply chains. (3) In the 1960s, firms in unrelated industries merged into huge conglomerates. (4) The 1980s were characterized by hostile takeovers and congeneric mergers. (5) In the 1990s, deregulation allowed mergers in once-sheltered industries (such as communications and financial services) and fostered cross-border mergers creating enormous multinational corporations.

Subsequent waves, in our opinions, are driven primarily by economic conditions. Figure 22-1 shows the value of worldwide mergers as a percentage of the world stock

FIGURE 22-1

Merger Activity

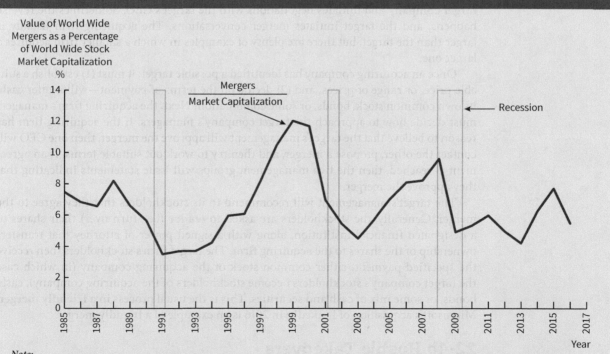

Note:

1. The shaded areas designate business recessions as defined by the National Bureau of Economic Research; see **www.nber.org/cycles**.

2. Data for merger activity are from the Institute for Mergers, Acquisitions and Alliances (IMAA): **https://imaa-institute.org/mergers-and-acquisitions-statistics/**.

3. Data for worldwide stock market capitalization (in 2016 dollars) are from **https://data.worldbank.org/indicator/CM.MKT.LCAP.CD?view=chart**.

4. The Consumer Price Index (CPI) is used to convert merger activity to 2016 dollars. See the U.S. Bureau of Economic Analysis and U.S. Bureau of the Census, Trade Balance: Goods and Services, Balance of Payments Basis [BOPGSTB], retrieved from FRED, Federal Reserve Bank of St. Louis, **https://fred.stlouisfed.org/series/BOPGSTB**.

market capitalization. Not surprisingly, increased merger activity tends to occur in periods of high economic growth and technological innovation, while decreases are driven by the same forces that lead to recessions.

Some mergers have been huge, such as the $161 billion merger of Vodafone AirTouch and Mannesmann in 2000, still the biggest merger ever as we write this in 2018. Other recent large mergers include Bayer's $63 billion acquisition of Monsanto in 2018, Abbott's $25 billion acquisition of St. Jude Medical, Inc., in 2017, and Microsoft's $26 billion acquisition of LinkedIn in 2016.

What major "merger waves" have occurred in the United States?

22-4 Hostile versus Friendly Takeovers

For some mergers, the senior executives of two firms agree that merging would be mutually beneficial. In other situations, one firm's executives fight tooth and nail to prevent the merger. The following sections describe both of these situations.

22-4a Friendly Mergers

In the vast majority of merger situations, an **acquiring company** wishes to purchase a **target company** and initiates negotiations with the target's CEO. Sometimes the reverse happens, and the target initiates merger conversations. The acquiring firm usually is larger than the target, but there are plenty of examples in which a smaller firm acquires a larger one.

Once an acquiring company has identified a possible target, it must (1) establish a suitable price, or range of prices, and (2) decide on the terms of payment—will it offer cash, its own common stock, bonds, or some combination? Next, the acquiring firm's managers must decide how to approach the target company's managers. If the acquiring firm has reason to believe that the target's management will approve the merger, then one CEO will contact the other, propose a merger, and then try to work out suitable terms. If an agreement is reached, then the two management groups will issue statements indicating that they approve the merger.

The target's management will recommend to its stockholders that they agree to the merger. Generally, the stockholders are asked to **tender** (i.e., turn over) their shares to a designated financial institution, along with a signed power of attorney that transfers ownership of the shares to the acquiring firm. The target firm's stockholders then receive the specified payment, either common stock of the acquiring company (in which case the target company's stockholders become stockholders of the acquiring company), cash, bonds, or some mix of cash and securities. This is the usual process in a **friendly merger**. Microsoft's acquisition of LinkedIn in 2016 is an example of a friendly merger.

22-4b Hostile Takeovers

Often, however, the target company's management resists, and the takeover attempt is called a **hostile merger**. If the acquiring company (often called a corporate raider) wishes to persist, it will make a **tender offer** directly to the target's shareholders, asking them to tender their shares in exchange for the offered price. The target's managers will urge stockholders not to tender their shares, generally claiming that the offer is too low.

Target firms may also employ other takeover defenses, such as changing the bylaws so that directors serve **staggered terms**, in which not all directors are elected at one time.

For example, only one-third of the seats are filled each year, and directors serve three-year terms. As described in Chapter 13, staggered terms make it harder for a hostile raider to purchase a minority stake in the company and then elect one of their allies to the board.

The target might also change the bylaws so that a merger must be approved by a *super majority* (such as 75% of the votes) rather than by a simple majority. Another tactic is to raise antitrust issues in the hope that the Justice Department will block the merger. Sometimes the target's senior executives will ask another company (with a more friendly CEO and board than the raider) to acquire them. If it agrees to try, the company is called a **white knight**; if it is successful, the result is a **defensive merger**. For example, Valent Pharmaceuticals International Inc. pursued a hostile takeover of Allergan Inc. (which manufactures Botox). However, Allergan fought the takeover and in 2015 was acquired by Activis PLC in a friendly merger. Alternatively, a target might seek out a **white squire** who is friendly to current management and can buy enough of the target firm's shares to block the merger.

As described in Chapter 13, the target might award the CEO a golden parachute, which is a very large payment made to executives who are forced out when a merger takes place. The target might adopt a poison pill defense, which is a shareholder rights provision allowing existing shareholders in the target to purchase additional shares of stock at a lower-than-market value if a potential acquirer purchases a controlling stake. Or it might resort to greenmail and buy back stock from the raider at a price that is higher than the market price. In return, the raider agrees to cease its acquisition attempt for a specified number of years.

Most hostile takeover attempts fail, at least initially. For example, in early 2016, Westlake Chemical Corp. made a $20 per share offer (part cash and part Westlake stock) for Axiall, another large chemical company. Axiall opposed the acquisition attempt even though the offer was almost double Axiall's current stock price. Other companies expressed an interest in acquiring Axiall, but Westlake offered $33 per share, all in cash, and completed the acquisition later that year.

SELF-TEST

What is the difference between a hostile and a friendly merger?

Describe some takeover defenses.

22-5 Merger Regulation

The following sections describe important federal and state laws regulating mergers.

22-5a Federal Regulation: The Williams Act

As we explained in Section 22-1a, Congress passed antitrust laws to protect consumers from higher prices resulting from mergers that reduced competition. These laws helped consumers but did little to protect shareholders during hostile takeover attempts. Hostile raiders often would make two-tier tender offers specifying that the acquirer would accept shareholder tenders in the order they were received, with an implicit threat to lower the bid price after 50% of the shares were in hand. The tender offers would expire within just a few days; if not enough shares were tendered, the raider could call off the deal. To make matters worse, the raider often failed to provide sufficient details for shareholders to determine the value of any stock or other securities to be received in exchange for tendering their shares.

To address these problems, Congress passed the Williams Act in 1968, requiring the following: (1) Acquirers must disclose their current holdings and future intentions within 10 days of amassing at least 5% of a company's stock. (2) Acquirers must disclose the source of the funds to be used in the acquisition. (3) The target firm's shareholders must be allowed at least 20 days to tender their shares; that is, the offer must be "open" for at least 20 days. (4) If the acquiring firm increases the offer price during the 20-day open period, then all shareholders who tendered prior to the new offer must receive the higher price. These provisions reduced the acquiring firm's ability to surprise management and to stampede target shareholders into accepting an inadequate offer.

22-5b State Regulations

States have also passed laws designed to deter hostile takeovers. For example, a raider often purchases enough of the target's stock to have a big impact on any shareholder votes, including those associated with the takeover. To limit this voting power, 27 states have passed *Control Share Acquisition* statutes.[7] For example, an Indiana law defined "control shares" as 20% or more of voting shares. If the threshold is exceeded by a raider, then it cannot vote unless approved by a majority (or supermajority) of shareholders who are not (1) officers or inside directors of the target or (2) associates of the raider. The statute usually gives the owner of control shares the right to call for such a vote within a specified number of days. A Control Share statute slows down the action and thus gives the target firm time to mount a defense.

Over 30 states have *Business Combination* statutes that come into effect if a minority shareholder, such as a raider, owns more than a specified percentage of voting shares. If that is the case, the statute forbids the raider from acquiring the target for a period that is often 3 to 5 years.

Over 30 states also have *Expanded Constituency* statutes that expressly permit the board to consider stakeholders other than shareholders, such as employees. In fact, some states have *Assumption of Labor Contracts* laws mandating that hostile acquirers continue to honor existing labor contracts.

Some states have *Fair Price Provisions* that require a raider to pay the same price in a two-tier tender offer instead of a high price in the first tier and a low price in the second. In fact, some companies have Fair Price bylaws requiring that any merger bid must meet or exceed a price that is determined from market conditions, such as the company's or industry's price/equity ratio.

Several states have a *Control Share Cash-Out* statute. Suppose a company or investor acquires enough stock in another company to exceed a threshold (such as 20% in Pennsylvania). Even if the purchaser doesn't plan on immediately attempting an acquisition, the target's remaining shareholders can require the purchaser to buy their shares at a fair price. This discourages investors from gaining a large minority interest unless they have immediate plans to acquire the company.

Instead of deterring takeovers, some state laws are designed to protect target shareholders from their *own* managers. For example, some state laws put limits on the use of golden parachutes, poison pills, and greenmail because these provisions enrich or entrench the target's senior executives at the expense of shareholders.

A Delaware court ruled that if multiple companies are bidding for a target, then the target must accept the bid with the highest price. Revlon, Inc. was the target in the court case, so the requirement is often called the "Revlon rule." This ruling protects shareholders from their own entrenched executives by making it more difficult for a target to take a lower offer from a white knight. About 10 states have adopted the Revlon rule. Interestingly, about the same number of states have adopted rulings that specifically *reject* the Revlon rule.

[7]See Matthew D. Cain, Stephen B. McKeon, and Steven Davidoff Solomon, "Do Takeover Laws Matter? Evidence from Five Decades of Hostile Takeovers," *Journal of Financial Economics*, 2017, pp. 464–485.

Is there a need to regulate mergers? Explain.

Do the states play a role in merger regulation, or is it all done at the national level? Explain.

22-6 Overview of Merger Analysis

An acquiring firm must answer two questions. First, how much would the target be worth after being incorporated into the acquirer? Notice that this may be quite different from the target's current value, which does not reflect any post-merger synergies or tax benefits. Second, how much should the acquirer offer for the target? Following sections discuss setting the offer's price and structure (cash versus stock), but for now we focus on estimating the post-merger value of the target.

There are two basic approaches used in merger valuation: discounted cash flow (DCF) techniques and market multiple analysis.[8] Survey evidence shows that virtually all investment banks use DCF techniques to estimate the current value of a target.[9] As part of the process, all respondents used constant growth models and market multiples to estimate the horizon value. The market multiple approach assumes that a target is directly comparable to the average firm in its industry. Because this procedure provides at best a ballpark estimate, we will focus on discounted cash flow approaches.

There are three widely used DCF methods: (1) the free cash flow corporate valuation method, (2) the compressed adjusted present value method, and (3) the free cash flow to equity method, which is also called the equity residual method. As explained in Chapter 21, the compressed adjusted value is the only appropriate model if there is a nonconstant capital structure during the explicit forecast period, something that often occurs in mergers. Therefore, we will use only the compressed APV approach in the following section to illustrate valuing a target and setting the bid price.

What are the two questions that an acquirer must answer?

What are four methods for estimating a target's value?

22-7 Estimating a Target's Value

Caldwell Inc., a large technology company, is evaluating the potential acquisition of a smaller company, Tutwiler Controls. (Tutwiler is the same company examined in Chapter 21.) If the acquisition takes place, it will occur on January 1, 2020, and so the valuation will be as of that date and will be based on the capital structure and synergies expected after the acquisition. Tutwiler's stock is trading at $15.40. Tutwiler has 10 million

---

[8]See Chapter 7 for an explanation of market multiple analysis.

[9]See W. Todd Brotherson, Kenneth M. Eades, Robert S. Harris, and Robert C. Higgins, "Company Valuation in Mergers and Acquisitions: How Is Discounted Cash Flow Applied by Leading Practitioners?" *Journal of Applied Finance*, No. 2, 2014, pp. 43–51. For additional survey evidence, see Tarun K. Mukherjee, Halil Kiymaz, and H. Kent Baker, "Merger Motives and Target Valuation: A Survey of Evidence from CFOs," *Journal of Applied Finance*, Fall/Winter 2004, pp. 7–23. For evidence on the effectiveness of market multiples and DCF approaches, see S. N. Kaplan and R. S. Ruback, "The Market Pricing of Cash Flow Forecasts: Discounted Cash Flow vs. the Method of 'Comparables,'" *Journal of Applied Corporate Finance*, Winter 1996, pp. 45–60. Also see Samuel C. Weaver, Robert S. Harris, Daniel W. Bielinski, and Kenneth F. MacKenzie, "Merger and Acquisition Valuation," *Financial Management*, Summer 1991, pp. 85–96; and Nancy Mohan, M. Fall Ainina, Daniel Kaufman, and Bernard J. Winger, "Acquisition/Divestiture Valuation Practices in Major U.S. Firms," *Financial Practice and Education*, Spring 1991, pp. 73–81.

outstanding shares, giving it a market cap of $154 million: 10($15.4) = $154. With $38 million of outstanding debt, Tutwiler's total market value is $192 million: $154 + $38 = $192.

Based on its debt and equity values, Tutwiler's current capital structure consists of almost 20% debt: $38/$192 = 19.79%. Caldwell intends to finance the acquisition with this same proportion of debt and plans to maintain a target capital structure of 20% debt and 80% equity throughout the projection period and thereafter.[10]

Tutwiler is a publicly traded company, and its market-determined beta is 1.4. Given a risk-free rate of 6% and a 5% market risk premium, the Capital Asset Pricing Model produces a required rate of return on equity, r_{sL}, of:

$$r_{sL} = r_{RF} + b(RP_M)$$
$$= 6\% + 1.4(5\%) = 13\%$$

Tutwiler's pre-tax cost of debt is 8%, and its federal-plus-state tax rate is 25%. Its WACC is:

$$WACC = w_d r_d(1 - T) + w_s r_{sL}$$
$$= 0.20(8\%)(1 - 0.25) + 0.80(13\%)$$
$$= 11.6\%$$

How much would Tutwiler be worth to Caldwell after the merger? The following sections answer this question.

22-7a Projecting Post-Merger Cash Flows

The first order of business is to estimate the post-merger cash flows that Tutwiler will produce. This is by far the most important task in any merger analysis. In a pure **financial merger**, defined as one in which no operating synergies are expected, the incremental post-merger cash flows are simply the target firm's expected cash flows. In an **operating merger**, in which the two firms' operations are to be integrated, forecasting future cash flows is obviously more difficult because potential synergies must be estimated. Managers from marketing, production, human resources, and accounting play leading roles here, with financial managers focusing on financing the acquisition and performing an analysis designed to determine whether the projected cash flows are worth the cost.

In this chapter, we take the projections as given and concentrate on how they are analyzed. Using the same techniques explained in *Web Extension 21A*, we have created post-merger projections for Tutwiler, taking into account all expected synergies and maintaining a constant capital structure; see worksheet *Explanation of Projections* in the file *Ch22 Tool Kit.xlsx*.[11] Both Caldwell and Tutwiler are in the 25% marginal federal-plus-state tax bracket. The cost of debt after the acquisition will remain at 8%. The projections assume that growth in the post-horizon period will be 5% due to synergies. Figure 22-2 shows these projections (keep in mind that these projections differ from those of Chapter 21 because they reflect the synergies expected in the acquisition).

Panel A of Figure 22-2 shows selected items from the projected financial statements. Panel B shows the calculations for free cash flow and the annual tax savings due to the deductibility of interest.

---

[10]Some mergers change the capital structure of the target. If Caldwell had chosen to do so, it would have used the forecasting techniques for a changing capital structure, as explained in Chapter 21 and *Web Extension 21A*.

[11]We rounded some of the projected values in the worksheet *Explanation of Projections* in *Ch22 Tool Kit.xlsx* for the sake of clarity.

FIGURE 22-2
Post-Merger Projections for the Tutwiler Subsidiary (Millions of Dollars)

	A	B	C	D	E	F	G	H
48			1/1/20	12/31/20	12/31/21	12/31/22	12/31/23	12/31/24
49	**Panel A: Selected Items from Projected**							
50		**Financial Statements**						
51	1. Net sales			$155.0000	$170.0000	$185.0000	$200.0000	$210.00000
52	2. EBIT			$24.0000	$28.0000	$32.0000	$34.0000	$36.54000
53	3. Interest expense[a]			$3.6380	$3.8696	$4.1697	$4.4566	$4.75273
54	4. Debt[b]		$45.4750	$48.3701	$52.1210	$55.7071	$59.4091	$62.37955
55	5. Total net op. capital		$114.8000	$120.9000	$132.6000	$144.3000	$156.0000	$163.80000
56	**Panel B: Compressed APV**							
57		**Model Cash Flows**						
58	6. NOPAT = EBIT(1-T)[c]			$18.0000	$21.0000	$24.0000	$25.5000	$27.40500
59	7. Less net investment in op. capital			$6.1000	$11.7000	$11.7000	$11.7000	$7.80000
60	8. Free cash flow			$11.9000	$9.3000	$12.3000	$13.8000	$19.60500
61	9. Interest tax savings = Interest(T)			$0.9095	$0.9674	$1.0424	$1.1141	$1.18818

Source: See the file *Ch22 Tool Kit.xlsx*. Numbers are reported as rounded values for clarity but are calculated using *Excel's* full precision. Thus, intermediate calculations using the figure's rounded values will be inexact.

Notes:

[a] Interest expense is based on Tutwiler's existing debt, new debt to be issued to finance the acquisition, and additional debt required to finance annual growth.

[b] Debt is existing debt plus additional debt required to maintain a constant capital structure. Caldwell will increase Tutwiler's debt by $7.475 million (from $38 million to $45.475 million) at the time of the acquisition in order to keep the capital structure constant. This increase occurs because the post-merger synergies make Tutwiler more valuable to Caldwell than it was on a stand-alone basis. Therefore, it can support more dollars of debt and still maintain the constant debt ratio.

[c] The tax rate is 25%.

Analysts should conduct sensitivity, scenario, and simulation analyses on the estimated cash flows, as shown in Chapter 11.[12] Indeed, risk analysis is an essential step in the due diligence process.

Following is the valuation of Tutwiler.

22-7b Valuation Using the Compressed APV Approach

The compressed APV approach requires an estimate of Tutwiler's unlevered cost of equity. As shown in Chapter 21, Tutwiler's unlevered cost of equity is:

$$r_{sU} = w_s r_{sL} + w_d r_d \qquad (22\text{-}1)$$

$$= 0.8(13\%) + 0.2(8\%)$$

$$= 12.00\%$$

---

[12] In actual merger valuations, the cash flow calculations would be much more complex, normally including such items as tax loss carryforwards, tax effects of plant and equipment valuation adjustments, and cash flows from the sale of some of the subsidiary's assets.

In other words, if Tutwiler had no debt, its cost of equity would be 12.00%.[13]

Alternatively, we can estimate the unlevered beta, b_U, and then calculate the unlevered cost of equity. We begin by estimating the beta for debt, b_d, as shown in Chapter 21:

$$b_d = (r_d - r_{RF})/RP_M \tag{22-2}$$

$$= (0.08 - 0.06)/0.05$$
$$= 0.4$$

As shown in Chapter 21, the unlevered beta is:

$$b_U = [b + b_d(w_d/w_s)]/[1 + (w_d/w_s)] \tag{22-3}$$

$$= [1.4 + 0.4(0.2/0.8)]/[1 + (0.2/0.8)]$$
$$= 1.2$$

Using the CAPM, the unlevered cost of equity is:

$$r_{sU} = r_{RF} + b_U(RP_M)$$
$$= 6\% + 1.2(5\%) = 12.00\%$$

This is exactly the unlevered cost previously estimated. Because this alternative approach requires that we assume the CAPM is the correct model and because it takes extra steps, we usually use the first method shown in Equation 22-1.

The horizon value of Tutwiler's unlevered cash flows ($HV_{U,2024}$) and tax shield ($HV_{TS,2024}$) can be calculated using the constant growth formula with the unlevered cost of equity as the discount rate, as shown in Chapter 21. The unlevered horizon value is $294.075 million:[14]

$$HV_{U,2024} = \frac{FCF_{2025}}{r_{sU} - g_L} = \frac{FCF_{2024}(1 + g_L)}{r_{sU} - g_L} \tag{22-4}$$

$$= \frac{\$19.6050(1.05)}{0.12 - 0.05} = \$294.075 \text{ million}$$

The horizon value of the tax shield is $17.823 million:

$$HV_{TS,2024} = \frac{TS_{2025}}{r_{sU} - g_L} = \frac{TS_{2024}(1 + g_L)}{r_{sU} - g_L} \tag{22-5}$$

$$= \frac{\$1.18818(1.05)}{0.12 - 0.05} = \$17.8227$$

---

[13]Notice that we do not use the Hamada equation to lever or unlever beta to determine the required return on equity because the Hamada equation assumes zero growth. Instead, we use Equation 22-1 to determine the unlevered cost of equity, which assumes that the growing debt tax shield is discounted at the unlevered cost of equity. See Chapter 21 for details of this process.

[14]All calculations are performed in the *Excel* file ***Ch22 Tool Kit.xls***, which uses the full nonrounded values.

Row 8 in Figure 22-2 shows the projected free cash flows. The unlevered value of operations is calculated as the present value of the free cash flows during the forecast period and the horizon value of the free cash flows:

$$V_{\text{Unlevered}} = \frac{\$11.9}{(1 + 0.12)^1} + \frac{\$9.3}{(1 + 0.12)^2} + \frac{\$12.3}{(1 + 0.12)^3}$$
$$+ \frac{\$13.8}{(1 + 0.12)^4} + \frac{\$19.605 + \$294.075}{(1 + 0.12)^5}$$
$$= \$213.6 \text{ million}$$

This shows that Tutwiler's operations would be worth a little over $213 million if it had no debt.

resource

See **Ch22 Tool Kit.xlsx** on the textbook's Web site for all calculations. Note that rounded intermediate values are shown in the text, but all calculations are performed in Excel using nonrounded values.

Row 9 shows the yearly interest tax savings. The value of the tax shield is calculated as the present value of the yearly tax savings and the horizon value of the tax shield:

$$V_{\text{Tax shield}} = \frac{\$0.9095}{(1 + 0.12)^1} + \frac{\$0.9674}{(1 + 0.12)^2} + \frac{\$1.0424}{(1 + 0.12)^3}$$
$$+ \frac{\$1.1141}{(1 + 0.12)^4} + \frac{\$1.1882 + \$17.8227}{(1 + 0.12)^5}$$
$$= \$13.8 \text{ million}$$

Tutwiler's total value of operations is the sum of its unlevered value and the value of the tax shield:

$$V_{\text{Ops}} = V_{\text{Unlevered}} + V_{\text{Tax shield}}$$
$$= \$213.6 + \$13.8 = \$227.4 \text{ million}$$

The value of the equity is equal to this total value less Tutwiler's outstanding debt:

$$V_{\text{Equity}} = V_{\text{Ops}} - \text{Debt}$$
$$= \$227.4 - \$38 = \$189.4 \text{ million}$$

As this analysis shows, Caldwell estimates that Tutwiler's equity would be worth about $189 million. How much should Caldwell offer to Tutwiler's shareholder? The answer is in the next section.

SELF-TEST

Why is the adjusted present value approach appropriate for situations with a changing capital structure?

Describe the steps required to apply the APV approach.

22-8 Setting the Bid Price

Under the acquisition plan, Caldwell would assume Tutwiler's debt and would also take on additional short-term debt as necessary to complete the purchase. The valuation model shows that $189.4 million is the most it should pay for Tutwiler's stock. If it paid more, then Caldwell's own value would be diluted. On the other hand, if it could get Tutwiler for less than $189.4 million, Caldwell's stockholders would gain value. Therefore, Caldwell should bid something less than $189.4 million when it makes an offer for Tutwiler.

Now consider the target company. As stated earlier, Tutwiler's market value of equity as an independent operating company is $154 million. If Tutwiler were acquired at a price greater than $154 million, then its stockholders would gain value, whereas they would lose value at any lower price.

The difference between $189.4 million and $154 million, which is about $35.4 million, is due to **synergistic benefits** expected from the merger. If there were no synergistic benefits, the maximum bid would be the current value of the target company. The greater the synergistic gains, the greater the gap between the target's current price and the maximum the acquiring company could pay.

The issue of how to divide the synergistic benefits is critically important. Obviously, both parties would want to get the best deal possible. In our example, if Tutwiler knew the maximum price Caldwell could pay, Tutwiler's management would argue for a price close to $189.4 million. Caldwell, on the other hand, would try to get Tutwiler at a price as close to $154 million as possible.

Where, within the range of $189.4 to $154 million, will the actual price be set? The answer depends on a number of factors, including whether Caldwell offers to pay with cash or securities, the negotiating skills of the two management teams, and, most importantly, the bargaining positions of the two parties as determined by fundamental economic conditions. Let's first consider bargaining power and then examine the mechanics of a cash offer versus a stock offer.

22-8a Relative Bargaining Power

To illustrate the relative bargaining power of the target and the acquirer, assume there are many companies similar to Tutwiler that Caldwell could acquire, but suppose that no company other than Caldwell could gain synergies by acquiring Tutwiler. In this case, Caldwell would probably make a relatively low, take-it-or-leave-it offer, and Tutwiler would probably take it because some gain is better than none.

On the other hand, if Tutwiler has some unique technology or other asset that many companies want, then once Caldwell announces its offer, others would probably make competing bids, and the final price would probably be close to $189.4 million. If some other company has a better synergistic fit or a more optimistic management team, then the offer price might be higher than the maximum of $189.4 million that Tutwiler might pay.

Caldwell would, of course, want to keep its maximum bid secret, and it would plan its bidding strategy carefully. If Caldwell thought other bidders would emerge or that Tutwiler's management might resist in order to preserve their jobs, Caldwell might make a high preemptive bid in hopes of scaring off competing bids or management resistance. On the other hand, it might make a lowball bid in hopes of "stealing" the company.[15]

22-8b Cash Offers versus Stock Offers

Most target stockholders prefer to sell their shares for cash rather than to exchange them for stock in the post-merger company. Following is a brief description of each payment method.

[15]For an interesting discussion of the after-effects of losing a bidding contest, see Mark L. Mitchell and Kenneth Lehn, "Do Bad Bidders Become Good Targets?" *Journal of Applied Corporate Finance*, Summer 1990, pp. 60–69.

CASH OFFERS

Tutwiler's pre-merger equity is worth $154 million. With 10 million shares outstanding, Tutwiler's stock price is $154/10 = $15.40. If the synergies are realized, then Tutwiler's equity will be worth $189.4 million to Caldwell, so $189.4/10 = $18.94 is the maximum price per share that Caldwell should be willing to pay to Tutwiler's stockholders. For example, Caldwell might offer something between $15.40 and $18.94, such as $16.40 cash for each share of Tutwiler stock.

STOCK OFFERS

In a stock offer, Tutwiler's stockholders exchange their Tutwiler shares for new shares in the post-merger company, which will retain the name Caldwell. Targets typically prefer cash offers to stock offers, all else equal, but taxation of the offer prevents all else from being equal. We discuss taxation in more detail in Section 22-10, but for now you should know that stock offerings are taxed more favorably than cash offerings. In this case, perhaps Caldwell should offer stock in the post-merger company that would be worth $16.80 per share. With 10 million outstanding Tutwiler shares, the Tutwiler shareholders must end up owning $16.80 × 10 million = $168 million worth of stock in the post-merger company. How many shares in the post-merger Caldwell-Tutwiler company must the Tutwiler shareholders be offered?

Suppose Caldwell has 20 million shares of stock outstanding (n_{Old}) prior to the merger and the stock price is $40.53 per share. Then the total pre-merger value of Caldwell's equity is $40.53 × 20 million = $810.6 million. As calculated previously, the post-merger value of Tutwiler to Caldwell is $189.4 million. Therefore, the total post-merger value of Caldwell-Tutwiler's equity will be $189.4 million + $810.6 = $1,000 million.

After the merger, Tutwiler's former stockholders should own $168/$1,000 = 0.168 = 16.8% of the post-merger company. With 20 million Caldwell shares outstanding, Caldwell must issue enough new shares, n_{New}, to the Tutwiler stockholders (in exchange for the Tutwiler shares) so that Tutwiler's former stockholders will own 16.8% of the post-merger stock:

$$\frac{\text{Percent required by}}{\text{target stockholders}} = \frac{n_{New}}{n_{New} + n_{Old}}$$

$$16.8\% = \frac{n_{New}}{n_{New} + 20}$$

$$n_{New} = \frac{20 \times 0.168}{1 - 0.168} = 4.04 \text{ million}$$

Tutwiler's former stockholders will exchange 10 million shares of stock in Tutwiler for 4.04 million new shares of stock in the post-merger company. Thus, the exchange ratio is 4.04/10 = 0.404.

After the merger, there will be 4.04 million new shares, for a total of 24.04 million shares. With a combined intrinsic equity value of $1,000 million, the resulting price per share will be $1,000/24.04 = $41.60. The total value owned by Tutwiler's shareholders is this price multiplied by their shares: $41.60 × 4.04 million = $168 million. Notice that this is exactly the value that Caldwell offered at the beginning of this analysis. Also notice that Caldwell's stock price will increase from $40.53 per share before the merger to $41.60 after the merger. In this example, it is a win–win outcome for all shareholders, assuming that the expected post-merger synergies are realized.

SELF-TEST

Explain the issues involved in setting the bid price.

22-9 Who Wins: The Empirical Evidence

Do mergers create value? Who wins in a merger, the acquirer or the target? What impact do federal or state regulations have on mergers? How effective are changes in bylaws in protecting entrenched executives? The following sections address these questions.

22-9a Value Created by Mergers

Are the decisions executives make about mergers in their shareholders' interests or in their own interests? To answer that question, researchers assume that investors' beliefs should affect stock price reactions when plans for a merger are announced. Researchers also know that market conditions will affect the stock prices of most companies, including bidders and targets. For example, if a merger was announced on a day when the entire market rose, then a rise in the target firm's price would not necessarily mean that the merger was expected to create value. Therefore, researchers must disentangle the portion of return due to the announced merger and the portion due to general market conditions. To do this, researchers first determine the expected return for the bidder and target on the announcement day using the CAPM, the Fama-French three-factor model, or even models with additional factors.[16] They subtract this expected return from the actual return to identify the *abnormal return* associated with the merger announcement. Using a large sample of mergers, researchers calculate the abnormal returns for the bidding company and the target.

Such *event studies* have examined nearly every acquisition involving publicly traded firms from the early 1960s to the present. The results are remarkably consistent: The average abnormal stock return for target firms is about 30% in hostile tender offers and 20% in friendly mergers. However, the average abnormal return is close to zero for acquiring firms whether the merger is friendly or hostile. Keep in mind that these results are for the *average* impact of mergers; some mergers create substantial value, and some destroy value. However, research strongly indicates that the average acquisition creates value but that the target firms' shareholders reap almost all of the benefits.

22-9b The Impact of Takeover Regulations and Bylaw Changes on Hostile Mergers

Cain, McKeon, and Solomon examined takeover regulations and hostile takeovers.[17] Following is a summary of their key findings.

Recall that the 1968 Williams Act required bidders to provide targets with more information and more time to respond. Before the Act, about 40% of mergers were hostile. By 2013, fewer than 9% of mergers were hostile, indicating major changes in the merger environment. The following sections identify which regulation and bylaw revisions contributed to the current merger environment.

Fair Price laws deter hostile takeover offers. This is as might be expected because Fair Price laws increase a raider's cost in a two-tiered offer. *Assumption of Labor Contracts* statutes also reduce hostile bids. This makes sense because raiders cannot reduce wages and benefits due under the target's current contracts. The Revlon rule encourages hostile takeovers, probably because it requires a target's board to accept the best price among multiple offers.

---

[16]See Chapter 6 for descriptions of the CAPM and the Fama-French three-factor model.

[17]See Cain, McKeon, and Solomon, op. cit., footnote 7.

Recall that under the *Control Share Cash-Out* statute, shareholders can require an investor with a large minority interest to purchase their shares at a fair price. This serves to discourage large minority ownership and instead stimulates hostile mergers. This may be due to the presence of dissatisfied target shareholders who sell additional shares to the minority owner because they want the change in leadership that often follows a hostile takeover.

Somewhat surprisingly, although restrictions on golden parachutes, poison pills, or greenmail make hostile takeovers less costly, none have a significant effect on takeovers. Neither do the other regulations and defenses described in Sections 22-4 and 22-5.

Cain, McKeon, and Solomon use results like those just described to create a Takeover Index measuring a company's susceptibility to a hostile takeover bid. They show that the value of a firm's stock is lower if the firm is less susceptible to a takeover, all else held equal. In other words, if executives are not worried about a hostile takeover, then their shareholders suffer. The researchers also show that if a firm is not very susceptible to a merger, then its executives have a strong bargaining position when a merger offer comes. As a result, a bid from an acquirer is at higher price than a bid for firms with higher susceptibility. Obviously, this discourages takeovers and adds insult to injury: Not only is a shareholder's stock less valuable, but also it will remain so until a generous bidder makes a high offer. This means that an acquirer must make a high offer to displace the target's entrenched executives.

SELF-TEST

Explain how researchers can study the effects of mergers on shareholder wealth.

Do mergers create value? If so, who profits from this value?

Do the research results discussed in this section seem logical? Explain.

22-10 The Role of Investment Bankers

Investment bankers are involved with mergers in five ways: (1) They help arrange mergers. (2) They help target companies develop and implement defensive tactics. (3) They help value target companies. (4) They help finance mergers. (5) They invest in the stocks of potential merger candidates.

22-10a Arranging Mergers

The major investment banking firms have merger and acquisition specialists who try to arrange mergers. They identify firms with excess cash that might want to buy other firms, companies that might be willing to be bought, and firms that might, for a number of reasons, be attractive to others. Sometimes dissident stockholders of firms with poor track records work with investment bankers to oust management by helping to arrange a merger.

22-10b Developing Defensive Tactics

Target firms that do not want to be acquired generally enlist the help of an investment banking firm along with a law firm that specializes in mergers. The investment bankers and lawyers help the target implement the takeover defenses described in Section 22-4b.

22-10c Establishing a Fair Value

If an acquirer pays a relatively low price for a target, then the target's shareholders might sue their executives and board for not acting in the shareholders' interests. The reverse is true if the price is high; the bidder's shareholders might sue their own executives and board. Therefore, the acquirer and target each usually hire an investment bank to estimate the target's fair value.

Because an investment bank's managers receive more compensation for a completed deal than for a failed takeover attempt, they have an incentive to estimate a "fair value" that is high enough to ensure that the target accepts the offer. However, research shows that overpricing hurts the investment bank in two ways. First, if an investment bank represented past acquirers that consistently had poor abnormal announcement returns (an indication of overpricing the offer), then that investment bank is much less likely to be retained as an advisor in subsequent deals or to be hired as an advisor by other acquirers in future deals. Second, if the investment bank is itself a publicly traded company and its client (i.e., an acquirer) has a positive abnormal announcement return, then the investment bank's own stock tends to have a positive return. The opposite is true if the client has a negative abnormal announcement return. Therefore, investment banks have an incentive to recommend an offer price that reflects the target's fair value.[18]

22-10d Financing Mergers

To be successful in the mergers and acquisitions (M&A) business, an investment banker must be able to offer a financing package to clients—whether they are acquirers who need capital to take over companies or target companies trying to finance stock repurchase plans or other defenses against takeovers. In fact, the fees that investment banks generate through issuing merger-related debt often dwarf their other merger-related fees.

22-10e Arbitrage Operations

Major brokerage houses, as well as some wealthy private investors, often purchase shares of likely takeover targets. They hope that a takeover soon will be announced, driving up the target's stock price. This is called **risk arbitrage**, even though true arbitrage is not risky.

SELF-TEST

What are some defensive tactics that firms can use to resist hostile takeovers?

What is the difference between pure arbitrage and risk arbitrage?

22-11 Other Business Combinations

The following sections describe mergers of equals, holding companies, and corporate alliances.

22-11a Merger of Equals

In a typical merger, a large firm acquires a smaller firm. However, in some situations it is hard to identify an "acquirer" and a "target" because shareholders and executives from both pre-merger companies have approximately the same amount of control in the post-merger company. Therefore, it is a "merger of equals" that consolidates the two companies.

For example, Office Depot, Inc. and OfficeMax Incorporated merged in 2013. After the merger, shareholders from OfficeMax held about 45% of the post-merger stock. The new board had an equal number of independent directors from each pre-merger company.

---

[18]See John J. McConnell and Valeriy Sibilkov, "Do Investment Banks Have Incentives to Help Clients Make Value-Creating Deals?" *Journal of Applied Corporate Finance*, 2016, No. 2, pp. 103–117.

Both of the pre-merger CEOs served as co-CEOs until later in the year when a new CEO was hired from outside both companies. This was a bit unusual because the CEO from one company often becomes the CEO of the merged company while the other CEO becomes the president.

22-11b Holding Companies

Holding companies are corporations formed for the sole purpose of owning the stocks of other companies. In this situation, the holding company is called a **parent company**, and the other companies are called **subsidiaries** or **operating companies**.

A holding company provides two principal advantages relative to a company that simply has different divisions. First, a holding company can control other companies through *fractional ownership*. For example, a holding company might buy enough shares of stock in another company to give it effective working control of the other company's operations. Working control might be possible even if the holding company owns less than 25% of the subsidiary's common stock. As they say on Wall Street, "If management thinks you can control the company, then you do."

A second advantage is the *isolation of risks*. Because the operating companies are separate legal entities, the obligations of one subsidiary are separate from those of the others. Therefore, other operating companies may be protected from claims arising if another incurs catastrophic losses or gigantic legal claims. This separation of risk sometimes can be pierced, particularly if lenders require the holding company to guarantee its subsidiaries' debt.

The main disadvantage incurred by a holding company is *partial multiple taxation of dividends* in which the holding company's shareholders are taxed on dividends received from the holding company, which itself might be taxed on dividends received from the operating companies. If the holding company owns less than 20% of the operating company, the holding company may deduct only 70% of the dividends it receives and is taxed on the remainder. If it owns more than 20% but less than 80%, it can deduct 80% of the dividends received. If it owns at least 80% of a subsidiary's voting stock, the IRS permits the filing of consolidated returns, in which case dividends received by the parent are not taxed

Holding companies can have high financial leverage that is not easily recognized by its shareholders. For example, suppose a holding company, Company A, raises $100 million in debt and $100 million in equity, giving it a total of $200 million in cash and a debt ratio of 50%. Suppose a second holding company, Company B, raises $200 million in equity from A and another $200 million in debt. Company B now has a total of $400 million in cash and a 50% debt ratio. Company A owns all of the equity in Company B.

Now suppose an operating company, Company C, raises $400 million in equity from Company B and raises another $400 million in debt, providing it with $800 million in cash and a 50% debt ratio. Company B owns all of the equity in C, and C invests the entire $800 million in operating assets.

Company A owns B and B owns C, so Company A owns all the stock in the chain and has complete control of the operating company, Company C. Even though each link in the chain has a 50% debt ratio, the entire chain's debt ratio is 87.5% ($700/$800 = 0.875 = 87.5%). Not only is the true debt ratio of 87.5% not very transparent, but even small losses by the operating company can trigger bankruptcy for the entire chain.

Because many utility companies went bankrupt due to levered chains, Congress passed the Public Utility Holding Company Act in 1935 to restrict such chains and reduce the risk of bankruptcy for utilities. In 2005, Congress repealed this Act, allowing pyramid structures in public utilities.

22-11c Corporate Alliances

Some companies strike cooperative deals, called **corporate alliances** or **strategic alliances**, which stop far short of merging. Whereas mergers combine all of the assets of the firms involved, as well as their ownership and managerial expertise, alliances allow firms to create combinations that focus on specific business lines that offer the most potential synergies. These alliances take many forms, from simple marketing agreements to joint ownership of worldwide operations.

One form of corporate alliance is the **joint venture**, in which parts of companies are joined to achieve specific, limited objectives. A joint venture is controlled by a management team consisting of representatives of the two (or more) parent companies. A study of corporate alliances found that about 43% of alliances were marketing agreements, 14% were R&D agreements, 11% were for licensing technology, 7% for technology transfers, and 25% for some combination of these four reasons.[19] The typical alliance lasted at least 5 years. When an alliance was announced, the average abnormal return for each partner was 0.64%. The market reacted most favorably when the alliance was for technology sharing between two firms in the same industry. In addition, the allied firms had better operating performance than their industry peers during the first 5 years of the alliance.

SELF-TEST

What is a merger of equals?

What is a holding company?

What are some of the advantages of holding companies? Identify a disadvantage.

What is the difference between a merger and a corporate alliance?

What is a joint venture? Give some reasons why joint ventures may be advantageous to the parties involved.

22-12 Divestitures

There are four types of **divestiture**. The first is a *sale of assets to another firm*. This generally involves the sale of an entire division or unit, usually for cash but sometimes for stock in the acquiring firm. The second type is a *liquidation*, where the assets of a division are sold off piecemeal to many purchasers rather than as a single operating entity to one purchaser.

In a **spin-off**, a firm's existing stockholders are given new stock representing separate ownership rights in the division that was divested. The division establishes its own board of directors and officers, and it becomes a separate company. The stockholders end up owning shares of two firms instead of one, but no cash has been transferred. For example, Biogen had a relatively stable business line focused on hemophilia and a more risky one directed toward neurological diseases. In 2017, Biogen spun off its hemophilia business into a newly created company, Bioverativ. Shareholders of Biogen kept their shares but also received two shares of Bioverativ. This spin-off increased investor transparency and managerial focus by separating the two different lines of business.

In an **equity carve-out**, a minority interest in a corporate subsidiary is sold to new shareholders, so the parent gains new equity financing yet retains control. For example, in 2016, Ashland Global Holdings, Inc. carved out its lubricant and oil change business (Valvoline, Inc.) with an initial public offering. Valvoline raised $759 million in the

---

[19] See Su Han Chan, John W. Kensinger, Arthur J. Keown, and John D. Martin, "When Do Strategic Alliances Create Shareholder Value?" *Journal of Applied Corporate Finance*, Winter 1999, pp. 82–87.

IPO and also raised $750 million in a separate debt offering. As part of the transaction, Valvoline transferred about $1.4 billion to Ashland, which retained an 83% ownership of Valvoline stock. Like most equity carve-outs, the parent (Ashland) received cash and still maintained a significant ownership in the newly separated company. The story doesn't end there: In 2017, Ashland distributed its Valvoline shares to Ashland shareholders, completely severing Ashland's ties to Valvoline.

In general, the empirical evidence shows that the market reacts favorably to divestitures, with the divesting company typically having a small increase in stock price on the day of the announcement. The announcement-day returns are largest for companies that "undo" previous conglomerate mergers by divesting businesses in unrelated areas.[20] Studies also show that divestitures generally lead to superior operating performance for both the parent and the divested company.[21]

SELF-TEST

What are some types of divestitures?

What are some motives for divestitures?

22-13 Merger Tax Treatments

Recall from Section 22-2 that there are three major acquisition methods. We show here that each is treated differently for tax purposes. First, if it is a stock offering to provide target shareholders with stock in the acquirer's post-merger company in exchange for their shares, then it is a *nontaxable exchange*.[22] Second, if it is a cash offer to purchase almost all of the assets from the target, then it is a *taxable purchase of assets* with a specific set of tax rules. Third, if it is a cash offer to purchase shares from the target's stockholders, then it is a *taxable purchase of shares* with a different set of tax rules. The following sections explain the tax treatment for mergers in these three categories. (Figure 22-3 is a flowchart of the tax treatments.) The sections also explain the impact of the 2017 TCJA on mergers.

22-13a Nontaxable Exchange of Stock

In a nontaxable deal, target shareholders who receive shares of the acquiring company's stock do not have to pay any taxes at the time of the merger. This also applies if the offer is a mix of cash and stock, so long as the offer is mostly stock. However, if the payment includes a significant amount of cash or bonds, then the IRS views it as a sale, and it is a taxable offer.

Shareholders receiving stock in a nontaxable exchange pay taxes only when they eventually sell their stock.[23] The amount of the gain is the sale price of their stock in the

---

[20]For details, see Jeffrey W. Allen, Scott L. Lummer, John J. McConnell, and Debra K. Reed, "Can Takeover Losses Explain Spin-off Gains?" *Journal of Financial and Quantitative Analysis*, December 1995, pp. 465–485.

[21]See Shane A. Johnson, Daniel P. Klein, and Verne L. Thibodeaux, "The Effects of Spin-offs on Corporate Investment and Performance," *Journal of Financial Research*, Summer 1996, pp. 293–307. Also see Steven Kaplan and Michael S. Weisbach, "The Success of Acquisitions: Evidence from Divestitures," *Journal of Finance*, March 1992, pp. 107–138.

[22]For more details, see J. Fred Weston, Mark L. Mitchell, and Harold Mulherin, *Takeovers, Restructuring, and Corporate Governance*, 4th ed. (Upper Saddle River, NJ: Prentice-Hall, 2004), especially Chapter 4. Also see Kenneth E. Anderson, Thomas R. Pope, and John L. Kramer, eds., *Prentice Hall's Federal Taxation 2017: Corporations, Partnerships, Estates, and Trusts*, 30th ed. (Upper Saddle River, NJ: Prentice-Hall, 2017), especially Chapter 7.

[23]This is a capital gain if it has been at least 1 year since they purchased their original stock in the target.

FIGURE 22-3
Merger Tax Effects

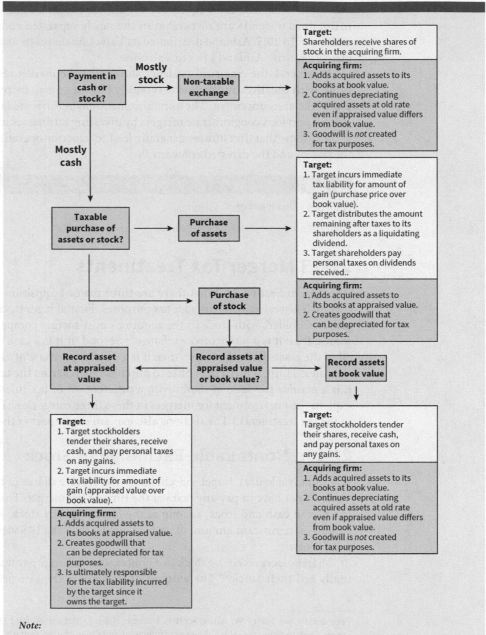

Note:

These are actual cash tax effects. However, the tax effects reported to shareholders will be different because shareholder statements must conform to GAAP conventions, not to federal Tax Code conventions.

acquiring company minus the price at which they purchased their original stock in the target company.

All else equal, stockholders prefer nontaxable offers because they can postpone taxes on their gains. Furthermore, if the target firm's stockholders receive stock, they will benefit from any synergistic gains produced by the merger. Most target shareholders are thus willing to give up their stock for a lower price in a nontaxable offer than in a taxable one. As a result, one might expect nontaxable bids to dominate. However, this is not the case: Roughly half of all mergers have been taxable. We explain why this is so by way of an example.

To keep the example simple, we assume the target has no debt. Suppose the target firm has assets with a book value of $100 million and an appraised value of $150 million. The stock offer by the acquiring firm is worth $220 million to the target's shareholders, and no tax is due until a shareholder sells his or her shares.

The acquiring firm simply adds the $100 million book value of the target's assets to its own assets and continues to depreciate the acquired assets using the target's existing depreciation schedule. Therefore, the acquirer might get a very small depreciation tax shield, especially if the target's assets are old. This is in contrast to larger depreciation tax shields that can result from other acquisition methods described in the following sections.

22-13b Taxable Purchase of Assets

If an offer is to purchase the target's assets, then the target's board of directors will evaluate the offer to determine whether the offer price is acceptable. If so, the board will recommend that shareholders vote to accept the offer; otherwise, they will recommend that shareholders reject the offer. The board's recommendation is not binding, and shareholders may vote as they choose.

If the shareholders accept the offer, the payment goes directly to the target corporation, which pays off any debt not assumed by the acquiring firm. The target firm pays corporate taxes on any gains that are due if the assets are sold for more than their book values. The target then distributes the remainder of the payment to the shareholders, often in the form of a liquidating dividend. The target firm is usually dissolved and no longer continues to exist as a separate legal entity, although its assets and workforce may continue to function as a division or as a wholly owned subsidiary of the acquiring firm. The acquisition of assets is a common form of takeover for small and medium-sized firms, especially those that are not publicly traded.

To illustrate the tax effects, suppose the acquirer in the previous example purchases the target's assets for $220 million instead of merging through an exchange of stock. The target's assets have a book value of $100 million, so the target firm must pay corporate tax on the $120 million gain: $220 − $100 = $120. Assuming the combined federal-plus-state corporate tax rate is 25%, this target will owe $30 million in taxes: 0.25($120) = $30.

This leaves the target with $190 million ($220 − $30 = $190) to distribute to its shareholders upon liquidation. The target's shareholders must also pay individual taxes on any of their own gains.[24] Recall from Chapter 2 that the tax rate on dividends for high-income individuals is 20%.[25] There is also the 3.8% Net Investment Income Tax (NIIT) on personal investment income. Therefore, the target's shareholders must pay taxes of $45.22 million: $190(20% + 3.8%) = $45.22. The total corporate tax and personal tax equals $75.22 million: $30 + $45.22 = $75.22. Therefore, the effective tax rate to the shareholders is 34.2%: $75.22/$220 = 34.2%. When we called this a taxable transaction, we weren't kidding!

In contrast to the selling firm's shareholders, the acquiring firm receives large tax benefits. First, the buyer adds the appraised value to its books and can depreciate this amount as though it is new property. This is not a new benefit for purchasers, but the TCJA made it even more valuable by allowing companies to depreciate 100% of the purchase in

---

[24]Our example assumes that the target is a publicly owned firm, which means that it must be a C corporation for tax purposes. However, if it is privately held, then it might be an S corporation, in which case only the stockholders would be taxed. This helps smaller firms use mergers as an exit strategy.

[25]See **Web Extension 2A** for an explanation of the tax rate on dividends if the recipient does not have a high-income.

2018–2022. This can significantly reduce taxable income and create large tax savings for the acquiring firm. Although firms cannot deduct 100% of the purchase price after 2022, the TCJA still provides generous first-year depreciation through 2026.[26]

Second, the acquirer records the difference between the purchase price and the appraised value in an asset account called **goodwill**. In the following sections, we explain the impact of goodwill on financial statements, but here we focus on taxes. The IRS allows an acquirer to amortize goodwill over 15 years using the straight-line method and then deduct the annual amortization expense from the taxable income it reports to the IRS.

We use the previous example to illustrate the acquirer's tax benefits. If the acquisition is completed before 2023, the acquirer will be able to deduct the full appraised value as bonus depreciation. Thus, it will immediately depreciate $150 million of assets. If the federal-plus-state corporate tax rate is 25%, then the acquirer will save $37.5 million in federal taxes by using bonus depreciation: 25%($150) = $37.5. In addition, the acquirer will be able to deduct $6.7 million in amortization expenses each year: $100/15 = $6.67. This deduction will reduce taxes in each of the next 15 years by $1.67 million: 25%($6.67) = $1.4.

Recall that in a stock purchase, the acquirer can only continue to depreciate the $100 million of book value using the target's existing depreciation schedule. As explained previously, the tax savings to the acquirer might be quite small.

22-13c Taxable Purchase of Shares

An offer for a target's stock rather than its assets can be made either directly to the shareholders, as is typical in a hostile takeover, or indirectly through the board of directors, which in a friendly deal makes a recommendation to the shareholders to accept the offer. In a successful offer, the acquiring firm will end up owning a controlling interest or perhaps even all the target's stock. Sometimes the target retains its identity as a separate legal entity and is operated as a subsidiary of the acquiring firm, and sometimes its corporate status is dissolved, and it is operated as one of the acquiring firm's divisions.

The acquirer can choose to record the target's assets at their book values or at their appraised values. Either way, the target shareholders must pay taxes on any gains. However, the methods differ with respect to the target firm's and the acquiring firm's tax treatments.

RECORD ASSETS AT BOOK VALUES

If the acquirer records the assets at their book values, then the acquirer continues to depreciate the acquired assets according to their previous depreciation schedules. Goodwill is not treated as a deductible expense. Note that the acquiring firm's tax treatment is the same as in Section 22-13a, in which the acquisition is by means of a stock exchange. As explained earlier, the annual tax deductions are relatively small for assets with long remaining lives.

RECORD ASSETS AT APPRAISED VALUES

If the acquirer records the assets at their appraised values, then the target incurs a tax liability for the difference between the appraised value and the book value. The acquiring firm will be responsible for this liability and pays these taxes after completing the acquisition. In contrast to this tax liability, the acquiring firm also receives a benefit because it can fully depreciate the appraised values of the assets and can deduct goodwill expenses from its taxable income.

---

[26]After 2022, the amount of the bonus depreciation in the first year falls by 20% per year: 80% in 2023, 60% in 2024, 40% in 2025, 20% in 2026, and 0% in 2027. This means that acquisitions will create significant tax savings for years to come.

What are three types of mergers regarding taxes?

How are targets and acquirers taxed in each type of merger?

22-14 Financial Reporting for Mergers

Although a detailed discussion of financial reporting is best left to accounting courses, the accounting implications of mergers cannot be ignored. Currently, mergers are handled using **purchase accounting**.[27] Keep in mind, however, that all large companies are required to keep two sets of books. The first is for the IRS, and it reflects the tax treatment of mergers as described in the previous section. The second is for financial reporting, and it reflects the treatment described here. As you will see, the rules for financial reporting differ from those for the IRS.

22-14a Purchase Accounting

Table 22-1 illustrates purchase accounting. Here, Firm A is assumed to have "bought" Firm B using A's stock. If the price paid is exactly equal to the acquired firm's *net asset value*, which is defined as its total assets minus its liabilities, then the consolidated balance sheet will be as if the two statements were combined into one. Normally, though, there is an important difference. If the price paid *exceeds* the net asset value, then asset values will be

TABLE 22-1

Accounting for Mergers: Firm A Acquires Firm B with Stock

	Firm A (1)	Firm B (2)	Post-Merger: Firm A $20 Paid[a] (3)	$30 Paid[a] (4)	$50 Paid[a] (5)
Current assets	$ 50	$25	$ 75	$ 75	$ 80[b]
Fixed assets	50	25	65[c]	75	80[b]
Goodwill[d]	0	0	0	0	10[d]
Total assets	$100	$50	$140	$150	$170
Liabilities	$ 40	$20	$ 60	$ 60	$ 60
Equity	60	30	80[e]	90	110[f]
Total claims	$100	$50	$140	$150	$170

Notes:

[a]The price paid is the *net asset value*—that is, total assets minus liabilities.

[b]Here we assume that Firm B's current and fixed assets are both increased to $30.

[c]Here we assume that Firm B's fixed assets are written down from $25 to $15 before constructing the consolidated balance sheet.

[d]*Goodwill* refers to the excess paid for a firm above the appraised value of the physical assets purchased. Goodwill represents payment both for intangibles such as patents and for "organization value," such as that associated with having an effective sales force. Beginning in 2001, purchased goodwill such as this may not be amortized for financial statement reporting purposes.

[e]Firm B's common equity is reduced by $10 prior to consolidation to reflect the fixed asset write-off.

[f]Firm B's equity is increased to $50 to reflect the above-book purchase price.

[27]In 2001, the Financial Accounting Standards Board (FASB) issued Statement 141, which eliminated the use of *pooling* accounting.

increased to reflect the price actually paid, whereas if the price paid is *less* than the net asset value, then assets must be written down when preparing the consolidated balance sheet.

Note that Firm B's net asset value is $30, which is also its reported common equity value. This $30 book value could be equal to the market value (which is determined by investors based on the firm's earning power), but book value could also be more or less than the market value. Three situations are considered in Table 22-1. First, in Column 3 we assume that Firm A gives stock worth $20 for Firm B. Thus, B's assets as reported on its balance sheet were overvalued, and A pays less than B's net asset value. The overvaluation could be in either fixed or current assets; an appraisal would be made, but we assume it is fixed assets that are overvalued. Accordingly, we reduce B's fixed assets and also its common equity by $10 before constructing the consolidated balance sheet shown in Column 3. Next, in Column 4, we assume that A pays exactly the net asset value for B. In this case, the financial statements are simply combined.

Finally, in Column 5 we assume that A pays more than the net asset value for B: $50 is paid for $30 of net assets. This excess is assumed to be partly attributable to undervalued assets (land, buildings, machinery, and inventories) and so, to reflect this undervaluation, current and fixed assets are each increased by $5. In addition, we assume that $10 of the $20 excess of market value over book value is due to a superior sales organization or to some other intangible factor, and we post this excess as goodwill. Firm B's common equity is increased by $20, the sum of the increases in current and fixed assets plus goodwill, and this markup is also reflected in Firm A's post-merger equity account.[28]

22-14b Income Statement Effects

A merger can have a significant effect on reported profits. If asset values are increased, as they often are under a purchase, then this must be reflected in higher depreciation charges (and also in a higher cost of goods sold if inventories are written up). This, in turn, will reduce reported profits. For financial reporting, but not for taxes, goodwill is subject to an annual **impairment test**. If the estimated fair market value of the goodwill has declined (i.e., been impaired) over the year, then the amount of the decline must be reported as an expense. However, if the goodwill's estimated fair market goes up, it cannot be reported as income.

Table 22-2 illustrates the income statement effects of the write-up of current and fixed assets. We assume A purchased B for $50, creating $10 of goodwill and $10 of higher physical asset value. As Column 3 indicates, the asset markups cause reported profits to be lower than the sum of the individual companies' reported profits because of the increased depreciation expense and the increased cost of goods sold.

The asset markup is also reflected in earnings per share. In our hypothetical merger, we assume that nine shares exist in the consolidated firm. (Six of these shares went to A's stockholders, and three went to B's.) The merged company's EPS is $2.92, whereas each of the individual companies' EPS was $3.00.

SELF-TEST

What is purchase accounting for mergers?

What is goodwill? What impact does goodwill have on the firm's balance sheet? On its income statement?

---

[28]This example assumes that additional debt was not issued to help finance the acquisition. If the acquisition were totally debt financed, then the post-merger balance sheet would show an increase in debt rather than an increase in the equity account. If it were financed by a mix of debt and equity, both accounts would increase. If the acquisition were paid for with cash on hand, then current assets would decrease by the amount paid, and the equity account would not increase.

TABLE 22-2
Income Statement Effects

	Pre-Merger		Post-Merger: Firm A
	Firm A (1)	Firm B (2)	Merged (3)
Sales	$ 100.0	$ 50.0	$150.00
Operating costs	72.0	36.0	109.00[a]
Operating income	$ 28.0	$ 14.0	$ 41.00[a]
Interest (10%)	4.0	2.0	6.00
Taxable income	$ 24.0	$ 12.0	$ 35.00
Taxes (25%)	6.0	3.0	8.75
Net income	$ 18.0	$ 9.0	$ 26.25
EPS[b]	$ 3.00	$ 3.00	$ 2.92

Notes:

[a]Operating costs are $1 higher than they otherwise would be; this reflects the higher reported costs (depreciation and cost of goods sold) caused by the physical asset markup at the time of purchase.

[b]Before the merger, Firm A had six shares and Firm B had three shares. Firm A gives one of its shares for each of Firm B's, so A has nine shares outstanding after the merger.

SUMMARY

- A **merger** occurs when two firms combine to form a single company. The primary motives for mergers are (1) synergy, (2) tax considerations, (3) purchase of assets below their replacement costs, (4) diversification, (5) gaining control over a larger enterprise, and (6) breakup value.
- Mergers can provide economic benefits through **economies of scale** and through putting assets in the hands of more efficient managers. However, mergers also have the potential for reducing competition, and for this reason they are carefully regulated by government agencies.
- In most mergers, one company (the **acquiring company**) initiates action to take over another (the **target company**).
- A **horizontal merger** occurs when two firms in the same line of business combine.
- A **vertical merger** combines a firm with one of its customers or suppliers.
- A **congeneric merger** involves firms in related industries but where no customer–supplier relationship exists.
- A **conglomerate merger** occurs when firms in totally different industries combine.
- In a **friendly merger**, the managements of both firms approve the merger, whereas in a **hostile merger**, the target firm's management opposes it.
- An **operating merger** is one in which the operations of the two firms are combined. A **financial merger** is one in which the firms continue to operate separately; hence, no operating economies are expected.
- In a typical merger analysis, the key issues to be resolved are (1) the price to be paid for the target firm and (2) the employment/control situation. If the merger is a consolidation of two relatively equal firms, at issue is the percentage of ownership that each merger partner's shareholders will receive.

- Four methods are commonly used to determine the value of the target firm: (1) market multiple analysis, (2) the free cash flow corporate valuation model, (3) the free cash flow to equity (FCFE) model, and (4) the compressed adjusted present value (CAPV) model. Of the discounted cash flow approaches, only the compressed APV model is appropriate if the capital structure is changing during the forecast period.
- **Purchase accounting** treats mergers as a purchase and is used for financial reporting.
- A **joint venture** is a **corporate alliance** in which two or more companies combine some of their resources to achieve a specific, limited objective.
- A **divestiture** is the sale of some of a company's operating assets. A divestiture may involve (1) selling an operating unit to another firm, (2) **spinning off** a unit as a separate company, (3) **carving out** a unit by selling a minority interest, or (4) the outright liquidation of a unit's assets.
- The reasons for divestiture include (1) settling antitrust suits, (2) improving the transparency of the resulting companies so that investors can more easily evaluate them, (3) enabling management to concentrate on a particular type of activity, and (4) raising the capital needed to strengthen the corporation's core business.
- A **holding company** is a corporation that owns sufficient stock in another firm to control it. The holding company is also known as the **parent company**, and the companies that it controls are called **subsidiaries** or **operating companies.**
- Holding company operations are advantageous because: (1) Control can often be obtained for a smaller cash outlay. (2) Risks may be segregated. (3) Regulated companies can operate separate subsidiaries for their regulated and unregulated businesses.
- The main disadvantage of a holding company is *partial multiple taxation of dividends* in which the holding company's shareholders are taxed on dividends received from the holding company, which itself might be taxed on dividends received from the operating companies.

QUESTIONS

(22-1) Define each of the following terms:
a. Synergy; merger
b. Horizontal merger; vertical merger; congeneric merger; conglomerate merger
c. Friendly merger; hostile merger; defensive merger; tender offer; target company; breakup value; acquiring company
d. Operating merger; financial merger
e. Purchase accounting
f. White knight; proxy fight
g. Joint venture; corporate alliance
h. Divestiture; spin-off
i. Holding company; operating company; parent company
j. Arbitrage; risk arbitrage

(22-2) Four economic classifications of mergers are (1) horizontal, (2) vertical, (3) conglomerate, and (4) congeneric. Explain the significance of these terms in merger analysis with regard to (a) the likelihood of governmental intervention and (b) possibilities for operating synergy.

(22-3) Firm A wants to acquire Firm B. Firm B's management agrees that the merger is a good idea. Might a tender offer be used? Why or why not?

(22-4) Distinguish between operating mergers and financial mergers.

(22-5) Explain why the APV model is suited for situations in which the capital structure is changing during the forecast period.

(ST-1)
Valuation of Target

Red Valley Breweries is considering an acquisition of Flagg Markets. Flagg currently has a cost of equity of 10%; 25% of its financing is in the form of 6% debt, and the rest is in common equity. Its federal-plus-state tax rate is 25%. After the acquisition, Red Valley expects Flagg to have the FCFs and interest payments for the next 3 years (in millions) shown in the following table. After the explicit forecast period, the free cash flows are expected to grow at a constant rate of 5%, and the capital structure will stabilize at 35% debt with an interest rate of 7%. Use the compressed adjusted present value approach to answer the following questions.

	Year 1	Year 2	Year 3
FCF	$10.00	$20.00	$25.00
Interest expense	28.00	24.00	20.28

a. What is Flagg's unlevered cost of equity? What are its levered cost of equity and cost of capital for the post-horizon period?
b. What is Flagg's value of operations to Red Valley?

EASY PROBLEMS 1–3

(22-1)
Unlevered Cost of Equity

Elliott's Cross Country Transportation Services has a capital structure with 25% debt at a 9% interest rate. Its beta is 1.6, the risk-free rate is 4%, and the market risk premium is 7%. Elliott's combined federal-plus-state tax rate is 25%.

a. What is Elliott's cost of equity?
b. What is its weighted average cost of capital?
c. What is its unlevered cost of equity?

(22-2)
Unlevered Value

Richter Manufacturing has a 10% unlevered cost of equity. Richter forecasts the following free cash flows (FCFs), which are expected to grow at a constant 3% rate after Year 3.

	Year 1	Year 2	Year 3
FCF	$715	$750	$805

a. What is the horizon value of the unlevered operations?
b. What is the total value of unlevered operations at Year 0?

(22-3)
Tax Shield Value

Wilde Software Development has a 12% unlevered cost of equity. Wilde forecasts the following interest expenses, which are expected to grow at a constant 4% rate after Year 3. Wilde's tax rate is 25%.

	Year 1	Year 2	Year 3
Interest expenses	$80	$100	$120

a. What is the horizon value of the interest tax shield?
b. What is the total value of the interest tax shield at Year 0?

INTERMEDIATE PROBLEMS 4–5

(22-4)
Intrinsic Value of Merger Target

Hasting Corporation is interested in acquiring Vandell Corporation. Vandell has 1.5 million shares outstanding and a target capital structure consisting of 30% debt; its beta is 1.4 (given its target capital structure). Vandell has $10.19 million in debt that trades at par and pays an 8% interest rate. Vandell's current free cash flow (FCF_0) is $2 million per year and is expected to grow at a constant rate of 5% a year. Vandell pays a 25% combined federal-plus-state tax rate, the same rate paid by Hastings. The risk-free rate of interest is 5%, and the market risk premium is 6%. Hasting's first step is to estimate the current intrinsic value of Vandell.

a. What is Vandell's cost of equity?
b. What is its weighted average cost of capital?
c. What is Vandell's intrinsic value of operations? (*Hint:* Use the free cash flow corporate valuation model from Chapter 7.)
d. Based on this analysis, what is the minimum stock price that Vandell's shareholders should accept?

(22-5)
Merger Valuation with Synergies

Hasting Corporation estimates that if it acquires Vandell Corporation, synergies will cause Vandell's free cash flows to be $2.5 million, $2.9 million, $3.4 million, and $3.57 million at Years 1 through 4, respectively, after which the free cash flows will grow at a constant 5% rate. Hasting plans to assume Vandell's $10.19 million in debt (which has an 8% interest rate) and raise additional debt financing at the time of the acquisition. Hastings estimates that interest payments will be $1.5 million each year for Years 1, 2, and 3. After Year 3, a target capital structure of 30% debt will be maintained. Interest at Year 4 will be $1.472 million, after which the interest and the tax shield will grow at 5%. As described in Problem 22-4, Vandell currently has 1.5 million shares outstanding and a target capital structure consisting of 30% debt; its current beta is 1.4 (i.e., based on its target capital structure). Vandell and Hastings each have a 25% combined federal-plus-state tax rate. The risk-free rate is 5% and the market risk premium is 6%.

a. What is Vandell's pre-acquisition levered cost of equity? What is its unlevered cost of equity? (*Hint:* You can use the pre-acquisition levered cost of equity you determined previously if you worked Problem 22-1.)
b. What is the intrinsic unlevered value of operations at $t = 0$ (assuming the synergies are realized)?
c. What is the value of the tax shields at $t = 0$?
d. What is the total intrinsic value at $t = 0$? What is the intrinsic value of Vandell's equity to Hasting? What is the maximum price per share that Hasting's should offer Vandell's shareholders?

CHALLENGING PROBLEM 6

(22-6)
Impact of Synergies and Capital Structure Changes

Crane Rafting Corporation is considering an acquisition of Frost Ski Supplies. Frost has a pre-merger 8% unlevered cost of equity, 6% pre-tax cost of debt, and 25% tax rate. Its pre-merger forecasted free cash flows and debt are expected to grow at a constant 5% rate after Year 4. Frost has 800 million outstanding shares.

If Crane makes the acquisition, synergies will increase Frost's free cash flows. Crane will also add debt at Frost's 6% rate. Crane's tax rate is 25%. The post-merger forecasted free cash flows and debt are expected to grow at a constant 5% rate after Year 4.

Data for Frost's pre-merger and post-merger FCF and debt are shown here:

Frost: Pre-merger	Year 0	Year 1	Year 2	Year 3	Year 4
FCF (millions)	$1,400	$1,600	$1,800	$1,900	$2,000
Debt (millions)	$7,700	$7,900	$8,100	$8,200	$8,300

Frost: Post-merger	Year 0	Year 1	Year 2	Year 3	Year 4
FCF (millions)	$1,400	$1,700	$2,000	$2,100	$2,200
Debt (millions)	$7,700	$22,000	$22,300	$22,400	$22,500

a. What is Frost's pre-merger unlevered horizon value? What is its Year-0 unlevered value?

b. What is Frost's pre-merger horizon value tax shield? What is its Year-0 tax shield value? Assume debt is added on the first day of the year; that is, calculate interest expenses for Year t based on debt at Year t.

c. What is Frost's current value of levered operations? What is its value of equity? What is the minimum stock price per share that Frost's shareholders should accept?

d. What is Frost's post-merger unlevered horizon value to Crane? What is its Year-0 unlevered value?

e. What is Frost's post-merger horizon value tax shield to Crane? What is its Year-0 tax shield value? Assume debt is added on the first day of the year; that is, calculate interest expenses for Year t based on debt at Year t.

f. What is Frost's post-merger Year-0 value of levered operations to Crane? What is its value of equity? (*Hint*: Remember that Crane assumes Frost's debt and subsequently issues more debt.) What is the maximum stock price per share that Crane should offer?

g. What percentage of Frost's pre-merger capital structure at Year 4 consisted of debt? (*Hint*: You already have the values you need to calculate the total value at the horizon.) What percentage after the merger? How much of Frost's post-merger increase in value to Crane is due to improved FCF? (*Hint*: You already have calculated the values you need to determine the answer to this question.) How much is due to the change in capital structure?

SPREADSHEET PROBLEM

(22-7)
Build a Model:
Merger Analysis

resource

Start with the partial model in the file *Ch22 P07 Build a Model.xlsx* on the textbook's Web site. Wansley Portal Inc., a large Internet service provider, is evaluating the possible acquisition of Alabama Connections Company (ACC), a regional Internet service provider. Wansley's analysts project the following post-merger data for ACC (in thousands of dollars):

	2020	2021	2022	2023	2024
Net sales	$500	$600	$700	$760	$806
Selling and administrative expense	60	70	80	90	96
Interest	30	40	45	60	74

If the acquisition is made, it will occur on January 1, 2020. All cash flows shown in the income statements are assumed to occur at the end of the year. ACC currently has a capital structure of 30% debt, which costs 9%, but Wansley would increase that over time to 40%, costing 10%, if the acquisition were made. ACC, if independent, would pay taxes at 25%, and its income would be taxed at 25% if it were consolidated. ACC's current market-determined beta is 1.4. The cost of goods sold, which includes depreciation, is expected to be 65% of sales. Required gross investment in operating capital is approximately equal to the depreciation charged, so there will be no investment in net operating capital. The risk-free rate is 7%, and the market risk premium is 6.5%. Wansley currently has $400,000 in debt outstanding. Use the compressed APV model to answer the following questions.

a. What is the unlevered cost of equity?
b. What are the horizon value of the tax shields and the horizon value of the unlevered operations? What are the value of ACC's operations and the value of ACC's equity to Wansley's shareholders?

MINI CASE

Hager's Home Repair Company, a regional hardware chain, which specializes in "do-it-yourself" materials and equipment rentals, is considering an acquisition of Lyon Lighting (LL). Doug Zona, Hager's treasurer and your boss, has been asked to place a value on the target and he has enlisted your help.

LL has 20 million shares of stock trading at $12 per share. Security analysts estimate LL's beta to be 1.25. The risk-free rate is 5.5% and the market risk premium is 4%. LL's capital structure is 20% financed with debt at an 8% interest rate; any additional debt due to the acquisition also will have an 8% rate. LL has a 25% federal-plus-state tax rate, which will not change due to the acquisition.

The following data incorporate expected synergies and required levels of total net operating capital for LL should Hager's complete the acquisition. The forecasted interest expense includes the combined interest on LL's existing debt and on new debt. After 2024, all items are expected to grow at a constant 6% rate.

	2019	2020	2021	2022	2023	2024
Net sales		$150	$170	$186	$200	$212
Cost of goods sold		$116	$128	$135	$148	$160
Selling/administrative expense		$ 22	$ 26	$ 27	$ 28	$ 32
Total net operating capital	$64	$ 75	$ 85	$ 93	$100	$106
Debt[a]	$30	$ 50	$ 52	$ 52	$ 53	$ 54

Note:

[a]Debt is added on the first day of the year, so the 2019 debt is LL's debt prior to the acquisition.

Hager's management is new to the merger game, so Zona has been asked to answer some basic questions about mergers as well as to perform the merger analysis. To structure the task, Zona has developed the following questions, which you must answer and then defend to Hager's board:

a. Several reasons have been proposed to justify mergers. Among the more prominent are (1) synergy, (2) tax considerations, (3) breakup value, (4) risk reduction through diversification, (4) purchase of assets at below-replacement cost, and (5) managerial incentives. In general, which of the reasons are economically justifiable? Which are not?
b. Briefly describe the differences between a hostile merger and a friendly merger.
c. What are the steps in valuing a merger using the compressed APV approach?

   d. Why can't we estimate LL's value to Hager's by discounting the FCFs at the WACC? What method is appropriate? Use the projections and other data to determine the LL division's free cash flows and interest tax savings for 2020 through 2024. Notice that the LL division's sales are expected to grow rapidly during the first years before leveling off at a sustainable long-term growth rate.
   e. Conceptually, what is the appropriate discount rate to apply to the cash flows developed in part d? What is your actual estimate of this discount rate?
   f. What is the estimated unlevered horizon value? What is the current unlevered operating value? What is the horizon value of the interest tax savings? What is the current value of the interest tax savings? What is the current total value of the acquisition to Hager's shareholders? Suppose another firm were evaluating Lyon Lighting as an acquisition candidate. Would they obtain the same value? Explain.
   g. Should Hager's make an offer for Lyon Lighting? If so, how much should it offer per share?
   h. Considerable research has been undertaken to determine whether mergers really create value and, if so, how this value is shared between the parties involved. What are the results of this research?
   i. What method is used to account for mergers?
   j. What merger-related activities are undertaken by investment bankers?
   k. What are the major types of divestitures? What motivates firms to divest assets?
   l. What are holding companies? What are their advantages and disadvantages?

SELECTED ADDITIONAL CASES

The following cases from CengageCompose cover many of the concepts discussed in this chapter and are available at **http://compose.cengage.com.**

Klein-Brigham Series:
Case 40, "Nina's Fashions, Inc."; Case 53, "Nero's Pasta, Inc."; and Case 70, "Computer Concepts/CompuTech."

CHAPTER 23

Enterprise Risk Management

On April 13, 2012, JPMorgan Chase CEO Jamie Dimon called rumors of impending trading losses a "tempest in a teapot." As time passed, the losses exceeded $6 billion and led to several criminal charges for hiding losses, making it a pretty big teapot!

Banks make loans to businesses, and JPMorgan is no exception. Many of its borrowers were exposed to difficult global economic conditions, including the Eurozone crises, which in turn exposed JPMorgan to risk. To offset potential losses on commercial lending, JPMorgan's Chief Investment Office in London took short positions on selected indexes that would pay off if some large companies, including some of their customers, defaulted on bank loans.[1] This is a classic hedge—if borrowers defaulted, JPMorgan's commercial lending group would lose money, but the London office would make money, and vice versa.

However, that is not the end of the story. The London office also took long positions on derivatives based on a broader credit index, the CDX.NA.IG.9. (Long positions meant that JPMorgan made commitments to buy at a fixed price.) Their intentions were to reduce expenses but also to hedge their short positions in the selected indexes, betting that the selected indexes were temporarily mispriced relative to the IG.9. JPMorgan continued to take long positions on the IG.9 during late 2011 and early 2012, until it became the biggest trader in this segment of the market. In fact, it is likely that JPMorgan's own trading activities artificially drove down the IG.9's price.

The low price of the IG.9 attracted hedge funds, and what goes down must come up. As the IG.9 price increased, JPMorgan began to lose money on its long positions and started liquidating some of its positions to prevent even bigger losses in the future. Keep this event in mind as you read the rest of the chapter.

---

[1] These indexes were actually composed of credit default swaps, so JPMorgan was going short in a derivative based on other derivatives.

Corporate Valuation and Risk Management

All companies are exposed to risk from volatility in product prices, demand, input costs, and other sources of business risk, such as the risk stemming from the choice of production technology. Many companies also are exposed to risk from volatility in exchange rates and interest rates.

Risk management can reduce firm risk, preventing catastrophes and leading to a lower cost of capital. In some instances, derivatives such as swaps can reduce the effective interest rate paid by a corporation, again reducing its cost of capital.

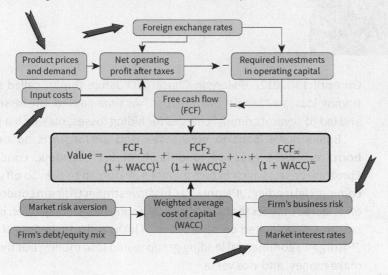

Defining risk management is simple: Identify events that could have adverse consequences and then take actions to prevent or minimize the damage caused by these events. Applying risk management is more difficult, but it is vital for a company's success, and perhaps even its survival. In this chapter we explain how risk management adds value to a corporation, describe an enterprise risk management framework, identify different categories of risks, explain how to measure selected risks, and show how to manage those risks.[2] We also illustrate how companies can use **derivatives**, which are securities whose values are determined by the market price of some other asset, to manage certain types of risk.

23-1 Reasons to Manage Risk

Does managing risk make a company more valuable? If so, how? If not, then why do companies manage risk? Consider the risk management tool **hedging**, in which a company can reduce or eliminate its exposure to a source of risk through the use of derivatives. Plastic Inc. manufactures dashboards, interior door panels, and other plastic components used by auto companies. Petroleum is the key feedstock for plastic and thus makes up a

---

[2]For excellent overviews of risk management, see Kenneth A. Froot, David S. Scharfstein, and Jeremy Stein, "A Framework for Risk Management," *Journal of Applied Corporate Finance*, Fall 1994, pp. 22–32; Brian Nocco and Rene Stultz, "Enterprise Risk Management, Theory and Practice," *Journal of Applied Corporate Finance*, Fall 2006, pp. 8–20; Walter Dolde, "The Trajectory of Corporate Financial Risk Management," *Journal of Applied Corporate Finance*, Fall 1993, pp. 33–41; and Marshall Blake and Nelda Mahady, "How Mid-Sized Companies Manage Risk," *Journal of Applied Corporate Finance*, Spring 1991, pp. 59–65.

large percentage of its costs. Plastic has a 3-year contract with an auto company to deliver 500,000 door panels each year at a price of $20 each. When the company recently signed this contract, oil sold for $100 per barrel and was expected to stay at that level for the next 3 years. If oil prices fell during this time, Plastic would have higher than expected profits and free cash flows, but if oil prices rose, profits would fall. Because Plastic's value depends on its profits and free cash flows, a change in the price of oil would cause stockholders to earn either more or less than they anticipated.

Now suppose that, shortly after signing the contract with its door panel supplier, Plastic announces that it plans to lock in a 3-year supply of oil at a guaranteed price of $100 per barrel *and* that the cost of this guarantee is zero. Would that cause its stock price to rise? At first glance, it seems the answer should be "yes," but that might not be correct. Recall that the value of a stock depends on the present value of its expected future free cash flows, discounted at the weighted average cost of capital (WACC). *Locking in the cost of oil will cause an increase in Plastic's stock price if and only if it either increases expected future free cash flows or decreases the WACC.*

Consider first the free cash flows. Before the announcement of guaranteed oil costs, investors had formed an estimate of the expected future free cash flows based on an expected oil price of $100 per barrel. Locking in the cost of oil at $100 per barrel will lower the *risk* of the expected future free cash flows, but it might not change the expected *size* of these cash flows because investors already expected a price of $100 per barrel. Of course, smaller than expected cash flows can disrupt a firm's operation and that disruption can, in turn, adversely affect cash flows.

Now what about the WACC? It will change only if locking in the cost of oil causes a change either in the cost of debt or equity or in the target capital structure. If the foreseeable increases in the price of oil are not enough to increase the threat of bankruptcy, then Plastic's cost of debt should not change and neither should its target capital structure. Regarding the cost of equity, recall from Chapter 6 that most investors hold well-diversified portfolios, which means that the cost of equity should depend only on systematic risk. Moreover, even though an increase in oil prices would have a negative effect on Plastic's stock price, it would not have a negative effect on all stocks. Indeed, oil producers should have higher than expected returns and stock prices. Assuming that Plastic's investors hold well-diversified portfolios that include stocks of oil-producing companies, we should have little reason to expect its cost of equity to decrease. The bottom line is this: If Plastic's expected future cash flows and WACC will not change significantly as a consequence of eliminating the risk of oil price increases, then neither should the value of its stock.

We discuss futures contracts and hedging in detail in the next section, but for now let's assume that Plastic has *not* locked in oil prices. Therefore, if oil prices increase, its stock price will fall. However, if its stockholders know this and prefer not to be exposed to this particular risk, they can build portfolios that contain oil futures whose values will rise or fall with oil prices and thus offset changes in the price of Plastic's stock. By choosing the correct amount of futures contracts, investors can thus "hedge" their portfolios and completely eliminate the risk due to changes in oil prices. There will be a cost to hedging, but that cost to large investors should be about the same as the cost to Plastic. Because stockholders can hedge away oil price risk themselves, why should they pay a higher price for Plastic's stock just because the company itself hedged away that risk?

The previous points notwithstanding, companies clearly believe that active risk management is important. A 1998 survey reported that 83% of firms with market values greater than $1.2 billion engage in risk management.[3] A more recent 2005 survey of CFOs

[3]See Gordon M. Bodnar, Gregory S. Hayt, and Richard C. Marston, "1998 Wharton Survey of Financial Risk Management by U.S. Non-Financial Firms," *Financial Management*, Winter 1998, pp. 70–91.

reported that 90% of the international and domestic firms responding considered risk in the planning process. The average of the estimates of the contribution that risk management made to the market value of the firm was 3.8%.[4] There are many reasons why companies manage their risks.

1. *Debt capacity.* Risk management can reduce the volatility of cash flows, which decreases the probability of bankruptcy. As we discussed in Chapter 15, firms with lower operating risks can use more debt, and this can lead to higher stock prices due to the interest tax savings.

2. *Maintaining the optimal capital budget over time.* Recall from Chapter 15 that firms are reluctant to raise external equity because of high flotation costs and market pressure. This means that the capital budget must generally be financed with a combination of debt and internally generated funds. In bad years, internal cash flows may be too low to support the optimal capital budget, causing firms to either slow investment below the optimal rate or else incur the high costs associated with external equity. By smoothing out the cash flows, risk management can alleviate this problem. This issue is most relevant for firms with large growth opportunities. A study by Professors Gerald Gay and Jouahn Nam found that such firms do in fact use derivatives more than low-growth firms.[5] Thus, maintaining an optimal capital budget is an important determinant of firms' risk management practices.

3. *Financial distress.* The stages of financial distress can range from stockholder concern and higher interest rates on debt to customer defections and bankruptcy. Any serious level of financial distress causes a firm to have lower cash flows than expected. Risk management can reduce the likelihood of low cash flows and hence of financial distress.

4. *Comparative advantages in hedging.* Most investors cannot hedge as efficiently as a company. First, firms generally incur lower transaction costs because of their larger volume of hedging activities. Second, there is the problem of asymmetric information: Managers know more about the firm's risk exposure than do outside investors, so managers can create more effective hedges. And third, effective risk management requires specialized skills and knowledge that firms are more likely to have.

5. *Borrowing costs.* As discussed later in the chapter, firms can sometimes reduce input costs—especially the interest rate on debt—through the use of derivative instruments called *swaps*. Any such cost reduction adds value to the firm.

6. *Tax effects.* The present value of taxes paid by companies with volatile earnings is higher than the present value of taxes paid by stable companies; this is due to the treatment of tax credits and the rules governing corporate loss carryforwards and interest expense deduction limits that are part of the 2017 Tax Cuts and Jobs Act (TCJA).[6] Moreover, if volatile earnings cause a company to declare bankruptcy, then the company often will lose the value of its tax loss carryforwards. Therefore, using risk management to stabilize earnings can reduce the present value of a company's tax burden.

---

[4]See Henri Servaes, Ane Tamayo, and Peter Tufano, "The Theory and Practice of Corporate Risk Management," *Journal of Applied Corporate Finance*, Fall 2009, pp. 60–78.

[5]See Gerald D. Gay and Jouahn Nam, "The Underinvestment Problem and Corporate Derivatives Use," *Financial Management*, Winter 1998, pp. 53–69.

[6]Recall from Chapter 2 that for 2019, 2020, and 2021, the TCJA reduced the annual allowable interest expense deduction to 30% of earnings before interest, taxes, depreciation, and amortization (EBITDA). For 2022 and subsequent years, the TCJA reduced the allowable interest expense deduction to 30% of earnings before interest and taxes (EBIT).

7. *Compensation systems.* Many compensation systems establish "floors" and "ceilings" on bonuses and also reward managers for meeting targets. To illustrate, suppose a firm's compensation system calls for a manager to receive no bonus if net income is below $1 million, a bonus of $10,000 if income is between $1 million and $2 million, or a bonus of $20,000 if income is $2 million or more. The manager will also receive an additional $10,000 if actual income is at least 90% of the forecasted level, which is $1 million. Now consider the following two situations. First, if income is stable at $2 million each year then the manager receives a $30,000 bonus each year, for a 2-year total of $60,000. However, if income is zero the first year and $4 million the second, the manager gets no bonus the first year and gets $30,000 the second, for a 2-year total of $30,000. So, even though the company has the same total income ($4 million) over the 2 years, the manager's bonus is higher if earnings are stable. Therefore, even if hedging does not add much value for stockholders, it may still benefit managers.

There are regulatory and economically driven reasons to manage risk. The following section describes a typical enterprise risk management framework.

SELF-TEST

Explain why finance theory, combined with well-diversified investors and "homemade hedging," might suggest that risk management should not add much value to a company.

List and explain some reasons companies might employ risk management techniques.

23-2 An Overview of Enterprise Risk Management

With the development of pricing models for derivatives, most companies began to actively manage their exposures to interest rates, exchange rates, and a wide variety of commodities. However, few companies employed a systematic approach to risk management. Instead, most companies had a risk management group in charge of insurance-related issues, but different groups in charge of managing each of the other specific risks. For example, one group might manage foreign exchange risk and another might manage commodity risk.

Regulation provided the impetus for a more comprehensive and systematic approach to risk management. In 1977, Congress passed the Foreign Corrupt Practices Act (FCPA) to address corporate bribery scandals. One of the provisions of this act requires companies to have an accounting system that can identify bribery. In 2002, Congress passed the Sarbanes-Oxley Act (SOX) to address the corporate fraud scandals involving Arthur Andersen, Tyco, and Enron. One of the provisions of this act requires senior management to address in the annual report the firm's internal control system and provide an assessment of its ability to detect fraud.

To address these and other accounting needs, a group of five accounting organizations formed the Committee of Sponsoring Organizations (COSO), which developed a framework for an internal control system designed to prevent fraudulent accounting. The framework satisfied the FCPA and SOX reporting requirements, so many companies adopted it. In 2004, COSO also issued a framework for enterprise risk management, which broadened the scope of the original internal control framework. Because many companies were already using the framework for internal controls, some adopted versions of the broader framework for enterprise risk management. Today, the COSO framework and similar frameworks are widely used.

COSO defines **enterprise risk management (ERM)** as follows:

> Enterprise risk management is a *process,* effected by an entity's *board of directors,* management and other personnel, applied in *strategy setting* and across the *enterprise,* designed to identify *potential events* that may affect the entity, and manage risk to be within its *risk appetite,* to provide reasonable *assurance* regarding the achievement of entity objectives.[7]

Notice how this definition differs from the traditional compartmentalization of risk management. The COSO framework is inclusive, starting with the board of directors in addition to managers and other employees; COSO is broad in defining risk, ranging from strategic choices to specific events; COSO is unambiguous, with the company explicitly choosing an acceptable level of risk; and COSO is transparent, requiring monitoring and reporting.

Another big regulatory wave, this time international in scope, also impacted risk management. The Basel Committee, headquartered in Switzerland, is composed of the heads of the central banks from well-developed economies. In the past 30 years, the Committee has introduced three major accords designed to control risk in the global financial system: Basel I (1988), Basel II (2004), and Basel III (introduced in 2010 and revised in 2011). There are similarities in all three accords, but we focus on Basel III because it is the most recent.

The essence of banking is raising funds (from sales of stock, issuances of debt, borrowing through short-term loans, and taking deposits) and then investing the funds in assets (such as business loans and derivatives). A bank experiences financial distress when its assets' cash flows and values aren't sufficient to cover its obligations to its creditors. To prevent a bank from experiencing financial distress (and then passing its problems on to taxpayers and the global financial system), Basel III seeks to ensure that a bank is not financed with too much debt relative to the risk of its assets. In addition to regulations regarding the types and proportions of capital a bank must maintain relative to its assets' risks, Basel III also requires adequate internal control systems to supervise a bank's risk and goes on to suggest particular techniques for measuring risk. We will describe several of these measures later in the chapter, including *value at risk* and *expected shortfall.*

SELF-TEST

Describe some regulatory actions that have influenced the evolution of risk management.

Define enterprise risk management.

23-3 A Framework for Enterprise Risk Management

No single framework is applicable to all companies, but the COSO framework (including modified versions) is widely used, so it provides an excellent example of an ERM framework.[8]

---

[7]We added the italics for emphasis. See page 2 of COSO, "Summary of Enterprise Risk Management—Integrated Framework," 2004, **www.coso.org/documents/coso_erm_executivesummary.pdf**.

[8]For more on the COSO framework, see The Committee of Sponsoring Organizations of the Treadway Commission, *Enterprise Risk Management—Integrated Framework*, 2004, available at **www.coso.org/guidance .htm**. A summary of the framework is available for free at the same Web site. Another widely used framework is ISO 3100:2009, published by the International Organization for Standardization (ISO), headquartered in Switzerland. For an ERM framework that is consistent with COSO and ISO, see **https://theirm.org/media/886062 /ISO3100_doc.pdf**, a report that is authored jointly by three major UK risk management associations.

23-3a The Committee of Sponsoring Organizations' (COSO) Framework for Enterprise Risk Management (ERM)

COSO designed its enterprise risk management framework with three dimensions. The first dimension is the organizational level. The COSO framework applies ERM at all levels of an organization, including the corporate level, division levels, business units, and subsidiaries.

The second dimension is the category of objectives. Each organizational level should define its objectives in each of four categories: (1) *strategic objectives,* which are based on the company's mission and overall goals; (2) *operating objectives,* which focus on the selection, implementation, and ongoing execution of projects and other applications of corporate resources; (3) *reporting objectives,* which seek to disseminate accurate and up-to-date information to decision makers inside the company and stakeholders outside the company (such as investors and regulators); and (4) *compliance objectives,* which seek to ensure the company complies with laws and regulatory requirements.

The third dimension is the process of risk management for an objective at a particular level within the organization. The risk management process for each objective has eight components, which we discuss in the following section.

23-3b The Components of the COSO Enterprise Risk Management Framework

The eight components of the COSO ERM process define the way in which an organization approaches and applies risk management.

COMPONENTS 1 AND 2: INTERNAL ENVIRONMENT AND OBJECTIVE SETTING

The first two components are related to a company's culture and mission, including the company's workplace environment, attitude toward risk, and goal-setting process. An important part of these processes is the identification of the amount of risk that a company is willing to take, which often is called the *risk appetite.*

COMPONENT 3: EVENT IDENTIFICATION

You can't manage a source of risk if you don't recognize it. A **risky event** is defined as any uncertain outcome that affects a company's previously defined objectives.[9] For example, risky events include increases in the prices of raw materials, an explosion at a factory, or a loss of customers to a competitor. To prevent overlooking risky events, ERM systems typically define categories and then identify the potential events within those categories. We will take a much closer look at risk categories later.

COMPONENT 4: RISK ASSESSMENT

After identifying a risk, a company should assess the risk. We will describe risk assessment in more detail later, but it always includes estimating both the probability that the event will occur and the resulting impact on the company's objectives. For example, an

---

[9]COSO defines risk as an event that negatively affects an objective, and an opportunity as an event that can positively affect an objective. We don't make that distinction—we define risk as uncertainty, which can result in positive or negative outcomes.

event might be an increase in interest rates, which would affect a company's cost when it issues debt. To assess this risk, the company would begin by forecasting the probabilities of different interest rates at the time it plans to issue the debt, and then estimate the cost of issuing debt at the different interest rates. As another example, an event might be a fire at a warehouse. In this case, a company would estimate the probability of a fire and the resulting cost. The insurance industry often uses the terms *loss frequency* and *loss severity* (the dollar value of each loss) for these concepts.

COMPONENT 5: RISK RESPONSE

After identifying and assessing a risky event, the next steps are to choose a response to the risk and implement that choice. There are several different types of responses, including the following.

Totally Avoid the Activity that Gives Rise to the Risk For example, a company might discontinue a product or service line because the risks outweigh the rewards. This often is the case with pharmaceutical products that have potentially harmful side effects or global expansion into countries with civil unrest.

Reduce the Probability of Occurrence of an Adverse Event The expected loss arising from any risk is a function of both the probability of occurrence and the dollar loss if the adverse event occurs. In some instances, it is possible to reduce the probability that an adverse event will occur. For example, the probability that a fire will occur can be reduced by instituting a fire prevention program, by replacing old electrical wiring, and by using fire-resistant materials in areas with the greatest fire potential.

Reduce the Magnitude of the Loss Associated with an Adverse Event In some instances, companies can take actions to reduce losses even if the event occurs. Continuing with the previous example, the dollar cost associated with a fire can be reduced by such actions as installing sprinkler systems, designing facilities with self-contained fire zones, and locating facilities close to a fire station.

Transfer the Risk to an Insurance Company Often, it is advantageous to insure against risk by transferring it to an insurance company. Even though an insured item's expected loss is the same for its owner and for the insurance company, the insurance company benefits from diversification. For example, an insurance company might provide coverage for tractors, harvesters, and other types of agricultural equipment, which often cost several hundred thousand dollars or more. If the insurance company has a large number of customers, it can predict quite accurately the amounts it will pay in claims and then can set premiums high enough to pay the claims and provide the return required by its investors. In addition, insurance companies can themselves insure parts of their risk by purchasing reinsurance from another insurance company. Therefore, the potential loss of a harvester might be quite risky to a farmer, but it may not be risky to a large insurance company.

However, just because something can be insured does not mean that a company should insure it. In many instances, it might be better for the company to *self-insure*, which means bearing the risk directly rather than paying another party to bear it. In fact, many large companies choose to self-insure, or to insure only the part of an asset's loss that exceeds a certain amount, which is equivalent to an individual who has a large deductible on car or home insurance.

Insurance typically excludes acts of war or terrorism, but this became a major issue after the September 11, 2001, attacks on the World Trade Center and the Pentagon.

Unless possible terrorist targets—including large malls, office buildings, oil refineries, airlines, and ships—can be insured against attacks, lenders may refuse to provide mortgage financing, and that would crimp the economy. Private insurance companies are reluctant to insure these projects, at least without charging prohibitive premiums, so the federal government has been asked to step in and provide terrorist insurance. However, losses due to terrorist attacks are potentially so large that they could bankrupt even strong insurance companies. Therefore, Congress passed the Terrorism Risk Insurance Act (TRIA) in 2002 and has extended it through 2020. Under the TRIA, the federal government and private insurers share the cost of benefits paid on insured losses caused by terrorists.

Transfer the Function that Produces the Risk to a Third Party For example, suppose a furniture manufacturer is concerned about potential liabilities arising from its ownership of a fleet of trucks used to transfer products from its manufacturing plant to various points across the country. One way to eliminate this risk would be to contract with a trucking company to do the shipping, thus passing the risks to a third party.

Share or Eliminate the Risk by Using Derivative Contracts Many companies use derivative contracts to reduce or eliminate an event's risk. For example, a cereal company may use corn or wheat futures to hedge against increases in grain prices. Similarly, financial derivatives can be used to reduce risks that arise from changes in interest rates and exchange rates. As we will describe later, the risk doesn't disappear—it is just taken on by the other party in the derivative contract.

Accept the Risk In some instances, a company will decide to accept a risk because the expected benefits are greater than the expected costs and because the risk doesn't exceed the company's risk appetite. Indeed, accepting risk is the nature of most businesses—if they were riskless, then investors would expect to receive a return only equal to the risk-free rate. Also, some stand-alone risks may be quite large, but they may not contribute much to the total corporate risk if they are not highly correlated with the company's other risks.

COMPONENTS 6, 7, AND 8: CONTROL ACTIVITIES, INFORMATION AND COMMUNICATION, AND MONITORING

The last three components focus on ensuring that risky events are in fact being treated as the risk management plan specifies—it doesn't do much good to develop strategies and tactics if employees don't follow them! For example, a single rogue trader lost €4.9 billion in 2008 at the French bank Société Générale, and another lost £1.5 billion in 2011 at the London branch of UBS (headquartered in Switzerland).

SELF-TEST

Define a risk event.

What are the two stages in risk assessment?

Describe some possible risk responses.

Should a firm insure itself against all of the insurable risks it faces? Explain.

23-4 Categories of Risk Events

Before addressing alternative risk responses to specific risk events, it will be helpful to describe ways to categorize risk.

23-4a Major Categories

Following is a typical list of major categories that are representative of those at several organizations.[10]

1. *Strategy and reputation.* A company's strategic choices simultaneously influence and respond to its competitors' actions, corporate social responsibilities, the public's perception of its activities, and its reputation among suppliers, peers, and customers. ERM addresses the risk inherent in these strategic choices.

2. *Control and compliance.* This category includes risk events related to regulatory requirements, litigation risks, intellectual property rights, reporting accuracy, and internal control systems.

3. *Hazards.* These include fires, floods, riots, acts of terrorism, and other natural or man-made disasters. Notice that hazards have only negative outcomes—an earthquake might destroy a factory, but it isn't going to build one.

4. *Human resources.* Success often depends upon a company's employees. ERM addresses risk events related to employees, including recruiting, succession planning, employee health, and employee safety.

5. *Operations.* A company's operations include supply chains, manufacturing facilities, existing product lines, and business processes. Risk events include supply chain disruptions, equipment failures, product recalls, and changes in customer demand.

6. *Technology.* Technology changes rapidly and is a major source of risk, including risk events related to innovations, technological failures, and IT reliability and security.

7. *Financial management.* This category includes risk events related to (1) foreign exchange risk, (2) commodity price risk, (3) interest rate risk, (4) project selection risk (including major capital expenditures, mergers, and acquisitions), (5) liquidity risk, (6) customer credit risk, and (7) portfolio risk (the risk that a portfolio of financial assets will decrease in value). For the remainder of the chapter, we will focus on the risk events related to financial management, but first we need to describe several other ways to think about risk.

23-4b Dimensions of Risk

Sometimes it is helpful to think about risk events based on different dimensions. For example, several risk management systems classify risk by whether it is driven by external forces or by internal decisions and activities. This is especially helpful in risk identification because it forces managers to look at a broader range of risk events.

Sometimes it is useful to classify risk by whether it is a pure risk that has only a downside (e.g., a hazard, such as a fire) or a speculative risk that has potential positive as well as negative outcomes (e.g., the exchange rate between dollars and euros can go up or down, which would have a big impact on the cash flows of U.S. importers). Most pure risks can be reduced or eliminated with insurance products.

When choosing among different risk responses, it is helpful to determine whether the source of risk is linear or nonlinear. For example, consider an agricultural company with access to a low-cost source of water for irrigation. The company grows corn and can

---

[10]To see the way that several organizations have categorized risk and the ways that surveyors categorize risk, see the following: Mark L. Frigo and Hans Læssøe, "Strategic Risk Management at the LEGO Group," *Strategic Finance*, February 2012, pp. 27–35; Henri Servaes, Ane Tamayo, and Peter Tufano, "The Theory and Practice of Corporate Risk Management," *Journal of Applied Corporate Finance*, Fall 2009, pp. 60–78; Celina Rogers, *The Risk Management Imperative* (Boston, MA: CFO Publishing LLC, 2010), **http://secure.cfo.com/whitepapers/index.cfm/download/14521624**; and Casualty Actuarial Society, *Overview of Risk Management*, 2003, **https://www.casact.org/area/erm/overview.pdf**.

predict its costs and the size of its harvest, but it is exposed to volatility in the price of corn. Notice that this is a linear risk—the company loses money when prices are low and makes money when they are high. We discuss the details later, but the company can enter into derivative contracts that provide positive cash flows when prices are low but create negative cash flows when prices are high. The derivative also has a linear payout, but its payouts are opposite those of the company. The combination of the company's internally generated cash flows from the harvest and its externally generated cash flows from the derivative can reduce or eliminate the company's risk.

In contrast, consider a company in the oil exploration and extraction industry.[11] The company will incur fixed costs and negative cash flows associated with continuing operations when oil prices are too low to justify additional exploration. When oil prices are high, the company incurs fixed costs and also variable costs associated with expanded exploration and extraction. However, when oil prices are high, the company will generate enough positive cash flow to cover its fixed costs and also the new variable costs associated with the additional exploration and extraction. Therefore, the company is exposed to nonlinear risk—it needs additional cash flow to support its ongoing operations only when oil prices are low but not when prices are high. In this situation, the company might be willing to buy a derivative that pays out only when oil prices are low. In other words, the company reduces its nonlinear risk with a nonlinear hedging strategy.

SELF-TEST

List and define the different major categories of risk events.

Should a firm insure itself against all of the insurable risks it faces? Explain.

Explain the difference between a linear risk and a nonlinear risk.

23-5 Foreign Exchange (FX) Risk

Foreign exchange (FX) risk occurs when a company's cash flows are affected by changes in currency exchange rates. This can occur if a company imports materials from other countries or sells its products in other countries. Some smaller companies manage FX risk for each transaction, but most large companies aggregate their transactions and manage their net exposures centrally. For example, if one division is selling goods denominated in Canadian dollars and another division is purchasing goods denominated in Canadian dollars, the company would net out the two transactions and just manage any remaining exposure.

The primary tool used to manage FX risk is a **forward contract**, which is an agreement in which one party agrees to buy an item at a specific price on a specific future date and another party agrees to sell the item at the agreed-upon terms. *Goods are actually delivered under forward contracts.* In the case of foreign exchange, the goods are the amount of foreign currency specified in the contract, paid for with the other currency specified in the contract.

Historically, FX trading has been directly between two parties using customized contracts with unique amounts and dates and no central market. This requires that both parties be morally and financially strong to minimize the danger that one party will default on the contract—this is called **counterparty risk**. In such contracts, major banks often act as counterparties for their customers. For example, a bank might agree to buy euros in 30 days at a price of 1.24 dollars per euro from one customer and agree to sell euros in 30 days at a rate of 1.25 dollars per euro to another customer. Depending on the change in

---

[11]See Kenneth A. Froot, David S. Scharfstein, and Jeremy Stein, "A Framework for Risk Management," *Journal of Applied Corporate Finance*, Fall 1994, pp. 22–32; also see the paper by Servaes et al., cited in footnote 9.

the euro exchange rate, the bank will make money on one of the contracts and lose money on the other, netting only the spread on the difference in prices. This matching of contracts allows banks to reduce their net exposure to exchange rate volatility, but the bank is still exposed to counterparty risk from the customers.

The failure to manage counterparty risk was one of the causes of the 2007 global financial crisis. For example, Lehman Brothers was a counterparty to many other financial institutions in a variety of derivative contracts, so Lehman's failure caused distress at financial institutions throughout the world. In response to this and other causes of the financial crisis, the Dodd-Frank Consumer Protection Act was passed in 2010. One of its provisions required the Commodities and Futures Trading Commission (CFTC) to establish, among other things, a mechanism for centralized clearing of foreign exchange derivatives contracts, such as forward contracts. The CME Group is one company that provides this clearing function in the United States and acts as the counterparty to all trades that it clears. As of mid-2017, the CME Group clears 26 cash-settled forward contracts involving 20 different currencies.[12]

Foreign exchange transactions are a big business. Contracts are based on the total amount of currency to be delivered at expiration, which is called the **notional value**. At the beginning of 2018, the notional value of over-the-counter FX derivatives was about $87 trillion![13] The total is even larger if customized FX contracts between two parties are considered.

To illustrate how foreign exchange contracts are used, suppose GE arranges to buy electric motors from a European manufacturer on terms that call for GE to pay 10 million euros in 180 days. GE would not want to give up the free trade credit, but if the euro appreciated against the dollar during the next 6 months, then the dollar cost of the 10 million euros would rise. GE could hedge the transaction by buying a forward contract under which it agreed to buy the 10 million euros in 180 days at a fixed dollar price, which would lock in the dollar cost of the motors. This transaction would probably be conducted through a money center bank, which would be GE's counterparty. The bank would also try to reduce its own risk from the transaction by finding a European company that needed dollars in 6 months.

SELF-TEST

What is a forward contract?

Explain how a company can use forward contracts to eliminate FX risk.

What is counterparty risk?

23-6 Commodity Price Risk

WWW

See the CME Group's Web site, www.cmegroup.com, for a wealth of information on the operation and history of the exchange.

Many companies use or produce commodities, including agricultural products, energy, metals, and lumber. Because commodity prices can be quite volatile, many companies manage their exposure to commodity price risk. Before describing specific ways to

---

[12]When a traditional forward for delivery contract expires, the two currencies are exchanged. In a cash-settled forward contract, however, the currencies are never exchanged. Rather, the difference between the contract price and the spot price at expiration is converted to U.S. dollars at the prevailing spot price and then these dollars are paid or received. The clearinghouse would require some form of collateral to reduce the risk that one of the parties didn't pay. In addition, cash-settled forward contracts can be "marked to market" every day like a futures contract, and this further reduces the clearinghouse's risk. See the CME Group's Web site, **www.CMEGroup.com**, for more information on their clearing mechanism and the products it clears.

[13]See the Bank for International Settlements, **www.bis.org/statistics/derstats.htm**.

manage commodity price risk, we begin with a brief overview of futures markets in the United States to illustrate some key concepts.

23-6a An Overview of Futures Markets

As we noted earlier, Midwest farmers in the early 1800s were concerned about the price they would receive for their wheat when they sold it in the fall, and millers were concerned about the price they would have to pay. Each party soon realized that the risks they faced could be reduced if they established a price earlier in the year. Accordingly, mill agents began going out to the Wheat Belt with contracts that called for the farmers to deliver grain at a predetermined price, and both parties benefited from the transaction in the sense that their risks were reduced. The farmers could concentrate on growing their crop without worrying about the price of grain, and the millers could concentrate on their milling operations.

These early agreements were between two parties who arranged the transactions themselves. Soon, though, intermediaries came into the picture. The Chicago Board of Trade, founded in 1848, was an early marketplace where *futures dealers* helped make a market in futures contracts.

A **futures contract** is similar to a forward contract in that two parties are involved, with one party taking a long position (which obligates the party to buy the underlying asset) and the other party taking a short position (which obligates the party to sell the asset). However, there are three key differences. First, gains and losses on futures contracts are recognized daily and the losing counterparty must pay the broker for the loss. This **mark-to-market** requirement for futures contracts greatly reduces the risk of default that exists with forward contracts because daily price changes are usually smaller than the cumulative change over the contract's life. For example, if a corn futures contract has a price of $4.00 per bushel and the price goes up to $4.10 the next day, a party with a short position must pay the $0.10 difference, and a party with a long position would receive the difference. This marking-to-market occurs daily until the delivery date. To see that this procedure does in fact lock in the price, suppose that the price doesn't change again. On the delivery date, the party with the short position would sell corn at the current price of $4.10. Because the short seller had already paid $0.10 from daily marking-to-market, the short seller's net cash flow is $4.00. The party with the long position would have to buy corn at the current price of $4.10, but because the purchaser had already received $0.10 from cumulative daily marking-to-market, the net purchase price would be $4.00.

The second major difference between a forward contract and a futures contract is that physical delivery of the underlying asset in a futures contract is virtually never taken—the two parties simply settle up with cash for the difference between the contracted price and the actual price on the expiration date. The third difference is that futures contracts are generally standardized instruments that are traded on exchanges, whereas forward contracts are usually tailor-made, negotiated between two parties, and not traded after they have been signed.

The needs of farmers and millers allowed a **natural hedge**, defined as a situation in which aggregate risk can be reduced by derivatives transactions between two parties. Natural hedges occur when futures are traded between cotton farmers and cotton mills, copper mines and copper fabricators, importers and foreign manufacturers for currency exchange rates, electric utilities and coal mines, and oil producers and oil users. In such situations, hedging reduces aggregate risk and thus benefits the economy.

There are two basic types of hedges: (1) **long hedges**, in which futures contracts are *bought* (obligating the hedger to purchase the underlying asset), providing protection against price increases, and (2) **short hedges**, where a firm or individual *sells* futures contracts (obligating the hedger to sell the underlying asset), providing protection against falling prices.

Not all participants in the futures markets are hedgers. **Speculation in derivatives** involves betting on future price movements, and futures are used instead of the commodities because of the leverage inherent in the contract. For example, a speculator might buy corn for $4 a bushel. If corn goes up to $4.40, the speculator has a 10% return (assuming rats don't eat the corn before it can be sold).

Now consider a speculator who takes a long position in a futures contract for 5,000 bushels at $4 per bushel. The exchange requires an investor to put up a **margin requirement** to ensure that the investor will not renege on the daily marking-to-market. However, the margin is quite small relative to the size of a contract. For this example, assume the margin is $1,100, but the total amount of corn is valued at $20,000 = $4(5,000).[14] If the price goes up to $4.40, the profit is $2,000 = ($4.40 − $4.00)(5,000). The rate of return on the invested margin is 82% = ($2,000 − $1,100)/$1,100. The 82% return on the futures contract is much greater than the 10% return on the underlying asset. Of course, any losses on the contract also would be magnified.

At first blush, one might think that the appearance of speculators would increase risk, but this is not necessarily true. Speculators add capital and players to the market. Thus, to the extent that speculators broaden the market and make hedging possible, they help decrease risk for those who seek to avoid it. Unlike the natural hedge, however, risk is not eliminated. Instead, it is transferred from the hedgers to the speculators.

Today, futures contracts are available on hundreds of real and financial assets traded on dozens of U.S. and international exchanges, the largest of which are the Chicago Board of Trade (CBOT) and the Chicago Mercantile Exchange (CME), both of which are now part of the CME Group. Futures contracts are divided into two classes, **commodity futures** and **financial futures**. Commodity futures include oil, various grains, oilseeds, livestock, meats, fibers, metals, and wood. Financial futures, which were first traded in 1975, include Treasury bills, notes, bonds, certificates of deposit, Eurodollar deposits, foreign currencies, and stock indexes. We describe how financial futures can reduce interest rate risk in a later section.

23-6b Using Futures Contracts to Reduce Commodity Price Exposure

We will illustrate commodity hedging at Porter Electronics, which uses large quantities of copper and several precious metals in its manufacturing operations. Suppose that in May 2019 Porter foresaw a need for 100,000 pounds of copper in March 2020 for use in fulfilling a fixed-price contract to supply solar power cells to the U.S. government. The spot price of copper in May is $4.08. Therefore, it would cost Porter $408,000 to purchase the

---

[14]The CME requires that an investor make an initial deposit at the time the investor takes a position in a contract. The dollar value of the initial margin might decline if the investor uses some of it to pay for daily marking-to-market. However, the investor must not let the amount on deposit drop below a specified amount, which is called the maintenance margin. The CME specifies the maintenance margin for each contract. For example, if you go to the CME Web site (**www.cmegroup.com**) and search for a contract, such as corn futures, you will be directed to a page with information about the contract, with an option to find the maintenance margin. For corn, it is $750 in 2017. For hedgers, the initial margin is set at 100% of the maintenance margin; for speculators, the initial margin is set at 110% of the maintenance margin (see **www.cmegroup.com/clearing/margins /initial-margin-requirements.html**). These margins requirement change over time as the value of the underlying commodity changes. For example, the corn margin was $3,750 in July of 2012, when corn spot prices were near record highs.

copper in March if the prices don't change: 100,000($4.08) = $408,000. However, Porter's managers are concerned that a strike by Chilean copper miners might occur, which would raise the price of copper in world markets and reduce Porter's expected profit.

Porter could go ahead and buy the copper it will need to fulfill the contract, but it would have to borrow money to pay for the copper and then pay for storage. As an alternative, Porter could hedge against increasing copper prices in the futures market. COMEX, a division of The New York Commodity Exchange, trades standard copper futures contracts of 25,000 pounds each. Thus, Porter could buy four contracts (go long) for delivery in March 2020. Suppose these contracts were trading in May 2019 for about $4.10 per pound.

What happens to Porter's cash flows if copper prices rise to $4.30 by the delivery date? Porter would have to spend $430,000 to buy the copper it needs. However, Porter would have made a profit on its futures contracts of $0.20 per pound ($4.30 − $4.10 = $0.20).[15] With contracts for 100,000 pounds, Porter's profit would be $20,000. Therefore, Porter's net cost to purchase the copper would be equal to the $430,000 it actually paid minus the $20,000 profit on the contract, which is a net cost of $410,000.

Now suppose copper prices fell to $4.00 per pound. Porter would have to pay $400,000 for the copper, but would have lost $10,000 on the futures contract: ($4.00 − $4.10) (100,000) = −$10,000. Porter's net cost would have been equal to the $400,000 it paid for the copper plus the $10,000 it lost on the futures contract, for a net cost of $410,000.

As this example shows, hedging in the copper futures market locks in Porter's net cost of raw materials at $410,000, eliminating any exposure to changes in copper prices. However, if copper prices had remained at their original spot price of $4.08, Porter would have paid only $408,000 for copper instead of its net cost of $410,000 with the hedge. Therefore, the hedge came with a cost: Porter locked in the price it paid for copper, but that fixed price might have been higher than the expected price.

Many other companies, such as Alcoa with aluminum and Archer Daniels Midland with grains, routinely use the futures markets to reduce the risks associated with price volatility.

23-6c Options and Options on Futures

Futures contracts and options are similar to one another—so similar that people often confuse the two. Therefore, it is useful to compare the two instruments. A *futures contract* is a definite agreement on the part of one party to buy something on a specific date and at a specific price, and the other party agrees to sell on the same terms. No matter how low or how high the market price goes, the two parties must trade at the agreed-upon contract price, and the losses of one party must exactly equal to the gains of the other. In addition, a dollar increase in the futures price has exactly the opposite effect of a dollar decrease in the futures price. A hedge constructed using futures contracts is called a **symmetric hedge** because of this feature—the payoff from an increase in the futures price is exactly opposite of the payoff from a decrease in the futures price. For this reason, symmetric hedges are typically used to provide a fixed transaction price at some date in the future and are ideal for managing a risk that is linear.

For an example using a futures contract to construct a symmetric hedge, suppose an agricultural company has access to a source of low-cost water for irrigation. The company can predict its costs and the size of its corn harvest but is exposed to price risk. The company could sell futures contracts (take a short position, which obligates it to sell corn) for delivery when the corn is harvested in 6 months. If the corn price (and hence the corn

---

[15]To focus the example on the primary impact of hedging, we have ignored daily marking-to-market.

futures price) decreases over the 6 months, then the company will receive less when selling the corn but will make up the difference when closing out the futures contract. If instead the corn price increases, then the company will make more money when selling the corn in 6 months but will lose money when closing out the futures contract. In this way the ending value of the position doesn't depend on the corn price in 6 months, and so the amount received for selling the corn in 6 months is locked in.

An *option*, on the other hand, gives someone the right to buy (call) or sell (put) an asset, but the holder of the option completes the transaction only if it is advantageous to do so. The payoff from a hedge constructed using options will be different from a futures hedge because of this option feature. As discussed in Chapter 8, the payoff from a call option increases as the price of the underlying asset increases, but if the underlying asset price decreases, then the most the option holder can lose is the amount invested in the option. That is, upside gains are unlimited but downside losses are capped at the amount invested in the option. For this reason, an option is said to create an **asymmetric hedge**— it hedges price changes in one direction more than price changes in the other. As such, options are ideal for managing nonlinear risks.

Options could be created and traded on tangible assets like 5,000 bushels of corn or 25,000 pounds of copper, but settlement when the options on commodities are exercised would be very expensive and cumbersome. Imagine exercising a call option on 25,000 pounds of copper and having to take delivery of the copper! Instead, the commodities exchanges trade options on futures contracts rather than options on the commodities themselves. So rather than purchasing a call option on 5,000 bushels of corn, a hedger or speculator would purchase an option on a corn futures contract. If the hedger exercises the call option, then a long futures contract plus the difference between the current futures price and the strike price on the option is delivered rather than the corn itself.

To see how a futures option works, suppose 6-month corn futures (May expiration) are trading at $4 per bushel. A 3-month call option on this futures contract with a strike price of $4.10 per bushel might sell for $0.20. Note the following: (1) The futures contract is for 5,000 bushels, so it would cost $0.20(5,000) = $1,000 to purchase this option. (2) The maturity of the option must be no longer than the maturity of the futures contract. (3) This option is out of the money; it can be exercised profitably only if the May corn futures price rises above $4.10.

If over the next 3 months, corn futures prices rise to $4.50 and the option is exercised, the holder of the option will receive from the seller a May corn futures contract at $4.50 plus a payment of ($4.50 − $4.10)(5,000) = $2,000. If the May corn futures price had, instead, declined, then the option would be allowed to expire without being exercised, and no cash or futures contracts would change hands.

For an example of an asymmetric hedge, suppose the agricultural company did not have access to irrigation but operated many farms in different states. A widespread drought would reduce the size of the harvest but probably would cause the price of corn to increase due to the lower supply. If this happened, the company's revenues would fall but would not be eliminated—the higher corn price would partially compensate for the smaller harvest. This means the company faces nonlinear risk with respect to corn prices. Instead of going long in a futures contract, the company might buy a put option on a corn futures contract, giving the company the right to sell a futures contract at a fixed price. If the price of corn decreased, the value of the put option would increase, and the profits on the option would offset the loss from selling the corn at the lower price. However, if corn prices increased, then the investor would let the put option expire and simply sell its smaller harvest at the higher price.

How does a futures contract differ from a forward contract?

What is a "natural hedge"? Give some examples of natural hedges.

Suppose a company knows the quantity of a commodity that it will produce. Describe how it might hedge using a futures contract.

23-7 Interest Rate Risk

Interest rates can be quite volatile, exposing a company to interest rate risk, especially if the company is planning to issue debt or if the company has floating-rate debt. The following sections describe ways to manage interest rate risk, but we begin with the London Interbank Offered Rate (LIBOR) and the Secured Overnight Financing Rate (SOFR).

23-7a The London Interbank Offered Rate (LIBOR) and the Secured Overnight Financing Rate (SOFR)

LIBOR might possibly be the most important number currently reported in financial markets because so many derivative contracts base payments on LIBOR. Some analysts estimate that over $370 trillion of derivatives are linked to LIBOR.

Before 2014, LIBOR was based on lending rates that selected banks reported to the British Bankers Association (BBA). To make a long story short, employees at some of these banks committed fraud when reporting the rates. Several bank CEOs lost their jobs and their banks were fined about $9 billion. Now the Intercontinental Exchange (ICE) publishes ICE LIBOR rates based on a more robust survey methodology. However, it is not clear whether any version of LIBOR will remain the rate of choice when setting contract terms.

As a potential replacement for LIBOR, the U.S. Federal Reserve created the **Secured Overnight Financing Rate (SOFR)**, which is based on actual transactions of overnight **repurchase agreements** which are commonly called **repos**. The typical overnight repo is a contract in which the owner of Treasury securities sells them to a counterparty but agrees to repurchase them the next day at a slightly higher price. The repo market is huge and SOFR is based on actual transactions, so no human judgement is involved. The Fed began publishing SOFR in April 2018 and swaps based on SOFR began trading several months later. Time will tell whether most derivatives are eventually based on the ICE LIBOR, SOFR, or some other rate.

23-7b Using Futures Contracts to Manage the Risk of Debt Issuances

To illustrate, assume that it is May and that Carson Foods is considering a plan to issue $10,000,000 of 20-year bonds in September to finance a capital expenditure program. The interest rate would be 9% paid semiannually if the bonds were issued today. However, the market interest rate might be higher when the bonds are actually issued. Carson would have to issue the bonds with a higher coupon rate than expected, causing Carson's financing costs to increase. Carson can protect itself against a rise in rates by hedging in the futures market using an interest rate futures contract.

INTEREST RATES FUTURES

To illustrate how interest rate futures work, consider the CBOT's contract on Treasury bonds. The basic contract is for $100,000 par value of a hypothetical 6% coupon,

TABLE 23-1
Example of Futures Prices (Treasury Bonds: $100,000; Pts. 32nds and ½ 32nds of 100%) in May

Delivery Month/Year (1)	Settle (2)	Change (3)	Open (4)	High (5)	Low (6)	Estimated Volume (7)	Open Interest (8)
Jun-20	128'120	0'140	128'060	129'110	127'300	500,000	640,000
Sep-20	127'110	0'150	127'010	127'310	126'280	300,000	95,000
Dec-20	126'160	0'170	126'160	126'160	126'160	0	50

semiannual payment Treasury bond with 20 years to maturity.[16] Table 23-1 shows illustrative quotes for Treasury bond futures.

The first column of Table 23-1 shows the delivery month and year. Column 2 shows the last price of the day, also called the *settlement* price, and the next column shows the change in price from the previous day. Treasury futures are quoted in percent of par plus 32nd of a percent of par with the smallest price increment ½ of a 32nd of a percent of par. For example, the settlement price for the September contract, 127'110, means 127 plus $^{11.0}$/$_{32}$, or 127.343750%, of par. The change was 0'150, which means the September 2020 contract's last price of the day was $^{15.0}$/$_{32}$ higher than the previous day's last trade, which must have been at 126'280. The next three columns show the opening, high, and low prices for the day. Column 7 shows the day's estimated trading volume. Notice that most of the trading occurs in the contract with the nearest delivery date. Finally, Column 8 shows the "open interest," which is the number of contracts outstanding.

To illustrate, we focus on the Treasury bonds for September delivery. The settlement price was 127.343750% of the $100,000 contract value. Thus, the price at which one could buy $100,000 face value of 6%, 20-year Treasury bonds to be delivered in December was 127.343750%($100,000) = $127,343.75.

The contract price increased by $^{15.0}$/$_{32}$ of 1% of $100,000 from the previous day's price, so if you had bought the contract yesterday, you would have made $468.75 = ($^{15.0}$/$_{32}$)(0.01) ($100,000). There were 95,000 contracts outstanding, representing a total value of about 95,000($127,343.75) ≈ $12 trillion.

Note that the contract increased by $^{15.0}$/$_{32}$ of a percent on this particular day. Why would the value of the bond futures contract increase? Bond prices increase when interest rates fall, so interest rates must have fallen on that day. Moreover, we can calculate the implied rate inherent in the futures price. Recall that the contract relates to a hypothetical 20-year, semiannual payment, 6% coupon bond. The settlement price was 127.343750% of par, so a $1,000 par bond would have a price of 127.343750%($1,000) = $1,273.4375. We can solve for r_d by using the following equation:

resource

See *Ch23 Tool Kit.xlsx* on the textbook's Web site for all calculations.

$$\sum_{t=1}^{40} \frac{\$30}{(1 + r_d/2)^t} + \frac{\$1,000}{(1 + r_d/2)^{40}} = \$1,273.4375$$

[16]The coupon rate on the hypothetical bond was changed to 6% from 8% in March 2000. The CBOT contract doesn't specify a 20-year bond but instead allows delivery of any noncallable bond with a remaining maturity greater than 15 years (or callable bond that is not callable for at least 15 years) and less than 25 years. Rather than simply deliver a bond, which might have an interest rate other than 6%, the actual bond price is adjusted by a conversion factor to make it equivalent to a 6% bond that is trading at par. Because the average maturity of bonds that are eligible for delivery is about 20 years, we use a 20-year maturity for the hypothetical bond in the futures contract. For even longer maturity hedging, the CBOT also has the Ultra T-Bond contract, which allows for delivery of a Treasury bond of at least 25 years to maturity.

Using *Excel* or a financial calculator, input N = 40, PV = −1273.4375, PMT = 30, and FV = 1000; then solve for I/YR = 2.0004%. This is the semiannual rate, which is equivalent to a nominal annual rate of 4.0007%, or approximately 4.00%.

The previous day's last (settlement) price was 126'280, or 126.87500%, for a bond price of $1,268.7500 = 126.87500%($1,000). Setting N = 40, PV = −1268.7500, PMT = 30, and FV = 1000 and then solving for I/YR = 2.0150% implies an annual yield of 4.0300%, or approximately 4.03%. Therefore, interest rates fell from 4.03% to 4.00%. This decline in rates was only 0.03 percentage points, but that was enough to increase the value of the contract by $468.75. Rather than discuss changes in percentage points, financial traders use **basis points**, with 100 basis points equal to 1 percentage point. Therefore, the decline in rates was 3 basis points.

At the time of the quotes in Table 23-1, which was May, the yield on a 20-year T-bond was about 3.90%. But as we just calculated, the implied yield on the September futures contract was about 4.00%. The September yield reflects investors' beliefs in May as to what the interest rate level will be in September: The marginal trader in the futures market is predicting a 10-basis-point increase in yields between May and September. That prediction could, of course, turn out to be incorrect.

For example, suppose that the implied yields in the futures market had fallen by 50 basis points from May to August—say, from 4.00% to 3.50%. Inputting N = 40, I/YR = 3.5/2 = 1.75, PMT = 30, and FV = 1000 and then solving for PV = −1,357.4279 shows that the September contract would be worth about $1,357.4279 per bond in August if implied yields fell by 50 basis points. Thus, the contract's value would have increased from $127,343.75 to $135,742.79, a gain of about $8,399: $135,742.79 − $127,343.75 ≈ $8,399.

HEDGING WITH TREASURY BOND FUTURES CONTRACTS

Recall that Carson Foods plans to issue $10,000,000 of 9% semiannual 20-year bonds in September and would like to protect itself from a possible increase in interest rates by using T-bond futures contracts. Rising interest rates cause bond prices to fall, and thus decrease the value of bond futures contracts. Therefore, Carson can guard against an *increase* in interest rates by taking a short position on a T-bond futures contract—if rates go up, Carson will receive a cash flow from the futures contract equal to the original futures price less the now-lower futures price.

resource

See Ch23 Tool Kit.xlsx on the textbook's Web site for all calculations.

Carson would choose a futures contract on the security most similar to the one it plans to issue, long-term bonds, and so would use the September Treasury bond futures. In the previous section, we calculated the price of a contract, which was $127,343.75. Because Carson plans to issue $10,000,000 of bonds and because each contract is worth $127,343.75, Carson will sell $10,000,000/$127,343.75 = 78.528 ≈ 79 contracts for delivery in September.[17] The total value of the contracts is 79($127,343.75) = $10,060,156, which is very close to the value of the bonds Carson wants to issue.

Now suppose that in September, when Carson issues its bonds, renewed fears of inflation have pushed interest rates up by 100 basis points. What would the bond proceeds be if Carson still tried to issue 9% coupon bonds when the market requires a 10% rate of return? We can find the total value of the offering with a financial calculator, inputting N = 40, I/YR = 5, PMT = −450000, and FV = −10000000 and then solving for PV = 9,142,046. Therefore, bonds with a 9% coupon, based upon its original plans, would bring proceeds of only $9,142,046, because investors now require a 10% return. Because Carson would have to issue $10 million worth of bonds at a 10% rate, Carson's proceeds would be less

---

[17]Carson will have to put up a margin and pay brokerage commissions. To keep the example focused on the primary issue, which is the impact of changing interest rates, we will ignore margins and commissions.

than expected: $857,954 = $10,000,000 − $9,142,046 as a result of delaying the financing. Therefore, Carson would have to issue additional bonds to raise the required $10,000,000. In other words, the increase in interest rates resulted in cost to Carson of $857,954.

Alternatively, we can estimate Carson's cost of delaying by calculating the present value of the incremental payments Carson must make. The increase in interest rates from 9% to 10% would cause the semiannual coupon payments to go up from $45 to $50 on a per-bond basis. For 10,000 bonds, the total incremental semiannual coupon payments are $50,000 = ($50 − $45)(10,000). We can find the present value of these incremental payments by inputting N = 40, I/YR = 5, PMT = −50000, and FV = 0 and then solving for PV = −857954 = −$857,954, which is the same cost found by the first method. Intuitively, this is because the first method identifies the difference between an asset's par value and its market value given a change in interest rates. This difference can be thought of as the extra amount of value that would need to be added to bring the market value up to par. One way to add value would be to increase the payments, which is what the second approach does.

Either way, Carson incurs a cost of $857,954 due to the increase in rates. However, the increase in interest rates would also bring about a change in the value of Carson's short position in the futures contract. When interest rates increase, the value of the futures contract will fall. If the interest rate on the futures contract also increased by the same full percentage point, from 4.0007% to 5.0007%, then the new contract value can be found by inputting N = 40, I/YR = 5.0007/2 = 2.50035, PMT = −3000, and FV = −100000 and then solving for PV = 112,541.86 per contract. With 79 contracts, the total value of the position is thus $8,890,806.94 = 79($112,541.86). Carson would then close its position in the futures market by repurchasing at a futures price of $8,890,806.94 the contracts that it earlier sold at $10,060,156.00, giving it a profit of $1,169,349.06.

Thus, Carson would offset the loss on the bond issue. In fact, in our example Carson more than offsets the loss, pocketing an additional $311,395.06 = $1,169,349.06− $857,954.[18] Of course, if interest rates had fallen, then Carson would have lost on its futures position, but this loss would have been offset because Carson could now sell its bonds with a lower coupon.

If futures contracts existed on Carson's own debt and if interest rates moved identically in the spot and futures markets, then the firm could construct a **perfect hedge** in which gains on the futures contract would exactly offset losses on the bonds. In reality, it is virtually impossible to construct perfect hedges, because in most cases the underlying asset is not identical to the futures asset; and even when the assets are identical, prices (and interest rates) may not move exactly together in the spot and futures markets.[19]

---

[18]Carson would have to pay taxes on the profit from the futures contract, so the after-tax value of the futures transaction can be found by multiplying the pre-tax profit by (1 − T). However, Carson would get to deduct the larger additional coupon payments from its income. To find the present value of the after-tax additional coupon payments, we multiply the additional pre-tax coupons by (1 − T) and calculate the present value. This gives the same result as first finding the present value of the additional pre-tax coupons and then multiplying the present value by (1 − T). In other words, the pre-tax cost of delaying and the pre-tax profit from the futures contract should be multiplied by (1 − T) to estimate the after-tax effectiveness of the hedge.

[19]In this example, Carson hedged a 20-year bond with a T-bond futures contract. Rather than simply matching on maturity, it would be more accurate to match on duration (see **Web Extension 5C**, available on the textbook's Web site, for a discussion of duration). A matching duration in the futures contracts could be accomplished by taking positions in the T-bond futures contract and in another financial futures contract, such as the 10-Year Treasury note contract. Because Carson's bond had a 20-year maturity, matching on maturity instead of duration provided a good hedge. If Carson's bond had a different maturity, then it would be essential to match on duration.

Observe also that if Carson had been planning an equity offering and if its stock tended to move fairly closely with one of the stock indexes, then the company could have hedged against falling stock prices by selling the index future. Even better, if options on Carson's stock were traded in the options market, then it could use options rather than futures to hedge against falling stock prices.

The futures and options markets permit flexibility in the timing of financial transactions: The firm can be protected, at least partially, against changes that occur between the time a decision is reached and the time the transaction is completed. However, this protection has a cost—the firm must pay commissions. Whether or not the protection is worth the cost is a matter of judgment. The decision to hedge also depends on management's risk aversion and on the company's strength and ability to assume the risk in question.[20]

23-7c Using Interest Rate Swaps: Managing Floating versus Fixed Rates

Suppose that Company S has a 20-year, $100 million floating-rate bond outstanding and that Company F has a $100 million, 20-year, fixed-rate issue outstanding. Thus, each company has an obligation to make a stream of interest payments, but one payment stream is fixed while the other will vary as interest rates change in the future. This situation is shown in Panel A of Figure 23-1.

Now suppose that Company S has stable cash flows and wants to lock in its cost of debt. Company F has cash flows that fluctuate with the economy, rising when the economy is strong and falling when it is weak. Recognizing that interest rates also move up and down with the economy, Company F has concluded it would be better off with variable-rate debt. Suppose the companies agreed to swap their payment obligations. Panel B of Figure 23-1 shows that the net cash flows for Company S are at a fixed rate and those for Company F are based on a floating rate. Company S would now have to make fixed payments, which are consistent with its stable cash inflows, and Company F would have a floating obligation, which for it is less risky.

In practice, the two companies would not deal with one another directly; instead, each company would enter into a swap with a large bank. For example, a bank might offer to swap LIBOR for a fixed payment of 2.5%.[21] In this example, Company S would pay the bank a fixed payment equal to 2.5% of the amount Company S borrowed at a floating rate, and the bank would pay Company S an amount equal to the current LIBOR rate multiplied by the amount Company S borrowed. Company F would enter into a similar contract with a bank, except Company F would make a floating rate payment to the bank (based on LIBOR), and the bank would make a fixed payment to Company F. Of course, the bank will charge a fee for this service.

A **swap** is just what the name implies—two parties agree to swap something, generally obligations to make specified payment streams.

The previous example, which is an **interest rate swap**, illustrates how swaps can reduce risks by allowing each company to match the variability of its interest payments with that of its cash flows. However, there are also situations in which swaps can reduce both the risk and the effective cost of debt. For example, Antron Corporation, which has a high

---

[20]For additional insights into the use of financial futures for hedging, see Mark G. Castelino, Jack C. Francis, and Avner Wolf, "Cross-Hedging: Basis Risk and Choice of the Optimal Hedging Vehicle," *The Financial Review,* May 1991, pp. 179–210.

[21]Recall from Chapter 1 that the U.K. authority responsible for regulating LIBOR announced in 2016 that it would cease to regulate LIBOR at the end of 2021. As a potential replacement, the U.S. Federal Reserve created the third rate, SOFR, which the Fed began publishing in April 2018.

FIGURE 23-1
Cash Flows under a Swap

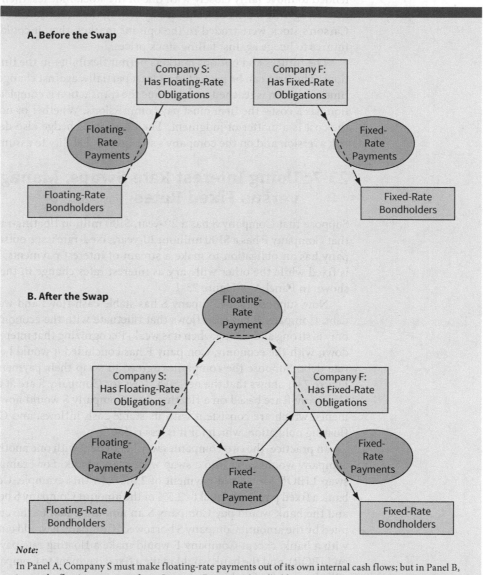

A. Before the Swap

Company S: Has Floating-Rate Obligations

Company F: Has Fixed-Rate Obligations

Floating-Rate Payments

Fixed-Rate Payments

Floating-Rate Bondholders

Fixed-Rate Bondholders

B. After the Swap

Floating-Rate Payment

Company S: Has Floating-Rate Obligations

Company F: Has Fixed-Rate Obligations

Floating-Rate Payments

Fixed-Rate Payment

Fixed-Rate Payments

Floating-Rate Bondholders

Fixed-Rate Bondholders

Note:

In Panel A, Company S must make floating-rate payments out of its own internal cash flows; but in Panel B, it uses the floating payments from Company F to pay its bondholders. Company F has a reversed position. After the swap, S has de facto fixed payments, which are consistent with its stable internal flows, and F has floating payments, which are consistent with its fluctuating flows.

credit rating, can issue either floating-rate debt at LIBOR + 1% or fixed-rate debt at 6%. Bosworth Industries is less creditworthy, so its cost for floating-rate debt is LIBOR + 1.5% and its fixed-rate cost is 6.4%. Owing to the nature of Antron's operations, its CFO has decided that the firm would be better off with fixed-rate debt; meanwhile, Bosworth's CFO prefers floating-rate debt. Paradoxically, both firms can benefit by issuing the type of debt they do not want and then swapping their payment obligations.

First, each company will issue an identical amount of debt, which is called the **notional principal**. Even though Antron wants fixed-rate debt, it issues floating-rate debt at LIBOR + 1%, and Bosworth issues fixed-rate debt at 6.4%. Next, the two companies enter

TABLE 23-2
Anatomy of an Interest Rate Swap

Antron's Payments: Borrows Floating, Swaps for Fixed		Bosworth's Payments: Borrows Fixed, Swaps for Floating	
Payment to lender	−(LIBOR + 1%)	Payment to lender	−6.40% fixed
Payment from Bosworth	+LIBOR	Payment from Antron	+4.95% fixed
Payment to Bosworth	−4.95% fixed	Payment to Antron	−LIBOR
Net payment by Antron	−5.95% fixed	Net payment by Bosworth	−(LIBOR + 1.45%)

into an interest rate swap.[22] Assume the debt maturities are 5 years, which means the length of this swap will also be 5 years. By convention, the floating-rate payments of most swaps are based on LIBOR, with the fixed rate adjusted upward or downward to reflect credit risk and the term structure. The riskier the company that will receive the floating-rate payments, the higher the fixed-rate payment it must make. In our example, Antron will be receiving floating-rate payments from Bosworth, and those payments will be set at LIBOR multiplied by the notional principal. Then, payments will be adjusted every 6 months to reflect changes in the LIBOR rate.

The fixed payment that Antron must make to Bosworth is set (that is, "fixed") for the duration of the swap at the time the contract is signed, and it depends primarily on two factors: (1) the level of fixed interest rates at the time of the agreement and (2) the relative creditworthiness of the two companies.

In our example, assume interest rates and creditworthiness are such that 4.95% is the appropriate fixed swap rate for Antron, so it will make 4.95% fixed-rate payments to Bosworth. In turn, Bosworth will pay the LIBOR rate to Antron. Table 23-2 shows the net rates paid by each participant, and Figure 23-2 graphs the flows. Note that Antron ends

FIGURE 23-2
The Antron/Bosworth Swap

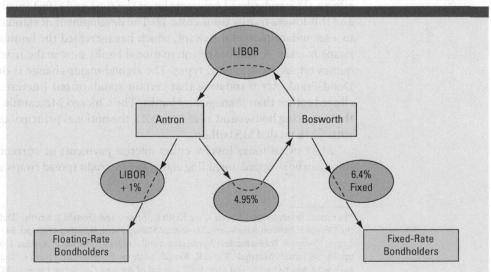

[22]Such transactions are generally arranged by large money center banks, and payments are made to the bank, which in turn pays the interest on the original loans. The bank assumes the credit risk and guarantees the payments should one of the parties default. For its services, the bank receives a percentage of the payments as its fee. In addition, the CME clears swaps similar to these.

up making fixed payments, which it desires, but because of the swap, the rate paid is 5.95% versus the 6% rate it would have paid had it issued fixed-rate debt directly. At the same time, the swap leaves Bosworth with floating-rate debt, which it wants, but at a rate of LIBOR + 1.45% versus the LIBOR + 1.50% it would have paid on directly issued floating-rate debt. As this example illustrates, swaps can sometimes lower the interest rate paid by each party.

Swaps like this are called "plain vanilla" swaps, and the CME Group now serves as a clearing agent for these types and other standardized swaps. This means that Antron and Bosworth would actually make payments to and receive payments from the CME Clearinghouse rather than to and from each other.

Currency swaps are special types of interest rate swaps. To illustrate, suppose Company A, an American firm, had issued $100 million of dollar-denominated bonds in the United States to fund an investment in Germany. Meanwhile, Company G, a German firm, had issued $100 million of euro-denominated bonds in Germany to make an investment in the United States. Company A would earn euros but be required to make payments in dollars, and Company G would be in the opposite situation. Thus, both companies would be exposed to exchange rate risk. However, both companies' risks would be eliminated if they swapped payment obligations.

Originally, swaps were arranged between companies by money center banks, which would match up counterparties. Such matching still occurs, but today most swaps are between companies and banks, with the Clearinghouse stepping in as counterparty to all transactions. For example, Citibank might arrange a swap with Company A. Company A would agree to make specified payments in euros to Citibank, while Citibank made dollar payments to Company A. Citibank would charge a fee for setting up the swap, and those charges would reflect the creditworthiness of Company A. To protect itself against exchange rate movements, the bank would hedge its position, either by lining up a European company that needed to make dollar payments or else by using currency futures.[23]

Major changes have occurred over time in the swaps market. First, standardized contracts have been developed for the most common types of swaps, which has had two effects: (1) Standardized contracts lower the time and effort involved in arranging swaps, and this lowers transactions costs. (2) The development of standardized contracts has led to a secondary market for swaps, which has increased the liquidity and efficiency of the swaps market. A number of international banks now make markets in swaps and offer quotes on several standard types. The second major change is due to a provision in the Dodd-Frank Act mandating that certain standardized interest rate swaps be centrally cleared rather than managed by banks. The Chicago Mercantile Group (CME) is one of these clearing houses and as of May 2017, the notional principal of the swaps outstanding with CME totaled $15 trillion.

Most swaps today involve either interest payments or currencies, but just about anything can be swapped, including equity swaps, credit spread swaps, and commodity swaps.[24]

---

[23]For more information on swaps, see Keith C. Brown and Donald J. Smith, "Default Risk and Innovations in the Design of Interest Rate Swaps," *Financial Management*, Summer 1993, pp. 94–105; Robert Einzig and Bruce Lange, "Swaps at Transamerica: Applications and Analysis," *Journal of Applied Corporate Finance*, Winter 1990, pp. 48–58; John F. Marshall, Vipul K. Bansal, Anthony F. Herbst, and Alan L. Tucker, "Hedging Business Cycle Risk with Macro Swaps and Options," *Journal of Applied Corporate Finance*, Winter 1992, pp. 103–108; and Laurie S. Goodman, "The Uses of Interest Rate Swaps in Managing Corporate Liabilities," *Journal of Applied Corporate Finance*, Winter 1990, pp. 35–47.

[24]In an equity swap, the cash flow based on an equity index is swapped for some other cash flow. In a commodity swap, the swapped cash flow is based on commodity prices. In a credit swap, the cash flow usually is based on the spread between a risky bond and a U.S. Treasury bond.

23-7d Inverse Floaters and Structured Notes

A floating-rate note has an interest rate that rises and falls with some interest rate index. For example, if the prime rate were currently 5.5%, then the interest rate on a $100,000 note at prime plus 1% would be 6.5% and the note's rate would move up and down with the prime rate. Because both the cash flows associated with the note and the discount rate used to value it would rise and fall together, the market value of the note would be relatively stable.

With an **inverse floater**, the rate paid on the note moves *counter* to market rates. Thus, if interest rates in the economy rise, the interest rate paid on an inverse floater will fall, reducing its cash interest payments. At the same time, the discount rate used to value the inverse floater's cash flows will rise along with other rates. The combined effect of lower cash flows and a higher discount rate would lead to a large decline in the value of the inverse floater. Thus, inverse floaters are exceptionally vulnerable to increases in interest rates. Of course, if interest rates fall then the value of an inverse floater will soar.

A **structured note** is part bond and part derivative. For example, it might consist of a bond with a specified maturity value and date but whose payments are linked to some other financial asset, including interest rate derivatives. Most structured notes are issued by financial institutions and there is not a liquid secondary market.

Could inverse floaters and structured notes be used for hedging purposes? The answer is "yes, perhaps quite effectively." These securities have a magnified effect, so not many are required to hedge a given position. However, because they are so volatile, they could make what is supposed to be a hedged position quite risky.

SELF-TEST

Explain how a company can use Treasury bond futures to hedge against rising interest rates.

What is an interest rate swap? Describe the mechanics of a fixed-rate to floating-rate swap.

A Treasury bond futures contract is selling for 94'160. What is the implied annual yield? **(6.5%)**

Messman Corporation issues fixed-rate debt at a rate of 9.00%. Messman agrees to an interest rate swap in which it pays LIBOR to Moore Inc. and Moore pays 8.75% to Messman. What is Messman's resulting net payment? **(LIBOR + 0.25%)**

23-8 Project Selection Risks

A project is any corporate undertaking that uses corporate assets such as cash, factories, buildings, equipment, IT infrastructure, intellectual property, and people. A successful project creates value by generating a return that is commensurate with the size and risk of the assets invested in the project. Perhaps the most important factor for a company's success is its ability to select value-adding projects and avoid value-destroying projects.

23-8a Using Monte Carlo Simulation to Evaluate Project Risk

When evaluating a potential project, a company should assess the project qualitatively and quantitatively using the three-step approach we described in Chapters 10 and 11: (1) Forecast the project's future cash flows. (2) Estimate the value of the cash flows. (3) Analyze the risk of the cash flows.[25] Small projects, such as the replacement of a single machine, require less analysis than large projects, which include major capital expenditures, product line extensions, new products, geographic expansion, acquisitions, and mergers.

---

[25]Recall from Chapter 10 that cash flow evaluation methods include the net present value (NPV), the internal rate of return (IRR), the modified internal rate of return (MIRR), the profitability index (PI), the payback period, and the discounted payback period.

For larger projects, it is absolutely vital to conduct a thorough risk analysis, including sensitivity analysis and scenario analysis, as described in Chapter 11. Very large projects require even more risk analysis, including Monte Carlo simulation, which is widely used in enterprise risk management—you can't manage a risk very well if you can't measure it!

We repeat here some of the results from the simulation analysis in Chapter 11, and we include some new results. Recall that the analysis in Chapter 11 was for the application of a radically new liquid nano-coating technology to a new type of solar water heater module. We projected cash flows for the project, calculated NPV and other evaluation measures, performed a sensitivity analysis, and did a scenario analysis; see Section 11-2 for the basic analysis and Sections 11-5 and 11-6 for the sensitivity and scenario analyses.

We conducted a Monte Carlo simulation analysis in Section 11-7. Recall that in a simulation analysis, a probability distribution is assigned to each input variable—sales in units, the sales price, the variable cost per unit, and so on. The computer begins by picking a random value for each variable from its probability distribution. Those values are then entered into the model, the project's NPV (and any other measures) is calculated, and the NPV is stored in the computer's memory. This is called a trial. After completing the first trial, a second set of input values is selected from the input variables' probability distributions, and a second NPV is calculated. This process is repeated until there are enough observations that the estimated NPV and any other outcome measures are stable.

We replicated the simulation analysis from Chapter 11 with 10,000 iterations; see **Ch23 Tool Kit.xlsx** and look in the worksheet **Simulation**. Figure 23-3 reports the estimated evaluation measures from Chapter 11 and some additional measures.[26] The measures from Chapter 11 for NPV include its average, standard deviation, maximum, minimum, median, and the probability that the NPV will be positive. Based on these measures, the project has a positive expected NPV and will at least break even about 55% of the time.

In addition to the evaluation measures from Chapter 11, enterprise risk management systems often use another measure called **value at risk (VaR)**. Using the trials from the simulation analysis, the company specifies a threshold, such as the bottom 1% or 5% of outcomes. The basic idea is to measure the value of the project if things go badly. For example, Figure 23-3 shows that there is a 5% chance that the project will lose $6.974 million or more (the values are reported in thousands) and a 1% chance that the project will lose $10.211 million or more.

The VaR measures are helpful, but they don't measure the extent of possible losses if things go badly. A measure that many companies now apply is the **conditional value at risk (CVaR)**; it is also called the **expected shortfall (ES)**, the expected tail loss (ETL), and the average value at risk (AVaR). The CVaR measures the average NPV of all outcomes below the threshold—it is the average NPV conditional upon the NPV being less than the threshold value.[27] For example, the CVaR for the 1% threshold is −$11.748 million, which means that if the worst 1% of outcomes occur, the expected loss is $11.748 million. Notice that the VaR calculation is not affected by the size of the losses below the threshold—it just tells you size of the loss *at* the threshold percentile. In contrast, the CVaR takes into account the size of the losses *below* the threshold—it shows the expected loss if things go badly.

Many companies now are applying simulation when they analyze mergers and acquisition. In addition to the quantitative output from a simulation analysis, the process of identifying sources of risk can help companies avoid costly mistakes.

---

[26]The values of the measures will be different in this figure than in Figure 11-7 since these results are from another run of 10,000 trials for the simulation. Each new run of the simulation will give slightly different results.

[27]This definition is correct when applying CVaR to the outcomes from a Monte Carlo simulation because there is an equal probability of each outcome. It is a little more complicated to calculate CVaR from a given probability distribution than it is from the outcomes of a simulation.

FIGURE 23-3
An Example of Monte Carlo Simulation Applied to Project Analysis (Thousands of Dollars)

	A	B	C	D	E	F	G
162	**Summary Statistics for**			**Number of Trials:**		**10,000**	
163	**Simulated Results**		**NPV**				
164	**Average**		**$738**		NPV at 5th percentile		−$6,974
165	**Standard deviation**		**$4,844**	Average NPV below 5th percentile			−$8,931
166	**Maximum**		**$20,131**		NPV at 1st percentile		−$10,211
167	**Minimum**		**−$15,398**	Average NPV below 1st percentile			−$11,748
168	**Median**		**$592**			Skewness	0.15
169	**Probability of NPV > 0**		**55.3%**				
170	**Coefficient of variation**		**6.56**				

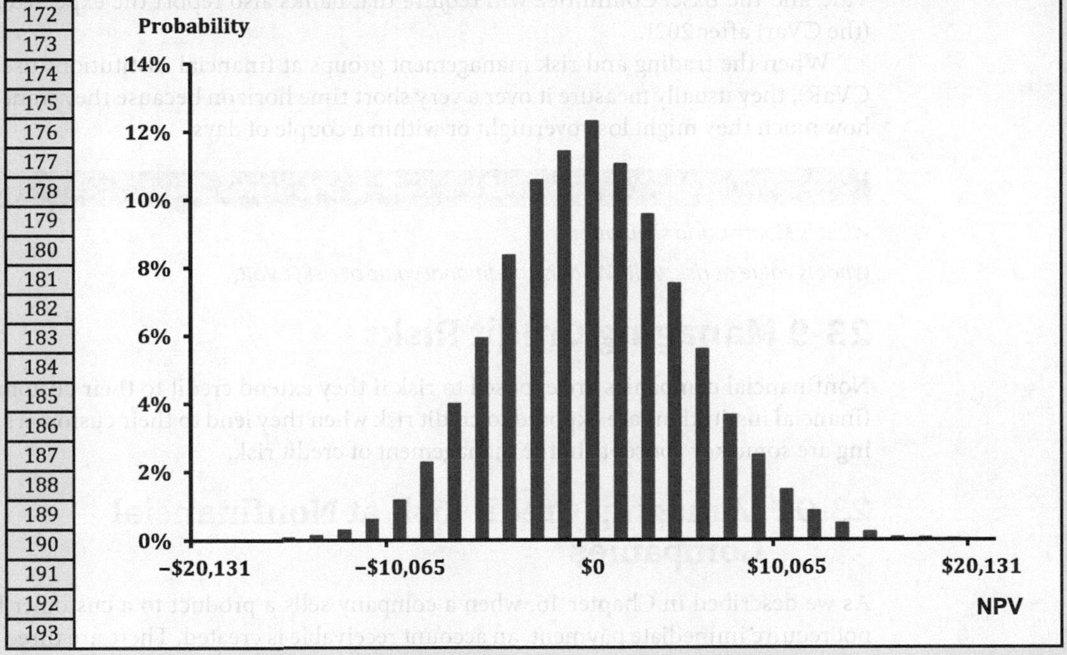

23-8b Using Monte Carlo Simulation to Evaluate Financing Risks

Companies use simulation for purposes other than project analysis. For example, the Danish maker of the popular plastic building-brick toys, the LEGO Group, also uses simulation in its budgeting process to show the possible outcomes. CFO Hans Læssøe reports that simulation analysis revealed that sales volatility has a much bigger impact than top managers previously understood.[28]

Simulation also is helpful when a company prepares a cash budget such as the one we described in Chapter 16. Rather than just showing the expected short-term financing requirements, simulation can show the probabilities of a larger financing requirement, allowing companies to plan for previously unexpected credit needs.

_____

[28]See the paper by Mark Frigo and Hans Læssøe cited in footnote 10.

23-8c Using Monte Carlo Simulation to Evaluate Portfolio Risks

Many companies are exposed to portfolio risk, which is the risk that a portfolio of financial assets will decrease in value. For example, many companies offer pension plans to their employees. Defined benefit plans have a portfolio of stocks, bonds, and other financial assets that is used to support promised pension benefits to its employees. Such companies are exposed to significant portfolio risk—if the value of the pension assets portfolio drops too much relative to the value of the promised pension benefits, then the company will have to use its other resources to make additional contributions to the plan.

Most financial institutions are also exposed to portfolio risk because they own financial assets and have financial liabilities. Simulation is a widely used tool for measuring a bank's portfolio risk. In fact, the Basel II and III accords require banks to report their VaR, and the Basel Committee will require that banks also report the expected shortfall (the CVar) after 2021.

When the trading and risk management groups at financial institutions use VaR (or CVaR), they usually measure it over a very short time horizon because they want to know how much they might lose overnight or within a couple of days.

SELF-TEST

What is Monte Carlo simulation?

What is value at risk, VaR? What is conditional value at risk, CVaR?

23-9 Managing Credit Risks

Nonfinancial companies are exposed to risk if they extend credit to their customers, and financial institutions are exposed to credit risk when they lend to their customers. Following are some key concepts in the management of credit risk.

23-9a Managing Credit Risk at Nonfinancial Companies

As we described in Chapter 16, when a company sells a product to a customer but does not require immediate payment, an account receivable is created. There are three primary tools that companies use to manage this credit risk.

First, a company evaluates its customers before extending credit. The company can do its own evaluation or purchase an evaluation from a third party. If the customer is an individual, credit evaluations are available from several companies, including Equifax, Experian, and TransUnion. Each of these companies provides a numerical score, with the FICO score being the most widely used. The score ranges from 300 to 850, with lower scores indicating that the customer is more likely to default.

When the customer is another company, the evaluation is conducted using many of the same ratios and analyses we described in Chapter 3. In addition, some companies create their own credit scoring models based on past experience or statistical models (such as multiple discriminant analysis).

A company can mitigate its credit risk by selling its accounts receivable to a third party in a process called factoring. Of course, the price a company receives from selling its receivables depends on the receivables' risk, with riskier receivables purchased for much less than their nominal value. A company can also buy insurance for some or all of its receivables. Many companies, including the LEGO Group, use simulation to estimate the risk of their receivables so that they can better negotiate with insurers.

23-9b Managing Credit Risk at Financial Institutions

In addition to the same techniques used at nonfinancial corporations (credit scoring models and simulation), many financial institutions use credit default swaps (CDS). Even though CDS are called swaps, they are like insurance. For example, an investor (which might be a financial institution) might purchase a CDS by making an annual payment to a counterparty to insure a particular bond or other security against default; if the bond defaults, the counterparty pays the purchaser the amount of the defaulted bond that was insured.

The CDS "price" is quoted in basis points and is called the "CDS spread." For example, the spread on Sprint Capital Corp., the wireless provider Sprint's debt financing subsidiary, was about 258 basis points in June 2017. An easy way to interpret the reported basis point spread is that it is the annual fee in dollars (or euros) to protect $10,000 (or euros) of the bond. Therefore, it would cost $258 per year to insure $10,000 of Sprint Capital Corp.'s bonds.

To protect $10 million of Sprint Capital Corp.'s debt, a buyer would pay $258,000 = 0.0258($10 million) per year. In contrast, the spread on the British financial services company Aviva's bonds was only 60 basis points, so insuring £10 million of Aviva's debt would cost only £60,000 per year. If the investors owned the bonds, then the purchase of the CDS would reduce the investors' risk.

There is an active secondary market for CDS, and it is not necessary to own the underlying security. In fact, most participants in the CDS market don't own the underlying securities. For example, a speculator might purchase a CDS on Sprint Capital Corp. for 258 basis points but purchase coverage for only 1 month, which would be a payment of $21,500 = $258,000/12. Now suppose the U.S. economy immediately worsened and drove Sprint Capital Corp.'s CDS spread up to 300 basis points. The investor could liquidate the position by selling 1-month credit protection for $25,000 = $300,000/12 and use the previously purchased CDS to offset the newly sold CDS. The investor's profit would be $3,500.

In addition to CDS for individual securities, there are CDS for indices. For example, the CDX.NA.IG is an index of 125 CDS for North American investment-grade debt. The index's movements are positively correlated with the overall level of default for many commercial loans—the index goes up when defaults increase. Therefore, a U.S. bank can protect itself from increasing default rates in its loan portfolio by taking a short position in the CDX.NA.IG. If defaults increase, then the index goes up, which means a short investor can profit by selling the now higher priced index at the lower price specified in the original short position. This is a situation in which the CDS help reduce a financial institution's risk—when defaults increase, the institution loses money on it loans but makes money on the index. Of course, if the index falls, then the bank loses on the short position but wins on its own loan portfolio because there are fewer defaults.

When banks and other major financial institutions take positions in swaps and CDS, they are themselves exposed to various risks, especially if their counterparties cannot meet their obligations. Furthermore, swaps are off–balance sheet transactions, making it impossible to tell just how large the swap market is or who has what obligation. The Bank of International Settlements estimates that in 2017 the notional value of all CDS was $9.3 trillion. As we write this in 2018, the SEC and the Commodity Futures Trading Commission (CFTC) continue implementation of provisions in Title VII of the 2010 Dodd-Frank Act to improve transparency in the swaps markets. Standardized interest-rate and credit-default swaps must now be centrally cleared and the market is working to develop new products that provide the same benefits as these swaps, but with lower counterparty risk.[29]

---

[29]See the U.S. Commodity Futures Trading Commission for updates and the current status of Dodd-Frank implementation: **www.cftc.gov/LawRegulation/DoddFrankAct/index.htm.**

FIGURE 23-4
Credit Default Swap Spreads for Sovereign Debt (September 14, 2018)

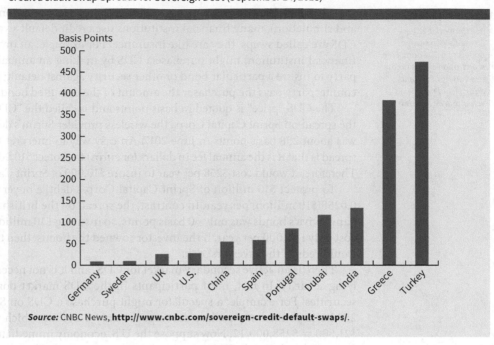

Source: CNBC News, **http://www.cnbc.com/sovereign-credit-default-swaps/**.

Credit default swaps are traded on government debt as well as corporate debt. Before 2008, a CDS on a 5-year U.S. Treasury bond was trading at less than 7 basis points, which would be a $7 annual fee to protect $10,000 of the bond. The CDS price increased to almost 100 basis points in 2009 and is currently (September 2018) trading around 28 basis points. Figure 23-4 shows the credit default spreads for the U.S. and selected European countries, some that have adopted the euro (Germany, France, Italy, Spain, and Portugal) and some that have not. The extremely high spreads for Eurozone debt indicate the problems facing these countries.

SELF-TEST

Describe some ways to manage credit risk at a nonfinancial company.

What are credit default swaps?

23-10 Risk and Human Safety

Risk management decisions, like all corporate decisions, should begin with a cost–benefit analysis for each feasible alternative. For example, suppose it would cost $50,000 per year to conduct a comprehensive fire safety training program for all personnel in a high-risk plant. Presumably, this program would reduce the expected value of future fire losses. An alternative to the training program would be to place $50,000 annually in a reserve fund set aside to cover future fire losses. Both alternatives involve expected cash flows, and from an economic standpoint the choice should be made on the basis of the lowest present value of future costs.

However, suppose a fire occurs and a life is lost. In situations involving safety and health, the trade-off between expected profits and expected losses is not sufficient for making sound decisions. Companies must always consider the impact their decisions have on the safety of their employees and customers. Ignoring safety and health is an ethical mistake, but it also is a business mistake because many companies have been forced out of business or suffered debilitating losses when they produced unsafe products.

Describe a situation in risk management that involves ethical as well as financial issues.

SUMMARY

The key concepts in enterprise risk management are listed here.

- **Enterprise risk management (ERM)** includes risk identification, risk assessment, and risk responses.
- A **derivative** is a security whose value is determined by the market price or interest rate of some other security.
- Risk management allows corporations (1) to increase their use of debt, (2) to maintain their capital budget over time, (3) to avoid costs associated with financial distress, (4) to utilize their comparative advantages in hedging relative to the hedging ability of individual investors, (5) to reduce both the risks and costs of borrowing, and (6) to reduce the higher taxes that result from fluctuating earnings. Managers may also want to stabilize earnings in order to boost their own compensation.
- Risk responses include (1) avoiding the activity, (2) reducing the probability of occurrence of an adverse event, (3) reducing the magnitude of the loss associated with an adverse event, (4) transferring the risk to an insurance company, (5) transferring the function that produces the risk to a third party, and (6) sharing the risk by purchasing a derivative contract.
- Major categories of risk include (1) strategy and reputation, (2) control and compliance, (3) hazards, (4) human resources, (5) operation, (6) technology, and (7) financial management.
- Types of financial risk include (1) foreign exchange risk, (2) commodity price risk, (3) interest rate risk, (4) project selection risk, (5) liquidity risk, (6) customer credit risk, and (7) portfolio risk.
- A **hedge** is a transaction that lowers risk. A **natural hedge** is a transaction between two **counterparties** whose risks are mirror images of each other.
- A **futures contract** is a standardized contract that is traded on an exchange and is marked-to-market daily, although physical delivery of the underlying asset usually does not occur.
- Under a **forward contract**, one party agrees to buy a commodity at a specific price and a specific future date and the other party agrees to make the sale; delivery does occur.
- A **swap** is an exchange of cash payment obligations. Swaps occur because the parties involved prefer the other's payment stream.
- **Financial futures** permit firms to create hedge positions to protect themselves against fluctuating interest rates, stock prices, and exchange rates.
- **Commodity futures** can be used to hedge against input price increases.
- **Long hedges** involve buying futures contracts to guard against price increases.
- **Short hedges** involve selling futures contracts to guard against price declines.
- **Symmetric hedges** protect against price increases and price decreases. Futures contracts are frequently used for symmetric hedges.

- **Asymmetric hedges** protect against price movements in one direction more than movements in another. Options are frequently used for asymmetric hedges.
- A **perfect hedge** occurs when the gain or loss on the hedged transaction exactly offsets the loss or gain on the unhedged position.

QUESTIONS

(23-1)   Define each of the following terms:
  - a. Derivatives
  - b. Enterprise risk management
  - c. Financial futures; forward contract
  - d. Hedging; natural hedge; long hedge; short hedge; perfect hedge; symmetric hedge; asymmetric hedge
  - e. Swap; structured note
  - f. Commodity futures

(23-2)   Give two reasons why stockholders might be indifferent between owning the stock of a firm with volatile cash flows and that of a firm with stable cash flows.

(23-3)   List six reasons why risk management might increase the value of a firm.

(23-4)   Discuss some of the techniques available to reduce risk exposures.

(23-5)   Explain how the futures markets can be used to reduce interest rate risk and input price risk.

(23-6)   How can swaps be used to reduce the risks associated with debt contracts?

SELF-TEST PROBLEM   SOLUTION SHOWN IN APPENDIX A

(ST-1)
Hedging

It is now March, and the current cost of debt for Wansley Construction is 12%. Wansley plans to issue $5 million in 20-year bonds (with coupons paid semiannually) in September, but it's afraid that rates will climb even higher before then. The following data are available:

Futures Prices: Treasury Bonds—$100,000; Pts. 32nds of 100%

Delivery Month (1)	Open (2)	High (3)	Low (4)	Settle (5)	Change (6)
Mar	96'28	97'13	97'22	98'05	+7
June	98'03	98'03	97'13	97'25	+8
Sept	97'03	97'17	97'03	97'13	+8

  - a. What is the implied interest rate on the September contract?
  - b. Construct a hedge for Wansley.
  - c. Assume all interest rates rise by 1 percentage point. What is the dollar value of Wansley's increased cost of issuing debt? What is Wansley's gain from the futures contract?

PROBLEMS   ANSWERS ARE IN APPENDIX B

EASY PROBLEMS 1–2

(23-1)
Swaps

Zhao Automotive issues fixed-rate debt at a rate of 7.00%. Zhao agrees to an interest rate swap in which it pays LIBOR to Lee Financial and Lee pays 6.8% to Zhao. What is Zhao's resulting net payment?

(23-2)
Futures

A Treasury bond futures contract has a settlement price of 89'08. What is the implied annual yield?

INTERMEDIATE PROBLEMS 3–4

(23-3)
Futures

What is the implied interest rate on a Treasury bond ($100,000) futures contract that settled at 100'160? If interest rates increased by 1%, what would be the contract's new value?

(23-4)
Swaps

Carter Enterprises can issue floating-rate debt at LIBOR + 2% or fixed-rate debt at 10%. Brence Manufacturing can issue floating-rate debt at LIBOR + 3.1% or fixed-rate debt at 11%. Suppose Carter issues floating-rate debt and Brence issues fixed-rate debt. They are considering a swap in which Carter makes a fixed-rate payment of 7.95% to Brence and Brence makes a payment of LIBOR to Carter. What are the net payments of Carter and Brence if they engage in the swap? Would Carter be better off if it issued fixed-rate debt or if it issued floating-rate debt and engaged in the swap? Would Brence be better off if it issued floating-rate debt or if it issued fixed-rate debt and engaged in the swap? Explain your answers.

CHALLENGING PROBLEM 5

(23-5)
Hedging

The Zinn Company plans to issue $10,000,000 of 20-year bonds in June to help finance a new research and development laboratory. The bonds will pay interest semiannually. It is now November, and the current cost of debt to the high-risk biotech company is 11%. However, the firm's financial manager is concerned that interest rates will climb even higher in coming months. The following data are available:

Futures Prices: Treasury Bonds—$100,000; Pts. 32nds of 100%

Delivery Month (1)	Open (2)	High (3)	Low (4)	Settle (5)	Change (6)	Open Interest (7)
Dec	94'280	95'130	94'220	95'050	+0'070	591,944
Mar	96'030	96'030	95'130	95'250	+0'080	120,353
June	95'030	95'170	95'030	95'170	+0'080	13,597

a. What is the implied yield on the June futures contract? How many futures contracts will be needed to hedge potential losses in bond proceeds (based on current market conditions) due to waiting (round up to the nearest integer)? What is the total value of the hedge position?

b. Assume that interest rates in general increase by 200 basis points. Suppose the bond's terms don't change and that the coupon rate is still 11%. How much would the proceeds be given the new market rates? What is the loss in proceeds based on the original target for proceeds?

c. Assume that Zinn had entered the hedge found in part a. What is the new price of the hedge position? What is the gain on the hedge? What is the net effect of the loss of proceeds and the gain on the hedge?

SPREADSHEET PROBLEM

(23-6)
Build a Model:
Hedging

resource

Start with the partial model in the file *Ch23 P06 Build a Model.xlsx* on the textbook's Web site. Use the following information and data.

F. Pierce Products Inc. is financing a new manufacturing facility with the issue in March of $20,000,000 of 20-year bonds with semiannual interest payments. It is now

October, and if Pierce were to issue the bonds now, the yield would be 10% because of Pierce's high risk. Pierce's CFO is concerned that interest rates will climb even higher in coming months and is considering hedging the bond issue. The following data are available:

Futures Prices: Treasury Bonds—$100,000; Pts. 32nds of 100%

Delivery Month (1)	Open (2)	High (3)	Low (4)	Settle (5)	Change (6)	Open Interest (7)
Dec	93'280	94'130	93'220	94'050	+0'060	723,946
Mar	95'030	95'030	94'130	94'250	+0'070	97,254

a. Create a hedge with the futures contract for Pierce's planned March debt offering of $20 million using the March Treasury Bond futures contract. What is the implied yield on the bond underlying the futures contract?

b. Suppose that interest rates fall by 300 basis points. What are the dollar savings from issuing the debt at the new interest rate? What is the dollar change in value of the futures position? What is the total dollar value change of the hedged position?

c. Create a graph showing the effectiveness of the hedge if the change in interest rates, in basis points, is −300, −200, −100, 0, 100, 200, or 300. Show the dollar cost (or savings) from issuing the debt at the new interest rates, the dollar change in value of the futures position, and the total dollar value change.

MINI CASE

Assume you have just been hired as a financial analyst by Tennessee Sunshine Inc. (TS), a mid-sized Tennessee company that specializes in creating exotic sauces from imported fruits and vegetables. The firm's CEO, Bill Stooksbury, recently returned from an industry corporate executive conference in San Francisco, and one of the sessions he attended was on the pressing need for companies to institute enterprise risk management programs. Because no one at Tennessee Sunshine is familiar with the basics of enterprise risk management, Stooksbury has asked you to prepare a brief report that the firm's executives could use to gain at least a cursory understanding of the topics.

To begin, you gathered some outside materials on derivatives and risk management and used these materials to draft a list of pertinent questions that need to be answered. In fact, one possible approach to the paper is to use a question-and-answer format. Now that the questions have been drafted, you have to develop the answers.

a. Why might stockholders be indifferent to whether or not a firm reduces the volatility of its cash flows?

b. What are six reasons risk management might increase the value of a corporation?

c. What is COSO? How does COSO define enterprise risk management?

d. Describe the eight components of the COSO ERM framework.

e. Describe some of the risks events within the following major categories of risk: (1) strategy and reputation, (2) control and compliance, (3) hazards, (4) human resources, (5) operations, (6) technology, and (7) financial management.

f. What are some actions that companies can take to minimize or reduce risk exposures?

g. What are forward contracts? How can they be used to manage foreign exchange risk?

h. Describe how commodity futures markets can be used to reduce input price risk.

i. It is January, and Tennessee Sunshine is considering issuing $5 million in bonds in June to raise capital for an expansion. Currently, the firm can issue 20-year bonds with a 7% coupon (with interest paid semiannually), but interest rates are on the rise and Stooksbury is concerned that long-term interest rates might rise by as much as 1% before June. You looked online and found that June T-bond futures are trading at 111'250. What are the risks of not hedging, and how might TS hedge this exposure? In your analysis, consider what would happen if interest rates all increased by 1%.

j. What is a swap? Suppose two firms have different credit ratings. Firm Hi can borrow fixed at 11% and floating at LIBOR + 1%. Firm Lo can borrow fixed at 11.4% and floating at LIBOR + 1.5%. Describe a floating versus fixed interest rate swap between firms Hi and Lo in which Lo also makes a "side payment" of 45 basis points to Firm L.

CHAPTER 24

Bankruptcy, Reorganization, and Liquidation

Lehman Brothers, Washington Mutual, Chrysler, and General Motors all filed for bankruptcy protection during the Great Recession. What did these four filings have in common with Australia? At the time of filings, the companies' assets totaled over $1.1 trillion dollars, which is about the same size as Australia's annual gross domestic product.

With $691 billion in assets, Lehman Brothers holds the record for the largest bankruptcy filing in history. Its operations and assets have been liquidated and sold piecemeal to other companies, including Barclays. Washington Mutual (WaMu) once was the largest S&L in the United States, with total assets of $328 billion in September 2008. But when it sustained enormous losses related to sub-prime mortgages, WaMu was placed into the Federal Deposit Insurance Corporation's (FDIC) receivership. The FDIC quickly sold WaMu's banking operations to JPMorgan Chase.

Chrysler filed for bankruptcy on April 30, 2009, and emerged from bankruptcy 40 days later on June 10, 2009. As part of the deal, Chrysler's new owners include its employees/retirees (through pension and health care funds), Fiat, and the U.S. government. Cerberus Capital, a private equity fund that was Chrysler's owner prior to the bankruptcy, lost its entire equity stake, and Chrysler's pre-bankruptcy debtholders are receiving pennies on the dollar.

When GM filed for bankruptcy on June 1, it became the largest manufacturer in U.S. history to fail. When GM emerged from bankruptcy 40 days later, the U.S. government owned 60.8% of the equity in the "new" GM, with the remaining equity owned by the Canadian government (11.7%), the UAW employee health care trust (17.5%), and former bondholders (10%). Notice that nothing was left for former stockholders.

As you read this chapter, think about the decisions that were made in the bankruptcy processes of these four companies.

Thus far, we have dealt with issues faced by growing, successful enterprises. However, many firms encounter financial difficulties, and some—including such big names as General Motors, Chrysler, Delta Air Lines, and Lehman Brothers—are forced into bankruptcy. When a firm encounters financial distress, its managers must try to ward off a total collapse and thereby minimize losses. The ability to hang on during rough times often means the difference between forced liquidation versus rehabilitation and eventual success. An understanding of bankruptcy is also critical to the executives of healthy firms, because they must know the best actions to take when their customers or suppliers face the threat of bankruptcy.

24-1 Financial Distress and Its Consequences

We begin with some background on financial distress and its consequences.[1]

24-1a Causes of Business Failure

A company's intrinsic value is the present value of its expected future free cash flows. Many factors can cause this value to decline. These include general economic conditions, industry trends, and company-specific problems such as shifting consumer tastes, obsolete technology, and changing demographics in existing retail locations. Financial factors, such as too much debt and unexpected increases in interest rates, can also cause business failures. The importance of the different factors varies over time, and most business failures occur because a number of factors combine to make the business unsustainable. Further, case studies show that financial difficulties are usually the result of a series of errors, misjudgments, and interrelated weaknesses that can be attributed directly or indirectly to management. In a few cases, such as Enron and MF Global Holdings, fraud leads to bankruptcy.

    As you might guess, signs of potential financial distress are generally evident in a ratio analysis long before the firm actually fails, and researchers use ratio analysis to estimate the probability that a given firm will go bankrupt. Financial analysts constantly are seeking ways to assess a firm's likelihood of going bankrupt. We discuss one method, multiple discriminant analysis (MDA), in **Web Extension 24A**.

24-1b The Business Failure Record

Over 22,000 companies went bankrupt in the year ending June 30, 2018.[2] Although bankruptcy is most frequent among smaller firms, several larger retailers declared bankruptcy in 2017, including Toys "R" Us, Inc., Sports Authority, Inc., and Nine West Holdings. Even extremely large firms are not immune from bankruptcy, as shown in Table 24-1. This was especially true in the Great Recession: Six of the largest bankruptcies occurred in 2008 and 2009.

    Bankruptcy obviously is painful for a company's shareholders, but it also can be harmful to the economy if the company is very large or is in a critical sector. For example, the failure of Lehman Brothers in September 2008 sparked a global run on financial institutions that froze credit markets and contributed to the ensuing global recession. It is not clear whether the damage to the world economy could have been mitigated if the government had intervened to prevent Lehman's failure, but the government subsequently decided not to take chances with many other troubled financial institutions. For example,

---

[1]Much of the current academic work in the area of financial distress and bankruptcy is based on writings by Edward I. Altman. See Edward I. Altman and Edith Hotchkiss, *Corporate Financial Distress and Bankruptcy: Predict and Avoid Bankruptcy, Analyze and Invest in Distressed Debt* (Hoboken, NJ: Wiley, 2006).

[2]There were over 750,000 personal bankruptcies in this same period.

TABLE 24-1
The Ten Largest Bankruptcies since 1980 (Billions of Dollars)

Company	Business	Assets	Date
Lehman Brothers Holdings Inc.	Investment banking	$691.1	September 15, 2008
Washington Mutual Inc.	Financial services	327.9	September 26, 2008
WorldCom, Inc.	Telecommunications	103.9	July 21, 2002
General Motors Corporation	Auto manufacturing	91.0	June 1, 2009
CIT Group Inc.	Financial services	80.4	November 1, 2009
Enron Corp.	Energy trading	63.4	December 2, 2001
Conseco Inc.	Financial services	61.4	December 17, 2002
Energy Future Holdings Corp.	Electric utility	50.0	April 29, 2014
MF Global Holdings Ltd.	Commodities	40.5	October 31, 2011
Chrysler LLC	Auto manufacturing	39.3	April 30, 2009

Source: **https://finance.yahoo.com/news/10-largest-bankruptcies-time-205509224.html.**

the government helped arrange the 2008 acquisition of Wachovia by Wells Fargo, the 2008 acquisition of Bear Stearns by JPMorgan Chase, and the 2009 acquisition of Merrill Lynch by Bank of America (despite Bank of America's misgivings). In addition, the government provided billions of dollars of capital to many major financial institutions in 2008, including AIG. In each of these cases, the government decided that a complete failure of these institutions might cause the entire financial system to collapse.

In other cases, the government has decided that a company was too important to the nonfinancial side of the economy to be allowed to go through liquidation. For example, in 2008 and 2009 the government provided billions of dollars of financing to General Motors and Chrysler. Even though these companies subsequently went through bankruptcy proceedings in 2009, they avoided liquidation, still have a significant number of employees, and remain major players in the automobile industry. In past years, the government also has intervened to support troubled firms in other critical sectors, such as Lockheed and Douglas Aircraft in the defense industry.

SELF-TEST

What are the major causes of business failure?

Do business failures occur evenly over time?

Which size of firm, large or small, is most prone to business failure? Why?

24-2 Issues Facing a Firm in Financial Distress

Financial distress begins when a firm is unable to meet scheduled payments or when cash flow projections indicate that it will soon be unable to do so. As the situation develops, five central issues arise.

1. Is the firm's inability to meet scheduled debt payments a temporary cash flow problem, or is it a permanent problem caused by asset values having fallen below debt obligations?
2. If the problem is temporary, then an agreement with creditors that gives the firm time to recover and to satisfy everyone may be worked out. However, if basic long-run asset values have truly declined, then economic losses have occurred. In this event, who should bear the losses, and who should get whatever value remains?

3. Is the company "worth more dead than alive"? That is, would the business be more valuable if it were liquidated and sold off in pieces or if it were maintained and continued in operation?

4. Should the firm file for protection under Chapter 11 of the Bankruptcy Act, or should it try to use informal procedures? (Both reorganization and liquidation can be accomplished either informally or under the direction of a bankruptcy court.)

5. Who should control the firm while it is being liquidated or rehabilitated? Should the existing management be left in charge, or should a trustee be placed in charge of operations?

In the remainder of the chapter, we discuss these issues in turn.

SELF-TEST

What five major issues must be addressed when a firm faces financial distress?

24-3 Settlements without Going through Formal Bankruptcy

When a firm experiences financial distress, its managers and creditors must decide whether the problem is temporary and the firm is financially viable or whether a permanent problem exists that endangers the firm's life. Then the parties must decide whether to try to solve the problem informally or under the direction of a bankruptcy court. Because of costs associated with formal bankruptcy—including the disruptions that occur when a firm's customers, suppliers, and employees learn that it has filed under the Bankruptcy Act—it is preferable to reorganize (or liquidate) outside of formal bankruptcy. We first discuss informal settlement procedures and then the procedures under a formal bankruptcy.

24-3a Informal Reorganization

In the case of an economically sound company whose financial difficulties appear to be temporary, creditors are generally willing to work with the company to help it recover and reestablish itself on a sound financial basis. Such voluntary plans, commonly called **workouts**, usually require a **restructuring** of the firm's debt, because current cash flows are insufficient to service the existing debt. Restructuring typically involves extension and/or composition. In an **extension**, creditors postpone the dates of required interest or principal payments, or both. In a **composition**, creditors voluntarily reduce their fixed claims on the debtor by accepting a lower principal amount, by reducing the interest rate on the debt, by taking equity in exchange for debt, or by some combination of these changes.

An **informal debt restructuring** begins with a meeting between the failing firm's managers and creditors. The creditors appoint a committee consisting of four or five of the largest creditors plus one or two of the smaller ones. This meeting is often arranged and conducted by an **adjustment bureau** associated with and run by a local credit managers' association.[3] The first step is for management to draw up a list of creditors that shows the amounts of debt owed. There are typically different classes of debt, ranging from first-mortgage holders to unsecured creditors. Next, the company develops information

---

[3]There is a nationwide group called the National Association of Credit Management, which consists of bankers and industrial companies' credit managers. This group sponsors research on credit policy and problems, conducts seminars on credit management, and operates local chapters in cities throughout the nation. These local chapters frequently operate adjustment bureaus.

showing the value of the firm under different scenarios. Typically, one scenario is going out of business, selling off the assets, and then distributing the proceeds to the various creditors in accordance with the priority of their claims, with any surplus going to the common stockholders. The company may hire an appraiser to get an appraisal of the value of the firm's property to use as a basis for this scenario. Other scenarios include continued operations, frequently with some improvements in capital equipment, marketing, and perhaps some management changes.

This information is then shared with the firm's bankers and other creditors. Frequently, the firm's debts exceed its liquidating value, and the legal fees and other costs associated with a formal liquidation under federal bankruptcy procedures will materially lower the net proceeds available to creditors. Furthermore, it generally takes at least a year (and often several years) to resolve matters in a formal proceeding, so the present value of the eventual proceeds will be lower still. This information, when presented in a credible manner, often convinces creditors they would be better off accepting something less than the full amount of their claims rather than holding out for the full face amount. If management and the major creditors agree that the problems can probably be resolved, then a more formal plan is drafted and presented to all the creditors, along with the reasons creditors should be willing to compromise on their claims.

In developing the reorganization plan, creditors prefer an extension because it promises eventual payment in full. In some cases, creditors may agree not only to postpone the date of payment but also to subordinate existing claims to vendors who are willing to extend new credit during the workout period. Similarly, creditors may agree to accept a lower interest rate on loans during the extension, perhaps in exchange for a pledge of collateral. Because of the sacrifices involved, the creditors must have faith that the debtor firm will be able to solve its problems.

In a composition, creditors agree to reduce their claims. Typically, creditors receive cash and/or new securities that have a combined market value that is less than the amounts owed them. The cash and securities, which might have a value of only 10% of the original claim, are taken as full settlement of the original debt. Bargaining will take place between the debtor and the creditors over the savings that result from avoiding the costs of legal bankruptcy: administrative costs, legal fees, investigative costs, and so on. In addition to escaping such costs, the debtor gains because the stigma of bankruptcy may be avoided. As a result, the debtor may be induced to part with most of the savings from avoiding formal bankruptcy.

Often, the bargaining process will result in a restructuring that involves both extension and composition. For example, the settlement may provide for a cash payment of 25% of the debt immediately plus a new note promising six future installments of 10% each, for a total payment of 85%.

Voluntary settlements are both informal and simple; they are also relatively inexpensive, because legal and administrative expenses are held to a minimum. Thus, voluntary procedures generally result in the largest return to creditors. Although creditors do not obtain immediate payment and may even have to accept less than is owed them, they generally recover more money, and sooner, than if the firm were to file for bankruptcy.

In recent years, the fact that restructurings can sometimes help creditors avoid showing a loss has motivated some creditors, especially banks and insurance companies, to agree to voluntary restructurings. Thus, a bank "in trouble" with its regulators over weak capital ratios may agree to extend loans that are used to pay the interest on earlier loans—in order to keep the bank from having to write down the value of those earlier loans. This particular type of restructuring depends on (1) the willingness of the regulators to go along with the process, and (2) whether the bank is likely to recover more by restructuring the debt than by forcing the borrower into bankruptcy immediately.

We should point out that informal voluntary settlements are not reserved for small firms. International Harvester (now Navistar International) avoided formal bankruptcy proceedings by getting its creditors to agree to restructure more than $3.5 billion of debt. Likewise, Chrysler's creditors accepted both an extension and a composition to help it through its bad years in the late 1970s before it merged with Daimler-Benz. The biggest problem with informal reorganizations is getting all the parties to agree to the voluntary plan. This problem, called the *holdout* problem, is discussed in a later section.

24-3b Informal Liquidation

When it is obvious that a firm is more valuable dead than alive, informal procedures can also be used to sell the firm's asset in a **liquidation**. **Assignment** is an informal procedure for liquidating a firm, and it usually yields creditors a larger amount than they would get in a formal bankruptcy liquidation. However, assignments are feasible only if the firm is small and its affairs are not too complex. An assignment calls for title to the debtor's assets to be transferred to a third party, known as an **assignee** or trustee. The assignee is instructed to liquidate the assets through a private sale or public auction and then to distribute the proceeds among the creditors on a pro rata basis. The assignment does not automatically discharge the debtor's obligations. However, the debtor may have the assignee write the requisite legal language on the check to each creditor so that endorsement of the check constitutes acknowledgment of full settlement of the claim.

Assignment has some advantages over liquidation in federal bankruptcy courts in terms of time, legal formality, and expense. The assignee has more flexibility in disposing of property than does a federal bankruptcy trustee, so action can be taken sooner, before inventory becomes obsolete or machinery rusts. Also, because the assignee is often familiar with the debtor's business, better results may be achieved. However, an assignment does not automatically result in a full and legal discharge of all the debtor's liabilities, nor does it protect the creditors against fraud. Both of these problems can be reduced by formal liquidation in bankruptcy, which we discuss in a later section.

SELF-TEST

Define the following terms: (1) restructuring, (2) extension, (3) composition, (4) assignment, and (5) assignee (trustee).

What are the advantages of liquidation by assignment versus a formal bankruptcy liquidation?

24-4 Federal Bankruptcy Law

U.S. bankruptcy laws were first enacted in 1898. They were modified substantially in 1938 and again in 1978, and some fine-tuning was done in 1986. In 2005, Congress further modified the bankruptcy code, speeding up bankruptcy proceedings for companies and making it more difficult for consumers to take advantage of provisions that can wipe out certain debts. The primary purpose of the bankruptcy law is to prevent individual creditors from forcing the liquidation of firms that are worth more as ongoing concerns, and thus causing harm to other stakeholders.

Currently, our bankruptcy law consists of eight odd-numbered chapters, plus one even-numbered chapter. (The old even-numbered chapters were deleted when the act was revised in 1978.) Chapters 1, 3, and 5 contain general provisions applicable to the other chapters. **Chapter 11**, which deals with **reorganization in bankruptcy**, is the most important section from a financial management viewpoint. **Chapter 7** details the procedures to be followed when liquidating a firm; generally, Chapter 7 does not come into play unless it has been determined that reorganization under Chapter 11 is not feasible. Chapter 9 deals with financially distressed municipalities; Chapter 12 covers special procedures for family-owned farms; Chapter 13 covers the adjustment of debts for "individuals with regular income"; and Chapter 15 sets up a system of trustees who help administer proceedings under the act.

A firm is officially bankrupt when it files for bankruptcy with a federal court. When you read that a company such as General Motors has "filed for court protection under Chapter 11," this means the company is attempting to reorganize under the supervision of a bankruptcy court. These **formal bankruptcy proceedings** are designed to protect both the firm and its creditors. On the one hand, if the problem is temporary insolvency, then the firm may use bankruptcy proceedings to gain time to solve its cash flow problems without asset seizure by its creditors. On the other hand, if the firm is truly bankrupt in the sense that liabilities exceed assets, then creditors can use bankruptcy procedures to stop the firm's managers from continuing to operate, lose more money, and thus deplete assets that should go to creditors.

Bankruptcy law is flexible in that it provides scope for negotiations between a company, its creditors, its labor force, and its stockholders. A case is opened by filing a **petition** with one of the 291 bankruptcy courts serving 90 judicial districts. The petition may be either **voluntary** or **involuntary**; that is, it may be filed either by the firm's management or by its creditors. After a filing, a committee of unsecured creditors is then appointed by the Office of the U.S. Trustee to negotiate with management for a reorganization, which may include the restructuring of debt. Under Chapter 11, a **trustee** will be appointed to take over the company if the court deems current management incompetent or if fraud is suspected. Normally, though, the existing management retains control. If no fair and feasible reorganization can be worked out, the bankruptcy judge will order that the firm be liquidated under procedures spelled out in Chapter 7 of the Bankruptcy Act, in which case a trustee will always be appointed.[4]

SELF-TEST

Define the following terms: bankruptcy law, Chapter 11, Chapter 7, trustee, voluntary bankruptcy, and involuntary bankruptcy.

How does a firm formally declare bankruptcy?

24-5 Reorganization in Bankruptcy (Chapter 11 of Bankruptcy Code)

It might appear that most reorganizations should be handled informally because informal reorganizations are faster and less costly than formal bankruptcy. However, two problems often arise to stymie informal reorganizations and thus force debtors into Chapter 11 bankruptcy: the common pool problem and the holdout problem.[5]

To illustrate these problems, consider a firm that is having financial difficulties. It is worth $9 million as a going concern (this is the present value of its expected future

---

[4]For a discussion of European bankruptcy laws, see Kevin M. J. Kaiser, "European Bankruptcy Laws: Implications for Corporations Facing Financial Distress," *Financial Management,* Autumn 1996, pp. 67–85.

[5]The issues discussed in this section are covered in more detail in Thomas H. Jackson, *The Logic and Limits of Bankruptcy Law* (Frederick, MD: Beard Group, 2001). Also see Stuart C. Gilson, "Managing Default: Some Evidence on How Firms Choose between Workouts and Chapter 11," *Journal of Applied Corporate Finance,* Summer 1991, pp. 62–70; and Yehning Chen, J. Fred Weston, and Edward I. Altman, "Financial Distress and Restructuring Models," *Financial Management,* Summer 1995, pp. 57–75.

free cash flows) but only $7 million if it is liquidated. The firm's debt totals $10 million at face value—ten creditors with equal priority each have a $1 million claim. Now suppose the firm's liquidity deteriorates to the point that it defaults on one of its loans. The holder of that loan has the contractual right to *accelerate* the claim, which means the creditor can *foreclose* on the loan and demand payment of the entire balance. Further, because most debt agreements have *cross-default provisions*, defaulting on one loan effectively places all loans in default.

The firm's market value is less than the $10 million face value of debt, regardless of whether it remains in business or liquidates. Therefore, it would be impossible to pay off all of the creditors in full. However, the creditors in total would be better off if the firm is not shut down, because they could ultimately recover $9 million if the firm remains in business but only $7 million if it is liquidated. The problem here, which is called the **common pool problem**, is that in the absence of protection under the Bankruptcy Act, individual creditors would have an incentive to foreclose on the firm even though it is worth more as an ongoing concern.

An individual creditor would have the incentive to foreclose because it could then force the firm to liquidate a portion of its assets to pay off that particular creditor's $1 million claim in full. The payment to that creditor would probably require the liquidation of vital assets, which might cause a shutdown of the firm and thus lead to a total liquidation. Therefore, the value of the remaining creditors' claims would decline. Of course, all the creditors would recognize the gains they could attain from this strategy, so they would storm the debtor with foreclosure notices. Even those creditors who understand the merits of keeping the firm alive would be forced to foreclose, because the foreclosures of the other creditors would reduce the payoff to those who do not. In our hypothetical example, if seven creditors foreclosed and forced liquidation, they would be paid in full, and the remaining three creditors would receive nothing.

With many creditors, as soon as a firm defaults on one loan, there is the potential for a disruptive flood of foreclosures that would make the creditors collectively worse off. In our example, the creditors would lose $9 − $7 = $2 million in value if a flood of foreclosures were to force the firm to liquidate. If the firm had only one creditor—say, a single bank loan—then the common pool problem would not exist. If a bank had loaned the company $10 million, it would not force liquidation to get $7 million when it could keep the firm alive and eventually realize $9 million.

Chapter 11 of the Bankruptcy Act provides a solution to the common pool problem through its **automatic stay** provision. *An automatic stay, which is forced on all creditors in a bankruptcy, limits the ability of creditors to foreclose to collect their individual claims.* However, the creditors can collectively foreclose on the debtor and force liquidation.

Although bankruptcy gives the firm a chance to work out its problems without the threat of creditor foreclosure, management does not have a completely free rein over the firm's assets. First, bankruptcy law requires the debtor firm to request permission from the court to take many actions, and the law also gives creditors the right to petition the bankruptcy court to block almost any action the firm might take while in bankruptcy. Second, **fraudulent conveyance** statutes, which are part of debtor–creditor law, protect creditors from unjustified transfers of property by a firm in financial distress.

To illustrate fraudulent conveyance, suppose a holding company is contemplating bankruptcy protection for one of its subsidiaries. The holding company might be tempted to sell some or all of the subsidiary's assets to itself (the parent company) for less than the true market value. This transaction would reduce the value of the subsidiary by the difference between the true market value of its assets and the amount paid, and the loss would be borne primarily by the subsidiary's creditors. Such a transaction would be voided by the courts as a fraudulent conveyance. Note also that transactions favoring one creditor at the expense of another can be voided under the same law. For example, a transaction in which an asset is sold and the proceeds are used to pay one creditor in full at the expense of other creditors could be voided. Thus, fraudulent conveyance laws also protect creditors from each other.[6]

The second problem that is mitigated by bankruptcy law is the **holdout problem**. To illustrate this, consider again our example firm with ten creditors owed $1 million each but with assets worth only $9 million. The goal of the firm is to avoid liquidation by remedying the default. In an informal workout, this would require a reorganization plan that is agreed to by each of the ten creditors. Suppose the firm offers each creditor new debt with a face value of $850,000 in exchange for the old $1,000,000 face value debt. If each of the creditors accepted the offer, the firm could be successfully reorganized. The reorganization would leave the equity holders with some value—the market value of the equity would be $9,000,000 − 10($850,000) = $500,000. Further, the creditors would have claims worth $8.5 million, much more than the $7 million value of their claims in liquidation.

Although such an exchange offer seems to benefit all parties, it might not be accepted by the creditors. Here's why: Suppose seven of the ten creditors tender their bonds; thus, seven creditors each now have claims with a face value of $850,000 each, or $5,950,000 in total, while the three creditors that did not tender their bonds each still have a claim with a face value of $1 million. The total face value of the debt at this point is $8,950,000, which is less than the $9 million value of the firm. In this situation, the three holdout creditors would receive the full face value of their debt. However, this probably would not happen, for two reasons: (1) All of the creditors would be sophisticated enough to realize this could happen. (2) Each creditor would want to be one of the three holdouts that gets paid in full. Thus, it is likely that none of the creditors would accept the offer. The holdout problem makes it difficult to restructure the firm's debts. Again, if the firm had a single creditor, there would be no holdout problem.

The holdout problem is mitigated in bankruptcy proceedings by the bankruptcy court's ability to lump creditors into classes. Each class is considered to have accepted a reorganization plan if two-thirds of the amount of debt and one-half the number of claimants vote for the plan, and the plan will be approved by the court if it is deemed to be "fair and equitable" to the dissenting parties. This procedure, in which the court mandates a reorganization plan in spite of dissent, is called a **cramdown provision**, because the court crams the plan down the throats of the dissenters. The ability of the court to force acceptance of a reorganization plan greatly reduces the incentive for creditors to hold out. Thus, in our example, if the reorganization plan offered each creditor a new claim worth $850,000 in face value along with information that each creditor would probably receive only $700,000 under the liquidation alternative, then reorganization would have a good chance of success.

It is easier for a firm with few creditors to reorganize informally than it is for a firm with many creditors. A 1990 study examined 169 publicly traded firms that experienced severe financial distress from 1978 to 1987.[7] About half of the firms reorganized without filing for bankruptcy, while the other half were forced to reorganize in bankruptcy. The firms that reorganized without filing for bankruptcy owed most of their debt to a few banks and had fewer creditors. Generally, bank debt can be reorganized outside of bankruptcy, but a publicly traded bond issue held by thousands of individual bondholders makes reorganization difficult.

---

[6]The bankruptcy code requires that all transactions undertaken by the firm in the 6 months prior to a bankruptcy filing be reviewed by the court for fraudulent conveyance, and the review can go back as far as 3 years.

[7]See Stuart Gilson, Kose John, and Larry Lang, "Troubled Debt Restructurings: An Empirical Study of Private Reorganization of Firms in Default," *Journal of Financial Economics*, October 1990, pp. 315–354.

Filing for bankruptcy under Chapter 11 has several other features that help the bankrupt firm.

1. Interest and principal payments, including interest on delayed payments, may be delayed without penalty until a reorganization plan is approved, and the plan itself may call for even further delays. This permits cash generated from operations to be used to sustain operations rather than be paid to creditors.

2. The firm is permitted to issue **debtor-in-possession (DIP) financing**. DIP financing enhances the ability of the firm to borrow funds for short-term liquidity purposes, because such loans are, under the law, senior to all previous unsecured debt.

3. The debtor firm's managers are given the exclusive right for 120 days after filing for bankruptcy protection to submit a reorganization plan, plus another 60 days to obtain agreement on the plan from the affected parties. The court may also extend these dates up to 18 months. After management's first right to submit a plan has expired, any party to the proceedings may propose its own reorganization plan.

Under the early bankruptcy laws, most formal reorganization plans were guided by the **absolute priority doctrine**.[8] This doctrine holds that creditors should be compensated for their claims in a rigid hierarchical order and that senior claims must be paid in full before junior claims can receive even a dime. If there were any chance that a delay would lead to losses by senior creditors, then the firm would be shut down and liquidated. However, an alternative position, the **relative priority doctrine**, holds that more flexibility should be allowed in a reorganization and that a balanced consideration should be given to all claimants. The current law represents a movement away from absolute priority toward relative priority.

The primary role of the bankruptcy court in a reorganization is to determine the **fairness** and the **feasibility** of the proposed plan of reorganization. The basic doctrine of fairness states that claims must be recognized in the order of their legal and contractual priority. Feasibility means that there is a reasonable chance that the reorganized company will be viable. Carrying out the concepts of fairness and feasibility in a reorganization involves the following steps:

1. Future sales must be estimated.
2. Operating conditions must be analyzed so that future earnings and cash flows can be predicted.
3. The appropriate capitalization rate must be determined.
4. This capitalization rate must then be applied to the estimated cash flows to obtain an estimate of the company's value.[9]
5. An appropriate capital structure for the company after it emerges from Chapter 11 must be determined.

---

[8]For more on absolute priority, see Lawrence A. Weiss, "The Bankruptcy Code and Violations of Absolute Priority," *Journal of Applied Corporate Finance,* Summer 1991, pp. 71–78; William Beranek, Robert Boehmer, and Brooke Smith, "Much Ado about Nothing: Absolute Priority Deviations in Chapter 11," *Financial Management,* Autumn 1996, pp. 102–109; and Allan C. Eberhart, William T. Moore, and Rodney Roenfeldt, "Security Pricing and Deviations from the Absolute Priority Rule in Bankruptcy Proceedings," *Journal of Finance,* December 1990, pp. 1457–1469.

[9]Several different approaches can be used to estimate a company's value. Market-determined multiples such as the price/earnings ratio, which are obtained from an analysis of comparable firms, can be applied to some measure of the company's earnings or cash flow. Alternatively, discounted cash flow techniques may be used. The key point here is that fairness requires the value of a company facing reorganization to be estimated so that potential offers can be evaluated rationally by the bankruptcy court.

6. The reorganized firm's securities must be allocated to the various claimants in a fair and equitable manner.

The primary test of feasibility in a reorganization is whether the fixed charges after reorganization will be adequately covered by earnings. Adequate coverage generally requires an improvement in earnings, a reduction of fixed charges, or both. Among the actions that must generally be taken are the following:

1. Debt maturities are usually lengthened, interest rates may be lowered, and some debt is usually converted into equity.
2. When the quality of management has been substandard, a new team must be given control of the company.
3. If inventories have become obsolete or depleted, they must be replaced.
4. Sometimes the plant and equipment must be modernized before the firm can operate and compete successfully.
5. Reorganization may also require an improvement in production, marketing, advertising, and/or other functions.
6. It is sometimes necessary to develop new products or markets to enable the firm to move from areas where economic trends are poor into areas with more potential for growth.
7. Labor unions must agree to accept lower wages and less restrictive work rules. This was a major issue for United Airlines (UAL) in 2003 as it attempted to emerge from Chapter 11 bankruptcy protection. By threatening liquidation, UAL was able to squeeze a $6.6 billion reduction in payroll costs from its pilots over 6 years and another $2.6 billion from its ground-crew workers. This wasn't enough, though, and UAL didn't emerge from bankruptcy for another 3 years.

These actions usually require at least some new money, so most reorganization plans include new investors who are willing to put up capital.

It might appear that stockholders have very little to say in a bankruptcy situation in which the firm's assets are worth less than the face value of its debt. Under the absolute priority rule, stockholders in such a situation should get nothing of value under a reorganization plan. In fact, however, stockholders may be able to extract some of the firm's value due to three reasons: (1) Stockholders generally continue to control the firm during the bankruptcy proceedings. (2) Stockholders have the first right (after management's 120-day window) to file a reorganization plan. (3) For the creditors, developing a plan and taking it through the courts would be expensive and time-consuming. Given this situation, creditors may support a plan under which they are not paid off in full and where the old stockholders will control the reorganized company, because the creditors want to get the problem behind them and to get some money in the near future.

24-5a Illustration of a Reorganization

Reorganization procedures may be illustrated with an example involving the Columbia Software Company, a regional firm that specializes in selling, installing, and servicing accounting software for small businesses.[10] Table 24-2 gives Columbia's balance sheet as of March 31, 2019. The company had been suffering losses running to $2.5 million a year, and (as the following discussion will make clear) the asset values in the balance sheet were overstated relative to their market values. The firm was **insolvent**, which means that the

---

[10]This example is based on an actual reorganization, although the company name has been changed and the numbers have been changed slightly to simplify the analysis.

TABLE 24-2
Columbia Software Company: Balance Sheet as of March 31, 2019 (Millions of Dollars)

Assets	
Current assets	$ 3.50
Net fixed assets	12.50
Other assets	0.70
Total assets	$16.70

Liabilities and Equity	
Accounts payable	$ 1.00
Accrued taxes	0.25
Notes payable	0.25
Other current liabilities	1.75
7.5% first-mortgage bonds, due 2026	6.00
9% subordinated debentures, due 2021[a]	7.00
Total liabilities	$16.25
Common stock ($1 par)	1.00
Paid-in capital	3.45
Retained earnings	(4.00)
Total liabilities and equity	$16.70

Note:

[a]The debentures are subordinated to the notes payable.

book values of its liabilities were greater than the market values of its assets, so it filed a petition with a federal court for reorganization under Chapter 11. Management filed a plan of reorganization with the court on June 13, 2019. The plan was subsequently submitted for review by the SEC.[11]

The plan concluded that the company could not be internally reorganized and that the only feasible solution would be to combine Columbia with a larger, nationwide software company. Accordingly, management solicited the interest of a number of software companies. Late in July 2019, Moreland Software showed an interest in Columbia. On August 3, 2019, Moreland made a formal proposal to take over Columbia's $6 million of 7.5% first-mortgage bonds, to pay the $250,000 in taxes owed by Columbia, and to provide 40,000 shares of Moreland common stock to satisfy the remaining creditor claims. The Moreland stock had a market price of $75 per share, so the value of the stock was $3 million. Thus, Moreland was offering $3 million of stock plus assuming $6 million of loans and $250,000 of taxes—a total of $9.25 million for assets that had a book value of $16.7 million.

Moreland's plan is shown in Table 24-3. As in most Chapter 11 plans, the secured creditors' claims are paid in full (in this case, the mortgage bonds are taken over by Moreland Software). However, the total remaining unsecured claims equal $10 million against only $3 million of Moreland stock. Thus, each unsecured creditor would be entitled to

[11]Reorganization plans must be submitted to the Securities and Exchange Commission (SEC) if two conditions hold: (1) The securities of the debtor are publicly held. (2) Total indebtedness exceeds $3 million. However, in recent years the only bankruptcy cases that the SEC has become involved in are those that set precedent or involve issues of national interest.

TABLE 24-3
Columbia Software Company: Reorganization Plan

Panel A: Senior Claims		
Senior Claimant	**Amount**	**Result**
Taxes	$ 250,000	Paid off by Moreland
Mortgage bonds	$6,000,000	Assumed by Moreland

The reorganization plan for the remaining $10 million of liabilities, based on 40,000 shares at a price of $75 for a total market value of $3 million, or 30% of the remaining liabilities, is as follows:

Panel B: Junior Claims					
Claimant **(1)**	**Original Amount** **(2)**	**30% of Claim Amount** **(3)**	**Claim after Subordination** **(4)**	**Number of Shares of Common Stock** **(5)**	**Percentage of Original Claim Received** **(6)**
Notes payable	$ 250,000	$ 75,000	$ 250,000[a]	3,333	100%
Unsecured creditors	2,750,000	825,000	825,000	11,000	30
Subordinated debentures	7,000,000	2,100,000	1,925,000[a]	25,667	28
	$10,000,000	$3,000,000	$3,000,000	40,000	30

Note:

[a]Because the debentures are subordinated to the notes payable, $250,000 − $75,000 = $175,000 must be redistributed from the debentures to the notes payable; this leaves a claim of $2,100,000 − $175,000 = $1,925,000 for the debentures.

receive 30% before the adjustment for subordination. Before this adjustment, holders of the notes payable would receive 30% of their $250,000 claim, or $75,000 in stock. However, the debentures are subordinated to the notes payable, so an additional $175,000 must be allocated to notes payable (see footnote a in Table 24-3). In Column 5, the dollar claims of each class of debt are restated in terms of the number of shares of Moreland common stock received by each class of unsecured creditors. Finally, Column 6 shows the percentage of the original claim that each group received. Of course, both the taxes and the secured creditors were paid off in full, while the stockholders received nothing.[12]

The bankruptcy court first evaluated the proposal from the standpoint of fairness. The court began by considering the value of Columbia Software as estimated by the unsecured creditors' committee and by a subgroup of debenture holders. After discussions with various experts, one group had arrived at estimated post-reorganization sales of $25 million per year. It further estimated that the profit margin on sales would equal 6%, thus producing estimated future annual earnings of $1.5 million.

This subgroup analyzed price/earnings ratios for comparable companies and arrived at 8 times future earnings for a capitalization factor. Multiplying 8 by $1.5 million gave an indicated equity value of the company of $12 million. This value was 4 times that of the 40,000 shares of Moreland stock offered for the remainder of the company. Thus, the subgroup concluded that the plan for reorganization did not meet the test of fairness. Note that, under both Moreland's plan and the subgroup's plan, the holders of common stock were to

[12]We do not show it, but $365,000 of fees for Columbia's attorneys and $123,000 of fees for the creditors' committee lawyers were also deducted. The current assets shown in Table 25-2 were net of these fees. Creditors joke (often bitterly) about the "lawyers first" rule in payouts in bankruptcy cases. It is often said, with much truth, that the only winners in bankruptcy cases are the attorneys.

receive nothing, which is one of the risks of ownership, while the holders of the first-mortgage bonds were to be assumed by Moreland, which amounts to being paid in full.

The bankruptcy judge examined management's plan for feasibility, observing that in the reorganization Moreland Software would take over Columbia's properties. The court judged that the direction and aid that Moreland could offer would remedy the deficiencies that had troubled Columbia. Whereas the debt/assets ratio of Columbia Software had become unbalanced, Moreland had only a moderate amount of debt. After consolidation, Moreland would still have a relatively low 27% debt ratio.

Moreland's net income before interest and taxes had been running at a level of approximately $15 million. The interest on its long-term debt after the merger would be $1.5 million and, taking short-term borrowings into account, would total a maximum of $2 million per year. The $15 million in earnings before interest and taxes would therefore provide an interest charge coverage of 7.5 times, exceeding the norm of 5 times for the industry.

Note that the question of feasibility would have been irrelevant if Moreland had offered $3 million in cash (rather than in stock) and payment of the bonds (rather than assuming them). It is the court's responsibility to protect the interests of Columbia's creditors. Because the creditors are being forced to take common stock or bonds guaranteed by another firm, the law requires the court to look into the feasibility of the transaction. However, if Moreland had made a cash offer, then the feasibility of its own operation after the transaction would not have been a concern.

Moreland Software was told of the subgroup's analysis and concern over the fairness of the plan. Further, Moreland was asked to increase the number of shares it offered. Moreland refused, and no other company offered to acquire Columbia. Because no better offer could be obtained and the only alternative to the plan was liquidation (with an even lower realized value), Moreland's proposal was ultimately accepted by the creditors despite some disagreement with the valuation.

One interesting aspect of this case concerned an agency conflict between Columbia's old stockholders and its management. Columbia's management knew when it filed for bankruptcy that the company was probably worth less than the amount of its debt and hence that stockholders would probably receive nothing. Indeed, that situation did materialize. If management has a primary responsibility to the stockholders, then why would it file for bankruptcy knowing that the stockholders would receive nothing? In the first place, management did not know for certain that stockholders would receive nothing. But they were certain that, if they did not file for bankruptcy protection, then creditors would foreclose on the company's property and shut the company down, which would surely lead to liquidation and a total loss to stockholders. Second, if the company were liquidated, then managers and workers would lose their jobs and the managers would have a black mark on their records. Finally, Columbia's managers thought (correctly) that there was nothing they could do to protect the stockholders, so they might as well do what was best for the workforce, the creditors, and themselves—and that meant realizing the most value possible for the company's assets.

Some of the stockholders felt betrayed by management—they thought management should have taken more heroic steps to protect them, regardless of the cost to other parties. One stockholder suggested management should have sold off assets, taken the cash to Las Vegas, and rolled the dice. Then, if they won, they should have paid off the debt and had something left for stockholders, leaving debtholders holding the bag if they lost. Actually, management had done something a bit like this in the year preceding the bankruptcy. Management realized the company was floundering, was likely to sink under its current operating plan, and that only a "big winner" project would save the company. Hence, they took on several risky, "bet the company" projects with negative expected NPVs but at least some chance for high profits. Unfortunately, those projects did not work out.

24-5b Prepackaged Bankruptcies

One type of reorganization combines the advantages of both the informal workout and formal Chapter 11 reorganization. This hybrid is called a **prepackaged bankruptcy**, or **pre-pack**.[13]

In an informal workout, a debtor negotiates a restructuring with its creditors. Even though complex workouts typically involve corporate officers, lenders, lawyers, and investment bankers, workouts are still less expensive and less damaging to reputations than are Chapter 11 reorganizations. In a prepackaged bankruptcy, the debtor firm gets all, or most, of the creditors to agree to the reorganization plan *prior* to filing for bankruptcy. Then, a reorganization plan is filed along with, or shortly after, the bankruptcy petition. If enough creditors have signed on before the filing, a cramdown can be used to bring reluctant creditors along.

A logical question arises: Why would a firm that can arrange an informal reorganization want to file for bankruptcy? The three primary advantages of a prepackaged bankruptcy are (1) reduction of the holdout problem, (2) preservation of creditors' claims, and (3) tax savings. Perhaps the biggest benefit of a prepackaged bankruptcy is the reduction of the holdout problem, because a bankruptcy filing permits a cramdown that would otherwise be impossible. By eliminating holdouts, bankruptcy forces all creditors in each class to participate on a pro rata basis, which preserves the relative value of all claimants. Also, filing for formal bankruptcy can at times have positive tax implications. First, in an informal reorganization in which the debtholders trade debt for equity, if the original equity holders end up with less than 50% ownership then the company loses its accumulated tax losses. In formal bankruptcy, in contrast, the firm may get to keep its loss carryforwards. Second, in a workout, when (say) debt worth $1,000 is exchanged for debt worth $500, the reduction in debt of $500 is considered to be taxable income to the corporation. However, if this same situation occurs in a Chapter 11 reorganization, the difference is not treated as taxable income.[14]

All in all, prepackaged bankruptcies make sense in many situations. If sufficient agreement can be reached among creditors through informal negotiations, a subsequent filing can solve the holdout problem and result in favorable tax treatment. For these reasons, the number of prepackaged bankruptcies has grown dramatically in recent years.

24-5c Reorganization Time and Expense

The time, expense, and headaches involved in a reorganization are almost beyond comprehension. Even in a small bankruptcy, such as one with assets valued between $2 million and $5 million, many people and groups are involved: lawyers representing the company, the U.S. Bankruptcy Trustee, each class of secured creditor, the general creditors as a group, tax authorities, and the stockholders if they are upset with management. There are time limits within which things are supposed to be done, but the process generally takes at least a year and usually much longer. The company must be given time to file its plan, and creditor groups must be given time to study and seek clarifications to it and then file

---

[13]For more information on prepackaged bankruptcies, see John J. McConnell and Henri Servaes, "The Economics of Pre-Packaged Bankruptcy," *Journal of Applied Corporate Finance,* Summer 1991, pp. 93–97; Brian L. Betker, "An Empirical Examination of Prepackaged Bankruptcy," *Financial Management,* Spring 1995, pp. 3–18; Sris Chatterjee, Upinder S. Dhillon, and Gabriel G. Ramirez, "Resolution of Financial Distress: Debt Restructurings via Chapter 11, Prepackaged Bankruptcies, and Workouts," *Financial Management,* Spring 1996, pp. 5–18; and John J. McConnell, Ronald C. Lease, and Elizabeth Tashjian, "Prepacks as a Mechanism for Resolving Financial Distress," *Journal of Applied Corporate Finance,* Winter 1996, pp. 99–106.

[14]Note that in both tax situations—loss carryforwards and debt value reductions—favorable tax treatment can be available in workouts if the firm is deemed to be legally insolvent—that is, if the market value of its assets is demonstrated to be less than the face value of its liabilities.

counterplans, to which the company must respond. Also, different creditor classes often disagree among themselves as to how much each class should receive, and hearings must be held to resolve such conflicts.

Management will want to remain in business, whereas some well-secured creditors may want the company liquidated as quickly as possible. Often, some party's plan will involve selling the business to another concern, as was the case with Columbia Software in our earlier example. Obviously, it can take months to seek out and negotiate with potential merger candidates.

The typical bankruptcy case takes about 2 years from the time the company files for protection under Chapter 11 until the final reorganization plan is approved or rejected. While all of this is going on, the company's business suffers. Sales certainly won't be helped, key employees may leave, and the remaining employees will be worrying about their jobs rather than concentrating on their work. Further, management will be spending much of its time on the bankruptcy rather than running the business, and it won't be able to take any significant action without court approval, which requires filing a formal petition with the court and giving all parties involved a chance to respond.

Even if its operations do not suffer, the company's assets surely will be reduced by its own legal fees and the required court and trustee costs. Good bankruptcy lawyers charge around $800 or more per hour, depending on the location, so those costs are not trivial. The creditors also will be incurring legal costs. Indeed, the sound of all of those meters ticking at $800 or so an hour in a slow-moving hearing can be deafening.

Note that creditors also lose the time value of their money. A creditor with a $100,000 claim and a 10% opportunity cost who ends up getting $50,000 after 2 years would have been better off settling for $41,500 initially. When the creditor's legal fees, executive time, and general aggravation are taken into account, it might make sense to settle for $25,000 or even $20,000.

Both the troubled company and its creditors know the drawbacks of formal bankruptcy, or their lawyers will inform them. Armed with knowledge of how bankruptcy works, management may be in a strong position to persuade creditors to accept a workout that may seem to be unfair and unreasonable. Or, if a Chapter 11 case has already begun, creditors may at some point agree to settle just to stop the bleeding.

One final point should be made before closing this section. In most reorganization plans, creditors with claims of less than $1,000 are paid off in full. Paying off these "nuisance claims" does not cost much money, and it saves time and gets votes to support the plan.[15]

SELF-TEST

Define the following terms: common pool problem, holdout problem, automatic stay, cramdown, fraudulent conveyance, absolute priority doctrine, relative priority doctrine, fairness, feasibility, debtor-in-possession financing, and prepackaged bankruptcy.

What are the advantages of a formal reorganization under Chapter 11?

What are some recent trends regarding absolute versus relative priority doctrines?

How do courts assess the fairness and feasibility of reorganization plans?

Why have prepackaged bankruptcies become so popular in recent years?

24-6 Liquidation in Bankruptcy

If a company is "too far gone" to be reorganized, then it must be liquidated. Liquidation should occur when the business is worth more dead than alive, or when the possibility of restoring it to financial health is remote and the creditors are exposed to a high risk

---

[15]For more information on bankruptcy costs, see Daryl M. Guffey and William T. Moore, "Direct Bankruptcy Costs: Evidence from the Trucking Industry," *The Financial Review*, May 1991, pp. 223–235.

of greater loss if operations are continued. Earlier we discussed assignment, which is an informal liquidation procedure. Now we consider **liquidation in bankruptcy**, which is carried out under the jurisdiction of a federal bankruptcy court.

Chapter 7 of the federal **Bankruptcy Reform Act of 1978** deals with liquidation. It (1) provides safeguards against fraud by the debtor, (2) provides for an equitable distribution of the debtor's assets among the creditors, and (3) allows insolvent debtors to discharge all their obligations and thus be able to start new businesses unhampered by the burdens of prior debt. However, formal liquidation is time-consuming and costly, and it extinguishes the business.

The distribution of assets under Chapter 7 is governed by the following **priority of claims in liquidation**.[16]

1. *Past-due property tax liens.*[17]
2. *Secured creditors, who are entitled to the proceeds of the sale of specific property pledged for a lien or a mortgage.* If the proceeds from the sale of the pledged property do not fully satisfy a secured creditor's claim, the remaining balance is treated as a general creditor claim (see Item 10 below).[18]
3. *Legal fees and other expenses to administer and operate the bankrupt firm.* These costs include legal fees incurred in trying to reorganize.
4. *Expenses incurred after an involuntary case has begun but before a trustee is appointed.*
5. *Wages due workers if earned within 180 days prior to the filing of the petition for bankruptcy.* The amount of wages is limited to $11,725 per employee.
6. *Claims for unpaid contributions to employee pension plans that should have been paid within 180 days prior to filing.* These claims, plus wages in Item 5, may not exceed the limit of $11,725 per wage earner.
7. *Unsecured claims for customer deposits.* These claims are limited to a maximum of $2,600 per individual.
8. *Taxes due to federal, state, county, and other government agencies.*
9. *Unfunded pension plan liabilities.* These liabilities have a claim above that of the general creditors for an amount up to 30% of the common and preferred equity, and any remaining unfunded pension claims rank with the general creditors.[19]

---

[16]See **www.law.cornell.edu/uscode/text/11/507** for a complete listing of the priority of claims.

[17]See **www.law.cornell.edu/uscode/text/11/724** for the priority rules regarding liens.

[18]Suppose a bank's customer borrows from the bank and then goes bankrupt. If the loan agreement stipulates that the bank has a first-priority claim on the customer's deposits, then the bank will use the deposits to offset all or part of the loan—in legal terms, this is "the right of offset." If the bank doesn't have a first-priority claim, the bank will attach the deposits and hold them for the general body of creditors, including the bank itself.

[19]Pension plan liabilities have a significant bearing on bankruptcy settlements. As we discuss in *Web Chapter 29*, pension plans may be *funded* or unfunded. With a *funded* plan, the firm makes cash payments to an insurance company or to a trustee (generally a bank), which then uses these funds (and the interest earned on them) to pay retirees' pensions. With an *unfunded* plan, the firm is obligated to make payments to retirees, but it does not provide cash in advance. Many plans are actually partially funded—some money has been paid in advance but not enough to provide full pension benefits to all employees.

If a firm goes bankrupt, the funded part of the pension plan remains intact and is available for retirees. Prior to 1974, employees had no explicit claims for unfunded pension liabilities, but under the Employees' Retirement Income Security Act of 1974 (ERISA), an amount up to 30% of the equity (common and preferred) is earmarked for employees' pension plans and has a priority over the general creditors, with any remaining pension claims having status equal to that of the general creditors. This means, in effect, that the funded portion of a bankrupt firm's pension plan is completely secured, whereas the unfunded portion ranks just above the general creditors. Obviously, unfunded pension liabilities should be of great concern to a firm's unsecured creditors.

10. *General, or unsecured, creditors.* Holders of trade credit, unsecured loans, the unsatisfied portion of secured loans, and debenture bonds are classified as general creditors. Holders of subordinated debt also fall into this category, but they must turn over required amounts to the senior debt.

11. *Preferred stockholders.* These stockholders can receive an amount up to the par value of their stock.

12. *Common stockholders.* These stockholders receive any remaining funds.[20]

To illustrate how this priority system works, consider the balance sheet of Whitman Inc., shown in Table 24-4. Assets have a book value of $90 million. The claims are shown on the right-hand side of the balance sheet. Note that the debentures are subordinated to the notes payable to banks. Whitman filed for bankruptcy under Chapter 11, but because no fair and feasible reorganization could be arranged, the trustee is liquidating the firm under Chapter 7.

The assets as reported in the balance sheet are greatly overstated; they are, in fact, worth less than half the $90 million that is shown. The following amounts are realized on liquidation:

From sale of current assets	$28,000,000
From sale of fixed assets	5,000,000
Total receipts	$33,000,000

TABLE 24-4
Whitman Inc.: Balance Sheet at Liquidation (Millions of Dollars)

Current assets	$80.0	Accounts payable	$20.0
Net fixed assets	10.0	Notes payable (to banks)	10.0
		Accrued wages (1,400 @ $500)	0.7
		Federal taxes	1.0
		State and local taxes	0.3
		Current liabilities	$32.0
		First mortgage	6.0
		Second mortgage	1.0
		Subordinated debentures[a]	8.0
		Total long-term debt	$15.0
		Preferred stock	2.0
		Common stock	26.0
		Paid-in capital	4.0
		Retained earnings	11.0
		Total equity	$43.0
Total assets	$90.0	Total liabilities and equity	$90.0

Note:

[a]The debentures are subordinated to the notes payable.

[20]Note that if different classes of common stock have been issued, then differential priorities may exist in stockholder claims.

The distribution of proceeds from the liquidation is shown in Table 24-5. The first-mortgage holders receive the $5 million in net proceeds from the sale of fixed property, leaving $28 million available to the remaining creditors, including a $1 million unsatisfied claim of the first-mortgage holders. Next are the fees and expenses of administering the bankruptcy, which are typically about 20% of gross proceeds (including the bankrupt firm's own legal fees); in this example, they are assumed to be $6 million. Next in priority are wages due workers, which total $700,000, and taxes due, which amount to $1.3 million. Thus far, the total amount of claims paid from the $33 million received from the asset sale is $13 million, leaving $20 million for the general creditors. In this example, we assume there are no claims for unpaid benefit plans or unfunded pension liabilities.

The claims of the general creditors total $40 million. Because $20 million is available, claimants will be allocated 50% of their claims initially, as shown in Column 3. However, the subordination adjustment requires that the subordinated debentures turn over to the notes payable all amounts received until the notes are satisfied. In this

TABLE 24-5

Whitman Inc.: Distribution of Liquidation Proceeds (Millions of Dollars)

Panel A: Distribution to Priority Claimants	
Proceeds from the sale of assets	$33.0
Less:	
1. First mortgage (paid from the sale of fixed assets)	5.0
2. Fees and expenses of bankruptcy	6.0
3. Wages due to workers within 3 months of bankruptcy	0.7
4. Taxes due to federal, state, and local governments	1.3
Funds available for distribution to general creditors	$20.0

	Panel B: Distribution to General Creditors			
General Creditors' Claims (1)	Amount of Claim[a] (2)	Pro Rata Distribution[b] (3)	Distribution after Subordination Adjustment[c] (4)	Percentage of Original Claim Received[d] (5)
Unsatisfied portion of first mortgage	$ 1.0	$ 0.5	$ 0.5	92%
Second mortgage	1.0	0.5	0.5	50
Notes payable (to banks)	10.0	5.0	9.0	90
Accounts payable	20.0	10.0	10.0	50
Subordinated debentures	8.0	4.0	0.0	0
Total	$40.0	$20.0	$20.0	

Notes:

[a]Column 2 is the claim of each class of general creditor. Total claims equal $40.0 million.

[b]From the top section of the table, we see that $20 million is available for distribution to general creditors. Because there is $40 million worth of general creditor claims, the pro rata distribution will be $20/$40 = 0.50, or 50 cents on the dollar.

[c]The debentures are subordinate to the notes payable, so up to $5 million could be reallocated from debentures to notes payable. However, only $4 million is available to the debentures, so this entire amount is reallocated.

[d]Column 5 shows the results of dividing the Column 4 final allocation by the original claim shown in Column 2—except for the first mortgage, where the $5 million received from the sale of fixed assets is included in the calculation.

situation, the claim of the notes payable is $10 million but only $5 million is available; the deficiency is therefore $5 million. After transfer of $4 million from the subordinated debentures, there remains a deficiency of $1 million on the notes; this amount will remain unsatisfied.

Note that 90% of the bank claim is satisfied, whereas a maximum of 50% of other unsecured claims will be satisfied. These figures illustrate the usefulness of the subordination provision to the security to which the subordination is made.

Because no other funds remain, the claims of the holders of preferred and common stocks, as well as the subordinated debentures, are completely wiped out. Studies of the proceeds in bankruptcy liquidations reveal that unsecured creditors receive, on the average, about 15 cents on the dollar, while common stockholders generally receive nothing.

SELF-TEST

Describe briefly the priority of claims in a formal liquidation.

What is the impact of subordination on the final allocation of proceeds from liquidation?

In general, how much do unsecured creditors receive from a liquidation? How much do stockholders receive?

24-7 Anatomy of a Bankruptcy: Transforming the GM *Corporation* into the GM *Company*

The General Motors *Corporation* was founded in 1908 and was the world's largest automobile manufacturer from 1931 until 2008. Despite its size and market power, GM lost a cumulative $82 billion from 2005 until 2008 and declared bankruptcy in 2009. Several factors contributed to GM's problems, including increased international competition, high costs associated with labor contracts (especially retirement benefits), the economic slowdown that began in 2007, and senior executives that the press labeled as out of touch.

In the years leading up to its bankruptcy, GM undertook several major restructuring efforts. During the 1980s, GM became a major player in the financial services industries, and by 2005 its financing and insurance operations had assets of $312 billion compared to its automotive business assets of $162 billion. By this measure, GM was a "bank" with an auto manufacturer and not an auto company with a "bank." However, in 2006 and 2007, facing declining sales and profits, GM moved to refocus on its core auto business and conserve cash. It halved its dividend, sold a 51% stake in its GMAC financing company, sold its stakes in other auto manufacturers, closed factories and reduced its workforce.

In 2007, during a United Auto Workers (UAW) strike, GM agreed to create a UAW-managed trust fund (a voluntary employees' beneficiary association, called a VEBA) that would fund retiree health care coverage in exchange for a lower wage structure. The liabilities associated with the retiree health care were estimated to be over $50 billion. GM agreed to put about $35 billion of assets into the VEBA (GM and the UAW assumed that the trust's $35 billion in assets would grow faster than the $50 billion in liabilities) and make the majority of its future contributions in the form of GM stock rather than cash.

Even after the restructurings and wage concessions, GM continued to lose money. In late 2008, the CEOs of GM, Chrysler, and Ford flew to Washington in private jets to ask for government assistance. The Bush administration broadened the Troubled Asset Relief

Program (TARP) to include the auto industry, and GM received a loan of $13.4 billion in December 2008. GMAC also received a TARP loan ($6 billion), as did Chrysler and its financial subsidiary. These loans required GM and Chrysler to submit turnaround plans to the government by February 17, 2009.[21]

An Obama administration task force reviewed and rejected the plans GM submitted and asked for and received the resignation of Rick Wagoner, GM's CEO. In addition, the government provided additional loans to GM and Chrysler, loans to their suppliers (who were reluctant to keep selling to the auto companies on credit) and created a program to ensure that customer warranty claims would be honored.

Ultimately, GM was unable to provide a turnaround plan that was acceptable to its debtholders, suppliers, dealers, and workforce, so it filed for Chapter 11 bankruptcy protection on June 1, 2009. As of the quarter ending March 31, 2009, GM listed $82 billion in assets, but more than twice that amount ($173 billion) in liabilities, including short-term debt of $26 billion, long-term debt of $29 billion, and retiree obligations of $47 billion.

Two days after filing for bankruptcy, TARP provided an additional $30 billion to GM; because GM had filed for bankruptcy, this loan was debtor-in-possession (DIP) financing. In total, TARP provided about $50 billion in financing to GM.

On July 10, 2009, GM emerged from bankruptcy as a new company—literally! GM and its creditors agreed to sell almost all of GM's assets to a new company, to be named the General Motors Company (instead of Corporation). In return, GM's creditors and stakeholders exchanged their old claims for new claims in the new GM Company. GM now had less than $16 billion in debt (compared to $55 billion before the bankruptcy) and $36 billion in retiree obligations (down from $47 billion). In addition to a much lower debt load, the bankruptcy plan called for GM to close over 10 factories, reduce the number of brands it sells, and reduce the number of its dealers.

GM emerged from bankruptcy with about $75 billion less in liabilities. What happened to all those claims? Senior secured loans and suppliers were paid in full. Subordinated bondholders were treated as senior unsecured debt and received about 1/8 the face value of their bonds. The common stockholders received nothing. As for other claimants, they received common stock in the new GM. The U.S. government received about 61% of the stock, the Canadian government received 11.7%, the VEBA trust received 17.5% (instead of the cash it was originally owed), and unsecured bondholders received 10%.

GM's shares were not publicly traded until November 18, 2010, when GM sold $20.1 billion in its IPO. GM's underwriters sold an additional $3 billion of stock, for a total of $23.1 billion, which made GM's IPO the biggest ever. GM didn't raise any cash in the IPO—all the shares were sold by existing stockholders, including the U.S. government, which reduced its ownership to about 33% of GM.

GM has been profitable since the IPO, but its stock price has been volatile, at one point falling to $19 from the IPO price of $33. The price eventually climbed past the IPO price but has lagged the stock market as a whole. In December 2013, the U.S. government sold the last of its GM stock, losing about $10 billion in the bailout.

SELF-TEST

What events preceded GM's bankruptcy?

What happened to the pre-bankruptcy stockholders and the claims of creditors?

---

[21]For a detailed treatment of the government's involvement in GM's bankruptcy, see a paper by Thomas H. Klier and James Rubenstein, "Detroit Back from the Brink? Auto Industry Crisis and Restructuring, 2008–11," *Economic Perspectives*, 2Q/2012, pp. 35–54.

24-8 Other Motivations for Bankruptcy

Normally, bankruptcy proceedings do not commence until a company has become so financially weak that it cannot meet its current obligations. However, bankruptcy law also permits a company to file for bankruptcy if its financial forecasts indicate that a continuation of current conditions would lead to insolvency.

Bankruptcy law has also been used to hasten settlements in major product liability suits. The Manville asbestos case is an example. Manville was being bombarded by thousands of lawsuits, and the very existence of such huge contingent liabilities made normal operations impossible. Further, it was relatively easy to demonstrate four salient facts: (1) If the plaintiffs won, the company would be unable to pay the full amount of the claims. (2) A larger amount of funds would be available to the claimants if the company continued to operate rather than liquidate. (3) Continued operations were possible only if the suits were brought to a conclusion. (4) A timely resolution of all the suits was impossible because of their vast number and variety.

Manville filed for bankruptcy in 1982, at that time the largest U.S. bankruptcy ever. The bankruptcy statutes were used to consolidate all the suits and to reach settlements under which the plaintiffs obtained more money than they otherwise would have received, and Manville was able to stay in business. (It was acquired in 2001 by Berkshire Hathaway.) The stockholders did poorly under these plans because most of the companies' future cash flows were assigned to the plaintiffs, but even so, the stockholders probably fared better than they would have if the suits had been concluded through the jury system.

SELF-TEST

What are some situations other than immediate financial distress that lead firms to file for bankruptcy?

24-9 Some Criticisms of Bankruptcy Laws

Although bankruptcy laws exist, for the most part, to protect creditors, many critics claim that current laws are not doing what they were intended to do. Before 1978, most bankruptcies ended quickly in liquidation. Then Congress rewrote the laws, giving companies more opportunity to stay alive on the grounds that this was best for managers, employees, creditors, and stockholders. Before the reform, 90% of Chapter 11 filers were liquidated, but now that percentage is less than 80%, and the average time between filing and liquidation has almost doubled. Indeed, large public corporations with the ability to hire high-priced legal help can avoid (or at least delay) liquidation, often at the expense of creditors and shareholders.

Critics believe that bankruptcy is great for businesses these days—especially for consultants, lawyers, and investment bankers, who reap hefty fees during bankruptcy proceedings, and for managers, who continue to collect their salaries and bonuses as long as the business is kept alive. The problem, according to critics, is that bankruptcy courts allow cases to drag on too long, depleting assets that could be sold to pay off creditors and shareholders. Too often, quick resolution is impossible because bankruptcy judges are required to deal with issues such as labor disputes, pension plan funding, and environmental liability—social questions that could be solved by legislative action rather than by bankruptcy courts.

Critics contend that bankruptcy judges ought to realize that some sick companies should be allowed to die—and die quickly. Maintaining companies on life support does not serve the interests of the parties that the bankruptcy laws were designed to protect. The 2005 changes to the bankruptcy code addressed this issue by limiting to 18 months the time that management has to file a reorganization plan. Prior to the change, judges could extend this time almost indefinitely. Now, creditors may propose a plan if an acceptable plan hasn't been filed by management within 18 months.

Other critics think the entire bankruptcy system of judicial protection and supervision needs to be scrapped. Some even have proposed an auction-like procedure, where shareholders and creditors would have the opportunity to gain control of a bankrupt company by raising the cash needed to pay the bills. The rationale here is that the market is a better judge than a bankruptcy court as to whether a company is worth more dead or alive.

SELF-TEST

According to critics, what are some problems with the bankruptcy system?

SUMMARY

This chapter discussed the main issues involved in bankruptcy and financial distress in general. The key concepts are listed here.

- The fundamental issue that must be addressed when a company encounters financial distress is whether it is "worth more dead than alive"; that is, would the business be more valuable if it continued in operation or if it were liquidated and sold off in pieces?
- In the case of a fundamentally sound company whose financial difficulties appear to be temporary, creditors will frequently work directly with the company, helping it to recover and reestablish itself on a sound financial basis. Such voluntary reorganization plans are called **workouts**.
- Reorganization plans usually require some type of **restructuring** of the firm's debts; this may involve an **extension**, which postpones the date of required payment of past-due obligations, and/or a **composition**, by which the creditors voluntarily reduce their claims on the debtor or the interest rate on their claims.
- When it is obvious that a firm is worth more dead than alive, informal procedures can sometimes be used to **liquidate** the firm. **Assignment** is an informal procedure for liquidating a firm, and it usually yields creditors a larger amount than they would receive in a formal bankruptcy liquidation. However, assignments are feasible only if the firm is small and its affairs are not too complex.
- Current bankruptcy law consists of nine chapters, designated by Arabic numbers. For businesses, the most important chapters are **Chapter 7**, which details the procedures to be followed when liquidating a firm, and **Chapter 11**, which contains procedures for formal reorganizations.
- Since the first bankruptcy laws, the **absolute priority doctrine** has guided most formal reorganization plans. This doctrine holds that creditors should be compensated for their claims in a rigid hierarchical order and that senior claims must be paid in full before junior claims can receive even a dime.
- Another position, the **relative priority doctrine**, holds that more flexibility should be allowed in a reorganization and that a balanced consideration should be given to all claimants. In recent years, there has been a shift away from absolute priority toward

relative priority. The primary effect of this shift has been to delay liquidations, giving managements more time to rehabilitate companies in an effort to provide value to junior claimants.

- The primary role of the bankruptcy court in a reorganization is to determine the **fairness** and the **feasibility** of proposed plans of reorganization.

- Even if some creditors or stockholders dissent and do not accept a reorganization plan, the plan may still be approved by the court if the plan is deemed to be "fair and equitable" to all parties. This procedure, in which the court mandates a reorganization plan in spite of dissent, is called a **cramdown**.

- A **prepackaged bankruptcy** (also called a **pre-pack**) is a hybrid type of reorganization that combines the advantages of both an informal workout and a formal Chapter 11 reorganization.

- The distribution of assets in a **liquidation** under Chapter 7 of the Bankruptcy Act is governed by a specific priority of claims.

- **Multiple discriminant analysis (MDA)** is a method to identify firms with high bankruptcy risk. We discuss MDA in *Web Extension 24A*.

QUESTIONS

(24-1) Define each of the following terms:
a. Informal restructuring; reorganization in bankruptcy
b. Assignment; liquidation in bankruptcy; fairness; feasibility
c. Absolute priority doctrine; relative priority doctrine
d. Bankruptcy Reform Act of 1978; Chapter 11; Chapter 7
e. Priority of claims in liquidation
f. Extension; composition; workout; cramdown; prepackaged bankruptcy; holdout

(24-2) Why do creditors usually accept a plan for financial rehabilitation rather than demand liquidation of the business?

(24-3) Would it be a sound rule to liquidate whenever the liquidation value is above the value of the corporation as a going concern? Discuss.

(24-4) Why do liquidations usually result in losses for the creditors or the owners, or both? Would partial liquidation or liquidation over a period limit their losses? Explain.

(24-5) Are liquidations likely to be more common for public utility, railroad, or industrial corporations? Why or why not?

SELF-TEST PROBLEM   SOLUTION SHOWN IN APPENDIX A

(ST-1)
Liquidation
At the time it defaulted on its interest payments and filed for bankruptcy, Medford Fabricators Inc. had the following balance sheet (in millions of dollars). The court, after trying unsuccessfully to reorganize the firm, decided that the only recourse was liquidation under Chapter 7. Sale of the fixed assets, which were pledged as collateral to the mortgage bondholders, brought in $750 million, while the current assets were sold for another $400 million. Thus, the total proceeds from the liquidation sale were $1,150 million. The trustee's costs amounted to $1 million; no single worker was due more than the maximum allowable wages per worker; and there were no unfunded pension plan liabilities.

Balance Sheet

Current assets	$ 800	Accounts payable		$ 100
		Accrued taxes		90
		Accrued wages		60
		Notes payable		300
		Total current liabilities		$ 550
Net fixed assets	1,100	First-mortgage bonds[a]		700
		Second-mortgage bonds[a]		400
		Debentures		500
		Subordinated debentures[b]		200
		Common stock		100
		Retained earnings		(550)
Total assets	$1,900	Total liabilities & equity		$1,900

Notes:

[a]All fixed assets are pledged as collateral to the mortgage bonds.

[b]Subordinated to notes payable.

a. How much of the proceeds from the sale of assets remains to be distributed to general creditors after distribution to priority claimants?

b. After distribution to general creditors and subordination adjustments are made, how much of the proceeds are received by the second-mortgage holders? By holders of the notes payable? By the subordinated debentures? By the common stockholders?

PROBLEMS   ANSWERS ARE IN APPENDIX B

EASY PROBLEM 1

(24-1)
Liquidation

Southwestern Wear Inc. has the following balance sheet:

Current assets	$1,875,000	Accounts payable	$ 375,000
Fixed assets	1,875,000	Notes payable	750,000
		Subordinated debentures	750,000
		Total debt	$1,875,000
		Common equity	1,875,000
Total assets	$3,750,000	Total liabilities & equity	$3,750,000

The trustee's costs total $281,250, and the firm has no accrued taxes or wages. The debentures are subordinated only to the notes payable. If the firm goes bankrupt and liquidates, how much will each class of investors receive if a total of $2.5 million is received from sale of the assets?

INTERMEDIATE PROBLEM 2

(24-2)
Reorganization

The Verbrugge Publishing Company's 2019 balance sheet and income statement are as follows (in millions of dollars):

Balance Sheet

Current assets	$300	Current liabilities	$ 40
Net fixed assets	200	Advance payments by customers	80
		Noncallable preferred stock, $6 coupon, $110 par value (1,000,000 shares)	110
		Callable preferred stock, $10 coupon, no par, $100 call price (200,000 shares)	200
		Common stock, $2 par value (5,000,000 shares)	10
		Retained earnings	60
Total assets	$500	Total liabilities & equity	$500

Income Statement

Net sales	$540
Operating expense	516
Net operating income	$ 24
Other income	4
EBT	$ 28
Taxes (25%)	7
Net income	$ 21
Dividends on $6 preferred	6
Dividends on $10 preferred	2
Income available to common stockholders	$ 13

Verbrugge and its creditors have agreed upon a voluntary reorganization plan. In this plan, each share of the noncallable preferred will be exchanged for 1 share of $2.40 preferred with a par value of $35 plus one 8% subordinated income debenture with a par value of $75. The callable preferred issue will be retired with cash generated by reducing current assets.

a. Assume that the reorganization takes place and construct the projected balance. Show the new preferred stock at its par value. What is the value for total assets? For debt? For preferred stock?
b. Construct the projected income statement. What is the income available to common shareholders in the proposed recapitalization?
c. What were the total cash flows received by the noncallable preferred stockholders prior to the reorganization? What were the total cash flows to the original noncallable preferred stockholders after the reorganization? What was the net income to common stockholders before the reorganization? After the reorganization.
d. *Required* pre-tax earnings are defined as the amount that is just large enough to meet fixed charges (debenture interest and/or preferred dividends). What are the required pre-tax earnings before and after the recapitalization?
e. How is the debt ratio (i.e., liabilities/total assets) affected by the reorganization? Suppose you treated preferred stock as debt and calculated the resulting debt ratios. How are these ratios affected? If you were a holder of Verbrugge's common stock, would you vote in favor of the reorganization? Why or why not?

CHALLENGING PROBLEMS 3–4

(24-3)
Liquidation

At the time it defaulted on its interest payments and filed for bankruptcy, the McDaniel Mining Company had the balance sheet shown here (in thousands of dollars). The court, after trying unsuccessfully to reorganize the firm, decided that the only recourse was liquidation under Chapter 7. Sale of the fixed assets, which were pledged as collateral to the mortgage bondholders, brought in $400,000, while the current assets were sold for another $200,000. Thus, the total proceeds from the liquidation sale were $600,000. The trustee's costs amounted to $50,000; no single worker was due more than the maximum allowable wages per worker; and there were no unfunded pension plan liabilities.

Balance Sheet (Thousands of Dollars)

Current assets	$ 400	Accounts payable	$ 50
Net fixed assets	600	Accrued taxes	40
		Accrued wages	30
		Notes payable	180
		Total current liabilities	$ 300
		First-mortgage bonds[a]	300
		Second-mortgage bonds[a]	200
		Debentures	200
		Subordinated debentures[b]	100
		Common stock	50
		Retained earnings	(150)
Total assets	$1,000	Total liabilities & equity	$1,000

Notes:

[a]All fixed assets are pledged as collateral to the mortgage bonds.

[b]Subordinated to notes payable only.

a. How much will McDaniel's shareholders receive from the liquidation?
b. How much will the first mortgage bondholders receive from collateralized assets? Will they receive their full claim? If not, how much is their remaining claim?
c. How much will the second mortgage bondholders receive from collateralized assets? Will they receive their full claim? If not, how much is their remaining claim?
d. Who are the other priority claimants (in addition to the mortgage bondholders)? How much will they receive from the liquidation?
e. Who are the remaining general creditors? How much will each receive from the distribution before subordination adjustment? How much will each receive after subordination? How much in total will the second mortgage holders receive (include the amount received from collateral).

(24-4)
Liquidation

The following balance sheet represents Boles Electronics Corporation's position at the time it filed for bankruptcy (in thousands of dollars):

Cash	$ 10	Accounts payable	$ 1,600
Receivables	100	Notes payable	500
Inventories	890	Wages payable	150
		Taxes payable	50
Total current assets	$ 1,000	Total current liabilities	$ 2,300
Net plant and property	4,000	Mortgage bonds	2,000
Net equipment	5,000	Subordinated debentures	2,500
		Preferred stock	1,500
		Common stock	1,700
Total assets	$10,000	Total liabilities & equity	$10,000

The mortgage bonds are secured by the plant but not by the equipment. The subordinated debentures are subordinated to notes payable. The firm was unable to reorganize under Chapter 11; therefore, it was liquidated under Chapter 7. The trustee, whose legal and administrative fees amounted to $200,000, sold off the assets and received the following proceeds (in thousands of dollars):

Asset	Proceeds
Plant	$1,600
Equipment	1,300
Receivables	50
Inventories	240
Total	$3,190

In addition, the firm had $10,000 in cash available for distribution. No single wage earner had claims exceeding the maximum allowable wages per worker, and there were no unfunded pension plan liabilities.

a. What is the total amount available for distribution to all claimants? What is the total of creditor and trustee claims? Will the preferred and common stockholders receive any distributions?
b. Determine the dollar distribution to each creditor and to the trustee. What percentage of each claim is satisfied?

SPREADSHEET PROBLEM

(24-5)
Liquidation

resource

Start with the partial model in the file **Ch24 P05 Build a Model.xlsx** on the textbook's Web site. Duchon Industries had the following balance sheet at the time it defaulted on its interest payments and filed for liquidation under Chapter 7. Sale of the fixed assets, which were pledged as collateral to the mortgage bondholders, brought in $900 million, while the current assets were sold for another $401 million. Thus, the total proceeds from the liquidation sales were $1,300 million. The trustee's costs amounted to $1 million; no single worker was due more than the maximum allowable wages per worker; and there were no unfunded pension plan liabilities. Determine the amount available for distribution to shareholders and all claimants.

Duchon Industries' Balance Sheets (Millions of Dollars)

Current assets	$ 400	Accounts payable	$ 50
Net fixed assets	600	Accrued taxes	40
		Accrued wages	30
		Notes payable	180
		Total current liabilities	$ 300
		First-mortgage bonds[a]	300
		Second-mortgage bonds[a]	200
		Debentures	200
		Subordinated debentures[b]	100
		Common stock	50
		Retained earnings	(150)
Total assets	$1,000	Total claims	$1,000

[a]All fixed assets are pledged as collateral to the mortgage bonds.

[b]Subordinated to notes payable only.

MINI CASE

Kimberly MacKenzie—president of Kim's Clothes Inc., a medium-sized manufacturer of women's casual clothing—is worried. Her firm has been selling clothes to Russ Brothers Department Store for more than 10 years, and she has never experienced any problems in collecting payment for the merchandise sold. Currently, Russ Brothers owes Kim's Clothes $65,000 for spring sportswear that was delivered to the store just 2 weeks ago. Kim's concern arose from reading an article in yesterday's *Wall Street Journal* that indicated Russ Brothers was having serious financial problems. Moreover, the article stated that Russ Brothers' management was considering filing for reorganization, or even liquidation, with a federal bankruptcy court.

Kim's immediate concern is whether her firm will collect its receivables if Russ Brothers goes bankrupt. In pondering the situation, Kim has also realized that she knows nothing about the process that firms go through when they encounter severe financial distress. To learn more about bankruptcy, reorganization, and liquidation, Kim has asked Ron Mitchell, her firm's chief financial officer, to prepare a briefing on the subject for the entire board of directors. In turn, Ron has asked you, a newly hired financial analyst, to do the groundwork for the briefing by answering the following questions:

a. (1) What are the major causes of business failure?
   (2) Do business failures occur evenly over time?
   (3) Which size of firm, large or small, is more prone to business failure? Why?
b. What key issues must managers face in the financial distress process?
c. What informal remedies are available to firms in financial distress? In answering this question, define the following terms:
   (1) Workout
   (2) Restructuring
   (3) Extension
   (4) Composition
   (5) Assignment
   (6) Assignee (trustee)
d. Briefly describe U.S. bankruptcy law, including the following terms:
   (1) Chapter 11
   (2) Chapter 7
   (3) Trustee
   (4) Voluntary bankruptcy
   (5) Involuntary bankruptcy
e. What are the major differences between an informal reorganization and reorganization in bankruptcy? In answering this question, be sure to discuss the following items:
   (1) Common pool problem
   (2) Holdout problem
   (3) Automatic stay
   (4) Cramdown
   (5) Fraudulent conveyance
f. What is a prepackaged bankruptcy? Why have prepackaged bankruptcies become more popular in recent years?
g. Briefly describe the priority of claims in a Chapter 7 liquidation.

h. Assume that Russ Brothers did indeed fail, and that it had the following balance sheet when it was liquidated (in millions of dollars):

Current assets	$40.0	Accounts payable	$10.0
Net fixed assets	5.0	Notes payable (to banks)	5.0
		Accrued wages	0.3
		Federal taxes	0.5
		State and local taxes	0.2
		Current liabilities	$16.0
		First-mortgage bonds	3.0
		Second-mortgage bonds	0.5
		Subordinated debentures[a]	4.0
		Total long-term debt	$ 7.5
		Preferred stock	1.0
		Common stock	13.0
		Paid-in capital	2.0
		Retained earnings	5.5
		Total equity	$21.5
Total assets	$45.0	Total claims	$45.0

[a]The debentures are subordinated to the notes payable.

The liquidation sale resulted in the following proceeds:

From sale of current assets	$14,000,000
From sale of fixed assets	2,500,000
Total receipts	$16,500,000

For simplicity, assume there were no trustee's fees or any other claims against the liquidation proceeds. Also, assume that the mortgage bonds are secured by the entire amount of fixed assets. What would each claimant receive from the liquidation distribution?

SELECTED ADDITIONAL CASE

The following case from CengageCompose covers many of the concepts discussed in this chapter and is available at **http://compose.cengage.com**.

Klein-Brigham Series:
Case 39, "Mark X Company (B)," which examines the allocation of proceeds under bankruptcy.

CHAPTER 25

Portfolio Theory and Asset Pricing Models

Americans love mutual funds. By 1985, they had invested about $495 billion in mutual funds, which is not exactly chicken feed. By December 2017, however, they had invested more than $18.7 trillion in mutual funds! Not only has the amount of money invested in mutual funds skyrocketed, but the variety of funds is astounding. You can buy funds that specialize in virtually any type of asset: funds that specialize in stocks from a particular industry, a particular continent, or a particular country. There are money market funds that invest only in Treasury bills and other short-term securities, and there are even funds that hold municipal bonds from a specific state.

For those with a social conscience, there are funds that refuse to own stocks of companies that pollute, sell tobacco products, or have workforces that are not culturally diverse. For others, there are "vice" funds, which invest only in brewers, defense contractors, tobacco companies, and the like.

You can buy an index fund, which simply holds a portfolio of stocks in an index such as the S&P 500. Index funds don't try to beat the market. Instead, they try to keep their expenses low and pass the savings on to investors. An exchange-traded fund, or ETF, has its own stock that is traded on a stock exchange. Different ETFs hold widely varied portfolios, ranging from the S&P 500 to gold-mining companies to Middle Eastern oil companies, and their fees to long-term investors are quite low. At the other extreme, hedge funds, which are pools of money provided by institutions and wealthy individuals, are very actively managed—even to the extent of taking over and then operationally managing firms in the portfolio—and they have relatively high expenses.

As you read this chapter, think about how portfolio theory has influenced the mutual fund industry.

Source: The Investment Company Institute publishes a *Fact Book* containing updated information on mutual funds. See **www.ici.org/research/stats/factbook**.

Intrinsic Value, Risk, and Return

In Chapter 1, we told you that managers should strive to make their firms more valuable and that the value of a firm is determined by the size, timing, and risk of its free cash flows (FCFs).

In Chapter 6, we discussed risk, which affects WACC and value. Now we provide additional insights into how to manage a portfolio's risk and measure a firm's risk.

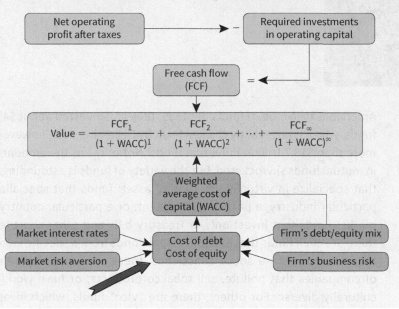

resource

The textbook's Web site contains an Excel file that will guide you through the chapter's calculations. The file for this chapter is **Ch25 Tool Kit.xlsx,** and we encourage you to open the file and follow along as you read the chapter.

In Chapter 6, we presented the key elements of risk and return analysis. There we saw that much of a stock's risk can be eliminated by diversification, so rational investors should hold portfolios of stocks rather than shares of a single stock. We also introduced the Capital Asset Pricing Model (CAPM), which links risk and required rates of return and uses a stock's beta coefficient as the relevant measure of risk. In this chapter, we extend these concepts and explain portfolio theory. We then present an in-depth treatment of the CAPM, including a more detailed look at how betas are calculated. We also describe the Arbitrage Pricing Theory model.

25-1 Efficient Portfolios

Recall from Chapter 6 the important role in portfolio risk that is played by the correlation between assets. One important use of portfolio risk concepts is to select **efficient portfolios,** defined as those portfolios that provide the highest expected return for any specified level of risk—or the lowest degree of risk for any specified level of return. We begin with the two-asset case and then extend it to the general case of N assets.

25-1a The Two-Asset Case

Consider two assets, A and B. Suppose we have estimated the expected returns ($\hat{r}_A$ and $\hat{r}_B$), the standard deviations (σ_A and σ_B) of returns, and the correlation coefficient (ρ_{AB}) for returns.[1]

---

[1]See Chapter 6 for definitions using historical data to estimate the expected return, standard deviation, covariance, and correlation.

The expected return and standard deviation (SD) for a portfolio containing these two assets are:

$$\hat{r}_p = w_A \hat{r}_A + (1 - w_A)\hat{r}_B \qquad \text{(25-1)}$$

and

$$\text{Portfolio SD} = \sigma_p = \sqrt{w_A^2 \sigma_A^2 + (1 - w_A)^2 \sigma_B^2 + 2w_A(1 - w_A)\rho_{AB}\sigma_A\sigma_B} \qquad \text{(25-2)}$$

Here w_A is the fraction of the portfolio invested in Security A, so $(1 - w_A)$ is the fraction invested in Security B.

To illustrate, suppose we can allocate our funds between A and B in any proportion. Suppose Security A has an expected rate of return of $\hat{r}_A = 5\%$ and a standard deviation of returns of $\sigma_A = 4\%$, while $\hat{r}_B = 8\%$ and $\sigma_B = 10\%$. Our first task is to determine the **feasible set** of portfolios, which are the ones that are *attainable* given the risk and expected return of Securities A and B. The second step is to examine the **attainable set** of portfolios and select the *efficient* subset.

To construct the attainable set, we need data on the degree of correlation between the two securities' expected returns, ρ_{AB}. Let us work with three different assumed degrees of correlation—namely, $\rho_{AB} = +1.0$, $\rho_{AB} = 0$, and $\rho_{AB} = -1.0$—and use them to develop the portfolios' expected returns, $\hat{r}_p$, and standard deviations, σ_p. (Of course, only one correlation can exist; our example simply shows three alternative situations that could occur.)

To calculate $\hat{r}_p$, we use Equation 25-1: Substitute the given values for $\hat{r}_A$ and $\hat{r}_B$, and then calculate $\hat{r}_p$ for different values of w_A. For example, if $w_A = 0.75$, then $\hat{r}_p = 5.75\%$:

$$\hat{r}_p = w_A \hat{r}_A + (1 - w_A)\hat{r}_B$$
$$= 0.75(5\%) + 0.25(8\%) = 5.75\%$$

Other values of $\hat{r}_p$ are found similarly and are shown in the third column of Figure 25-1.

resource

See Ch25 Tool Kit.xlsx on the textbook's Web site for all calculations.

FIGURE 25-1

$\hat{r}_p$ and σ_p under Various Assumptions

	A	B	C	D	E	F
					σ_p	
143 144 145 146	**Proportion of Portfolio in Security A (Value of w_A)**	**Proportion of Portfolio in Security B (Value of $1 - w_A$)**	$\hat{r}_p$	Case 1 $\rho_{AB} = +1.0$	Case 2 $\rho_{AB} = 0.0$	Case 3 $\rho_{AB} = -1.0$
147	1.00	0.00	5.00%	4.0%	4.0%	4.0%
148	0.86	0.14	5.41%	4.8%	3.7%	2.1%
149	0.75	0.25	5.75%	5.5%	3.9%	0.5%
150	0.71	0.29	5.86%	5.7%	4.0%	0.0%
151	0.50	0.50	6.50%	7.0%	5.4%	3.0%
152	0.25	0.75	7.25%	8.5%	7.6%	6.5%
153	0.00	1.00	8.00%	10.0%	10.0%	10.0%

Source: See the file **Ch25 Tool Kit.xlsx**. Numbers are reported as rounded values for clarity but are calculated using Excel's full precision. Thus, intermediate calculations using the figure's rounded values will be inexact.

Next, we use Equation 25-2 to find σ_p. Substitute the given values for σ_A, σ_B, and ρ_{AB}, and then calculate σ_p for different values of w_A. For example, if $\rho_{AB} = 0$ and $w_A = 0.75$, then $\sigma_p = 3.9\%$:

$$\sigma_p = \sqrt{w_A^2\sigma_A^2 + (1 - w_A)^2\sigma_B^2 + 2w_A(1 - w_A)\rho_{AB}\sigma_A\sigma_B}$$

$$= \sqrt{(0.75^2)(0.04^2) + (1 - 0.75)^2(0.10^2) + 2(0.75)(1 - 0.75)(0)(0.04)(0.10)}$$

$$= \sqrt{0.0009 + 0.000625 + 0} = \sqrt{0.001525} = 0.039 = 3.9\%$$

Figure 25-1 gives $\hat{r}_p$ and σ_p values for several different values of w_A; Figure 25-2 plots $\hat{r}_p$ and σ_p for each set of weights and correlations. For any given set of weights, the graphs show the feasible set of portfolios. Note the following points:

1. Panel A shows the feasible expected portfolio returns for three different values of correlation: (1) Case 1, with $\rho_{AB} = +1$; (2) Case 2, with $\rho_{AB} = 0$; and (3) Case 3, with $\rho_{AB} = -1$. Notice that these graphs are identical for each of the three cases: The portfolio return, $\hat{r}_p$, is a linear function of w_A, and it does not depend on the correlation coefficients. This is also seen from the $\hat{r}_p$ column in Figure 25-1. This should not be surprising because Equation 25-1 shows that a portfolio's expected return is a weighted average of the individual expected returns.

2. Panel B shows how risk is affected by the asset mix in the portfolio. For Case 1, where $\rho_{AB} = +1$, portfolio risk (σ_p) changes linearly as the portfolio weights change. In other words, portfolio risk is a weighted average of the individual standard deviations. However, the graphs for Cases 2 and 3 paint a very different picture. Portfolio risk is a nonlinear function of the weights, with the risk for these cases being lower than the risk for Case 1. This shows that if the stocks are not perfectly positively correlated (i.e., $\rho_{AB} \neq +1$), then combining stocks in a portfolio can diversify away some of its risk. In fact, if $\rho_{AB} = -1$, then risk can be completely diversified away! Thus, a portfolio's risk (σ_p), unlike a portfolio's expected return ($\hat{r}_p$), *does* depend on correlation.

3. Panel C has graphs plotting a portfolio's expected return versus its risk. Unlike the other panels, which plotted return and risk versus the portfolio's composition, each of these three graphs in Panel C is plotted from pairs of $\hat{r}_p$ and σ_p. For example, Point A (in the first graph of Panel C) is the point $\hat{r}_p = 5\%$ and $\sigma_p = 4\%$, corresponding to $w_A = 100\%$ from Panels A and B for Case 1 (i.e., $\rho_{AB} = +1$). Notice that the relationship between risk and return is linear for Case 1 but not for Cases 2 and 3 in which correlation is not equal to +1.

4. Are all portfolios in the feasible set equally good? The answer is "No." Only that part of the feasible set from Y to B in Cases 2 and 3 is defined as *efficient*. The part from A to Y is inefficient because, for any degree of risk on the line segment AY, a higher return can be found on segment YB. Thus, no rational investor would hold a portfolio that lies on segment AY. In Case 1, however, the entire feasible set is efficient—no combination of the securities can be ruled out.

5. We rarely encounter $\rho_{AB} = -1.0$, 0.0, or +1.0. Generally, ρ_{AB} is in the range of +0.3 to +0.6 for most stocks. Case 2 (zero correlation) produces graphs that, pictorially, most closely resemble real-world examples.

From these examples we see that in one extreme case ($\rho = -1.0$), risk can be diversified away completely, while in the other extreme case ($\rho = +1.0$), higher expected returns always have higher risk. Between these extremes, combining two stocks into a portfolio can reduce but does not eliminate the risk inherent in the individual stocks.

FIGURE 25-2
Illustrations of Portfolio Returns, Risk, and the Feasible Set of Portfolios

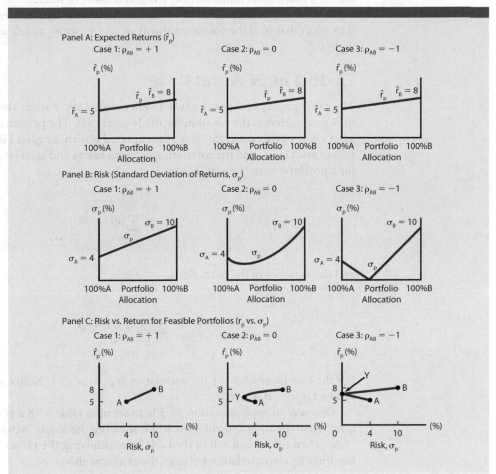

Panel C of Figure 25-2 shows that there exists a minimum possible risk portfolio (Y) for Cases 2 and 3 (i.e., for $\rho \neq +1.0$). How can we determine the weights for the minimum risk portfolio? Differentiate Equation 25-2 with respect to w_A, set the derivative equal to zero, and then solve for w_A. This identifies the fraction of the portfolio that should be invested in Security A if we wish to form the least-risky portfolio. Here is the equation:

$$\text{Minimum risk portfolio: } w_A = \frac{\sigma_B(\sigma_B - \rho_{AB}\sigma_A)}{\sigma_A^2 + \sigma_B^2 - 2\rho_{AB}\sigma_A\sigma_B} \qquad (25\text{-}3)$$

A value of w_A that is negative means that Security A is sold short; if w_A is greater than 1, B is sold short. In a short sale, you borrow shares of stock from a broker and then sell them, expecting to buy shares of stock back later (at a lower price) in order to repay the person from whom you borrowed the stock. If you sell short and the stock price rises, then you lose, but you win if the price declines. If the stock pays a dividend, you must pay the dividend to the broker, who passes it on to the client who provided the shares. Therefore, selling a share short is like owning a negative share of stock.

To find the minimum risk portfolio if short sales are not used, limit w_A to the range 0 to +1.0; that is, if the solution value is $w_A > 1.0$, set w_A to 1.0, and if w_A is negative, set w_A to 0.0.

25-1b The N-Asset Case

The same principles from the two-asset case also apply when the portfolio is composed of N assets. Here is the notation for the N-asset case: The percentage of the investment in asset i (the portfolio weight) is w_i, the expected return for asset i is $\hat{r}_i$, the standard deviation of asset i is σ_i, and the correlation between asset i and asset j is ρ_{ij}. The expected return for a portfolio with N assets is then:

$$\hat{r}_p = \sum_{i=1}^{N} w_i \hat{r}_i \qquad (25\text{-}4)$$

and the variance of the portfolio is:

$$\sigma_p^2 = \sum_{i=1}^{N} \sum_{j=1}^{N} w_i w_j \sigma_i \sigma_j \rho_{ij} \qquad (25\text{-}5)$$

For the case in which i = j, the correlation is $\rho_{ij} = \rho_{ii} = 1$. Notice also that when i = j, the product $\sigma_i \sigma_j = \sigma_i \sigma_i = \sigma_i^2$.

One way to apply Equation 25-5 is to set up a table with a row and column for each asset. Give the rows and columns labels showing the assets' weights and standard deviations. Then fill in each cell in the table by multiplying the values in the row and column headings by the correlation between the assets, as shown here:

	$w_1\sigma_1$ (1)	$w_2\sigma_2$ (2)	$w_3\sigma_3$ (3)
$w_1\sigma_1$ (1)	$w_1\sigma_1 w_1\sigma_1 \rho_{11} = w_1^2\sigma_1^2$	$w_1\sigma_1 w_2\sigma_2 \rho_{12}$	$w_1\sigma_1 w_3\sigma_3 \rho_{13}$
$w_2\sigma_2$ (2)	$w_2\sigma_2 w_1\sigma_1 \rho_{21}$	$w_2\sigma_2 w_2\sigma_2 \rho_{22} = w_2^2\sigma_2^2$	$w_2\sigma_2 w_3\sigma_3 \rho_{23}$
$w_3\sigma_3$ (3)	$w_3\sigma_3 w_1\sigma_1 \rho_{31}$	$w_3\sigma_3 w_2\sigma_2 \rho_{32}$	$w_3\sigma_3 w_3\sigma_3 \rho_{33} = w_3^2\sigma_3^2$

The portfolio variance is the sum of the nine cells. For the diagonal, we have substituted the values for the case in which i = j. Notice that some of the cells have identical values. For example, the cell for Row 1 and Column 2 has the same value as the cell for Column 1 and Row 2. This suggests an alternative formula:

$$\sigma_p^2 = \sum_{i=1}^{N} w_i^2\sigma_i^2 + \sum_{i=1}^{N} \sum_{\substack{j=1 \\ j \neq i}}^{N} w_i\sigma_i w_j\sigma_j \rho_{ij} \qquad (25\text{-}5a)$$

The main thing to remember when calculating portfolio standard deviations is simply this: Do not leave out any terms. Using a table like the one shown here can help.

What does the term "attainable set" mean?

Within this set, which portfolios are "efficient"?

Stock A has an expected return of 10% and a standard deviation of 35%. Stock B has an expected return of 15% and a standard deviation of 45%. The correlation coefficient between Stocks A and B is 0.3. What are the expected return and standard deviation of a portfolio invested 60% in Stock A and 40% in Stock B? **(12.0%; 31.5%)**

25-2 Choosing the Optimal Portfolio

With only two assets, the feasible set of portfolios is a line or curve, as shown in Figure 25-2, Panel C. However, by increasing the number of assets, we obtain an area, such as the shaded region in Figure 25-3. Points A, H, G, and E represent single securities (or portfolios containing only one security). All the other points in the shaded area and its boundaries, which comprise the feasible set, represent portfolios of two or more securities. Each point in this area represents a particular portfolio with a risk of σ_p and an expected return of $\hat{r}_p$. For example, Point X represents one such portfolio's risk and expected return, as does each of Points B, C, and D.

Given the full set of potential portfolios that could be constructed from the available assets, which portfolio should actually be held? This choice involves two separate decisions: (1) determining the efficient set of portfolios and (2) choosing from the efficient set the single portfolio that is best for the specific investor.

25-2a The Efficient Frontier

In Figure 25-3, the boundary line BCDE defines the **efficient set** of portfolios, which is also called the **efficient frontier**.[2] Portfolios to the left of the efficient set are not possible

FIGURE 25-3
The Efficient Set of Investments

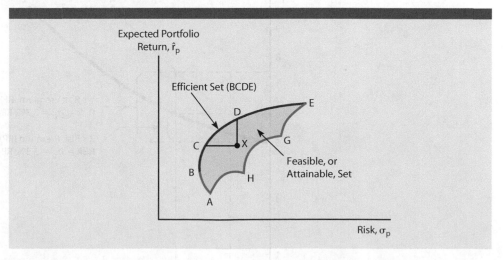

[2] A computational procedure for determining the efficient set of portfolios was developed by Harry Markowitz and first reported in his article "Portfolio Selection," *Journal of Finance*, March 1952, pp. 77–91. In this article, Markowitz developed the basic concepts of portfolio theory, and he later won the Nobel Prize in economics for his work.

because they lie outside the attainable set. Portfolios to the right of the boundary line (interior portfolios) are inefficient because some other portfolio would provide either a higher return for the same degree of risk or a lower risk for the same rate of return. For example, Portfolio X is *dominated* in this sense by all portfolios on the curve CD.

25-2b Risk–Return Indifference Curves

Given the efficient set of portfolios, which specific portfolio should an investor choose? To determine the optimal portfolio for a particular investor, we must know the investor's attitude toward risk as reflected in his or her risk–return trade-off function, or **indifference curve**.

An investor's risk–return trade-off function is based on the standard economic concepts of utility theory and indifference curves, which are illustrated in Figure 25-4. The curves labeled I_Y and I_Z represent the indifference curves of two individuals, Ms. Y and Mr. Z. Ms. Y's curve indicates indifference between the riskless 5% portfolio, a portfolio with an expected return of 6% but a risk of $\sigma_p = 1.4\%$, and so on. Mr. Z's curve indicates indifference between a riskless 5% return, an expected 6% return with risk of $\sigma_p = 3.3\%$, and so on.

Note that Ms. Y requires a higher expected rate of return as compensation for any given amount of risk; thus, Ms. Y is said to have more **risk aversion** than Mr. Z. Her higher risk aversion causes Ms. Y to require a higher **risk premium**—defined here as the difference between the 5% riskless return and the expected return required to compensate for any specific amount of risk—than Mr. Z requires. Thus, Ms. Y requires a risk premium

FIGURE 25-4
Risk–Return Indifference Curves

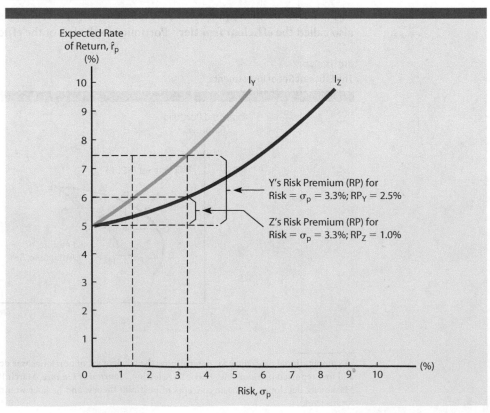

(RP_Y) of 2.5% to compensate for a risk of $\sigma_p = 3.3\%$, whereas Mr. Z's risk premium for this degree of risk is only $RP_Z = 1.0\%$. *In general, an indifference curve with a steeper slope means that the investor is more risk averse.* Thus, Ms. Y is more risk averse than Mr. Z.

Each individual has a "map" of indifference curves; the indifference maps for Ms. Y and Mr. Z are shown in Figure 25-5. The higher curves denote a greater level of satisfaction (or utility). Thus, I_{Z2} is better than I_{Z1} because, for any level of risk, Mr. Z has a higher expected return and hence greater utility. An infinite number of indifference curves could be drawn in the map for each individual, and each individual has a unique map.

25-2c The Optimal Portfolio for an Investor

Figure 25-5 also shows the feasible set of portfolios for the two-asset case, under the assumption that $\rho_{AB} = 0$, as it was developed in Figure 25-2. The **optimal portfolio** for each investor is found at the tangency point between the efficient set of portfolios and one of the investor's indifference curves. This tangency point marks the highest level of satisfaction the investor can attain. Ms. Y, who is more risk averse than Mr. Z, chooses a portfolio with a lower expected return (about 6%) but a risk of only $\sigma_p = 4.2\%$.

FIGURE 25-5
Selecting the Optimal Portfolio of Risky Assets

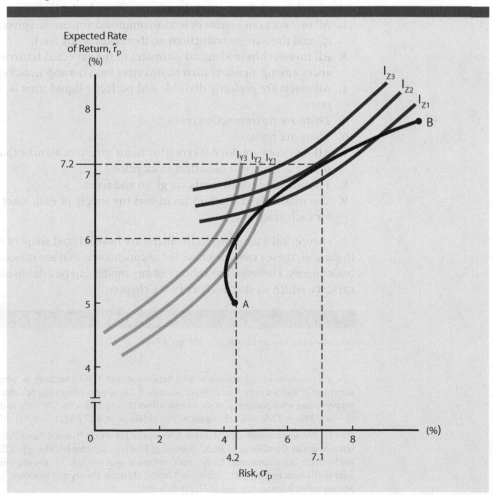

Mr. Z picks a portfolio that provides an expected return of about 7.2% but has a risk of about $\sigma_p = 7.1\%$. Ms. Y's portfolio is more heavily weighted with the less risky security, while Mr. Z's portfolio contains a larger proportion of the more risky security.[3]

SELF-TEST

What is the efficient frontier?

What are indifference curves?

Conceptually, how does an investor choose his or her optimal portfolio?

25-3 The Basic Assumptions of the Capital Asset Pricing Model

The **Capital Asset Pricing Model (CAPM)**, which was introduced in Chapter 6, specifies the relationship between risk and required rates of return on assets when they are held in well-diversified portfolios. The assumptions underlying the CAPM's development are summarized in the following list:[4]

1. All investors focus on a single holding period, and they seek to maximize the expected utility of their terminal wealth by choosing among alternative portfolios on the basis of each portfolio's expected return and standard deviation.
2. All investors can borrow or lend an unlimited amount at a given risk-free rate of interest, r_{RF}, and there are no restrictions on short sales of any asset.
3. All investors have identical estimates of the expected returns, variances, and covariances among all assets (that is, investors have homogeneous expectations).
4. All assets are perfectly divisible and perfectly liquid (that is, marketable at the going price).
5. There are no transaction costs.
6. There are no taxes.
7. All investors are price takers (that is, all investors assume that their own buying and selling activity will not affect stock prices).
8. The quantities of all assets are given and fixed.
9. The market is in equilibrium in that the supply of each asset is equal to the demand for each asset.

Theoretical extensions in the literature have relaxed some of these assumptions, and, in general, these extensions have led to conclusions that are reasonably consistent with the basic theory. However, the validity of any model can be established only through empirical tests, which we discuss later in the chapter.

SELF-TEST

What are the key assumptions of the CAPM?

---

[3]Ms. Y's portfolio would contain 67% of Security A and 33% of Security B, whereas Mr. Z's portfolio would consist of 27% of Security A and 73% of Security B. These percentages can be determined with Equation 25-1 by simply seeing what percentage of the two securities is consistent with $\hat{r}_p = 6.0\%$ and 7.2%. For example, $w_A(5\%) + (1 - w_A)(8\%) = 7.2\%$, and, solving for w_A, we obtain $w_A = 0.27$ and $(1 - w_A) = 0.73$.

[4]The CAPM was originated by William F. Sharpe in his article "Capital Asset Prices: A Theory of Market Equilibrium under Conditions of Risk," *Journal of Finance,* September 1964, pp. 425–442. Professor Sharpe won the Nobel Prize in economics for his work on capital asset pricing. The assumptions inherent in Sharpe's model were spelled out by Michael C. Jensen in "Capital Markets: Theory and Evidence," *Bell Journal of Economics and Management Science,* Autumn 1972, pp. 357–398.

25-4 The Capital Market Line and the Security Market Line

Figure 25-5 showed the set of portfolio opportunities for the two-asset case, and it illustrated how indifference curves can be used to select the optimal portfolio from the feasible set. In Figure 25-6, we show a similar diagram for the many-asset case, but here we also include a **risk-free asset** with a return r_{RF}. By *risk-free* we mean *default-free*. The riskless asset by definition has zero risk, $\sigma = 0\%$, so it is plotted on the vertical axis.

The figure shows both the feasible set of portfolios of risky assets (the shaded area) and a set of indifference curves (I_1, I_2, I_3) for a particular investor. Point N, where indifference curve I_1 is tangent to the efficient set, represents a possible portfolio choice; it is the point on the efficient set of risky portfolios where the investor obtains the highest possible return for a given amount of risk and the smallest degree of risk for a given expected return.

However, the investor can do better than Portfolio N by reaching a higher indifference curve. In addition to the feasible set of risky portfolios, we now have a risk-free asset that provides a riskless return, r_{RF}. Given the risk-free asset, investors can create new portfolios that combine the risk-free asset with a portfolio of risky assets. This enables them to achieve any combination of risk and return on the straight line connecting r_{RF} with M, the point of tangency between that straight line and the efficient frontier of risky asset portfolios.[5] Some portfolios on the line $r_{RF}MZ$ will be preferred to most risky portfolios on the efficient frontier BNME, so the points on the line $r_{RF}MZ$ now represent the best attainable combinations of risk and return.

Given the new opportunities along line $r_{RF}MZ$, our investor will move from Point N to Point R, which is on her highest attainable risk–return indifference curve. Note that any point on the old efficient frontier BNME (except the point of tangency M) is dominated by some point along the line $r_{RF}MZ$. In general, because investors can purchase some of the

---

[5]The risk–return combinations between a risk-free asset and a risky asset (a single stock or a portfolio of stocks) will always be linear. To see this, consider the following equations, which were developed earlier, for return $(\hat{r}_p)$ and risk (σ_p) for any combination w_{RF} and $(1 - w_{RF})$:

$$\hat{r}_p = w_{RF}r_{RF} + (1 - w_{RF})\hat{r}_M \qquad \text{(25-1a)}$$

and

$$\sigma_p = \sqrt{w_{RF}^2\sigma_{RF}^2 + (1 - w_{RF})^2\,\sigma_M^2 + 2w_{RF}(1 - w_{RF})\rho_{RF,M}\sigma_{RF}\sigma_M} \qquad \text{(25-2a)}$$

Equation 25-1a is linear. As for Equation 25-2a, we know that r_{RF} is the risk-free asset, so $\sigma_{RF} = 0$; hence, σ_{RF}^2 is also zero. Using this information, we can simplify Equation 25-2a as follows:

$$\sigma_p = \sqrt{(1 - w_{RF})^2\sigma_M^2} = (1 - w_{RF})\sigma_M \qquad \text{(25-2b)}$$

Thus, σ_p is also linear in w_{RF} when a riskless asset is combined with a portfolio of risky assets.

If expected returns, as measured by $\hat{r}_p$, and risk, as measured by σ_p, are both linear functions of w_{RF}, then the relationship between $\hat{r}_p$ and σ_p, when graphed as in Figure 25-6, must also be linear. For example, if 100% of the portfolio is invested in r_{RF} with a return of 8%, then the portfolio return will be 8% and σ_p will be 0. If 100% is invested in M with $r_M = 12\%$ and $\sigma_M = 10\%$, then $\sigma_p = 1.0(10\%) = 10\%$ and $\hat{r}_p = 0(8\%) + 1.0(12\%) = 12\%$. If 50% of the portfolio is invested in M and 50% in the risk-free asset, then $\sigma_p = 0.5(10\%) = 5\%$ and $\hat{r}_p = 0.5(8\%) + 0.5(12\%) = 10\%$. Plotting these points will reveal the linear relationship given as $r_{RF}MZ$ in Figure 25-6.

FIGURE 25-6
Investor Equilibrium: Combining the Risk-Free Asset with the Market Portfolio

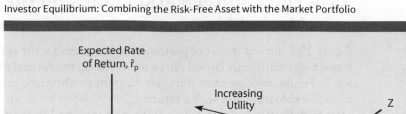

risk-free security and some of the risky portfolio (M), it will be possible to move to a point such as R. In addition, if the investor can borrow as well as lend (lending is equivalent to buying risk-free debt securities) at the riskless rate r_{RF}, then it is possible to move out on the line segment MZ; an investor would do so if his or her indifference curve were tangent to r_{RF}MZ, to the right of Point M.[6]

All investors should hold portfolios lying on the line r_{RF}MZ under the conditions assumed in the CAPM. This implies that they should hold portfolios that are combinations of the risk-free security and the risky Portfolio M. Thus, the addition of the risk-free asset totally changes the efficient set: The efficient set now lies along line r_{RF}MZ rather than along the curve BNME. Note also that if the capital market is to be in equilibrium, then M must be a portfolio that contains every risky asset in exact proportion to that asset's fraction of the total market value of all assets. In other words, if Security i is X percent of the total market value of all securities, then X percent of the market portfolio M must consist of Security i. (That is, M is the market value–weighted portfolio of *all* risky assets in the economy.) Thus, all investors should hold portfolios that lie on the line

---

[6]An investor who is highly risk averse will have a steep indifference curve and will end up holding only the riskless asset or perhaps a portfolio at a point such as R (i.e., holding some of the risky market portfolio and some of the riskless asset). An investor who is only slightly averse to risk will have a relatively flat indifference curve, which will cause her to move out beyond M toward Z, borrowing to do so. This investor might buy stocks on margin, which means borrowing and using the stocks as collateral. If individuals' borrowing rates are higher than r_{RF}, then the line r_{RF}MZ will tilt down (i.e., be less steep) beyond M. This condition would invalidate the basic CAPM, or at least require it to be modified. Therefore, the assumption of being able to borrow or lend at the same rate is crucial to CAPM theory.

$r_{RF}MZ$, with the particular location of a given individual's portfolio being determined by the point at which his indifference curve is tangent to the line.

The line $r_{RF}MZ$ in Figure 25-6 is called the **Capital Market Line (CML)**. It has an intercept of r_{RF} and a slope of $(\hat{r}_M - r_{RF})/\sigma_M$.[7] The equation for the Capital Market Line may be expressed as follows:

$$\text{CML: } \hat{r}_p = r_{RF} + \left(\frac{\hat{r}_M - r_{RM}}{\sigma_M}\right)\sigma_p \qquad (25\text{-}6)$$

The expected rate of return *on an efficient portfolio* is equal to the riskless rate plus a risk premium that is equal to $(\hat{r}_M - r_{RF})/\sigma_M$ multiplied by the portfolio's standard deviation, σ_p. Thus, the CML specifies a linear relationship between an efficient portfolio's expected return and risk, where the slope of the CML is equal to the expected return on the market portfolio of risky stocks $(\hat{r}_M)$ *minus* the risk-free rate (r_{RF}), which is called the **market risk premium**, all divided by the standard deviation of returns on the market portfolio, σ_M:

$$\text{Slope of the CML} = (\hat{r}_M - r_{RF})/\sigma_M$$

For example, suppose $r_{RF} = 10\%$, $\hat{r}_M = 15\%$, and $\sigma_M = 15\%$. In this case, the slope of the CML would be $(15\% - 10\%)/15\% = 0.33$, and if a particular efficient portfolio had $\sigma_p = 10\%$, then its $\hat{r}_p$ would be:

$$\hat{r}_p = 10\% + 0.33(10\%) = 13.3\%$$

A (riskier) portfolio with $\sigma_p = 20\%$ would have $\hat{r}_p = 10\% + 0.33(20\%) = 16.6\%$.

The CML is graphed in Figure 25-7. It is a straight line with an intercept at r_{RF} and a slope equal to the market risk premium $(\hat{r}_M - r_{RF})$ divided by σ_M. The slope of the CML reflects the aggregate attitude of investors toward risk.

Recall that an efficient portfolio is well diversified; hence, all of its unsystematic risk has been eliminated, and its only remaining risk is market risk. Therefore, unlike individual stocks, the risk of an efficient portfolio is measured by its standard deviation, σ_p. The CML equation specifies the relationship between risk and return for such efficient portfolios—that is, for portfolios that lie on the CML—and in the CML equation and graph, risk is measured by portfolio standard deviation.

The CML specifies the relationship between risk as measured by standard deviation and expected return for an efficient portfolio, but investors and managers are more concerned about the relationship between risk and required return for *individual assets*.[8] To develop the risk–return relationship for individual securities, note in Figure 25-6 that all investors are assumed to hold Portfolio M, so M must be the market portfolio (i.e., the one that contains all stocks). Note also that M is an *efficient* portfolio, so there are no attainable portfolios that have both a smaller standard deviation and a larger expected return.

---

[7]Recall that the slope of any line is measured as $\Delta Y/\Delta X$, or the change in height associated with a given change in horizontal distance. Here, r_{RF} is at 0 on the horizontal axis, so $\Delta X = \sigma_M - 0 = \sigma_M$. The vertical axis difference associated with a change from r_{RF} to $\hat{r}_M$ is $\hat{r}_M - r_{RF}$. Therefore, slope $= \Delta Y/\Delta X = (\hat{r}_M - r_{RF})/\sigma_M$.

[8]Recall that an asset's *expected* return is the return that an investor expects to receive from it, while the *required* return is the minimum expected return that will induce the investor to hold the asset. Since the CAPM assumes that markets are in equilibrium and all investors agree on expected returns, the required return on a stock is equal to its expected return.

FIGURE 25-7
The Capital Market Line (CML)

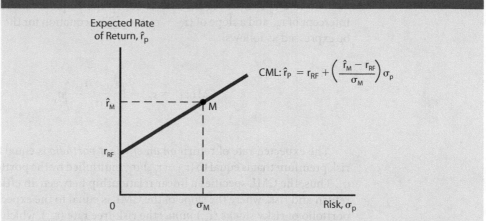

Note: We did not draw it in, but you can visualize the shaded space shown in Figure 25-6 in this graph and the CML as the line formed by connecting r_{RF} with the tangent to the shaded space.

These two observations can be combined using a little bit of algebra to give the relationship between an individual stock's expected return and its risk as:[9]

$$\hat{r}_i = r_{RF} + \frac{(\hat{r}_M - r_{RF})}{\sigma_M}\left(\frac{Cov(r_i, r_M)}{\sigma_M}\right)$$

$$= r_{RF} + (\hat{r}_M - r_{RF})\left(\frac{Cov(r_i, r_M)}{\sigma_M^2}\right)$$

(25-7)

The CAPM defines Company i's **beta coefficient, b_i**, as follows:

$$b_i = \frac{\text{Covariance between Stock i and the market}}{\text{Variance of market returns}} = \frac{Cov(r_i, r_M)}{\sigma_M^2}$$

$$= \frac{\rho_{iM}\sigma_i\sigma_M}{\sigma_M^2} = \rho_{iM}\left(\frac{\sigma_i}{\sigma_M}\right)$$

(25-8)

Recall that the risk premium for the market, RP_M, is $\hat{r}_M - r_{RF}$. Using this definition and substituting Equation 25-8 into Equation 25-7 gives:

$$\hat{r}_i = r_{RF} + (\hat{r}_M - r_{RF})b_i$$

$$= r_{RF} + (RP_M)b_i$$

(25-9)

---

[9]For consistency with most investment textbooks, we let $Cov(r_i, r_M)$ denote the covariance between the returns of assets i and M. Using the notation in Chapter 6, we would have denoted the covariance as $COV_{i,M}$. For an accessible derivation of Equation 25-7, see Chapter 9 in *Investments*, 11th Edition, by Zvi Bode, Alex Kane, and Alan Marcus (McGraw-Hill Education, 2018).

Equation 25-9 shows how expected return and beta should be related under the CAPM assumptions. Since the CAPM also assumes markets are in equilibrium, it must also be the case that each stock's expected return, $\hat{r}_i$, is equal to its required return, r_i, and the market's expected return, $\hat{r}_M$, is equal to its required return, r_M. Noting this gives the **Security Market Line (SML)** equation that relates required return to beta and the market risk premium:[10]

$$
\begin{aligned}
\text{SML: } r_i &= r_{RF} + (r_M - r_{RF})b_i \\
&= r_{RF} + (RP_M)b_i
\end{aligned}
\tag{25-10}
$$

The SML tells us that an individual stock's required return is equal to the risk-free rate plus a premium for bearing risk. The premium for risk is equal to the risk premium for the market, RP_M, multiplied by the risk of the individual stock, as measured by its beta coefficient. The beta coefficient measures the amount of risk that the stock contributes to the market portfolio.

Unlike the CML for a well-diversified portfolio, the SML tells us that the standard deviation (σ_i) of an individual stock should not be used to measure its risk because some of the risk as reflected by σ_i can be eliminated by diversification. Beta reflects risk after taking diversification benefits into account, and so beta, rather than σ_i, is used to measure individual stocks' risks to investors. Be sure to keep in mind the distinction between the SML and the CML and why that distinction exists.

SELF-TEST

Draw a graph showing the feasible set of risky assets, the efficient frontier, the risk-free asset, and the CML.

Write out the equation for the CML and explain its meaning.

Write out the equation for the SML and explain its meaning.

What is the difference between the CML and the SML?

The standard deviation of stock returns of Park Corporation is 60%. The standard deviation of the market return is 20%. If the correlation between Park and the market is 0.40, what is Park's beta? **(1.2)**

25-5 Calculating Beta Coefficients

Equation 25-8 defines beta, but recall from Chapter 6 that this equation for beta is also the formula for the slope coefficient in a regression of the stock return against the market return. Therefore, beta can be calculated by plotting the historical returns of a stock on the y-axis of a graph versus the historical returns of the market portfolio on the x-axis and then fitting the regression line. In his 1964 article that set forth the CAPM, Sharpe called this regression line the **characteristic line**. Thus, a stock's beta is the slope of its characteristic line.

In Chapter 6, we estimated MicroDrive's beta using 4 years of monthly returns. In this chapter, we estimate betas using 1 year of weekly returns because this is another often used approach. In addition to estimating the beta of a company in this chapter (Apple), we also estimate the beta of a mutual fund (Fidelity's Magellan Fund) to illustrate the impact

---

[10]You will see the market risk premium written as $r_M - r_{RF}$ and as $\hat{r}_M - r_{RF}$. These are the same under the CAPM assumption that markets are in equilibrium. For practical purposes, though, only the expected return on the market, $\hat{r}_M$, can be estimated from market data. See **Web Extension 9A** for a discussion of how to estimate the expected return on the market.

TABLE 25-1
Summary of Data for Calculating Beta (Weekly Returns from 9/22/2017 to 9/14/2018)

	r_M, Market Return (S&P 500 Index)	r_i, Apple Return	r_p, Vanguard Mid-Cap Value Index Fund Investor Shares Return	r_{RF}, Risk-Free Rate (Yield on 3-Month T-Bill)
Average return (annualized)	15.9%	38.9%	11.9%	1.647%
Standard deviation (annual)	12.9%	27.4%	12.0%	0.048%
Correlation with market return, ρ		0.50	0.95	−0.03

Source: See the file *Ch25 Tool Kit.xlsx*. Returns are based on adjusted prices from Yahoo! Finance, and T-bill yields are from the Federal Reserve Bank of St. Louis's FRED® Economic Data.

that portfolio diversification has on confidence intervals for estimated betas. In addition, we examine a modified estimation approach using excess returns, which are the assets' returns in excess of the risk-free rate.

25-5a Calculating the Beta Coefficient for a Single Stock: Apple

resource

See Ch25 Tool Kit.xlsx on the textbook's Web site.

Table 25-1 shows a summary of the data used in this analysis; the full data set is in the file ***Ch25 Tool Kit.xlsx*** and has 52 weekly returns for September 22, 2017 to September 14, 2018. Table 25-1 shows the market returns (defined as the percentage price change of the S&P 500), the stock returns for Apple, and the returns on the Vanguard Mid-Cap Value Index Fund Investor Shares[11] (which is a well-diversified portfolio). The table also shows the risk-free rate, defined as the yield on a short-term (3-month) U.S. Treasury bill, which we will use later in this analysis.

As Table 25-1 shows, Apple had an average annual return of 38.9% during the time period, while the market had an average annual return of 15.9%. As we have noted, it is usually unreasonable to think that the future expected return for a stock will equal its average historical return over a relatively short period, such as 52 weeks. However, we might well expect past volatility to be a reasonable estimate of future volatility, at least during the next year. Observe that the standard deviation for Apple's return during this period was 27.4%, versus 12.9% for the market. Thus, the market's volatility is much less than that of Apple. This is what we would expect because the market is a well-diversified portfolio, and thus much of its risk has been diversified away. The correlation between Apple's stock returns and the market returns is about 0.5, which is a little higher than the correlation for a typical stock.

Figure 25-8 shows a plot of Apple's returns against the market's returns. We used the *Excel* Trendline feature to plot the trendline and show the estimated regression equation on the chart. We also used *Excel*'s regression analysis feature (Data, Data Analysis, Regression) to estimate the regression equation. Table 25-2 reports some of these regression results for Apple. Its estimated beta, which is the slope coefficient in the regression, is about 1.37.

As with all regression results, Apple's estimated beta of 1.06 is just an estimate, not necessarily the true value of beta. Table 25-2 also shows the t-statistic and the probability that the true beta is zero. For Apple, this probability is approximately equal to zero. This means that there is virtually a zero chance that the true beta is equal to zero. Because this probability is less than 5%, statisticians would say that the slope coefficient, beta, is

---

[11]This portfolio has over 200 stocks and is invested in stocks with market valuations around $14 billion. Its strategy is to purchase stocks that might be undervalued based on several ratios. See **https://investor .vanguard.com/mutual-funds/profile/portfolio/vmvix** for more details.

FIGURE 25-8
Calculating a Beta Coefficient for Apple

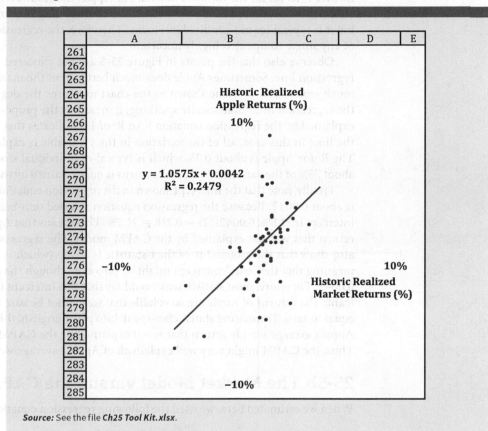

Source: See the file *Ch25 Tool Kit.xlsx*.

TABLE 25-2
Regression Results for Calculating Beta

	Regression Coefficient	t-Statistic	Probability of t-Statistic	Lower 95% Confidence Interval	Upper 95% Confidence Interval
Panel A: Apple (Market model)					
Intercept	0.0042	0.91	36.84%	−0.005	0.014
Slope (beta)	1.0575	4.06	0.02%	0.534	1.581
Panel B: Vanguard Fund (Market model)					
Intercept	−0.0004	−0.53	59.86%	−0.002	0.001
Slope (beta)	0.8821	20.99	0.00%	0.798	0.966
Panel C: Apple (CAPM: Excess returns)					
Intercept	0.0043	0.91	36.48%	−0.005	0.014
Slope (beta)	1.0566	4.06	0.02%	0.533	1.580

Source: See the file *Ch25 Tool Kit.xlsx*.

Note: The market model uses actual historical returns; the CAPM model uses returns in excess of the risk-free rate.

"statistically significant." The output of the regression analysis also gives us the 95% confidence interval for the estimate of beta. For Apple, the results tell us that we can be 95% confident that the true beta is between 0.534 and 1.581. This is an extremely wide range, but it is typical for most individual stocks. Therefore, the regression estimate for the beta of any single company is highly uncertain.

Observe also that the points in Figure 25-8 are not clustered very tightly around the regression line. Sometimes Apple does much better than the market; other times, it does much worse. The R^2 value shown in the chart measures the degree of dispersion about the regression line. (Statistically speaking, it measures the proportion of variation that is explained by the regression equation.) An R^2 of 1.0 indicates that all points lie exactly on the line; in this case, all of the variation in the y-variable is explained by the x-variable. The R^2 for Apple is about 0.25, which is typical of individual stocks. This indicates that about 75% of the variation in Apple's returns is *not* explained by the overall market return.

Finally, note that the intercept shown in the regression equation displayed on the chart is about 0.0042. Because the regression equation is based on weekly data, the annualized intercept is 21.8%: $0.0042(52) = 0.218 = 21.8\%$. This means that Apple had a 21.8% annual return that was *not* explained by the CAPM model. The regression results in Table 25-2 also show that the probability of the t-statistic is 36.8% (which is much greater than 5%), meaning that the "true" intercept might be zero even though the estimated intercept was 0.0042. Therefore, most statisticians would say that this intercept is not statistically significant: The returns of Apple are so volatile that we cannot be sure the true intercept is not equal to zero. Translating statistician-speak into plain English, this means that the part of Apple's average weekly return that is *not* explained by the CAPM could, in fact, be zero. Thus, the CAPM might very well explain all of Apple's average weekly returns.

25-5b The Market Model versus the CAPM

When we estimated beta, we used the following regression equation:

$$\bar{r}_{i,t} = a_i + b_i \bar{r}_{M,t} + e_{i,t} \qquad \text{(25-11)}$$

where

$$\begin{aligned}
\bar{r}_{i,t} &= \text{Historical (realized) rate of return on Stock i in period t} \\
\bar{r}_{M,t} &= \text{Historical (realized) rate of return on the market in period t} \\
a_i &= \text{Vertical axis intercept term for Stock i} \\
b_i &= \text{Slope, or beta coefficient, for Stock i} \\
e_{i,t} &= \text{Random error, reflecting the difference between the actual return on Stock} \\
&\quad \text{i in a given period and the return as predicted by the regression line}
\end{aligned}$$

Equation 25-11 is called the **market model**, because it regresses the stock's return against the market's return. However, the SML of the CAPM for realized returns is a little different from Equation 25-11:

$$\text{SML for realized returns: } \bar{r}_{i,t} = \bar{r}_{RF,t} + b_i(\bar{r}_{M,t} - \bar{r}_{RF,t}) + e_{i,t} \qquad \text{(25-12)}$$

where $\bar{r}_{RF,t}$ is the historical (realized) risk-free rate in period t.

In order to use the CAPM to estimate beta, we must rewrite Equation 25-12 as a regression equation by adding an intercept, a_i. The result is:

$$(\bar{r}_i - \bar{r}_{RF,t}) = a_i + b_i(\bar{r}_{M,t} - \bar{r}_{RF,t}) + e_{i,t} \qquad (25\text{-}13)$$

Therefore, to be theoretically correct when estimating beta, we should use the stock's return in excess of the risk-free rate as the y-variable and use the market's return in excess of the risk-free rate as the x-variable. We did this for Apple using the data in *Ch25 Tool Kit.xlsx* (which are summarized in Table 25-1); the results are reported in Panel C of Table 25-2. Note that there are no appreciable differences between the results in Panel A, the market model, and in Panel C, the CAPM model. This typically is the case, so we will use the market model in the rest of the book.

25-5c Calculating the Beta Coefficient for a Portfolio: The Vanguard Mid-Cap Value Index Fund Investor Shares

Let's calculate beta for the Vanguard Mid-Cap Value Index Fund Investor Shares, a well-diversified portfolio. Figure 25-9 shows the plot of the fund's weekly returns versus the market's weekly returns. Note the differences between this chart and the one for Apple

FIGURE 25-9
Calculating a Beta Coefficient for the Vanguard Mid-Cap Value Index Fund Investor Shares

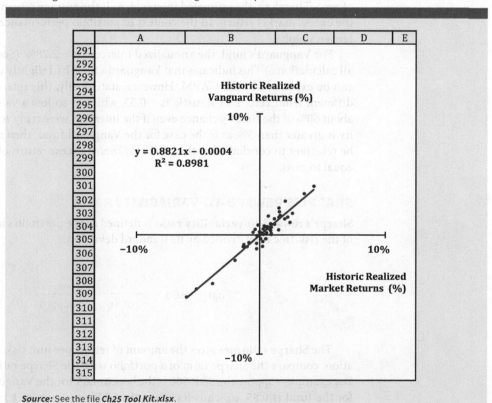

Source: See the file *Ch25 Tool Kit.xlsx*.

shown in Figure 25-8. The points for the fund are tightly clustered around the regression line, indicating that the vast majority of the fund's variability is explained by the stock market. The R^2 of about 0.90 confirms this visual conclusion. We can also see from Table 25-1 that the fund has a standard deviation of 12.0%, which is similar to the 12.9% standard deviation of the market.

As Table 25-2 shows, the fund's estimated beta is 0.882, and the 95% confidence interval is from 0.798 to 0.996, which is much tighter than the confidence interval for Apple's estimated beta. The fund's intercept is virtually zero, and the probability of the intercept's t-statistic is much greater than 5%. Therefore, the intercept is statistically insignificant, indicating that the CAPM explains the average weekly return of the fund very well.

25-5d Performance Measures

resource

See Ch25 Tool Kit.xlsx on the textbook's Web site for all calculations for these performance measures.

Mutual fund managers are often evaluated by their risk-adjusted performance. The three most widely used measures are *Jensen's alpha, Sharpe's reward-to-variability ratio,* and *Treynor's reward-to-volatility ratio.*

JENSEN'S ALPHA

Consider the intercept in the CAPM regression of excess returns, shown in Equation 25-13 and repeated here for convenience:

$$(\bar{r}_i - \bar{r}_{RF,t}) = a_i + b_i(\bar{r}_{M,t} - \bar{r}_{RF,t}) + e_{i,t}$$

For regression equations that have an intercept, the error terms (e_{it}) have an average value of zero. Therefore, the estimated intercept, a_i, is the average return that is not explained by the excess market return. In the context of portfolio performance, this intercept is called **Jensen's alpha**.

For Vanguard's fund, the annualized intercept is −2.28%. (See **Ch25 Tool Kit.xlsx** for all calculations.) This indicates that Vanguard's fund had slightly worse performance than can be explained by the CAPM. However, statistically, this intercept is not significantly different from zero. Its t-statistic is −0.53, which is so low a value that it could happen about 60% of the time by chance even if the intercept were truly zero. When this probability is greater than 5%, as is the case for the Vanguard fund, then most statisticians would be reluctant to conclude that the fund's *estimated* excess return of −2.28% is not *actually* equal to zero.

SHARPE'S REWARD-TO-VARIABILITY RATIO

Sharpe's reward-to-variability ratio is defined as the portfolio's average return (in excess of the risk-free rate) divided by its standard deviation:

$$\text{Sharpe ratio} = \frac{r_{p,Avg} - r_{RF,Avg}}{\sigma \text{ of } (r_{p,Avg} - r_{RF,Avg})} \tag{25-14}$$

The Sharpe ratio measures the amount of return per unit risk. For performance evaluation, compare the Sharpe ratio of a portfolio with the Sharpe ratio of a benchmark asset. For example, suppose the S&P 500 is the benchmark for the Vanguard fund. Sharpe's ratio for the fund is 0.85, which is less than the S&P's measure of 1.1. This indicates that the fund earned a lower return per unit risk than the S&P 500 earned.

TREYNOR'S REWARD-TO-VOLATILITY RATIO

Treynor's reward-to-volatility ratio is defined as the portfolio's average return (in excess of the risk-free rate) divided by its beta:

$$\text{Treynor's ratio} = \frac{r_{p,Avg} - r_{RF,Avg}}{b_p} \qquad (25\text{-}15)$$

The Treynor ratio measures the return per unit of risk as measured by beta. For Vanguard, the Treynor ratio is 11.6%, which is worse than the S&P 500's ratio of 14.2%. All in all, the Vanguard fund seems to have slightly underperformed the market but perhaps not by a statistically significant amount. Although it's pretty clear that Vanguard did not "beat the market," it did dramatically reduce the risk faced by investors as compared with the risk inherent in a randomly chosen individual stock.

25-5e Additional Insights into Risk and Return

The CAPM provides some additional insights into the relationship between risk and return.

1. The relationship between a stock's total risk, market risk, and diversifiable risk can be expressed as follows:

$$\text{Total risk} = \text{Variance} = \text{Market risk} + \text{Diversifiable risk}$$
$$\sigma_i^2 = b_i^2 \sigma_M^2 + \sigma_{e_i}^2 \qquad (25\text{-}16)$$

Here σ_i^2 is the variance (or total risk) of Stock i, σ_M^2 is the variance of the market, b_i is Stock i's beta coefficient, and $\sigma_{e_i}^2$ is the variance of Stock i's regression error term.

2. If all the points in Figure 25-8 had plotted exactly on the regression line, then the variance of the error term, $\sigma_{e_i}^2$, would have been zero, and all of the stock's risk would have been market risk. On the other hand, if the points were widely scattered about the regression line, then much of the stock's total risk would be diversifiable. The shares of a large, well-diversified mutual fund will plot very close to the regression line.

3. Beta is a measure of relative market risk, but the *actual* market risk of Stock i is $b_i^2 \sigma_M^2$. Market risk can also be expressed in standard deviation form, $b_i \sigma_M$. Therefore, stocks with higher betas have greater market risk. If beta were zero, the stock would have no market risk, whereas if beta were 1.0, then the stock would be exactly as risky as the market—assuming the stock is held in a diversified portfolio—and the stock's market risk would be σ_M.

25-5f Modifying the Historical Beta

Betas are generally estimated from the stock's characteristic line by running a linear regression between past returns on the stock in question and past returns on some market index. We define betas developed in this manner as **historical betas**. However, in most situations, it is the *future* beta that is needed. This has led to the development of two different types of betas: (1) adjusted betas and (2) fundamental betas.

Adjusted betas grew largely out of the work of Marshall E. Blume, who showed that true betas tend to move toward 1.0 over time.[12] Therefore, we can begin with a firm's pure historical statistical beta, make an adjustment for the expected future movement toward 1.0, and produce an adjusted beta that will, on average, be a better predictor of the future beta than the unadjusted historical beta would be. *Value Line* publishes betas based on approximately this formula:

$$\text{Adjusted beta} = 0.67(\text{Historical beta}) + 0.35(1.0) \quad (25\text{-}17)$$

Consider American Camping Corporation (ACC), a retailer of supplies for outdoor activities. ACC's historical beta is 1.2. Therefore, its adjusted beta is:

$$\text{Adjusted beta} = 0.67(1.2) + 0.35(1.0) = 1.15$$

Other researchers have extended the adjustment process to include such fundamental risk variables as financial leverage, sales volatility, and the like. The end product here is a **fundamental beta**, which is constantly adjusted to reflect changes in a firm's operations and capital structure. In contrast, such changes might not be reflected in historical betas (including adjusted ones) until several years after the company's "true" beta had changed.

Adjusted betas obviously are heavily dependent on unadjusted historical betas, and so are fundamental betas as they are actually calculated. Therefore, the plain old historical beta, calculated as the slope of the characteristic line, is important even if one goes on to develop a more exotic version.

25-5g Choice of Estimation Period, Holding Period, and Market Index

When calculating betas from past returns, you must choose the sample estimation period, which is the amount of calendar time over which you gather past returns. You must also choose the holding period over which you measure returns, such as weekly returns. Finally, you must choose an index to represent the market portfolio. Following is a discussion of each choice.

LENGTH OF ESTIMATION PERIOD

Betas can be based on historical periods of different lengths. For example, data for the past 1 year, 3 years, 5 years, or even 10 years may be used. Estimated betas can vary significantly for different choices of estimation periods. For example, the beta estimated from 1 year of data might be very different from the beta estimated from 5 years of data, especially if the company has undergone operating changes or shifts in capital structure during the 5-year period. Because changes in a company's operations or financing can change its beta, most analysts use only 1 to 3 years of past data to estimate beta.

HOLDING PERIOD FOR MEASURING RETURNS

Returns may be calculated over holding periods of different lengths—a day, a week, a month, a quarter, a year, and so on. For example, if data on NYSE stocks are analyzed over a 2-year period, then we might obtain $52(2) = 104$ weekly returns for a stock and for the market index. Alternatively, we could use monthly returns, which would provide

---

[12]See Marshall E. Blume, "Betas and Their Regression Tendencies," *Journal of Finance*, June 1975, pp. 785–796; and Marshall E. Blume, "On the Assessment of Risk," *Journal of Finance*, March 1971, pp. 1–10.

24 observations in the sample period: 12(2) = 24. Or we could use daily returns, which would provide about 504 observations in the 2-year period (there are about 252 trading days in a year).

Given the choice of holding period for returns and length of the estimation period, the stock returns would be regressed on the corresponding market returns to obtain the stock's beta. In statistical analysis, it is generally better to have more rather than fewer observations because using more observations generally leads to greater statistical confidence. This suggests the use of weekly returns and, say, 5 years of data for a sample size of 260, or even daily returns for a still larger sample size. However, the shorter the holding period, the more likely the data are to exhibit random "noise." Also, the greater the number of years of data, the more likely the company's basic risk position has changed. Thus, the choice of both the number of years of data and the length of the holding period for calculating rates of return involves trade-offs between the preference for many observations and a desire to rely on more recent and thus more relevant data.

CHOICE OF MARKET INDEX

The value used to represent "the market" is also an important consideration because the index that is used can have a significant effect on the calculated beta. Many analysts today use the New York Stock Exchange Composite Index (based on more than 2,000 common stocks, weighted by the value of each company), but others use the S&P 500 Index. In theory, a broader index yields a more theoretically correct estimate of beta. Indeed, the theoretical index should include returns on all stocks, bonds, leases, private businesses, real estate, and even "human capital." As a practical matter, however, we cannot get accurate returns data on most other types of assets, so measurement problems largely restrict us to stock indexes.

OUR RECOMMENDATION

Where does this leave financial managers regarding the proper beta? We recommend estimating your own beta using daily returns for 1 to 2 years. This seems to be the "sweet" spot that provides the tightest confidence intervals for the estimated betas. Shorter estimation periods don't have enough observations, whereas longer estimation periods have problems associated with betas changing during the estimation period. We also recommend adjusting the estimated beta using Equation 25-17.

If you don't estimate your own betas, we recommend *Value Line* because it estimates betas similarly to the way we recommend. Alternatively, you could get betas from several online sources and average them together for a final estimate.

SELF-TEST

Explain the meaning and significance of a stock's beta coefficient. Illustrate your explanation by drawing, on one graph, the characteristic lines for stocks with low, average, and high risk. (Hint: Let your three characteristic lines intersect at $\bar{r}_i = \bar{r}_M = 6\%$, the assumed risk-free rate.)

What is a typical R^2 for the characteristic line of an individual stock? For a portfolio?

What is the market model? How is it different from the SML for the CAPM?

How are total risk, market risk, and diversifiable risk related?

25-6 Empirical Tests of the CAPM

Does the CAPM's SML produce reasonable estimates for a stock's required return? The literature dealing with empirical tests of the CAPM is quite extensive, so we can give here only a synopsis of some of the key work.

25-6a Tests of the Stability of Beta Coefficients

According to the CAPM, the beta used to estimate a stock's market risk should reflect investors' estimates of the stock's *future* variability in relation to that of the market. Obviously, we do not know now how a stock will be related to the market in the future, nor do we know how the average investor views this expected future relative variability. All we have are data on past variability, which we can use to plot the characteristic line and to calculate *historical betas*. If historical betas have been stable over time, then there would seem to be reason for investors to use past betas as estimators of future variability. For example, if Stock i's beta had been stable in the past, then its historical b_i would probably be a good proxy for its *ex ante,* or expected, beta. By "stable" we mean that if b_i were calculated with data from the period of, say, 2015 to 2019, then this same beta (approximately) should be found from 2020 to 2024.

Robert Levy, Marshall Blume, and others have studied in depth the question of beta stability.[13] Levy calculated betas for individual securities, as well as for portfolios of securities, over a range of time intervals. He reached two conclusions: (1) The betas of individual stocks are unstable, and hence past betas for *individual securities* are *not* good estimators of their future risk. (2) Betas of portfolios of ten or more randomly selected stocks are reasonably stable, and hence past *portfolio* betas are good estimators of future portfolio volatility. In effect, the errors in individual securities' betas tend to offset one another in a portfolio. The work of Blume and others supports this position.

The conclusion that follows from the beta stability studies is that the CAPM is a better concept for structuring investment portfolios than it is for estimating the required return for individual securities.[14]

25-6b Tests of the CAPM Based on the Slope of the SML

The CAPM states that a linear relationship exists between a security's required rate of return and its beta. Moreover, when the SML is graphed, the vertical axis intercept should be r_{RF}, and the required rate of return for a stock (or portfolio) with $b = 1.0$ should be r_M, the required rate of return on the market. Various researchers have attempted to test the validity of the CAPM by first calculating betas and then plotting subsequent realized rates of return in graphs such as that in Figure 25-10. Second, researchers then determine whether the results conform to three CAPM implications: (1) Is the intercept equal to r_{RF}? (2) Is the plot linear or curved? (3) Is the slope of the line equal to $r_M - r_{RF}$? Monthly or daily historical rates of return are generally used for stocks, and both 30-day Treasury bill rates and long-term Treasury bond rates have been used to estimate the value of r_{RF}. Also, most of the studies actually analyzed portfolios rather than individual securities because security betas are so unstable.

Before discussing the results of the tests, it is critical to recognize that although the CAPM is an *ex ante,* or forward-looking, model, the data used to test it are entirely historical. This presents a problem, for there is no reason to believe that *realized* rates of return over past holding periods are necessarily equal to the rates of return to *expect*

---

[13]See Robert A. Levy, "On the Short-Term Stationarity of Beta Coefficients," *Financial Analysts Journal,* November/December 1971, pp. 55–62; and Marshall E. Blume, "Betas and Their Regression Tendencies," *Journal of Finance,* June 1975, pp. 785–796.

[14]For more on beta stability, see Robert W. Kolb and Ricardo J. Rodriguez, "The Regression Tendencies of Betas: A Reappraisal," *The Financial Review,* May 1989, pp. 319–334. Also see Robert Kolb, "Is the Distribution of Betas Stationary?" *Journal of Financial Research,* Winter 1990, pp. 279–283.

FIGURE 25-10
Tests of the CAPM

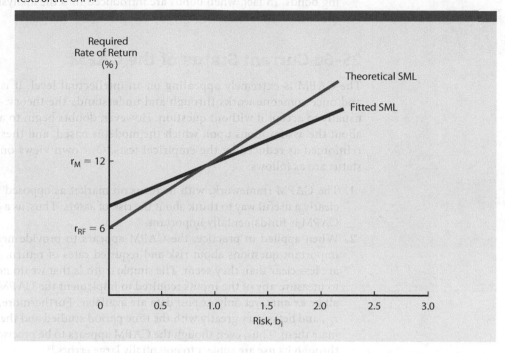

in the future. Also, historical betas may or may not reflect expected future risk. This lack of *ex ante* data makes it extremely difficult to test the CAPM, but here is a summary of the key results.

1. The evidence generally shows a significant positive relationship between realized returns and beta. However, the intercept usually is a bit higher than predicted by the CAPM, and the slope usually is smaller than that predicted by the CAPM.

2. The relationship between risk and return appears to be linear. Empirical studies give no evidence of significant curvature in the risk–return relationship.

3. Tests that attempt to assess the relative importance of market- and company-specific risk do not yield conclusive results. The CAPM implies that company-specific risk should not be relevant, yet both kinds of risk appear to be positively related to security returns; that is, higher returns seem to be required to compensate for diversifiable as well as market risk. However, it may be that the observed relationships reflect statistical problems rather than the true nature of capital markets.

4. Richard Roll has questioned whether it is even conceptually possible to test the CAPM.[15] Roll showed that the linear relationship that prior researchers had observed in graphs like Figure 25-10 resulted from the mathematical properties of the models being tested; therefore, a finding of linearity would prove nothing whatsoever about the CAPM's validity. Roll's work did not disprove the CAPM, but it did demonstrate the virtual impossibility of proving that investors behave in accordance with its predictions.

---

[15]See Richard Roll, "A Critique of the Asset Pricing Theory's Tests," *Journal of Financial Economics*, March 1977, pp. 129–176.

5. If the CAPM were completely valid, then it should apply to all financial assets, including bonds. In fact, when bonds are introduced into the analysis, they do *not* plot on the SML. This is worrisome, to say the least.

25-6c Current Status of the CAPM

The CAPM is extremely appealing on an intellectual level: It is logical and rational, and once someone works through and understands the theory, his or her reaction is usually to accept it without question. However, doubts begin to arise when one thinks about the assumptions upon which the model is based, and these doubts are as much reinforced as reduced by the empirical tests. Our own views on the CAPM's current status are as follows:

1. The CAPM framework, with its focus on market as opposed to stand-alone risk, is clearly a useful way to think about the risk of assets. Thus, as a conceptual model, the CAPM is fundamentally important.
2. When applied in practice, the CAPM appears to provide neat, precise answers to important questions about risk and required rates of return. However, the answers are less clear than they seem. The simple truth is that we do not know precisely how to measure any of the inputs required to implement the CAPM. These inputs should all be *ex ante,* yet only *ex post* data are available. Furthermore, historical data on $\bar{r}_M$, r_{RF}, and betas vary greatly with the time period studied and the methods used to estimate them. Thus, even though the CAPM appears to be precise, estimates of r_i found through its use are subject to potentially large errors.[16]
3. Because the CAPM is logical in the sense that it represents the way risk-averse people ought to behave, the model is a useful conceptual tool.
4. It is appropriate to think about many financial problems in a CAPM framework. However, it is also important to recognize the limitations of the CAPM when using it in practice.

SELF-TEST

What are the two major types of tests that have been performed to test the validity of the CAPM? **(beta stability; slope of the SML)** *Explain their results.*

Are there any reasons to question the validity of the CAPM? Explain.

25-7 Arbitrage Pricing Theory

The CAPM is a single-factor model; that is, it specifies risk as a function of only one factor, the security's beta coefficient. Perhaps the risk–return relationship is more complex, with a stock's required return a function of more than one factor. For example, what if investors, because personal tax rates on capital gains are lower than those on dividends, value capital gains more highly than dividends? Then, if two stocks had the same market risk, the stock paying the higher dividend would have the higher required rate of return. In that case, required returns would be a function of two factors: market risk and dividend policy.

---

[16]For an article supporting a positive link between market risk and expected return, see Felicia Marston and Robert S. Harris, "Risk and Return: A Revisit Using Expected Returns," *The Financial Review,* February 1993, pp. 117–137.

Further, what if many factors are required to specify the equilibrium risk–return relationship rather than just one or two? Stephen Ross has proposed an approach called the **Arbitrage Pricing Theory (APT)**.[17] The APT can include any number of risk factors, so the required return could be a function of two, three, four, or more factors. We should note at the outset that the APT is based on complex mathematical and statistical theory that goes far beyond the scope of this text. Also, although the APT model is widely discussed in academic literature, practical usage to date has been limited. However, such use may increase, so students should at least have an intuitive idea of what the APT is all about.

The SML states that each stock's required return is equal to the risk-free rate plus the product of the market risk premium times the stock's beta coefficient. If stocks are in equilibrium, then the required return will be equal to the expected return:

$$\hat{r}_i = r_i = r_{RF} + (r_M - r_{RF})b_i$$

The historical realized return, $\bar{r}_i$, which will generally be different from the expected return, can be expressed as follows:[18]

$$\bar{r}_i = \hat{r}_i + (\bar{r}_M - \hat{r}_M)b_i + e_i \qquad \text{(25-18)}$$

Thus, the realized return, $\bar{r}_i$, will be equal to the expected return, $\hat{r}_i$, plus a positive or negative increment, $(\bar{r}_M - \hat{r}_M)b_i$, which depends jointly on the stock's beta and on whether the market did better or worse than was expected, plus a random error term, e_i.

The market's realized return, $\bar{r}_M$, is in turn determined by a number of factors, including domestic economic activity as measured by gross domestic product (GDP), the strength of the world economy, the level of inflation, changes in tax laws, and so forth. Further, different groups of stocks are affected in different ways by these fundamental factors. So, rather than specifying a stock's return as a function of one factor (return on the market), one could specify required and realized returns on individual stocks as a function of various fundamental economic factors. If this were done, we would transform Equation 25-18 into Equation 25-19:

$$\bar{r}_i = \hat{r}_i + (\bar{F}_1 - \hat{F}_1)b_{i1} + \cdots + (\bar{F}_j - \hat{F}_j)b_{ij} + e_i \qquad \text{(25-19)}$$

Here:

$\bar{r}_i$ = Realized rate of return on Stock i

$\hat{r}_i$ = Expected rate of return on Stock i

$\bar{F}_j$ = Realized value of economic Factor j

$\hat{F}_j$ = Expected value of Factor j

b_{ij} = Sensitivity of Stock i to economic Factor j

e_i = Effect of unique events on the realized return of Stock i

---

[17]See Stephen A. Ross, "The Arbitrage Theory of Capital Asset Pricing," *Journal of Economic Theory,* December 1976, pp. 341–360.

[18]To avoid cluttering the notation, we have dropped the subscript t to denote a particular time period.

Equation 25-19 shows that the realized return on any stock is the sum of (1) the stock's expected return; (2) increases or decreases that depend on unexpected changes in fundamental economic factors, multiplied by the sensitivity of the stock to these changes; and (3) a random term that reflects changes unique to the firm.

Certain stocks or groups of stocks are most sensitive to Factor 1, others to Factor 2, and so forth, and every portfolio's returns depend on what happened to the different fundamental factors. Theoretically, one could construct a portfolio that is riskless and that requires a zero net investment. (Some stocks would be sold short, with the proceeds from the short sales being used to buy the stocks held long.) Such a zero-investment portfolio must have a zero expected return, or else arbitrage operations would occur and cause the prices of the underlying assets to change until the portfolio's expected return became zero. Using this key insight and the hypothesized risk–return relationship for *actual* returns in Equation 25-19, the APT determines the risk–return relationship for *required* returns (i.e., equivalent of the CAPM's Security Market Line):[19]

$$r_i = r_{RF} + (r_1 - r_{RF})b_{i1} + \cdots + (r_j - r_{RF})b_{ij} \tag{25-20}$$

Here, r_j is the required rate of return on a portfolio that is sensitive only to economic Factor j ($b_{pj} = 1.0$) and has zero sensitivity to all other factors. Thus, for example, $(r_2 - r_{RF})$ is the risk premium on a portfolio with $b_{p2} = 1.0$ and all other $b_{pj} = 0.0$. Note that Equation 25-20 is identical in form to the SML, but it permits a stock's required return to be a function of multiple factors.

To illustrate the APT concept, assume that all stocks' returns depend on only three risk factors: inflation, industrial production, and the aggregate degree of risk aversion (the cost of bearing risk, which we assume is reflected in the spread between the yields on Treasury and low-grade bonds). Further, suppose the following: (1) The risk-free rate is 8.0%. (2) The required rate of return is 13% on a portfolio with unit sensitivity (b = 1.0) to inflation and zero sensitivities (b = 0.0) to industrial production and degree of risk aversion. (3) The required return is 10% on a portfolio with unit sensitivity to industrial production and zero sensitivities to inflation and degree of risk aversion. (4) The required return is 6% on a portfolio (the risk-bearing portfolio) with unit sensitivity to the degree of risk aversion and zero sensitivities to inflation and industrial production. Finally, assume that Stock i has factor sensitivities (betas) of 0.9 to the inflation portfolio, 1.2 to the industrial production portfolio, and −0.7 to the risk-bearing portfolio. Stock i's required rate of return, according to the APT, would be 16.3%:

$$r_i = 8\% + (13\% - 8\%)0.9 + (10\% - 8\%)1.2 + (6\% - 8\%)(-0.7)$$
$$= 16.3\%$$

Note that if the required rate of return on the market were 15.0% and if Stock i had a CAPM beta of 1.1, then its required rate of return, according to the SML, would be 15.7%:

$$r_i = 8\% + (15\% - 8\%)1.1 = 15.7\%$$

The primary theoretical advantage of the APT is that it permits several economic factors to influence individual stock returns, whereas the CAPM assumes that the effect of all factors, except those that are unique to the firm, can be captured in a single measure:

[19]See Thomas E. Copeland, J. Fred Weston, and Kuldeep Shastri, *Financial Theory and Corporate Policy*, 4th ed. (Reading, MA: Addison-Wesley, 2005).

the variability of the stock with respect to the market portfolio. Also, the APT requires fewer assumptions than the CAPM and hence is more general. Finally, the APT does not assume that all investors hold the market portfolio, a CAPM requirement that is clearly not met in practice.

However, the APT faces several major hurdles in implementation, the most severe of which is that the theory does not actually identify the relevant factors. The APT does not tell us what factors influence returns, nor does it indicate how many factors should appear in the model. There is some empirical evidence that only three or four factors are relevant—perhaps inflation, industrial production, the spread between low- and high-grade bonds, and the term structure of interest rates—but no one knows for sure.

The APT's proponents argue that it is not necessary to identify the relevant factors. Researchers use a statistical procedure called "factor analysis" to develop the APT parameters. Basically, they start with hundreds or even thousands of stocks and then create several different portfolios, where the returns on each portfolio are not highly correlated with returns on the other portfolios. Thus, each portfolio is apparently more heavily influenced by one of the unknown factors than are the other portfolios. Then, the required rate of return on each portfolio becomes the estimate for that unknown economic factor, shown as r_j in Equation 25-20. The sensitivities of each individual stock's returns to the returns on that portfolio are the factor sensitivities (betas). Unfortunately, the results of factor analysis are not easily interpreted; hence, it does not provide significant insights into the underlying economic determinants of risk.[20]

SELF-TEST

What is the primary difference between the APT and the CAPM?

What are some disadvantages of the APT?

An analyst has modeled the stock of Brown Kitchen Supplies using a two-factor APT model. The risk-free rate is 5%, the required return on the first factor (r_1) is 10%, and the required return on the second factor (r_2) is 15%. If $b_{i1} = 0.5$ and $b_{i2} = 1.3$, what is Brown's required return? **(20.5%)**

SUMMARY

The primary goal of this chapter was to extend your knowledge of risk and return concepts. The key concepts covered are listed here.

- The **feasible set** of portfolios represents all portfolios that can be constructed from a given set of assets.
- An **efficient portfolio** is one that offers the most return for a given amount of risk or the least risk for a given amount of return.
- The **optimal portfolio** for an investor is defined by the investor's highest possible **indifference curve** that is tangent to the **efficient set** of portfolios.
- The **Capital Asset Pricing Model (CAPM)** describes the relationship between market risk and required rates of return.

[20]For additional discussion of the APT, see Edward L. Bubnys, "Simulating and Forecasting Utility Stock Returns: Arbitrage Pricing Theory vs. Capital Asset Pricing Model," *The Financial Review*, February 1990, pp. 1–23; David H. Goldenberg and Ashok J. Robin, "The Arbitrage Pricing Theory and Cost-of-Capital Estimation: The Case of Electric Utilities," *Journal of Financial Research*, Fall 1991, pp. 181–196; and Ashok Robin and Ravi Shukla, "The Magnitude of Pricing Errors in the Arbitrage Pricing Theory," *Journal of Financial Research*, Spring 1991, pp. 65–82.

- The **Capital Market Line (CML)** describes the risk–return relationship for efficient portfolios—that is, for portfolios consisting of a mix of the market portfolio and a riskless asset.
- Stock i's **beta coefficient, bi**, is a measure of the stock's market risk. Beta measures the variability of a security's returns relative to the stock market.
- The beta coefficient is measured by the slope of the stock's **characteristic line**, which is found by regressing past stock returns versus past market returns.
- The **Security Market Line (SML)** is an integral part of the CAPM, and it describes the risk–return relationship for individual assets. The required rate of return for any Stock i is equal to the risk-free rate plus the **market risk premium** multiplied by the stock's beta coefficient: $r_i = r_{RF} + (r_M - r_{RF})b_i$.
- In contrast to the CAPM, the **Arbitrage Pricing Theory (APT)** hypothesizes that expected stock returns are due to more than one factor.

QUESTIONS

(25-1)   Define the following terms, using graphs or equations to illustrate your answers wherever feasible:

      a. Portfolio; feasible set; efficient portfolio; efficient frontier
      b. Indifference curve; optimal portfolio
      c. Capital Asset Pricing Model (CAPM); Capital Market Line (CML)
      d. Characteristic line; beta coefficient, b
      e. Arbitrage Pricing Theory (APT)

(25-2)   Security A has an expected rate of return of 6%, a standard deviation of returns of 30%, a correlation coefficient with the market of −0.25, and a beta coefficient of −0.5. Security B has an expected return of 11%, a standard deviation of returns of 10%, a correlation with the market of 0.75, and a beta coefficient of 0.5. Which security is more risky? Why?

SELF-TEST PROBLEM   SOLUTION SHOWN IN APPENDIX A

(ST-1)   You are planning to invest $200,000. Two securities are available, A and B, and you
Risk and Return   can invest in either of them or in a portfolio with some of each. You estimate that the following probability distributions of returns are applicable for A and B:

Security A		Security B	
P_A	r_A	P_B	r_B
0.1	−10.0%	0.1	−30.0%
0.2	5.0	0.2	0.0
0.4	15.0	0.4	20.0
0.2	25.0	0.2	40.0
0.1	40.0	0.1	70.0
	$\hat{r}_A = ?$		$\hat{r}_B = 20.0\%$
	$\sigma_A = ?$		$\sigma_B = 25.7\%$

a. The expected return for Security B is $\hat{r}_B = 20\%$, and $\sigma_B = 25.7\%$. Find $\hat{r}_A$ and σ_A.

b. Use Equation 25-3 to find the value of w_A that produces the minimum risk portfolio. Assume $\rho_{AB} = -0.5$ for parts b and c.

c. Construct a table giving $\hat{r}_p$ and σ_p for portfolios with $w_A = 1.00, 0.75, 0.50, 0.25, 0.0$, and the minimum risk value of w_A. (Hint: For $w_A = 0.75$, $\hat{r}_p = 16.25\%$ and $\sigma_p = 8.5\%$; for $w_A = 0.5$, $\hat{r}_p = 17.5\%$ and $\sigma_p = 11.1\%$; for $w_A = 0.25$, $\hat{r}_p = 18.75\%$ and $\sigma_p = 17.9\%$.)

d. Graph the feasible set of portfolios and identify the efficient frontier of the feasible set.

e. Suppose your risk–return trade-off function, or indifference curve, is tangent to the efficient set at the point where $\hat{r}_p = 18\%$. Use this information, together with the graph constructed in part d, to locate (approximately) your optimal portfolio. Draw in a reasonable indifference curve, indicate the percentage of your funds invested in each security, and determine the optimal portfolio's σ_p and $\hat{r}_p$. (Hint: Estimate σ_p and $\hat{r}_p$ graphically; then use the equation for $\hat{r}_p$ to determine w_A.)

f. Now suppose a riskless asset with a return $r_{RF} = 10\%$ becomes available. How would this change the investment opportunity set? Explain why the efficient frontier becomes linear.

g. Given the indifference curve in part e, would you change your portfolio? If so, how? (Hint: Assume that the indifference curves are parallel.)

h. What are the beta coefficients of Stocks A and B? (Hint: Recognize that $r_i = r_{RF} + b_i(r_M - r_{RF})$ and then solve for b_i; assume that your preferences match those of most other investors.)

PROBLEMS   ANSWERS ARE IN APPENDIX B

EASY PROBLEMS 1–2

(25-1)
Beta

The standard deviation of stock returns for Stock A is 40%. The standard deviation of the market return is 20%. If the correlation between Stock A and the market is 0.70, then what is Stock A's beta?

(25-2)
APT

An analyst has modeled the stock of Crisp Trucking using a two-factor APT model. The risk-free rate is 6%, the expected return on the first factor (r_1) is 12%, and the expected return on the second factor (r_2) is 8%. If $b_{i1} = 0.7$ and $b_{i2} = 0.9$, what is Crisp's required return?

INTERMEDIATE PROBLEMS 3–4

(25-3)
Two-Asset Portfolio

Stock A has an expected return of 12% and a standard deviation of 40%. Stock B has an expected return of 18% and a standard deviation of 60%. The correlation coefficient between Stocks A and B is 0.2. What are the expected return and standard deviation of a portfolio invested 30% in Stock A and 70% in Stock B?

(25-4)
SML and CML Comparison

The beta coefficient of an asset can be expressed as a function of the asset's correlation with the market as follows:

$$b_i = \frac{\rho_{iM}\sigma_i}{\sigma_M}$$

a. Substitute this expression for beta into the Security Market Line (SML), Equation 25-10. This results in an alternative form of the SML.

b. Compare your answer to part a with the Capital Market Line (CML), Equation 25-6. What similarities do you observe? What conclusions can you draw?

CHALLENGING PROBLEMS 5–6

(25-5)
Characteristic
Line and Security
Market Line

You are given the following set of data:

	Historical Rates of Return	
Year	NYSE	Stock X
1	−26.5%	−14.0%
2	37.2	23.0
3	23.8	17.5
4	−7.2	2.0
5	6.6	8.1
6	20.5	19.4
7	30.6	18.2

a. Use a spreadsheet (or a calculator with a linear regression function) to determine Stock X's beta coefficient.

b. Determine the arithmetic average rates of return for Stock X and the NYSE over the period given. Calculate the standard deviations of returns for both Stock X and the NYSE.

c. Assume that the situation during Years 1 to 7 is expected to prevail in the future (i.e., $\hat{r}_X = \bar{r}_{X,\text{Average}}$, $\hat{r}_M = \bar{r}_{M,\text{Average}}$, and both σ_X and b_X in the future will equal their past values). Also assume that Stock X is in equilibrium—that is, it plots on the Security Market Line. What is the risk-free rate?

d. Plot the Security Market Line.

e. Suppose you hold a large, well-diversified portfolio and are considering adding to that portfolio either Stock X or another stock, Stock Y, which has the same beta as Stock X but a higher standard deviation of returns. Stocks X and Y have the same expected returns: $\hat{r}_X = \hat{r}_Y = 10.6\%$. Which stock should you choose?

(25-6)
Characteristic Line

You are given the following set of data:

	Historical Rates of Return	
Year	NYSE	Stock Y
1	4.0%	3.0%
2	14.3	18.2
3	19.0	9.1
4	−14.7	−6.0
5	−26.5	−15.3
6	37.2	33.1
7	23.8	6.1
8	−7.2	3.2
9	6.6	14.8
10	20.5	24.1
11	30.6	18.0
	Mean = 9.8%	9.8%
	σ = 19.6%	13.8%

a. Construct a scatter diagram showing the relationship between returns on Stock Y and the market. Use a spreadsheet or a calculator with a linear regression function to estimate beta.

b. Give a verbal interpretation of what the regression line and the beta coefficient show about Stock Y's volatility and relative risk as compared with those of other stocks.

c. Suppose the regression line were exactly as shown by your graph from part b but the scatter plot of points was more spread out. How would this affect (1) the firm's risk if the stock is held in a one-asset portfolio and (2) the actual risk premium on the stock if the CAPM holds exactly?

d. Suppose the regression line were downward sloping and the beta coefficient were negative. What would this imply about (1) Stock Y's relative risk, (2) its correlation with the market, and (3) its probable risk premium?

SPREADSHEET PROBLEM

(25-7)
Feasible Portfolios

resource

Start with the partial model in the file **Ch25 P07 Build a Model.xlsx** from the textbook's Web site. Following is information for the required returns and standard deviations of returns for A, B, and C:

Stock	r_i	σ_i
A	7.0%	33.11%
B	10.0	53.85
C	20.0	89.44

The correlation coefficients for each pair are shown in the following matrix, with each cell in the matrix giving the correlation between the stock in that row and column. For example, $\rho_{AB} = 0.1571$ is in the row for A and the column for B. Notice that the diagonal values are equal to 1 because a variable is always perfectly correlated with itself.

	A	B	C
A	1.0000	0.1571	0.1891
B	0.1571	1.0000	0.1661
C	0.1891	0.1661	1.0000

a. Suppose a portfolio has 30% invested in A, 50% in B, and 20% in C. What are the expected return and standard deviation of the portfolio?

b. The partial model lists six different combinations of portfolio weights. For each combination of weights, find the required return and standard deviation.

c. The partial model provides a scatter diagram showing the required returns and standard deviations already calculated. This provides a visual indicator of the feasible set. If you seek a return of 10.5%, then what is the smallest standard deviation that you must accept?

MINI CASE

You have been hired at the investment firm of Bowers & Noon. One of its clients doesn't understand the value of diversification or why stocks with the biggest standard deviations don't always have the highest expected returns. Your assignment is to address the client's concerns by showing the client how to answer the following questions:

a. Suppose Asset A has an expected return of 10% and a standard deviation of 20%. Asset B has an expected return of 16% and a standard deviation of 40%. If the correlation between A and B is 0.35, what are the expected return and standard deviation for a portfolio consisting of 30% Asset A and 70% Asset B?

b. Plot the attainable portfolios for a correlation of 0.35. Now plot the attainable portfolios for correlations of +1.0 and −1.0.

c. Suppose a risk-free asset has an expected return of 5%. By definition, its standard deviation is zero, and its correlation with any other asset is also zero. Using only Asset A and the risk-free asset, plot the attainable portfolios.

d. Construct a plausible graph that shows risk (as measured by portfolio standard deviation) on the x-axis and expected rate of return on the y-axis. Now add an illustrative feasible (or attainable) set of portfolios and show what portion of the feasible set is efficient. What makes a particular portfolio efficient? Don't worry about specific values when constructing the graph—merely illustrate how things look with "reasonable" data.

e. Add a set of indifference curves to the graph created for part b. What do these curves represent? What is the optimal portfolio for this investor? Add a second set of indifference curves that leads to the selection of a different optimal portfolio. Why do the two investors choose different portfolios?

f. Now add the risk-free asset. What impact does this have on the efficient frontier?

g. Write out the equation for the Capital Market Line (CML), and draw it on the graph. Interpret the plotted CML. Now add a set of indifference curves and illustrate how an investor's optimal portfolio is some combination of the risky portfolio and the risk-free asset. What is the composition of the risky portfolio?

h. What is the Capital Asset Pricing Model (CAPM)? What are the assumptions that underlie the model? What is the Security Market Line (SML)?

i. What is a characteristic line? How is this line used to estimate a stock's beta coefficient? Write out and explain the formula that relates total risk, market risk, and diversifiable risk.

j. What are two potential tests that can be conducted to verify the CAPM? What are the results of such tests? What is Roll's critique of CAPM tests?

k. Briefly explain the difference between the CAPM and the Arbitrage Pricing Theory (APT).

SELECTED ADDITIONAL CASE

The following case from CengageCompose covers many of the concepts discussed in this chapter and is available at **http://compose.cengage.com**.

Klein-Brigham Series:
Case 2, "Peachtree Securities, Inc. (A)."

CHAPTER 26

Real Options

In addition to its speedy shoes, Adidas AG has manufacturing facilities so speedy that Adidas named them "Speedfactories." What is the need for speed? Consumers want customized products that are personalized to meet their individual needs. This is not possible with traditional manufacturing facilities, so Adidas is changing the way it makes shoes and clothing.

A conventional factory produces large quantities of a single item before changing over to make another product. These changeovers take time, often several days. In contrast, an Adidas Speedfactory can make much faster changeovers because it uses smart machines, such as 3D printers, robots, and software-controlled equipment. The payoffs are greater customer satisfaction, quicker deliveries, and lower labor costs.

Think about the flexibility option of the Speedfactory as you read about real options in this chapter.

Source: Mariana Cid De Leon Ovalle, "Adidas Speedfactory to Improve Manufacturing Process," *Boss Magazine,* at **https://thebossmagazine.com/adidas-speedfactory/**.

resource

The textbook's Web site contains an Excel file that will guide you through the chapter's calculations. The file for this chapter is Ch26 Tool Kit.xlsx, and we encourage you to open the file and follow along as you read the chapter.

Traditional discounted cash flow (DCF) analysis—in which an asset's cash flows are estimated and then discounted to obtain the asset's NPV—has been the cornerstone for valuing all types of assets since the 1950s. Accordingly, most of our discussion of capital budgeting has focused on DCF valuation techniques. However, in recent years, academics and practitioners have demonstrated that DCF valuation techniques do not always tell the complete story about a project's value and that rote use of DCF can, at times, lead to incorrect capital budgeting decisions.[1]

DCF techniques were originally developed to value securities such as stocks and bonds. Securities are passive investments: Once they have been purchased, most investors have no influence over the cash flows they produce. However, real assets are not passive investments, because managerial actions after an investment has been made can influence its results. Furthermore, investing in a new project often brings with it the potential for increasing the firm's future investment opportunities. Such opportunities are, in effect, options—the right (but not the obligation) to take some action in the future. As we demonstrate in the next section, options are valuable, so projects that expand the firm's set of opportunities have positive **option values**. Similarly, any project that reduces the set of future opportunities destroys option value. A project's impact on the firm's opportunities, or its option value, may not be captured by conventional NPV analysis, so this option value should be considered separately, as we do in this chapter.

26-1 Valuing Real Options

Recall from Chapter 13 that **real options** are opportunities for management to change the timing, scale, or other aspects of an investment in response to changes in market conditions. These opportunities are options in the sense that management can, if it is in the company's best interest, undertake some action; management is not *required* to undertake the action. These opportunities are real (as opposed to financial) because they involve decisions regarding real assets—such as plants, equipment, and land—rather than financial assets like stocks or bonds. Four examples of real options are investment timing options, growth options, abandonment options, and flexibility options. This chapter provides an example of how to value an investment timing option and a growth option. **Web Extension 26A** on the textbook's Web site shows how to value an **abandonment option**, which allows a company to reduce a project's capacity or drop the project entirely if market conditions deteriorate.

Valuing a real option requires judgment, both to formulate the model and to estimate the inputs. Does this mean the answer won't be useful? Definitely not. For example, the models used by NASA only approximate the centers of gravity for the moon, the Earth, and other heavenly bodies, yet even with these "errors" in their models, NASA has been able to put astronauts on the moon. As one professor said, "All models are wrong, but some are still quite useful." This is especially true for real options. We might not be able to find the exact value of a real option, but the value we find can be helpful in deciding whether or not to accept the project. Equally important, the process of looking for and then valuing real options often identifies critical issues that might otherwise go unnoticed.

---

[1]For an excellent general discussion of the problems inherent in discounted cash flow valuation techniques as applied to capital budgeting, see Avinash K. Dixit and Robert S. Pindyck, "The Options Approach to Capital Investment," *Harvard Business Review,* May/June 1995, pp. 105–115.

Five possible procedures can be used to deal with real options. Starting with the simplest, they are as follows:

1. Use discounted cash flow (DCF) valuation and ignore any real options by assuming their values are zero.
2. Use DCF valuation and include a qualitative recognition of any real option's value.
3. Use decision-tree analysis.
4. Use a standard model for a financial option.
5. Develop a unique, project-specific model using financial engineering techniques.

The following sections illustrate these procedures.

List the five possible procedures for dealing with real options.

26-2 The Investment Timing Option: An Illustration

resource

*All calculations for the analysis of the investment timing option are shown in **Ch26 Tool Kit.xlsx** on the textbook's Web site.*

There is frequently an alternative to investing immediately—the decision to invest or not can be postponed until more information becomes available. By waiting, a better-informed decision can be made, and this **investment timing option** adds value to the project and reduces its risk.

Murphy Systems is considering a project for a new type of handheld device that provides wireless Internet connections. The cost of the project is $50 million, but the future cash flows depend on the demand for wireless Internet connections, which is uncertain. Murphy believes there is a 25% chance that demand for the new device will be high, in which case the project will generate cash flows of $33 million each year for 3 years. There is a 50% chance of average demand, with cash flows of $25 million per year, and a 25% chance that demand will be low and annual cash flows will be only $5 million. A preliminary analysis indicates that the project is somewhat riskier than average, so it has been assigned a cost of capital of 14% versus 12% for an average project at Murphy Systems. Here is a summary of the project's data:

Demand	Probability	Annual Cash Flow	NPV of Scenario
High	0.25	$33 million	$26.61 million
Average	0.50	25 million	8.04 million
Low	0.25	5 million	−38.39 million
Expected annual cash flow		$22 million	
Project's cost of capital	14%		
Life of project	3 years		
Initial investment	$50 million		
NPV = Expected NPV	$1.08 million		

Murphy could accept the project and implement it immediately; however, because the company has a patent on the device's core modules, it could also choose to delay the decision until next year, when more information about demand will be available. The cost will still be $50 million if Murphy waits, and the project will still be expected to generate the indicated cash flows, but each flow will be pushed back 1 year. However, if Murphy waits, then it will know which of the demand conditions—and hence which set of cash flows—will occur. If Murphy waits, then it will, of course, make the investment only if demand is sufficient to yield a positive NPV.

Observe that this real timing option resembles a call option on a stock. A call gives its owner the right to purchase a stock at a fixed strike price, but only if the stock's price is higher than the strike price will the owner exercise the option and buy the stock. Similarly, if Murphy defers implementation, then it will have the right to "purchase" the project by making the $50 million investment if the NPV as calculated next year, when new information is available, is positive.

26-2a Approach 1: DCF Analysis Ignoring the Timing Option

Based on probabilities for the different levels of demand, the expected annual cash flows are $22 million per year:

$$\text{Expected cash flow per year} = 0.25(\$33) + 0.50(\$25) + 0.25(\$5)$$
$$= \$22 \text{ million}$$

Ignoring the investment timing option, the traditional NPV is $1.08 million, found as follows:

$$\text{NPV} = -\$50 + \frac{\$22}{(1 + 0.14)^1} + \frac{\$22}{(1 + 0.14)^2} + \frac{\$22}{(1 + 0.14)^3} = \$1.08$$

The present value of the cash inflows is $51.08 million while the cost is $50 million, leaving an NPV of $1.08 million.

Based just on this DCF analysis, Murphy should accept the project. Note, however, that if the expected cash flows had been slightly lower—say, $21.5 million per year—then the NPV would have been negative and the project would have been rejected. Also, note that the project is risky: There is a 25% probability that demand will be weak, in which case the NPV will turn out to be a negative $38.4 million.

26-2b Approach 2: DCF Analysis with a Qualitative Consideration of the Timing Option

The discounted cash flow analysis suggests that the project should be accepted, but just barely, and it ignores the existence of a possibly valuable real option. If Murphy implements the project now, it gains an expected (but risky) NPV of $1.08 million. However, accepting now means that it is also giving up the option to wait and learn more about market demand before making the commitment. Thus, the decision is this: Is the option Murphy would be giving up worth more or less than $1.08 million? If the option is worth more than $1.08 million, then Murphy should not give up the option, which means deferring the decision—and vice versa if the option is worth less than $1.08 million.

Based on the discussion of financial options in Chapter 8, what qualitative assessment can we make regarding the option's value? Put another way: Without doing any additional calculations, does it appear that Murphy should go forward now or wait? In thinking about this decision, first note that the value of an option is higher if the current value of the underlying asset is high relative to its strike price, other things held constant. For example, a call option with a strike price of $50 on a stock with a current price of $50 (an at-the-money call) is worth more than if the current stock price were $20 (an out-of-the-money call). The strike price of the project is $50 million, and our first guess at the value of its cash flows is $51.08 million. We will calculate the exact value of Murphy's underlying asset later, but the DCF analysis does suggest that the underlying asset's value will be close to the strike price, so the option should be valuable. We also know that an option's value is higher the longer its time to expiration. Here the option has a 1-year life, which is fairly long for an option, and this also suggests that the option is probably valuable. Finally, we know that the value of an option increases with the risk of the underlying asset. The data used in the DCF analysis indicate that the project is quite risky, which again suggests that the option is valuable.

Thus, our qualitative assessment indicates that the option to delay might well be more valuable than the expected NPV of $1.08 if we undertake the project immediately. This conclusion is subjective, but the qualitative assessment suggests that Murphy's management should go on to make a quantitative assessment of the situation.

26-2c Approach 3: Scenario Analysis and Decision Trees

Part 1 of Figure 26-1 presents a scenario analysis and decision tree similar to the examples in Chapter 13. Each possible outcome is shown as a "branch" on the tree. Each branch shows the cash flows and probability of a scenario laid out as a time line. Thus, the top line, which gives the payoffs of the high-demand scenario, has positive cash flows of $33 million for the next 3 years, and its NPV is $26.61 million. The average-demand branch in the middle has an NPV of $8.04 million, while the NPV of the low-demand branch is a negative $38.39 million. Because Murphy will suffer a $38.39 million loss if demand is weak, and there is a 25% probability of weak demand, the project is clearly risky.

The expected NPV is the weighted average of the three possible outcomes, where the weight for each outcome is its probability. The weighted sum in the last column in Part 1 shows that the expected NPV is $1.08 million, the same as in the original DCF analysis. Part 1 also shows a standard deviation of $24.02 million for the NPV and a coefficient of variation (defined as the ratio of standard deviation to the expected NPV) of 22.32, which is extremely large. Clearly, the project is quite risky under the analysis thus far.

Part 2 is set up similarly to Part 1 except that it shows what happens if Murphy delays the decision and then implements the project only if demand turns out to be high or average. No cost is incurred now at Year 0—here, the only action is to wait. Then, if demand is average or high, Murphy will spend $50 million at Year 1 and receive either $33 million or $25 million per year for the following 3 years. If demand is low, as shown on the bottom branch, Murphy will spend nothing at Year 1 and will receive no cash flows in subsequent years. The NPV of the high-demand branch is $23.35 million and that of the average-demand branch is $7.05 million. Because all cash flows under the low-demand scenario are zero, the NPV in this case will also be zero. The expected NPV if Murphy delays the decision is $9.36 million.

This analysis shows that the project's expected NPV will be much higher if Murphy delays than if it invests immediately. Also, because there is no possibility of losing money under the delay option, this decision also lowers the project's risk. This plainly indicates that the option to wait is valuable; hence, Murphy should wait until Year 1 before deciding whether to proceed with the investment.

Before we conclude the discussion of decision trees, note that we used the same cost of capital, 14%, to discount cash flows in the "proceed immediately" scenario analysis in Part 1 and under the "delay 1 year" scenario in Part 2. However, this is not appropriate for three reasons. First, because there is no possibility of losing money if Murphy delays, the investment under that plan is clearly less risky than if Murphy charges ahead today. Second, the 14% cost of capital might be appropriate for risky cash flows, yet the investment in the project at Year 1 in Part 2 is known with certainty. Perhaps, then, we should discount it at

FIGURE 26-1
DCF and Decision-Tree Analysis for the Investment Timing Option (Millions of Dollars)

	A	B	C	D	E	F	G	H
41	**Part 1. Scenario Analysis: Proceed with Project Today**							
42								
43					**Future Cash Flows**			**NPV of This**
44	**Now: Year 0**		**Probability**	**Year 1**	**Year 2**	**Year 3**		**Scenario[a]**
45								
46		→ High →	0.25	$33	$33	$33		$26.61
47	↗							
48	–$50	→ Average →	0.50	$25	$25	$25		$8.04
49	↘							
50		→ Low →	0.25	$5	$5	$5		–$38.39
51			1.00					
52						Expected value of NPV[b] =		$1.08
53						Standard deviation[b] =		$24.02
54						Coefficient of variation[c] =		22.32
55								
56	**Part 2. Decision-Tree Analysis: Implement in One Year Only if Optimal**							
57								
58					**Future Cash Flows**			**NPV of This**
59	**Now: Year 0**		**Probability**	**Year 1**	**Year 2**	**Year 3**	**Year 4**	**Scenario[d]**
60								
61		→ High →	0.25	–$50	$33	$33	$33	$23.35
62	↗							
63	**Wait**	→Average →	0.50	–$50	$25	$25	$25	$7.05
64	↘							
65		→ Low →	0.25	$0	$0	$0	$0	$0.00
66			1.00					
67						Expected value of NPV[b] =		$9.36
68						Standard deviation[b] =		$8.57
69						Coefficient of variation[c] =		0.92

Source: See the file ***Ch26 Tool Kit.xlsx***. Numbers are reported as rounded values for clarity but are calculated using *Excel*'s full precision. Thus, intermediate calculations using the figure's rounded values will be inexact.

Notes:

[a] The WACC is 14%.

[b] The expected value and standard deviation are calculated as explained in Chapter 2.

[c] The coefficient of variation is the standard deviation divided by the expected value.

[d] The NPV in Part 2 is as of Year 0. Therefore, each of the project cash flows is discounted back 1 more year than in Part 1.

the risk-free rate.[2] Third, the project's cash inflows (excluding the initial investment) are different in Part 2 than in Part 1 because the low-demand cash flows are eliminated. This suggests that if 14% is the appropriate cost of capital in the "proceed immediately" case, then some lower rate would be appropriate in the "delay decision" case.

---

[2] For a more detailed explanation of the rationale behind using the risk-free rate to discount the project cost, see Timothy A. Luehrman, "Investment Opportunities as Real Options: Getting Started on the Numbers," *Harvard Business Review,* July/August 1998, pp. 51–67. This paper also provides a discussion of real option valuation. Professor Luehrman also wrote a follow-up paper that provides an excellent discussion of the ways real options affect strategy: "Strategy as a Portfolio of Real Options," *Harvard Business Review,* September/October 1998, pp. 89–99.

In Figure 26-2, Part 1, we repeat the "delay decision" analysis but with two changes. First, we treat the Year-1 investment differently from the project's subsequent *operating cash flows*. The cash flows that remain we will call *operating cash flows*. We discount the Year-1 investment at the risk-free rate of 6% because the cost is known with certainty. However, we discount the subsequent operating cash flows at the 14% WACC. This increases the PV of the cost, which lowers the NPV from $9.36 million to $6.88 million.

FIGURE 26-2
Decision-Tree and Sensitivity Analysis for the Investment Timing Option (Millions of Dollars)

	A	B	C	D	E	F	G	H	I
80	**Part 1. Decision-Tree Analysis: Implement in One Year Only if Optimal**								
81	**(Discount Cost at the Risk-Free Rate and Operating Cash Flows at the WACC)**								
82									
83					**Future Cash Flows**			**NPV of This**	
84	**Now: Year 0**		**Probability**	**Year 1**	**Year 2**	**Year 3**	**Year 4**	**Scenario**[a]	
85									
86		**→ High →**	**0.25**	**-$50**	**$33**	**$33**	**$33**	**$20.04**	
87		↗							
88	**Wait**	**→Average →**	**0.50**	**-$50**	**$25**	**$25**	**$25**	**$3.74**	
89		↘							
90		**→ Low →**	**0.25**	**$0**	**$0**	**$0**	**$0**	**$0.00**	
91			**1.00**						
92					**Expected value of NPV**[b] **=**			**$6.88**	
93					**Standard deviation**[b] **=**			**$7.75**	
94					**Coefficient of variation**[c] **=**			**1.13**	
95									
96	**Part 2. Sensitivity Analysis of NPV to Changes in the Cost of Capital Used to**								
97	**Discount Cost and Cash Flows**								
98									
99			**Cost of Capital Used to Discount the Year-1 Cost**						
100			3%	4%	5%	6%	7%	8%	9%
101	**Cost of Capital Used to Discount the Year-2 through Year-4 Operating Cash Flows**	8%	**$13.1**	**$13.5**	**$13.8**	**$14.1**	**$14.5**	**$14.8**	**$15.1**
102		9%	**$11.8**	**$12.1**	**$12.5**	**$12.8**	**$13.1**	**$13.5**	**$13.8**
103		10%	**$10.5**	**$10.9**	**$11.2**	**$11.5**	**$11.9**	**$12.2**	**$12.5**
104		11%	**$9.3**	**$9.6**	**$10.0**	**$10.3**	**$10.6**	**$11.0**	**$11.3**
105		12%	**$8.1**	**$8.4**	**$8.8**	**$9.1**	**$9.5**	**$9.8**	**$10.1**
106		13%	**$6.9**	**$7.3**	**$7.6**	**$8.0**	**$8.3**	**$8.6**	**$9.0**
107		14%	**$5.9**	**$6.2**	**$6.5**	**$6.9**	**$7.2**	**$7.5**	**$7.9**
108		15%	**$4.8**	**$5.1**	**$5.5**	**$5.8**	**$6.2**	**$6.5**	**$6.8**
109		16%	**$3.8**	**$4.1**	**$4.5**	**$4.8**	**$5.1**	**$5.5**	**$5.8**
110		17%	**$2.8**	**$3.1**	**$3.5**	**$3.8**	**$4.1**	**$4.5**	**$4.8**
111		18%	**$1.8**	**$2.2**	**$2.5**	**$2.9**	**$3.2**	**$3.5**	**$3.8**

Source: See the file ***Ch26 Tool Kit.xlsx***. Numbers are reported as rounded values for clarity but are calculated using *Excel*'s full precision. Thus, intermediate calculations using the figure's rounded values will be inexact.

Notes:

[a] The operating cash flows in Year 2 through Year 4 are discounted at the WACC of 14%. The cost in Year 1 is discounted at the risk-free rate of 6%.

[b] The expected value and standard deviation are calculated as explained in Chapter 2.

[c] The coefficient of variation is the standard deviation divided by the expected value.

Because we don't know the precise WACC for this project—the 14% we used might be too high or too low for the operating cash flows in Year 2 through Year 4.[3] Therefore, in Part 2 of Figure 26-2 we show a sensitivity analysis of the NPV in which the discount rates used for both the operating cash flows and for the project's cost vary. This sensitivity analysis shows that, under all reasonable WACCs, the NPV of delaying is greater than $1.08 million. This confirms that the option to wait is more valuable than the $1.08 million NPV resulting from immediate implementation. Therefore, Murphy should wait rather than implement the project immediately.

26-2d Approach 4: Valuing the Timing Option with the Black-Scholes Option Pricing Model

The decision-tree approach, coupled with a sensitivity analysis, may provide enough information for a good decision. However, it is often useful to obtain additional insights into the real option's value, which means using the fourth procedure, an option pricing model. To do this, the analyst must find a standard financial option that resembles the project's real option.[4] As noted earlier, Murphy's option to delay the project is similar to a call option on a stock. Hence, the Black-Scholes option pricing model can be used. This model requires five inputs: (1) the risk-free rate, (2) the time until the option expires, (3) the strike price, (4) the current price of the stock, and (5) the variance of the stock's rate of return. Therefore, we need to estimate values for those five inputs.

First, if we assume that the rate on a 52-week Treasury security is 6%, then this rate can be used as the risk-free rate. Second, Murphy must decide within a year whether or not to implement the project, so there is 1 year until the option expires. Third, it will cost $50 million to implement the project, so $50 million can be used for the strike price. Fourth, we need a proxy for the value of the underlying asset, which in Black-Scholes is the current price of the stock. Note that a stock's current price is the present value of its expected future cash flows. For Murphy's real option, the underlying asset is the project itself, and its current "price" is the present value of its expected future cash flows. Therefore, as a proxy for the stock price we can use the present value of the project's future cash flows. And fifth, the variance of the project's return can be used to represent the variance of the stock's return in the Black-Scholes model.

Figure 26-3 shows how to estimate the present value of the project's cash inflows. We need to find the current value of the underlying asset—that is, the project. For a stock, the current price is the present value of all expected future cash flows, including those that are expected even if we do not exercise the call option. Note also that the strike price for a call option has no effect on the stock's current price.[5] For our real option, the underlying asset is the delayed project, and its current "price" is the present value of all its future expected cash flows. Just as the price of a stock includes all of its future cash flows, so should the present value of the project include all of its possible future cash flows. Moreover, because the price of a stock is not affected by the strike price of a call option,

---

[3]Murphy might gain information by waiting, which could reduce risk, but if a delay would enable others to enter and perhaps preempt the market, this could increase risk. In our example, we assumed that Murphy has a patent on critical components of the device, precluding the entrance of a competitor that could preempt its position in the market.

[4]In theory, financial option pricing models apply only to assets that are continuously traded in a market. Even though real options usually don't meet this criterion, financial option models often provide a reasonably accurate approximation of the real option's value.

[5]The company itself is not involved with traded stock options. However, if the option were a warrant issued by the company, then the strike price would affect the company's cash flows and hence its stock price.

FIGURE 26-3
Estimating the Input for Stock Price in the Option Analysis of the Investment Timing Option (Millions of Dollars)

	A	B	C	D	E	F	G	H
140					**Future Cash Flows**			**PV of This**
141	Now: Year 0		**Probability**	**Year 1**	**Year 2**	**Year 3**	**Year 4**	**Scenario**[a]
142								
143		→ High →	0.25	$0	$33	$33	$33	$67.21
144	↗							
145	"P₀" →	→Average →	0.50	$0	$25	$25	$25	$50.91
146	↘							
147		→ Low →	0.25	$0	$5	$5	$5	$10.18
148			1.00					
149							Expected value of PV[b] =	$44.80
150							Standard deviation[b] =	$21.07
151							Coefficient of variation[c] =	0.47

Source: See the file **Ch26 Tool Kit.xlsx**. Numbers are reported as rounded values for clarity but are calculated using *Excel*'s full precision. Thus, intermediate calculations using the figure's rounded values will be inexact.

Notes:

[a] Here we find the PV, not the NPV, because the project's cost is ignored. The WACC is 14%. All cash flows in this scenario are discounted back to Year 0.

[b] The expected value and standard deviation are calculated as explained in Chapter 2.

[c] The coefficient of variation is the standard deviation divided by the expected value.

we ignore the project's "strike price" (i.e., the project's implementation cost) when we find the project's present value. Figure 26-3 shows the expected cash flows if the project is delayed. The PV of these cash flows as of now (Year 0) is $44.80 million, and this is the input we should use for the current price in the Black-Scholes model.

The last required input is the variance of the project's return. Three different approaches could be used to estimate this input. First, we could use judgment—an educated guess. Here, we would begin by recalling that a company is a portfolio of projects (or assets), with each project having its own risk. Because returns on the company's stock reflect the diversification gained by combining many projects, we might expect the variance of the stock's returns to be lower than the variance of one of its average projects. The variance of an average company's stock return is about 0.12, so we might expect the variance for a typical project to be somewhat higher, say, 0.15 to 0.25. Companies in the Internet infrastructure industry are riskier than average, so we might subjectively estimate the variance of Murphy's project to be in the range of 0.18 to 0.30.

The second approach, called the *direct* method, is to estimate the rate of return for each possible outcome and then calculate the variance of those returns. First, Part 1 in Figure 26-4 shows the PV for each possible outcome as of Year 1, the time when the option expires. Here, we simply find the present value of all future operating cash flows discounted back to Year 1, using the WACC of 14%. The Year-1 present value is $76.61 million for high demand, $58.04 million for average demand, and $11.61 million for low demand. Then, in Part 2, we show the percentage return from the current time until the option expires for each scenario, based on the $44.80 million starting "price" of the project at Year 0 as calculated in Figure 26-3. If demand is high, we will obtain a return of 71.0%: ($76.61 − $44.80)/$44.80 = 0.710 = 71.0%. Similar calculations show returns of 29.5% for

FIGURE 26-4
Estimating the Input for Variance in the Option Analysis of the Investment Timing Option (Millions of Dollars)

	A	B	C	D	E	F	G	H
160	**Part 1. Find the Value and Risk of Future Cash Flows at the Time the Option Expires**							
161								
162								PV in Year 1
163					**Future Cash Flows**			for This
164	Now: Year 0		Probability	Year 1	Year 2	Year 3	Year 4	Scenario[a]
165								
166		→ High →	0.25		$33	$33	$33	$76.61
167	↗				↗			
168	Scenario	→Average →	0.50	"P₁" →	$25	$25	$25	$58.04
169	↘				↘			
170		→ Low →	0.25		$5	$5	$5	$11.61
171			1.00					
172							Expected value of PV[b] =	$51.08
173							Standard deviation[b] =	$24.02
174							Coefficient of variation[c] =	0.47
175								
176	**Part 2. Direct Method: Use the Scenarios to Directly Estimate the Variance of the Project's Return**							
177								
178	Price$_{Year\,0}$[d]		Probability	PV$_{Year\,1}$[e]	Return$_{Year\,1}$[f]			
179								
180		→ High →	0.25	$76.61	71.0%			
181	↗							
182	$44.80	→Average →	0.50	$58.04	29.5%			
183	↘							
184		→ Low →	0.25	$11.61	−74.1%			
185			1.00					
186								
187				Expected return[b] =	14.0%			
188				Variance of return[b] =	0.287			
189								
190	**Part 3. Indirect Method: Use the Scenarios to Indirectly Estimate the Variance of the Project's Return**							
191								
192			Expected "price" at the time the option expires[g] =			$51.08		
193			Std. dev. of expected "price" at the time the option expires[h] =			$24.02		
194			Coefficient of variation (CV) =			0.47		
195			Time (in years) until the option expires (t) =			1.00		
196			Variance of the project's expected return = $\ln(CV^2+1)/t$ =			0.200		

Source: See the file **Ch26 Tool Kit.xlsx**. Numbers are reported as rounded values for clarity but are calculated using *Excel*'s full precision. Thus, intermediate calculations using the figure's rounded values will be inexact.

Notes:

[a] The WACC is 14%. The Year-2 through Year-4 cash flows are discounted back to Year 1.

[b] The expected value, variance, and standard deviation are calculated as explained in Chapter 2.

[c] The coefficient of variation is the standard deviation divided by the expected value.

[d] The Year-0 price is the expected PV from Figure 26-3.

[e] The Year-1 PVs are from Part 1.

[f] The returns for each scenario are calculated as $(PV_{Year\,1} - Price_{Year\,0})/Price_{Year\,0}$.

[g] The expected "price" at the time the option expires is taken from Part 1.

[h] The standard deviation of expected "price" at the time the option expires is taken from Part 1.

average demand and −74.1% for low demand. The expected percentage return is 14%, the standard deviation is 53.6%, and the variance is 0.287.[6]

The third approach for estimating the variance of the annual rate of return is also based on the scenario data, but the data are used in a different manner. First, we know that demand is not really limited to three scenarios, which means the direct approach in Figure 26-4 isn't necessarily reliable. We could overcome this problem by estimating thousands of scenarios, but that would require a lot of effort. Fortunately, there is a simple shortcut we can use. From Part 1 of Figure 26-4, we have estimates of the expected value of the project and its standard deviation at the time the option expires. Using this information (and a lot of complicated mathematics), we can estimate the variance of the project's annual rate of return, σ^2, with this formula:[7]

$$\sigma^2 = \frac{\ln(CV^2 + 1)}{t} \qquad \text{(26-1)}$$

Here CV is the coefficient of variation of the underlying asset's price at the time the option expires, and t is the time until the option expires. Although the three outcomes in the scenarios represent a small sample of the many possible outcomes, we can still use the scenario data to estimate the variance that the project's rate of return would have if there were an infinite number of possible outcomes. For Murphy's project, this indirect method produces the following estimate of the variance of the project's return:

$$\sigma^2 = \frac{\ln(0.47^2 + 1)}{1} = 0.20 \qquad \text{(26-1a)}$$

Which of the three approaches is best? Obviously, they all involve judgment, so an analyst might want to consider all three. In our example, all three methods produce similar estimates, but for illustrative purposes we will simply use 0.20 as our initial estimate for the variance of the project's rate of return.

In Part 1 of Figure 26-5, we calculate the value of the option to defer investment in the project based on the Black-Scholes model, and the result is $7.04 million. Because this is significantly higher than the $1.08 million NPV under immediate implementation and because the option would be forfeited if Murphy goes ahead right now, we conclude as before that the company should defer the final decision until more information is available.

Many inputs were based on subjective estimates, so it is important to determine how sensitive the final outcome is to key inputs. Therefore, in Part 2 of Figure 26-5 we show the sensitivity of the option's value to different estimates of the variance. It is reassuring to see that, for all reasonable estimates of variance, the option to delay remains more valuable than immediate implementation.

---

[6]For use in the Black-Scholes model, we need a percentage return calculated as shown, not an IRR return. The IRR is not used in the option pricing approach. Second, the expected return comes to 14%, the same as the WACC. This is because the Year-0 price and the Year-1 PVs were all calculated using the 14% WACC and because we measured return over only 1 year. If we measure the compound return over more than 1 year, then the average return generally will not equal 14%.

[7]For a more detailed discussion of the relationship between the variance of a stock's price and the variance of its return, see David C. Shimko, *Finance in Continuous Time* (Miami, FL: Kolb Publishing, 1992).

FIGURE 26-5
Estimating the Value of the Investment Timing Option Using a Standard Financial Option (Millions of Dollars)

	A	B	C	D	E	F	G	H	I
210	**Part 1. Find the Value of a Call Option Using the Black-Scholes Model**								
211									
212		**Inputs for Real "Call" Option:**							
213		r_{RF} = k-free interest rate				=		6%	
214		t = ntil the option expires				=		1	
215		X = implement the project				=		$50.00	
216		P = ıt value of the project				=		$44.80 [a]	
217		σ^2 = the project's rate of return				=		0.20 [b]	
218		**Intermediate Calculations:**							
219		$d_1 = \{ [r_{RF} + (\sigma^2/2)] t \} / (\sigma\, t^{1/2})$				=		0.1124	
220		$d_2 = d_1 - \sigma(t^{1/2})$				=		−0.3348	
221		$N(d_1)$ = of d_1 in Normal PD function				=		0.5447	
222		$N(d_2)$ = of d_2 in Normal PD function				=		0.3689	
223									
224		$V =$	$-Xe^{-(\text{risk-free rate})(t)} [N(d_2)]$			=		$7.04	
225									
226	**Part 2. Sensitivity Analysis of Option Value to Changes in Variance**								
227									
228			Variance	Option Value					
229			0.12	$5.24					
230			0.14	$5.74					
231			0.16	$6.20					
232			0.18	$6.63					
233			0.20	$7.04					
234			0.22	$7.42					
235			0.24	$7.79					
236			0.26	$8.15					
237			0.28	$8.49					
238			0.30	$8.81					
239			0.32	$9.13					

Source: See the file **Ch26 Tool Kit.xlsx**. Numbers are reported as rounded values for clarity but are calculated using *Excel*'s full precision. Thus, intermediate calculations using the figure's rounded values will be inexact.

Notes:

[a] The current value of the project is taken from Figure 26-3.

[b] The variance of the project's rate of return is taken from Part 3 of Figure 26-4.

26-2e Approach 5: Financial Engineering

Sometimes an analyst might not be satisfied with the results of a decision-tree analysis and cannot find a standard financial option that corresponds to the real option. In such a situation the only alternative is to develop a unique model for the specific real option being analyzed, a process called **financial engineering**. When financial engineering is applied on Wall Street, where it was developed, the result is a newly designed financial product.[8] When it is applied to real options, the result is the value of a project that contains embedded options.

---

[8] Financial engineering techniques are widely used for the creation and valuation of derivative securities.

Although financial engineering was originally developed on Wall Street, many financial engineering techniques have been applied to real options during the last 20 years. We expect this trend to continue, especially in light of the rapid improvements in computer processing speed and spreadsheet software capabilities. One financial engineering technique is called **risk-neutral valuation**. This technique uses simulation, and we discuss it in *Web Extension 14B*. Most other financial engineering techniques are too complicated for a course in financial management, so we leave a detailed discussion of them to a specialized course.

S E L F - T E S T

What is a decision tree?

In a qualitative analysis, what factors affect the value of a real option?

26-3 The Growth Option: An Illustration

As we saw with the investment timing option, there is frequently an alternative to merely accepting or rejecting a static project. Many investment opportunities, if successful, lead to other investment opportunities. The production capacity of a successful product line can later be expanded to satisfy increased demand, or distribution can be extended to new geographic markets. A company with a successful name brand can capitalize on its success by adding complementary or new products under the same brand. These opportunities are **growth options**, which add value to a project and explain, for example, why companies are flocking to make inroads into the very difficult business environment in China.

Kidco Corporation designs and manufactures products aimed at the preteen market. Most of its products have a very short life, given the rapidly changing tastes of preteens. Kidco is now considering a project that will cost $30 million. Management believes there is a 25% chance that the project will "take off" and generate operating cash flows of $34 million in each of the next 2 years, after which preteen tastes will change and the project will be terminated. There is a 50% chance of average demand, in which case cash flows will be $20 million annually for 2 years. Finally, there is a 25% chance that preteens won't like the product at all, and it will generate cash flows of only $2 million per year. The estimated cost of capital for the project is 14%.

Based on its experience with other projects, Kidco believes it will be able to launch a second-generation product if demand for the original product is average or above. This second-generation product will cost the same as the first-generation product, $30 million, and the cost will be incurred at Year 2. However, given the success of the first-generation product, Kidco believes that the second-generation product would be just as successful as the first-generation product.

This growth option resembles a call option on a stock, because it gives Kidco the opportunity to "purchase" a successful follow-on project at a fixed cost if the value of the project is greater than the cost. Otherwise, Kidco will let the option expire by not implementing the second-generation product.

The following sections apply the first four valuation approaches: (1) DCF, (2) DCF and qualitative assessment, (3) decision-tree analysis, and (4) analysis with a standard financial option.

26-3a Approach 1: DCF Analysis Ignoring the Growth Option

Based on probabilities for the different levels of demand, the expected annual operating cash flows for the project are $19 million per year:

$$0.25(\$34) + 0.50(\$20) + 0.25(\$2) = \$19.00$$

Ignoring the growth option, the traditional NPV is $1.29 million:

$$NPV = -\$30 + \frac{\$19}{(1 + 0.14)^1} + \frac{\$19}{(1 + 0.14)^2} = \$1.29$$

Based on this DCF analysis, Kidco should accept the project.

26-3b Approach 2: DCF Analysis with a Qualitative Consideration of the Growth Option

Although the DCF analysis indicates that the project should be accepted, it ignores a potentially valuable real option. The option's time to maturity and the volatility of the underlying project provide qualitative insights into the option's value. Kidco's growth option has 2 years until maturity, which is a relatively long time, and the cash flows of the project are volatile. Taken together, this qualitative assessment indicates that the growth option should be quite valuable.

26-3c Approach 3: Decision-Tree Analysis of the Growth Option

Part 1 of Figure 26-6 shows a scenario analysis for Kidco's project. The top line, which describes the payoffs for the high-demand scenario, has operating cash flows of $34 million for the next 2 years. The NPV of this branch is $25.99 million. The NPV of the average-demand branch in the middle is $2.93 million, and it is −$26.71 million for the low-demand scenario. The sum in the last column of Part 1 shows the expected NPV of $1.29 million. The coefficient of variation is 14.54, indicating that the project is very risky.

Part 2 of Figure 26-6 shows a decision-tree analysis in which Kidco undertakes the second-generation product only if demand is average or high. In these scenarios, shown on the top two branches of the decision tree, Kidco will incur a cost of $30 million at Year 2 and receive operating cash flows of either $34 million or $20 million for the next 2 years, depending on the level of demand. If the demand is low, shown on the bottom branch, Kidco has no cost at Year 2 and receives no additional cash flows in subsequent years. All operating cash flows (which do not include the cost of implementing the second-generation project at Year 2) are discounted at the WACC of 14%. Because the $30 million implementation cost is known, it is discounted at the risk-free rate of 6%. As shown in Part 2 of Figure 26-6, the expected NPV is $4.70 million, indicating that the growth option is quite valuable.

The option itself alters the risk of the project, which means that 14% is probably not the appropriate cost of capital. Figure 26-7 presents the results of a sensitivity analysis in which the cost of capital for the operating cash flows varies from 8% to 18%. The sensitivity analysis also allows the rate used to discount the implementation cost at Year 2 to vary from 3% to 9%. The resulting NPV is positive for all reasonable combinations of discount rates.

26-3d Approach 4: Valuing the Growth Option with the Black-Scholes Option Pricing Model

The fourth approach is to use a standard model for a corresponding financial option. As we noted earlier, Kidco's growth option is similar to a call option on a stock, so we will use the Black-Scholes model to find the value of the growth option. The time until the growth option expires is 2 years. The rate on a 2-year Treasury security is 6%, and this provides a good estimate of the risk-free rate. Implementing the project will cost $30 million, which is the strike price.

The input for stock price in the Black-Scholes model is the current value of the underlying asset. For the growth option, the underlying asset is the second-generation project,

FIGURE 26-6

Scenario Analysis and Decision-Tree Analysis for the Kidco Project (Millions of Dollars)

	A	B	C	D	E	F	G	H
281	**Part 1. Scenario Analysis of Kidco's First-Generation Project**							
282								
283				**Future Cash Flows**			**NPV of This**	
284	**Now: Year 0**		**Probability**	**Year 1**	**Year 2**		**Scenario**[a]	
285								
286		→ High →	25%	$34	$34		$25.99	
287	↗							
288	–$30.00	→Average →	50%	$20	$20		$2.93	
289	↘							
290		→ Low →	25%	$2	$2		–$26.71	
291								
292					**Expected value of NPV**[b] **=**		$1.29	
293					**Standard deviation**[b] **=**		$18.70	
294					**Coefficient of variation**[c] **=**		14.54	
295								
296	**Part 2. Decision-Tree Analysis of the Growth Option**							
297								
298				**Future Cash Flows**				**NPV of This**
299	**Now: Year 0**		**Probability**	**Year 1**	**Year 2**[d]	**Year 3**	**Year 4**	**Scenario**[e]
300								
301			25%	$34	$34	$34	$34	$42.37
302		→ High →			–$30			
303	↗							
304	–$30.00	→Average →	50%	$20	$20	$20	$20	$1.57
305	↘				–$30			
306	↘							
307		→ Low →	25%	$2	$2	$0	$0	–$26.71
308			1.00					
309								
310					**Expected value of NPV**[b] **=**			$4.70
311					**Standard deviation**[b] **=**			$24.62
312					**Coefficient of variation**[c] **=**			5.24

Source: See the file ***Ch26 Tool Kit.xlsx**. Numbers are reported as rounded values for clarity but are calculated using *Excel's* full precision. Thus, intermediate calculations using the figure's rounded values will be inexact.

Notes:

[a] The operating cash flows are discounted by the WACC of 14%.

[b] The expected value, standard deviation, and variance are calculated as in Chapter 2.

[c] The coefficient of variation is the standard deviation divided by the expected value.

[d] The total cash flows at Year 2 are equal to the operating cash flows for the first-generation product minus the $30 million cost to implement the second-generation product, if the firm chooses to do so. For example, the Year-2 cash flow in the high-demand scenario is $34 − $30 = $4 million. Based on Part 1, it makes economic sense to implement the second-generation product only if demand is high or average.

[e] The operating cash flows in Year 1 through Year 2, which do not include the $30 million cost of implementing the second-generation project at Year 2 for the high-demand and average-demand scenarios, are discounted at the WACC of 14%. The $30 million implementation cost at Year 2 for the high-demand and average-demand scenarios is discounted at the risk-free rate of 6%.

and its current value is the present value of its cash flows. The calculations in Figure 26-8 show that this value is $24.07 million. Because the strike price of $30 million is greater than the current "price" of $24.07 million, the growth option is currently out-of-the-money.

Figure 26-9 shows the estimates for the variance of the project's rate of return using the two methods described earlier in the chapter for the analysis of the investment

FIGURE 26-7
Sensitivity Analysis of the Kidco Decision-Tree Analysis in Figure 26-6 (Millions of Dollars)

	A	B	C	D	E	F	G	H	I
329			Cost of Capital Used to Discount the $30 Million Implementation						
330			Cost in Year 2 of the Second-Generation Project						
331			3%	4%	5%	6%	7%	8%	9%
332		8%	$11.0	$11.4	$11.8	$12.1	$12.5	$12.9	$13.2
333		9%	$9.6	$10.0	$10.4	$10.8	$11.2	$11.5	$11.9
334		10%	$8.3	$8.7	$9.1	$9.5	$9.9	$10.2	$10.6
335		11%	$7.0	$7.4	$7.8	$8.2	$8.6	$9.0	$9.3
336		12%	$5.8	$6.2	$6.6	$7.0	$7.4	$7.7	$8.1
337		13%	$4.7	$5.1	$5.5	$5.8	$6.2	$6.6	$6.9
338		14%	$3.5	$3.9	$4.3	$4.7	$5.1	$5.4	$5.8
339		15%	$2.4	$2.8	$3.2	$3.6	$4.0	$4.3	$4.7
340		16%	$1.4	$1.8	$2.2	$2.5	$2.9	$3.3	$3.6
341		17%	$0.3	$0.7	$1.1	$1.5	$1.9	$2.3	$2.6
342		18%	−$0.7	−$0.3	$0.1	$0.5	$0.9	$1.3	$1.6

(Column A label, spanning rows 332–342: "Cost of Capital Used to Discount the Year-1 through Year-4 Operating Cash Flows[a]")

Source: See the file *Ch26 Tool Kit.xlsx*. Numbers are reported as rounded values for clarity but are calculated using *Excel*'s full precision. Thus, intermediate calculations using the figure's rounded values will be inexact.

Note:

[a] The operating cash flows do not include the $30 million implementation cost of the second-generation project in Year 2.

FIGURE 26-8
Estimating the Input for Stock Price in the Growth Option Analysis of the Investment Timing Option (Millions of Dollars)

	A	B	C	D	E	F	G	H
350				Future Cash Flows				PV of This
351	Now: Year 0		Probability	Year 1	Year 2	Year 3	Year 4	Scenario[a]
352								
353		→ High →	25%	$0	$0	$34	$34	$43.08
354	↗							
355	"P$_0$" →	→Average →	50%	$0	$0	$20	$20	$25.34
356	↘							
357		→ Low →	25%	$0	$0	$2	$2	$2.53
358			1.00					
359						Expected value of PV[b] =		$24.07
360						Standard deviation[b] =		$14.39
361						Coefficient of variation[c] =		0.60

Source: See the file *Ch26 Tool Kit.xlsx*. Numbers are reported as rounded values for clarity but are calculated using *Excel*'s full precision. Thus, intermediate calculations using the figure's rounded values will be inexact.

Notes:

[a] The WACC is 14%. All cash flows in this scenario are discounted back to Year 0.

[b] The expected value, standard deviation, and variance are calculated as in Chapter 2.

[c] The coefficient of variation is the standard deviation divided by the expected value.

FIGURE 26-9
Estimating the Input for Stock Return Variance in the Growth Option Analysis (Millions of Dollars)

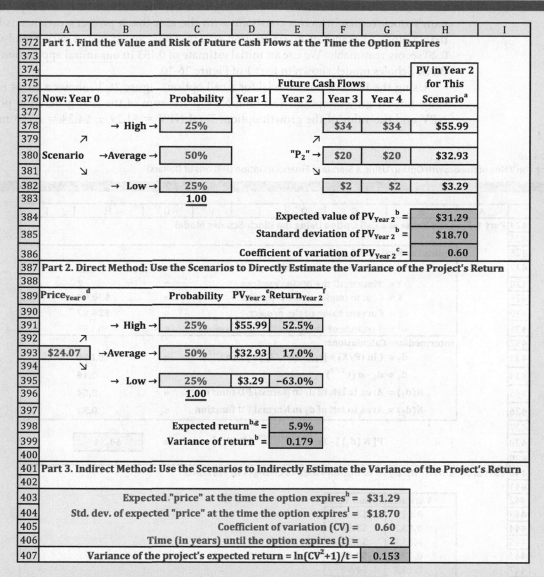

	A	B	C	D	E	F	G	H	I
372	**Part 1. Find the Value and Risk of Future Cash Flows at the Time the Option Expires**								
373									
374								**PV in Year 2**	
375					**Future Cash Flows**			**for This**	
376	Now: Year 0		Probability	Year 1	Year 2	Year 3	Year 4	**Scenario**[a]	
377									
378		→ High →	25%			$34	$34	$55.99	
379	↗				↗				
380	Scenario	→Average →	50%		"P_2" →	$20	$20	$32.93	
381	↘				↘				
382		→ Low →	25%			$2	$2	$3.29	
383			1.00						
384					Expected value of $PV_{Year\ 2}$[b] =			$31.29	
385					Standard deviation of $PV_{Year\ 2}$[b] =			$18.70	
386					Coefficient of variation of $PV_{Year\ 2}$[c] =			0.60	
387	**Part 2. Direct Method: Use the Scenarios to Directly Estimate the Variance of the Project's Return**								
388									
389	$Price_{Year\ 0}$[d]		Probability	$PV_{Year\ 2}$[e]	$Return_{Year\ 2}$[f]				
390									
391		→ High →	25%	$55.99	52.5%				
392	↗								
393	$24.07	→Average →	50%	$32.93	17.0%				
394	↘								
395		→ Low →	25%	$3.29	−63.0%				
396			1.00						
397									
398			Expected return[b,g] =		5.9%				
399			Variance of return[b] =		0.179				
400									
401	**Part 3. Indirect Method: Use the Scenarios to Indirectly Estimate the Variance of the Project's Return**								
402									
403			Expected "price" at the time the option expires[h] =		$31.29				
404			Std. dev. of expected "price" at the time the option expires[i] =		$18.70				
405			Coefficient of variation (CV) =		0.60				
406			Time (in years) until the option expires (t) =		2				
407			Variance of the project's expected return = $\ln(CV^2+1)/t$ =		0.153				

Source: See the file **Ch26 Tool Kit.xlsx**. Numbers are reported as rounded values for clarity but are calculated using *Excel*'s full precision. Thus, intermediate calculations using the figure's rounded values will be inexact.

Notes:

[a] The WACC is 14%. The Year-3 through Year-4 cash flows are discounted back to Year 2.

[b] The standard deviation, variance, and expected value are calculated as in Chapter 2.

[c] The coefficient of variation is the standard deviation divided by the expected value.

[d] The Year-0 price is the expected PV from Figure 26-8.

[e] The Year-2 PVs are from Part 1.

[f] The annualized returns for each scenario are calculated as $(PV_{Year\ 2}/Price_{Year\ 0})^{0.5} - 1$.

[g] The expected annualized return is not equal to the cost of capital, 14%. However, if you do the calculations, then you'll see that the expected 2-year return is 29.26%, which is equal to the 2-year compounded cost of capital: $(1.14)^2 - 1 = 29.26\%$.

[h] The expected "price" at the time the option expires is taken from Part 1.

[i] The standard deviation of the expected "price" at the time the option expires is taken from Part 1.

timing option. The direct method, shown in Part 2 of the figure, produces an estimate of 0.179 for the variance of return. The indirect method, in Part 3, estimates the variance as 0.153. Both estimates are somewhat higher than the 0.12 variance of a typical company's stock return, which is consistent with the idea that a project's variance is higher than a stock's because of diversification effects. Thus, an estimated variance of 0.15 to 0.20 seems reasonable. We use an initial estimate of 0.153 in our initial application of the Black-Scholes model, shown in Part 1 of Figure 26-10.

Using the Black-Scholes model for a call option, Figure 26-10 shows a $4.34 million value for the growth option. The total NPV is the sum of the first-generation project's NPV and the value of the growth option: Total NPV = $1.29 + $4.34 = $5.63 million,

FIGURE 26-10
Estimating the Value of the Growth Option Using a Standard Financial Option (Millions of Dollars)

	A	B	C	D	E	F	G	H	I
424	**Part 1. Find the Value of a Call Option Using the Black-Scholes Model**								
425									
426		**Inputs for Real "Call" Option:**							
427		r_{RF} = **Risk-free interest rate**					=	6%	
428		t = **Time until the option expires**					=	2	
429		X = **Cost to implement the project**					=	$30.00	
430		P = **Current value of the project**					=	$24.07 [a]	
431		σ^2 = **Variance of the project's rate of return**					=	0.153 [b]	
432		**Intermediate Calculations:**							
433		$d_1 = \{\ln(P/X) + [r_{RF} + (\sigma^2/2)]t\} / (\sigma t^{1/2})$					=	0.095	
434		$d_2 = d_1 - \sigma(t^{1/2})$					=	-0.46	
435		$N(d_1)$ = **Area to left of d_1 in Normal PD function**					=	0.54	
436		$N(d_2)$ = **Area to left of d_2 in Normal PD function**					=	0.32	
437									
438		V =	$P[N(d_1)] - Xe^{-(\text{risk-free rate})(t)}[N(d_2)]$					$4.34	
439									
440	**Part 2. Sensitivity Analysis of Option Value to Changes in Variance**								
441									
442			**Variance**	**Option Value**					
443			0.113	$3.60					
444			0.133	$3.98					
445			0.153	$4.34					
446			0.173	$4.68					
447			0.193	$4.99					
448			0.213	$5.29					
449			0.233	$5.57					
450			0.253	$5.84					
451			0.273	$6.10					
452			0.293	$6.35					
453			0.313	$6.59					

Source: See the file **Ch26 Tool Kit.xlsx**. Numbers are reported as rounded values for clarity but are calculated using *Excel's* full precision. Thus, intermediate calculations using the figure's rounded values will be inexact.

Notes:

[a] The current value of the project is taken from Figure 26-8.

[b] The variance of the project's rate of return is taken from Part 3 of Figure 26-9.

which is much higher than the NPV of the first-generation project alone. As this analysis shows, the growth option adds considerable value to the original project. In addition, the sensitivity analysis in Part 2 of Figure 26-10 indicates that the growth option's value is large for all reasonable values of variance. Kidco should therefore accept the project.

For an illustrative valuation of an abandonment option, see *Web Extension 26A*.

SELF-TEST

Explain how growth options are like call options.

26-4 Concluding Thoughts on Real Options

We don't deny that real options can be complicated. Keep in mind, however, that 60 years ago very few companies used NPV because it seemed too complicated. Now NPV is a basic tool used by virtually all companies and taught in all business schools. A similar but more rapid pattern of adoption is occurring with real options. Very few companies used real options before 1990, but a survey of CFOs reported that by 2001 more than 26% of companies used real option techniques when evaluating projects.[9] Just as with NPV, it's only a matter of time before virtually all companies use real option techniques.

We have provided you with some basic tools for evaluating real options, starting with the ability to identify real options and make qualitative assessments regarding a real option's value. Decision trees are another important tool, because they facilitate an explicit identification of the embedded options, which is critical in the decision-making process. Keep in mind that since the decisions change the risk of the project, the original project's cost of capital is probably not the correct cost to use in the decision tree. However, finance theory has not yet provided a way to estimate the appropriate cost of capital for a decision tree in situations like this so sensitivity analysis should be used to identify the effect that different costs of capital have on the project's value.

Many real options can be analyzed using a standard model for an existing financial option, such as the Black-Scholes model for calls and puts. There are also other financial models for a variety of options. These include the option to exchange one asset for another, the option to purchase the minimum or the maximum of two or more assets, the option on an average of several assets, and even an option on an option.[10] In fact, there are entire textbooks that describe even more options.[11] Given the large number of standard models for existing financial options, it is often possible to find a financial option that resembles the real option being analyzed.

Sometimes there are some real options that don't resemble any financial options. But the good news is that many of these options can be valued using techniques from financial engineering. This is frequently the case if there is a traded financial asset that matches the risk of the real option. For example, many oil companies use oil futures

---

[9]See John R. Graham and Campbell R. Harvey, "The Theory and Practice of Corporate Finance: Evidence from the Field," *Journal of Financial Economics,* May 2001, pp. 187–243.

[10]See W. Margrabe, "The Value of an Option to Exchange One Asset for Another," *Journal of Finance,* March 1978, pp. 177–186; R. Stulz, "Options on the Minimum or Maximum of Two Risky Assets: Analysis and Applications," *Journal of Financial Economics,* Vol. 10, 1982, pp. 161–185; H. Johnson, "Options on the Maximum or Minimum of Several Assets," *Journal of Financial and Quantitative Analysis,* September 1987, pp. 277–283; P. Ritchken, L. Sankarasubramanian, and A. M. Vijh, "Averaging Options for Capping Total Costs," *Financial Management,* Autumn 1990, pp. 35–41; and R. Geske, "The Valuation of Compound Options," *Journal of Financial Economics,* March 1979, pp. 63–81.

[11]See John C. Hull, *Options, Futures, and Other Derivatives,* 10th ed. (Boston, MA: Pearson, 2018).

contracts to price the real options that are embedded in various exploration and leasing strategies. With the explosion in the markets for derivatives, there are now financial contracts that span an incredible variety of risks. This means that an ever-increasing number of real options can be valued using these financial instruments. Most financial engineering techniques are beyond the scope of this book, but *Web Extension 14B* on the textbook's Web site describes one particularly useful financial engineering technique called risk-neutral valuation.[12]

How widely used is real option analysis?

What techniques can be used to analyze real options?

SUMMARY

In this chapter we discussed some topics that go beyond the simple capital budgeting framework, including the following:

- Investing in a new project often brings with it a potential increase in the firm's future opportunities. Opportunities are, in effect, options—the right but not the obligation to take some future action.
- A project may have an **option value** that is not accounted for in a conventional NPV analysis. Any project that expands the firm's set of opportunities has positive option value.
- **Real options** are opportunities for management to respond to changes in market conditions and involve "real" rather than "financial" assets.
- There are five possible procedures for valuing real options: (1) DCF analysis only, and ignore the real option; (2) DCF analysis and a qualitative assessment of the real option's value; (3) decision-tree analysis; (4) analysis with a standard model for an existing financial option; and (5) financial engineering techniques.
- Many **investment timing options** and **growth options** can be valued using the Black-Scholes call option pricing model.
- See *Web Extension 26A* on the textbook's Web site for an illustration of valuing the **abandonment option**.
- See *Web Extension 26B* on the textbook's Web site for a discussion of **risk-neutral valuation**.

---

[12]For more on real options, see Martha Amram, *Value Sweep: Mapping Corporate Growth Opportunities* (Boston, MA: Harvard Business School Press, 2002); Martha Amram and Nalin Kulatilaka, *Real Options: Managing Strategic Investment in an Uncertain World* (Boston, MA: Harvard Business School Press, 1999); Michael Brennan and Lenos Trigeorgis, *Project Flexibility, Agency, and Competition: New Developments in the Theory and Application of Real Options* (New York: Oxford University Press, 2000); Eduardo Schwartz and Lenos Trigeorgis, *Real Options and Investment Under Uncertainty* (Cambridge, MA: MIT Press, 2001); Han T. J. Smit and Lenos Trigeorgis, *Strategic Investment: Real Options and Games* (Princeton, NJ: Princeton University Press, 2004); Lenos Trigeorgis, *Real Options in Capital Investment: Models, Strategies, and Applications* (Westport, CT: Praeger, 1995); and Lenos Trigeorgis, *Real Options: Managerial Flexibility and Strategy in Resource Allocation* (Cambridge, MA: MIT Press, 1996).

QUESTIONS

(26-1)   Define each of the following terms:

   a. Real option; managerial option; strategic option; embedded option
   b. Investment timing option; growth option; abandonment option; flexibility option
   c. Decision tree

(26-2)   What factors should a company consider when it decides whether to invest in a project today or to wait until more information becomes available?

(26-3)   In general, do timing options make it more or less likely that a project will be accepted today?

(26-4)   If a company has an option to abandon a project, would this tend to make the company more or less likely to accept the project today?

SELF-TEST PROBLEM   SOLUTION SHOWN IN APPENDIX A

(ST-1)
Real Options

Katie Watkins, an entrepreneur, believes that consolidation is the key to profit in the fragmented recreational equine industry. In particular, she is considering starting a business that will develop and sell franchises to other owner-operators, who will then board and train hunter-jumper horses. The initial cost to develop and implement the franchise concept is $8 million. She estimates a 25% probability of high demand for the concept, in which case she will receive cash flows of $13 million at the end of each year for the next 2 years. She estimates a 50% probability of medium demand, with annual cash flows of $7 million for 2 years, and a 25% probability of low demand, with annual cash flows of $1 million for 2 years. She estimates the appropriate cost of capital is 15%. The risk-free rate is 6%.

   a. Find the NPV of each scenario, and then find the expected NPV.
   b. Now assume that the expertise gained by taking on the project will lead to an opportunity at the end of Year 2 to undertake a similar venture that will have the same cost as the original project. The new project's cash flows would follow whichever branch resulted for the original project. In other words, there would be an $8 million cost at the end of Year 2 and then cash flows of $13 million, $7 million, or $1 million for Years 3 and 4. Use decision-tree analysis to estimate the combined value of the original project and the additional project (but implement the additional project only if it is optimal to do so). Assume that the $8 million cost at Year 2 is known with certainty and should be discounted at the risk-free rate of 6%.
   (*Hint:* Do one decision tree that discounts the operating cash flows at the 15% cost of capital and another decision tree that discounts the costs of the projects—that is, the costs at Year 0 and Year 2—at the risk-free rate of 6%; then sum the two decision trees to find the total NPV.)
   c. Instead of using decision-tree analysis, use the Black-Scholes model to estimate the value of the growth option. Assume that the variance of the project's rate of return is 0.15. Find the total value of the project with the option to expand—that is, the sum of the original expected value and the growth option. (*Hint:* You will need to find the expected present value of the additional project's operating cash flows in order to estimate the current price of the option's underlying asset.)

INTERMEDIATE PROBLEMS 1–5

(26-1)
Investment Timing Option: Decision-Tree Analysis

Kim Hotels is interested in developing a new hotel in Seoul. The company estimates that the hotel would require an initial investment of $20 million. Kim expects the hotel will produce positive cash flows of $3 million a year at the end of each of the next 20 years. The project's cost of capital is 13%.

a. What is the project's net present value?

b. Kim expects the cash flows to be $3 million a year, but it recognizes that the cash flows could actually be much higher or lower, depending on whether the Korean government imposes a large hotel tax. One year from now, Kim will know whether the tax will be imposed. There is a 50% chance that the tax will be imposed, in which case the yearly cash flows will be only $2.2 million. At the same time, there is a 50% chance that the tax will not be imposed, in which case the yearly cash flows will be $3.8 million. Kim is deciding whether to proceed with the hotel today or to wait a year to find out whether the tax will be imposed. If Kim waits a year, the initial investment will remain at $20 million. Assume that all cash flows are discounted at 13%. Use decision-tree analysis to determine whether Kim should proceed with the project today or wait a year before deciding.

(26-2)
Investment Timing Option: Decision-Tree Analysis

The Karns Oil Company is deciding whether to drill for oil on a tract of land the company owns. The company estimates the project would cost $8 million today. Karns estimates that, once drilled, the oil will generate positive net cash flows of $4 million a year at the end of each of the next 4 years. Although the company is fairly confident about its cash flow forecast, in 2 years it will have more information about the local geology and about the price of oil. Karns estimates that if it waits 2 years then the project would cost $9 million. Moreover, if it waits 2 years, then there is a 90% chance that the net cash flows would be $4.2 million a year for 4 years and a 10% chance that they would be $2.2 million a year for 4 years. Assume all cash flows are discounted at 10%.

a. If the company chooses to drill today, what is the project's net present value?

b. Using decision-tree analysis, does it make sense to wait 2 years before deciding whether to drill?

(26-3)
Investment Timing Option: Decision-Tree Analysis

Wansley Lumber is considering the purchase of a paper company, which would require an initial investment of $300 million. Wansley estimates that the paper company would provide net cash flows of $40 million at the end of each of the next 20 years. The cost of capital for the paper company is 13%.

a. Should Wansley purchase the paper company?

b. Wansley realizes that the cash flows in Years 1 to 20 might be $30 million per year or $50 million per year, with a 50% probability of each outcome. Because of the nature of the purchase contract, Wansley can sell the company 2 years after purchase (at Year 2 in this case) for $280 million if it no longer wants to own it. Given this additional information, does decision-tree analysis indicate that it makes sense to purchase the paper company? Again, assume that all cash flows are discounted at 13%.

c. Wansley can wait for 1 year and find out whether the cash flows will be $30 million per year or $50 million per year before deciding to purchase the company. Because of the nature of the purchase contract, if it waits to purchase, Wansley can no longer sell the company 2 years after purchase. Given this additional information, does decision-tree analysis indicate that it makes sense to purchase the paper company? If so, when? Again, assume that all cash flows are discounted at 13%.

(26-4)
Real Options:
Decision-Tree
Analysis

Utah Enterprises is considering buying a vacant lot that sells for $1.2 million. If the property is purchased, the company's plan is to spend another $5 million today ($t = 0$) to build a hotel on the property. The after-tax cash flows from the hotel will depend critically on whether the state imposes a tourism tax in this year's legislative session. If the tax is imposed, the hotel is expected to produce after-tax cash inflows of $600,000 at the end of each of the next 15 years, versus $1,200,000 if the tax is not imposed. The project has a 12% cost of capital. Assume at the outset that the company does not have the option to delay the project. Use decision-tree analysis to answer the following questions.

a. What is the project's NPV if the tax is imposed?

b. What is the project's NPV if the tax is not imposed?

c. Given that there is a 50% chance that the tax will be imposed, what is the project's expected NPV if the company proceeds with it today?

d. Although the company does not have an option to delay construction, it does have the option to abandon the project if the tax is imposed. If it abandons the project, it would complete the sale of the property 1 year from now at an expected price of $6 million. If the company decides to abandon the project, it won't receive any cash inflows from it except for the selling price. If all cash flows are discounted at 12%, would the existence of this abandonment option affect the company's decision to proceed with the project today?

e. Assume there is no option to abandon or delay the project but that the company has an option to purchase an adjacent property in 1 year at a price of $1.5 million. If the tourism tax is imposed, then the present value of future development opportunities for this property (as of $t = 1$) is only $300,000 (so it wouldn't make sense to purchase the property for $1.5 million). However, if the tax is not imposed, then the present value of the future opportunities from developing the property would be $4 million (as of $t = 1$). Thus, under this scenario it would make sense to purchase the property for $1.5 million. Given that cash flows are discounted at 12% and that there's a 50-50 chance the tax will be imposed, how much would the company pay today for the option to purchase this property 1 year from now for $1.5 million?

(26-5)
Growth Option:
Decision-Tree
Analysis

Fethe's Funny Hats is considering selling trademarked, orange-haired curly wigs for University of Tennessee football games. The purchase cost for a 2-year franchise to sell the wigs is $20,000. If demand is good (40% probability), then the net cash flows will be $25,000 per year for 2 years. If demand is bad (60% probability), then the net cash flows will be $5,000 per year for 2 years. Fethe's cost of capital is 10%.

a. What is the expected NPV of the project?

b. If Fethe makes the investment today, then it will have the option to renew the franchise fee for 2 more years at the end of Year 2 for an additional payment of $20,000. In this case, the cash flows that occurred in Years 1 and 2 will be repeated (so if demand was good in Years 1 and 2, it will continue to be good in Years 3 and 4). Write out the decision tree and use decision-tree analysis to calculate the expected NPV of this project, including the option to continue for an additional 2 years. (*Note:* The franchise fee payment at the end of Year 2 is known, so it should be discounted at the risk-free rate, which is 6%.)

CHALLENGING PROBLEMS 6–8

(26-6)
Investment
Timing Option:
Option Analysis

Rework Problem 26-1 using the Black-Scholes model to estimate the value of the option. Assume that the variance of the project's rate of return is 0.0687 and that the risk-free rate is 8%.

(26-7) **Investment** **Timing Option:** **Option Analysis**	Rework Problem 26-2 using the Black-Scholes model to estimate the value of the option. Assume that the variance of the project's rate of return is 0.111 and that the risk-free rate is 6%.
(26-8) **Growth Option:** **Option Analysis**	Rework Problem 26-5 using the Black-Scholes model to estimate the value of the option. Assume that the variance of the project's rate of return is 0.2025 and that the risk-free rate is 6%.

SPREADSHEET PROBLEM

(26-9) **Build a Model:** **Real Options**	Start with the partial model in the file **Ch26 P09 Build a Model.xlsx** on the textbook's Web site. Bradford Services Inc. (BSI) is considering a project with a cost of $10 million and an expected life of 3 years. There is a 30% probability of good conditions, in which case the project will provide a cash flow of $9 million at the end of each of the next 3 years. There is a 40% probability of medium conditions, in which case the annual cash flows will be $4 million, and there is a 30% probability of bad conditions with a cash flow of −$1 million per year. BSI uses a 12% cost of capital to evaluate projects like this.

a. Find the project's expected present value, NPV, and the coefficient of variation of the present value.

b. Now suppose that BSI can abandon the project at the end of the first year by selling it for $6 million. BSI will still receive the Year-1 cash flows, but will receive no cash flows in subsequent years.

c. Now assume that the project cannot be shut down. However, expertise gained by taking it on would lead to an opportunity at the end of Year 3 to undertake a venture that would have the same cost as the original project, and the new project's cash flows would follow whichever branch resulted for the original project. In other words, there would be a second $10 million cost at the end of Year 3 followed by cash flows of either $9 million, $4 million, or −$1 million for the subsequent 3 years. Use decision-tree analysis to estimate the value of the project, including the opportunity to implement the new project at Year 3. Assume that the $10 million cost at Year 3 is known with certainty and should be discounted at the risk-free rate of 6%.

d. Now suppose the original project (no abandonment option or additional growth option) could be delayed a year. All the cash flows would remain unchanged, but information obtained during that year would tell the company exactly which set of demand conditions existed. Use decision-tree analysis to estimate the value of the project if it is delayed by 1 year. (*Hint:* Discount the $10 million cost at the risk-free rate of 6% because the cost is known with certainty.)

e. Go back to part c. Instead of using decision-tree analysis, use the Black-Scholes model to estimate the value of the growth option. The risk-free rate is 6%, and the variance of the project's rate of return is 0.22.

MINI CASE

Assume you have just been hired as a financial analyst by Tropical Sweets Inc., a mid-size California company that specializes in creating exotic candies from tropical fruits such as mangoes, papayas, and dates. The firm's CEO, George Yamaguchi, recently returned from an industry corporate executive conference in San Francisco, and one of the sessions he attended addressed real options. Because no one at Tropical Sweets is familiar with the basics of real options, Yamaguchi has asked you to prepare a brief report that the firm's executives can use to gain a cursory understanding of the topic.

To begin, you gathered some outside materials on the subject and used these materials to draft a list of questions that need to be answered. Now that the questions have been drafted, you must develop the answers.

a. What are some types of real options?

b. What are five possible procedures for analyzing a real option?

c. Tropical Sweets is considering a project that will cost $70 million and will generate expected cash flows of $30 million per year for 3 years. The cost of capital for this type of project is 10%, and the risk-free rate is 6%. After discussions with the marketing department, you learn that there is a 30% chance of high demand with associated future cash flows of $45 million per year. There is also a 40% chance of average demand with cash flows of $30 million per year as well as a 30% chance of low demand with cash flows of only $15 million per year. What is the expected NPV?

d. Now suppose this project has an investment timing option, because it can be delayed for a year. The cost will still be $70 million at the end of the year, and the cash flows for the scenarios will still last 3 years. However, Tropical Sweets will know the level of demand and will implement the project only if it adds value to the company. Perform a qualitative assessment of the investment timing option's value.

e. Use decision-tree analysis to calculate the NPV of the project with the investment timing option.

f. Use a financial option pricing model to estimate the value of the investment timing option.

g. Now suppose that the cost of the project is $75 million and the project cannot be delayed. However, if Tropical Sweets implements the project, then the firm will have a growth option: the opportunity to replicate the original project at the end of its life. What is the total expected NPV of the two projects if both are implemented?

h. Tropical Sweets will replicate the original project only if demand is high. Using decision-tree analysis, estimate the value of the project with the growth option.

i. Use a financial option model to estimate the value of the project with the growth option.

j. What happens to the value of the growth option if the variance of the project's return is 0.142? What if it is 0.50? How might this explain the high valuations of many start-up high-tech companies that have yet to show positive earnings?

Solutions to Self-Test Problems

CHAPTER 2

ST-1

a.

	EBIT	$4,000,000
	Interest	1,000,000
	EBT	$3,000,000
	Taxes (25%)	750,000
	Net income	$2,250,000

b.
$$\text{NCF} = \text{NI} + \text{DEP \& AMORT}$$
$$= \$2,250,000 + \$1,000,000 = \$3,250,000$$

c.
$$\text{NOPAT} = \text{EBIT}(1 - \text{T})$$
$$= \$4,000,000(0.75)$$
$$= \$3,000,000$$

d.
$$\text{NOWC} = \text{Operating current assets} - \text{Operating current liabilities}$$
$$= (\text{Cash} + \text{Accounts receivable} + \text{Inventory})$$
$$- (\text{Accounts payable} + \text{Accruals})$$
$$= \$14,000,000 - \$4,000,000$$
$$= \$10,000,000$$

$$\text{Total net operating capital} = \text{NOWC} + \text{Operating long-term assets}$$
$$= \$10,000,000 + \$15,000,000$$
$$= \$25,000,000$$

e.
$$\text{FCF} = \text{NOPAT} - \text{Net investment in operating capital}$$
$$= \$3,000,000 - (\$25,000,000 - \$24,000,000)$$
$$= \$2,000,000$$

f.
$$\text{ROIC} = \text{NOPAT}/(\text{Total net operating capital})$$
$$= \$3,000,000/\$25,000,000$$
$$= 12\%$$

g.
$$\text{EVA} = \text{NOPAT} - (\text{Total net operating capital})(\text{After-tax cost of capital})$$
$$= \$3,000,000 - (\$25,000,000)(0.10)$$
$$= \$3,000,000 - \$2,500,000 = \$500,000$$

CHAPTER 3

ST-1 Argent has $120 million in debt. With $150 million in total liabilities and $210 million in total common equity, Argent has $150 + $210 = $360 million in total liabilities and equity. Therefore, Argent also has $360 million in total assets (because balance sheets must balance). Argent's debt-to-assets ratio is:

$$\text{Debt-to-assets} = \frac{\text{Total debt}}{\text{Total assets}} = \frac{\$120}{\$360} = 33.33\%$$

Argent's debt-to-equity ratio is:

$$\text{Debt-to-equity} = \frac{\text{Total debt}}{\text{Total common equity}}$$

$$= \frac{\$120}{\$210} = 57.14\%$$

ST-2 a. In answering questions such as this, always begin by writing down the relevant definitional equations and then start filling in numbers. (*Note:* All dollar values are in millions.)

(1) $$\text{DSO} = \frac{\text{Accounts receivable}}{\text{Sales}/365}$$

$$40 = \frac{\text{AR}}{\text{Sales}/365}$$

$$\text{AR} = 40(\$14,600/365) = \$1,600$$

(2) $$\text{Quick ratio} = \frac{\text{Current assets} - \text{Inventories}}{\text{Current liabilities}} = 2.0$$

$$\text{Quick ratio} = \frac{\text{Cash} + \text{AR}}{\text{Current liabilities}} = 2.0$$

$$\text{Current liabilities} = \frac{\text{Cash} + \text{AR}}{\text{Quick ratio}}$$

$$\text{Current liabilities} = (\$400 + \$1,600)/2 = \$1,000$$

(3) $$\text{Current ratio} = \frac{\text{Current assets}}{\text{Current liabilities}} = 3.0$$

$$\text{Current asset} = (\text{Current ratio})(\text{Current liabilities})$$

$$\text{Current assets} = 3.0(\$1,000) = \$3,000$$

(4) $$\text{Total assets} = \text{Current assets} + \text{Fixed assets}$$

$$= \$3,000 + \$4,300 = \$7,300$$

(5) $$\text{ROA} = \frac{\text{Net income}}{\text{Total assets}}$$

$$\text{ROA} = \frac{\$730}{\$7,300} = 0.10 = 10\%$$

(6) $$\text{ROE} = \frac{\text{Net income}}{\text{Equity}} = 12.5\%$$

$$\text{Equity} = \frac{\text{Net income}}{\text{ROE}}$$

$$\text{Equity} = \$730/0.125 = \$5,840 \text{ million}$$

(7)   Total assets = Total claims = $7,300
           Total assets = Current liabilities + Long-term debt + Equity
           Long-term debt = Total assets − Current liabilities − Equity
           Long-term debt = $7,300 − $1,000 − $5,840 = $460

(8) Equity multiplier = $\dfrac{\text{Total assets}}{\text{Equity}} = \dfrac{\$7,300}{\$5,840} = 1.25$

(9) Profit margin = $\dfrac{\text{Net income}}{\text{Sales}} = \dfrac{\$730}{\$14,600} = 0.05 = 5\%$

(10) Total asset turnover = $\dfrac{\text{Sales}}{\text{Total assets}} = \dfrac{\$14,600}{\$7,300} = 2$

The DuPont equation is:
           ROE = (Profit margin)(Total assets turnover)(Equity multiplier)
           ROE = (5%)(1.25)(2)
               = $12.5%

CHAPTER 4

ST-1   a.

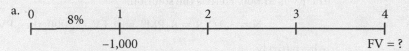

$1,000 is being compounded for 3 years, so your balance at Year 4 is $1,259.71:

$$FV_N = PV(1 + I)^N = \$1,000(1 + 0.08)^3 = \$1,259.71$$

Alternatively, using a financial calculator, input N = 3, I/YR = 8, PV = −1000, and PMT = 0; then solve for FV = $1,259.71.

b.

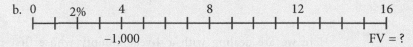

There are 12 compounding periods from Quarter 4 to Quarter 16.

$$FV_N = PV\left(1 + \frac{I_{NOM}}{M}\right)^{NM} = FV_{12} = \$1,000(1.02)^{12} = \$1,268.24$$

Alternatively, using a financial calculator, input N = 12, I/YR = 2, PV = −1000, and PMT = 0; then solve for FV = $1,268.24.

c.

```
     0    8%   1        2        3        4
     ├─────────┼────────┼────────┼────────┤
              250      250      250      250
                                       FV = ?
```

$$FVA_4 = \$250\left[\frac{(1 + 0.08)^4}{0.08} - \frac{1}{0.08}\right] = \$1,126.53$$

Using a financial calculator, input N = 4, I/YR = 8, PV = 0, and PMT = −250; then solve for FV = $1,126.53.

d.

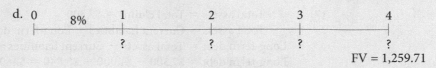

$$PMT\left[\frac{(1 + 0.08)^4}{0.08} - \frac{1}{0.08}\right] = \$1{,}259.71$$

$$PMT(4.5061) = \$1{,}259.71$$

$$PMT = \$279.56$$

Using a financial calculator, input $N = 4$, $I/YR = 8$, $PV = 0$, and $FV = 1259.71$; then solve for $PMT = -\$279.56$.

ST-2   a.   Set up a time line like the one in the preceding problem:

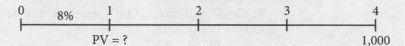

Note that your deposit will grow for 3 years at 8%. The deposit at Year 1 is the PV, and the FV is \$1,000. Here is the solution:

$$N = 3, I/YR = 8, PMT = 0, FV = 1000; \text{ then } PV = \$793.83.$$

Alternatively,

$$PV = \frac{FV_N}{(1 + I)^N} = \frac{\$1{,}000}{(1 + 0.08)^3} = \$793.83$$

b.

Here we are dealing with a 4-year annuity whose first payment occurs 1 year from today and whose future value must equal \$1,000. Here is the solution: $N = 4$; $I/YR = 8$; $PV = 0$; $FV = 1000$; then $PMT = \$221.92$. Alternatively,

$$PMT\left[\frac{(1 + 0.08)^4}{0.08} - \frac{1}{0.08}\right] = \$1{,}000$$

$$PMT(4.5061) = \$1{,}000$$

$$PMT = \$221.92$$

c.   This problem can be approached in several ways. Perhaps the simplest is to ask this question: "If I received \$750 1 year from now and deposited it to earn 8%, would I have the required \$1,000 4 years from now?" The answer is "no":

$$FV_3 = \$750(1.08)(1.08)(1.08) = \$944.78$$

This indicates that you should let your father make the payments rather than accept the lump sum of \$750.

You could also compare the $750 with the PV of the payments:

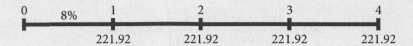

$$N = 4, I/YR = 8, PMT = -221.92, FV = 0; \text{ then } PV = \$735.03.$$

Alternatively,

$$PVA_4 = \$221.92 \left[\frac{1}{0.08} - \frac{1}{(0.08)(1 + 0.08)^4} \right] = \$735.03$$

This is less than the $750 lump sum offer, so your initial reaction might be to accept the lump sum of $750. However, it would be a mistake to do so. The problem is that, when you found the $735.03 PV of the annuity, you were finding the value of the annuity *today*. You were comparing $735.03 today with the lump sum of $750 in 1 year. This is, of course, invalid. What you should have done was take the $735.03, recognize that this is the PV of an annuity as of today, multiply $735.03 by 1.08 to get $793.83, and compare this $793.83 with the lump sum of $750. You would then take your father's offer to make the payments rather than take the lump sum 1 year from now.

d.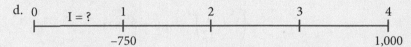

$$N = 3, PV = -750, PMT = 0, FV = 1000; \text{ then } I/YR = 10.0642\%.$$

e.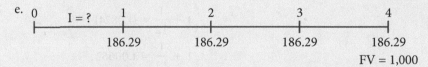

$$N = 4, PV = 0, PMT = -186.29, FV = 1000; \text{ then } I/YR = 19.9997\%.$$

You might be able to find a borrower willing to offer you a 20% interest rate, but there would be some risk involved—he or she might not actually pay you your $1,000!

f.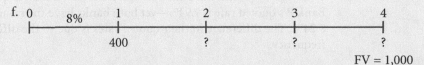

Find the future value of the original $400 deposit:

$$FV_6 = PV(1 + I)^6 = 400(1 + 0.04)^6 = \$400(1.2653) = \$506.12.$$

This means that, at Year 4, you need an additional sum of $493.88: $1,000.00 − $506.12 = $493.88. This amount will be accumulated by making 6 equal payments that earn 8% compounded semiannually, or 4% each 6 months: N = 6, I/YR = 4, PV = 0, FV = 493.88; then PMT = \$74.46. Alternatively,

$$\text{PMT}\left[\frac{(1 + 0.04)^6}{0.04} - \frac{1}{0.04}\right] = \$493.88$$

$$\text{PMT}(6.6330) = \$493.88$$

$$\text{PMT} = \$74.46$$

g.

$$\text{EFF\%} = \left(1 + \frac{I_{\text{NOM}}}{M}\right)^M - 1.0$$

$$= \left(1 + \frac{0.08}{2}\right)^2 - 1.0$$

$$= 1.0816 - 1 = 0.0816 = 8.16\%$$

ST-3   Bank A's effective annual rate is 8.24%:

$$\text{EFF\%} = \left(1 + \frac{0.08}{4}\right)^4 - 1.0$$

$$= 1.0824 - 1 = 0.0824 = 8.24\%$$

Now Bank B must have the same effective annual rate:

$$\left(1 + \frac{I}{12}\right)^{12} - 1.0 = 0.0824$$

$$\left(1 + \frac{I}{12}\right)^{12} = 1.0824$$

$$1 + \frac{I}{12} = (1.0824)^{1/12}$$

$$1 + \frac{I}{12} = 1.00662$$

$$\frac{I}{12} = 0.00662$$

$$I = 0.07944 = 7.94\%$$

Thus, the two banks have different quoted rates—Bank A's quoted rate is 8%, whereas Bank B's quoted rate is 7.94%—yet both banks have the same effective annual rate of 8.24%. The difference in their quoted rates is due to the difference in compounding frequency.

CHAPTER 5

ST-1   a. Pennington's bonds were sold at par; therefore, the original YTM equaled the coupon rate of 12%.

b.

$$V_B = \sum_{t=1}^{50} \frac{\$120/2}{\left(1 + \frac{0.10}{2}\right)^t} + \frac{\$1,000}{\left(1 + \frac{1.10}{2}\right)^{50}}$$

$$= \$60\left[\frac{1}{0.05} - \frac{1}{0.05\,(1 + 0.05)^{50}}\right] + \frac{\$1,000}{(1 + 0.05)^{50}}$$

$$= \$1,182.56$$

Alternatively, with a financial calculator, input the following: N = 50, I/YR = 5, PMT = 60, and FV = 1000; solve for PV = −$1,182.56.

c.   Current yield = Annual coupon payment ÷ Price
                     = $120/$1,182.56
                     = 0.1015 = 10.15%

Capital gains yield = Total yield − Current yield
                     = 10% − 10.15% = −0.15%

Total yield = Current yield + Capital gains yield
                     = 10.15% + (−0.15%) = 10.00%

d. $$\$916.42 = \sum_{t=1}^{13} \frac{\$60}{(1 + r_d/2)^t} + \frac{\$1,000}{(1 + r_d/2)^{13}}$$

With a financial calculator, input the following: N = 13, PV = −916.42, PMT = 60, and FV = 1000; then solve for = I/YR = $r_d/2$ = 7.00%. Therefore, r_d = 14.00%.

Current yield = $120/$916.42   = 13.09%
Capital gains yield = 14% − 13.09% = 0.91%
                          Total yield = 14.00%

e. The following time line illustrates the years to maturity of the bond:

1/1/20   6/30/20   12/31/20   6/30/21   12/31/21   12/31/26
├────┼────┼──────────┼──────────┼──────────┼ ··· ──┤
       3/1/20

Thus, on March 1, 2020, there were 13⅔ periods left before the bond matured. Bond traders actually use the following procedure to determine the price of the bond.

(1) Find the price of the bond immediately after the first coupon is paid on June 30, 2020:

$$V_B = \$60\left[\frac{1}{0.0775} - \frac{1}{0.0775(1 + 0.0775)^{13}}\right] + \frac{\$1,000}{(1 + 0.0775)^{13}}$$

= $859.76

Using a financial calculator, input N = 13, I/YR = 7.75, PMT = 60, and FV = 1000; then solve for PV = −$859.76.

(2) Add the coupon, $60, to the bond price to get the total value, TV, of the bond on the next interest payment date: TV = $859.76 + $60.00 = $919.76.

(3) Discount this total value back to the purchase date:

$$\text{Value at purchase date (March 1, 2020)} = \frac{\$919.76}{(1 + 0.0775)^{(4/6)}}$$

= $875.11

Using a financial calculator, input N = 4/6, I/YR = 7.75, PMT = 0, and FV = 919.76; then solve for PV = $875.11.

(4) Therefore, you would have written a check for $875.11 to complete the transaction. Of this amount, $20 = (⅓)($60) would represent accrued interest, and $855.11 would represent the bond's basic value. This breakdown would affect both your taxes and those of the seller.

(5) This problem could be solved *very* easily using a spreadsheet or a financial calculator with a bond valuation function.

CHAPTER 6

ST-1   a. The average rate of return for each stock is calculated simply by averaging the returns over the 5-year period. The average return for Stock A is:

$$r_{Avg\,A} = (-18\% + 44\% - 22\% + 22\% + 34\%)/5$$

$$= 12\%$$

The realized rate of return on a portfolio made up of Stock A and Stock B would be calculated by finding the average return in each year as:

$$r_A(\% \text{ of Stock A}) + r_B(\% \text{ of Stock B})$$

and then averaging these annual returns:

Year	Portfolio AB's Return, r_{AB}
2012	−21%
2013	34
2014	−13
2015	15
2016	45
	$r_{Avg} = \underline{\underline{12\%}}$

b. The standard deviation of returns is estimated as follows:

$$\text{Estimated } \sigma = S = \sqrt{\dfrac{\displaystyle\sum_{t=1}^{N} (\bar{r}_t - \bar{r}_{Avg})^2}{N-1}}$$

For Stock A, the estimated σ is about 30%:

$$\sigma_A = \sqrt{\dfrac{\begin{array}{c}(-0.18 - 0.12)^2 + (0.44 - 0.12)^2 + (-0.22 - 0.12)^2 + \\ (0.22 - 0.12)^2 + (0.34 - 0.12)^2\end{array}}{5-1}}$$

$$= 0.30265 \approx 30\%$$

The standard deviations of returns for Stock B and for the portfolio are similarly determined, and they are as follows:

	Stock A	Stock B	Portfolio AB
Standard deviation	30%	30%	29%

c. Because the risk reduction from diversification is small (σ_{AB} falls only from 30% to 29%), the most likely value of the correlation coefficient is 0.8. If the correlation coefficient were −0.8, then the risk reduction would be much larger. In fact, the correlation coefficient between Stocks A and B is 0.8.

d. If more randomly selected stocks were added to a portfolio, σ_p would decline to somewhere in the vicinity of 20%. The value of σ_p would remain constant only if the correlation coefficient were +1.0, which is most unlikely. The value of σ_p would decline to zero only if $\rho = -1.0$ for some pair of stocks or some pair of portfolios.

ST-2 a. $b = (0.6)(0.70) + (0.25)(0.90) + (0.1)(1.30) + (0.05)(1.50)$
$= 0.42 + 0.225 + 0.13 + 0.075 = 0.85$

b. $r_{RF} = 6\%; RP_M = 5\%; b = 0.85$
$r_p = 6\% + (5\%)(0.85)$
$= 10.25\%$

c. $b_N = (0.5)(0.70) + (0.25)(0.90) + (0.1)(1.30) + (0.15)(1.50)$
$= 0.35 + 0.225 + 0.13 + 0.225$
$= 0.93$
$r = 6\% + (5\%)(0.93)$
$= 10.65\%$

CHAPTER 7

ST-1 The first step is to solve for g, the unknown variable, in the constant growth equation. Because D_1 is unknown but D_0 is known, substitute $D_0(1 + g_L)$ as follows:

$$\hat{P}_0 = P_0 = \frac{D_1}{r_s - g_L} = \frac{D_0(1 + g_L)}{r_s - g_L}$$

$$\$36 = \frac{\$2.40(1 + g_L)}{0.12 - g_L}$$

Solving for g_L, we find the growth rate to be 5%:

$$\$4.32 - \$36g_L = \$2.40 + \$2.40g_L$$
$$\$38.4g_L = \$1.92$$
$$g_L = 0.05 = 5\%$$

The next step is to use the growth rate to project the stock price 5 years hence:

$$\hat{P}_5 = \frac{D_0(1 + g_L)^6}{r_s - g_L}$$

$$= \frac{\$2.40(1.05)^6}{0.12 - 0.05}$$

$$= \$45.95$$

(Alternatively, $\hat{P}_5 = \$36(1.05)^5 = \$45.95$.) Therefore, Ewald Company's expected stock price 5 years from now, $\hat{P}_5$, is $45.95.

ST-2 a. (1) Calculate the PV of the dividends paid during the supernormal growth period:

$$D_1 = \$1.1500(1.15) = \$1.3225$$
$$D_2 = \$1.3225(1.15) = \$1.5209$$
$$D_3 = \$1.5209(1.13) = \$1.7186$$

PV of Div. $= \$1.3225/(1.12) + \$1.5209/(1.12)^2 + \$1.7186/(1.12)^3$
$= \$3.6167 \approx \$3.62$

(2) Find the PV of Snyder's stock price at the end of Year 3:

$$\hat{P}_3 = \frac{D_4}{r_s - g} = \frac{D_3(1 + g)}{r_s - g}$$

$$= \frac{\$1.7186(1.06)}{0.12 - 0.06}$$

$$= \$30.36$$

$$\text{PV of } \hat{P}_3 = \$30.36/(1.12)^3 = \$21.61$$

(3) Sum the two components to find the value of the stock today:

$$\hat{P}_0 = \$3.62 + \$21.61 = \$25.23$$

Alternatively, the cash flows can be placed on a time line as follows:

```
0        12%      1            2            3            4
├─────────────────┼────────────┼────────────┼────────────┤
   g = 15%          g = 15%       g = 13%       g = 6%

       1.3225        1.5209        1.7186        1.8217
                                                   │
                                                   ▼
```

$$30.3617 = \frac{\$1.8217}{0.12 - 0.06}$$

$$\underline{32.0803}$$

Enter the cash flows into the cash flow register ($CF_0 = 0$, $CF_1 = 1.3225$, $CF_2 = 1.5209$, $CF_3 = 32.0803$) and I/YR = 12; then press the NPV key to obtain $\hat{P}_0 = \$25.23$.

b. $\hat{P}_1 = \$1.5209/(1.12) + \$1.7186/(1.12)^2 + \$30.36/(1.12)^2$
    $= \$26.9311 \approx \$26.93$
    (Calculator solution: $26.93)

    $\hat{P}_2 = \$1.7186/(1.12) + \$30.36/(1.12)$
    $= \$28.6429 \approx \$28.64$
    (Calculator solution: $28.64)

c.

Year	Dividend Yield	+	Capital Gains Yield	=	Total Return
1	$\frac{\$1.3225}{\$25.23} \approx 5.24\%$	+	$\frac{\$26.93 - \$25.23}{\$25.23} \approx 6.74\%$	$\approx$	12%
2	$\frac{\$1.5209}{\$26.93} \approx 5.65\%$	+	$\frac{\$28.64 - \$26.93}{\$26.93} \approx 6.35\%$	$\approx$	12%
3	$\frac{\$1.7186}{\$28.64} \approx 6.00\%$	+	$\frac{\$30.36 - \$28.64}{\$28.64} \approx 6.00\%$	$\approx$	12%

ST-3   a. $V_{op} = \dfrac{FCF(1 + g)}{WACC - g} = \dfrac{\$100,000(1 + 0.07)}{0.11 - 0.07} = \$2,675,000$

b. Total value = Value of operations + Value of nonoperating assets
                = \$2,675,000 + \$325,000 = \$3,000,000

c. Value of equity = Total value − Value of debt
$$= \$3{,}000{,}000 - \$1{,}000{,}000 = \$2{,}000{,}000$$

d. Price per share = Value of equity ÷ Number of shares
$$= \$2{,}000{,}000/50{,}000 = \$40$$

CHAPTER 8

ST-1   The option will pay off $60 − $42 = $18 if the stock price is up. The option pays off nothing ($0) if the stock price is down. Find the number of shares in the hedge portfolio:

$$N = \frac{C_u - C_d}{P_u - P_d} = \frac{\$18 - \$0}{\$60 - \$30} = 0.60$$

With 0.6 shares, the stock's payoff will be either 0.6($60) = $36 or 0.6($30) = $18. The portfolio's payoff will be $36 − $18 = $18, or $18 − 0 = $18.

The present value of $18 at the daily compounded risk-free rate is PV = $18/[1 + (0.05/365)]^{365} = $17.12. Or use a financial calculator and enter N = 365, I/YR = 5/365, PMT = 0, and FV = −18; solve for PV = 17.12. The option price is the current value of the stock in the portfolio minus the PV of the payoff:

$$V = 0.6(\$40) - \$17.12 = \$6.88$$

ST-2
$$d_1 = \frac{\ln(P/X) + [r_{RF} + (\sigma^2/2)]t}{\sigma\sqrt{t}}$$

$$= \frac{\ln(\$22/\$20) + [0.05 + (0.49/2)](0.5)}{0.7\sqrt{0.5}}$$

$$= 0.4906$$

$$d_2 = d_1 - \sigma(t)^{0.5} = 0.4906 - 0.7(0.5)^{0.5} = -0.0044$$

$N(d_1) = 0.6881$ (from *Excel* NORMSDIST function)

$N(d_2) = 0.4982$ (from *Excel* NORMSDIST function)

$$V = P[N(d_1)] - Xe^{-r_{RF}t}[N(d_2)]$$

$$= \$22(0.6881) - \$20e^{(-0.05)(0.5)}(0.4982)$$

$$= \$5.42$$

CHAPTER 9

ST-1   a. Component costs are as follows:

Debt at $r_d = 8\%$:

$$r_d(1 - T) = 8\%(1 - 0.25) = 6\%$$

Preferred with F = 5%:

$$r_{ps} = \frac{\text{Preferred dividend}}{P_{ps}(1 - F)} = \frac{\$9}{\$100(0.95)} = 9.5\%$$

Common with dividend growth approach:

$$r_s = \frac{D_1}{P_0} + g = \frac{\$3.922}{\$60} + 6\% = 12.5\%$$

Common with CAPM:

$$r_s = 6\% + 1.3(5\%) = 12.5\%$$

b. $\text{WACC} = w_d r_d (1 - T) + w_{ps} r_{ps} + w_s r_s$

$= 0.25(8\%)(1 - 0.25) + 0.15(9.5\%) + 0.60(12.5\%)$

$= 10.425\%$

CHAPTER 10

ST-1   a. **Payback:**

To determine the payback, construct the cumulative cash flows for each project as follows:

Year	Cumulative Cash Flows	
	Project X	**Project Y**
0	−$10,000	−$10,000
1	−3,500	−6,500
2	−500	−3,000
3	2,500	500
4	3,500	4,000

$$\text{Payback}_X = 2 + \frac{\$500}{\$3,000} = 2.17 \text{ years}$$

$$\text{Payback}_Y = 2 + \frac{\$3,000}{\$3,500} = 2.86 \text{ years}$$

Net Present Value (NPV):

$$\text{NPV}_X = -\$10,000 + \frac{\$6,500}{(1.12)^1} + \frac{\$3,000}{(1.12)^2} + \frac{\$3,000}{(1.12)^3} + \frac{\$1,000}{(1.12)^4} = \$966.01$$

$$\text{NPV}_Y = -\$10,000 + \frac{\$3,500}{(1.12)^1} + \frac{\$3,500}{(1.12)^2} + \frac{\$3,500}{(1.12)^3} + \frac{\$3,500}{(1.12)^4} = \$630.72$$

Alternatively, using a financial calculator, input the cash flows into the cash flow register, enter I/YR = 12, and then press the NPV key to obtain $\text{NPV}_X = \$966.01$ and $\text{NPV}_Y = \$630.72$.

Internal Rate of Return (IRR):

To solve for each project's IRR, find the discount rates that equate each NPV to zero:

$$\text{IRR}_X = 18.0\%$$
$$\text{IRR}_Y = 15.0\%$$

Modified Internal Rate of Return (MIRR):

To obtain each project's MIRR, begin by finding each project's terminal value (TV) of cash inflows:

$$TV_X = \$6,500(1.12)^3 + \$3,000(1.12)^2 + \$3,000(1.12)^1 + \$1,000 = \$17,255.23$$
$$TV_Y = \$3,500(1.12)^3 + \$3,500(1.12)^2 + \$3,500(1.12)^1 + \$3,500 = \$16,727.65$$

Now, each project's MIRR is the discount rate that equates the PV of the TV to each project's cost, $10,000:

$$MIRR_X = 14.61\%$$
$$MIRR_Y = 13.73\%$$

Profitability Index (PI):

To obtain each project's PI, divide its present value of future cash flows by its initial cost. The PV of future cash flows can be found from the NPV calculated earlier:

$$PV_X = NPV_X + \text{Cost of X} = \$966.01 + \$10,000 = \$10,966.01$$
$$PV_Y = NPV_Y + \text{Cost of Y} = \$630.72 + \$10,000 = \$10,630.72$$
$$PI_X = PV_X/\text{Cost of X} = \$10,966.01/\$10,000 = 1.097$$
$$PI_Y = PV_Y/\text{Cost of Y} = \$10,630.72/\$10,000 = 1.063$$

b.   The following table summarizes the project rankings by each method:

	Project That Ranks Higher
Payback	X
NPV	X
IRR	X
MIRR	X

Note that all methods rank Project X over Project Y. Because both projects are acceptable under the NPV, IRR, and MIRR criteria, both should be accepted if they are independent.

c.   In this case, we would choose the project with the higher NPV at r = 12%, or Project X.

d.   To determine the effects of changing the cost of capital, plot the NPV profiles of each project. The crossover rate occurs at about 6% to 7% (6.2%). See the graph following part e.

     If the firm's cost of capital is less than 6.2%, then a conflict exists because $NPV_Y > NPV_X$ but $IRR_X > IRR_Y$. Therefore, if r were 5% then a conflict would exist. Note, however, that when r = 5.0% we have $MIRR_X = 10.64\%$ and $MIRR_Y = 10.83\%$; hence, the modified IRR ranks the projects correctly even if r is to the left of the crossover point.

e.   The basic cause of the conflict is differing reinvestment rate assumptions between NPV and IRR: NPV assumes that cash flows can be reinvested at the cost of capital, whereas IRR assumes that reinvestment yields the (generally) higher IRR. The high reinvestment rate assumption under IRR makes early cash flows especially valuable, so short-term projects look better under IRR.

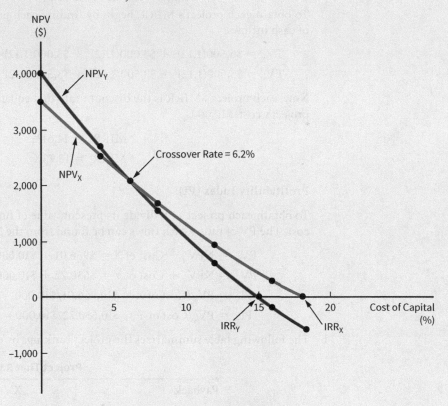

NPV Profiles for Projects X and Y

Cost of Capital	NPV$_X$	NPV$_Y$
0%	$3,500	$4,000
4	2,545	2,705
8	1,707	1,592
12	966	631
16	307	(206)
18	5	(585)

CHAPTER 11

ST-1   a. **Estimated Investment Requirements:**

Price	−$50,000
Modification	−10,000
Change in net working capital	−2,000
Total Year 0 cash flow	−$62,000

b. **Operating Cash Flows:**

	Year 1	Year 2	Year 3
1. After-tax cost savings[a]	$15,000.0	$15,000.0	$15,000.0
2. Depreciation[b]	19,998.0	26,670.0	8,886.0
3. Depreciation tax savings[c]	4,999.5	6,667.5	2,221.5
Operating cash flow (1 + 3)	$19,999.5	$21,667.5	$17,221.5

[a]$20,000(1 − T) = $20,000(1 − 0.25) =$15,000.

[b]Depreciable basis = Price + Modification = $60,000; the MACRS percentage allowances are 0.3333, 0.4445, and 0.1481 in Years 1, 2, and 3, respectively; hence, depreciation in Year 1 = 0.3333($60,000) = $19,998, Year 2 = 0.4445 ($60,000) = $26,670, and Year 3 = 0.1481 ($60,000) = $8,886. The remaining book value at Year 3 will be $4,446 = 0.0741($60,000).

[c]Depreciation tax savings = T(Depreciation) = 0.25($19,998) = $4,999.5 in Year 1, and so forth.

c. **Termination Cash Flow:**

Salvage value	$20,000.0
Tax on salvage value[a]	−3,888.5
Net working capital recovery	2,000.0
Termination cash flow	$ 18,111.5

[a]Calculation of tax on salvage value:

Book value = Depreciation basis − Accumulated depreciation
= $60,000 − $55,554 = $4,446

Sales price	$20,000.0
Less book value	4,446.0
Taxable income	$15,554.0
Tax at 25%	$ 3,888.5

d. **Project NPV:**

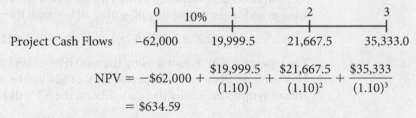

	0	10%	1	2	3
Project Cash Flows	−62,000		19,999.5	21,667.5	35,333.0

$$NPV = -\$62,000 + \frac{\$19,999.5}{(1.10)^1} + \frac{\$21,667.5}{(1.10)^2} + \frac{\$35,333}{(1.10)^3}$$

$$= \$634.59$$

Alternatively, using a financial calculator, input the cash flows into the cash flow register, enter I/YR = 10, and then press the NPV key to obtain NPV = $634.59. Because the earth mover has a positive NPV, it should be purchased.

ST-2   a. First, find the expected cash flows:

Year		Expected Cash Flows			
0	0.2(−$100,000)	+ 0.6(−$100,000)	+ 0.2(−$100,000)	=	−$100,000
1	0.2($20,000)	+ 0.6($30,000)	+ 0.2($40,000)	=	$30,000
2	0.2($20,000)	+ 0.6($30,000)	+ 0.2($40,000)	=	$30,000
3	0.2($20,000)	+ 0.6($30,000)	+ 0.2($40,000)	=	$30,000
4	0.2($20,000)	+ 0.6($30,000)	+ 0.2($40,000)	=	$30,000
5	0.2($20,000)	+ 0.6($30,000)	+ 0.2($40,000)	=	$30,000
5*	0.2($0)	+ 0.6($20,000)	+ 0.2($30,000)	=	$18,000

	0	10%	1	2	3	4	5
	−$100,000		30,000	30,000	30,000	30,000	48,000

Next, determine the NPV based on the expected cash flows:

$$NPV = -\$100{,}000 + \frac{\$30{,}000}{(1.10)^1} + \frac{\$30{,}000}{(1.10)^2} + \frac{\$30{,}000}{(1.10)^3}$$

$$+ \frac{\$30{,}000}{(1.10)^4} + \frac{\$48{,}000}{(1.10)^5} = \$24{,}900$$

Alternatively, using a financial calculator, input the cash flows in the cash flow register, enter I/YR = 10, and then press the NPV key to obtain NPV = \$24,900.

b. For the worst case, the cash flow values from the cash flow column farthest on the left are used to calculate NPV:

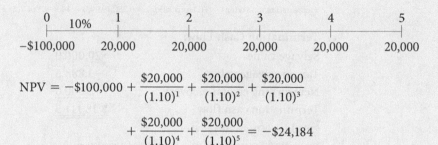

0	1	2	3	4	5
10%					
−\$100,000	20,000	20,000	20,000	20,000	20,000

$$NPV = -\$100{,}000 + \frac{\$20{,}000}{(1.10)^1} + \frac{\$20{,}000}{(1.10)^2} + \frac{\$20{,}000}{(1.10)^3}$$

$$+ \frac{\$20{,}000}{(1.10)^4} + \frac{\$20{,}000}{(1.10)^5} = -\$24{,}184$$

Similarly, for the best case, use the values from the column farthest on the right. Here the NPV is \$70,259.

   If the cash flows are perfectly dependent, then the low cash flow in the first year will mean a low cash flow in every year. Thus, the probability of the worst case occurring is the probability of getting the \$20,000 net cash flow in Year 1, or 20%. If the cash flows are independent, then the cash flow in each year can be low, high, or average and so the probability of getting all low cash flows will be:

$$(0.2)(0.2)(0.2)(0.2)(0.2) = 0.2^5 = 0.00032 = 0.032\%$$

c. The base-case NPV is found using the most likely cash flows and is equal to \$26,142. This value differs from the expected NPV of \$24,900 because the Year-5 cash flows are not symmetric. Under these conditions, the NPV distribution is as follows:

P	NPV
0.2	−\$24,184
0.6	26,142
0.2	70,259

Thus, the expected NPV is 0.2(−\$24,184) + 0.6(\$26,142) + 0.2(\$70,259) = \$24,900. As is always the case, the expected NPV is the same as the NPV of the expected cash flows found in part a. The standard deviation is \$29,904:

$$\sigma_{NPV}^2 = 0.2(-\$24{,}184 - \$24{,}900)^2 + 0.6(\$26{,}142 - \$24{,}900)^2$$
$$+ 0.2(\$70{,}259 - \$24{,}900)^2$$
$$= \$894{,}261{,}126$$
$$\sigma_{NPV} = \sqrt{\$894{,}261{,}126} = \$29{,}904$$

The coefficient of variation, CV, is \$29,904/\$24,900 = 1.20.

CHAPTER 12

ST-1   To solve this problem, we first define ΔS as the change in sales and g as the growth rate in sales. Then we use the three following equations:

$$\Delta S = S_0 g$$

$$S_1 = S_0(1 + g)$$

$$AFN = (A^*/S_0)(\Delta S) - (L^*/S_0)(\Delta S) - MS_1(1 - \text{Payout ratio})$$

Set AFN = 0; substitute in known values for A^*/S_0, L^*/S_0, M, d, and S_0; and then solve for g:

$$
\begin{aligned}
0 &= 1.6(\$100g) - 0.4(\$100g) - 0.10[\$100(1 + g)](0.55) \\
&= \$160g - \$40g - 0.055(\$100 + \$100g) \\
&= \$160g - \$40g - \$5.5 - \$5.5g \\
\$114.5g &= \$5.5 \\
g &= \$5.5/\$114.5 = 0.048 = 4.8\% \\
&= \text{Maximum growth rate without external financing}
\end{aligned}
$$

ST-2   Assets consist of cash, marketable securities, receivables, inventories, and fixed assets. Therefore, we can break the A^*/S_0 ratio into its components—cash/sales, inventories/sales, and so forth. Then,

$$\frac{A^*}{S_0} = \frac{A^* - \text{Inventories}}{S_0} + \frac{\text{Inventories}}{S_0} = 1.6$$

We know that the inventory turnover ratio is sales/inventories = 3 times, so inventories/sales = 1/3 = 0.3333. Further, if the inventory turnover ratio can be increased to 4 times, then the inventory/sales ratio will fall to 1/4 = 0.25, a difference of 0.3333 − 0.2500 = 0.0833. This, in turn, causes the A^*/S_0 ratio to fall from A^*/S_0 = 1.6 to A^*/S_0 = 1.6 − 0.0833 = 1.5167. This change has two effects: First, it changes the AFN equation; and second, it means that Barnsdale currently has excessive inventories. Because it is costly to hold excess inventories, Barnsdale will want to reduce its inventory holdings by not replacing inventories until the excess amounts have been used. We can account for this by setting up the revised AFN equation (using the new A^*/S_0 ratio), estimating the funds that will be needed next year if no excess inventories are currently on hand, and then subtracting out the excess inventories that are currently on hand:

Present Conditions:

$$\frac{\text{Sales}}{\text{Inventories}} = \frac{\$100}{\text{Inventories}} = 3$$

so

$$\text{Inventories} = \$100/3 = \$33.3 \text{ million at present}$$

New Conditions:

$$\frac{\text{Sales}}{\text{Inventories}} = \frac{\$100}{\text{Inventories}} = 4$$

so

$$\text{New level of inventories} = \$100/4 = \$25 \text{ million}$$

Therefore,

$$\text{Excess inventories} = \$33.3 - \$25 = \$8.3 \text{ million}$$

Forecast of Funds Needed, First Year:

$$\Delta S \text{ in first year} = 0.2(\$100 \text{ million}) = \$20 \text{ million}$$

$$\begin{aligned} \text{AFN} &= 1.5167(\$20) - 0.4(\$20) - 0.1(0.55)(\$120) - \$8.3 \\ &= \$30.3 - \$8 - \$6.6 - \$8.3 \\ &= \$7.4 \text{ million} \end{aligned}$$

Forecast of Funds Needed, Second Year:

$$\Delta S \text{ in second year} = gS_1 = 0.2(\$120 \text{ million}) = \$24 \text{ million}$$
$$\begin{aligned} \text{AFN} &= 1.5167(\$24) - 0.4(\$24) - 0.1(0.55)(\$144) \\ &= \$36.4 - \$9.6 - \$7.9 \\ &= \$18.9 \text{ million} \end{aligned}$$

ST-3   a. Full capacity sales $= \dfrac{\text{Current sales}}{\substack{\text{Percentage of capacity at which} \\ \text{FA were operated}}} = \dfrac{\$36,000}{0.75} = \$48,000$

$$\text{Percentage increase} = \frac{\text{New sales} - \text{Old sales}}{\text{Old sales}} = \frac{\$48,000 - \$36,000}{\$36,000} = 0.33 = 33\%$$

Therefore, sales could expand by 33% before Van Auken Lumber would need to add fixed assets.

b. First, forecast the income statement using the projected sales growth rate and the projected ratio of operating costs to projected sales. Because new debt is added at the end of the year, the projected interest expense is equal to the product of the interest rate and the previous year's debt.

Van Auken Lumber: Projected Income Statement for December 31, 2020 (Thousands of Dollars)

	2019	Forecast Basis	2020
Sales	$36,000	1.25(Sales$_{19}$)	$45,000
Operating costs	30,600	85%(Sales$_{20}$)	38,250
EBIT	$ 5,400		$ 6,750
Interest	720	10%(Debt$_{19}$)	850
EBT	$ 4,680		$ 5,900
Taxes (25%)	1,170		1,475
Net income	$ 3,510		$ 4,425
Dividends (60%)	$ 2,106		$ 2,655
Additions to RE	$ 1,404		$ 1,770

Project cash, receivables, inventories, accounts payable, and accruals as a percent of projected sales. Project the retained earnings based on the projected income statement. Plug in the amount of the line of credit that makes the balance sheets balance.

Van Auken Lumber: Projected Balance Sheet for December 31, 2020 (Thousands of Dollars)

	2019	Percent of 2019 Sales	Additions[a]	2020	LOC	2020 after AFN
Cash	$ 1,800	5%		$ 2,250		$ 2,250
Receivables	10,800	30		13,500		13,500
Inventories	12,600	35		15,750		15,750
Total current assets	$25,200			$ 31,500		$31,500
Net fixed assets	$21,600			$21,600b		$21,600
Total assets	$46,800			$ 53,100		$53,100
Accounts payable	$ 7,200	20		$ 9,000		$ 9,000
Notes payable	3,500			3,500		3,500
Line of credit	0			0	$2,100	2,100
Accruals	2,520	7		3,150		3,150
Total current liabilities	$13,220			$ 15,650		$ 17,750
Long-term bonds	5,000			5,000		5,000
Common stock	2,000			2,000		2,000
Retained earnings	26,580		1,770	28,350		28,350
Total liabilities and equity	$46,800			$ 51,000		$53,100
Financing deficit =				$ 2,100		

[a]See income statement for additions to retained earnings.

[b]From part a, we know that sales can increase by 33% before additions to fixed assets are needed.

CHAPTER 14

ST-1 a.

Capital investments	$6,000,000
Projected net income	$5,000,000
Required equity = 60%(Capital investment)	$3,600,000
Available residual	$1,400,000
Shares outstanding	1,000,000

DPS = $1,400/1,000,000 shares = $1.40

b. EPS = $5,000,000/1,000,000 shares = $5.00
Payout ratio = DPS/EPS = $1.4/$5 = 28%, or
Total dividends ÷ NI = $1,400,000/$5,000,000 = 28%

ST-2 a.

Value of operations	$2,100
+ Value of ST investments	$100
Total intrinsic value of firm	$2,200
− Debt	$ 200
− Preferred stock	$0
Intrinsic value of equity	$2,000
÷ Number of shares	100
Intrinsic price per share	$ 20

b.
Value of operations	$2,100
+ Value of ST investments	$0
Total intrinsic value of firm	$2,100
− Debt	$ 200
− Preferred stock	$0
Intrinsic value of equity	$1,900
÷ Number of shares	100
Intrinsic price per share	$ 19

c. The price before the repurchase, during the repurchase, and after the repurchase doesn't change. So the number of shares after the repurchase is the value of equity after the repurchase divided by the original price: n_{Post} = $1,900/$20 = 95.

Value of operations	$2,100
+ Value of ST investments	$0
Total intrinsic value of firm	$2,100
− Debt	$200
− Preferred stock	$0
Intrinsic value of equity	$1,900
÷ Number of shares	95
Intrinsic price per share	$ 20

CHAPTER 15

ST-1 a. $S = P(n) = \$30(600,000) = \$18,000,000$
$V = D + S = \$2,000,000 + \$18,000,000 = \$20,000,000$

b. $w_d = D/V = \$2,000,000/\$20,000,000 = 0.10$
$w_s = S/V = \$18,000,000/\$20,000,000 = 0.90$
$\text{WACC} = w_d\,r_d(1 - T) + w_s\,r_s$
$\quad\quad\quad = (0.10)(10\%)(0.75) + (0.90)(15\%) = 14.25\%$

c. $\text{WACC} = (0.50)(12\%)(0.75) + (0.50)(18.5\%) = 13.75\%$
Since $g = 0$, it follows that FCF = NOPAT.
$V_{opNew} = \text{FCF/WACC} = \text{EBIT}(1 - T)/0.1375 = \$4,700,000(0.75)/0.1375$
$\quad\quad = \$25,636,363.636$
$D = w_d(V_{op}) = 0.50(\$25,636,363.636) = \$12,818,181.818$

Since it started with $2 million debt, it will issue:

$D_{New} - D_{Old} = \$12,818,181.818 - \$2,000,000 = \$10,818,181.818$
$S_{Post} = V_{opNew} - D_{New} = \$25,636,363.636 - \$12,818,181.818 = \$12,818,181.818$
(Alternatively, $S_{Post} = w_s(V_{opNew}) = 0.50(\$25,636,363.636) = \$12,818,181.818$)

$$n_{Post} = n_{Prior}\left[\frac{V_{opNew} - D_{New}}{V_{opNew} - D_{Old}}\right]$$

$$= 600,000\left[\frac{\$25,636,363.636 - \$12,818,181.818}{\$25,636,363.636 - \$2,000,000}\right]$$

$$= 600,000\left[\frac{\$12,818,181.818}{\$23,636,363.636}\right]$$

$$= 325,384.615$$

$$P_{Post} = (V_{opNew} - D_{Old})/n_{Prior}$$
$$= (\$25,636,363.636 - \$2,000,000)/600,000$$
$$= \$39.394$$

Alternatively, after issuing debt and before repurchasing stock, the firm's equity, $S_{Prior} = V_{opNew} + (D_{New} - D_{Old}) - D_{New} = V_{opNew} + - D_{Old} = \$25,636,363.636 - \$2,000,000 = \$23,636,363.636$. The stock price prior to the repurchase is $P_{Prior} = S_{Prior}/n_{Prior} = \$23,636,363.636/600,000 = \$39.3939$. The firm used the proceeds of the new debt, \$10,818,181.818, to repurchase X shares of stock at a price of \$39.393939 per share. The number of shares it will repurchase is $X = \$10,818,181.818/\$39.393939 = 274,615.3874$. Thus, there are $600,000 - 274,615.3874 = 325,384.6126$ shares remaining. As a check, the stock price should equal the market value of equity (S) divided by the number of shares: $P_0 = \$12,818,181.818/325,384.6126 = \$39.39$.

ST-2   a. LIC's current cost of equity is:

$$r_s = 6\% + 1.5(4\%) = 12\%$$

b. LIC's unlevered beta is:

$$b_U = 1.5/[1 + (1 - 0.25)(25\%/75\%)] = 1.5/1.25 = 1.20$$

c. LIC's levered beta at D/S = 60%/40% = 1.5 is:

$$b = 1.20[1 + (1 - 0.25)(60/40)] = 2.55$$

LIC's new cost of capital will be:

$$r_s = 6\% + (2.55)(4\%) = 16.2\%$$

CHAPTER 16

ST-1   The Calgary Company: Alternative Balance Sheets

	Restricted (40%)	Moderate (50%)	Relaxed (60%)
Current assets (% of sales)	$1,200,000	$1,500,000	$1,800,000
Fixed assets	600,000	600,000	600,000
Total assets	$1,800,000	$2,100,000	$2,400,000
Debt	$ 900,000	$1,050,000	$1,200,000
Equity	900,000	1,050,000	1,200,000
Total liabilities and equity	$1,800,000	$2,100,000	$2,400,000

The Calgary Company: Alternative Income Statements

	Restricted	Moderate	Relaxed
Sales	$3,000,000	$3,000,000	$3,000,000
EBIT	400,000	400,000	400,000
Interest (10%)	90,000	105,000	120,000
Earnings before taxes	$ 310,000	$ 295,000	$ 280,000
Taxes (25%)	77,500	73,750	70,000
Net income	$ 232,500	$ 221,250	$ 210,000
ROE	25.8%	21.1%	17.5%

ST-2   a and b.

Income Statements for Year Ended December 31, 2020 (Thousands of Dollars)

	Part a.		Part b.	
	Van Press	**Herr Publishing**	**Van Press**	**Herr Publishing**
EBIT	$ 30,000	$ 30,000	$ 30,000	$ 30,000
Interest	4,500	3,300	5,500	8,300
Taxable income	$ 25,500	$ 26,700	$ 24,500	$ 21,700
Taxes (25%)	6,375	6,675	6,125	5,425
Net income	$ 19,125	$ 20,025	$ 18,375	$ 16,275
Equity	$140,000	$140,000	$140,000	$140,000
Return on equity	13.66%	14.30%	13.13%	11.63%

Herr Publishing has a higher ROE when short-term interest rates are high (part a), whereas Van Press does better when short-term rates are lower (part b).

c. Herr's position is riskier. First, its profits and return on equity are much more volatile than Van's. Second, Herr must renew its large short-term loan every year, and if the renewal comes up at a time when money is tight or when its business is depressed or both, then Herr could be denied credit, which could put it out of business.

CHAPTER 17

ST-1 $$\frac{\text{Euros}}{\text{C\$}} = \frac{\text{Euros}}{\text{US\$}} \times \frac{\text{US\$}}{\text{C\$}}$$

$$= \frac{0.98}{\$1} \times \frac{\$1}{1.5} = \frac{0.98}{1.5} = 0.6533 \text{ euros per Canadian dollar}$$

CHAPTER 18

ST-1   a. Using Equation 18-4:

$$n_{New} = \frac{(\% \text{ owned by new investors})n_{Existing}}{1 - (\% \text{ owned by new investors})}$$

$$= [0.20(20 \text{ million})]/(1 - 0.20) = 5 \text{ million.}$$

b. Intrinsic stock price per share before the IPO = $V_{Pre\text{-}IPO}/n_{Existing}$

$$= (\$500)/20 = \$25.00$$

c. Using Equation 18-6:

$$P_{Offer} = \left[\frac{V_{Pre-IPO}}{F(n_{New}) + n_{Existing}} \right] = \$500/[(0.07)(5) + 20] = \$24.57$$

ST-2   a. Net proceeds per share = $(1 - 0.07)(\$20) = \$18.60$
         Required proceeds after direct costs: $30 million + $800,000 = $30.8 million
         Number of shares = $30.8 million/$18.60 per share = 1.656 million shares

b. Amount left on table = (Closing price − offer price)(Number of shares)
= ($22 − $20)(1.656 million) = $3.312 million

c. Underwriting cost = 0.07($20)(1.656) = $2.318 million
Total costs = $0.800 + $2.318 + $3.312 = $6.430 million

CHAPTER 19

ST-1   a. **Cost of Leasing:**

	Year 0	Year 1	Year 2	Ye ar 3	Year 4
Lease payment	−$10,000	−$10,000	−$10,000	−$10,000	$0
Payment tax savings	$2,500	$2,500	$2,500	$2,500	$0
Net cash flow	−$7,500	−$7,500	−$7,500	−$7,500	$0
PV of leasing @ 7.5% =	−$27,004				

b. **Cost of Owning:**
Our first step is to calculate the depreciation tax savings.

Year	Year 0	Year 1	Year 2	Year 3	Year 4
Depr. Rate		0.3333	0.4445	0.1481	0.0741
Depr.		$13,332	$17,780	$5,924	$2,964
Depr. tax savings		$3,333	$4,445	$1,481	$741

In our solution, we will consider the $40,000 cost as a Year-0 outflow rather than including all the financing cash flows. The net effect is the same because the PV of the financing flows, when discounted at the after-tax cost of debt, is the cost of the asset.

	Year 0	Year 1	Year 2	Year 3	Year 4
Purchase price	−$40,000				
Maintenance cost		−$1,000	−$1,000	−$1,000	−$1,000
Maintenance tax savings		$250	$250	$250	$250
Depreciation tax savings		$3,333	$4,445	$1,481	$741
Residual value					$10,000
Residual value tax					−$2,500
Net cash flow	−$40,000	$2,583	$3,695	$731	$7,491
PV of owning @ 7.5% =	−$28,202				

Since the present value of leasing is better than the present value of owning, the tractor should be leased. Specifically, the NAL is: −$27,004 − (−$28,202) = $1,198.

CHAPTER 20

ST-1   a. First issue: 10-year straight bonds with a 6% coupon.

Second issue: 10-year bonds with 4.5% annual coupon with warrants. Both bonds issued at par $1,000. Value of warrants = ?

First issue: N = 10, PV = −1000, PMT = 60, and FV = 1000; then solve for I/YR = r_d = 6%. (Since it sold for par, we should know that r_d = 6%.)

Second issue: $1,000 = Bond + Warrants. This bond should be evaluated at 6% (since we know the first issue sold at par) in order to determine its present value: N = 10, I/YR = r_d = 6, PMT = 45, and FV = 1000; then solve for PV = $889.60.

The value of the warrants can be determined as the difference between $1,000 and the second bond's present value:

$$\text{Value of warrants} = \$1,000 - \$889.6 = \$110.40$$

CHAPTER 21

ST-1   a. $HV_{U,2} = [FCF_2(1 + g_L)]/(r_{sU} - g_L) = [\$120(1.04)]/0.08 - 0.4) = \$3,120$

b. $V_U = FCF_1/(1 + r_{sU}) + (FCF_2 + HV_{U,2})/(1 + r_{sU})^2$

$= (100/1.08) + (\$120 + \$3,120)/(1.08)^2 = \$2,870.37$

c. $TS_1 = r_d\, D\, T = 0.05(\$800)(0.25) = \$10$

$TS_2 = TS_1 = \$10$

d. $HV_{TS,2} = [TS_2(1 + g_L)]/(r_{sU} - g_L) = [\$10(1.04)]/0.08 - 0.4) = \$260$

e. $V_{\text{Tax shield}} = TS_1/(1 + r_{sU}) + (TS_2 + HV_{TS,2})/(1 + r_{sU})^2$

$= (10/1.08) + (\$10 + \$260)/(1.08)^2 = \$240.74$

f. $V_{op} = V_U + V_{\text{Tax shield}} = \$2,870.37 + \$240.74 = \$3,111.11$

CHAPTER 22

ST-1   a. The unlevered cost of equity based on the pre-merger required rate of return and pre-merger capital structure is:

$$r_{sU} = w_d r_d + w_s r_s$$
$$= 0.25(6\%) + 0.75(10\%)$$
$$= 9\%$$

The post-horizon levered cost of equity is

$$r_{sL} = r_{sU} + (r_{sU} - r_d)(D/S)$$
$$= 9\% + (9\% - 7\%)(0.35/0.65)$$
$$= 10.077\%$$
$$WACC = w_d r_d(1 - T) + w_s r_s$$
$$= 0.35(7\%)(1 - 0.40) + 0.65(10.077\%)$$
$$= 8.02\%$$

b. The horizon value of unlevered operations is

$$HV_{U,3} = FCF_3(1 + g)/(r_{sU} - g)$$
$$= [\$25(1.05)]/(0.09 - 0.05)$$
$$= \$656.250 \text{ million}$$

$$\text{Unlevered } V_{ops} = \frac{\$10}{(1.09)^1} + \frac{\$20}{(1.09)^2} + \frac{\$25 + \$656.25}{(1.09)^3}$$

$$= \$552.058 \text{ million}$$

Tax shields in Years 1 through 3 are:

$$\text{Tax shield} = \text{Interest} \times T$$
$$TS_1 = \$28.00(0.40) = \$11.200 \text{ million}$$
$$TS_2 = \$24.00(0.40) = \$9.600 \text{ million}$$
$$TS_3 = \$20.28(0.40) = \$8.112 \text{ million}$$
$$HV_{TS,3} = TS_3(1 + g)/(r_{sU} - g)$$
$$= [\$8.112(1.05)]/(0.09 - 0.05)$$
$$= \$212.940 \text{ million}$$

$$\text{Value of tax shield} = \frac{\$11.2}{(1.09)^1} + \frac{\$9.6}{(1.09)^2} + \frac{\$8.112 + \$212.940}{(1.09)^3}$$

$$= \$189.048 \text{ million}$$
$$\text{Total value} = \text{Unlevered V}_{ops} + \text{Value of tax shield}$$
$$= \$552.058 + \$189.048$$
$$= \$741.106$$

CHAPTER 23

ST-1   a. The hypothetical bond in the futures contract has an annual coupon of 6% (paid semiannually) and a maturity of 20 years. At a price of 97'13 (this is the percent of par), a $1,000 par bond would have a price of $1,000(97 + 13/32)/100 = $974.0625. To find the yield: N = 40, PMT = 30, FV = 1000, PV = −974.0625; then I = 3.1143% per 6 months. The nominal annual yield is 2(3.1143%) = 6.2286%.

b. In this situation, the firm would be hurt if interest rates were to rise by September, so it would use a short hedge or sell futures contracts. Because futures contracts are for $100,000 in Treasury bonds, the value of a futures contract is $97,406.25 and the firm must sell $5,000,000/$97,406.25 = 51.33 ≈ 51 contracts to cover the planned $5,000,000 September bond issue. Because futures maturing in June are selling for 97 13/32 of par, the value of Wansley's futures is about 51($97,406.25) = $4,967,718.75. Should interest rates rise by September, Wansley will be able to repurchase the futures contracts at a lower cost, which will help offset their loss from financing at the higher interest rate. Thus, the firm has hedged against rising interest rates.

c. The firm would now pay 13% on the bonds. With a 12% coupon rate, the PV of the new issue is only $4,646,361.83 (N = 40, I = 13/2 = 6.5, PMT = −0.12/2(5000000) = −300000, FV = −5000000; then solve for PV). Therefore, the new bond issue would bring in only $4,646,361.83, so the cost of the bond issue that is due to rising rates is $5,000,000 − $4,646,361.83 = $353,638.17.

     However, the value of the short futures position began at $4,967,718.75. Now, if interest rates increased by 1 percentage point, then the yield on the futures would go up to 7.2286% (7.2286 = 6.2286 + 1). To find the value of the futures contract, enter N = 40, I = 7.2286/2 = 3.6143 (from part a), PMT = 3000, and FV = 100000; then solve for PV = $87,111.04 per contract. With 51 contracts, the value of the futures position is $4,442,663.04. (*Note:* If you don't round off in any previous calculations, then the PV comes to $4,442,668.38.)

     Because Wansley Company sold the futures contracts for $4,967,718.75 and will, in effect, buy them back at $4,442,668.04, the firm would make a profit of $4,967,718.75 − $4,442,668.04 = $525,050.71 profit on the transaction (if we ignore transaction costs).

     Thus, the firm gained $525,050.71 on its futures position, but lost $353,638.17 on its underlying bond issue. On net, it gained $525,050.71 − $353,638.17 = $171,412.54.

CHAPTER 24

ST-1   a. Distribution to priority claimants (millions of dollars):

Total proceeds from the sale of assets	$1,150
Less:	
1. First mortgage (paid from sale of fixed assets)	700
2. Second mortgage (paid from sale of fixed assets after satisfying first mortgage: $750 − $700 = $50)	50
3. Fees and expenses of bankruptcy	1
4. Wages due to workers	60
5. Taxes due	90
Funds available for distribution to general creditors	$ 249

b. Distribution to general creditors (millions of dollars):

General Creditor Claims	Amount of Claim	Pro Rata Distribution[a]	Distribution after Subordinate Adjustment[b]	% of Original Claim Received
Unsatisfied second mortgage	$ 350	$ 60	$ 60	28%[c]
Accounts payable	100	17	17	17
Notes payable	300	52	86	29
Debentures	500	86	86	17
Subordinated debentures	200	34	0	0
Total	$1,450	$249	$249	

Notes:

[a]Pro rata distribution: $249/$1,450 = 0.172 = 17.2%.

[b]Subordinated debentures are subordinated to notes payable. Unsatisfied portion of notes payable is greater than subordinated debenture distribution, so subordinated debentures receive $0.

[c]Includes $50 from sale of fixed assets received in priority distribution.

Total distribution to second mortgage holders: $50 + $60 = $110 million.

Total distribution to holders of notes payable: $86 million.

Total distribution to holders of subordinated debentures: $0 million.

Total distribution to common stockholders: $0 million.

CHAPTER 25

ST-1   a. For Security A:

P_A	r_A	$P_A r_A$	$(r_A - \hat{r}_A)$	$(r_A - \hat{r}_A)^2$	$P_A(r_A - \hat{r}_A)^2$
0.1	−10%	−1.0%	−25%	625	62.5
0.2	5	1.0	−10	100	20.0
0.4	15	6.0	0	0	0.0
0.2	25	5.0	10	100	20.0
0.1	40	4.0	25	625	62.5
		$\hat{r}_A = 15.0\%$			$\sigma_A = \sqrt{165.0} = 12.8\%$

b. $w_A = \dfrac{\sigma_B(\sigma_B - \rho_{AB}\sigma_A)}{\sigma_A^2 + \sigma_B^2 - 2\rho_{AB}\sigma_A\sigma_B}$

$= \dfrac{25.7[25.7 - (-0.5)(12.8)]}{(12.8)^2 + (25.7)^2 - 2(-0.5)(12.8)(25.7)}$

$= \dfrac{824.97}{1{,}153.29} = 0.7153.$

or 71.53% invested in A and 28.47% invested in B.

c. $\sigma_p = \sqrt{(w_A\sigma_A)^2 + (1 - w_A)^2(\sigma_B)^2 + 2w_A(1 - w_A)\rho_{AB}\sigma_A\sigma_B}$

$= \sqrt{(0.75)^2(12.8)^2 + (0.25)^2(25.7)^2 + 2(0.75)(0.25)(-0.5)(12.8)(25.7)}$

$= \sqrt{92.16 + 41.28 - 61.68}$

$= \sqrt{71.76} = 8.47\%$ when $w_A = 75\%$

$\sigma_p = \sqrt{(0.7153)^2(12.8)^2 + (0.2847)^2(25.7)^2 + 2(0.7153)(0.2847)(-0.5)(12.8)(25.7)}$

$= 8.38\%$ when $w_A = 71.53\%$ (this is the minimum σ_p)

$\sigma_p = \sqrt{(0.5)^2(12.8)^2 + (0.5)^2(25.7)^2 + 2(0.5)(0.5)(-0.5)(12.8)(25.7)}$

$= 11.3\%$ when $w_A = 50\%$

$\sigma_p = \sqrt{(0.25)^2(12.8)^2 + (0.75)^2(25.7)^2 + 2(0.25)(0.75)(-0.5)(12.8)(25.7)}$

$= 17.89\%$ when $w_A = 25\%$

% in A	% in B	$\hat{r}_p$	σ_p
100.00%	0.00%	15.00%	12.8%
75.00	25.00	16.25	8.5
71.53	28.47	16.42	8.4
50.00	50.00	17.50	11.1
25.00	75.00	18.75	17.9
0.00	100.00	20.00	25.7

Calculations for preceding table:

$r_p = w_A(\hat{r}_A) + (1 - w_A)(\hat{r}_B)$

$= 0.75(15) + (0.25)(20)$ $= 16.25\%$ when $w_A = 75\%$

$= 0.7153(15) + 0.2847(20)$ $= 16.42\%$ when $w_{A0} = 71.53\%$

$= 0.5(15) + 0.5(20)$ $= 17.50\%$ when $w_A = 50\%$

$= 0.25(15) + 0.75(20)$ $= 18.75\%$ when $w_A = 25\%$

d. See the following graph:

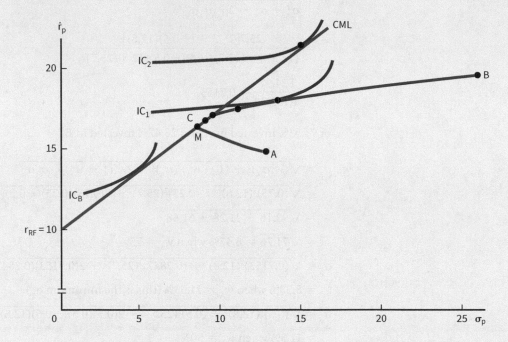

e. See indifference curve IC_1 in the preceding graph. At the point where $\hat{r}_p = 18\%$, $\sigma_p = 13.5\%$.

$$\hat{r}_p = w_A(\hat{r}_A) + (1 - w_A)(\hat{r}_B)$$
$$18 = w_A(15) + (1 - w_A)(20)$$
$$= 15w_A + 20 - 20w_A$$
$$5w_A = 2$$
$$w_A = 0.4 \text{ or } 40\%$$

Therefore, to an approximation, your optimal portfolio would have 40% in A and 60% in B, with $\hat{r}_p = 18\%$ and $\sigma_p = 13.5\%$. (We could get an exact σ_p by using $w_A = 0.4$ in the equation for σ_p.)

f. The existence of the riskless asset would enable you to go to the CAPM. We would draw in the CML as shown on the graph in part d. Now you would hold a portfolio of stocks, borrowing on margin to hold more stocks than your net worth, and move to a higher indifference curve, IC_2.

You can put all of your money into the riskless asset, all in A, all in B, or some in each security. The most logical choices are (1) hold a portfolio of A and B plus some of the riskless asset, (2) hold only a portfolio of A and B, or (3) hold a portfolio of A and B and borrow to leverage the portfolio, assuming you can borrow at the riskless rate.

Reading from the graph, we see that your $\hat{r}_p$ at the point of tangency between your IC_2 and the CML is about 22%. We can use this information to find out how much you invest in the market portfolio and how much you invest in the riskless asset. (It will turn out that you have a *negative* investment in the riskless asset, which means that you borrow rather than lend at the risk-free rate.)

$$\hat{r}_P = w_{RF}(r_{RF}) + (1 - w_{RF})(\hat{r}_M)$$
$$22 = w_{RF}(10) + (1 - w_{RF})(16.8)$$
$$= 10w_{RF} + 16.8 - 16.8w_{RF}$$
$$-6.8w_{RF} = 5.2$$
$$w_{RF} = -0.76 \text{ or } -76\% \text{ (which means that you borrow)}$$
$$1 - W_{RF} = 1.0 - (-0.76)$$
$$= +1.76 \text{ or } 176\% \text{ in the market portfolio}$$

Hence this investor, with $200,000 of net worth, buys stock with a value of $200,000(1.76) = $352,000 and borrows $152,000.

The risk of this leveraged portfolio is:

$$\sigma_P = \sqrt{(-0.76)^2(0)^2 + (1.76)^2(8.5)^2 + 2(-0.76)(1.76)(0)(8.5)(0)}$$
$$= \sqrt{(1.76)^2(8.5)^2}$$
$$= (1.76)(8.5) = 15\%$$

Your indifference curve suggests that you are not very risk averse. A risk-averse investor would have a steep indifference curve (visualize a set of steep curves that were tangent to CML to the left of Point C). This investor would hold some of A and B, combined to form portfolio M, and some of the riskless asset.

g. Given your assumed indifference curve, you would, when the riskless asset becomes available, change your portfolio from the one found in part e (with $\hat{r}_P = 18\%$ and $\sigma_P = 13.5\%$) to one with $\hat{r}_P \approx 22.0\%$ and $\sigma_P \approx 15.00\%$.

h.
$$r_A = r_{RF} + (r_M - r_{RF})b_A$$
$$15 = 10 + (16.8 - 10)b_A$$
$$= 10 + (6.8)b_A$$
$$b_A = 0.74$$
$$20 = 10 + (6.8)b_B$$
$$b_B = 1.47$$

Note that the 16.8% value for r_M was approximated from the graph. Also, this solution *assumes* that you can borrow at $r_{RF} = 10\%$. This is a basic—but questionable—CAPM assumption. If the borrowing rate is *above* r_{RF}, then the CML would turn down to the right of Point M.

CHAPTER 26

ST-1   a. NPV of each demand scenario:

0	Probability	Future Cash Flows		NPV of This Scenario	Probability × NPV
		Year 1	Year 2		
		$13	$13	$13.13	$3.28
	25%				
−$8	50%	$7	$7	$3.38	$1.69
	25%				
		$1	$1	−$6.37	−$1.59

Expected NPV of future CFs = $\boxed{\$3.38}$

NPV under high-demand scenario:

$$\text{NPV} = -\$8 + \frac{\$13}{(1 + 0.15)^1} + \frac{\$13}{(1 + 0.15)^2} = \$13.13$$

NPV under medium-demand scenario:

$$\text{NPV} = -\$8 + \frac{\$7}{(1 + 0.15)^1} + \frac{\$7}{(1 + 0.15)^2} = \$3.38$$

NPV under low-demand scenario:

$$\text{NPV} = -\$8 + \frac{\$1}{(1 + 0.15)^1} + \frac{\$1}{(1 + 0.15)^2} = -\$6.37$$

Expected NPV = 0.25($13.13) + 0.50($3.38) + 0.25(−$6.37) = $3.38 million.

b. NPV of operating cash flows if the additional project is implemented only when optimal:

Probability	Future Operating Cash Flows (Discount at WACC)				NPV of This Scenario	Probability × NPV
	Year 1	Year 2	Year 3	Year 4		
	$13	$13	$13	$13	$37.11	$9.28
25%						
50%	$7	$7	$7	$7	$19.98	$9.99
25%						
	$1	$1	$0	$0	$1.63	$0.41

Expected NPV of future operating CFs = $\boxed{\$19.68}$

NPV of operating cash flows under high-demand scenario:

$$\text{NPV} = \frac{\$13}{(1 + 0.15)^1} + \frac{\$13}{(1 + 0.15)^2} + \frac{\$13}{(1 + 0.15)^3} + \frac{\$13}{(1 + 0.15)^4} = \$37.11$$

NPV of operating cash flows under medium-demand scenario:

$$NPV = \frac{\$7}{(1 + 0.15)^1} + \frac{\$7}{(1 + 0.15)^2} + \frac{\$7}{(1 + 0.15)^3} + \frac{\$7}{(1 + 0.15)^4} = \$19.98$$

NPV of operating cash flows under low-demand scenario:

$$NPV = \frac{\$1}{(1 + 0.15)^1} + \frac{\$1}{(1 + 0.15)^2} = \$1.63$$

Expected NPV of operating cash flows = 0.25($37.11) + 0.50($19.98) + 0.25($1.63)
= $19.68 million

Find NPV of costs, discounted at risk-free rate:

0	Probability	Year 1	Year 2	NPV of This Scenario	Probability × NPV
		$0	−$8	−$15.12	−$3.78
	25%				
−$8	50%	$0	−$8	−$15.12	−$7.56
	25%				
		$0	$0	−$8.00	−$2.00

Expected NPV of future operating CFs = $\boxed{−\$13.34}$

NPV of costs under high-demand scenario:

$$NPV = -\$8 + \frac{\$0}{(1 + 0.06)^1} + \frac{-\$8}{(1 + 0.06)^2} = -\$15.12$$

NPV of costs under medium-demand scenario:

$$NPV = -\$8 + \frac{\$0}{(1 + 0.06)^1} + \frac{-\$8}{(1 + 0.06)^2} = -\$15.12$$

NPV of costs under low-demand scenario:

$$NPV = -\$8 + \frac{\$0}{(1 + 0.06)^1} + \frac{\$0}{(1 + 0.06)^2} = -\$8.00$$

Expected NPV of costs = 0.25(−$15.12) + 0.50(−$15.12) + 0.25(−$8.00)
= −$13.34 million

$$\begin{matrix} \text{Expected NPV} \\ \text{of project} \end{matrix} = \begin{matrix} \text{Expected NPV of} \\ \text{operating cash flows} \end{matrix} - \begin{matrix} \text{Expected NPV} \\ \text{of costs} \end{matrix}$$

$$= \$19.68 - \$13.34 = \$6.34$$

c. Find the expected NPV of the additional project's operating cash flows, which is analogous to the "stock price" in the Black–Scholes model:

0	Probability	Year 1	Year 2	Year 3	Year 4	NPV of This Scenario	Probability × NPV
		$0	$0	$13	$13	$15.98	$4.00
	25%						
	50%	$0	$0	$7	$7	$8.60	$4.30
	25%						
		$0	$0	$1	$1	$1.23	$0.31

$$\text{Expected NPV of future operating CFs} = \boxed{\underline{\$8.60}}$$

NPV of operating cash flows under high-demand scenario:

$$\text{NPV} = \frac{\$0}{(1 + 0.15)^1} + \frac{\$0}{(1 + 0.15)^2} + \frac{\$13}{(1 + 0.15)^3} + \frac{\$13}{(1 + 0.15)^4} = \$15.98$$

NPV of operating cash flows under medium-demand scenario:

$$\text{NPV} = \frac{\$0}{(1 + 0.15)^1} + \frac{\$0}{(1 + 0.15)^2} + \frac{\$7}{(1 + 0.15)^3} + \frac{\$7}{(1 + 0.15)^4} = \$8.60$$

NPV of operating cash flows under low-demand scenario:

$$\text{NPV} = \frac{\$0}{(1 + 0.15)^1} + \frac{\$0}{(1 + 0.15)^2} + \frac{\$1}{(1 + 0.15)^3} + \frac{\$1}{(1 + 0.15)^4} = \$1.23$$

$$\begin{array}{l} \text{Expected NPV of additional project's} \\ \text{operating cash flows} \end{array} = 0.25(\$15.98) + 0.50(\$8.60) + 0.25(\$1.23)$$

$$= \$8.60 \text{ million}$$

The inputs for the Black–Scholes model are: $r_{RF} = 0.06$, $X = 8$, $P = 8.6$, $t = 2$, and $\sigma^2 = 0.150$. Using these inputs, the value of the option, V, is

$$d_1 = \frac{\ln(P/X) + \left[r_{RF} + \dfrac{\sigma^2}{2}\right] \times t}{\sigma\sqrt{t}} = \frac{\ln(8.6/8) + \left[0.06 + \dfrac{0.150}{2}\right] \times 2}{\sqrt{0.15}\sqrt{2}} = 0.62499$$

$$d_2 = d_1 - \sigma\sqrt{t} = 0.62499 - \sqrt{0.15}\sqrt{2} = 0.07727$$

Use *Excel*'s NORMSDIST function to calculate $N(d_1)$ and $N(d_2)$:

$$N(d_1) = 0.73401$$
$$N(d_2) = 0.53079$$

$$V = P[N(d_1)] - Xe^{-r_{RF}t}[N(d_2)] = 8.6(0.73401) - 8e^{-0.06(2)}(0.53079) = \$2.55 \text{ million}$$

The total value is the value of the original project (from part a) and the value of the growth option:

$$\text{Total value} = \$3.38 + \$2.55 = \$5.93 \text{ million}$$

Answers to End-of-Chapter Problems

We present here some intermediate steps and final answers to selected end-of-chapter problems. Please note that your answer may differ slightly from ours because of rounding differences. Also, although we hope not, some of the problems may have more than one correct solution, depending on what assumptions are made when working the problem. Finally, many of the problems involve some verbal discussion as well as numerical calculations; this verbal material is not presented here.

2-1 5.76%.

2-2 31.25%.

2-3 $3,000,000.

2-4 $3,000,000.

2-5 $3,600,000.

2-6 $25,000,000.

2-7 $3,000,000.

2-8 $22,000,000.

2-9 $14,000,000.

2-10 Taxable income = $322,500;
Tax = $67,725;
NI = $262,275.

2-11 a. $10,500,000.
b. $210,000.
c. $105,000.

2-12 AT&T bond = 5.214%;
AT&T preferred stock = 5.370%;
Florida bond = 5.000%.

2-13 NI = $592,500;
NCF = $792,500.

2-14 a. NI = $1,185,000;
Net CF = $2,685,000.
b. NI = $0;
Net CF = $3,000,000.
c. NI = $1,177,500;
Net CF = $2,527,500.

2-15 $60,000.

2-16 $1,390 million.

2-17 $14 million.

2-18 a. NOPAT = $756 million.

b. $NOWC_{19}$ = $3.0 billion;
$NOWC_{20}$ = $3.3 billion.

c. Op. capital$_{19}$ = $6.5 billion;
Op. capital$_{20}$ = $7.15 billion.

d. FCF = $106 million.

e. ROIC = 10.57%.

f. Answers in millions:
A-T int. = $90;
Inc. in debt = −$284;
Div. = $202;
Rep. stock = $88;
Purch. ST inv. = $10.

2-19 a. Taxable income = $20,000;
Remaining losses = $420,000.

b. Taxable income = $60,000;
Remaining losses = $180,000.

c. Taxable income = $170,000;
Remaining losses = $0.

3-1 AR = $400,000.

3-2 Debt ratio = Debt-to-assets ratio = 15%.

3-3 M/B = 10.

3-4 P/E = 16.0.

3-5 ROE = 12%.

3-6 S/TA = 2.4; TA/E = 1.67.

3-7 CL = $2,000,000;
Inv = $1,000,000.

3-8 Net profit margin = 3.33%;
L/A = 42.86%;
Debt ratio = 21.43%.

3-9 $262,500; 1.19.

3-10 TIE = 3.5.

3-11 Sales = $600,000;
COGS = $450,000;
Cash = $28,000;
AR = $60,000;
Inv. = $120,000;
FA = $192,000;
AP = $110,000;
Common stock = $140,000;
TL & Equity = $400,000.

3-12 Sales = $2,580,000.

3-13 a. Current ratio = 2.39;
DSO = 77 days;
Inv TO = 5.67;
FA turnover = 5.56;
TA turnover = 1.754;
PM = 1.52%;
ROA = 2.67%;
ROE = 4.30%;
Total debt/Total assets = 11.70%;
TL/TA = 38.01%.

   b. Lozano: DuPont ROE = 4.3%;
Industry: DuPont ROE = 9.0%.

3-14 Quick ratio = 0.85;
Current ratio = 2.33;
Inv. TO = 4.00;
DSO = 37.35 days;
FA TO = 9.95;
TA TO = 2.34;
ROA = 5.90%;
ROE = 13.07%;
PM = 2.53%;
Debt-to-assets ratio = 27.47%;
TL/TA = 54.81%;
PE ratio = 5.00;
M/B ratio = 0.65.

4-1 FV_5 = $16,105.10.

4-2 PV = $1,292.10.

4-3 I/YR = 8.01%.

4-4 N = 11.01 years.

4-5 N = 11 years.

4-6 FVA_5 = $1,725.22;
$FVA_{5\,Due}$ = $1,845.99.

4-7 PV = $923.98;
FV = $1,466.24.

4-8 PMT = $444.89;
EAR = 12.6825%.

4-9 a. $530.

   b. $561.80.

   c. $471.70.

   d. $445.00.

4-10 a. $895.42.

   b. $1,552.92.

   c. $279.20.

   d. $160.99.

4-11 a. N = 10.24 ≈ 10 years.

   b. N = 7.27 ≈ 7 years.

   c. N = 4.19 ≈ 4 years.

   d. N = 1.00 ≈ 1 year.

4-12 a. $6,374.97.

   b. $1,105.13.

   c. $2,000.00.

   d. (1) $7,012.46.
(2) $1,160.38.
(3) $2,000.00.

4-13 a. $2,457.83.

   b. $865.90.

   c. $2,000.00.

   d. (1) $2,703.61.
(2) $909.19.
(3) $2,000.00.

4-14 a. PV_A = $1,251.25;
PV_B = $1,300.32.

   b. PV_A = $1,600;
PV_B = $1,600.

4-15 a. 7%.

   b. 7%.

   c. 9%.

   d. 15%.

4-16 a. $881.17.

   b. $895.42.

   c. $903.06.

   d. $908.35.

4-17 a. $279.20.

   b. $276.84.

   c. $443.72.

4-18 a. $5,272.32.

   b. $5,374.07.

4-19 a. Universal, EAR = 7%;
Regional, EAR = 6.14%.

4-20 a. PMT = $6,594.94;
   Interest$_1$ = $2,500;
   Interest$_2$ = $2,090.51.

    b. $13,189.87.

    c. $8,137.27.

4-21 a. I = 14.87% ≈ 15%.

4-22 I = 7.18%.

4-23 I = 9%.

4-24 a. $33,872.11.

    b. (1) $26,243.16.
      (2) $0.

4-25 N = 14.77 ≈ 15 years.

4-26 6 years; $1,106.01.

4-27 (1) $1,428.57.
     (2) $714.29.

4-28 $893.16.

4-29 $984.88.

4-30 57.18%.

4-31 a. $1,432.02.

    b. $93.07.

4-32 I$_{NOM}$ = 15.19%.

4-33 PMT = $36,949.61.

4-34 First PMT = $9,736.96.

5-1 $928.39.

5-2 12.48%.

5-3 8.55%.

5-4 7%; 7.33%.

5-5 2.5%.

5-6 0.3%.

5-7 $1,085.80.

5-8 YTM = 6.62%; YTC = 6.49%.

5-9 a. 5%: V_L = $1,518.98;
          V_S = $1,047.62.

      8%: V_L = $1,171.19;
          V_S = $1,018.52.

      12%: V_L = $863.78;
          V_S = $982.14.

5-10 a. YTM at $829 = 13.98%;
       YTM at $1,104 = 6.50%.

5-11 14.82%.

5-12 a. 10.37%.

    b. 10.91%.

    c. −0.54%.

    d. 10.15%.

5-13 8.65%.

5-14 10.78%.

5-15 YTC = 6.47%.

5-16 a. 10-year, 10% coupon = 6.75%;
      10-year zero = 9.75%;
      5-year zero = 4.76%;
      30-year zero = 32.19%;
      $100 perpetuity = 14.29%.

5-17 C_0 = $1,012.79; Z_0 = $693.04;
     C_1 = $1,010.02; Z_1 = $759.57;
     C_2 = $1,006.98; Z_2 = $832.49;
     C_3 = $1,003.65; Z_3 = $912.41;
     C_4 = $1,000.00; Z_4 = $1,000.00.

5-18 5.8%.

5-19 1.5%.

5-20 6.0%.

5-21 a. $1,251.22.

    b. $898.94.

5-22 a. 8.02%.

    b. 7.59%.

5-23 a. r_1 = 9.20%; r_5 = 7.20%.

6-1 b = 1.08.

6-2 r_s = 10.40%.

6-3 r_M = 12%;
    r_{sB} = 16.9%.

6-4 16.96%.

6-5 r̂ = 11.40%; σ = 26.69%.

6-6 a. r̂$_M$ = 13.5%; r̂$_j$ = 11.6%.

    b. σ$_M$ = 3.85%; σ$_j$ = 6.22%.

6-7 a. b_A = 1.40.

    b. r_A = 15%.

6-8 a. r_i = 14.8%.

    b. (1) r_M = 13%;
        r_i = 15.8%.

      (2) r_M = 11%;
        r_i = 13.8%.

    c. (1) r_i = 17.6%.
      (2) r_i = 13.4%.

6-9 $b_N = 1.25$.

6-10 $b_p = 0.7625$;

$r_p = 12.1\%$.

6-11 $b_N = 1.1250$.

6-12 4.5%.

6-13 a. $\bar{r}_A = 11.80\%$;

$\bar{r}_B = 11.80\%$.

b. $\bar{r}_p = 11.80\%$.

c. $\sigma_A = 25.3\%$;

$\sigma_B = 24.3\%$;

$\sigma_p = 16.3\%$.

6-14 a. $b_X = 1.3471$;

$b_Y = 0.6508$.

b. $r_X = 12.7355\%$;

$r_Y = 9.254\%$.

c. $r_p = 12.04\%$.

7-1 a. $\text{Sales}_1 = \$880$ million;

$\text{Sales}_2 = \$924$ million.

b. $\text{NOPAT}_1 = \$88.00$ million;

$\text{NOPAT}_2 = \$92.40$ million.

c. $\text{OpCap}_1 = \$704.00$ million;

$\text{OpCap}_2 = \$739.20$ million.

e. FCF = \$57.20 million.

7-2 $V_{op} = \$6,000,000$.

7-3 V_{op} at 2022 = \$15,900 million.

7-4 \$9,357.80 million.

7-5 \$62.00.

7-6 $D_1 = \$1.5750$;

$D_3 = \$1.7364$;

$D_5 = \$2.1011$.

7-7 $\hat{P}_0 = \$21.43$.

7-8 $\hat{P}_1 = \$24.20$; $\hat{r}_s = 16.00\%$.

7-9 \$50.50. You will get \$50.53 if you carry out all decimal places in D_3 and in calculating the horizon value.

7-10 $r_{ps} = 10\%$.

7-11 (1) \$15.83.

(2) \$23.08.

(3) \$39.38.

(4) \$110.00.

7-12 a. $HV_2 = \$2,700,000$.

b. \$2,303,571.43.

7-13 a. \$713.33 million.

b. \$527.89 million.

c. \$43.79.

7-14 \$32.00.

7-15 9%.

7-16 $\hat{P}_3 = \$43.08$.

7-17 a. 11.67%.

b. 8.75%.

c. 7.00%.

d. 5.00%.

7-18 13%; \$25.03.

7-19 $\hat{P}_0 = \$10.76$.

7-20 a. \$125.

b. \$83.33.

7-21 a. 7%.

b. 5%.

c. 12%.

7-22 a. $D_3 = \$1.79$.

b. PV = \$3.97.

c. \$18.74.

d. \$22.71.

7-23 a. $\text{FCF}_1 = \$2.01$ million;

$\text{FCF}_2 = \$2.31$ million;

$\text{FCF}_3 = \$2.66$ million;

$\text{FCF}_4 = \$3.06$ million;

$\text{FCF}_5 = \$3.52$ million.

b. \$52.80 million.

c. \$29.96 million.

d. \$9.48 million.

e. \$39.44 million.

7-24 a. $\hat{P}_0 = \$78.3482$.

b. \$84.50.

c. (1) 4.148%.

(2) 7.852%.

(3) 12.00%.

d. (1) 5.00%.

(2) 7.00%.

(3) 12.00%.

8-1 \$5;

\$2.

8-2 $27.00;
$37.00.

8-3 $1.67.

8-4 $3.70.

8-5 $1.89.

8-6 $2.39.

8-7 $1.91.

9-1 a. 13%.

b. 10.4%.

c. 8.45%.

9-2 6.3%.

9-3 9%.

9-4 5.41%.

9-5 13.33%.

9-6 10.4%.

9-7 9.44%.

9-8 12%.

9-9 9%.

9-10 a. 16.3%.

b. 15.4%.

c. 16%.

9-11 a. 8%.

b. $2.81.

c. 15.81%.

9-12 a. $g = 3\%$.

b. $EPS_1 = \$5.562$.

9-13 16.1%.

9-14 6.91%;
7.64%.

9-15 a. $15,000,000.

b. 9.0%.

9-16 Short-term debt = 11.14%;
Long-term debt = 22.03%;
Common equity = 66.83%.

9-17 a. $w_d = 20\%$;
$w_{ps} = 4\%$;
$w_s = 76\%$.

b. 8.85%.

c. 10.4%.

d. 14%

e. $g = 8\%$;
$r_s = 13.4\%$.

f. 14.8%.

g. 12.826%.

10-1 NPV = $2,409.77.

10-2 IRR = 12.84%.

10-3 MIRR = 11.93%.

10-4 PI = 1.06.

10-5 4.44 years.

10-6 6.44 years.

10-7 a. 5%: $NPV_A = \$16,108,952$;
$NPV_B = \$18,300,939$.

10%: $NPV_A = \$12,836,213$;
$NPV_B = \$15,954,170$.

15%: $NPV_A = \$10,059,587$;
$NPV_B = \$13,897,838$.

b. $IRR_A = 43.97\%$;
$IRR_B = 82.03\%$.

10-8 $NPV_T = \$409$;
$IRR_T = 15\%$; $MIRR_T = 14.54\%$;
Accept.
$NPV_P = \$3,318$;
$IRR_P = 20\%$; $MIRR_P = 17.19\%$;
Accept.

10-9 $NPV_E = \$3,861$; $IRR_E = 18\%$;
$NPV_G = \$3,057$; $IRR_G = 18\%$;
Purchase electric-powered forklift because
it has a higher NPV.

10-10 $NPV_S = \$814.33$;
$NPV_L = \$1,675.34$;
$IRR_S = 15.24\%$;
$IRR_L = 14.67\%$;
$MIRR_S = 13.77\%$;
$MIRR_L = 13.46\%$;
$PI_S = 1.081$;
$PI_L = 1.067$.

10-11 $MIRR_X = 17.49\%$;
$MIRR_Y = 18.39\%$.

10-12 a. NPV = $136,578;
IRR = 19.22%.

10-13 b. $IRR_A = 20.7\%$;
$IRR_B = 25.8\%$.

c. 10%: $NPV_A = \$478.83$;
$NPV_B = \$372.37$.

17%: $\text{NPV}_A = \$133.76$;
        $\text{NPV}_B = \$173.70$.

d. (1) $\text{MIRR}_A = 14.91\%$;
              $\text{MIRR}_B = 17.35\%$.

  (2) $\text{MIRR}_A = 18.76\%$;
              $\text{MIRR}_B = 21.03\%$.

e. Crossover rate $= 14.76\%$.

10-14 a. $\$0$; $-\$10,250,000$;
    $\$1,750,000$.

b. 16.07%.

10-15 a. $\text{NPV}_A = \$18,108,510$;
    $\text{NPV}_B = \$13,946,117$;
    $\text{IRR}_A = 15.03\%$;
    $\text{IRR}_B = 22.26\%$;

b. $\text{NPV}_\Delta = \$4,162,393$;
    $\text{IRR}_\Delta = 11.71\%$.

10-16 Extended $\text{NPV}_A = \$12.76$ million;
  Extended $\text{NPV}_B = \$9.26$ million.
  $\text{EAA}_A = \$2.26$ million;
  $\text{EAA}_B = \$1.64$ million.

10-17 Extended $\text{NPV}_A = \$4.51$ million:
  $\text{EAA}_A = \$0.85$ million;
  $\text{EAA}_B = \$0.69$ million.

10-18 NPV of 360-6 $= 22,256$;
  Extended NPV of 190-3 $= 20,070$;
  EAA of 360-6 $= \$5,723.30$;
  EAA of 190-3 $= \$5,161.02$.

10-19 d. 7.61%; 15.58%.

10-20 a. Undefined.

b. $\text{NPV}_C = -\$911,067$;
    $\text{NPV}_F = -\$838,834$.

10-21 a. $A = 2.67$ years;
    $B = 1.5$ years.

b. $A = 3.07$ years;
    $B = 1.825$ years.

c. $\text{NPV}_A = \$12,739,908$;
    $\text{IRR}_A = 27.27\%$;
    $\text{NPV}_B = \$11,554,880$;
    $\text{IRR}_B = 36.15\%$;
    Choose both.

d. $\text{NPV}_A = \$18,243,813$;
    $\text{NPV}_B = \$14,964,829$;
    Choose A.

e. $\text{NPV}_A = \$8,207,071$;
    $\text{NPV}_B = \$8,643,390$;
    Choose B.

f. 13.53%.

g. $\text{MIRR}_A = 21.93\%$;
    $\text{MIRR}_B = 20.96\%$.

10-22 a. 3 years; $\text{NPV}_3 = \$1,307$.

b. No.

11-1 a. $22.00 million.

b. $22.00 million.

c. $23.50.

11-2 $7.75 million.

11-3 $3.75 million.

11-4 NPV $= \$6,746.78$.

11-5 a. Straight line: $425,000 per year.
    MACRS: $566,610; $755,650; $251,770;
    $125,970.

b. MACRS, $16,902.26 higher.

11-6 a. $-\$955,500$.

b. $306,326 , $332,458 , $262,804.

c. 407,913.50.

d. NPV $= \$60,441.11$;
    Purchase.

11-7 a. $-\$89,000$.

b. $25,832.63, $28,195.63, $21,897.13.

c. $28,074.63.

d. $-\$4,669.11$.

11-8 a. PV of future CFs $= \$275,000$;
    NPV $= \$105,000$.

b. $-\$5,000$.

11-9 NPV of replace $= \$3,544.60$.

11-10 NPV of replace $= \$\$26,285$.

11-11 E[NPV] $= \$3$ million;
  $\sigma_{\text{NPV}} = \$23.622$ million;
  $\text{CV}_{\text{NPV}} = 7.874$.

11-12 a. NPV $= \$37,661$;
    IRR $= 13.72\%$;
    MIRR $= 12.07\%$;
    Payback $= 3.63$ years.

b. $100,209; −$24,887.

c. E[NPV] = $34,322;
σ_{NPV} = $53,730;
CV = 1.57.

11-13 a. −$86,875.

b. $31,124; $34,460; $25,568; $23,348; $6,125.

c. −$2,243.

11-14 a. −$561,250.

b. Depreciation tax shield: $16,250; $39,500; $14,700; −$180; −$180.

c. $89,910.

d. CF = −$561,250; $155,000; $178,250; $153,450; $138,570; $228,480.
NPV = $46,175.

11-15 a. Expected CF_A = $6,750;
Expected CF_B = $7,650;
CV_A = 0.0703.

b. NPV_A = $10,036;
NPV_B = $11,624.

11-16 a. IRR = 22.62%.

b. NPV = $1,048,236.70.

c. (2) Annual CF:
Year 0 = −$4,000,000
Year 1 = $637,500
Year 2 = $975,000
Year 3 = $562,500

(3) NPV = −$2,338,599.

11-17 a. $117,779.

b. σ_{NPV} = $445,060;
CV_{NPV} = 3.78.

12-1 $283,800.

12-2 $1,100.

12-3 $2,200.

12-4 ΔS = $202,312.

12-5 a. $590,000; $1,150,000.

b. $238,563.

12-6 AFN = $360.

12-7 a. $13.44 million.

b. 6.38%.

c. LOC = $13.44 million.

12-8 a. $2,300.

b. $1,740.

c. $1,305.

d. $783.

e. $19,044.

f. $33,534.

g. $10,380.

h. $2,511.

12-9 $98,000.

14-1 Payout = 33.33%.

14-2 Payout = 20%.

14-3 Payout = 52%.

14-4 V_{op} = $175 million;
n = 8.75 million.

14-5 P_0 = $80.

14-6 $6.90 million.

14-7 n = 4,000;
EPS = $5.00;
DPS = $1.50;
P = $40.00.

14-8 D_0 = $4.25.

14-9 Payout = 17.89%.

14-10 a. (1) $4.32.

(2) $5.12.

(3) $7.85.

(4) Regular = $4.32;
Extra = $3.53.

14-11 a. $10,500,000.

b. DPS = $0.50;
Payout = 4.55%.

c. $9,000,000.

d. No.

e. 40%.

f. $1,500,000.

g. $12,875,143.

14-12 a. $848 million.

b. $450 million.

c. $30.

d. 1 million;
14 million.

e. $420 million;
$30.

15-1 20,000.

15-2 1.0.

15-3 3.6%.

15-4 $50 billion.

15-5 $425 billion.

15-6 $515.83 billion.

15-7 $300 million.

15-8 $30.

15-9 40 million.

15-10 a. ΔProfit = $850,000;
Return = 21.25% > r_s = 15%.

b. $Q_{BE,Old}$ = 40;
$Q_{BE,New}$ = 45.45.

15-11 a. V_{op} = $4,500,000;
P = $22.50;
EPS = $2.25.

b. WACC = 9.975;
V = $4,511,278.195;
D = $1,353,383.459.

c. P = $22.5564 ≈ $22.56;
n = 140,000;
EPS = $2.71.

15-12 30% debt:
WACC = 11.14%;
V = $101.023 million.

50% debt:
WACC = 11.25%;
V = $100 million.

70% debt:
WACC = 11.94%;
V = $94.255 million.

15-13 a. 0.8421.

b. b = 1.2632;
r_s = 11.0528%.

c. WACC = 9.3317%;
V = $128.60 million.

15-14 WACC at optimal debt level: 9.61%.

15-15 a. V = $80.594 million.

b. D = $19.406 million;
Yield = 9.93%.

c. V = $74.385 million;
D = $25.615 million;
Yield = 6.92%.

16-1 $3,000,000.

16-2 AR = $59,500.

16-3 r_{NOM} = 75.26%;
EAR = 109.84%.

16-4 EAR = 8.49%.

16-5 $7,500,000.

16-6 a. DSO = 38 days.

b. AR = $156,164.

c. DSO = 34.5 days;
AR = $141,781.

16-7 a. 73.74%.

b. 14.90%.

c. 32.25%.

d. 21.28%.

e. 29.80%.

16-8 a. 32.25%.

b. 45.15%.

16-9 Nominal cost = 14.90%;
Effective cost = 15.89%.

16-10 EAR = 14.91%.

16-11 a. 60 days.

b. $420,000.

c. 7.3.

16-12 a. 56.8 days.

b. (1) 2.7082.

(2) 18.96%.

c. (1) 36.6 days.

(2) 2.95.

(3) 20.68%.

16-13 a. ROE_T = 11.79%;
ROE_M = 11.00%;
ROE_R = 9.64%.

16-14 a. December loan = $4,400;
January loan = $11,200;
February surplus = $2,000.

b. $164,400.

16-15 a. $100,000.

b. No.

c. (1) $300,000.

(2) Nominal cost = 37.24%;
Effective cost = 44.59%.

d. Nominal cost = 24.83%;
Effective cost = 27.86%.

16-16 a. 14.35%.

16-17 a. $300,000.

b. $2,000.

c. (1) $322,500.

(2) $26,875.

(3) 13.57%.

(4) 14.44%.

17-1 12.3589 yen per peso.

17-2 f_t = $0.00907.

17-3 1 euro = $0.9091 or $1 = 1.1 euros.

17-4 0.6667 euros per dollar.

17-5 1.5152 Swiss francs.

17-6 2.4 Swiss francs per pound.

17-7 $r_{NOM-U.S.}$ = 9.30%.

17-8 117 pesos.

17-9 +$500,000.

17-10 $24,500.

17-11 a. $1,658,925.

b. $1,646,091.

c. $2,000,000.

17-12 f_t = 1.3990 dollars per euro; discount.

17-13 $322 million.

17-14 a. $89,357; 20%.

b. 1,039.90 won per U.S. dollar and 1,029.95 won per U.S. dollar.

c. 78,150,661 won; 18.85%.

18-1 a. $700,000.

b. $3,700,000.

c. −$2,300,000.

18-2 964,115 shares.

18-3 10,000 shares at $20 per share.

18-4 a. (1) $31,286,800;

(2) $22,016,893;

(3) $20,016,893;

(4) $40.03.

b. (1) Abercrombie: D/A 30.43%;
P/E 15.91;
M/B 2.19;
ROE 13.8%;
P/FCF 21.47.

(2) Gunter: D/A 20.00%;
P/E 15.02;
M/B 2.35;
ROE 15.7%;
P/FCF 18.50.

(3) B&C:
D/A 18.18%;
P/E 15.40;
M/B 2.22;
ROE 14.4%;
P/FCF 20.02.

c. (1) Price based on: Abercrombie P/E $41.36; Gunter P/E $39.04.

(2) Price based on: Abercrombie M/B $39.38; Gunter M/B $42.30.

(3) Price based on: Abercrombie P/FCF $42.94; Gunter P/FCF $37.01.

18-5 $14.74;

$13,708,200.

19-1 −$56,234.

19-2 −$155,945.

19-3 $1,557.2.

19-4 a. $36,027.47.

b. $36,027.47.

c. $7,846.36.

d. $49,039.78.

e. $50,925.93.

f. $49,039.78.

19-5 a. $98,079.56.

b. $98,079.56.

c. $7,846.36.

d. $49,039.78.

e. $50,925.93.

f. $49,039.78.

19-6 a. −$1,072,090.25.

b. −$925,787.40.

c. $146,302.85.

19-7 a. −$793,716.27

b. −$706,073.42

c. $87,642.85

d. $353,163

20-1 $182.16.

20-2 20 shares.

20-3 a. (1) $0.

(2) $0.

(3) $5.

(4) $75.

b. 9.992%;
$99.92.

20-4 Premium = 10%: $46.20;
Premium = 30%: $54.60.

20-5 a. 14.1%.

b. $12 million before taxes.

c. $330.89.

d. Value as a straight bond = $699.25;
Value in conversion = $521.91.

f. Value as a straight bond = $1,000.00;
Value in conversion = $521.91.

20-6 a. *Alternative 1:*
Long-term debt = $0;
Common stock ($1 par) = $162,500;
Paid-in capital = $437,500.

Alternative 2:
Long-term debt = $0;
Common stock ($1 par) = $150,000;
Paid-in capital = $450,000.

Alternative 3:
Long-term debt (8%) = $500,000;
Common stock ($1 par) = $150,000;
Paid-in capital = $450,000.

b. Plan 1, 49%;
Plan 2, 53%;
Plan 3, 53%.

c. Plan 1, $0.74;
Plan 2, $0.80;
Plan 3, $1.10.

d. Plan 1, 19%;
Plan 2, 19%;
Plan 3, 50%.

20-7 a. Year = 7;
CV_7 = $1,210.422;
CF_7 = $1,290.422.

b. 10.20%.

21-1 $500 million.

21-2 $815 million.

21-3 $809.375 million.

21-4 $57.00.

21-5 $2,100.

21-6 a. b_u = 1.2.

b. r_{sL} = 16%.

c. Debt = $2, r_{sL} = 17.14%;
Debt = $4, r_{sL} = 18.82%;
Debt = $6, r_{sL} = 21.54%.

d. r_{sL} = 21.54%.

21-7 a. V_U = 12;
V_L = 16.

b. r_{sU} = 10%; r_{sL} = 15%.

c. $7.5 million.

d. WACC for levered company = 8.57%.

21-8 a. $10,000,000.

b. V_L = $11,750,000; r_{sL} = 17.44%.

c. V_L = $11,250,000;
Stock = $9.5 million;
r_{sL} = 16.60%.

21-9 a. $713.33 million.

b. $563.29 million.

c. $71.33 million.

d. $57.86 million.

e. $621.15 million.

22-1 a. r_{sL} = 15.2%.

b. WACC = 13.0875%.

c. r_{sU} = $13.65%.

22-2 a. HV_U = $11,845.

b. V_U = $10,774.

22-3 a. HV_{TS} = $390.

b. V_{TS} = $336.7347.

22-4 a. r_{sL} = 13.4%.

b. WACC = 11.18%.

c. V_{ops} = $33.98 million.

d. P_0 = $15.86 per share.

22-5 a. r_{sL} = 13.4%;
r_{sU} = 11.78%.

b. V_U = $44.692 million.

c. V_{TSs} = $4.790 million.

d. V_{ops} = $49.482 million;

V_s = $39.292 million;
P_0 = $26.20 if no rounding in
intermediate steps.

22-6 a. $70,000;
$57,455.122.

b. $4,357.5;

$3,605.934.

c. $61,061.056;
$53,361.056;
$66.70.

d. $77,000;
$63,170.164.

e. $11,812.5;
$9,789.6757.

f. $72,959.8397;
$65,259.8397;
$81.57.

g. 11.2%;
25.3%;
$5,715.04;
$6,183.74.

23-1 Net payment = LIBOR + 0.2%.

23-2 r_d = 7.01%.

23-3 r_d = 5.96%;
Futures = $89,748.54.

23-4 Net to Carter = 9.95% fixed;

Net to Brence = LIBOR + 3.05% floating.

23-5 a. Yield =6.3992%;
Sell 105 contracts;
Total hedge position = $10,030,781.25.

b. Bond proceeds = $8,585,447.31;
Loss on proceeds = $1,414,552.69.

c. New total hedge position = $8,079,283.80;
Futures = $1,951,497.45;
Net = +$536,945.

24-1 AP = $375,000;
NP = $750,000;
SD = $750,000;

Stockholders = $343,750.

24-2 a. TA: $300 million;
D = $75 million;
PS = $35 million.

b. Income: $14.1 million.

c. Noncallable before: $6 million; total after:
$8.4 million;
NI before: $13 million; after: $14.1.

d. Before: $10.67 million;
After: $9.2 million.

e. D/TA: before = 24%;
after = 65%.
(D + PS)/TA: before = 86%;

after = 76.67%.

24-3 a. $0.

b. $300,000; yes; $100,000; $0.

c. $100,000; no; $100,000 as general
claimant.

d. Trustee's expenses: $50,000;
Wages due: $30,000;
Taxes due: $40,000.

e. *Before subordination:*
Accounts payable = $6,350;
Notes payable = $22,860;
Second mortgage = $12,700;
Debentures = $25,400;
Subordinated debentures = $12,700.

After subordination:
Notes payable = $35,560;
Subordinated debentures = $0.
Total received by second mortgage
holders = $112,700.

24-4 a. Available = $3,200; Claims = $7,000;
$0 for stockholders.

b. AP = 24%;
NP = 100%;
WP = 100%;
TP = 100%;
Mortgage = 85%;
Subordinated debentures = 9%;
Trustee = 100%.

25-1 1.4.

25-2 12%.

25-3 16.2%; 45.9%.

25-4 a. Alternative SML:

$$r_i = r_{RF} + \left(\frac{r_M - r_{RF}}{\sigma_M} \right) r_{iM} \sigma_i.$$

25-5 a. b = 0.56.

b. X: 10.6%; 13.1%;

M: 12.1%; 22.6%.

c. 8.6%.

25-6 a. b = 0.62.

26-1 a. $1.074 million.

b. $2.96 million.

26-2 a. $4.68 million.

b. $3.21 million.

26-3 a. −$19 million.

b. $10.28 million.

c. $22.67 million. Wait to purchase.

26-4 a. −$2.113 million.

b. $1.973 million.

c. −$70,222.

d. $565,090.

e. $1.116 million.

26-5 a. $2,562.

b. E[NPV] = $9,786; Value of growth option = $7,224.

26-6 P = $18.650 million;
X = $20 million;
t = 1;
r_{RF} = 0.08;
s^2 = 0.0687;
V = $2.03 million.

26-7 P = $10.479 million;
X = $9 million;
t = 2; r_{RF} = 0.06;
σ^2 = 0.111;
V = $3.239 million.

26-8 P = $18,646;
X = $20,000;
t = 2;
V = $5,009.

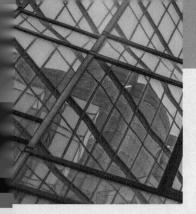

Selected Equations

CHAPTER 1

$$\text{Value} = \frac{FCF_1}{(1 + WACC)^1} + \frac{FCF_2}{(1 + WACC)^2} + \frac{FCF_3}{(1 + WACC)^3} + \cdots + \frac{FCF_\infty}{(1 + WACC)^\infty}$$

CHAPTER 2

EBIT = Earnings before interest and taxes = Sales revenues − Operating costs

EBITDA = Earnings before interest, taxes, depreciation and amortization

= EBIT + Depreciation + Amortization

Net cash flow = Net income + Depreciation and amortization

NOWC = Net operating working capital

= Operating current assets − Operating current liabilities

$$= \left(\begin{array}{c} \text{Cash + Accounts receivable} \\ \text{+ Inventories} \end{array}\right) - \left(\begin{array}{c} \text{Accounts payable} \\ \text{+ Accruals} \end{array}\right)$$

Total net operating capital = Net operating working capital + Operating long-term assets

NOPAT = Net operating profit after taxes = EBIT(1 − Tax rate)

Free cash flow (FCF) = NOPAT − Net investment in operating capital

$$= \text{NOPAT} - \left(\begin{array}{cc} \text{Current year's total} & \text{Previous year's total} \\ \text{net operating capital} & \text{net operating capital} \end{array}\right)$$

$$\text{FCF} = \text{Operating cash flow} - \frac{\text{Gross investment}}{\text{in operating capital}}$$

$$\text{Return on invested capital (ROIC)} = \frac{\text{NOPAT}}{\text{Total net operating capital}}$$

$$\text{Operating profitability ratio (OP)} = \frac{\text{NOPAT}}{\text{Sales}}$$

$$\text{Capital requirement ratio (CR)} = \frac{\text{Total net operating capital}}{\text{Sales}}$$

MVA = Market value of stock − Equity capital supplied by shareholders

= (Shares outstanding)(Stock price) − Total common equity

MVA = Total market value − Total investor-supplied capital

$$= \left(\begin{array}{c} \text{Market value of stock} \\ \text{+Market value of debt} \end{array}\right) - \text{Total investor-supplied capital}$$

$$\text{EVA} = \begin{pmatrix} \text{Net operating profit} \\ \text{after taxes} \end{pmatrix} - \begin{pmatrix} \text{After-tax dollar cost of capital} \\ \text{used to support operations} \end{pmatrix}$$

$$= \text{EBIT}(1 - \text{Tax rate}) - (\text{Total net operating capital})(\text{WACC})$$

$$\text{EVA} = (\text{Total net operating capital})(\text{ROIC} - \text{WACC})$$

CHAPTER 3

$$\text{Current ratio} = \frac{\text{Current assets}}{\text{Current liabilities}}$$

$$\text{Quick, or acid test, ratio} = \frac{\text{Current assets} - \text{Inventories}}{\text{Current liabilities}}$$

$$\text{Inventory turnover ratio} = \frac{\text{Cost of goods sold}}{\text{Inventories}}$$

$$\text{DSO} = \text{Days sales outstanding} = \frac{\text{Receivables}}{\text{Average sales per day}} = \frac{\text{Receivables}}{\text{Annual sales}/365}$$

$$\text{Fixed assets turnover ratio} = \frac{\text{Sales}}{\text{Net fixed assets}}$$

$$\text{Total assets turnover ratio} = \frac{\text{Sales}}{\text{Total assets}}$$

$$\text{Debt ratio} = \frac{\text{Total debt}}{\text{Total assets}}$$

$$\text{Liabilities-to-assets ratio} = \frac{\text{Total liabilities}}{\text{Total assets}}$$

$$\text{Market debt ratio} = \frac{\text{Total debt}}{\text{Total liabilities} + \text{Market value of equity}}$$

$$\text{Debt-to-equity ratio} = \frac{\text{Total debt}}{\text{Total common equity}}$$

$$\text{Equity multiplier} = \frac{\text{Total assets}}{\text{Common equity}}$$

$$\text{Times-interest-earned (TIE) ratio} = \frac{\text{EBIT}}{\text{Interest charges}}$$

$$\text{EBITDA coverage ratio} = \frac{\text{EBITDA} + \text{Lease payments}}{\text{Interest} + \text{Principal payments} + \text{Lease payments}}$$

$$\text{Net profit margin} = \frac{\text{Net income available to common stockholders}}{\text{Sales}}$$

$$\text{Operating profit margin} = \frac{\text{EBIT}}{\text{Sales}}$$

$$\text{Gross profit margin} = \frac{\text{Sales} - \text{Cost of goods sold}}{\text{Sales}}$$

$$\text{Return on total assets (ROA)} = \frac{\text{Net income available to common stockholders}}{\text{Total assets}}$$

$$\text{Basic earning power (BEP) ratio} = \frac{\text{EBIT}}{\text{Total assets}}$$

$$\text{ROA} = \text{Profit margin} \times \text{Total assets turnover} = \frac{\text{Net income}}{\text{Sales}} \times \frac{\text{Sales}}{\text{Total assets}}$$

$$\text{Return on common equity (ROE)} = \frac{\text{Net income available to common stockholders}}{\text{Common equity}}$$

$$\text{ROE} = \text{ROA} \times \text{Equity multiplier}$$

$$= \text{Profit margin} \times \text{Total assets turnover} \times \text{Equity multiplier}$$

$$= \frac{\text{Net income}}{\text{Sales}} \times \frac{\text{Sales}}{\text{Total assets}} \times \frac{\text{Total assets}}{\text{Common equity}}$$

$$\text{Price/earnings (P/E) ratio} = \frac{\text{Price per share}}{\text{Earnings per share}}$$

$$\text{Price/cash flow ratio} = \frac{\text{Price per share}}{\text{Cash flow per share}}$$

$$\text{Book value per share} = \frac{\text{Common equity}}{\text{Shares outstanding}}$$

$$\text{Market/book (M/B) ratio} = \frac{\text{Market price per share}}{\text{Book value per share}}$$

CHAPTER 4

$$FV_N = PV(1 + I)^N$$

$$PV = \frac{FV_N}{(1 + I)^N}$$

$$\text{PV of a perpetuity} = \frac{PMT}{I}$$

$$FVA_N = PMT\left[\frac{(1 + I)^N}{I} - \frac{1}{I}\right] = PMT\left[\frac{(1 + I)^N - 1}{I}\right]$$

$$FVA_{Due} = FVA_{Ordinary}(1 + I)$$

$$PVA_N = PMT\left[\frac{1}{I} - \frac{1}{I(1 + I)^N}\right] = PMT\left[\frac{1 - \dfrac{1}{(1 + I)^N}}{I}\right]$$

$$PVA_{Due} = PVA_{Ordinary}(1 + I)$$

$$PV_{\text{Uneven stream}} = \sum_{t=1}^{N} \frac{CF_t}{(1 + I)^t}$$

$$FV_{\text{Uneven stream}} = \sum_{t=1}^{N} CF_t(1 + I)^{N-t}$$

$$I_{PER} = \frac{I_{NOM}}{M}$$

$$APR = I_{PER}(M)$$

$$\text{Number of periods} = N(M)$$

$$FV_N = PV(1 + I_{PER})^{\text{Number of periods}} = PV\left(1 + \frac{I_{NOM}}{M}\right)^{MN}$$

$$EFF\% = (1 + I_{PER})^M - 1.0 = \left(1 + \frac{I_{NOM}}{M}\right)^M - 1.0$$

CHAPTER 5

$$V_B = \sum_{t=1}^{N} \frac{INT}{(1 + r_d)^t} + \frac{M}{(1 + r_d)^N}$$

$$\text{Semiannual payments: } V_B = \sum_{t=1}^{2N} \frac{INT/2}{(1 + r_d/2)^t} + \frac{M}{(1 + r_d/2)^{2N}}$$

$$\text{Yield to maturity: Bond price} = \sum_{t=1}^{N} \frac{INT}{(1 + YTM)^t} + \frac{M}{(1 + YTM)^N}$$

$$\text{Price of callable bond (if called at N)} = \sum_{t=1}^{N} \frac{INT}{(1 + r_d)^t} + \frac{\text{Call price}}{(1 + r_d)^N}$$

$$\text{Current yield} = \frac{\text{Annual interest}}{\text{Bond's current price}}$$

$$\text{Current yield} + \text{Capital gains yield} = \text{Yield to maturity}$$

$$r_d = r^* + IP + MRP + DRP + LP$$

$$IP_N = \frac{I_1 + I_2 + \cdots + I_N}{N}$$

CHAPTER 6

$$\text{Expected rate of return} = \hat{r} = \sum_{i=1}^{n} p_i r_i$$

$$\text{Historical average, } \bar{r}_{Avg} = \frac{\sum_{t=1}^{T} \bar{r}_t}{n}$$

$$\text{Variance} = \sigma^2 = \sum_{i=1}^{n} (r_i - \hat{r})^2 p_i$$

$$\text{Standard deviation} = \sigma = \sqrt{\sum_{i=1}^{n} (r_i - \hat{r})^2 p_i}$$

$$\text{Historical estimated } \sigma = S = \sqrt{\dfrac{\displaystyle\sum_{t=1}^{T} (\bar{r}_t - \bar{r}_{Avg})^2}{T - 1}}$$

$$\hat{r}_p = \sum_{i=1}^{n} w_i \hat{r}_i$$

$$\sigma_p = \sqrt{\sum_{i=1}^{n} (r_{pi} - \hat{r}_p)^2 P_i}$$

$$\text{Historical estimated } \rho = R = \dfrac{\displaystyle\sum_{t=1}^{T} (\bar{r}_{i,t} - \bar{r}_{i,Avg})(\bar{r}_{j,t} - \bar{r}_{j,Avg})}{\sqrt{\displaystyle\sum_{t=1}^{T} (\bar{r}_{i,t} - \bar{r}_{i,Avg})^2 \sum_{t=1}^{T} (\bar{r}_{j,t} - \bar{r}_{j,Avg})^2}}$$

$$COV_{iM} = \rho_{iM}\sigma_i\sigma_M$$

$$b_i = \left(\dfrac{\sigma_i}{\sigma_M}\right)\rho_{iM} = \dfrac{COV_{iM}}{\sigma_M^2}$$

$$b_p = \sum_{i=1}^{n} w_i b_i$$

Required return on stock market $= r_M$

Market risk premium $= RP_M = r_M - r_{RF}$

$RP_i = (r_M - r_{RF})b_i = (RP_M)b_i$

$SML = r_i = r_{RF} + (r_M - r_{RF})b_i = r_{RF} + RP_M b_i$

Fama-French: $(\bar{r}_{i,t} - \bar{r}_{RF,t}) = a_i + b_i(\bar{r}_{M,t} - \bar{r}_{RF,t}) + c_i(\bar{r}_{SMB,t}) + d_i(\bar{r}_{HML,t}) + e_{i,t}$

CHAPTER 7

V_{op} = Value of operations

  = PV of expected future free cash flows

$$= \sum_{t=1}^{\infty} \dfrac{FCF_t}{(1 + WACC)^t}$$

$$V_{op} \text{ (constant growth)} = \dfrac{FCF_1}{WACC - g_L} = \dfrac{FCF_0(1 + g_L)}{WACC - g_L}$$

$$V_{op} \text{ (for a perpetuity)} = \dfrac{FCF}{WACC}$$

$$\text{Horizon value (at time t)} = HV_t = V_{op} \text{ (at time t)} = \dfrac{FCF_t(1 + g_L)}{WACC - g_L} = \dfrac{FCF_{t+1}}{WACC - g_L}$$

Total intrinsic entity value $= V_{op}$ + Value of nonoperating assets

Intrinsic value of equity = Total intrinsic entity value − Preferred stock − Debt

$$V_{op} \text{ (at Horizon Year T)} = OpCap_T \left[1 + \frac{\left((1 + g_L) \dfrac{OP_T}{CR_T} - WACC \right)}{WACC - g_L} \right]$$

$$V_{op} \text{ (at Horizon Year T)} = OpCap_T \left[1 + \frac{(1 + g_L) ROIC_T - WACC}{WACC - g_L} \right]$$

$$\hat{P}_0 = \text{PV of expected future dividends} = \sum_{t=1}^{\infty} \frac{D_t}{(1 + r_s)^t}$$

Constant growth: $\hat{P}_0 = \dfrac{D_0(1 + g_L)}{r_s - g_L} = \dfrac{D_1}{r_s - g_L}$

Constant growth: $\hat{r}_s = \dfrac{D_1}{P_0} + g_L$

Expected dividend yield $= \dfrac{D_1}{P_0}$

Expected capital gains yield $= \dfrac{\hat{P}_1 - P_0}{P_0}$

$\hat{r}_s$ = Expected rate of return on stock = Expected dividend yield + Expected capital gains yield

$$= \frac{D_1}{P_0} + \frac{\hat{P}_1 - P_0}{P_0}$$

$\bar{r}_s$ = Actual dividend yield + Actual capital gains yield

For a zero growth stock, $\hat{P}_0 = \dfrac{D}{r_s}$

Horizon value of stock $= \hat{P}_T = \dfrac{D_{T+1}}{r_s - g_L} = \dfrac{D_T(1 + g_L)}{r_s - g_L}$

$$V_{ps} = \frac{D_{ps}}{r_{ps}}$$

$$\hat{r}_{ps} = \frac{D_{ps}}{V_{ps}}$$

CHAPTER 8

Exercise value = MAX[Current price of stock − Strike price, 0]

Number of stock shares in hedged portfolio $= N = \dfrac{C_u - C_d}{P_u - P_d}$

$$V_C = P[N(d_1)] - Xe^{-r_{RF}t}[N(d_2)]$$

$$d_1 = \frac{\ln(P/X) + [r_{RF} + (\sigma^2/2)]t}{\sigma\sqrt{t}}$$

$$d_2 = d_1 - \sigma\sqrt{t}$$

Put–call parity: Put option $= V_C - P + Xe^{-r_{RF}t}$

V of put $= P[N(d_1) - 1] - Xe^{-r_{RF}t}[N(d_2) - 1]$

CHAPTER 9

After-tax component cost of debt $= r_d(1 - T)$

$$M(1 - F) = \sum_{t=1}^{N} \frac{INT(1 - T)}{[1 + r_d(1 - T)]^t} + \frac{M}{[1 + r_d(1 - T)]^N}$$

$$r_{ps} = \frac{D_{ps}}{P_{ps}(1 - F)}$$

Market equilibrium: $\dfrac{\text{Expected}}{\text{rate of return}} = \hat{r}_M = \dfrac{D_1}{P_0} + g_L = r_{RF} + RP_M = r_M = \dfrac{\text{Required}}{\text{rate of return}}$

(*Note:* D_1, P_0, and g_L are for the market, not an individual company.)

Rep/Div = ratio of payouts via repurchases to payouts via dividends

$$r_M = \hat{r}_M = (1 + \text{Rep/Div})\frac{D_1}{P_0} + g_L$$

(*Note:* g_L is long-term growth rate in total payouts for the market; D_1 and P_0 are for the market, not an individual company.)

CAPM: $r_s = r_{RF} + b_i(RP_M)$

Dividend growth approach: $r_s = \hat{r}_s = \dfrac{D_1}{P_0} + $ Expected g in dividends per share

Own-bond yield-plus-judgmental-risk-premium: $r_s = \dfrac{\text{Company's own}}{\text{bond yield}} + \dfrac{\text{Judgmental}}{\text{risk premium}}$

g = (Retention rate)(ROE) = (1.0 − Payout rate)(ROE)

$$r_e = \hat{r}_e = \frac{D_1}{P_0(1 - F)} + g_L$$

$$WACC = w_d r_d(1 - T) + w_{std} r_{std}(1 - T) + w_{ps} r_{ps} + w_s r_s$$

CHAPTER 10

$$NPV = CF_0 + \frac{CF_1}{(1 + r)^1} + \frac{CF_2}{(1 + r)^2} + \cdots + \frac{CF_N}{(1 + r)^N}$$

$$= \sum_{t=0}^{N} \frac{CF_t}{(1 + r)^t}$$

IRR: $CF_0 + \dfrac{CF_1}{(1 + IRR)^1} + \dfrac{CF_2}{(1 + IRR)^2} + \cdots + \dfrac{CF_N}{(1 + IRR)^N} = 0$

$$NPV = \sum_{t=0}^{N} \frac{CF_t}{(1 + IRR)^t} = 0$$

MIRR: PV of costs = PV of terminal value

$$\sum_{t=0}^{N} \frac{COF_t}{(1+r)^t} = \frac{\sum_{t=0}^{N} CIF_t(1+r)^{N-t}}{(1+MIRR)^N}$$

$$PV \text{ of costs} = \frac{\text{Terminal value}}{(1+MIRR)^N}$$

$$PI = \frac{PV \text{ of future cash flows}}{\text{Initial cost}} = \frac{\sum_{t=1}^{N} \frac{CF_t}{(1+r)^t}}{CF_0}$$

$$\text{Payback} = \begin{array}{c} \text{Number of} \\ \text{years prior to} \\ \text{full recovery} \end{array} + \frac{\begin{array}{c} \text{Unrecovered cost} \\ \text{at start of year} \end{array}}{\begin{array}{c} \text{Cash flow during} \\ \text{full recovery year} \end{array}}$$

CHAPTER 11

$$\text{Project cash flow} = FCF = \begin{array}{c} \text{Investment outlay} \\ \text{cash flow} \end{array} + \begin{array}{c} \text{Operating} \\ \text{cash flow} \end{array} + \begin{array}{c} \text{NOWC} \\ \text{cash flow} \end{array} + \begin{array}{c} \text{Salvage} \\ \text{cash flow} \end{array}$$

$$\text{Expected NPV} = \sum_{i=1}^{n} P_i(NPV_i)$$

$$\sigma_{NPV} = \sqrt{\sum_{i=1}^{n} P_i(NPV_i - \text{Expected NPV})^2}$$

$$CV_{NPV} = \frac{\sigma_{NPV}}{E(NPV)}$$

CHAPTER 12

$$\begin{array}{c} \text{Additional} \\ \text{funds} \\ \text{needed} \end{array} = \begin{array}{c} \text{Required} \\ \text{asset} \\ \text{increase} \end{array} - \begin{array}{c} \text{Spontaneous} \\ \text{liability} \\ \text{increase} \end{array} - \begin{array}{c} \text{Increase in} \\ \text{retained} \\ \text{earnings} \end{array}$$

$$AFN = (A^*/S_0)\Delta S - (L^*/S_0)\Delta S - MS_1(1 - \text{Payout ratio})$$

$$\text{Self-supporting } g = \frac{M(1 - POR)(S_0)}{A_0^* - L_0^* - M(1 - POR)(S_0)}$$

$$\begin{array}{c} \text{Full} \\ \text{capacity} \\ \text{sales} \end{array} = \frac{\text{Actual sales}}{\begin{array}{c} \text{Percentage of capacity} \\ \text{at which fixed assets} \\ \text{were operated} \end{array}}$$

$$\text{Target fixed assets/Sales} = \frac{\text{Actual fixed assets}}{\text{Full capacity sales}}$$

$$\begin{array}{c} \text{Required level} \\ \text{of fixed assets} \end{array} = (\text{Target fixed assets/Sales})(\text{Projected sales})$$

CHAPTER 14

Residual distribution = Net income − [(Target equity ratio)(Total capital budget)]

Number of shares repurchased = $n_{Prior} - n_{Post} = \dfrac{Cash_{Rep}}{P_{Prior}}$

$$n_{Post} = n_{Prior} - \dfrac{Cash_{Rep}}{P_{Prior}} = n_{Prior} - \dfrac{Cash_{Rep}}{S_{Prior}/n_{Prior}} = n_{Prior}\left(1 - \dfrac{Cash_{Rep}}{S_{Prior}}\right)$$

CHAPTER 15

$$V_{op} = \sum_{t=1}^{\infty} \dfrac{FCF_t}{(1 + WACC)^t}$$

$$WACC = w_d(1 - T)r_d + w_s r_s$$

$$ROIC = \dfrac{NOPAT}{Capital} = \dfrac{EBIT(1 - T)}{Capital}$$

$$EBIT = PQ - VQ - F$$

$$Q_{BE} = \dfrac{F}{P - V}$$

MM, no taxes, Proposition I: $V_L = S_L + D$

MM, no taxes: $V_L = V_U$

MM, no taxes, Proposition II: $r_{sL} = r_{sU} + (r_{sU} - r_d)(D/E)$

MM, corporate taxes: $V_L = V_U + TD$

MM, corporate taxes, Proposition II: $r_{sL} = r_{sU} + (r_{sU} - r_d)(1 - T)(D/S)$

Miller, corporate and personal taxes: $V_L = V_U + \left[1 - \dfrac{(1 - T_c)(1 - T_s)}{(1 - T_d)}\right]D$

Hamada: $b = b_U[1 + (1 - T)(D/S)] = b_U[1 + (1 - T)(w_d/w_s)]$

Hamada: $b_U = b/[1 + (1 - T)(D/S)] = b/[1 + (1 - T)(w_d/w_s)]$

$r_s = r_{RF} + RP_M(b)$

$r_s = r_{RF}$ + Premium for business risk + Premium for financial risk

If g = 0: $V_{op} = \dfrac{FCF}{WACC} = \dfrac{NOPAT}{WACC} = \dfrac{EBIT(1 - T)}{WACC}$

Total corporate value = V_{op} + Value of short-term investments

S = Total corporate value − Value of all debt

$D = w_d V_{op}$

$S = (1 - w_d)V_{op}$

Cash raised by issuing debt = $D - D_0$

$P_{Prior} = S_{Prior}/n_{Prior}$

$$P_{Post} = P_{Prior}$$

$$n_{Post} = n_{Prior}\left[\frac{V_{opNew} - D_{New}}{V_{opNew} - D_{Old}}\right]$$

$$n_{Post} = n_{Prior} - (D_{New} - D_{Old})/P_{Prior}$$

$$P_{Post} = \frac{V_{opNew} - D_{Old}}{n_{Prior}}$$

$$V_0 = P[N(d_1)] - Xe^{-r_{RF}t}[N(d_2)]$$

$$d_1 = \frac{\ln(P/X) + (r_{RF} + \sigma^2/2)t}{\sigma\sqrt{t}} \text{ and } d_2 = d_1 - \sigma\sqrt{t}$$

$$EPS = NI/n$$

$$NI = (EBIT - r_d D)(1 - T)$$

CHAPTER 16

$$\text{Inventory conversion period} = \frac{\text{Inventory}}{(\text{Cost of goods sold})/365}$$

$$\text{Average collection period (ASO)} = \text{Days sales outstanding (DSO)} = \frac{\text{Receivables}}{\text{Daily Sales}}$$

$$\text{Payables deferral period} = \frac{\text{Payables}}{(\text{Cost of goods sold})/365}$$

$$\begin{matrix} \text{Cash} \\ \text{conversion} \\ \text{cycle} \end{matrix} = \begin{matrix} \text{Inventory} \\ \text{conversion} \\ \text{period} \end{matrix} + \begin{matrix} \text{Average} \\ \text{collection} \\ \text{period} \end{matrix} - \begin{matrix} \text{Payables} \\ \text{deferral} \\ \text{period} \end{matrix}$$

$$\begin{matrix} \text{Accounts} \\ \text{receivable} \end{matrix} = \begin{matrix} \text{Credit sales} \\ \text{per day} \end{matrix} \times \begin{matrix} \text{Length of} \\ \text{collection period} \end{matrix}$$

$$\text{Receivables} = (\text{Daily sales})(\text{DSO})$$

$$\begin{matrix} \text{Nominal annual cost} \\ \text{of trade credit} \end{matrix} = \frac{\text{Discount percentage}}{100 - \begin{matrix}\text{Discount}\\\text{percentage}\end{matrix}} \times \frac{365}{\begin{matrix}\text{Days credit is}\\\text{outstanding}\end{matrix} - \begin{matrix}\text{Discount}\\\text{period}\end{matrix}}$$

CHAPTER 17

$$\text{Single-period interest rate parity: } \frac{\text{Forward exchange rate}}{\text{Spot exchange rate}} = \frac{1 + r_h}{1 + r_f}$$

$$\text{Expected t-year forward exchange rate} = (\text{Spot rate})\left(\frac{1 + r_h}{1 + r_f}\right)^t$$

$$P_h = (P_f)(\text{Spot rate})$$

$$\text{Spot rate} = \frac{P_h}{P_f}$$

CHAPTER 18

Amount left on table = (Closing price – Offer price)(Number of shares)

$$\text{Percentage shares owned by new investors} = \frac{n_{New}}{n_{New} + n_{Existing}}$$

$$n_{New} = \frac{(\% \text{ owned by new investors}) n_{Existing}}{1 - (\% \text{ owned by new investors})}$$

$$V_{Post\text{-}IPO} = V_{Pre\text{-}IPO} + P_{Offer}(1 - F)n_{New}$$

$$P_{Offer} = \left[\frac{V_{Pre-IPO}}{F(n_{New}) + n_{Existing}} \right]$$

$$\% \text{ of shares required by new investors} = \frac{\text{Investment}}{(1 - F)\,\text{Investment} + V_{Pre-IPO}}$$

CHAPTER 19

NAL = PV cost of owning − PV cost of leasing

CHAPTER 20

$$\begin{array}{l}\text{Price paid for} \\ \text{bond with warrants}\end{array} = \begin{array}{l}\text{Straight-debt} \\ \text{value of bond}\end{array} + \begin{array}{l}\text{Value of} \\ \text{warrants}\end{array}$$

$$\text{Conversion price} = P_c = \frac{\text{Par value of bond given up}}{\text{Shares received}}$$

$$= \frac{\text{Par value of bond given up}}{\text{CR}}$$

$$\text{Conversion ratio} = CR = \frac{\text{Par value of bond given up}}{P_c}$$

CHAPTER 21

MM, no taxes:

$$V_L = V_U = \frac{EBIT}{WACC} = \frac{EBIT}{r_{sU}}$$

$$r_{sL} = r_{sU} + \text{Risk premium} = r_{sU} + (r_{sU} - r_d)(D/S)$$

MM, corporate taxes:

$$V_L = V_U + TD$$

$$V_U = S = \frac{EBIT(1 - T)}{r_{sU}}$$

$$r_{sL} = r_{sU} + (r_{sU} - r_d)(1 - T)(D/S)$$

General adjusted present value (APV):

$$V_L = V_U + V_{\text{Tax shield}}$$

$$V_{\text{Tax shield}} = \frac{r_d TD}{r_{TS} - g}$$

$$V_L = V_U + \left(\frac{r_d}{r_{TS} - g}\right) TD$$

Compressed adjusted present value (APV), $r_{TS} = r_{sU}$:

$$V_L = V_U + \left(\frac{r_d TD}{r_{sU} - g}\right)$$

$$r_{sL} = r_{sU} + (r_{sU} - r_d)\frac{D}{S}$$

$$b = b_U + (b_U - b_D)\frac{D}{S}$$

$$r_{sU} = w_s r_{sL} + w_d r_d$$

Tax savings = (Interest expense)(Tax rate)

$$\begin{array}{l}\text{Horizon value of} \\ \text{unlevered firm}\end{array} = HV_{U,N} = \frac{FCF_{N+1}}{r_{sU} - g} = \frac{FCF_N(1 + g)}{r_{sU} - g}$$

$$\begin{array}{l}\text{Horizon value of} \\ \text{tax shield}\end{array} = HV_{TS,N} = \frac{TS_{N+1}}{r_{sU} - g} = \frac{TS_N(1 + g)}{r_{sU} - g}$$

$$V_{\text{Unlevered}} = \sum_{t=1}^{N} \frac{FCF_t}{(1 + r_{sU})^t} + \frac{HV_{U,N}}{(1 + r_{sU})^N}$$

$$V_{\text{Tax shield}} = \sum_{t=1}^{N} \frac{TS_t}{(1 + r_{sU})^t} + \frac{HV_{TS,N}}{(1 + r_{sU})^N}$$

Value of operations = $V_{op} = V_{\text{Unlevered}} + V_{\text{Tax shield}}$

Free cash flow to equity:

$$FCFE = \begin{array}{c}\text{Free} \\ \text{cash flow}\end{array} - \begin{array}{c}\text{After-tax} \\ \text{interest expense}\end{array} - \begin{array}{c}\text{Principal} \\ \text{payments}\end{array} + \begin{array}{c}\text{Newly issued} \\ \text{debt}\end{array}$$

$$= \begin{array}{c}\text{Free} \\ \text{cash flow}\end{array} - \begin{array}{c}\text{Interest} \\ \text{expense}\end{array} + \begin{array}{c}\text{Interest} \\ \text{tax shield}\end{array} + \begin{array}{c}\text{Net change} \\ \text{in debt}\end{array}$$

$$FCFE = \text{Net income} - \begin{array}{c}\text{Net investment in} \\ \text{operating capital}\end{array} + \begin{array}{c}\text{Net change} \\ \text{in debt}\end{array}$$

$$HV_{FCFE,N} = \frac{FCFE_{N+1}}{r_{sL} - g} = \frac{FCFE_N(1 + g)}{r_{sL} - g}$$

$$V_{FCFE} = \sum_{t=1}^{N} \frac{FCFE_t}{(1 + r_{sL})^t} + \frac{HV_{FCFE,N}}{(1 + r_{sL})^N}$$

$$S = V_{FCFE} + \text{Nonoperating assets}$$

CHAPTER 22

$$\frac{\text{Total value of shares to target shareholders}}{\text{Total post-merger value of equity}} = \frac{\text{Percent required by}}{\text{target stockholders}} = \frac{n_{New}}{n_{New} + n_{Old}}$$

CHAPTER 25

$$\hat{r}_p = w_A \hat{r}_A + (1 - w_A)\hat{r}_B$$

Portfolio SD = $\sigma_p = \sqrt{w_A^2 \sigma_A^2 + (1 - w_A)^2 \sigma_B^2 + 2w_A(1 - w_A)\rho_{AB}\sigma_A\sigma_B}$

Minimum-risk portfolio: $w_A = \dfrac{\sigma_B(\sigma_B - \rho_{AB}\sigma_A)}{\sigma_A^2 + \sigma_B^2 - 2\rho_{AB}\sigma_A\sigma_B}$

$$\hat{r}_p = \sum_{i=1}^{N} (w_i \hat{r}_i)$$

$$\sigma_p^2 = \sum_{i=1}^{N} \sum_{j=1}^{N} (w_i w_j \sigma_i \sigma_j \rho_{ij})$$

$$\sigma_p^2 = \sum_{i=1}^{N} w_i^2 \sigma_i^2 + \sum_{i=1}^{N} \sum_{\substack{j=1 \\ j \neq i}}^{N} w_i \sigma_i w_j \sigma_j \rho_{ij}$$

$$\sigma_p = \sqrt{(1 - w_{RF})^2 \sigma_M^2} = (1 - w_{RF})\sigma_M$$

CML: $\hat{r}_p = r_{RF} + \left(\dfrac{\hat{r}_M - r_{RF}}{\sigma_M}\right)\sigma_p$

$$r_i = r_{RF} + \frac{(r_M - r_{RF})}{\sigma_M}\left(\frac{\text{Cov}(r_i, r_M)}{\sigma_M}\right) = r_{RF} + (r_M - r_{RF})\left(\frac{\text{Cov}(r_i, r_M)}{\sigma_M^2}\right)$$

$$b_i = \frac{\text{Covariance between Stock i and the market}}{\text{Variance of market returns}} = \frac{\text{Cov}(r_i, r_M)}{\sigma_M^2} = \frac{\rho_{iM}\sigma_i\sigma_M}{\sigma_M^2} = \rho_{iM}\left(\frac{\sigma_i}{\sigma_M}\right)$$

SML = $r_i = r_{RF} + (r_M - r_{RF})b_i = r_{RF} + (RP_M)b_i$

Sharpe reward-to-variability ratio = $\dfrac{r_{p,Avg} - r_{RF,Avg}}{\sigma \text{ of }(r_{p,Avg} - r_{RF,Avg})}$

Treynor reward-to-volatility ratio = $\dfrac{r_{p,Avg} - r_{RF,Avg}}{b_p}$

$$\sigma_i^2 = b_i^2 \sigma_M^2 + \sigma_{e_i}^2$$

APT: $r_i = r_{RF} + (r_1 - r_{RF})b_{i1} + \cdots + (r_j - r_{RF})b_{ij}$

CHAPTER 26

$$CV = \frac{\sigma(\text{PV of future CF})}{E(\text{PV of future CF})}$$

Variance of project's rate of return: $\sigma^2 = \dfrac{\ln(CV^2 + 1)}{t}$

Glossary

A

2017 Tax Cut and Jobs Creation Act The unofficial name of an Act of Congress signed into law in December 2017. Among its many changes, the Act replaces the previous graduated corporate tax brackets (which had a top rate of 35%) with a flat tax of 21%. The Act also suspends for 2018–2025 the 2017 personal brackets and rates of 2017 and temporarily replaces them with brackets and rates that reduce taxes for most personal filers, especially for those with very high income. In 2026, the Act returns brackets and rates set to their 2017 levels (after adjusting for inflation).

401(k) retirement plan Employees' contributions, matching contributions from the sponsoring employer (if these are included in the plan), and profits on the investments are not taxable until withdrawn.

501(c)(3) corporation A charitable organization that meets the IRS requirements for tax-exempt status under the tax code section 501(c)(3).

abandonment option Allows a company to reduce the capacity of its output in response to changing market conditions. This includes the option to contract production or abandon a project if market conditions deteriorate too much.

abnormal yield curve A downward-sloping yield curve. Also called an inverted yield curve.

absolute priority doctrine States that claims must be paid in strict accordance with the priority of each claim, regardless of the consequence to other claimants.

accelerated depreciation method Depreciation method that has larger depreciation rates in the early years when compared to straight-line depreciation and has smaller depreciation rates in the latter years.

account payable Represents the amount a company owes a supplier when purchasing a product or service with credit extended by the seller. It is a current liability from the purchaser's perspective and a current asset from the

seller's. The balance of the account payable is reduced to zero when the company actually pays its supplier. Often just called payables.

account receivable Represents the amount a customer owes a company when the company extends credit to the purchaser of a product or service. It is a current asset from the selling company's perspective and a current liability from the purchaser's. The balance of the account receivable is reduced to zero when the company collects a cash payment from the purchaser. Often just called receivables.

accounting beta Estimated by using *accounting return on assets* instead of stock returns.

accounting beta method Method of estimating a divisional beta by running a regression of the division's *accounting return on assets* against the *average return on assets* for the market.

accounting income Income as defined by Generally Accepted Accounting Principles (GAAP) and reported on the income statement. Also called accounting profit, earnings, net income, or profit.

accounting profit Income as defined by Generally Accepted Accounting Principles (GAAP) and reported on the income statement. Also called accounting income, earnings, net income, or profit.

Accounting Standards Update (ASU) 2016-02 A change in FASB accounting standards that requires virtually all leases of more than 1 year in length to be capitalized.

accredited investors Officers and directors of a privately held company, high-wealth individuals, and institutional investors. Allowed to purchase securities in a nonregistered private placement, but cannot subsequently sell their securities in the secondary market to the general public.

accruals Amounts owed (i.e., accrued) for expense but that have not yet been paid. Common examples are wages and taxes, which are paid periodically rather than daily.

acid test ratio Indicates the extent to which current liabilities are covered by the most liquid current assets; it is found by subtracting inventories from current assets and then dividing this difference by current liabilities. It is also called the quick ratio.

acquiring company A company that seeks to acquire another firm.

actively managed fund Mutual fund that has higher fees than a passively managed fund but that seeks to invest in undervalued securities within a particular category, such as growth stocks.

actual rate of return on stock, $\bar{r}_s$ The actual rate of return on a share of stock during a particular holding period. Also called the realized rate of return on stock.

actuarial rate of return the discount rate used to determine the present value of future benefits under a defined benefits pension plan.

additional funds needed (AFN) Amount of financing required to implement an operating plan, given the preliminary choices of capital structure and dividend payout.

additional funds needed (AFN) equation A simplified method to forecast external financing requirements for only 1 year ahead. It assumes that all asset-to-sales ratios are identical, all spontaneous liabilities-to-sales ratios are identical, and all cost-to-sales ratios are identical. Given these assumptions, the AFN is equal to the required increase in assets minus the increase in spontaneous liabilities minus the increase in retained earnings.

add-on interest Interest is calculated over the life of the loan as the product of the initial amount borrowed, the number of years until full repayment, and the annual rate on the loan. This total interest charge is added to the loan amount to get the total amount of payments. The total amount of payments is divided by the number of payments periods to get an equal "installment" payment each period. This raises the effective cost of the loan.

adjustable rate preferred stock Instead of fixed dividends, has dividend payments that are linked to rates on Treasury securities.

adjusted beta Adjustment to historical beta that reflects knowledge of the distribution of true betas (i.e., average beta is equal to 1). If estimated beta is greater than 1, then adjusted beta is between 1 and the estimated beta; if the estimated beta is less than 1, the adjusted beta is between the estimated beta and 1.

adjusted present value approach (APV) The value of an unlevered firm plus the value of side effects due to leverage. These often include the present value of annual tax savings each year and the present value of any expected financial distress costs.

adjustment bureau Group sponsored by a local credit managers' association for the purpose of helping creditors and borrowers work out problems without having to go through formal bankruptcy proceedings.

after-tax cost of debt, $(1 - T)r_d$ A company's after-tax cost of providing the required rate of return on debt.

agency conflict Conflicts between owners, managers, employees, and creditors occurring when one of these groups acts on its own behalf at the expense of one or more of the other groups.

agency cost An expense, either direct or indirect, that is borne by a principal as a result of having delegated authority to an agent. An example is the costs borne by shareholders to encourage managers to maximize a firm's stock price rather than act in their own self-interests. These costs may also arise from lost efficiency and the expense of monitoring management to ensure that debtholders' rights are protected.

agency debt Debt issued by federal agencies such as the Tennessee Value Authority. Agency debt is not officially backed by the full faith and credit of the U.S. government, but investors assume that the government implicitly guarantees this debt, so these bonds carry interest rates only slightly higher than Treasury bonds.

agency problem Occurs when owners, managers, employees, and creditors can act to benefit themselves at the expense of others.

agency relationship Arises whenever someone (the principal) hires someone (an agent) to perform a service and gives the agent decision-making authority to act on behalf of the principal.

agent A person or organization to whom a principal has delegated decision-making authority, usually with the intent for the agent to act on behalf of the principal.

aggressive approach (for short-term financing) Refers to a policy in which a firm finances all of its fixed assets with long-term capital but part of its permanent current assets with short-term bank loans.

aging schedule Breaks down accounts receivable according to how long they have been outstanding. This gives the firm a more complete picture of the structure of accounts receivable than that provided by days sales outstanding.

alternative minimum tax (AMT) A provision of the U.S. Tax Code to ensure that a filer cannot use tax loopholes to avoid paying any personal tax at all. Before 2018, there was a corporate AMT, but it was eliminated in the 2017 Tax Cut and Jobs Act.

alternative trading system (ATS) A type of trading venue that can be registered with the SEC but that does not have as stringent requirements as a registered stock exchange. Commonly called "dark pools" because they do not have to report any pre-trade quotes.

American option An option which may be exercised on or before the exercise date.

amortization expense A noncash charge on the income statement to reflect a decrease in value of an intangible asset, such as goodwill.

amortization schedule A table that breaks down the periodic fixed payment of an installment loan into its principal and interest components.

amortized loan A loan that is repaid in equal periodic amounts (or "killed off") over time.

anchoring bias Occurs when predictions of future events are influenced too heavily by recent events.

angel investors Wealthy individual investors providing early external financing for a start-up company by purchasing equity. Often have helpful experience and industry contacts.

annual compounding When interest is compounded once per year.

annual percentage rate (APR) The rate required to be reported by the Truth in Lending Act. It is the nominal annual interest rate found by multiplying the periodic rate by the number of periods.

annual report A report issued annually by a corporation to its stockholders. It contains basic financial statements as well as management's opinion of the past year's operations and the firm's future prospects.

annual vesting A certain percentage of the options in a grant vest each year. For example, one-third of the options in the grant might vest each year.

annuity A series of payments of a fixed amount for a specified number of periods.

annuity due An annuity with payments occurring at the beginning of each period.

APR The rate required to be reported by the Truth in Lending Act. It is the nominal annual interest rate found by multiplying the periodic rate by the number of periods.

arbitrage The simultaneous buying and selling of the same commodity or security in two different markets at different prices, thus yielding a risk-free return. The person engaging in arbitrage has no personal funds invested, has no risk, and has a guaranteed payoff.

Arbitrage Pricing Theory (APT) An approach to measuring the equilibrium risk–return relationship for a given stock as a function of multiple factors, rather than the single factor (the market return) used by the CAPM. The APT is based on complex mathematical and statistical theory, and it can account for several factors (such as GNP and the level of inflation) in determining the required return for a particular stock.

arrearages Preferred dividends that have not been paid and hence are "in arrears."

ask quote (or ask price) Lowest price among the investors that are willing to sell a particular stock or other security.

asset allocation models Used by pension fund managers to make funding and investment decisions; these models use computer simulations to examine the risk/return characteristics of portfolios with various mixes of assets.

asset management ratios A set of ratios that measure how effectively a firm is managing its assets. Also called efficiency ratios.

asset-backed security A new security that represents a claim on a specific portfolio of financial assets, such as a portfolio of credit card debts or mortgages.

assignee (in informal liquidation) Third party in an informal liquidation, to whom title of debtor's assets is transferred for the purpose of liquidating the assets.

assignment (in informal liquidation) An informal procedure for liquidating debts that transfers title to a debtor's assets to a third person, known as an assignee or trustee, who then sells the assets.

asymmetric hedge Occurs for a derivative in which the payoff from a dollar increase in the underlying asset does not have exactly the opposite effect of a dollar decrease in the underlying asset. For example, consider a call option's payoffs when the current price of the underlying asset is equal to the option's strike price. A $1 increase in the asset's price causes a $1 increase in the option's payoff, whereas a $1 decline in the asset's price doesn't change the payoff.

asymmetric information When managers have more information than investors. This can cause investors to interpret new stock issues as signals that managers believe the stock is overvalued, which in turn causes managers to have a preferred "pecking order" of financing: (1) retained earnings, followed by (2) debt, and then (3) new common stock.

at par A bond trades at par when its price is equal to its face value.

attainable set Represents all portfolios that can be constructed from a given set of stocks. Also known as the feasible set.

automated matching engine Part of a computer system in which buyers and sellers post orders and then let the computer automatically match and execute trades.

automated trading platform Computer system in which buyers and sellers post orders. Trades are automatically executed for matching orders.

automatic stay (in bankruptcy) Bankruptcy provision forced on all lenders to prevent any from foreclosing to collect on their loans. Allows borrowing firm to remain a going concern.

average collection period (ACP) Used to appraise accounts receivable and indicates the length of time the firm must wait after making a sale before receiving cash. It is found by dividing receivables by average daily sales. Also called the days sales outstanding and receivables conversion period.

average return, $\bar{r}_{Avg}$ The average return from a sample period of past actual returns.

average tax rate Calculated by taking the total amount of tax paid divided by taxable income.

B

bait and switch Strategy of raising funds through debt financing and investing the funds in riskier projects than anticipated by the lenders.

balance of trade Level of imports relative to exports. A deficit occurs when businesses and individuals in the United States import more goods from foreign countries than are exported. A surplus occurs when exports are greater than imports. Also called the foreign trade balance and the trade balance.

balance sheet A statement of the firm's financial position at a specific point in time. The firm's assets are listed on the left-hand side of the balance sheet; the right-hand side shows its liabilities and equity, or the claims against these assets.

banker's acceptance Created when an importer's bank promises to accept a postdated check written to an exporter even if there are insufficient funds in the importer's account. If the bank is strong, then this financial instrument virtually eliminates credit risk.

bankruptcy Economic bankruptcy occurs when a company is insolvent because (1) its debt and other claims exceed the market value of it's assets or (2) it does not have enough cash to meet its interest and principal payments. Legal bankruptcy occurs when a company or its creditors file for bankruptcy in the United States Bankruptcy Court.

bankruptcy costs Direct costs from bankruptcy filings, including legal expenses, accounting expenses, and liquidation of assets at below-market value. Indirect costs include other financial distress costs, including employee turnover, reduced employee productivity, reduced product quality due to cost-cutting measures, reduction in credit provide by suppliers, loss of customers, and higher interest rates demanded by lenders.

Bankruptcy Reform Act of 1978 Enacted to speed up and streamline bankruptcy proceedings. This law represented a shift to a relative priority doctrine of creditors' claims.

basic earning power (BEP) ratio Calculated by dividing earnings before interest and taxes by total assets. This ratio shows the raw earning power of the firm's assets before the influence of taxes and leverage.

basis point Equal to 1/100 of a percentage point. For example, 0.25 percentage points are equal to 25 basis points. A decline in interest rates from 4.45% to 4.20% means that rates have fallen by 25 basis points.

Baumol model A model for establishing the firm's target cash balance that closely resembles the economic ordering quantity model used for inventory. The model assumes (1) that the firm uses cash at a steady, predictable rate, (2) that the firm's cash inflows from operations also occur at a steady, predictable rate, and

(3) that its net cash outflows therefore also occur at a steady rate. The model balances the opportunity cost of holding cash against the transactions costs associated with replenishing the cash account.

b_d, debt beta A measure of the amount of risk that debt contributes to a well-diversified portfolio. Calculated as $b_d = (\sigma_d/\sigma_M)\rho_{d,M}$, where σ_d is the standard deviation of debt's return, σ_M is the standard deviation of the market return, and $\sigma_{d,M}$ is the correlation between debt and the market.

behavioral finance A field of study that analyzes investor behavior as a result of psychological traits. It does not assume that investors necessarily behave rationally and instead focuses on irrational, but predictable, financial decisions.

benchmark company A leading competitor that is selected by a company for comparative purposes.

benchmarking When a firm compares its ratios to other leading (benchmark) companies in the same industry.

benefit corporation (B-Corp) Corporate form that expands directors' fiduciary responsibilities to include other interests than shareholders'.

best efforts basis A type of contract with an investment banker when issuing stock. In a best efforts sale, the investment banker is only committed to making every effort to sell the stock at the offering price. In this case, the issuing firm bears the risk that the new issue will not be fully subscribed.

beta coefficient, b_i A measure of the amount of risk that an individual Stock i contributes to a well-diversified portfolio. Calculated as $b_i = (\sigma_i/\sigma_M)\rho_{i,M}$, where σ_i is the standard deviation of Stock i's return, σ_M is the standard deviation of the market return, and $\sigma_{i,M}$ is the correlation between Stock i and the market.

beta risk The risk that an individual stock's beta (or an individual project's beta) contributes to a well-diversified portfolio. Also called market risk.

b_i, beta coefficient A measure of the amount of risk that an individual Stock i contributes to a well-diversified portfolio. Calculated as $b_i = (\sigma_i/\sigma_M)\rho_{i,M}$, where σ_i is the standard deviation of Stock i's return, σ_M is the standard deviation of the market return, and $\sigma_{i,M}$ is the correlation between Stock i and the market.

bid quote (or bid price) Price at which investor is willing to buy a stock or other security.

bid-ask spread The ask price minus the bid price for a security.

binomial approach A method of determining an option's value by assuming that the underlying asset's value can change to only one of two values at the end of a time period. For example, the binomial method might assume that a stock's price can only go up by 15% or down by 10% during the next year.

binomial lattice Occurs when an underlying asset's value can change to only one of two values at the end of a time period. Changes in subsequent periods depend upon the changes in previous periods. The resulting path of possible values resembles a lattice.

bird-in-the-hand theory Assumes that investors value a dollar of dividends more highly than a dollar of expected capital gains, because a certain dividend is less risky than a possible capital gain. This theory implies that a high-dividend stock has a higher price and lower required return, all else held equal.

Black-Scholes option pricing model A model to estimate the value of a call option. It is widely used by options traders.

blocked currency A currency that cannot be traded freely in the international currency markets and cannot be exchanged at current market rates but must be exchanged at a rate set by the country's government. Often called a soft currency or a nonconvertible currency.

board of trustees Group of community leaders who control a tax-exempt, charitable organization. Members of the board of trustees must have no direct economic interest in the organization.

bond A promissory note issued by a business or a governmental unit.

bond covenant Provisions in a bond indenture that cover such points as the conditions under which the issuer can pay off the bonds prior to maturity, the levels at which certain ratios must be maintained if the company is to issue additional debt, and restrictions against the payment of dividends unless earnings meet certain specifications. Also called a covenant or a restrictive covenant.

bond insurance Protects investors against default by the issuer and provides credit enhancement to the bond issue.

bond rating Reflects the probability that a bond will go into default. Bonds rated AAA have the least probability of defaulting.

bond spread The difference between the yield of a bond relative to another bond with less risk.

bonus depreciation Allows projects to be depreciated even more quickly than the Modified Accelerated Cost Recovery System (MACRS). Congress occasionally changes the tax code to temporarily add bonus depreciation, so it is not a permanent depreciation method.

book-building (IPO) Process of investment banker recording the number of shares each investor is willing to buy in an IPO.

book value Values of assets, liabilities, or equity as reported on financial statements.

book value per share Common equity divided by the number of shares outstanding.

branch of decision tree A possible path in a decision tree arising.

break-even analysis A form of sensitivity analysis that identifies the level of an input that produces an output of exactly zero. Often used to find the value of a project's input needed for the project to have an NPV of zero.

break-even point The level of unit sales at which costs equal revenues. Also called the operating break-even point.

breakup value A firm's value if its assets are sold off in pieces.

broker Person or organization that registers with the SEC to buy and sell stocks on behalf of clients. Brokers must also follow state and industry licensing and registration requirements.

brokerage firm A company that employs registered brokers buy and sell stocks on behalf of clients.

broker-dealer A broker that also is registered so that it can buy and sell for itself when it acts as a market maker. Broker-dealers can be individuals, companies, or subsidiaries of a larger financial service company company.

broker-dealer network A network in which a broker-dealer makes a market, usually bypassing stock exchanges. The broker-dealer can trade for its clients or for itself.

b_{TS}, tax shield beta A measure of the amount of risk that the tax shield contributes to a well-diversified portfolio. Calculated as $b_{TS} = (\sigma_{TS}/\sigma_M)\rho_{TS,M}$, where σ_{TS} is the

standard deviation of the tax shield, σ_M is the standard deviation of the market return, and $\rho_{TS,M}$ is the correlation between the tax shield and the market.

b_U, unlevered beta The beta that a firm would have if it had no debt. Can be estimated using the Hamada equation: $b_U = b/[1 + (1 - T)(D/S)] = b/[1 + (1 - T)(w_d/w_s)]$.

business risk The risk inherent in the operations of the firm, prior to the financing decision. Thus, business risk is the uncertainty inherent in future operating income or earnings before interest and taxes. Business risk is caused by many factors; two of the most important are sales variability and operating leverage.

buy forward (in a forward contract) Taking a long position to buy a specified amount of an asset (such as wheat) at a specified price and a specified time.

bylaws Set of rules drawn up by the founders of the corporation to specify how it will be governed.

C

call option An option that allows the holder to buy the asset at some predetermined price within a specified period of time.

call premium The extra amount above the par value that a company must pay if it calls a bond that has a call provision. The premium generally declines over time.

call protection Feature stating that a callable bond may not be called until a specified number of years after issue have passed. This is also known as a deferred call provision.

call provision Gives the issuing corporation the right to call the bonds for redemption. The call provision generally states that if the bonds are called then the company must pay the bondholders an amount greater than the par value, or a call premium. Most bonds contain a call provision.

callable bond Bond that gives the issuing corporation the right to call the bonds for redemption. The call provision generally states that if the bonds are called then the company must pay the bondholders an amount greater than the par value, or a call premium. Most bonds contain a call provision.

cannibalization A type of externality in capital budgeting in which the introduction of a new product causes the sales of existing products in the firm to decrease.

Capital Asset Pricing Model (CAPM) A model based on the proposition that any stock's required rate of return is equal to the risk-free rate of return plus a risk premium reflecting only the risk remaining after diversification. The CAPM equation is $r_i = r_{RF} + b_i(r_M - r_{RF})$.

capital assets Assets such as stocks, bonds, and real estate.

capital budget Outlines the planned expenditures on fixed assets.

capital budgeting The whole process of analyzing projects and deciding whether they should be included in the planned expenditures on fixed assets.

capital components Sources of investor-supplied capital used to determine the weighted average cost of capital, including common stock, preferred stock, and long-term debt. Short-term debt is a capital component for those companies using it as a permanent source of financing.

capital gain (loss) The profit (loss) from the sale of a capital asset for more (less) than its purchase price. If an asset is purchased and sold within a year, then it is a short-term gain (or loss); otherwise, it is a long-term gain (or loss).

capital gains yield Results from changing prices and is calculated as $(P_1 - P_0)/P_0$, where P_0 is the beginning-of-period price and P_1 is the end-of-period price.

capital gains yield (on a bond) The rate of return due to a change in a bond's price. The total yield on a bond is equal to the sum of the current yield and the expected capital gains yield.

capital intensity ratio, $A_0{}^*/S_0$ The dollar amount of assets required to produce a dollar of sales, defined as the assets at Time 0 (A_0) divided by the sales at Time 0 (S_0). If all assets are used in operations (i.e., there are no short-term investments), the capital intensity ratio is the reciprocal of the total assets turnover ratio.

capitalize (a lease) Report a lease on the balance sheets. Calculate the present value of future lease payments and add to balance sheets both as a liability and as an asset.

capital lease Covers the entire expected life of the equipment; does not provide for maintenance service, is not cancellable, and is fully amortized. Also called a financial lease.

capital market Capital markets are the financial markets for long-term debt and corporate stocks. The New York Stock Exchange is an example of a capital market.

Capital Market Line (CML) Shows the relationship between the expected return and standard deviation for the set of optimal portfolios: $\hat{r}_p = r_{RF} + [(\hat{r}_M - r_{RF})/\sigma_M] \sigma_p$.

capital rationing Occurs when management places a constraint on the size of the firm's capital budget during a particular period.

capital requirement (CR) ratio Total net operating capital divided by sales. Measures how much total net operating must be tied up to generate a dollar of sales.

capital structure The manner in which a firm's assets are financed; that is, the right side of the balance sheet. Capital structure is normally expressed as the percentage of each type of capital used by the firm such as debt, preferred stock, and common equity.

capital structure decision Company's choice of a target capital structure, average maturity of its debt, and the specific types of financing it decides to use at any particular time.

capital surplus The difference between the amount investors paid for newly issues stock shares and the par value of those shares. Also called paid-in capital.

CAPM, Capital Asset Pricing Model A model based on the proposition that any stock's required rate of return is equal to the risk-free rate of return plus a risk premium reflecting only the risk remaining after diversification. The CAPM equation is $r_i = r_{RF} + b_i(r_M - r_{RF})$.

carried interest A type of compensation received by the manager of a venture capital fund, hedge fund, or private equity fund. It is defined as a percentage, often 20%, of any profits generated by the fund's investments even though the fund manager usually invests a very small amount (around 1% to 2%) of the total investment. phones. It is in addition to the fund manager's annual compensation that is usually about 2% of the total invested capital under management.

carrying cost Cost that generally rises in direct proportion to the average amount of inventory carried, such as financing costs, storage costs, spoilage, and obsolescence.

cash balance plan A type of defined benefits plan in which benefits are defined in terms of the cash balance in the employee's account rather than monthly salary.

cash budget A schedule showing net cash flows (receipts, disbursements), actual cash balances, and target cash balances for a firm over a specified period.

cash conversion cycle The length of time between the firm's actual cash expenditures on productive resources (materials and labor) and its own cash receipts from the sale of products (that is, the length of time between paying for labor and materials and collecting on receivables). Thus, the cash conversion cycle equals the length of time the firm has funds tied up in current assets.

cash discounts (in credit terms) A provision in credit terms: A percentage reduction in the sales price if the purchaser pays in cash before the end of the specified discount period. Otherwise, the full price is due at the end of the regular credit period. Also called discounts, cash discounts, or trade discounts.

CDO, collateralized debt obligation Created when large numbers of mortgages are bundled into pools to create new securities that are then sliced into tranches; the tranches are re-combined and re-divided into securities called CDOs.

CDS, credit default swap Derivative in which a counterparty pays if a specified debt instrument goes into default; similar to insurance on a bond.

certainty equivalent method A method of discounting risky cash flows by finding the risk-free cash flow that is worth the same to the investor as the risky cash flow. This certainty equivalent cash flow is then discounted at the risk-free rate.

Chapter 11 bankruptcy The 11th chapter of the bankruptcy statutes, regulates reorganization in a bankruptcy. Filed by a borrower to prevent a lender from filing a bankruptcy claim and seizing assets.

Chapter 7 bankruptcy The 7th chapter of the bankruptcy statutes, regulates liquidation in a bankruptcy. Filed by a borrower to prevent a lender from filing a bankruptcy claim and seizing assets.

characteristic line Obtained by regressing the historical returns on a particular stock against the historical returns on the general stock market. The slope of the characteristic line is the stock's beta, which measures the amount by which the stock's expected return increases for a given increase in the expected return on the market.

charitable contributions One way that not-for-profit businesses raise equity capital. Individuals and firms make these contributions for a variety of reasons including concern for the well-being of others, the recognition that accompanies large donations, and tax deductibility.

charter The legal document that is filed with the state to incorporate a company.

civil law A legal system that is based on detailed rules and regulations. France has a civil law system.

classified boards A board of directors with staggered terms. For example, a board with one-third of the seats filled each year and directors serving three-year terms.

classified stock Sometimes created by a firm to meet special needs and circumstances. Generally, when special classifications of stock are used, one type is designated "Class A," another as "Class B," and so on. For example, Class A might be entitled to receive dividends before dividends can be paid on Class B stock. Class B might have the exclusive right to vote. Also known as dual class stock if there are two classes.

cleanup clause A clause in a line of credit that requires the borrower to reduce the loan balance to zero at least once a year.

clearing (payment process) Occurs when: (1) a payer's bank verifies that the payer has sufficient funds and (2) the payer's bank receives confirmation (usually through the Federal Reserve) that it has sufficient funds. Clearing must occur before the payer's account and the payee's account can be settled.

clientele effect The attraction of companies with specific dividend policies to those investors whose needs are best served by those policies. Thus, companies with high dividends will have a clientele of investors with low marginal tax rates and strong desires for current income. Conversely, companies with low dividends will have a clientele of investors with high marginal tax rates and little need for current income.

cliff vesting All the options in a grant vest on the same date.

closely held corporation Refers to companies that are so small that their common stocks are not actively traded; they are owned by only a few people, usually the companies' managers.

closely held stock Refers to stock in a closely held company. The stock is not actively traded and is owned by only a few people, usually the companies' managers.

coefficient of variation (CV) Equal to the standard deviation divided by the expected return; it is a standardized risk measure that allows comparisons between investments having different expected returns and standard deviations.

collateralized debt obligation (CDO) Created when large numbers of mortgages are bundled into pools to create new securities that are then sliced into tranches; the tranches are re-combined and re-divided into securities called CDOs.

collection policy The procedure for collecting accounts receivable. A change in collection policy will affect sales, days sales outstanding, bad debt losses, and the percentage of customers taking discounts.

collections float Float created while funds from customers' checks are being deposited and cleared through the check collection process.

combination lease Combines some aspects of both operating and financial leases. For example, a financial lease that contains a cancellation clause—normally associated with operating leases—is a combination lease.

commercial bank Financial intermediary whose primary purpose is to take deposits and make loans to businesses and individuals.

commercial paper Unsecured, short-term promissory notes of large firms, usually issued in denominations of $100,000 or more and having an interest rate somewhat below the prime rate.

commitment fee Fee paid by a borrower to a bank to establish a formal, committed line of credit even if borrower doesn't draw on the line of credit.

commodity futures Futures contracts that involve the sale or purchase of various commodities, including grains, oilseeds, livestock, meats, fiber, metals, and wood.

common equity (net worth) The cumulative sum of capital supplied by common stockholders—capital stock, paid-in capital, retained earnings, and (occasionally) certain reserves. Paid-in capital is the difference between the stock's par value and what stockholders paid when they bought newly issued shares.

common law A legal system that is based on prior court decisions rather than on detailed specific rules and laws. Common law systems have better shareholder protections than civil law systems. The United States and Britain have common law systems.

common life (replacement chain) approach A method of comparing mutually exclusive projects that have unequal lives. Each project is replicated so that they will both terminate in a common year. If projects with lives of 3 years and 5 years are being evaluated,

then the 3-year project would be replicated 5 times and the 5-year project replicated 3 times; thus, both projects would terminate in 15 years.

common pool problem Can happen in bankruptcy if the value of the borrowing firm is worth more as a going concern than in liquidation. Caused by individual creditors wishing to collect on their own debt even if it means borrower must sell vital assets needed to keep the company as a going concern. Leads to liquidation, which results in less total value to remaining creditors.

common size analysis Analysis in which all income statement items are divided by sales and all balance sheet items are divided by total assets. Thus, a common size income statement shows each item as a percentage of sales, and a common size balance sheet shows each item as a percentage of total assets.

common stock account Cumulative proceeds reported on a company's financial statement due to sales of common stock. It is the sum of the par value and paid-in capital.

comparative ratio analysis Compares a firm's own ratios to other leading companies in the same industry. This technique is also known as benchmarking.

compensating balance (CB) A minimum checking account balance that some banks require a firm to maintain to compensate the bank for services rendered or for making a loan; generally equal to 10%–20% of the loans outstanding.

competitive bids (security offerings) A security offering in which investment banks submit bids to the issuing company regarding the fees for underwriting the issuance. Occurs primarily with frequent debt offerings from large utilities.

composition Creditors voluntarily reduce their fixed claims on the debtor by accepting a lower principal amount, reducing the interest rate on the debt, accepting equity in place of debt, or some combination of these changes.

compound interest The interest that is earned (or charged) on interest as well as on principal.

compounding The process of finding the future value of a single payment or series of payments. The compounding is based on periodic interest rates unless using continuous compounding.

compressed adjusted present value (CAPV) approach The APV approach but where the tax shield is discounted at the unlevered cost of equity. In this way, the FCF and the tax shield can be added together and then discounted together rather than calculating separately the unlevered value of operations and the value of the tax shield.

computer/telephone network A computer/telephone network that links buyers and sellers. It may or may not automatically execute trades.

conditional value at risk (CVaR) The average portfolio value (or loss) conditional upon the portfolio value being less than a specified threshold value (or threshold percentile). It can also be defined as the average NPV conditional upon the NPV being less than a specified threshold value (or threshold percentile). It is also called the expected shortfall (ES).

congeneric merger Involves firms that are interrelated but do not have identical lines of business. One example is Prudential's acquisition of Bache & Company.

conglomerate merger Occurs when unrelated enterprises combine, such as Mobil Oil and Montgomery Ward.

conservative approach (for short-term financing) Refers to using permanent capital to finance all permanent asset requirements as well as to meet some or all of the seasonal demands.

consol A type of perpetuity. Consols were originally bonds issued by England in the mid-1700s to consolidate past debt.

constant dividend growth model Formula for the present value of an infinite stream of constantly growing dividends. Sometimes called just the dividend growth model. Also called the Gordon model (or Gordon growth model) due to Myron J. Gordon.

constant growth model Formula for the present value of an infinite stream of constantly growing cash flows.

constant yield method A method of amortizing bond discount or premium to calculate the interest deduction allowed each period. The amount of discount or premium amortized each period is calculated to be the amount required so the interest payment plus amortized discount, or the interest payment minus the amortized premium, results in a return on the bond's resulting basis each period equal to the bond's yield to maturity at purchase.

consumer credit markets Lending for consumer use, such as loans for autos, appliances, education, and vacations.

continuing value The present value of all free cash flows beyond the horizon date discounted back to the horizon date. Also called the horizon value (because it is at the horizon date) or the called the terminal value (because it is at the end of the explicit forecast period).

continuous compounding The process of finding the future value of a single payment or series of payments assuming that interest is incurred continuously rather than periodically.

continuous probability distribution Probability distribution having an infinite number of possible outcomes. Often shown as a graph with outcomes on the x-axis having values that might range from $-\infty$ to $+\infty$ (although many probability distributions do not have an infinite range of possible outcomes). The values on the y-axis are a continuous curve that begin with a value of zero (or tangent to zero), are always positive, and end with a value of zero (or tangent to zero). Also, the area under this curve must be equal to 100% (this is a probability density function). Sometimes shown with cumulative probabilities on the y-axis (i.e., the probability that an outcome will be less than or equal to the value on the x-axis; this is a cumulative density function).

conversion price, P_c The effective price per share of stock if conversion occurs; the par value of the convertible security divided by the conversion ratio.

conversion ratio, CR The number of shares of common stock received upon conversion of one convertible security.

conversion value The value of the stock that the investor would receive if conversion occurred; the market price per share times the conversion ratio.

convertible bond Bond that is convertible into shares of common stock, at a fixed price, at the option of the bondholder.

convertible currency A currency that can be traded in the international currency markets and can be exchanged at current market rates. Often called a hard currency, freely convertible currency, or a fully convertible currency.

convertible security Bonds or preferred stocks that can be exchanged for (converted into) common stock, under specific terms, at the option of the holder. Unlike the exercise of warrants, conversion of a convertible security does not provide additional capital to the issuer.

corporate alliance A cooperative deal that stops short of a merger but still allows firms to create combinations that focus on specific business lines that offer the most potential synergies. Also called a strategic alliance.

corporate beta The measure of risk a project has when considered as a part of a larger company rather than as a part of a well-diversified portfolio.

corporate bond Debt issued by corporations and exposed to default risk. Different corporate bonds have different levels of default risk, depending on the issuing company's characteristics and on the terms of the specific bond.

corporate governance The set of rules that control a company's behavior toward its directors, managers, employees, shareholders, creditors, customers, competitors, and community.

corporate risk The variability a project contributes to a corporation's stock returns; also called within-firm risk.

corporation A corporation is a legal entity created by a state. The corporation is separate and distinct from its owners and managers.

correlation The tendency of two variables to move together.

correlation coefficient, ρ (rho) A standardized measure of how two random variables covary. A correlation coefficient (ρ) of $+1.0$ means that the two variables move up and down in perfect synchronization, whereas a coefficient of -1.0 means the variables always move in opposite directions. A correlation coefficient of zero suggests that the two variables are not related to each other; that is, they are independent.

cost of common stock, r_s A firm's cost to provide r_s, the return required by the firm's common stockholders.

cost of debt after taxes, $(1 - T)r_d$ A company's after-tax cost of providing the required rate of return on debt.

cost of equity The price of using equity capital.

cost of goods sold (COGS) Includes labor, raw materials, and other expenses directly related to the production or purchase of the items or services sold.

cost of new external common equity, r_e A project financed with external equity must earn a higher rate of return because it must cover the flotation costs. Thus, the cost of new common equity is higher than that of common equity raised internally by reinvesting earnings.

cost of preferred stock, r_{ps} The return required by the firm's preferred stockholders. The cost of preferred stock, r_{ps}, is the cost to the firm of issuing new preferred stock. For perpetual preferred, it is the preferred dividend, D_{ps}, divided by the net issuing price per share after flotation costs, $(1 - F)P_{ps}$.

costly trade credit The extra credit taken from the end of the discount period to the end of the full credit period. It is costly because the payment to the seller is higher than it would have been if payment had been made during the discount period.

counterparty risk Risk that one of the two parties involved in a derivative position will not honor its financial obligations should an event call for a payment.

coupon interest rate Stated rate of interest on a bond; defined as the coupon payment divided by the par value.

coupon payment Dollar amount of interest paid to each bondholder on the interest payment dates.

covenant Provisions in a bond indenture that cover such points as the conditions under which the issuer can pay off the bonds prior to maturity, the levels at which certain ratios must be maintained if the company is to issue additional debt, and restrictions against the payment of dividends unless earnings meet certain specifications. Also called a bond covenant or a restrictive covenant.

covered call option The situation when a person owns a share of stock and then writes a call option on the stock. If the option is exercised, then the writer is "covered" because the writer doesn't have to buy a share of stock in the market to be able to sell the share to the owner of the call option.

cramdown provision Reorganization plans that are mandated by the bankruptcy court and binding on all parties, which means all creditors must accept the plan even if they disagree.

credit default swap (CDS) Derivative in which a counterparty pays if a specified debt instrument goes into default; similar to insurance on a bond.

credit enhancement Enables a bond's rating to be upgraded to AAA when the issuer purchases bond insurance. The bond insurance company guarantees that bondholders will receive the promised interest and principal payments. Therefore, the bond carries the credit rating of the insurance company rather than that of the issuer.

credit period A provision in credit terms: The length of time for which credit is extended. For example, "net 30" means full payment is due in 30 days. If the credit period is lengthened then sales will generally increase, as will accounts receivable. This will increase the firm's financing needs and possibly increase bad debt losses. A shortening of the credit period will have the opposite effect.

credit policy The firm's policy on granting and collecting credit. There are four elements of credit policy: credit period, discounts, credit standards, and collection policy.

credit standards The financial strength and creditworthiness that qualifies a customer for a firm's regular credit terms.

credit terms Statement specifying the terms under which a customer may not be required to make immediate cash payment, including the discount percentage rate (if offered), discount period (if offered), and the credit period at which full payment is due. For example, "2/10, net 30" means that a purchaser can deduct 2% of the sales price by paying in cash within 10 days; otherwise, the full price is due in 30 days.

credit union Cooperative associations that take deposits from members and then make loans only to other members, generally for auto purchases, home-improvement loans, and home mortgages

cross rate The exchange rate between two non-U.S. currencies.

crossover rate The cost of capital at which the NPV profiles for two projects intersect. One project has a higher NPV below the crossover rate but the other project has a higher NPV above the crossover rate.

cumulative preferred dividends A protective feature on preferred stock that requires all past preferred dividends to be paid before any common dividends can be paid.

currency appreciation Occurs to a particular currency when it increases in value relative to another particular currency. For example, if the exchange rate of 1.0 dollar per euro changes to 1.1 dollars per euro, then euro has appreciated against the dollar by 10%.

currency depreciation Occurs to a particular currency when it decreases in value relative to another particular currency. For example, if the exchange rate of 1.0 dollar per euro changes to 0.9 dollars per euro, then euro has depreciated against the dollar by 10%.

currency manipulator Designation of a foreign government by the U.S. Treasury when the country has a large trade surplus with the United States, a large current account balance, and repeated large currency interventions in one direction.

currency swap A company makes a payment in denoted in a specified currency to a counterparty and the counterparty make a payment to the company in a different currency—the two parties "swap" payments denoted in different currencies.

current ratio Is the ratio of current assets to current liabilities. It Indicates the extent to which current liabilities are covered by current assets.

current yield (on a bond) The annual coupon payment divided by the current market price.

D

dark pool A type of trading venue that can be registered as an alternative trading system (ATS) with the SEC and is called a "dark pool" because it does not have to report any pre-trade quotes.

days sales outstanding (DSO) Used to appraise accounts receivable and indicates the length of time the firm must wait after making a sale before receiving cash. It is found by dividing receivables by average daily sales. Also called the average collection period and receivables conversion period.

DCF (discounted cash flow) analysis The method of determining today's value of a cash flow to be received in the future. Because a dollar in the future is worth less than a dollar today, the process of equating today's dollars with future dollars is called discounting. Also called the time value of money analysis. DCF analysis can be used to estimate a financial asset's value by finding the present value of the asset's expected cash flows when discounted at rate that reflects the asset's risk. This method can be applied to the cash flows from bonds, stocks, entire companies, and specific projects.

dealer market In a dealer market, a dealer holds an inventory of the security and makes a market by offering to buy or sell. Others who wish to buy or sell can see the offers made by the dealers and can contact the dealer of their choice to arrange a transaction.

debenture An unsecured bond; as such, it provides no lien against specific property as security for the obligation. Debenture holders are therefore general creditors whose claims are protected by property not otherwise pledged.

debt beta (b$_d$) A measure of the amount of risk that debt contributes to a well-diversified portfolio. Calculated as b$_d$ = (σ_d/σ_M)$\rho_{d,M}$, where σ_d is the standard deviation of debt's return, σ_M is the standard deviation of the market return, and $\sigma_{d,M}$ is the correlation between debt and the market.

debt management ratios Used to identify (1) the extent to which the firm is financed with debt and (2) a firm's ability to pay interest. Also called leverage ratios.

debt ratio The ratio of total debt provided by investor to total assets, it measures the percentage of funds provided by investors other than preferred or common shareholders. Also called the debt-to-assets ratio.

debt service requirements The total amount of principal and interest that must be paid on a bond issue.

debtor-in-possession (DIP) financing Provision in bankruptcy law making any additional funds borrowed for short-term liquidity purposes senior to all previous unsecured debt. This allows the borrowing firm to continue operations during the bankruptcy proceedings.

debt-to-assets ratio The ratio of total debt provided by investors to total assets, it measures the percentage of funds provided by investors other than preferred or common shareholders. Also called the debt ratio.

debt-to-equity ratio Ratio of total debt provided by investors divided by total equity.

decision node A place in a decision tree at which managers can make a decision based on the situation occurring at that point. Called a node because additional paths branch out, with each branch corresponding to the possible decisions.

decision tree A form of project analysis in which possible future *possible* scenarios for cash flows are identified for each year in the project's life *and* in which managers can make decisions at future dates depending on the *actual* scenario occurring at that future date. It is called a decision tree because there are branches beginning at Year 0 (e.g., three possible scenarios) and because managers can make a decision at a future time (e.g., abandon the project or increase capacity, depending on the level of demand at that time), which leads to additional branches based on that decision.

declaration date The date on which a firm's directors issue a statement declaring a dividend. The dollar value of the declared payment is reported as a liability on the balance sheet and the retained earnings account is reduced by that amount.

deductible expense An expense that reduces taxable income. For example, a company may deduct the salaries it pays employees but may not deduct the dividends that it pays shareholders.

default risk The risk that a borrower may not pay the interest and/or principal on a loan when it becomes due. If the issuer defaults, investors receive less than the promised return on the bond. Default risk is influenced by the financial strength of the issuer and also by the terms of the bond contract, especially whether collateral has been pledged to secure the bond. The greater the default risk, the higher the bond's yield to maturity.

default risk premium (DRP) The premium added to the real risk-free rate to compensate investors for the risk that a borrower may fail to pay the interest and/or principal on a loan when they become due.

defensive merger Occurs when the management of an acquisition target seek out a friendly company to acquire their company.

deferred annuity An annuity with a fixed number of equal payments occurring at the end of each period. Also called an ordinary annuity.

deferred call Feature stating that a callable bond may not be called until a specified number of years after issue have passed. This is also known as call protection.

defined benefit (DB) retirement plan Retirement plan in which the sponsoring employer agrees to pay retirement benefits based on the employee's length of service, salary, or other factors; i.e., the benefits are defined by the plan.

defined contribution plan Retirement plan in which employers agree to make specific payments into a retirement fund and retirees receive benefits that depend on the plan's investment success.

degree of financial leverage (DFL) Percentage change in earnings per share that results from a percentage change in EBIT.

degree of operating leverage (DOL) Percentage change in operating income that results from a percentage change in sales.

degree of total leverage Percentage change in earnings per share that results from a percentage change in sales. Is equal to (DOL)(DFL).

delivery date Date on which a person with a short position in a forward contract must deliver the contract's asset.

de minimis The minimum amount of discount on a bond's issue price that qualifies for linear amortization of the bond discount. This is 0.25% × Maturity in years × Par value. If the bond discount is greater than de minimis, then the constant yield method is used to amortize the bond discount.

depreciation expense A noncash charge against tangible assets, such as buildings or machines. It is taken for the purpose of showing an asset's estimated dollar cost of the capital equipment used up in the production process.

derivatives Claims whose value depends on what happens to the value of some other asset. Futures and options are two important types of derivatives, and their values depend on what happens to the prices of other assets. Therefore, the value of a derivative security is derived from the value of an underlying real asset or other security.

detachable warrant A warrant that can be detached and traded separately from the underlying security. Most bonds with warrants have detachable warrants.

devaluation The lowering, by governmental action, of the price of its currency relative to another currency. For example, in 1967 the British pound was devalued from $2.80 per pound to $2.50 per pound.

development bond A tax-exempt bond sold by state and local governments whose proceeds are made available to corporations for specific uses deemed (by Congress) to be in the public interest.

direct quote When discussing exchange rates, the number of U.S. dollars required to purchase one unit of a foreign currency. For example, EUR/USD 1.20 is a direct quote meaning that the rate is 1.20 dollars per euro.

disbursement float Float created before checks written by a firm have cleared and been deducted from the firm's account; disbursement float causes the firm's own checkbook balance to be smaller than the balance on the bank's records.

discount bond Bond prices and interest rates are inversely related; that is, they tend to move in the opposite direction from one another. A fixed-rate bond will sell at par when its coupon interest rate is equal to the going rate of interest, r_d. When the going rate of interest is above the coupon rate, a fixed-rate bond will sell at a "discount" below its par value. If current interest rates are below the coupon rate, a fixed-rate bond will sell at a "premium" above its par value.

discounted cash flow (DCF) analysis The method of determining today's value of a cash flow to be received in the future. Because a dollar in the future is worth less than a dollar today, the process of equating today's dollars with future dollars is called discounting. Also called the time value of money analysis. DCF analysis can be used to estimate a financial asset's value by finding the present value of the asset's expected cash flows when discounted at rate that reflects the asset's risk. This method can be applied to the cash flows from bonds, stocks, entire companies, and specific projects.

discounted payback period The number of years it takes a firm to recover its project investment based on discounted cash flows.

discount (foreign currency forward rate) When the foreign currency indirect spot rate is less than the forward rate; i.e., the foreign currency is expected to depreciate (based on forward rates) with respect to the home currency.

discount interest Interest that is calculated on the face amount of a loan but is paid in advance.

discount percentage (credit) A provision in credit terms: The percentage reduction in the sales price if the purchaser pays in cash before the end of the specified discount period. For example, "2/10" means a 2% discount if paid within 10 days. Otherwise, the full price is due at the end of the regular credit period.

discount period (credit) A provision in credit terms: The number of days a purchaser is given to make a payment and still get the discount. For example, "2/10" means a 2% discount if paid within 10 days, so 10 days is the discount period. Otherwise, the full price is due at the end of the regular credit period.

discounting The process of finding the present value of a single payment or series of payments.

discounts (in credit terms) A provision in credit terms: A percentage reduction in the sales price if the purchaser pays in cash before the end of the specified discount period. Otherwise, the full price is due at the end of the regular credit period. Also called "cash discounts" or "trade discounts."

discrete compounding A method of compounding with a periodic interest rate for a particular period of time, such as a year or month.

discrete probability distribution Probability distribution having a finite number of outcomes. Often presented as a listing, chart, or graph showing all possible outcomes with a probability assigned to each outcome. This listing of outcomes and probabilities is a probability density function.

discriminant function The boundary line in a multiple discriminant analysis that separates the parameter values that predict a company will go bankrupt from the values that predict it will not.

distribution policy Sets the level of cash distributions (the dollar amount) and the form of the distributions (dividends and stock repurchases).

distribution ratio Percentage of net income distributed to shareholders through cash dividends or stock repurchases.

diversifiable risk Refers to that part of a security's total risk associated with random events not affecting the market as a whole. This risk can be eliminated by proper diversification. Also known as company-specific risk.

diversification The reduction in risk due to holding a portfolio of assets that are not perfectly correlated.

divestiture The opposite of an acquisition. That is, a company sells a portion of its assets—often a whole division—to another firm or individual.

dividend capitalization method Method of estimating a stock's cost of equity as the sum of its expected dividend yield and constant growth rate. Often called the dividend growth approach. Sometimes called the dividend-yield-plus-growth-rate approach or the discounted cash flow (DCF) approach.

dividend growth approach Method of estimating a stock's cost of equity as the sum of its expected dividend yield and constant growth rate. Often called the dividend capitalization model. Sometimes called the dividend-yield-plus-growth-rate approach or the discounted cash flow (DCF) approach.

dividend growth model Formula for the present value of an infinite stream of constantly growing dividends. Sometimes called the constant dividend growth model. Also called the Gordon model (or Gordon growth model) due to Myron J. Gordon.

dividend irrelevance theory Holds that dividend policy has no effect on either the price of a firm's stock or its cost of capital.

dividend reinvestment plan (DRIP) Allows stockholders to automatically purchase shares of common stock of the paying corporation in lieu of receiving cash dividends. There are two types of plans: one involves only stock that is already outstanding; the other involves newly issued stock. In the first type, the dividends of all participants are pooled and the stock is purchased on the open market. Participants benefit from lower transaction costs. In the second type, the company issues new shares to the participants. Thus, the company issues stock in lieu of the cash dividend.

dividend tax penalty Occurs if dividends are taxed more highly than capital gains.

dividend yield Defined as either the end-of-period dividend divided by the beginning-of-period price or as the ratio of the current dividend to the current price. Valuation formulas use the former definition.

divisional cost of capital The appropriate cost of capital to use when evaluating the typical project of a division or line of business. It may differ from the company's overall cost of capital if division's risk or debt capacity differ from those of the company.

Dodd-Frank Wall Street Reform and Consumer Protection Act Passed by Congress in 2010 to prevent financial crises similar to the ones triggering the great recession of 2007.

domestic currency The currency from a local perspective. For example, in the United States, the local perspective means the dollar is the home currency; in India, the local perspective means the home currency is the rupee. Also called the home currency.

dual class shares Classified stock with two classes having different dividend rights or voting rights.

due diligence A detailed investigation of a target of a potential acquisition, including financial statements, legal liabilities, etc.

DuPont equation A formula showing that the rate of return on equity can be found as the profit margin multiplied by the product of total assets turnover and the equity multiplier.

duration (bond) Measures the average number of years that a bond's PV of cash flows (coupons and principal payments) remains outstanding. If the term structure is flat and can only shift up or down, then duration also measures the percentage change in a bond's price due to a percentage change in interest rates.

E

earnings Income as defined by Generally Accepted Accounting Principles (GAAP) and reported on the income statement. Also called accounting income, accounting profit, net income, or profit.

earnings before interest and taxes (EBIT) A firm's sales minus its cost of goods sold and other operating expenses.

earnings before taxes (EBT) Usually equal to sales revenue minus all allowable costs, including depreciation and allowable interest expenses. Also called taxable income or pre-tax income.

EBITDA Earnings before interest, taxes, depreciation, and amortization.

EBITDA coverage ratio The sum of pre-tax earnings available to pay leases and debt obligations divided by the sum of lease and debt obligations. In practice, this is often defined as the sum of EBITDA and lease payments divided by the sum of lease payments, interest payments, and required principal payments.

ECN, electronic communication network A type of alternative trading system that uses an automated trading platform and that publicly reported order book information in much the same way as registered stock exchange.

economic life The number of years a project should be operated to maximize its net present value; often less than the maximum potential life.

economic ordering quantity (EOQ) The order quantity that minimizes the costs of ordering and carrying inventories.

Economic Value Added (EVA) A method used to measure a firm's true profitability. EVA is found by taking the firm's after-tax operating profit and subtracting the annual cost of all the capital a firm uses. If the firm generates a positive EVA, its management has created value for its shareholders. If the EVA is negative, management has destroyed shareholder value.

economies of scale Phenomenon in which larger companies can reduce costs, increase sales, or both.

effective (or equivalent) annual rate (EAR or EFF%) The effective annual rate is the rate that, under annual compounding, would have produced the same future value at the end of 1 year as was produced by more frequent compounding, say quarterly. If the compounding occurs annually, then the effective annual rate and the nominal rate are the same. If compounding occurs more frequently, then the effective annual rate is greater than the nominal rate.

efficiency ratios A set of ratios that measure how effectively a firm is managing its assets. Also called asset management ratios.

efficient frontier The set of efficient portfolios out of the full set of potential portfolios. On a graph, the efficient frontier constitutes the boundary line of the set of potential portfolios. Also called the efficient set.

Efficient Markets Hypothesis (EMH) States (1) that stocks are always in equilibrium and (2) that it is impossible for an investor to consistently "beat the market" by getting a higher return than is justified by the stock's risk. The EMH assumes that all important information regarding a stock is reflected in the price of that stock.

efficient portfolio Provides the highest expected return for any specified level of risk. The efficient portfolio also provides the lowest degree of risk for any specified level of expected return.

efficient set The set of efficient portfolios out of the full set of potential portfolios. On a graph, the efficient set constitutes the boundary line of the set of potential portfolios. Also called the efficient frontier.

embedded options Options that are a part of another project. Also called real options, managerial options, and strategic options.

embedded rate (for debt) The average coupon rate on a company's outstanding debt; also called the historical rate. Used in rate case hearings for public utilities but not for valuation.

Employee Retirement Income Security Act (ERISA) The federal law passed in 1974 that governs the structure and administration of corporate pension plans.

Employee Stock Ownership Plan (ESOP) A type of retirement plan in which employees own stock in the company.

engineering life of project The maximum potential life of a project; also called physical life. This can exceed the optimal economic life.

enterprise risk management (ERM) A process that includes risk identification, risk assessment, and risk responses. ERM requires the participation of all levels within an organization.

entity multiple For a group of comparable firms, the average ratio of the observed market entity value to a particular metric that applies to a whole firm, such as sales, EBITDA, number of subscribers, or any other metric that applies to the entity values of the target firm and the comparable firms.

entity valuation model Estimates the total value of a corporation rather than just the values of debt or stock.

entity value The total value of a corporation, including its common stock, preferred stock, and debt.

entrenchment Occurs when a company has such a weak board of directors and has such strong anti-takeover provisions in its corporate charter that senior managers feel there is little chance of being removed.

EOQ model The equation used to find the economic ordering quantity: $EOQ = \sqrt{[2(F)(S)]/[(C)(P)]}$, where F is the fixed cost per order, S is annual sales, C is the annual carrying cost expressed as a percentage of average inventory value, and P is the purchase price per unit of inventory.

EOQ range The range around the optimal ordering quantity that may be ordered without significantly affecting total inventory costs.

equilibrium The condition under which the intrinsic value of a security is equal to its price; also, when a security's expected return is equal to its required return. Also known as market equilibrium.

equity carve-out IPO in which a parent company creates a new publicly traded company from a subsidiary and sells some of the stock to the public. Parent companies typically retain at least 80% of the subsidiary's common stock to maintain control and to preserve their ability to file a consolidated tax return. Also called a partial public offering or a spin-out.

equity multiplier A set of ratios that measure how effectively a firm is managing its assets. Also called asset management ratios.

equity premium, RP_M Expected market return minus the risk-free rate; also called market risk premium or equity risk premium

equity residual model Discounts free cash flow to equity by the levered cost of equity. Also called the free cash flow to equity model.

equity risk premium, RP_M Expected market return minus the risk-free rate; also called market risk premium or equity premium

equivalent annual annuity (EAA) method Use to compare mutually exclusive projects with different lifespans. Convert the unequal annual cash flows of a project into a constant cash flow stream (i.e., an annuity) whose NPV is equal to the NPV of the initial stream. Do for both projects and compare the annuities.

ESOP (Employee Stock Ownership Plan) A type of retirement plan in which employees own stock in the company.

ETF, exchange-traded fund A special type of mutual fund that allows investors to sell their shares at any time during normal trading hours. ETFs usually have very low management expenses.

euro The currency used by nations in the European Monetary Union.

Eurobond Any bond sold in some country other than the one in whose currency the bond is denominated. Thus, a U.S. firm selling dollar bonds in Switzerland is selling Eurobonds.

Eurodollar A U.S. dollar on deposit in a foreign bank or a foreign branch of a U.S. bank. Eurodollars are used to conduct transactions throughout Europe and the rest of the world.

European option An option which may be exercised only at expiration. In contrast, an American option may be exercised on or before the expiration date.

event risk The chance that some sudden event will occur and increase the credit risk of a company, hence lowering the firm's bond rating and the value of its outstanding bonds. Some bonds reduce event risk by including a super poison put in the bond's covenant.

exchange rate Specifies the number of units of a given currency that can be purchased for one unit of another currency. For example, USD/JPY 80 means that 1 U.S. dollar can purchase 80 Japanese yen. Also called the foreign exchange rate, the FX rate, and the FOREX rate.

exchange rate risk Risk that a transaction in a foreign currency will be more costly than anticipated due to possible future fluctuations in exchange rates.

exchange-traded fund (ETF) A special type of mutual fund that allows investors to sell their shares at any time during normal trading hours. ETFs usually have very low management expenses.

ex-dividend date The date when the right to the dividend leaves the stock. This date was established by stockbrokers to avoid confusion, and it is two business days prior to the holder-of-record date. If the stock sale is made prior to the ex-dividend date, then the dividend is paid to the buyer; if the stock is bought on or after the ex-dividend date, the dividend is paid to the seller.

exercise price The price stated in the option contract at which the security can be bought (or sold). Also called the strike price.

exercise value Equal to payoff of the option if it is in-the-money or zero if it is not in-the-money. For a call option that is in the money, the exercise value is the current price of the stock (underlying the option) minus the strike price of the option.

expectations theory States that the slope of the yield curve depends on expectations about future inflation rates and interest rates. Thus, if the annual rate of inflation and future interest rates are expected to increase, then the yield curve will be upward sloping; the curve will be downward sloping if the annual rates are expected to decrease.

expected rate of return on a portfolio, $\hat{r}_p$ The rate of return expected on a portfolio given its current price and expected future cash flows.

expected rate of return, $\hat{r}_s$ The rate of return expected on a stock given its current price and expected future cash flows. If the stock is in equilibrium, the required rate of return will equal the expected rate of return.

expected return The mean of the probability distribution of returns.

expected shortfall (ES) The average portfolio value conditional upon the portfolio value being less than a specified threshold value (or threshold percentile). It can also be defined as the average NPV conditional upon the NPV being less than a specified threshold value (or threshold percentile). It is also called the conditional value at risk (CVaR).

expiration date Date after which an option may not be exercised.

expropriation risk The risk that a host government will seize property.

ex-rights day The first day a trader purchasing a stock that has had a rights offering will not receive the right. Currently, 2 business days prior to the rights offering date of record.

extension A form of debt restructuring in which creditors postpone the dates of required interest or principal payments, or both.

externality The effect a project has on other parts of the firm or on the environment.

extra dividend A dividend paid, in addition to the regular dividend, when earnings permit. Firms with volatile earnings may have a low regular dividend that can be maintained even in years of low profit (or high capital investment) but is supplemented by an extra dividend when excess funds are available. Also called a special dividend.

F

F, percentage flotation cost for debt and preferred stock The total dollar value of flotation costs divided by the total par value of the issue. Flotation costs include commissions, legal expenses, fees, and any other costs that a company incurs when it issues new securities.

face value (stock or bond) The value printed on the "face" of a stock or bond certificate, Also called the par value. A stock's face value is not related to its market value, even at the time it is issued. In contrast, a bond's face value usually is the amount that the firm promises to repay at some future date.

factoring Selling accounts receivable.

fairness (in bankruptcy) The standard of fairness states that claims must be recognized in the order of their legal and contractual priority. In simpler terms, the reorganization must be fair to all parties.

Fama-French three-factor model Includes one factor for the excess market return (the market return minus the risk-free rate), a second factor for size (defined as the return on a portfolio of small firms minus the return on a portfolio of big firms), and a third factor for the book-to-market effect (defined as the return on a portfolio of firms with a high book-to-market ratio minus the return on a portfolio of firms with a low book-to-market ratio).

FASB (Financial Accounting Standards Board) Determines rules for financial statement reporting based on GAAP.

feasibility (in bankruptcy) The standard of feasibility states that there must be a reasonably high probability of successful rehabilitation and profitable future operations.

feasible set Represents all portfolios that can be constructed from a given set of stocks; also known as the attainable set.

FIFO (first-in, first-out) The first-in, first-out inventory accounting method that estimates production costs and the value of remaining inventory by assuming that the first items placed in inventory are the first ones used in production.

finance lease Covers the entire expected life of the equipment; does not provide for maintenance service, is not cancellable, and is fully amortized. Also called a capital lease.

Financial Accounting Standards Board (FASB) Determines rules for financial statement reporting based on GAAP.

financial analysis Set of tools for evaluating opportunities to exchange cash now for claims on future cash.

financial asset market Market for stocks, bonds, notes, mortgages, derivatives, and other financial instruments.

financial distress costs Incurred when a leveraged company's value or cash flow declines to such an extent that the probability of bankruptcy becomes imminent. Costs include employee turnover, reduced employee productivity, reduced product quality due to cost-cutting measures, reduction in credit provide by suppliers, loss of customers, and higher interest rates demanded by lenders.

financial engineering Use of option pricing and derivative pricing techniques to create and determine the value of a new financial security or to determine the value of a real option embedded in a project.

financial futures Provide for the purchase or sale of a financial asset at some time in the future, but at a price that is established today. Financial futures exist for Treasury bills, Treasury notes and bonds, certificates of deposit, Eurodollar deposits, foreign currencies, and stock indexes.

Financial Industry Regulatory Authority (FINRA) A private non-profit organization that acts on behalf of investors by: (1) licensing brokers and (2) monitoring trading activities of brokers and brokerage firms.

financial instrument A claim on a future cash flow.

financial intermediary Intermediary that buys securities with funds that it obtains by issuing its own securities. An example is a common stock mutual fund that buys common stocks with funds obtained by issuing shares in the mutual fund.

financial leverage Ratio of total assets to common equity. Shows the factor by which ROA is scaled up to determine ROE. Is the magnifying effect that debt has on ROE and shareholder risk.

financial markets Ways of connecting providers of cash today with users of cash by exchanging the cash now for claims on future cash.

financial merger A merger in which the companies will not be operated as a single unit and for which no operating economies are expected.

financial risk The risk added by the use of debt financing. Debt financing increases the variability of earnings before taxes (but after interest); thus, along with business risk, it contributes to the uncertainty of net income and earnings per share. Business risk plus financial risk equals total corporate risk.

financial security A claim that is standardized and regulated by the government.

financial services company A company that offers a wide range of financial services, such as brokerage operations, insurance, and commercial banking.

financing deficit The shortfall of spontaneous liabilities, planned change in external financing (total changes of debt, preferred stock, and common stock from the preliminary financing plan), and internal funds (net income less planned dividends) relative to additional assets required by the operating plan.

financing feedback Circularity created when additional debt causes additional interest expense, which reduces the addition to retained earnings, which in turn requires a higher level of debt, which causes still more interest expense, causing the cycle to be repeated.

financing surplus The excess of spontaneous liabilities, planned change in external financing (total changes of debt, preferred stock, and common stock from the preliminary financing plan), and internal funds (net income less planned dividends) relative to additional assets required by the operating plan.

first-mortgage bond Has higher priority claim on the issuer's asset than subsequently issued bonds. Also called a senior bond.

fixed assets turnover ratio The ratio of sales to net fixed assets; it measures how effectively the firm uses its plant and equipment.

fixed exchange rate system The system in effect from the end of World War II until August 1971. Under the system, the U.S. dollar was linked to gold at the rate of $35 per ounce, and other currencies were then tied to the dollar.

flexibility option Permits a firm to alter operations depending on how conditions change during the life of the project, such as the ability to produce different products to match changing demand.

float Difference between the balance shown in a firm's (or individual's) checkbook and the balance on the bank's records.

floating exchange rates Exchange rates that change with market forces of supply and demand, having little or no government intervention.

floating-rate bond A bond whose coupon payment may vary over time. The coupon rate is usually linked to the rate on some other security, such as a Treasury security, or to some other rate, such as the prime rate or LIBOR.

flotation costs (for issuing securities) The commissions, legal expenses, fees, and any other costs that a company incurs when it issues new securities, including any difference between the price at which an underwriter sells the issue versus the price that the underwriter pays the issuing company (i.e., the spread). The flotation costs often are expressed on a percentage basis, denoted by F, and defined as the total flotation costs divided by the net proceeds. For bonds issued at par, F is equal to the total flotation costs divided by the total par value of the bonds being issued.

forecast horizon The last year in a cash flow forecast. Cash flows may grow unevenly during the forecast period, but are assumed to grow at a constant rate for all periods after the forecast horizon. Also called the horizon date or the terminal date because it is at the end of the explicit forecast period.

forecasted financial statements (FFS) method Approach to financial planning in which a company forecasts its complete set of financial statements to determine the value of operations and the additional external funding that may be needed. Many items on the income statement and balance sheets are assumed to increase proportionally with sales. As sales increase, these items that are tied to sales also increase, and the values of these items for a particular year are estimated as percentages of the forecasted sales for that year.

foreign bond A bond sold by a foreign borrower but denominated in the currency of the country in which the issue is sold. Thus, a U.S. firm selling bonds denominated in Swiss francs in Switzerland is selling foreign bonds.

foreign currency Any currency other than the home (or domestic) currency. For example, from a perspective in the United States, all currencies other than the dollar are foreign currencies.

foreign exchange (FX) risk The risk that a change in a currency exchange rate might adversely affect a company.

foreign exchange rate Specifies the number of units of a given currency that can be purchased for one unit of another currency. For example, USD/JPY 80 means that 1 U.S. dollar can purchase 80 Japanese yen. Also called the exchange rate, the FX rate, and the FOREX rate.

foreign trade balance Level of imports relative to exports. A deficit occurs when businesses and individuals in the United States import more goods from foreign countries than are exported. A surplus occurs when exports are greater than imports. Also called the trade balance and the balance of trade.

FOREX rate Specifies the number of units of a given currency that can be purchased for one unit of another currency. For example, USD/JPY 80 means that 1 U.S. dollar can purchase 80 Japanese yen. Also called the exchange rate, the foreign exchange rate, and the FX rate.

formal bankruptcy proceedings When a company files for bankruptcy under Chapter 7 or Chapter 11 of the federal bankruptcy code.

forward contract A contract to buy or sell some item at some time in the future at a price established when the contract is entered into.

forward exchange rate The foreign exchange rate for exchange (delivery) at some agreed-upon future date, which is usually 30, 90, or 180 days from the day the transaction is negotiated.

forward price The price specified in a forward contract at which the underlying asset must be sold (or bought) at the delivery date. The forward price usually will be different from the actual market price at the time of delivery.

founders' shares Stock owned by the firm's founders that have sole voting rights but restricted dividends for a specified number of years.

fraudulent conveyance (in bankruptcy) Provision in bankruptcy law to protect creditors from unjustified transfers of property by a firm in financial distress, such as selling assets at low prices to a firm's stockholders.

free cash flow (FCF) The cash flow actually available for distribution to a company's investors (shareholders and creditors) after the company has made all investments in fixed assets and working capital necessary to sustain ongoing operations. Defined as net operating profit after taxes (NOPAT) minus the investment in total net operating capital.

free cash flow (FCF) valuation model Defines the total value of a company as the present value of its expected free cash flows discounted at the weighted average cost of capital (i.e., the value of operations) plus the value of nonoperating assets such as T-bills.

free cash flow to equity (FCFE) Free cash flow available to equity holders. Defined as free cash flow plus any increase in debt minus after-tax interest expense.

free cash flow to equity model Discounts free cash flow to equity by the levered cost of equity. Also called the equity residual model.

freely convertible currency A currency that can be traded in the international currency markets and can be exchanged at current market rates. Also called a fully convertible currency, a hard currency, or a convertible currency.

free trade credit Credit a purchaser receives during the discount period. If the purchaser pays after the discount period, the purchase must make a higher payment.

friendly merger Occurs when the target company's management agrees to the merger and recommends that shareholders approve the deal.

fully convertible currency A currency that can be traded in the international currency markets and can be exchanged at current market rates. Also called a freely convertible currency, a hard currency, or a convertible currency.

fully funded pension plan The present value of all expected retirement benefits is equal to assets on hand.

fund capital Not-for-profit business equivalent of equity capital. It consists of retained profits and charitable contributions.

fundamental beta Incorporates adjustments to historical beta that address impact of current variables such as operating leverage, financial leverage, and sales volatility.

fundamental value Value of company or financial security (such as a share of stock) that incorporates all relevant information regarding expected future cash flows and risk. Also called intrinsic value.

funding strategy Necessary for a defined benefit plan and involves two decisions: how fast should any unfunded liability be reduced and what rate of return should be assumed in the actuarial calculations.

future value, FV The value that a payment (or series of payments) will grow to at a future date.

future value interest factor, FV_N The future value of $1 in N periods invested at a rate of i% per period.

future value interest factor for an annuity, $FVIFA_{I,N}$ The future value of $1 to be received at the end of each of N periods invested at a rate of i% per period.

future value of annuity, FVA The future value of a stream of annuity payments.

futures contract A derivative contract in which one party agrees to purchase something at a pre-determined price and in which the second party agrees to sell the same item at the same price. In contrast to a forward contract, the two parties must settle up each day as the price of the futures contract changes, a process called marking-to-market.

futures market For assets whose delivery is at some future date, such as 6 months or a year into the future

FVA_N The future value of a stream of annuity payments, where N is the number of payments of the annuity.

$FVIFA_{I,N}$, future value interest factor for an annuity The future value interest factor for an ordinary annuity of N periodic payments paying I percent interest per period.

$FVIF_{I,N}$, future value interest factor The future value interest factor for a lump sum left in an account for N periods paying I percent interest per period.

FV_N The future value of an initial single cash flow, where N is the number of periods the initial cash flow is compounded.

FX rate Specifies the number of units of a given currency that can be purchased for one unit of another currency. For example, USD/JPY 80 means that 1 U.S. dollar can purchase 80 Japanese yen. Also called the exchange rate, the foreign exchange rate, and the FOREX rate.

G

GAAP (Generally Accepted Accounting Principles) A set of standards for financial reporting established by the accounting profession.

GASB (Government Accounting Standards Board) Promulgates standards for issues pertaining to governmental entities.

general obligation bonds Type of municipal bonds which are secured by the full faith and credit of a government unit; that is, backed by the full taxing authority of the issuer.

general partner General partners in a limited partnership have unlimited liability and control of decisions made by the partnership.

Generally Accepted Accounting Principles (GAAP) A set of standards for financial reporting established by the accounting profession.

Glass-Steagall Act Passed in 1933 by Congress with the intent of preventing another great depression. It was fully repealed in 1999.

global corporation A corporation that operates in an integrated fashion in more than one country. Also called multinational corporation, multinational enterprise, and transnational corporation.

going interest rate The annual rate of interest stated in a contract, quoted for a security, or reported by the press. It is also called the market interest rate, the quoted rate, and the nominal annual interest rate.

going private Transaction in which the entire equity of a publicly held firm is purchased by a small group of investors, ending public trading of the stock.

going public The act of selling stock to the public at large by a closely held corporation or its principal stockholders.

golden parachute A payment made to executives who are forced out when a merger takes place.

gold standard A monetary system in which the currency that can be redeemed for gold from the government's treasury.

goodwill An accounting intangible asset created when a company acquires another company but pays more than the assets are worth. The difference is called goodwill.

Gordon model Formula for the present value of an infinite stream of constantly growing dividends, named after Myron J. Gordon. Also called the Gordon growth model or the constant dividend growth model.

greenmail Targeted share repurchases that occur when a company buys back stock from a potential acquirer at a higher than fair-market price. In return, the potential acquirer agrees not to attempt to take over the company.

gross proceeds Total amount raised during an IPO. It is equal to the offer price multiplied by the number of new shares issued (n_{New}).

gross profit margin Ratio of gross profit (sales minus cost of goods sold) divided by sales.

growing annuity A series of payments that grow at a constant rate. Although an annuity payment is constant, the expression "growing annuity" is widely used.

growth option Occurs if an investment creates the opportunity to make other potentially profitable investments that would not otherwise be possible, including options to expand output, to enter a new geographical market, and to introduce complementary products or successive generations of products.

growth rate, g, g_L, or $g_{t,t+1}$ Growth rate of sales, free cash flows, or any other specified item. The rate can be over the next period (g), can be the long-term constant rate for all future periods (gL), or can be from period t to period t + 1 ($g_{t,t+1}$).

GSE (government-sponsored enterprise) debt Debt issued by government-sponsored enterprises (GSEs) such as the Tennessee Valley Authority or the Small Business Administration; not officially backed by the full faith and credit of the U.S. government.

guideline lease Meets all of the Internal Revenue Service (IRS) requirements for a genuine lease. If a lease meets the IRS guidelines, the IRS allows the lessor to deduct the asset's depreciation and allows the lessee to deduct the lease payments. Also called a tax-oriented lease or a true lease.

H

half-year convention Used in calculating depreciation expenses for tax purposes as though the asset is placed into service halfway through the year even if the asset was placed into service at some other point in the year. The first-year's depreciation expense is half of what is would have been if the half-year convention were not used. An extra half-year of depreciation is allowed after the end of the asset's tax life. For example, a project with a 5-year life would report 6 years of depreciation expenses.

Hamada equation Shows the effect of debt on the beta coefficient—increases in debt increase beta, and decreases in debt reduce beta: $b = b_U[1 + (1 - T)(D/S)] = b/[1 + (1 - T)(w_d/w_s)]$.

hard currency A currency that can be traded in the international currency markets and can be exchanged at current market rates. Also called a freely convertible currency, a fully convertible currency, or a convertible currency.

hedge fund Raises money from institutional investors and a relatively small number of high net-worth individuals, then engages in a variety of investment activities.

hedge portfolio A portfolio, usually consisting of a call option and shares of stock, that will have a constant payoff at expiration no matter what the stock price is at expiration.

hedging A risk management technique in which a company can reduce or eliminate its exposure to a source of risk through the use of derivatives.

herding Occurs when groups of investors emulate other successful investors and chase asset classes that are doing well. Also occurs when analysts go along with other analysts rather than state their true opinions.

high-frequency trading (HFT) Occurs when a trader buys (or sells) stock and then immediately sells (or buys) the stock, usually within milliseconds. Unlike broker-dealer internalization, high-frequency traders do not provide any infrastructure or other direct service for other buyers and sellers.

historical beta Beta as estimated using historical data for the past returns on the stock and market portfolio. Often estimated by a regression with the stock's returns (or return in excess of the risk-free rate) on the y-axis and the market's returns (or excess returns) on the x-axis.

historical rate (for debt) The average coupon rate on a company's outstanding debt; also called the embedded rate. Used in rate case hearings for public utilities but not for valuation.

holder-of-record date If a company lists the stockholder as an owner on the holder-of-record date, then the stockholder receives the dividend.

holding company A corporation formed for the sole purpose of owning stocks in other companies. A holding company differs from a stock mutual fund in that holding companies own sufficient stock in their operating companies to exercise effective working control.

holdout problem (in bankruptcy) Occurs in informal bankruptcy reorganizations when all involved parties do not agree to the voluntary plan. Holdouts are usually made by creditors in an effort to receive full payment on claims.

home currency The currency from a local perspective. For example, in the United States, the local perspective means the dollar is the home currency; in India, the local perspective means the home currency is the rupee. Also called the domestic currency.

horizon date The last year in a cash flow forecast. Cash flows may grow unevenly during the forecast period, but are assumed to grow at a constant rate for all periods after the horizon date. Also called the forecast horizon or the terminal date because it is at the end of the explicit forecast period.

horizon value The present value of all free cash flows beyond the horizon date discounted back to the horizon date. Also called the terminal value (because it is at the end of the explicit forecast period) or the continuing value (because it is the value if operations continue to be used rather than be liquidated).

horizontal merger A merger between two companies in the same line of business.

hostile merger Occurs when the management of the target company resists the offer.

hurdle rate The rate used to discount a project's cash flows after taking into consideration firm's overall cost of capital, the divisional cost of capital and any additional subjective risk assessments for the particular project, including its impact on the firm's debt capacity. Also called the project cost of capital and the risk-adjusted cost of capital.

I

immunized When a bond portfolio is selected so that its sensitivity to reinvestment rate risk and interest rate risk offset one another.

impairment test The standard by which goodwill is reduced for financial reporting (but not for federal tax reporting) purposes. Goodwill is not amortized. It is reduced only when it is deemed "impaired."

improper accumulation The retention of earnings by a business for the purpose of enabling stockholders to avoid personal income taxes on dividends.

income bond Pays interest only if the interest is earned. These securities cannot bankrupt a company, but from an investor's standpoint, they are riskier than "regular" bonds.

income statement Summarizes the firm's revenues and expenses over an accounting period. Net sales are shown at the top of each statement, after which various costs, including income taxes, are subtracted to obtain the net income available to common stockholders. The bottom of the statement reports earnings and dividends per share.

incremental cash flow Those cash flows that arise solely from the asset that is being evaluated. Equal to the cash flows of the company with the project minus the cash flows without the project.

indentures A legal document that spells out the rights of both bondholders and the issuing corporation.

independent projects Projects that can be accepted or rejected individually.

index fund Passively managed fund designed to replicate the returns on a particular market index, such as the S&P 500.

indexed bond The interest rate of such a bond is based on an inflation index such as the consumer price index (CPI), so the interest paid rises automatically when the inflation rate rises, thus protecting the bondholders against inflation. The final principal payment is also linked to inflation. Also called a purchasing power bond.

indifference curve The risk–return trade-off function for a particular investor; reflects that investor's attitude toward risk. An investor would be indifferent between any pair of assets on the same indifference curve. In risk–return space, the greater the slope of the indifference curve, the greater is the investor's risk aversion.

indirect quote When discussing exchange rates, the number of units of foreign currency that can be purchased for one unit of home currency. For example, from the U.S. perspective, USD/JPN 80 is an indirect quote meaning that the rate is 80 yen per dollar.

inflation premium (IP) The premium added to the real risk-free rate of interest to compensate for the expected loss of purchasing power. The inflation premium is the average rate of inflation expected over the life of the security.

informal debt restructuring An agreement between a troubled firm and its creditors to change existing debt terms. An extension postpones the required payment date; a composition is a reduction in creditor claims.

information content hypothesis A theory hypothesizing that investors regard dividend changes as "signals" of management forecasts. Thus, when dividends are raised, this is viewed by investors as recognition by management of future earnings increases. Therefore, if a firm's stock price increases with a dividend increase, the reason may not be investor preference for dividends but rather expectations of higher future earnings. Conversely, a dividend reduction may signal that management is forecasting poor earnings in the future. Also called the signaling hypothesis for dividends.

initial public offering (IPO) Occurs when a closely held corporation or its principal stockholders sell stock to the public at large.

I_{NOM} The nominal, or quoted, annual interest rate. This is the rate used in a time line if the cash flows occur annually. If cash flows occur more frequently, it should not be used in a time line.

inside directors Board members who hold managerial positions within the company, such as the CFO.

insiders The officers, directors, and employees of a publicly traded company. Insiders at privately held companies also include major stockholders.

insolvent Condition that occurs if (1) a company's total debt and other claims exceed the market value of its assets or (2) a company does not have enough cash to meet its interest and principal payments.

interest coverage ratio Also called the times-interest-earned (TIE) ratio; determined by dividing earnings before interest and taxes by the interest expense.

interest rate The price of using debt.

interest rate parity Holds that investing in a domestic risk-free bond should provide the same return as converting cash into a foreign currency while simultaneously purchasing a risk-free bond in the foreign country and taking a position in a forward contract to convert the bond payment from the foreign into the original domestic currency. Otherwise, investors would be able engage in arbitrage.

interest rate risk Arises from the fact that bond prices decline when interest rates rise. Under these circumstances, selling a bond prior to maturity will result in a capital loss; the longer the term to maturity, the larger the loss.

interest rate swap A company makes a floating rate payment to a counterparty (usually based on the current LIBOR rate) and the counterparty makes a fixed payment to the company, or vice versa. In other words, the company and the counterparty swap fixed payments for floating rate payments.

interest tax savings (TS$_t$) Annual tax savings due to the deductibility of interest from taxable income. Because the deduction reduces taxable income, taxes are lower than they otherwise would have been. Also called tax savings due to interest.

interest tax shield (V$_{\text{Tax shield}}$) Present value of all expected future annual tax savings due to the deductibility of interest expenses. Also called the tax shield.

interlocking boards of directors Occur when the CEO of Company A sits on the board of Company B while B's CEO sits on A's board.

internal rate of return (IRR) method The discount rate that equates the present value of the expected future cash inflows and outflows. IRR measures the rate of return on a project, but it assumes that all cash flows can be reinvested at the IRR rate.

internalization A pair of trades in which a broker-dealer is the counterparty for both clients—the broker-dealer buys from one client and sells to the other.

international bond Any bond sold outside of the country of the borrower. There are two types of international bonds: Eurobonds and foreign bonds.

International Monetary Fund (IMF) An organization created in 1944 by the Bretton Woods Convention whose purpose was to promote international trade and prosperity by stabilizing exchange rates, by reducing restrictions on currency exchanges, and by providing short-term financial help to countries with financial crises.

interstate public offering Occurs when securities are registered for sale in more than one state; regulated by the SEC unless it is a very small offering.

in-the-money option An option that would have a positive payoff if exercised immediately. For example, a call option is in-the-money if the stock price is greater than the strike price.

intrinsic value (or price) Value of company or financial security (such as a share of stock) that incorporates all relevant information regarding expected future cash flows and risk. Also called fundamental value.

inventory blanket lien In inventory financing, gives the lending institution a lien against all the borrower's inventories.

inventory conversion period The average length of time to convert materials into finished goods and then to sell them; calculated by dividing total inventory by daily costs of goods sold.

inventory turnover ratio Cost of goods sold (which includes depreciation) divided by inventories.

inverse floater Floating rate security with interest payments that move counter to market rates. If the market interest rate (usually LIBOR) goes up, the floating rate payment goes down, and vice versa if the market interest rate falls.

inverted (abnormal) yield curve A downward-sloping yield curve. Also called an abnormal yield curve.

investment bank A firm that assists in the design of an issuing firm's corporate securities and in the sale of the new securities to investors in the primary market.

Investment-grade bond Securities with ratings of Baa/BBB or above.

investment strategy Deals with the question of how the pension assets portfolio should be structured given the assumed actuarial rate of return.

investment timing option Gives companies the option to delay a project rather than implement it immediately. This option to wait allows a company to reduce the uncertainty of market conditions before it decides to implement the project.

investor-supplied capital Total amount of short-term debt, long-term debt, preferred stock, and total common equity shown on a balance sheet. It is the amount of financing that investors have provided to a company. It also called total investor-supplied capital.

investor-supplied operating capital The total amount of short-term debt, long-term debt, preferred stock, and total common equity shown on a balance sheet, less the amount of short-term investments shown on the balance sheet. It is the amount of financing used in operations that investors have provided to a company. It also called total investor-supplied operating capital. It is also equal to the total amount of net operating capital.

involuntary petition (in bankruptcy) Filing by creditor of petition in bankruptcy court.

irregular cash flow stream A stream of cash flows that cannot be represented by an annuity. Also called an uneven cash flow stream.

J

Jensen's alpha Measures the vertical distance of a portfolio's return above or below the Security Market Line; first suggested by Professor Michael Jensen, it became popular because of its ease of calculation. It measures the average return that cannot be explained by the CAPM.

joint venture Involves the joining together of parts of companies to accomplish specific, limited objectives. Joint ventures are controlled by the combined management of the two (or more) parent companies.

junior mortgage bond Secured by the same assets as senior mortgage bonds. In the event of liquidation, holders of junior mortgage bonds receive payments only after the senior bondholders have been paid in full. Also called second-mortgage bonds.

junk bond High-risk, high-yield bond issued to finance leveraged buyouts, mergers, or troubled companies.

just-in-time (JIT) inventory system Process in which delivery of components is tied to the speed of the assembly line, with delivery to production facility occurring just before the parts are needed. Reduces the need to carry large inventories, but requires a great deal of coordination between the manufacturer and its suppliers.

K

keiretsus Form of corporate organization in Japan having combinations of companies with cross-ownership of stock among the member companies.

L

lead arranger Bank that provides some funding for a syndicated loan, but other lenders also join the syndicate and provide additional funds.

lead underwriter Investment bank that sets up a security offering and forms a syndicate to help sell it. Also called managing underwriter.

lease liability A balance sheet liability entry that represents the remaining unamortized portion of the capitalized value of a lease, including operating leases and financial leases. It is also equal to right-of-use asset.

lessee The party leasing the property.

lessor The party receiving the payments from the lease (that is, the owner of the property).

leveraged buyout (LBO) A transaction in which a firm's publicly owned stock is acquired in a mostly debt-financed tender offer, resulting in a privately owned, highly leveraged firm. Often, the firm's own management initiates the LBO.

leveraged lease The lessor borrows a portion of the funds needed to buy the equipment to be leased.

leverage ratios Used to identify (1) the extent to which the firm is financed with debt and (2) a firm's ability to pay interest. Also called debt management ratios.

levered beta The beta of a levered firm (i.e., a firm partially financed with debt).

levered firm's stock, S_L Value of stock in company with debt. It reflects any side effects due to leverage or other factors.

levered value of a firm, V_L The total value of a firm with debt: $V_L = \text{Stock} + \text{Debt} = S_L + \text{Debt}$. Also called value of a levered firm.

liabilities-to-assets ratio The ratio of total liabilities to total assets, it measures the percentage of funds provided by other than preferred and common shareholders.

LIBOR (London Interbank Offered Rate) Reported rate that U.K. banks charge one another. Many financial contracts have rates based on LIBOR, such as

LIBOR + 2%. Due to misreporting scandals, the British Banking Authority lost its role as LIBOR's administrator in 2014. LIBOR is now called ICE LIBOR and is administered by an American firm, Intercontinental Exchange. The U.K. Financial Conduct Authority will regulate ICE LIBOR only through the end of 2020, but ICE LIBOR will continue to have a role in financial markets.

lien The right of a creditor to claim a specific asset in the event of default on the debt.

life insurance company Takes premiums from customers, invests these funds in stocks, bonds, real estate, and mortgages, and then makes payments to beneficiaries.

LIFO (last-in, last out) The last-in, first-out inventory accounting method that estimates production costs and the value of remaining inventory by assuming that the last items (i.e., the most recent) placed in inventory are the first ones used in production.

limit order Order sent to a broker in which the buyer or seller specifies limits with respect to the bid or ask price and duration for which the order is in effect.

limited liability company (LLC) Combines the limited liability advantage of a corporation with the tax advantages of a partnership.

limited liability partnership (LLP) Combines the tax advantages of a partnership with the limited liability advantage of a corporation.

limited partners Limited partners' liabilities, investment returns, and control are limited in a limited partnership.

limited partnership A partnership in which limited partners' liabilities, investment returns, and control are limited; general partners have unlimited liability and control.

line of credit (LOC) An arrangement in which a bank agrees now to lend up to a specified maximum amount of funds during a future designated period. Most banks charge a fee for setting up the line of credit in addition to interest on funds that are borrowed. The LOC often has a cleanup clause requiring the balance to be zero at least once a year.

linear programming for capital budgeting Technique to find maximum (or minimum) value of a linear objective function subject to linear constraints. Can be used to select the optimal mix of projects if constraints preclude accepting all projects with positive NPVs.

liquid asset One that trades in an active market, so it can be converted quickly to cash at the going market price.

liquidation in bankruptcy The sale of the assets of a firm and the distribution of the proceeds to the creditors and owners in a specific priority. Can be informal or formal (via Chapter 7 of the bankruptcy code).

liquidity (corporation) Liquidity refers to a firm's cash and marketable securities position and to its ability to meet maturing obligations.

liquidity (security) The degree to which a security can be quickly sold at its "fair" value. Active markets provide liquidity.

liquidity premium (LP) A liquidity premium is added to the real risk-free rate of interest, in addition to other premiums, if a security is not liquid.

liquidity ratio A ratio that shows the relationship of a firm's cash and other current assets to its current liabilities.

listed stock A company's stock that an SEC-registered stock exchange accepts for listing after the company has registered with the SEC to have its stock traded publicly. A company can be listed on only one exchange, but can be traded on many.

lockbox system A cash management tool in which incoming checks for a firm are sent to post office boxes rather than to corporate headquarters. Several times a day, a local bank will collect the contents of the lockbox and deposit the checks into the company's local account.

London Interbank Offered Rate (LIBOR) Rate that U.K. banks charge one another. Many financial contracts have rates based on LIBOR, such as LIBOR + 2%.

long hedges Obligates the party to purchase the underlying asset at a predetermined price, providing protection against price increases. For example, bread manufacturer might go long in wheat to protect itself from increases in wheat prices.

long position (in forward contract) Obligates person in a long position to buy a specified amount of an asset (such as wheat) at a specified price and at a specified time.

Long-Term Equity AnticiPation Security (LEAPS) An option with an expiration date that is longer than that of a typical option. LEAPS can have up to 3 years before expiring.

loss aversion A behavioral phenomenon occurring when investors dislike a loss more than they like a gain of the same amount. For example, an investor dislikes a loss of $100 more than a gain of $100.

low-regular-dividend-plus-extras policy Dividend policy in which a company announces a low regular dividend that it is sure can be maintained; if extra funds are available, the company pays a specially designated extra dividend or repurchases shares of stock.

lumpy assets Those assets that cannot be acquired smoothly and instead require large, discrete additions. For example, an electric utility that is operating at full capacity cannot add a small amount of generating capacity, at least not economically.

M

MACRS (modified accelerated cost recovery system) An accelerated depreciation method in which property is assigned to a particular category (based on its useful life) for which the IRS has specified annual depreciation rates. These rates are applied to the basis, which is the acquisition cost.

make-whole call provision Allows a company to call a bond, but it must pay a call price that is essentially equal to the market value of a similar noncallable bond. This provides companies with an easy way to repurchase bonds as part of a financial restructuring, such as a merger.

managed floating rate An exchange rate system in which the currency floats, but there is significant government intervention to manage supply and demand.

managerial options Options that give opportunities to managers to respond to changing market conditions. Also called real options.

managing underwriter Investment bank that sets up a security offering and forms a syndicate to help sell it. Also called lead underwriter.

margin call Occurs when the stock prices falls and an investor had borrowed a percentage of the stock's price in order to buy the stock. The margin call requires the investor either to put up more money (i.e., pay of some of the borrowed money) or have their margined stock sold to pay off their loans.

margin requirement (for futures) Amount that a futures exchange requires from an investor to ensure that the investor will not renege on the daily marking to market.

margin requirement (for stock) The margin is the percentage of a stock's price that an investor has borrowed in order to purchase the stock. The Securities and Exchange Commission sets margin requirements, which is the maximum percentage of debt that can be used to purchase a stock.

marginal cost of capital The cost of capital associated with the next dollar of investment. It may increase if new external funds have flotation costs or other incremental costs in addition to the required rate of return.

marginal rate (for debt) The required rate of return on new debt, which is the yield to maturity on existing debt and the coupon rate on new debt issued at par.

marginal tax rate The tax rate on the last unit of income.

market auction preferred stock Resets dividend rates every 7 weeks at an auction. Also called money market preferred stock.

market capitalization Total market value of a firm's stock, found by multiplying the price per share by the number of shares. Also called market cap.

market debt ratio The ratio of the market value of total debt provided by investor to the total market value of debt and equity. If the market value of debt is not available, then then many analysts use the book value of debt as reported on the financial statements.

market equilibrium The condition under which the intrinsic value of a security is equal to its price; also, when a security's expected return is equal to its required return. Also known as equilibrium.

market interest rate The annual rate of interest stated in a contract, quoted for a security, or reported by the press. It is also called the going interest rate, the quoted rate, and the nominal annual interest rate.

market model A regression with a stock's returns on the y-axis and the market's returns on the x-axis.

market multiple method Used to estimate the value of a company. First identifies a sample of comparable firms and calculates for each comparable firm the ratio of its observed market value to a particular metric, which can be net income, earnings per share, sales, book value, number of subscribers, or any other metric that applies to the target firm and the comparable firms. Then calculates the average ratio from the sample and multiplies the result by the metric of the target firm, resulting in the target firm's estimated value.

market order Order asking broker to trade at the market price.

market portfolio A portfolio consisting of all shares of all stocks.

market price The price of the most recent transaction as observed in a financial market. Sometimes the current quoted ask price is called the market price because the ask price is the one at which an investor could buy the asset.

market risk That part of a security's (or project's) total risk that cannot be eliminated by diversification; measured by the beta coefficient and often called beta risk. In the context of project analysis, it is the risk of the project as viewed by a well-diversified stockholder who owns many different stocks, which is the project's impact on the firm's beta coefficient.

market risk premium, RP_M The difference between the expected return on the market and the risk-free rate. This is the extra rate of return that investors require to invest in the stock market rather than purchase risk-free securities. It is also called the equity premium or the equity risk premium.

market value Values of financial assets as determined in the markets—the price that a willing buyer will pay to a willing seller.

Market Value Added (MVA) The difference between the market value of the firm (that is, the sum of the market value of common equity, the market value of debt, and the market value of preferred stock) and the book value of the firm's common equity, debt, and preferred stock. If the book values of debt and preferred stock are equal to their market values, then MVA is also equal to the difference between the market value of equity and the amount of equity capital that investors supplied.

market value ratios Relate the firm's stock price to its earnings and book value per share.

market/book (M/B) ratio The stock price per share (i.e., the market value per share) divided by the book value per share; alternative, the total market value of equity divided by the total common equity reported on the balance sheet. Show how much current shareholders value the firm relative to the total cumulative amount of cash the firm has raised from shareholders either directly through stock issuances or indirectly by reinvesting net income rather than paying it all out as dividends.

marketable securities Can be converted to cash on very short notice and provide at least a modest return.

mark-to-market The process whereby the daily profit or loss on a futures contract is added to or subtracted from the investor's brokerage account. Recognizing losses on a daily basis rather than all at once at the contract's expiration reduces the risk of default.

maturity date The date when the bond's par value is repaid to the bondholder. Maturity dates generally range from 10 to 40 years from the time of issue.

maturity matching approach (for short-term financing) A policy that matches asset and liability maturities. It is also referred to as the self-liquidating approach.

maturity risk premium (MRP) The net effect upon a bond's yield due to interest rate risk and reinvestment risk. Interest rate risk seems to dominate, because investors usually require a higher yield for bonds with longer maturities.

merger The joining of two firms to form a single firm.

merger waves The empirical observation that mergers tend to cluster in time, becoming frequent in some years and infrequent in other years.

Miller model Introduces the effect of personal taxes into the valuation of a levered firm, which reduces the advantage of corporate debt financing:

$$V_L = V_U + \left[1 - \frac{(1 - T_c)(1 - T_s)}{(1 - T_d)} \right] D.$$

minimum annual cash contribution The sum of (1) the amount needed to fund projected future benefit payments that were accrued during the current period, (2) the amount that must be contributed to make up for not having funded all benefits for service that occurred prior to the current period, and (3) an additional amount required to offset unexpected deviations from the plan's actuarial assumptions, especially deviations in the earned rate of return and in employee turnover and wage rates.

MM Proposition I States that if there are no taxes, then $V_L = V_U = EBIT/r_{sU}$. Since both EBIT and r_{sU} are constant, firm value is also constant and capital structure is irrelevant. If there are corporate taxes, states that $V_L = V_U + TD$. Thus, firm value increases with leverage and the optimal capital structure is virtually all debt.

MM Proposition II States that if there are no taxes, then the required return on stock increases so that the WACC remains constant: $r_{sL} = r_{sU} + (r_{sU} - r_d)(D/S)$.

If there are corporate taxes, states that the WACC falls as debt is added and that the required rate of return on stock is: $r_{sL} = r_{sU} + (r_{sU} - r_d)(1 - T)(D/S)$.

moderate policy (current assets) A policy under which operating current assets are not allowed to be excessively high nor restrictively low.

modified accelerated cost recovery system (MACRS) An accelerated depreciation method in which property is assigned to a particular category (based on its useful life) for which the IRS has specified annual depreciation rates. These rates are applied to the basis, which is the acquisition cost.

Modified Internal Rate of Return (MIRR) method Assumes that cash flows from all projects are reinvested at the cost of capital, not at the project's own IRR. This makes the modified internal rate of return a better indicator of a project's true profitability.

money left on the table The increase in the stock price the first day of trading over the issue price during an IPO.

money market A financial market for debt securities with maturities of less than 1 year (short-term). The New York money market is the world's largest.

money market fund A mutual fund that invests in short-term debt instruments and offers investors check-writing privileges; thus, it amounts to an interest-bearing checking account.

money market preferred stock Resets dividend rates every 7 weeks at an auction. Also called market option preferred stock.

monopoly A market structure in which a single firm has enough market power to deter new competitors from entering the market. Without competition, a firm with monopoly power can maximize its profits by increasing prices until decreasing sales offset its gains.

Monte Carlo simulation analysis A risk analysis technique in which a computer is used to simulate probable future events and thus to estimate the likely profitability and risk of a project. Often called just simulation analysis. Can be applied to cash management systems as a means of estimating the appropriate target cash balance.

mortgage bond A bond for which a corporation pledges certain assets as security. All such bonds are written subject to an indenture.

mortgage market For loans on residential, agricultural, commercial, and industrial real estate.

multinational corporation A corporation that operates in an integrated fashion in more than one country. Also called global corporation, multinational enterprise, and transnational corporation.

multinational enterprise (MNE) A corporation that operates in an integrated fashion in more than one country. Also called global corporation, multinational corporation, and transnational corporation.

multiple discriminant analysis (MDA) A statistical technique used to determine the likelihood that a company will go bankrupt based on financial statement measures.

multiple IRRs Existence of more than one internal rate of return based on a project's cash flows and can occur when a project has nonnormal cash flows. In this situation, none of the calculated IRRs provide useful information.

multistage valuation model Approach to find the present value of cash flows that grow at a nonconstant rate for multiple periods before eventually beginning to grow at a constant growth rate for infinity. Is the sum of the present values of all cash flows during the forecast period plus the present value of the horizon value.

municipal bond Issued by state and local governments. The interest earned on most municipal bonds is exempt from federal taxes and also from state taxes if the holder is a resident of the issuing state.

municipal bond insurance An insurance company guarantees to pay the coupon and principal payments should the issuer of the bond (the municipality) default. This reduces the risk to investors who are willing to accept a lower coupon rate for an insured bond issue compared to an uninsured issue.

mutual fund A corporation that sells shares in the fund and uses the proceeds to buy stocks, long-term bonds, or short-term debt instruments. The resulting dividends, interest, and capital gains are distributed to the fund's shareholders after the deduction of operating expenses. Some funds specialize in certain types of securities, such as growth stocks, international stocks, or municipal bonds.

mutual savings bank Similar to S&Ls, but they operate primarily in the northeastern states.

mutually exclusive projects Projects that cannot be performed at the same time. A company could choose either Project 1 or Project 2, or it can reject both, but it cannot accept both projects.

N

naked call option The situation when a person writes a call option on a stock but does not own shares of the stock. If the option is exercised, then the writer must buy a share of stock in the market to be able to sell the share to the owner of the call option.

NASDAQ Stock Market (NASDAQ) A registered U.S. stock exchange with the most company listings. NASDAQ stands for National Association of Securities Dealers Automated Quotations, although the exchange is not owned by the NASD and the NASD is now part of the Financial Industry Regulatory Authority (FINRA).

National Best Bid and Offer (NBBO) The overall best (highest) bid price and best (lowest) ask price (the price at which an investor offers to sell stock) from among all registered stock exchanges. The NBBO represents the best prices at which an investor could buy or sell on any registered exchange.

natural hedge A transaction between two counterparties where both parties' risks are reduced, such as a farmer going short in wheat and a baker going long in wheat.

negatively correlated With assets, the correlation between the two assets is negative. Their returns tend to move opposite to each other.

negotiated deals (security offerings) A security offering in which an investment bank negotiates with the issuing company regarding its fees for underwriting the issuance. Occurs with most stock and debt offerings.

net advantage to leasing (NAL) The dollar value of the lease to the lessee. It is the net present value of leasing minus the net present value of owning.

net cash flow The sum of net income plus noncash adjustments.

net float The difference between a firm's disbursement float and collections float.

net income Income as defined by Generally Accepted Accounting Principles (GAAP) and reported on the income statement. Also called accounting income, accounting income, earnings, or profit.

net investment in operating capital The change in total net operating capital from the previous year, which represents the net amount that the company has spent on operating capital during the year.

net issue price (for a bond) The price per bond that the company actually receives. It is equal to the issue price minus the flotation costs.

net operating capital The sum of net operating working capital and operating long-term assets, such as net plant and equipment. Net operating capital is also called total net operating capital. It is also equal to the net amount of investor-supplied operating capital.

net operating profit after taxes (NOPAT) The amount of profit a company would generate if it had no debt and no financial assets.

net operating working capital (NOWC) Operating current assets minus operating current liabilities. Operating current assets are the current assets used to support operations, such as cash, accounts receivable, and inventory. They do not include short-term investments. Operating current liabilities are the current liabilities that are a natural consequence of the firm's operations, such as accounts payable and accruals. They do not include notes payable or any other short-term debt that charges interest.

net present value (NPV) The present value of the project's expected future cash flows, discounted at the appropriate cost of capital. NPV is a direct measure of the value of the project to shareholders.

net present value (NPV) profile Graph showing a project's NPV on the y-axis for different costs of capital on the x-axis.

net proceeds Amount raised during an IPO that goes to the issuing company after the investment banker receives the underwriting spread.

net profit margin Calculated by dividing net income by sales; gives the profit per dollar of sales. Also called the profit margin on sales or just the profit margin. Often denoted by M for margin.

net working capital Current assets minus current liabilities. Different from net *operating* working capital, because current assets and current liabilities may contain nonoperating accounts such as short-term investments and short-term loans.

net worth or shareholders' net worth The value of common equity shown on a balance sheet, which is the value of total assets less the value of liabilities and preferred stock.

new-issue bond Describes a bond that has been issued recently, usually within one month. Such bonds are actively traded, whereas bonds that have been issued further in the past often have very little trading because they are held in portfolios until maturity.

New York Stock Exchange (NYSE) Oldest registered stock exchange in the Unites States. NYSE is the largest exchange when measured by the market value of its listed stocks.

nominal rate of return (r_n) or nominal annual interest rate The annual rate of interest stated in a contract, quoted for a security, or reported by the press. When used in a time line with annual cash flows, it is called I_{NOM}. When referring to debt, the nominal annual rate is called the required rate of return on debt, r_d. When used in the context of expected inflation, the nominal rate is the rate that actually is observed in financial markets and is often denoted by r_n (for nominal)—it is the rate you see, whereas expected inflation and the real rate (i.e., the one that would exist if there were no inflation) are not directly observable. In the context of project analysis, if net cash flows from a project include increases due to expected future inflation, then the cash flows should be discounted at the nominal cost of capital to estimate NPV, and the internal rate of return resulting should be compared with the nominal cost of capital. The nominal rate is also called the going interest rate, the market interest rate, and the quoted interest rate.

nominal risk-free interest rate (r_{RF}) The quoted interest rate on a U.S. Treasury security, which is default-free and very liquid. It is equal to the real risk-free rate plus a premium for expected inflation. In the context of bond yields, it is the rate on either a short-term or long-term U.S. Treasury bond. In the context of the Capital Asset Pricing Model, it is the rate on a long-term Treasury bond (often the 10-year T-bond). Also called the risk-free rate of return or risk-free rate of interest.

nonconstant growth model An asset pricing model in which the cash flows do not grow at a constant growth rate until the horizon.

nonconvertible currency A currency that cannot be traded freely in the international currency markets and cannot be exchanged at current market rates but must be exchanged at a rate set by the country's government. Often called a soft currency or a blocked currency.

nonnormal cash flow projects Projects with cash flows that change signs more than once. For example, cash flow is negative at beginning of project, becomes positive, and then becomes negative again. Nonnormal cash flows can have multiple internal rates of return.

nonoperating assets Include investments in marketable securities and noncontrolling interests in the stock of other companies.

nonoperating current assets Short-term investments or any other current assets not used in operations.

nonpecuniary benefits Perks that are not actual cash payments, such as lavish offices, memberships at country clubs, corporate jets, and excessively large staffs.

non-tax-oriented lease Does not meet Internal Revenue Service (IRS) requirements for a genuine lease. Therefore, the lessee cannot deduct the full lease payment for tax purposes but instead can deduct depreciation and the implied interest portion of the lease payment.

NOPAT (net operating profit after taxes) The amount of profit a company would generate if it had no debt and no financial assets.

normal cash flow project A project with one or more cash outflows (costs) followed by a series of cash inflows. Note that the signs of the cash flows change only once, when they go from negative to positive (or from positive to negative).

normal distribution A widely used continuous probability distribution that resembles a bell-shaped curve.

normal yield curve When the yield curve slopes upward it is said to be "normal," because it is like this most of the time.

not-for-profit corporation A tax-exempt charitable organization. The tax code defines a charitable organization as any corporation, community chest, fund, or foundation that is organized and operated exclusively for religious, charitable, scientific, public safety, literary, or educational purposes. This standard may be expanded to include an organization that provides health care services provided other requirements are met.

notional principal For interest rate swaps, the principal amount used by the swapped interest rates to determine the dollar value of swapped payments.

notional value For forward and futures contracts, the amount to be delivered under the contract's terms.

O

off–balance sheet financing A financing technique in which a firm uses partnerships and other arrangements to (in effect) borrow money while not reporting the liability on its balance sheet. For example, for many years neither leased assets nor the liabilities under lease contracts appeared on the lessees' balance sheets. To correct this problem, the Financial Accounting Standards Board issued FASB Statement 13.

offer price Price at which the investment banking syndicate sells stocks to investors in an IPO.

off-exchange transaction The purchase or sale of a stock or other security that is not executed through a registered exchange. Also called an over-the-counter trade.

official statement Contains information about municipal bond issues. It is prepared before the issue is brought to market.

oligopoly A market structure in which several firms dominate an industry and choose not to compete on the basis of prices. The firms jointly behave much like a monopoly, leading to higher consumer prices.

on-the-run bond Describes a bond that has been issued recently, usually within one month. Such bonds are actively traded, whereas bonds that have been issued further in the past often have very little trading because they are held in portfolios until maturity.

open outcry auction A method of matching buyers and sellers in which the buyers and sellers are face-to-face, all stating a price at which they will buy or sell.

operating break-even point The level of unit sales at which costs equal revenues. Also called the break-even point.

operating capital The sum of net operating working capital and operating long-term assets, such as net plant and equipment. Operating capital is also called net operating capital and total net operating capital. It is also equal to the net amount of investor-supplied operating capital.

operating company A company controlled by a holding company.

operating current assets The current assets used to support operations, such as cash, accounts receivable, and inventory. It does not include short-term investments.

operating current assets financing policy The way a firm chooses to finance permanent and temporary operating current assets.

operating current liabilities The current liabilities that are a natural consequence of the firm's operations, such as accounts payable and accruals. It does not

include notes payable or any other short-term debt that charges interest.

operating lease Provides for both financing and maintenance. Generally, the operating lease contract is written for a period considerably shorter than the expected life of the leased equipment and contains a cancellation clause; sometimes called a service lease.

operating leverage The extent to which fixed costs are used in a firm's operations. If a high percentage of a firm's total costs are fixed costs, then the firm is said to have a high degree of operating leverage. Operating leverage is a measure of one element of business risk but does not include the second major element, sales variability.

operating merger Occurs when the operations of two companies are integrated with the expectation of obtaining synergistic gains. These may occur in response to economies of scale, management efficiency, or a host of other factors.

operating profit margin Ratio of earnings before interest and taxes divided by sales.

operating profitability (OP) ratio Net operating profit after taxes divided by sales. Measures how many dollars of operating profit are generated per dollar of sales.

opportunity cost A cash flow that a firm must forgo in order to accept a project. For example, if the project requires the use of a building that could otherwise be sold, then the market value of the building is an opportunity cost of the project.

opportunity cost rate The rate of return available on the best alternative investment of similar risk.

optimal capital budget Set of projects that maximizes the value of the firm.

optimal capital structure The capital structure (relative amounts of debt and equity financing) that maximizes the total value of the firm. It is also the capital structure that minimizes the weighted average cost of capital (WACC).

optimal distribution policy The distribution policy that maximizes the value of the firm by choosing the optimal level and form of distributions (dividends and stock repurchases).

optimal portfolio The point at which the efficient set of portfolios—the efficient frontier—is just tangent to the investor's indifference curve. This point marks the highest level of satisfaction an investor can attain given the set of potential portfolios.

option A contract that gives its holder the right to buy or sell an asset at some predetermined price within a specified period of time.

option value (of project) Value of opportunities to modify a project after its implementation, including expansion, contraction, or delay. Also includes additional opportunities that a project provides to a firm, such as introduction of complementary product line.

order book A trading venue's record of all limit orders still in effect.

ordering cost Cost of placing and receiving an order, including time spent on interoffice memos, long-distance telephone calls, setting up a production run, and taking delivery.

ordinary annuity An annuity with a fixed number of equal payments occurring at the end of each period. Also called a deferred annuity.

original issue discount (OID) bond In general, any bond originally offered at a price that is significantly below its par value.

original maturity A bond's number of years until maturity at the time it is issued.

out-of-the money option An option which would not have a positive payoff if exercised immediately. For example, a call option is out-of-the-money if the stock price is less than the strike price.

outside directors Board members who are not employed by the company and who have no other affiliations or financial interests in the company.

outsourcing The practice of purchasing components rather than making them in-house.

outstanding bond Describes a bond that has not been issued within the past month or two. Such bonds usually are not actively traded because they often are held in portfolios until maturity.

overfunded pension plan The assets on hand exceed the present value of all expected retirement benefits.

oversubscribed (IPO) Occurs in IPO when investors wish to purchase more shares than are available. Investment bank will allocate shares to the investors.

over-the-counter (OTC) trade The purchase or sale of a stock or other security that is not executed through a registered exchange.

P

paid-in-capital The difference between the amount investors paid for newly issues stock shares and the par value of those shares. Also called capital surplus.

par value (of a bond) The value printed on a bond certificate. A bond's par value, also called its face value, usually is the amount that the firm promises to repay at the bond's maturity date. The par value of a bond is often $1,000, but it can be $5,000 or more.

par value (of a stock) The value printed on a stock certificate. A stock's par value is not related to its market value, even at the time it is issued.

parent company Another name for a holding company. A parent company will often have control over many subsidiaries.

partial public offering IPO in which a parent company creates a new publicly traded company from a subsidiary and sells some of the stock to the public. Parent companies typically retain at least 80% of the subsidiary's common stock to maintain control and to preserve their ability to file a consolidated tax return. Also called an equity carve-out or a spin-out.

partially convertible currency A currency that trades in international Forex markets but whose conversion faces significant government restrictions.

partnership A partnership exists when two or more persons associate to conduct a business.

passively managed fund Mutual fund that holds a group of stocks in a particular category and then minimizes expenses by rarely trading.

pass-through entity A business whose income is not taxed at the business level but is instead passed through to its owners, where it is taxed at their individual personal tax rates.

payables deferral period (PDP) The average length of time between a firm's purchase of materials and labor and the payment of cash for them. It is calculated by dividing accounts payable by credit purchases per day (i.e., cost of goods sold ÷ 365).

payback period The number of years it takes a firm to recover its project investment. Payback does not capture a project's entire cash flow stream and is thus not the preferred evaluation method. Note, however, that the payback does measure a project's liquidity, so many firms use it as a risk measure.

payment date The date on which a firm actually pays a cash dividend to those owning the stock two business days prior to the holder of record date.

payment-in-kind (PIK) bonds Don't pay cash coupons but pay coupons consisting of additional bonds (or a percentage of an additional bond).

payment (PMT) Equal to the dollar amount of an equal or constant cash flow (an annuity).

payout ratio Percentage of net income paid as a cash dividend. Often denoted by POR.

payroll taxes Taxes other than income taxes that are deducted from a paycheck. These include Social Security taxes and Medicare taxes.

pecking order hypothesis A preferred sequence (i.e., a pecking order) of financing: (1) reinvested earnings, followed by (2) debt, and then (3) new common stock. This avoids a negative signal caused by investors' assumptions that managers have more information and will issue stock when it is overvalued. Higher flotation costs for debt than equity also imply a pecking order.

pegged exchange rates Rates that are fixed against a major currency such as the U.S. dollar. Consequently, the values of the pegged currencies move together over time.

Pension Benefit Guarantee Corporation (PBGC) Established by ERISA to insure corporate defined benefits plans; PBGC steps in and takes over payments to retirees of bankrupt companies with underfunded pension plans.

pension fund Retirement plan funded completely or partially by a corporation or government agency.

percentage change analysis Analysis in which percentage changes for all income statement items and balance sheet accounts are calculated relative to the items' values in the base year. Shows how different items change over time.

percentage flotation cost for debt and preferred stock, F The total dollar value of flotation costs divided by the total par value of the issue. Flotation costs include commissions, legal expenses, fees, and any other costs that a company incurs when it issues new securities.

perfect hedge A hedge in which the gain or loss on the hedged transaction exactly offsets the loss or gain on the unhedged position.

periodic compounding When interest is compounded once per period. The period is usually some period other than a year.

periodic rate, I_{PER} The rate charged by a lender or paid by a borrower each period. It can be a rate per year, per 6-month period, per quarter, per month, per day, or per any other time interval (usually 1 year or less).

permanent net operating working capital The NOWC required when the economy is weak and seasonal sales are at their low point. Thus, this level of NOWC always requires financing and can be regarded as permanent.

permanent operating current assets The level of current assets required when the economy is weak and seasonal sales are at their low point. Thus, this level of current assets always requires financing and can be regarded as permanent.

perpetuity A series of payments of a fixed amount that continue indefinitely.

petition (in bankruptcy) Initiation of formal bankruptcy proceeds via filing with bankruptcy court. Can be initiated by creditor (an involuntary petition) or borrower (voluntary petition).

physical asset market Market for tangible or "real" assets like as wheat, autos, real estate, computers, and machinery.

physical life of project The maximum potential life of a project; also called engineering life. This can exceed the optimal economic life.

physical location exchanges Exchanges, such as the New York Stock Exchange, that facilitate trading of securities at a particular location.

PIPE Private investment in public equity. Occurs when a public company sells shares of its stock directly to an investor, such as an insurance company or a pension fund.

plan sponsor The company that pays into a retirement fund for employee retirement benefits.

pledging of accounts receivable Putting accounts receivable up as security for a loan.

poison pills Shareholder rights provisions that allow existing shareholders in a company to purchase additional shares of stock at a lower-than-market value if a potential acquirer purchases a controlling stake in the company.

political risk Refers to the possibility of expropriation and the unanticipated restriction of cash flows to the parent by a foreign government.

pollution control bond A tax-exempt bond sold by state and local governments whose proceeds are made available to corporations for pollution control projects deemed (by Congress) to be in the public interest.

pooling of interests A method of accounting for a merger in which the consolidated balance sheet is constructed by simply adding together the balance sheets of the merged companies. This is no longer allowed.

portability A pension plan that an employee can carry from one employer to another.

portable pension plan A portable pension plan is one that the employee can carry from one employer to another.

portfolio Collection of assets, such as stocks or bonds, held in combination. An asset that would be relatively risky if held in isolation may have little or no risk if held in a well-diversified portfolio.

portfolio companies (in VC fund) Companies in which a venture capital fund invests, comprising the fund's portfolio of investments.

portfolio insurance A hedging technique that limits the possible downside losses on a portfolio.

portfolio risk The risk a stock adds to an already well diversified portfolio. This is also called beta risk.

portfolio weight The percentage of a portfolio's value that an asset makes up.

positively correlated With assets, the correlation between the two assets is positive. Their returns tend to move together.

post-audit The final aspect of the capital budgeting process. The post-audit is a feedback process in which the actual results are compared with those predicted in the original capital budgeting analysis. The post-audit has several purposes, of which the most important are to improve forecasts and operations.

precautionary balance A cash balance held in reserve for random, unforeseen fluctuations in cash inflows and outflows.

preemptive right Gives the current shareholders the right to purchase any new shares issued in proportion to their current holdings. The preemptive right enables current owners to maintain their proportionate share of ownership and control of the business.

preemptive rights offering Occurs when a corporation sells a new issue of common stock to its existing stockholders. Each stockholder receives a certificate, called a stock purchase right, giving the stockholder the

option to purchase a specified number of the new shares. The rights are issued in proportion to the amount of stock that each shareholder currently owns. Also called a just a rights offering.

preferred stock A hybrid security that is similar to bonds in some respects and to common stock in other respects. Preferred dividends are similar to interest payments on bonds in that they are fixed in amount and generally must be paid before common stock dividends can be paid. If the preferred dividend is not earned, the directors can omit it without throwing the company into bankruptcy.

preliminary prospectus A preliminary prospectus that may be distributed to potential buyers prior to approval of the registration statement by the Securities and Exchange Commission. After the registration has become effective, the securities—accompanied by the prospectus—may be offered for sale. Also called a red herring.

premium bond Bond prices and interest rates are inversely related; that is, they tend to move in the opposite direction from one another. A fixed-rate bond will sell at par when its coupon interest rate is equal to the going rate of interest, r_d. When the going rate of interest is above the coupon rate, a fixed-rate bond will sell at a "discount" below its par value. If current interest rates are below the coupon rate, a fixed-rate bond will sell at a "premium" above its par value.

premium (foreign currency forward rate) When the foreign currency indirect spot rate is greater than the forward rate; i.e., the foreign currency is expected to appreciate (based on forward rates) with respect to the home currency.

prepackaged bankruptcy (or pre-pack) A type of re-organization that combines the advantages of informal workouts and formal Chapter 11 reorganization.

present value interest factor The present value of $1 to be received in N periods discounted at a rate of i% per period.

present value interest factor for an annuity The present value of $1 to be received at the end of each of N periods discounted at a rate of i% per period.

present value of annuity, PVA The value today of a stream of annuity payments.

present value, PV The value today of a payment (or series of payments) that will be received in the future. It is also the beginning amount that will grow to some future value.

pre-tax earnings or pre-tax income The amount of earnings (or income) that is subject to taxes. It is also equal to earnings before interest and taxes (EBIT) less the interest expense. It is sometimes called earnings before taxes (EBT) or taxable income.

price improvement Occurs when a broker's client gets better deal than the posted NBBO quotes would indicate.

price/earnings (P/E) ratio Calculated by dividing price per share by earnings per share. This shows how much investors are willing to pay per dollar of reported profits.

price/EBITDA ratio The ratio of price per share divided by per share earnings before interest, depreciation, and amortization.

price/free cash flow (P/FCF) ratio Calculated by dividing price per share by free cash flow per share. This shows how much investors are willing to pay per dollar of free cash flow.

primary market Markets in which newly issued securities are sold for the first time, including IPOs and seasoned offerings.

prime rate Published by a bank as the rate it charges its strongest customers. However, very large and strong customers often can borrow at a lower rate.

principal (agency relationships) A person or organization to which has delegated decision-making authority to an agent, usually with the intent for the agent to act on behalf of the principal.

principal (debt) The amount of debt a borrower owes to a lender.

priority of claims in liquidation Established in Chapter 7 of the Bankruptcy Act. It specifies the order in which the debtor's assets are distributed among the creditors.

private equity (PE) fund Raises money from institutional investors and a relatively small number of high net-worth individuals. Private equity funds primarily invest in stock of private companies.

private investment in public equity (PIPE) When a public company sells shares of its stock directly to an investor, such as an insurance company or a pension fund.

private markets Markets in which transactions are worked out directly between two parties and structured

in any manner that appeals to them. Bank loans and private placements of debt with insurance companies are examples of private market transactions.

private placement The sale of stock to only one or a few investors, usually institutional investors. The advantages of private placements are lower flotation costs and greater speed, since the shares issued are not subject to Securities and Exchange Commission registration.

pro forma financial statement Shows how a future statement would look if certain assumptions are realized. Also called a projected financial statement.

probability distribution (continuous) Probability distribution having an infinite number of possible outcomes. Often shown as a graph with outcomes on the x-axis having values that might range from $-\infty$ to $+\infty$ (although many probability distributions do not have an infinite range of possible outcomes). The values on the y-axis are a continuous curve that begin with a value of zero (or tangent to zero), are always positive, and end with a value of zero (or tangent to zero). Also, the area under this curve must be equal to 100% (this is a probability density function). Sometimes shown with cumulative probabilities on the y-axis (i.e., the probability that an outcome will be less than or equal to the value on the x-axis; this is a cumulative density function).

probability distribution (discrete) Probability distribution having a finite number of outcomes. Often presented as a listing, chart, or graph showing all possible outcomes with a probability assigned to each outcome. This listing of outcomes and probabilities is a probability density function.

professional association (PA) Participants are not relieved of professional (malpractice) liability, but have most of the benefits of incorporation.

professional corporation (PC) Has most of the benefits of incorporation but the participants are not relieved of professional (malpractice) liability.

profit Income as defined by Generally Accepted Accounting Principles (GAAP) and reported on the income statement. Also called accounting income, accounting profit, earnings, or net income.

profit margin (on sales) Calculated by dividing net income by sales; gives the profit per dollar of sales. Also called the net profit margin or just the profit margin. Often denoted by M for margin.

profit sharing plan Under this type of pension plan, employers make payments into the retirement fund but the payments to retirees vary with the level of corporate profits.

profitability index Found by dividing the project's present value of future cash flows by its initial cost. A profitability index greater than 1 is equivalent to a project's having positive net present value.

profitability ratios Ratios that show the combined effects of liquidity, asset management, and debt on operating *and* financial results.

progressive tax A tax system in which the higher one's income, the larger the percentage paid in taxes.

project cash flows The incremental cash flows of a proposed project. Equal to the cash flows of the company with the project minus the cash flows without the project.

project cost of capital, r The rate used to discount a project's cash flows after taking into consideration firm's overall cost of capital, the divisional cost of capital and any additional subjective risk assessments for the particular project, including its impact on the firm's debt capacity. Also called the hurdle rate and the risk-adjusted cost of capital.

project financing Financing method in which the project's creditors do not have full recourse against the borrowers; the lenders and lessors must be paid from the project's cash flows and equity.

project net cash flows Same as project cash flows. The incremental cash flows of a proposed project.

projected financial statement Shows how a future statement would look if certain assumptions are realized. Also called a pro forma financial statement.

promissory note A document specifying the terms and conditions of a loan, including the amount, interest rate, and repayment schedule.

proprietorship A business owned by one individual.

prospectus Summarizes information about a new security issue and the issuing company. Is part of the S-1 registration statement.

proxy A document giving one person the authority to act for another, typically the power to vote shares of common stock.

proxy fight An attempt to take over a company in which an outside group solicits existing shareholders' proxies,

which are authorizations to vote shares in a shareholders' meeting, in an effort to overthrow management and take control of the business.

public markets Markets in which standardized contracts are traded on organized exchanges. Securities that are issued in public markets, such as common stock and corporate bonds, are ultimately held by a large number of individuals.

public offering An offer of new common stock to the general public.

publicly owned corporation Corporation in which the stock is owned by a large number of investors, most of whom are not active in management.

purchase accounting A method of accounting for a merger in which the merger is handled as a purchase. In this method, the acquiring firm is assumed to have "bought" the acquired company in much the same way it would buy any capital asset.

purchasing power bond The interest rate of such a bond is based on an inflation index such as the consumer price index (CPI), so the interest paid rises automatically when the inflation rate rises, thus protecting the bondholders against inflation. The final principal payment is also linked to inflation. Also called an index bond.

purchasing power parity (PPP) Implies that the level of exchange rates adjusts so that identical goods have the same true cost in different countries. For example, if converting domestic currency into foreign currency and purchasing a foreign product should have the same cost as purchasing an identical domestic product. Sometimes referred to as the "law of one price."

pure expectations theory States that the slope of the yield curve depends on expectations about future inflation rates and interest rates. Thus, if the annual rate of inflation and future interest rates are expected to increase, then the yield curve will be upward sloping; the curve will be downward sloping if the annual rates are expected to decrease.

pure play method Method of estimating a divisional beta as the average of betas from other companies that compete only in the division's line of business.

put option Allows the holder to sell the asset at some predetermined price within a specified period of time.

put–call parity relationship States that the value of a portfolio consisting of a put option and a share of stock must equal the value of a portfolio consisting of a call option (with the same strike price and expiration date as the put option) and cash, where the amount of cash is equal to the present value of the strike price.

PV The value today of a payment (or series of payments) that will be received in the future. PV is also the beginning amount that will grow to some future value.

PVA$_N$ The value today of a future stream of N equal payments at the end of each period (an ordinary annuity).

PVIFA$_{I,N}$ The present value interest factor for an ordinary annuity of N periodic payments discounted at I percent interest per period.

PVIF$_{I,N}$ The present value interest factor for a lump sum received N periods in the future discounted at I percent per period.

Q

quantity discount Reduction in unit price when a large number of units are purchased.

quick ratio Indicates the extent to which current liabilities are covered by the most liquid current assets; it is found by dividing current assets less inventories by current liabilities. It is also called the acid test ratio.

quiet period (IPO) Begins when an IPO registration statement is made effective; lasts for 40 days after the stock begins trading. Its purpose is to create a level playing field for all investors by ensuring that they all have access to the same information.

quoted interest rate The annual rate of interest stated in a contract, quoted for a security, or reported by the press. It is also called the going interest rate, the market interest rate, and the nominal annual interest rate.

R

ρ (rho), correlation coefficient A standardized measure of how two random variables covary. A correlation coefficient (ρ) of +1.0 means that the two variables move up and down in perfect synchronization, whereas a coefficient of −1.0 means the variables always move in opposite directions. A correlation coefficient of zero suggests that the two variables are not related to each other; that is, they are independent.

rating (bond) Reflects the probability that a bond will go into default. Bonds rated AAA have the least probability of defaulting.

$\bar{r}_{Avg}$, **average return** The average return from a sample periods of past actual returns.

r$_d$, required rate of return on debt The rate of return that fairly compensates an investor for purchasing or holding debt, taking into consideration its risk, timing, and the returns available on other similar investments. When referring to debt, r$_d$ is also called the yield, the quoted market interest rate, the going rate, and the nominal interest rate.

real options Occur when managers can influence the size and risk of a project's cash flows by taking different actions during the project's life. They are referred to as real options because they deal with real as opposed to financial assets. They are also called managerial options because they give opportunities to managers to respond to changing market conditions. Sometimes they are called strategic options because they often deal with strategic issues. Finally, they are also called embedded options because they are a part of another project.

real rate of return, r$_r$ Return that reflects actual growth in future purchasing power when there is inflation. For example, suppose you invest $100 now and receive $110 in 1 year. The nominal rate of return is 10%. If inflation has caused prices to go up by 10%, then your investment will not provide any additional purchasing power relative to the amount that your initial $100 could have purchased. Therefore, the investment's real rate of return is zero. In the context of project analysis, if net cash flows from a project do not include increases due to expected future inflation, then the cash flows should be discounted at the real cost of capital to estimate NPV and the internal rate of return resulting should be compared with the real cost of capital.

real risk-free interest rate (r*) The rate that a hypothetical riskless security pays each moment if zero inflation were expected. The real risk-free rate is not constant—r* changes over time depending on economic conditions.

realized rate of return on stock, $\bar{r}_s$ The rate of return that was actually realized on a share of stock during a particular holding period. Also called the actual rate of return.

realized rate of return, $\bar{r}_t$ The actual return an investor receives on his or her investment during period t. It can be quite different than the expected return.

rebalance Changing the assets and their weights in a portfolio.

recapitalization When a firm undertakes a wholesale change in its capital structure. This is usually increasing the level of debt and using the proceeds to repurchase stock or pay a dividend or issuing equity and using the proceeds to retire debt. Also called a recap.

receivables conversion period The average length of time required to convert a firm's receivables into cash. It is calculated by dividing accounts receivable by sales per day. Also called the average collection period or the days sales outstanding.

recourse When pledging accounts receivable for a loan, if the buyer who owes money on the account receivable doesn't pay, the lender can get the money back from the company that borrowed it.

red herring prospectus A preliminary prospectus that may be distributed to potential buyers prior to approval of the registration statement by the Securities and Exchange Commission. After the registration has become effective, the securities—accompanied by the prospectus—may be offered for sale. Called a red herring because it is marked in red.

redeemable at par Gives investors the right to sell the bonds back to the corporation at a price that is usually close to the par value. If interest rates rise, then investors can redeem the bonds and reinvest at the higher rates.

red-line method Determines the reorder times for inventory items stocked in a bin by drawing a red line inside of the bin at the level of the reorder point. The inventory manager places an order when the red line shows.

refunding operation Occurs when a company issues debt at current low rates and uses the proceeds to repurchase one of its existing high–coupon rate debt issues. Often these are callable issues, which means the company can purchase the debt at a call price lower than the market price.

registered stock exchange A trading venue that is registered as a stock exchange with the SEC. Must display quotes as well as report transactions.

registration statement (S-1) Required by the Securities and Exchange Commission before a company's securities can be offered to the public. This statement is used to summarize various financial and legal information about the company.

regression line A plot of the regression equation.

regular interest The situation when interest is not compounded; that is, interest is earned (or charged) only on principal and not on interest. Also called simple interest. Divide the nominal interest rate by 365 and multiply by the number of days the funds are borrowed to find the interest for the term borrowed.

Regulation D A provision in the Code of Federal Regulations that permits the sale of securities to accredited investors but places restrictions on the subsequent trading of those securities.

Regulation National Market System (Reg NMS) A set of rules designed by the SEC to protect investors and foster competition among exchanges and other trading venues. The order protection rule is intended to prevent an investor from buying or selling stock on one exchange when a better price is available on another exchange.

reinvestment rate risk Occurs when a short-term debt security must be "rolled over." If interest rates have fallen then the reinvestment of principal will be at a lower rate, with correspondingly lower interest payments and ending value.

relative priority doctrine More flexible than absolute priority. Gives a more balanced consideration to all claimants in a bankruptcy reorganization than does the absolute priority doctrine.

relaxed policy (current assets) A policy under which excessive amounts of cash and inventories are carried, and under which sales are stimulated by a liberal credit policy, resulting in a high level of receivables.

relevant risk An asset's contribution to a well-diversified portfolio's risk.

reorder point The inventory level at which a new order is placed.

reorganization (in bankruptcy) Restricting a lender's debt terms so that a borrower's company can continue to operate if the company is more valuable as a going concern than if it were liquidated. Can be informal or formal (via Chapter 11 of the bankruptcy code). A formal court-approved reorganization must adhere to the standards of fairness and feasibility.

repatriation The cash flow, usually in the form of dividends or royalties, from the foreign branch or subsidiary to the parent company. These cash flows must be converted to the currency of the parent and thus are subject to future exchange rate changes. A foreign government may restrict the amount of cash that may be repatriated. In addition, the parent's country may impose additional taxes on repatriated profits if the parent country has a higher tax rate than the foreign country.

replacement chain (common life) approach A method of comparing mutually exclusive projects that have unequal lives. Each project is replicated so that they will both terminate in a common year. If projects with lives of 3 years and 5 years are being evaluated, then the 3-year project would be replicated 5 times and the 5-year project replicated 3 times; thus, both projects would terminate in 15 years.

replicating portfolio A portfolio of assets whose prices are known and whose future payoffs identical to the payoffs of another asset. Because the payoffs of the portfolio and other asset are identical, the values of the portfolio and the other asset must also be identical.

repo Slang for a repurchase agreement, which is a contract in which the owner of Treasury securities sells them to a counterparty but agrees to repurchase them at a fixed date and price. Most repos are for 1 day and are called overnight repos.

repurchase (stock) Occurs when a firm purchases its own stock that it had previously issued. These shares of stock are then referred to as treasury stock.

repurchase agreement Contract in which the owner of Treasury securities sells them to a counterparty but agrees to repurchase them at a fixed date and price. Also called repos. Most repos are for 1 day and are called overnight repos.

required rate of return The rate of return that fairly compensates an investor for purchasing or holding a particular investment after considering its risk, timing, and the returns available on other similar investments. An investor requires the prospect of this return before investing.

required rate of return on a portfolio, r_p The minimum acceptable rate of return on a portfolio, considering both its risk and the returns available on other investments. With the Capital Asset Pricing model, the required rate of return is equal to the risk-free rate plus the extra return (i.e., the risk premium) needed to induce an investor to hold the portfolio. The required rate of return on a portfolio is the weighted average of the required rates of returns of the stocks comprising the portfolio.

required rate of return on debt, r_d The rate of return that fairly compensates an investor for purchasing or holding debt, taking into consideration its risk, timing, and the returns available on other similar investments. When referring to debt, r_d is also called the yield, the quoted market interest rate, the going rate, and the nominal interest rate.

required rate of return on Stock i, r_i The minimum acceptable rate of return on Stock i, considering both its risk and the returns available on other investments. With the Capital Asset Pricing model, the required rate of return is equal to the risk-free rate plus the extra return (i.e., the risk premium) needed to induce an investor to hold the stock.

required rate of return on stock, r_s Rate that shareholders require to be fairly compensated for the risk they bear. Also equal to the cost of common stock because it is the cost a company incurs to provide the required rate of return.

reserve borrowing capacity Exists when a firm uses less debt under "normal" conditions than called for by the trade-off theory, giving it the flexibility to use debt in the future when additional capital is needed. This avoids a negative signal caused by investors assuming that managers have more complete information and will issue stock when it is overvalued.

residual distribution model In this model, firms should pay dividends only when more earnings are available than needed to support the optimal capital budget.

residual value The market value of the leased property at the expiration of the lease. The estimate of the residual value is one of the key elements in lease analysis.

restricted charitable contributions Donations that can be used only for designated purposes.

restricted policy (current assets) A policy under which current assets are minimized by reducing holdings of cash, short-term investments, inventories, and receivables.

restricted stock awards (or grants) Compensation provided in the form of stock shares. The recipient receives dividends and may vote but may not sell the shares until they have vested.

restricted stock share unit (RSU) Compensation that provides that recipient a share of stock (or the equivalent in cash) after vesting. The recipient does not receive dividends or voting rights during vesting period.

restricted voting rights A provision that automatically deprives a shareholder of voting rights if the shareholder owns more than a specified amount of stock.

restrictive covenant Provisions in a bond indenture that cover such points as the conditions under which the issuer can pay off the bonds prior to maturity, the levels at which certain ratios must be maintained if the company is to issue additional debt, and restrictions against the payment of dividends unless earnings meet certain specifications. Also called a bond covenant or a covenant.

restructuring (of debt terms) Changing the terms of debt in an informal reorganization to avoid formal bankruptcy. Usually involves: (1) extending the time until the interest and/or principal payments are due; and (2) reducing the composition of the terms by reducing the interest and/or principal payments.

retained earnings The portion of the firm's earnings that have been saved rather than paid out as dividends.

retention growth equation Shows how growth is related to reinvestment and is expressed as follows: g = ROE(Retention ratio).

retention ratio Percentage of net income retained; i.e., the percent *not* paid as a cash dividend.

retiree health benefits a major issue for employers because of the escalating costs of health care and a recent FASB ruling forcing companies to accrue the retiree health care liability rather than expensing the cash flows as they occur.

return on assets (ROA) Found by dividing net income by total assets; also called the return on total assets. Measure how much net income is generated per dollar of assets.

return on common equity (ROE) Found by dividing net income by common equity; also called return on equity. Measures shareholders' rate of return after incorporating the impact of financial leverage.

return on equity (ROE) Found by dividing net income by common equity; also called return on common equity. Measures shareholders' rate of return after incorporating the impact of financial leverage.

return on invested capital (ROIC) Net operating profit after taxes divided by total net operating capital. Provides

a measure of how well the company is operating because it excludes the impact of financial leverage.

return on total assets (ROA) Found by dividing net income by total assets; also called the return on assets. Measure how much net income is generated per dollar of assets.

revaluation Occurs when the relative price of a currency is increased. It is the opposite of devaluation.

revenue bonds Type of municipal bonds which are secured by the revenues derived from projects such as roads and bridges, airports, water and sewage systems, and not-for-profit health care facilities.

reverse split Situation in which shareholders exchange a particular number of shares of stock for a smaller number of new shares.

revolving credit agreement A formal, committed line of credit extended by a bank or other lending institution. Borrower often must pay a commitment fee even if borrower doesn't draw on the line of credit.

r$_i$, required rate of return on Stock i The minimum acceptable rate of return on Stock i, considering both its risk and the returns available on other investments. With the Capital Asset Pricing model, the required rate of return is equal to the risk-free rate plus the extra return (i.e., the risk premium) needed to induce an investor to hold the stock.

right-of-use asset A balance sheet asset entry that represents the remaining unamortized portion of the capitalized value of a lease, including operating leases and financial leases. It is also equal to the lease liability.

rights offering Occurs when a corporation sells a new issue of common stock to its existing stockholders. Each stockholder receives a certificate, called a stock purchase right, giving the stockholder the option to purchase a specified number of the new shares. The rights are issued in proportion to the amount of stock that each shareholder currently owns. Also called a preemptive rights offering.

rights-on When a share will receive the stock purchase right in a rights offering. Stock purchased prior to the ex-rights date will receive the right.

right (stock purchase) Certificate issued in a rights offering that gives the holder the right to purchase a specified number of new shares at a specified price. Often called a stock purchase right.

risk Exposure to the chance of an unfavorable event.

risk-adjusted cost of capital, r The rate used to discount a project's cash flows after taking into consideration firm's overall cost of capital, the divisional cost of capital and any additional subjective risk assessments for the particular project, including its impact on the firm's debt capacity. Also called the project cost of capital and the hurdle rate.

risk-adjusted discount rate, r The rate used to discount a project's cash flows after taking into consideration firm's overall cost of capital, the divisional cost of capital and any additional subjective risk assessments for the particular project, including its impact on the firm's debt capacity. Also called the project cost of capital, the risk-adjusted cost of capital, and the hurdle rate.

risk arbitrage The practice of purchasing stock in companies (in the context of mergers) that may become takeover targets.

risk aversion A risk-averse investor dislikes risk and requires a higher rate of return as an inducement to buy riskier securities.

risk-free asset An asset with a zero probability of default. Although nothing is truly risk-free, most investors consider a short-term U.S. Treasury security to be a risk-free asset.

risk-free interest rate, r_{RF} Usually estimated as the quoted interest rate on a U.S. Treasury security, which is default-free and very liquid. It is equal to the real risk-free rate plus a premium for expected inflation. In the context of bond yields, it is the nominal risk-free rate on either a short-term or long-term U.S. Treasury bond. In the context of the Capital Asset Pricing Model, it is the rate on a long-term Treasury bond (often the 10-year T-bond). It is also called the risk-free rate of return or the nominal risk-free rate.

risk-free interest rate (the nominal long-term rate) Usually estimated as the quoted interest rate on a long-term U.S. Treasury bond, which is default-free, very liquid, and has a long time until maturity. It is exposed to inflation risk. It is also exposed to price volatility caused by interest rate volatility. The quoted risk-free rate of interest on a short-term U.S. Treasury bond, which is which is default-free and very liquid. Note that r_{T-bond} includes the premium for expected inflation and interest rate volatility related to maturity: $r_{T-bond} = r^* + IP + MRP$.

risk-free interest rate (the nominal short-term rate) The quoted risk-free rate of interest rate on a short-term U.S. Treasury bill, which is default-free, very liquid, and has a short time until maturity. Includes the premium for expected inflation and is approximated by $r_{T-bill} = r^* + IP$ It is exposed to inflation risk.

risk-free nominal rate of interest rate, r_{RF} The quoted interest rate on a U.S. Treasury security, which is default-free and very liquid. In the context of short-term securities, the risk-free rate refers to a U.S. Treasury bill, which is default-free, very liquid, and has a short time until maturity (although it still is exposed to inflation risk). In the context of long-term securities, the risk-free rate refers to a U.S. Treasury, bond, which is default-free, very liquid, and has a long time until maturity (although it still is exposed to inflation risk and price volatility caused by interest rate volatility). The real risk-free rate plus a premium for expected inflation. The short-term nominal risk-free rate is usually approximated by the U.S. Treasury bill rate, and the long-term nominal risk-free rate is approximated by the rate on U.S. Treasury bonds.

risk-free rate of return, r_{RF} Usually estimated as the quoted interest rate on a U.S. Treasury security, which is default-free and very liquid. It is equal to the real risk-free rate plus a premium for expected inflation. In the context of bond yields, it is the nominal risk-free rate on either a short-term or long-term U.S. Treasury bond. In the context of the Capital Asset Pricing Model, it is the rate on a long-term Treasury bond (often the 10-year T-bond). Also called the risk-free interest rate or the nominal risk-free rate.

risk-neutral valuation Method of derivative valuation that replaces the actual growth rates of asset values with the risk-free rate and then discounts the resulting cash flows at the risk-free rate. The result is the correct value of the asset (in the sense that there will be no arbitrage opportunities if asset is priced with the result of the risk-neutral valuation technique).

risk premium The additional expected return on a higher risk investment relative to a lower risk investment. A higher expected return is required by investors as compensation for bearing higher risk.

risk premium for individual Stock i, RP_i Product of the stock's beta and the market risk premium: $RP_i = b_i (RP_M)$.

risky event An uncertain outcome that adversely affects a company's objectives.

x1124 Glossary

roadshow Before an IPO, the senior management team and the investment banker make presentations to potential investors. They make three to five presentations daily over a 2-week period in 10 to 20 cities.

roll-up merger A type of horizontal merger in which a company acquires a number of other companies in the same industry and consolidates them to create a single brand.

$\hat{r}_p$, **expected rate of return on a portfolio** The rate of return expected on a portfolio given its current price and expected future cash flows.

r_p, **required rate of return on a portfolio** The minimum acceptable rate of return on a portfolio, considering both its risk and the returns available on other investments. With the Capital Asset Pricing Model, the required rate of return is equal to the risk-free rate plus the extra return (i.e., the risk premium) needed to induce an investor to hold the portfolio. The required rate of return on a portfolio is the weighted average of the required rates of returns of the stocks comprising the portfolio.

RP_i, **risk premium for individual Stock i** Product of the stock's beta and the market risk premium: $RP_i = b_i (RP_M)$.

RP_M, **market risk premium** The difference between the expected return on the market and the risk-free rate. This is the extra rate of return that investors require to invest in the stock market rather than purchase risk-free securities. It is also called the equity premium or the equity risk premium.

r^*, **real risk-free interest rate** The rate that a hypothetical riskless security pays each moment if zero inflation were expected. The real risk-free rate is not constant—r^* changes over time depending on economic conditions.

r, **real rate of return** Return that reflects actual growth in future purchasing power when there is inflation. For example, suppose you invest $100 now and receive $110 in 1 year. The nominal rate of return is 10%. If inflation has caused price to go up by 10%, then your investment will not provide any additional purchasing power relative to the amount that your initial $100 could have purchased. Therefore, the investment's real rate of return is zero. In the context of project analysis, if net cash flows from a project do not include increases due to expected future inflation, then the cash flows should be discounted at the real cost of capital to estimate NPV and the internal rate of return resulting should be compared with the real cost of capital.

r_{RF}, **risk-free rate of return** The quoted interest rate on a U.S. Treasury security, which is default-free and very liquid. It is equal to the real risk-free rate plus a premium for expected inflation. In the context of bond yields, it is the nominal risk-free rate on either a short-term or long-term U.S. Treasury bond. In the context of the Capital Asset Pricing Model, it is the rate on a long-term Treasury bond (often the 10-year T-bond). Also called the risk-free interest rate or the nominal risk-free rate.

$\hat{r}$, **expected rate of return** The rate of return expected on a stock given its current price and expected future cash flows. If the stock is in equilibrium, the required rate of return will equal the expected rate of return.

$\bar{r}_s$, **realized rate of return on stock** The rate of return that was actually realized on a share of stock during a particular holding period.

r_s, **required rate of return on stock** Rate that shareholders require to be fairly compensated for the risk they bear. Also equal to the cost of common stock because it is the cost a company incurs to provide the required rate of return.

RSU (restricted stock share unit) Compensation that provides that recipient a share of stock (or the equivalent in cash) after vesting. The recipient does not receive dividends or voting rights during vesting period.

r_{sU}, **unlevered cost of equity** Cost of equity for a firm with no debt.

r_{TS}, **tax shield discount rate** Rate that is used to discount the annual tax savings due to interest (TS_t).

$\bar{r}_t$, **realized rate of return** The actual return an investor receives on his or her investment during period t. It can be quite different than the expected return.

Rule of 78 Method of allocating a payment's portions of interest and principal. The portion due to interest for a payment is defined as the number of remaining payments (not including the current payment) divided by the sum of the payment numbers. For example, with 12 payments, the sum of 1 through 12 is 78 and the interest allocation in the first payment is 12/78.

S

safety stock Inventory held to guard against larger-than-normal sales and/or shipping delays.

sale-and-leaseback A type of financial lease in which the firm owning the property sells it to another firm, often a financial institution, while simultaneously entering into an agreement to lease the property back from the firm.

salvage value The market value at which a used asset can be sold.

savings and loan association (S&L) A financial institution that takes in most of its deposits from members of their community and makes most if its loans to homeowners and consumers.

scenario analysis Assumes several possible scenarios, including the inputs and the probability of occurrence for each scenario. Uses the scenario's inputs to calculate key results (such as NPV), and then uses the probabilities to estimate the expected value and standard deviation of each key result.

seasonal dating Setting an invoice date to correspond with the beginning of the time the goods are likely to be sold rather than when the goods are actually shipped.

seasonal effects on ratios Seasonal factors can distort ratio analysis. At certain times of the year, a firm may have excessive inventories in preparation of a "season" of high demand. Therefore, an inventory turnover ratio taken at this time will be radically different than one taken after the season.

seasoned bond Describes a bond that has not been issued within the past month or two. Such bonds usually are not actively traded because they often are held in portfolios until maturity.

seasoned equity offering The sale of additional shares of stock by a public company after its initial public offering.

secondary market Markets in which securities are resold after initial issue in the primary market. The New York Stock Exchange is an example.

second-mortgage bond Secured by the same assets as first-mortgage bonds. In the event of liquidation, holders of second-mortgage bonds receive payments only after the first-mortgage bondholders have been paid in full. Also called junior mortgage bonds.

secured basis loan A loan backed by collateral, which is often in the form of inventories or receivables.

secured debt Debt for which a corporation pledges certain assets as security.

Secured Overnight Financing Rate (SOFR) Introduced by the U.S. Federal Reserve to be a replacement for

LIBOR. The SOFR is based on actual overnight loans that use Treasury securities as collateral.

Securities and Exchange Commission (SEC) A government agency which regulates the sales of new securities and the operations of securities exchanges. The SEC, along with other government agencies and self-regulation, helps ensure stable markets, sound brokerage firms, and the absence of stock manipulation.

securitization The process whereby financial instruments that were previously thinly traded are converted to a form that creates greater liquidity. Securitization also applies to the situation where specific assets are pledged as collateral for securities, thus creating asset-backed securities. One example of the former is junk bonds; an example of the latter is mortgage-backed securities.

security instrument In inventory financing, a document that acknowledges that the goods in inventory are held in trust for the lender. Also called a trust receipt.

Security Market Line (SML) Represents, in a graphical form, the relationship between the risk of an asset as measured by its beta and the required rates of return for individual securities. The SML equation is one of the key results of the CAPM:
$$r_i = r_{RF} + b_i(r_M - r_{RF}) = r_{RF} + b_i(RP_M).$$

self-liquidating approach (for short-term financing) A policy that matches asset and liability maturities. It is also referred to as the maturity matching approach.

sell forward (in a forward contract) Taking a short position to sell a specified amount of an asset (such as wheat) at a specified price and a specified time.

selling group All members of an underwriting syndicate plus additional dealers usually selling to retail customers.

semiannual compounding When interest is compounded twice per year.

semistrong form of market efficiency States that current market prices reflect all publicly available information. Therefore, the only way to gain abnormal returns on a stock is to possess inside information about the company's stock.

senior mortgage bond Has higher priority claim on the issuer's asset than subsequently issued bonds. Also called a first-mortgage bond.

sensitivity analysis Indicates exactly how much net present value will change in response to a given change in an input variable, other things held constant. Sensitivity analysis is sometimes called "what if" analysis because it answers this type of question.

Separate Trading of Registered Interest and Principal of Securities (STRIPS) Zero coupon bonds created from coupon-paying Treasury bonds by stripping the T-bonds' coupon payments and principal payment and then selling each one as an individual security.

settlement (payment process) Occurs when the payer's bank actually deducts the payment amount from the account balance and the payee's bank actually deposits the amount into the payees account.

shareholder rights provision Allows existing shareholders in a company to purchase additional shares of stock at a lower-than-market value if a potential acquirer purchases a controlling stake in the company. Also called a poison pill.

Sharpe's reward-to-variability ratio Asset's average return (in excess of the risk-free rate) divided by its standard deviation. Measure the return per unit of risk as defined by standard deviation.

shelf registration Frequently, companies will file a master registration statement and then update it with a short form statement just before an offering. This procedure is termed shelf registration because companies put new securities "on the shelf" and then later sell them when cash is needed and market conditions are favorable.

short hedges Obligates the party to sell the underlying asset at a predetermined price, providing protection against price decreases. For example, a farming company might go short in wheat to protect itself from decreases in wheat prices.

short position (in forward contract) Obligates person in a short position to sell a specified amount of an asset (such as wheat) at a specified price and a specified time.

signal An action taken by a firm's management that reveals information to investors about its future prospects.

signaling hypothesis (dividends) A theory hypothesizing that investors regard dividend changes as "signals" of management forecasts. Thus, when dividends are raised, this is viewed by investors as recognition by management of future earnings increases. Therefore, if a firm's stock price increases with a dividend increase, the reason may not be investor preference for dividends but rather expectations of higher future earnings. Conversely, a dividend reduction may signal that management is forecasting poor earnings in the future. Also called the dividend information content hypothesis.

signaling theory (capital structure) Assumes managers have more information than investors and will issue stock when it is overvalued, causing a stock issue to be a negative signal. Leads to a preferred "pecking order" of financing: (1) retained earnings, followed by (2) debt, and then (3) new common stock.

simple interest The situation when interest is not compounded; that is, interest is earned (or charged) only on principal and not on interest. Also called regular interest. Divide the nominal interest rate by 365 and multiply by the number of days the funds are borrowed to find the interest for the term borrowed.

simulation analysis A risk analysis technique in which a computer is used to simulate probable future events and thus to estimate the likely profitability and risk of a project. Often called Monte Carlo simulation analysis.

sinking fund Facilitates the orderly retirement of a bond issue. This can be achieved in one of two ways: (1) the company can call in for redemption (at par value) a certain percentage of bonds each year; or (2) the company may buy the required amount of bonds on the open market.

S$_L$, levered firm's stock value Value of stock in a company with debt. It reflects side effects due to leverage or other factors.

social value Projects of not-for-profit businesses are expected to provide a social value in addition to an economic value.

SOFR (Secured Overnight Financing Rate) Introduced by the U.S. Federal Reserve to be a replacement for LIBOR. The SOFR is based on actual overnight loans that use Treasury securities as collateral.

soft currency A currency that cannot be traded freely in the international currency markets and cannot be exchanged at current market rates but must be exchanged at a rate set by the country's government. Often called a nonconvertible currency.

special dividend A dividend paid, in addition to the regular dividend, when earnings permit. Firms with volatile earnings may have a low regular dividend that can be maintained even in years of low profit (or high capital investment) but is supplemented by an extra dividend when excess funds are available.

special purpose entity (SPE) Created when a company establishes a separate legal entity but provides a guarantee of the entity's liabilities. This guarantee allows the entity to borrow money and then purchase financial or physical assets. Because the entity is separate from the creating company, the entity's assets and liabilities are reported on its own balance sheets and not those of the creating company. The entity usually has a narrow purpose, such as purchasing an asset and leasing it to the creating company.

special tax bonds Type of municipal bonds which are secured by a specified tax, such as a tax on utility services.

specific identification Inventory accounting method in which a unique cost is attached to each item in inventory. When an item is sold, the inventory value is reduced by that specific amount.

speculation in derivatives Occurs when one of the counterparties is not hedging away risk but is instead entering the derivatives contract in the hopes of making a profit on the contract.

speculative balances Funds held by a firm in order to have cash for taking advantage of bargain purchases or growth opportunities.

spin-off Occurs when a holding company distributes the stock of one of the operating companies to its shareholders, thus passing control from the holding company to the shareholders directly.

spin-out IPO in which a parent company creates a new publicly traded company from a subsidiary and sells some of the stock to the public. Parent companies typically retain at least 80% of the subsidiary's common stock to maintain control and to preserve their ability to file a consolidated tax return. Also called a partial public offering or an equity carve-out.

spontaneous liabilities Liabilities which grow with sales, such as accounts payable and accruals.

spontaneous liabilities-to-sales ratio, L_0^*/S_0 The ratio of spontaneous liabilities at Time 0 (L_0) divided by the sales at Time 0 (S_0). This is the amount of spontaneous liabilities generated by a dollar of sales, which reduces the need for external financing to support sales.

spot markets Where assets are bought or sold for "on-the-spot" delivery (literally, within a few days).

spot rate (foreign exchange) Specifies the number of units of a given currency that can be purchased for one unit of another currency for immediate (on the spot) delivery.

spread, bond yield The difference between the yield of a bond relative to another bond with less risk.

spread, underwriting The difference between the offer price at which an underwriter sells the stock in an initial public offering and the proceeds that the underwriter passes on to the issuing firm; the fee collected by the underwriter. It is often about 7% of the offering price.

staged decision tree A type of capital budgeting analysis that models the decisions that management can make about the project after the project has started as a decision tree.

staggered terms The structure of a corporate board in which not all of the directors are elected at the same time.

stakeholders All parties that have an interest, financial or otherwise, in a company. This includes employees and the communities in which the company does business.

stand-alone risk The risk an investor would take by holding only one asset. In the context of project analysis, it is the risk a company would have if the company had only one project and it is caused by variability in a project's cash flows. The standard deviation is used often to measure stand-alone risk.

standard deviation, σ A statistical measure of how dispersed a set of observations are about the mean of the observations. It is the square root of the variance.

statement of cash flows Reports the impact of a firm's operating, investing, and financing activities on cash flows over an accounting period.

statement of stockholders' equity Statement showing the beginning stockholders' equity, any changes due to stock issues/repurchases, the amount of net income that is retained, and the ending stockholders' equity.

stepped-up strike (or exercise) price A provision in a warrant that increases the strike price over time. This provision is included to encourage owners to exercise their warrants.

stock dividend Increases the number of shares outstanding but at a slower rate than splits. Current shareholders receive additional shares on some proportional basis. Thus, a holder of 100 shares would receive 5 additional shares at no cost if a 5% stock dividend were declared.

stock exchange (registered) A trading venue that is registered as a stock exchange with the SEC. Must display quotes as well as report transactions.

stock option A contract that gives its holder the right to buy or sell a share of stock at some predetermined price within a specified period of time. For example, a call option on a stock allows the option's owner to purchase a share of stock at a fixed price, called the strike price or the exercise price, no matter what the actual price of the stock is. Stock options always have an expiration date, after which they cannot be exercised.

stock option compensation plan An additional form of employee compensation above and beyond cash salaries and cash bonuses in which the employee is granted call options on the firm's stock. Typical plans do not vest immediately but require that the employee stay with the company a specified period before exercising the option is permitted.

stock purchase right Certificate issued in a rights offering that gives the holder the right to purchase a specified number of new shares at a specified price. Often just called a right.

stock repurchase Occurs when a firm purchases its own stock that it had previously issued. These shares of stock are then referred to as treasury stock.

stock split Current shareholders are given some number (or fraction) of shares for each stock share owned. Thus, in a 3-for-1 split, each shareholder would receive three new shares in exchange for each old share, thereby tripling the number of shares outstanding. Stock splits usually occur when the stock price is outside of the optimal trading range.

stock-out cost (inventory) The cost of running short of inventory and subsequently losing sales.

straight-line depreciation method Depreciation method for financial reporting purposes that calculates depreciation basis as the acquisition cost minus the expected salvage and then divides the basis by the number of years until salvage to determine the annual depreciation rate that can be applied to the basis.

strategic alliance A cooperative deal that stops short of a merge but still allow firms to create combinations that focus on specific business lines that offer the most potential synergies. Also called a corporate alliance.

strategic options Options that often deal with strategic issues. Also called real options, embedded options, and managerial options.

stretching accounts payable The practice of deliberately paying accounts late.

strike (or exercise) price The price stated in the option contract at which the security can be bought (or sold).

STRIPS (Separate Trading of Registered Interest and Principal of Securities) Zero coupon bonds created from coupon-paying Treasury bonds by stripping the T-bonds' coupon payments and principal payment and then selling each one as an individual security.

strong form of market efficiency Assumes that all information pertaining to a stock, whether public or inside information, is reflected in current market prices. Thus, no investors would be able to earn abnormal returns in the stock market.

structured note Security that usually consists of a bond with a specified maturity value and date but whose payments are linked to some other financial asset, such as stocks, commodities, foreign currencies, or even other interest rate derivatives.

subordinated debenture Debentures that have claims on assets, in the event of bankruptcy, only after senior debt (as named in the subordinated debt's indenture) has been paid off. Subordinated debentures may be subordinated to designated notes payable or to all other debt.

subsidiary A company whose stock is owned by other companies. If all the stock is owned by one company, it is called a wholly owned subsidiary.

sunk cost A cost that has already occurred and is not affected by the capital project decision. Sunk costs are not relevant to capital budgeting decisions.

super poison put Enables a bondholder to turn in, or "put," a bond back to the issuer at par in the event of a takeover, merger, or major recapitalization.

supply chain The network of organizations that convert materials and labor into products or services that ultimately are purchased by consumers.

swap An exchange of cash payment obligations. Usually occurs because the parties involved prefer someone else's payment pattern or type.

sweetener A feature that makes a security more attractive to some investors, thereby inducing them to accept a lower current yield. Convertible features and warrants are examples of sweeteners.

symmetric hedge Occurs for a derivative in which the payoff from a dollar increase in the underlying asset has exactly the opposite effect of a dollar decrease in the underlying asset. For example, forward contracts and futures have symmetric payoffs.

symmetric information When investors have the same information as managers.

synchronization of cash flows Occurs when firms are able to time cash receipts to coincide with cash requirements.

syndicated loan A loan in which a group of financial institutions act jointly to fund the loan.

synergistic benefits Difference between the value of a company to an acquirer (which reflects synergy) and the value to the target if not acquired.

synergy Occurs when the whole is greater than the sum of its parts. When applied to mergers, a synergistic merger occurs when the post-merger earnings exceed the sum of the separate companies' pre-merger earnings.

synthetic lease Version of an operating lease in which a company established a special purpose entity to borrow funds in the financial markets, purchase an asset with the borrowed funds, and then lease the asset to the creating company.

T

takeover An action whereby a person or group succeeds in ousting a firm's management and taking control of the company.

tapping fund assets Deals with the issue of allowing a corporation to invest its pension fund assets to the corporation's own advantage.

target capital structure Percentages of the different sources of capital the firm plans to use on a regular basis, with the percentages based on the market values of those sources. These percentages are used to estimate the weighted average cost of capital.

target cash balance The desired cash balance that a firm plans to maintain in order to conduct business.

target company A firm that another company seeks to acquire.

target distribution ratio Percentage of net income distributed to shareholders through cash dividends or stock repurchases. The actual distribution ratio can vary from the target year to year, but the average actual distribution ratio over time should match the target.

targeted share repurchases Also known as greenmail, occurs when a company buys back stock from a potential acquirer at a price that is higher than the market price. In return, the potential acquirer agrees not to attempt to take over the company.

target payout ratio Percentage of net income that company seeks to pay as a cash dividend. The actual payout ratio can vary from the target year to year, but the average actual payout ratio over time should match the target.

target stock or targeting stock A class of stock with dividends tied to a particular part of a company. Also called tracking stock.

taxable income (for companies) Usually equal to sales revenue minus all allowable costs, including depreciation and allowable interest expenses. It is also called pre-tax income, pre-tax earnings, or earnings before taxes (EBT).

taxable income (for individuals) Gross income less a set of exemptions and deductions that are spelled out in the instructions to the tax forms that individuals must file.

Tax Cuts and Jobs Act (TCJA) The unofficial name of an Act of Congress signed into law in December 2017. Among its many changes, the Act replaces the previous graduated corporate tax brackets (which had a top rate of 35%) with a flat tax of 21%. The Act also suspends for 2018–2025 the 2017 personal brackets and rates of 2017 and temporarily replaces them with brackets and rates that reduce taxes for most personal filers, especially for those with very high income. In 2026, the Act returns individual brackets and rates to their 2017 levels (after adjusting for inflation).

tax effect theory Proposes that investors prefer capital gains over dividends, because capital gains taxes can be deferred into the future but taxes on dividends must be paid as the dividends are received.

tax-exempt bonds Bonds issued by industrial development agencies and pollution control agencies whose proceeds are made available to corporations for uses deemed (by Congress) to be in the public interest. The interest paid to investors is exempt from federal income taxes.

tax loss carryforward Prior cumulative operating losses may be carried forward indefinitely and may be used to offset up to 80% of the taxable income for a particular year.

tax-oriented lease Meets all of the Internal Revenue Service (IRS) requirements for a genuine lease. If a lease meets the IRS guidelines, the IRS allows the lessor to deduct the asset's depreciation and allows the lessee to deduct the lease payments. Also called a guideline lease and a true lease.

tax savings due to interest, TS_t Year-t tax savings due to the deductibility of interest from taxable income. Because the deduction reduces taxable income, taxes are lower than they otherwise would have been. Also called interest tax savings.

tax shield, $V_{Tax\ shield}$ Present value of all expected future annual tax savings due to deductibility of interest expenses. Also called the interest tax shield.

tax shield beta, b_{TS} A measure of the amount of risk that the tax shield contributes to a well-diversified portfolio. Calculated as $b_{TS} = (\sigma_{TS}/\sigma_M)\rho_{TS,M}$, where σ_{TS} is the standard deviation of tax shield, σ_M is the standard deviation of the market return, and $\sigma_{TS,M}$ is the correlation between the tax shield and the market.

tax shield discount rate, r_{TS} Rate that is used to discount the annual tax savings due to interest (TS_t). In the Modigliani and Miller models, $r_{TS} = r_d$. In the compressed adjusted present value (CAPV) model, $r_{TS} = r_{sU}$.

T-bill A Treasury bill, which is a short-term security issued by the federal government. A T-bill has a maturity of 52 weeks or less at the time of issue, and it makes no payments at all until it matures. Thus, T-bills are sold initially at a discount to their face, or maturity, value. T-bills have no default risk.

T-bond Treasury bonds issued by the federal government. A T-bond makes an equal payment every 6 months until it matures, at which time it makes an additional lump-sum payment of its par value. If the maturity at the time of issue is less than 10 years, the

security is called a note rather than a bond. T-bonds have no default risk.

TCJA See Tax Cuts and Jobs Act.

technical analysts Stock analysts who believe that past trends or patterns in stock prices can be used to predict future stock prices.

TED spread The 3-month LIBOR rate minus the 3-month T-bill rate. It is a measure of risk aversion and measures the extra compensation that banks require to induce them to lend to one another.

temporary net operating working capital The NOWC required above the permanent level when the economy is strong and/or seasonal sales are high.

temporary operating current assets The operating current assets required above the permanent level when the economy is strong and/or seasonal sales are high.

tender When stockholders of a merger target turn over their shares to a designated financial institution, along with a signed power of attorney that transfers ownership of the shares to the acquiring firm.

tender offer The offer of one firm to buy the stock of another by going directly to the stockholders, frequently over the opposition of the target company's management.

terminal date The last year in a cash flow forecast. Cash flows may grow unevenly during the forecast period, but are assumed to grow at a constant rate for all periods after the terminal date. Also called the forecast horizon or the horizon date.

terminal value The present value of all free cash flows beyond the horizon date discounted back to the horizon date. Also called the horizon value (because it is at the horizon date) or the continuing value (because it is the value if operations continue to be used rather than be liquidated).

term structure of interest rates The relationship between yield to maturity and term to maturity for bonds of a single risk class.

time line A graphical representation used to show the timing of cash flows.

time value of an option The difference between an option's price and its exercise value.

time value of money (TVM) analysis The method of determining today's value of a cash flow to be received in the future. Also called discounted cash flow analysis.

times-interest-earned (TIE) ratio Determined by dividing earnings before interest and taxes by the interest charges. This ratio measures the extent to which operating income can decline before the firm is unable to meet its annual interest costs.

TIPS (Treasury Inflation-Protected Security) A bond issued by the U.S. government with a principal amount that is based on an inflation index such as the consumer price index (CPI). This causes interest rates and the final principal payment to automatically rise when the inflation rate rises, thus protecting the bondholders against inflation.

tornado diagram A chart resembling a tornado because it shows the results of a sensitivity analysis with the range in possible outcomes for each variable drawn as horizontal bars arranged from the widest bar (i.e., the range for the input to which the output is most sensitive) at the top and the smallest bar at the bottom.

total assets turnover ratio Measures the turnover of all the firm's assets; it is calculated by dividing sales by total assets.

total carrying cost (TCC) The costs of carrying inventory.

total inventory costs (TIC) The sum of ordering and carrying costs.

total net discount (for a bond issue) An original issue discount bond's issue price minus its flotations costs. Also, can occur if an original issue bond's issue price minus its flotation cost is less than par.

total net operating capital The sum of net operating working capital and operating long-term assets, such as net plant and equipment. Total net operating capital is also called net operating capital. It is also equal to the net amount of investor-supplied operating capital.

total net premium (for a bond issue) An original issue premium bond's issue price minus its flotations costs. If this total is less than par, then the bond has a total net discount instead of a total net premium.

total net present value (TNPV) Equal to net present value plus net present social value in a not-for-profit business.

total ordering cost (TOC) The costs of ordering inventory.

tracking stock A class of stock with dividends tied to a particular part of a company. Also called target stock or targeting stock.

trade balance Level of imports relative to exports. A deficit occurs when businesses and individuals in the United States import more goods from foreign countries than are exported. A surplus occurs when exports are greater than imports. Also called the foreign trade balance and the balance of trade.

trade balance (deficit or surplus) Deficit occurs when a country imports more goods from abroad than it exports; surplus is the reverse and occurs when a country exports more than it imports.

trade credit Arising from credit sales and is the amount of the sale price that is not paid in cash at the time of the purchase; recorded as an account receivable by the seller and as an account payable by the buyer.

trade discounts A provision in credit terms: A percentage reduction in the sales price if the purchaser pays in cash before the end of the specified discount period. Otherwise, the full price is due at the end of the regular credit period. Also called "cash discounts" or just "discounts."

trade-off theory The addition of financial distress and agency costs to either the MM tax model or the Miller model. In this theory, the optimal capital structure can be visualized as a trade-off between the benefit of debt (the interest tax shelter) and the costs of debt (financial distress and agency costs).

trading venue A site (geographical or electronic) where secondary market trading occurs, including stock exchanges, alternative trading systems, and broker-dealer networks.

transactions balance The cash balance associated with payments and collections; the balance necessary for day-to-day operations.

transfer price Price a subsidiary pays a parent for raw materials, finished goods, or other goods and services.

transnational corporation A corporation that operates in an integrated fashion in more than one country. Also called global corporation, multinational corporation, and multinational enterprise.

Treasury bill (T-bill) A short-term security issued by the federal government. A T-bill has a maturity of 52 weeks or less at the time of issue, and it makes no payments at all until it matures. Thus, T-bills are sold initially at a discount to their face, or maturity, value. T-bills have no default risk.

Treasury bond (T-bond) Bonds issued by the federal government; sometimes called T-bonds or government bonds. A T-bond makes an equal payment every 6 months until it matures, at which time it makes an additional lump-sum payment of its par value. If the maturity at the time of issue is less than 10 years, the security is called a note rather than a bond. T-bonds have no default risk.

Treasury Inflation-Protected Security (TIPS) A bond issued by the U.S. government with a principal amount that is based on an inflation index such as the consumer price index (CPI). This causes interest rates and the final principal payment to automatically rise when the inflation rate rises, thus protecting the bondholders against inflation.

trend analysis An analysis of a firm's financial ratios over time. It is used to estimate the likelihood of improvement or deterioration in its financial situation.

Treynor's reward-to-volatility ratio Asset's average return (in excess of the risk-free rate) divided by its beta. Measure the return per unit of risk as defined by beta.

triangular probability distribution Has a peak at the most likely outcome and the probability of occurrence declines in each direction from the most likely outcome.

true lease Meets all of the Internal Revenue Service (IRS) requirements for a genuine lease. If a lease meets the IRS guidelines, the IRS allows the lessor to deduct the asset's depreciation and allows the lessee to deduct the lease payments. Also called a guideline lease and a tax-oriented lease.

trust receipt In inventory financing, a document that acknowledges that the goods in inventory are held in trust for the lender. Also called a security instrument.

trustee (for bond indenture) Official (usually a bank) who represents the bondholders and makes sure the terms of the indenture are carried out.

trustee (in bankruptcy) Third party appointed by bankruptcy court to manage the company during the bankruptcy period; only happens if the court deems current management incompetent or if fraud is suspected.

two-bin method Determines the reorder times for inventory items stocked in two bins. When the working bin is empty, an order is placed and inventory is drawn from the second bin until the new inventory arrives.

U

uncollected balances schedule Reports each month's remaining receivables as a percentage of the month's sales. Adds together the monthly percentages for a given period, such as each quarter, and provides a comparison of this sum over time. Avoids misleading signals that are given by the DSO and aging schedule when sales are seasonal.

underfunded pension plan The present value of expected retirement benefits exceeds the assets on hand.

underinvestment problem A type of agency problem that can cause managers to forgo risky projects even if they have positive NPVs. High debt levels or the need to finance a project with debt exacerbates the problem. Occurs because a bankruptcy or other failure damages the manager's reputation and future earnings.

underwrite An investment bank underwrites a security offering when it guarantees to buy (at a fixed price) all stock a company offers in an IPO.

underwriter (of IPO) Investment bank which agrees to buy all stock in an initial public offering from issuing company at a set price and then resell the stock to investors at the offering price. Underwriter bears risk of selling the issue.

underwriting spread (F) The difference between the offer price at which an underwriter sells the stock in an initial public offering and the proceeds that the underwriter passes on to the issuing firm; the fee collected by the underwriter. It is often about 7% of the offering price.

underwriting syndicate Group of investment banks that underwrites a security issuance; minimizes the risk each individual bank faces.

underwritten arrangement Contract between a firm and an investment banker when stock is issued. An investment banker agrees to buy the entire issue at a set price and then resells the stock at the offering price. Thus, the risk of selling the issue rests with the investment banker.

uneven cash flow stream A stream of cash flows that cannot be represented by an annuity. Also called an irregular cash flow stream.

unfunded pension liability Pension plan obligations whose present value exceed the assets designated to fund the obligations.

unicorn A company in a venture capitalist's portfolio whose estimated worth is at least $1 billion even though it has no history of profitable operations.

uniform probability distribution A probability distribution in which each discrete outcome has the same probability. If a continuous distribution, then two outcome ranges have the same probability if the sizes of the ranges are the same.

unlevered beta, b_U The beta that a firm would have if it had no debt. Can be estimated using the Hamada equation: $b_U = b/[1 + (1 - T)(D/S)] = b/[1 + (1 - T)(w_d/w_s)]$.

unlevered cost of equity, r_{sU} Cost of equity for a firm with no debt.

unlevered value of a firm, V_U Value of a firm's equity if it had no debt. Also called the value of an unlevered firm.

unsyndicated offering Offering in which the managing underwriter—acting alone—sells the issue entirely to a group of institutional investors.

V

value at risk (VaR) The dollar value that defines a specified percentile in the probability distribution of portfolio's loss or a project's NPV. For example, if the specified percentile is 5%, a VaR of −$1 million means that there is a 5% probability that the portfolio will lose $1 million or more.

value-based management Systematic use of the free cash flow valuation model to identify value drivers and to guide managerial and strategic decisions.

value drivers Inputs to the free cash flow valuation model that managers are able to influence through strategic choices and execution of business plans. These include the revenue growth rate, the operating profitability ratio, the capital requirement ratio, and the weighted average cost of capital.

value of an unlevered firm, V_U Value of a firm's equity if it had no debt. Also called the unlevered value of a firm.

value of levered firm, V_L The total value of a firm with debt: $V_L = Stock + Debt = S_L + Debt$. Also called levered value of a firm.

value of operations, V_{op} The present value of all expected future free cash flows when discounted at the weighted average cost of capital.

value of preferred stock, V_{ps} The constant fixed dividend (D_{ps}) divided by the preferred stock's required rate of return (r_{ps}).

variance, σ^2 A measure of a distribution's variability. It is the sum of the weighted squared deviations from the expected value, where the weights are the probabilities of the deviations' occurrences.

venture capital fund Private limited partnership which typically raises cash from a relatively small group of primarily institutional investors and then purchases equity in start-up companies.

venture capitalist The manager of a venture capital fund. The fund raises most of its capital from institutional investors and invests in start-up companies in exchange for equity.

vertical merger Occurs when a company acquires another firm that is "upstream" or "downstream"; for example, an automobile manufacturer acquires a steel producer.

vested Retirement benefits that the employee can keep even after leaving the company.

vesting If an employee has the right to receive pension benefits even if they leave the company prior to retirement, their rights are said to be vested.

vesting period Period during which employee stock options cannot be exercised.

V_L (levered value of a firm) The total value of a firm with debt: $V_L = Stock + Debt = S_L + Debt$.

Volcker rule A part of the Dodd-Frank Act named after former Fed chairman Paul Volcker. It seeks to limit a bank's proprietary trading, such as investing the banks' own funds into hedge funds.

voluntary petition (in bankruptcy) Filing by borrower of petition in bankruptcy court.

V_{ps}, value of preferred stock The constant fixed dividend (D_{ps}) divided by the preferred stock's required rate of return (r_{ps}).

$V_{Tax\ shield}$, value of tax shield Present value of all expected future annual tax savings due to deductibility of interest expenses. Also called the interest tax shield and just the tax shield.

V_U, unlevered value of a firm Value of a firm's equity if it had no debt. Also called value of an unlevered firm.

W

warehouse receipt financing A way to finance inventory that uses inventory as a security for the loan and requires field warehousing.

warrant A call option, issued by a company, that allows the holder to buy a stated number of shares of stock from the company at a specified price. Warrants are generally distributed with debt, or preferred stock, to induce investors to buy those securities at lower cost.

weak form of market efficiency Assumes that all information contained in past price movements is fully reflected in current market prices. Thus, information about recent trends in a stock's price is of no use in selecting a stock.

weighted average cost of capital (WACC) The weighted average of the after-tax component costs of capital—debt, preferred stock, and common equity. Each weighting factor is the proportion of that type of capital in the optimal, or target, capital structure.

weighted average inventory valuation method Determines the weighted average unit cost of goods available for sale from inventory based on past purchases and past usage of inventory.

well-diversified portfolio A portfolio that has enough assets that are sufficiently uncorrelated with one another that diversifiable risk has been reduced to near zero.

white knight A friendly competing bidder that a target management likes better than the company making a hostile offer; the target solicits a merger with the white knight as a preferable alternative.

white squire An investor who is friendly to current management and can buy enough of the target firm's shares to block a merger.

window dressing Techniques employed by firms to make their financial statements look better than they really are.

wire transfer Direct online transfers from one bank account to another, which were first conducted via telegraph.

within-firm risk The variability a project contributes to a corporation's returns; also called corporate risk.

working capital A firm's investment in short-term assets—cash, marketable securities, inventory, and accounts receivable.

workout Voluntary reorganization plans arranged between creditors and generally sound companies experiencing temporary financial difficulties. Workouts typically require some restructuring of the firm's debt.

writing an option The act of creating an option and then selling it to someone else. The writer of the option is obligated to honor its terms if the purchaser of the option decides to exercise the option. For example, the writer of a call option might receive $4 from an investor for an option with a strike price of $20. If the option expires out-of-the-money (the price at expiration is less than $20), the writer has a $4 profit. However, if the stock price is $25 when the investor exercises the option, then the writer must sell a share of stock that is worth $25 to the investor for the price of $20. In this case, the writer would have received $4 from writing the option but would have lost $5 when it was exercised, for a net loss of $1.

Y

Yankee bonds Bond issued by a foreign borrower denominated in dollars and sold in the United States under SEC regulations

yield The rate of return that fairly compensates an investor for purchasing or holding debt, taking into consideration its risk, timing, and the returns available on other similar investments. It is also called the required rate of return on debt (r_d), the quoted market interest rate, the going rate, and the nominal interest rate.

yield curve The curve that results when yield to maturity is plotted on the y-axis with term to maturity on the x-axis.

yield to call (YTC) The rate of interest earned on a bond if it is called. If current interest rates are well below an outstanding callable bond's coupon rate, then the YTC may be a more relevant estimate of expected return than the YTM because the bond is likely to be called.

yield to maturity (YTM) The rate earned on a bond if it is held to maturity.

Z

Z score The fitted value in a multiple discriminant analysis that is used to determine whether a company is likely to go bankrupt.

zero coupon bonds (zeros) Pay no coupons at all but are offered at a substantial discount below par value and hence provide capital appreciation rather than interest income.

zero working capital target Managerial objective to set: Inventories + Receivables − Payables = 0. Frees up cash, speeds up production, and helps businesses operate more efficiently.

zone of ignorance A Z score from multiple discriminant analysis that is in the range ±0.3. In bankruptcy prediction, a score in this range means that the analysis does not provide a clear indication as to whether the firm is likely or unlikely to fail.

Name Index

In this index, n indicates entries that can be found in notes and t indicates entries that can be found in tables.

Subject Index

In this index, *f* represents figure, *t* represents table, and n indicates entries that can be found in notes.

A

AAA-rated companies, 226
AAII. *See* American Association of Individual Investors (AAII)
Abandonment option, 479
Abbott Labs, 226
Abbott Labs acquisition of St. Jude Medical, 866
Abercrombie & Fitch, 548
Abnormal yield curve, 228
Absolute priority doctrine, 940
Accelerated cost recovery system (ACRS), 495
Accelerated depreciation, 464, 495
Accounting beta, 398
Accounting beta method, 398
Accounting frauds, 540n2
Accounting income, 62
Accounting profit, 62
Accounting Standards Update (ASU 2016-02), 781–782
Accounts payable, 57, 59, 667–670
Accounts receivable, 58, 651
    See also Receivables management
Accredited investor, 748
Accrual accounting method, 59
Accruals, 667
Accumulated depreciation, 59
ACH. *See* Automated clearing house (ACH)
Acid test ratio, 112
ACP. *See* Average collection period (ACP)
Acquiring company, 866
ACRS. *See* Accelerated cost recovery system (ACRS)
Actively managed fund, 26
Activis PLC, 867
Add-on interest, 174
Add-on interest loan, 682–683
Additional financing needed (AFN), 514, 526
Additional financing needed (AFN) equation, 520–522, 526
Adidas, 997
Adidas Speedfactory, 997
Adjustable-rate mortgage (ARM), 44, 180

Adjustable rate preferred stock (ARP), 807
Adjusted beta, 984
Adjusted present value (APV) approach, 834–837
    example valuation, 848–850
    levered beta, 836–837
    levered cost of equity, 836
    overview, 845t
    tax shield discount rate, 837
    value of levered firm, 834–836
Adjustment bureau, 934
ADR. *See* American depository receipt (ADR)
AerCap Holdings NV, 779
Aetna Incorporated, 833
AFN. *See* Additional financing needed (AFN)
AFN equation. *See* Additional financing needed (AFN) equation
After-tax cost of debt, 377–381
After-tax cost of long-term debt, 378–379
After-tax cost of short-term debt, 377–378
Agency conflicts, 538–541
Agency costs, 538, 820–821
Agency debt, 197
Agency relationship, 538
Agent, 538
Aggressive approach, 654f, 655
Aging schedule, 666, 666t
AIG, 47, 933
Airbnb, 750
Airbus, 779
Alcoa, 649, 909
Alibaba, 8, 726
Allena Pharmaceuticals, 757
Allergan Inc., 867
Alt-A mortgage, 42
Alternate minimum tax (AMT), 87, 88
Alternative trading system (ATS), 37
"Alternative Trading Systems: Description of ATS Trading in National Market System Stocks," 37n19
Altria Group Inc., 567t
Amazon.com, 3, 262t, 567t, 662
American Association of Individual Investors (AAII), 127

American depository receipt (ADR), 726
American DG Energy, 864
American option, 345
American Recovery and Reinvestment Act (2009), 48
American Stock Exchange, 32
Amortization expense, 60
Amortization schedule, 178, 178f
Amortized loan, 176–180
AMT. *See* Alternate minimum tax (AMT)
Analysis of financial statements. *See* Financial analysis
Analyzing project proposals. *See* Capital budgeting
Anchoring bias, 282
Andreessen Horowitz, 750
Angel investors, 748
Anheuser-Busch InBev, 726
Annual compounding, 171
Annual percentage rate (APR), 174
Annual report, 56
Annual Statement Studies, 125
Annual vesting, 546
Annuity
    deferred, 156
    defined, 156
    growing, 181–183
    ordinary. *See* Ordinary annuity
    variable, 163
Annuity due
    defined, 156
    future value, 159–160
    present value, 162
Anthem, 860–861
Antron/Bosworth swap, 915–918
AOL Time Warner, 61n3
Apollo Global Management, LLC, 26
Apple, 3, 5, 55, 65, 71, 119, 125, 262t, 417n3, 455, 561, 563, 649, 651, 662, 675, 679, 698, 736, 978–980
APR. *See* Annual percentage rate (APR)
APT. *See* Arbitrage pricing theory (APT)
APV. *See* Adjusted present value (APV) approach
Arbitrage, 352, 707, 878
Arbitrage pricing theory (APT), 988–991
Archer Daniels Midland, 909